Adobe® Dreamweaver® CS6 Bible

Adobe® Dreamweaver® CS6 BIBLE

Joseph Lowery

WILEY
John Wiley & Sons, Inc.

Adobe® Dreamweaver® CS6 Bible

Published by
John Wiley & Sons, Inc.
10475 Crosspoint Boulevard
Indianapolis, IN 46256
www.wiley.com

Published simultaneously in Canada

ISBN: 978-1-118-17063-2
ISBN: 978-1-118-22779-4 (ebk)
ISBN: 978-1-118-23977-3 (ebk)
ISBN: 978-1-118-26447-8 (ebk)

Manufactured in the United States of America

10 9 8 7 6 5 4 3 2 1

For general information on our other products and services please contact our Customer Care Department within the United States at (877) 762-2974, outside the United States at (317) 572-3993 or fax (317) 572-4002.

Wiley publishes in a variety of print and electronic formats and by print-on-demand. Some material included with standard print versions of this book may not be included in e-books or in print-on-demand. If this book refers to media such as a CD or DVD that is not included in the version you purchased, you may download this material at http://booksupport.wiley.com. For more information about Wiley products, visit www.wiley.com.

Library of Congress Control Number: 2012936416

For all the readers who took a chance on one of my books, thank you for giving me this opportunity to do what I love most.

About the Author

Joseph Lowery has been writing about computers and new technology since 1981. He is the author of the previous editions of *Dreamweaver Bible*, as well as the recent *HTML5 24-Hour Trainer, Adobe CS4 Web Workflows, Adobe CS3 Web Workflows*, and *CSS Hacks and Filters* (all published by Wiley). He is also the author of *Joseph Lowery's Beyond Dreamweaver, Dreamweaver MX 2004 Killer Tips* (with Angela Buraglia), and *Dreamweaver MX 2004 Web Application Recipes* and *Dreamweaver 8 Recipes* (with Eric Ott), all published by New Riders. He has also written books on HTML and on using the Internet for business. His books are international best sellers, having sold more than 400,000 copies worldwide in 11 different languages. Joe is also a consultant and trainer, as well as a multi-course author with Lynda.com. He has presented at Seybold in both Boston and San Francisco, Adobe conferences in the United States and Europe, and ThunderLizard's Web Design World. He is currently building websites for a number of designers and is also the Vice President of Yggdrasil Ink, LLC.

About the Technical Editor

Colin Macdonald's interest in computers began when he first witnessed the power of VisiCalc running on an Apple II computer, and his interest intensified when he designed the print collateral for the first commercial spell-checking program for personal computers. He began using and teaching most of the Adobe and Macromedia programs from their introduction—including Dreamweaver, when it came with a 146-page manual. He has been a record company art director, university creative director, professor, consultant, and trainer in both North America and Asia.

Colin enjoys sharing his experiences and knowledge with and learning from others. He instituted the first multimedia courses at the University of Hawaiis Department of Communication, where he taught multimedia design and development for over a decade. He is a core faculty member of Pacific New Media, the premier digital and media education center in Hawaii.

When Colin isn't creating websites, consulting, or training, he enjoys photography, live music, hiking, and traveling to other countries. He calls Honolulu, Hawaii, home and can be found on the Internet at `http://www.macbinary.com`.

Credits

Executive Editor
Carol Long

Senior Project Editor
Adaobi Obi Tulton

Technical Editor
Colin Macdonald

Production Editor
Daniel Scribner

Copy Editor
Nancy Rapoport

Editorial Manager
Mary Beth Wakefield

Associate Director of Marketing
David Mayhew

Marketing Manager
Ashley Zurcher

Business Manager
Amy Knies

Production Manager
Tim Tate

Vice President and Executive Group Publisher
Richard Swadley

Vice President and Executive Publisher
Neil Edde

Associate Publisher
Jim Minatel

Project Coordinator, Cover
Katie Crocker

Compositor
James D. Kramer, Happenstance Type-O-Rama

Proofreader
Nicole Hirschman

Indexer
Ron Strauss

Cover Designer
Ryan Sneed

Cover Image
© Aleksandar Velasevic / iStockPhoto

Contents at a Glance

Introduction xxxiii

Part I: Laying the Groundwork in Dreamweaver 1

Chapter 1: Introducing Dreamweaver CS6 3
Chapter 2: Touring Dreamweaver 35
Chapter 3: Setting Your Preferences 89
Chapter 4: Setting Up Sites and Servers 127

Part II: Designing and Crafting Basic Pages 167

Chapter 5: Accessing the Code Directly 169
Chapter 6: Building Style Sheet Web Pages 237
Chapter 7: Working with Text 291
Chapter 8: Inserting Images 347
Chapter 9: Establishing Web Links 379

Part III: Adding Advanced Design Features 399

Chapter 10: Working with Layouts 401
Chapter 11: Using Behaviors 449
Chapter 12: Setting Up Tables 485
Chapter 13: Enabling User Interaction with Forms 521
Chapter 14: Creating Lists 559
Chapter 15: Using Frames and Framesets 587
Chapter 16: Powering Ajax Pages with Spry 619
Chapter 17: Working with JavaScript Frameworks 669

Part IV: Incorporating Dynamic Data 695

Chapter 18: Establishing Connections and Recordsets 697
Chapter 19: Making Data Dynamic 729
Chapter 20: Managing Data 751
Chapter 21: Working with Dynamic Live View 765
Chapter 22: Crafting Multi-Page Applications 781
Chapter 23: Using Web Content Management Systems 819

Part V: Including Multimedia Elements 837

Chapter 24: Adobe Photoshop, Fireworks, and Bridge Integration 839
Chapter 25: Inserting Flash Elements 867
Chapter 26: Adding Video to Your Web Page 877
Chapter 27: Using Audio on Your Web Page 897

Part VI: Enhancing Productivity and Website Management 911
Chapter 28: Using Dreamweaver Templates 913
Chapter 29: Using Library Items and Server-Side Includes 965
Chapter 30: Maximizing Cross-Browser Compatibility 983
Chapter 31: Building Websites with a Team 997
Chapter 32: Integrating XML and XSLT 1031

Part VII: Extending Dreamweaver 1055
Chapter 33: Customizing Dreamweaver 1057
Chapter 34: Handling Server Behaviors 1083
Chapter 35: Creating Adobe AIR Applications 1115

Appendix A: What's on the Website? 1129

Index 1133

Contents

Introduction. xxxiii

Part I: Laying the Groundwork in Dreamweaver 1

Chapter 1: Introducing Dreamweaver CS6 3

The Dynamic World of Dreamweaver 3
Designing for multiple screens 4
Connecting to the world's data 5
True page representation 5
Integrated visual and text editors 5
World-class code editing 7
Website maintenance tools 8
Team-oriented site building 9
The Dreamweaver Interface 9
Easy text entry 9
Drag-and-drop data fields 10
One-stop object modification 10
Accessing and managing resources 10
Complete custom environment 12
Managing keyboard shortcuts 12
Simple selection process 12
Enhanced layout options 13
Plugin media preview 13
Extended find and replace 14
Up-to-Date Code Standards 14
Cutting-edge CSS support 14
Addressing accessibility 15
Straightforward text and graphics support 16
Enhanced table capabilities 16
Easy form entry 17
Multimedia enhancements 17
Next-Generation Features 18
Multiple Screen Design 18
Content management system support 19
Ajax spoken here 19
Dynamic style updates 20
Photoshop, Flash, and Fireworks integration 20
Server-side behaviors 21
XML and XSLT integration 21
CSS layout control 22

JavaScript behaviors....23
Mobile app development....24
Program Extensibility....24
Objects and behaviors....24
Server Behavior Builder....25
Commands and floating panels....26
Adjustable Insert panels....26
Custom tags, translators, and Property inspectors....26
Automation Enhancements....27
Rapid application development with Data objects....27
Importing Office documents....28
Reference panel....29
History panel....29
Site Management Tools....29
Object libraries....29
Supercharged templates....30
Browser targeting....31
Verifying links....32
FTP publishing....32
File Check In/Check Out....32
Summary....33

Chapter 2: Touring Dreamweaver....35

Choosing a Workspace Layout....35
Viewing the Document Window....40
Switching views in the Document window....41
Design and Code views....42
Live View and Live Code....43
Working with the status bar....45
Tag Selector....45
Select, Hand, and Zoom tools....46
Window Size options....47
Download Indicator....49
Accessing the Toolbars....50
The Application bar....50
The Related Files bar....51
The Document toolbar: Design view....51
Setting up for multiple screen design....52
Previewing your file....53
Managing files....53
Validating your site pages....54
Checking for browser errors....54
Easy refresh and viewing options....55
Document Toolbar: Live View....56
The Standard toolbar....58
The Style Rendering toolbar....59
The Coding toolbar....60
Selecting from the Insert Panel....63
Common objects....64

Layout objects 66
Forms objects 67
Data objects 68
Spry objects 69
jQuery Mobile objects 71
InContext Editing objects 73
Text objects 73
Favorites 75
ASP objects 76
CFML and CFForm objects 76
PHP objects 76
XSLT objects 76
Getting the Most Out of the Property Inspector 76
Manipulating the Property inspector 77
Property inspector elements 78
Customizing Your Workspace with Dockable Panels 80
Hiding and showing panels 80
Customizing panel groups 84
Accessing the Menus 85
Summary 87

Chapter 3: Setting Your Preferences. 89

Customizing Your Environment 89
General preferences 89
Document Options 90
Editing Options 92
Preferences for invisible elements 95
Highlighting preferences 96
Window Size preferences 98
Window sizes 98
Connection Speed option 99
File Types/Editors preferences 99
Open In Code View option 100
External Code Editor option 100
Enable BBEdit Integration (Macintosh only) option 100
Reload Modified Files option 100
Save On Launch option 100
Fireworks option 101
Defining editors for different file types 101
Copy/Paste preferences 102
New Document preferences 103
Default Document option 104
Default Extension option 104
Default Document Type option 104
Encoding options 104
Show New Document Dialog Box On Ctrl+N (Command+N) option 104
Adjusting Advanced Features 105
Accessibility preferences 105
Show Attributes When Inserting option 105

Keep Focus In The Panel When Opening option (Windows only) 105
Offscreen Rendering option (Windows only) 105
AP Elements preferences 106
Visibility option 106
Width and Height options 106
Background Color option 107
Background Image option 107
Nesting option 108
CSS Styles preferences 108
Making Online Connections 110
Site preferences 110
Always Show Local/Remote Files On The Right/Left option 110
Dependent Files options 111
FTP Connection: Disconnect After __ Minutes Idle option 111
FTP Time Out option 111
FTP Transfer option: Select Default Action In Dialogs After __ Seconds 111
Firewall Host and Firewall Port options 112
Put options 112
Move options 112
Manage Sites button 112
Preview In Browser preferences 112
Customizing Your Code 114
Fonts preferences 114
Code Hints preferences 116
Close Tags option 116
Options: Enable Code Hints 117
Code Rewriting preferences 117
Fix Invalidly Nested And Unclosed Tags option 118
Rename Form Items When Pasting option 118
Remove Extra Closing Tags option 118
Warn When Fixing Or Removing Tags option 118
Never Rewrite Code preferences 119
Special Characters Encoding preferences 119
URL Encoding preferences 119
Code Coloring preferences 119
Code Format preferences 121
Indent control options 121
Line control options 122
Case control options 122
CSS Source Format preferences 123
W3C Validator preferences 124
Summary 125

Chapter 4: Setting Up Sites and Servers 127

Planning Your Site 128
Deciding what you want to say 128
Targeting your audience 128
Determining your resources 128
Mapping Dynamic Pages for Web Applications 129

Defining a Site....130
Working with Site Setup....130
Establishing local connections....130
Specifying a remote server....134
Defining a testing server....138
Cloaking Site Folders....140
Managing Site Info....142
Creating and Saving New Pages....143
Starting Dreamweaver....143
Opening existing files....144
Opening a new file....144
Saving your file....145
Closing the file....146
Quitting the program....146
Creating New Documents....146
Using the New Document dialog box....147
Creating a new default document....149
Previewing Your Web Pages....149
Previewing in your browsers....150
Displaying pages with BrowserLab....151
Putting Your Pages Online....153
Transferring with FTP....154
Using the FTP Log panel....156
Getting Online with Business Catalyst....157
Creating a new site with Business Catalyst....158
Working with your Business Catalyst site online....159
Integrating Business Catalyst Code in Dreamweaver....161
Inserting a Module....162
Styling a Module's Output....163
Summary....165

Part II: Designing and Crafting Basic Pages 167

Chapter 5: Accessing the Code Directly....169

The Structure of a Web Page....170
Expanding into XHTML....171
doctype and doctype Switching....172
Defining <head> Elements....173
Establishing Page Properties....174
Appearance (CSS)....175
Appearance (HTML)....175
Links (CSS)....176
Headings (CSS)....176
Title/Encoding....178
Tracing Image....178
Understanding <meta> and other <head> tags....180
Inserting tags with the Meta object....180
Aiding search engines with the Keywords and Description objects....182

Refreshing the page and redirecting users....183
Changing bases....185
Linking to other files....185
Adding to the <body>....187
Logical styles....187
Physical styles....188
Working with Code View and the Code Inspector....188
Printing code....191
Coding HTML5 Structural Tags....191
Integrating Live View, Related Files, and Code Navigator Features....195
Enhanced workflow with Live View....196
Incorporating Live Code....198
Setting Live View options....199
Accessing Related Files....200
Navigating with the Code Navigator....201
Using the Coding Toolbar....203
Code collapse....203
Code selection and highlight....205
Commenting code....206
Wrapping tags and inserting snippets....206
Manipulating CSS....207
Enhancing Code Authoring Productivity....208
Code Hints and Tag Completion....208
Modifying blocks of code....211
Inserting code with the Tag Chooser....212
Adding Code Through the Snippets Panel....214
Using the Reference Panel....216
Modifying Code with the Tag Inspector....218
Rapid Tag Modification with the Quick Tag Editor....219
Insert HTML mode....221
Wrap Tag mode....222
Edit Tag mode....224
Adding Java Applets....225
Managing JavaScript and VBScript....227
Inserting JavaScript and VBScript....228
Editing JavaScript and VBScript....228
Extracting JavaScript....230
Inserting Symbols and Special Characters....231
Named characters....232
Decimal characters and UTF-8 encoding....232
Using the Character objects....233
Summary....235

Chapter 6: Building Style Sheet Web Pages....237

Understanding Cascading Style Sheets....238
Grouping properties....239
Inheritance of properties....239
Cascading characteristics....240
Defining new class and ID selectors for extended design control....240

Specificity ... 241
How styles are applied ... 242
External style sheets ... 242
Embedded styles ... 243
Inline styles ... 243
Working with the CSS Styles Panel ... 244
All mode ... 244
Current mode ... 246
Creating and Applying Styles ... 248
Generating new styles ... 248
Class ... 251
ID ... 251
Tag ... 251
Compound ... 251
Descendants and other advanced selectors ... 252
Applying styles through the Property inspector ... 253
Inserting multiple classes ... 253
Attaching an external style sheet ... 254
Choosing a media type ... 255
Rendering different styles ... 256
Applying, changing, and removing a style ... 256
Changing styles ... 258
Removing applied styles ... 258
Editing and managing style sheets ... 260
CSS Styles panel ... 260
CSS Styles panel Properties pane ... 262
Applying Enhanced CSS3 Styles ... 263
Handling vendor-specific CSS properties ... 264
Toggling CSS properties ... 265
Managing CSS rules ... 266
Debugging your applied CSS ... 268
Styles and Their Attributes ... 271
Type options ... 271
Background options ... 273
Block options ... 275
Box options ... 277
Border options ... 278
List options ... 279
Positioning options ... 279
Extensions options ... 281
Transition options ... 282
Animating CSS Transitions ... 285
Design-Time Style Sheets ... 288
Summary ... 289

Chapter 7: Working with Text ... 291

Starting with Headings ... 291
Working with Paragraphs ... 294
Inserting text ... 295

Cutting, copying, and pasting ... 296
Using drag-and-drop ... 297
Inserting text from other text applications ... 297
Copying and pasting code ... 298
Undo, redo, and the History panel ... 298
Checking Your Spelling ... 300
Using Find and Replace ... 301
Finding on the visual page ... 302
Searching the code ... 306
Looking for text in the code ... 306
Using advanced text options in Find and Replace ... 307
Replacing HTML tags and attributes ... 309
Concentrating your search with regular expressions ... 311
Wildcard characters ... 312
Matching character positions and repeating characters ... 313
Matching character ranges ... 314
Using grouping with regular expressions ... 315
Controlling Whitespace ... 316
Indenting text ... 316
Working with preformatted text ... 317
The <br> tag ... 318
Working with Microsoft Office Documents ... 319
Importing Office documents ... 319
Copying and pasting Office content ... 320
Dragging and dropping Word and Excel files ... 321
Importing Word HTML ... 322
Styling Your Text ... 324
Depicting various styles ... 324
Using the <address> tag ... 327
Adding abbreviations and acronyms ... 328
Modifying Text Format ... 328
Adjusting font size ... 328
Adding font color ... 330
Assigning a specific font ... 333
About HTML fonts ... 334
Selecting a font ... 335
Editing the font list ... 335
Aligning text ... 337
Quoting entire paragraphs ... 338
Implementing Web Fonts ... 338
About @font-face ... 339
Applying web fonts in Dreamweaver ... 340
Incorporating Dates ... 342
Commenting Your Code ... 344
Summary ... 346

Chapter 8: Inserting Images ... 347

Using Images Inline ... 348
Inserting images ... 348

Relative to Document 350
Relative to Site Root 351
Dragging images from the Assets panel 352
Optimizing and altering images 356
Cropping graphics 357
Resampling after resizing 359
Affecting brightness and contrast 360
Sharpening graphic lines 360
Employing the Optimize Image command 361
Editing images 362
Modifying image attributes 363
Naming your image 364
Adjusting height and width 364
Adding image descriptions 365
Bordering a graphic 366
Working with alignment options 367
Horizontal alignment 367
Vertical alignment 367
Wrapping text 368
Adding Background Images 369
Dividing the Web Page with Horizontal Rules 372
Including Banner Ads 373
Inserting Rollover Images 375
Summary 377

Chapter 9: Establishing Web Links 379

Understanding URLs 379
Surfing the Web with Hypertext 381
Eliminating underlines from links 383
Inserting URLs from the Assets panel 385
Pointing to a file 386
Addressing types 387
Checking links 388
Adding an E-mail Link 390
Navigating with Anchors 391
Moving within the same document 393
Using named anchors in a different page 394
Creating null links 394
Targeting Your Links 396
Summary 397

Part III: Adding Advanced Design Features 399

Chapter 10: Working with Layouts 401

Divs and AP Elements 101 403
Placing <div> Tags 405
Defining a CSS rule for a <div> tag 405
Inserting the <div> tag 406

Visualizing <div> tags....408
CSS Inspect....409
CSS layout backgrounds....410
CSS Layout Box Model....410
CSS Layout Outlines....412
Designing fluid layouts with a grid....414
Working with a fluid grid layout....415
Fluid grid layout helper files....418
Creating AP Elements with Dreamweaver....419
Inserting an AP element object....419
Using the Insert ➪ Layout Objects ➪ AP Div option....420
Setting default characteristics of an AP element....421
Choosing relative instead of absolute positioning....422
Using the Relative attribute....422
Using nested AP elements....423
Modifying an AP Element....423
Selecting an AP element....423
Resizing an AP element....423
Moving an AP element....424
Using the CSS-P Property inspector....425
ID....426
Tag attribute....428
Visibility....428
Overflow....429
Clipping....430
Z-index....430
Background image or color....431
The AP Elements panel....431
Modifying properties with the AP Elements panel....431
Nesting with the AP Elements panel....432
Aligning AP elements....433
Using the ruler....433
Working with guides....434
Aligning objects with the grid....438
Adding elements to an AP element....439
Forms and AP elements....439
Using the Tracing Image Feature with AP Elements....440
Adding the Tracing Image to your page....440
Moving the Tracing Image....441
Activating AP Elements with Behaviors....442
Drag AP Element....442
Set Text of Container....444
Show-Hide Elements....446
Summary....447

Chapter 11: Using Behaviors....449

Understanding Behaviors, Events, and Actions....449
Attaching a Behavior....450
Using the Behaviors panel....451
Adding a behavior....452

Managing events 453
Standard actions 456
Call JavaScript..456
Change Property..457
Check Plugin 458
Drag AP Element..459
Go to URL...462
Jump Menu and Jump Menu Go 463
Open Browser Window 464
Popup Message 465
Preload Images 465
Set Text of Container 467
Set Text of Frame...468
Set Text of Status Bar 469
Set Text of Text Field 470
Show-Hide Elements 470
Swap Image and Swap Image Restore...471
Validate Form 472
Spry effects in Dreamweaver 474
Appear/Fade..474
Blind 475
Grow/Shrink...476
Highlight 478
Shake 479
Slide..479
Squish 480
Installing, Managing, and Modifying Behaviors 481
Altering the parameters of a behavior 482
Sequencing behaviors 482
Deleting behaviors...483
Summary 484

Chapter 12: Setting Up Tables 485

HTML Table Fundamentals...485
Rows...487
Cells 487
Column and row headings..488
Inserting Tables in Dreamweaver 489
Modifying Tables..494
Selecting table elements 494
Selecting in Expanded Tables mode..495
Selecting an entire table...495
Selecting a row or column 496
Selecting cells..497
Editing a table's contents 497
Moving through a table...498
Cutting, copying, and pasting in tables..499
Working with table properties 502
Setting alignment 502
Resizing a table..504

Inserting rows and columns 506
Deleting rows and columns 507
Setting table borders and backgrounds 508
Working with cell spacing and cell padding 509
Merging and splitting cells 509
Setting cell, column, and row properties 512
Horizontal alignment 513
Vertical alignment 513
Cell wrap 514
Table header cells 514
Cell width and height 514
Color elements 515
Sorting Tables 515
Importing Tabular Data 516
Summary 518

Chapter 13: Enabling User Interaction with Forms 521

How HTML Forms Work 522
Inserting a Form in Dreamweaver 524
Using Text Fields 526
Inserting text fields 526
Creating password fields 528
Inserting multiline text areas 528
Providing Checkboxes and Radio Buttons 531
Checkboxes 531
Radio buttons 532
Creating Form Lists and Menus 535
Drop-down menus 535
Menu values 537
Scrolling lists 538
Navigating with a Jump Menu 541
Modifying a jump menu 542
Activating Go buttons 544
Activating Your Form with Buttons 545
Submit, Reset, and Command buttons 545
Graphical buttons 546
Using Hidden and File Fields 547
The hidden input type 547
The file input type 548
Improving Accessibility 548
Exploring HTML5 Form Elements 550
Enhanced HTML5 attributes 551
HTML5-specific input types 551
Next-gen form controls 552
Styling Forms with CSS 553
Highlighting the form 553
Altering input fields 554
Distinguishing lists and menus 555
Changing labels and legends 556
Highlighting focus 557
Summary 558

Chapter 14: Creating Lists 559

Creating Unordered (Bulleted) Lists 559
Editing unordered lists 561
List tags.. 561
Using other bullet symbols.. 564
Styling lists with CSS.. 564
Mastering Ordered (Numbered) Lists 565
Editing ordered lists 566
Using other numbering styles.. 568
Creating Navigation Buttons from Lists 569
Step 1: Preparing background graphics.. 570
Step 2: Creating the list and containing <div>.. 571
Step 3: Building the CSS styles 573
Step 4: Applying the CSS 578
Making Definition Lists.. 579
Using Nested Lists 581
Accessing Special List Types.. 583
Menu lists.. 583
Directory lists 584
Summary 584

Chapter 15: Using Frames and Framesets 587

Frames and Framesets: The Basics.. 588
Creating a Frameset and Frames.. 589
Creating a new frameset file 589
Creating a frameset visually 591
Creating framesets quickly with frame objects.. 593
Adding More Frames.. 595
Using the menus.. 596
Using the mouse 596
Selecting, Saving, and Closing Framesets 597
Selecting framesets and frames 597
Saving framesets and frames.. 598
Closing framesets 599
Working with the Frameset Property Inspector 600
Resizing frames in a frameset.. 601
Manipulating frameset borders 602
Enabling borders.. 602
Border color options.. 603
Modifying a Frame.. 603
Page properties.. 603
Working with the Frame Property inspector.. 604
Naming your frames.. 604
Opening a web page into a frame 605
Setting borders.. 605
Adding scroll bars.. 606
Resizing.. 607
Setting margins.. 608
Modifying content.. 608
Deleting frames 608

Targeting Frame Content 609
Targeting sections of your frameset 609
Targeting specific frames in your frameset 610
Updating two or more frames at once 610
Handling Frameless Browsers 612
Investigating iframes 614
Summary 616

Chapter 16: Powering Ajax Pages with Spry 619

Understanding Ajax and Spry 620
What is Ajax? 620
What is Spry? 621
Integrating XML or HTML Data with Spry 622
Merging HTML data into web pages 622
Connecting to XML data 628
Defining Spry regions 631
Binding data to the page 634
Repeating Spry regions 636
Enhancing Your Site with Spry Widgets 641
Validating form fields 642
Spry Validation Text Field 643
Spry Validation Textarea 647
Spry Validation Select 649
Spry Validation Checkbox 650
Spry Validation Password 652
Spry Validation Confirm 654
Spry Validation Radio Group 655
Extending layout options 657
Spry Menu Bar 657
Spry Tabbed Panel 660
Spry Accordion Panel 661
Spry Collapsible Panel 663
Spry Tooltip 665
Spry Effects 666
Summary 667

Chapter 17: Working with JavaScript Frameworks 669

Using JavaScript Frameworks 670
Integrating Framework Functions 671
Implementing a Web Widget 675
Installing and using legacy web widgets 676
Working with the Widget Browser 678
Building Apps with jQuery Mobile 682
Creating a jQuery Mobile page 683
Inserting jQuery objects 685
Styling with jQuery themes 688
Working with PhoneGap 691
Summary 693

Part IV: Incorporating Dynamic Data 695

Chapter 18: Establishing Connections and Recordsets. 697

Data Source Basics ... 698
Understanding How Active Content Pages Work ... 701
Opening a Connection to a Data Source ... 703
Using data source names ... 705
ASP ... 707
ColdFusion ... 708
PHP ... 712
Specifying connection strings ... 712
DSN-less connections for ASP ... 712
OLE DB ... 714
PHP ... 715
Managing Connections ... 717
Extracting Recordsets ... 718
Building simple recordsets ... 718
Writing advanced SQL statements ... 721
Working with recordsets ... 725
Summary ... 727

Chapter 19: Making Data Dynamic 729

Working with Dynamic Text ... 729
Inserting dynamic text ... 729
Viewing dynamic data ... 731
Formatting Dynamic Data ... 733
Data formatting ... 734
Editing and creating new data formats ... 739
Making Images Dynamic ... 741
Integrating Flash and Other Dynamic Media ... 747
Summary ... 748

Chapter 20: Managing Data. 751

Displaying Data Conditionally ... 751
Repeating data ... 751
Showing and hiding page elements ... 756
Handling Record Navigation ... 758
Building record navigation links ... 758
Using Data objects for record navigation ... 760
Tracking record status ... 761
Summary ... 764

Chapter 21: Working with Dynamic Live View 765

Engaging Live View ... 766
How Live View works ... 766
Setting up for Live View ... 766
Entering and exiting Live View ... 768
Making changes in Live View ... 769

HTTP Request Settings 770
Getting the query string 770
Posting responses with HTTP Request Settings 772
Previewing an Application in the Browser 775
Using the Server Debug Panel with ColdFusion (Windows Only) 776
Summary 779

Chapter 22: Crafting Multi-Page Applications 781

Using the URL to Pass Parameters 781
Sending parameters 782
Receiving parameters 784
Filtering a detail page recordset in Simple mode 784
Filtering a detail page recordset in Advanced mode 786
Using a server behavior to filter a recordset 786
Automating Master-Detail Page production 787
Getting Values from a Form 791
Passing single values from a form 792
Passing multiple values from a form 793
Passing form and URL values to a related page 794
Establishing Dynamic Form Elements 797
Text fields 797
Checkboxes 798
Radio buttons 799
List/menus 800
Managing Data Sources Online 801
Inserting data 801
Inserting data manually 802
Inserting data with the Record Insertion Form 803
Updating data 804
Creating an update page 805
Using the Record Update Form object 806
Deleting data 807
Inserting Variables 808
Application and session variables 809
Request and other variables 809
Connecting to the Customer 812
Logging in existing customers 812
Restricting access 813
Helping users log out 816
Adding new customers 816
Summary 817

Chapter 23: Using Web Content Management Systems 819

Understanding Web Content Management Systems 819
Working with WordPress 821
Installing WordPress 823
Discovering dynamically related files 828
Customizing your WordPress site 830
Adjusting graphics in a WordPress site 833
Summary 835

Part V: Including Multimedia Elements 837

Chapter 24: Adobe Photoshop, Fireworks, and Bridge Integration 839

Bringing in Photoshop Images 841
- Inserting Photoshop files 841
- Copying and pasting from Photoshop 843
- Updating a Photoshop Smart Object 844

Integrating Fireworks 847
- Modifying a Fireworks image 847
- Editing an image in Fireworks 851
- Replacing an image placeholder using Fireworks 853

Applying Sprites 854

Inserting Rollovers 856
- Using Dreamweaver's behaviors 857
- Using Fireworks' code 859
- Modifying sliced images 862

Working with Bridge 863

Summary 865

Chapter 25: Inserting Flash Elements 867

Including SWF Files in Dreamweaver Projects 867

Designating SWF Attributes 870
- Setting Scale in Flash movies 871
- Additional parameters for Flash 872

Configuring MIME Types 872

Editing SWF Files from Within Dreamweaver 873

Adding Shockwave Files 874

Summary 876

Chapter 26: Adding Video to Your Web Page 877

The Flash Video Revolution 878
- Encoding video 878
- Progressive download versus streaming 879
- Inserting Flash video 880
  - Including a progressive download FLV file 881
  - Adding a streaming FLV file 882
- Publishing Flash video files 883
- Modifying Flash video parameters 884

Working with Video Clips 886
- Linking to video 887
- Embedding video 888

Playing Videos in Dreamweaver 888

Inserting QuickTime Movies 889

Integrating HTML5 Video Code 893

Summary 895

Chapter 27: Using Audio on Your Web Page 897

Linking to Audio Files 898

Embedding Sounds and Music 899

Playing Background Music....901
Targeting Specific Plugins....902
Windows Media Player audio....903
Using embed with ActiveX....905
Integrating Podcasts....905
Podcast XML feeds....906
Linking to podcasts and feeds....907
Coding an HTML5 Player for Audio....908
Summary....910

Part VI: Enhancing Productivity and Website Management 911

Chapter 28: Using Dreamweaver Templates....913

Understanding Templates....914
Creating Your Own Templates....915
Using Editable Regions....916
Marking existing content as editable....916
Inserting a new editable region....918
Creating links in templates....918
Recommended linking technique....918
Handling special template workflows....919
Locking an editable region....920
Adding Content to Template Documents....920
Making Attributes Editable....924
Setting Editable Attributes....926
Enabling Repeating Regions....928
Modifying a repeating region....929
Constructing a repeating table....930
Establishing Optional Regions....933
Combining editable and optional regions....936
Setting optional region properties....937
Evaluating template expressions....937
Template expression language and object model....938
Multiple-if template expressions....941
Template expression examples....941
Alternating row background colors....941
Automatic row numbering....943
Computing values in a table....944
Sequential navigation links....946
Nesting Templates....947
Working with Templates in the Assets Panel....949
Creating a blank template....951
Opening and deleting templates....951
Applying templates....952
Mapping inconsistent template regions....952
Updating Templates....954
Removing Template Markup....955
Deleting template markup individually....955

Removing template markup from an entire page 955
Exporting a site without template markup 956
Changing the Default Document 957
Editing Content in the Browser 957
Setting up InContext Editing templates 958
Adding an editable region 959
Repeating page sections 962
Summary 963

Chapter 29: Using Library Items and Server-Side Includes 965

Dreamweaver Library Items 966
Using the Library Assets Panel 967
Adding a Library item 968
Moving Library items to a new site 969
Inserting a Library item in your web page 969
Deleting an item from the Library 971
Renaming a Library item 972
Editing a Library Item 974
Updating Your Websites with Libraries 975
Applying Server-Side Includes 978
Adding server-side includes 979
Editing server-side includes 981
Summary 981

Chapter 30: Maximizing Cross-Browser Compatibility 983

Converting Pages in Dreamweaver 983
Validating Your Code 985
Setting W3C Validator preferences 986
Checking Your Page for Compatibility 988
Checking your pages 991
Excluding page elements from issue checking 992
Viewing and correcting issues 993
Using the results of the Browser Compatibility Check 994
Summary 996

Chapter 31: Building Websites with a Team 997

Following Check In/Check Out Procedures 998
Check In/Check Out overview 998
Enabling Check In/Check Out 1000
Checking files in and out 1001
Keeping Track with Design Notes 1003
Setting up for Design Notes 1003
Setting the status with Design Notes 1005
Creating custom Design Notes 1006
Viewing Design Notes 1006
Browsing File View Columns 1007
Generating Reports 1009
Outputting HTML reports 1012
Using Workflow reports 1012

Administering Adobe Contribute Sites ... 1014
Setting up Contribute compatibility ... 1015
Entering sitewide administrator settings ... 1017
Rolling back a Contribute page in Dreamweaver ... 1018
Communicating with WebDAV ... 1020
Version Control with Subversion ... 1021
Connecting to a Subversion server ... 1022
Managing files in the repository ... 1023
Viewing local and repository files ... 1024
Getting the latest version ... 1025
Committing files ... 1026
Getting latest versions ... 1026
Locking and unlocking files ... 1027
Managing revisions ... 1028
Resolving conflicts ... 1029
Summary ... 1029

Chapter 32: Integrating XML and XSLT ... 1031

Understanding XML ... 1031
Exporting XML ... 1033
Importing XML ... 1036
Styling with XSL ... 1037
Including XSLT fragments ... 1038
Binding XSL data to the page ... 1038
Repeating XSL data ... 1040
Filtering XSL data ... 1041
Showing XSL data conditionally ... 1043
Styling XSLT fragments ... 1045
Adding XSLT fragments to web pages ... 1045
Building full XSLT pages ... 1046
Client-side pages ... 1047
Server-side pages ... 1051
Summary ... 1052

Part VII: Extending Dreamweaver 1055

Chapter 33: Customizing Dreamweaver ... 1057

Adding New Commands ... 1058
Understanding Dreamweaver commands ... 1058
The Apply Source Formatting and Apply Source Formatting To Selection commands ... 1059
The Clean Up HTML and Clean Up XHTML commands ... 1059
Recording and replaying commands ... 1061
Scripting commands ... 1064
Managing Menus and Keyboard Shortcuts ... 1066
Handling History panel commands ... 1066
Using the Keyboard Shortcut editor ... 1067
Adjusting the menus.xml file ... 1070

Generic shortcuts 1070
Menubar definitions 1072
Building menu commands 1074
Working with Custom Tags 1075
Customizing Your Tag Libraries 1078
Editing tag libraries, tags, and attributes 1078
Creating and deleting tag libraries, tags, and attributes 1080
Importing a DTD or schema to create a new tag library 1081
Summary 1081

Chapter 34: Handling Server Behaviors 1083
Understanding Server Behaviors 1083
Applying and Managing Server Behaviors 1085
Inserting and removing server behaviors 1085
Editing the parameters 1085
Standard Server Behaviors 1086
Recordset (Query) 1087
Repeat Region 1088
Recordset Paging 1089
Move To Specific Record 1090
Show Region 1091
Go To Detail Page 1092
Go To Related Page (ASP only) 1093
Insert Record 1094
Update Record 1095
Delete Record 1096
User authentication 1097
Log In User 1097
Restrict Access To Page 1098
Log Out User 1099
Check New Username 1100
Dynamic elements 1101
Dynamic Text 1101
Dynamic List/Menu 1102
Dynamic Text Field 1103
Dynamic CheckBox 1104
Dynamic Radio Buttons 1105
Stored procedure/command/callable 1106
Installing Additional Server Behaviors 1108
Creating Custom Server Behaviors 1109
Summary 1113

Chapter 35: Creating Adobe AIR Applications 1115
About Adobe AIR 1115
Installing AIR into Dreamweaver 1117
Designing for AIR 1118
Packaging Your AIR Application 1122
Summary 1126

Appendix A: What's on the Website? 1129
Visiting the Book's Website 1129
Files and Programs on the Website 1129
Dreamweaver extensions 1130
Dreamweaver Techniques files... 1130
Dreamweaver CS6 Bible code examples 1130
Web resource directory... 1130
Troubleshooting 1131

Index. 1133

Introduction

What's in a name? In the case of Adobe's Dreamweaver, you find one of the most appropriate product names around. Web page design is a blend of art and craft; whether you're a deadline-driven professional or a vision-filled amateur, Dreamweaver provides an intuitive way to make your web visions a reality and excels at producing multifaceted web pages that bring content locked in a data store to the surface.

What's New in Dreamweaver CS6

To slightly stretch a metaphor, today's web design ball is clearly in the HTML and CSS court. And how has the Dreamweaver team reacted? With Dreamweaver CS6, they've taken the ball and run with it! The surge of mobile computing—complete with the increasing ubiquity of web-enabled phones and tablets—has placed a new, profound emphasis on the latest versions of core web technologies, HTML5 and CSS3, and supplanted the dominance of plugin-driven content for advanced features. Dreamweaver CS6 offers enhanced support for the foundation languages, new tools to build upon the foundation, and new workflows to take advantage of the updated toolset.

Modern CSS styling

The ever-quickening browser updates have brought a bounty of advanced CSS support. Now, web designers have an embarrassment of riches for their palette: shadows, gradients, rounded corners, web fonts, animated transitions, and much more. Dreamweaver CS6 includes baseline code hinting support for virtually all CSS3 properties, as well as easy-to-use interfaces for key ones, such as `border-radius`, `text-shadow`, and `box-shadow`. This latest version of Dreamweaver also makes it drop-dead simple to include web fonts in your sites. Last, and certainly not least, Dreamweaver CS6 provides a path to CSS-based animation through the new CSS Transitions panel and other user interface elements.

Enhanced CSS3 support

Web designers never had it so good. Thanks to CSS3 and the ever-widening support for advanced properties, the designer's tool chest is overflowing with new possibilities. Many visual elements, previously only applicable by a graphics program, can now be programmatically added to the page. You can, for example, add a nice drop shadow to highlight a boxed area with rounded corners with a few lines of code. Dreamweaver CS6 not only renders these cutting-edge effects in Live View but will help you write the code with the improved user interface elements you see in Figure I-1.

Because CSS3 support in browsers is rapidly evolving, designers need a way to make their pages as compatible as possible. Dreamweaver CS6 includes full code hinting capabilities for the full spectrum of vendor-specific properties, such as `-webkit-border-radius`. Just start typing with a dash and all the vendor options are at your fingertips.

FIGURE I-1

Take advantage of Dreamweaver's updated CSS3 support to create box shadows.

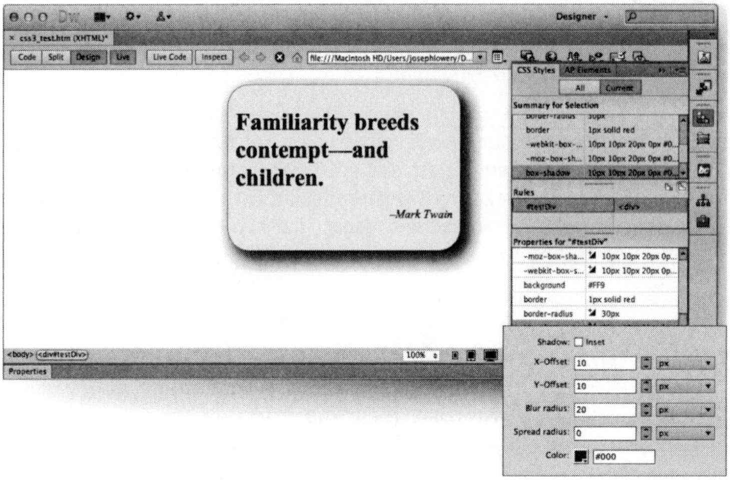

Web fonts support

This is near the top of my personal wish list for designing web pages: escape from Boring Font Hell. After being stuck with the same limited set of system fonts (you know them all too well: Arial, Helvetica, Times, Georgia, Verdana . . . yawn) from when the web was known importantly as the World Wide Web, the ability to use downloadable web fonts is just plain wonderful.

What's even better is that Dreamweaver has made it amazingly straightforward to use. All you need to do is to download a folder of web fonts in a range of formats, along with a style sheet to set them up using the `@font-face` statement, and you're good to go. Wait, I hear you saying—that doesn't sound easy at all! Ah, but it is, especially since Dreamweaver recognizes the exact same folder structure output by Font Squirrel (`http://www.fontsquirrel.com/`) and numerous other web font outlets. Simply download the font package and store the uncompressed files in your site's designated web font folder. Now you're ready to assign your new web font to any text selector, like the `<h1>` tag shown in Figure I-2, through any of Dreamweaver's standard CSS interfaces.

CSS3 transitions

While Adobe Flash is far from gone, its use is no longer mandatory to create simple animations. With CSS3's transition properties, you can easily rotate, grow, shrink, fade in, or fade out any HTML element. Admittedly the code, mostly due to the required presence of vendor-specific properties, can be a bit overwhelming at present. Happily, however, Dreamweaver CS6 brings point-and-click usability to the animator's metaphoric light table.

In Dreamweaver CS6's new CSS Transitions panel (see Figure I-3) and associated interfaces, you're given a number of ways to work. You can either set the same key values—such as duration of animation and how long it is in effect—for all properties you want to animate to achieve a consistent motion graphics approach or define different values for each property, should you prefer to mix it up.

FIGURE I-2

Web fonts keep text like "Win a Trip to Saturn" searchable and selectable while opening the floodgates of design potential.

FIGURE I-3

Create a new transition to animate any of the almost 50 different CSS properties with the New Transition dialog box.

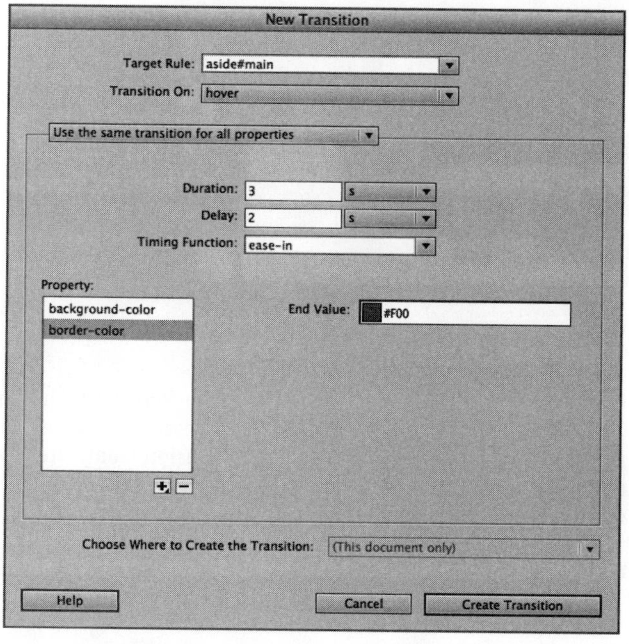

Responsive designs for multiple screens

Since mobile computing—by which I mean accessing the web by any wireless device—has really taken off, designers have been struggling with the increased challenge of creating sites that look their best on a variety of screen sizes. A number of techniques have emerged, the first of which uses media queries Dreamweaver embraced in version CS6.5, with the Multiscreen Preview dialog box. This method is great for folks who are retrofitting an existing desktop layout to work with tablets and phones. However, it's not so great if you're taking a "mobile first" approach and trying to adhere to the responsive web design philosophy, which has attracted a great many adherents.

To help designers hit the ground running with their responsive web designs, Dreamweaver CS6 includes the capability to create a fluid grid layout (see Figure I-4). The idea of this layout is to set up your page structure to align to a percentage-based grid so that small changes in screen size—such as going from an iPhone to an Android phone—are handled smoothly. You can easily resize and drag the fluid grid layout <div> tags to create the desired design. Different grid layouts—triggered by media queries—are possible for phone, tablet, and desktop screens. Dreamweaver CS6 also has handy window size icons on the Status bar now so you can quickly shift between the three major screen variants.

FIGURE I-4

Dreamweaver displays a background grid with flexible containers to help you develop a responsive layout.

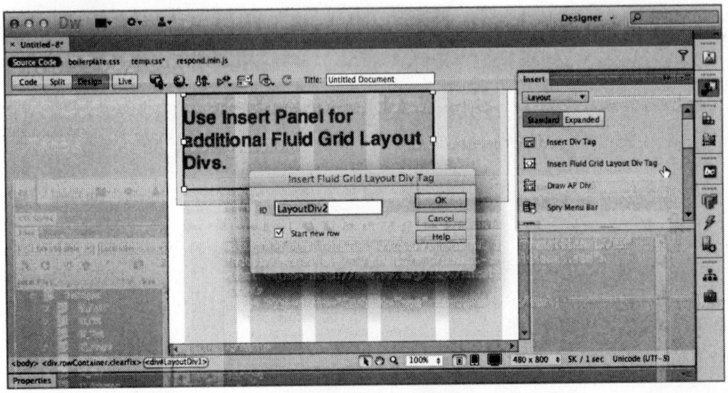

Developing mobile applications

Website designers have a whole new market to address: mobile applications. With the same tools used daily to create websites—HTML, CSS, and JavaScript—web professionals can expand their reach to one of the hottest growth areas going. On the mobile app design front, Dreamweaver CS6.5 started the ball rolling with its integration of jQuery Mobile objects, and Dreamweaver CS6 picks up speed with the enhanced design options brought by jQuery Mobile swatches. Adobe's acquisition of Nitobi, creators of PhoneGap, has allowed Dreamweaver to greatly expand and simplify its supported mobile app platforms with a direct connection to PhoneGap Build.

jQuery Mobile swatches

Anyone who's ever scratched the surface of the jQuery framework site knows that one of the coolest features there is the jQuery ThemeRoller (`http://jqueryui.com/themeroller`). Designers can play for hours with this visual tool as they create just the right look and feel for their site—and instantly download the CSS code for a custom, consistent theme palette. When jQuery Mobile was introduced, the framework for theming was built-in, but there were just five standard themes. Now, jQuery Mobile has its own ThemeRoller. Not surprisingly, given the fact that it was built with the assistance of Dreamweaver engineers, Dreamweaver CS6 offers a seamless integration with the new theming tool. Now, through the jQuery Mobile Swatches panel (see Figure I-5), Dreamweaver users can apply a new theme—custom-built in ThemeRoller—to their mobile apps.

FIGURE I-5

Apply a custom theme to your jQuery Mobile web app through the new jQuery Mobile Swatches panel.

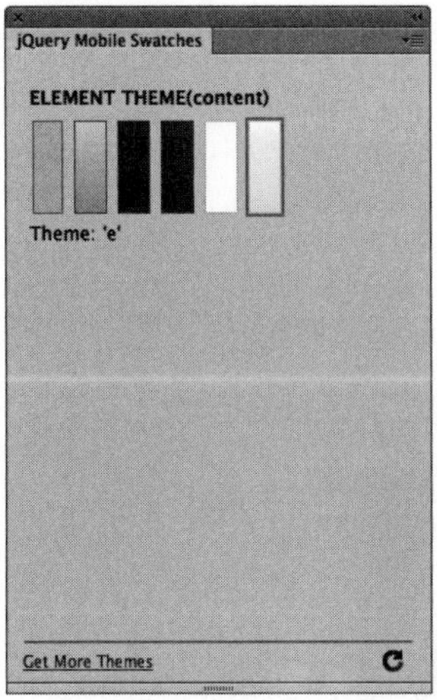

PhoneGap Build

The previous version of Dreamweaver lurched toward the creation of mobile apps by integrating PhoneGap support for iOS and Android devices. Unfortunately, the fast-moving world of mobile development often left Dreamweaver playing catch-up, which resulted in components that were difficult to install and incomplete at best. But sometimes daddy brings home the bacon. The previously-mentioned Adobe acquisition of Nitobi opened the door for much more extensive—and far easier—mobile app creation in Dreamweaver CS6.

Instead of the burdensome and prone-to-failure task of downloading and installing Android and iOS SDKs, Dreamweaver now connects directly with an online service, PhoneGap Build (see Figure I-6). With PhoneGap Build, you can directly upload your Dreamweaver mobile app project files, compile in the cloud, and download working apps for a wide range of mobile platforms, including Android, iOS, Windows 7, and Blackberry.

FIGURE I-6

Connect to the cloud-based service PhoneGap Build right from within Dreamweaver and output mobile apps for a variety of platforms.

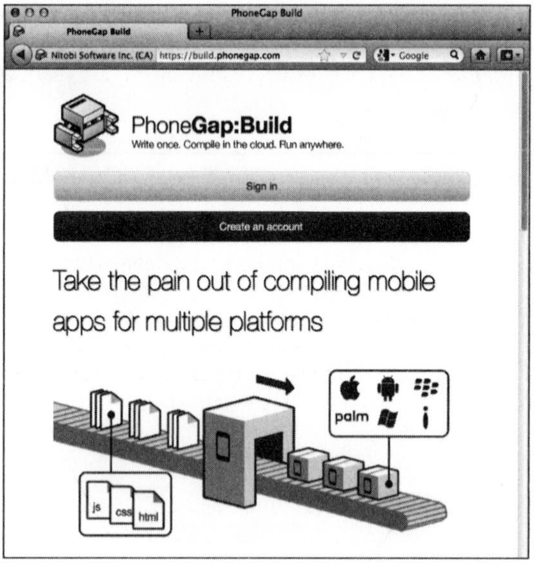

Improved Program Functionality

As I've pointed out before, Dreamweaver is a big program with a lot of moving parts—and sometimes those parts need a little love to perform at peak efficiency again. While everybody loves new whiz-bang features, the working web professional truly appreciates program enhancements that make his or her everyday life a little easier. In Dreamweaver CS6, the improvements impact a range of areas from the never-ending chore of uploading files to updating the basic user interface.

W3C validation

Validating your web pages is not only something your mother says you should do but actually good for you! Seriously, making sure your pages validate is a critical step in debugging and should be practiced at various stages of development. Dreamweaver CS6 just made that onerous chore simplicity itself by integrating W3C validation into the program. Now you can send any page—static or dynamic—to the official body of web standards, `http://www.w3.org/`, with a single command. You'll get back a full list of warnings and errors, if any are encountered, pointing directly to the offending line of code. Awesome!

FTP enhancements

Transferring files from one computer to another is a fact of life for web developers. It's such a critical task that Dreamweaver has included a built-in tool for handling file transfer protocol (FTP) since version 1. Unfortunately, Dreamweaver's FTP program has not been regarded as the most robust solution and is often criticized for relative slowness and a lack of features. Dreamweaver CS6 makes great strides in addressing those concerns by significantly ramping up the transfer speed, allowing for enhanced background processing, and increasing the transfer reporting. Now, when you move a group of files from your local to remote site (or vice versa), you have a much clearer idea of where you are in the process thanks to the greatly improved progress bar. The first time you push a site live with Dreamweaver CS6, it will be obvious that a great deal of effort has gone into upgrading the program's file transfer engine for this latest version.

User interface updates

Numerous aspects of Dreamweaver's user interface have been given a facelift for CS6, including a major overhaul for the Mac version. You'll notice a big change when you open the Manage Sites dialog box (see Figure I-7). The interface has been given a more modern look and feel in addition to the expanded functionality of working with Business Catalyst sites. New panels have been added to handle CSS transitions and jQuery Mobile swatches, and the Properties pane of the CSS Styles panel has been extended to make it easier to work with advanced CSS3 properties. In addition, there have been a good number of minor adjustments as well; perhaps the most visible is the integration of the Browser Navigation toolbar into the Document toolbar. Now, browser navigation elements become available when you switch to Live View.

FIGURE I-7

The new Manage Sites dialog box is sleeker, with more robust functionality.

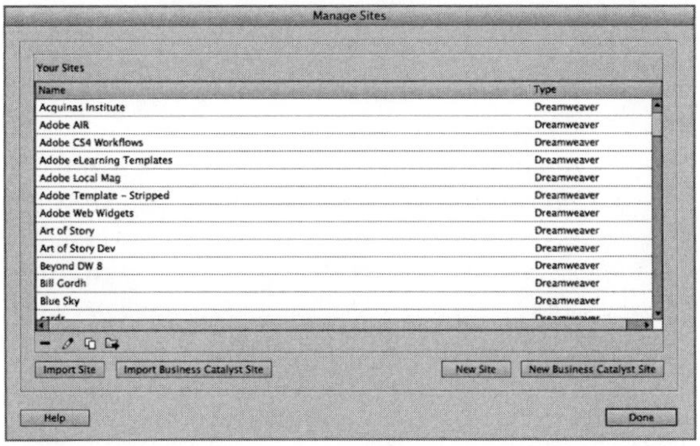

But Mac users will notice the biggest change from a user-interface perspective. The entire front-end of the program was re-coded from the ground up to take advantage of Mac OS updates. The option to apply an application frame is perhaps the most important addition on the Mac side. Designers now have the choice of working in the classic Mac style where the desktop and other programs are visible behind Dreamweaver or invoking Window ➪ Application Frame and setting up a neutral background to isolate their work.

Deeper Business Catalyst integration

Business Catalyst is, at its core, a web hosting business. However, it's a web host with a big difference: functionality. Once you set up your site on Business Catalyst, a huge range of possibilities opens up for you, including, but not limited to e-Commerce, e-mail marketing, visitor tracking and reporting, blogs, mobile device support, and social media integration. Adobe acquired Business Catalyst a few years ago, and Dreamweaver has slowly been increasing its connections to it. Dreamweaver CS6 takes the plunge and brings Business Catalyst to the forefront of its website creation, design, and maintenance capabilities.

You'll notice the tighter Business Catalyst integration the moment you install Dreamweaver CS6. The Business Catalyst panel is prominently displayed in virtually all workspaces, which display an invitation to learn more or sign in. Once you've logged in through the panel, you can import existing Business Catalyst sites or create new ones. Business Catalyst is now fully integrated right out of the box—you no longer have to download an extension to get started.

As noted in an earlier section, the Manage Sites dialog box now sports tools for working with Business Catalyst sites. Once you've opened such a site, the Business Catalyst panel offers a host of modules for drag-and-drop functionality, as shown in Figure I-8. Completed pages are easily put to the remote site—which is automatically set up for you when you create your Business Catalyst site. Additional changes can be made through the Business Catalyst portal or in Dreamweaver, depending on how you like to work.

FIGURE I-8

The Business Catalyst panel makes it easy to add advanced functionality by inserting any of the numerous modules.

The increased connectivity between Dreamweaver and Business Catalyst is ultimately a boon to average Dreamweaver users, making it possible for them to offer clients a greater range of website applications without having to dive into the code. And that's a win-win for everyone.

Who Should Read This Book

Dreamweaver attracts a wide range of web developers. Because it's the first web authoring tool that doesn't rewrite original code, veteran designers are drawn to using Dreamweaver as their first visual editor. Because it also automates complicated effects, beginning web designers are interested in Dreamweaver's power and performance. *Dreamweaver CS6 Bible* addresses the full spectrum of web professionals, providing basic information on HTML if you're just starting, as well as advanced tips and tricks for seasoned pros. Moreover, this book is a complete reference for everyone working with Dreamweaver on a daily basis.

How This Book Is Organized

Dreamweaver CS6 Bible can take you from raw beginner to full-fledged professional if read cover to cover. However, you're more likely to read each section as needed, taking the necessary information and coming back later. To facilitate this approach, *Dreamweaver CS6 Bible* is divided into seven major task-oriented parts. After you're familiar with Dreamweaver, feel free to skip around the book, using it as a reference guide as you increase your own knowledge base.

The early chapters present the basics, and all chapters contain clearly written steps for the tasks you need to perform. In most chapters, you encounter two special sections: Dreamweaver Quickstarts and Dreamweaver Techniques. A Dreamweaver Quickstart is just as it sounds: a few quick steps that show you how to achieve a targeted goal, such as creating a link. Dreamweaver Techniques are step-by-step instructions for accomplishing specific web designer tasks; taken together, the Dreamweaver Techniques constitute an entire how-to course. These step-by-step instructions are self-contained in each chapter, so you're free to explore them in any order you choose. You'll find all the practice files for working on the Techniques on the website, both as starting points and as completed files. Naturally, you can also use the Dreamweaver Techniques as stepping-stones for your own explorations into web page creation.

Part I: Laying the Groundwork in Dreamweaver CS6

Part I begins with an overview of Dreamweaver's philosophy and design. To get the most out of the program, you need to understand the key advantages it offers over other authoring programs and how Dreamweaver addresses the deficiencies of those programs. Part I takes you all the way to setting up your first site.

Part II: Designing and Crafting Basic Pages

Although Dreamweaver is partly a visual design tool, its roots derive from the language of the web: HTML. Part II gives you a solid foundation in the basics of HTML, even if you've never seen code. It also shows you how to get the most out of Dreamweaver's code environment with any language. Chapter 6 describes what you need to know about the overall structure of a web page, including best practices for coding with HTML5.

Reflecting the current emphasis in web design on Cascading Style Sheets, Chapter 5 lays the foundation to CSS. In this chapter, you learn the basics of CSS, as well as how to define and apply styles in Dreamweaver. Following the introduction to CSS, you learn the three fundamentals of static web pages: text, images, and links. In Chapters 7, 8, and 9, you explore how to completely incorporate these elements.

Part III: Adding Advanced Design Features

After you master the basics, you're ready to learn about some of Dreamweaver's true power tools in Part III. First up is one of the most important constructs of an HTML page: layout. Chapter 10 examines this brave new world of design, including fluid grid layouts. Chapter 11 offers an in-depth look at the capabilities of Dreamweaver behaviors. These bring a great deal of interactivity to page elements specifically and to your web page in general. Each standard behavior is covered in detail with step-by-step instructions.

Chapter 12 explores the various uses of tables—from a clear presentation of data to organizing entire web pages. Here you learn how to use Dreamweaver's visual table editing capabilities to resize and reshape your HTML tables quickly. Forms are an essential element in dynamic web page design, and you learn all about them in Chapter 13. Chapter 14 presents another fundamental HTML option: lists. You study the list in all its forms: numbered lists, bulleted lists, definition lists, nested lists, and more. Chapter 15 investigates the somewhat complex and outdated world of frames.

Chapter 16 takes the web to a whole new level of JavaScript functionality. With the introduction of the Spry framework, Adobe has made the sophisticated inner-workings of Ajax accessible to every web developer. This chapter explains what Ajax is and how Spry fits into the picture before diving into the wide range of Spry tools available in Dreamweaver CS6, including Spry Data, Spry Widgets, and Spry Effects. Chapter 17 broadens Dreamweaver's scope to incorporate other JavaScript frameworks such as jQuery, YUI, or MooTools, as well as working jQuery Mobile when building web apps for phones and tablets.

Part IV: Incorporating Dynamic Data

Chapter 18 begins an in-depth investigation of Dreamweaver's power to create dynamic web pages by describing how to set up your basic connections and recordsets. Chapter 19 explains how to insert text from a data source onto your web page and how to format it after it's incorporated. You also see how to relate other web page elements—such as images, Flash movies, and other media files—to a data source. Chapter 20 continues the exploration by delving into Dreamweaver's powerful Repeat Region server behavior, as well as discussing techniques for hiding and showing your data at will.

One of Dreamweaver's most useful features, the Live View, is examined extensively in Chapter 21, through the lens of application development. Chapter 22 enters the world of multipage applications and explains how variables and other data can be passed from one page to another. The final chapter in this part, Chapter 23, dives into the brave new world of content management systems with step-by-step instructions for setting up and integrating WordPress into your Dreamweaver workflow.

Part V: Including Multimedia Elements

In recent years, the web has moved from a relatively static display of text and simple images to a full-blown multimedia circus with streaming video, background music, and interactive animations. Part V contains the power tools for incorporating various media files into your website.

Graphics remain the key medium on the web today, and Adobe's graphics programs are the world leaders. Chapter 24 delves into methods for incorporating both Adobe Photoshop Smart objects and Adobe Fireworks graphics, as well as graphics management through Adobe Bridge. Special focus is given to the Dreamweaver-to-Photoshop and Dreamweaver-to-Fireworks communication links and how your web production efforts can benefit from it.

In addition to Dreamweaver, Adobe is perhaps best known for one other contribution to web multimedia: Adobe Flash. Chapter 25 explores the possibilities offered by incorporating Flash and Shockwave movies into Dreamweaver-designed web pages and includes everything you need to know about configuring MIME types.

Chapter 26 covers digital video in its many forms—Flash video, downloadable AVI files, streaming RealVideo displays, panoramic QuickTime movies, and the newest, hottest media: the HTML5 `<video>` tag. Chapter 27 focuses on digital audio, with coverage of standard MP3, WAV, and MIDI sound files, as well as the newer playback method via the HTML5 `<audio>` tag.

Part VI: Enhancing Productivity and Website Management

Although web page design gets all the glory, website management pays the bills. In Part VI, you see how Dreamweaver makes this essential part of any webmaster's day easier to handle. Chapter 28 starts off with a look at the use of Dreamweaver Templates and how they can speed up production while ensuring a unified look and feel across your website, along with the in-browser site modifications possible with the InContext Editing service. Chapter 29 covers the Library, which can significantly reduce any webmaster's workload by providing reusable—and updatable—page elements. Chapter 30 describes Dreamweaver's built-in tools for maintaining cross- and backward-browser compatibility, including the essential Browser Compatibility Check, which reviews your page for rendering issues in a number of modern browsers.

Individual web developers have often been stymied when attempting to work in a team development environment. File locking was all too easily subverted, allowing team members to inadvertently overwrite revisions. Site reports were difficult to compile, and, worst of all, version control was nonexistent. Dreamweaver CS6 tackles all these concerns while laying a foundation for future connectivity. In Chapter 31, you see how you can tie Dreamweaver into an existing Subversion or WebDAV version control system. Other features covered include custom file view columns and enhanced Design Notes accessibility.

I can't think of any technology on the web that has gained widespread acceptance as quickly as XML. In a nutshell, XML (short for Extensible Markup Language) enables you to create your own custom tags that make the most sense for your business or profession. Chapter 32 shows you how to apply this broad-reaching technology in Dreamweaver, with a special section on Dreamweaver CS6's XML/XSLT technology.

Part VII: Extending Dreamweaver

Dreamweaver is a program with immense capabilities for expanding its own power. Chapter 33 explores the exciting world of Dreamweaver extensibility, with complete coverage of using and building commands, as well as custom tags, translators, floaters, and C-level extensions. With its own set of objects and behaviors, Dreamweaver complements HTML's extensibility. Finally, Chapter 34 examines server behaviors, describing every standard one in detail and then exploring the use of the Server Behavior Builder, Dreamweaver's tool for creating custom server behaviors. Finally, in Chapter 35, you can see how Dreamweaver is on the cutting edge of producing Adobe AIR applications.

Appendix

Appendix A describes the contents of *Dreamweaver CS6 Bible*'s companion website, `http://www.wiley.com/go/dreamweavercs6bible`. Throughout this book, whenever you encounter a reference to files or programs on the website, please check this appendix for more information.

Conventions and features

There are many different organizational and typographical features throughout this book designed to help you get the most of the information.

Windows and Macintosh conventions

Because Dreamweaver CS6 Bible is a cross-platform book, it gives instructions for both Windows and Macintosh users when keystrokes for a particular task differ. Throughout this book, the Windows keystrokes are given first; the Mac's are given second in parentheses, as follows:

> To undo an action, press Ctrl+Z (Command+Z).

The first action instructs Windows users to press the Ctrl and Z keys in combination, and the second action (in parentheses) instructs Macintosh users to press the Command and Z keys together.

Key combinations

When you are instructed to press two or more keys simultaneously, each key in the combination is separated by a plus sign. For example:

> Ctrl+Alt+T (Command+Option+T)

The preceding tells you to press the three listed keys for your system at the same time. You can also hold down one or more keys and then press the final key. Release all the keys at the same time.

Mouse instructions

When instructed to click an item, move the mouse pointer to the specified item and click the mouse button once. Windows users use the left mouse button unless otherwise instructed. Double-clicking means clicking the mouse button twice in rapid succession.

When instructed to select or choose an item, you can click it once as previously described. If you are selecting text or multiple objects, click the mouse button once, press Shift, and then move the mouse to a new location and click again. The color of the selected item or items inverts to indicate the selection. To clear the selection, click once anywhere on the web page.

When instructed to drag an item, like a sizing handle surrounding a selected image, click-and-hold the mouse button and then move it across the screen.

Menu commands

When instructed to select a command from a menu, you see the menu and the command separated by an arrow symbol. For example, when instructed to execute the Open command from the File menu, you see the notation File ➪ Open. Some menus use submenus, in which case you see an arrow for each submenu, as follows: Insert ➪ Form Object ➪ Text Field.

Typographical conventions

I use *italic* type for new terms and for emphasis and **boldface** type for text that you need to type directly from the computer keyboard.

Code

A special typeface indicates HTML or other code, as demonstrated in the following example:

```
<html>
<head>
<title>Untitled Document</title>
</head>
<body bgcolor="#FFFFFF">
</body>
</html>
```

This code font is also used within paragraphs to designate HTML tags, attributes, and values such as `<body>`, `bgcolor`, and `#FFFFFF`. All HTML tags are presented in lowercase, as written by Dreamweaver, although browsers are not generally case-sensitive in terms of HTML.

Dreamweaver Quickstarts

Located right at the start of many chapters, Dreamweaver Quickstarts give you just the details you need to accomplish common web design tasks. A Dreamweaver Quickstart is great for folks who are familiar with a given web element such as tables or lists and want to know how to use it in Dreamweaver.

Dreamweaver Techniques

A Dreamweaver Technique section provides the steps you need to try out a specific Dreamweaver task. An interactive simulation of each technique is included in download material on this book's website.

Tips, Notes, and Cautions

Whenever I want to bring something important to your attention, the information will appear in a Tip, Note, or Caution.

TIP

Tips generally are used to provide information that can make your work easier—special shortcuts or methods for doing something easier than the norm.

NOTE

Notes provide additional, ancillary information that is helpful, but somewhat outside of the current presentation of information.

CAUTION

This information is important and is set off in a separate paragraph with a special icon. Cautions provide information about things to watch out for, whether simply inconvenient or potentially hazardous to your data or systems.

Cross-references point you to other places in the book that have additional information relative to the current topic.

Minimum Requirements

Dreamweaver CS6 Bible includes coverage of Dreamweaver CS6. Written to be platform-independent, this book covers both Macintosh and Windows versions of Dreamweaver CS6.

Macintosh

Adobe recommends the following minimum requirements for running Dreamweaver on a Macintosh:

- Multicore Intel processor
- Mac OS 10.5.8 – 10.7.*x*
- 512MB of available RAM
- 1.8GB of available disk space
- 16-bit video card capable of 1280 × 800 resolution
- DVD-ROM drive
- Broadband Internet connection required for online services and to validate Subscription Edition (if applicable) on an ongoing basis

Windows

Adobe recommends the following minimum requirements for running Dreamweaver on a Windows system:

- Intel Pentium 4 or AMD Athlon 64 processor
- Windows XP SP3 or Vista Home Premium, Business, Enterprise, Ultimate SP1, or Windows 7
- 512MB of available RAM
- 1GB of available disk space
- 16-bit video card capable of 1280 × 800 resolution
- DVD-ROM drive
- Broadband Internet connection required for online services and to validate Subscription Edition (if applicable) on an ongoing basis

These are the minimum requirements. As with all graphics-based design tools, more capability is definitely better for using Dreamweaver, especially in terms of memory and processor speed.

Further Information

You can find more help for specific problems and questions by investigating several websites. Adobe's own Dreamweaver website is the best place to start:

`http://www.adobe.com/products/dreamweaver/`

I heartily recommend that you visit and participate in the official Dreamweaver forums:

`http://forums.adobe.com/community/dreamweaver`

You can also e-mail me at `jlowery@idest.com`.

I can't promise instantaneous turnaround, but I answer all my mail to the best of my ability.

Part I

Laying the Groundwork in Dreamweaver

IN THIS PART

Chapter 1
Introducing Dreamweaver CS6

Chapter 2
Touring Dreamweaver

Chapter 3
Setting Your Preferences

Chapter 4
Setting Up Sites and Servers

CHAPTER 1

Introducing Dreamweaver CS6

IN THIS CHAPTER

Understanding the Dreamweaver philosophy

How Dreamweaver is designed

Connecting to data in Dreamweaver

Accessing next-generation features

Automating web application production

Maintaining your website with Dreamweaver

Adobe Dreamweaver CS6 is a professional website development program for creating both standard web pages and dynamic applications. In its latest incarnation, Dreamweaver has rededicated itself to professional coding practices and web standards, while pushing its capabilities into mobile web development. In addition to creating standards-based HTML pages with enhanced Cascading Style Sheets (CSS) rendering, it is also suitable for coding a wide range of web formats, including JavaScript, XML, and ActionScript—even those incorporating Web 2.0 methods, such as Ajax, and responsive web design. Among its many other distinctions, it was the first web authoring tool capable of addressing multiple server models. This feature makes it equally easy for developers of ASP, ColdFusion, or PHP to use it.

Dreamweaver is truly a tool designed by web developers for web developers. Designed from the ground up to work the way professional web designers do, it speeds site construction and streamlines site maintenance. Because web designers rarely work in a vacuum, Dreamweaver integrates smoothly with the leading media programs: Adobe Photoshop, Adobe Fireworks, and Adobe Flash. This chapter describes the philosophical underpinnings of the program and provides a sense of how Dreamweaver blends traditional HTML and other web languages with cutting-edge server-side techniques and CSS design standards. You also learn some of the advanced features that it offers to help you manage a website.

The Dynamic World of Dreamweaver

Dreamweaver is a program very much rooted in the real world. Web applications are developed for a variety of different server models, and Dreamweaver writes code for the most widely used ones. Because the real world is also a changing world, its extensible architecture opens the door for custom or third-party server models as well. The current version, for example, provides new techniques for working with content management systems such as WordPress.

Moreover, Dreamweaver recognizes the real-world problem of incompatible browser commands and addresses that by producing code that is compatible across browsers. It includes browser-specific HTML validation so that you can see how your existing or new code works in a particular browser. Even better, Dreamweaver checks your page for common rendering problems and provides immediate solutions and in-depth discussion via a community-developed resource, the CSS Advisor mini-site on Adobe.com (`http://www.adobe.com/go/cssadvisor`).

Dreamweaver CS6 extends this real-world approach to the workplace. Dreamweaver's CSS rendering is top of the line and lets you design with web standards for multiple screens like no other program. Live View incorporates an actual browser engine, WebKit (the rendering engine powering Safari, iOS, Android, and Google Chrome), to render pages with complete fidelity. The advanced Design view makes it possible to quickly structure whole pages during the production stage, while maintaining backward compatibility with browsers when the pages are published. Features such as the Assets panel streamline the production and maintenance process on large websites. Dreamweaver's Commands capability enables web designers to automate their most difficult web creations, and its Server Behavior Builder enables them to easily insert frequently used custom code.

Designing for multiple screens

For today's world, where more and more devices are Internet-ready, Dreamweaver has developed a robust multiple-screen framework for creating responsive websites. The modern web designer needs to create sites that work for desktops but also for tablets and phones. Dreamweaver CS6 offers a new way of building a structure for flexible websites with the Fluid Grid Layout feature, shown in Figure 1-1.

FIGURE 1-1

Get a jump start on building your web pages for desktop, tablet, and phone with Dreamweaver's Fluid Grid Layout feature.

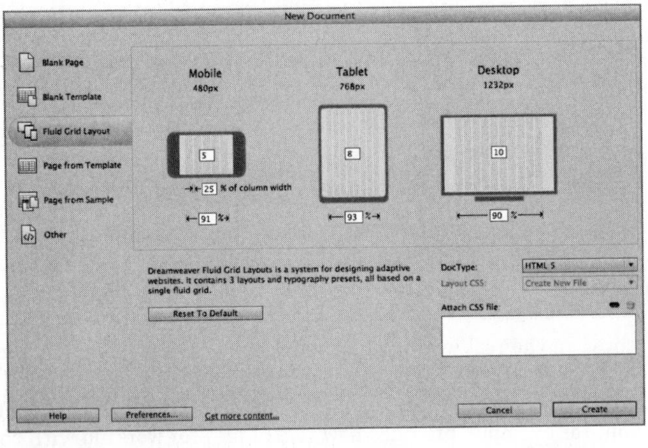

Once the fluid grid layout is created, the site design changes according to the screen on which it is viewed. You can use Dreamweaver's Multiscreen Preview to see up to three designs simultaneously or switch quickly from one device size to another with the convenient Window Size option.

Connecting to the world's data

Connectivity is more than a buzzword in Dreamweaver; it's an underlying concept. Moreover, Dreamweaver makes it possible to connect to any data source supported by the most widely used application servers: ASP, ColdFusion, PHP, and even XML. A special set of features is available for transforming XML data into a browser-ready format using Extensible Stylesheet Transformation (XSLT) technology. The Spry toolset takes advantage of Adobe's market-leading work in the Ajax (Asynchronous JavaScript and XML) workspace and the advanced Spry Data Set feature opens the door to incorporating data in any structured HTML format, such as tables, lists, or divs. Dreamweaver offers a choice of languages for a number of application servers, and a collection of expertly designed CSS-based layouts.

Dreamweaver accesses standard recordsets—subsets of a database—as well as more sophisticated data sources, such as session or application variables and stored procedures. Through their implementation of cookies and server-side code, web applications designed in Dreamweaver can track visitors or deny them entrance.

With Dreamweaver's Live View Navigation facility, you can navigate entire sites on the web and inspect their page designs right from within Dreamweaver. Open up Code view and you can even get an inside peek into how they are constructed.

You also find support in Dreamweaver for high-end technologies such as web services and ColdFusion components. Dreamweaver enables you to examine elements of all technologies so that coders can quickly grasp the syntax, methods, and functions required.

True page representation

One of Dreamweaver's truly innovative features integrates the actual data requested with the web page—while still in the design phase. The Live View mode uses the same rendering engine found in many of today's browsers, for both the desktop and mobile devices, so you can work with a high-fidelity page rendition. If you have a Testing server defined, Live View sends the page-in-process to the application server to depict records from the data source within the page, as shown in Figure 1-2. You can alter the dynamic data's formatting and see those changes instantly applied. Live View shortens the work cycle by showing the designer exactly what the user will see. In addition, the page can be viewed under different conditions through the Live View Settings feature.

Integrated visual and text editors

In the early days of the World Wide Web, most developers hand-coded their web pages using simple text editors such as Notepad and SimpleText. The second generation of web authoring tools brought visual design, or WYSIWYG (what you see is what you get), editors to market. What these products furnished in ease of layout, they lacked in completeness of code. Professional web developers were required to hand-code their web pages, even with the most sophisticated WYSIWYG editor.

Dreamweaver acknowledges this reality and has integrated a real-world browser engine in Live View, as well as a superb visual editor with its browser-like Design view. You can work graphically in Design view or programmatically in Code view. You even have the option of a split-screen view, which shows Design view and Code view simultaneously, either horizontally or vertically as shown in Figure 1-3. Any change made in the Design view is reflected in the Code view and vice versa. If you prefer to work with a code editor you're more familiar with, Dreamweaver enables you to work with any text editor. Whichever route you choose, Dreamweaver enables a natural, dynamic flow between the visual editors and the code editors.

FIGURE 1-2

When in Live View, you can style the web page to best display the actual data used.

FIGURE 1-3

Dreamweaver enables you to work with a visual WYSIWYG editor and a code editor simultaneously, side by side.

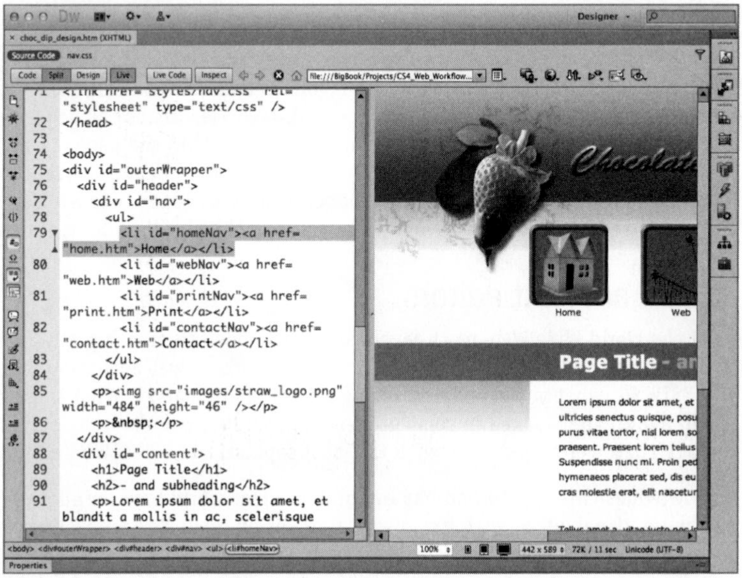

Dreamweaver further tightens the integration between the visual design and the underlying code with the Quick Tag Editor. Web designers frequently adjust the HTML code minutely—changing an attribute here or adding a single tag there. The Quick Tag Editor, which appears as a small pop-up window in Design or Code view, makes these code tweaks quick and easy.

World-class code editing

Coding is integrally tied to web page development, and Dreamweaver's coding environment is second to none. If you're hand-coding, you'll appreciate the Code Hints (see Figure 1-4), code collapse, and code completion features that Dreamweaver offers. Many of these elements have been encapsulated into a Coding toolbar displayed along the side of Code view. Not only do all these features speed development of HTML pages, but Dreamweaver's underlying Tag Libraries also extend their use to the full range of other code formats such as JavaScript, ActionScript, and XML. Dreamweaver also supports imported JavaScript frameworks such as jQuery or Prototype with immediately available code hinting.

FIGURE 1-4

Code Hints speed hand-coding by displaying all the attributes available for a specific tag, including color.

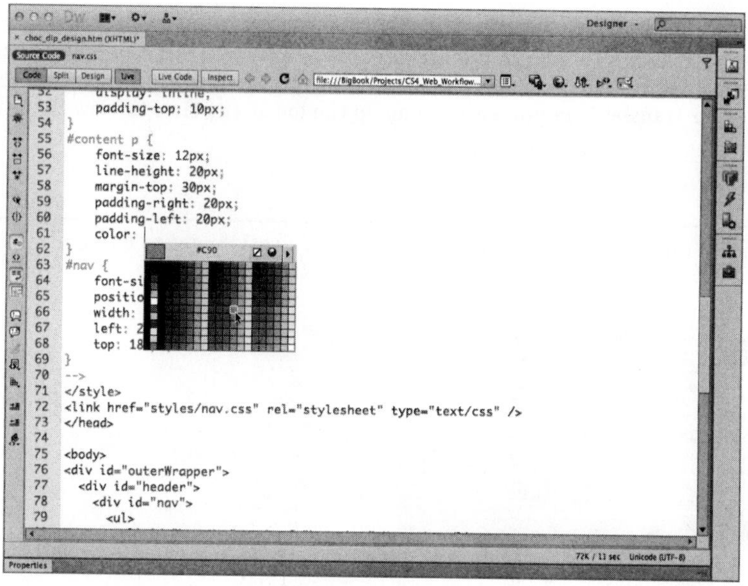

Dreamweaver's Code view is easy on the eyes as well with syntax coloring that can be turned off and on at will. To get around the page quickly, use either the standard line-numbering facility or the advanced Code Navigation feature; Code Navigation lists all the functions found on a page and instantly jumps to that code when a function is selected.

Veterans and novices alike find Dreamweaver's Tag Chooser and Tag inspector indispensable. As the name implies, the Tag Chooser enables the coder to select a tag from a full list of tags in the various web markup languages including HTML, CFML, PHP, ASP, and more.

The Tag inspector gives a complete overview of all the aspects of a selected tag. Not only do you get to see a full array of all the associated properties—far more than could ever fit in the Property inspector—but you can also modify their values in place. Any applied JavaScript behaviors are also displayed in the Tag inspector. Perhaps the most innovative feature of this inspector is a CSS-related one, which displays any style impacting on a tag with completely modifiable properties and values. Select a CSS style and the Tag inspector becomes the Rule inspector for quick and easy CSS editing.

Code is far more than just a series of individual tags, of course. Dreamweaver's Snippets panel stores the most commonly used sections of code just a drag-and-drop away. Dreamweaver comes with many snippets ready to use—and gives you a way to add your own at any time.

Website maintenance tools

Dreamweaver's creators also understand that creating a site is only a part of the webmaster's job. Maintaining the website can be an ongoing, time-consuming chore. Dreamweaver simplifies the job with a group of site management tools, including a library of repeating elements and a file-locking capability for easy team updates.

Dreamweaver's built-in FTP transfer engine is quite robust and now better fits the designer's workflow with its capability to work in the background, as shown in Figure 1-5. Designers are now free to begin a large publishing operation and return to Dreamweaver to continue crafting pages while the FTP transfer is in process or bring up the log at any time to view the details.

FIGURE 1-5

Start to upload an entire site and get back to work right away, thanks to FTP background processing.

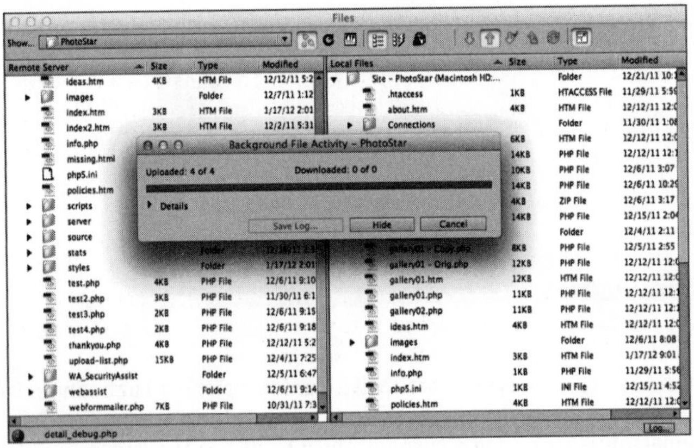

Overall in Dreamweaver, website maintenance is easier than ever. Links are updated automatically or, if a file moves from one directory to another, are under user control. Moreover, not only can you access a library of repeating elements to be inserted in the page, but you can also define templates to control the entire look and feel of a website—and modify a single template to update all the pages sitewide.

Team-oriented site building

Dreamweaver CS6 supports an industry-standard source control system—WebDAV—and a widely accepted version control system, Subversion. More important, Adobe has developed the source-control solution as a system architecture, enabling other third-party content management or version control developers to use Dreamweaver as their front end.

The Subversion version control system is more robust than the standard check in/check out system and allows multiple developers to work on the same code base safely. After connecting to the Subversion (or SVN) server, the repository of files is presented in the Files panel. Dreamweaver makes it easy to get files from and commit files to the repository. If two team members attempt to commit the same file and there are differences, the file is locked until the conflict is resolved. With Subversion support, you can easily review previous versions of files.

ColdFusion developers have long enjoyed the benefits of Remote Development Services (RDS)—and RDS connectivity is available in Dreamweaver. Through RDS, teams of developers can work on the same site stored on a remote server. Moreover, you can connect directly to an RDS server without creating a site.

Extensible architecture also underlies Dreamweaver's site reporting facility. Dreamweaver ships with the capability to generate reports on usability issues (such as missing Alt text) or workflow concerns (such as who has what files checked out). Users can also develop custom reports on a project-by-project basis.

The Dreamweaver Interface

When creating a web page, webmasters do two things repeatedly: They insert an element—whether text, image, or AP element—and then they modify it. Dreamweaver excels at such web page creation. The Dreamweaver workspace combines a series of windows, panels, and inspectors to make the process as fluid as possible, thereby speeding up the web designer's work.

Easy text entry

Although much of the web's glitz comes from multimedia elements such as images and sound, web pages are primarily a text-based medium. Dreamweaver recognizes this and makes the text cursor the default tool. To add text, just click in Dreamweaver's main workspace—the Document window—and start typing. The Property inspector even enables you to change characteristics of the text, such as the size, font, position, or color by assigning a Cascading Style Sheets (CSS) rule (see Figure 1-6). Dreamweaver even helps you by creating a CSS rule if none has been previously assigned or modifying the properties if one has.

FIGURE 1-6

Use the Text Property inspector to change the format of the selected text with CSS.

Drag-and-drop data fields

It's one thing to make a connection to a data source; it's quite another to actually insert the dynamic data in the proper place on the web page. Dreamweaver makes drag-and-drop easy with the Bindings panel. All the available data sources for a page are displayed in an expandable tree outline in the Bindings panel, as shown in Figure 1-7. You can insert an instance of any dynamic field displayed in the panel onto the page by either dropping it into place or clicking the Insert button.

One-stop object modification

You can select web page elements other than text from the Insert panel. Adding a picture to a web page is as easy as clicking the Image icon from the Insert panel. Dreamweaver asks you to select the file for the image, and your image appears at your current cursor position. After your graphic is onscreen, selecting it brings up the appropriate Property inspector to enable you to make modifications. The same technique works for all inserted elements—from `<div>` tags to Shockwave movies.

Accessing and managing resources

One standout addition to Dreamweaver's interface is the Assets panel, shown in Figure 1-8. The Assets panel gathers all the various elements used in an individual site: images, background and text colors, external URLs, included scripts, FLV (Flash video), SWF (Flash movies), and QuickTime media, as well as Dreamweaver templates and library items. Resizable thumbnails of graphics and media are displayed in the preview pane of the Assets panel—you can even play Flash, Shockwave, and QuickTime elements in preview before dragging them onto the page. Moreover, often-used resources can be listed in a Favorites category, distinguishing them from the rest of the assets found in the site.

FIGURE 1-7

Drag any field from the Bindings panel onto a selected placeholder phrase to quickly turn a static page into a dynamic one.

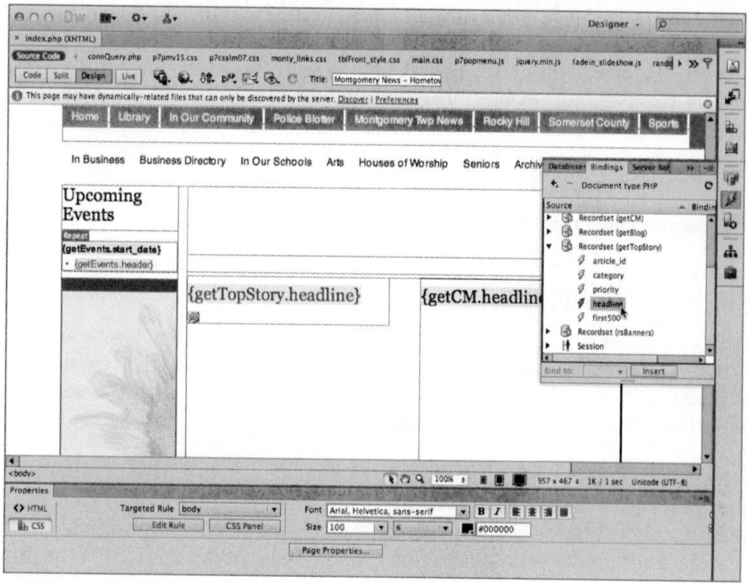

FIGURE 1-8

You can preview an image with the Assets panel before placing it on the Dreamweaver page.

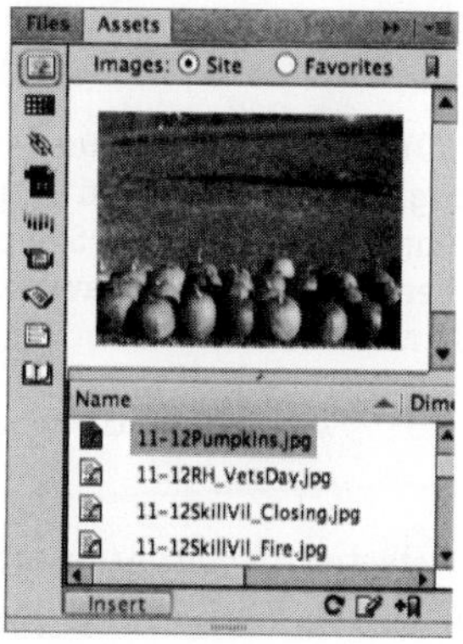

Complete custom environment

Dreamweaver enables you to customize your workspace to suit yourself. Much of Dreamweaver's power derives from the various windows, panels, and inspectors, all of which are movable. Just drag them wherever you want them onscreen or keep them docked to the side. You can even iconify them to maximize your screen real estate. Want to see your page by itself? You can hide all windows at the touch of a function button; press it again, and your controls are revealed. Got your working environment just the way you like it? Create a custom workspace and reset it at any time with a simple menu selection from the Workspace Switcher.

Dreamweaver's customization capabilities extend even further. If you find that you are repeatedly inserting something, such as a QuickTime video or WAV sound file, you can add that element to your Insert panel. Dreamweaver even enables you to add a specific element—a Home button, for example—to the Insert panel. In fact, you can add entire categories of objects if you like. Moreover, Dreamweaver CS6 exposes the entire menu structure for customization—not only can you change keyboard shortcuts, you can also add custom menus.

For more information about customizing your Insert panel, see Chapter 33.

Managing keyboard shortcuts

Keyboard shortcuts are great in theory: Just press a key combination to activate an essential feature. Unfortunately, in reality, there are too many essential features, too few single-purpose keys on the keyboard, and, most important, too few brain cells to retain all the widely varied keyboard combinations that the working designer must master.

Adobe has taken steps to ease keyboard-shortcut overload across its entire product line, and Dreamweaver is no exception. Dreamweaver offers a Keyboard Shortcut Editor that enables you to both standardize and customize the key combinations used in the program. Choose from the Dreamweaver standard set or use sets taken from BBEdit, Dreamweaver MX 2004, or HomeSite.

If you're a ColdFusion Studio user switching to Dreamweaver, you'll really appreciate the capability to add keyboard shortcuts to snippets. You can even select a set from an entirely different program such as HomeSite or BBEdit. Best of all, any keyboard shortcut can be personalized to represent a combination that's easy for you to remember.

Simple selection process

As with most modern layout programs, to modify anything in Dreamweaver, you must select it first. The usual process to do this is to click an object to highlight it or to click and drag over a block of text to select it. Dreamweaver adds another selection option with the Tag Selector feature. Click anywhere on a web page under construction and then look at Dreamweaver's status bar. The applicable tags appear on the left side of the status bar.

In the example in Figure 1-9, the Tag Selector shows `<body> <div#wrapper> <div#content> <div.categoryImage><p><a><img>`.

Click one of these tags, and the corresponding elements are selected on your page, ready for modification. The Tag Selector is a terrific time-saver; throughout this book, I point out how you can use it in various circumstances.

FIGURE 1-9

Choosing a tag (a div tag in this example) in Dreamweaver's Tag Selector is a quick and easy way to highlight a particular section of your web page.

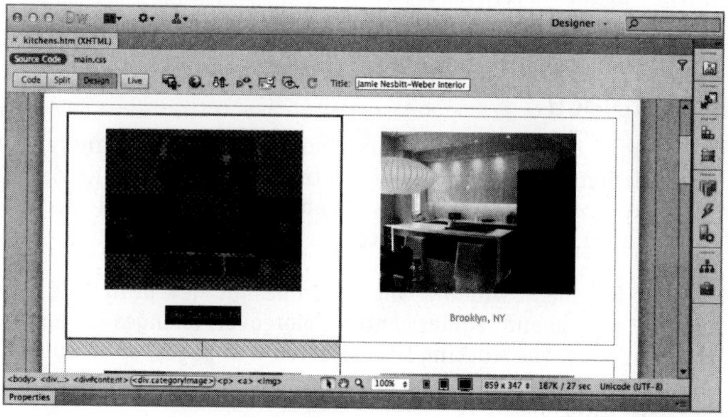

If you're working in Code view, your selection options increase significantly. With a click of the Select Parent button on the Coding toolbar, you can easily highlight the parent tag of the current selection. Click again to select the next parent. There are also options for simultaneously selecting and collapsing code sections.

Enhanced layout options

Dreamweaver works much more like a desktop publishing program than do many other visual HTML editors. Today's browser capabilities permit images and text to be placed in specific locations on the web page—a concept known as *absolute positioning*. To enable you to take full advantage of this power, Dreamweaver includes guides, rulers, and grids. Both vertical and horizontal guides are supported. You can specify the type of measurement to be used (inches, pixels, or centimeters), as well as the spacing and appearance of the grid lines. You can even have objects snap to the guides or grid for easy alignment.

The capability to magnify all or any portion of the page is available, complementing Dreamweaver's other layout tools. Choose from a select set of magnifications from a menu or keyboard shortcut or use the Zoom tool to magnify a desired area. You can also opt to view the full page or home in on any selected object.

To find out more about absolute positioning, guides, and grids, see Chapter 10.

Plugin media preview

For a browser to display anything beyond standard format graphics, a plugin is generally required. Plugins extend the capability of most browsers to show animations, play music, or even explore 3D worlds. Dreamweaver was one of the first web authoring tools to enable you to design your web page with an active plugin playing the extended file; with all other systems, you have to preview your page in a browser to see the active content.

The active content feature in Dreamweaver enables the playback of plugins such as Adobe Flash, Shockwave, and others. However, this feature extends beyond that. Many web pages are coded with server-side includes, which traditionally require the page to be viewed through a web server. Dreamweaver translates much of the server-side information so that the entire page—server-side includes and all—can be viewed in its entirety at design time.

Extended find and replace

The web is a fluid medium. Pages are constantly in flux, and because changes are relatively easy to effect, corrections and additions are the norm. Quite often, a web designer needs to update or alter an existing page—or series of pages. Dreamweaver's enhanced Find and Replace feature is a real power tool when it comes to making modifications.

Find and Replace works in the Document window, whether in Design view or in Code view, as well as in the Code inspector to alter code and regular content. Moreover, changes are applicable to a selected section, the current page, the working site, selected web pages, or an entire folder of pages, regardless of the number. Complex Find and Replace queries can be stored and retrieved later to further automate your work.

Up-to-Date Code Standards

Most web pages are created in HyperText Markup Language (HTML). This programming language—really a series of tags that modify a text file—is standardized by an organization known as the World Wide Web Consortium, or W3C (`http://www.w3.org`). Each new release of HTML incorporates an enhanced set of commands and features. All browsers in use today recognize the current version, HTML 4. Dreamweaver writes clear, easy-to-follow, real-world, browser-compatible HTML version 4.01 code whenever you insert or modify an element in the visual editor. Dreamweaver also includes the ability to create pages with an HTML 5 doctype, although that standard has, as of this writing, not been finalized.

If you're working in Extensible HyperText Markup Language (XHTML), Dreamweaver has you covered as well, with a number of tools. When coding from the ground up, you can set any page type—static or dynamic—to be XHTML-compliant. In fact, the default page type is today's recognized standard, XHTML 1.0 Transitional. If you need to bring legacy pages into compliance, Dreamweaver converts an existing page from HTML to XHTML with one operation.

Additionally, Dreamweaver includes complete Unicode support. Unicode is an encoding standard that enables web browsers to display characters from almost any language worldwide. Dreamweaver displays Unicode properly at design time and runtime.

Cutting-edge CSS support

Browser support for Cascading Style Sheets (CSS) is now solid across the board, and Dreamweaver has greatly enhanced its own support in response. In addition to enhanced rendering of advanced CSS effects such as @font-face and 2-D transitions, Dreamweaver has made it far simpler to apply CSS from the ground up.

Dreamweaver offers a wide spectrum of layout starting points—all professionally crafted with standards-based CSS. Choose a variety of layout designs: fixed, which stay the same width regardless, or liquid, which flow with the browser window size. The CSS used in each starting point file is heavily commented as well—perfect for web designers beginning to climb the rather steep CSS learning curve.

In Dreamweaver, editing a CSS style is just as easy as applying one. The CSS Styles panel (see Figure 1-10) displays all the current styles—both internal and external—with detailed characteristics. Double-click any style to modify it. Properties of any style can be disabled or re-enabled with the click of a mouse. Moreover, defined CSS rules can easily be moved within the style sheet or to another one with a simple drag-and-drop action.

FIGURE 1-10

The CSS Styles panel is your one-stop shop to create, apply, and modify styles, whether from an embedded or an external style sheet.

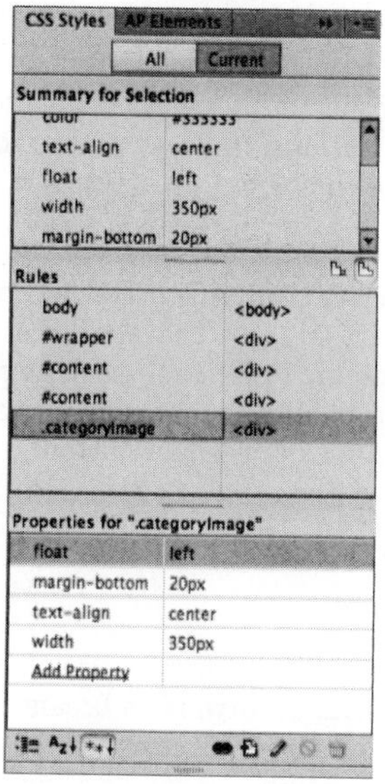

CSS has become the standard approach to web design, and it pervades every aspect of Dreamweaver. CSS rules can be applied—and created—right from the CSS tab of the Property inspector. When you are creating a new CSS rule, Dreamweaver suggests the correct descendent selector, which you can make less specific, if desired. In Live View, Dreamweaver properly renders the more advanced CSS properties, such as float and fixed background, so that designers can truly concentrate on the look of a site rather than wrestling with code hacks.

Addressing accessibility

Accessibility is an issue of great concern to many web developers. Increasingly, many designers labor under a mandate to produce accessible sites, especially in consideration of Section 508 of the Federal Rehabilitation Act. To help designers create accessible pages, Dreamweaver optionally displays additional attributes for key web page objects such as tables, forms, images, media, and frames. These attributes—like the summary attribute for the <table> tag—are always available through the Tag inspector when enabled through Dreamweaver's Preferences.

In addition, Dreamweaver is accessible as a tool itself. A number of screen readers, including JAWS for Windows and Window Eyes, are supported. Furthermore, the entire Dreamweaver interface can be navigated without using the mouse.

Straightforward text and graphics support

Text is a basic building block of any web page, and Dreamweaver makes formatting your text a snap. After you've inserted your text, by either typing it directly or pasting it from another program, you can change its appearance. Apply the standard HTML formats, such as the H1 through H6 headings and their relative sizes, or a paragraph tag, either of which can be quickly styled in CSS.

Chapter 7 shows you how to work with text in Dreamweaver.

Additional text support in Dreamweaver enables you to add both numbered (ordered) and bulleted (unordered) lists to your web page. The Text Property inspector provides buttons for both kinds of lists. Some elements, including lists, offer extended options. In Dreamweaver, clicking the Property inspector's Expander arrow opens a section from which you can access additional controls.

Graphics are handled in much the same easy-to-use manner. Select the image or its placeholder to enable the Image Property inspector. From there, you can modify any available attributes, including the image's source, or its width or height. Many simple graphic functions—such as cropping and rescaling—can be handled right from within Dreamweaver. Need to touch up your image more precisely? Send it to your favorite graphics program with just a click of the Edit button.

You learn all about adding and modifying images in Chapter 8.

Enhanced table capabilities

Other features—standard, yet more advanced—are similarly straightforward in Dreamweaver. Tables remain a key component in today's web pages, and Dreamweaver gives you full control over all their functionality. It changes the work of resizing the column or row of a table, previously a dreary hand-coding task, into an easy click-and-drag motion. Likewise, you can delete all the width and height values from a table with the click of a button. The Table Property inspector centralizes many of these options in Dreamweaver.

The nitty-gritty of table editing is often tedious and tricky: Grabbing just the right selection in a tightly formatted table row is meticulous work. Dreamweaver's Expanded mode takes the guesswork out of precise selection by visually exploding the table at design time to make all the elements far more accessible, as shown in Figure 1-11. You can switch between Standard and Expanded modes at the click of the mouse.

Tables are flexible in Dreamweaver. CSS class changes can be applied to any number of selected cells, rows, or columns. Tabular data, maintained in a spreadsheet such as Microsoft Excel or output from a database like Microsoft Access, is easily imported. A standard command enables you to automatically sort your table data as well.

You can find all you need to know about tables in Chapter 12.

FIGURE 1-11

By temporarily displaying borders with increased cell padding and cell spacing, Expanded mode makes table editing far easier.

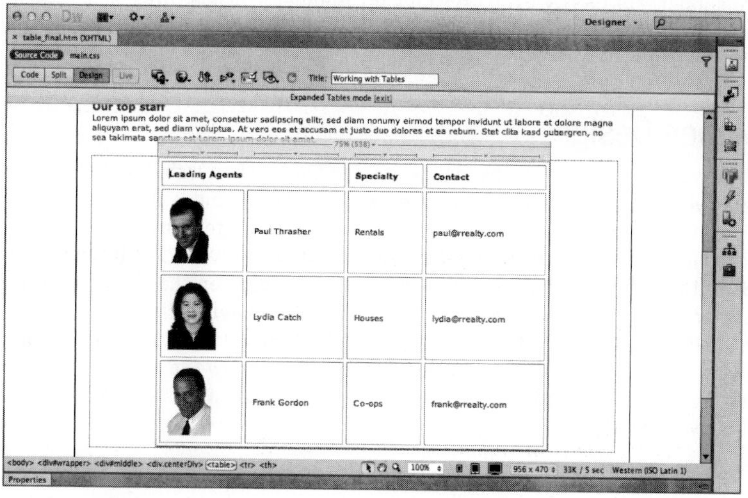

Easy form entry

Forms, the basic vehicle for web page data exchange, are just as easy to implement as tables in Dreamweaver. Switch to the Forms category of the Insert panel and insert any of the available elements: text boxes, radio buttons, checkboxes, and even drop-down or scrolling lists. With the Spry form validation widgets, you can easily specify any field as a required field and check to ensure that the requested type of information has been entered—and tell the user how to fix the problem—all with a single object.

Multimedia enhancements

Dreamweaver enables you to drop in any number of multimedia extensions, plugins, applets, or controls. Just click the appropriate button on the Insert panel and modify with the Property inspector. Two multimedia elements, Flash SWF and FLV files—both from Adobe—warrant special consideration in Adobe's Dreamweaver. When you insert either of these objects, Dreamweaver automatically includes the necessary HTML code to ensure the widest browser acceptance, and you can edit all the respective properties and then preview directly in the workspace.

Dreamweaver fully supports a wide range of multimedia output through custom objects that enable complex images, audio, and presentations to be easily inserted and displayed in web pages.

Next-Generation Features

Dreamweaver was among the first web authoring tools to work with the capabilities brought in by the 4.0 generation of browsers—and now, it's the first to support the enhanced options of Web 2.0 and state-of-the-art content management systems such as WordPress. The latest browsers all support variations of Ajax, and Dreamweaver makes it easy to implement this cutting-edge functionality. Moreover, the current generation of browsers adheres to the CSS standards, rapidly growing support for CSS3 with its options for rounded corners, drop-shadows, and animation effects. Dreamweaver gives web developers an interface that translates these advanced possibilities into reality.

Multiple Screen Design

Nobody's felt the revolution brought on by mobile devices harder than web designers. Now, instead of creating one slowly evolving screen—the ever-growing desktop—suddenly, there were two other design spaces demanding attention: tablet and phone. Dreamweaver's response has been full-throated, with complete support of CSS media queries, which allow styles to be conditionally applied, so you can specify distinct widths, backgrounds, font sizes, and more depending on the size of the target screen. To help the designer visualize these differences, the Multiscreen Preview dialog box shows three different designs simultaneously, as shown in Figure 1-12. Additionally, the Document Window, when in Design or Live View, applies any defined media queries, so you can view the modified styles by clicking one of the Quick Size icons, choosing another entry from the adjacent Window Sizes list, or simply resizing the window manually.

FIGURE 1-12

The Multiscreen Preview feature shows your web designs for phone, tablet, and desktop.

Content management system support

The prevalence and ease of use of low- or no-cost content management systems (CMS) have changed the way many websites are developed and deployed. WordPress, Drupal, and Joomla are among the most widely used CMS platforms. While these systems started as blogging tools, they quickly spread to more general use.

Dreamweaver CS6 recognizes the importance of the CMS platforms in the web designer's palette and includes functionality to work with them directly. The Dynamic Related Files feature examines the code to uncover any linked files and make them accessible to the Dreamweaver coding environment. If the files are installed on your system, you can quickly modify them—which makes styling CMS pages with their deeply buried CSS styles a dream. Remote files can be explored in Code view to reveal their underlying structure.

Ajax spoken here

An Ajax-driven page easily provokes the most "Wow! How'd they do that?" comments—and Dreamweaver brings Ajax capabilities within reach of everyday designers. With Ajax, you can integrate dynamic information into your pages without application servers.

A key Web 2.0 technique is to update part of the page, revealing new data, without refreshing the entire page. Dreamweaver includes key data manipulation tools to build this type of functionality into your sites through the Adobe-created Spry framework. Moreover, Spry makes it possible to incorporate advanced JavaScript layout widgets such as accordion, collapsible, and tabbed panels (see Figure 1-13).

In addition to adding next-generation data and layout capabilities, Spry brings a full slate of JavaScript behavior effects to the designer's palette. The Spry effects—including appearing/fading, shrinking/growing, shaking, and sliding—can all be triggered by your choice of event: a user's click of a link, a page loading, or tabbing away from a form.

Get all the information you'll need on Ajax and Spry functionality in Chapter 16.

FIGURE 1-13

Sophisticated layout features such as tabbed panels are easily inserted and modified with Spry widgets.

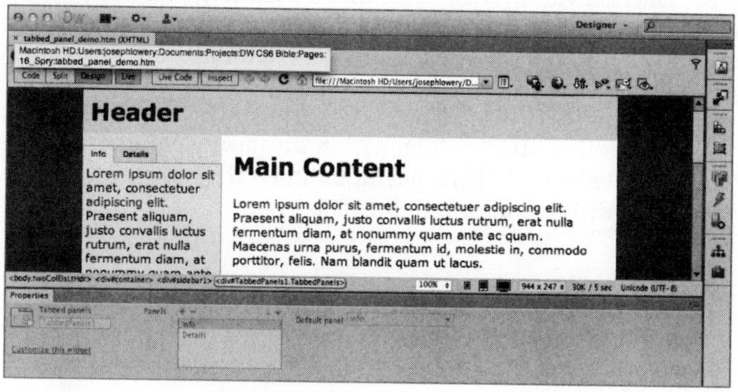

Dynamic style updates

Dreamweaver completely supports the Cascading Style Sheets (CSS) specification agreed upon by the World Wide Web Consortium. CSS gives web designers more flexible control over almost every element on their web pages. Dreamweaver applies CSS capabilities as if they were styles in a word processor. For example, you can make all the `<h1>` tags blue and italic, and put them in small caps. If your site's color scheme changes, you can make all the `<h1>` tags red—and you can do this throughout your website with one command. Dreamweaver gives you style control over type, background, blocks, boxes, borders, lists, and positioning.

By linking a CSS change to a user-driven event such as moving the mouse, text can be highlighted or de-emphasized, screen areas can be lit up, and figures can even be animated. Moreover, it can all be done without repeated trips to the server or huge file downloads.

Details about using Cascading Style Sheets begin in Chapter 6.

Photoshop, Flash, and Fireworks integration

Dreamweaver has upped the ante for integration with Adobe's graphics powerhouse, Photoshop. Copy any selection from Photoshop and paste it directly in Dreamweaver, easily converting it to a web-compatible format on the way. Once the converted image is inserted, it becomes a Smart Object and indicates if the source Photoshop file is modified; if so, you can update it with the click of a button.

You're also free to use Adobe's web graphics engine, Fireworks; designed specifically for the web, Fireworks provides all the web optimization you need for your graphic work. Images derived directly from Fireworks are identified as such, both in the Property inspector and in the Assets panel. Graphics can be optimized to alter the file size, cropping, transparency, or many other aspects right from within Dreamweaver.

Dreamweaver has picked up a couple of tricks from its close association with Fireworks and can now handle basic graphics editing on its own. Use Dreamweaver to crop, resample, brighten, darken, or sharpen any GIF or JPEG image. All the tools are immediately accessible from the Image Property inspector. If more extensive modification is required, click the Edit button to send the graphic back to Photoshop or Fireworks, whichever is your designated graphics editor.

Video on the web has a common feature, largely because of the ubiquity of Flash video. Dreamweaver has embraced the Flash video format, FLV, whole-heartedly, and web page designers have a clear path for easily inserting instant-on videos in their site, as shown in Figure 1-14. Flash video is available in either a progressive download or a streaming format, both of which are fully supported in Dreamweaver. The emerging HTML5 `<video>` tag is also supported in Code view.

You can send Flash movies to be edited directly from within Dreamweaver, just as you can with Fireworks. After you have completed your editing operation in Flash, just click Done, and your revised movie is republished and inserted back into Dreamweaver.

FIGURE 1-14

Add Flash video to any Dreamweaver web page, complete with full-screen capabilities.

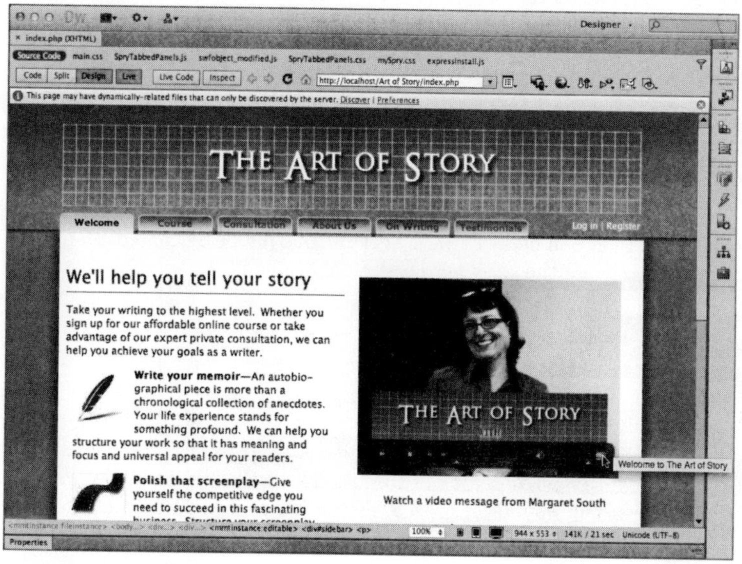

Server-side behaviors

The driving forces behind Dreamweaver's web application creation are its server behaviors. A *server behavior* is code written in a language understood by the particular server model that is executed on the server. Dreamweaver comes standard with a wide variety of useful server behaviors, ranging from one that replicates records on a page to another that restricts access to a page.

You apply and manage server behaviors from the Server Behaviors panel, shown in Figure 1-15. Unlike the Bindings panel, from which you drag fields onto the page, the main area of the Server Behaviors panel indicates which server behaviors have been inserted into the page. If the server behavior has user-defined parameters, they can be altered by double-clicking the entry in the panel.

XML and XSLT integration

Extensible Markup Language (XML) has piqued the interest of many web designers, intranet developers, and corporate users because of its underlying customizable nature. With XML, tags are created to describe the use of the information, rather than its appearance. Another standards-based technology, Extensible Stylesheet Transformation (XSLT) controls the data styling.

Dreamweaver has taken the next step with XML and made it possible for almost any designer to incorporate XML data right into her own web pages. Through the use of XSLT, Dreamweaver displays XML data from RSS feeds and other sources. Dreamweaver's implementation exposes this technology on both client-side and server-side, widening its appeal to a range of designers.

FIGURE 1-15

Quickly identify the page elements affected by a server behavior by selecting the entry in the Server Behaviors panel.

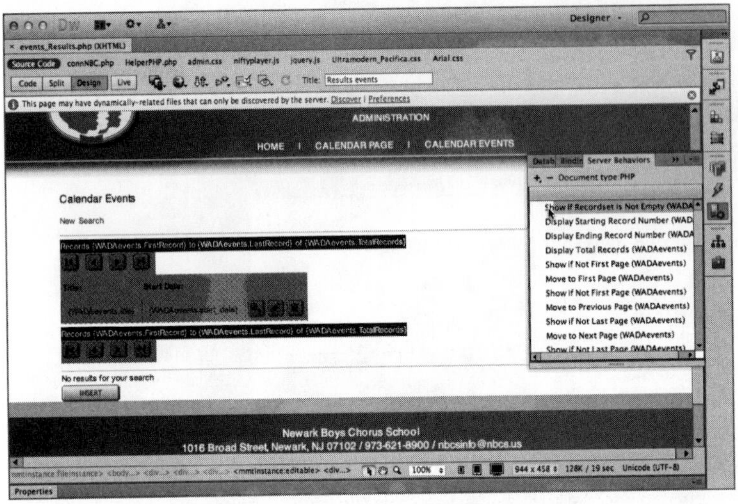

Dreamweaver is capable of exporting and importing XML tags, no matter what the tag definition. You can also create, modify, and validate XML files in Dreamweaver. As XML grows in popularity, Dreamweaver is ready to handle the work.

CSS layout control

The majority of web designers now use CSS to create their page layouts. This process keeps the layout properties (the CSS rules) separate from the content and makes for simpler maintenance. Dreamweaver offers an easy-to-apply `<div>` tag object, right from the Insert panel's Common category (see Figure 1-16).

Another way to create a similar container in Dreamweaver is by clicking the Draw AP Div button on the Insert panel. Dreamweaver pairs the necessary CSS with the AP element, typically a `<div>` or `<span>` tag. After they are created, AP elements can be positioned anywhere on the page by clicking and dragging the selection handle. As with other Dreamweaver objects, you can modify an AP element through the Property inspector.

Dreamweaver also now provides a path for designers to create their web pages with a fluid grid layout, best suited for sites viewed on mobile devices and desktops. Handy screen-size widgets allow you to switch quickly between phone, tablet, and desktop.

See Chapter 10 for detailed information about using `<div>` tags, AP elements, and fluid grid layouts in Dreamweaver.

FIGURE 1-16

Position your content through <div> tags or drawn layers—with Dreamweaver, it's up to you.

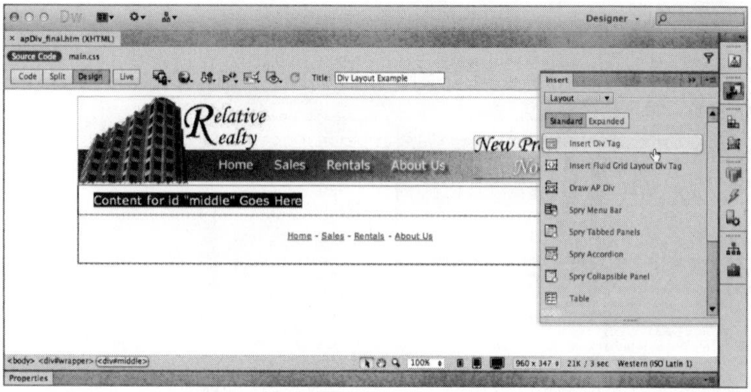

JavaScript behaviors

Through the development of JavaScript behaviors, Dreamweaver combines the power of JavaScript with the ease of a point-and-click interface. A *behavior* is defined as a combination of an event and an action—whenever your web page user does something that causes something else to happen, that's a behavior. What makes behaviors extremely useful is that they require no programming whatsoever.

TIP

The previously mentioned Spry effects are all, essentially, behaviors and can be found in the Behaviors panel under the Effects listing.

Behaviors are JavaScript-based, and this is significant because JavaScript is supported to varying degrees by existing browsers. You simply select the web page element that you want to use to control the action and open the Behaviors panel. Next, you choose from a full list of available actions, such as go to a URL, play a sound, pop up a message, or open a browser window (see Figure 1-17). You can also assign multiple actions to an event and even determine when they occur.

For complete details about working with JavaScript behaviors, see Chapter 11.

CAUTION

Once you've developed and tested your page, you can extract the JavaScript and place it in an external file for a cleaner source code page. The Externalize JavaScript command gives you the option of just moving the JavaScript functions or also employing an unobtrusive JavaScript technique, which replaces the trigger attributes, such as `onClick`, with external DOM functions.

FIGURE 1-17

Easily add common JavaScript code with Dreamweaver behaviors.

Mobile app development

Creating apps for mobile devices has really taken off, and Dreamweaver is ready to blast into orbit so that you can prototype and test apps for Android and iOS devices. You can create a mobile app project right from scratch through the built-in jQuery Mobile framework, creating separate pages for your project quickly and easily. When you're ready to pull in advanced functionality, access PhoneGap Build to compile your code and preview in a range of devices, like the one shown in Figure 1-18.

Program Extensibility

One of Dreamweaver's primary strengths is its extensibility. Virtually no two websites are alike, in either their design or their execution. With such a tremendous variety of results, the more flexible a web authoring tool, the more useful it is to a larger group of designers. Dreamweaver runs the gamut of extensibility: from objects and behaviors that are easily customizable to more advanced work with custom floaters, commands, translators, and Property inspectors. The basic underpinnings of Dreamweaver can even be extended with C-Level Extensibility options.

Objects and behaviors

In Dreamweaver parlance, an *object* is a bit of HTML code that represents a specific image or HTML tag, such as a `<table>` or a `<form>`. Dreamweaver's objects are completely open to user customization, or even out-and-out creation. For example, if you'd rather import structured data into a table without a border instead of with the standard 1-pixel border, you can easily make that modification to the Insert Tabular Data object file—right from within Dreamweaver—and every subsequent table is similarly inserted. Objects are accessed from the Insert panel, as well as through the menus.

FIGURE 1-18

Apply a standardized interface via jQuery Mobile and test in mobile simulators, right from within Dreamweaver.

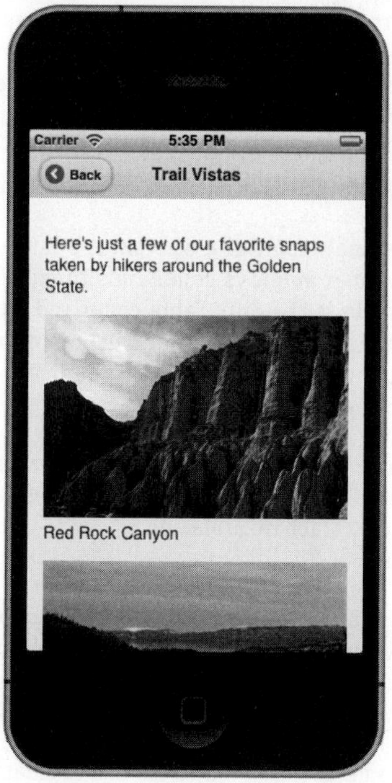

Objects are terrific time-saving devices, essentially enabling you to drop in significant blocks of HTML code at the click of a mouse. Likewise, Dreamweaver behaviors enable even novice web designers to insert complex JavaScript functions designed to propel pages to the cutting edge. Dreamweaver ships with a full array of standard behaviors—but that's only the tip of the behavior iceberg. Because behaviors are also customizable and can be built by anyone with a working knowledge of JavaScript, many Dreamweaver designers have created custom behaviors and made them publicly available.

TIP

You can find a large assortment of custom objects, behaviors, and commands on the website for this book at `http://www.wiley.com/go/dreamweavercs6bible`.

Server Behavior Builder

Server behaviors are key to Dreamweaver's success as a web application authoring tool. Although Dreamweaver provides a full palette of server behaviors for handling many of the required tasks, the needs of web developers are diverse and numerous. Dreamweaver cannot supply a server behavior for every occasion. Enter Dreamweaver's Server Behavior Builder, a terrific tool for creating custom server behaviors.

The Server Behavior Builder is engineered to handle a wide range of circumstances. Some server behaviors can be encapsulated in a single line of code repeated verbatim, whereas others require multiple blocks of programming involving several user-supplied parameters—you can construct almost any kind of code with the Server Behavior Builder. After you create the custom server behavior, you can apply and modify it just like any of the standard Dreamweaver server behaviors.

Commands and floating panels

Objects and behaviors are great ways to help build the final result of a web page, but what about automating the work of producing that page? Dreamweaver employs commands to modify the existing page and streamline production. A great example is the Sort Table command, standard with Dreamweaver. If you've ever had to sort a large table by hand—meticulously moving data, one row at a time—you can appreciate the power of this option the first time you use a command to alphabetize or otherwise sort a table.

Commands hold great promise—they are, in effect, more powerful than either objects or behaviors combined. In fact, some of the more complex objects, such as some of the Business Catalyst interfaces, are actually commands. Commands can also extract information sitewide and offer a powerful programmable language within Dreamweaver.

Creating a Dreamweaver command is easy for anyone, thanks to the History panel. Aside from displaying every action you undertake as you build your web page, the History panel enables you to select any number of those actions and save them as a command. Your new command is instantly available to be called from the menu whenever you need it.

After only a few moments with Dreamweaver, you become accustomed to its use of floating panels. You can even create custom floating panels, perhaps to show existing resources or to provide a whole new interface for modifying an HTML element.

Adjustable Insert panels

With the Insert panel designers can quickly see all the available object categories and switch to them with a single click. More important—from an extensibility standpoint—new categories can be developed and integrated into the Dreamweaver workspace on a contextual basis. In other words, if you create a category for SMIL, you can set the preferences so that it displays only when you are working on an SMIL file.

The Insert panel is quite accessible to new users. You can even switch between the different categories being available as a drop-down list or as a series of tabs when in the Classic workspace. The ultimate in accessibility, however, has to be the Insert panel's Favorites category. You can personalize the Favorites category and display just those objects you use most frequently, in the order you choose.

Custom tags, translators, and Property inspectors

In Dreamweaver, almost every part of the user interface can be customized—including the tags themselves. You can easily add new tags and specify how they should be formatted via the Tag

Library Editor; you can even import entire tag sets represented by DTDs. After you've developed your custom third-party tags, you can display and modify their current properties with a custom Property inspector. Moreover, if your custom tags include content not typically shown in Dreamweaver's Document window, you can build a custom translator, enabling the content to be displayed.

Programs such as Dreamweaver are usually built in the programming language called C or C++, which must be compiled before it is used. Generally, the basic functions of a C program are frozen solid; there's no way that you can extend them. This is not the case with Dreamweaver, however, which offers a C-Level Extensibility feature that permits programmers to create libraries to install new functionality into the program. Translators, for example, normally rely on new C libraries to display content in Dreamweaver that could not be shown otherwise. Companies can use the C-Level Extensibility feature to integrate Dreamweaver into their existing workflow and maximize productivity.

Automation Enhancements

Website design is the dream job; website production is the reality. After a design has been finalized, its execution can become repetitive and burdensome. Dreamweaver offers a number of ways to automate the production work, keeping the look of the web pages consistent—with minimum work required.

Rapid application development with Data objects

Although it's true that almost every active website has one or more unique situations that require some custom coding, it's equally true that the same type of web application is used repeatedly. It's hard to find an e-commerce–enabled site that doesn't use some variation of the master-detail web application in which a search returns a list of matches (the master page), each of which links to a page with more information (the detail page). Likewise, every intranet administration application requires the capability to add, edit, and remove records. To speed the development of these types of applications, Dreamweaver includes a series of Data objects, some of which reduce a 20-step operation to a single dialog box, like the one shown in Figure 1-19.

Here are some of the Data objects that come standard with Dreamweaver:

- Dynamic Table
- Master Detail Page Set
- Recordset Navigation Bar
- Recordset Navigation Status
- Record Insertion Form
- Record Update Form

Although they vary in complexity, all are guaranteed time-savers. In addition to creating pages as needed, Data objects can also insert dynamic data and apply server behaviors.

FIGURE 1-19

The Master Detail Page Set Data object provides rapid development for a common web application.

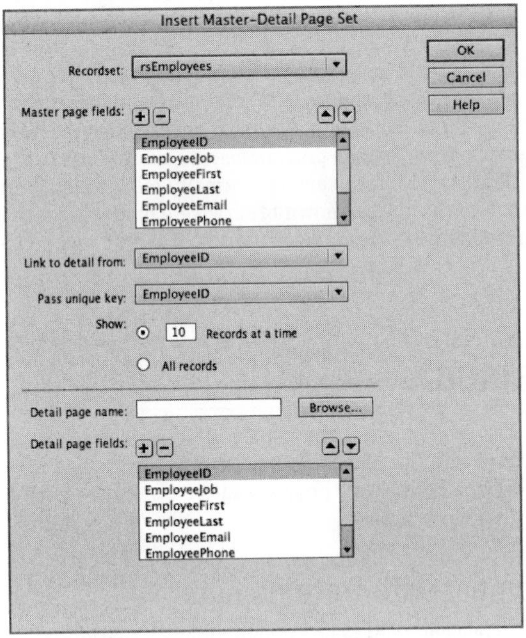

Importing Office documents

Much of the web's content originates from other sources—in-house documents produced by a word processor or spreadsheet program. Dreamweaver bridges the gap between the offline and the online worlds with a variety of useful import features.

Microsoft Word, perhaps the most widely used word processor, is great at creating and storing word processing documents but not so accomplished at outputting standard HTML. An HTML file derived from Word is, to put it mildly, bloated with extraneous and repetitive code.

Content from Word can be simply copied and pasted into Dreamweaver. Dreamweaver handles the conversion from Word to HTML, automatically retaining most formatting in clean HTML. The same copy/paste functionality applies to Excel.

For full documents, you can use Dreamweaver's Clean Up Word HTML command. This feature strips out the unnecessary code and even permits you to format the code as you format your other Dreamweaver files. The Clean Up Word HTML command offers a wide range of options for cleaning up the code.

Of course, not all web content derives from word processing documents—databases and spreadsheets are the other two legs of the modern office software triangle. With the Import Tabular

Data command, Dreamweaver offers the capability to incorporate data from any source that can export structured text files. Just save your spreadsheet or database as a comma-, tab-, or otherwise-delimited file and bring it directly into Dreamweaver in the table style of your choice.

Reference panel

Even the most advanced coder needs a reference when including seldom-used HTML tags or arcane JavaScript functions. Dreamweaver includes built-in references with HTML, JavaScript, and Cascading Style Sheets. Dreamweaver's guide is context-sensitive; highlight a tag or function in Code view and press Shift+F1 to get a breakdown on syntax and browser compatibility.

In addition to the resources already noted, you can use a couple of ColdFusion Markup Language references from Adobe or a wide range of guides from O'Reilly on everything from ASP to XSLT. Furthermore, UsableNet has contributed a valuable guide to accessibility issues.

History panel

Building a website is often a matter of entering the same series of commands over and over. You might, for example, need to change a list of names from a first name followed by last name format to one where the last name appears initially, separated by a comma from the first name. Rather than laboriously cutting and pasting each name and entering the extra characters, you can perform the actions once and save that action as a repeatable command.

You can find the feature that brings this degree of automation to Dreamweaver in the History panel. The History panel shows each step taken by a designer as the page is developed. Although this visual display is great for complex, multilevel undo actions, the capability to save any number of your steps as an instantly available command is truly time-saving.

Site Management Tools

Updates and revisions are ongoing for nearly every website. For this reason, site management tools are as important to a web authoring program as site creation tools. Dreamweaver delivers on both counts.

Object libraries

In addition to site management functions that have become traditional, such as FTP publishing, Dreamweaver adds a whole new class of functionality called *libraries*. One of the truisms of web page development is that if you repeat an element across your site, you're sure to have to change it—on every page. Dreamweaver libraries eliminate that drudgery. You can define almost anything as a library element: a paragraph of text, an image, a link, a table, a form, a Java applet, an ActiveX control, and so on. Just choose the item and open the Library category of the Assets panel (see Figure 1-20). After you've created the library entry, you can reuse it throughout your website. Each website can have its own library, and you can copy entries from one library to another.

FIGURE 1-20

Use Dreamweaver's library feature to simplify the task of updating elements repeated across many web pages.

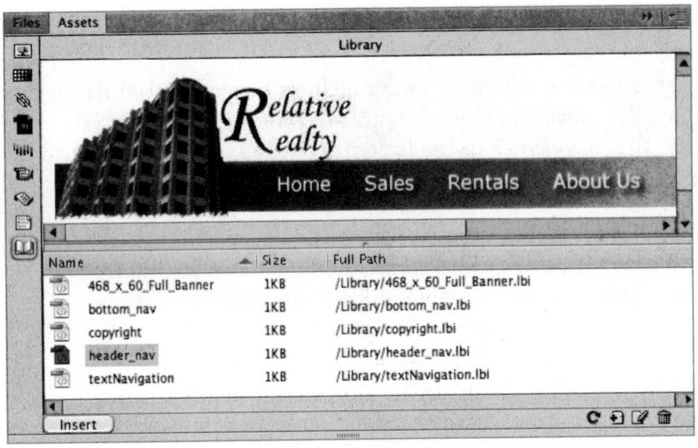

Being able to include boilerplate web elements is one issue; being able to update them across the site simultaneously is quite another! You can easily change a library entry through the Library category of the Assets panel. After the change is complete, Dreamweaver detects the modification and asks if you want to update your site. Imagine updating copyright information across a 400+ page website in the blink of an eye, and you start to understand the power of Dreamweaver libraries.

To find out more about making sitewide changes with library items, see Chapter 29.

Supercharged templates

The more your website grows, the more you find yourself using the same basic format for different pages. Dreamweaver enables the use of web page templates to standardize the look and feel of a website and to cut down on the repetitive work of creating new pages. A Dreamweaver template can hold the basic structure for the page—an image embedded in the CSS background, a navigation bar along the left side, or a set-width table in the center for holding the main text, for example—with as many elements predefined as possible.

Dreamweaver templates are far more than just molds for creating pages, however. Basically, templates work with a series of locked and editable regions. To update an entire site based on a template, all you have to do is alter one or more of the template's locked regions. Dreamweaver stores any template that you create in the same folder, so that your templates are accessible through the Templates category of the Assets panel.

You can find more about using and creating templates in Chapter 28.

Dreamweaver templates are much more than just editable and uneditable regions, however. Dreamweaver gives the designer a high degree of control with such features as repeating regions—which, for example, enable a table row to be repeated as many times as needed but constrain the other areas of a table. You're also able to hide and show areas of a page conditionally with optional regions, as shown in Figure 1-21. Dreamweaver's template power extends to nested templates, so that changes can ripple down through a series of locked and editable regions.

CAUTION

Dreamweaver also offers a different kind of template for the Adobe InContext Editing service. With InContext Editing, site owners can quickly make changes to the editable sections of their web pages directly in the browser. These editable regions are defined in Dreamweaver; once they are assigned, you can define the degree to which the user can make changes, from just changing the text to full-on styling. Dreamweaver also includes a repeating region object for InContext Editing to handle a series of web page items.

FIGURE 1-21

This template contains editable and optional regions.

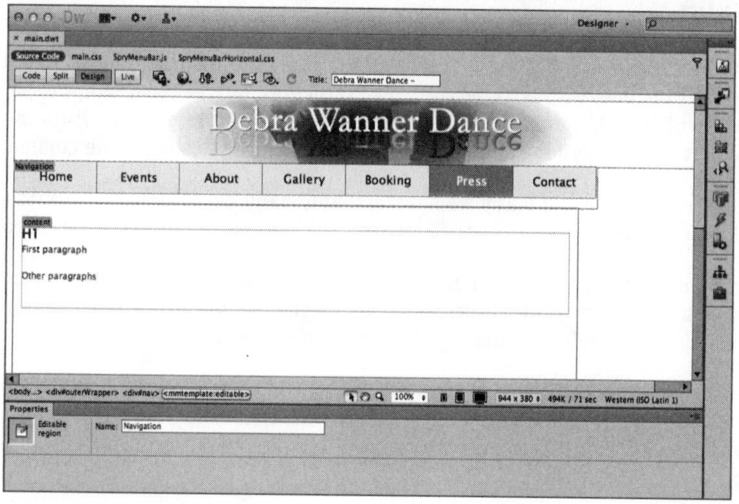

Browser targeting

Browser targeting is another site management innovation from Dreamweaver. One of the major steps in any site development project is to test the web pages in various browsers to look for inconsistencies and invalid code. Dreamweaver's Browser Targeting function enables you to check your HTML against any existing browser's profile. Dreamweaver includes predefined profiles for several browsers, and you can create a profile for any browser you'd like to check.

To learn how you can set up your own profile for Browser Targeting, see Chapter 30.

You can also preview your web page in any number of browsers. Dreamweaver enables you to specify primary and secondary browsers that can display your page at the press of a function key. You can install up to 18 other browsers for previewing your web page. The entire list of browsers is available through the Preview In Browser command in the File menu.

For the widest range of testing, use the built-in access to the Adobe BrowserLab service. With BrowserLab, you can get a quick snapshot of any page as rendered on the full spectrum of OS configurations and browser combinations. What's more, you can compare two browser tests side-by-side or even overlayed with onionskinning transparency for pixel-precise alignment.

Verifying links

Websites are ever-evolving entities. Maintaining valid connections and links amid all that diversity is a constant challenge. Dreamweaver includes a built-in Link Checker so you can verify the links on a page, in a directory, or across your entire site. The Link Checker quickly shows you which files have broken links, which files have links to external sites, and which files may have been *orphaned* (so that no other file connects with them).

FTP publishing

The final step in web page creation is publishing your page on the Internet. As any webmaster knows, this step is one that happens repeatedly as the site is continually updated and maintained. Dreamweaver includes an FTP (File Transfer Protocol) publisher that simplifies the work of posting your site; FTP publishing is now handled as a background process. More important, Dreamweaver enables you to synchronize your local and remote sites with one command.

Security is a prime concern among many webmasters, and many developers have switched to using Secure FTP (SFTP). Dreamweaver lists SFTP among its supported file-transfer flavors.

Not all the files found in your local site need to be uploaded to the remote site. Dreamweaver includes a feature called *cloaking*, which permits the designer to designate folders and particular file types that should be excluded during synchronization operations.

You can work with sites originating from a local folder, such as one on your own hard drive. Or, in a collaborative team environment, you can work with sites being developed on a remote server. Dreamweaver enables you to set up an unlimited number of sites to include the source and destination directories, FTP usernames, passwords, and more.

The Dreamweaver Files panel, shown in Figure 1-22, is a visual interface in which you can click and drag files or select a number of files and transfer them with the Get (download) and Put (upload) buttons. You can even set the preferences so the system automatically disconnects after remaining idle for a user-definable period of time.

File Check In/Check Out

On larger web projects, more than one person is usually responsible for creation and daily upkeep of the site. An editor may need to include the latest company press release, or a graphic artist may have to upload a photo of the newest product—all on the same page. To avoid conflicts with overlapping updates, Dreamweaver has devised the Check In/Check Out system by which web pages can be marked as checked out and locked to prevent any other corrections until the file is once again checked in.

FIGURE 1-22

The Files panel enables you to publish the files that make up your website directly from within Dreamweaver to your application server with Put or to transfer files from the server to your HD with Get.

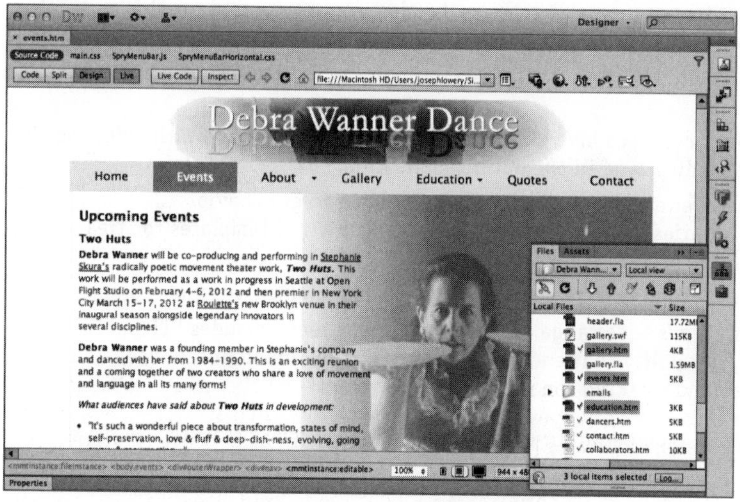

Dreamweaver places a green checkmark over a file's icon in the Site Files window when you have checked it out and a red checkmark if another member of your team has checked it out. In addition, so you won't have to guess who that team member is, Dreamweaver displays the name of the person next to the filename. You can also keep track of who last checked out a particular web page (or image)—Dreamweaver keeps an ongoing log listing the file, person, date, and time of the checkout.

Summary

Building any website—whether static or dynamic—is half craft and half art, and Dreamweaver is the perfect tool for blending these often dueling disciplines. Dreamweaver's visual editor enables quick and artful page creation, and at the same time, its integrated text editors offer the detail-oriented focus required by programmers. Dreamweaver's key advantages include the following:

- Dreamweaver works the way professional web developers do, with integrated visual and text editors. Dreamweaver won't convert your code when it's used with pre-existing web pages (unless you want it to).
- It supports standard HTML commands with easy entry and editing of text, graphics, tables, and multimedia elements.

- Dreamweaver provides straightforward yet robust connectivity to data sources and access to the most popular server models.
- It makes cutting-edge features, such as Ajax, Dynamic HTML, and Cascading Style Sheets, easy to use.
- Dreamweaver connects directly to the most commonly used graphic and motion tools, including Photoshop, Fireworks, and Flash.
- A supercharged editor features advanced options such as code completion and Code Hints.
- With Dreamweaver's Live View, you can construct your page while viewing the actual data to be displayed in the online application.
- Dreamweaver offers you a variety of reusable server behaviors, JavaScript behaviors, object libraries, commands, Application objects, and templates to streamline your web page creation.
- Enhanced templates are possible with optional and conditional regions.
- Dreamweaver's wide range of site management tools includes FTP publishing, a file-locking capability that encourages team creation and maintenance, a built-in Link Checker, and cloaking capabilities.

In the next chapter, you get an in-depth tour of Dreamweaver's features.

CHAPTER

2

Touring Dreamweaver

IN THIS CHAPTER

- Choosing a workspace layout
- Comparing workspace layouts
- Working in the Document window
- Accessing common commands on the toolbars
- Inserting elements with the Insert panel
- Modifying tag properties with the Property inspector
- Working with dockable panels
- Stepping through the menus
- Accessing online services

Dreamweaver's user interface is efficient, powerful, and flexible. By offering a wide variety of customizable tools and controls, Dreamweaver helps you tailor its workspace to your specific preferences and needs so that you can focus on the task of creating your website. This chapter provides a detailed overview of the Dreamweaver workspace so you know where all the tools are when you need to use them.

Choosing a Workspace Layout

One of Dreamweaver's greatest strengths is its flexibility. The makers of Dreamweaver realize that not everyone works in the same way, and they have created a product that you can customize to maximize your efficiency. By default, Dreamweaver provides a range of different workspace layouts and even allows you to customize your own.

You can access these options by choosing Window ➪ Workspace Layout or by choosing the Workspace switcher in the Applications bar and selecting one of the available choices.

The default layout option is referred to as the Designer workspace. Here, the most design-oriented of Dreamweaver's many panels are organized into groups and docked on the right side of the window, with the panel names exposed. The Designer workspace is illustrated in Figure 2-1.

A variation on the Designer workspace is the Coder workspace option. Here, the panels are docked on the left side of the window rather than the right. With this option, when you first open documents, you are presented with the code for the document rather than a view that reflects what the page will look like when viewed in a browser. Figure 2-2 shows the Coder workspace layout.

FIGURE 2-1

Dreamweaver's Designer workspace places docked panel groups on the right.

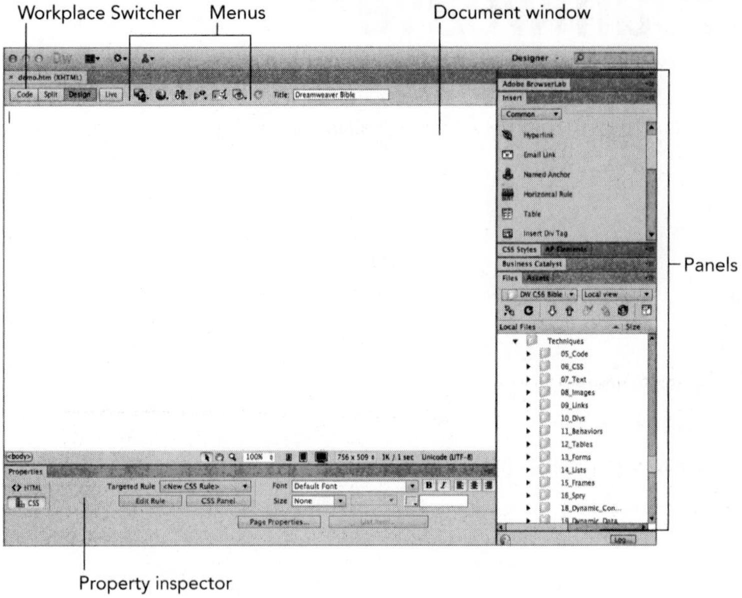

FIGURE 2-2

The Coder style workspace opens documents in Code view and docks panels on the left.

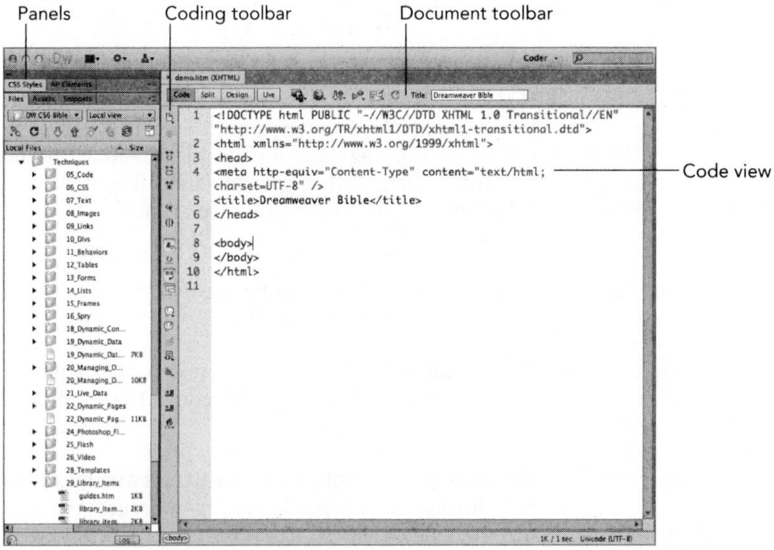

You have numerous options for customizing Dreamweaver. Later in this chapter, you learn how to move the panels and toolbars; dock or float the panels; hide, show, or resize panels; and more. Chapter 3 systematically covers many additional customization options, referred to within Dreamweaver, as with most programs, as *preferences*.

Another option, Dual Screen, is useful if you have two monitors for the same computer. When invoked, the Dual Screen layout undocks all the major components (Property inspector, panel groups, and Code inspector) so that they can be positioned exactly how you like.

Other layout options are detailed in Table 2-1.

If you ever adjust a standard layout and want to return to its default settings, choose Reset *Workspace*, where *Workspace* is the name of the workspace from either the Window ➪ Workspace Layout menu or the Workspace switcher.

TABLE 2-1 Default Layout Options

Layout	Panels on Left	Panels on Right	Property Inspector	View
App Developer	CSS Styles, AP Elements Databases, Bindings, Server Behaviors Files, Assets, Snippets [Labels without icons]		No	Split
App Developer Plus	CSS Styles, AP Elements Files, Assets, Snippets [Labels without icons]	Adobe BrowserLab Insert Databases, Bindings, Server Behaviors [Labels with icons]	Yes	Code
Business Catalyst	Files, Assets	Insert, CSS Transitions, Business Catalyst, CSS Styles	Yes	Code
Classic Insert panel presented as Insert bar along top of Document window as with Dreamweaver CS3		Adobe BrowserLab CSS Styles, AP Elements, Tag Inspector Databases, Bindings, Server Behaviors Files, Assets, Snippets [Labels without icons]	Yes	Design

Continues

TABLE 2-1 *(continued)*

Layout	Panels on Left	Panels on Right	Property Inspector	View
Coder	CSS Styles, AP Elements Files, Assets, Snippets [Labels without icons]		No	Code
Coder Plus	Files, Assets, Snippets [Labels without icons]	Adobe BrowserLab Insert CSS Styles, AP Elements [Labels with icons]	No	Code
Designer		Adobe BrowserLab Insert CSS Styles, AP Elements Business Catalyst Files, Assets [Labels without icons]	Yes	Design
Designer Compact		Adobe BrowserLab Insert CSS Styles, AP Elements Business Catalyst Files, Assets [Labels with icons]	Yes	Design
Dual Screen	Adobe BrowserLab Insert CSS Styles, AP Elements Business Catalyst Databases, Bindings, Server Behaviors Assets, Snippets [Grouped together but undocked, labels without icons] Files [Expanded mode in undocked panel]	Code inspector [Undocked panel]	Yes	Design
Fluid Layout		Insert CSS Styles Files, Assets	Yes	Design

Layout	Panels on Left	Panels on Right	Property Inspector	View
Mobile Applications	Files, Assets	Insert, CSS Transitions jQuery Mobile Swatches CSS Styles	Yes [Collapsed]	Code

TIP

If you aren't sure which workspace works best for you, don't worry; you can switch workspaces at any time and even completely customize a workspace so that it works the way you do.

2

All customized layouts can be saved for later retrieval. Once you've set up the desired layout, you can choose Window ➪ Workspace Layout ➪ New Workspace or, from the Workspace switcher, New Workspace, to store your customized environment. When you opt to create a new workspace, a dialog box appears for you to name your layout; after confirming your choice by clicking OK, your new layout option is displayed in the Workspace Layout submenu. Select Window ➪ Workspace Layout ➪ Manage Workspaces to delete or rename your custom layouts; the same command is available from the Workspace switcher.

NEW FEATURE

Dreamweaver offers Mac users the capability to enable the Application Frame (enabled by default), a boxed-in version of the application that blocks the view through to the Desktop with a Windows-like gray background. To revert to the previous user interface with separate panels, Document window, and Property inspector (see Figure 2-3), toggle Window ➪ Application Frame.

As you can see in Figures 2-1, 2-2, and 2-3, all the workspaces comprise variations of the same basic elements even though they are laid out differently on the screen. For the most part, you work with those elements in the same way, regardless of workspace; the only major differences among the workspaces are the location of the tools onscreen and which panels are open. The basic elements of Dreamweaver include the following:

- Document window
- Toolbars
- Insert panel
- Property inspector
- Panels
- Menus

The rest of this chapter takes you on a tour of each of these basic interface elements.

FIGURE 2-3

The workspace for Mac enables users to position panels wherever they would like while still being able to see the Desktop.

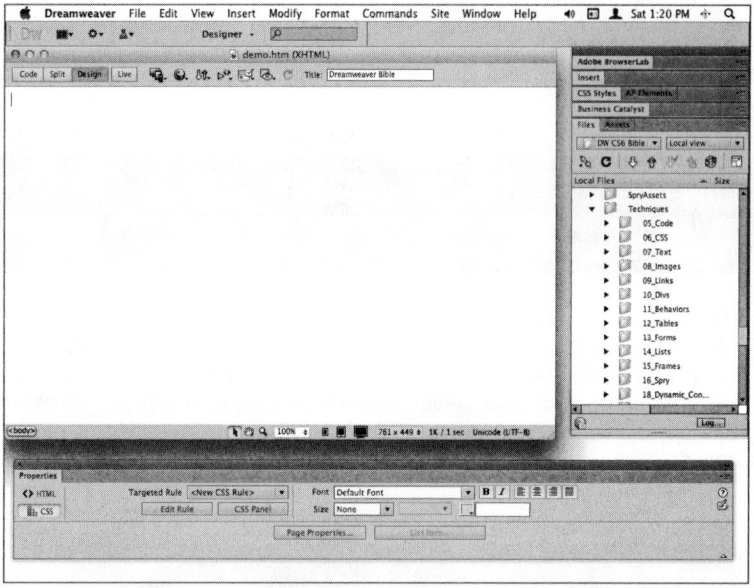

Viewing the Document Window

Dreamweaver's primary work area is the Document window. When you first create a new page in Dreamweaver, you see what is essentially an empty canvas surrounded by tool panels and toolbars. This canvas is where you create your web pages by typing headlines and paragraphs; inserting images and links; and creating tables, forms, and other HTML elements.

You can open more than one document at once in Dreamweaver, and all of your documents are viewed within the same window. If the documents are not maximized, you can see more than one document at once using the various window manipulation commands on the Window menu. If you want to separate documents, choose Window ➪ Cascade, Window ➪ Arrange Horizontally, or Window ➪ Arrange Vertically (Window ➪ Cascade, Window ➪ Tile, and Window ➪ Combine as Tabs on the Mac). This adds a great deal of flexibility because you can have multiple documents open in tabs in multiple document windows.

TIP

For maximum flexibility with documents on the Mac, make sure Window ➪ Application Frame is not selected.

If you maximize one document, all the open documents are maximized. Switch between the open documents by clicking the appropriate tab for the document, located near the top of the window, or by choosing Window ➪ Next Document/Previous Document. The buttons to minimize, restore, and close a maximized document on Windows are located in the upper-right corner of the Dreamweaver Document window. On a Mac, the buttons to close, minimize, and restore a group of tabbed documents remain in the upper left of the document window. To close one document, click the close widget to the right of the filename on each tab. You can also right-click a document tab and choose Close from the context menu to close the document. Figure 2-4 illustrates maximized documents within the Mac workspace.

TIP

To change the order in which your documents are displayed in tabs, drag a tab to the desired position.

If you open more documents than Dreamweaver can show, it displays a double-angle bracket indicator on the far right of the tab list that displays a drop-down list of files to choose from.

FIGURE 2-4

In the Dreamweaver workspace use tabs to switch between maximized documents.

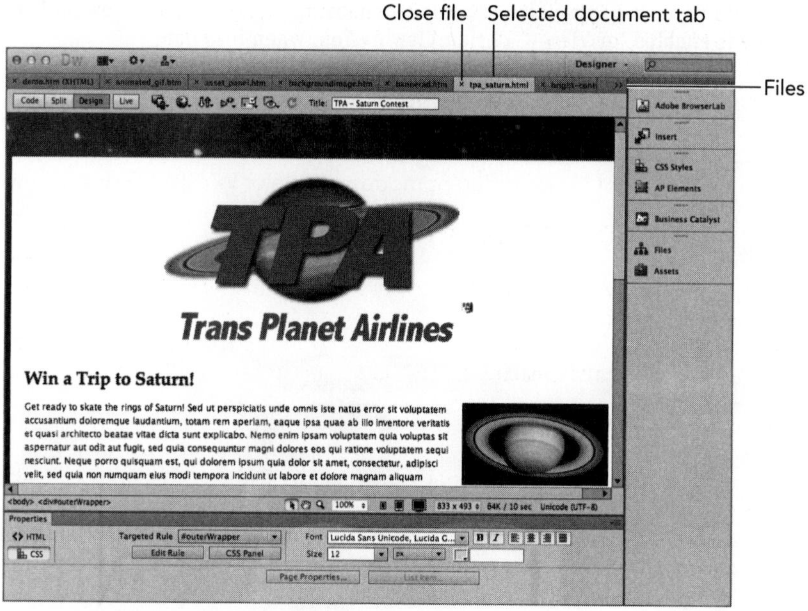

Switching views in the Document window

Typical web design tasks consist of visually creating a page in Dreamweaver, perhaps tweaking the underlying code to achieve the exact effect you want, and making sure your standard web page or application is performing as expected. You can do all these things without ever leaving the Dreamweaver Document window, simply by switching the view of the page you are editing.

Design and Code views

In Design view, you lay out a page visually. As your web page begins to take shape, Design view shows you a close representation of how the page looks when viewed through a browser such as Firefox or Internet Explorer. You can even see active elements, such as QuickTime movies or Shockwave and Flash files in your web page as you're building it. You can switch to Design view with the View ➪ Design menu command or by clicking the Show Design View button on the Document toolbar, described in the section "Accessing the Toolbars" later in this chapter.

As the name suggests, Code view displays the underlying code used to create the document, whether that is HTML, CSS style definitions, or JavaScript—whatever code is used to create the page is visible to you in Code view. If you are working in the Coder style workspace, Code view is the default view; but you can also switch to Code view by choosing the View ➪ Code menu command or by clicking the Show Code View button on the Document toolbar. When in Code view, you have the ability to examine the code from the same page in two different windows by choosing View ➪ Split Code. This option replaces Design view, if open.

You can choose View ➪ Code and Design to split the Document window, so that both Code view and Design view are visible at the same time (see Figure 2-5). You can also do this by clicking the Split button on the Document toolbar. Once in Split view, you can orient Code view and Design view horizontally by deselecting View ➪ Split Vertically. You also have the option of repositioning Design view to the left or on top by choosing View ➪ Design View on Left, when Split Vertically is enabled, or View ➪ Design View on Top, when it is not.

FIGURE 2-5

Quickly edit your document in two different modes—code or WYSIWYG design—with Split view.

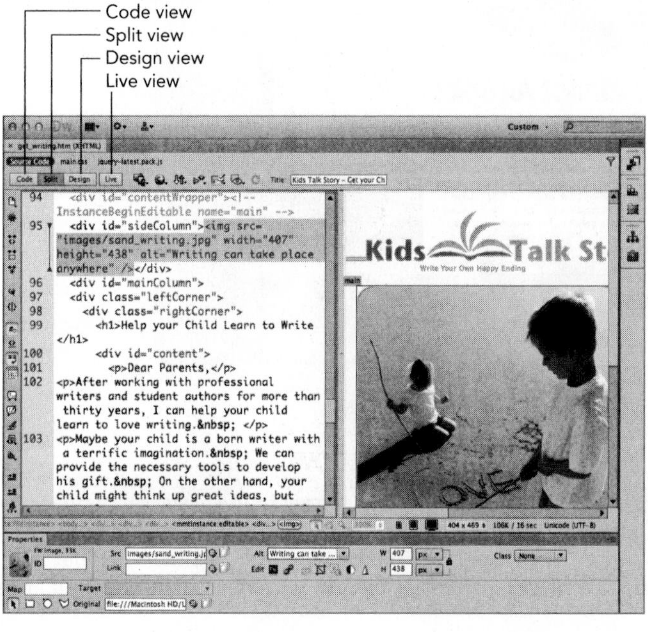

When you switch document views, the switch applies to the currently active open document and to any subsequent documents you open. It does not, however, change the view of other open documents.

Live View and Live Code

Whereas Design view gives you an editable, browser-approximate display of your web page, Live View is an actual real-world browser rendering. Although Live View is not editable, it is tightly integrated with Code view, so that any changes made to the code are immediately rendered when you refresh the page.

Live View is based on Apple's open source browser engine, WebKit, which is the basis for Apple's Safari and Google's Chrome browsers. Live View brings a whole new workflow to Dreamweaver, one that is well-suited to the modern web designer's task of crafting complex web pages that integrate external JavaScript, CSS, or server-side include files. Live View not only displays web pages accurately according to up-to-date web standards but also provides basic interactivity so you can test your CSS or JavaScript rollovers right within Dreamweaver.

Live View is best used in conjunction with Code view. The typical workflow is to switch to Live View once your basic page has been completed and you are fine-tuning the code. At this stage, click Live View in the Document toolbar or choose View ➪ Live View and then choose Split from the Document toolbar, as shown in Figure 2-6, or choose View ➪ Design and Code. Then, make any desired changes in Code view and, when you're ready, click Refresh Design View in the Document toolbar, choose View ➪ Refresh Design View, or press F5. Although page elements in Live View are not editable, you can click any area to navigate to the related code block. In addition to Code view, you can also make changes in other Dreamweaver panels, most notably the CSS Styles panel.

FIGURE 2-6

Live View is built on the open source WebKit browser engine for real-world rendering.

When you enter into Live View, the Live Code feature becomes available. Like Live View, Live Code gives you a real-world, albeit uneditable, window into your web page, but on the code side. You can easily tell you're in Live Code by the yellow highlighted code. Certain JavaScript or server-side functions may rewrite the HTML sent to the browser to be rendered. With Live Code enabled, you can see the exact code used. Moreover, you can interact with the page in Live View and then stop the interactivity by choosing View ➪ Live View Options ➪ Freeze JavaScript, choosing Freeze JavaScript from the Live View menu button, or pressing F6. Once the JavaScript is frozen, you can examine the current state in Live Code or Live View and make changes in the CSS Styles panel.

Enhanced features such as Related files and the Code Navigator, as well as the capability to freeze JavaScript, are all part of the Live View and Live Code workflow. To learn more about how to use Live View with these features, see Chapter 5.

If you are creating a web application that includes dynamic elements from a database, Live View can also serve you well. When you invoke Live View while the current page uses the PHP, ASP, or ColdFusion server model, Dreamweaver displays your page with data from your data source. The live data that Dreamweaver displays replaces data source placeholders such as `{rs.employeeID}` with the selected information pulled from the database's designated field, as shown in Figure 2-7.

To use Live View with a dynamic page, you'll need a connection to a testing server, either local or remote, to be properly established in the Site Definition dialog box. If Dreamweaver is unable to complete the connection, an error message appears with several possible solutions listed.

Live View is extremely helpful in building your web applications. Find out more about how to use this important feature in Chapter 21.

FIGURE 2-7

Live View lets you work on a dynamic web page—altering the CSS styles—while displaying the actual data from your application.

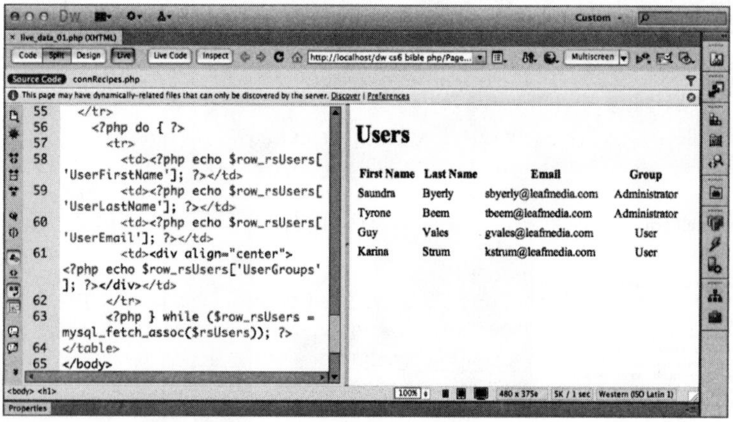

Working with the status bar

The status bar is found at the bottom of the Document window. Embedded here are several important tools: the Tag Selector, Zoom tool, Window Size pop-up menu, and Download Indicator. These helpful status bar tools provide the web designer with several time-saving utilities.

Tag Selector

The Tag Selector is an excellent example of Dreamweaver's elegant design approach. On the left side of the status bar, you see a listing of the current HTML tags. When you first open a blank page in Dreamweaver, you see only the <body> tag. If you type a line of text and then press Enter (Return), the paragraph tag <p> appears. Your cursor's position in the document determines which tags are displayed in the Tag Selector. The Tag Selector keeps continuous track of where you are in the HTML document by displaying the tags surrounding your current cursor position. This becomes especially important when you are building complex web pages that use such features as nested <div> tags.

2

As its name implies, the Tag Selector does more than just indicate a position in a document. Using the Tag Selector, you can quickly choose any of the elements surrounding your current cursor. After an element is selected, you can modify or delete it. If you have the Property inspector (described later in this chapter) onscreen, choosing a different code from the Tag Selector makes the corresponding options available in the Property inspector.

TIP

If you want to quickly clear most of your HTML page, choose the <body> tag in the Tag Selector and press Delete. All graphics, text, and other elements you have inserted through the Document window are erased. Left intact is any HTML code in the <head> section, including your title, <meta> tags, and any preliminary JavaScript. The <body> tag is also left intact.

In a more complex web page section, such as the one shown in Figure 2-8, the Tag Selector shows a wider variety of HTML tags. As you move your pointer over individual codes in the Tag Selector, they are highlighted; click one, and the code becomes bold. Tags are displayed from left to right in the Tag Selector—starting on the far left with the most inclusive (in this case, the <body> tag) and proceeding to the narrowest selection (here, the italic <h1> tag) on the far right.

As a web page developer, you're constantly selecting elements in order to modify them. Rather than rely on the click-and-drag method to highlight an area—which often grabs unwanted sections of your code, such as <td> tags—use the Tag Selector to unerringly pick just the code you want. Dreamweaver's Tag Selector is a subtle but extremely useful tool that can speed up your work significantly.

Right-clicking (Control+clicking) an item in the Tag Selector displays a menu that contains several tag-editing commands. Using this menu in Design view, you can remove the tag or select a `class` or `id` attribute for the tag. From either Design view or Code view, you can also modify the tag by choosing Edit Tag from the context menu.

FIGURE 2-8

The Tag Selector enables you to highlight just the code you want. If you select the <h1> tag here, the complete tag and its contents are chosen.

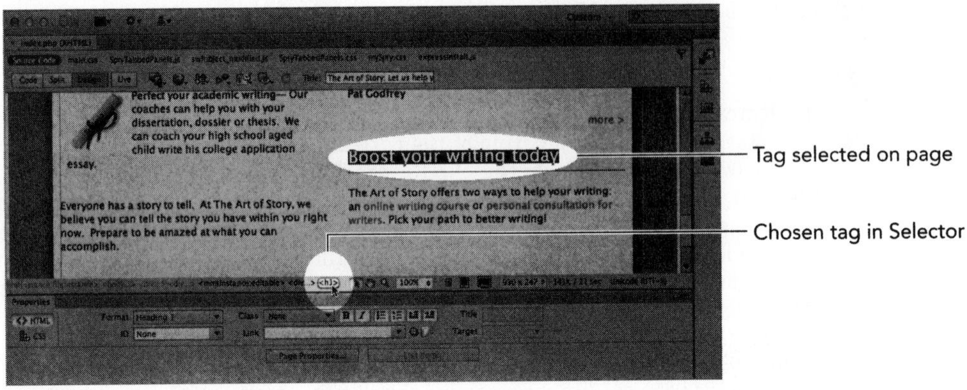

Select, Hand, and Zoom tools

With the greater layout flexibility made possible by CSS positioning comes the need for more powerful design tools. The first set of tools on the right side of the status bar offers Dreamweaver designers a number of options for viewing and interacting with the page at design time.

With the Zoom enhancement, Dreamweaver offers designers the ability to magnify a page for finer design control. This set of tools—Select, Hand, Zoom, and the Set Magnification pop-up menu—works together. In the typical design session, Dreamweaver is generally in Select mode, which allows the selection and manipulation of any and all page elements. Choose the Hand tool to pan around a page that is larger than the Document window, whether or not the page is magnified.

The Zoom tool works in a multifaceted fashion similar to graphic applications such as Photoshop and Fireworks. Once you've selected the Zoom tool, you can:

- Magnify a specific section of the page by clicking that area; each click increasing the magnification according to the values in the Set Magnification pop-up menu. For example, one click magnifies the area from 100 to 150 percent and then another goes to 200 percent magnification and so on. Hold Alt (Option) while clicking to zoom out of an area.
- Drag a rectangle around the area to magnify to view that section at the highest magnification, as shown in Figure 2-9.

To zoom in or out by a preset amount, select a value from the Set Magnification pop-up menu. Magnification options range from 6 to 6,400 percent. You can also opt to zoom in on a specific selection by choosing Fit Selection, view the width of the page by choosing Fit Width, or view the entire page by choosing Fit All. If you prefer to view the page at a specific magnification not found on the Set Magnification pop-up menu, you can enter the value directly in the field and press Tab; there's no need to enter the percent symbol, %.

FIGURE 2-9

Get in tight for close-up work with Dreamweaver's magnification tools.

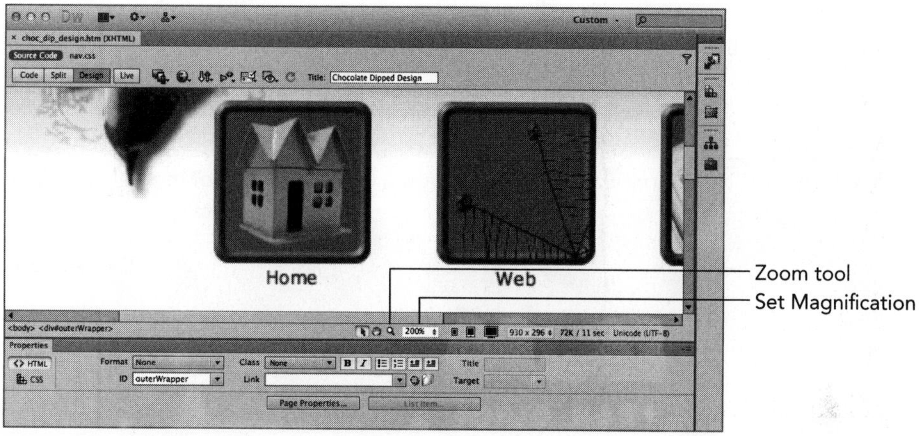

2

> **TIP**
>
> If you're zoomed in or out of a page, you can double-click either the Zoom or the Pointer tool to return to 100 percent magnification. To quickly begin selecting in standard magnification, double-click the Pointer tool.

Keyboard shortcuts are also available for zooming in and out of the page. Press Ctrl+= (Command+=) to zoom in and Ctrl+– (Command+–) to zoom out.

To return to editing the page—at any magnification level—click the Select tool.

Window Size options

The universality of the Internet enables virtually any type of computer system from anywhere in the world to access publicly available web pages. Although this accessibility is a boon to global communication, it forces web designers to be aware of how their creations look under various circumstances—especially different screen sizes.

> **NEW FEATURE**
>
> A number of window size options give designers a sense of how their pages look on different monitors. Three screen icons allow you to quickly flip from one common target to another: mobile, tablet, and desktop. An example design for a mobile phone is shown in Figure 2-10.

For a wider range of possibilities, use the Window Size pop-up menu. Located just right of the three screen-size icons, the Window Size pop-up menu indicates the screen size of the current Document window, in pixels, in *width* × *height* format. If you resize your Document window, the

Window Size indicator updates instantly. This indicator gives you an immediate check on the dimensions of the current page.

To select a different screen size, click once on the expander arrow to the right of the displayed dimensions to bring up a menu listing the standard sizes. Click a size from the menu.

FIGURE 2-10

The Window Size options can quickly give you a design preview of multiple screen layouts.

> **NOTE**
>
> If no sizes are listed in the status bar, you may be in Code view, described later in this chapter. Select View ➪ Design to gain access to the Window Size pop-up menu. If you can see the menu, but the options are disabled, your Document window is maximized (this happens only in the Dreamweaver integrated workspace for Windows users).

The standard sizes, and their most common uses, are as follows:

- 240 × 320 Feature Phone
- 320 × 480 Smart Phone
- 480 × 800 Smart Phone
- 592
- 768 × 1024 Tablet
- 1000 × 620 (1024 × 768, Maximized)

- 1260 × 875 (1280 × 1024, Maximized)
- 1420 × 750 (1440 × 900, Maximized)
- 1580 × 1050 (1600 × 1200, Maximized)

The fourth option, 592, is the only option that does not change the height and the width. Instead, this option uses the current window height and alters only the width.

TIP

You can set up your own custom screen settings by choosing Edit Sizes from the Window Size pop-up menu. This option opens the Status Bar category of the Preferences dialog box. Chapter 3 describes how to modify the pop-up list.

The dimensions offered by the Window Size pop-up menu describe the entire editable area of a page.

2

Download Indicator

So, you've built your web masterpiece, and you've just finished uploading the HTML, along with the 23 JPEGs, 8 audio files, and 3 Flash movies that make up the page. You open the page over the Internet and—surprise!—it takes five minutes to download. Okay, this example is a tad extreme, but every web developer knows that opening a page from your hard drive and opening a page over the Internet are two vastly different experiences. Dreamweaver has taken the guesswork out of loading a page from the web by providing the Download Indicator.

The Download Indicator is located to the right of the Window Size item on the status bar. As illustrated in Figure 2-11, Dreamweaver gives you two values, separated by a slash character:

FIGURE 2-11

Find the Download Indicator in the status bar.

- The cumulative size of the page, including all the associated graphics, plugins, and multimedia files, measured in kilobytes (KB)
- The time it takes to download at a particular connection speed, measured in seconds (sec)

TIP

You can check the download size of any individual graphic by selecting it and looking at the Property inspector—you can find the file size in kilobytes next to the thumbnail image on the left.

The Download Indicator is a handy real-world check. As you build your web pages, it's a good practice to monitor your file's download size—in both kilobytes and seconds. As a web designer, you ultimately have to decide what your audience will deem is worth the wait and what will have it reaching for that Stop button. Remember that all the component parts of a page make up the total file weight shown in the Download Indicator.

Not everybody has the same connection speed. If you are working with an intranet or on a broadband site, you can set your connection speed far higher. Likewise, if your site gets a lot of traffic from mobile users, you can lower the connection speed. Change the anticipated download speed through Dreamweaver's Preferences dialog box, as explained in Chapter 3.

Accessing the Toolbars

Regardless of the job—whether it's hanging a picture or fixing a faucet—work goes faster when your tools are at your fingertips. The same principle holds true for website building: The easier it is to accomplish the most frequently required tasks, the more productive you'll be as a web designer. Dreamweaver puts a number of repetitive tasks, such as previewing your page in a browser, just a function key away. However, there are far more necessary operations than there are function keys. In an effort to put needed functionality right up front, Dreamweaver incorporates four toolbars—Standard, Document, Browser Navigation, and Style Rendering—located across the top of the Document window. One other toolbar is available only when you are in Live Data view and another when you're in Code or Split view. In addition, Dreamweaver has two other bars built into the interface that provide essential functionality: the Application and Related Files bars.

The Application bar

The Application bar, so-called because of the identifying application icon on the left side, is common to all Adobe Creative Suite software programs. In addition to the menus, you can also find the following user interface elements in the Application bar, shown in Figure 2-12.

FIGURE 2-12

The goal of the Application bar is to surface commonly used features such as creating a new site or searching help.

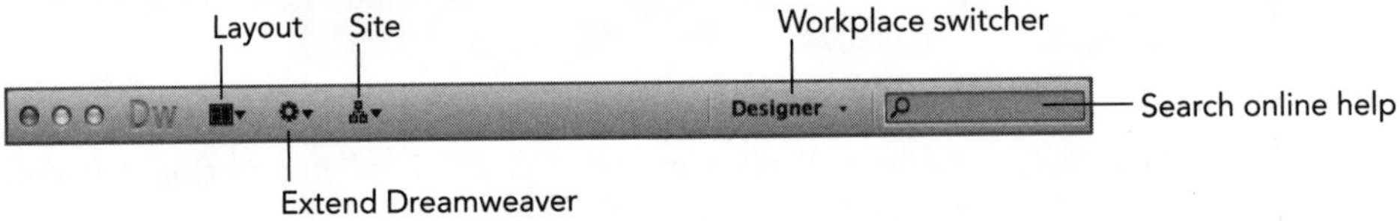

- **Layout:** The Layout menu button gives you quick access to the various document views including Code, Split Code, Design, and Code and Design (a.k.a. Split view); you can also toggle the Split Vertically and Design View On Left options from the Layout menu button.
- **Extend Dreamweaver:** Dreamweaver is wonderfully extensible, and you can add many time-saving capabilities through the free and commercial extensions available. Under the Extend Dreamweaver menu button, you'll find quick access to the Extension Manager, the Creative Suites tool for inserting and managing extensions. Two other menu items give you direct access to some of the available extensions. Browse For Web Widgets opens your primary browser to the Adobe Exchange page dedicated to JavaScript web widgets compatible with Dreamweaver, and Browse For Other Dreamweaver Extensions takes you to the main Adobe Exchange page for Dreamweaver.

- **Site:** The Site menu button offers two options. New Site opens the Site Definition dialog box so you can define a new local and/or remote site. Manage Sites displays the full-featured Manage Sites dialog box, which allows you to edit, duplicate, or remove existing sites; import or export site settings; or set up new sites or direct server connections.
- **Workspace switcher:** As described earlier in this chapter, the Workspace switcher is used to modify your Dreamweaver environment. You can either choose from default workspaces or create your own custom ones.
- **Search:** The search field included in the Application bar allows you to perform online searches of the Dreamweaver Help system. Enter a term and then press Enter (Return) or click the magnifying glass icon to load the search results in your primary browser.

The Related Files bar

The Related Files bar is located between the filename tab and the Document toolbar if the current file contains links to any external CSS, JavaScript, or server-side file. Any such documents, or related files, are listed in the order they are included in the primary web page, after a Source Code link, which, when clicked, displays the primary web page in Code view.

The beauty of the Related Files feature is that you can click the entry for a related file to open it in Code view while continuing to display the complete web page in Design or Live Data view. Any updates made to the code—whether in CSS, JavaScript, or server-side code includes—can be immediately displayed in Live View. If you're not already in Split view, choosing one of the related files will switch to that mode.

CAUTION

Some web pages can include a great number of related files—often too many to deal with practically. Dreamweaver provides a filtering mechanism to show just the files you want to work with, whether they're CSS, PHP, or JavaScript. Just click the Filter icon found on the far right of the Related Files bar and toggle on just the file types you need. You can even create a custom filter to restrict the related files displayed to a common file name or extension.

Should you prefer to open related files as separate documents rather than in Code view all the time, there is an option for doing so in the General category of Preferences. To open a related file just once, right-click (Control+click) the related file link and choose Open as Separate File.

To make the most out of the Related Files feature and its companion features (Live Data view and Code Navigator), see Chapter 5.

The Document toolbar: Design view

The Document toolbar gives you quick access to commands that affect the entire document. As with the Standard toolbar, you can hide and show the Document toolbar with a menu command: View ➪ Toolbars ➪ Document. The Document toolbar actually has two modes. This first is displayed when Dreamweaver is in Design view. One of the Document toolbar's best features in Design view is the quick and easy access it offers for changing your web page's title, as shown in Figure 2-13.

FIGURE 2-13

The Document toolbar offers easy access to an important element of a web page, the title.

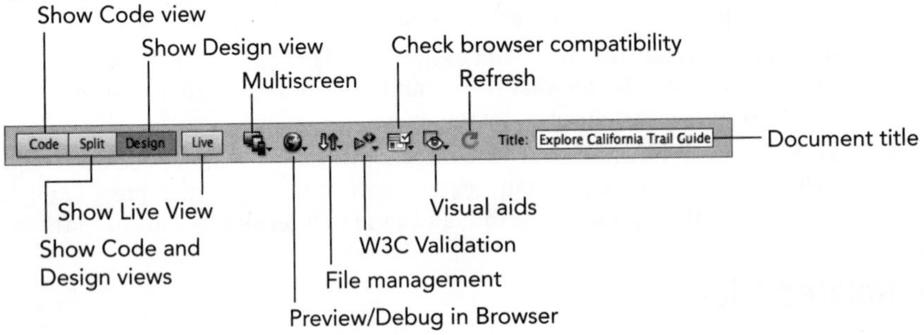

The first set of buttons in the Document toolbar in both modes is dedicated to the various views: Code, Split, and Design. These buttons are mutually exclusive because only one view can be shown at a time.

To the right of the first three buttons is another view-related button: Live View. As previously explained, when Live View is selected, Dreamweaver renders the page with the built-in browser, and it also invokes the second mode of the Document toolbar. For more details, see the section "Document Toolbar: Live View." The following subsections describe additional functionality found on both Document toolbar modes.

Setting up for multiple screen design

Today's world is rife with an ever-increasing number of mobile devices capable of browsing the web as easily as a desktop. For Dreamweaver users, this means designs should be flexible enough to fit well on a number of differently sized screens. To meet this need, Dreamweaver has introduced a workflow that uses media queries—CSS statements that allow styles to be applied conditionally. The Multiscreen Preview dialog box, accessible from the Document toolbar, is designed to assign these media queries to the appropriate style sheets and compare the results, side by side.

When you first click the Multiscreen icon (to the right of the four view buttons when in Design view, and after Live View Options when in Live View), you're presented with a very large dialog box and three identical displays. The main area on the bottom shows the current desktop view while the upper left shows what a phone-sized screen would show, and the upper right shows a tablet view. Click the Media Queries button within the dialog box to set up your style sheet conditions. After you've added custom styles to the appropriate style sheets, Multiscreen Preview will reflect those differences, as shown in Figure 2-14.

To learn more about media queries and designing layouts for multiple screens, see Chapter 6.

FIGURE 2-14

Review the custom layouts for three different devices in the Multiscreen Preview.

Previewing your file

Although Dreamweaver gives you a good representation of what your page looks like when rendered in a browser, it's not perfect—even with Live View. So many variations exist among the different browser programs—not to mention versions—that you absolutely must test your page throughout the development process.

Selecting the Preview in Browser button on the Document toolbar (next to Multiscreen) presents a dynamic list of available browsers. All the browsers entered in Preferences appear first, with the primary and secondary browsers leading the list.

The final entry under the toolbar's Preview/Debug in Browser button is Edit Browser List. When invoked, this command opens the Preview in Browser category of Preferences, enabling you to add, remove, or otherwise manage the browsers on your system in relation to Dreamweaver.

See Chapter 3 for details about working with the Preview in Browser preferences.

Managing files

At the far right end of the Document toolbar is the Title text field for displaying and altering the title of your document. Dreamweaver, by default, titles every new page *Untitled Document*. Not only is it considered bad form to keep this default title, search engines need a relevant title to properly index a site. To change a page title, enter the new text in the Title field and press Enter (Return) to confirm your modification.

The File Management button (up and down arrows), which contains web-publishing–related commands, is to the right of the Title field when in Live View and to its left when in normal view. While maintaining a website, you'll often be required to make small alterations such as changing a bit of text or rescaling an image. I prefer to post these changes as quickly as possible to get the work off my virtual desk. The Get and Put options, along with the Check In and Check Out options, found on the Document toolbar under File Management, greatly simplify the process and speed up my work. Note that these commands are available only if you have defined a remote site as part of your site definition.

The File Management button offers these options:

- **Turn Off Read Only:** Unlocks the current file for editing. This command is enabled only if the current document is marked as read-only. (On the Mac, the Turn Off Read Only option is called Unlock.)
- **Get:** Transfers the remote file to the local site.
- **Check Out:** Marks the file as checked out and gets the remote file.
- **Put:** Transfers the local file to the remote site.
- **Check In:** Marks the file as checked in and puts the file to the remote site.
- **Undo Check Out:** Replaces the local version of the page with the remote version, effectively undoing any changes made on the local file.
- **Show Checked Out By:** Displays a dialog box that allows you to filter files checked out by a specific user.
- **Design Notes:** Opens the Design Notes dialog box for the current page.
- **Locate In Site:** Selects the current page in the file listings of the Site panel. This command is enabled only if the current file has been saved.

Validating your site pages

A key technique to make sure that your website pages are compatible across the board is to validate them. Dreamweaver now makes it possible to validate your pages with the W3C—the authority responsible for creating the HTML, CSS, and other specifications—without leaving the program. To start the process, click W3C Validation and choose Validate Current Document (W3C). Results are shown in the Validation window. Dynamic pages can also be validated by entering into Live View and choosing Validate Live Document (W3C). The W3C Validation menu also includes the Settings option, which displays the Validation category of Preferences.

To find out more about W3C Validation in Dreamweaver, see Chapter 30.

Checking for browser errors

With the wide range of browsers on the market today—many with different rendering capabilities—web designers need to keep a close eye on their page from start to finish. Dreamweaver offers a handy debugging feature known as Check Browser Compatibility. As mentioned earlier, the Check Browser Compatibility button is found to the right of the File Management button.

Check Browser Compatibility relies on the web-building community for its expertise. With the Check Browser Compatibility feature, Dreamweaver currently inspects the page for 26 different CSS issues that affect a full range of modern browsers. In addition to pinpointing the problematic code on your page and describing the error in the Results panel, the Check Browser Compatibility feature also provides a link to the relevant page on Adobe's CSS Advisor site.

For details on each of the CSS rendering issues checked by Dreamweaver, see Chapter 30.

Dreamweaver checks the page against whichever browsers you specify in the Target Browsers dialog box, opened by choosing Settings from the Browser Check menu. You have the option of choosing any or all of six different browsers and specifying the minimum acceptable browser version.

The Check Browser Compatibility menu offers these options:

- **Check Browser Compatibility:** Checks the current page against the browser versions selected in the Settings dialog box.
- **Next Issue:** Displays the first (or next) problem Dreamweaver found in Split view with the cause of the error marked with a wavy red underline. Mouse over the error to see an explanation of the error in a tooltip; Dreamweaver also lists the browser or browsers in which the error occurs.
- **Previous Issue:** Displays the prior error, again marked with a red wavy underline.
- **Show All Issues:** Opens the Target Browser Check category of the Results panel with a list of all the problems found in the document. Double-click an entry to highlight that error in Split view.
- **Edit Ignored Issue List:** Opens the `Exceptions.xml` file, which contains the browser check errors you want Dreamweaver to ignore during the checking process.
- **Check Spelling:** Displays the Check Spelling dialog box and begins spell-checking the current document.
- **Check CSS Advisor Website For New Issues:** Opens the CSS Advisor site on Adobe.com in your primary browser.
- **Report A Browser Rendering Issue:** Displays the page on the CSS Advisor site to submit a new post; you'll need to be registered with Adobe.com and signed in to file a new report.
- **Settings:** Opens the Target Browsers dialog box where you specify which browser and browser version you want Dreamweaver to check.

I find it helpful to run the Browser Compatibility Check after each major CSS addition (layout, text styling, and so on) during the design stage rather than wait until the page is fully completed. By keeping a close eye on browser compatibility, I keep the debugging compartmentalized and easier to solve.

Easy refresh and viewing options

The next two items on the Document toolbar are the Visual Aids and the Refresh Design View buttons. Use the Refresh Design View button when you've altered code directly in the Code view and you're ready to apply those changes in the Design view; this option is especially useful when the split-screen Code and Design view is in operation.

The layout-oriented Visual Aids are only available in Design view. A series of options toggle web page–focused helper tools on and off. One command, Show/Hide All Visual Aids, displays or conceals all of them at once. The Visual Aids are:

- Hide All Visual Aids
- Fluid Grid Layout Guides
- CSS Layout Backgrounds
- CSS Layout Box Model
- CSS Layout Outlines
- AP Element Outlines
- Table Widths
- Table Borders
- Frame Borders
- Image Maps
- Invisible Elements

Document Toolbar: Live View

Next to the three initial view buttons (Code, Split, and Design) is a fourth: Live, for invoking Live View. Dreamweaver's Live View is, at its heart, a full-fledged web browser. And, like other web browsers, Live View can be used to jump from one page to another via links or by direct URL input. You can control how you move through a site—and the code displayed—through the Document toolbar when in Live View. Entering Live View displays another mode of the Document toolbar, exposing buttons like Live Code and Inspect, as shown in Figure 2-15. Choose Live Code to reveal the code as processed by the browser.

FIGURE 2-15

Extended options are available on the Document toolbar when in Live View.

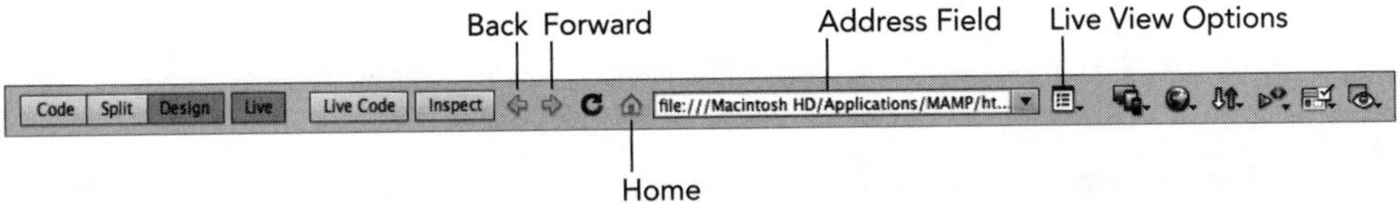

Adjacent to Live View is the Inspect button. Click Inspect to display color-coded backgrounds for the margins (yellow), padding (purple), border (green), and content (blue) areas of any element you hover over while in Live View. If you're not in Live View when you click Inspect, Dreamweaver automatically shifts into that mode.

TIP

You'll get the most out of the Inspect feature if your CSS panel is open in Current mode. Depending on the situation, you might also find it helpful to have Live Code enabled in Split view.

Much of the Document toolbar's functionality when in Live View is given over to mimicking a traditional browser. There are back and forward buttons, an easy way to refresh the page, an address field for quick URL entry, and even a home icon to get you back where you started. More Dreamweaver-specific commands that, for example, allow you to freeze JavaScript and reveal generated code, are handily grouped under a menu button. The key elements of the Browser Navigation toolbar are:

- **Back and Forward:** Browser-like buttons for moving to and from a previously selected web page.
- **Refresh:** Reloads the current page.
- **Home:** Displays the initially loaded page in Live View.
- **Address:** Shows the current pages URL and can be used to enter a new web address.
- **Live View options:** Contains a collection of commands related to Live View.

Once Live View is engaged, the additional icons on the Document toolbar become active, and the current page's file URL is shown in the Address field, like `file:///C|/inetpub/wwwroot/Ellen%20Celli%20Jewelry/index.htm` or, on the Mac, `file:///Macintosh%20HD/Users/josephlowery/Sites/markofthejoe/index.htm`. Amazingly, you can enter any standard URL in the Address field, press Enter (Return), and, assuming you're online, display that web page in Dreamweaver. Moreover, if you click Live Code, you can even see how it's built, as shown in Figure 2-16.

FIGURE 2-16

Reveal the underlying code as used by the browser in Live Code.

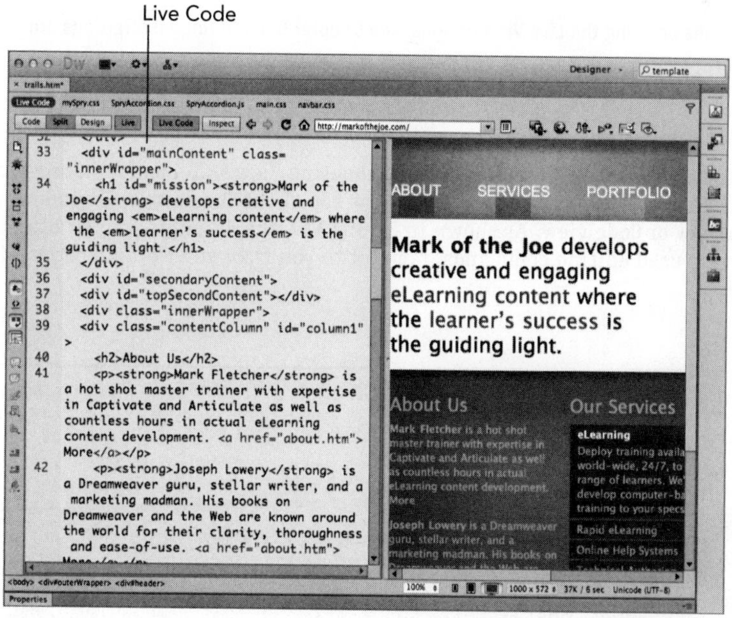

The Live View Options menu offers a variety of commands, all geared toward helping you make the most of Live View:

- **Freeze JavaScript:** Stops JavaScript from functioning so you can inspect the current state in Live Code.
- **Disable JavaScript:** Turns JavaScript off, as a user might, to display the page under that condition.
- **Disable Plugins:** Turns off any plugin, such as the Flash Player, so you can test your page output in that scenario.
- **Highlight Changes In Live Code:** Adds a background color to source code during user interactivity.
- **Edit The Live View Page In A New Tab:** Opens the current page, navigated to in Live View, in a new Document Window.
- **Follow Link (Ctrl+Click/Cmd+Click Link):** Displays linked pages in Live View when the listed keys are pressed and the link clicked.
- **Follow Links Continuously:** Displays related pages when the link is clicked without requiring a modifier key.
- **Automatically Sync Remote Files:** Includes related files that are hosted remotely automatically.
- **Use Testing Server For Document Source:** Pulls the linked pages from the designated testing server in the Site dialog box.
- **Use Local Files For Document Links:** Relies on files saved locally to displayed linked pages.
- **HTTP Request Settings:** Opens a dialog box for setting URL and form parameters.

For more details on using the Live View options, see Chapter 5. HTTP Request Settings are covered in Chapter 21.

The Standard toolbar

You can toggle the Standard toolbar on and off by choosing View ➪ Toolbars ➪ Standard. When first enabled, the Standard toolbar appears across the top of the Dreamweaver window, whether you're in Design view or Code view. As shown in Figure 2-17, the Standard toolbar offers some of the most frequently used editing commands, familiar to you from any word processing program.

FIGURE 2-17

The Standard toolbar contains frequently used editing commands.

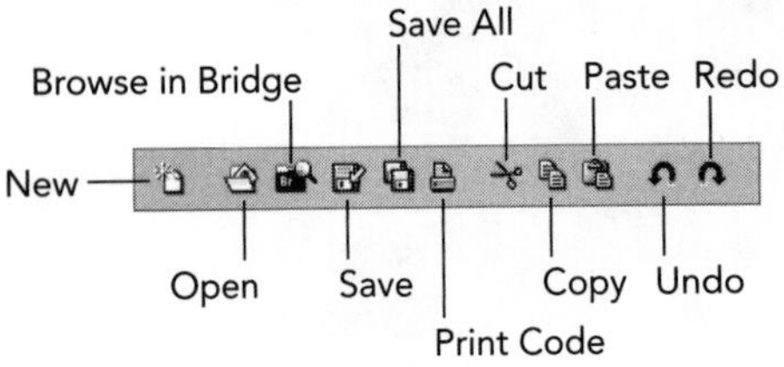

The first group of buttons you find on the Standard toolbar includes New, Open, Browse in Bridge (Adobe's visual file browser), Save, Save All, and Print Code. These create a new document, open an existing document, display available assets in Adobe Bridge, save the current document, save all open documents, and print the code of the current document, respectively. The next group of buttons includes Cut, Copy, and Paste. These enable you to place a selected item on the clipboard and then paste it into another location. The final group of buttons on the Standard toolbar includes the all-important Undo and Redo. Undo removes the effects of the last action you performed, and Redo repeats the most recent action or performs an undone action again.

For more details on how to use Bridge with Dreamweaver, see Chapter 24.

In Windows, you can reposition the Standard toolbar by clicking one of the separator bars between the toolbar buttons and then dragging. If you drag the Standard toolbar away from the edge of the window, it becomes a floating toolbar. You can dock the Standard toolbar by dragging it to the top or bottom edge of the window. On a Mac, the Standard toolbar cannot be repositioned.

The Style Rendering toolbar

One of the reasons CSS is increasingly used for layout is its capability to target different media types. Although web designers most frequently do not specify a media type at all—which is the same as using one style sheet for all output devices—savvy designers take the time to optimize their pages for both screen and printer at a minimum.

The W3C specification recognizes many different media types including Screen, Print, Handheld, Projection, TTY, and TV. Through the Style Rendering toolbar (see Figure 2-18), Dreamweaver allows designers to switch from one type to another, if defined. This feature is extremely helpful when the designer needs to add a print-friendly style sheet. As web designers restyle their content to fit other devices, such as handhelds, the Style Rendering toolbar becomes indispensable.

FIGURE 2-18

The Style Rendering toolbar allows you not only to quickly switch between CSS media types but also to toggle CSS rendering on and off.

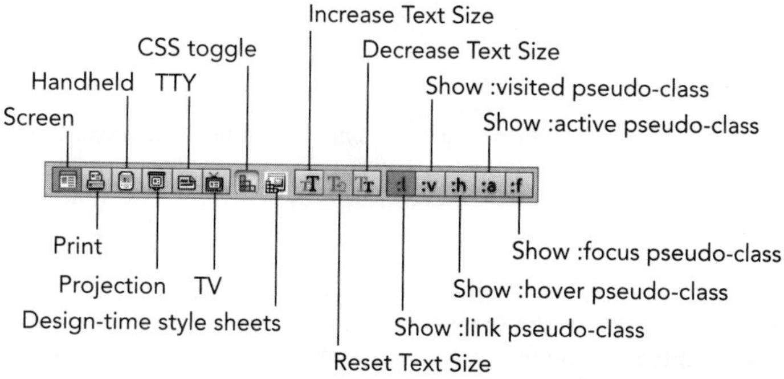

2

The next button on the Style Rendering toolbar toggles the rendering of CSS. This capability is extremely helpful when optimizing your CSS; for example, without CSS layout, you can quickly tell how a screen reader would approach your page and determine if content needs to be repositioned to make it more understandable.

The Style Rendering toolbar's next button, Design-Time Style Sheets, allows the designer to include or exclude CSS style sheets to be rendered in the development phase; that is, design time. This is a powerful feature that can help fine-tune Dreamweaver's rendering capabilities without affecting the final published output.

Modern browsers all make it relatively easy for users to change the text size of the web page they're looking at. The next three buttons on the Style Rendering toolbar—Increase Text Size, Reset Text Size, and Decrease Text Size—help you simulate that effect so you can gauge how your layout is affected.

NOTE

Changing text size by itself isn't used as much these days as all major browsers now support page zoom, which increases the size of both text and images together.

The final set of buttons on the Style Rendering toolbar is great for displaying another browser feature, link states. Hyperlinks have five different states possible:

- **Link:** The initial state of the hyperlink when the page first loads.
- **Visited:** How the link looks after it has been clicked.
- **Hover:** The appearance displayed when the user's mouse rolls over the link.
- **Active:** The state invoked when the user's mouse clicks a link and the mouse button is held down.
- **Focus:** The state triggered by the user tabbing to a particular link.

In CSS, these states are referred to as pseudo-classes because, like a standard CSS class, they can be assigned to any number of page elements, but unlike the typical class, they are dependent on the user's actions and not the designer's coding. These pseudo-class buttons are mutually exclusive, and you can display only one at a time.

The Coding toolbar

The Coding toolbar is quite different from the other toolbars in a number of ways. First, it's only available in Code view, and second, it's a vertical rather than horizontal toolbar. The Coding toolbar also cannot be repositioned in either Windows or Mac. These differences, however, quickly fall by the wayside once coders understand the power inherent in the toolbar.

Much of the functionality is unique to the Coding toolbar (see Figure 2-19), although a few commands are replicated from elsewhere in the Dreamweaver interface for ease of use. The very top button, Open Documents, falls into the former category; click the Open Documents button to see a list of all files currently open. What distinguishes this button from other file listings—on the document tabs and under the Window menu—is the listing of the full path to the file rather than just the filename. The first time you have four files from separate folders, all named `index.html`, open at the same time, you'll immediately grasp the value of this feature.

FIGURE 2-19

The Coding toolbar hugs the left edge of Code view, easily accessible to the power coder.

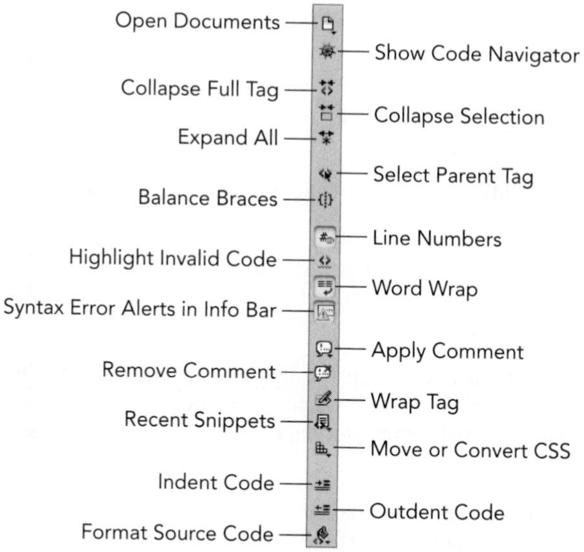

TIP

The Code Navigator allows you to quickly move to any code functions related to or affecting the current selection. When Show Code Navigator—a nautically themed ship's wheel icon—is clicked, the Code Navigator window appears with a series of links. Click any link to go directly to the code.

The next group of functions relate to Dreamweaver's Code Collapse functionality. Included in this group are Collapse Full Tag, Collapse Selection, and Expand All. When clicked, Collapse Full Tag expands the current selection to the immediate tag and collapses the code. Press Alt (Option) while clicking either Collapse Full Tag or Collapse Selection to collapse all except the current tag or selection, respectively; a very useful feature when you're trying to focus on one aspect of your code.

The following group of buttons helps coders verify proper code. Select Parent Tag quickly highlights the tag surrounding the current selection, clicking it again highlights its parent's tag, and Balance Braces selects code within the matching set of parentheses, braces, or square brackets. Both Line Numbers and Highlight Invalid Code can also be found in the Visual Aids menu option of the Document toolbar.

CAUTION

Dreamweaver reads your code as you write it or make any changes in Code view. If any errors are found in the syntax of your code, a yellow info bar appears at the top of the document with the line number of a possible problem in your code if the Syntax Error Alerts In Info Bar option is enabled. If you're making a number of changes, you might want to disable this option to prevent being alerted to a series of false positives.

Comments are an essential building block of any programming language, and Dreamweaver supports a wide range of them. Under the Apply Comments button, you'll find the option to insert HTML, JavaScript, CSS comments, and more. The different types of comments available are:

- `<!-- HTML Comments -->`
- `/* CSS or JavaScript block style comments */`
- `// CSS or JavaScript single line style comments`
- `'Visual Basic single line style comments`
- ASP, ASP.NET, JSP, PHP, or ColdFusion style comments, depending on the application server used

Each of the comment options wraps a selection in the chosen comment style; in the case of single line style comments, the comments are placed at the start of each selected line. If no code is highlighted, an empty comment of the desired type is inserted.

Paired with the Apply Comment button is another option for deleting them: Remove Comment. The Remove Comment feature uncomments any selected code and will remove multiple comments unless they are nested. In the case of nested comments, only the outer comments are deleted.

Need a quick way to add a parent tag to a selection? Choose Wrap Tag and you can easily enter the desired outer element, along with any desired attributes and values. Press Enter (Return) to confirm your choices and the parent tag code is inserted.

You can wrap content with much more than a single tag through the Recent Snippets button. The Recent Snippets feature lists the 10 most recently used snippets, which can be either wrap or block type.

The next button, Move or Convert CSS, includes two CSS management functions: Convert Inline CSS to Rule and Move CSS Rules. The Convert Inline CSS to Rule extracts styles that are defined within a selected tag (or *inline*), like this:

```
<div id="pullQuote" style="float: right; margin: 5px;">
```

to a new rule, like this:

```
pullQuote {
  float: right;
  margin: 5px;
}
```

You'll have an opportunity to choose whether the new rule should be saved in the `<head>` section of the current document or in an external style sheet. Inline styles are harder to manage and more limited in their effect and, under most circumstances, should be converted to rules.

The clearly named Move CSS Rules does just that: moves selected CSS rules from the current page or style sheet to an external style sheet. You can specify an existing style sheet or create a new one to hold your rules. This command is especially beneficial for designers who—like me—prefer to embed CSS rules when first creating a new layout.

The final buttons on the Coding toolbar are used for styling your code. The Indent Code and Outdent Code buttons move selected code blocks in or out according to the options set in the Code Format category of Preferences. The final button, Format Source Code, allows you to style either the entire document or a selection of your code according to the Code Format Settings, which, along with another code style option, Tag Libraries, is also available under this menu.

Selecting from the Insert Panel

The Insert panel holds the items most frequently used—the primary colors, as it were—when designing web pages. You can select everything from images to ActiveX plugins to HTML comments from the Insert panel.

The Insert panel is divided into separate categories of objects: Common, Layout, Forms, Data, Spry, jQuery Mobile, InContext Editing, Text, and Favorites. Additional advanced categories are available for various server-side scripting languages: ASP, CFML Basic, CFML Flow, CFML Advanced, PHP, and XSLT. These advanced categories are available only when the currently open document is of the relevant file type, as determined by its file extension. Table 2-2 shows the file extensions related to each category.

TABLE 2-2 File Types for Advanced Categories

Insert Panel Category	Related File Extensions
ASP	.asp
CFML Basic	.cfm, .cfc
CFML Flow	.cfm, .cfc
CFML Advanced	.cfm, .cfc
PHP	.php, .php3
XSLT	.xsl

The initial view is of the Common category. Switch from one category to another by selecting the appropriate choice from the category menu (see Figure 2-20).

TIP

If you yearn for the good old days pre-CS4, when the Insert panel was an Insert bar, fear not. From the Workspace switcher, choose Classic to move the Insert panel to its former position above the Document window. Once the change is made, if you prefer the menu view rather than the Insert panel tab view, choose Show As Menu from the bottom of the category menu. To switch back, right-click and choose Show As Tabs, as shown in Figure 2-21.

FIGURE 2-20

Switch categories from the pop-up menu on the Insert panel.

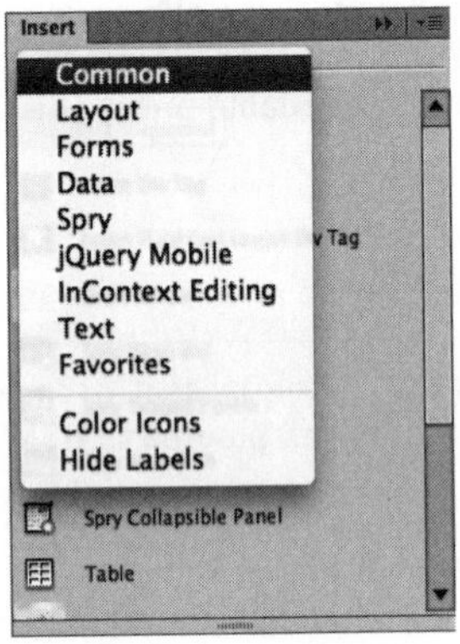

FIGURE 2-21

You can switch your Insert panel view from menus to tabs and back again when in the Classic workspace.

If the Insert panel is not available when you first start Dreamweaver, you can enable it by choosing Window ➪ Insert, View ➪ Toolbars ➪ Insert, or by pressing the keyboard shortcut, Ctrl+F2 (Command+F2). Likewise, choosing Window ➪ Insert, View ➪ Toolbars ➪ Insert, or the shortcut again, closes the Insert panel.

TIP

The icons in Dreamweaver's Insert panel are intentionally grayscale in appearance to keep focus on the web page under development. When you hover over them with your cursor, they change to a colored icon. If you'd prefer to have the icons always appear in color, right-click (Control+click) and choose Colored Icons from the pop-up menu.

The following sections describe each category in the Insert panel.

Common objects

The most frequently used HTML elements, aside from text, are accessible through the Common category of the Insert panel.

The Insert panel in Dreamweaver uses menu buttons in each category, like the Images and Media menus in the Common category. Menu buttons are identifiable by a small downward-pointing arrow to the right of the button. Numerous objects are contained within each menu group; when you choose an object, that object becomes the default item for the menu. For example, if you choose Image Placeholder from the Images menu group, the icon for that menu item is displayed in the Insert panel. Image Placeholder then becomes the default until another item from the group, such as Image or Fireworks HTML, is chosen. The first time any menu button is accessed, no default object yet exists, and you must choose an object from the menu group.

The Common category contains five submenus: Images, Media, Head, Script, and Templates. Everything from basic images to the navigation bar is available from the Images group, as shown in Figure 2-22. Dreamweaver facilitates the inclusion of external elements—such as multimedia animations, Java applets, plugins, and ActiveX controls—through the Media group of the Insert panel's Common category. Under the Head menu button, you'll find tags that affect or describe the entire document, such as `keywords` and `description`, and that are inserted in the <head> area of the page. The Script group contains only two objects—Script and No Script—that give the designer the option of including JavaScript external files or functions or telling the browser what to display if the user does not have JavaScript enabled. Templates are special Dreamweaver documents that define the layout and visual design of a page. The most common template options are found under the Template menu on the Insert panel's Common category.

2

FIGURE 2-22

Graphics-related objects are grouped under the Images menu in the Common category.

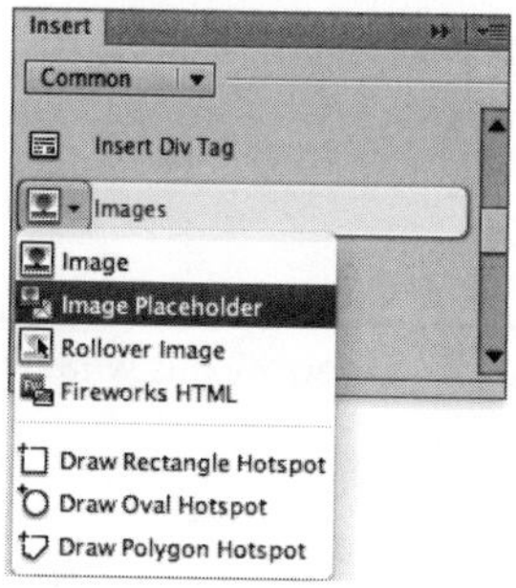

Many of the common objects open a dialog box that enables you to browse for a file or specify parameters. If you prefer to enter all your information (including the necessary filenames) through the Property inspector or in Code view, you can turn off the automatic appearance of the dialog box for some objects when inserted through the Insert panel or the menus. Choose Edit ➪ Preferences (Dreamweaver ➪ Preferences) and, from the General category, clear the Show Dialog When Inserting Objects option. In the Common category, this option affects the Hyperlink, Email Link, Named Anchor, Insert Table, Image, and Image Placeholder, as well as all the Head elements and Flash objects.

NOTE

Additional Preferences settings, located in the Accessibility category of the Preferences dialog box, also cause dialog boxes to appear when you insert an object using the Insert panel. These accessibility dialog boxes appear even if the Show Dialog When Inserting Objects option is clear.

General document information—such as the title and any descriptive keywords about the page—is written into the <head> section of an HTML document. The Head menu objects enable web designers to drop in these bits of code in a handy object format. Although Dreamweaver enables you to see the <head> objects onscreen via the View ➪ Head Content menu option, you don't have to have the Head Content visible to drop in the objects. Simply click any of the objects, and a dialog box opens, prompting you for the needed information.

Script menu objects simplify the task of adding custom scripts or server-side includes to your page.

Layout objects

You use the Layout category of the Insert panel to work with tables, <div> tags, AP elements, and Fluid Grid Layout Divs—objects that enable you to define the layout of your page. You can even insert advanced JavaScript-controlled elements through the four Spry widgets available here: the Spry Menu Bar, Spry Tabbed Panels, Spry Accordion, and Spry Collapsible Panel. These objects are explained a bit later in this chapter in the section covering the Spry category, "Spry Objects."

Dreamweaver offers you two ways to work with tables. You can use Standard mode (where you define the structure of a table using dialog boxes, menu commands, and the Property inspector), or you can use Expanded Table mode (where the table structure is made more obvious for easy modification). Switch between these mutually exclusive modes by clicking their buttons in the Layout category.

You'll also find objects for manipulating table structure, such as those for adding a row or column, as shown in Figure 2-23.

FIGURE 2-23

Whether you are working with <divs> or <table> tags, the Layout category has what you need.

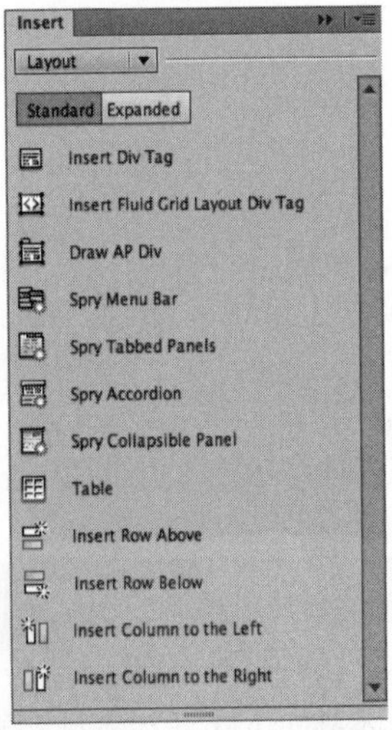

NOTE

Because of the visual nature of tables and AP elements, many of the objects in the Layout category can be used only in Design view.

Forms objects

Forms are the primary method for implementing HTML interactivity. The Forms category of the Insert panel gives you the basic building blocks for creating your web-based form—including the Form tag, Text field, Checkbox, and Radio buttons—as shown in Figure 2-24.

FIGURE 2-24

Implementing forms is a key aspect of web applications; not shown are the various Spry Validation form objects.

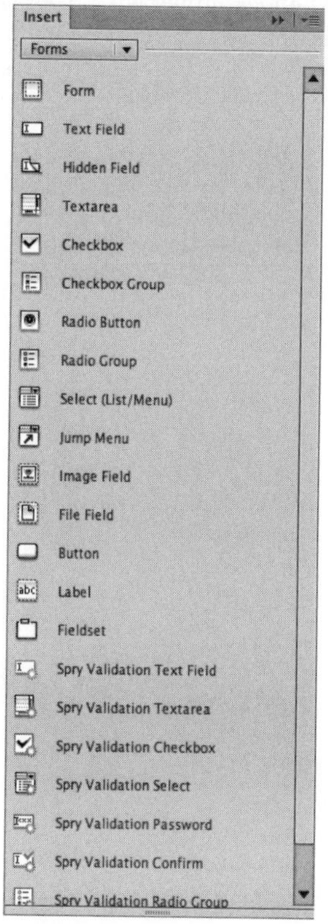

As with the Layout category, the Forms category has several JavaScript-driven objects. These Spry-based elements provide form validation and the basic form object. For more details, see the section "Spry Objects" later in this chapter.

Data objects

Although the layout of a web page and the dynamic content that fills it may vary widely, much of the code underlying basic web data operations remains the same. For example, the basic code that is used to insert employee records into a Human Resources database may also be used to add a new entry into a database that maintains a DVD collection. Dreamweaver removes much of the tedium of scripting common web applications by supplying objects in the Data category of the Insert panel. Additionally, you'll also find objects for handling data in non-dynamic formats, including importing tabular data and applying Spry data sets. For more information about the Spry elements, see the following section.

With a single Data object, you can build an entire web application that displays a list of records, enables you to navigate through them, displays which records are currently onscreen, and links to another page with detailed information from a selected record. In general, Dreamweaver's Data objects can be used separately or together. The Master Detail Page Set object includes two other Data objects: the Recordset Navigation Bar object and the Recordset Navigation Status object.

Data objects, shown in Figure 2-25, are particularly powerful when combined with Dreamweaver's template feature. It's possible, for example, to create a basic Master Detail Page Set with the Data object and then apply a template to give the page a specific look and feel, thereby integrating it into a site. Numerous menu buttons bring almost all of Dreamweaver's server-side power to the Insert panel.

FIGURE 2-25

Common web data, such as the Master Detail Page Set, are created in one action with Dreamweaver's Data objects.

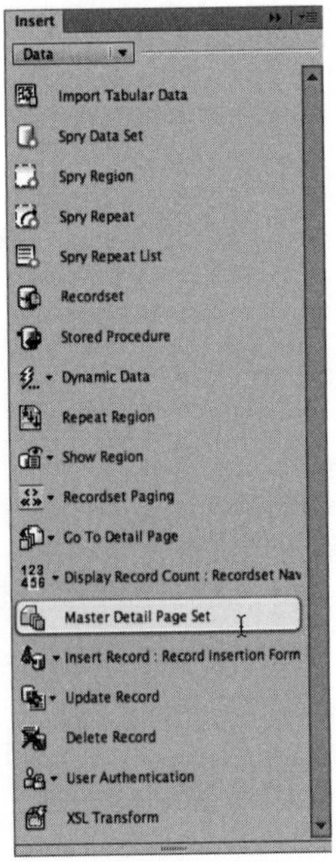

Spry objects

Spry is an Ajax (Asynchronous JavaScript and XML) framework developed by Adobe. The Spry objects in Dreamweaver make it easy to apply the more powerful facets of Ajax, including the capability to update data in a portion of the page without refreshing the entire page.

The Spry category of the Insert panel, shown in Figure 2-26, is divided into three groups: data, forms, and layout. As noted earlier, these objects are also available from each of the Insert panel's corresponding categories. The Dreamweaver team decided to take this multiple access approach to both highlight the new Spry technologies and emphasize where the various components fit in the web designer's workflow.

You'll find a full chapter devoted to the world of Ajax and the Spry implementation in Chapter 16.

FIGURE 2-26

Spry objects make it possible to include advanced JavaScript and XML technologies with the click of a mouse.

The Spry data objects work with associated HTML or XML files to selectively display just the data requested by the user. The first object in the group, Spry Data Set, is a wizard that establishes the connection to the data and, optionally, lays out the elements. The other objects are components of this process and can be applied separately. Table 2-3 details the individual Spry data objects.

TABLE 2-3 Spry Data Objects

Icon	Name	Description
	Spry Data Set	Identifies an HTML or XML data source and data columns to work with.
	Spry Region	Sets an HTML tag, typically <div> or <span>, to work with a specified Spry data set.
	Spry Repeat	Establishes a repeating region for Spry data within <div> or <span> tags.
	Spry Repeat List	Repeats Spry data for list-related tags, such as <ol>, <ul>, or <dl>.

The Spry form objects add client-side validation to a range of form elements. With validation enabled, users are immediately informed if they enter their information in the wrong format. Table 2-4 lists the available Spry form objects.

TABLE 2-4 Spry Form Objects

Icon	Name	Description
	Spry Validation Text Field	Inserts a standard text field with 13 different validation types.
	Spry Validation Textarea	Inserts a textarea form element that can be required or restricted to a certain number of characters.
	Spry Validation Checkbox	Includes a checkbox form element to the page that can be required or, if multiple checkboxes are used, restricted to a minimum or maximum selected.
	Spry Validation Select	Adds a menu select list to the page that checks to see if a choice or invalid selection has been made.
	Spry Validation Password	Inserts a password field with masked input, which can require a defined number of letters, numbers, uppercase letters, and special characters.
	Spry Validation Confirm	Adds a password or text field where the input value is required to match the input value of another such field on the form.
	Spry Validation Radio Group	Includes two or more radio buttons, which can be required.

The four Spry layout objects bring enhanced layout possibilities to every designer's palette. Each of the Spry layout options—from the Menu Bar to the Accordion panel—are easily customizable in Design view with the help of the dedicated Property inspectors. Table 2-5 provides details about the Spry layout objects.

TABLE 2-5 Spry Layout Objects

Icon	Name	Description
	Spry Menu Bar	Inserts a standards-based vertical or horizontal navigation bar, capable of supporting multiple levels.
	Spry Tabbed Panels	Adds a series of content areas to the page, each made visible by selecting the corresponding tab.
	Spry Accordion	Initially includes two sliding content areas, which can be opened and closed interactively by the page visitor; additional areas can easily be added.
	Spry Collapsible Panel	Inserts a pod-like region that can be expanded or collapsed with a mouse click. Multiple panels, independently controlled, can be applied to a page.
	Spry Tooltip	Adds a completely customizable tooltip to any page selection, which can be configured with various effects, such as fade and blind.

jQuery Mobile objects

The jQuery framework has, for several years, been among the most popular JavaScript libraries for web development in general, and the recently introduced jQuery Mobile framework looks to achieve the same success for the mobile platform. jQuery Mobile gives a common look and feel across a wide spectrum of mobile device operating systems, including iOS, Android, Blackberry, and Windows, among others. Dreamweaver makes it easy to set up and implement a mobile-optimized site or mobile app with the jQuery Mobile objects, as shown in Figure 2-27.

FIGURE 2-27

Take advantage of the mobile platform's advanced functionality by adding an object from the jQuery Mobile category.

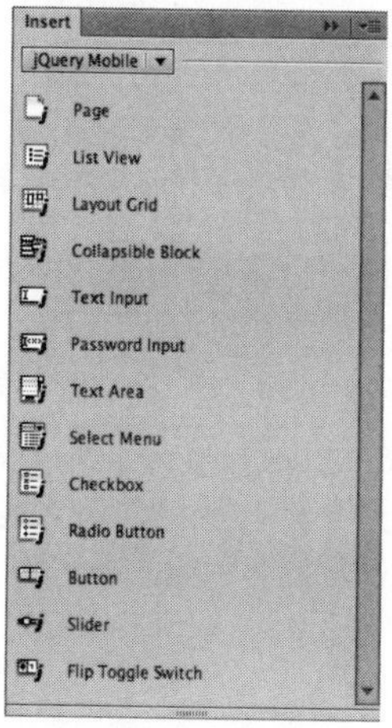

When you first insert a jQuery Mobile object, Dreamweaver presents you with a dialog box that sets up the framework for you, copying files and inserting code where needed. You have the option of working with locally or remotely hosted JavaScript and CSS files or even using another version entirely.

The jQuery Mobile objects cover a great deal of functionality, from core layout to enhanced user controls. Unlike standard websites, which typically rely on a separate HTML file for each page, a jQuery Mobile site can use a single file for numerous pages. This basic division is set up with the Page object. The page is often structured using a List View for navigation, and a Layout Grid or Collapsible Block for content. A full array of form controls is included, each within its own contained area that combines label and field. You'll find details about the complete collection of jQuery Mobile objects in Table 2-6.

TABLE 2-6 jQuery Mobile objects

Icon	Name	Description
	Page	Inserts code for a <div> tag with a data-role attribute of page with optional header and footer sections.
	List View	Adds code for an unordered or ordered list with a data-role attribute of listview and a variety of options.
	Layout Grid	Inserts code for a user-definable grid of layout <div> tags.
	Collapsible Block	Includes code for creating a jQuery-driven collapsing and expanding area.
	Text Input	Adds a <label> tag and <input> text field within a <div> tag with a data-role attribute of fieldcontain.
	Password Input	Same as Text Input, but the <input> tag is set to type=password.
	Text Area	Same as Text Input, with a <textarea> instead of <input> tag.
	Select Menu	Same as Text Input, with a <select> instead of <input> tag.
	Checkbox	Same as Text Input, but the <input> tag is set to type=checkbox.
	Radio Button	Same as Text Input, but the <input> tag is set to type=radio.
	Button	Inserts code for one or more links, <button> or <input> tags that act as buttons.
	Slider	Same as Text Input, but the <input> tag is set to type=range.
	Flip Toggle Switch	Same as Select Menu with two options specified (Off and On) and data-role=slider.

To learn more about the exciting possibilities of the jQuery Mobile objects, see Chapter 17.

InContext Editing objects

InContext Editing allows anyone to make updates to specific areas of their web pages directly through the browser, without installing any additional software. Offered as part of the Business Catalyst hosting, InContext Editing is perfect for those clients who want control of their content but lack the technical expertise to create and modify the pages in a web authoring tool like Dreamweaver. The InContext Editing editable areas are inserted and managed through the objects found in the Insert panel InContext Editing category, shown in Figure 2-28. In addition to an object for creating an editable region, this category also includes another for generating a repeating region.

FIGURE 2-28

InContext Editing objects make it possible to modify web pages directly in the browser.

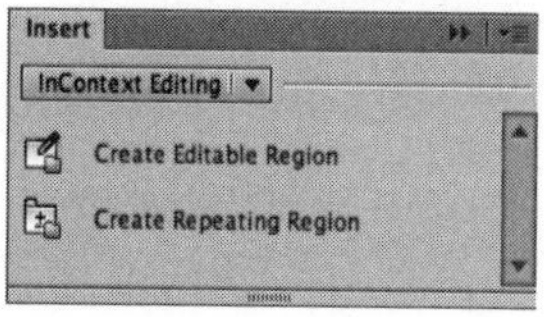

InContext Editing is covered in depth in Chapter 28.

Text objects

The text objects represent the most commonly used text formatting HTML tags, such as those needed to emphasize text or create bulleted lists (see Figure 2-29).

The Text objects behave differently, depending on whether you are working in Design view or Code view. If you are working in Code view, Dreamweaver puts you in charge and simply surrounds whatever text is selected with the appropriate HTML tags. If no text is selected, the tag pair is inserted at the current text insertion point.

In Design view, Dreamweaver also surrounds selected text with the appropriate tag pair. But in some situations, Dreamweaver does more than blindly surround the selected text with the specified HTML tags. The following examples illustrate the additional processing that occurs in Design view:

- In Design view, the Paragraph, Preformatted Text, Heading 1, Heading 2, and Heading 3 objects are treated as mutually exclusive. If you select text that is formatted as a Heading 1, and then you click the Heading 2 button on the Insert panel, Dreamweaver not only surrounds the selected text with `<h2></h2>` tags but also removes the `<h1></h1>` tags that were there before. In Code view, Dreamweaver simply adds the `<h2></h2>` tags without automatically removing the `<h1></h1>` tags. This is inappropriate coding and should be avoided.

- When you select one or more paragraphs of text in Design view and then click the Unordered List button, Dreamweaver creates a bulleted list by inserting `<ul></ul>` tags around the selected text, as in Code view. But in Design view, Dreamweaver additionally converts each paragraph to a separate item in that list by inserting the appropriate `<li></li>` tags. The same is true for Ordered lists and Definition lists.

FIGURE 2-29

Change the format of selected text by choosing a Text object.

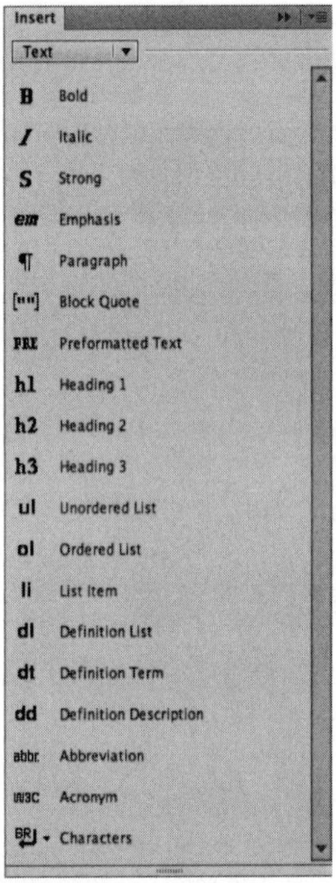

In Design view, if no text is selected when you click one of the text formatting buttons in this category, no tags are added until you start typing. This feature helps prevent the inclusion of empty tag pairs within your document.

The Text category contains a single menu button: Characters. Certain special characters—such as the copyright symbol (©)—are represented in HTML by codes called *character entities*. Dreamweaver eases the entry of these complex, hard-to-remember codes with the Characters objects. The most commonly used characters are included as separate objects, and another button opens a dialog box with additional special characters from which to choose. The Characters category also contains objects for inserting a line break and a nonbreaking space.

Favorites

Because you can choose from an overwhelming number of objects on the Insert panel, the Favorites category is a welcome and productive addition to Dreamweaver. Initially, no objects are displayed in the Favorites category—it's up to you to choose which objects to include. All modification of the Favorites category is handled through the Customize Favorite Objects dialog box (see Figure 2-30), which shows all the available objects on the left and the selected objects on the right. Objects can be grouped through use of a dotted-line separator.

To add, remove, or modify objects in the Favorites category, follow these steps:

1. Choose Favorites from the Insert panel menu or tab.
2. Right-click (Control+click) and choose Customize Favorites from the context menu. You can actually perform the same action from any category/tab of the Insert panel to open the Customize Favorite Objects dialog box.
3. In the Customize Favorite Objects dialog, select the category holding the object you want to display in the Favorites category from the drop-down list under Available Objects. The All category displays every available object, sorted by category. If you know what category your object is in, it's quicker to select that category from the list.

FIGURE 2-30

Use the Customize Favorite Objects dialog box to personalize your Insert panel for maximum productivity.

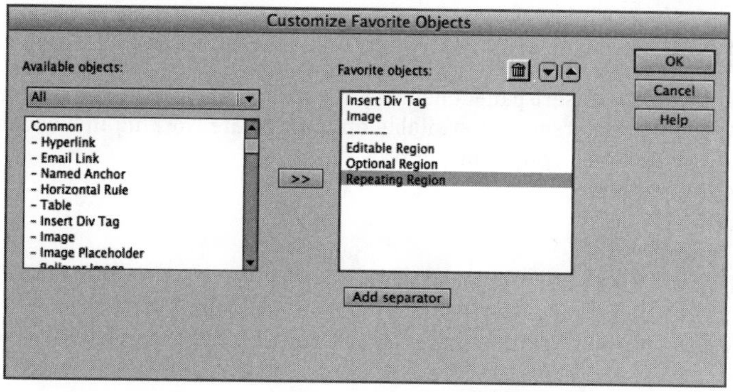

4. Choose an object from those listed in the Available Objects area and select the double-arrow button. The selected item moves to the Favorite Objects list.
5. Repeat Steps 3 and 4 to declare additional objects as favorites.
6. Change the order in which the objects are displayed by selecting an object and then clicking Up or Down to move the object left or right, respectively.
7. To delete an object from the Favorites list, select it and choose Remove.
8. To group objects together, choose Add Separator to insert a dotted-line divider.
9. When you're finished, click OK.

The objects you've selected, in the order you've specified, appear in the Favorites category. You can modify these objects at any time by re-opening the Customize Favorite Objects dialog box.

ASP objects

If you are creating Active Server Pages, the ASP category of the Insert panel can speed up the development of your code. Only available when the current document is named with an extension of `.asp`, this category contains the building blocks of an ASP page.

CFML and CFForm objects

The CFML and CFForm categories of the Insert panel give you access to the most frequently used objects in the ColdFusion toolbox. These categories are available on the Insert panel only if the active document has a file extension of `.cfm` or `.cfc`. In addition to the standard objects, there are a couple of menu buttons. The first is Flow, which inserts ColdFusion markup tags that alter the flow of control through the code. The second is Advanced, which provides numerous advanced functions, such as those that enable you to transfer files and data using a variety of protocols.

TIP

You can find detailed descriptions of the ColdFusion tags in the Reference panel. To view the ColdFusion documentation, select Window ⇨ Reference, and then select Adobe CFML Reference from the Book drop-down list.

PHP objects

The PHP category of the Insert panel enables you to insert code used in the PHP server-side scripting language. This category is available only if you are working in a document with the extension of `.php`, `.php3`, `.php4`, or `.php5`.

XSLT objects

If you're building either an XSLT fragment or a full page, you'll have access to the XSLT object category of the Insert panel. This category replicates features available from the Insert ⇨ XSLT Objects menu and includes Dynamic Text, Repeat Region, Conditional Region, Multiple Conditional Region, and XSL Comment.

Getting the Most Out of the Property Inspector

Dreamweaver's Property inspector is your primary tool for specifying an object's particulars. What exactly those particulars are—in HTML, they are known as *attributes* and in CSS, *properties*—depends on the object itself. The contents of the Property inspector vary depending on which object is selected and which button, HTML or CSS, is selected. For example, click anywhere on a blank web page, and the Property inspector set to HTML shows text attributes for format, bold, italic, and so on. When in CSS mode, the same selection displays the targeted rule, font name, size, color, and so on. You can see the differences between the two modes in Figure 2-31. If, however, you click an image, the Property inspector displays a small thumbnail of the picture, and the image's attributes for height and width, image source, link, and alternative text. There is no HTML or CSS option.

FIGURE 2-31

The Property inspector takes many forms, depending on the HTML element you select and, if text, whether you're in HTML (top) or CSS mode (bottom).

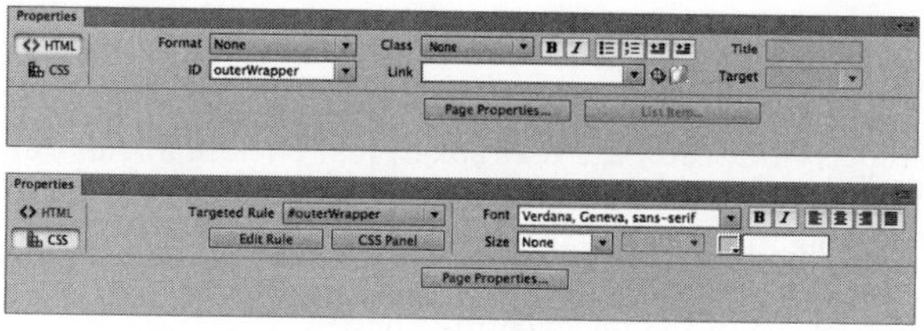

Manipulating the Property inspector

You can enable the Property inspector by choosing Window ➪ Properties or selecting the keyboard shortcut Ctrl+F3 (Command+F3). As with the Insert panel, the Property inspector can be closed by clicking the Close button (available only if the Property inspector is floating), unchecking Window ➪ Properties, or choosing the keyboard shortcut again. You can also close the Property inspector by selecting Close Panel Group from the panel menu, which is accessed by clicking the gray button at the right side of the Property inspector's title bar (see Figure 2-31).

CAUTION

For text—whether in a paragraph, heading, or table cell—the Property inspector can switch between two modes: HTML and CSS. You move from one mode to the other by clicking the HTML or CSS button on the far left of the Property inspector. When in HTML mode, you can choose a standard text format, such as paragraph or any of the heading tags, set a class or ID, provide a link, add a `<strong>` or `<em>` tag through the Bold and Italic buttons, or change to an ordered or unordered list. Enter CSS mode to redefine text-based properties of applied rules, such as font-family, color, font-size, font-weight, font-style, and text-align. The CSS mode is also an efficient way to initially define a new style for a selection.

For more information about applying the HTML attributes and CSS properties to text, see Chapter 7.

You can reposition the Property inspector in one of the following ways:

- If the Property inspector is floating, you can click and drag the drag bar that appears along the left edge of the window and move it to a new location.
- You can also click and drag any open gray area in the floating inspector itself, a difference between it and the Insert panel. This technique is handy for quickly moving the inspector aside, out of your way.
- When you move the floating inspector near the edge of the screen or near a window border, the Property inspector snaps to the edge of the window or screen.

The Property inspector initially displays the most typical attributes for a given element. Virtually all the inserted objects have additional parameters that can be modified. Unless you're tight on screen real estate, it's a good idea to keep the Property inspector expanded so you can see all your options.

TIP

You can reveal (or hide) the expanded attributes by double-clicking any open gray area of the Property inspector.

Property inspector elements

Many of the attributes in the Property inspector are text boxes; just click in any one and enter a value. If a value already appears in the text box, whether a number or a name, double-click it (or click and drag over it) to highlight the information and then enter your new data—the old value is immediately replaced. You can see the effect of your modification by pressing the Tab key to move to the next attribute or by clicking in the Document window.

For several attributes, the Property inspector also provides drop-down list boxes that offer a limited number of options. To open the drop-down list of available options, click the arrow button to the right of the list box. Then choose an option by highlighting it.

TIP

Some options on the Property inspector are a combination drop-down list and text box–you can select from available options or type in your own values. For example, when text is selected, the font name and size are combination list/text boxes.

If you see a folder icon next to a text box, you have the option of browsing for a filename on your local or networked drive or manually inputting a filename. Clicking the folder opens a standard Open File dialog box (called Select File in Dreamweaver); after you've chosen your file and clicked OK (Open or Choose on the Mac), Dreamweaver inputs the filename and any necessary path information in the correct attribute.

Dreamweaver enables you to quickly select an onscreen file (in either a Document window or the Files panel) as a link, with its Point to File icon, found next to the folder icon. Just click and drag the Point to File icon until it touches the file (or the filename from the Files panel) that you want to reference. The path is automatically written into the Link text box.

Certain objects such as text, AP elements, and table cells enable you to specify a color attribute. The Property inspector alerts you to these options with a small color box next to the text box. You can type in a color's name (such as **blue**) or its three- or six-figure hexadecimal value (such as **#3366FF** or **#666**), or select the color box. Choosing the color box opens a color picker, shown in Figure 2-32, which displays the so-called *browser-safe* colors. You can go outside of this range by clicking the System Color Picker icon in the upper-right corner of the color picker. Selecting this icon opens a full-range Color dialog box in which you can choose a color visually or enter its red, green, and blue values or its hue, saturation, and brightness values.

FIGURE 2-32

Dreamweaver's color picker enables you to choose from a wide selection of colors, from the palette or right off the desktop, with the Eyedropper tool.

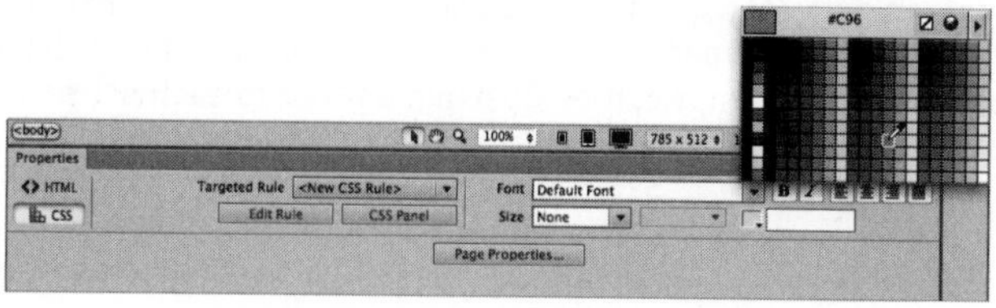

The color picker in Dreamweaver is very flexible. Not only can you choose from a series of color swatches, but you can also select any color onscreen with Dreamweaver's Eyedropper tool. If you'd like to access the system color picker, the color wheel button opens it for you. You can also use the Default Color tool, which deletes any color choice previously inserted. Finally, you can use the color picker's context menu to change the swatch set shown. By default, the Color Cubes view is shown, but you can also view swatches in a Continuous Tone configuration or in Windows OS, Mac OS, or Grayscale colors. Although the web designer may not use these options frequently, Adobe standardized the color picker across its product line to make it easier to switch between applications.

TIP

To close the color picker without selecting a color, click in the empty gray area at the top of the color picker.

The Property inspector also includes a panel menu. Open this context-sensitive menu by clicking the panel menu icon, located in the upper-right corner of the Property inspector. The commands on this menu vary depending on what type of object has been selected in the Document window. Some basic commands, however, are always available, regardless of what has been selected, such as the following:

- **Help:** Opens a Help topic for the current Property inspector.
- **Close:** Closes the Property inspector.
- **Close Tab Group:** Closes the Property inspector and any other panels it may be grouped with.

NOTE

Two additional commands that are typically available for panels, Group Properties With and Maximize Panel Group, are disabled for the Property inspector. You cannot dock the Property inspector with other panels, and you cannot change the height of the Property inspector.

Customizing Your Workspace with Dockable Panels

Dreamweaver is known for its powerful set of tools: behaviors, AP elements, and so much more. Dreamweaver presents its tools in a variety of panels, as shown in Figure 2-33. Panels can be combined into the same window; when grouped together in this way, each panel is displayed as a tab within the panel group. The panel groups can be floating, docked to each other, or docked within the Dreamweaver window.

FIGURE 2-33

Dreamweaver's many tools reside in panels, which can float anywhere on the screen or be docked within the Document window.

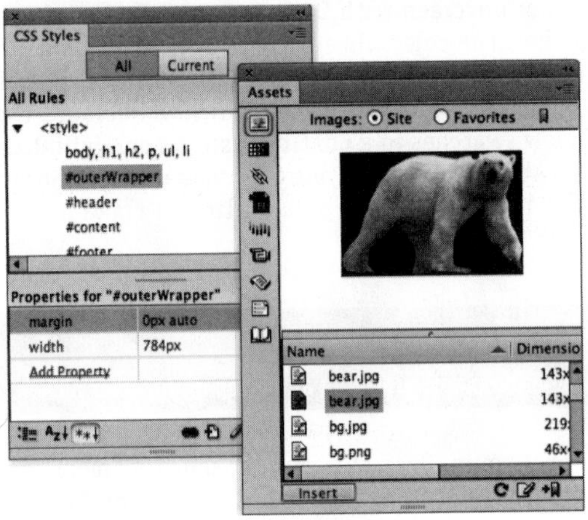

Table 2-7 lists each of the panels available in Dreamweaver, along with a description and a cross-reference to chapters in this book that provide more information about the panel. It also lists a keyboard shortcut that you can use to open the panel. If the keyboard shortcut is different between Mac and Windows platforms, the Mac shortcut is listed in parentheses after the Windows shortcut. If the Mac shortcut is not available, the initials N/A are displayed in the parentheses.

Hiding and showing panels

Because of the large number of panels available in Dreamweaver, your workspace can become cluttered very quickly. To reduce the amount of screen real estate taken up by the individual panels but still utilize their power, Dreamweaver enables you to group multiple panels in a single window. These groups of related panels are called, not surprisingly, *panel groups*. Whenever one panel is docked with another in a panel group, each panel becomes accessible by clicking its representative tab. Selecting the tab brings the panel to the front.

TABLE 2-7 Dreamweaver Panels

Panel	Keyboard Shortcut	Description	Detailed Information
Adobe BrowserLab	Ctrl+Shift+F12 (Command+Shift+F12)	Connects to the Adobe BrowserLab service for rendering pages in multiple browsers.	See Chapter 4.
CSS Styles	Shift+F11 (N/A)	Enables you to create external and embedded CSS style sheets.	See Chapter 6.
jQuery Mobile Swatches	None	Applies jQuery Mobile themes to selected elements.	See Chapter 17.
AP Elements	None	Enables you to view and change some characteristics of AP elements.	See Chapter 10.
Business Catalyst	Ctrl+Shift+B (Command+Shift+B)	Connects you to the Business Catalyst service.	See Chapter 4.
Databases	Ctrl+Shift+F10 (Command+Shift+F10)	Provides a bird's-eye view of all the connections currently defined for your site, enabling you to add new connections; browse tables, views, and stored procedures for each database; and add the necessary server-side include to use that connection.	See chapters in Part IV.
Bindings	Ctrl+F10 (Command+F10)	Enables you to create recordsets and datasets and display that information on your page. You can also bind data to tag attributes and form elements and set the formatting for dynamic elements.	See chapters in Part IV.
Server Behaviors	Ctrl+F9 (Command+F9)	Gives you access to prewritten server-side scripts that are used in applications. For example, you can use server behaviors to create, update, or delete records.	See Chapter 34.
Components	Ctrl+F7 (Command+F7)	Enables you to quickly add new ColdFusion components.	See Chapter 19.
CSS Transitions		Applies and manages CSS transitions for animating page elements.	See Chapter 7.
Files	F8 (Command+Shift+F)	Manages the files in your local, remote, and testing sites.	See Chapter 4.

Continues

2

TABLE 2-7 *(continued)*

Panel	Keyboard Shortcut	Description	Detailed Information
Assets	None	Gives you access to many components that make up your site, including images, colors, URLs, Flash and Shockwave objects, movies, scripts, templates, and library items.	See the following: Images: Chapter 8 Colors: Chapter 7 URLs: Chapter 9 Flash: Chapter 25 Shockwave: Chapter 25 Movies: Chapter 26 Scripts: Chapter 5 Templates: Chapter 28 Library: Chapter 29.
Snippets	Shift+F9 (N/A)	Gives you access to prewritten snippets of code for common scenarios.	See Chapter 5.
Tag Inspector	F9 (Option+Shift+F9)	Displays a collapsible outline of the tags used on the current page, enabling you to quickly determine if tags are correctly nested and to view and change tag attributes.	See Chapter 5.
Behaviors	Shift+F4	Enables you to create Dynamic HTML effects.	See Chapter 11.
History	Shift+F10 (N/A)	Tracks each change you make, enabling you to undo and redo multiple steps at a time.	See Chapter 7.
Frames	Shift+F2	Enables you to select and rename frames within a frameset.	See Chapter 15.
Code Inspector	F10 (Option+F10)	Provides an alternative to Code view in a floating window.	See Chapter 5.
Results ➪ Search	F7 to open the Results panel and then choose the Search category	Shows the results of a Find All request.	See Chapter 7.
Results ➪ Reference	F7 to open the Results panel and then choose the Reference category	Presents extensive reference documentation for HTML, CSS, JavaScript, accessibility guidelines, and a variety of server-side scripting languages.	See Chapter 5.
Results ➪ Validation	F7 to open the Results panel and then choose the Validation category	When you validate a document, the results are displayed in this panel.	See Chapter 30.

Panel	Keyboard Shortcut	Description	Detailed Information
Results ➪ Browser Compatibility	F7 to open the Results panel and then choose the Browser Compatibility category	Displays results of a Browser Compatibility check.	See Chapter 30.
Results ➪ Link Checker	F7 to open the Results panel and then choose the Link Checker category	Shows the results when you check for broken links within your site.	See Chapter 9.
Results ➪ Site Reports	F7 to open the Results panel and then choose the Site Reports category	Displays the output from a variety of site reports.	See Chapter 31.
Results ➪ FTP Log	F7 to open the Results panel and then choose the FTP Log category	Lists the results of FTP operations.	See Chapter 4.
Results ➪ Server Debug (Windows only)	F7 to open the Results panel and then choose the Server Debug category	Enables you to browse your page directly in Dreamweaver's Design window as if it were a web browser. This is different from Live Data view because the page is not editable.	See Chapter 34.
Extensions ➪ Adobe BrowserLab	None	Connects to the service for pre-viewing current page in a variety of web browsers and operating systems.	See Chapter 4.

2

You can also display individual panels by using the keyboard shortcuts listed in Table 2-6 or by using commands in the Window menu; a separate command opens each panel. Using any of these methods opens the panel or brings it to the top if it is hidden; if the panel is already on top, any of these actions collapses the panel group so that only its title bar is showing.

Tip

One very important keyboard shortcut to remember is the F4 key, which hides all panels. This shortcut immediately clears the screen of all panels, including the Property inspector. Pressing F4 again restores all the hidden interfaces.

To maximize your Document window, you can reduce panels to an icon representation when closed. Simply make the panel smaller by dragging a panel's left or right edge; if the panel or panel group is docked, you'll need to drag the edge furthest from the program border. Once iconified, a click on the icon opens up the panel fully.

A panel can be set to remain open or automatically close once you click outside of it. To expose your options, right-click the dark gray border area. From the pop-up menu, choose Auto-collapse Iconic Panels to automatically close your panel; leave this option unchecked to keep the panel open.

The panel groups may be docked along the edges of the Dreamweaver window. In this situation, you can collapse all the panel groups to maximize your work area by clicking the double-triangle button that appears at the top of the panel, as shown in Figure 2-34. This action collapses only the panel groups docked on one edge of the screen, leaving intact toolbars, floating panels, or even panels docked along a different edge of the window.

FIGURE 2-34

You can collapse all the panel groups along one edge of the screen with the click of a single button.

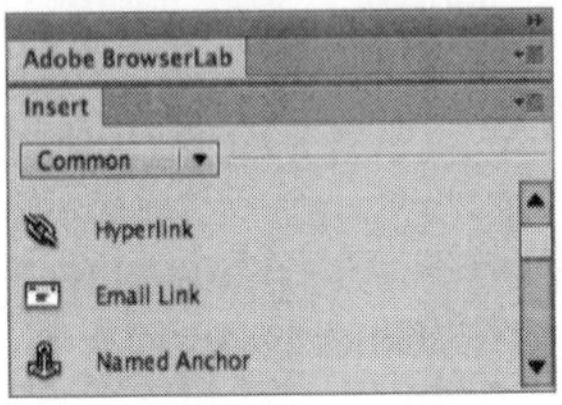

In any workspace, you can collapse an individual panel group so that just its title bar is showing. To do this, double-click the panel group name in the title bar. To resize any floating panel, click and drag its borders. If the panel groups are docked together, you can drag the border of the panel area to resize all the panel groups in that area.

Finally, if you want to close a panel group entirely so that even its title bar is not visible, click the panel menu located on the right of the title bar in an open panel group, and then select Close Panel Group from the drop-down list. You can also right-click (Control+click) in the title bar and select Close Tab Group, even if the panel group is collapsed. The next time you open any panel within the group, the entire panel group opens automatically.

NOTE

The panel menu also gives you access to Help for the currently displayed panel and may contain additional commands specific to the panel that is open.

Customizing panel groups

Dreamweaver comes with related panels already combined into panel groups. However, you're not limited to the predefined panel groups. In fact, the panel groups are completely customizable, giving you optimum control over your workflow. Moving panels from one group to another, creating new groups, and renaming panel groups are straightforward operations. If you want, you can also remove little-used panels from groups and reorder the panels within a group.

To move a panel from one group to another, drag the panel's name tab and drop it into place; Dreamweaver displays a blue border to indicate where the panel will be positioned. If the blue border appears as a thin line below existing docked panels, the moved panel will appear in its own panel group. If the blue border is displayed on a panel group's separator, the panel will be incorporated into that group. Finally, if the blue border appears to one side of the panel group, the panel will be docked to the side of the group. Why might you want to have two or more docked sets of panels? Dreamweaver (and all Creative Suite applications) allows only one panel in a docked panel group to be visible at one time. If you ever need to display two panels simultaneously, you can either establish them as individual panels or dock them in different panel groups.

TIP

To reorder panels within a panel group, simply drag them by their tabs into new positions.

How do you remove a panel from a panel group? Simply drag it away. You can move a panel group by dragging the panel's tab (see Figure 2-35) and dragging the group to any location on the screen.

FIGURE 2-35

Drag the gray area to remove a panel from its dock.

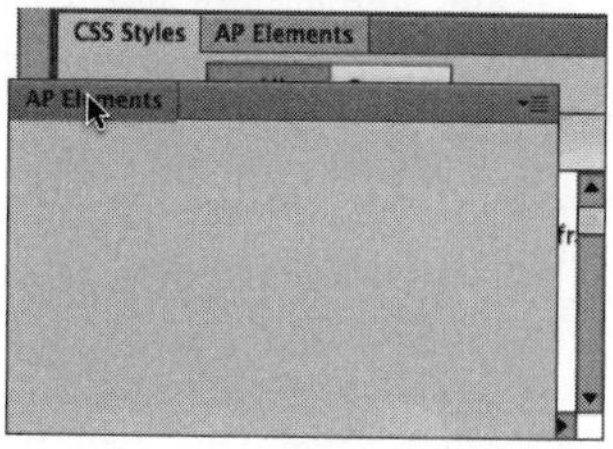

Accessing the Menus

Like many programs, Dreamweaver's menus duplicate most of the features accessible through panels. Certain features, however, are available only through the menus in the Document window or through a corresponding keyboard shortcut. This section offers a reference guide to the menus when you need a particular feature or command. (Note to Windows users: The menus referred to here are those for the Document window and not the Files panel; the menu options particular to the Files panel are covered in Chapter 4.)

TIP

Almost every element placed in the Document window has a shortcut menu associated with it. To access a shortcut menu, right-click (Control+click) any area or object. The shortcut menus are context-sensitive and vary according to which object or area is selected. Using the shortcut menus can enhance your productivity tremendously.

Following is a glance at the various Dreamweaver Document window menus. You can find explanations of each command (along with its keyboard shortcuts for Windows and Mac) on this book's website.

- **File menu:** Contains commands for file handling and overall site management. All import, export, and convert features are also found in this menu.
- **Edit menu:** Provides the commands necessary to quickly modify your page—or recover from a devastating accident. Many of the commands (Cut, Copy, and Paste, for example) are standard in other programs; others, such as Select Parent Tag, are unique to Dreamweaver.
- **View menu:** As you build your web pages, you may find that it's helpful to be able to turn certain features on and off. The View menu centralizes all these commands and switches between Design view and Code view. One of the handiest commands hides all the visual aids with a keyboard shortcut, Ctrl+Shift+I (Command+Shift+I).
- **Insert menu:** Contains the same items available through the Insert panel. In fact, if you add additional objects, you can see your objects listed on the Insert menu the next time you start Dreamweaver. All objects selected from the Insert menu are added to the page at the current cursor position.
- **Modify menu:** Inserting objects is less than half the battle of creating a web page. Most web designers spend most of their time adjusting, experimenting with, and tweaking the various elements. The Modify menu lists all Dreamweaver's commands for altering existing selections.
- **Format menu:** The Internet was initially an all-text medium, and despite all the multimedia development, the World Wide Web hasn't traveled far from those beginnings. The Format menu commands cover overall formatting and provide access to the Color dialog box.
- **Commands menu:** Commands are user-definable code capable of affecting almost any tag, attribute, or item on the current page—or even the current site. Commands increase your productivity by automating many of the mundane, repetitive tasks in web page creation.

  Dreamweaver comes with several handy commands, but they are truly just the tip of the iceberg. Commands are written in a combination of HTML and JavaScript and can be created and modified by any capable JavaScript programmer.

  The first few items on the Commands menu enable you to create, add, and manage custom commands. The additional items represent standard commands that come with Dreamweaver. If you add custom commands to Dreamweaver, they also appear in this menu.
- **Site menu:** Web designers spend a good portion of the day directly interacting with a web server: putting up new files, getting old ones, and generally maintaining the site. To ease the workflow, Dreamweaver groups site-management commands in their own menu.
- **Window menu:** Manages both program and user-opened windows. Through this menu you can open, close, arrange, bring to the front, or hide all the additional Dreamweaver screens.

TIP

The commands for Dreamweaver's various windows, panels, and inspectors are toggles. Select a command once to open the window; select it again to close it.

- **Help menu:** Provides access to Dreamweaver's excellent offline and online Help, as well as special examples and lessons.

Summary

In this chapter, you were introduced to some of the power of Dreamweaver and had a look at its well-designed layout. From the Insert panel to the various customizable panels, Dreamweaver offers you an elegant, flexible workspace for creating next-generation websites. Here are some of the key points covered in this chapter:

- Users can choose from 11 default workspace layouts or choose to structure their workspace in whatever manner best suits their workflow. The same basic tools are available in each layout; the primary difference involves where the panels are located and whether you have more than one display.
- The Document window is your main canvas for visually designing your Dreamweaver web pages. This window includes simple, powerful tools such as the Tag Selector, Zoom, and the Window Size pop-up menu.
- Frequently used tools are available on Dreamweaver's various toolbars. The toolbars can be displayed or hidden depending on your personal preferences.
- The Insert panel is Dreamweaver's toolbox. Highly customizable, the Insert panel holds the elements you need most often, grouped into useful categories. You can customize one category of the Insert panel, Favorites, and place your own most commonly used objects together.
- Dreamweaver's mechanism for assigning details and attributes to an HTML object is the Property inspector. The Property inspector is context-sensitive, and its options vary according to the object selected.
- Many of Dreamweaver's tools reside in separate panels, which can be combined into panel groups. Panel groups can be docked or floated, hidden or shown, depending on your workflow.
- Dreamweaver's full-featured menus offer complete file manipulation, a wide range of insertable objects, the tools to modify them, and extensive online—and on the web—help. The most commonly used menu items can be invoked through keyboard shortcuts.
- Dreamweaver offers a direct connection to Adobe's robust hosting service, Business Catalyst. Once you've signed up to Business Catalyst, you can create and modify sites from within Dreamweaver.

In the next chapter, you learn how to customize Dreamweaver to work the way you work by establishing your own preferences for the program and its interface.

CHAPTER 3

Setting Your Preferences

IN THIS CHAPTER

Dreamweaver made to order

Customizing Dynamic HTML specs

Extending preferences outside Dreamweaver

Specifying your code formatting

Everyone works differently. Whether you need to conform to a corporate style sheet handed down from the powers that be or you think, "It just looks better that way," Dreamweaver offers you the flexibility to shape your web page tools and your code output. This chapter describes the options available in Dreamweaver's Preferences and then details how you can instruct Dreamweaver to format source code your way.

Customizing Your Environment

The vast majority of Dreamweaver's settings are controlled through the Preferences dialog box. You can open Preferences by choosing Edit ➪ Preferences (Dreamweaver ➪ Preferences) or by using the keyboard shortcut Ctrl+U (Command+U). Within Preferences, you find 19 different subjects listed on the left side of the screen. As you switch from one category to another by selecting a name from the Category list, the options available for that category appear in the main area of the dialog box. Most changes to Preferences take effect immediately after you close the window by clicking OK. This chapter covers all the options available in each category; the categories are grouped by function rather than by order of appearance in the Category list.

General preferences

Dreamweaver's General preferences, shown in Figure 3-1, cover the program's appearance, user operation, and fundamental file settings. The appearance of the program's interface may seem to be a trivial matter, but Dreamweaver is a program for designers and coders, to whom work environment is extremely important. These user-operation options, described in the following sections, are based purely on how you, the user, work best.

FIGURE 3-1

Dreamweaver's General Preferences enable you to change your program's appearance and certain overall operations.

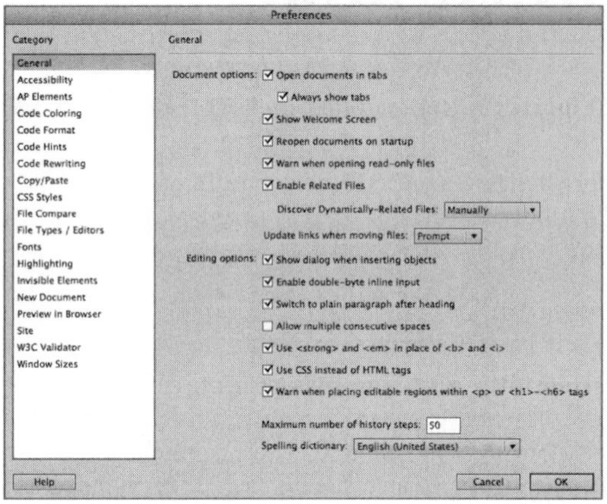

Document Options

The first area of the General category, Document Options, determines how you work with HTML and other files.

> **TIP**
>
> In choosing all the preferences, including the General ones, you can work in two ways. If you are a seasoned web designer, you probably want Dreamweaver to work in your established manner to minimize the learning curve. If you're just starting out as a web page creator, work with the default options for a while and then try other options. You should know right away which style works for you.

Open Documents In Tabs option

This Macintosh-only checkbox tells Dreamweaver whether you want files to open in tabs instead of separate windows. Documents in tabs keep the workspace orderly and allow you to easily switch between open files. If you click the additional Always Show Tabs option, Dreamweaver will display every document with a tab, even if there is only one.

Show Welcome Screen option

The welcome screen is a very helpful innovation that gets you up and running right away in Dreamweaver—whether you're just starting out or in the middle of editing a full site. If you're new to the program, Dreamweaver's welcome screen gives you quick access to tutorials and a tour of the key features. After you've worked with the program for a while, you'll appreciate the immediate access to the more recently opened files and one-click creation of static or dynamic pages. The welcome screen displays when Dreamweaver launches or when no document is currently open.

The welcome screen is extremely handy, but if it doesn't fit with your workflow, you can disable it. Clear the Show Welcome Screen checkbox and, depending on your other settings and actions, the next time Dreamweaver opens you see either a blank, documentless environment or your previously opened files.

The welcome screen changes from time to time because it includes a Flash movie (located in the lower-right corner) that uses dynamically set parameters to display different information if you're connected to the Internet when running Dreamweaver.

Reopen Documents On Startup option

In an ideal world, a web designer works on one page at a time, carefully crafting each and every detail. Well, it's far from an ideal world, and often designers are working on several pages simultaneously—and over multiple sessions. If your workflow fits into this real-world model, the Reopen Documents On Startup option makes your life a little easier.

When I'm working on a web application, I often have four to six pages (or more) open simultaneously. If I'm continuing my work from one day to the next, the first thing I do is to make sure I've opened all the files that I need. With the Reopen Documents On Startup option selected, Dreamweaver automatically opens any files left unclosed when I last quit the program. If this option is left unselected, you see either the welcome screen or a documentless environment.

Warn When Opening Read-Only Files option

Read-only files have been locked to prevent accidental overwriting. Optionally, Dreamweaver can warn you when such a file is opened. The warning is actually more than just an alert, however. Dreamweaver provides an option on the warning dialog box to make the file writable (or check it out if you're using the Check In/Check Out feature). Alternatively, you can just view the file.

See Chapter 31 for more on the Check In/Check Out feature.

Although Dreamweaver enables you to edit the file either way, if the document is still read-only when you save your changes, the Save As dialog box opens, and you're prompted to store the file under a new name.

Enable Related Files option

With the Enable Related Files option selected, Dreamweaver displays a link to any file referenced in the primary source document in the Related Files bar. Click any related file link to view its source code while continuing to show the rendered main page in Display or Live view. Related files can be CSS external files, server-side includes, Library items, JavaScript source files, or any other type of file that is linked, included, or imported.

The associated Discover Dynamically-Related Files list determines whether you want Dreamweaver to process the server-side code in a PHP, ColdFusion, or ASP page to identify any additional related files on demand (the default Manually option), all the time (Automatically), or never (Disabled). Most content management systems such as WordPress, Drupal, or Joomla rely on server-side code to combine files for needed functionality. With the Discover Dynamically-Related Files option, you can locate specific functions or styles that would otherwise remain hidden.

Chapter 5 has all the details on how to make the most of the Related Files feature.

Update Links option

As your site grows in complexity, keeping track of the various links is an increasingly difficult task. Dreamweaver has several enhanced features to help you manage links, and the Update Links When Moving Files option is one of them. Dreamweaver can check each link on a page when a file is moved—whether it is the web page you're working on or one of the support files, such as an image, that goes on the page. The Update Links option determines how Dreamweaver reacts when it notes an altered link.

By default, the Update Links When Moving Files option is set to Prompt, which causes Dreamweaver to alert you to any link changes and requires you to verify the code alterations by clicking the Update button, as shown in Figure 3-2. To leave the files as they are, click the Don't Update button. You can elect to have Dreamweaver automatically keep your pages up-to-date by selecting the Always option from the Update Links drop-down list. Finally, you can select the Never option, and Dreamweaver ignores the link changes necessary when you move, rename, or delete a file.

As a general rule, I keep my Update Links option set to Always. It is a very rare circumstance when I intentionally maintain a bad link on my web page. Likewise, I recommend using the Never option with extreme caution.

FIGURE 3-2

Dreamweaver offers to update all links when a file is moved or renamed.

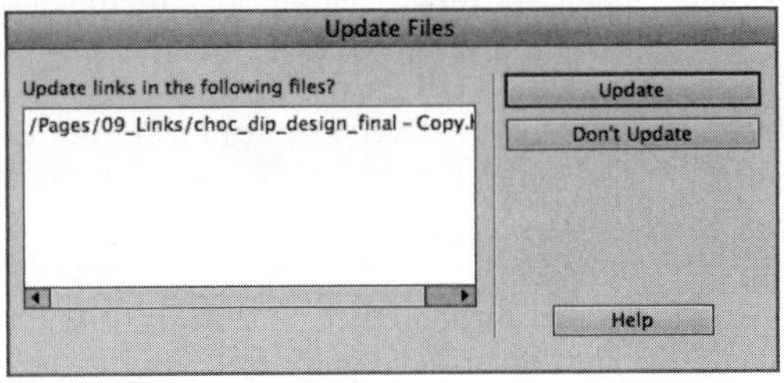

Editing Options

The second main section of the General category of the Preferences dialog box consists of numerous checkbox options you can turn on or off. Overall, these options fall into the user-interaction category, reflecting how you like to work. Consider the Show Dialog When Inserting Objects option, for example. Some web creators prefer to enter all their attributes at one time through the Property inspector and would rather not have dialog boxes appear for every inserted object. Others want to get their file sources in immediately and modify the rest later. The choice depends on how you want to work. The following sections describe various other options.

Show Dialog When Inserting Objects option

By default, almost all the objects that Dreamweaver inserts—via either the Insert panel or the Insert menu—open an initial dialog box to gather needed information. In some cases, the dialog box enables you to input a URL or browse for a source file. Turning off the Show Dialog When Inserting Objects option causes Dreamweaver to insert a default-sized object, or a placeholder, for the object in this circumstance. You must then enter all attributes through the Property inspector.

TIP

To selectively avoid the prompts, leave this option checked, but press Ctrl+click (Option+click) on an object to skip the prompt.

Enable Double-Byte Inline Input option

Some computer representations of languages, primarily Asian languages, require more raw descriptive power than others. The ideogram for *snow*, for example, is far more complex than a four-letter word. These languages need twice the number of bytes per character and are known as *double-byte* languages. In versions of Dreamweaver before 2, all double-byte characters had to go through a separate text-input window, instead of directly into the Document window.

Dreamweaver simplifies the page creation process for double-byte languages with the Enable Double-Byte Inline Input option. If selected, this option enables double-byte characters to be entered directly into the Document window. To use the old method of inserting such characters, deselect this option.

Switch To Plain Paragraph After Heading option

This may seem like a small thing, but this nifty little feature is one of my favorites. If the Switch To Plain Paragraph After Heading option is not enabled, pressing Enter (Return) after a heading tag (`<h1>` or `<h2>`, for example) causes the next line to maintain the heading style. Select the Switch To Plain Paragraph After Heading option so that the next line is a standard paragraph (`<p>`) tag.

Use this option to speed up your workflow. You'll almost always want a heading followed by a plain paragraph. This option gets rid of one more click of the mouse or shortcut key, making your workflow that much faster.

Allow Multiple Consecutive Spaces option

Some designers prefer adding two spaces after every period, or they like to use multiple spaces to indent paragraphs to maintain a print-type appearance. Without this option selected, this type of spacing requires that you press Ctrl+Shift+Space (Command+Shift+Space) to add an ` ` to the document. Select the Allow Multiple Consecutive Spaces option, and Dreamweaver adds the necessary code for you, without requiring the additional keyboard shortcut.

TIP

This option may seem wonderful at first, but I recommend leaving it unchecked. Having a single space after a sentence is the standard online and is standard practice in print applications. (You'll find no double spaces in this little tome.) Enabling this option only encourages bad habits.

Use <strong> And <em> In Place Of <b> And <i> option

In recent HTML and XHTML standards, the `<b>` and `<i>` tags were deprecated because they don't imply any structural significance to the text they surround. Many screen readers may even completely ignore the `<b>` and `<i>` tags. Check the Use <strong> And <em> In Place Of <b> And <i> box to use the more syntactically correct `<strong>` and `<em>` tags in their place.

The option to use `<strong>` and `<em>` tags enables you to create more semantically correct HTML code. Individuals using screen readers benefit, and you make your code more syntactically correct, further separating style from content.

Warn When Placing Editable Regions Within <p> Or <h1>–<h6> Tags option

Sometimes Dreamweaver adheres a bit too strictly to the rules for my taste—and this preference addresses one of those times. In Dreamweaver templates, editable regions define areas of the page that can be altered in the pages derived from templates. Most often, designers wrap editable regions around block elements such as headings or paragraphs. However, there are occasions when it is advantageous to make just the content within block tags editable and lock the surrounding tags themselves. I, for example, apply this technique when I want a template-derived page to always start with a single `<h1>` heading but know that the heading will always be different. Dreamweaver regards this approach with suspicion because such an editable region will not allow the user to press Enter (Return) and add more block-level tags.

To prevent novices from inadvertently limiting the expansion of content within an editable region, Dreamweaver displays an alert whenever a template is saved that has an editable region within a block element. You can continue the save—and the subsequent updating of template-derived pages—or you can cancel and correct the situation. In previous versions, Dreamweaver displayed this error without recourse, even when the coding it was protesting was intentional. By disabling the Warn When Placing Editable Regions Within <p> Or <h1>–<h6> Tags option, you can avoid having to repeatedly dismiss the alert.

If you're new to Dreamweaver and its template technology, I recommend that you enable this option. Doing so will likely save you grief on your initial template-derived pages and prevent you from having to redo the templates. However, once you've worked with templates for a while, I suggest you disable this option; the technique of embedding editable regions within block tags is a common one and not having to acknowledge the alert over and over again is a major time-saver.

Maximum Number Of History Steps option

Almost every Dreamweaver action, except the mouse click, is listed in the History panel. These steps can be undone by moving the slider on the History panel or choosing Edit ➪ Undo. A limit exists, however, to the number of steps that can be tracked. By default, this option is set to 50.

Although 50 history steps are more than enough for most systems, you can alter this number by changing the Maximum Number Of History Steps value. When the maximum number of history steps is exceeded, the oldest actions are wiped from memory and made unrecoverable. The history steps are not discarded when a file is saved.

Spelling Dictionary option

The Spelling Dictionary option enables you to select a spell-checking dictionary from any of those installed. In addition to the standard English-language version, which has 3 alternatives—English (American), English (British), and English (Canadian)—there are 33 other languages including Finnish, French, German (Classic), German (New Spelling), Italian, Norwegian (Bokml), Portuguese (Brazilian), Portuguese (Iberian), Spanish, and Swedish.

To select a different dictionary for spell-checking, select the Dictionary option button and choose an item from the drop-down list. Dreamweaver also maintains a personal dictionary (although it's not visible on the list) to hold any words you want Dreamweaver to learn during the spell-checking process. So the next time you spell-check a technical document, just click Add for each word Dreamweaver catches that you want it to remember. That word is added to the personal dictionary, and you never have to worry about it again.

Preferences for invisible elements

By their nature, all HTML markup tags remain unseen to one degree or another when presented for viewing through the browser. You may want to see certain elements while designing a page, however. For example, adjusting line spacing is a common task, and turning on the visibility of the line break tag `<br>` can help you understand the layout.

Dreamweaver enables you to control the visibility of 13 different codes, as well as dynamic data and server-side includes—or rather their symbols, as shown in Figure 3-3. When, for example, a named anchor is inserted, Dreamweaver shows you a small gold shield with an anchor emblem. Not only does this shield indicate the anchor's position, but you can also manipulate the code with cut-and-paste or drag-and-drop techniques. Moreover, clicking a symbol opens the pertinent Property inspector and enables quick changes to the tag's attributes.

3

FIGURE 3-3

You can show or hide any or all of the 13 invisible elements listed in the Preferences dialog box and determine the appearance of recordset fields and includes.

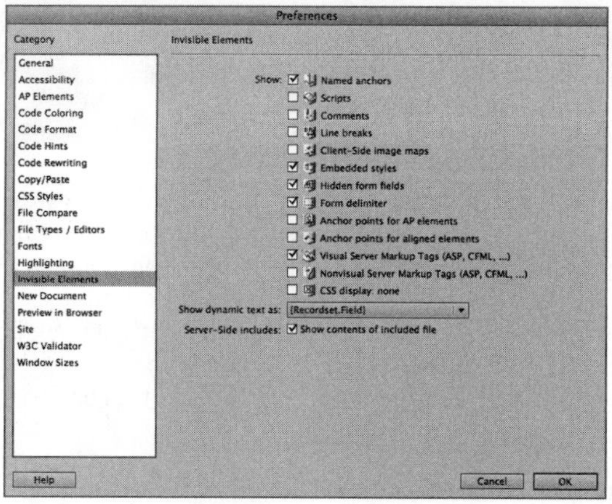

TIP

Temporarily hide all invisible elements by deselecting View ➪ Visual Aids ➪ Invisible Elements.

The 13 items controlled through the Invisible Elements panel are as follows:

- Named Anchors
- Scripts
- Comments
- Line Breaks
- Client-Side Image Maps
- Embedded Styles
- Hidden Form Fields
- Form Delimiter
- Anchor Points For AP Elements
- Anchor Points For Aligned Elements
- Visual Server Markup Tags (ASP, CFML, . . .)
- Nonvisual Server Markup Tags (ASP, CFML, . . .)
- CSS Display: None

Most of the Invisible Elements options display or hide small symbols in Dreamweaver's visual Document window. Several options, however, show an outline or another type of highlight. Turning off Form Delimiter, for example, removes the dashed line that surrounds a form in the Document window.

TIP

You may have noticed that the PHP, ColdFusion, Active Server Page, and .NET tags are combined into one symbol, Visual Server Markup Tags. Dreamweaver's capability to handle dynamic pages generated by databases makes these invisible elements essential. I generally leave the Nonvisual Server Markup Tags option unchecked because these icons flag server-side coding in the page and tend to interrupt the flow of the design.

Dreamweaver-developed pages often include references to *dynamic text*. Dynamic text is replaced by an entry from a recordset when the page is processed by the application server. Dreamweaver uses what is called *dot notation* in programming circles to fully display these names, such as `{rsMaillist.EmailAddress}`, enclosed in curly braces. When you are designing a page, you may have field names that are longer than the actual data, and the full dot notation becomes a visual hindrance rather than an aid. In these situations, you may want to use Dreamweaver's alternative dynamic text syntax, an empty pair of curly braces: `{}`. Enable this option from the Show Dynamic Text As drop-down list on the Invisible Elements panel.

When designing dynamic sites you may often use server-side includes to speed development and updates. Unfortunately, rendering these in the design window can often cause problems if you are conditionally including multiple files. Clear the Show Contents Of Included File option to disable rendering your server-side includes.

Highlighting preferences

Dreamweaver is extremely extensible—custom functions are automatically incorporated, server-side markup is more acceptable, and more third-party tags are supported. Many of these features depend on hidden capabilities that are not noticeable in the final HTML page. The web designer, however, must consider them. Dreamweaver employs user-selectable highlighting to mark areas on a web page under construction.

- Mouse-Over
- Editable Regions
- Nested Editable Regions
- Locked Regions
- Library Items
- Third-Party Tags
- Untranslated Live Data
- Translated Live Data

The Highlighting panel of the Preferences dialog box, shown in Figure 3-4, enables you to choose the highlight color for eight different types of extended objects.

FIGURE 3-4

Use the Highlighting preferences to control how template regions, library items, and third-party tags appear in the Document window.

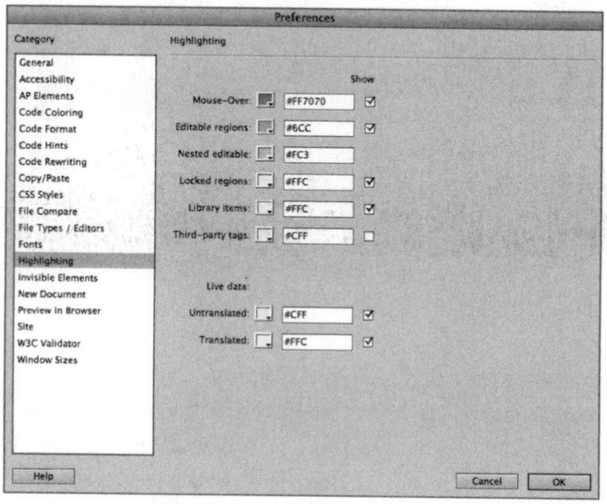

In each case, select the color swatch to open Dreamweaver's color picker and choose a highlight color. Then, use the Eyedropper to pick a color from the web-safe palette or from the desktop. After you've chosen an appropriate color, be sure to select the related Show checkbox so that the highlighting is displayed; all but the highlighting for nested editable regions can be toggled to be shown or hidden.

NOTE

You can see the Locked Region highlighted in Templates only if you open the Code view; the Display view highlights Editable Regions only. You see the Live Data highlighting only while actually viewing your page in Live Data mode.

Window Size preferences

The list at the top of the Window Sizes category, as seen in Figure 3-5, shows the current options for the Window Size pop-up menu. This list is completely user-editable and enables you to add new window sizes, modify existing dimensions, add descriptions, or delete rarely used measurements.

Window sizes

As discussed in Chapter 2, the Window Size pop-up is a Dreamweaver feature that enables you to instantly change your screen size so that you can view and build your page under different monitor conditions. To change any of the current dimensions, simply click the measurement you want to alter and enter a new value. You can also change any description of the existing widths and heights by clicking in the Description column and entering your text. Although you can enter as much text as you like, it's not practical to enter more than about 15 to 20 characters.

FIGURE 3-5

Use the Status Bar category to evaluate your real-world download times and control the size of your Document window.

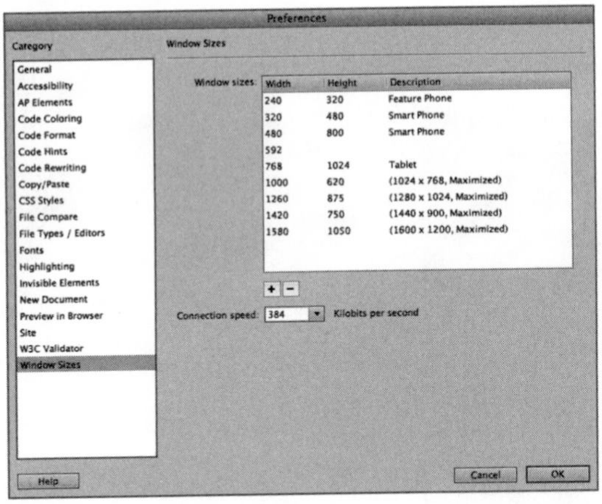

To enter a new set of dimensions in the Window Sizes list box, follow these steps:

1. From the Window Sizes category of the Preferences dialog box, click the Add button.
2. Click once in the Width column on the line below the last entry.
3. Enter the desired width of the new window size in pixels.
4. Press Tab to move to the Height column.
5. Enter the desired height for the new window size.
6. Press Tab again.
7. Optionally, you can enter short, descriptive text in the Description column, and then press Tab when you're finished.
8. To continue adding new sizes, repeat Steps 2 through 6. Click OK when you finish.

CAUTION

You don't have to enter the word "pixels" or the abbreviation "px" after your values in the Width and Height columns of the Window Sizes list box, but you can. If you enter any dimensions under 20, Dreamweaver converts the measurement to its smallest possible window size, 20 pixels.

Connection Speed option

Dreamweaver understands that not all access speeds are created equal, so the Connection Speed option enables you to check the download time for your page (or the individual images) at a variety of rates. The Connection Speed setting evaluates the download statistics in the status bar. You can choose from seven preset connection speeds, all in kilobits per second: 56, 128, 384, 768, 1,500, 6,000, and 10,000. The lower speeds (14.4 through 56) represent various dial-up modem connection rates—if you are building a page for the mass market, you might still consider selecting 56. Use the 128 setting if your audience connects through an ISDN line. If you know that everyone will view your page through a direct LAN connection, change the connection speed to 1,500. You are not limited to these preset settings. You can type any desired speed directly into the Connection Speed text box. If you find yourself designing for an audience using DSL or cable modems, change the Connection Speed to 150 or higher.

File Types/Editors preferences

Refinement is often the name of the game in web design, and quick access to your favorite modification tools—whether you're modifying code, graphics, or other media—is one of Dreamweaver's key features. The File Types/Editors category, shown in Figure 3-6, is where you specify the program you want Dreamweaver to call for any file type you define.

FIGURE 3-6

Assign your favorite HTML, graphics editors, and more through the File Types/Editors category of the Preferences dialog box.

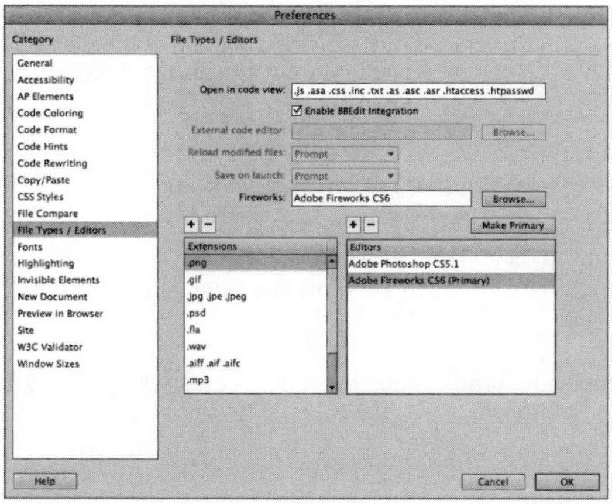

Open In Code View option

It's not just an HTML world—many code types are commonly found on a web designer's palette such as XML, XSL, PHP, and Perl. Dreamweaver's internal code is full-featured enough to handle a wide variety of code, and with the Open In Code View option, you can determine which types you'd like it to handle. By default, JavaScript (`.js`), text (`.txt`), and Active Server Application (`.asa`) files are automatically opened in Code view. Dreamweaver attempts to open any other selected file type in Design view.

If you find yourself hand-editing other file types, such as XML files, you can add their extension to the Open In Code View field. Separate extensions with a space, and be sure to begin each one with a period.

External Code Editor option

Dreamweaver recognizes the importance of your choice of a text editor. Although Dreamweaver ships with an excellent built-in code editor, you can opt to use any other program. To select your editor, enter the path in the External Code Editor text box or click the Browse button to choose the appropriate executable file.

Enable BBEdit Integration (Macintosh only) option

Dreamweaver for Macintosh ships with this option activated. If you prefer to use another editor, deselect this option. Clear this box to enable the External Code Editor fields.

Reload Modified Files option

The drop-down list for the Reload Modified Files setting offers three choices for working with an external editor:

- **Prompt:** Detects when files are updated by another program and enables you to decide whether to update them within Dreamweaver.
- **Always:** Updates the file in Dreamweaver automatically when the file is changed in an outside program.
- **Never:** Assumes that you want to make all updates from within Dreamweaver yourself.

Personally, I prefer to have Dreamweaver always update my files. I find that it saves a couple of mouse clicks—not to mention time.

Save On Launch option

Any external HTML editor—even the integrated BBEdit—opens and reads a previously saved file. So, if you make any changes in Dreamweaver's visual editor and switch to your editor without saving, the editor shows only the most recently saved version. You have three options to control this function:

- **Prompt:** Determines that unsaved changes have been made and asks you to save the file. If you do not, the external editor reverts to the last saved version.
- **Always:** Saves the file automatically before opening it in the external editor.
- **Never:** Disregards any changes made since the last save, and the external editor opens the previously saved file.

Here, again, as with Reload Modified Files, I prefer to always save my files when switching back and forth.

TIP

If you try to open a file that has never been saved in an external editor, Dreamweaver prompts you to save it regardless of your preference settings. If you opt not to save the file, the external editor is not opened, because it has no saved file to display.

Fireworks option

Dreamweaver enjoys a tight integration with its sister graphics program, Adobe Fireworks. To empower Dreamweaver with Fireworks capabilities, such as Launch and Edit, Dreamweaver has to know where Fireworks is installed. If you install CS6, the path to Fireworks is prefilled for you and shown in this option. If you install Fireworks separately, you'll need to click Browse and locate the Fireworks executable.

Defining editors for different file types

Dreamweaver has the capability to call an editor for any specified type of file at the click of a button. For example, when you import a graphic, you often need to modify its color, size, shape, transparency, or another feature to make it work correctly on the web page. Rather than starting your graphics program independently, you load the image, make the changes, and resave the image. Dreamweaver enables you to send any selected image directly to your editor. After you've made your modifications and saved the file, the altered image appears automatically in Dreamweaver.

The capability to associate different file types with external editors applies to more than just images in Dreamweaver. You can link one or more editors to any type of media—images, audio, video, even specific kinds of code. The defined external editor is invoked when the file is double-clicked in the Files panel. Because the editors are assigned according to file extension, as opposed to media type, one editor can be assigned to GIF files and another to JPEGs. The selection is completely customizable.

NOTE

If you have the same file type both defined to Open In Code View and set up in the editor list, the file defaults to opening in Code view.

When you double-click a file in the Files panel, that file type's primary editor runs. Dreamweaver offers the capability to define multiple editors for any file extension. You might, for instance, prefer to open certain JPEGs in Fireworks and others in Photoshop. To choose an alternative editor, right-click (Control+click) the filename in the Files panel and select the desired program from the Open With menu option. The Open With option also enables you to browse for a program.

To assign an editor to an existing file type, follow these steps:

1. Select the file type from the Extensions list.
2. Click the Add (+) button above the Editors list. The Add External Editor dialog box opens.

3. Locate the application file of the editor and click Open when you're ready. You can also select a shortcut to or alias for the application.
4. If you want to select the editor as the primary editor, click Make Primary while the editor is highlighted.

To add a new file type, click the Add (+) button above the Extensions list and enter the file extension—including the period—in the field displayed at the bottom of the list. For multiple file extensions, separate each extension with a space, as shown here:

```
.doc .dot .rtf
```

TIP

Looking for a good, almost-all-purpose media editor? QuickTime 7 Pro (*not* Quicktime X) makes a great addition to Dreamweaver as the editor for AIFF, AU, WAV, MP3, AVI, and MOV, among other, file types. The Pro Player is wonderful for quick edits and optimization, especially with sound files. It's available from the Apple website (`www.apple.com/quicktime/extending/`) for both platforms for around $30.

Finally, to remove an editor or a file extension, select it and click the Delete (–) button above the corresponding list. Note that removing a file extension also removes the associated editor.

Make sure that your graphics program is adept at handling the three graphic formats used most on the web: GIFs, JPEGs, and PNG images. One optimal choice is Adobe Fireworks, a graphics editor designed specifically for the web, which integrates seamlessly with Dreamweaver. In fact, it integrates so nicely that this book includes an entire chapter on it, Chapter 24.

Copy/Paste preferences

Dreamweaver has a robust featureset when it comes to copying and pasting text. When a copied section of any text document—including those from Microsoft Office—is pasted into Dreamweaver, Dreamweaver automatically converts the formatting to HTML, preserving the full range of original formatting. Moreover, you can even drag entire documents right onto the Dreamweaver web page—what happens next depends on the settings in the Copy/Paste preferences, shown in Figure 3-7.

With the Copy/Paste options, you can determine how text from documents outside of Dreamweaver is added to the page. Best of all, this feature works hand in glove with the new Paste Special command, which gives you the opportunity to change the settings on a case-by-case basis.

The four main Copy/Paste options are:

- **Text Only:** Pastes completely unformatted text; even line breaks or paragraphs are removed.
- **Text With Structure:** Pastes unstyled text while retaining structured elements such as lists, paragraphs, line breaks, and tables.
- **Text With Structure Plus Basic Formatting:** Adds simple formatting, such as bold, italic, and underline, to structured text. If the text is copied from an HTML document, the pasted text retains any HTML text style tags, including `<b>`, `<i>`, `<u>`, `<strong>`, `<em>`, `<abbr>`, and `<acronym>`.
- **Text With Structure Plus Full Formatting:** Pasted text keeps all structure and formatting. If the copied text retains inline CSS styles, Dreamweaver pastes them as well.

FIGURE 3-7

The Copy/Paste settings affect any text pasted into Dreamweaver.

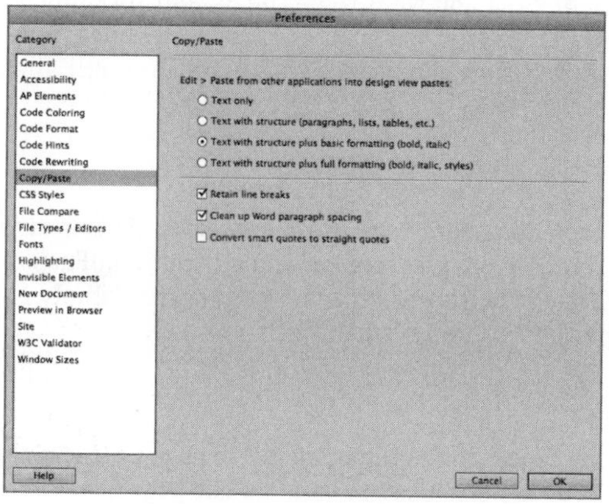

Two other options are available for modifying your copy/paste preferences. The Retain Line Breaks option maintains line breaks in pasted text; if you choose Text Only, this option is disabled. The Clean Up Word Paragraph Spacing option works with the Text With Structure and Text With Structure Plus Basic Formatting choices to remove additional space between paragraphs.

New Document preferences

Dreamweaver has greatly improved the New Document interface. You can now quickly choose which type of document you want to create, as well as select from built-in page designs and CSS. The New Document dialog box appears each time you press Ctrl+N (Command+N) or choose File ⇨ New. Use the New Document preferences (shown in Figure 3-8) to refine how you interact with the New Document dialog box.

FIGURE 3-8

Choose your default document extensions, encoding, and HTML version.

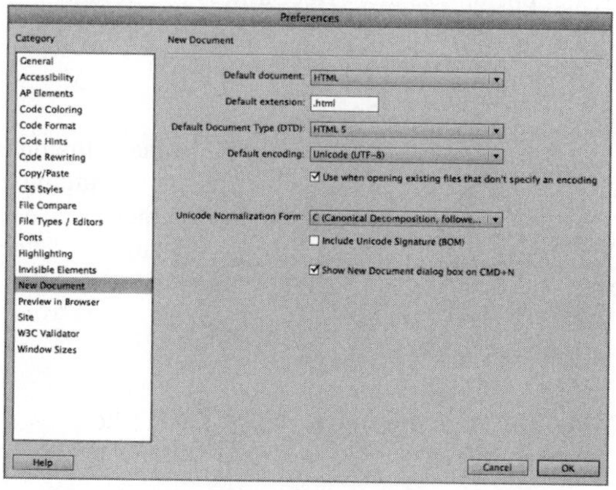

Default Document option

The Default Document menu contains all the default document types in the New Document dialog box (File ➪ New). Choose the document type you want to be the default for quickly creating new documents. If you design ASP applications more often than plain HTML files, just choose ASP VBScript rom the list menu. You can also choose templates, XML files, and PHP files; the list goes on.

Default Extension option

You can define a default extension for each document type in Dreamweaver. This means that if your server requires all ASP files to have the `.dan` extension and all your ColdFusion pages to have the `.joe` extension, you can change the extension to fit your needs. Simply enter the desired file extension, with a leading period, in the Default Extension field.

Default Document Type option

A document type, or DTD, is a line of code found at the top of an HTML page that lets the browser know how to render the following file. DTDs are also used to validate the page against a chosen set of specifications.

The Default Document Type option enables you to select which DTD, if any, you'd like to include by default. This option is originally set to XHTML 1.0 Transitional, a standard now among many web designers. You can choose from other XHTML and HTML selections including HTML 5. You can always change the DTD by choosing File ➪ Convert and then selecting one of the entries presented in the sub-list.

Encoding options

The Encoding options determine the character set in which you want your web page to be displayed. The Default Encoding option for the English version of Dreamweaver is initially set to Unicode (UTF-8). New pages use whatever choice you make from the Default Encoding list; however, the encoding can be altered in the Page Properties on a per-page basis. When you are opening existing pages without an encoding, the selected encoding is added if the accompanying option (Use When Opening Existing Files That Don't Specify An Encoding) is checked.

The Unicode Normalization Form list enables you to choose how the Unicode characters are converted to binary format. The Include Unicode Signature option determines whether a byte order mark (BOM) is attached to the file. Neither option has any effect unless the Default Encoding is set to Unicode (UTF-8).

Show New Document Dialog Box On Ctrl+N (Command+N) option

If you consistently use the same document type, clear the Show New Document Dialog Box On Control+N (Command+N) box to prevent the New Document dialog box from coming up when you press Ctrl+N (Command+N). This can measurably speed up creating new documents. Leave this box checked to see the New Document dialog box every time you create a new document. Selecting File ➪ New will always present the New Document dialog box.

Adjusting Advanced Features

Evolution of the web and its language, HTML, never ends. New features emerge, often from leading browser developers. A developer often introduces a feature similar to those marketed by his competitors but that works in a slightly different way. The HTML standards organization—the World Wide Web Consortium, also known as the W3C—can then endorse one approach or introduce an entirely new method of reaching a similar goal. Eventually, one method usually wins the approval of the marketplace and becomes the accepted coding technique.

To permit the widest range of features, Dreamweaver enables you to designate how your code is written to accommodate the latest web features: accessibility options, AP elements, and style sheets. The default preferences for these elements offer the highest degree of cross-browser and backward compatibility. If your web pages are intended for a more specific audience, Dreamweaver enables you to take advantage of a more specific feature set. Furthermore, Dreamweaver also gives you control over its Layout mode, enabling you to set options globally or on a site-by-site basis.

Accessibility preferences

Dreamweaver offers much improved support for accessibility options. With the passing of the Section 508 statute (`http://www.usdoj.gov/crt/508/508home.html`), all government agencies are required to make their sites as accessible as possible (and making your own site accessible isn't such a bad idea). Dreamweaver makes that transition just a little easier for you by allowing you to manage which accessibility options you want to enable by using the accessibility preferences, as shown in Figure 3-9.

Show Attributes When Inserting option

Check the box next to each tag for which you want to view additional accessible options when you insert that object into your page. If you check the box next to Form Objects, you get an expanded dialog box the next time you insert any form element, such as a text field or checkbox.

Inserting a form element with the accessibility options enabled gives you a much wider range of options, including labels and the capability to set an access key and tab index. The same holds true for frames, media, and images.

Keep Focus In The Panel When Opening option (Windows only)

When Dreamweaver opens a panel, such as the Files panel or CSS Styles panel, it typically returns focus to the Document window, in either Design view or Code view. If you're using a screen reader, you'd then need to locate and select the opened panel to work in it. Apply the Keep Focus In The Panel When Opening option to maintain selection in the opened panel.

Offscreen Rendering option (Windows only)

Dreamweaver uses double buffering (drawing into an off-screen bitmap before drawing to the screen) to prevent flickering. Unfortunately, this confuses screen readers, devices that help blind people use applications (such as Dreamweaver). If you're using a screen reader, disable this option.

FIGURE 3-9

Choose the tags where you want additional accessibility options to appear while you are coding.

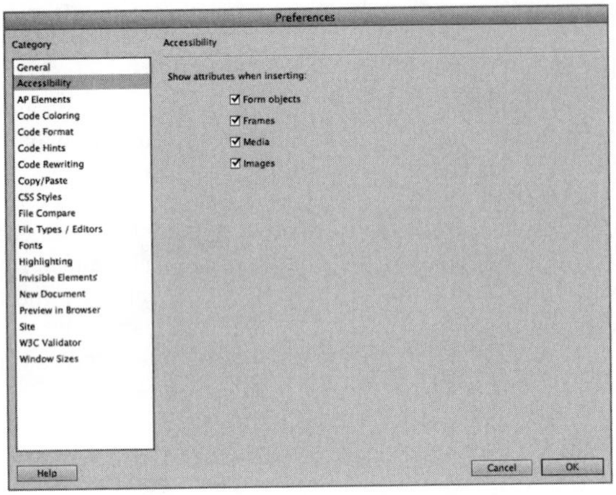

AP Elements preferences

Aside from helping you control the underlying coding method for producing AP elements, Dreamweaver enables you to define the default AP element. An AP element is a page element, often a <div> tag that is absolutely positioned. This capability is especially useful during a major production effort in which the web development team must produce hundreds of AP elements spread over a website. Being able to specify in advance the initial size, color, background, and visibility saves numerous steps—each of which would have to be repeated for every AP element. Figure 3-10 shows the layout of the AP Elements category of the Preferences dialog box. The controls accessible through the AP Elements category are described in the following sections.

Visibility option

AP elements can be either visible or hidden when the web page is first loaded. An AP element created using the default visibility option is always displayed initially; however, no specific information is written into the code. Selecting Visible forces Dreamweaver to include a `visibility:visible` line in your AP element code. Likewise, if you select Hidden from the Visibility options, the AP element is initially hidden.

Use the Inherit option when creating nested AP elements. Creating one AP element inside another makes the outer AP element the parent and the inner AP element the child. If the parent AP element is visible and the child AP element is set to `visibility:inherit`, the child is also visible. This option makes it possible to affect the visibility of many AP elements with one command—hide the parent AP element, and all the inheriting child AP elements disappear as well.

Width and Height options

When you choose Draw AP Div from the Insert panel, you drag out the size and shape of your AP element. Choosing Insert ➪ Layout Objects ➪ AP Div puts an AP element of a default size and shape at your current cursor position. The Width and Height options enable you to set these defaults. Select the text boxes and type in your new values. Dreamweaver's default is an AP element that is 200 pixels wide and 115 pixels high.

FIGURE 3-10

In the AP Elements category of Preferences, you can predetermine the structure of the default Dreamweaver AP element.

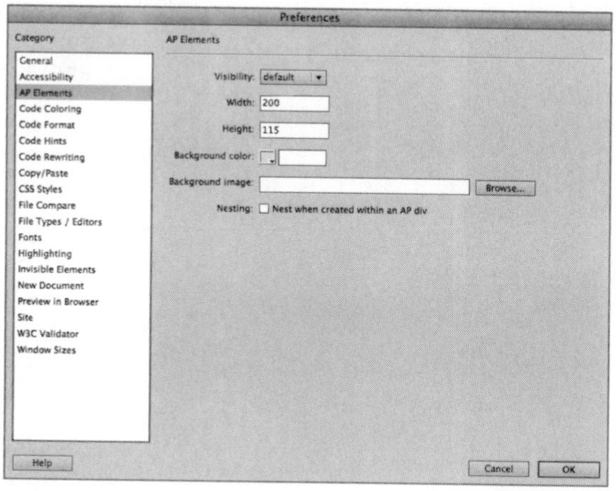

Background Color option

AP elements can have their own background colors independent of the web page's overall background color (which is set as a <body> attribute). You can define the default background color of any inserted AP element through either the Insert menu or the Insert panel. For this preference setting, type a color, either by its standard name or as a hexadecimal triplet, directly into the text box. You can also click the color swatch to display the Dreamweaver browser-safe color picker.

CAUTION

Note that although you can specify a different background color for the AP element, you can't alter the AP element's default text and link colors (except on an AP-element-by-AP-element basis) as you can with a page. If your page and AP element background colors are highly contrasting, be sure your text and links are readable in both environments. A similar caveat applies to the use of an AP element's background image, as explained in the next section.

Background Image option

Just as you can pick a specific background color for AP elements, you can select a different background image for AP elements. You can type a file source directly into the Background Image text box or select your file from a dialog box by clicking the Browse button. The AP element's background image supersedes the AP element background color, just as it does in the HTML page. Similarly, just as the page's background image tiles to fill the page, so does the AP element's background image.

Nesting option

The two best options regarding AP elements seem to be directly opposed: overlapping and nesting AP elements. You can design AP elements to appear one on top of another, or you can code AP elements so that they are within one another. Both techniques are valuable options, and Dreamweaver enables you to decide which one should be the overriding method. The AP Elements panel is capable of displaying both approaches, as shown in Figure 3-11.

If you are working primarily with nested AP elements and plan to use the inheritance facility, check the Nest When Created Within An AP Div option. If your design entails a number of overlapping but independent AP elements, make sure this option is turned off. Regardless of your preference, you can reverse it on an individual basis by pressing the Ctrl (Command) key when drawing out your AP elements.

FIGURE 3-11

Nested AP elements are shown in the AP Elements panel as child entries, and unnested ones are depicted on the same level.

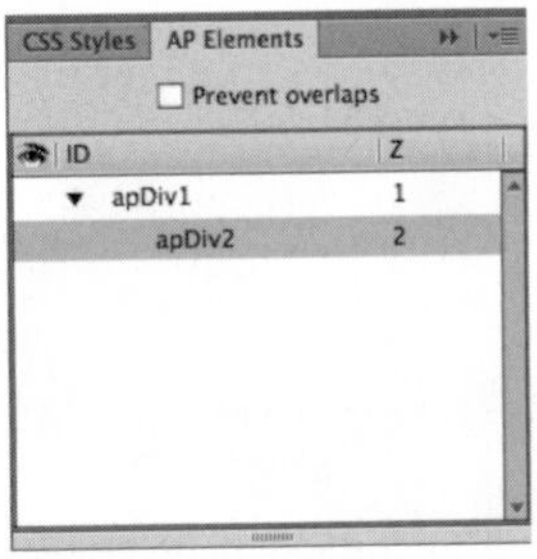

CSS Styles preferences

The CSS Styles category (see Figure 3-12) is entirely devoted to how your code is written. As specified by the W3C, CSS declarations—the specifications of a style—can be written in several ways. One method displays a series of items, separated by semicolons:

```
H1 {
  font-family: Arial, Helvetica, sans-serif;
  font-size: 12pt;
  line-height: 14pt;
  font-weight: bold;
}
```

Certain properties (such as Font) have their own grouping shorthand, developed to be more readable to designers coming from a traditional print background. A second, shorthand method of rendering the preceding declaration follows:

```
H1 { font: bold 12px/14px Arial, Helvetica, sans-serif; }
```

FIGURE 3-12

The CSS Styles category enables you to code the style sheet sections of your web pages in a graphics designer–friendly manner.

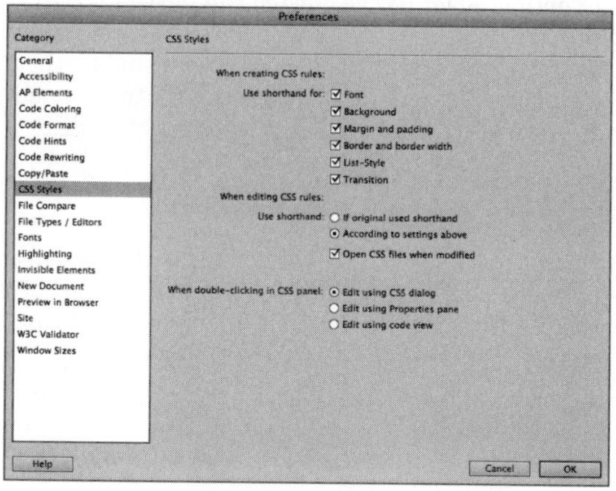

With the CSS Styles category, you can enable the shorthand method for any or all the six different properties that permit it. Select any of the checkboxes under Use Shorthand For to have Dreamweaver write your style code in this fashion.

The second option on the CSS Styles category determines how Dreamweaver edits styles in previously coded pages. If you want to retain the format of the original page, click Use Shorthand If Original Used Shorthand. If you want Dreamweaver to write new code in the manner that you specify, select Use Shorthand According To Settings Above.

The final option in this group, Open CSS Files When Modified, gives the designer a bit of a safety net when working with external CSS files. With this option enabled, Dreamweaver does indeed open the CSS file when you make a change in any of the CSS rules, whether through the CSS Style definition dialog box or the Relevant CSS panel; however, it's important to understand why the CSS file is opened. If the file is not opened, Dreamweaver cannot undo the CSS modification. It's not necessary to switch to the CSS file and undo the changes from that document; Dreamweaver handles the modifications from any page linked to the external CSS file. You must, however, save the CSS file when you're done, confirming the final styles being used. Although it may seem a bit awkward to have an external file open while working on another, I recommend selecting the Open CSS Files When Modified option.

Dreamweaver gives designers the option to modify CSS styles the way they prefer. The fastest technique for beginning the modification process is to double-click a selector in the CSS Styles panel; what happens next depends on the settings of the final group of options in this preference category. Under the When Double-Clicking In CSS Panel options, there are three choices. The first, Edit Using CSS Dialog, opens Dreamweaver's standard CSS Definition dialog box. The second, Edit Using Properties Pane, reveals the Properties pane of the CSS Styles panel, if necessary, and puts the focus on the first property's value. The final option, Edit Using Code View, displays the selected rule in Code view whether it is contained in the current document or in an external file.

Making Online Connections

Dreamweaver's visual layout editor offers an approximation of your web page's appearance in the real world of browsers—offline or online. After you've created the initial draft of your web page, you should preview it through one or more browsers. And when your project nears completion, you should transfer the files to a server for online, real-time viewing and further testing through a File Transfer Protocol (FTP) program. Dreamweaver gives you control over all these stages of web page development through the Site and Preview In Browser categories.

Site preferences

As your web site takes shape, you spend more time with the Files panel portion of Dreamweaver. The Site category, shown in Figure 3-13, enables you to customize the look and feel of your site, as well as to enter essential connection information. The available Site preferences are described in the following sections.

FIGURE 3-13

Options for Dreamweaver's Files panel are handled through the Site category.

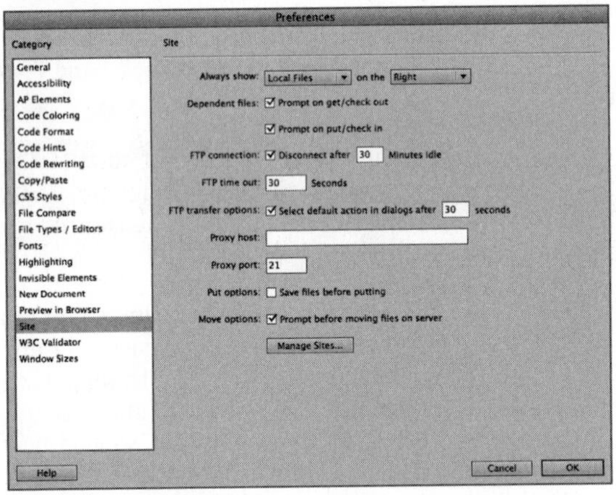

Always Show Local/Remote Files On The Right/Left option

The expanded Files panel is divided into two panes: one showing local files and one showing remote files on the server. By default, Dreamweaver puts the local pane on the right and the remote pane on the left. However, Dreamweaver enables you to customize that option. Like many designers, I'm used to using other FTP programs in which the remote files are on the right and the local files on the left; Dreamweaver enables me to work the way I'm used to working.

To switch the layout of your expanded Files panel, switch to expanded mode and open the Site preferences. Select the file location you want to change to (Local Files or Remote Files) from the

Always Show drop-down list or select the panel you want to change to (Right or Left) from the On The drop-down list. Be careful not to switch both options or you end up where you started!

Dependent Files options

Web pages are seldom just composed of single HTML files. Any graphic—whether it's in the background, part of your main logo, or used on a navigational button—is uploaded as a separate file. The same is true for any additional multimedia add-ons such as audio or video files. If you've enabled File Check In/Check Out when defining your site, Dreamweaver can also track these so-called dependent files.

Enabling the Prompt checkboxes causes Dreamweaver to ask you if you'd like to move the dependent files when you transfer an HTML file. Choose to see the dialog box for Get/Check Out, Put/Check In, or both.

TIP

You're not stuck with your Dependent Files choice. If you turn off the Dependent Files prompt, you can make it appear by pressing the Alt (Option) key while clicking the Get or Put button.

FTP Connection: Disconnect After __ Minutes Idle option

You can easily forget you're online when you are busy modifying a page. You can set Dreamweaver to automatically disconnect you from an FTP site after a specified interval. The default is 30 minutes; if you want to set a different interval, you can select the FTP Connection value in the Disconnect After text box. Dreamweaver then asks if you want to continue to wait or to disconnect when the time limit is reached, but you can maintain your FTP connection regardless by deselecting this option.

FTP Time Out option

Client-server communication is prone to glitches. Rather than hanging up your machine while trying to reach a server that is down or slow, Dreamweaver alerts you to an apparent problem after a set period. You can determine the number of seconds you want Dreamweaver to wait by altering the FTP Time Out value. The default is 30 seconds.

FTP Transfer option: Select Default Action In Dialogs After __ Seconds

I often start a large FTP process (like uploading an entire site) and then go for my morning blast of coffee. Unfortunately, this means that I sometimes miss a prompt, such as "Do you want to overwrite this file?" or "Do you want to upload all dependent files?" With earlier versions of Dreamweaver, I'd come back an hour later (I drink a lot of coffee) and nothing would be done. Check this handy option to have Dreamweaver accept the default action for the prompt after a set number of seconds.

CAUTION

This action is enabled by default, but be sure you know what the default values for most dialog boxes are before checking this box. The default action for uploading files is to include dependent files. If you have out-of-date files on your local machine, the latest awesome logo your graphic designer uploaded last night might be overwritten.

Firewall Host and Firewall Port options

Dreamweaver enables users to access remote FTP servers outside their network firewalls. A firewall is a security component that protects the internal network from unauthorized outsiders while enabling Internet access. To enable firewall access, enter the Proxy Host and Proxy Port numbers in the appropriate text boxes; if you do not know these values, contact your network administrator.

TIP

If you're having trouble transferring files through the firewall via FTP, make sure to select the Use Proxy, As Defined In option in the Site Definition dialog box for your site: Servers ➪ Edit Existing Server (pencil icon) ➪ More Options.

Put options

Certain site operations, such as putting a file on the remote site, are available in the Document window. It's common to make an edit to your page and then quickly choose the Site ➪ Put command—without saving the file first. In this situation, Dreamweaver prompts you with a dialog box to save your changes. However, you can avoid the dialog box and automatically save the file by choosing the Save Files Before Putting option.

Move options

Every now and then sites need to be restructured. To make sure that all the appropriate dependent files are transferred when an HTML file is moved, select the Prompt Before Moving Files On Server option.

Manage Sites button

Dreamweaver offers access to your site definitions from the Preferences dialog box. Just click the Manage Sites button to open the Manage Sites dialog box. This option is the same as choosing Manage Sites from the Sites pop-up on the Files panel.

See Chapter 4 to learn how to use the site definitions.

Preview In Browser preferences

Browser testing is an essential stage of web page development. Previewing your web page within the environment of a particular browser gives you a more exact representation of how it looks when viewed online. Because each browser renders the HTML with slight differences, you should preview your work in several browsers. Dreamweaver enables you to select both a primary and a secondary browser, which can both be called by pressing a function key. You can name up to 18 additional browsers through the Preview In Browser category shown in Figure 3-14. This list of preferences is also called when you choose File ➪ Preview In Browser ➪ Edit Browser List.

FIGURE 3-14

The Preview In Browser category lists browsers currently available for preview and enables you to modify the list.

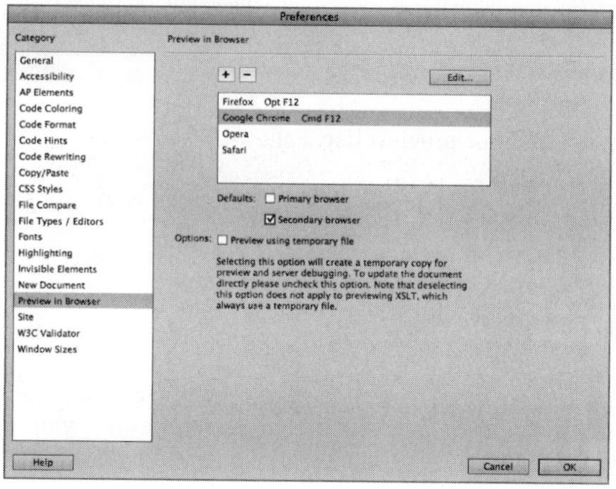

To add a browser to your preview list, follow these steps:

1. Choose Edit ➪ Preferences (Dreamweaver ➪ Preferences) or press the keyboard shortcut Ctrl+U (Command+U).
2. Select the Preview In Browser category.
3. Click the Add (+) button.
4. Enter the path to the browser file in the Path text box or click the Browse button to pick the file from the Select Browser dialog box.
5. After you have selected your browser application, Dreamweaver fills in the Name field. You can alter this name if you want.
6. If you want to designate this browser as your primary or secondary browser, select one of those checkboxes in the Defaults section.
7. Click OK when you're finished.
8. You can continue to add browsers (up to a total of 20) by following Steps 3 through 7. Click OK when you're finished.

After you've added a browser to your list, you can modify your selection by following these steps:

1. Open the Preview In Browser category and highlight the browser you want to alter.
2. Click the Edit button to open the Edit Browser dialog box.
3. After you've made your modifications, click OK to close the dialog box.

3

TIP

You can quickly designate a browser as your primary or secondary previewing choice without going through the Edit screen. From the Preview In Browser category, select the desired browser and check either Primary Browser or Secondary Browser. Note that if you already have a primary or secondary browser defined, this action overrides your previous choice.

You can also easily remove a browser from your preview list. Follow these steps:

1. Open the Preview In Browser category and choose the browser you want to delete from the list.
2. Click the Remove (-) button and click OK.

Dreamweaver can use temporary files for previewing your work in a browser. The temporary files generally have `TMPXXXXX.html`-type names and are automatically deleted when you quit Dreamweaver. With this option selected, Dreamweaver previews a temporary version of the file, displaying the file in its current state; with it unchecked, Dreamweaver requires you to save your file before it can be previewed in a browser. This option is unchecked by default.

CAUTION

If you have this checkbox selected, and Dreamweaver does not shut down normally, the temporary files are not deleted. Feel free to delete them the next time you launch Dreamweaver.

Customizing Your Code

For all its multimedia flash and visual interactivity, the web is based on code. The more you code, the more particular about your code you are likely to become. Achieving a consistent look and feel to your code enhances its readability and, thus, your productivity. In Dreamweaver, you can even design the HTML code that underlies a web page's structure.

Every time you open a new document, the default web page already has several key elements in place, such as the language in which the page is to be rendered. Dreamweaver also enables you to customize your work environment by selecting default fonts and even the colors of your HTML code.

Fonts preferences

In the Fonts category, shown in Figure 3-15, you can control the basic language of the fonts as seen by a user's browser and the fonts that you see when programming. The Font Settings section enables you to choose Western-style fonts for web pages to be rendered in English, one of the Asian languages—Japanese, Traditional Chinese, Simplified Chinese, Thai, or Korean—or another language, such as Arabic, Cyrillic, Greek, Hebrew, or Turkish. If you change the Font Settings in the Page Properties for a document, the font sizes defined in these preferences are used.

FIGURE 3-15

Use the Fonts category to set the default font encoding for each web page and the fonts you use when programming.

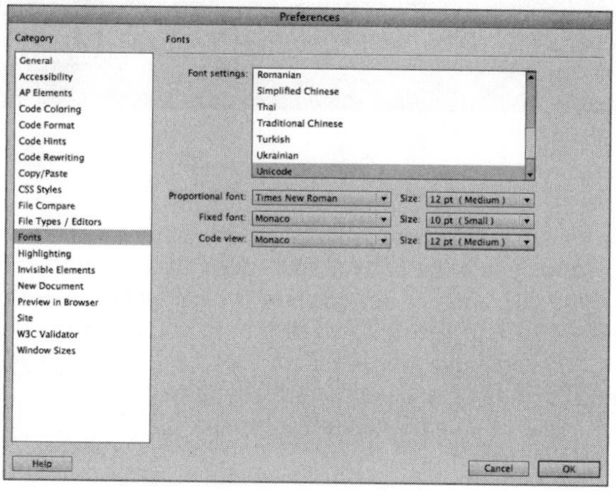

Dreamweaver now offers 15 encoding options on Windows and 19 on the Mac. The default encoding, UTF-8, has platform-specific configurations, so be sure to check the options before you make a selection.

In the bottom portion of the Fonts category, you can alter the default font and size for three different fonts:

- **Proportional Font:** This font option sets the default font used in Dreamweaver's Document window to depict paragraphs, headings, and lists.
- **Fixed Font:** In a fixed font, every character is allocated the same width. Dreamweaver uses your chosen fixed font to depict preformatted-styled text.
- **Code View:** The Code View font is used by Dreamweaver's built-in text editor. You should probably use a monospaced font such as Courier or Monaco. A monospaced font makes it easy to count characters, which is often necessary when debugging your code.

For all font options, select your font by clicking the list and highlighting your choice of font. Change the font size by selecting the value in the Size text box or by typing in a new number.

In Windows, if you select Unicode from the Font Settings list, a special option, Use Dynamic Font Mapping, appears. When this option is selected, Dreamweaver examines the current font-family to make sure all the required glyphs are available. If they are not, the font-family is replaced with a similar one that does keep the unknown character symbol—the blank rectangle—from appearing. It is recommended that you enable this option to preserve readability. The Macintosh always relies on dynamic mapping for the Unicode setting.

CAUTION

Don't be misled into thinking that by changing your Proportional Font preference to Arial or another font, you cause all your web pages to appear automatically in that typeface. Changing these font preferences affects only the default fonts that you see when developing the web page; the default font that the user sees is controlled by the user's browser. To ensure that a different font is used, you have to specify it for any selected text through the Text Properties inspector.

Code Hints preferences

With Code Hints, your work in Code view is much more productive. You can now start typing a tag in Code view, and Dreamweaver shows you a list of available codes. Start typing `<b` and a list appears with `<b>` highlighted. Type `<bl` and `<blockquote>` is highlighted. After the tag you want is highlighted, just press Enter (Return) to insert the proper tag. But wait, there's more. The Code Hints also include all the available attributes for each tag, and when you add the closing > symbol, the matching closing tag can be automatically inserted for you. The Code Hints preferences shown in Figure 3-16 determine how Code Hints work for you.

FIGURE 3-16

Code Hints speed your coding while keeping your entries accurate, whether you're working in HTML or CSS.

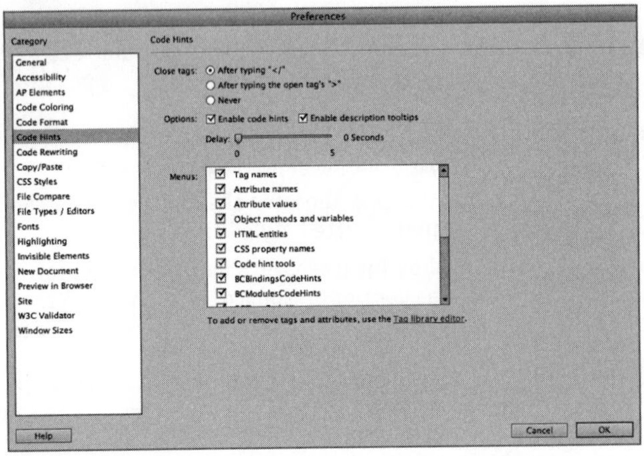

Close Tags option

Dreamweaver gives you two ways to handle code completion. The first option, After Typing "</", works by inserting the closing tag after you enter these first two characters. This has become my preferred technique because it allows me to enter the opening tag and the enclosed code and then to close it with just two characters.

If you prefer the legacy method, choose the After Typing The Open Tag's ">" option. With this option selected, after I type <b> into Code view, the corresponding </b> will be added as soon as I type the last > in the bold tag.

Auto Tag Completion is one of my favorite features in Dreamweaver, and it definitely keeps me from forgetting those pesky closing tags. Whichever method suits you best, I recommend you select one of them and speed up your coding.

Options: Enable Code Hints

This checkbox determines whether you get the new Dreamweaver Code Hints. If you have this box enabled, you can set the delay before the Code Hints drop-down menu appears. I leave the delay set to 0 so that Code Hints display as soon as I start typing.

Code Rewriting preferences

The exception to Dreamweaver's policy of not altering imported code occurs when HTML or other code is incorrectly structured. Dreamweaver automatically fixes tags that are nested in the wrong order or have additional, unnecessary closing tags—unless you tell Dreamweaver otherwise by setting up the Code Rewriting preferences accordingly (see Figure 3-17).

FIGURE 3-17

The Code Rewriting category can be used to protect nonstandard HTML from being automatically changed by Dreamweaver.

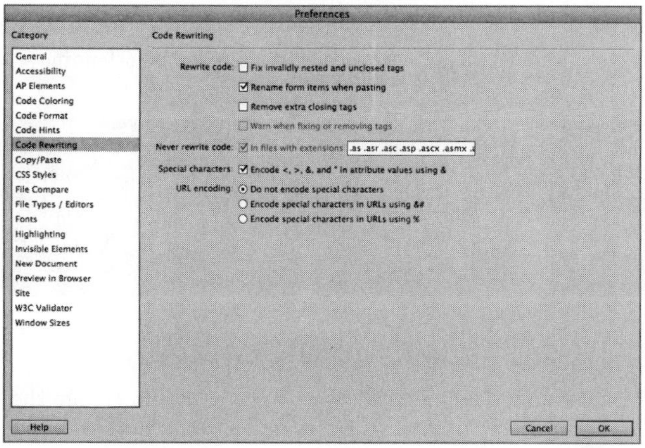

Dreamweaver accommodates many different types of markup languages, not just HTML, through the Never Rewrite Code In Files With Extensions option. Moreover, you can prevent Dreamweaver from encoding special characters such as spaces, tildes, and ampersands in URLs or attribute values. Dreamweaver is now extremely flexible. The following sections describe each of the options available through the Code Rewriting category.

Fix Invalidly Nested And Unclosed Tags option

When enabled, this option repairs incorrectly placed tags. For example, if a file contains the following line:

```
<h3><strong>Welcome to the Monkey House!</h3></strong>
```

Dreamweaver rewrites it as follows:

```
<h3><strong>Welcome to the Monkey House!</strong></h3>
```

Open that same file with this option turned off, and Dreamweaver highlights the misplaced code in the Document window. Double-clicking the code brings up a window with a brief explanation.

Rename Form Items When Pasting option

In general, static web pages require each form element to be uniquely named; with this option selected, you can quickly insert a series of text fields with similar attributes and be assured that they are individually named. However, with dynamic applications, the names may be supplied dynamically, and you don't want that code overwritten. Uncheck this box to prevent Dreamweaver from renaming all your form elements.

Remove Extra Closing Tags option

When you're editing your code by hand, it's fairly easy to miss a closing tag. Dreamweaver cleans up such code if you enable the Remove Extra Closing Tags option. You may, for example, have the following line in a previously edited file:

```
<p>And now back to our show...</p></em>
```

Notice that the closing emphasis tag, `</em>`, has no matching opening partner. If you open this file in Dreamweaver with the Remove option enabled, Dreamweaver plucks out the offending `</em>`.

TIP

In some circumstances, you want to ensure that your pages remain as originally formatted. If you edit pages in Dreamweaver that have been preprocessed by a server unknown to Dreamweaver (prior to displaying the pages), be sure that you disable both the Fix Invalidly Nested And Unclosed Tags option, where possible, and the Remove Extra Closing Tags option.

Warn When Fixing Or Removing Tags option

If you're editing a lot of web pages created on another system, you should enable the Warn When Fixing Or Removing Tags option. If this setting is turned on, Dreamweaver displays a list of changes that have been made to your code in the HTML Corrections dialog box. The changes can be quite extensive when Dreamweaver opens what it regards as a poorly formatted page.

CAUTION

Remember that after you've enabled these Rewrite Code options, the fixes occur automatically. If this sequence happens to you by mistake, immediately close the file (without saving it!), disable the Code Rewriting preferences options, and reopen the document.

Never Rewrite Code preferences

Many of the database connectivity programs, such as ColdFusion, use proprietary tags embedded in a regular web page to communicate with their servers. Dreamweaver enables you to explicitly protect file types identified with a particular file extension.

To enter a new file type in the Never Rewrite Code options, select the In Files With Extensions field. Enter the file extension of the file type, including the period, at the end of the list. Be sure to separate your extensions from the others in the list with a space on either side.

Special Characters Encoding preferences

By encoding special characters such as `<`, `>`, `&`, and `"` in attribute values, Dreamweaver ensures that the characters are interpreted correctly by the browser. This works well for static pages, but many dynamic pages use the same characters in their server-side code. If you find that your application server is misinterpreting attributes with these characters, disable the Encode <, >, &, And " In Attribute Values Using & option.

URL Encoding preferences

In addition to the rewriting of proprietary tags, many middleware vendors face another problem when trying to integrate with Dreamweaver. By default, earlier versions of Dreamweaver encoded all URLs so that Unix servers could understand them. The encoding converted all special characters to their decimal equivalents, preceded by a percent sign. Spaces became `%20`, tildes (~) became `%7E`, and ampersands were converted to `&`. Although this is valid for Unix servers and helps to make the Dreamweaver code more universal, it can cause problems for many other types of application servers.

Dreamweaver gives you the option to disable the URL encoding, if necessary, or choose the type of encoding you prefer for special characters. If you choose to encode them using &#, Dreamweaver uses numeric character entities; the default option is not to encode them. Select the Encode Special Characters In URLs Using % option and Dreamweaver uses decimal equivalents.

In general, however, it's best to leave the URL encoding option set to the default unless you find your third-party tags being rewritten destructively.

Code Coloring preferences

HTML code is a combination of the tags that structure the language and the text that provides the content. A web page designer often has difficulty distinguishing swiftly between the two—and finding the right code to modify. Dreamweaver enables you to set color preferences for the code as it appears in Code view or the Code inspector. You can not only alter colors for the background, default tags, and text and general comments but also specify certain tags to get certain colors.

Dreamweaver enables you to specify color-coding for individual document types. If you want different code coloring in VBScript documents, HTML, and PHP documents, you can customize the coloring for each individually. The only color on the main dialog box is the default background color. This isn't the page background color, but the Code view background color.

To modify any of the elements for a specific document type, select the document type as illustrated in Figure 3-18 and click Edit Coloring Scheme.

After you click Edit Coloring Scheme, you get the Edit Coloring Scheme For HTML dialog box, which enables you to change every facet of Dreamweaver's color coding, as shown in Figure 3-19.

FIGURE 3-18

Use the Code Coloring category to custom color-code the HTML inspector.

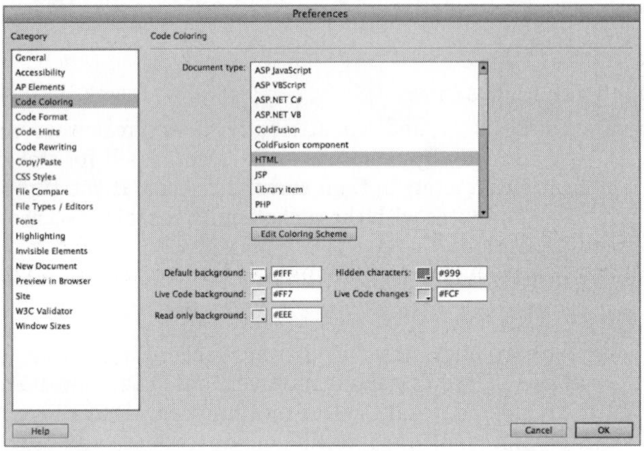

FIGURE 3-19

The Edit Coloring Scheme dialog box provides a method to completely customize the way you view your raw page code.

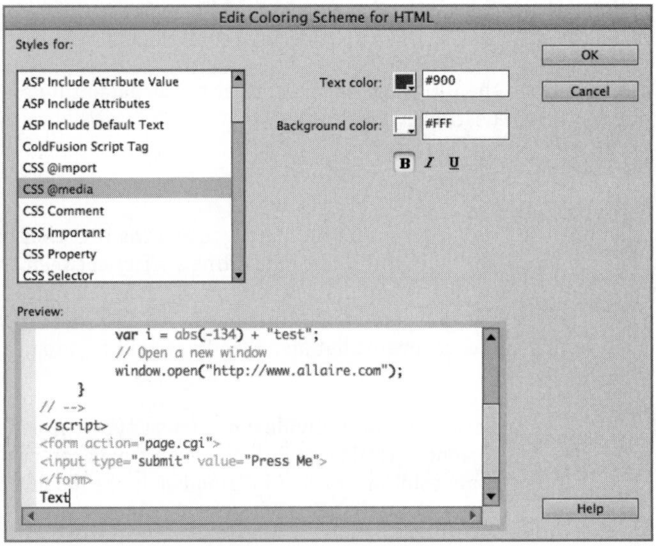

The left-hand Styles For box contains every type of tag you could ever want to color. Just select a tag type and then click the color swatch to select one of the 216 colors displayed in the color picker. After the color picker opens, you can also choose the small palette icon to select from the full range of colors available to your system. The color picker also enables you to use the Eyedropper tool to pick a color from the Document window.

As you change colors, you can see a preview of how your code looks in the Preview window.

Code Format preferences

Dreamweaver includes a fantastic tool for customizing your HTML with the easy-to-use, point-and-click preferences category called Code Format. Most of your HTML code parameters can be controlled through the Code Format category.

In the Code Format category, you can also decide whether to use indentations—and if so, whether to use spaces or tabs and how many of each. You can also globally control the case of your HTML tags and their attributes. As you can see in Figure 3-20, the Code Format category is full-featured.

To examine the available options in the Code Format category, let's separate them into four areas: indent control, line control, case control, and CSS source format options.

FIGURE 3-20

The Code Format category enables you to shape your HTML to your own specifications.

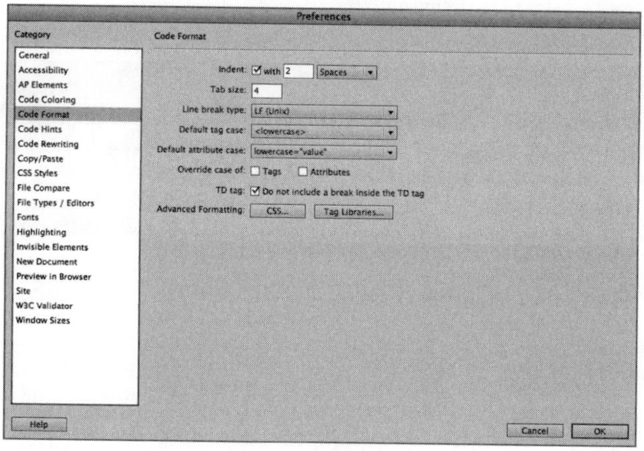

Indent control options

Indenting your code generally makes it more readable. Dreamweaver defaults to indenting most HTML tags with two spaces. All these parameters can be altered through the Code Format category of the Preferences dialog box.

The first indent option enables indenting, and you can switch from spaces to tabs. To permit indenting, make sure a checkmark is displayed in the Indent checkbox. If you prefer your code to be displayed flush left, turn off the Indent option altogether.

To use tabs instead of the default spaces, select Tabs from the drop-down list. If you anticipate transferring your code to a word processing program for formatting and printing, you should use tabs; otherwise, stay with the default spaces.

The other two items in the indent control section of the Code Format preferences category are Indent and Tab Size. Change the value in Indent to establish the size of indents using spaces. To alter the size of tab indents, change the Tab Size value.

Line control options

The browser is responsible for ultimately formatting an HTML page for viewing. This formatting includes wrapping text according to each user's screen size and the placement of the paragraph tags (`<p> . . . </p>`). Therefore, you control how your code wraps in your HTML editor. You can turn off the automatic wrapping feature or set it for a particular column through the line control options of the Code Format category.

The Line Break Type setting determines which line break character is appended to each line of the page. Each of the major operating systems employs a different ending character: Macintosh uses a carriage return (CR), Unix uses a line feed (LF), and Windows uses both (CR LF). If you know the operating system for your remote server, choosing the corresponding line break character ensures that the file has the correct appearance when viewed online. Click the drop-down arrow next to Line Break Type to select your system.

CAUTION

The operating system for your local development machine may be different from the operating system of your remote server. If so, using the Line Break Type option may cause your HTML to appear incorrect when viewed through a simple text editor (such as Notepad or TextEdit). Dreamweaver's Code view and Code inspector, however, do render the code correctly.

Case control options

The case of HTML tags is becoming more and more important. In XHTML, all tags and attribute names must be in lowercase. If you're coding in regular HTML, case is only a personal preference among web designers. That said, some webmasters consider case a serious preference and insist that their code be all uppercase, all lowercase, or a combination of uppercase and lowercase. Personally, I fall in the lowercase camp. Dreamweaver gives you control over the tags and attributes it creates, as well as over case conversion for files that Dreamweaver imports. The Dreamweaver default for both tags and attributes is lowercase.

TIP

Lowercase tags and attributes are also less fattening, according to the W3C. Files with lowercase tag names and attributes compress better and thus transmit faster.

You can also use Dreamweaver to standardize the letter case in tags of previously saved files. To alter imported files, select the Override Case Of Tags and/or the Override Case Of Attributes options. When enabled, these options enforce your choices made in the Case For Tags and Case For Attributes option boxes in any file Dreamweaver loads. Again, be sure to save your file to keep the changes.

The TD Tag option ensures that there is no line break after the `<td>` tag in your document. Putting a line break after the `<td>` can create display anomalies in some browsers, such as unwanted space. I recommend leaving this one checked.

CSS Source Format preferences

Just as the format of HTML code matters to many web designers, so does the format of the embedded or attached CSS code. Clicking the CSS button opens the CSS Source Format Options dialog box (see Figure 3-21), which offers a range of controls to stylize your style sheets.

FIGURE 3-21

Control your CSS look and feel with the CSS Source Format Options.

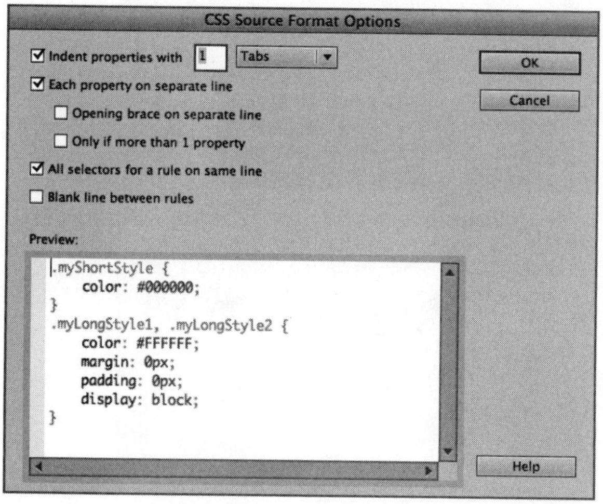

Most designers find that, like HTML code, CSS code is easier to read if it is indented. The Indent Properties option enables you to set the amount of tabs or spaces to use for each indentation. Readability is also enhanced by selecting the Each Property On Separate Line option, which has two related options: You can force the opening brace ({) onto a separate line if you prefer and restrict the rule to a single line if there is only one property. You'll also have the choice to keep all your selectors on the same line and to place a blank line between defined rules.

The format of your CSS, perhaps even more than your HTML, is completely up to the designer's personal preferences. I try to strike a balance between readability and compactness by selecting all the options except Opening Brace On Separate Line and Blank Line Between Rules.

Not only can you customize your general code and CSS preferences, but with Dreamweaver's Tag Library Editor you can modify all the various tags individually—as well as import entire new tag sets. For details on how the Tag Library Editor works, see Chapter 33.

W3C Validator preferences

Dreamweaver offers the capability to validate against multiple HTML schemes and server-side languages. You can even choose which types of errors you'd like Dreamweaver to warn you about. In the W3C Validator preferences, shown in Figure 3-22, notice that you can choose just the specs you want to support.

FIGURE 3-22

The W3C Validator preferences enable you to validate against one or multiple HTML schemes or server-side languages.

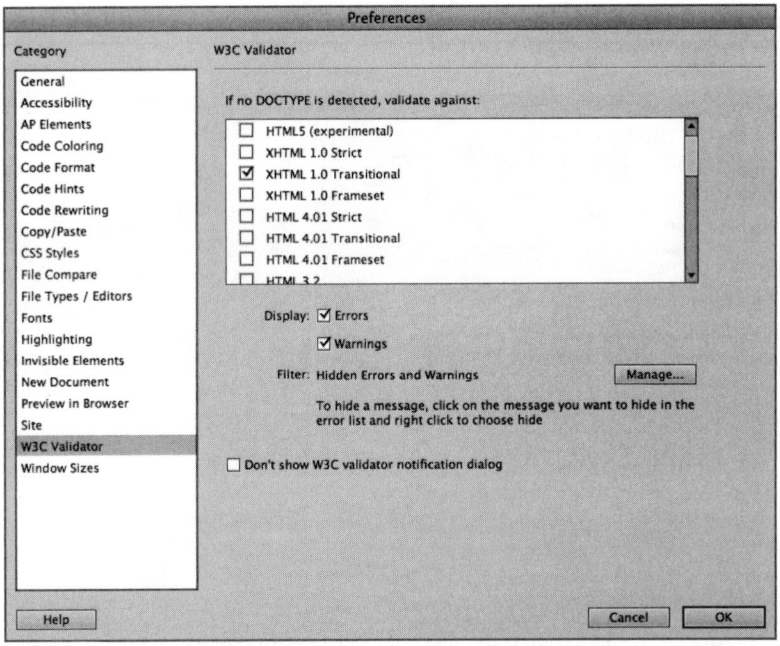

The Validate Against list includes the following entries:

- HTML5 (Experimental)
- XHTML 1.0 Strict
- XHTML 1.0 Transitional
- XHTML 1.0 Frameset
- HTML 4.0.1 Strict
- HTML 4.0.1 Transitional
- HTML 4.0.1 Frameset
- HTML 3.2
- HTML 2.0
- ISO/IEC 15445:2000 ("ISO HTML")

- XHTML 1.1
- XHTML + RDFa
- XHTML Basic 1.0
- XHTML Basic 1.1
- XHTML Mobile-Profile 1.2
- XHTML-Print 1.0
- XHTML 1,1 plus MathML 2.0
- XHTML 1.1 plus MathML 2.0 plus SVG 1.1
- MathML 2.0
- SVG 1.0
- SVG 1.1
- SVG 1.1 Tiny
- SVG 1.1 Basic
- SMIL 1.0
- SMIL 2.0

Dreamweaver allows you to hide errors or warnings generated by the W3C Validation procedure. Click Manage to review errors and warnings, select any you don't want displayed, and then choose hide.

Summary

Creating web pages, like any design job, is easier when the tools fit your hands. Through Preferences, you can make Dreamweaver work the way you work. When you're examining and setting Dreamweaver's preferences, keep these points in mind:

- Dreamweaver enables you to customize your web page design and HTML coding environment through a series of easy-to-use, point-and-click categories.
- Dreamweaver's startup options include a welcome screen that brings your recent documents within one-click reach, as well as the opportunity to automatically reopen all your documents from your previous session.
- You can decide how best to use most layout features, such as AP elements and style sheets, depending on the degree of cross-browser and backward compatibility you need.
- Dreamweaver gives you plenty of elbow room for previewing and testing by providing for 20 selections on your browser list.
- Set the level of validation you want to strive for through the Validator preferences.

In the next chapter, you learn how to define a site in Dreamweaver.

Summary

CHAPTER

4

Setting Up Sites and Servers

IN THIS CHAPTER

Making a local site

Dreamweaver Technique: Setting Up Your Site

Generating and saving pages

Previewing your website

Publishing online

Working with Business Catalyst

Websites—especially those integrating web applications—are far more than collections of HTML documents. Every image—from the smallest navigational button to the largest background image—is a separate file that must be uploaded with your HTML page. Moreover, if you use any additional elements, such as an included script, background sound, digital video, or Java applet, these files must be transferred as well. To preview the website locally and view it properly on the Internet, you have to organize your material in a particular manner.

While you can code individual pages in Dreamweaver, for a great many of Dreamweaver's features, you'll need to define a site. As I describe in this chapter, each time you begin developing a new site, you define several initial parameters, including the chosen server model (provided, of course, you are creating a dynamically driven site, such as a web application). These steps lay the groundwork for Dreamweaver to properly link your local development site with a remote online site, as well as to link properly to your data sources (again, for dynamically driven sites). This chapter begins with a brief description of approaches to online design, aimed primarily at those who are just starting to create websites. The remainder of the chapter is devoted to the mechanics of setting up your site and basic file manipulation. You also learn how to connect directly to servers, without establishing a local site.

Dreamweaver QUICKSTART

Ready to jump in and start building sites with Dreamweaver? It's really easy to define a simple site and start designing. Here's how:

1. Choose Site ➪ New Site.
2. When the Site Setup dialog box opens, enter a name for your site in the Site Name field.
3. Click the folder icon next to the Local Site Folder field.
4. In the Choose Root Folder dialog box, navigate to the folder you want to contain your site and click Select (Choose).
5. When you return to the Site Setup dialog box, click Save.

That's it! Of course, there's a lot more you can do pertaining to sites in Dreamweaver, all of which is covered in the rest of this chapter.

Planning Your Site

Planning in web design, just as in any other design process, is essential. Not only does careful planning cut your development time considerably, but it makes it far easier to achieve a uniform look and feel for your website—making it friendlier and easier to use. This section briefly covers some of the basics of website design: what to focus on, what options to consider, and what pitfalls to avoid. If you are an established website developer who has covered this ground before, feel free to skip this section.

Even before you choose the overarching structure for your site (as discussed in the following sections), you need to address the all-important issues of message, audience, and budget.

Deciding what you want to say

If I had to pick one overriding concern for website design, it would be to answer the following question: What are you trying to say? The clearer you are about your message, the more focused your website will be. To this end, I find it useful to try to state the purpose of the website in one sentence. "Creating the coolest website on the planet" doesn't count. Although it could be regarded as a goal, it's too open-ended to be useful. Here are some examples of clearly stated website concepts:

- To provide the best small-business resource center focused on Adobe software
- To chronicle the world's first voyage around the world by hot air balloon
- To advertise music lessons offered by a collective of keyboard teachers in New York City

Targeting your audience

Right behind a site's concept in terms of importance—some would say neck and neck with it—is the site's audience. Who are you trying to reach? Quite often, a site's style is heavily influenced by a clear vision of the site's intended audience. Take, for example, a small site I developed for my wife's dance work, `http://debrawannerdance.com`. This site is pitched to the intended audience of folks interested in modern dance based in New York City. Hence, the site is a bit snazzy but focuses on being informative and locally oriented.

In contrast, a site that is devoted to mass-market e-commerce must work with a very different group in mind: shoppers. Everyone at one time or another falls into this category, so I am really talking about a state of mind, rather than a profession. Many shopping sites use a very straightforward page design that is easily maneuverable, comforting in its repetition—where visitors can quickly find what they are looking for and, with as few impediments as possible, buy it.

Determining your resources

Unfortunately, websites aren't created in a vacuum. Virtually all development work happens under real-world constraints of some kind. A professional web designer is accustomed to working within a budget. In fact, the term "budget" can apply to several concepts.

First, you have a monetary budget—how much is the client willing to spend? This translates into a combination of development time (for designers and programmers), materials (custom graphics, stock photos, and the like), and ongoing maintenance. You can build a large site with many pages that pulls dynamically from an internal database and requires very little hands-on upkeep. Alternatively, you can construct a small, graphics-intensive site that must be updated by hand weekly. It's entirely possible that both sites end up costing the same.

Second, "budget" also applies to the amount of time you can afford to spend on any given project. The professional web designer is quick to realize that time is an essential commodity. The resources needed when undertaking a showcase for yourself when you have no deadline are very different from those needed when you sign a contract on June 30 for a job that must be ready to launch on July 4.

The third real-world budgetary item to consider is bandwidth. The web, with faster Internet connections and an improved infrastructure, is slowly shedding its image as the World Wide Wait. However, users accessing the web via their wireless devices may be working with bandwidth limit, which means that webmasters must keep a steady eye on a page's weight—how long it takes to download under the most typical modem rates. Of course, you can always decide to include that animated video masterpiece that takes 8 minutes to download on a cable modem—you just can't expect everyone to wait to see it.

In conclusion, when you are trying to define your web page, filter it through these three ideas: message, audience, and the various faces of the budget. The time spent visualizing your web pages in these terms is time decidedly well spent.

Mapping Dynamic Pages for Web Applications

Many, if not most, web applications require more than one web page. One variation on a search engine, for example, might use the following:

- An entry page containing the form elements (text field, list boxes, and so on) that make up the search criteria.
- A results page that displays the list of items matching the search criteria; each of the items typically provides a link to a detail page and more information.
- A detail page (or pages) that provides more information—this page is linked from the results page.
- An error page, if the initial search criteria do not have any matches.

The experienced web developer maps out the structure for all the anticipated web applications in the site before beginning the building process. In addition to providing a truer picture of the work involved, mapping the required pages highlights potentially redundant pages—for example, the same error page may be used throughout the site—and pinpoints areas that would benefit from dynamic data application. The web application map can also serve as a workflow schematic that shows which pages are static HTML and could be built by an HTML designer with little or no coding experience (typically, the entry and error pages) and which pages are dynamic web pages that require data-aware designers.

Defining a Site

Now that you've decided on a design and mapped your site, you're ready to set it up in Dreamweaver. When you define a site, you are telling Dreamweaver where to store your web pages locally, where to transfer them to remotely, and the style of code in which to write them. Defining a site is an essential first step.

The Site Setup dialog box offers a multi-tiered approach that allows you to define just what you need and nothing more. You can create a local site in just two steps and quickly get started designing pages with nothing more. Or, if you already know the login and other details for your web host, you can define a remote server as well. In addition, there are numerous details, such as version control, that can be specified if necessary.

Working with Site Setup

The Site Setup dialog box comprises three main categories—Site, Servers, and Version Control—and a fourth category, Advanced Settings, with a variety of site-level properties. You can set up a basic local site by accessing just the Site category.

NOTE **The sub-categories in the Site Setup dialog box Advanced Settings category (Local info, Cloaking, Design Notes, File View Columns, Contribute, Templates, Spry, and WebFonts) are especially helpful for working in a team environment. You can find more information on these features later in this chapter and on team website building in Chapter 31.**

The three main steps for fully defining a site in Dreamweaver are:

1. Locate the folder to be used for the local development site.
2. Enter the remote site information.
3. If you are creating a web application, specify the testing server model to be used for the site.

While these steps can be taken one stage at a time, the first step of defining a local folder must be taken first and is essential in Dreamweaver.

Establishing local connections

After your site is on your web server and fully operational, it consists of many files—plain HTML, style sheets, JavaScript, graphics, and other media files—that make up the individual web pages. All these associated files are kept on the remote server in one folder, with, likely, one or more subfolders. This main folder is called the *remote site folder*. In order for Dreamweaver to properly display your linked pages and embedded images—just as they are displayed online—the program maintains a mirror of your remote site on your local development system. This primary mirror folder on your system is known as the local site folder.

You must establish the local site folder at the beginning of a project. This ensures that Dreamweaver duplicates the complete structure of the web development site when it comes time to publish your pages to the web. One of Dreamweaver's key site-management features enables you to select just the HTML pages for publication; Dreamweaver then automatically transfers all the associated files, creating any needed folders in the process. The mirror images of your local and remote site folders are critical to Dreamweaver's capability to expedite your workload in this way.

TIP

If you do decide to transfer an existing website to a new Dreamweaver local site folder, run Dreamweaver's Link Checker after you've consolidated all your files. Choose Site ➪ Check Links Sitewide or press the keyboard shortcut Ctrl+F8 (Command+F8). The Link Checker informs you of broken links and orphan files.

To set up a local site folder in Dreamweaver, follow these steps:

1. Choose Site ➪ New Site.
2. The Site Setup dialog box opens, as shown in Figure 4-1.

FIGURE 4-1

Defining a basic website is very straightforward with Dreamweaver's Site Setup dialog box.

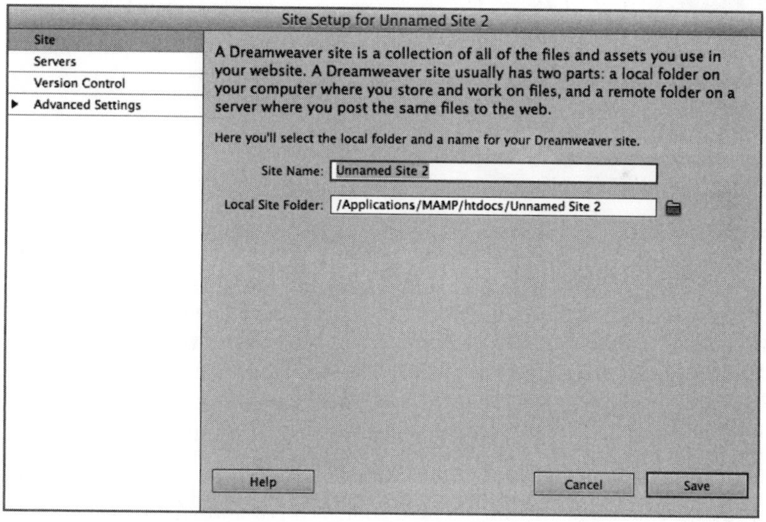

3. From the Site category, enter a name for your site in the Site Name text field. This is the name that appears in the Sites drop-down list and the Edit Sites dialog box.
4. Specify the folder to serve as the local site folder by either typing the pathname directly into the Local Site Folder field or clicking the folder icon to open the Choose Root Folder dialog box. Click New Folder if needed. When you've made your choice there, click the Select (Choose) button.
5. Click Save.

NOTE

The Choose Root Folder dialog boxes look somewhat different on the PC than on the Mac, but you can make sure you're designating the folder you want with a single technique. On both operating systems, the current folder is listed at the top of the dialog box. Verify that the desired folder is displayed before you click Select on the PC and Choose on the Mac.

Your new site appears in the Files panel, as shown in Figure 4-2, with any files in the folder, collapsed under the site name. Any defined site can be accessed by selecting it from the list at the top of the Files panel.

FIGURE 4-2

Previously created folders—as well as files, if any—in the chosen local site folder appear in the Files panel after the site is set up.

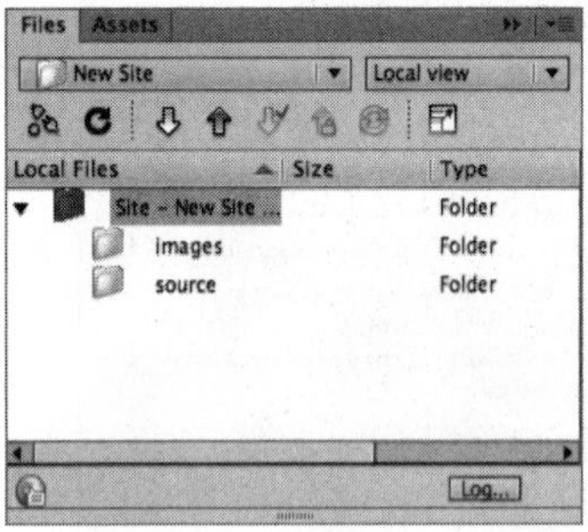

While the details entered in the Site category are all you need to get started creating a local site with Dreamweaver, there are a few more settings you can specify to make working with a local site easier and customized to your liking. These settings are contained under Advanced Settings in the Local Info subcategory. You can easily modify these properties after you've created your site.

1. Choose Site ➪ Manage Sites.
2. When the Manage Sites dialog box appears, make sure the site you want to modify is chosen in the list and click Edit.
3. When the Site Setup dialog box appears, expand the Advanced Settings category and choose Local Info (see Figure 4-3).
4. If your site is to have a dedicated images folder, specify it in the Default Images Folder text box. Note that your Default Images Folder can have subfolders.

   Any images that you select from outside your local site folder will need to be copied to the site root. If you have a Default Images Folder established, Dreamweaver will automatically copy those files there, saving you the step of selecting it each time.

5. If you plan on using a CSS file that contains links to media query statements, enter its path in the Site-Wide Media Query File field or click the Browse For File icon to select the file.

NOTE

Media queries are used to change the CSS styles depending on browser width and other factors. For more information on using media queries, see Chapter 6.

6. Choose which type of links you'd prefer to use by default: Document or Site Root. If you're unsure, leave the standard option, Document.
7. Enter the full URL for your site in the web URL text field. This field is unavailable if a remote server has already been defined.

FIGURE 4-3

Speed up your web page development by specifying settings in the Local info category.

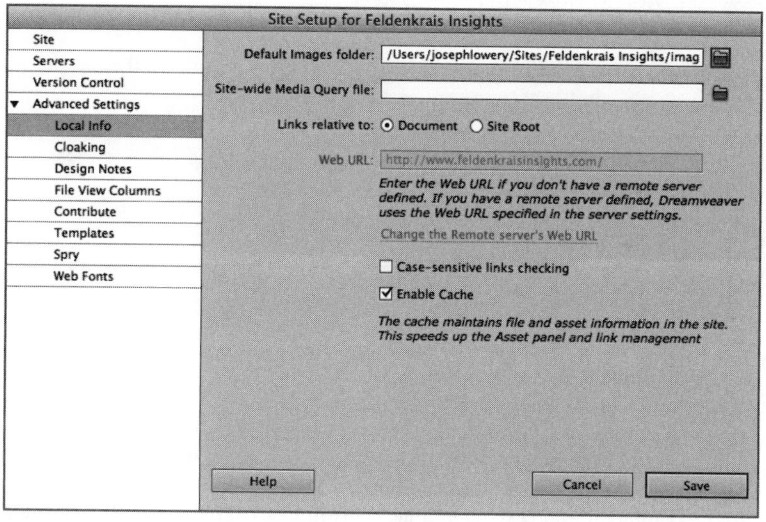

When checking links for your website, Dreamweaver uses the web URL to determine whether absolute links, such as `www.idest.com/dreamweaver/index.htm`, reference external files or files on your site.

8. If you'd like to make sure that your links match files names, including their case, choose the Case-Sensitive Links Checking option. This option is most helpful when your site is hosted on a Unix server that relies on case-sensitive filenames.
9. For fastest performance, select the Enable Cache option. Having a site cache enables Dreamweaver to store information that makes certain key site tasks, such as link updates, run faster.

Dreamweaver TECHNIQUE

Setting Up Your Site

In this Technique, you set up a site that is used throughout this book in the other Dreamweaver Techniques. The process is simple, but essential.

1. If you haven't already downloaded the Dreamweaver Technique Simulation files from the book's website to your system, visit `http://www.wiley.com/go/dreamweavercs6bible` and download the `.zip` file now. Uncompress the `.zip` file and copy/move the resulting folder named Techniques to wherever you store, or plan to store, sites you create on your computer.

TIP

If Mac users aren't planning on serving web pages directly from their computers, the Sites folder, located in the user's Home folder, is a logical place to put the Techniques folder.

2. Choose Site ➪ New Site from within Dreamweaver.
3. In the Site tab of the Site Setup dialog box, enter **Techniques** in the Site Name field.
4. Select the folder icon next to the Local Site Folder field.
5. In the Choose Local Root Folder dialog box, locate and select the Techniques folder; click Select (Choose) when you're done.
6. Click OK to create the site. This doesn't modify anything in the Techniques folder; it simply sets Dreamweaver up so that it knows where the referenced files are located.

In Dreamweaver Techniques found in subsequent chapters, you'll be directed to open files in the Techniques site just established.

Specifying a remote server

To share your site with others—whether globally through the World Wide Web or more specifically via an intranet or other network—you can define one or more servers. A *remote* server is connected to the Internet and publicly accessible; files are typically transferred to a remote server via FTP (File Transfer Protocol) or SFTP (Secure File Transfer Protocol). A testing server is intended to be used for development and testing and most often is accessed through a closed network.

NOTE

Dreamweaver allows you to define as many servers as you need, whether remote or testing, and then access them whenever you'd like. In the simplest scenario, a designer would establish a remote server with the information provided from the web host. For sites that require server-side coding, such as PHP or ColdFusion, many Dreamweaver developers create a testing server on their development system, as well as a remote server. Team-developed sites might add another testing server to which designers post their pages for additional testing. At the appropriate time, the network administrator exports the files from the testing server to the remote server; alternatively, if you have sufficient access, you can handle the transfer yourself. For any server–testing or remote–a remote site folder is created on the server that acts as a mirror to the local site folder.

You'll need various bits of information to establish a server, particularly if you post your material to a remote site via FTP. In addition to the FTP host's name—used by Dreamweaver to find the server on the Internet—you also need, at a minimum, the username and password to log on to the server. The host's technical support staff can provide you with this and any other necessary information.

To set up a connection to a remote server, follow these steps:

1. Choose Window ➪ Manage Sites.
2. In the Manage Sites dialog box, select the site you want to add a remote server to and click Edit.

TIP

To open your site definition directly, double-click the site name in the Files panel.

3. In the Site Setup dialog box, choose Servers.

   The Servers category screen displays all the servers currently defined and allows you to add new ones, as well as edit existing definitions, or remove any you no longer need (see Figure 4-4).

FIGURE 4-4

Set up and manage both remote and testing servers through the Servers category.

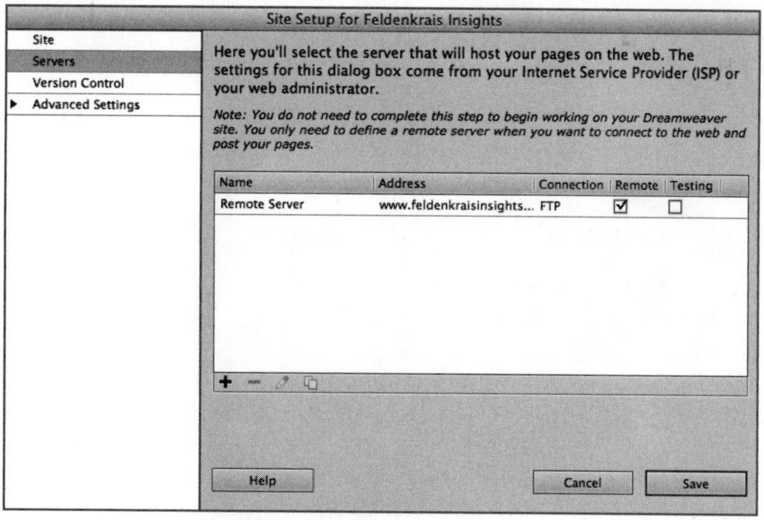

4. Click Add New Server, the plus sign.
5. In the Basic tab, enter how you want to identify your remote server in the Server Name field.

6. From the Connect Using list, choose the access description that applies to your site; FTP is shown in Figure 4-5:
   - **FTP:** Select this option if you connect to your web server via File Transfer Protocol (FTP).
   - **SFTP:** Choose this option to connect using Secure File Transfer Protocol (SFTP).
   - **FTP Over SSL/TLS (Implicit Encryption):** Select this option to connect using a Secure Sockets Layer (SSL) connection as part of the Transport Layer Security (TLS) protocol. The security is enabled automatically when the connection is made to an FTP server.
   - **FTP Over SSL/TLS (Explicit Encryption):** Select this option to connect using a Secure Sockets Layer (SSL) connection as part of the Transport Layer Security (TLS) protocol. Here, the security is enabled on demand when a request is made to the FTP server.
   - **Local/Network:** Select this option if you are running a local web server and want to store your remote site on your local drive, or if your web server is mounted as a network drive.
   - **WebDAV:** Choose this option to store your files remotely in a Web-based Distributed Authoring and Versioning (WebDAV) system.
   - **RDS:** Choose this option if you are working with a ColdFusion site that has Remote Development Services (RDS) enabled.

FIGURE 4-5

You'll need configuration details from your web host to create an FTP connection.

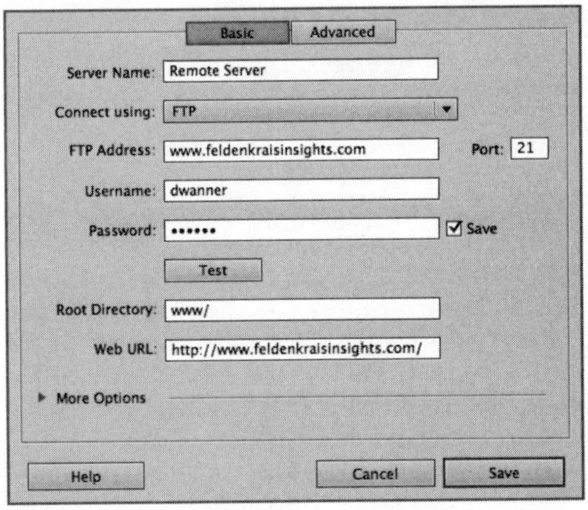

7. If you selected FTP for access, complete the following options:
   - **FTP Address:** Enter the host name of the FTP connection for your web server, which is usually in the form `ftp.sitename.com`. Do not include the full URL, such as `ftp://ftp.sitename.com`.

- **Port:** The default FTP port number is `21`; change this value if necessary.
- **Username:** Enter the login name you have been assigned for access to the web server.
- **Password:** Enter the password necessary for you to gain access to the web server. Note that many servers are case-sensitive when it comes to usernames and passwords.
- **Save:** Dreamweaver automatically selects this option after you enter a password. Deselect it only if you and others access the server from the current system.
- **Test:** After you've specified all your FTP parameters, you can click the Test button to verify that Dreamweaver can connect successfully to your web server.
- **Root Directory:** Enter the directory in which publicly accessible documents are stored on the server. Typical host directory names are `www/`, `public/`, `docs/`, and `public_html/`. Your remote site folder is a subfolder of the host directory. If you are unsure of the exact name of the host directory, check with your web server administrator. Often, the FTP host connects to the correct directory automatically, and you can leave this field blank.
- **Web URL:** Enter the web address for your site.

8. If the connection test is unsuccessful, expand the More Options link and choose from the following options shown in Figure 4-6.

FIGURE 4-6

Additional options are available if you are unable to make an FTP connection.

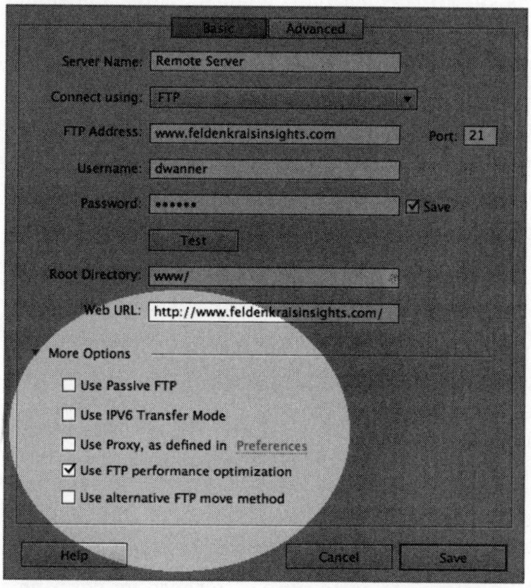

- **Use Passive FTP:** Passive FTP establishes the FTP connection through the local software, rather than the server. Certain firewall configurations use passive FTP; check with your network administrator to see if you need it.

- **Use IPv6 Transfer Mode:** IPv6 (Internet Protocol version 6) is the most recent networking communication standard enjoying widespread adoption. Select this option if you need to connect to an IPv6-enabled FTP server.
- **Use Proxy:** This option is automatically selected if you've set the Preferences with the correct firewall host/port information (to access this information, click the Preferences button).
- **Use FTP Performance Optimization:** On by default, disable this option if the test is unsuccessful and try again.
- **Use Alternative FTP Move Method:** Select this option only if errors occur when transferring files or using Contribute rollbacks. The alternative method is an older, slower one and should be avoided if possible.

9. If you're working with a team or are interested in other remote server options, click the Advanced tab to access the following choices:
   - **Maintain Synchronization Information:** With this option selected (as it is by default), Dreamweaver automatically stores details for files in both the local and the remote sites to determine which is the most recent.
   - **Automatically Upload Files To Server On Save:** Choose this option to store files locally and remotely simultaneously. Under most circumstances, I do not recommend that this option be selected because the risk for uploading unfinished work is too great.
   - **Enable File Check Out:** Select this option when working with other designers or contributors on a site. If this option is enabled, three additional choices are activated:
     - **Check Out Files When Opening:** When selected, Dreamweaver will automatically check out any files when they are opened; if not selected, Dreamweaver asks if you'd like to check out the file or just make it viewable.
     - **Check-Out Name:** Enter the name you want to appear in the Files panel for checked-out files.
     - **Email Address:** Enter the e-mail address to associate with a checked-out file.
10. When you're done, click Save.
11. On the Servers category screen, the new server is listed; make sure the Remote checkbox is selected and click Save once again.

As with other elements of the Site Setup dialog box, the Servers category is multi-layered with numerous options available if needed. In most situations, the best strategy is to start with the default options and modify only if necessary.

Defining a testing server

The steps for setting up a testing server are quite similar to those for defining a remote server. In fact, if you put files on your testing server by using FTP, it can be exactly the same except you select the Testing checkbox instead of the Remote checkbox in the Servers category. However, many Dreamweaver users create their testing server on a local or networked system, which can speed up the development and testing process.

To define a local testing server, follow these steps:

1. Choose Window ➪ Manage Sites.
2. In the Manage Sites dialog box, select the site you want to add a remote server to and click Edit.
3. In the Site Setup dialog box, choose Servers.
4. Click Add New Server, the plus sign.
5. In the Basic tab, enter the name you want to identify your testing server in the Server Name field.
6. From the Connect Using list choose Local/Network (see Figure 4-7).

FIGURE 4-7

The only info you'll need to create a local testing server is a folder location and an optional web URL on the Basic tab; be sure to click the Advanced tab and select your server model.

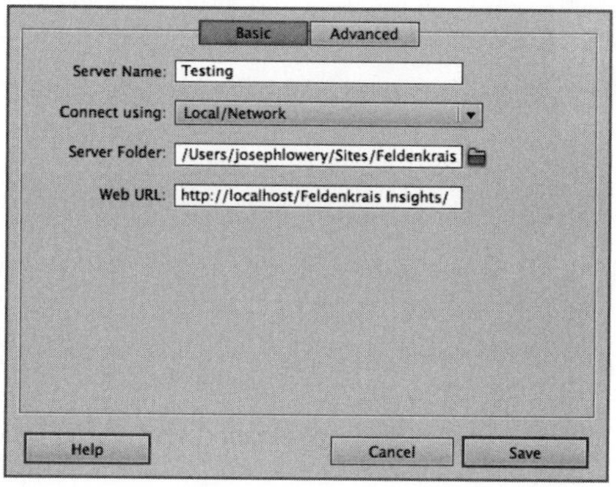

7. Click the Remote Folder icon to choose a local or networked folder for the remote testing site.

TIP

Web servers running on both primary operating systems automatically recognize folders in specific locations as sites, easily located in a browser with an `http://localhost/` address. If you're on a PC, choose a subfolder within the c:\inetpub\www\ folder; on the Mac, select a subfolder in the Sites folder located within your [username] folder.

8. In the Web URL field, enter the web address for your site, if available.
9. If you're working with a server model such as PHP or ColdFusion, click the Advanced tab and make your choice from the Server Model list.

   Available server models in the list are: ASP JavaScript, ASP VBScript, ASP.NET C#, ASP.NET VB, ColdFusion, JSP, PHP MySQL, or None. Dreamweaver creates code for ASP VBScript, ColdFusion, and PHP.

10. Click Save to return to the Server category.
11. If necessary, choose the Testing checkbox.
12. Click Save.

After you've defined your servers, you can access them directly by choosing the one you want from the list on the top right of the Files panel, as shown in Figure 4-8.

FIGURE 4-8

Work with your defined server files in the Files panel.

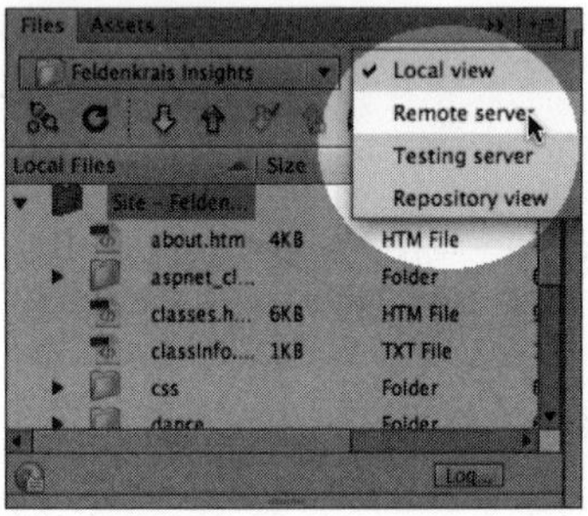

Cloaking Site Folders

Dreamweaver supports *site cloaking*, which enables you to exclude (cloak) specified site folders from operations such as Put, Get, Check In/Out, Synchronize, and so on. (For a full list of cloaked operations, see the following paragraphs.) The site cloaking feature can save you a significant amount of upload/maintenance time. Suppose that you're working on a site that contains several dozen large MP3 files, all stored in a folder named mp3s. You can cloak the mp3s folder, so that when you put (upload) your site files at the end of the day, you don't end up re-putting all those MP3 files, which most likely haven't changed, anyway.

NOTE

A site's folder-cloaking settings are sticky; after you've specified them, Dreamweaver remembers them whenever you work on the site.

Cloaking excludes cloaked folders from the following operations:

- Put, Get
- Check In, Check Out
- Reports
- Select Newer Local, Select Newer Remote

- Sitewide commands, such as Check Links Sitewide and Find And Replace Entire Site
- Synchronize
- Asset panel contents
- Template and library updating

Cloaking and uncloaking site folders is a breeze. Follow these steps:

1. In the Files panel, select the desired site from the drop-down list box. Note that this site must have cloaking enabled in the Site Setup dialog box, which is the default site setting. If, however, you need to enable cloaking for a site, choose Site ⇨ Cloaking ⇨ Enable Cloaking.
2. Select the folder(s) you want to cloak or uncloak.
3. From the Options menu of the Files panel, choose Site ⇨ Cloaking ⇨ Cloak or Site ⇨ Cloaking ⇨ Uncloak. Alternatively, you can right-click (Control+click) a selected folder and use the context menu. A red, diagonal line across the selected folders appears or disappears to show that they are cloaked or uncloaked, as shown in Figure 4-9.

   To uncloak all site folders (and files), choose Site ⇨ Cloaking ⇨ Uncloak All from the panel menu or the pop-up context menu.

CAUTION

When you uncloak an entire site, you cannot undo it! If you want to recloak folders, you have to do so manually.

FIGURE 4-9

You can easily cloak or uncloak your site folders.

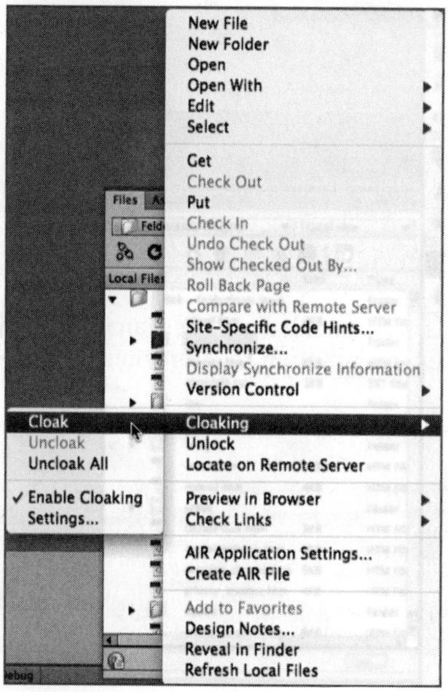

Managing Site Info

You can change any of the information associated with your local site folders by choosing Site ➪ Manage Sites (see Figure 4-10). Select the site you want to modify from the Manage Sites dialog box and click the Edit button; you see the corresponding information, which you can edit.

After your participation in a project has ended, you can remove the site from your list. In the Edit Sites dialog box, choose the site you want to remove, and click the Remove button. Note that this action removes the site only from Dreamweaver's internal site list; it *does not* actually delete any files or folders from your hard drive.

FIGURE 4-10

Create new sites, edit existing ones, or remove unwanted ones with the Manage Sites dialog box.

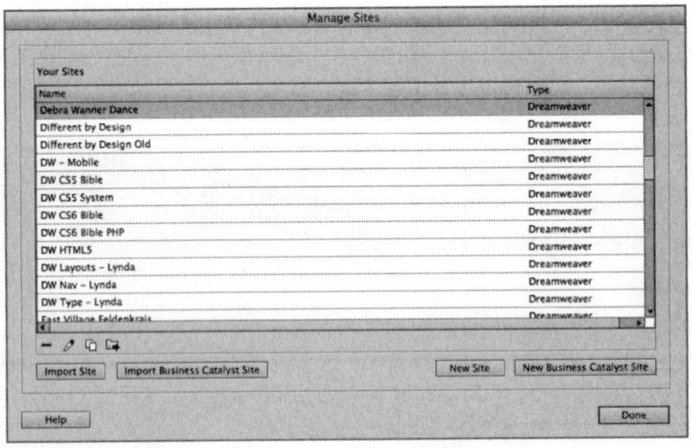

TIP

Before you remove a site, make sure you export the site settings by choosing Export from the Manage Sites dialog box (Site ➪ Manage Sites). The exported file preserves all the connection information and can be imported through the Manage Sites dialog box at a later date.

In addition to editing existing site details, you can also use the Manage Sites dialog box to start a new Dreamweaver site or import the setup information for a previously created site.

NEW FEATURE

The Manage Sites dialog box not only is your central station for handling sites created in Dreamweaver but also can be used for managing your Business Catalyst sites. As with Dreamweaver sites, you can create new Business Catalyst ones or import existing ones. When you click either Import Business Catalyst Site or New Business Catalyst Site, you're presented with an opportunity to log in to your Business Catalyst account or, if you're new to the system, a chance to sign up. For more about Business Catalyst, see the section "Getting Online with Business Catalyst" later in this chapter.

Creating and Saving New Pages

You've considered message, audience, and budget issues. You've chosen a design. You've set up your site and its address. All the preliminary planning is completed, and now you're ready to really rev up Dreamweaver and begin creating pages. This section covers the basic mechanics of opening and saving web pages during development.

Building Placeholder Pages

One technique you might find helpful—and especially so with the use of *document-relative* addressing in Dreamweaver web projects—is what I call *placeholder pages*. These placeholder pages provide an effortless way to include links as you create web pages.

Suppose, for example, you've just finished laying out most of the text and graphics for your home page and you want to put in some links to internal pages. You drop in your text and images and align them just so. All that's missing are the links. If you're using document-relative addressing, the best way to assign a link is to click the Browse For File button in the Property inspector and select your file. But what do you do if you haven't created any other pages yet and there aren't any files to select? That's when you can put placeholder pages to work.

After you've designed the basics of your site and created your local site folder, as described previously in this chapter, start with a blank Dreamweaver page. Type a single identifying word on the page and save it in the local site folder. Repeat this step for all the web pages in your plan. When it comes time to make your links, all you have to do is point and click to the appropriate placeholder page. This arrangement also gives you an immediate framework for link testing. When it comes time to work on the next page, just open up the correct placeholder page and start to work.

Another style of working involves using the Files panel as your base of operations, rather than the Document window. It's very easy in Dreamweaver to choose File ➪ New File from the Files panel menu several times and create the basic files of your site.

Starting Dreamweaver

4

Start Dreamweaver as you would any other program. Double-click the Dreamweaver program icon, or single-click if you are using Internet Explorer's Desktop Integration feature in Windows or if you have Dreamweaver's icon in your Dock on OS X. After the splash screen, Dreamweaver opens with the Welcome screen, which lists 10 of your previously opened documents and also offers a full range of new document types. Choose HTML from the Welcome screen to create a new blank page. This page is created from the `Default.html` file found in Dreamweaver's Configuration/DocumentTypes/NewDocuments folder. Of course, you may want to replace the original `Default.html` file with one of your own—perhaps with your copyright information. All your blank pages are then created from the template that you've designed.

TIP

If you do decide to create your own Default template, it's probably a good idea to rename the Dreamweaver Default template—as `Original-Default.html` or something similar—prior to creating your new, personalized Default template.

Opening existing files

To open an existing file that belongs to a site you've defined in Dreamweaver, select the site in the Files panel and double-click the file icon. Recently opened files, regardless of their origin, are available through the Welcome screen or from the File ➪ Open Recent menu.

To open an existing file that does not belong to a site defined in Dreamweaver—or that was created in a different program—choose File ➪ Open or Ctrl+O (Command+O), and choose the file from the File Open dialog box.

TIP

You can enable/disable Dreamweaver from automatically repairing HTML syntax errors in your files when it opens them. Choose Edit ➪ Preferences (Dreamweaver ➪ Preferences) to open the Preferences dialog box, select the Code Rewriting category, and check/uncheck the desired options: Fix Invalidly Nested And Unclosed Tags, Rename Form Items When Pasting, Remove Extra Closing Tags, and so on. To have Dreamweaver report its syntax repairs, select the Warn When Fixing Or Removing Tags option.

Opening a new file

You can work on as many Dreamweaver files as your system memory can sustain. When you choose File ➪ New or the keyboard shortcut Ctrl+N (Command+N) and select a file type from the New Document dialog box, Dreamweaver opens a new blank file of your specified type. (For more on this, see the section "Creating New Documents" later in this chapter.)

TIP

If you are working with maximized documents, you can easily switch among open files by clicking their respective tabs at the top of the Document window or by using the Windows menu.

Each time you open a new file, Dreamweaver temporarily names the file `Untitled-`*n*, where *n* is the next number in the sequence. This naming convention prevents you from accidentally overwriting a new file opened in the same session.

NOTE

Using the New Document dialog box to create new documents of all types (HTML, JavaScript, ASP, ColdFusion, and so on) is discussed in detail later in this chapter in the section "Creating New Documents."

Opening Other Types of Files

Dreamweaver defaults making HTML files with an extension of `.htm`, `.html`, or `.xhtml` accessible. To look for other types of files, expand the Files Of Type (Enable) list. Dreamweaver allows several other file types, including server-side includes (`.shtml`, `.shtm`, `.stm`, or `.ssi`), Active Server Pages (`.asp`), and ColdFusion (`.cfm`, `.cfml`, or `.cfc`). To load a valid HTML file with a different extension, select the All Files (All Documents) option.

If you are working consistently with a different file format, you can add your own extensions and file types to Dreamweaver's Open dialog box. In the Configuration folder, open an editable text file called `Extensions.txt` in Dreamweaver or in your favorite text editor to make any additions. The syntax must follow the format of the standard `Extensions.txt` file:

```
HTM,HTML,SHTM,SHTML,HTA,HTC,XHTML,STM,SSI,JS,AS,ASC,ASR,XML,XSL,XSD,DTD,
    XSLT,RSS,RDF,LBI,DWT,ASP,ASA,ASPX,ASCX,ASMX,CONFIG,CS,CSS,CFM,CFML,
    CFC,TLD,TXT,PHP,PHP3,PHP4,PHP5,JSP,WML,TPL,LASSO,JSF,VB,VBS,VTM,VTML,
    INC,SQL,JAVA,EDML,MASTER,INFO,INSTALL,THEME,CONFIG,MODULE,
    PROFILE,ENGINE:All Documents
HTM,HTML,HTA,HTC,XHTML:HTML Documents
SHTM,SHTML,STM,SSI,INC:Server-Side Includes
JS,JSON:JavaScript Documents
XML,DTD,XSD,XSL,XSLT,RSS,RDF:XML Files
LBI:Library Files
DWT:Template Files
CSS:Style Sheets
ASP,ASA:Active Server Pages
ASPX,ASCX,ASMX,CS,VB,CONFIG,MASTER:Active Server Plus Pages
CFM,CFML,CFC:ColdFusion Templates
AS:ActionScript Files
ASC:ActionScript Communication Files
ASR:ActionScript Remote Files
TXT:Text Files
PHP,PHP3,PHP4,PHP5,TPL,PHP-DIST,PHTML:PHP Files
LASSO:Lasso Files
JSP,JST:Java Server Pages
JSF:Fireworks Script
TLD:Tag Library Descriptor Files
JAVA:Java Files
SQL:SQL Files
ASX:Windows Media Advanced Stream Redirector
WML:WML Files
EDML:EDML Files
VBS:VBScript Files
VTM,VTML:VTML Files
```


Saving your file

Saving your work is very important in any computer-related task, and Dreamweaver is no exception. To initially save the current file, choose File ➪ Save or use the keyboard shortcut Ctrl+S (Command+S). The Save dialog box opens; you can enter a filename and, if you wish, a different path.

By default, all HTML files are saved with an `.html` filename extension. Different file formats are saved with different extensions; XML documents, for example, are stored with an `.xml` extension. To save your file with another extension, such as `.shtml` or `.xhtml`, change the Save As Type option to the specific file type and then enter your full filename *with* the extension.

CAUTION
Although it may seem kind of backward in this age of long filenames, it's still a good idea to choose all-lowercase names for your files without spaces or punctuation other than an underscore or hyphen. Not all servers read the filename correctly, and you can encounter problems linking your pages.

Closing the file

When you're done working on a file, you can close it by choosing File ➪ Close or by using the keyboard shortcut Ctrl+W (Command+W). If you've made any changes to your file since last saving it, Dreamweaver prompts you to save it. Click Yes to save the file or No to close it without saving your changes.

NOTE
You can easily tell whether a file has been altered since the last save by looking at the title bar. Dreamweaver places an asterisk after the filename in the title bar for modified files. Dreamweaver is even smart enough to properly remove the asterisk should you reverse your changes with the Undo command or the History panel.

Quitting the program

When you're finished working for the day—or, more often, the late, late night—you can close Dreamweaver by choosing File ➪ Exit (File ➪ Quit) or by using the standard keyboard shortcut Ctrl+Q (Command+Q).

TIP
Have to stop work in the middle of a session and want to get back to work ASAP? Leave one or more documents open when you close Dreamweaver and they'll reappear when the program next launches. To enable this feature, choose the Reopen On Startup option from the General category of Preferences.

Creating New Documents

Dreamweaver provides three methods for creating new documents:

- Select your preferred document type from the Create New column of the Dreamweaver Welcome screen.
- You can use the New Document dialog box to create a new document of a type that you select from a comprehensive list, including HTML, XSLT, ActionScript, CSS, JavaScript, ASP VBScript, ColdFusion, and PHP. If you work with multiple document types, this is the way to go.
- You can create a new document of a default type that you've specified in the Preferences dialog box. If you work mostly with one document type—HTML, ColdFusion, or ASP, for example—this method can prove very convenient.

Using the New Document dialog box

Dreamweaver offers a wide range of starting points through the New Document dialog box: You can start off with anything from a completely blank page to the basic HTML code to a fully CSS compliant, 3-column elastic design with header and footer.

All of the layouts listed in the New Document dialog box when the Blank Page ➪ HTML (or any of the dynamic page types) is chosen are expertly crafted with carefully commented code. Not only do these CSS layouts provide an excellent jumping off point for designs, but they also serve as a terrific learning resource.

To create a new document using the New Document dialog box, follow these steps:

1. Choose File ➪ New to open the New Document dialog box, as shown in Figure 4-11.
2. In the New Document dialog box, select the category of new document that you want to create: Blank Page, Blank Template, Fluid Grid Layout, Page From Template, Page From Sample, or Other.

   The adjoining columns and page preview change according to the New Document category selected. The following steps assume that the Blank Page category has been selected.

NOTE

The Fluid Grid Layout option is new to Dreamweaver CS6. To learn more about this responsive web design feature, see Chapter 10.

FIGURE 4-11

Choose the type of new file you want to start with through the New Document dialog box.

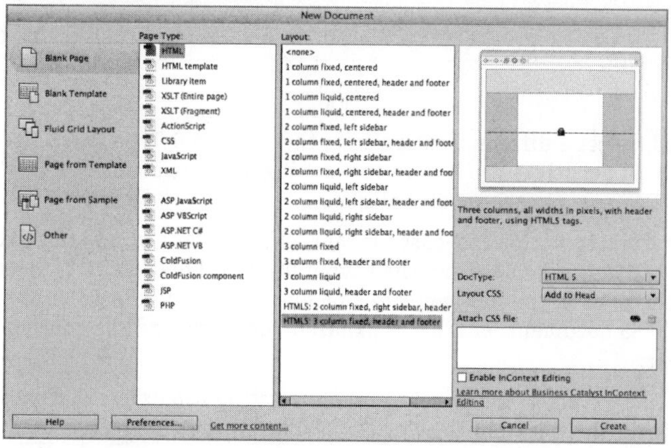

3. In the Page Type list, select the specific type of document you want to create: HTML, HTML Template, Library Item, and so on. The page types are grouped into static page types, which do not require an additional application server, and dynamic page types, which do.

4. From the Layout column, choose the basic page design. Select <none> for a blank HTML page. Select any layout to view the illustrated preview and read a brief description of the design. Two key terms are used to identify layout characteristics:
   - **Fixed:** Notes a column or other page component where the width is defined in pixels. A fixed width layout does not expand or contract.
   - **Liquid:** Indicates a column or other page component where the width is defined as a percentage, so the column or page component expands or contracts depending on the width of your browser window, as shown in Figure 4-12.

FIGURE 4-12

This liquid design adjusts to changes in browser window width.

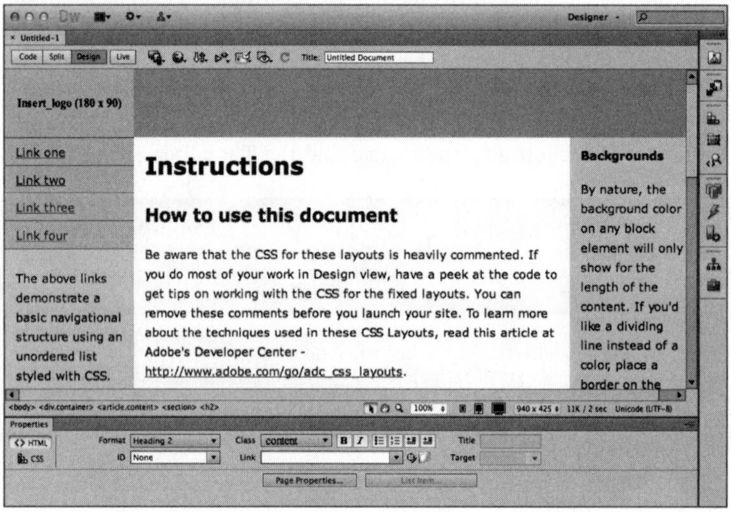

5. If desired, select a different option from the Document Type (DTD) list. Note that this setting does not stick; you'll need to reset it each time or select a new DTD option in the New Document category of Preferences.
6. If you're working with a CSS-based layout, choose where you would like to store the predesigned CSS layout rules from the Layout CSS list. Choose Add To Head if you'd like to embed the rules in the newly created document, Create A New File to put them in a new external CSS document, or Link To Existing File to append the rules to an existing CSS document.
7. If you'd like to link or import one or more existing CSS external style sheets, click the Attach Style Sheet icon in the Attach CSS File section. You can attach as many external CSS style sheets as you'd like. If you'd like to delete one from the list, select it and click Remove (the trash can icon).
8. Click Create to create a new, blank document of the selected category/type.

If you want to create a new document based on a custom template, use the Page From Template—rather than the Blank Page—category. For more information on creating and using templates, see Chapter 28.

To learn more about the CSS layouts available from the New Document dialog box, see Chapter 6.

Creating a new default document

If you often create one type of document—HTML or ColdFusion files, for example—you can take advantage of Dreamweaver's default document feature to save yourself some document creation time and trouble. By using the techniques described in this section, you can open a new document of your default type (HTML, ColdFusion, and so on) with one quick keyboard shortcut—in other words, without having to work your way through the New Document dialog box.

To create a new default document, follow these steps:

1. Choose Edit ➪ Preferences (Dreamweaver ➪ Preferences) to open the Preferences dialog box, and select the New Document category. If the document type you want is not already defined as the Default Document Type, define it now.

   Note the Show New Document Dialog On Ctrl+N (Command+N) option. Clear this box if you want Ctrl+N (Command+N) to create a new default document without showing the New Document dialog box; check it if you want Ctrl+N (Command+N) to show the New Document dialog box.

TIP

If you are a Windows user, no matter what Show New Document Dialog On Ctrl+N setting you choose, Ctrl+Shift+N always creates a new default document *without showing the New Document dialog box.*

   If desired, select a different option from the Document Type (DTD) list. When you're finished, click OK to close the Preferences dialog box.

2. After you perform the preceding step, you're done. To create a new default document, simply press Ctrl+Shift+N (Windows only). If you turned off the Show New Document Dialog On Ctrl+N option, you can also press Ctrl+N (Command+N).

NOTE

If, when defining your site, you specified a server model to be used, the new default document is the file type that corresponds to that server model—despite the Preferences dialog box setting you have chosen.

Previewing Your Web Pages

When using Dreamweaver or any other web authoring tool, it's important to frequently check your progress in one or more browsers. Dreamweaver's Document window offers a near-browser view of your web page, but because of the variations among the different browsers, it's imperative that you preview your page early and often. Dreamweaver offers you easy access to a maximum of 20 browsers—and they're just a function key away.

Previewing in your browsers

You add a browser to your preview list by choosing File ➪ Preview in Browser ➪ Edit Browser List or by choosing the Preview In Browser category from the Preferences dialog box. Both actions open the Preview In Browser category of the Preferences. The steps for editing your browser list are described in detail in Chapter 3. Here's a brief recap:

1. Choose File ➪ Preview in Browser ➪ Edit Browser List to open the Preview In Browser Preferences category.
2. To add a browser (up to 20), click the Add (+) button and fill out the following fields in the Add Browser dialog box (see Figure 4-13):
   - **Name:** When you choose the browser application, Dreamweaver automatically provides a name for the browser. You can accept this name, or change it by typing a new name in the Name field.
   - **Application:** Type in the path to the browser program or click the Browse button to locate the browser executable (`.exe`) file.
   - **Primary Browser/Secondary Browser:** If you want, select one of these checkboxes to designate the current browser as such.
3. After you add a browser to your list, you can easily edit or delete it. Reopen the Preview In Browser Preferences category and highlight the browser you want to modify or delete.
4. To alter your selection, click the Edit button. To delete your selection, click the Remove (–) button.
5. After you finish your modifications, click OK to close the dialog box.

FIGURE 4-13

It's best to leave the Name field blank until you choose the browser executable in the Application field; Dreamweaver automatically fills in the name and removes any previously entered value.

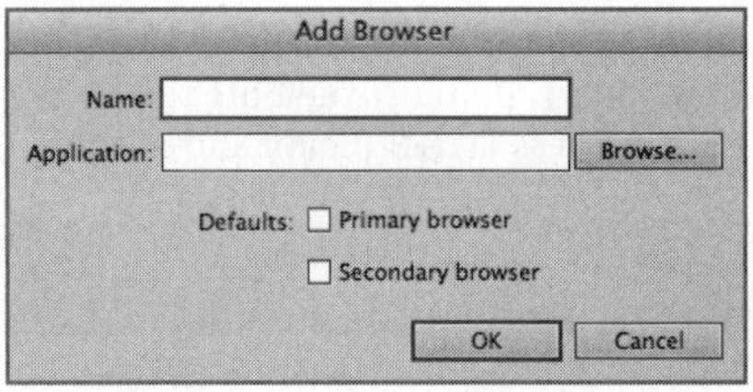

After you add one or more browsers to your list, you can preview the current page in these browsers. Choose File ➪ Preview in Browser ➪ *BrowserName*, where *BrowserName* indicates the particular program. If the Preview using Temporary File option is selected in Preferenes, Dreamweaver saves the page to a temporary file, starts the browser, and loads the page; if the option is not selected, the browser loads the current page.

In order to view any changes you've made to your web page under construction, you must select the Preview In Browser menu option again (or press one of the function keys for primary/secondary browser previewing, described in the following paragraph). Clicking the Refresh/Reload button in your browser does not load in any modifications. The temporary preview files are deleted when you quit Dreamweaver.

TIP

Dreamweaver saves preview files with a filename like the following: `TMP5c34jymi4q.asp`; a unique name is generated with each preview to ensure that the browser does not load the page from the cache. If Dreamweaver unexpectedly quits, these TMP files are not deleted. Feel free to delete any such TMP files you find in your site, or use them as backups to restore unsaved work should a crash occur.

You can also use keyboard shortcuts to preview two different browsers by pressing a function key. Press F12 (Option+F12) to preview the current Dreamweaver page in your primary browser, and Ctrl+F12 (Command+F12) to preview the same page in your secondary browser. These are the primary and secondary browser settings you establish in the Preview In Browser Preferences panel, explained in Chapter 3.

You can easily reassign your primary and secondary browsers. Go to the Preview In Browser Preferences category, select the desired browser, and select the appropriate checkbox to designate the browser as primary or secondary. In the list of browsers, you see the indicator of F12 (Option+F12) or Ctrl+F12 (Command+F12) appear next to the browser's name.

Displaying pages with BrowserLab

In addition to checking your web page output on a variety of browsers on your system, it's also a good idea to preview the page on other platforms. If you're designing on a Macintosh, try to view your pages on a Windows system, and vice versa. Watch out for some not-so-subtle differences between the two environments in terms of screen resolution. If you don't have easy access to another operating system and a wide range of browsers, Adobe BrowserLab can come to your rescue.

NOTE

BrowserLab is an online rendering service capable of displaying your web pages in a variety of browser versions and operating systems. A page can be viewed in a single browser/OS configuration, such as Firefox 5.0/Windows; two configurations side by side; or one configuration overlying another, with variable transparency. BrowserLab makes it possible to quickly preview your pages on the most commonly used browsers and OS combinations.

It's important to understand that BrowserLab displays an image of your web page, not the page itself. Although you can scroll the window to see the entire page, no interactivity—such as links, hover states, or JavaScript effects—is possible. However, you can trigger any JavaScript in Dreamweaver's Live View, freeze JavaScript by pressing F6, and then preview the result in BrowserLab.

NOTE

As with other Adobe services, you'll need an Adobe account to use BrowserLab. Adobe accounts are free and easy to get: Just visit any page on the Adobe website, including `www.adobe.com`, and click the Your Account link in the top navigation. When the login page appears, click the Create an Adobe Account link and fill out the simple form and your account is immediately available.

To preview a Dreamweaver page in BrowserLab, follow these steps:

1. Choose File ➪ Preview ➪ Preview in Adobe BrowserLab or select Preview in Adobe BrowserLab from the Preview/Debug in Browser menu button on the Document toolbar.
2. When the Adobe BrowserLab panel appears, choose Local from the list if you want to render the currently displayed page, or Server if you want to render the version of the current page that resides on the active server.
3. Click Preview.

   Adobe BrowserLab will open in your primary browser. Before you can proceed, you'll need to log in.
4. If you are not currently logged into Adobe, enter your e-mail and password.

Once you are logged in, the selected page will render in BrowserLab with the default browser and operating system configuration, as shown in Figure 4-14. Viewing a single page on BrowserLab is known as 1-up View. You can change views by selecting from the list in the upper-left corner of the BrowserLab window. Available options are:

- **1-up View:** Displays a single browser/OS configuration.
- **2-up View:** Displays two browser/OS configurations side by side (see Figure 4-15).
- **Onion skin View:** Shows two browser/OS configurations, one on top of another with a variable transparency so you can compare pages on the pixel level. A slider at the top of the page controls the transparency of the two rendered pages.
- **Show/Hide Rulers:** Displays rulers for any rendered pages.

FIGURE 4-14

BrowserLab can render your web pages in a dozen browser/OS combinations.

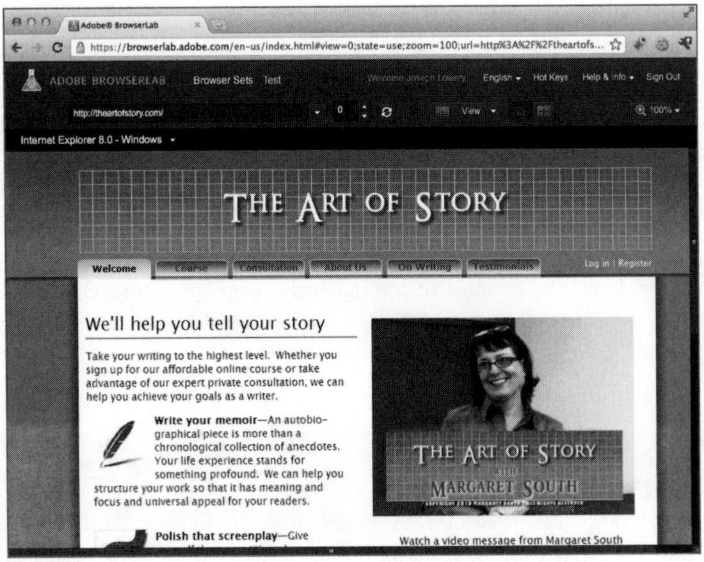

FIGURE 4-15

Easily compare the same page on two different browser/OS configurations with 2-up View.

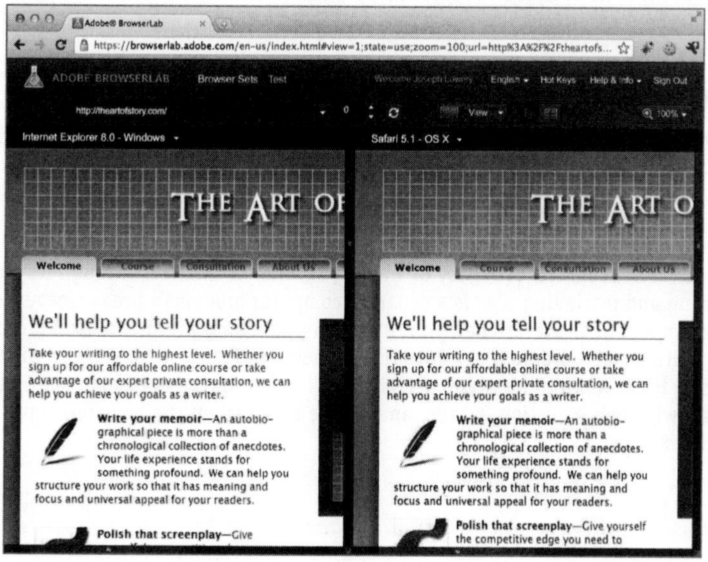

BrowserLab allows you to customize the browser/OS configurations you'd like to incorporate in your testing. Click Browser Sets and choose the combinations you want to use from the Available Browsers list: Your chosen browsers will appear in the column on the right. You can reorder the browsers by simply clicking and dragging them. Any number of custom browser sets can be created in this manner.

NOTE

Adobe BrowserLab is a commercial service. As of this writing, the details on how much BrowserLab will cost, if anything, have not been announced.

Putting Your Pages Online

The final phase of setting up your Dreamweaver site is publishing your pages to the web. When you begin, this publishing process is up to you. Some web designers wait until everything is absolutely perfect on the local development site and then upload everything at once. Others like to establish an early connection to the remote site and extend the transfer of files over a longer period of time.

I fall into the latter camp. When I start transferring files at the beginning of the process, I find that I catch my mistakes earlier and avoid having to make massive changes to the site after everything is up. For example, in developing one large site, I started out using mixed-case filenames, as in `ELFhome.html`. After publishing some early drafts of a few web pages, however, I discovered that the host had switched servers; on the new server, filenames had to be entirely lowercase. Had I waited until the last moment to upload everything, I would have been faced with an unexpected and laborious search-and-replace job.

Transferring with FTP

After you've established your local site folder—and you've included your remote site's FTP information in the setup—the actual publishing of your files to the web is a very straightforward process.

Putting and getting files to and from your server, while easy, can be incredibly time-consuming. Dreamweaver frees its users from the drudgery of waiting for files to transfer through its background FTP feature. Uploading and retrieving files is a separate computer process in Dreamweaver, distinct from working in Design and Code view. When you initiate a publishing event, the Background File Activity dialog box with a small progress bar appears, as shown in Figure 4-16. You can dismiss the dialog box by clicking Hide; when hidden, file activity can be seen in the bottom of the Files panel. An ongoing log is shown when you click Details, and can be saved when the transfers have been completed by clicking Save Log.

FIGURE 4-16

Dreamweaver transfers files through a background FTP process so you can continue working while files are being published.

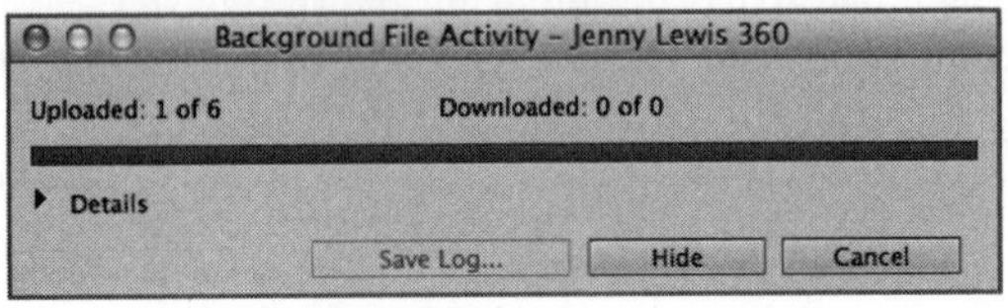

To transfer your local web pages to an online site, follow these steps:

1. Choose Window ➪ Files or press F8 to open the Files panel, and select the desired site from the Site drop-down list.
2. In the Files panel, click the Connect button. (You may need to connect to the Internet first.) Dreamweaver displays a message box showing the progress of the connection.
3. If you didn't enter a password in the Remote Info category when you defined the site, or if you entered a password but didn't opt to save it, Dreamweaver asks you to type in your password. When the connection is complete, the directory listing of the remote site appears in the Files panel.
4. Click the Expand/Collapse button to expand the Files panel into its two-pane view: Remote pane on the left, Local pane on the right. In the Local pane (green icons), select the folder(s) and file(s) you want to upload—or, to upload the entire site, select the site folder (at the top of the list)—and then click the Put File(s) button, as shown in Figure 4-17.

5. If Dreamweaver asks if you would like to move the dependent files as well, click Yes to transfer all embedded graphics and other objects, or No if you'd prefer to move these yourself. You can also select the Don't Ask Me Again checkbox to make transfers of dependent files automatic in the future.

FIGURE 4-17

Use the Put File(s) button in the Files panel to transfer files, folders, and entire sites.

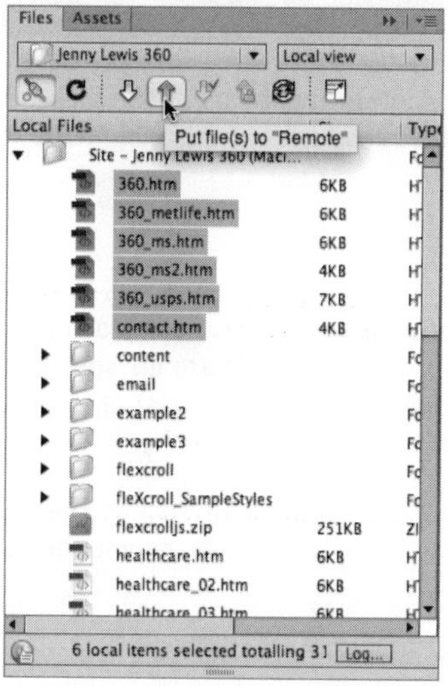

6. The Background File Transfer dialog box appears. Click Hide to hide the dialog box and continue working in Dreamweaver; click Details to see the files being transferred. If it's hidden, you can restore the Background File Transfer dialog box by clicking the globe icon at the bottom of the Files panel.
7. After each file has successfully transferred, Dreamweaver places a checkmark next to its icon—provided that File Check In/Out is enabled in the site's Remote Info category.
8. When you finish transferring your files, click the Disconnect button.
9. If you'd like to store the log file, display the Background File Transfer dialog box (if necessary) and click Save Log.

4

NOTE

Dreamweaver provides an FTP Log panel that displays all your FTP file transfer activity (Puts, Gets, and so on). This panel is particularly useful for troubleshooting FTP transfer errors. For more information, see the next section, "Using the FTP Log Panel."

Remember that the only files you have to highlight for transfer to the remote site are the HTML files. As noted previously, Dreamweaver automatically transfers any dependent files (if you allow it), which means that you'll never forget to move a GIF again. (Nor will you ever move an unnecessary file, such as an earlier version of an image, by mistake.) Moreover, Dreamweaver automatically creates any subfolders necessary to maintain the site's integrity. Combine these two features to save substantial time and worry.

CAUTION
Be aware that Dreamweaver does not always know to include files that are used within scripts; you might need to upload these files manually.

Now you have made your site a reality, from the planning stages to the local site folder and onto the web. Congratulations—all that's left is to fill those pages with insightful content, amazing graphics, and wondrous code.

Using the FTP Log panel

Like all data transfers on the Internet, FTP file transfers sometimes go awry: Servers are busy or down, file/directory permissions are improperly set, passwords are misspelled, and so on. If you run into an FTP transfer problem with your Dreamweaver Put File(s) or Get File(s) command, you can use the FTP Log panel to find out exactly what went wrong.

The FTP Log panel displays all your FTP file-transfer activity. To display the FTP Log panel, first choose Windows ⇨ Results or use the keyboard shortcut F7. Then, select the FTP Log category from the Results panel.

FTP logs may seem complex and indecipherable, but the information they contain is invaluable for troubleshooting FTP errors. Figure 4-18, for example, displays the FTP log that results from Putting (uploading) a file to a remote server.

FIGURE 4-18

The FTP Log generates a blow-by-blow description of actions taken.

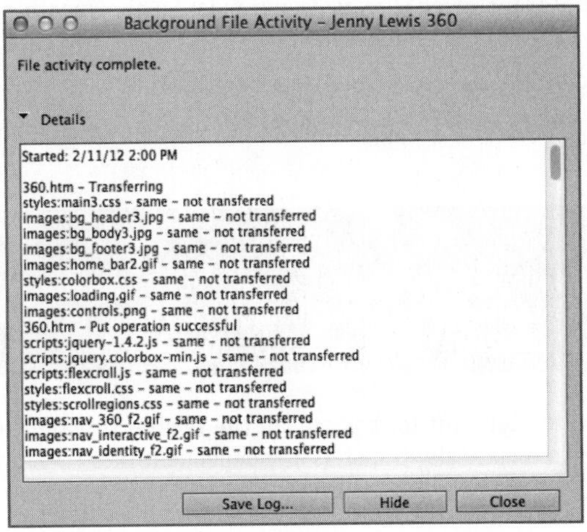

Getting Online with Business Catalyst

Business Catalyst is a website hosting service managed by Adobe that offers web developers and store owners a one-stop shop for full-featured online businesses. When you sign up for a Business Catalyst account, you're still able to design your site exactly the way you want to, you just don't have to do any of the coding in order to add application functionality such as e-mail auto-responders, search and result pages, and event registration—even a completely functioning online store. Business Catalyst makes it easy to track your site visitors, customers, and sales with built-in reporting tools.

Initially, the Business Catalyst panel displays a Get Started button with a link to an informational website. If you click Get Started, you're presented with a dialog box that allows you to sign up for a new account, or—if you're already registered—log in to your account. Business Catalyst offers new users a free site for 30 days so you can try out its system.

Once you set up a site, the Business Catalyst panel displays a list of available modules, as well as the data settings for a selected module. The Business Catalyst modules are the real power tools of the system and with them, you can easily add functionality for everything from blogs to e-commerce, as shown in Figure 4-19. The Business Catalyst service is great for web designers who need to create sites with server-side functionality that is beyond their level of technical expertise.

FIGURE 4-19

Drag-and-drop robust functionality through the Business Catalyst modules.

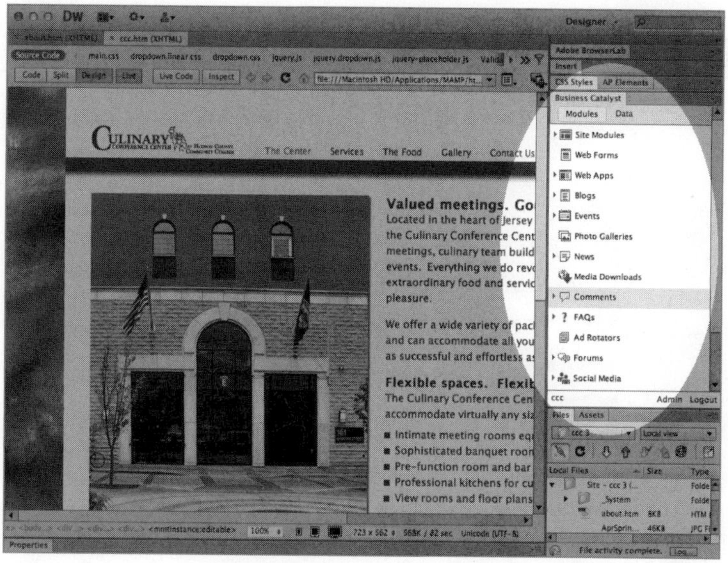

Creating a new site with Business Catalyst

One of the great advantages of working with Business Catalyst is how fast you can get a new site up and running—without any additional cost! Business Catalyst allows you to set up a new site for free using its templates or your own designs; all you need is an Adobe ID.

To set up a new Business Catalyst site, follow these steps:

1. Choose Site ➪ New Business Catalyst Site.
2. When the Business Catalyst dialog box opens, shown in Figure 4-20, complete the following entries:
   - **Site Name:** Enter the name for your site.
   - **URL:** Enter the name of the BusinessCatalyst.com subdomain.
   - **Country:** Choose the country your site is based in.
   - **Data Center:** Select the location of the hosting center closest to your country from the three options: United States, European Union, and Australia.
   - **Time Zone:** Select the time zone for your site.
3. If you want to work on your site locally in Dreamweaver, check the Automatically Download The Entire Business Catalyst Site Locally option.
4. Click Create Free Temporary Site.

   After you've clicked Create Free Temporary Site, the site will be set up on the designated server.

FIGURE 4-20

Quickly set up a free Business Catalyst site to try out its features or highlight your own work.

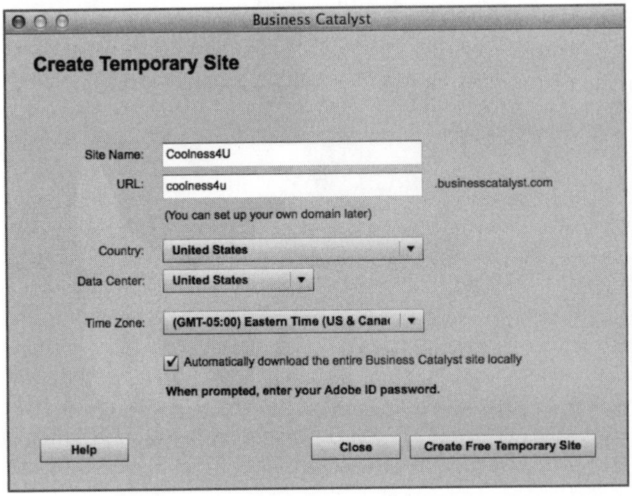

5. **When the Select Folder dialog appears, choose a location for your new site. You can select an existing folder or create a new one.**
6. **In the Enter Password dialog box, enter a password for the site and choose the Remember Password option to avoid having to re-enter the password every time you open the site.**

Once the site set-up is complete, Dreamweaver gets all the initial files for your new site and, if you selected the Automatically Download The Entire Business Catalyst Site Locally option, copy them to your local site root. You can open up the index.htm file in Live View and see the "Coming Soon" graphic on your new home page (Figure 4-21).

FIGURE 4-21

A new Business Catalyst site includes a range of layouts and module templates, as well as a Coming Soon temporary home page.

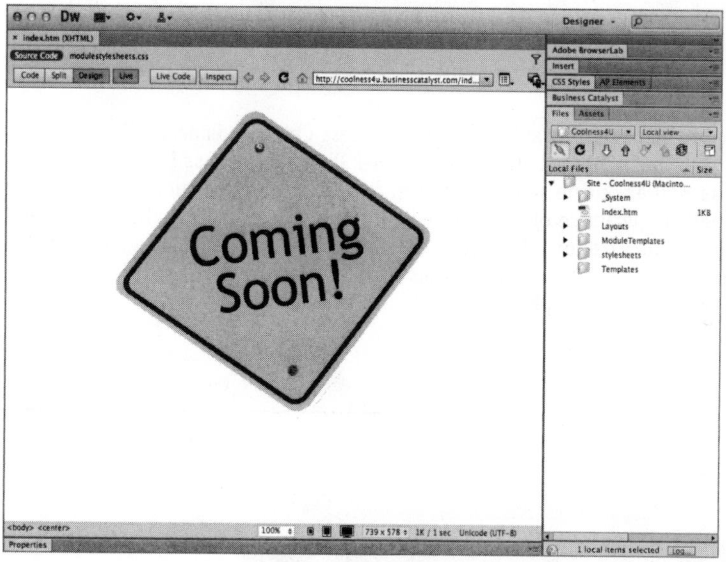

Your new site will also be listed in the Manage Sites dialog box and designated as a Business Catalyst (versus a Dreamweaver) site, as shown in Figure 4-22. You can use the Manage Sites dialog box to view, modify, or export your Business Catalyst site settings just as you could any standard Dreamweaver site. If you choose to edit your site settings, you'll notice that a server has been set up to handle both testing and remote services.

Working with your Business Catalyst site online

After you've created your Business Catalyst site, you'll also receive an e-mail, sent to the account registered with your Adobe ID, that provides site details such as public and administrative URLs. You can log in to the site with your Adobe ID and password.

FIGURE 4-22

Business Catalyst sites are easily identified in the Manage Sites dialog box.

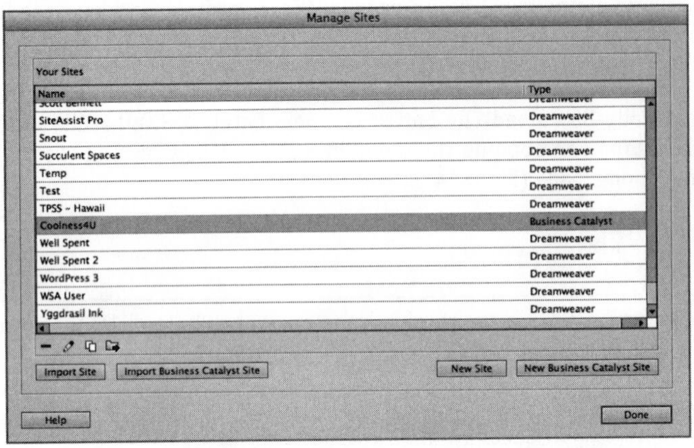

Your initial view of the administrative side of Business Catalyst is accessible by two tabs, one for Development and the other, Business (Figure 4-23). The Business Dashboard shows an overview of visitors, as well as online sales, inquiries, forum posts, and much more. You can replicate the business owner's experience of working with Business Catalyst by choosing from the main options along the top navigation: Manage Site, Site Editor, and File Manager. A fourth option, Partner Portal, is available to you as a Business Catalyst partner. The navigation on the left changes according to the main option selected.

FIGURE 4-23

Clients can get a quick take on how a site is doing through the Development tab of the Business Catalyst dashboard.

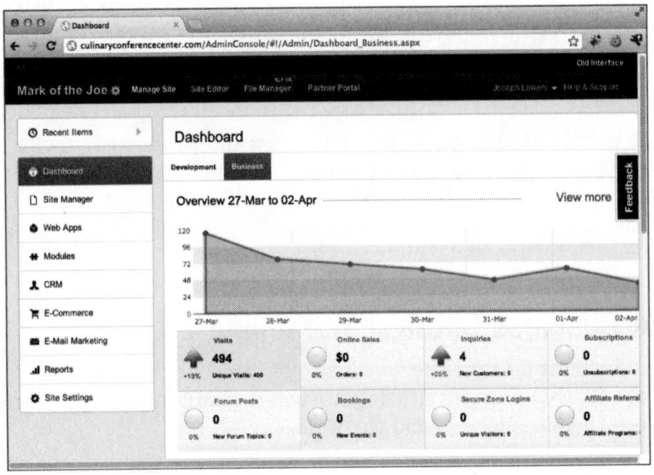

The Manage Site section allows authorized users to modify pages, set up e-mail campaigns, and even set up products for sale in the online store. Business owners can also view reports on site activity and e-mail campaigns.

The Site Editor opens the existing site for direct in-browser modification using an Adobe developed system called InContext Editing. With the Site Editor, you can navigate to any page on the site and, unless the content is locked, make edits to the text or images right in the browser (Figure 4-24).

FIGURE 4-24

With Business Catalyst's Site Editor, your clients can make changes online through their browser.

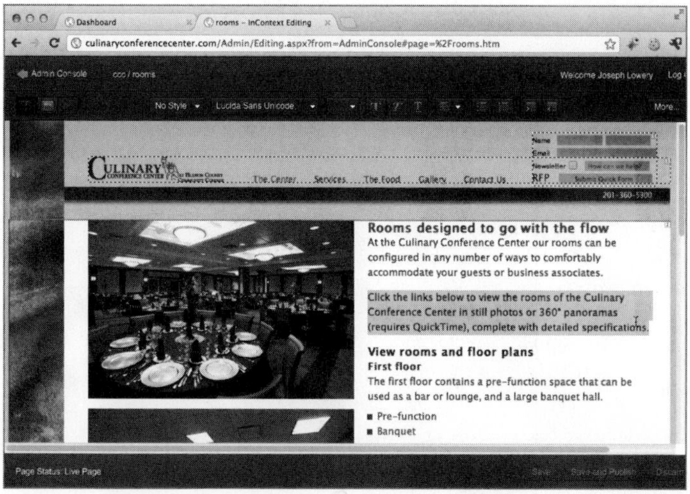

NOTE

Unfortunately, not all browsers work with the Business Catalyst Site Editor. You (or your client) can use Safari, Chrome, or Internet Explorer, but not Firefox.

The File Manager (in Alpha at the time of this writing) provides full-featured access to all your site files in either Code or Design view. Files can be uploaded, created, or renamed, as well as edited. The File Manager's Code view provides color coding and formatting similar to Dreamweaver's. You can also use the File Manager to quickly insert or modify Business Catalyst modules for adding and controlling special functionality like blogs or ad rotators.

Integrating Business Catalyst Code in Dreamweaver

With the Business Catalyst site established, you can pretty much develop your site just as you would a standard Dreamweaver one by creating pages in HTML and CSS. However, one of the key advantages of working with Business Catalyst is the advanced functionality that can be easily integrated. The advanced functionality is contained in what Business Catalyst calls Modules.

Inserting a Module

There are currently 16 different major modules that cover everything from ad rotators to web forms (Figure 4-25). Adding any of them works pretty much the same way:

1. From the Business Catalyst panel, make sure you're in Modules tab and expand the specific module you want to work with.
2. From the available options for a particular module, double-click the desired one.
3. Dreamweaver will contact the Business Catalyst server to retrieve any data already entered for the chosen module. There may be several levels of data to choose from, depending on the module.
4. When you've targeted the desired module data, click Insert Module.

FIGURE 4-25

Access advanced Business Catalyst functionality from the available modules.

The inserted code is added to the page; the code is delineated with curly braces like this one for listing FAQs:

```
{module_faq,a,}
```

You can view the rendered module code by entering into Live View, previewing it in a browser, or putting the page on your remote site and viewing it through the browser.

Styling a Module's Output

Because Business Catalyst is completely integrated with Dreamweaver, you can easily revamp the HTML layout. All of the modules come with their own layout pages that can be downloaded to your local site and modified as needed.

TIP

Unlike working with standard web pages, you'll find it more useful to work in Design view rather than Live View with Business Catalyst modules. Live View cannot currently render data output from a module as you would see it in a browser. However, in Design view, you can select Business Catalyst code to enable a custom Property inspector that grants quick access to the layout template (within Dreamweaver) and the module data (either in Dreamweaver or, if not available, in your primary browser from the hosted site).

Module layouts are contained in the site root folder aptly named Layouts. Within the Layouts folder is a subfolder for each module. If you open any of these subfolders, you'll see one or more HTML files. Each file contains the HTML and CSS used for rendering the output, along with any Business Catalyst specific code.

For example, let's say I want to change the way that the FAQ output is handled. By default, when you insert an FAQ module, the initial display is of a series of questions; click on any question to see the answer and an associated comment form. If I wanted to restyle the question itself, I can open the list.html file found in the Faq folder and see that the Business Catalyst code `{tag_question}` is contained within a `<div>` tag with a class of `faq-question`, like this:

```
<div class="faq-question">{tag_question}</div>
```

Therefore, to add a bit of space between each question I could define a CSS rule like this:

```
.faq-question { padding-bottom: .8em; }
```

Although I could embed this new CSS rule in the list.html page, it'd be better to store it with all the other module styles in the ModuleStyleSheets.css file located at site root folder StyleSheets.

You're not limited to modifying a module's CSS: You can just as easily restructure its HTML. For example, the comment form displayed with the FAQ answer includes, among other fields, an optional field for entering a website URL, shown in Figure 4-26.

To remove the website field, you'd follow these steps:

1. From the Files panel, expand the Layouts folder.
2. Expand the Faq folder.
3. Open the details.html file.
4. Select the `<div>` tag surrounding the website label (Figure 4-27) and field and press Delete.
5. Save and upload the details.html file.

Now, whenever the FAQ answer and comment form is displayed, the unwanted field would not be shown.

FIGURE 4-26

Access advanced Business Catalyst functionality from the available modules.

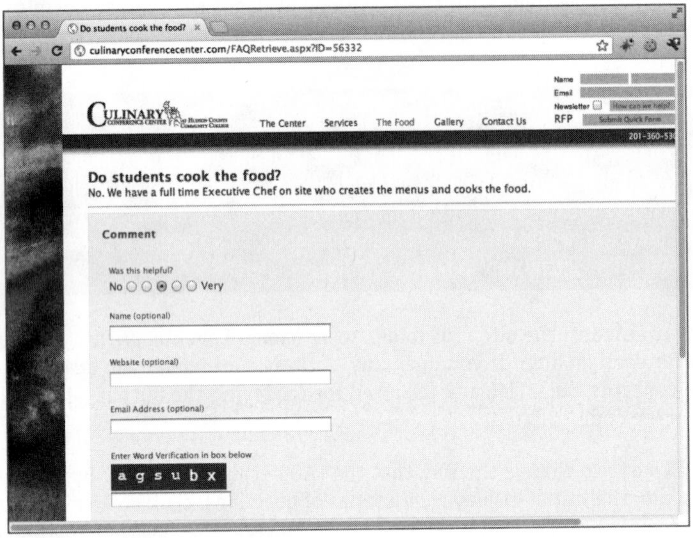

FIGURE 4-27

Open the HTML files within the Layouts subfolders to modify the displayed elements of a Business Catalyst module.

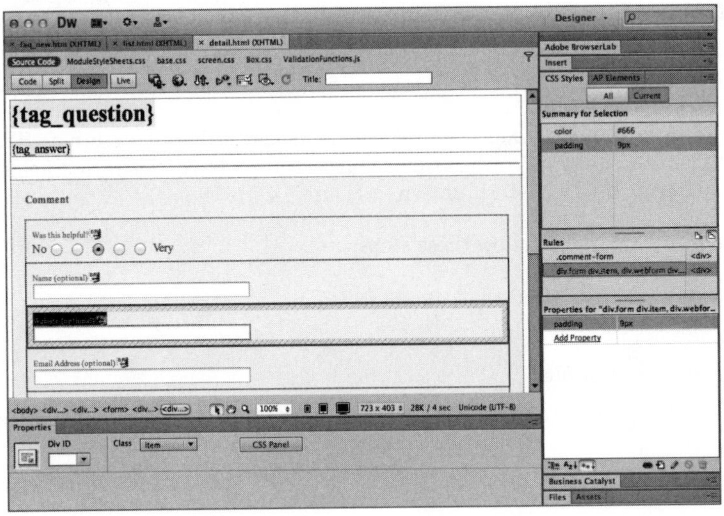

Summary

In this chapter, you learned some options for planning your website and what you need to do in Dreamweaver to initialize the site. As you plan your site and set up your servers, keep these points in mind:

- Put as much time into planning your site as possible. The more clearly conceived the site, the cleaner the execution.
- Set up your local site folder in Dreamweaver right away. The local site folder is essential for Dreamweaver to properly publish your files to the remote site later.
- Establish as many servers as your development process requires, whether to connect to your remote server on the web or to a local or networked testing server.
- If you are creating a web application, choose one server model per site and set it when you define your site. This step is needed so that Dreamweaver knows the type of server code to write.
- Get started quickly with any of the 18 CSS-based layouts, available through the New Document dialog box.
- Preview early, often, and with various browsers. Dreamweaver gives you quick function-key access to a primary (F12/Option+F12) and secondary (Ctrl+F12/Command+F12) browser. Check your pages frequently in these browsers and then spend some time checking your pages against other available browsers and browser versions.
- Dreamweaver also gives you the option to check your page with browsers and operating systems not available on your local system through Adobe BrowserLab. You can compare your page designs in up to two browser configurations side by side or even overlaid on top of one another.
- Establish an early connection to the web and use it frequently. You can begin publishing your local site through Dreamweaver's Site window almost immediately.
- Dreamweaver offers a direct connection to Adobe's robust hosting service, Business Catalyst. Once you've signed up to Business Catalyst, you can create and modify sites from within Dreamweaver.

In the next chapter, you learn how to use Dreamweaver to begin coding your web pages.

Part II

Designing and Crafting Basic Pages

IN THIS PART

Chapter 5
Accessing the Code Directly

Chapter 6
Building Style Sheet Web Pages

Chapter 7
Working with Text

Chapter 8
Inserting Images

Chapter 9
Establishing Web Links

CHAPTER 5

Accessing the Code Directly

IN THIS CHAPTER

- Laying the code foundation
- Working with the <head> section
- Developing the <body> section
- Exploring Code view
- Incorporating HTML5 tags
- Working with Live View and Live Code view
- Using related and dynamically related files
- Accessing the Code Navigator
- Consolidating code with the JavaScript Extractor
- Dreamweaver Technique: Collapsing and Moving Code
- Adding special characters

As far as most designers are concerned, in a perfect world, you could lay out a complex website with a visual authoring tool and never have to see the HTML and other code, much less modify it. Dreamweaver takes you a long way toward this goal—in fact, you can create many types of web pages using only Dreamweaver's Design and Live views. As your pages become more complex, however, you may need to tweak your code in one way or another.

Programmers, on the other hand, are happiest working directly with the code. To accomplish their goals efficiently, coders need a responsive, flexible editor capable of handling a wide range of computer languages. Just how much assistance is required is a matter of personal taste: Some code writers want all the help they can get, with features such as syntax coloring, code completion, and Code Hints, among others. Other programmers just want the editor to stay out of their way.

Dreamweaver tries to give coders the best of both worlds by providing a full-featured editor with numerous options. In addition to the features mentioned in the preceding paragraph, Dreamweaver includes full tag libraries in numerous languages: HTML, CFML, ASP.NET, JSP, and PHP to name a few. Both hand-coders and visual designers can enjoy the benefits of Dreamweaver tools such as the Snippets panel, for adding chunks of code via drag-and-drop, and the Tag inspector, for displaying all the attributes of a chosen tag—and making them editable as well. This chapter covers all these features and more.

Although the Internet is made up of a plethora of technologies, HTML is still at the heart of a web page. This chapter gives you a basic understanding of how HTML works and provides you with the specific building blocks to begin creating web pages. This chapter also gives you your first look at a Dreamweaver innovation: Code view, for altering the code side by side with the visual environment. The other Dreamweaver-specific material in this chapter—which primarily describes how Dreamweaver sets and modifies page properties—is suitable for even the most accomplished web designers. Armed with these fundamentals, you are ready to begin your exploration of web page creation.

The Structure of a Web Page

To understand what HTML is, you simply need to know what it stands for: Hypertext Markup Language. *Hypertext* refers to one of the web's main properties—the capability to jump from one page to another, no matter where the pages are located on the web. *Markup Language* means that a web page is actually a heavily annotated text file. The basic building blocks of HTML, such as `<strong>` and `<p>`, are known as *markup elements*, or *tags*. The terms *element* and *tag* are used interchangeably.

An HTML page, then, is a set of instructions (the tags) suggesting to your browser how to display the enclosed text and images. The browser knows what kind of page it is handling based on the tag that opens the page, `<html>`, and the tag that closes the page, `</html>`. The great majority of HTML tags come in such pairs, in which the closing tag always has a forward slash before the keyword. Two examples of tag pairs are `<p> . . . </p>` and `<title> . . . </title>`. A few important tags are represented by a single element: the image tag `<img>`, for example.

The HTML page is divided into two primary sections: the `<head>` and the `<body>`. Information relating to the entire document goes in the `<head>` section: the title, description, keywords, and any language subroutines called from within the `<body>`. The content of the web page is found in the `<body>` section. All the text, graphics, embedded animations, Java applets, and other elements of the page are found between the opening `<body>` and the closing `</body>` tags.

When you start a new document in Dreamweaver, the basic format is already laid out for you. Listing 5-1 shows the code from a blank Dreamweaver web page.

LISTING 5-1 The HTML for a New Dreamweaver Page

```
<!DOCTYPE HTML PUBLIC "-//W3C//DTD HTML 4.01 Transitional//EN">
<html>
<head>
<title>Untitled Document</title>
<meta http-equiv="Content-Type" content="text/html; charset=iso-8859-1">
</head>

<body>

</body>
</html>
```

I cover the opening <!DOCTYPE> tag in the section "doctype and doctype Switching" a little later in the chapter. First, you should notice how the <head> . . . </head> pair is separate from the <body> . . . </body> pair and that both are contained within the <html> . . . </html> tags.

Notice also that the <meta> tag has two additional elements:

```
http-equiv="Content-Type"
```

and

```
content="text/html; charset=iso-8859-1"
```

These types of elements are known as *attributes*. Attributes modify the basic tag and can be either equal to a value or stand-alone. I cover the specifics of the <meta> tag later in this chapter; for now, you should focus on just the syntax. Attributes are made up of name/value pairs where the attribute is set to be equal to some value, typically in quotes. Not all tags have attributes, but when they do, the attributes are specific.

One last note about an HTML page: You are free to use carriage returns, spaces, and tabs as needed to make your code more readable. The interpreting browser ignores all but the included tags and text to create your page. I point to some minor, browser-specific differences in interpretation of these elements throughout the book, but generally you can indent or space your code as you wish.

The style in which Dreamweaver inserts code is completely customizable. See Chapter 3 for details on changing your code preferences and Chapter 33 to see how you can adjust your tags more specifically with the Tag Library Editor.

Expanding into XHTML

There is a series of HTML versions known as XHTML, short for Extensible HTML. XHTML is based on XML and, as such, has a more rigid syntax than HTML. For example, tags that do not enclose content—the so-called *empty tags*—are written differently. In HTML, a line-break tag is:

```
<br>
```

whereas in XHTML, the line-break tag is:

```
<br />
```

Notice the additional space and the closing slash. Other differences include an opening XML declaration, as well as a specific doctype tag placed before the opening <html> tag. All tags must be in lowercase, and all attribute values must appear in quotes (but not necessarily lowercase) as follows:

```
<table align="RIGHT">
```

Dreamweaver makes it easy to code in XHTML and even to convert existing pages from HTML to XHTML. To work in XHTML from the ground up, you don't have to do anything: It's the default new document type. If, however, you want to change the Document Type Definition (DTD) option to one of the other XHTML options available on the New Document category of Preferences (available when you choose Edit ➪ Preferences on Windows or Dreamweaver ➪ Preferences on a Mac). Selecting this option automatically sets an identical option on the New Document dialog box (File ➪ New), which you can change on a case-by-case basis, if necessary. After a document has been set as an XHTML file, all the tags are written in the proper style.

To change an HTML page into an XHTML one, choose File ➪ Convert ➪ XHTML. The conversion is automatically applied to the current document; no standard method exists to convert an entire site.

Because Dreamweaver has taken the pain out of using XHTML, the question is: Should you code in XHTML or HTML? As in most situations, it depends. Many larger companies that work extensively in XML require well-formed XHTML pages.

doctype and doctype Switching

The very first element of an HTML page—even before the `<html>` tag—is a `doctype` declaration. As the name implies, a `doctype` declaration specifies the language or, more specifically, the DTD (Document Type Definition) in use for the file that follows. To validate their page, many authors include `doctype` statements like the following:

```
<!DOCTYPE HTML PUBLIC "-//W3C//DTD HTML 4.01 Transitional//EN">
```

This `doctype` is inserted by default when Dreamweaver creates a new static HTML page.

NOTE

As of this writing, the latest version of HTML to complete the recommendation process by the W3C is 4.01. After this version, the W3C recommended the switch to XHTML. Another revision of HTML, HTML5, is in the works and almost at the recommendation stage: HTML5 allows you to use either HTML or XHTML syntax.

Some browser versions inspect the `doctype` element in order to determine how the page should be rendered. Engaging in a practice known as `doctype` switching, these browsers (Internet Explorer 5.*x* and Safari 1.*x* or higher on a Mac, Internet Explorer 6 on Windows, and Netscape 6 or higher) work in two modes: strict (also known as standard) and regular (also called quirks mode). When a browser is in strict mode, a page must be well-formed and validate without error to be rendered properly. Strict rendering is more consistent across browsers. The regular mode is far looser and more forgiving in how the page is coded; however, the page is more likely to be rendered differently in the varying browser versions. It is highly recommended that you work in strict mode whenever possible.

You can ensure that your pages are rendered in the regular mode in a number of ways:

- Do not include a `doctype` declaration at all.
- Use a `doctype` declaration that specifies an HTML version earlier than 4.0.
- Use a `doctype` declaration that declares a transitional DTD of HTML 4.01 but does not include a URL to the DTD.

To trigger a browser's strict rendering mode:

- Use a `doctype` declaration for XML or XHTML.
- Use a `doctype` declaration that declares a strict DTD of HTML 4.01.
- Use a `doctype` declaration that declares a transitional DTD of HTML 4.01 that includes a URL to the DTD.

When including a URL to the DTD, the `doctype` looks as follows:

```
<!DOCTYPE HTML PUBLIC "-//W3C//DTD HTML 4.01 Transitional//EN"
"http://www.w3.org/TR/html4/loose.dtd">
```

You have several alternatives in Dreamweaver for including whichever `doctype` you choose. Hand-coding is a sure but tedious method; the `doctype` statement is somewhat cumbersome and certainly not easy to remember precisely. You could also alter the standard HTML page by changing the `Default.html` file found in your Dreamweaver CS6\Configuration\DocumentTypes\NewDocuments folder.

For more details on altering the default page template, see Chapter 28.

Another approach is to create a custom snippet that enables you to drag the desired code right onto the page on a case-by-case basis. Use of the Snippets panel is covered later in this chapter in the section "Adding Code Through the Snippets Panel."

TIP

The doctype for HTML5 is simplicity itself:

```
<!doctype html>
```

HTML5 does not support any sort of doctype switching.

Which approach you take—strict or regular—depends, as with HTML and XHTML, on your audience. If a significant portion of your site's audience uses older browsers, stay with a regular `doctype`. If the statistics for your site indicate that a high percentage of visitors are using more current browsers, go with a strict `doctype`. Of course, some clients or managers may mandate that their designers use a specific `doctype`.

Defining <head> Elements

Information pertaining to the web page overall is contained in the `<head>` section of an HTML page. Browsers read the `<head>` to determine how to render the page—for example, is the page to be displayed using the Western, the Chinese, or some other character set? Search engine spiders also read this section to quickly glean a summary of the page.

When you begin inserting JavaScript (or code from another scripting language such as VBScript) into your web page, all the subroutines and document-wide declarations generally go into the `<head>` area. Dreamweaver uses this format by default when you insert a JavaScript behavior.

Dreamweaver enables you to insert, view, and modify <head> content without opening an HTML editor. Dreamweaver's View Head Content capability enables you to work with <meta> tags and other <head> HTML code as you do with the regular content in the visual editor.

Establishing Page Properties

When you first open a page in Dreamweaver, your default web page is untitled, with no background image and only a plain, white background. You can change any of these properties and more through Dreamweaver's Page Properties dialog box.

As usual, Dreamweaver gives you more than one method for accessing the Page Properties dialog box. You can choose Modify ➪ Page Properties, or you can use the keyboard shortcut Ctrl+J (Command+J).

TIP

Here's another way to open the Page Properties dialog box: Click the Page Properties button of the Text Property inspector.

The Page Properties dialog box, shown in Figure 5-1, gives you easy control over the overall look and feel of the HTML page.

NOTE

If you set options in the Appearance (HTML) category, the values you assign through the Page Properties dialog box are applied to the <body> tag. However, because values assigned in Appearance (CSS), the preferred way of working, result in CSS rules embedded in the document's <head> area, this topic is covered here.

The main categories of the Page Properties dialog box are Appearance (CSS), Appearance (HTML), Links (CSS), Headings (CSS), Title/Encoding, and Tracing Image. The Appearance (HTML) category should be used only on legacy pages that have not been converted to CSS styling.

FIGURE 5-1

Change your web page's overall appearance through the Page Properties dialog box.

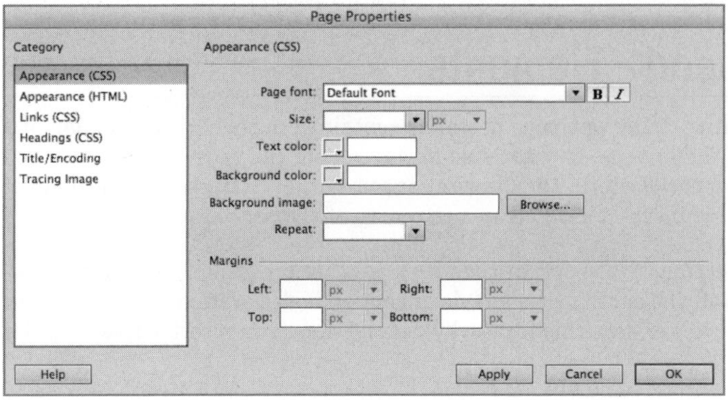

Appearance (CSS)

The Appearance (CSS) category controls the overall look and feel of the current document as CSS rules. The Appearance (CSS) options, shown in Figure 5-1, include:

- **Page Font:** Set the font family from the drop-down list or select Edit Font List to make more options available. Fonts can optionally be set to bold and/or italic.
- **Size:** Choose a default size from the list or enter a specific value. Both absolute (9, 10, 12, and so on) and relative (xx-small, medium, larger, and so on) are available. If an absolute value is used, any of the standard measurement systems such as pixels, points, or ems can be chosen.
- **Text Color:** Click this color swatch to control the color of default text.
- **Background Color:** Click this color swatch to change the background color of the web page. Select one of the browser-safe colors from the drop-down list, or enter its name or hexadecimal representation (for example, `#FFFFFF`) directly into the text field.
- **Background Image:** Select the graphic displayed in the page background. The path to the source file can be either entered in the field directly or chosen by clicking the Browse button. If the image is smaller than your content requires, the browser tiles the image to fill out the page; in such a circumstance, specifying a large background image (or repeating an image) may hide any selection in the Background Color field, although the background-color value will appear wherever the image does not.
- **Repeat:** Define whether the background image is repeated along the X or Y axis, both, or not at all. If no Repeat option is specified, the background image repeats horizontally and vertically to fill the page.
- **Margins:** Enter values here to change the page margin settings. As with the text size, the various measurement systems are available.

TIP

To gain greater control over your background image, set the parameters through the CSS Rule Definition dialog box when defining a CSS rule for the `<body>` tag. Through CSS, you can control the background image placement and the attachment options (fixed or scroll).

NOTE

If you set the Preferences to use HTML tags rather than CSS, you enter the margin settings into the `<body>` tag.

Appearance (HTML)

The Appearance (HTML) category defines the background and margin properties like the equivalent settings in the Appearance (CSS) category, but writes the code as attributes in the `<body>` tag. This category includes:

- **Background Color:** Click this color swatch to change the background color of the web page. Select one of the browser-safe colors from the drop-down list, or enter its name or hexadecimal representation (for example, `#FFFFFF`) directly into the text field.

- **Background Image:** Select the graphic displayed in the page background. The path and source filename can be either entered in the field directly or chosen by clicking the Browse button. If the image is smaller than your content requires, the browser tiles the image to fill out the page; specifying a background image overrides any selection in the Background Color field.
- **Margins:** Enter values here to change the page margin settings. As with the text size, the various measurement systems are available.

NOTE

If you set the Preferences to use HTML tags rather than CSS, you enter the margin settings into the `<body>` tag.

Links (CSS)

Hyperlinks are a critical aspect of any web page, and the Links (CSS) category of the Page Properties dialog box sets their initial and interactive appearance. This category has the following options (see Figure 5-2):

- **Link Font:** Set the typeface for links. The default choice is to use the same font as the rest of the page, an option set in the Appearance (CSS) category. You can also opt to bold or italicize a link.
- **Size:** Set the font size for the link. If you do not enter a value, links are displayed in the same size as the standard font.
- **Link Color:** Click this color swatch to modify the color of any text designated as a link or the border around an image link.
- **Visited Links:** Click this color swatch to select the color that linked text changes to after a visitor to your web page has selected that link and then returned to your page.
- **Rollover Links:** Select the color you want to appear when the user's mouse moves over the link.
- **Active Links:** Click this color swatch to choose the color to which linked text changes briefly when a user selects the link. The active link flashes very briefly during a normal operation, and many designers don't bother specifying this parameter.
- **Underline Style:** Determine how the link uses underlines. Designers have the choice of always underlining the link, never underlining it, displaying the underline only on rollover, or hiding it during rollover.

Headings (CSS)

Dreamweaver enables you to control the headings on a page separately from the paragraph text, if you so desire. By default, all headings (tags `<h1>` through `<h6>`) share the same font as set for the page, but you can choose a new font from the Heading Font list. Any font chosen here applies to all headings, but sizes and colors for each heading may be set independently, as shown in Figure 5-3.

TIP

Again, if you want more control, use the CSS Style Definition dialog box to define a style for any heading tag.

FIGURE 5-2

Make links as obvious or subtle as you like by changing their font, size, color, and underline style.

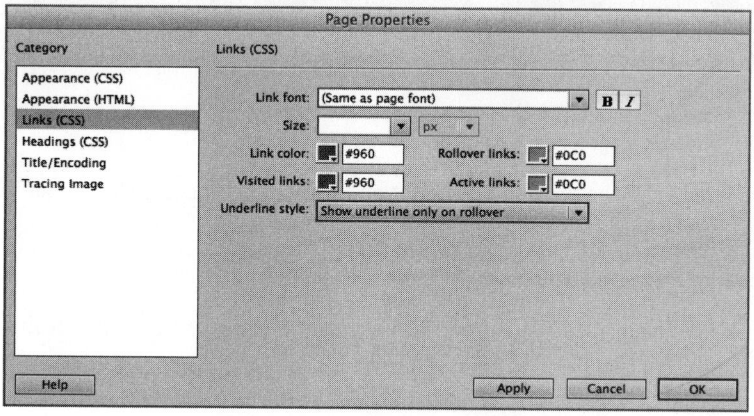

FIGURE 5-3

Although you can use a different font for your headings in many designs, be careful not to define too many color and size variations.

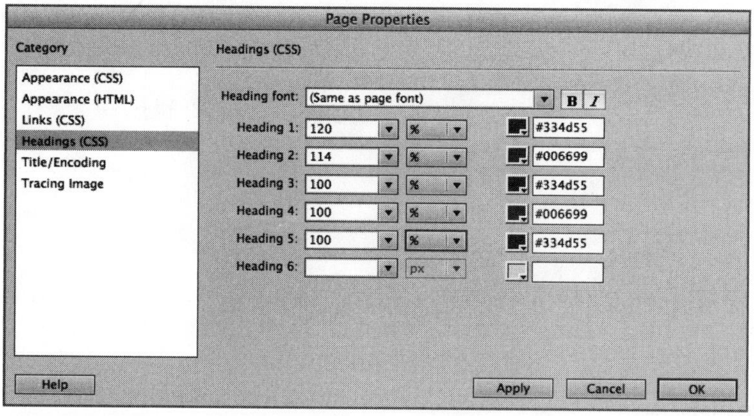

5

Title/Encoding

Fundamental aspects of the web page are set in the Title/Encoding category. Use the Title field to enter the web page title; what you enter here appears in the browser's title bar when your page is viewed. Search engine spiders also read the title as one of the important indexing cues.

TIP

You can also change the document title in Dreamweaver's Document toolbar. Just enter the information in the Title field and press Enter (Return) to confirm the modification. You see the new title appear in the program's title bar and whenever you preview the page in a browser.

The Encoding options determine the character set in which you want your web page to be displayed. The default option for the English version of Dreamweaver is Unicode (UTF-8).

If Unicode is selected, both the Unicode Normalization Form list and the Include Unicode Signature (BOM) option become available, as shown in Figure 5-4. The Unicode Normalization Form list chooses how the Unicode characters are converted to binary format. The Unicode Signature option determines whether a byte order mark (BOM) is attached to the file.

The Page Properties dialog box also displays the document folder if the page has been saved and the current site root folder if one has been selected.

FIGURE 5-4

Unicode support in Dreamweaver is vital for developing multilanguage websites.

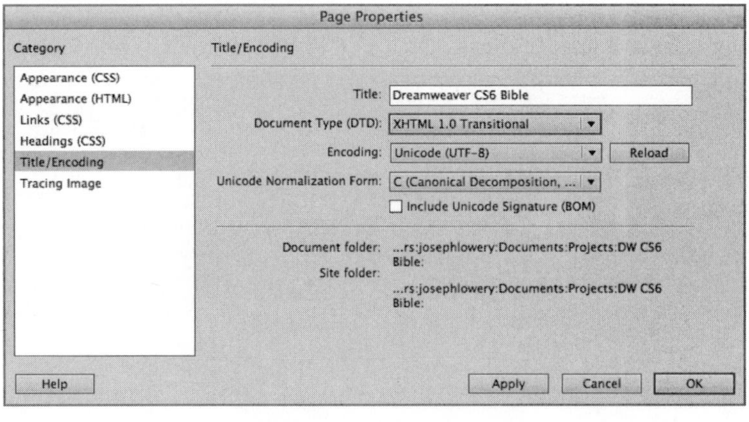

Tracing Image

The Tracing Image category enables you to pick a graphic that can be used as a layout guide; the tracing image is displayed only in Dreamweaver. Select the file by clicking the Browse button and locating a GIF, JPG, PNG, or PSD file; if you choose a Photoshop (PSD) document, Dreamweaver converts it to a web-ready format. After you've selected your file, you can set the degree of opaqueness by changing the Transparency slider, shown in Figure 5-5.

The Tracing Image option is a powerful feature for quickly building a web page based on design comps. For details about this feature and how to use it with Dreamweaver AP elements, see Chapter 10.

FIGURE 5-5

The tracing image is only visible at design time.

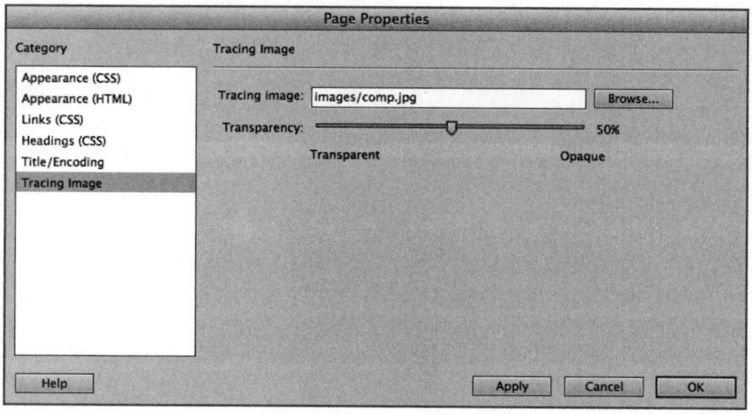

Choosing Colors from an Onscreen Image

One of the features found throughout Dreamweaver, the Eyedropper tool, is especially useful in the Page Properties options. The Eyedropper tool appears whenever you open any of Dreamweaver's color swatches, such as those attached to the Background, Text, and Links colors. You can not only pick a color from the web-safe palette that appears but also use the Eyedropper to select any color on your screen—including system colors such as those found in dialog boxes and menu strips.

To use the Eyedropper tool to choose a color for the background (or any of the other options) from an onscreen image, follow these steps:

1. Insert your image on the page and, using the vertical scroll bar, position the Document window so that the image and the Page Properties dialog box can be viewed simultaneously.

   If your image is too big to fit both it and the Page Properties dialog box on the same screen, temporarily resize your image by dragging its sizing handles. You can restore the original image size when you have finished by clicking the Refresh button on the Image Property inspector.

2. Open the Page Properties dialog box by choosing Modify ➪ Page Properties or using the keyboard shortcut Ctrl+J (Command+J).
3. Drag the Page Properties dialog box to a place where the image can be seen.
4. Select the Background color swatch (or whichever one you want to change). The Dreamweaver color picker opens, and the pointer becomes an eyedropper.

Continues

continued

5. Move the Eyedropper tool over the image until you find the correct color. (In Windows, you must hold down the mouse button as you drag the Eyedropper off the Dreamweaver dialog box to the image.) As you move the Eyedropper over an image, its colors are reflected in the color well, and its hex value is shown on the color picker. Click once when you've found the appropriate color. The color picker closes.
6. Repeat Steps 4 and 5 to grab other colors from the screen for other color swatches. Click OK when you've finished modifying the page properties.

You don't have to keep the image on your page to get its color. Just insert it temporarily and then delete it after you've used the Eyedropper to grab the shade you want.

Understanding <meta> and other <head> tags

Summary information about the content of a page—and a lot more—is conveyed through `<meta>` tags used within the `<head>` section. The `<meta>` tag can be read by the server to create a header file, which makes it easier for indexing software used by search engines to catalog sites. Numerous different types of `<meta>` tags exist, and you can insert them in your document just like other objects.

One `<meta>` tag is included by default in every Dreamweaver page. The Document Encoding option of the Page Properties dialog box determines the character set used by the current web page and is displayed in the `<head>` section as follows:

```
<meta http-equiv="Content-Type" content="text/html; charset=iso-8859-1">
```

The preceding `<meta>` tag tells the browser that this page is, in fact, an HTML page and that the page should be rendered using the specified character set (the `charset` attribute). The key attribute here is `http-equiv`, which is responsible for generating a server response header.

After you've determined your `<meta>` tags for a website, the same basic `<meta>` information can go on every web page. Dreamweaver provides a way to avoid having to insert the same lines repeatedly: templates. After you've set up the `<head>` elements the way you like them, choose File ➪ Save As Template. To add `<meta>` or any other `<head>` tags to an existing template, you can edit the template and then update the affected pages. For more information about templates, turn to Chapter 28.

In Dreamweaver, you can insert a `<meta>` tag or any other tag using the `<head>` tag objects, which you access via the Head menu in the Insert panel's Common category (see Figure 5-6) or the Insert ➪ Common ➪ Head Tags menu option. The `<head>` tag objects are described in Table 5-1 and in subsequent subsections.

Inserting tags with the Meta object

The Meta object is used to insert tags that provide information for the web server through the `HTTP-equiv` attribute, and to include other overall data that you want in your web page but not made visible to the casual browser. Some web pages, for example, have built-in expiration dates after which the content is to be considered outmoded. In Dreamweaver, you can use the Meta object to insert a wide range of descriptive data.

FIGURE 5-6

Quick access to hidden code is available through the Head menu of the Insert panel's Common category.

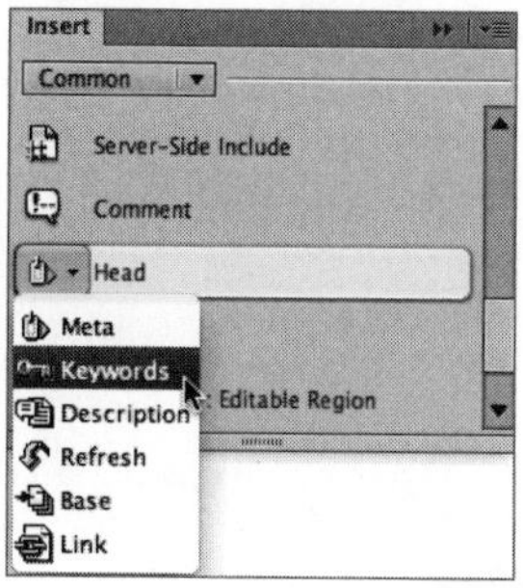

TABLE 5-1 **Head Tag Objects**

Object	Description
Meta	Inserts information that describes or affects the entire document.
Keywords	Includes a series of words used by some search engines to index the current web page and/or site.
Description	Includes a text description of the current web page and/or site.
Refresh	Reloads the current document or loads a new URL within a specified number of seconds.
Base	Establishes a reference for all other URLs in the current web page.
Link	Inserts a link to an external document, such as a style sheet.

You can access the Meta object in the Head menu in the Common category of the Insert panel or via the Insert menu by choosing Insert ➪ HTML ➪ Head Tags ➪ Meta. As with all the Head objects, you don't have to have the Head Content visible to insert the Meta object, although you do have to choose View ➪ Head Content if you want to edit the object. To insert a Meta object, follow these steps:

1. Choose Insert ➪ HTML ➪ Head Tags ➪ Meta or select the Meta object from the Head menu in the HTML category of the Insert panel. Your current cursor position is irrelevant. The Meta dialog box opens, as shown in Figure 5-7.
2. Choose the attribute `Name` or an HTTP equivalent from the Attribute list box. Press Tab.
3. Enter the value for the selected attribute in the Value text box. Press Tab.
4. Enter the value for the content attribute in the Content text box.
5. Click OK when you have finished.

5

FIGURE 5-7

The Meta object enables you to enter a full range of <meta> tags in the <head> section of your web page.

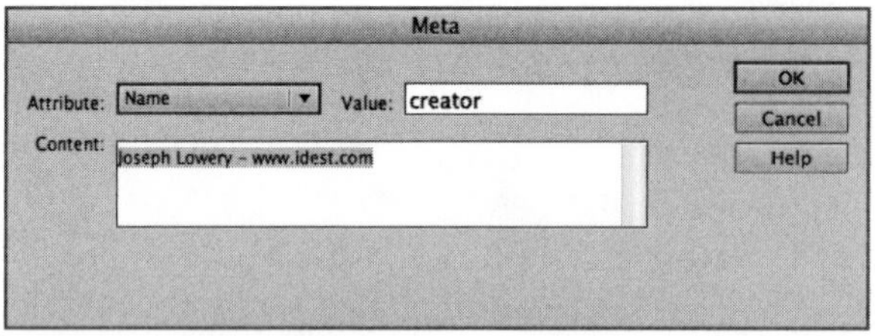

You can add as many Meta objects as you want by repeating Steps 1 through 4. To edit an existing Meta object, you must first choose View ➪ Head Content to reveal the <head> code, indicated by the various icons. Click the Meta icon and make your changes in the Property inspector.

Built-in Meta Commands

Although Dreamweaver presents six different Head objects, <meta> tags form the basis of four of them: Meta, Keywords, Description, and Refresh. By specifying different name attributes, the purpose of the <meta> tags changes. For example, a Keywords object uses the following format:

```
<meta name="keywords" content="dreamweaver, web, authoring,
HTML, DHTML, CSS, Adobe">
```

whereas a Description object inserts this type of code:

```
<meta name="description" content="This site is devoted to
extensions made possible by Adobe's Dreamweaver, the
premier Web authoring tool.">
```

It is possible to create all your <meta> tags with the Meta object by specifying the name attribute and giving it the pertinent value, but it's easier to just use the standard Dreamweaver Head objects.

Aiding search engines with the Keywords and Description objects

Take a closer look at the tags that convey indexing and descriptive information to some search engine spiders. Those chores are handled by the Keywords and Description objects. As noted in the sidebar "Built-in Meta Commands," the Keywords and Description objects output specialized <meta> tags.

Both objects are straightforward to use. Choose Insert ➪ HTML ➪ Head Tags ➪ Keywords or Insert ➪ HTML ➪ Head Tags ➪ Description. You can also choose the corresponding objects from the Head menu in the Text category of the Insert panel. After they are selected, these objects open similar dialog boxes with a single entry area, a large text box, as shown in Figure 5-8. Enter the values—whether keywords or a description—in the text box and click OK. You can edit the Keywords and Description objects, like the Meta object, by clicking their icons in the Head area of the Document window, revealed by choosing View ➪ Head Contents.

CAUTION

Although you can enter paragraph returns in your Keywords and Description objects, you have no reason to. Browsers ignore all such formatting when processing your code.

What types of keywords should you use? Suppose, for example, that you want to categorize your web page as an homage to the music of the early seventies; you could enter the following in the Content area of the Keywords object:

```
music, 70s, 70's, eagles, ronstadt, bee gees, pop, rock
```

In the preceding case, the content list is composed of words or phrases, separated by commas. Use sentences in the Description object, as follows:

```
The definitive look back to the power pop rock stylings of early
1970s music, with special sections devoted to the Eagles, Linda
Ronstadt, and the Bee Gees.
```

FIGURE 5-8

Entering information through the Keywords object helps search engines correctly index your web page.

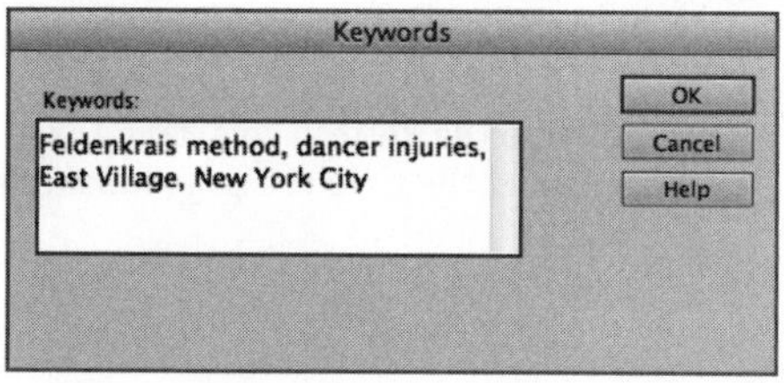

Keep in mind that the content in the Description should complement and extend both the Keywords and the web page title. You have more room in both the Description and the Keywords objects—actually, an unlimited amount—than in the page title, which should be on the short side in order to fit into the browser's title bar.

CAUTION

When using `<meta>` tags with the Keywords or Description objects, don't stuff the `<meta>` tags repeatedly with the same word. The search engines are engineered to reject too many instances of the same words, and your description will not get the attention it deserves.

Refreshing the page and redirecting users

The Refresh object forces a browser to reload the current page or to load a new page after a designer-set interval. The web page visitor usually controls refreshing a page; if, for some reason, the display has become garbled, the user can choose Reload or Refresh from the menu to redraw the screen. Impatient web surfer that I am, I often stop a page from loading to see what text links are available and then—if I don't see what I need—I hit Reload to bring in the full page. The code inserted by the Refresh object tells the server, not the browser, to reload the page. This can be a powerful tool, but it can lead to trouble if used improperly.

To insert a Refresh object, follow these steps:

1. Choose Insert ➪ HTML ➪ Head Tags ➪ Refresh or select the Insert Refresh object from the Head menu in the Common category of the Insert panel. The Refresh dialog box, shown in Figure 5-9, opens.

FIGURE 5-9

Use the Refresh object to redirect visitors from an outdated page.

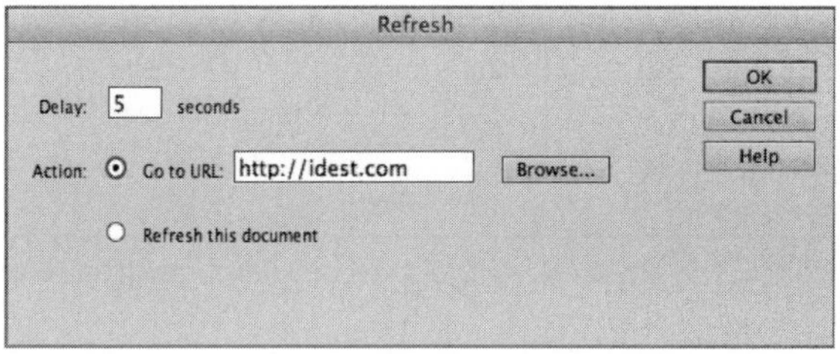

2. Enter the number of seconds you want to wait before the Refresh command takes effect in the Delay text box. The Delay value is calculated from the time the page finishes loading.
3. Select the desired Action:
   - Go To URL
   - Refresh This Document
4. If you selected Go To URL, enter a path to another page in the text box or click the Browse button to select a file.
5. Click OK when you have finished.

The Refresh object is most often used to redirect a visitor to another web page. The web is a fluid place, and sites often move from one address to another. Typically, a page at the old address contains the Refresh code that automatically takes the user to the new address. It's good practice to include a link to your new URL on the change-of-address page because not all browsers support the Refresh option. One other tip: Keep the number of seconds to a minimum—there's no point in waiting for something to happen automatically when you could click a link.

CAUTION

If you elect to choose the Refresh This Document option, use extreme caution, for several reasons. First, you can easily set up an endless loop for your visitors in which the same page is constantly being refreshed. If you are working with a page that updates often, enter a longer Refresh value, such as 300 or 500. You should be sure to include a link to another page to enable users to exit from the continually refreshed page. You should also be aware that many search engines will not index pages using the `<meta>` refresh tag because of widespread abuse by certain industries on the web.

Changing bases

Through the Base object, the <head> section enables you to exert fundamental control over the basic HTML element: the link. The code inserted by this object specifies the base URL for the current page. If you use relative addressing (covered in Chapter 9), you can switch all your links to another directory—even to another website—with one command. The Base object takes two attributes: `href`, which redirects all the other relative links on your page, and `target`, which specifies where the links are rendered.

To insert a Base object in your page, follow these steps:

1. Choose Insert ➪ HTML ➪ Head Tags ➪ Base or select the Base object from the Head menu of the Text category of the Insert panel. The Base dialog box opens.
2. Input the path that you want all other relative links to be based on in the Href text box or click the Browse button to pick the path.
3. If you want, enter a default target for all links without a specific target to be rendered in the Target text box.
4. Click OK when you've finished.

How does a `<base>` tag affect your page? Suppose you define one link as follows:

```
images/backgnd.gif
```

Normally, the browser looks in the same folder as the current page for a subfolder named images. A different sequence occurs, however, if you set the `<base>` tag to another URL in the following way:

```
<base href="http://www.testsite.com/client-demo01/">
```

With this `<base>` tag, when the same `images/backgnd.gif` link is activated, the browser looks for its file in the following location:

```
http://www.testsite.com/client-demo01/images/backgnd.gif
```

CAUTION

Because of the all-or-nothing capability of `<base>` tags, many webmasters use them cautiously, if at all.

Linking to other files

The Link object indicates a relationship between the current page and another page or file. Although many other intended uses exist, the `<link>` tag is most commonly used to apply an external Cascading Style Sheet (CSS) to the current page. This code is entered automatically in Dreamweaver when you create a new linked style sheet (as described in Chapter 6), or you can add the attributes yourself with the Link object. The `<link>` tag can also be used to connect to alternative or relative content for the current page.

5

To insert a Link object, first choose Insert ➪ HTML ➪ Head Tags ➪ Link or select the Insert Link object from the Head group on the Common category of the Insert panel. This action opens the Link dialog box, shown in Figure 5-10.

TIP

One other popular use of the `<link>` tag is to create *favicons*. A favicon is a small icon that appears in the Address bar or Favorites menu of some browsers when you mark a site as a Favorite or bookmarked. To have a favicon appear, create a favicon using one of the tools listed at `http://www.favicon.cc` and upload that image file to your site. Then put a tag like this on your page in the `<head>` section:

```
<link rel="SHORTCUT ICON" href="/images/fav.ico">
```

where `fav.ico` is the name of the icon file, here stored in the images folder at the root of the site.

FIGURE 5-10

The Link object can be used to add a fav icon to your web page.

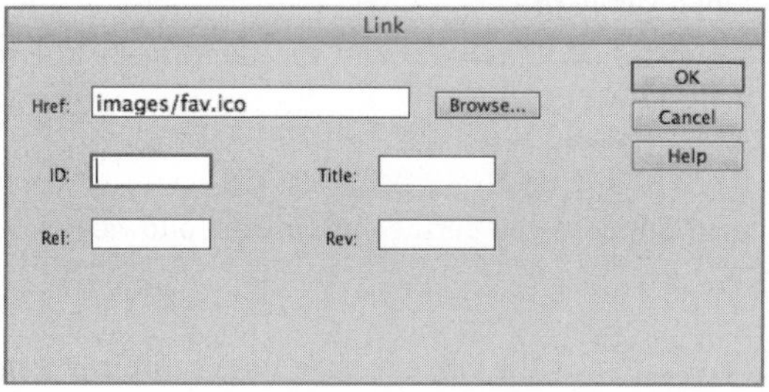

Next, enter the necessary attributes, as shown in Table 5-2.

NOTE

Aside from the style sheet use, little browser support exists for the other link functions. However, the World Wide Web Consortium (W3C) supports an initiative to use the `<link>` tag to address other media, such as speech synthesis and Braille devices, and it's entirely possible that the Link object will be used for this purpose in the future.

TABLE 5-2 Attributes for the Link Object

Attribute	Description
href	Path to the file being linked. Use the Browse button to open the Select File dialog box.
id	Used by scripts to identify this particular object and affect it if need be.
title	Gives the title of the link.
rel	Keyword that describes the relationship of the linked document to the current page. For example, an external style sheet uses the keyword stylesheet.
rev	Like rel, also describes a relationship, but in the reverse. For example, if home.html contained a link tag with a rel attribute set to intro.html, intro.html could contain a link tag with a rev attribute set to home.html.

Adding to the <body>

The content of a web page—the text, images, links, and plugins—is all contained in the <body> section of an HTML document. The great majority of <body> tags can be inserted through Dreamweaver's visual layout interface.

To use the <body> tags efficiently, you need to understand the distinction between logical styles and physical styles used in HTML. An underlying philosophy of HTML is to keep the web as universally accessible as possible. Web content is intended to be platform- and resolution-independent, but the content itself can be styled by its intent as well. This philosophy is supported by the existence of logical <body> tags (such as <code> and <cite>), with which a block of text can be rendered according to its meaning, and physical style tags for directly italicizing or underlining text. HTML enables you to choose between logical styles, which are relative to the text, or physical styles, which can be regarded as absolute.

Logical styles

Logical styles are contextual, rather than explicit. Choose a logical style when you want to ensure that the meaning, rather than a specific look, is conveyed. Table 5-3 shows a listing of logical style tags and their most common usage. Tags not supported through Dreamweaver's visual interface are noted.

Logical styles are the standard approach to using Cascading Style Sheets. Style sheets make it possible to combine the best elements of both logical and physical styles. With CSS, you can easily make the text within your <code> tags blue, and the variables, denoted with the <var> tag, green.

TABLE 5-3 HTML Logical Style Tags

Tag	Usage
<cite>	Citations, titles, and references; usually shown in italic.
<code>	For showing programming code, usually displayed in a monospaced font.
<dfn>	Defining instance; used to mark the introduction of a new term.
<em>	Emphasis; usually depicted as underlined or italicized text.
<kbd>	Keyboard; used to render text to be entered exactly.
<samp>	Sample; a sequence of literal characters.
<strong>	Strong emphasis; usually rendered as bold text.
<var>	Variable; used to distinguish variables from other programming code.

TIP

By default, Dreamweaver is now set to use the logical styles <strong> and <em> whenever you click the Bold and Italic buttons on the Property inspector, respectively. Choose Edit ➪ Preferences (Dreamweaver ➪ Preferences) and, in the General category of the Preferences dialog box, deselect the Use <strong> And <em> In Place Of <b> And <i> option if you'd prefer not to use the logical styles.

5

Physical styles

HTML picked up the use of physical styles from modern typography and word processing programs. Use a physical style when you want something to be absolutely bold, italic, or underlined (or, as we say in HTML, <b>, <i>, and <u>, respectively). You can apply the bold and the italic tags to selected text through the Property inspector or by choosing Text ➪ Style; the underline style is available only through the Text menu.

Working with Code View and the Code Inspector

Although Dreamweaver offers many options for using the visual interface of the Document window, sometimes you just have to tweak the code by hand. Dreamweaver's acceptance by professional coders is due in large part to the easy access to the underlying code. Dreamweaver includes several methods for directly viewing, inputting, and modifying code for your web page. For large-scale additions and changes, you might consider using an external HTML editor such as BBEdit or Homesite, but for many situations, the built-in Code view and Code inspector are perfectly suited and much faster to use.

Code view is one of the coolest tools in Dreamweaver's code-savvy toolbox. You can view your code full-screen either in the Document window, split-screen with Design view, or in a separate panel, the Code inspector. The underlying engine for all Code views is the same.

You can use either of the following methods to display the full-screen Code view:

- Choose View ➪ Code.
- Click the Show Code View button on the toolbar. Code view displays, as shown in Figure 5-11.

FIGURE 5-11

Code view is easily accessible from the Document toolbar.

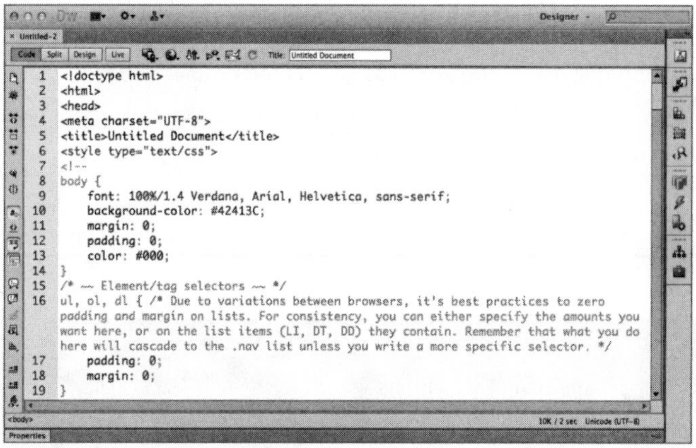

You can access the split-screen Code and Design view with either of the following methods:

- Choose View ➪ Code and Design.
- Click the Show Code and Design Views (Split) button on the Document toolbar.

In recent years, monitors have gotten wider, and Dreamweaver's previously default horizontal Split view seemed to be wasting space. Now, Dreamweaver in Split view defaults to placing the code in a vertical window, so you see Code and Design view side by side rather than one on top of the other. Dreamweaver even offers a quick menu alternative if you'd prefer to switch your Design view position, View ➪ Design View on Left. If you prefer to see the two views horizontally, deselect View ➪ Split Vertically.

To change the relative size of the Code and Design views, drag the splitter bar. In the split-screen Code and Design view, Code view is shown to the left of the Design view. You can reverse that order by choosing View ➪ Design View On Left. If you've chosen to split the screen horizontally, Code view is normally on the top and can be switched by choosing View ➪ Design View On Top.

Another coding option is the Code inspector. You have two ways to open the Code inspector. You can either choose Window ➪ Code Inspector or use the keyboard shortcut F10 (Option+F10). After you open it, the Code inspector (see Figure 5-12) behaves like any other floating panel in Dreamweaver: The Code inspector can be resized, moved, hidden, and, on Windows, docked above or below the Document window or grouped with other panels. When the Code inspector is opened initially, it is automatically selected.

FIGURE 5-12

To update Design view while still working in the Code view, click the handy Refresh button—on either the Document toolbar or the Property inspector—or press F5.

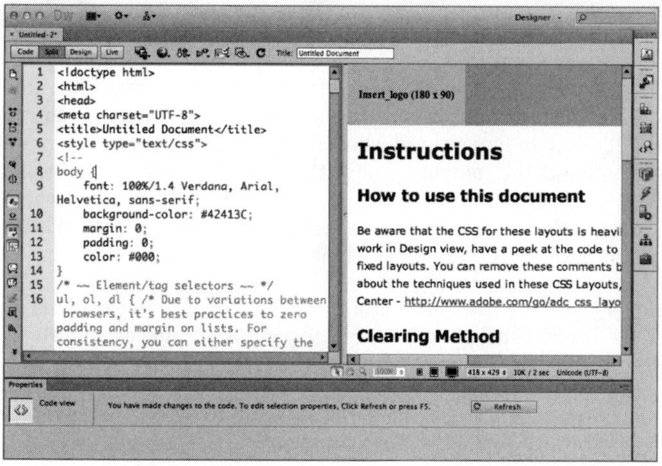

In all Code views, Dreamweaver does not update the Design view of the document immediately—whereas changes in Design view are instantly reflected in any open Code view. This delay is enforced to enable the code to be completed before being applied. To apply modifications made in the code, switch to Design view; if Design view is open, click anywhere in it to give it focus. Should Dreamweaver detect any invalid HTML, such as an improperly closed tag, the offending code is flagged with a yellow highlight in both Design and Code views. Select the marked tag to see an explanation and suggestions for correcting the problem in the Property inspector.

You can also apply code changes to Design view by saving the document or by clicking the Refresh button on the toolbar or the Property inspector. The Refresh button becomes active only when modifications are made in any Code view. You also have a keyboard and menu alternative: Pressing F5 has the same effect as choosing View ➪ Refresh Design View.

Generally, the Code view and Code inspector act like a regular text editor. Simply click anywhere in the inspector to add or modify code. Double-click a word to select it. Select an entire line by moving your pointer to the left edge of the code—where the pointer becomes a right-pointing arrow—and clicking once. Multiple lines can be selected in this same fashion by dragging the right-pointing arrow. After a section of code is selected, you can drag and drop it into a new location; pressing the Ctrl (Option) key while dragging makes a copy of the selection. You can move from word to word by pressing Ctrl (Command) in combination with any of the arrow keys.

You can also easily change the indentation—in or out—for selected blocks of code. To further indent a block of code, select it and press Tab. To decrease the level of indentation for a selected code block, press Shift+Tab. Alternatively, you can choose Edit ➪ Indent Code or use the keyboard shortcut Ctrl+. (Shift+Command+.) to indent a code block. Similarly, you choose Edit ➪ Outdent Code or use the keyboard shortcut Ctrl+, (Shift+Command+,) to outdent it.

TIP

Although the keyboard shortcuts for indenting and outdenting code may seem arbitrary at first, they're actually easy to remember. The period and comma used in those shortcuts are on the same key as the left angle bracket (>) and right angle bracket (<), respectively—which indicates the direction of the code shift.

As a further aid to help you find your way through a maze of code, Dreamweaver includes the Balance Braces command. JavaScript is notorious for using parentheses, brackets, and curly braces to structure its code—and it's easy to lose sight of where one enclosing brace begins and its closing mate ends. Dreamweaver highlights the content found within the closest pair of braces to the cursor when you choose Edit ➪ Balance Braces or use the keyboard shortcut Ctrl+' (Command+'). If you select the command again, the selection expands to the set of surrounding braces. When the selection is not enclosed by parentheses, brackets, or curly braces, Dreamweaver sounds an alert.

Although most web designers who use the code editor in Dreamweaver prefer to manually enter their code, the power of the Insert panel is still at your disposal for rapid code development. Any element available from the Insert panel can be inserted directly into Code view or the inspector. To use the Insert panel, you must first position your cursor where you would like the code for the object to appear. Then select the element or drag and drop the element from the Insert panel to Code view or the inspector.

Keep in mind that Dreamweaver's code editor is highly customizable. You can change the way the lines wrap by using indents for certain tag pairs; you can even control the amount of indentation. All the preferences are outlined for you in Chapter 3.

Printing code

Although you may spend the vast majority of your time writing, modifying, and debugging your code onscreen, there are times when you need to see it in hard copy.

Dreamweaver offers the option of printing out your code—even in color! Just choose File ➪ Print Code to open the standard operating system Print dialog box. You have the option to print all the code or a selection; you cannot, however, print individual pages of your code. Optionally, you can press the keyboard shortcut Ctrl+P (Command+P) to open the Print dialog box. If you'd prefer to print your code in black and white, deselect the Syntax Coloring option under the View ➪ Code View Options menu.

Coding HTML5 Structural Tags

HTML5—although not a completed specification—is gaining use quickly in the web design community. Although HTML5 made a big splash with the `<video>` and `<audio>` tags providing plugin-free media players, this update to the markup language also includes other tags that, with less fanfare, offer fundamental changes to the way designers structure a page with code.

Prior to HTML5, designers typically used a series of `<div>` tags, each identified with an ID and/or class to create a page, like this:

```
<div id="header">
  <div id="nav">
  </div> <!-- End nav -->
</div> <!-- End header -->
<div id="mainContent">
</div> <!-- End mainContent -->
<div id="sideContent">
</div> <!-- End sideContent -->
<div id="footer">
</div> <!-- End footer -->
```

There's no hard-and-fast rule about what IDs or classes to apply—I could just have easily used `<div id="angel">` as my content container as `<div id="mainContent">`. It doesn't matter at all to the browsers. Where it *does* matter—increasingly so—is to other devices (whether desktop, tablet, or phone) that are trying to reuse that content. Increasingly, content is syndicated and re-published on a variety of outlets. The spread of information is a good thing, both in general and specifically for the sites from which the content comes. To make such syndication possible, a common standard must be applied to the page structure so content that can be re-published is easily recognized. HTML5 incorporates such a standard through its structural or semantic tags.

The most commonly used HTML5 structural tags are:

- `<header>`: Used to denote the top section of a page or of a section.
- `<nav>`: Contains the primary and secondary navigational elements of a page.
- `<section>`: Holds thematically related content that is not intended to be syndicated in its entirety, such as a chapter of a book or section of a newspaper.

- <article>: Used for content that is targeted for syndication, such as a blog post or comment.
- <aside>: Contains non-essential page content like that found in sidebars and pull quotes.
- <footer>: Holds material typically displayed at the bottom of a document or section.

NEW FEATURE

So much for theory—how do you work with these tags in Dreamweaver? Currently, the only method available is entering them directly in Code view. But wait, it's not as bad as it sounds! Dreamweaver provides full code hinting support for all HTML5 tags and attributes. This facility greatly flattens your learning curve and simplifies the coding. All you need to remember is the how the tag starts, and Dreamweaver prompts you with the rest.

If you're developing an HTML5 page from scratch, I recommend working from the outside in, especially in the <body> area. Here's a bare-bones HTML5 page to start with:

```
<!doctype html>
<html>
<head>
<meta charset="UTF-8">
<title>Untitled Document</title>
</head>
<body>
</body>
</html>
```

NOTE

I included the single <meta> tag, <meta charset="UTF-8">, to highlight the new charset attribute, which defines the character set for the page. This meta tag is highly recommended to future-proof your page as the web continues to evolve and access is available globally in many areas that may not use your specific character set by default.

While it may seem counterintuitive, the very first tag pair I insert within the <body> area is a <div> tag. It's important to understand that while HTML5 has a new slate of structural tags, the <div> tag is still very much a part of the syntax. The HTML5 specification recommends that you use <div> tags for positioning or styling content—and my initial <div> tag is used to contain the entire page so I can position it where I want on the screen and control its overall width with CSS. Here's the developing page with the new code in bold:

```
<!doctype html>
<html>
<head>
<meta charset="UTF-8">
<title>Untitled Document</title>
</head>
<body>
  <div id="outerWrapper">
  </div>
</body>
</html>
```

Now it's time to add one of our structural tags, <header>:

```
<!doctype html>
<html>
<head>
<meta charset="UTF-8">
<title>Untitled Document</title>
</head>
<body>
  <div id="outerWrapper">
    <header>
    </header>
  </div>
</body>
</html>
```

When you begin typing the tag, Dreamweaver's code hinting feature leaps into action, as shown in Figure 5-13, as well as its code completion (if enabled in Preferences).

FIGURE 5-13

Dreamweaver offers complete code hinting support for all HTML5 tags and attributes.

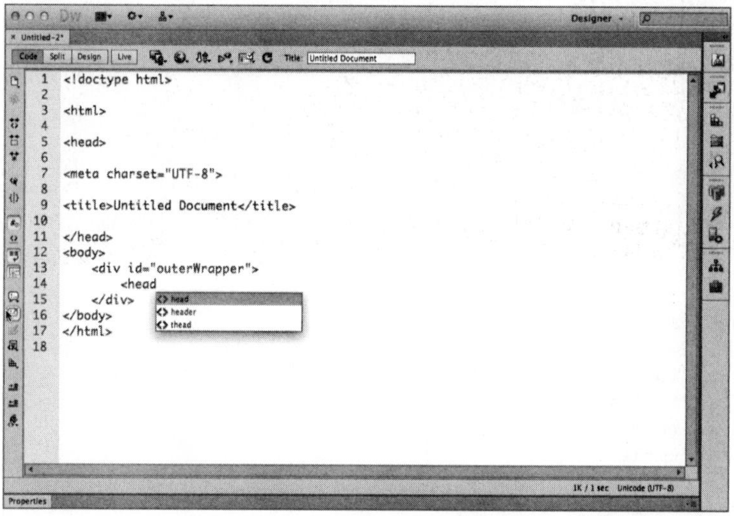

Continue adding HTML5 tags to build out the structure of the page. Typically, the <header> contains the navigation and is followed by the content area, like this:

```
<!doctype html>
<html>
<head>
<meta charset="UTF-8">
```

```
<title>Untitled Document</title>
</head>
<body>
  <div id="outerWrapper">
    <header>
      <nav>
      </nav>
    </header>
    <div id="contentWrapper">
    </div>
  </div>
</body>
</html>
```

TIP

If you nest tags, like the <nav> tag is nested within the <header> tag, Dreamweaver will automatically indent the code for easier reading if you choose Apply Source Formatting from the last icon on the Coding toolbar, Format Source Code.

Unsurprisingly, content goes within the `contentWrapper` div. HTML5 authors can use <section>, <article>, and <aside> tags as their primary content structures:

```
<!doctype html>
<html>
<head>
<meta charset="UTF-8">
<title>Untitled Document</title>
</head>
<body>
  <div id="outerWrapper">
    <header>
      <nav>
      </nav>
    </header>
    <div id="contentWrapper">
      <section>
        <article>
        </article>
        <article>
        </article>
      </section>
      <aside>
      </aside>
    </div>
  </div>
</body>
</html>
```

Feel free to use as many discreet <article> tags as necessary to hold content intended for syndication. The final element added to a basic page should be the <footer> tag:

```
<!doctype html>
<html>
Stet - jl
<head>
<meta charset="UTF-8">
<title>Untitled Document</title>
</head>
<body>
  <div id="outerWrapper">
    <header>
      <nav>
      </nav>
    </header>
    <div id="contentWrapper">
      <section>
        <article>
        </article>
        <article>
        </article>
      </section>
      <aside>
      </aside>
    </div>
    <footer>
    </footer>
  </div>
</body>
</html>
```

Note that the <footer> tag is outside of the contentWrapper div, but inside the outerWrapper div.

NOTE

There's a lot more to learn about HTML5. If you're just starting out with the code, you might be interested in a basic primer I wrote with Mark Fletcher, *HTML5 24-Hour Trainer*, published by Wiley.

Integrating Live View, Related Files, and Code Navigator Features

The great majority of what appear to be single web pages are really a collection of multiple files (CSS, JavaScript, XML, and PHP or other server-side coding) interwoven into a master HTML source file. From the designer's and the browser's perspective, all of these files are not separate documents but parts of the whole: the completed web page. Managing and editing these multiple but connected documents are difficult tasks for the modern web designer.

To answer the challenge of editing and managing all of these elements, Dreamweaver CS6 provides a way of working with three interrelated features: Live View, Related Files, and Code Navigator. The first of these features, Live View, accurately displays the complex requirements for CSS in the modern browser—because it is a modern browser! Based on WebKit, the open source engine used by Apple's Safari and Google's Chrome browsers, Live View gives you a fully rendered page right in Dreamweaver, complete with JavaScript interactivity. Unlike Design view, the visual representation in Live View is not editable. However, Code view remains completely available and active. Moreover, not only can you edit the HTML source in Code view while reviewing real-world results in Live View, you can also modify any of the associated document through the second associated feature, Related Files. Just choose the link to any external code from the Related Files bar to open it in Code view, ready for editing.

Code Navigator completes the circuit begun with the Live View and Related Files features. While clicking a link in the Related Files bar displays that page for editing, Code Navigator goes from your source HTML (in Code or Design view) directly to the targeted code block.

The following sections offer detailed explanations of these three interrelated features to help you more effectively design and re-design your multi-part web pages.

Enhanced workflow with Live View

Up to a point, Live View lets you view and interact with your web page within Dreamweaver as if it were on a live web server. You'll still need to test your website and pages fully in a range of browsers before they can be pushed live, but Live View does give you the capability to review your page in Dreamweaver while making changes to the code. Any modifications to the code can be immediately displayed by refreshing the page by pressing F5, clicking Refresh in the Document toolbar, or clicking into the Live View display.

With Live View, you can:

- Click named anchor links contained within the same page
- Review rollover effects where one image source is replaced by another
- See `onLoad` events, such as a portion of a page fading into view
- Trigger Ajax-based partial page updates, like those developed with Spry data sets
- Display CSS-based interactions, including menu hover states
- Show both inline and CSS-based JavaScript events such as tooltips
- Display server-side code output as HTML output, with a proper testing server set up

What you can't do with Live View:

- Pop open browser windows
- Submit and process forms
- Preview the page in a specific browser

To work in Live View, follow these steps:

1. Enter into Live View by doing one of the following:
   - Clicking Live View in the Document toolbar
   - Choosing View ➪ Live View
   - Pressing Alt+F11 (Option+F11)
2. Interact with your page by moving your mouse over linked text, images, or CSS-based interactive elements.
3. To make a change to the page, enter Split view by clicking Split in the Document toolbar or choosing View ➪ Split, as shown in Figure 5-14.
4. Modify your code.

FIGURE 5-14

Live View gives you the capability to make code changes and see the real-world browser representation immediately.

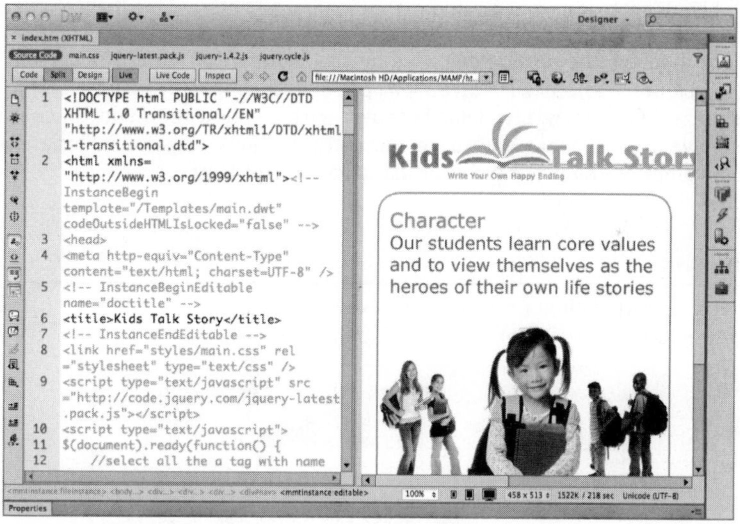

5. Refresh the rendered page by doing one of the following:
   - Clicking Refresh Design View in the Document toolbar
   - Clicking Refresh in the Property inspector
   - Clicking anywhere in Live View
   - Choosing View ➪ Refresh Design View
   - Pressing F5

6. To leave Live View, do one of the following:
   - Clicking Live View in the Document toolbar
   - Choosing View ➪ Live View
   - Pressing Alt+F11 (Option+F11)

TIP

Not only is Code view available for modifications when you're in Live View, but a number of Dreamweaver panels are also available. You can, for example, make a change to a property in the CSS Styles panel and it will be applied to Live View when the page is refreshed. Additionally, both the Tag inspector and the Behaviors panel remain active while in Live View. If you click into Code view, all panels become available.

Incorporating Live Code

Browsers, of course, base their rendered display of web pages on their reading of the source code. Source code can change dynamically during a visitor's session. JavaScript functions can rewrite entire blocks of code to swap CSS classes or images, XML data can be swapped in and out, and server-side coding can completely update the page. Dreamweaver includes a companion feature to Live View to give you an under-the-hood perspective: Live Code.

Live Code displays the actual code used by the browser to render the current display in Live View (see Figure 5-15). As with Live View, the Live Code display is not editable. To distinguish it from standard Code view, Live Code is shown with a yellow highlight. Once it is displayed, you can use Live Code to debug your page. For instance, JavaScript variables are revealed as their runtime values, without the need for using JavaScript alerts.

FIGURE 5-15

Use Live Code in conjunction with Live View to debug portions of your page that dynamically update, including JavaScript, XML, CSS, or server-side changes.

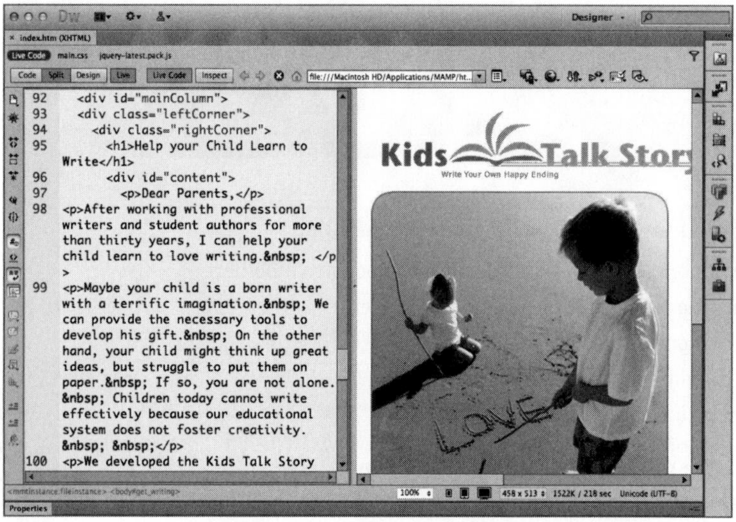

You must be in Live View to access the Live Code mode. Working with Live Code is very straightforward:

1. Once you're in Live View, do one of the following:
   - Click Live Code in the Document toolbar.
   - Choose View ➪ Live Code.
2. Interact with the page to review any code changes.
3. To exit Live Code, either click Live Code in the Document toolbar or choose View ➪ Live Code again.

Setting Live View options

Dreamweaver includes a number of options to enhance Live View functionality. One of the most useful options is the ability to freeze the JavaScript in its current state so you can review the code more closely. This feature makes it possible to modify the effects of JavaScript rollovers and other interactions. A simple press of the keyboard shortcut, F6, while in Live View freezes the JavaScript. You can then modify any code and, once you refresh the page, review your rendered changes. Press F6 again to unfreeze JavaScript.

To access the Live View options, choose the Live View menu button, shown in Figure 5-16, or select View ➪ Live View Options.

FIGURE 5-16

The Live View options are available from the Live View menu button on the Document toolbar.

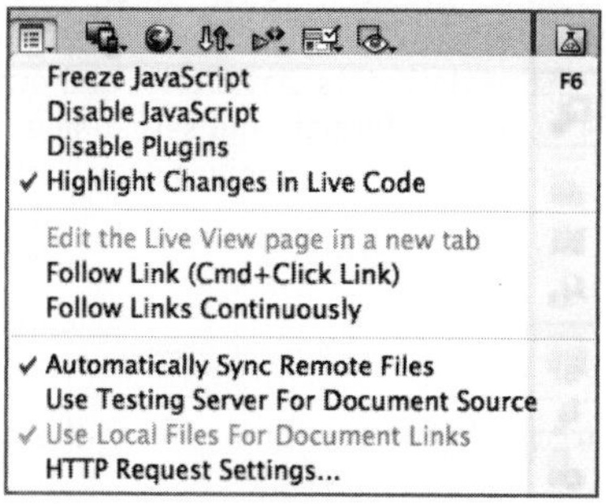

The available Live View options include:

- **Freeze JavaScript:** Pauses JavaScript interaction and displays elements in their current state. Can be invoked with the keyboard shortcut F6.
- **Disable JavaScript:** Turns off JavaScript and re-renders the page with JavaScript enabled.
- **Disable Plugins:** Turns off plugins and re-renders the page without the plugins enabled.
- **Highlight Changes in Live Code:** Changes the background color for code that is dynamically written, such as changing classes or IDs.

- **Edit The Live View Page In A New Tab:** If you've followed a link to a page, when this option is selected, it will open for editing in a new document tab.
- **Follow Link (Ctrl/Cmd+Click Link):** Manually follow any link when Ctrl+clicked (Cmd+clicked).
- **Follow Links Continuously:** Automatically follow links when clicked.
- **Automatically Sync Remote Files:** Allows remote files to be displayed if a link to that file is clicked.
- **Use Testing Server For Document Source:** Relies on the current page as stored on the staging server to render in Live View. This option is enabled by default for dynamic sites using PHP, ColdFusion, or ASP.
- **Use Local Files For Document Links:** Sets Live View to use files stored in your Local Site Root as the related files. This option is enabled by default for standard, non-dynamic sites; if it is not checked, Dreamweaver uses files found on the Testing server.
- **HTTP Request Settings:** Opens a dialog box for setting the method (Get or Post) and defining URL parameter variables and values, such as those displayed after a question mark in the URL, that is, `http://www.your_blue_sky.com?ID=23`. The settings can optionally be stored with the document for rapid development and testing.

Accessing Related Files

As noted earlier, the modern web page is often, essentially, a compound document with external files of various types, like CSS and JavaScript, integrated in the main HTML source code. The Related Files feature makes it possible to quickly navigate to any of these external files and make any changes in Code view while reviewing the rendered page in Dreamweaver's Design view or Live View.

All included files—as well as a link to the HTML source code—are displayed in the Related Files bar, located below the filename tab and the Document toolbar, as shown in Figure 5-17. Dreamweaver recognizes four different types of related files: external CSS style sheets, JavaScript and other client-side scripting files, Spry data set sources in either HTML or XML format, and server-side includes. Related Files support for external CSS style sheets is so good, it even recognizes nested style sheets, where one is imported in another.

FIGURE 5-17

Click any external file in the Related Files toolbar to quickly make edits; refresh the page to re-render it in Design view or Live View.

With the Related Files functionality, you can discover deeply nested related files that are dynamically included. The Dynamically Related Files feature makes it possible to work with popular content management systems (CMS)—such as WordPress, Drupal, and Joomla—from within Dreamweaver. Dreamweaver is now capable of working with so many related files, in fact, that an additional capability to set a filter for only those desired files has also been added to the program. With the filter "wide-open," it's possible for Dreamweaver to discover well over 100 files related to a single web page. The Dynamically Related Files feature works only with PHP pages.

The recommended method for getting the most out of the Related Files feature is to enable Live View and enter into Split view to display both the code and the rendered page simultaneously. Dreamweaver will enter Split view automatically if you're in Live View and click any of the related files, including Source Code.

TIP

If you'd prefer to open your external files as a separate document, you have two options. To do so on a case-by-case basis, right-click (Control+click) the related file link and choose Open as Separate File. To turn off the Related Files feature, clear the Enable Related Files checkbox in the General category of Preferences.

If you're working with a PHP page, Dreamweaver will display a message in the Info bar at the top of the Document Window that notifies you that there may be dynamically related files that can only be revealed by server-side processing. Clicking the Discover link in the Info bar submits the page to a testing or live server, which allows Dreamweaver to identify additional related files that fit into these categories:

- **Nested server-side includes:** Server-side includes referenced in another server-side include.
- **Dynamically generated includes:** Files linked via paths created through a combination of variables and server-side language processing. For example, a path to a configuration file might be constructed by combining the `conf_path()` variable with the filename `settings.php`.
- **Included External Files:** CSS and JavaScript files referenced in a dynamically generated server-side include.

By default, Dreamweaver will only discover dynamically related files manually—that is, if you click the Discover link. You can, however, set Dreamweaver to discover dynamically related files automatically through the General category of Preferences.

For more in-depth information on how to get the most out of the Dynamically Related Files feature, see Chapter 23.

Navigating with the Code Navigator

If the Related Files bar is the Ferrari that gets you to your external file quickly, the Code Navigator is the Ducati motorcycle that zips directly to your code block. With the Code Navigator, you can quickly see what code is affecting the current selection and reveal that precise code chunk for immediate editing.

When activated, the Code Navigator displays as a pop-up window with a series of clickable links, as shown in Figure 5-18. Pertinent to the current selection, the Code Navigator displays related CSS rules (internal and external), external JavaScript files, server-side includes, template parents, library files, and iframe source files. Best of all, access to the Code Navigator is pretty much ubiquitous

5

in Dreamweaver: You can invoke the Code Navigator in Live View and Design, Code, Split, and Live Code views. Click the icon that resembles a ship's steering wheel, which appears over the current selection to open the Code Navigator. Alternatively, you can Alt+click (Command+Option+click) to display the Code Navigator.

FIGURE 5-18

In the Code Navigator, the CSS rules affecting the current selection are presented in the cascade order so you can determine the most relevant.

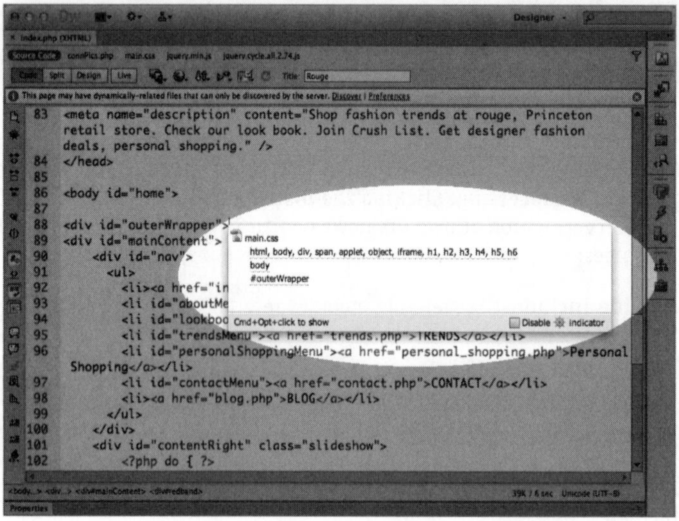

To use the Code Navigator, follow these steps:

1. Place your cursor in the code you want to inspect and click the Code Navigator indicator (the steering wheel icon) that appears.

   Another approach is to Alt+click (Command+Option+click) the code you want to investigate.
2. When the Code Navigator window opens, move your mouse over any of the CSS selectors to see a pop-up window with the rule's properties and values.
3. Click any link to open the containing file and go to the associated code block.
4. After you've modified the code, click Refresh in the Document toolbar, pressing F5 or clicking in Design view or Live View to see the updated page.

If you find that the Code Navigator indicator is getting in your way, you can hide it by choosing the Disable Indicator option in the Code Navigator window.

TIP

When a link to a CSS rule, JavaScript file, or server-side include is clicked in the Code Navigator, the code appears as a related file in Split view. Files that cannot be displayed as a related file—including templates, library items, and iframe source files—are opened as a separate document.

Using the Coding Toolbar

Much of the special tools and functionality aimed at helping the coder are concentrated in the Coding toolbar. The Coding toolbar, enabled by default, is attached to the left side of Code view. In all, there are 19 different buttons and menu buttons that greatly enhance the coding experience in Dreamweaver.

The Coding toolbar's functions are a combination of old and new; some of the features have been placed on the Coding toolbar for ease of use, whereas others cannot be found anywhere else in Dreamweaver. The top button, Open Documents, falls into the latter category and brings some much needed access when working with multiple files. Select Open Documents to see a listing of all files currently open. Unlike the tabs or the list in the Windows menu, the Open Documents list shows the full path of each entry, as shown in Figure 5-19; this is an essential distinction for designers who want pages from multiple directories, and even multiple sites, open at the same time.

FIGURE 5-19

The Coding toolbar's Open Documents feature displays the full path for all currently available files.

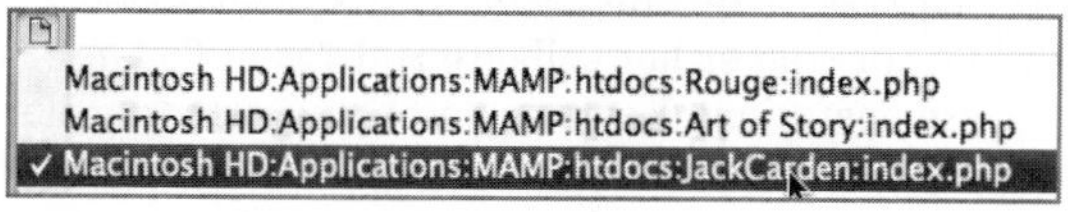

Access to the Code Navigator (discussed in the previous section) is available through the second button in the Coding toolbar. The next series of buttons control a feature called code collapse.

Code collapse

Code collapse is the focus of the next group of buttons in the Coding toolbar. Code collapse allows you to home in on your work by temporarily condensing specific sections of the code into a single line or, alternatively, condensing all but the selection. Hover your cursor over the collapsed element to see the first 10 lines of code in a tooltip (see Figure 5-20).

The three buttons in this group work in concert with your cursor position and selection in Code view:

- **Collapse Full Tag:** Expands the current selection or cursor position to the immediately surrounding tag and collapses the code

- **Collapse Selection:** Reduces the current selection to a collapsed single line
- **Expand All:** Extends all condensed portions of code in the current document

FIGURE 5-20

Code collapse lets you concentrate on just the code you're working on, while keeping the hidden code accessible via tooltips.

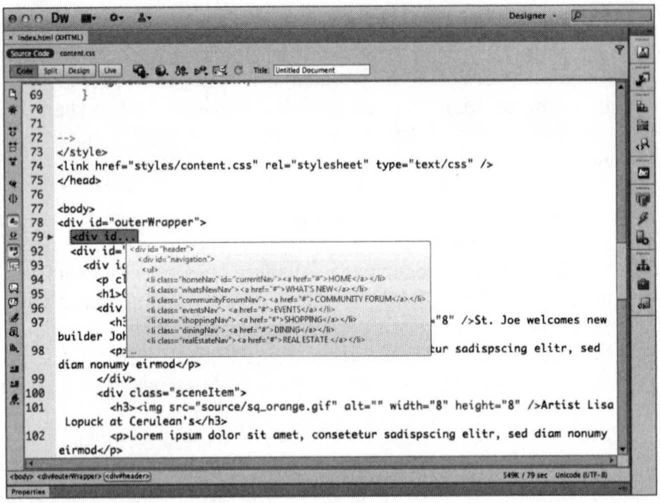

Any code marked as collapsed retains that state after the document has been saved, closed, or re-opened. If you press Alt (Option) while clicking either Collapse Full Tag or Collapse Selection, Dreamweaver inverses the normal collapse operation. For example, if your cursor is placed in a `<div>` tag and you press Alt (Option) while clicking Collapse Full Tag, all the code outside of the current `<div>` tag is collapsed.

You can also expand and collapse code outside of the Coding toolbar. Whenever you select any portion of the code, handles appear at the top and bottom of your selection to the left of the code. Click either of the handles to collapse the code; click the single collapsed handle again to expand it. As noted earlier, you can hover over the collapsed code to see the first 10 lines in a tooltip.

Dreamweaver TECHNIQUE

Collapsing and Moving Code

In this Technique, you use various features of the Coding toolbar, including Dreamweaver's code collapse feature, to make it easy to move code from one place on the page to another.

1. In the Techniques site, expand the 05_Code folder and open the `code_start.htm` file.
2. While in Design view, place your cursor in the first heading, Relative Realty Benefits.
3. Switch to Code view.

4. From the Coding toolbar, click Select Parent Tag (located below the Code Collapse group) once to select the `<h1>` tag and then again to select its parent, `<div id="benefits">`.
5. Click Collapse Full Tag from the Coding toolbar.

   Hover your cursor over the collapsed code to see the hidden code in the tooltip.
6. Place your cursor in the code for the next div, `<div id="reasons">`.
7. Choose Collapse Full Tag again.

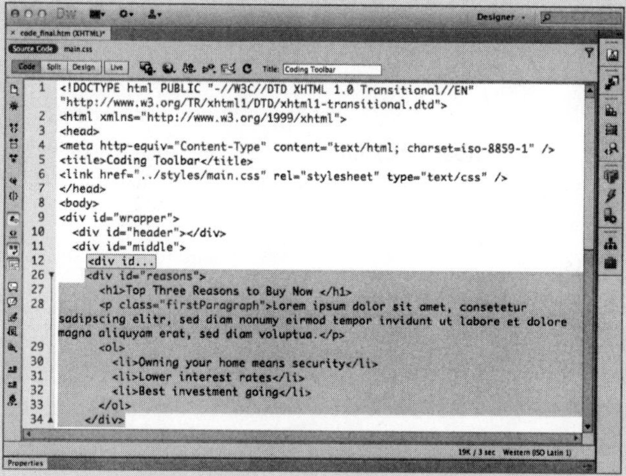

8. Select the code line containing the just-collapsed tag and drag it in front of the first collapsed code.
9. From the Coding toolbar, click Expand All.

   The two different sections of the page have now been switched. One last operation will clean up the look of the code.
10. From the bottom of the Coding toolbar, choose Format Source Code ➪ Apply Source Formatting.
11. Switch to Design view and save your page.

Familiarity with the functions of the Coding toolbar will greatly help your coding productivity.

Code selection and highlight

Coders will appreciate the capability to quickly select and identify different groups of code with the next series of buttons on the Coding toolbar:

- **Select Parent Tag:** Expands the selection from the current cursor position to enclose the surrounding tag.

5

- **Balance Braces:** Selects code within the matching set of parentheses, braces, or square brackets; if the code is nested, click again to select the parentheses, braces, or square brackets.
- **Word Wrap:** Wraps the code at the edge of the Document window.
- **Syntax Error Alerts In Info Bar:** Shows or hides errors in the code in a bar along the top of the Document window.
- **Line Numbers:** Toggles the line numbers on the left of Code view.
- **Highlight Invalid Code:** Marks broken code with a yellow highlight.

The last four options are also found in the View ➪ Code Options menu.

Commenting code

The next two buttons of the Coding toolbar focus on comments. Because Dreamweaver is a web page editor, you'll find a variety of different types of comments available under the first menu button, Apply Comments:

- <!-- HTML Comments -->
- /* CSS or JavaScript block style comments */
- // CSS or JavaScript single line style comments
- ' Visual Basic single line style comments
- ASP-, ASP.NET-, JSP-, PHP-, or ColdFusion-style comments, depending on the application server used

Each of the comment options wraps a selection in the chosen comment style; in the case of single-line style comments, the comments are placed at the start of each selected line. If no code is highlighted, an empty comment of the desired type is inserted.

The Remove Comment button follows Apply Comment. To use, select the entire commented area, including both opening and closing comment tags, and then click Remove Comment. The Remove Comment feature uncomments any selected code and will remove multiple comments unless they are nested. In the case of nested comments, only the outer comments are deleted.

Wrapping tags and inserting snippets

Need a quick way to add a parent tag to a selection? Choose Wrap Tag and you can easily enter the desired outer element, along with any desired attributes and values. Press Enter (Return) to confirm your choices and the parent tag code is inserted.

NOTE

Although the Wrap Tag function resembles the Quick Tag Editor, you cannot use it to toggle between the three different modes as you can in the Quick Tag Editor.

You can wrap content with much more than a single tag through the Recent Snippets button. A snippet is a block of code that has been stored by Dreamweaver and can be inserted at any point. The Recent Snippets feature lists the 10 most recently used snippets, which can be either wrap or block type. For more information about Snippets, see the section "Adding Code Through the Snippets Panel" later in the chapter.

The final buttons on the Coding toolbar are used for styling your code. The Indent Code and Outdent Code buttons move selected code blocks in or out according to the options set in the Code Format category of Preferences. The final button, Format Source Code, allows you to style either the entire document or a selection of your code according to the Code Format Settings—which, along with another code style option, Tag Libraries—is also available under this menu.

Manipulating CSS

CSS has become an integral element of the web designer's tool chest, and its code is frequently entwined with the page's HTML. This, however, is not always a desirable situation, and the Coding toolbar provides two tools to help separate CSS from the code: Convert Inline CSS to Rule and Move CSS.

In the highly pressured work environment that often typifies the creation of a full-featured site, web designers don't always follow best practices. It's not uncommon for designers to temporarily apply an inline style to a tag to try out a particular look. However, by the time the page is pushed live on the web, it's almost always best to move your inline styles to standard rules. The Convert Inline CSS to Rule command is the perfect clean-up tool for just this type of situation.

Your cursor will need to be within a tag that includes an inline style for the Move or Convert CSS ⇨ Convert Inline CSS to Rule command to become active. To refresh your memory, an inline style looks like this:

```
<div id="logoLayer" style="position:absolute; width:232px;
height:39; z-index:2; left: 5px; top: 0px; visibility: visible">
```

Once the command is invoked, the Convert Inline CSS dialog box appears (see Figure 5-21). With it, you can choose to store the inline CSS in a new class, the current tag, or a new CSS selector. You'll also have options for creating the new rule in an existing style sheet or the `<head>` tag of the document.

FIGURE 5-21

Move your inline styles to new rules with the Convert Inline CSS to Rule command.

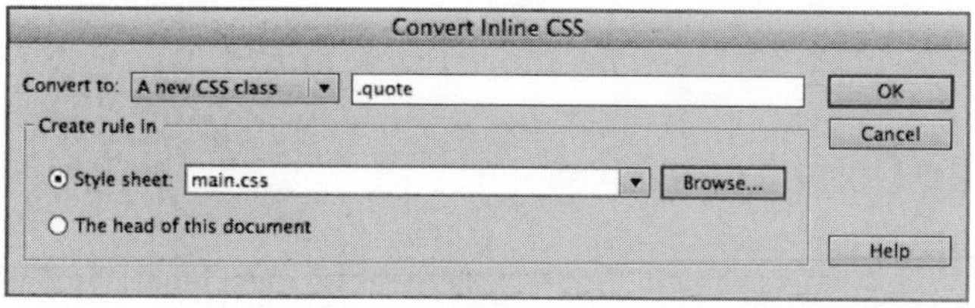

The Move CSS command handles another common pre-launch task: moving embedded styles to an external style sheet. Many designers use embedded styles during the design phase for quicker debugging; for maximum effectiveness, the final styles are removed from the <head> of the document and placed in an external style sheet. The Move CSS command—as the name implies—exports CSS rules from the current location to the external style sheet of your choosing.

To access the Move or Convert CSS ➪ Move CSS command, your cursor must be in or selecting a CSS rule. Typically, the rules you want to move are found in a `<style>` in the head section of the document. The Move CSS command, however, can also be used to move selected styles from one external style sheet to another. Once you have invoked the command, the Move To External Style Sheet dialog box (see Figure 5-22) enables you to select an existing style sheet or a new one. If you choose to create a new style sheet, a Save Style Sheet File As dialog box appears for you to enter a filename and path; the new style sheet is then opened for editing.

FIGURE 5-22

Quickly move your embedded styles to an external style sheet with the Move CSS feature.

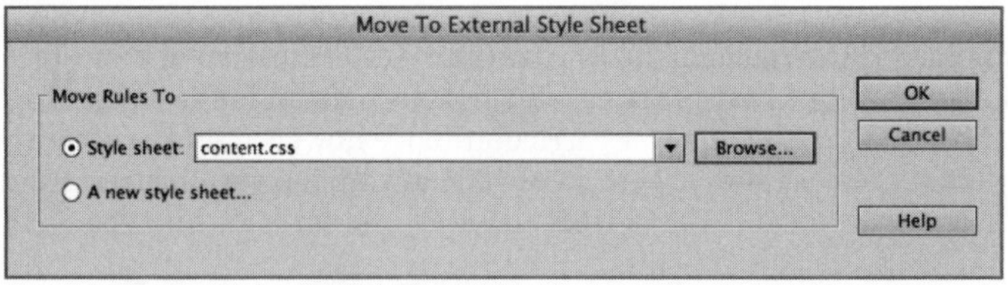

Enhancing Code Authoring Productivity

One of the reasons why the web grew so quickly is that the basic tool for creating web pages was ubiquitous: Any text editor would do. That's still true, but just as you can cut down any tree with a handsaw, that doesn't make it the right tool—the most efficient tool—for the job. Dreamweaver includes numerous features and options that make it a world-class code editor and not just for HTML. The Tag Library feature makes Dreamweaver a terrific code-editing environment for almost any web language, including XHTML, XML, ColdFusion, ASP, ASP.NET, JSP, and PHP. Moreover, the database structure underlying the tag libraries means that the libraries can be expanded or modified at any time. New tags, attributes, and even entire languages can be added by hand or imported in a number of methods, including from a DTD schema.

Dreamweaver's tag libraries offer numerous benefits that greatly enhance the coding experience. Chief among these benefits are Code Hints and Tag Completion.

Code Hints and Tag Completion

Writing code is an exact art. If you enter `<blickquote>` instead of `<blockquote>`, neither Dreamweaver nor the browser renders the tag properly. Perhaps an even bigger problem than misspelling tags and attributes is remembering them all. As more and more developers of static web pages go dynamic, many are finding that the sheer amount of information they need is quite daunting. Don't worry hand-coders: Dreamweaver's Code Hints feature helps you avoid those misspellings and prompts your memory—making you more efficient in the process.

The Code Hints tool is a valuable aid to all web designers, even beginners. It's a quick way to develop a tag as you type it by displaying a pop-up list of tags (as shown in Figure 5-23), attributes, and, in some cases, even values for each tag. Best of all, Code Hints work the way you want to work. If you're a touch-typist, your hands never have to leave the keyboard to accept a particular tag or attribute. If you prefer to use the mouse, you can easily double-click to select your entry. If you like, Dreamweaver even completes your code with an ending tag.

The Code Hints that appear are stored in Dreamweaver's Tag Library database and can be modified by choosing Edit ➪ Tag Libraries. Code Hints are available for the web languages HTML (including XHTML), CFML, ASP.NET, JSP, JRun Custom Library, ASP, PHP, and WML, as well as Dreamweaver templates tags.

FIGURE 5-23

Master the use of the Code Hints feature to give your code writing a major productivity boost.

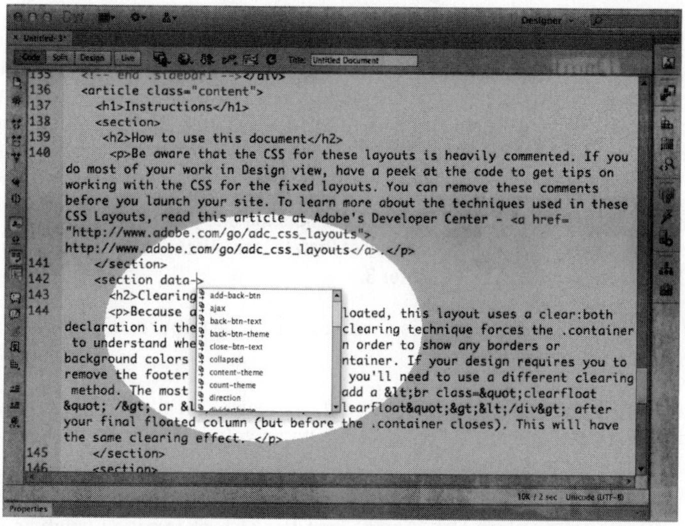

> **Code Hints are enabled by default. To disable them or to control the speed with which the pop-up list appears, choose Edit ➪ Preferences (Dreamweaver ➪ Preferences) and select the Code Hints category. See Chapter 3 for a detailed explanation of all the options.**

When Code Hints is turned on, follow these steps to use this helpful feature:

1. In Code view, enter the opening tag bracket, <. The Code Hint pop-up list instantly shows all the tags for the document type of the current page.
2. To move down the list, type the first letter of the tag. With each letter that you type, Dreamweaver homes in on the indicated tag.
3. When the proper tag is highlighted, press Enter (Return) and the code is inserted. Alternatively, you can scroll down the list and double-click the desired tag to insert it.

4. To add attributes to the tag, enter a space. The attribute list for the current tag is displayed.
5. As with the tag, type until the desired attribute is highlighted in the list and then press Enter (Return). Attributes are, for the most part, followed by an equal sign and a pair of quotes for the value. The cursor is positioned between the quotes.
6. Enter the desired value for the attribute.
7. If the attribute can accept only a certain range of values, such as the `align` attribute, the accepted values also appear in the Code Hints pop-up list. If you choose one of the specified values, the cursor moves to the end of the name-value pair after the closing quote.
8. Enter a space to continue adding attributes or enter the closing tag bracket, >.
9. Insert any content to follow the opening tag.
10. When you're ready to add the closing tag, just type the first two characters </ and Dreamweaver adds the rest of the tag.

Dreamweaver's Tag Completion feature is really quite intelligent and can easily handle any number of nested tags. For example, let's say you start with an opening `<div>` tag and then begin to enter your headings and `<p>` tags. As you enter the closing characters </ after each tag, Dreamweaver completes the proper tag. If you type the closing characters after all other tags are closed, Dreamweaver will finish the final `</div>` tag automatically.

There are actually a couple of different styles of Code Completion and you can choose which one you'd prefer—or none at all—from the Code Hints category of Preferences. All the various options are covered in the section "Customizing Your Code" in Chapter 3.

In addition to straight text, Dreamweaver offers several types of attribute values, each with its own special type of drop-down list:

- **Color:** When a color-related attribute is entered, Dreamweaver displays a color palette and eyedropper cursor for sampling the color. When a color is picked, its corresponding hexadecimal value is entered into the code.
- **Font:** For attributes requiring the name of a font, such as the `<font>` tag's `face` attribute, Dreamweaver displays the current font list of font families (such as Arial, Helvetica, sans serif), as well as an option to edit that list.
- **Style:** Enter the class attribute in almost any tag, and you see a complete list of available CSS styles defined for the current page. Other CSS controls, such as Edit Style Sheet and Attach Style Sheet, are also available.
- **File:** Should an attribute require a filename, Dreamweaver opens the standard Select File dialog box to enable you to easily locate a file or choose a data source.

Code Hints aren't just for entering new tags; you can take advantage of their prompting when modifying existing code as well. To add an attribute, place your cursor just before the closing bracket and press the spacebar to trigger the Code Hints pop-up menu. To change an entered value, delete both the value and the surrounding quotes; the pop-up options appear after the opening quote is entered.

Modifying blocks of code

When it comes to coding, mindless repetition is one big time-killer. Quite often, you repeat the same function—such as converting all the tags to lowercase—for a section of your code. These types of procedures quickly become tedious, and performing them one at a time is grossly inefficient. For commonly performed operations, Dreamweaver has a far better way.

The Selection menu is activated in Dreamweaver's shortcut menu whenever a section of code is highlighted. Twenty-seven varied, but extremely useful, functions are available, as shown in Figure 5-24. All the procedures take effect immediately and require no further dialog box or interaction. Just select the code and choose the operation, and you're done. The Selection functions are especially helpful when cleaning imported code or when converting code to text or vice versa.

The Selection menu includes the following:

- **Collapse Selection:** Collapses the selected code
- **Collapse Outside Selection:** Collapses all but the selected code
- **Expand Selection:** Expands any collapsed code inside the selection
- **Collapse Full Tag:** Collapses the nearest parent tag
- **Collapse Outside Full Tag:** Collapses all but the nearest parent tag
- **Expand All:** Expands all collapsed code in the document
- **Apply HTML Comment:** Inserts an HTML comment: <!-- -->

FIGURE 5-24

Quickly alter the formatting or modify the code itself of any selected code block through the Selection commands.

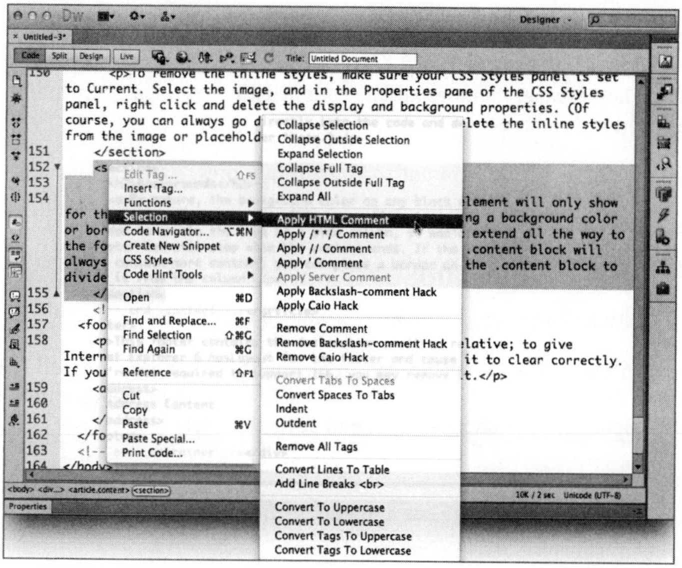

- **Apply /* */ Comment:** Inserts a multiline JavaScript/CSS comment: `/* */`.
- **Apply // Comment:** Inserts a single-line JavaScript/CSS comment at the start of a code line: `//`.
- **Apply ' Comment:** Inserts a single-line ASP comment at the start of a code line: `'`.
- **Apply Server Comment:** Inserts a comment applicable to the current server model.
- **Apply Backslash-Comment Hack:** Adds a CSS hack to hide styles from Internet Explorer for the Mac 4.x.
- **Apply Caio Hack:** Adds a CSS hack to hide styles from Netscape 4.x.
- **Remove Comment:** Removes any kind of comment in the current selection.
- **Remove Backslash-Comment Hack:** Removes a previously applied Backslash-comment hack.
- **Remove Caio Hack:** Removes a previously applied Caio hack.
- **Convert Tabs To Spaces:** Changes every tab used for indenting to four spaces.
- **Convert Spaces To Tabs:** Substitutes a tab for every four spaces.
- **Indent:** Indents the code block one tab stop.
- **Outdent:** Outdents the selected code one tab stop.
- **Remove All Tags:** Strips all tags from a code block, leaving the content.
- **Convert Lines To Table:** Places each individual line, separated by a carriage return, into a table row and the entire code selection in a table.
- **Add Line Breaks <br>:** Inserts a `<br>` tag at the end of every line; if the page is XHTML-compliant, the `<br />` tag is used instead.
- **Convert To Uppercase:** Changes the selected code block—both tags and content—to uppercase.
- **Convert To Lowercase:** Lowercases the selection of code, including all the tags and content.
- **Convert Tags To Uppercase:** Uppercases only the tags in the current selection; all code within the tag, including attributes and values, are uppercased.
- **Convert Tags To Lowercase:** Changes all the code within tags (again, including attributes and values) to lowercase.

If the results of your Selection operation are not to your liking, press Ctrl+Z (Command+Z) to undo the command.

Inserting code with the Tag Chooser

If you'd rather point and click than type, Dreamweaver has you covered.

With the Dreamweaver Tag Chooser, you have access to all the standard tags in HTML/XHTML, CFML, ASP.NET, JSP, JRun Custom Library, ASP, PHP, and WML, and the Adobe-specific tags for Dreamweaver templates. Open the Tag Chooser in one of several ways:

- Choose Insert ➪ Tag.
- Right-click (Control+click) in Code view and choose Insert Tag from the context menu.
- Press the keyboard shortcut Ctrl+E (Command+E).

- Position your cursor where you'd like the tag to appear—in either Code or Design view—and select Tag Chooser from the Insert panel's Common category.
- Drag the Tag Chooser button from the Insert panel's Common category to the appropriate place in either Code or Design view.

The tags are grouped under their respective languages. Select any of the languages from the list on the left and all the available tags display on the right. Most of the languages have a plus sign or disclosure triangle that, when selected, expands the chosen language and displays various functional groupings of tags, such as Page Composition, Lists, and Tables, as shown in the background of Figure 5-25. Under HTML Tags, you can expand the tag groupings further to see, in some cases, tags separated into additional categories such as General, Browser-Specific, and Deprecated.

If you're confused about what a specific tag is for or how it's used, click the Tag Info button. The bottom half of the dialog box converts to a context-sensitive reference panel. Exactly what information is available depends on the tag itself. For most HTML tags, you find a description, examples, and a list of browsers in which the tag is recognized. Much of the information available is also available in the Reference panel (covered later in this chapter); however, not all tags are covered.

When you've chosen a tag and either double-clicked it or selected Insert, the Tag Editor opens. Each tag has its own user interface with full accessibility and CSS options. As shown in Figure 5-25, selecting a category from the list on the left displays the available options on the right.

FIGURE 5-25

When you select your page element from the Tag Chooser (background), you have a wealth of options in the Tag Editor (foreground).

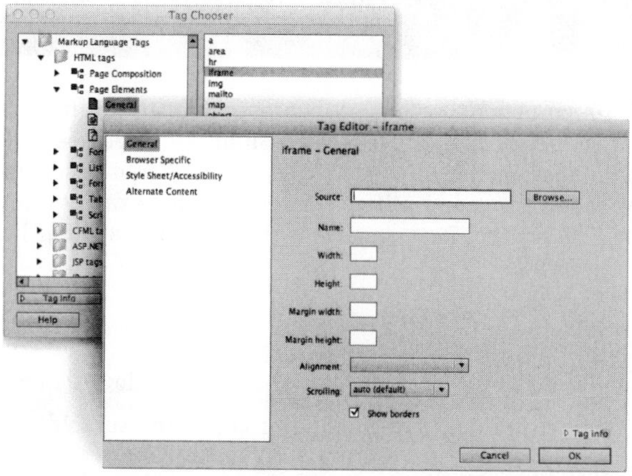

NOTE
Custom tags or attributes entered into the Tag Library are not displayed in the Tag Chooser.

5

After you enter all the desired parameters in the Tag Editor, click OK to insert the code into the page with the cursor in between the opening and the closing tags (or after the tag if it is empty). The Tag Chooser uses a nonmodal window and remains open until Close is selected.

CAUTION

Because the Tag Chooser is nonmodal, you may not realize that you have already inserted the desired tag, causing you to select Insert again. Dreamweaver does not prevent you from entering multiple versions of the same tag.

Adding Code Through the Snippets Panel

Using the valuable Snippets feature, you can save portions of HTML code for easy recall in other files. It's a lot easier than copying and pasting blocks of code from various files. Tag snippets range from a single tag, such as an HTML comment, to a full navigation layout. Commonly used JavaScript and other language functions and methods are also good candidates to be turned into snippets for later use.

Dreamweaver provides a notable assortment of snippets, but the most important aspect of this feature is that it's extensible. Coders and noncoders alike can easily add any commonly used section of code for later reuse. Snippets work in one of two different ways: A snippet either inserts a solid code block at the cursor point or wraps a selection with before and after code.

NOTE

Code snippets that include deprecated tags (such as `<font>`) or outdated JavaScript routines have been relocated to the ~Legacy folder in the Snippets panel.

By default, the Snippets panel is found under the Code panel group; to open it directly, choose Window ➪ Snippets or use the keyboard shortcut Shift+F9. The Snippets panel (see Figure 5-26) shows a preview of the selected snippet. If the snippet itself is not rendered onscreen, like a JavaScript function, the preview shows the code itself; otherwise, you see exactly what the code looks like on the page, minus any CSS styling. Rearrange your snippets by dragging them within the panel, from folder to folder, if you like.

To insert a snippet, follow these steps:

1. Display the Snippets panel if it's not already open by choosing Window ➪ Snippets.
2. Find the desired snippet by expanding the folder and, if necessary, subfolders.
3. To insert a snippet as a block of code:
   a. Position the cursor where you'd like the code to appear.
   b. Double-click the snippet (or Snippet icon) or select the snippet and click Insert.

   Alternatively, you can drag the snippet into position in either Code view or Design view.

FIGURE 5-26

Use the handy Snippets panel to quickly reuse portions of your code.

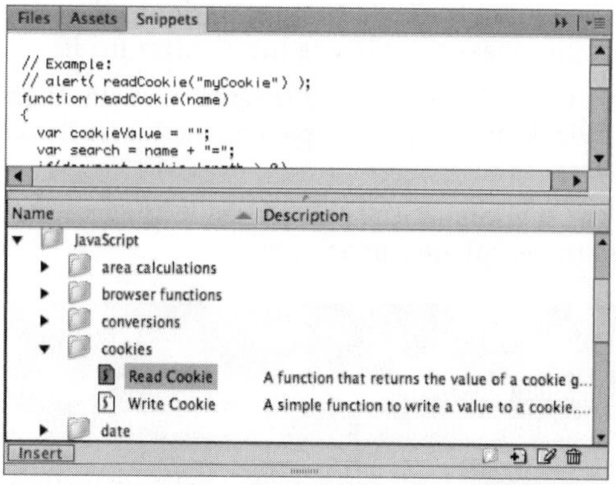

4. To wrap a snippet around some existing code or page elements:
   a. Select the code or elements.
   b. Double-click the snippet or select the snippet and click Insert.

   Again, you can drag the snippet onto the selected code.

> **TIP**
> You can quickly hide a section of a page by selecting it and then choosing the Comment, Multiline snippet from the Comments category of the Snippets panel.

Although Dreamweaver's standard code snippets are handy, you don't realize the real value of the Snippets panel until you begin adding your own snippets. To help you manage your snippets, Dreamweaver enables you to create new folders, rename existing ones, or delete ones no longer needed. All this functionality is available through the options menu on the Snippets panel, as well as through the context menu. Snippets, as well as folders, can be renamed, deleted, edited, and, of course, created.

> **TIP**
> Before you begin to create your own code snippet, select it first. The Snippets dialog box is modal, and you cannot access other Dreamweaver windows while it is open. The selected code is copied to the Insert Before text field.

To save code as a snippet, follow these steps:

1. Click the New Snippet button on the bottom of the Snippets panel.
2. Enter a name to be displayed in the Snippets panel in the Name field.
3. If you like, you can enter a brief description of the snippet in the Description field.

5

4. Choose the type of snippet you're creating: Wrap Selection or Insert Block. The dialog box changes depending on your choice.
5. If you chose Wrap Selection, enter the code to appear prior to the selection in the Insert Before field, and the code to appear after in the Insert After field.
6. If you chose Insert Block, enter the code in the Insert Code field. If you switch from Wrap Selection to Insert Block, Dreamweaver appends the Insert Before field with the contents of the Insert After field.
7. Choose how you would like the snippet to be displayed in the preview area of the Snippets panel, rendered in Design view or as code.

CAUTION

If you choose the Design preview option for code that does not display in a browser, such as a JavaScript function, it won't be as readable. You still see the code in the preview area, but it does not appear in a monospace font, and all whitespace formatting (such as tabs) appears to be lost.

8. Click OK when you're finished.

You'll remember that when hand-coding, the last 10 used snippets are available directly from the Coding toolbar's Recent Snippets command.

Using the Reference Panel

Pop quiz: What value of a form tag's `enctype` attribute should you use if the user is submitting a file?

A. `application/x-www-form-urlencoded`

B. `multipart/form-data`

C. `multipart/data-form`

Unless you've recently had to include such a form in a web page, you probably had to pull down that well-worn HTML reference book you keep handy and look up the answer. All code for the web—including HTML, JavaScript, and Cascading Style Sheets (CSS)—must be precisely written or it is, at best, ignored; at worst, an error is generated whenever the user views the page. Even the savviest of web designers can't remember the syntax of every tag, attribute, and value in HTML, every function in JavaScript; or every style rule in CSS. A good reference is a necessity in web design. (By the way, the answer to the pop quiz is B.)

Adobe has lightened the load on your bookshelf considerably with the addition of the Reference panel, shown in Figure 5-27. With the Reference panel, you can quickly look up any HTML tag and its attributes, as well as JavaScript objects and CSS style rules. Dynamic site builders can rely on references for CFML, ASP, PHP, JSP, XML, and XSLT. In addition, the panel contains a complete reference on web-related accessibility issues from UsableNet. Not only does the Reference panel offer the proper syntax for any code in question, it also displays the level of browser support available in most situations. Moreover, you don't have to dig through the tag lists to find the information you need—just highlight the tag or object in question and press the keyboard shortcut Shift+F1.

FIGURE 5-27

To quickly look up a tag, select it in the Tag Selector or in Code view and then press Shift+F1 to open the Reference panel.

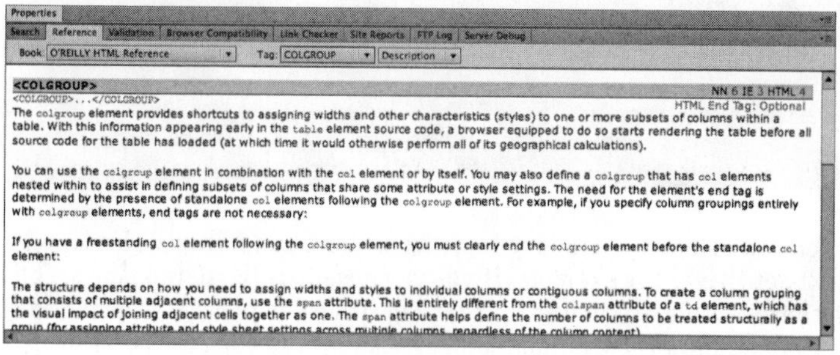

You have three different ways to open the Reference panel:

- Choose Window ➪ Reference.
- Click the Reference button on the toolbar.
- Use the Shift+F1 keyboard shortcut.

TIP

To find reference details for the attributes of an HTML tag, a JavaScript object, or a CSS style rule included on a web page, open Code view and select the code in question prior to choosing Shift+F1 or clicking the Reference button on the toolbar.

To look for information about code not included in the page, follow these steps:

1. Display the Reference panel by choosing Window ➪ Results ➪ Reference or using the keyboard shortcut Shift+F1. The Reference panel appears as a tab in the Results panel.
2. Select the required guide from the Book drop-down list. The standard options are as follows:
   - Adobe ColdFusion Function Reference
   - Adobe CFML Reference
   - O'Reilly ASP Reference
   - O'Reilly ASP.NET Reference
   - O'Reilly CSS Reference
   - O'Reilly HTML Reference
   - O'Reilly JavaScript Reference
   - O'Reilly JSP Reference
   - O'Reilly PHP Pocket Reference
   - O'Reilly SQL Language Reference
   - O'Reilly XML in a Nutshell
   - O'Reilly XSLT Reference
   - UsableNet Accessibility Reference

3. Choose the primary topic from the Style/Tag/Object drop-down list. The list heading changes depending on which book is selected.

TIP

You can move quickly to a topic by selecting the drop-down list and then pressing the key for the first letter of the term being sought. Then you can use the down arrow to move through items that start with that letter. For example, if you were looking for information about the JavaScript regular expressions object, you could press r and then the down arrow to reach RegExp.

4. If desired, you can select a secondary topic from the second drop-down list. The second list is context-sensitive. For example, if you've chosen an HTML tag, the secondary list displays all the available attributes for that tag. If you've chosen a JavaScript object, the secondary list shows the available properties for that object. The information shown depends, naturally, on the book, topic, and subtopic chosen.

The Reference panel's context menu enables you to switch between three different font sizes: small, medium, and large. This capability is especially useful when working at resolutions higher than 800 × 600. You also have an option to connect directly to O'Reilly Books Online.

TIP

Any code in the Reference panel can be copied by right-clicking (Control-clicking) and choosing Copy. Dreamweaver automatically selects the entire code block with a single click, ready to be copied.

Modifying Code with the Tag Inspector

Since Dreamweaver's beginning, one of my favorite features has been the Property inspector. I really appreciate how it adapts for a selected tag. However, the Property inspector is not without its drawbacks. The feature's main deficiency is key to its design—the Property inspector has only a limited amount of room. To encompass the full range of possible attributes for all the possible tags, Dreamweaver needs a more wide-open solution. Enter the Tag inspector.

The Tag inspector (Window ➪ Tag Inspector) is a panel that, like the Property inspector, displays the attributes of the selected tag. The Tag inspector, however, presents the attributes and values in the same two-column layout regardless of the selection: attributes on the left and values on the right. Any displayed attribute can be modified through the Tag inspector—simply click into the attribute's value field to make a change. After you've clicked elsewhere or pressed Enter (Return) to move to the next attribute, the attribute/value pair is written into your tag.

Value fields are not just simple text fields, although you can enter the attribute by hand if you want. The value fields change according to the type of attribute. Attributes that can use a predefined value display a pop-up list with all the possible values; for example, click an `<a>` tag and the pop-up value list for the `lang` attribute contains entries for all the possible languages, including `en` for English (as shown in Figure 5-28). Such pop-up lists are also editable—which means you can enter a value not in the list. Color-type attributes, such as `bgcolor`, offer the Adobe standard color picker, whereas attributes requiring a filename display both Browse To File (the folder) and Point To File (the crosshairs) icons. All value fields include a lightning bolt icon for inserting dynamic data, such as a field, from a recordset.

You can view the attributes in one of two ways: by category or alphabetically. Two buttons at the top of the panel control the view; click the one on the left to see a breakdown of attributes by categories (General, CSS/Accessibility, Language, ICE, Spry, jQueryMobile, GlobalAttributes, Accessibility, and Uncategorized). The A-to-Z button on the right lists the attributes alphabetically.

FIGURE 5-28

Use the Tag inspector to quickly modify any or all attributes of any tag on the page.

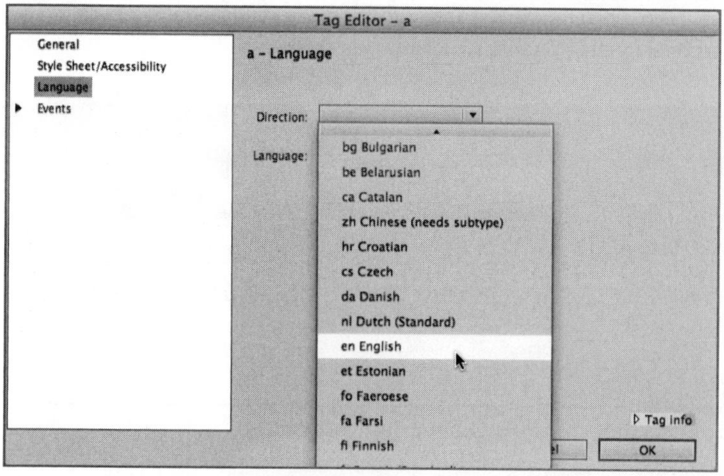

TIP

Attributes that Dreamweaver is unaware of can be added by entering them into the last row of the Tag inspector. To remove an existing attribute, select it and press Backspace (Delete).

Rapid Tag Modification with the Quick Tag Editor

I tend to build web pages in two phases. Generally, I first lay out my text and images to create the overall design, and then I add details and make alterations to get the page just right. The second phase of web page design often requires that I make a small adjustment to the HTML code, typically through the Property inspector, but occasionally I need to go right to the source—the code.

Dreamweaver offers a feature for making minor, but essential, alterations to the code: the Quick Tag Editor. The Quick Tag Editor is a small pop-up window that appears in the Document window and enables you to edit an existing tag, add a new tag, or wrap the current selection in a tag.

5

One other feature makes the Quick Tag Editor even quicker to use: A handy list of tags or attributes cuts down on typing.

To call up the Quick Tag Editor, use any of the following methods:

- Choose Modify ➪ Quick Tag Editor.
- Press the keyboard shortcut Ctrl+T (Command+T).
- Click the Quick Tag Editor icon on the Property inspector.

The Quick Tag Editor has three modes: Insert HTML, Wrap Tag, and Edit HTML. Although you can get to all three modes from any situation, which mode appears initially depends on the current selection. The Quick Tag Editor's window (see Figure 5-29) appears above the current selection when you use either the menu or the keyboard method of opening it or next to the Property inspector when you click the icon. In either case, you can move the Quick Tag Editor window to a new location onscreen by dragging its title bar.

TIP

Regardless of which mode the Quick Tag Editor opens in, you can toggle to the other modes by pressing the keyboard shortcut Ctrl+T (Command+T).

The Quick Tag Editor offers built-in code hinting, just like that found in Code view. See the sidebar "Working with the Hint List" later in this chapter for details about this feature.

FIGURE 5-29

The Quick Tag Editor is great for quickly tweaking your code.

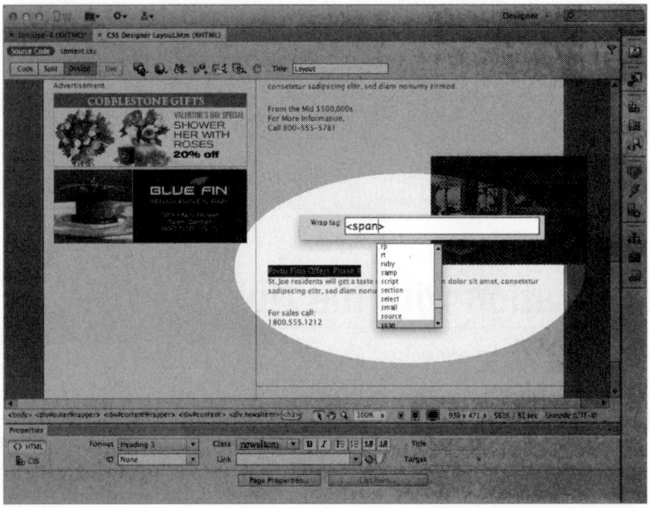

Insert HTML mode

The Insert HTML mode of the Quick Tag Editor is used for adding new tags and code at the current cursor position; it is the initial mode when nothing is selected. The Insert HTML mode starts with a pair of angle brackets enclosing a blinking cursor. You can enter any tag—whether standard HTML or custom XML—and any attribute or content within the new tag. When you're finished, just press Enter (Return) to confirm your addition.

To add new tags to your page using the Quick Tag Editor Insert HTML mode, follow these steps:

1. Position your cursor where you would like the new code to be inserted.
2. Choose Modify ➪ Quick Tag Editor or use the keyboard shortcut Ctrl+T (Command+T) to open the Quick Tag Editor. The Quick Tag Editor opens in Insert HTML mode, as shown in Figure 5-30.
3. Enter your HTML or XML code.

FIGURE 5-30

Use the Quick Tag Editor's Insert HTML mode to add tags not available through Dreamweaver's visual interface.

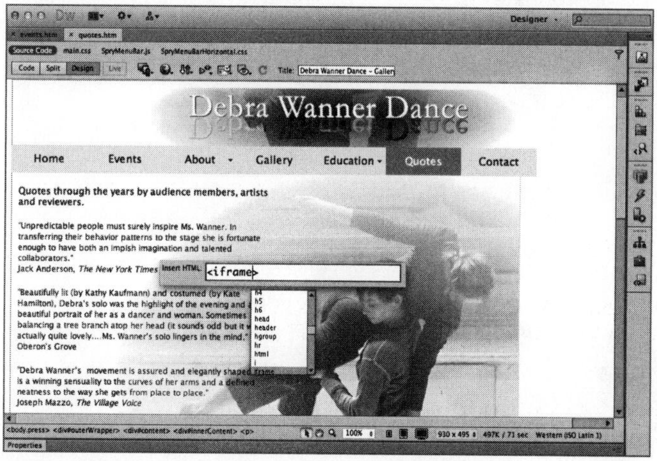

> **TIP**
> Use the right arrow key to move quickly past the closing angle bracket and add text after your tag.

4. If you pause while typing, the hint list appears, selecting the first tag that matches what you've typed so far. Use the arrow keys to select another tag in the list and press Enter (Return) to select a tag.
5. Press Enter (Return) when you're finished.

5

The Quick Tag Editor is fairly intelligent and tries to help you write valid HTML. If, for example, you leave off a closing tag, such as `</strong>`, the Quick Tag Editor automatically adds it for you.

Wrap Tag mode

Part of the power and flexibility of HTML is the capability to wrap one tag around other tags and content. To make a phrase appear bold and italic—or as the best web practices have it, strong and emphasized, respectively—the code is written as follows:

```
<strong><em>On Sale Now!</em></strong>
```

Note how the inner `<em> . . . </em>` tag pair is enclosed by the `<strong> . . . </strong>` pair. The Wrap Tag mode of the Quick Tag Editor surrounds any selection with your entered tag in one easy operation.

Working with the Hint List

The Quick Tag Editor has a rather nifty feature referred to as the *hint list*. To make it even quicker to use the Quick Tag Editor, a list of tags pops up when you pause in your typing. When you're entering attributes within a tag, a list of appropriate parameters pops up instead of tags. These lists are tied to what, if anything, you've already typed. Suppose, for instance, you've begun to enter `blockquote` and have only gotten as far as typing `b` and `l`. When the hint list appears, it scrolls to blink—the first tag in the list starting with those two letters. If you continue typing `o`, `blockquote` is selected. All you have to do to insert it into your code is press Enter (Return).

Following are a few other hint list hints:

- Scroll to a tag by using the up or down arrow keys.
- Double-clicking the selected hint list item also inserts it into the code.
- After the hint list is open, press Esc if you decide not to enter the selected tag or attribute.
- If an attribute has a set series of values that can be applied (for example, the `<div>` tag's `align` attribute can only be set to left, right, or center), those values are accessible via the hint list.
- Control how quickly the hint list appears—or even whether it appears at all—by altering the Quick Tag Editor preferences.

The Wrap Tag mode appears initially when you have selected just text (with no surrounding tags) or an incomplete tag (the opening tag and contents, but no closing tag). The Wrap Tag mode is visually similar to the Insert HTML mode, as you can see in Figure 5-31.

However, rather than just include exactly what you've entered into the Quick Tag Editor, Wrap Tag mode also inserts a closing tag that corresponds to your entry. For example, you want to apply a tag not available as an object: the subscript, or `<sub>`, tag. After highlighting the text that you want to mark up as subscript (the 2 in the formula H_2O, for example), you open the Quick Tag Editor and enter `sub`. The resulting code looks like the following:

```
H<sub>2</sub>0
```

CAUTION

You can enter only one tag in Wrap Tag mode; if more than one tag is entered, Dreamweaver displays an alert informing you that the tag you've entered appears to be invalid HTML. The Quick Tag Editor is then closed, and the selection is cleared.

FIGURE 5-31

Enclose any selection with a tag by using the Quick Tag Editor's Wrap Tag mode.

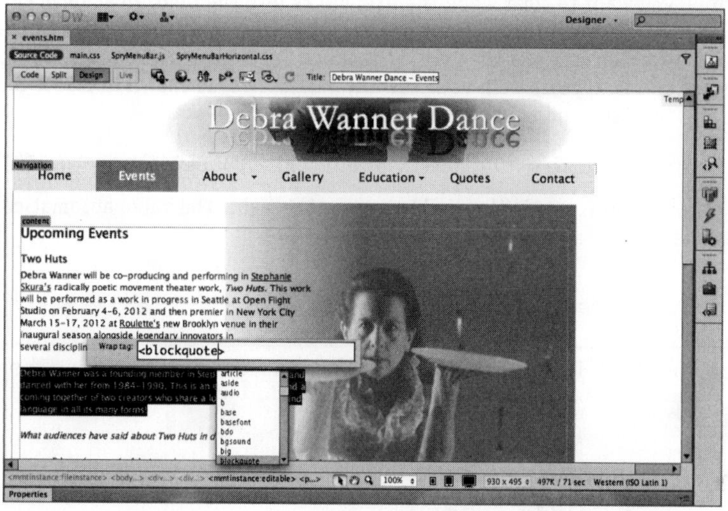

To wrap a tag with the Quick Tag Editor, follow these steps:

1. Select the text or tags you want to enclose in another tag.
2. Choose Modify ⇨ Quick Tag Editor or use the keyboard shortcut Ctrl+T (Command+T) to open the Quick Tag Editor.
3. If you select a complete tag, the Quick Tag Editor opens in Edit Tag mode; press the keyboard shortcut Ctrl+T (Command+T) to toggle to Wrap Tag mode.
4. Enter the tag you want.
5. If you pause while typing, the hint list appears. It selects the first tag that matches what you've typed so far. Use the arrow keys to select another tag in the list and press Enter (Return) to select a tag from the hint list.
6. Press Enter (Return) to confirm your tag.

   The Quick Tag Editor closes, and Dreamweaver places the tag before your selection and a corresponding closing tag after it.

5

Edit Tag mode

If a complete tag—either a single tag, such as `<img>`, or a tag pair, such as `<h1> ... </h1>`—is selected, the Quick Tag Editor opens in Edit Tag mode. Unlike the other two modes (in which you are presented with just open and closing angle brackets and a flashing cursor), the Edit Tag mode displays the entire selected tag with all its attributes, if any. You can always invoke the Edit Tag mode when you start the Quick Tag Editor by clicking its icon in the Property inspector.

The Edit Tag mode has many uses. It's excellent for adding a parameter not found on Dreamweaver's Property inspector. For example, when you are building a form, some text fields have pre-existing text in them—which you want to clear when the user clicks into the field. To achieve this effect, you add a minor bit of JavaScript, a perfect use for the Edit Tag mode. Therefore, you can just select the `<i>` tag from the Tag Selector and then click the Quick Tag Editor icon to open the Quick Tag Editor. The `<imgnput>` tag appears with your current parameters, as shown in Figure 5-32. After you have opened it, tab to the end of the tag and enter this code:

```
onFocus="if(this.value=='Email Required')this.value='';"
```

In this example, `Email Required` is the visible text in the field. The value automatically clears when the field is selected.

FIGURE 5-32

In Edit Tag mode, the Quick Tag Editor shows the entire tag, with attributes and their values.

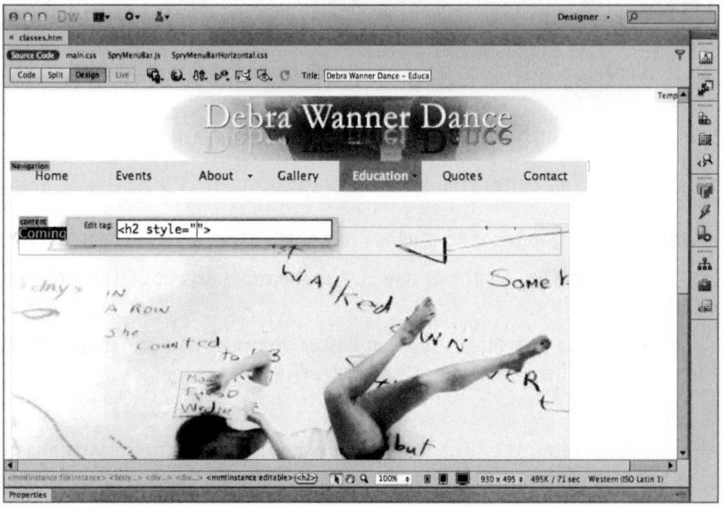

To use the Quick Tag Editor in Insert HTML mode, follow these steps:

1. Select an entire tag by clicking its name in the Tag Selector.
2. Choose Modify ➪ Quick Tag Editor.

3. To change an existing attribute, tab to the current value and enter a new one.
4. To add a new attribute, tab and/or use the arrow keys to position the cursor after an existing attribute or after the tag, and enter the new parameter and value.

TIP

If you don't close the quotation marks for a parameter's value, Dreamweaver does it for you.

5. If you pause briefly while entering a new attribute, the hint list appears with attributes appropriate for the current tag. If you select an attribute from the hint list, press Enter (Return) to accept the parameter.
6. When you've finished editing the tag, press Enter (Return).

In addition to this capability to edit complete tags, Dreamweaver has a couple of navigational commands to help select just the right tag. The Select Parent Tag command—keyboard shortcut Ctrl+[(Command+[)—highlights the tag immediately surrounding the present tag. Going in the other direction, the Select Child Tag—keyboard shortcut Ctrl+] (Command+])—selects the next tag, if any, contained within the current tag. Both commands are available under the Edit menu. Exercising these commands is equivalent to selecting the next tag in the Tag Selector to the left (parent) or right (child).

CAUTION

Although it works well in Design view, unfortunately the Select Child command does not function in Code view.

Adding Java Applets

Java is a platform-independent programming language originally developed by Sun Microsystems. Although Java can also be used to write entire applications, its most frequent role is on the web in the form of an applet. An *applet* is a self-contained program that can be run within a web page.

Java is a compiled programming language similar to C++. After a Java applet is compiled, it is saved as a class file. Web browsers call Java applets through, aptly enough, the `<applet>` tag. When you insert an applet, you refer to the primary class file much as you call a graphic file for an image tag.

Each Java applet has its own unique set of parameters—and Dreamweaver enables you to enter as many as necessary in the same manner as plugins and ActiveX controls. In fact, the Applet object works almost identically to the Plugin and ActiveX objects.

CAUTION

Keep two caveats in mind if you're planning to include Java applets in your website. First, most (but not all) browsers support some version of Java—the newest release has the most features, but the least support. Second, all the browsers that support Java offer the user the option of disabling it because of security issues. Be sure to use the `Alt` property to designate an alternative image or some text for display by browsers that do not support Java.

A Java applet can be inserted in a web page with a bare minimum of parameters: the code source and the dimensions of the object. Java applets derive much of their power from their configurability, and most of these little programs have numerous custom parameters. As with plugins and ActiveX controls, Dreamweaver enables you to specify the basic attributes through the Property inspector and the custom ones via the Parameters dialog box.

To include a Java applet in your web page, follow these steps:

1. Position the cursor where you want the applet to originate and choose Insert ➪ Media ➪ Applet. You can also click the Insert Applet button from the Media group on the Common category of the Insert panel. The Insert Applet dialog box opens.
2. From the Select File dialog box, enter the path to your class file in the File Name text box or click the Browse button to locate the file. An Applet object placeholder appears in the Document window. In the Applet Property inspector (see Figure 5-33), the selected source file appears in the Code text box, and the folder appears in the Base text box.

FIGURE 5-33

Use the Insert Applet button to insert a Java Applet object and display the Applet Property inspector.

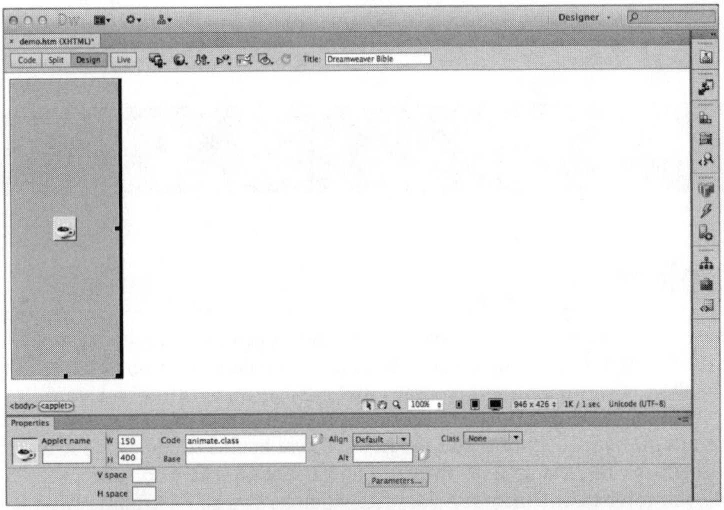

NOTE

The path to your Java class files cannot be expressed absolutely; it must be given as an address relative to the web page that is calling it.

3. Enter the height and width of the Applet object in the H and W text boxes, respectively. You can also resize the Applet object by clicking and dragging any of its three sizing handles.
4. You can enter any of the usual basic attributes, such as a name for the object, as well as values for Align, V, and/or H Space in the appropriate text boxes in the Property inspector.

5. If you want, enter the online directory where the applet code can be found in the Base text box. If none is specified, the document's URL is assumed to be this attribute, known as the *codebase*.
6. To display an alternative image if the Java applet is unable to run (typically, because the user's browser does not support Java or the user has disabled Java), enter the path to the image in the Alt field. You can use the folder icon to locate the image as well. Text may also serve as the alternative content if you don't want to use an image. Any text entered into the Alt field is displayed in the browser as a tooltip.
7. To enter any custom attributes, click the Parameters button to open the Parameters dialog box.
8. Click the Add (+) button and enter the first parameter. Press Tab to move to the Value column.
9. Enter the value for the parameter, if any. Press Tab.
10. Continue entering parameters in the left column, with their values in the right. Click OK when you've finished.

TIP

Because of the importance of displaying alternative content for users not running Java, Dreamweaver provides a method for displaying something for everyone. To display an image, enter the URL to a graphics file in the Alt text box. To display text and an image, you have to do a little hand-coding. First select a graphics file to insert in the Alt text box and then open Code view. In the `<img>` tag found between the `<applet>` tags, add an `alt="your_message"` attribute by hand (where the text you want to display is the value for the `alt` attribute). Now your Java applet displays an image for browsers that are graphics-enabled but not Java-enabled, and text for text-only browsers such as Lynx. In this sample code, I've bolded the additional `alt` attribute.

```
<applet code="animate.class" width="100" height="100"><param name="img1"
    value="/images/1.jpg"><param name="img2" value="/images/2.jpg"><img
    src="animation.gif" alt="Animate for Life!" width="100" height="100"></applet>
```

Some Java class files have additional graphics files. In most cases, you store both the class files and the graphics files in the same folder.

Managing JavaScript and VBScript

When initially developed by Netscape, JavaScript was called LiveScript. This browser-oriented language did not gain importance until Sun Microsystems joined the development team and the product was renamed JavaScript. Although the rechristening was a stroke of marketing genius, it has caused endless confusion among beginning programmers—JavaScript and Java have almost nothing in common outside of their capability to be incorporated in a web page. JavaScript is used primarily to add functionality on the client-side of the browser (for tasks such as verifying form data and adding interactivity to interface elements). Java, on the other hand, is an application-development language that can be used for a wide variety of tasks.

Conversely, VBScript is a full-featured Microsoft product. Both VBScript and JavaScript are scripting languages, which means that you can write the code in any text editor and compile it at runtime.

JavaScript enjoys more support than VBScript. JavaScript can be rendered by all modern browsers, whereas VBScript is read only by Internet Explorer on Windows systems and is rarely used today. In Dreamweaver, both types of code are inserted in the web page in the same manner.

Inserting JavaScript and VBScript

If only mastering JavaScript or VBScript were as easy as inserting the code in Dreamweaver! Simply go to the Script menu on the Common category of the Insert panel and click the Script button, or choose Insert ➪ HTML ➪ Script Objects ➪ Script and enter your code in the Insert Script dialog box. After you click OK, a Script icon appears in place of your script.

Of course, JavaScript or VBScript instruction is beyond the scope of this book, but every working web designer must have an understanding of what these languages can do. Both languages refer to and, to varying degrees, manipulate the information on a web page. Over time, you can expect significant growth in the capabilities of the JavaScript and VBScript disciplines.

Dreamweaver behaviors have been instrumental in making JavaScript useful for nonprogrammers. To learn more about behaviors, see Chapter 11.

Use the Script Property inspector (see Figure 5-34) to select an external file for your JavaScript or VBScript code. You can also set the language type by opening the Language drop-down list from the Script window and choosing either JavaScript or VBScript. Because different features are available in the various releases of JavaScript, you can also specify JavaScript 1.1 through 1.5. Choose a specific version of JavaScript when you initially insert the script—you cannot change the setting from the Script Property inspector. Naturally, you can also make the adjustment in Code view.

When you choose JavaScript or VBScript as your Language type, Dreamweaver writes the code accordingly. Both languages use the `<script>` tag pair, and each is specified in the `language` attribute, as follows:

```
<script language="JavaScript">alert("Look Out!")</script>
```

With Dreamweaver, you are not restricted to inserting code in just the `<body>` section of your web page. Many JavaScript and VBScript functions must be located in the `<head>` section. To insert this type of script, first choose View ➪ Head Content. Next, select the now visible `<head>` window and choose Insert ➪ HTML ➪ Script Objects ➪ Script, or click the Insert Script object. Enter your script as described earlier in this section and then select the main Document window, or choose View ➪ Head Content again to deselect it.

You can also indicate whether your script is based on the client-side or server-side by choosing the Type option from the Property inspector. If you choose server-side, your script is enclosed in `<server> ... </server>` tags and is interpreted by the web server hosting the page.

Editing JavaScript and VBScript

Dreamweaver provides a large editing window for modifying your script code. To open this Script Properties window, select the placeholder icon for the script you want to modify and then click the Edit button on the Script Property inspector. You have the same functionality in the Script Properties window as in the Script Property inspector; namely, you can choose your language or link to an external script file (see Figure 5-35).

FIGURE 5-34

The generous Script dialog box provides plenty of room for modifying your JavaScript or VBScript.

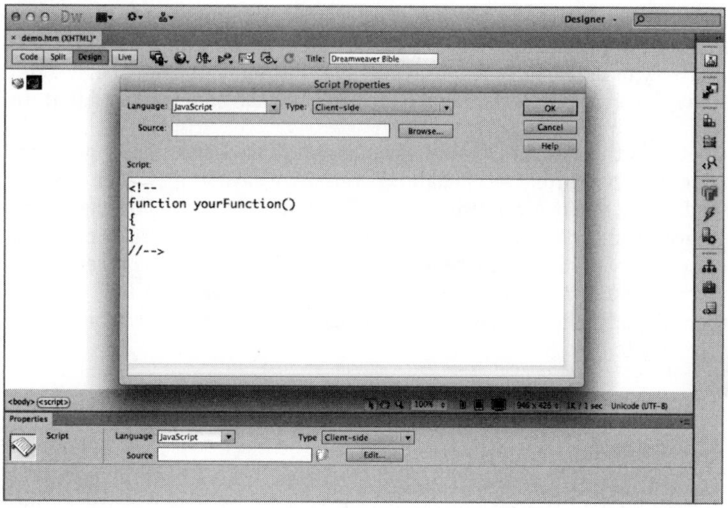

FIGURE 5-35

Insert either JavaScript or VBScript using the Insert panel's Script object.

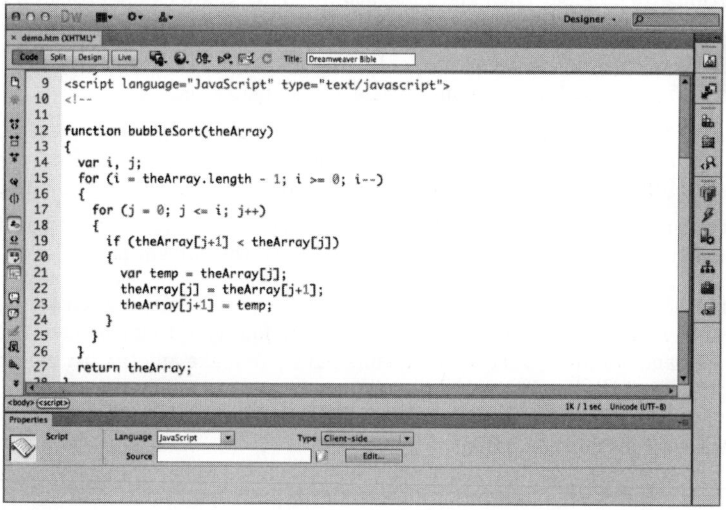

Extracting JavaScript

Many of today's web designers have noted the benefits brought by working with external CSS style sheets—including clarity of code and easier maintenance—and looked for a way to apply the same techniques to JavaScript. By moving all the JavaScript functions into an external file, the core HTML source code loads faster and is easier to review, and the same external page can govern the interactivity of multiple pages. Dreamweaver has long created a barrier to this ideal because all of its JavaScript behaviors are embedded in the page containing the interactivity.

To bridge the gap between the standard Dreamweaver approach to client-side scripting and the more modern method, Dreamweaver offers a command: Externalize JavaScript. When the Externalize JavaScript command is run, you're given two options. You can either move just the JavaScript functions from the `<head>` to an external file or move the functions and also remove the triggers, such as `onClick` or `onMouseOver`. The implementation of this latter technique is referred to as *unobtrusive JavaScript* and uses a combination of CSS ID selectors and JavaScript DOM (Document Object Model) manipulation. Happily, the Dreamweaver team has made this very powerful and sophisticated command extremely easy to use.

To extract JavaScript from your page, follow these steps:

1. Choose Commands ➪ Externalize JavaScript.
2. Choose the desired option:
   - **Only Externalize JavaScript:** This option exports all JavaScript functions in the `<head>` of the document to an external document and links to that document. Script tags in the `<body>`, with the exception of Spry widgets, are not removed.
   - **Externalize JavaScript And Attach Unobtrusively:** In addition to the preceding functionality, triggers (also known as event handlers) are deleted from `<a>` tags and replaced with a JavaScript file with DOM functions and CSS IDs.
3. If you chose to externalize JavaScript only, Dreamweaver lists a single option, Remove JavaScript From Head. Leave the option selected and click OK.
4. If you chose to externalize JavaScript and attach unobtrusively, Dreamweaver displays all the attributes that act as triggers and suggested IDs, as shown in Figure 5-36. To remove all of the triggers, leave all options selected; modify any desired ID, and click OK.
5. Dreamweaver reports the results of the operation, including the names of new files that have been created and will need to be published with the current page; click OK.

Be aware of some trade-offs when externalizing your JavaScript, especially when you select the unobtrusive option. After Dreamweaver makes this conversion, client-side behaviors can no longer be re-opened and modified from the Behaviors panel. To make any further modifications, you'd need to open one of the newly created files (*`current_file`*`.js` where *`current_file`* is the name of the file from which the JavaScript was extracted) in either Code or Split view and edit the final series of functions by hand.

The other drawback to extracting JavaScript affects either path you decide to take; externalize JavaScript only or externalize and unobtrusively connect. Once the conversion is complete, it can be undone only after the page is closed. You can, however, reverse your decision by choosing Edit ➪ Undo up until that point.

FIGURE 5-36

Dreamweaver can extract all the JavaScript and replace any selected trigger attribute so that the client-side scripting is not apparent in the code.

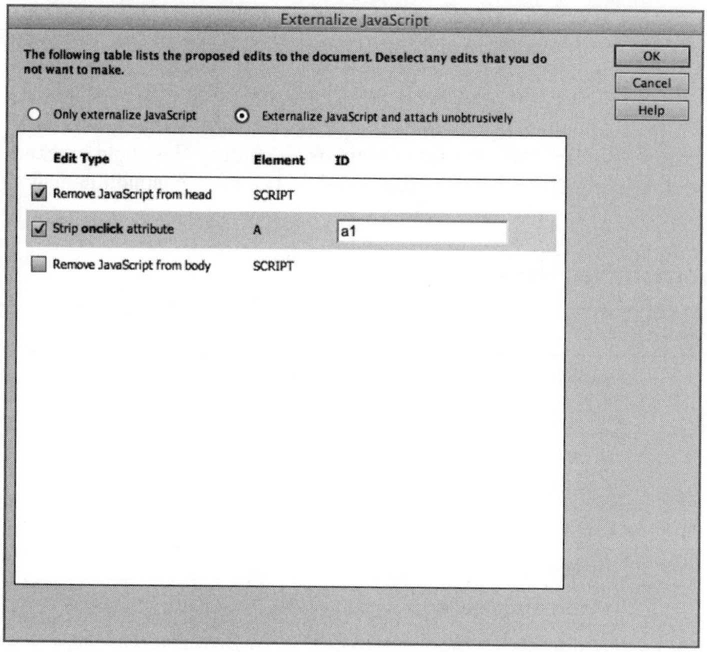

Inserting Symbols and Special Characters

When working with Dreamweaver, you're usually entering text directly from your keyboard, one keystroke at a time, with each keystroke representing a letter, number, or other keyboard character. Some situations, however, require special letters that have diacritics or common symbols, such as the copyright symbol, which are outside of the regular, standard character set represented on your keyboard. HTML enables you to insert a full range of such character entities through two systems. The more familiar special characters have been assigned a mnemonic code name to make them easy to remember; these are called *named characters*. Less typical characters must be inserted by entering a numeric code; these are known as *decimal characters*. For the sake of completeness, named characters also have a corresponding decimal character code.

Both named and decimal character codes begin with an ampersand (`&`) symbol and end with a semicolon (`;`). For example, the HTML code for an ampersand symbol is:

```
&amp;
```

Its decimal character equivalent is:

```
&#38;
```

CAUTION

If, during the browser-testing phase of creating your web page, you suddenly see an HTML code onscreen rather than a symbol, double-check your HTML. The code could be just a typo; you may have left off the closing semicolon, for instance. If the code is correct and you're using a named character, however, switch to its decimal equivalent.

Named characters

HTML coding conventions require that certain characters, including the angle brackets that surround tags, be entered as character entities. Table 5-4 lists the most common named characters.

TABLE 5-4 Common Named Characters

Named Entity	Symbol	Description
<	<	A left angle bracket or the less-than symbol
>	>	A right angle bracket or the greater-than symbol
&	&	An ampersand
"	"	A double quotation mark
	∞	A nonbreaking space
©	©	A copyright symbol
®	®	A registered mark
™	™	A trademark symbol, which cannot be previewed in Dreamweaver but is supported in Internet Explorer

TIP

Those characters that you can type (like &) or insert directly into Dreamweaver's Document window are automatically translated into the correct named characters in HTML. Try this when in split-screen Code and Design view. You can also enter a nonbreaking space in Dreamweaver by pressing Ctrl+Shift+spacebar (Command+Shift+Spacebar) or by choosing the Nonbreaking Space object.

Decimal characters and UTF-8 encoding

Diacritical marks—such as á, ñ, or â—can be entered directly in the Document window, if supported in the keyboard and UTF-8 encoding is in use. Dreamweaver handles the conversion to character entities. As mentioned in the preceding section, decimal characters take the form of `&#number;`, where the number can range from 00 to 255. Not all numbers have matching symbols; the sequence from 14 through 31 is currently unused. The upper range (127 through 159), only partially supported by modern browsers such as Firefox, Safari, and Chrome, is now deemed invalid by the W3C. In addition, not all fonts have characters for every entity.

Dreamweaver uses UTF-8 encoding for characters higher than 127. UTF-8 is an ASCII-compatible version of the Unicode character set. Unicode provides a unique number for every character in every language; however, the raw Unicode number is rendered in 15-bit words, unreadable by browsers—a problem solved by UTF-8.

UTF-8 also uses numbers, but does away with the upper limit of 255. For example, the UTF-8 encoding for the trademark symbol is `™`, whereas the no-longer-used number entity is `™`. Fortunately, you don't have to remember complex codes—all you have to do is use the Character objects.

Using the Character objects

Not only is it difficult to remember the various name or number codes for the specific character entities; it's also time-consuming to enter the code by hand. The Dreamweaver engineers recognized this problem and created a series of Character objects, which are found under the Characters menu of the Insert panel's Text category or the Insert ➪ HTML ➪ Special Characters submenu.

Ease of use is the guiding principle for the new Character objects. Twelve of the most commonly used symbols, such as © and ®, are instantly available as separate objects. Inserting the single Character objects is a straightforward point-and-click affair. Either drag the desired symbol to a place in the Document window or position your cursor and select the object. The individual Character objects are described in Table 5-5.

TABLE 5-5 Character Objects

Icon	Name	HTML Code Inserted
	Line Break	
	NonBreaking Space	
	Copyright	©
	Registered	®
	Trademark	™
	Pound	£
	Yen	¥
	Euro	€
	Left Quote	“
	Right Quote	”

Continues

TABLE 5-5 *(continued)*

Icon	Name	HTML Code Inserted
	Em-Dash	—
	En-Dash	–

NOTE

You may notice that the Character objects insert a mix of named and number character entities. Not all browsers recognize the easier-to-identify named entities, so for the widest compatibility, Dreamweaver uses the number codes for a few objects.

The final object in the Characters menu is used for inserting these or any other character entity. The Insert Other Character object displays a large table with symbols for 99 different characters, as shown in Figure 5-37. Simply select the desired symbol, and Dreamweaver inserts the appropriate HTML code at the current cursor position. By the way, the very first character—which appears to be blank—actually inserts the code for a nonbreaking space, also accessible via the keyboard shortcut Ctrl+Shift+spacebar (Command+Shift+spacebar). The nonbreaking space is also available in the Characters menu in the Common category of the Insert panel.

NOTE

Keep in mind that the user's browser must support the character entity for it to be visible to the user; again, testing is essential.

FIGURE 5-37

Use the Insert Other Character object to insert the character entity code for any of 99 different symbols.

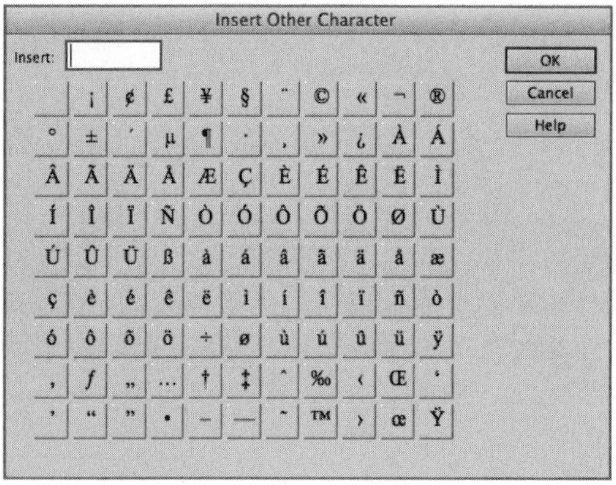

Summary

Creating web pages with Dreamweaver is a special blend of using visual layout tools and HTML coding. Regardless, you need to understand the basics of HTML so that you have the knowledge and the tools to modify your code when necessary. This chapter covered the following key areas:

- An HTML page is divided into two main sections: the `<head>` and the `<body>`. Information pertaining to the entire page is kept in the `<head>` section; all the actual content of the web page goes in the `<body>` section.
- You can change the color and background of your entire page, as well as set its title, through the CSS categories in the Page Properties dialog box.
- Use `<meta>` tags to summarize your web page so that search engines can properly catalog it. In Dreamweaver, you can use the View Head Contents feature to easily alter these and other `<head>` tags.
- The Live View, Related Files, and Code Navigator features all work together to provide an enhanced workflow with real-world browser rendering and quick access to code in external files.
- Java applets can be inserted as Applet objects in a Dreamweaver web page. Java source files, called *classes*, can be linked to the Applet object through the Property inspector.
- Dreamweaver offers a simple method for including both JavaScript and VBScript code in the `<body>` section of your HTML page. Script functions that you want to insert in the `<head>` section can now be added by choosing View ⇨ Head Content.
- To separate content from presentation, consider extracting your JavaScript with the Externalize JavaScript command. Remember, however, that if you choose to replace the trigger attributes with unobtrusive JavaScript, your Dreamweaver behaviors no longer are editable in the Behaviors panel.
- Special extended characters such as symbols and accented letters require the use of HTML character entities, which can be either named (as in `"`) or in decimal format (as in `"`).

In the next chapter, you learn how to work with Cascading Style Sheets—also known as CSS—to style and lay out your web pages in Dreamweaver.

CHAPTER

6

Building Style Sheet Web Pages

IN THIS CHAPTER

Cascading Style Sheets basics

Using external style sheets

Applying style sheet attributes

Animating with CSS3

Dreamweaver Technique: Applying External Style Sheet Styles

Defining and inserting styles

Dreamweaver Technique: Crafting a Print Style Sheet

Understanding style properties

Specifying design-time style sheets

All publications, whether on paper or the web, need a balance of style and content to be effective. Style without content is all flash with no real information. Content with no style is flat and uninteresting, thus losing the substance. Traditionally, HTML has tied style to content wherever possible, preferring logical tags, such as `<strong>` to indicate emphasis, to physical tags, such as `<b>` for bold. But although this emphasis on the logical worked for many single documents, its imprecision made achieving style consistency across a broad range of web pages unrealistic, if not impossible.

The Cascading Style Sheets specification has changed this situation—and much more. As support for Cascading Style Sheets (CSS) has grown, web designers have been able to alter the display of font faces, type size, spacing, and many other page elements with a single block of CSS code—and have the effect ripple not only throughout the page but also throughout a website.

Dreamweaver was one of the first web authoring tools to make the application of Cascading Style Sheets user-friendly—and in this latest version, Dreamweaver has integrated CSS throughout the program and taken it to the next level with support for the latest version, CSS3. Through Dreamweaver's intuitive interface, the web designer can access more than 100 different CSS settings, affecting everything from type specs to multimedia-like transitions. Dreamweaver enables you to work the way you want: Create your complete style sheet first and then link it when you're ready, or make up your styles one by one as you build your web page. Dreamweaver's advanced CSS rendering helps you create the design you visualize every step of the way; best of all, Dreamweaver renders CSS according to the W3C specifications, today's standard for web designers.

In this chapter, you find out how CSS works and why you need it. As you work through a Dreamweaver Technique to remove underlines from links, you also walk through a typical style sheet session. With that experience under your belt, you're ready for the later sections with detailed information on the current CSS rules—and how to apply those rules to your web page and site. Also, the section on defining styles helps you understand what's what in the Style Definition dialog box. You learn how you can create external style sheets to establish—and maintain—the look and feel of an entire website with a single document. Finally, you see how Dreamweaver's special CSS features, including design-time style sheets, make the CSS promise a reality.

Dreamweaver QUICKSTART

If you're already well-versed in CSS and just want to know how to create a CSS rule with Dreamweaver, here's one quick method:

1. If available, select the object or text you want to style.
2. From the CSS Styles panel, choose New CSS Rule.

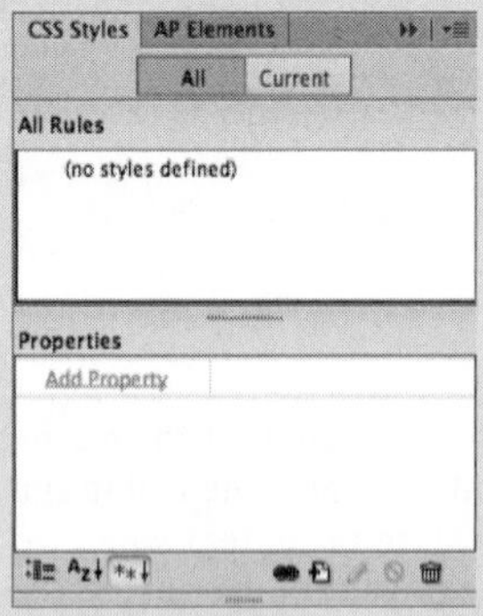

3. When the New CSS Rule dialog box opens, choose the Selector Type and the Selector Name, and determine where you want to place the code from the Rule Definition list. Click OK.
4. In the CSS Rule Definition dialog box, choose the desired properties and values you need in the various categories. When you're done, click OK.

Content in tags are immediately restyled. To apply an existing class to a selection, choose it from the Class list in the Property inspector; enter an ID in the Property inspector's ID field (without the leading pound sign). There's a great deal more to learn about CSS in Dreamweaver, and it's all covered in this chapter.

Understanding Cascading Style Sheets

The Cascading Style Sheets system significantly increases the design capabilities for a website. If you are a designer used to working with desktop publishing tools, you may recognize many familiar features in CSS, including the following:

- Commands for specifying and applying font characteristics

- Traditional layout measurement systems and terminology
- Pinpoint precision for page layout

Cascading Style Sheets are able to apply many features with a simple syntax that is easy to understand. If you're familiar with the concept of using styles in a word processing program, you'll have no trouble grasping style sheets.

Here's how the process works: CSS instructions are given in rules; a style sheet is a collection of these rules. A rule is a statement made up of an HTML or custom identifier, called a *selector*, and its defined properties and values. For example, a CSS rule that makes the contents of all `<h1>` tags (the selector) red (#FF0000 in hexadecimal, the value) in color (the property) looks like the following:

```
h1 {
   color: #FF0000;
}
```

A CSS property and its associated value are collectively referred to as a *declaration*.

In the following sections, you see the various characteristics of CSS—grouping, inheritance, and cascading—working together to give style sheets their flexibility and power.

Grouping properties

A web designer often needs to change several style properties at once. CSS enables you to group declarations by separating them with semicolons. For example:

```
h1 {
  color:#FF0000;
  font-family:Arial,Helvetica,sans-serif;
  font-size:18pt;
}
```

The Dreamweaver interface provides a wide range of options for styles. If you look at the code, you find that Dreamweaver groups your selections exactly as shown in the preceding example. You can group selectors, as well as declarations. Separate grouped selectors with commas rather than semicolons. For example:

```
h1, h2, p, em {
  color:green;
  text-align:left;
}
```

Inheritance of properties

CSS rules can also be applied to more than one tag through inheritance. The HTML tags enclosed within the CSS selector can inherit most, but not all, CSS declarations. Suppose you set all `<p>` tags to the color red. Any tags included within a `<p> . . . </p>` tag pair then inherit that property and are also colored red unless they have a separate, conflicting definition.

Inheritance is also at work within HTML tags that involve a parent-child relationship, such as a list. Whether numbered (ordered, `<ol>`) or bulleted (unordered, `<ul>`), a list comprises any number of list items, designated by <li> tags. Each list item is considered a child of the parent tag, <ol> or <ul>. Look at the following example:

```
ol {
  color:#FF0000;
}
ul {
  color:#0000FF;
}
```

Using the preceding example, all ordered list items appear in red (#FF0000); all unordered list items appear in blue (#0000FF). One major benefit to this parent-child relationship is that you can change the font for an entire page with one CSS rule. The following statement accomplishes this change:

```
body {
  font-family: Verdana, Arial, Helvetica, sans-serif;
}
```

The change is possible in the previous example because the <body> tag is considered the parent of every HTML element on a page.

Cascading characteristics

The term *cascading* describes the capability of a local style to override a general style. Think of a stream flowing down a mountain; each ledge encountered by the stream has the potential to change its direction. The last ledge determines the final direction of the stream. In the same manner, one CSS rule applying generally to a block of text can be overridden by another rule applied to a more specific part of the same text.

For example, you've defined, using style sheets, all normal paragraphs—<p> tags—as a particular font in a standard color, but you mark one section of the text using a little-used tag such as <samp>. If you make a CSS rule altering both the font and the color of the <samp> tag, the section takes on the characteristics of that rule.

The cascading aspect of style sheets also works on a larger scale. One of the key features of CSS is the capability to define external style sheets that can be linked to individual web pages, acting on their overall look and feel. Indeed, you can use the cascading behavior to fine-tune the overall website style based on a particular page or range of pages. Your company may, for instance, define an external style sheet for the entire company intranet; each division could then build upon that overall model for its individual web pages. For example, suppose that the company style sheet dictates that all <h2> headings are in Arial and black. One department could output its web pages with <h2> tags in Arial, but colored red rather than black, whereas another department could make them blue.

Defining new class and ID selectors for extended design control

Redefining existing HTML tags is a step in the right direction toward consistent design, but the real power of CSS comes into play when you define custom selectors. One type of custom selector is called a *class*; class selector names always begin with a period. To style all copyright notices at the bottom of all pages of a website to display in 8 pixel Helvetica all caps, you could define a tag as in this simple example:

```
.cnote {
  font-family:Helvetica, sans-serif;
  font-size:8px;
  font-transform:uppercase
}
```

If you define this style in an external style sheet and apply it to all 999 pages of your website, you have to alter only one line of code (instead of all 999 pages) when the edict comes down from management to make all the copyright notices a touch larger. After a new class has been defined, you can apply it to any range of text, from one word to an entire page.

Classes can be applied to more than one element on a page. You could, for example, have more than one paragraph styled as a copyright notice in various parts of the page. A custom tag intended to be applied to a single element, such as a `<div>` tag that contains the footer content, is called an *ID selector*. An ID selector is identified by its beginning pound sign—technically called an octothorpe—for example, `#footer`. If you want the footer content to really stand out, you could style it with white type against a black background with a red border. The CSS rule looks like this:

```
#footer {
   color: #FFFFFF;
   background: #000000;
   border: thin solid #FF0000;
}
```

An ID selector is applied to a tag through the self-named `id` attribute, minus the pound sign. Thus, the `<div>` tag that holds the footer content is coded like this:

```
<div id="footer">Footer content goes here</div>
```

Designers use a combination of class and ID selectors—as well as other types of selectors—when laying out the page. It's considered a best practice to avoid using class selectors when the CSS rule is intended to be applied only once on the page; in those situations, an ID selector is the better choice.

Specificity

The specificity of a CSS rule determines which rule takes effect when two or more rules conflict. For example, let's say you have one rule that sets the color of an `<h1>` tag to dark gray, like this:

```
h1 { color: #333333; }
```

and another rule that sets the color of a class called `.alert` to bright red:

```
.alert { color: #FF0000; }
```

What would happen when the browser encounters code like this:

```
<h1 class="alert">Attention all shoppers!</h1>
```

As you might suspect, the .alert rule would be applied and the <h1> tag would appear red. This occurs because the .alert selector is more specific than the <h1> tag selector. The W3C CSS specification (no relation) provides a different weight for each kind of selector.

A rule's specificity is noted with four comma-separated values. For example, the specificity for the <h1> rule is

```
0,0,0,1
```

because there is one tag element in the selector, whereas the specificity for the .alert rule is

```
0,0,1,0
```

because there is one class element in the selector. Any positive value in the second-to-last column outweighs any value in the last column.

The formula for creating specificity is as follows:

```
Total inline styles, total ID selectors, total class and
pseudo-class selectors, total tag elements
```

Inline styles are the most specific—and the most rarely used these days—so they trump any other type of selector. If two rules have the same specificity and are applied to the same selection, the rule that comes later in the style sheet—because it is physically closer to the code—wins.

How styles are applied

CSS applies style formatting to your page in one of three ways:

- Via an external, linked style sheet
- Via an embedded style
- Via inline style rules

External style sheets

An external style sheet is a file containing the CSS rules; it links one or more web pages. One benefit of linking to an external style sheet is that you can customize and change the appearance of a website quickly and easily from one file.

Two different methods exist for working with an external style sheet: the link method and the import method. Dreamweaver initially defaults to the link method, but you can also choose import if you prefer.

For the link method, a line of code is added outside of the <style> tags, as follows:

```
<link href="mainstyle.css" rel="style sheet" type="text/css">
```

The import method writes code within the style tags, as follows:

```
<style type="text/css">
@import url("newstyles.css");
</style>
```

When using an external style sheet, all `@import` rules must precede all other rules, except the `@charset` rule, if present.

If you compare the `link` and the `import` methods, you see that the `link` method was previously better supported among browsers, but all major browsers support both techniques now. As a general rule, many developers use the HTML element `<link>` to attach external style sheets to an HTML page and the CSS `@import` property from a CSS file to import other CSS documents.

Embedded styles

Embedded styles are those typically written into the actual file at the top of a web page within a `<style> ... </style>` tag pair. Placing style sheets within the header tags has become a convention that many designers use, although you can also apply a style sheet anywhere on a page.

The `<style>` tag for a Cascading Style Sheet identifies the `type` attribute as `text/css`. A sample embedded Class listing looks like the following:

```
<style type="text/css">
<!--
p {
  font-family: "Arial, Helvetica, sans-serif";
  color: #000000;
}
.cnote {
  font: 8pt "Arial, Helvetica, sans-serif";
  text-transform: uppercase;
}
h1 {
  font: bold 18pt Arial, Helvetica, sans-serif;
  color: #FF0000;
}
-->
</style>
```

The HTML comment tags `<!--` and `-->` prevent older browsers that can't read style sheets from displaying the CSS rules.

Inline styles

The final method of applying a style inserts it within HTML tags using the `style` attribute—a technique known as *inline styles*. This method is the most local of all the techniques; that is, it is closest to the tag it is affecting and, therefore, has ultimate control—because of the cascading nature of style sheets as previously discussed.

> **CAUTION**
> As my mother used to say, "Just because you can do something, doesn't mean you should." Generally, inline styles are not used because they exert such a high level of control, and modifying the style must be done on an item-by-item basis, which defeats much of the purpose of CSS.

When you create an AP element within Dreamweaver, you notice that the positioning attribute creates an embedded Cascading Style Sheet rule like the following:

```
#apDiv1 {
  position: absolute;
  left: 560px;
  top: 474px;
  width: 154px;
  height: 66px;
  z-index: 1;
}
```

For all its apparent complexity, the Cascading Style Sheets system becomes straightforward in Dreamweaver. Often, you won't have to write a single line of code. But even if you don't have to write code, you should understand the CSS fundamentals of grouping, inheritance, and cascading.

Dreamweaver gives anyone working with CSS layouts a big boost with the newly introduced starter pages available through the Layout category of the New Document dialog box. With a full array of layout variations, you can quickly get a solid head start without touching a single CSS rule. Naturally, you're free—and encouraged—to customize the styles. For more details about creating a new page based on the CSS layouts, see Chapter 4.

Working with the CSS Styles Panel

The CSS Styles panel is Dreamweaver's central point for establishing, modifying, and learning about Cascading Style Sheets. It is, by far, the most complex and sophisticated of any of Dreamweaver's panels and requires a bit of explanation to help you to understand how best to use it. You can open the CSS Styles panel by choosing Window ➪ CSS Styles or use the keyboard shortcut, Shift+F11; the CSS Styles panel is available by default and its title bar can be double-clicked to expose it as well.

The CSS Styles panel can be viewed in two separate ways: All mode and Current mode. In brief, All mode displays the embedded and external CSS styles contained in the current page; it does not display inline styles. Current mode shows every style rule affecting the current selection on the page, regardless of whether the source is defined in an inline, embedded, or external style rule.

Personally, I tend to work in All mode during the initial development of a page and then switch to Current when I need to drill down into a particular style. Both modes allow for rapid modification of any defined CSS properties and the equally speedy setting of new attributes.

All mode

Enter All mode by selecting All at the top of the CSS Styles panel. Once it is selected, you'll note that the panel is divided into two parts, the All Rules pane and the Properties pane. The All Rules pane shows every embedded and external style rule associated with the current page. Select any rule to see its properties and values in the Properties pane (see Figure 6-1).

Dreamweaver's All mode enables you to tell, at a glance, where a custom style is from—whether it's from a linked external style sheet or included in the current document. The CSS Styles panel displays the containing tag `<style>` if the styles are embedded or imported; expand the `<style>` entry to determine if it contains styles or an imported sheet or both. You may recall that the code for importing a style sheet is placed within a `<style>` tag. Linked style sheets are shown with just the filename, as you can see in Figure 6-1.

> **NOTE**
> **The style rules are presented in the order they appear in the embedded style tag or external style sheet. To adjust the order of the rules, drag the style rule you want to move to its new location.**

FIGURE 6-1

Use All mode to see the full list of embedded and external style rules for the current page.

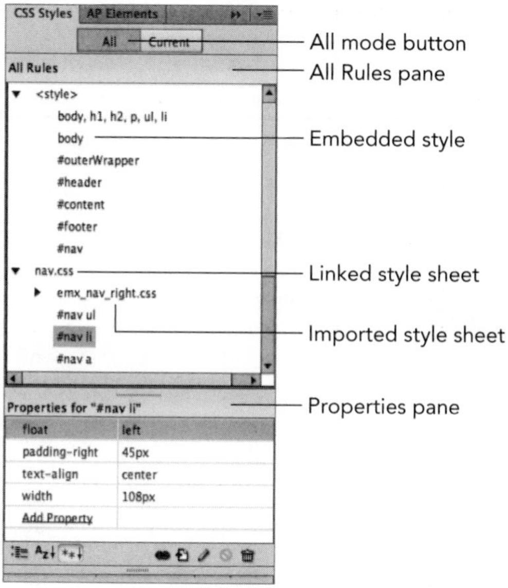

Select any rule in the All Rules pane to see its properties and values in the Properties pane. By default, only the currently set properties are displayed. There are two other ways to display the properties, Category view and List view. You can choose the way you'd like to see the properties by selecting from one of the buttons on the bottom left of the Properties pane:

- **Category View:** Separates the CSS properties and values into the same nine categories found in the CSS Rule Definition dialog box: Font, Background, Block, Border, Box, List, Positioning, Tables, Content Quotes; User Interfaces, Multi-Column Layout, Text, Line Layout, Animations, Transformations, and Transitions. This view is useful when you want to add one or more new properties in a specific category.

- **List View:** Shows an alphabetical listing of the properties with the applied ones listed first. Use this view when you know the name of a property but don't want to enter it by hand.
- **Show Only Set Properties:** Displays only the currently set properties, as well as an option to add a new one. Once you've gained familiarity with CSS properties, you'll find this view the most efficient because it both isolates your current properties and provides a direct route to defining new ones.

For any property displayed, you can modify the current value directly. Details are provided in a later section in this chapter, "Editing and Managing Style Sheets."

Current mode

As the name implies, Current mode focuses on the current selection (see Figure 6-2); click Current to enter into this mode. Current mode has three separate panes rather than the two for All mode—you can change the height of any by dragging the separating border up or down within the CSS Styles panel.

FIGURE 6-2

Get detailed information and control over the current selection by entering Current mode.

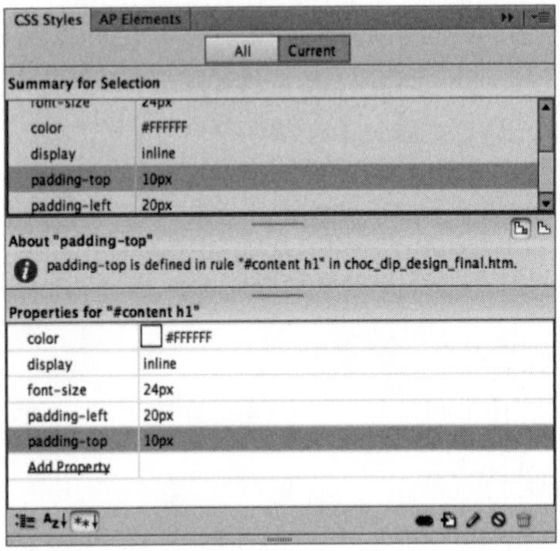

Choose any entry in the Tag Selector or select any section of the page and the CSS Styles panel under Current mode displays all the properties applicable to that selection, regardless of their origin, in the top section known as the Summary for Selection pane. The next area on the panel is the Rules pane, which shows either information about the property currently selected in the Summary for Selection pane or all the rules affecting the current selection; two buttons on the Rules pane title bar allow you to switch between views. The final area in Current mode—the Properties pane—works the same way as it does in All mode.

The Summary for Selection pane lists both properties and values; each entry is listed in order of specificity, the property with lowest specificity appearing first. Furthermore, if there are two conflicting properties, only the one with the highest specificity is shown. Although subtle, these applications of specificity are a valuable debugging and teaching tool.

For instance, let's say you're trying to change the line height of a particular paragraph where the property is declared in two different rules: `p` and `.openingParagraph`. If you try to change the line height for the `p` rule, you won't see a difference in either Dreamweaver or your browser. A glance at the Summary for Selection pane while the paragraph in question is selected will show just the property for the `.openingParagraph` rule.

How do you tell which rule a displayed property is from? Dreamweaver offers a number of methods. Hover your cursor over any property in the Summary for Selection pane and the property's location—both rule and document—appear in a tooltip. The Rules pane provides another alternative. Click any property in the Summary for Selection pane and, if the Rules pane is in the About view, you'll see a brief sentence describing the property's location. When you are in Rules view, the Rules pane shows a cascade of all of the—you guessed it—rules affecting the current selection; the rule containing the property selected in the Summary for Selection pane is highlighted, as shown in Figure 6-3. You switch between the About view and the Rules view by clicking the Show Information About Selected Property button and the Show Cascade Of Rules For Selected Tag button, respectively, located on the right of the Rules pane title bar.

TIP

Move your cursor over any property in the Rules pane while in Rules view to see the tooltip that notes both the property's location and its specificity.

FIGURE 6-3

Find out where a property is defined through the About view and see the cascade of rules in the Rules view.

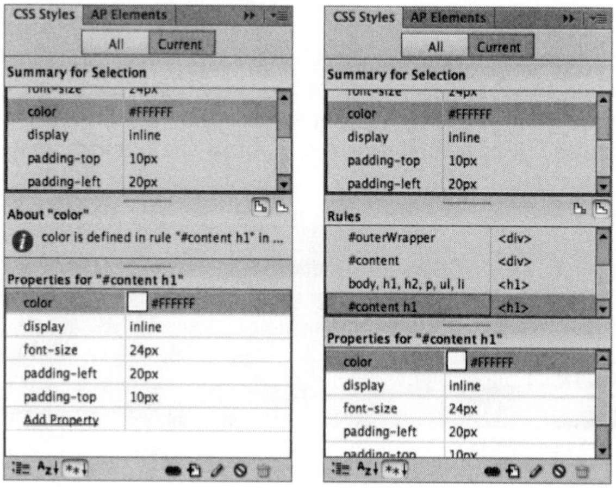

The final pane, Properties, is almost exactly the same in the Current mode as it is in All mode. Again, the Show Only Set Properties option is the default, and you can, if desired, switch to either Category or List view by using the buttons at the bottom of the CSS Styles panel.

The Properties pane in Current mode differs from the same pane in All mode in one respect: Both applied and irrelevant properties are displayed. The irrelevant properties are noted with a strikethrough. If you place your cursor over the property, Dreamweaver displays a tooltip explaining why the property is not relevant. The two most common reasons for a property to be marked as irrelevant are that it is overridden by another rule or not inherited.

Creating and Applying Styles

Dreamweaver uses four primary tools to implement Cascading Style Sheets: the CSS tab of the Property inspector, the CSS Styles panel, the Edit Style Sheet dialog box, and the Style Definition dialog box. The CSS tab of the Property inspector is available when text is selected and is a great vehicle for applying styles and reviewing and modifying related properties, such as font-family, size, and color—you can also create new CSS rules for selected text. You use the CSS Styles panel to view all the styles available or those that are being applied to the currently selected HTML tag; the CSS Styles panel also provides a direct link to modifying any property or for adding properties to any rule. The Edit Style Sheet dialog box is useful for managing groups of styles and style sheets, whereas the Style Definition dialog box defines the CSS rules themselves. With these interfaces, you can accomplish the following:

- Link or import all your styles from an external style sheet
- Create new selectors and specify their rules
- Apply styles to selected text or to a particular tag surrounding that text
- Modify any styles you create

Generating new styles

The world of CSS can be overwhelming to the novice designer: How do you even begin to master this complex set of rules and concepts? Dreamweaver offers many routes to explore CSS, but perhaps the easiest entry is through the Property inspector. Set a font, font size, or color on any bit of text and Dreamweaver applies your formatting either as a modification of an existing rule or as a new style that is added to the list of available styles, right in the Property inspector.

CAUTION

Dreamweaver CS6 is much smarter about the creation of new styles through the Property inspector than in previous versions. Dreamweaver no longer automatically inserts generically named classes—such as Style1, Style2, and so on—into the head of your document. Instead, Dreamweaver intelligently guides you to proper CSS rule creation with appropriate selectors or class names of your choosing, stored where you specify: embedded in the document or within an external style sheet.

Walk through the following steps to see how Dreamweaver helps you build styles correctly:

1. Switch to the CSS tab in the Property inspector.
2. Select the text you want to style, by either highlighting it or choosing the tag from the Tag Selector.

   Dreamweaver selects any CSS rule previously defined that specifically targets the selection in the Targeted Rule list. If no such rule exists, `<New CSS Rule>` is selected in the Targeted Rule list, as shown in Figure 6-4.

FIGURE 6-4

If there is no specific rule for the current selection, Dreamweaver automatically prepares the way for you to create a new style by setting the <New CSS Rule> in the Targeted Rule list.

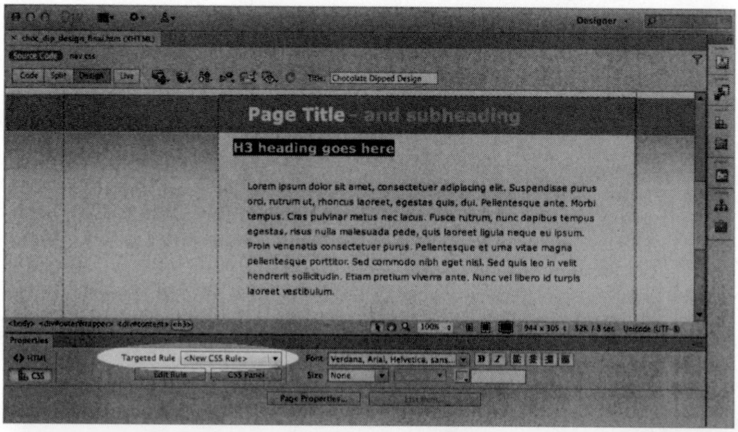

TIP

If you select a portion of text rather than the entire tag, the style is applied to a `<span>` tag surrounding your selection; otherwise, the style is applied to the containing element, such as a `<p>` or heading tag such as `<h3>`.

3. Change any property in the Property inspector, including font name, size, color, or alignment, or select the Bold or Italic options.
4. Dreamweaver displays the New CSS Rule dialog box.

   The type of selector and the selector name displayed depends on—you guessed it—your selection. If you have chosen a range of text, Dreamweaver sets the Selector Type to Class and gives you the opportunity to enter a new class name. If you've chosen a tag from the Tag Selector, the Selector Type becomes Compound and the Selector Name is a descendant selector (covered later in this chapter), such as `#outerWrapper #content h3`, as shown in Figure 6-5. The descendant selector represents where the selected tag is in the CSS cascade.

Dreamweaver even provides a plain-language translation of how the rule is applied, as in the following:

```
This selector name will apply your rule to
all <h3> elements
that are within any HTML elements with id "content"
that are within any HTML elements with id "outerWrapper".
```

FIGURE 6-5

When a tag is selected for a new rule, Dreamweaver puts the most specific descendant selector possible in the Selector Name field.

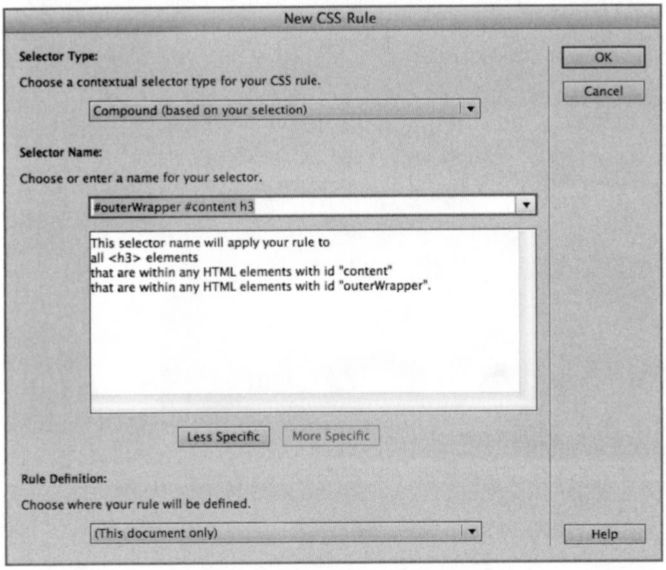

5. If the current selector is too specific and you want the rule to be more generally applicable, click Less Specific. Each time you click Less Specific, the leftmost selector (`#outerWrapper` in this example) is removed.

   Once you choose Less Specific, the More Specific button is enabled. You can restore the leftmost selector by clicking More Specific. The plain-language translation is adjusted accordingly.

6. Choose where you want your new rule stored from the Rule Definition list and click OK.

Dreamweaver's mechanism for creating new CSS rules through the Property inspector is extremely powerful, from both workflow and learning perspectives. Not only does Dreamweaver help you create appropriate CSS rules, but it provides insight into a key CSS concept, the cascade, when working with Compound selectors.

The following sections explain the four selector types—Class, ID, Tag, and Compound—in depth.

Class

Making a custom style is the most flexible way to define a style on a page. The first step in creating a custom style is to give it a name; this name is used in the `class` attribute. The name for your class must start with a period followed by a letter and must be alphanumeric without punctuation or special characters. If you do not begin the name of your custom style with a period, Dreamweaver inserts one for you. Here are some typical names you can use:

```
.master
.pagetitle
.bodytext
```

CAUTION

Although you can give your classes names such as **`body`**, **`title`**, or any other HTML tag, this approach is not a good idea. Dreamweaver warns you of the conflict if you try this method. It's best to name classes (or IDs) based on function rather than appearance. Also you should be aware that class names are case-sensitive.

ID

An ID selector is applied through the `id` attribute, available for almost all HTML tags. Each ID selector is intended to be unique for each page. In other words, you apply an ID rule once per page. An ID selector is identified by an initial pound sign, as in `#footer`.

Tag

The third option in the Selector Type list is Tag. This type of style provides an excellent tool for making quick, global changes to existing web pages. Essentially, the Tag style enables you to modify the features of your existing HTML tags. When you select this option, the drop-down list displays more than 90 HTML tags in alphabetical order. Select a tag from the drop-down list and click OK. As you become more familiar with HTML, you're free to simply enter the tag into the Tag field.

Compound

Because of its flexibility, you may find that you use the Compound option frequently. Enter the selector directly in the Compound field; Dreamweaver allows almost any type of input, whether or not it recognizes the selector type. In addition to ID and descendant selectors, you can also group selectors when applying a single style to multiple tags and/or classes. If, for example, you want to create a style for the `<body>`, `<td>`, and `<th>` tags, you enter the tag names in the Compound field (without their delimiters) in a comma-separated list like this:

```
body,td,th
```

The Compound option is also useful for defining *pseudo-classes* and *pseudo-elements*. A pseudo-class represents dynamic states of a tag that may change under user action or over time. Several standard pseudo-classes associated with the `<a>` tag are used to style hypertext links. When you choose Compound, the drop-down list box contains four customization options, which can all be categorized as pseudo-classes:

- `a:link`—Customizes the style of a link that has not yet been visited
- `a:visited`—Customizes the style of a link to a page that has been visited

- `a:hover`—Customizes the style of a link while the user's cursor is over it
- `a:active`—Customizes the style of a link when it is selected by the user

TIP

Dreamweaver does not preview pseudo-class styles (except for `a:link`), although they can be previewed through a supported browser.

A pseudo-element, on the other hand, gives you control over contextually defined page elements: For example, `p:first-letter` styles the first letter in every paragraph tag, enabling a drop-cap design. Because of their specific nature, Dreamweaver does not display any pseudo-elements in the Compound list. You can, however, enter your own—Dreamweaver does a fine job of rendering both the `:first-letter` and the `:first-line` pseudo-elements.

NOTE

Dreamweaver does not render the lesser-used pseudo-elements `:before` and `:after` in the Design view; however, they are displayed properly in Live View.

Descendants and other advanced selectors

Dreamweaver also enables you to enter some of the more advanced additions to the CSS selector palette through the Compound selector type.

One such selector is the *descendant* selector. Descendant selectors are contextual selectors because they specify one tag within another. A descendant selector, for example, permits you to target the anchor tag within a specific unorder list, with a selector like this: `nav ul li a`.

For example, to style text within nested blockquotes, enter the following in the Compound field of the New CSS Rule dialog box:

```
blockquote blockquote
```

In essence, you are creating a custom style for a set of HTML tags used in your document. This type of CSS selector acts like an HTML tag that has a CSS style applied to it; that is, all page elements fitting the criteria are automatically styled. You can also combine custom styles with redefined HTML styles in a descendant selector.

Other advanced selectors that you can enter in the Compound field include:

- **Child:** Selects an element that is a *direct* child of another element. For example, in a `div` tag with nested `div` elements, `div > p` selects the paragraphs in the outermost `div` tag only.
- **Adjacent-sibling:** Selects an element that immediately follows another. For example, in an unordered list with two list items, `li + li` selects the second list item, but not the first.

- **Universal:** Selects any element. This selector may be used to skip one or more generations of tags. Use `body * p` to select paragraphs contained within `div` elements that are children of the `body` tag, for example.
- **Attribute:** Selects tags with specified attributes. You can select tags if they either contain the attribute (`p[align]`) or contain an attribute set to a specific value (`p[align="left"]`).

Best of all, these selectors are rendered correctly in Dreamweaver's Design view and Live View. Most modern browsers (such as Firefox, Internet Explorer 7 and higher, or Safari) properly render these selectors as well.

NOTE

Dreamweaver warns you if you enter what it considers an invalid selector type; however, you are given the option to use the selector if you choose.

Applying styles through the Property inspector

In addition to automatically creating CSS styles, Dreamweaver also enables you to apply any defined style directly through the Property inspector. The immediate availability of CSS styles is a major boon to productivity and is extremely helpful for designers working in a site fully committed to using Cascading Style Sheets.

To apply a class style from the Property inspector, switch to the HTML tab, select a page element, and then make your choice from the Class list, as shown in Figure 6-6; to make it simpler for you, a style is previewed in the Class list. If the tag allows an ID to be assigned, all available ID selectors are listed in a similar list. However, unlike class selectors, after an ID selector has been assigned to a tag, Dreamweaver no longer displays it in the ID list.

FIGURE 6-6

CSS styles are previewed and applied from the Property inspector.

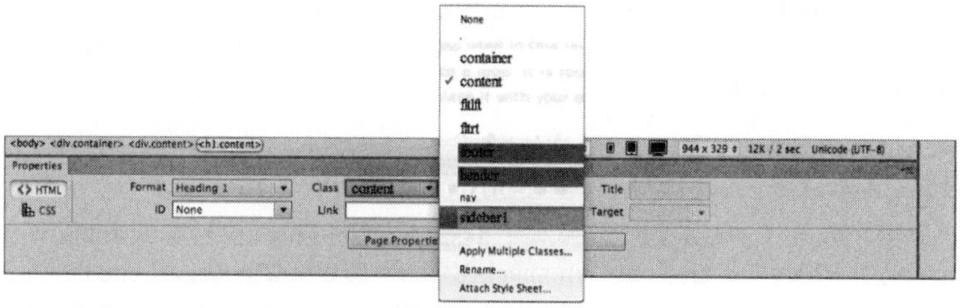

Inserting multiple classes

One of the unique properties of classes is that you can assign more than one to an element. In code, multiple classes are separated by a space, like this:

```
<div class="pullQuote mainStory onSale">
```

Dreamweaver gives you the power to achieve this same goal without touching the code, right from the Property inspector. To assign more than one class to a selection, follow these steps:

1. From the HTML tab of the Property inspector, expand the Class list.
2. Choose Apply Multiple Classes.
3. When the Multiclass Selection dialog box opens (see Figure 6-7), check the box for any listed class to select it.
4. To add an undefined class, enter its name in the open field, separating each class with a space.
5. Click OK when you're done.

FIGURE 6-7

Quickly select any predefined style to add multiple classes to a selector.

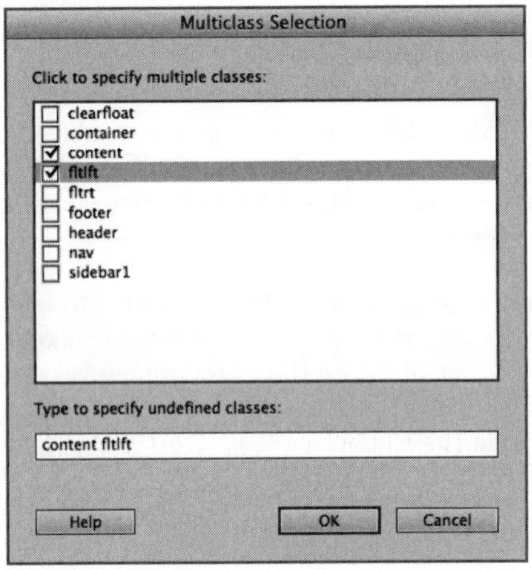

Multiple classes are rendered by browsers following the principles of the cascade. In other words, if you apply two classes, each with the same property defined, the value in the class defined later in the style sheet is rendered.

Attaching an external style sheet

Now that CSS-enabled browsers dominate, more web designers are encountering clients with existing external style sheets. To apply the site's design specifications to a new page, all the designer needs do is connect the current page to the CSS document. Dreamweaver provides a streamlined method for doing just that.

The Attach Style Sheet button, found on the CSS Styles panel, is a straightforward solution for linking external style sheets to the current document. When Attach Style Sheet is selected, the Attach External Style Sheet dialog box, shown in Figure 6-8, appears. Here, you can choose between the two previously discussed methods for attaching an external style sheet: Link or Import. You'll also have the option to target your style sheet for a specific media type.

FIGURE 6-8

You can use either the Link or the Import method to attach an external style sheet.

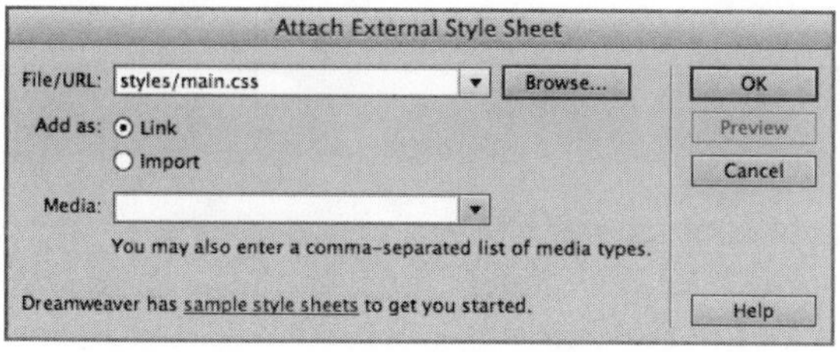

If you're not sure which style sheet is the appropriate one, you can check it out before applying it. Just select the existing style sheet and click Preview. Dreamweaver applies the selected style sheet to the current page. If you choose another style sheet or click Cancel, the sheet is removed.

Click Browse to locate a previously existing style sheet. When it is selected, a standard Select File dialog box appears with the `*.css` filter set. Simply locate the style sheet and select it: Dreamweaver inserts the necessary code into the `<head>` of your document. If any HTML tags—such as `<p>` or any of the heading tags—on your page are defined in the style sheet, you see an immediate change in your document.

TIP

If you don't have an external style sheet and want to create one, just enter the path and filename in the text field, making sure to use the `.css` extension. Dreamweaver notes that the file cannot be found and asks if you want to proceed. Click OK, and, when you create your first style, Dreamweaver also creates the CSS file with the requested filename.

The final option on the Attach External Style Sheet dialog box, the Media list, is discussed in the next section.

Choosing a media type

One of the most important facets of the Cascading Style Sheet specification is the ability to style a page for a specific *media type*. A media type is a means of communication, such as a computer screen, printer, or TTY device. The W3C identifies 10 different media types for CSS 2.1: `all`, `braille`, `embossed`, `handheld`, `print`, `projection`, `screen`, `speech`, `TTY`, and `TV`. If no media type is declared, the style sheet is applied to all devices that render the page. If one is declared, a `media` attribute is added to the code, like this (addition bolded for emphasis):

```
<link href="Techniques/styles/main.css" rel="style sheet"
type="text/css" media="screen" />
```

The bulk of today's designers do not apply a media type at all. However, an increasing number have started to create different style sheets: one to be viewed on the computer screen and another to be printed. Dreamweaver makes this easy by including a media list on the Attach External Style Sheet dialog box. The list includes the nine media types recognized by the W3C, as well as another one from the specification, `all`. It's considered a best practice to add a media attribute to your page and recommended to use `all` to cover every media type, `screen` for computer screen, and `print` for printer.

TIP

If you'd like to declare your style sheet for multiple media types, enter the desired types in a comma-separated list through the Media field of the Attach External Style Sheet dialog box.

Rendering different styles

Dreamweaver's Style Rendering toolbar complements the development of separate style sheets. After you've defined a style sheet for a specific media type, such as print, you can use the Style Rendering toolbar to select the desired media type and Dreamweaver will render your page as if it were that medium. To display the Style Rendering toolbar (see Figure 6-9), choose View ➪ Toolbars ➪ Style Rendering or right-click (Control+click) any other visible toolbar and choose Style Rendering. Three media types—`speech`, `embossed`, and `Braille`—are not included in the Style Rendering toolbar because their rendition is beyond Dreamweaver's scope.

FIGURE 6-9

The Style Rendering toolbar quickly changes the media type for Dreamweaver to emulate.

Another option on the Style Rendering toolbar is to disable CSS rendering altogether. Select the Toggle Rendering Of CSS Displays option in the middle of the toolbar to view the page without CSS; select again to enable CSS rendering. This feature is extremely helpful for both debugging CSS pages and viewing the order in which screen readers will present the page.

You also have the possibility of designing while displaying various pseudo-classes, typically used for styling the various link states. There are five mutually exclusive buttons for toggling pseudo-classes on the Style Rendering toolbar: `:link`, `:visited`, `:hover`, `:active`, and `:focus`. These are very useful for checking the look and feel of your design without having to enter into Live View or preview in a browser.

Applying, changing, and removing a style

As noted, any HTML tags redefined as CSS styles in an attached style sheet are automatically applied to your document. However, any custom CSS style must be applied on a case-by-case basis. Most web designers use a combination of HTML and custom CSS styles. Only custom CSS styles appear in the CSS Styles panel in Apply Styles mode or in the Class list in the HTML tab of the Property inspector.

In Dreamweaver, you can apply a style in four main ways: from the Property inspector, the menus, the Tag Selector, or the CSS Styles panel.

To apply an existing custom style using the Property inspector, follow these steps:

1. To apply the style to a section of the page enclosed by an HTML tag, select the tag from the Tag Selector; if you're applying the style to text, you can also highlight the text without entirely selecting the containing tag.
2. Select the custom style from the Class list in the HTML tab of the Property inspector for class styles or from the ID list for ID selectors, if available. Dreamweaver applies the custom style by setting either the `class` or the `id` attribute of the selected tag to the custom style. If you select only text and not an enclosing tag, Dreamweaver wraps a `<span>` tag around the selection.

The second approach is to use the menus to apply a style to your pages. Follow these steps:

1. Highlight the text to which you're applying the style, either by using the Tag Selector or by using the mouse.
2. Choose Format ➪ CSS Styles ➪ Your Style. The same dynamic CSS Class list is maintained in the Set Class entry of the context menu, accessible through a right-click (Control+click) on the selected text, as shown in Figure 6-10.

FIGURE 6-10

Dreamweaver collects all the classes available to the current document, whether from embedded styles or from external style sheets, and displays them alphabetically—and graphically—in the Tag Selector's Set Class list.

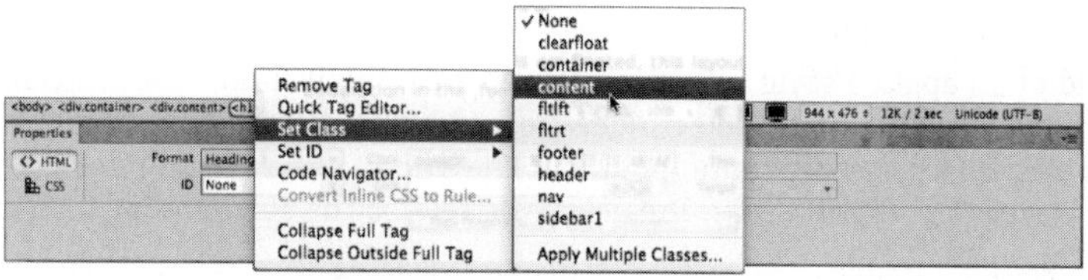

The third approach is to use the Tag Selector exclusively. Right-click (Control+click) the selected tag name in the Tag Selector and choose the style from either the Set Class or the Set ID submenus.

Finally, you can use the CSS Styles panel itself to apply a style:

1. Select the tag or text to which you want to apply your style.
2. In the CSS Styles panel, right-click (Control+click) the style and choose Apply from the context menu.

Changing styles

Changing from one applied custom style to another is extremely straightforward in Dreamweaver. Just place your cursor anywhere within the styled text and select a different custom style from the Class list on the Property inspector. Dreamweaver changes the old style to the new instantly. You get the same results if you switch styles from the Tag Selector or use the menus.

But what if you want to apply a new style to a text range within an existing <span> tag? Dreamweaver, by design, avoids nested <span> tags. Here's how it works. Suppose that you're working with the following code:

```
<span class="bodyCopy">Developing strategies to survive requires industry
insight and forward thinking in this competitive marketplace.</span>
```

If you apply a custom style called `hype` to the phrases `industry insight` and `forward thinking` by first selecting those phrases and then choosing `hype` from the Class list, the code looks like this:

```
<span class="bodyCopy">Developing strategies to survive
requires </span><span class="hype">industry insight</span>
<span class="bodyCopy"> and </span><span class="hype">forward
thinking</span><span class="bodyCopy"> in this competitive marketplace.</span>
```

Dreamweaver wraps each phrase in a distinct <span> tag so that nesting is entirely avoided. This behavior enables the style of each phrase to be altered more easily.

CAUTION

Although the use of the `<span>` tag is unavoidable under some circumstances, be careful not to overuse it. It's far better to apply a logical tag that makes sense in the context, such as `<em>` (emphasis) or `<cite>`, and then to create a CSS style that formats those tags for the look you want.

Removing applied styles

Getting rid of an applied style is just as easy as changing it. Now, just position your cursor anywhere in the stylized text and select None from the Class list. Dreamweaver also removes the no-longer-needed `class` attribute for all but the <span> tag. If you remove the class from a selection marked by <span> tags, Dreamweaver deletes the surrounding <span> tags.

NOTE

Be sure your cursor is *positioned within* the styled text and not selecting any of the text. Selecting None from the Class list on the Property inspector when just text—not tags—is highlighted forces Dreamweaver to remove the style from the tag and apply it to `<span>` tags on either side of the now unstyled text.

Styles can also be removed through the Tag Selector—just right-click (Control+click) any styled tag on the Tag Selector and choose Set Class ➪ None or Set ID ➪ None.

Dreamweaver TECHNIQUE

Applying External Style Sheet Styles

In this Technique, you attach an existing style sheet to a page and assign styles to various page elements.

1. In the Technique site, expand the 06_css folder and open `css_start.htm`.
2. If necessary, choose Window ⇨ CSS Styles to expose the CSS Styles panel.
3. At the bottom of the CSS Styles panel, click Attach Style Sheet.
4. When the Attach External Style Sheet dialog box opens, click the Browse button.
5. In the Select Style Sheet dialog box, browse to the styles folder in the root of the site and select `primary.css`.
6. From the Media list of the Attach External Style Sheet dialog box, choose All; click OK when you're ready.

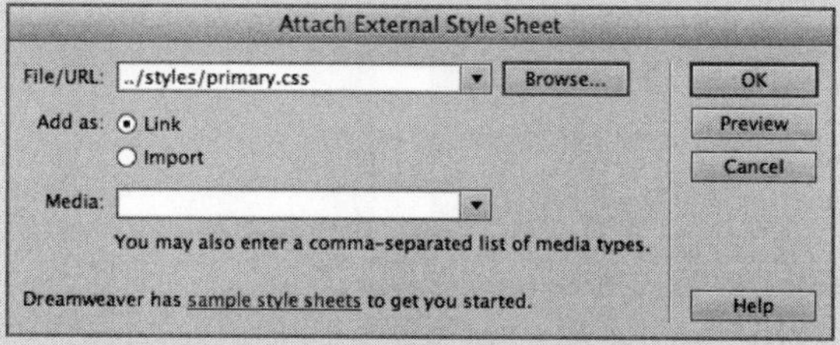

You'll notice that certain parts of the page, like the headings and paragraphs, are automatically styled because the style sheet includes rules for those tags. Now, let's apply some styles to specific page elements.

1. Place your cursor in the first heading, Coming attractions.
2. From the Tag Selector, choose the `<div>` tag to the left of the `<h1>` tag.
3. In the Property inspector, select middle from the Div ID list.

   The `#middle` style adds an outside border and increases the padding. Now, add a class to differentiate the first paragraph under each heading.
4. Place your cursor in the first paragraph beneath the initial heading.
5. Right-click the `<p>` tag in the Tag Selector and choose Set Class ⇨ firstParagraph.
6. Repeat the preceding Steps 1 and 2 for each of the remaining paragraphs under the different headings.

   Finally, apply classes to the images to help the page flow.
7. Select the first image on the page.
8. From the Property inspector's Class list, choose `.imageLeft`.

Continues

continued

9. Repeat the preceding Steps 1 and 2 for the remaining images, alternating between the `.imageLeft` and the `.imageRight` classes.
10. When you're done, save your page.

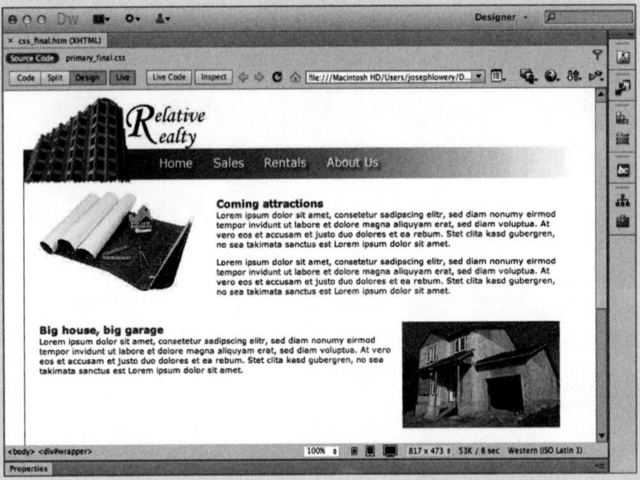

The two image-related styles align the image differently and add additional padding to complete the effect.

Editing and managing style sheets

Style sheets, like most elements of a web page, are almost never set in stone. Designers need to be able to modify style rules—whether they're embedded or from an external style sheet—at a moment's notice. Through the CSS Styles panel's Edit Styles mode, Dreamweaver provides near-immediate access.

CSS Styles panel

As discussed earlier, the CSS Styles panel in All mode displays all the styles attached to the current page, whether embedded or external. Presented in a collapsible outline (see Figure 6-11), Dreamweaver shows the styles in the order in which they are defined in the code. The Class list is more than just a pretty display—it's a direct pipeline to editing each style. You can select any style and click the Edit Style button, and Dreamweaver displays the CSS Rule Definition dialog box with the current style's settings.

If you'd prefer to work directly with the CSS code, double-click the style. Dreamweaver goes to the style selected in the editing option of your choice, as defined in the CSS Styles category of the Preferences. You can choose between using the Edit CSS dialog box, the Properties pane, or Code view.

FIGURE 6-11

Both embedded and external styles are shown in the Edit Styles mode of the CSS Styles panel.

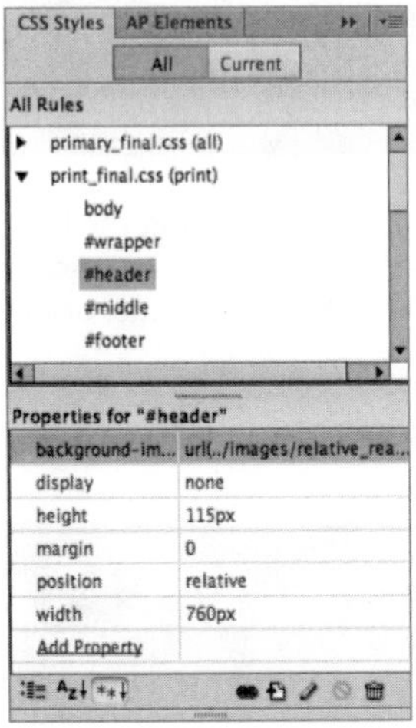

6

Applying CSS Hacks

As any designer beginning to work with CSS knows, not all browsers are created equal. In fact, browsers vary wildly in their CSS support. To achieve cross-browser compatibility with CSS, designers have resorted to using what are referred to as *CSS hacks*. A CSS hack is the use of CSS code in an unintended fashion to make CSS elements unavailable to certain browsers. In other words, a CSS hack acts as a filter. Dreamweaver includes two of the most common hacks that allow you to hide CSS from two of the most problematic browsers: Netscape 4.*x* and Internet Explorer 5 for Mac. Both hacks are available only from within Code view through the context menu; commands for applying and removing each hack are included.

To hide a CSS rule from Netscape 4.*x*, use the Caio hack. In Code view, select the CSS code you want to make sure that Netscape 4.*x* does not attempt to render and right-click (Control+click). From the context menu that appears, choose Selection ➪ Apply Caio Hack. Dreamweaver wraps your selection with the following code:

```
/*/*/
/* */
```

The first line starts hiding code from Netscape 4.*x* and the second line stops the hiding.

You can hide CSS rules from Internet Explorer 5 for Mac in a similar fashion with the Backslash-Comment hack. To hide particular rules, select them and then right-click (Control+click) to bring up the context menu. Choose Selection ➪ Apply Backslash-Comment Hack; Dreamweaver wraps your selection with the following code:

```
/*Start hiding from IE Mac \*/
/*Stop hiding from IE Mac */
```

To remove either of these hacks, select the entire code block, including the opening and closing hack lines, and choose Selection ➪ Remove Backslash-Comment Hack or Selection ➪ Remove Caio.

TIP

Modifying or deleting a style in an external style sheet causes that style sheet to open. Dreamweaver does this so that the modification or deletion can be undone. You can force the style sheet not to open by unchecking the Open CSS Files When Modified option in the CSS Styles category of the Preferences; but, if you do, changes to the style sheet cannot be undone.

If you have an external CSS editor such as TopStyle or Style Master defined—and the Use External Editor option selected—double-clicking a style opens the style sheet in that editor. Access the Use External Editor option by right-clicking (Control+clicking) in the CSS Styles panel or by selecting the CSS Styles panel menu.

To delete a style, select the style and click the Delete CSS Rule button.

NOTE

If you're looking for a single reference on CSS hacks, check out *CSS Hacks and Filters* written by me and published by Wiley. For more details, visit `www.idest.com/csshacks/`.

CSS Styles panel Properties pane

Although the CSS Rule Definition dialog box is helpful when establishing CSS rules, it's not the most direct route for modifying them. Dreamweaver supplies a much quicker facility for viewing and changing existing styles: the Properties pane of the CSS Styles panel (see Figure 6-12).

To change the value of a property, click into the corresponding field on the right of the CSS Properties tab. Color-based properties, such as `background-color`, include a standard Dreamweaver color picker to simplify your selection; properties requiring a URL offer both Point-To-File and Browse-For-File icons. Those properties that use specific keywords, such as `display`, provide a list of acceptable values. In all cases, the value can also be entered by hand. This is especially useful when working with properties that accept compound values, such as `border`, for which entering the values in proper order (style, color, width) is valid. Hover over a property value to see a code hint. After you've inserted your new value, press Enter (Return) or click anywhere to confirm the change; Dreamweaver immediately renders the results.

To add a new property to an existing rule in the Properties pane, follow these steps:

1. In the Properties pane, click Add New Property.
2. Enter the property in the blank field that appears. Alternatively, you can choose a property from the drop-down list.
3. Press Tab or Enter (Return) to move to the second column.
4. Enter the value for the new property.

To remove a property from the Properties pane, select it and press Delete.

FIGURE 6-12

Insert a new property directly into a rule through the Properties pane's Add Property link.

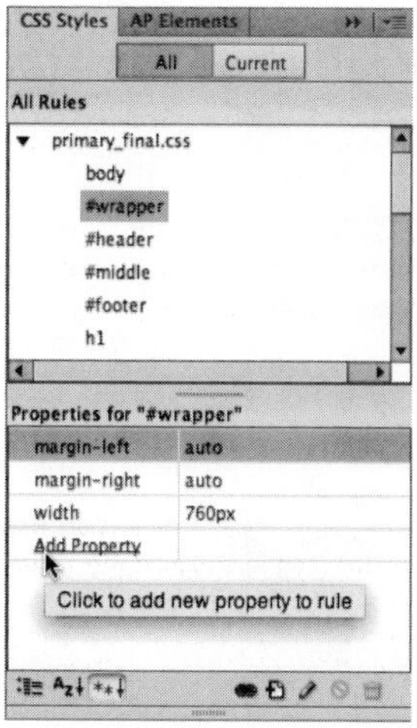

You can add new properties through the CSS Styles panel in either All or Current modes. All mode works best when you're editing CSS from a top-down perspective. If you'd prefer a bottom-up approach, switch to Current mode and select the tag containing the existing style rather than the style itself.

Applying Enhanced CSS3 Styles

CSS3 has brought a host of new web design possibilities, including rounded corners, drop shadows, and gradient backgrounds. Dreamweaver has full code support for CSS3 properties with a good number of them definable through special mechanisms in the CSS Styles panel Properties pane.

Let's look at the `box-shadow` property, which allows you to add a drop-shadow (as well as many other varieties) to an element like a `<div>` tag. This versatile property includes parameters for X and Y offsets, blur radius, spread distance, and color. You can even make the shadow appear within a box via the `inset` keyword. Naturally, Dreamweaver provides complete code-hinting support for this property, but it also offers an enhanced interface in the Properties pane of the CSS Styles panel. Click the plus-triangle symbol to expand the additional user interface shown in Figure 6-13. As you can see, all values can be entered directly and the effect is shown immediately in Live View.

Other CSS3 properties that have been given the expanded interface treatment in Dreamweaver include `border-image`, `border-radius`, `text-shadow`, and the vendor-specific properties (explained in the next section) for these elements.

FIGURE 6-13

No need to add a drop shadow in a graphics program with the CSS3 box-shadow property.

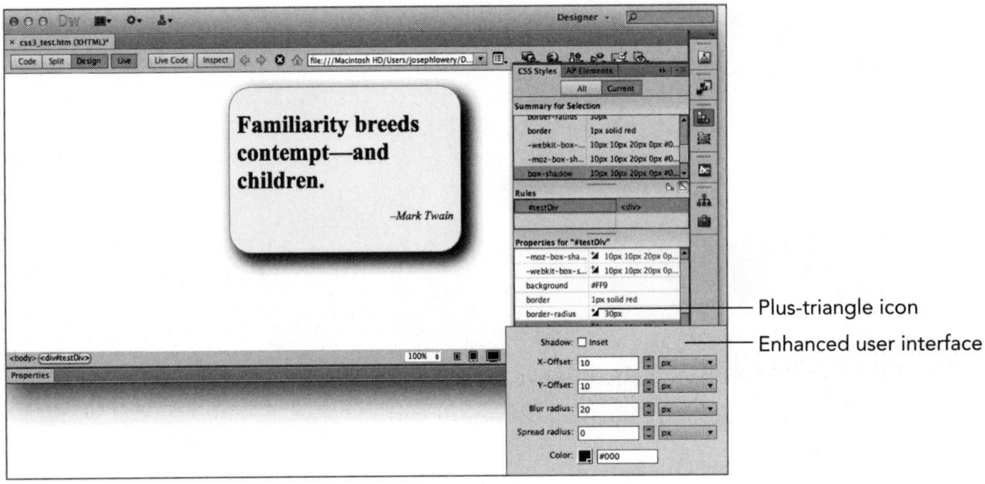

Handling vendor-specific CSS properties

Although many enhanced CSS3 properties enjoy surprisingly good support in modern browsers, the CSS3 specification is still in flux and some of the effects can only be rendered using properties with vendor-specific prefixes. Vendor-specific prefixes include:

- `-webkit`: For browsers that use the WebKit rendering engine such as Safari and Chrome (and Dreamweaver's Live View).
- `-moz`: For Mozilla-based browsers such as Firefox.
- `-o`: For the Opera browser.
- `-ms`: For Microsoft browsers, that is, Internet Explorer.

If you know the syntax, you can enter vendor-specific properties and values directly in the Properties pane. If you're not sure, use Code view and take advantage of Dreamweaver's robust code hinting.

The best way to write the code for properties that include vendor specific options is to be sure to list the generic CSS3 property last so that—if and when—the standard CSS3 property gains full browser support, it will take precedence. Here's an example of the `border-radius` property, with vendor-specific options for WebKit and Mozilla browsers:

```
-webkit-border-radius: 20px;
-moz-border-radius: 20px;
border-radius: 20px;
```

Although recent versions of most browsers render the CSS3 `border-radius` property, many designers continue to include vendor-specific properties to extend backwards-compatibility.

Toggling CSS properties

Have you ever had to pinpoint which circuit breaker controlled which part of your home? Typically, you end up turning them off and on, one at a time, to see which lights went out when. Similarly, it's easy to lose sight of what properties in the various rules are having what effect, and temporarily removing them is a good testing technique. Dreamweaver provides a point-and-click method for easily disabling and enabling any CSS property.

> **TIP**
>
> Move your cursor over the far-left column of the properties in the CSS Styles panel and you'll see the universal "no" symbol (a circle with the line through it) appear in gray. Click once to turn the symbol red and disable the associated property (see Figure 6-14); click again to enable the property again. The ability to enable/disable CSS properties is available in the Properties pane for both All and Current mode, as well as the Current mode's Summary pane.

FIGURE 6-14

Temporarily disable a CSS property to better understand how it affects your page.

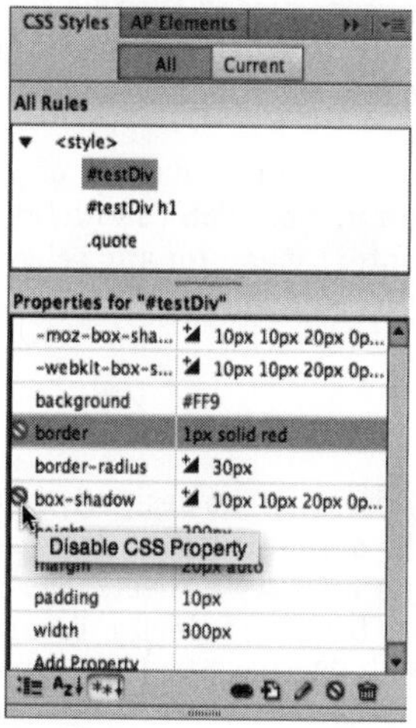

When you disable a property, Dreamweaver comments it out of the code using a special syntax. For example, let's say there is a `background-color` property that is coded like this:

```
background-color: #fff;
```

If you disable the property in the CSS styles panel, the code changes to this:

```
/* [disabled]background-color: #FFF; */
```

In CSS, surrounding your code with `/*` and `*/` converts it to a comment. Within that comment, Dreamweaver inserts the `[disabled]` keyword to distinguish any toggled-off property from any comments entered manually in the code. But what if you already have a comment following a property? CSS doesn't permit nested comments, so Dreamweaver will take code like this:

```
background-color: #fff; /* Make sure the bg is white */
```

and comment out just the property and value, thereby leaving your comment intact:

```
/* [disabled]background-color: #FFF; */ /* Make sure the bg is white */
```

Should you enable the property again, Dreamweaver removes its comment indicators and restores your code as before.

TIP

Any property that has been disabled is also identified with the universal "no" symbol in the Code Navigator.

If you have disabled a number of properties in a CSS rule, you can re-enable them all at once with a single command. Simply right-click (Control+click) any properties in the rule or the rule itself and choose Enable All Disabled in Selected Rule from the context menu. This option is also available from the panel menu button in the upper-right of the CSS Styles panel.

Conversely, let's say you've completed your testing and you've discovered a number of properties that have no impact and are currently disabled. You can clean up your CSS rules by removing these unneeded properties in one operation. Bring up the context menu for any selected rule via the panel menu button or right-clicking (Control+clicking) the rule or property and choosing Delete All Disabled in Selected Rule.

Managing CSS rules

The development of the CSS rules for a site is an evolutionary process. The designer may start by embedding CSS layout rules in the basic page and, when the design is locked down, elect to move the rules to an external sheet. Or, before publishing the final style sheets, the designer may prefer to clean them up, grouping similar styles together for added clarity. Dreamweaver offers a number of key tools to help designers manipulate their CSS rules however they choose.

Managing your CSS rules in Dreamweaver is both intuitive and fast. You can, for example, simply drag-and-drop a CSS rule from one location in your style sheet to another—right in the CSS Styles panel. Highlight any rule while in All mode and drag it to its new location. Rules can easily be moved to any embedded or attached style sheet; any unopened style sheet affected is opened and marked as modified. You can move a single rule at a time or select any number of them to drag to a new location.

CSS rules can also be moved to an unattached or new style sheet. Right-click any selected rules and choose Move CSS Rules to begin the process. When the Move To External Style Sheet dialog box opens, as shown in Figure 6-15, you have the option to choose an existing style sheet or store the selected rules in a new one. If you decide to use a new style sheet, a Save Style Sheet As dialog box appears when you click OK.

FIGURE 6-15

Move any style rules selected in the CSS Styles panel to a current external style sheet or a brand-new one.

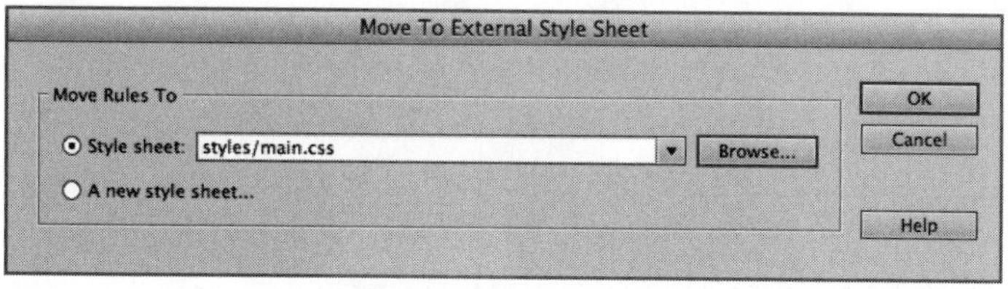

The Move CSS Rules feature is also available in the Coding toolbar along with another powerful, albeit more specialized, CSS management command: Convert Inline CSS To Rule. As the name implies, the Convert Inline CSS To Rule feature moves style attributes within a tag like this:

```
<div id="legalDisclaimer" style="font-size: smaller;">
```

to a separate rule, like this:

```
#legalDisclaimer { font-size: smaller; }
```

TIP

The Convert Inline CSS To Rule command is terrific for cleaning up legacy pages where the use of inline styles in absolutely positioned `<div>` tags was the rule rather than the exception.

The contextual menu in the CSS Styles panel offers a number of other management tools in addition to the Move CSS Rules command. Beyond the traditional cut/copy/paste options is the Go To Code feature. As you might suspect, Go To Code goes directly to the CSS code defining the selected rule, whether the rule is in the current page or an external style sheet. Go To Code lets you dive right into the heart of your CSS, quickly and easily.

The Duplicate command is another CSS rule management power tool and one that I personally use all the time. Often I find that a rule I need to create has similar properties to an existing rule—and it's much faster to duplicate the rule than re-create it. When you choose to duplicate a selected rule, a dialog box with all the options of the New CSS Rule dialog box appears (see Figure 6-16). This featureset allows you to copy the properties of any rule and, if you choose, change the selector to anything you desire. You could, for example, duplicate a rule with an ID selector and save your new rule as a class. You can even save the duplicated rule in a different style sheet or the current page. Once you select the name of your duplicated rule, as well as the selector, the style is added to the specified location; however, unlike when creating a new style, the CSS Rule Definition dialog box does not appear.

FIGURE 6-16

Duplicate any rule to quickly repurpose already defined properties under a different name, selector, and/or location.

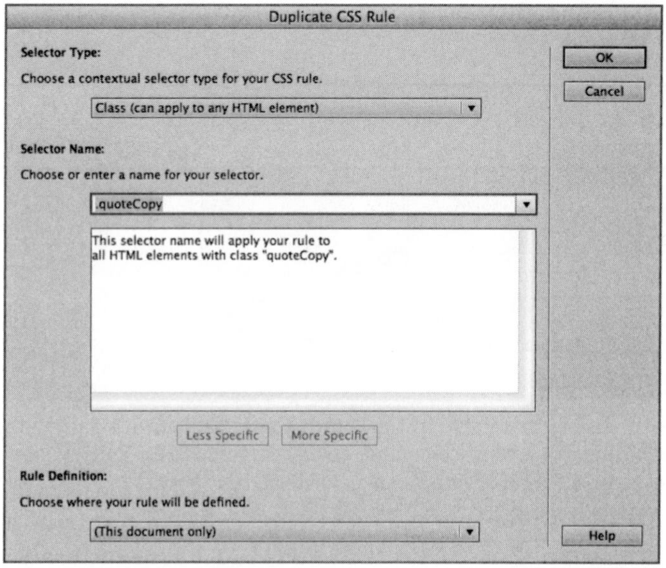

Debugging your applied CSS

Anyone working with CSS for any amount of time has experienced the frustration of seeing his or her Dreamweaver-perfect page break in one or more browsers. Real-world browser testing is a tried-and-true technique, but a tedious and time-consuming one with no clear solutions. Dreamweaver offers a real alternative: Check Browser Compatibility.

With the Check Browser Compatibility feature, your page is quickly reviewed for 26 different, common browser rendering issues. Better yet, the command offers full relief for the identified problems, both its in an immediate form through the Results panel and in a more full-featured fashion via the web. Debugging your CSS styled pages just got a whole lot easier.

To begin the CSS debugging process, choose File ➪ Check Page ➪ Browser Compatibility or select Check Browser Compatibility from the Document toolbar. The current page is immediately reviewed, and if any issues are found, they are listed in the Results panel, as shown in Figure 6-17. Each listing displays the line number, the name, and a brief description of the problem, as well as browsers affected. The Learn More link opens your primary browser to the relevant page on Adobe's CSS Advisor mini-site (`http://www.adobe.com/go/cssi`) where a community-recognized solution is available. Users can contribute to the site to help build the knowledge base as new problems and answers arise.

You can find a detailed discussion of the Check Browser Compatibility feature, including which CSS bugs are detected and establishing command settings, in Chapter 30.

FIGURE 6-17

Run Check Browser Compatibility for any page to identify CSS rendering issues in any of the supported browsers.

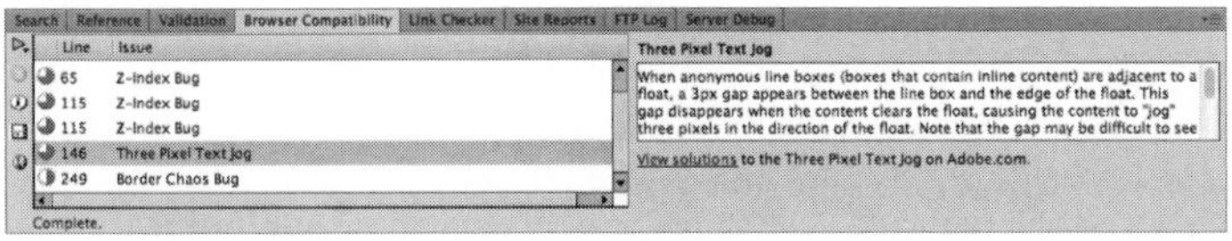

Dreamweaver TECHNIQUE

Crafting a Print Style Sheet

In this Technique, you attach a print style sheet to a page and change the styles so that the document is more printer-friendly.

1. In the Technique site, expand the 06_css folder and open `print_start.htm`.
2. From the CSS Styles panel, click Attach Style Sheet.
3. When the Attach External Style Sheet dialog box opens, click the Browse button.
4. In the Select Style Sheet dialog box, browse to the styles folder in the root of the site and select `print.css`.
5. From the Media list of the Attach External Style Sheet dialog box, choose Print; click OK when you're ready.

To see the changes you'll make take effect, you'll need to switch to print style rendering:

1. Choose View ➪ Toolbars ➪ Style Rendering.
2. From the Style Rendering toolbar, click Render Print Media Type, or choose View ➪ Style Rendering ➪ Screen Media Type.
3. In the CSS Styles panel, make sure you're in All mode; if not, click All.

For your first change to the print style sheet, hide those page elements that are not relevant in print: the header and footer.

1. In the CSS Styles panel, expand the `print.css` entry and select the `#header` style.
2. Click Edit Style at the bottom of the CSS Styles panel.
3. When the CSS Rule Definition dialog box opens, switch to the Block category and, from the Display list, choose None.
4. Repeat Steps 1–3, selecting the `#footer` style from the CSS Styles panel instead.

Now, you need to adjust certain styles so they are more suitable for print:

1. In the CSS Styles panel, select the `#wrapper` style.
2. From the Properties pane, click in the value column next to the width property and enter **auto**; press Enter (Return) when you're done.
3. In the CSS Styles panel, select the `h1` style.

Continues

continued

4. From the Properties pane, click in the color swatch next to the color property and select black (#000000) from the pop-up color picker.
5. Select the value next to the `font-size` property and enter **14pt**; press Enter (Return) to confirm your choice.
6. Repeat Steps 3–5, selecting the `p, td, th` style and changing the `font-size` property to **12pt**.
7. With the `p, td, th` style still selected, click Add Property and enter **line-height**; press Enter (Return) and then enter **18pt**.

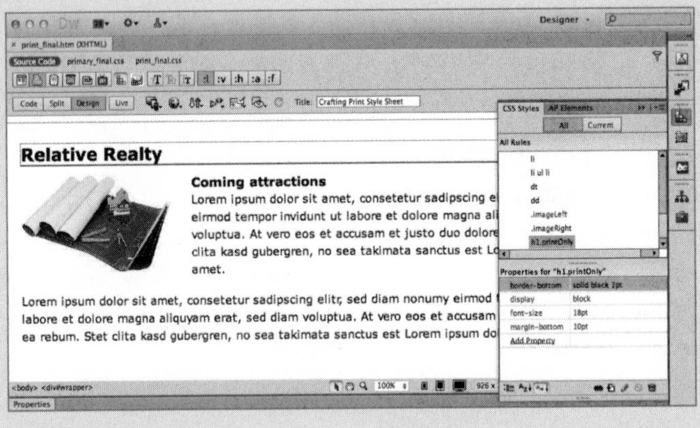

The final step is to add a heading that appears only in the print version of the page. To accomplish this, you'll need to hide the content in the screen-oriented style sheet.

1. Place your cursor on the first image on the page and switch to Code view.
2. Press the left-arrow button to move the cursor in front of the `<img>` tag and enter the following code: **<h1>Relative Realty</h1>**. Return to Design view when you're done.
3. Place your cursor in the new `<h1>` tag and, from the Property inspector's Class list, choose `printOnly`.
4. In the Style Rendering toolbar, choose Switch To Render Screen Media Type, or choose View ➪ Style Rendering ➪ Screen Media Type.

   You'll notice that the heading—redundant in screen mode—is also visible here. You can change that by adding a style.
5. In the CSS Styles panel, select the `primary.css` entry and click New CSS Rule.
6. In the New CSS Rule dialog box, switch the Selector Type set to Class and change the Name field to `.printOnly`; click OK when you're ready.
7. Switch to the Block category and, from the Display list, choose None; click OK to confirm the change and close the dialog box.
8. Select File ➪ Save All to store all the changes.

You can easily see the differences by switching between the Screen and the Print icons on the Style Rendering toolbar.

Styles and Their Attributes

After you've selected a type and name for a new style or chosen to edit an existing style, the CSS Rule Definition dialog box opens. A Category list from which you select a style category (just as you select a category of preferences in Dreamweaver's Preferences dialog box) is located on the left side of this dialog box.

Dreamweaver offers you nine categories of CSS styles to help you define your style sheet:

- Type
- Background
- Block
- Box
- Border
- List
- Positioning
- Extensions
- Transitions

You can define styles from one or all categories. The following sections describe each style category and its available settings.

Type options

The Type category specifies the appearance and layout of the typeface for the page in the browser window. The Type category, shown in Figure 6-18, is one of the most widely used and supported categories—it can be rendered in all current browser versions.

Table 6-1 explains the settings available in this category.

FIGURE 6-18

The Type category includes some of the most frequently used CSS attributes.

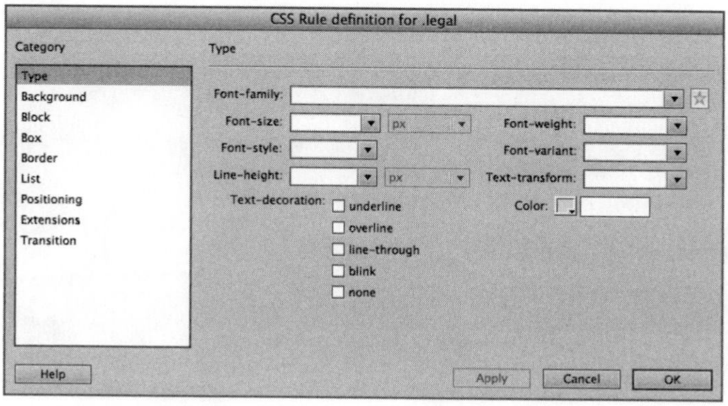

TABLE 6-1 CSS Type Attributes

Type Setting	Description
Font	Specifies the font or a collection of fonts, known as a font *family*. You can edit the font list by selecting Edit Font List from the drop-down list. (This sequence opens the Edit Font List dialog box, as described in Chapter 7.)
Size	Selects a size for the selected font. If you enter a value, you can then select the measurement system in the adjacent text box (the default is pixels). The relative sizes, such as small, medium, and large, are set relative to the parent element. Values can be selected from the drop-down list or entered by hand.
Style	Specifies a normal, italic, or oblique attribute for the font. An oblique font may have been generated in the browser by electronically slanting a normal font.
Line Height	Sets the line height of the line (similar to *leading* in traditional layout). Typically, line height is a point or two more than the font size, although you can set the line height to be the same as or smaller than the font size for an overlapping effect.
Decoration	Changes the decoration for text. Options include underline, overline, line-through, blink, and none. The blink decoration is displayed only in Netscape 4.*x* and earlier browsers but is deprecated in HTML5 and, as the W3C notes, "No, really, don't use it. It's simply evil."
Weight	Sets the boldness of the text. You can use the relative settings (normal, lighter, bold, and bolder) or apply a numeric value. Normal is around 400; bold is 700.
Variant	Switches between normal and small caps. Small caps is a font style that displays text in all uppercase, but the letters that you style as capitals appear slightly larger.
Text-Transform	Forces a browser to render the text as capitalized, uppercase, lowercase, or none.
Color	Sets a color for the selected font. Enter a color name or select the color swatch to choose a browser-safe color from the color picker or, new to CS6, with the Color Format options (provide details if necessary).

NOTE

Although it is not listed in the CSS Definition dialog box, Dreamweaver supports a CSS3 property that renders a shadow on any text element, aptly called `text-shadow`. The `text-shadow` property takes up to four values: horizontal offset, vertical offset, blur distance, and color. Here's what the property looks like in code:

```
text-shadow: 2px -2px 6px #000;
```

As shown, negative offsets are allowed. You can also include multiple shadows by separating value sets with commas, like this:

```
text-shadow: 2px 2px 1px #000, -2px -2px 1px #000;
```

Enter the `text-shadow` property in Dreamweaver's CSS Styles panel Properties pane or in Code view.

Background options

Background images and background color are a key option in the designer's tool chest. Thanks to CSS Background attributes, designers can use background images and color with increased control. CSS backgrounds can be specified for a single paragraph or any other CSS selector; for example, to set a background for the entire page, apply the style to the <body> tag. Moreover, instead of an image automatically tiling to fill the browser window, CSS backgrounds can be made to tile horizontally, vertically, or not at all (see Figure 6-19). You can even position the image relative to the selected element.

FIGURE 6-19

You can achieve a number of different tiling effects by using the Repeat attribute of the CSS Background category.

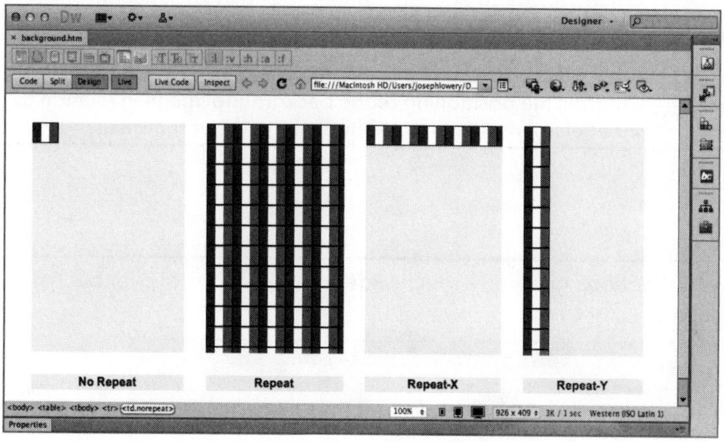

The current versions of browsers support the CSS Background attributes shown in Figure 6-20 and described in Table 6-2.

TABLE 6-2 CSS Background Attributes

Background Setting	Description
Background Color	Sets the background color for a particular style. Note that this setting enables you to set background colors for individual paragraphs or other elements.
Background Image	Specifies a background image. The background image appears closer to the viewer than does the background color (if any).

Continues

TABLE 6-2 *(continued)*

Background Setting	Description
Repeat	Determines the tiling options for a graphic: ■ **no repeat** displays the image in the upper-left corner of the applied style. ■ **repeat** tiles the background image horizontally and vertically across the applied style. ■ **repeat-x** tiles the background image horizontally across the applied style. ■ **repeat-y** tiles the background image vertically down the applied style.
Attachment	Determines whether the background image remains fixed in its original position or scrolls with the page. This setting is useful for positioned elements. If you use the overflow attribute, you often want the background image to scroll in order to maintain layout control.
Horizontal Position	Controls the positioning of the background image in relation to the style sheet elements (text or graphics) along the horizontal axis.
Vertical Position	Controls the positioning of the background image in relation to the style sheet elements (text or graphics) along the vertical axis.

FIGURE 6-20

The CSS Background options give you a much wider range of control over background images and color.

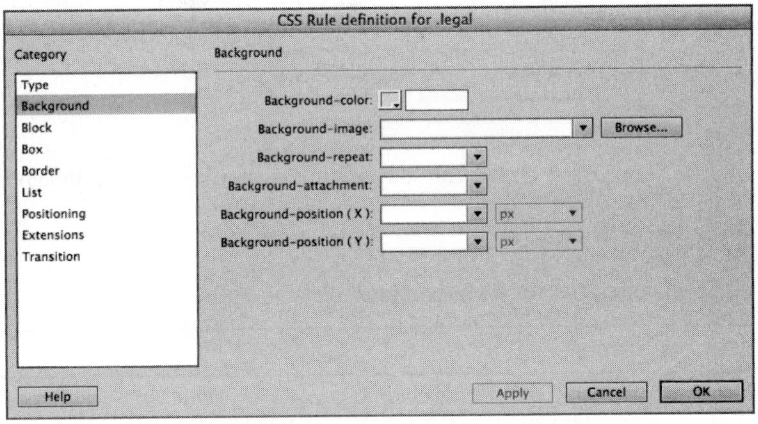

NOTE

One of the most exciting CSS3 developments is the introduction of gradients to the CSS coder's palette. Graphic designers make great use of gradients in page and element backgrounds, as well as navigation buttons, among other areas. While CSS3 gradients aren't intended to replace your graphic programs gradient fill feature, they're certainly helpful in reducing image downloads and speeding page load.

As with `text-shadow`, CSS gradients are supported in Dreamweaver only through Code view and the Properties pane of the CSS Styles panel. The syntax, however, is significantly more complex, especially if you want to extend support to Internet Explorer browsers. Luckily, a number of tools have emerged that will handle the heavy code lifting for you—all you need to do is copy and paste. One superlative online tool, the Ultimate CSS Gradient Generator, can be found at `http://www.colorzilla.com/gradient-editor/`. Another option is the latest release of Adobe Fireworks CS6. Its CSS Properties panel can pick up many different CSS properties, including gradients. Here's the code from a simple linear gradient:

```
/* Firefox v3.6+ */
background-image:-moz-linear-gradient(50% 0% -90deg,rgb(153,255,255)
0%,rgb(0,76,102) 100%);
/* Safari v4.0+ and by Chrome v3.0+ */
background-image:-webkit-gradient(linear,50% 0%,50% 100%,color-stop(0,
rgb(153,255,255)),color-stop(1, rgb(0,76,102)));
/* Chrome v10.0+ and by Safari nightly build*/
background-image:-webkit-linear-gradient(-90deg,rgb(153,255,255) 0%,rgb
(0,76,102) 100%);
/* Opera v11.10+ */
background-image:-o-linear-gradient(-90deg,rgb(153,255,255) 0%,rgb
(0,76,102) 100%);
background-image:linear-gradient(-90deg,rgb(153,255,255) 0%,rgb
(0,76,102) 100%);width:643px;
height:152px;
filter:progid:DXImageTransform.Microsoft.gradient( startColorstr =
#ff99ffff,endColorstr =#ff004c66,GradientType = 0);
-ms-filter:"progid:DXImageTransform.Microsoft.gradient( startColorstr =
#ff99ffff,endColorstr =#ff004c66,GradientType = 0)";
```

Although this example uses just two color stops, you can use as many color stops as desired, as well as variable opacity.

Block options

One of the most common formatting effects in traditional publishing is justified text—text that appears as a solid block. Justified text is possible with the `Text Align` attribute, one of the seven options available in the CSS Block category, as shown in Figure 6-21. Indented paragraphs are also a possibility.

Dreamweaver includes an option for setting the `Display` attribute. As the name implies, the `Display` attribute determines how an element should be presented. `Display` accepts a wide range of values—19 in all—but only a few are currently supported by even the latest browsers. That said, the supported values—`block`, `inline`, and, curiously enough, `none`—are very important indeed. Setting a `Display` attribute to `None` effectively hides the element to which the CSS attribute is applied; setting the same attribute to `Block` or `Inline` reveals the element. Many collapsible/expandable lists depend on the `Display` attribute to achieve their effects.

Table 6-3 lists the CSS Block options.

FIGURE 6-21

The Block options give the web designer enhanced text control.

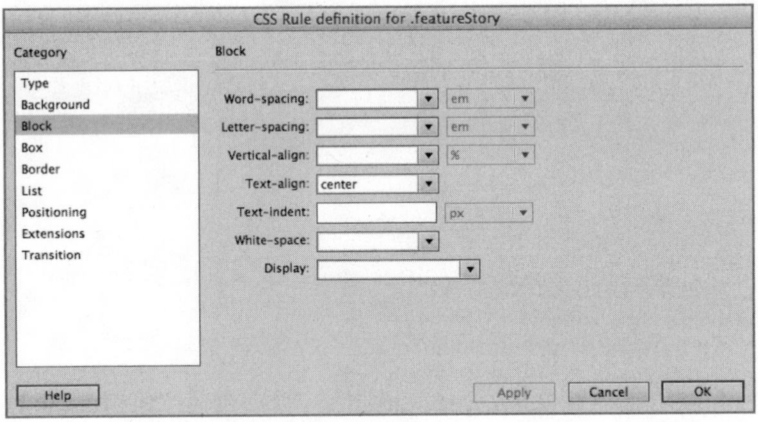

TABLE 6-3 CSS Block Attributes

Block Setting	Description
Word Spacing	Defines the spacing between words. You can increase or decrease the spacing with positive and negative values, set in ems by default. (In CSS, 1 *em* is equal to the height of a given font.) If you have a 12 pt. font, to increase the spacing between words to 24 pts., set the Word Spacing value to 2 ems.
Letter Spacing	Defines the spacing between the letters of a word. You can increase or decrease the spacing with positive and negative values, set in ems by default.
Vertical Alignment	Sets the vertical alignment of the style. Choose from baseline, sub, super, top, text-top, middle, bottom, or text-bottom, or add your own value.
Text Align	Sets text alignment (left, right, center, and justified).
Text Indent	Indents the first line of text on a style by the amount specified (negative values can also be used).
Whitespace	Controls display of spaces and tabs. The normal option causes all whitespace to collapse. The Pre option behaves similarly to the <pre> tag; all whitespace is preserved. The Nowrap option enables text to wrap if a tag is detected.
Display	Determines how a tag is represented. Possible values include none, inline, block, list-item, run-in, inline-block, compact, marker, table, inline-table, table-row-group, table-header-group, table-footer-group, table-row, table-column-group, table-column, table-cell, table-caption, and inherit.

Box options

The Box attribute defines the placement and settings for elements on a page. Many of the controls (shown in Figure 6-22) emulate spacing behavior similar to that found in `<table>` attributes, which are described in Table 6-4.

> **TIP**
>
> To have the same padding or margins all around a box area, check the Same For All option. This option allows you to set one value—Top—to use for all four sides.

FIGURE 6-22

The CSS Box attributes define the placement of HTML elements on the web page.

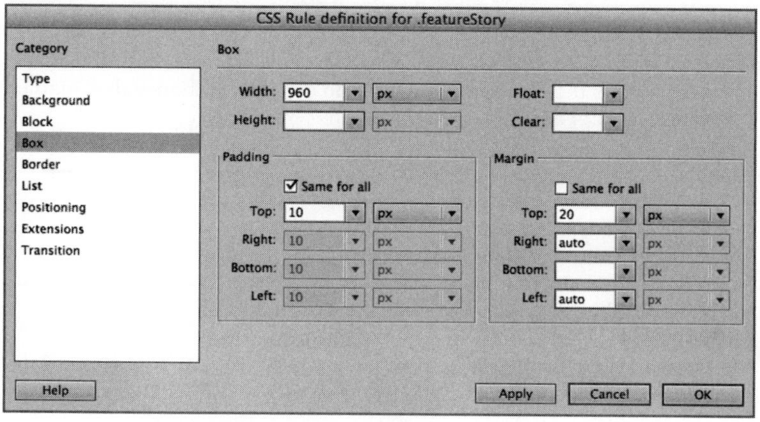

TABLE 6-4 CSS Box Attributes

Box Setting	Description
Width	Sets the width of the element.
Height	Defines the height of the element.
Float	Places the element at the left or right of the containing block's edge or the edge of another float. Any text that encounters the element wraps around its side.
Clear	Sets the side on which floated elements cannot be displayed next to the element. If a floated element is encountered, the element with the `Clear` attribute places itself beneath the element and stops the text from wrapping.
Margin	Defines the amount of space between the borders of the element and other elements in the page.
Padding	Sets the amount of space between the element and the border or margin, if no border is specified. You can control the padding for the top, right, bottom, or left independently.

Border options

With Cascading Style Sheets, you can specify many parameters for borders surrounding text, images, and other elements such as Java applets. In addition to specifying separate colors for any of the four box sides, you can also choose the width of each side's border, as shown in the CSS Border category (see Figure 6-23). You can use eight different types of border lines, including solid, dashed, inset, and ridge. As with the `Padding` and `Margin` attributes in the Box category, Dreamweaver includes a Same For All option under the `Style`, `Width`, and `Color` attributes to save you the work of having to enter the same value for all four sides. Table 6-5 lists the Border options.

TABLE 6-5 CSS Border Attributes

Border Setting	Description
Style	Sets the style of the border. You can use any of the following border styles: dotted, dashed, solid, double, groove, ridge, inset, and outset.
Width	Determines the width of the border on each side. Choose thin, medium, or thick, or enter a number to set a width.
Color	Sets the color of the border on each side.

FIGURE 6-23

Borders are useful to highlight a section of text or a graphic.

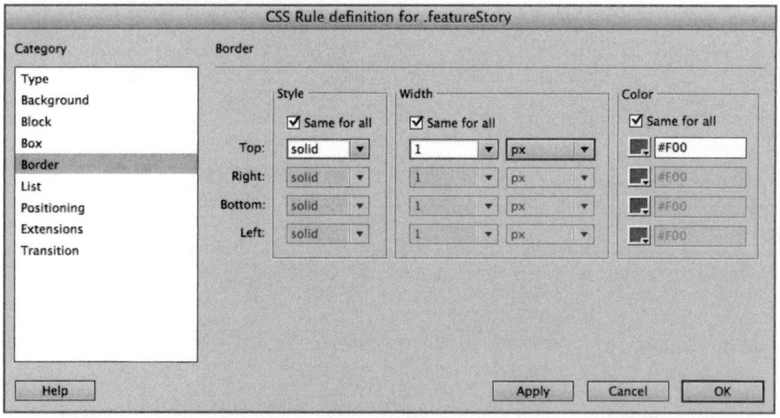

> **TIP**
> CSS Border attributes are especially useful for highlighting paragraphs of text with a surrounding box. Use the Box category's `Padding` attributes to inset the text from the border.

List options

CSS gives you greater control over bulleted points. With Cascading Style Sheets, you can now display a specific bulleted point based on a graphic image, or you can choose from the standard built-in bullets, including disc, circle, and square. The CSS List category also enables you to specify the type of ordered list, including decimal, Roman numerals, or A-B-C order. Figure 6-24 shows, and Table 6-6 describes, the settings for lists.

TABLE 6-6 List Category for Styles

List Setting	Description
Type	Selects a built-in bullet type. The options include disc, circle, square, decimal, lowercase Roman, uppercase Roman, lowercase alpha, uppercase alpha, and none.
Bullet Image	Sets an image to be used as a custom bullet. Enter the path to the image in the text box.
Position	Determines whether the list item wraps to the outside (the default) or to the inside (second lines of text align with the list marker).

FIGURE 6-24

Use the CSS List category to specify a graphic to use as a bullet.

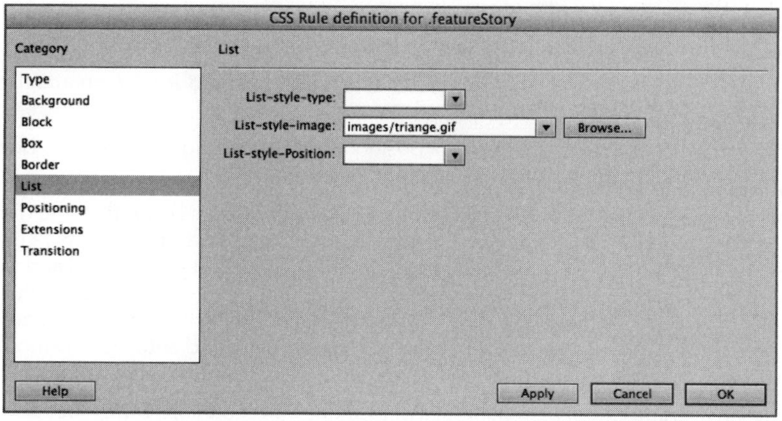

Positioning options

For many designers, positioning has increased creativity in page layout design. With positioning, you have exact control over where an element is placed on a page. The positioning attributes are often applied to targeted `div` tags to place them precisely on the page. Figure 6-25 shows the various attributes that provide this pinpoint control of your page elements. The options are described in Table 6-7.

FIGURE 6-25

Control over the placement of elements on a page is handled through CSS positioning.

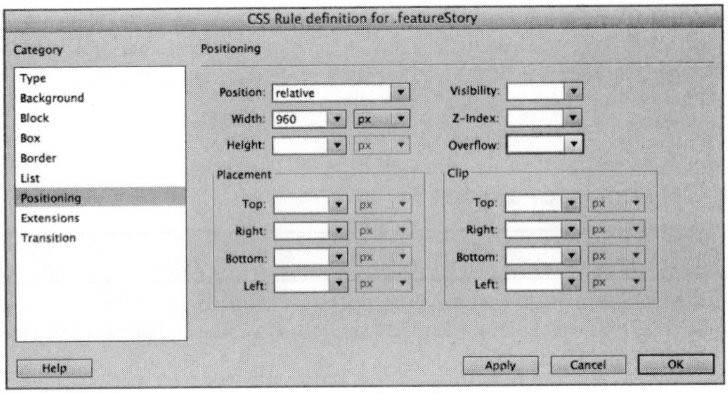

TABLE 6-7 CSS Positioning Attributes

Positioning Setting	Description
`Type`	Determines whether an element's position is absolute, relative, or static on a page. The fourth option, static, is the default positioning value and renders elements in the normal document flow.
`Width`	Sets the width of the element.
`Height`	Sets the height of the element.
`Visibility`	Determines whether the element is visible or hidden, or inherits the property from its parent.
`Z-Index`	Sets the stack order of a positioned element. Higher values are closer to the top.
`Overflow`	Specifies how the element is displayed when it's larger than the dimensions of the element. Options include the following: `visible`, `hidden`, `scroll`, and `auto`. `Visible`, where the element is displayed and the dimensions are disregarded; `hidden`, where content outside of the element's dimensions are not shown; `scroll`, which inserts scroll bars to display the overflowing portion of the element; and auto, which automatically displays scrollbars if content exceeds the element's dimensions.
`Placement`	Sets the styled element's placement with the `top`, `right`, `bottom`, or `left` attributes.
`Clip`	Sets the visible portion of the element through the top, right, bottom, and left attributes.

Dreamweaver's AP elements are built upon the foundation of CSS positioning. For a complete explanation of AP elements and their attributes, see Chapter 10.

Extensions options

The specifications for Cascading Style Sheets are rapidly evolving, and Dreamweaver has grouped some cutting-edge features in the Extensions category. As of this writing, most of the Extensions attributes (see Table 6-8) are supported by all major browsers with the exception of filters, which are rendered only by Internet Explorer. The Extensions settings shown in Figure 6-26 affect three different areas: page breaks for printing, the user's cursor, and special effects called *filters*.

TABLE 6-8 CSS Extensions Attributes

Extensions Setting	Description
Pagebreak	Inserts a point on a page where a printer sees a page break. This feature is partially supported only by most modern browsers and fully supported by Opera 9.2 or higher.
Cursor	Defines the type of cursor that appears when the user moves the cursor over an element. Currently supported by most modern browsers.
Filter	Filters enable you to customize the look and transition of an element without having to use graphic or animation files. Currently supported only by Internet Explorer 4.0 and above.

FIGURE 6-26

The CSS Extensions category enables some terrific effects, which, unfortunately, are not well supported across the board.

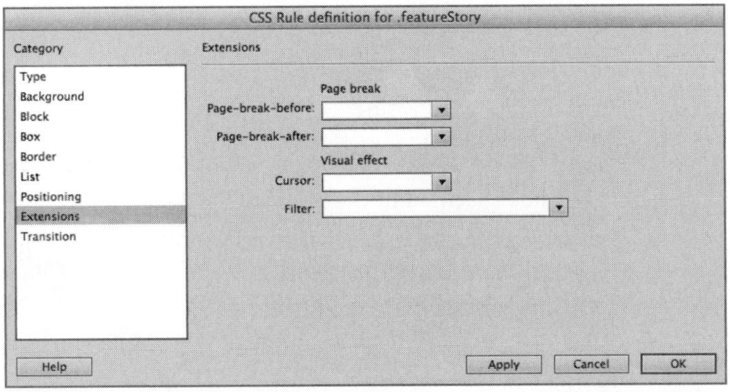

NOTE

One of the problems with the web's never-ending evolution of page design is evident when you begin to print the page. The `Pagebreak` attribute alleviates this problem by enabling the designer to designate a style that forces a page break when printing; the break can occur either before or after the element is attached to the style. This attribute is especially important for print media styles.

The `Filter` attribute offers 16 different special effects that can be applied to an element. Many of these effects, such as Wave and Xray, are quite stunning, although their overall effectiveness is muted with just Internet Explorer support. Several effects involve transitions, as well. Table 6-9 details these effects.

Transition options

The Transition category of the CSS Rule Definition dialog box allows you to animate a wide range of CSS properties. Typically the transitions are applied to a selector with a user-driven pseudo-class such as `:hover` or `:focus`. The Transition category allows you to set the the same duration, delay how the transition is applied over time to all properties that can be animated within the selector, or define separate values for individual properties, as shown in Figure 6-27. Once you clear the All Animatable Properties checkbox and click Add (+), a list of properties appears. Select any one to set its particular values. Once a property is set, it becomes unavailable from the Add list.

FIGURE 6-27

To set different values for individual properties, clear the All Animatable Properties checkbox and select your properties from the Add icon.

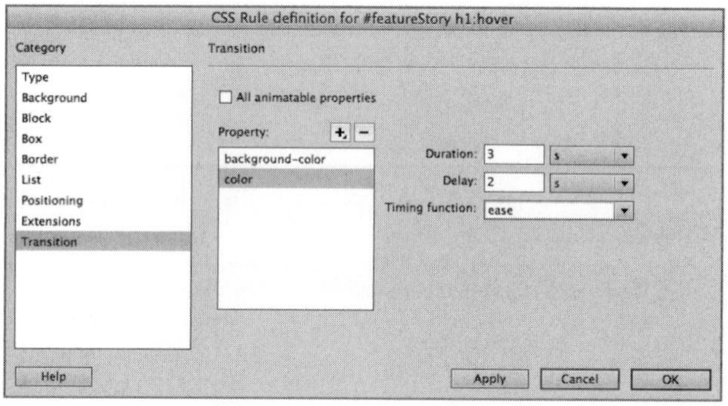

There are three properties that can be specified in the Transition category: Duration, Delay, and Timing Function. Both Duration and Delay can be set in seconds (s) or milliseconds (ms). The Timing Function defines how the transition is applied during the duration period. These options can give a transition a more-or-less mechanical feel. The six available options are:

- **cubic-bezier (x1, y1, x2, y2):** Allows for custom definition of the transition by specifying four values in the generated code from 0 to 1.
- **ease:** Starts the animation slow, picks up speed, and then slows down before finishing.
- **ease-in:** Sets the transition to start slowly and then finish evenly.
- **ease-in-out:** Defines the transition to start and finish slowly.
- **ease-out:** Starts the transition quickly and finishes slowly.
- **linear:** Sets the transition to use the same speed from start to finish.

TABLE 6-9 CSS Filters

Filter	Syntax	Description
`Alpha`	`Alpha (Opacity=`*`opacity`*`, FinishOpacity=`*`finishopacity`*`, Style=`*`style`*`, StartX=`*`startX`*`, StartY=`*`startY`*`, FinishX=`*`finishX`*`, FinishY=`*`finishY`*`)` ■ *`opacity`* is a value from 0 to 100, where 0 is transparent and 100 is fully opaque. ■ *`startX`*, *`startY`*, *`finishX`*, and *`finishY`* are pixel values indicating where the effect should start and end. ■ *`style`* can be 0 (uniform), 1 (linear), 2 (radial), or 3 (rectangular).	Sets the opacity of a specified gradient region. This can have the effect of creating a burst of light in an image.
`BlendTrans`	`blendTrans (Duration=`*`duration`*`)` ■ *`duration`* is a time value for the length of the transition, in the format of *seconds.milliseconds*.	Causes an image to fade in or out over a specified time.
`Blur`	`blur (Add=`*`add`*`, Direction=`*`direction`*`, Strength=`*`strength`*`)` ■ *`add`* is any integer other than 0. ■ *`direction`* is any value from 0 to 315 in increments of 45. ■ *`strength`* is any positive integer representing the number of pixels affected.	Emulates motion blur for images.
`Chroma`	`chroma (Color= `*`color`*`)` ■ *`color`* must be given in hexadecimal form—for example, #rrggbb.	Makes a specific color in an image transparent.
`DropShadow`	`Dropshadow (Color=`*`color`*`, OffX=`*`offX`*`, OffY=`*`offY`*`, Positive=`*`positive`*`)` ■ *`color`* is a hexadecimal triplet. ■ *`offX`* and *`offY`* are pixel offsets for the shadow. ■ *`positive`* is a Boolean switch; use 1 to create shadow for nontransparent pixels and 0 to create shadow for transparent pixels.	Creates a drop shadow of the applied element, either image or text, in the specified color.
`FlipH`	`FlipH`	Flips an image or text horizontally.
`FlipV`	`FlipV`	Flips an image or text vertically.
`Glow`	`Glow (Color=`*`color`*`, Strength=`*`strength`*`)` ■ *`positive`* is a Boolean switch; use 1 to create shadow for nontransparent pixels and 0 to create shadow for transparent pixels. ■ *`color`* is a hexadecimal triplet. ■ *`strength`* is a value from 0 to 100.	Adds radiance to an image in the specified color.

Continues

TABLE 6-9 *(continued)*

Filter	Syntax	Description
`Gray`	`Gray`	Converts an image in grayscale.
`Invert`	`Invert`	Reverses the hue, saturation, and luminance of an image.
`Light*`	`Light`	Creates the illusion that an object is illuminated by one or more light sources.
`Mask`	`Mask (Color=`*`color`*`)` ■ *`color`* is a hexadecimal triplet.	Sets all the transparent pixels to the specified color and converts the nontransparent pixels to the background color.
`RevealTrans*`	`RevealTrans (Duration=`*`duration`*`, Transition=`*`style`*`)` ■ *`duration`* is a time value that the transition takes, in the format of seconds.milliseconds. ■ *`style`* is one of 23 different transitions.	Reveals an image using a specified type of transition over a set period of time.
`Shadow`	`Shadow (Color=`*`color`*`, Direction=`*`direction`*`)` ■ *`color`* is a hexadecimal triplet. ■ *`direction`* is any value from 0 to 315 in increments of 45.	Creates a gradient shadow in the specified color and direction for images or text.
`Wave`	`Wave (Add=`*`add`*`, Freq=`*`freq`*`, LightStrength=`*`lightstrength`*`, Phase=`*`phase`*`, Strength=`*`strength`*`)` ■ *add* is a Boolean value, where 1 adds the original object to the filtered object and 0 does not. ■ *`freq`* is an integer specifying the number of waves. ■ *`lightstrength`* is a percentage value. ■ *`phase`* specifies the angular offset of the wave, in percentage (for example, 0% or 100% = 360 degrees, 25% = 90 degrees). ■ *`strength`* is an integer value specifying the intensity of the wave effect.	Adds sine wave distortion to the selected image or text.
`Xray`	`Xray`	Converts an image to inverse grayscale for an X-rayed appearance.

If you choose the cubic-bezier option for your timing function, you'll need to change the placeholder values generated by Dreamweaver. Here's the code Dreamweaver outputs:

```
-webkit-transition-timing-function: cubic-bezier(x1,y1,x2,y2);
-moz-transition-timing-function: cubic-bezier(x1,y1,x2,y2);
-ms-transition-timing-function: cubic-bezier(x1,y1,x2,y2);
-o-transition-timing-function: cubic-bezier(x1,y1,x2,y2);
transition-timing-function: cubic-bezier(x1,y1,x2,y2);
```

You'll need to modify the `(x1,y1,x2,y2)` values to the same set of values in each of the five declarations. As noted earlier, these values need to be between 0 and 1 for older browser support; if you're just working with newer browsers, you can go below 0 and above 1. Here's one example that gives a bounce effect when viewed in supporting browsers:

```
-webkit-transition-timing-function: cubic-bezier(0, 1.4, 1, -.560);
-moz-transition-timing-function: cubic-bezier(0, 1.4, 1, -.560);
-ms-transition-timing-function: cubic-bezier(0, 1.4, 1, -.560);
-o-transition-timing-function: cubic-bezier(0, 1.4, 1, -.560);
transition-timing-function: cubic-bezier(0, 1.4, 1, -.560);
```

Dreamweaver also includes a dedicated panel and dialog box for creating CSS-driven changes (called transforms) and transitions, covered in the following section.

Animating CSS Transitions

Until CSS3 gained wide browser support, creating simple animations required complex JavaScript coding or a plugin like Adobe Flash—but the game has definitely changed. Now, one can interactively change background colors, fade images in and out, and even fly page elements across the screen, all with just a bit of CSS3 coding.

New Feature

Dreamweaver has greatly simplified the somewhat daunting task of animating CSS properties with the CSS Transitions panel. Now you can easily animate any (or all) of the 50 available CSS properties, and set the duration, delay, timing function, and final value (whether it's a window width, font size, or background color) all at once. Moreover, the animations are easily modifiable and widely supported—and Dreamweaver handles all the coding for you.

To create a CSS transition, follow these steps:

1. Choose Window ➪ CSS Transitions.
2. When the CSS Transitions panel opens, click Add (+).
3. In the New Transition dialog box, shown in Figure 6-28, select the desired rule from the Target Rule list.
4. Choose the triggering event from the Transition On list.

FIGURE 6-28

Define as many animated properties as desired in the New Transition dialog box.

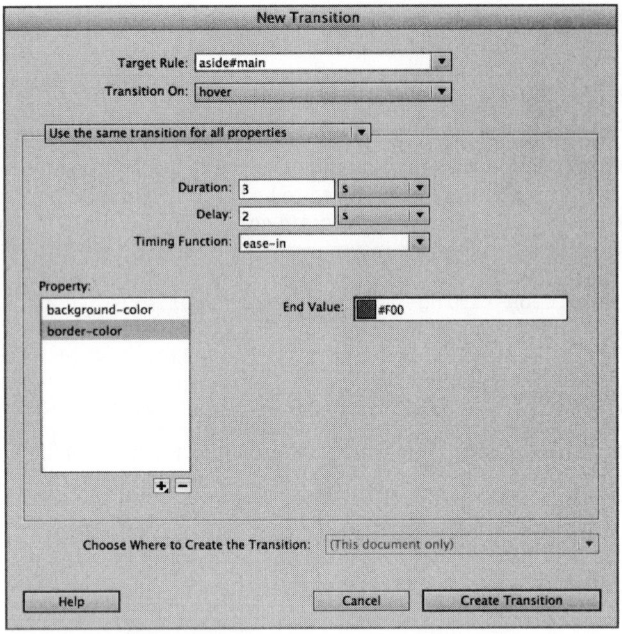

The available options in the Transition On list are:

- `active`: Invoked when the mouse is pressed down on a link.
- `checked`: Triggered by the selection of a checkbox.
- `disabled`: Set when a form element is disabled.
- `enabled`: Set when a form element is enabled.
- `focus`: Triggered when a page element is given focus, by being either clicked on or tabbed into.
- `hover`: Invoked when the user's mouse is positioned over an element.
- `indeterminate`: Set when none of the radio buttons in a collection are selected.
- `target`: Triggered when an ID of a page element matches a hash tag in the current URL, like `home.htm#news`.

5. Decide whether you're using the same transition for all properties or a different one for each and choose the desired option from the list.

   This is an important decision, as it determines the workflow for the remainder of the steps.

6. If you're setting transitions for all properties, do the following:

   a. Enter the desired time you want the animation to take in the Duration field, in either seconds or milliseconds.

   b. Enter the length of time you want the effect to remain in place in the Delay field, in either seconds or milliseconds.

c. Choose the type of animation from the Timing Function list. (See the previous section for a discussion of the timing function options.)

d. Click Add (+) to select a property to animate.

e. Enter the final value in the End Value field.

f. Repeat Steps d and e for any additional properties.

7. If you're setting transitions for each individual property, do the following:

   a. Click Add (+) to select a property to animate.

   b. Enter the desired time you want the animation to take in the Duration field, in either seconds or milliseconds.

   c. Enter the length of time you want the effect to remain in place in the Delay field, in either seconds or milliseconds.

   d. Choose the type of animation from the Timing Function list. (See the previous section for a discussion of the timing function options.)

   e. Enter the final value in the End Value field.

   f. Repeat Steps a through e for any additional properties.

8. If available, set where you'd like the code written from the Choose Where To Create the Transition list.

9. Click OK.

Dreamweaver then writes out the code and lists the transitions, complete with rule, trigger, and affected element in the CSS Transitions dialog box (see Figure 6-29).

FIGURE 6-29

Transitions are organized by CSS rule in the CSS Transitions dialog box.

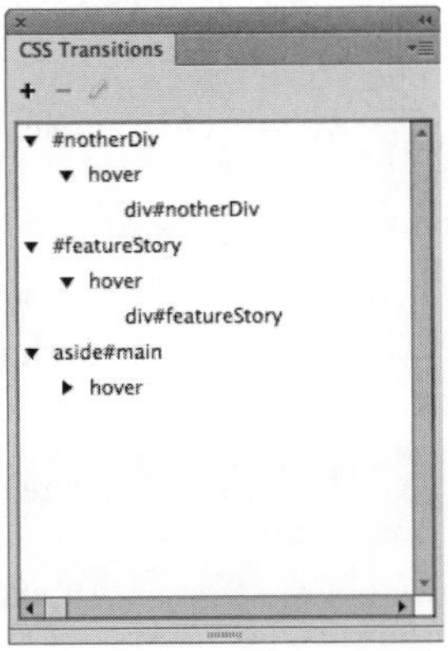

You can edit any transition at any time by selecting it and choosing Edit or simply double-clicking its name. To delete a transition, select it and click Remove (-). When you opt to delete a transition, you're given an opportunity to choose which parts you'd like to remove: the rule, the properties, or the triggers (Remove Transitions On).

TIP

As long as the CSS rules exist in your code, you can create a transition for it. If the rule has not been applied yet—if, for example, you have a rule for an uncreated `<div>` tag—Dreamweaver will note the transition as Not Applied Yet in the CSS Transition panel and update the code and panel when the rule is applied or the element is created.

Dreamweaver writes out all the CSS declarations in the specified location. Transition-related properties, including all vendor-specific varieties, are entered into the selected rule. A new rule is created with the triggering pseudo-class, like `#featureStory:hover`, that includes the defined property to animate and an end value.

Design-Time Style Sheets

Cascading Style Sheets give the designer an awesome flexibility with respect to the overall look and feel of a site. In fact, it's entirely possible for sites to be designed with multiple style sheets, each one applicable to a particular condition. With a little JavaScript or server-side coding, different style sheets can be applied according to which browser is being used, the platform employed, even the screen resolution at work. How does Dreamweaver know which style sheet to use? With the Design-Time Style Sheets feature, of course. The Design-Time Style Sheets feature enables you to show a specific style sheet while hiding others as you work. One key use of this command is to utilize a style sheet that is linked from your page dynamically at runtime. Your style sheets, in other words, do not have to be specifically attached to your page for you to be able to use them.

To set up design-time style sheets, follow these steps:

1. From the CSS Styles panel menu, choose Design-Time Style Sheets. Alternatively, choose Format ⇨ CSS Styles ⇨ Design Time or, from the Style Rendering toolbar, click Design-Time Style Sheets. Whichever method you choose, the Design-Time Style Sheets dialog box, shown in Figure 6-30, is displayed.
2. To show a specific style sheet, click the Add (+) button above the Show Only At Design Time list area and select an external style sheet from the Select File dialog box.
3. To hide a specific style sheet, click the Add (+) button above the Hide At Design Time list area and select an external style sheet from the Select File dialog box.
4. To delete a listed style sheet from either list, select the entry and click the Remove (–) button above the list.

CAUTION

The Design-Time Style Sheet information is stored in a design note; make sure that you do not unwittingly delete any such design note file.

5. Click OK when you're finished.

FIGURE 6-30

Use the Design-Time Style Sheets feature to display a variety of style sheets while you're creating the page.

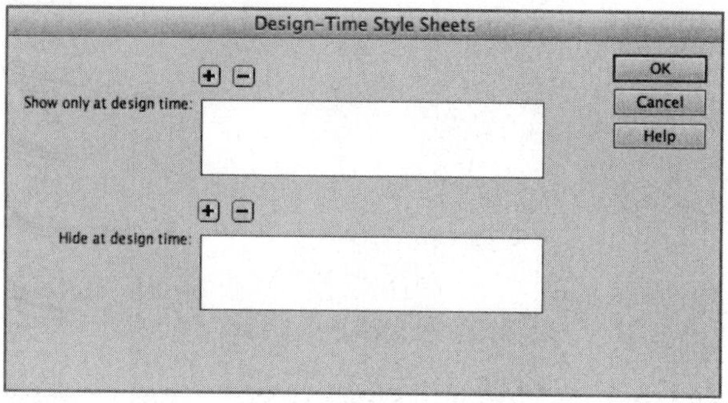

Summary

In this chapter, you discovered how you can easily and effectively add and modify Cascading Style Sheets. With CSS, you can now accomplish all the following:

- Define external style sheets to control the look and feel of an entire site
- Create styles automatically when working with the CSS tab of the Property inspector
- Update and change styles easily with the CSS Styles panel
- Easily apply generated styles to an element on a page
- Position fonts and elements, such as images, with pinpoint accuracy
- Exercise control over the layout, size, and display of fonts on a page
- Set up style sheets so that they're visible only at design time

In the next chapter, you learn how to insert and format text in Dreamweaver.

CHAPTER

7

Working with Text

IN THIS CHAPTER

- Creating headlines in Dreamweaver
- Adding and editing paragraphs
- Dreamweaver Technique: Entering and Pasting Text
- Running the spell checker
- Automating your work with Find and Replace
- Handling whitespace
- Bringing Office documents online
- Using special text formats
- Working with CSS styles
- Changing fonts, font size, and font color in CSS
- Integrating web fonts
- Formatting dates
- Inserting HTML comments

If content is king on the web, then certainly style is queen; together they rule hand in hand. Entering, editing, and formatting text on a web page is a major part of a webmaster's job. Dreamweaver gives you the tools to make the task as clear-cut as possible. From headlines to comments, this chapter covers the essentials of working with basic text; inserting and formatting dynamic data are covered in Chapter 19.

When the web first came online, web designers didn't have many options for manipulating text. However, the majority of browsers now understand a number of text-related commands, and the designer can specify the font and its color and size through Cascading Style Sheets (CSS). Moreover, Dreamweaver includes a range of text-manipulation tools. All these topics are covered in this chapter, along with details on working with text from other sources, such as Microsoft Office applications, including Word and Excel.

Starting with Headings

Text in HTML is primarily composed of headings and paragraphs. Headings separate and introduce major sections of the document, just as a newspaper uses headlines to announce a story and subheads to highlight essential details. HTML has six levels of headings; the syntax for the heading tags is <h*n*>, where *n* is a number from 1 to 6. The largest heading is <h1>, and the smallest is <h6>.

Dreamweaver QUICKSTART

It's very easy to start entering text with Dreamweaver—in fact, it's Dreamweaver's default mode. If you're new to Dreamweaver, the first thing you'll need to know about text is how to differentiate between headings and paragraphs. Here's how you enter a heading:

1. Place your cursor where you'd like your heading to appear.
2. From the HTML tab of the Property inspector, select the Format list and choose any of the options from Heading 1 to Heading 6.

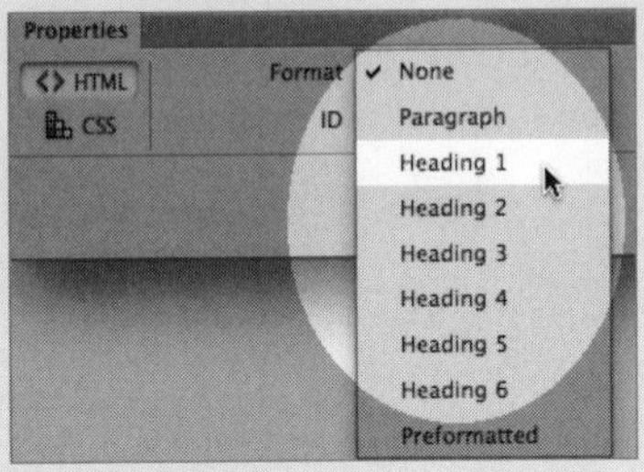

3. Type your heading.
4. Press Enter (Return) when you're done.

Dreamweaver, by default, sets the next line to be a paragraph. To get the same style without initially creating a headline, choose Paragraph from the Format list.

NOTE

Although Dreamweaver is capable of outputting several different types of web pages—ASP, ColdFusion, and so on—after the page has been executed on the application server, straight HTML is returned to the visitor's browser. You'll find numerous references to HTML pages throughout this chapter, and even though the pages may be stored as ASP pages or other types, HTML is the result.

Headings are not linked to any specific size, unlike type produced in a page layout or word processing program. Without CSS targeted rules, headings in a web document are sized relative to one another, and their final, exact size depends on the browser used. The sample headlines in Figure 7-1 depict the basic headings as rendered through Dreamweaver in Live View and as compared to the default paragraph font size. As you can see, some headings are rendered in type smaller than that used for the default paragraph. Headings are usually displayed with a bold weight.

Several methods set text as a particular heading size in Dreamweaver. In all cases, you first select the text you want to affect. If you are styling a single line or paragraph as a heading, just position the cursor anywhere in the paragraph to select it. If you want to convert more than one paragraph, click and drag out your selection.

FIGURE 7-1

Standard HTML allows six headings of different importance.

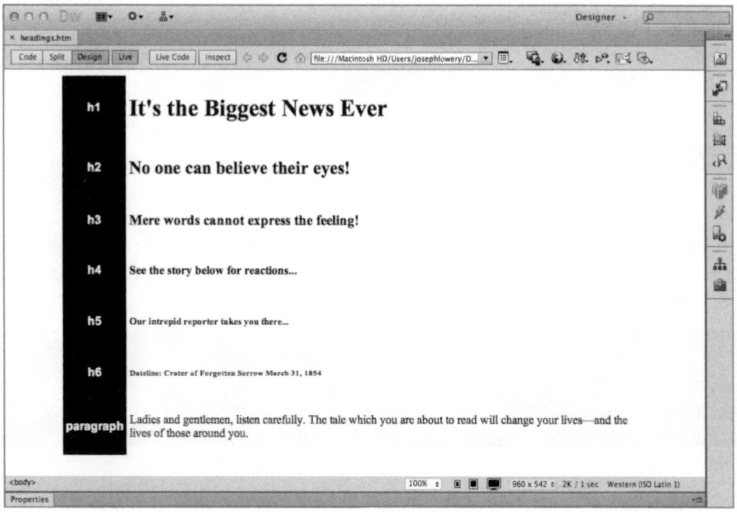

TIP

You can't mix heading levels in a single paragraph. That is, you can't have a word with an <h1> heading in the same line as a word styled with an <h4> heading. Furthermore, headings belong to a group of HTML elements called *block elements*. All block elements are rendered on a single line, which isolates (blocks) the text. To work around both of these restrictions, use Cascading Style Sheets, described in Chapter 6, to achieve the effect of varying sizes for words within the same line or for lines of different sizes close to one another.

After the text for the heading is selected, choose your heading level in one of the following ways:

- Choose Format ➪ Paragraph Format and then one of the Headings (1 through 6) from the submenu.
- Click the Heading 1, Heading 2, or Heading 3 button from the Text category of the Insert panel.
- Make your selection from the Text Property inspector HTML tab. (If it's not already open, display the Text Property inspector by selecting Window ➪ Properties and, if necessary, choose the HTML tab instead of CSS.) In the Text Property inspector, open the Format drop-down list (see Figure 7-2) and choose one of the six headings.

TIP

You can also use keyboard shortcuts for assigning headings. Headings 1 through 6 correspond to Ctrl+1 through Ctrl+6 (Command+1 through Command+6). The Paragraph option is rendered with Ctrl+Shift+P (Command+Shift+P); remove all formatting with Ctrl+0 (Command+0).

FIGURE 7-2

You can convert any paragraph or line into a heading through the Format options in the Text Property inspector HTML tab.

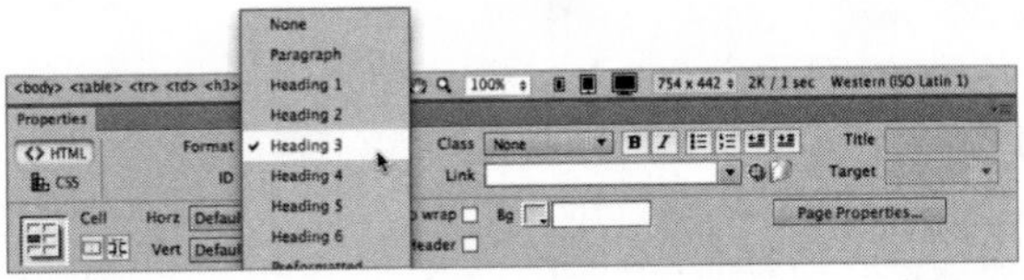

Headings are best applied in a hierarchical fashion, h1 to h6. This web standard ensures that your page is structured correctly. You can use CSS to vary the size of the headings, as needed.

CAUTION

Be careful when using the smallest headings, <h4> to <h6>, without styling them with CSS; they are likely to be difficult to read on any resolution higher than 800 x 600.

Working with Paragraphs

Usually the bulk of text on any web page is composed of paragraphs. Paragraphs in HTML are denoted by the <p> and </p> pair of tags. When your web page is processed, the browser formats everything between those two tags as one paragraph, word wrapping as needed within the available margins. Any additional line breaks and unnecessary whitespace (beyond one space between words and between sentences) in the HTML code are ignored.

Dreamweaver starts a new paragraph every time you press Enter (Return) when composing text in the Document window. If you have the Code view or the Code inspector open when you work, you can see that Dreamweaver inserts the following code with each new paragraph:

```
<p> </p>
```

The code between the tags creates a nonbreaking space that enables the new line to be visible. You won't see the new line if you have just the paragraph tags with nothing in between (neither a character nor a character entity, such as):

```
<p></p>
```

When you continue typing, Dreamweaver replaces the nonbreaking space with your input, unless you press Enter (Return) again. Figure 7-3 illustrates two paragraphs with text followed by paragraphs with the nonbreaking space still in place.

You can easily change text from most other formats, such as a heading, to paragraph format. First, select the text you want to alter. Then, in the Property inspector's HTML tab, open the Format drop-down list and choose Paragraph. You can also choose Format ➪ Paragraph Format ➪ Paragraph from the menu or use the keyboard shortcut Ctrl+Shift+P (Command+Shift+P).

FIGURE 7-3

Dreamweaver automatically wraps any text inserted into the Document window. If you press Enter (Return) without entering text, Dreamweaver enters paragraph tags surrounding a non-breaking space (in HTML).

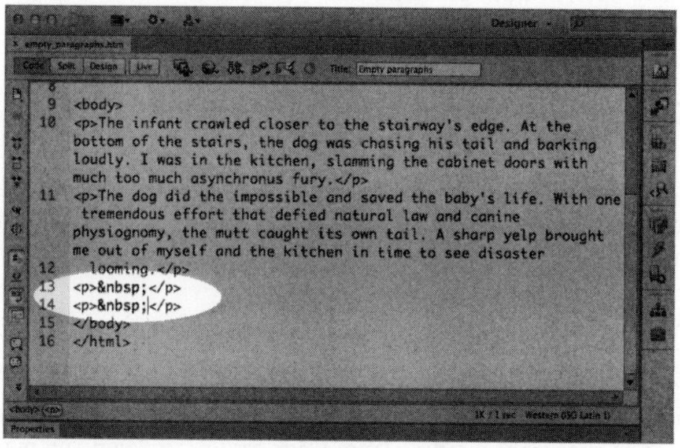

All paragraphs are initially rendered on the browser page in the default font at the default size. The user can designate these defaults through the browser preferences, although most people don't bother to alter them. If you want to change the font name or the font size for selected paragraphs explicitly, use the techniques described in the upcoming section "Modifying Text Format" or use Cascading Style Sheets, described in Chapter 6.

TIP

Remember that you can always use the Tag Selector on the status bar to select and highlight any tag surrounding your current cursor position. This method makes it easy to see exactly what a particular tag is affecting.

By and large, the editing features of Dreamweaver are similar to other modern word processing programs—with one or two web-oriented twists. Like other programs, Dreamweaver has Cut, Copy, and Paste options, as well as Undo and Redo commands.

The twists come from the relationship between the Design and Code views of the Document window, which give Dreamweaver special functionality for copying and pasting text and code. You learn how that works in the following sections.

Inserting text

You've already seen how you can position the cursor on the page and directly enter text. In this sense, Dreamweaver acts like a word processing program rather than a page layout program. On a blank page, the cursor starts at the top-left corner of the page. Words automatically wrap to the next line when the text exceeds the right margin. Press Enter (Return) to end the current paragraph and start the next one.

By default, after you type in text formatted as a heading and then press Enter (Return), the next line is formatted as a paragraph. This makes sense because you don't normally want to follow one heading with another. You can, however, control this behavior through Dreamweaver Preferences. Select Edit ➪ Preferences, click the General category, and then deselect the Switch To Plain Paragraph After Heading option. Now, pressing Enter (Return) after a heading creates another heading.

Cutting, copying, and pasting

Text can be moved from one place to another—or from one web document to another—using the standard cut-and-paste techniques. No surprises here: Before cutting or copying anything, you must select it. Select by clicking the mouse at the beginning of the text you want to cut or copy, drag the highlight to the end of your selection, and then release the mouse button.

Here are some other selection methods:

- Double-click a word to select it; triple-click to select an entire paragraph.
- Move the pointer to the left margin of the text until the pointer changes to a right-facing arrow. Click once to highlight a single line. Click and drag down the margin to select a group of lines.
- Position the cursor at the beginning of your selection. Hold down the Shift key and then click once at the end of the selection.
- Select everything in the body of your document by using Edit ➪ Select All or the keyboard shortcut Ctrl+A (Command+A).
- Use the Tag Selector in the status bar to select text or other objects contained within specific tags.
- You can also select text by holding down the Shift key and using the right or left arrow key to select one character at a time. If you hold down Ctrl+Shift (Command+Shift), press the right or left arrow key to select one word at a time.
- Hold down the Shift key and then press the up or down arrow key to select a line at a time. Pressing Ctrl+Shift (Command+Shift) as you press the up or down arrow key selects a paragraph at a time.

Dreamweaver provides quick access to the most common editing commands, such as Cut, Copy, and Paste, through the Standard toolbar. To enable the toolbar, choose View ➪ Toolbars ➪ Standard.

When you want to move a block of text, first select it and then use Edit ➪ Cut, the Cut button on the Standard toolbar, or the keyboard shortcut Ctrl+X (Command+X). This sequence places the text on your system's clipboard. To paste the text, move the pointer to the new location, click once to place the cursor, and then select Edit ➪ Paste or use the keyboard shortcut Ctrl+V (Command+V). The text is copied from the clipboard to its new location. You can continue pasting this same text from the clipboard until another block of text is copied or cut.

The procedure is much the same to copy text. Select the text using one of the preceding methods and then use Edit ➪ Copy, the Copy button on the Standard toolbar, or Ctrl+C (Command+C). The selected text is copied to the clipboard, and the original text is left in place. You then position the cursor in a new location and select Edit ➪ Paste (or use the keyboard shortcut).

Using drag-and-drop

The other, quicker method for moving or copying text is the drag-and-drop technique. After you've selected your text, release the mouse button and move the cursor over the highlighted area. The cursor changes from an I-beam to an arrow. To move the text, click the selected area with the arrow cursor and drag your mouse to a new location. The arrow cursor now has a box attached to it, indicating that it is carrying something. As you move your cursor, a bar (the insertion point) moves with you, indicating where the text will be positioned. Release the mouse button to drop the text.

You can duplicate text in the same manner by holding down the Ctrl (Option) key as you drag-and-drop your selected text. When copying this way, the box attached to the cursor is marked with a plus sign.

To completely remove text, select it and then choose Edit ➪ Clear or press Delete. The only way to recover deleted text is to use the Undo feature described later in this section.

Inserting text from other text applications

The Paste command can also insert text from another program into Dreamweaver. If you cut or copy text from a file in any other program—whether it is a word processor, spreadsheet, or database program—Dreamweaver inserts it at the cursor position. The results of an ordinary Paste operation may be undesirable, however. To more closely control the text inserted into Dreamweaver, use Paste Special.

Paste Special allows you to choose exactly how you'd like the copied text inserted into your document. Choose from a range of options that give you the flexibility to add straight text, structured text, structured text with simple formatting, or fully formatted text. The options can be preset in the Copy/Paste category of the Preferences and adjusted on a case-by-case basis.

After you've copied text in another application, choose Edit ➪ Paste Special. You're presented with a dialog box with four options:

- **Text Only:** Pastes completely unformatted text; even line breaks or paragraphs are removed.
- **Text With Structure:** Pastes unstyled text while retaining structured elements such as lists, paragraphs, line breaks, and tables.
- **Text With Structure Plus Basic Formatting:** Includes everything from the Text With Structure option but also retains simple formatting, such as bold, italic, and underline. If the text is copied from an HTML document, the pasted text retains any HTML text style tags, including `<b>`, `<i>`, `<u>`, `<strong>`, `<em>`, `<abbr>`, and `<acronym>`.
- **Text With Structure Plus Full Formatting:** Pasted text keeps all structure and formatting. If the copied text retains inline CSS styles or Word styles, Dreamweaver pastes them as well.

Two other options are available for modifying your paste output. The Retain Line Breaks option maintains line breaks in pasted text; if you choose Text Only, this option is disabled. The Clean Up Word Paragraph Spacing option works with the Text With Structure and Text With Structure Plus Basic Formatting choices to remove additional space between paragraphs.

If you use the standard Paste command, Dreamweaver can insert only plain, unformatted text—any bold, italic, or other styling in the original document is not retained in Dreamweaver. Paragraph breaks, however, are retained and reproduced in two different ways. A single paragraph return becomes a line break (a `<br>` tag) in Dreamweaver, whereas text separated by two returns is formatted into two HTML paragraphs, using the `<p> ... </p>` tag pair.

Copying and pasting code

As mentioned earlier in this chapter, Dreamweaver includes a couple of twists to the standard Cut, Copy, and Paste operations. Dreamweaver's Design and Code views enable you to copy and paste both text and code.

Put simply, to copy only text from Dreamweaver to another application, use the Edit ➪ Copy command in Design view; to copy both text and code, use the Edit ➪ Copy command in Code view.

Within Dreamweaver itself, content copied from Design view and pasted in Code view using Edit ➪ Paste appears as plain text without any code. To insert text and code, you'd need to use the Edit ➪ Paste Special command and select either of the options that include formatting: Text With Structure Plus Basic Formatting or Text With Structure Plus Full Formatting.

Undo, redo, and the History panel

The Undo command has to be one of the greatest inventions of the twentieth century. Make a mistake? Undo! Want to experiment with two different options? Undo! Change your mind again? Redo! The Undo command reverses your last action, whether you changed a link, added a graphic, or deleted the entire page. The Redo command enables you to reverse your Undo actions.

To use the Undo command, choose Edit ➪ Undo, select Undo from the Standard toolbar, or press the keyboard shortcut Ctrl+Z (Command+Z); any of these commands undoes a single action at a time. Dreamweaver displays all your previous actions on the History panel, so you can easily see what steps you took. Choose Window ➪ History to view the History panel. To undo multiple actions, drag the slider in the History panel to the last action you want to keep, or just click in the slider track at that action.

Dreamweaver's implementation of the Undo command enables you to back up as many steps as set in Maximum Number Of History Steps, found in the General category of Preferences. The History steps can even undo actions that took place before a document was saved. Note that the History panel has additional features besides multiple applications of the Undo command.

The complement to the Undo command is the Redo command. To reverse an Undo command, choose Edit ➪ Redo, click the Redo button on the Standard toolbar, or press Ctrl+Y (Command+Y). To reverse several Undo commands, drag the slider in the History panel back over the grayed-out steps; alternatively, click once in the slider track at the last of the steps you'd like to redo.

Tip

The best use I've found for the Redo command is in concert with Undo. When I'm trying to decide between two alternatives, such as two different images, I'll replace one choice with another and then use the Undo/Redo combination to go back and forth between them. Because Dreamweaver replaces any selected object with the current object from the clipboard—even if one is a block of text and the other is an AP element—you can easily view two separate options with this trick. The History panel enables you to apply this procedure to any number of steps.

Dreamweaver TECHNIQUE

Entering and Pasting Text

In this Technique, you practice entering headings and pasting text copied from another application into Dreamweaver.

NOTE
The following technique requires Microsoft Word.

1. In the Techniques site, expand the 07_Text folder and open `text_start.htm`.
2. Highlight and delete the placeholder text, *Content for id "middle" Goes Here*.
3. Enter the heading **Neighborhood Watch: East Side**.
4. With your cursor still in the heading, from the Property inspector's Format list, choose `h1`.

   If you don't see the Format list, you're probably in the CSS tab of the Property inspector; switch to the HTML tab.
5. Make sure your cursor is at the end of the heading and press Enter (Return).

   A new paragraph is created. Rather than type in a paragraph of text, use Dreamweaver's advanced copy/paste capabilities to bring in formatted text.
6. In Microsoft Word, choose File Open and select `neighborhood.rtf` from the 07_Text folder.
7. Select all the text and copy it.
8. Back in Dreamweaver, place your cursor on the line below the heading.
9. Choose Edit ➪ Paste Special.
10. In the Paste Special dialog box, choose the Text Plus Basic Formatting option; make sure the Clean Up Word Paragraph Spacing option is selected and click OK.

    Dreamweaver converts the copied text to HTML and inserts it into the page.

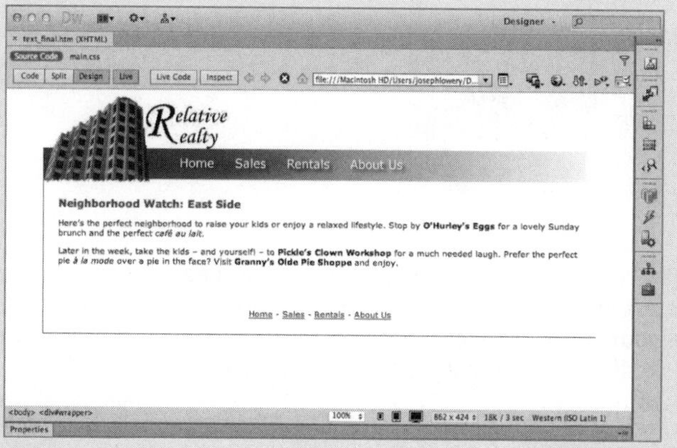

11. Save your page.

The next time you open the Paste Special dialog box, the chosen setting will be remembered.

A variation of the Redo command is the Repeat command. When your last action was the Undo command, the Edit menu shows the Redo command. But if the last action you performed was not Undo, the Edit menu shows the Repeat command, which allows you to repeat your last action. You can use the same button on the Standard toolbar to Repeat and Redo. In addition, the Repeat command has the same keyboard shortcut as Redo: Ctrl+Y (Command+Y). The Repeat command is useful, for example, when you need to create several links to the same location. To do this, create the first link, and then select the next text you want to link and use the Repeat command to add the next link.

Checking Your Spelling

A typo can make a significant impression, and not the one you want to make. Not many things are more embarrassing than showing a new website to a client and having that client point out a spelling error. Dreamweaver includes an easy-to-use spell checker to avoid such awkward moments. Make it a practice to spell check every web page before it's posted online.

You start the process by choosing Commands ➪ Check Spelling or pressing the keyboard shortcut Shift+F7. This sequence opens the Check Spelling dialog box, as shown in Figure 7-4.

FIGURE 7-4

Dreamweaver's spell checker double-checks your spelling and can find the typos on any web page.

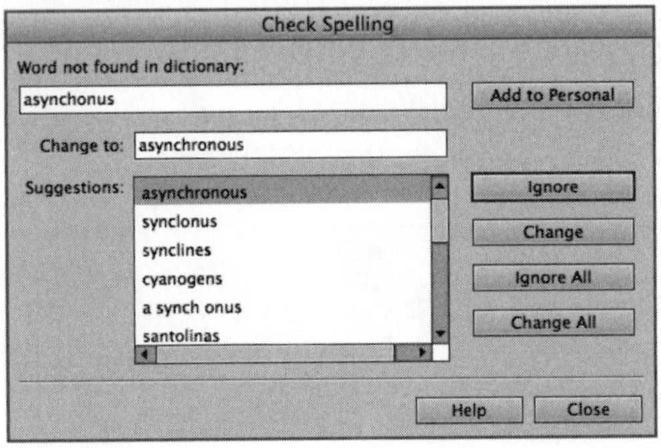

After you've opened the Check Spelling dialog box, Dreamweaver begins searching your text for errors. Unless you have selected a portion of your document, Dreamweaver checks the full document, regardless of where your cursor is placed. When text is selected, Dreamweaver checks the selection first and then asks if you'd like to do the entire document.

Dreamweaver checks your web page text against two dictionaries: a standard dictionary for your chosen language and a personal dictionary to which you can add words. If the spell checker finds any text that is not in either of the program's dictionaries, the text is highlighted in the Document window and appears in the Word Not Found In Dictionary field of the dialog box. A list of suggested corrections appears in the Suggestions list box, with the topmost one highlighted and also displayed in the Change To box. If Dreamweaver cannot find any suggestions, the Change To box is left blank. At this point, you have the following options:

- **Add To Personal:** Click this button to include the word in your personal dictionary and prevent Dreamweaver from tagging it as an error in the future.
- **Ignore:** Click this button when you want Dreamweaver to leave the currently highlighted word alone and continue searching the text.
- **Change:** If you see the correct replacement among the list of suggestions, highlight it and click the Change button. If no suggestion is appropriate, type the correct word into the Change To text field and then click this button.
- **Ignore All:** Click this button when you want Dreamweaver to disregard all occurrences of this word in the current document.
- **Change All:** Click this button to replace all instances of the current word within the document with the word in the Change To text field.

Spell-Checking in Non-English Languages

A variety of language dictionaries are built into Dreamweaver, so you can check spelling in a number of languages, including Danish, Dutch, English (American), English (British), English (Canadian), Finnish, French, German (Classic Spelling), German (New Spelling), Italian, Norwegian, Portuguese (Brazilian), Portuguese (Iberian), Spanish, and Swedish among many others.

Open Preferences by choosing Edit ➪ Preferences (Dreamweaver ➪ Preferences) and, in the General category, expand the Spelling Dictionary list. Choose the new language from the drop-down list, and you're ready to spell correctly in another tongue.

Using Find and Replace

Dreamweaver's Find and Replace feature is both time-saving and lifesaving (well, almost). You can use Find and Replace to cut your input time substantially by searching for abbreviations and expanding them to their full state. You can also find a client's incorrectly spelled name and replace it with the correctly spelled version—that's a lifesaver! However, that's just the tip of the iceberg when it comes to what Find and Replace can really do. The Find and Replace engine should be considered a key power tool for any web developer. Not only can you search multiple files, but you can also easily check the code separately from the content.

Here's a short list of what the Find and Replace feature makes possible:

- Search the Document window to find any type of text.
- Search the underlying HTML to find tags, attributes, or text enclosed within tags.
- Look for text within specific tags with specific attributes—or look for text that's outside of a specific tag with specific attributes.
- Find and replace patterns of text, using wildcard characters called *regular expressions*.
- Apply any of the preceding Find and Replace operations to just the selected text, the current document, the current site, any folder, or any group of selected files.

The basic command, Find and Replace, is found with its companion, Find Next/Again, under the Edit menu. You can use both commands in either Dreamweaver's Design or Code view. Although invoked by a single command, the Find feature can be used independently or in conjunction with Replace.

Find and Replace operations can be applied to one or a series of documents. In addition to searching all or part of the current document, you can also apply Find and Replace to all the files in a folder or an entire site. Furthermore, individual files selected in the Files panel are also searchable.

Finding on the visual page

The most basic method of using Find and Replace takes place in the Document window. Whenever you need to search for any text that can be seen by the public on your web page—whether it's to correct spelling or change a name—Dreamweaver makes it fast and simple.

The Find and Replace dialog box, unlike most of Dreamweaver's dialog boxes, is actually a *non-modal window*. This technical term just means that you can easily move back and forth between your Document window and the Find and Replace dialog box without having to close the dialog box first, as you do with the other Dreamweaver dialog boxes.

Whether you are working with a long, involved document or you just want to look in a particular area, you'll welcome Dreamweaver's capability to search a selection. Just highlight the text you want to search and, in the Find and Replace dialog box, choose Selected Text from the Find In drop-down list. You can search just selected code, too.

To find some text on your web page, follow these steps:

1. From the Document window, choose Edit ➪ Find and Replace or use the keyboard shortcut Ctrl+F (Command+F). If the Search panel (Window ➪ Results ➪ Search) is open, you can also click the Find and Replace button (the small green triangle) on the panel.
2. In the Find and Replace dialog box, shown in Figure 7-5, make sure that Text is the selected Search option.
3. In the text field next to the Search option, type the word or phrase you're looking for.

FIGURE 7-5

The Find and Replace dialog box can search your browser-rendered text or the source code.

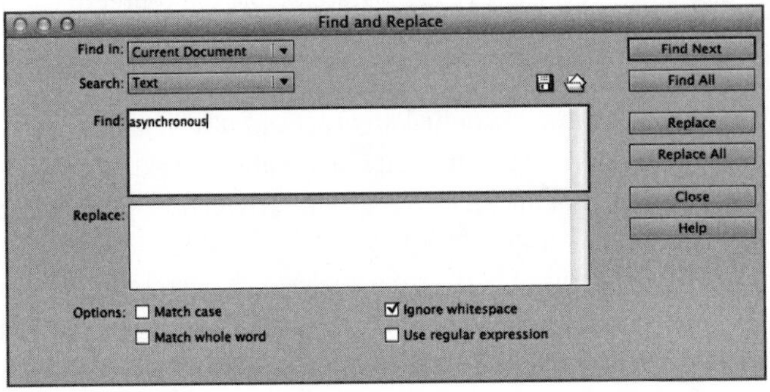

TIP

If you select your text *before* launching the Find dialog box, it automatically appears in the Search text field. Should you select text containing a greater number of characters, Dreamweaver assumes you want to search the selection and keeps the Search field clear.

4. Select the appropriate search options, if any:
   - If you want to find an exact replica of the word as you entered it, select the Match Case checkbox; otherwise, Dreamweaver searches for all variations of your text, regardless of case.
   - To force Dreamweaver to disregard any whitespace variations, such as additional spaces, hard spaces, or tabs, select the Ignore Whitespace option. For most situations, it's a good idea to leave this default option enabled.
   - Selecting Use Regular Expression enables you to work with Dreamweaver's wildcard characters (discussed later in this section). Use Regular Expression and Ignore Whitespace are mutually exclusive options.

5. Click the Find Next button to begin the search from the cursor's current position.
   - If Dreamweaver finds the selected text, it highlights the text in the Document window.
   - If Dreamweaver doesn't find the text in the remaining portion of the document, it automatically continues the search from the beginning of the document until the entire document has been checked.
   - If Dreamweaver doesn't locate the search term, it displays a message saying the term has not been found.
6. If you want to look for the next occurrence of your selected text, click the Find Next button again.
7. You can enter other text to search or exit the Find dialog box by clicking the Close button.

The text you enter in the Find and Replace dialog box is kept in memory until it's replaced by your next use of the Find feature. After you have executed the Find command once, you can continue to search for your text without redisplaying the Find and Replace dialog box by selecting Edit ➪ Find Next or by using the keyboard shortcut F3 (Command+G). If Dreamweaver finds your text, it is highlighted just as it is when the Find and Replace dialog box is open. However, the Edit ➪ Find Next/Again command searches indefinitely through your document; no message displays after it has searched the entire file. The Find Next command gives you a quick way to search through a long document—especially when you put the F3 (Command+G) key to work.

Instead of locating one instance of your text at a time, you can also look for all occurrences of your text at once. To do this, open and set up the Find and Replace dialog box as previously described, but choose Find All instead of Find Next. When you choose Find All, Dreamweaver closes the Find and Replace dialog box and opens the Search panel. The Search panel displays each found occurrence on a separate line, as shown in Figure 7-6. A message at the bottom of the Search panel also tells you how many occurrences of your selection, if any, were found. If you want to search for a different term, click the Find and Replace button (the small green triangle) in the Search panel to reopen the Find and Replace dialog box.

FIGURE 7-6

The Search panel displays results of a Find All command.

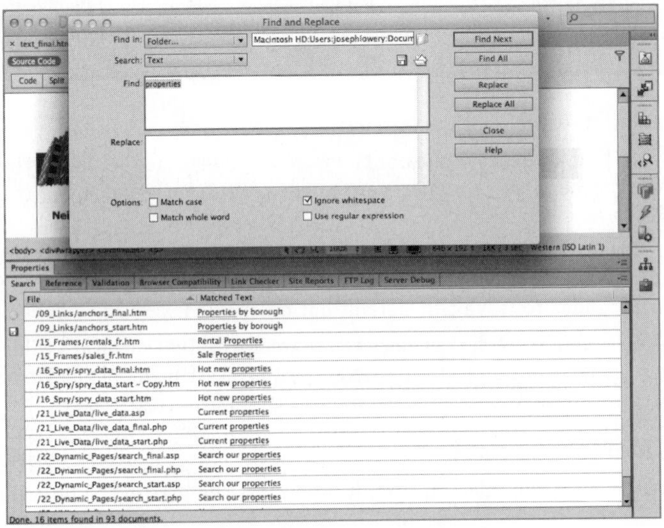

TIP

To quickly move from one found selection to another in the Document window, double-click an entry in the Search panel. Dreamweaver highlights the selection, scrolling the Document window, if necessary. Note, however, that the results listed in the Search panel may take you to the wrong location if you add or remove content in the document after you perform the search.

If you perform two Find All operations in a row, the Search panel automatically clears the results of the first search and replaces them with the results of the new search. To manually clear the Search panel, right-click (Control+click) and choose Clear Results.

CAUTION

If you edit the document after performing a Find All, the results of the search may no longer be valid. In this situation, double-clicking an item in the Search panel may no longer take you to the correct place in the document. If you have added or removed text in the document after performing a Find All, perform the search again by clicking the Find and Replace button (the small green triangle) in the Search panel to reopen the Find and Replace dialog box. If no text is selected in the Document window before you open the Find and Replace dialog box, the search parameters should automatically be set up; you just click Find All again.

When you replace text in the Document window, it is replaced regardless of its formatting. For example, suppose you have the following paragraph:

> Mary's accusation reminded Jon of studying synchrones in high school. *Synchrones*, he recalled, were graphs in which the lines constantly approached zero, but never made it. "Yeah," he thought, "That's me, all right. I'm one big **synchrone**."

Upon discovering that *synchrone* should actually be *asymptote*, you could use the Find and Replace feature to replace all the plain, italic, and bold versions of the *synchrone* text simultaneously.

TIP

It's possible to alter formatting as well—to change all the formatting to bold only, for example—but for that you need to perform your Find and Replace operations on the underlying code, as discussed in the following section.

Follow these steps to use Dreamweaver's Replace feature in the Document window:

1. Choose Edit ➪ Find and Replace or use the keyboard shortcut Ctrl+F (Command+F).
2. In the Find and Replace dialog box, make sure that Text is the selected Search option and then, in the text field next to the Search option, type the word or phrase you're looking for. You can also copy and paste text from the Document window into the Search field.
3. In the Replace With text field, type the substitute text.

TIP

Need more room for your Find or Replace entries? The Find and Replace dialog box can be widened or deepened by dragging the border as you would a window; Mac users should drag the lower-right corner as usual.

4. Click the Find Next button. Dreamweaver begins searching from the current cursor position. If Dreamweaver finds the text, it is highlighted.
5. To replace the highlighted occurrence of the text, click the Replace button. Dreamweaver replaces the found text with the substitute text and then automatically searches for the next occurrence.
6. If you want to replace all instances of the Search text, click the Replace All button. When Dreamweaver has found all the occurrences of your Search text, it displays a message telling how many replacement operations were made.

CAUTION

The Search panel applies to Find operations but not to Replace operations. When you click Replace All, Dreamweaver does not update the Search panel to list items that have been replaced. Further, if you click Find All and then perform a Replace All, the previous results in the Search panel may no longer correctly reflect the location of the text you just replaced, and changed items in the Search panel are not flagged.

TIP

To rerun individual Find and Replace operations, highlight the appropriate step in the History panel (choose Window ➪ History) and click the Replay button. You cannot, however, use the History panel to repeat a Find All operation.

Storing and Retrieving Queries

Dreamweaver enables you to develop extremely complex search queries. Rather than forcing you to repeatedly re-enter Find and Replace queries, Dreamweaver enables you to save and load them when needed. Dreamweaver saves the queries with a `.dwr` file extension.

To save a query, select the Diskette icon on the Find and Replace dialog box. The standard Save Query (Save Query To File) dialog box appears for you to enter a filename; the appropriate file extension is appended automatically. To load a previously saved query, click the Folder icon on the Find and Replace dialog box to open the Load Query dialog box. Although only queries with a `.dwr` extension are being saved in the current version, you can still load both `.dwq` and `.dwr` files saved from previous Dreamweaver versions.

Although saving and opening queries is an obvious advantage when working with complex wildcard operations, you can also make it work for you in an everyday situation. If, for example, you have a set series of acronyms or abbreviations that you must convert repeatedly, you can save your simple text queries and use them as needed without having to remember all the details.

Searching the code

The power curve ramps up significantly when you start to explore Dreamweaver's Find and Replace capabilities for HTML code. Should your client (newly acquired by another company) need to change the company's name throughout the 300-page site, you can accommodate him with a few keystrokes—instead of hours of mind-numbing grunt work.

You can perform three different types of searches that use the HTML in your web page:

- You can search for text anywhere in the HTML code. With this capability, you can look for text within `alt` or any other attribute—and change it.
- You can search for text relative to specific tags. Sometimes you need to change just the text contained within the `<b>` tag and leave all other matching text alone.
- You can search for specific HTML tags and/or their attributes. Dreamweaver's Find and Replace feature gives you the capability to insert, delete, or modify tags and attributes.

Looking for text in the code

Text that appears onscreen is often replicated in various sections of your off-screen HTML code. It's not uncommon, for example, to use the `alt` attribute in an `<img>` tag that repeats the caption under the picture. What happens if you replace the wording using the Find and Replace dialog box with the Search field set to Text? You're still left with the task of tracking down the `alt` attribute and making that change as well. Dreamweaver enables you to act on both content and programming text in one operation—a major savings in time and effort, not to mention aggravation.

To find and replace text in both the content and the code, follow these steps:

1. Choose Edit ⇨ Find and Replace to open the Find and Replace dialog box.
2. Select the parameters of your search from the Find In option: Selected Text, Current Document, Open Documents, Folder, Selected Files In Site, or Entire Current Local Site. If you choose Selected Files In Site, select the files of interest in the Site panel.

3. From the Search drop-down list, select the Source Code option.
4. Enter the text you're searching for in the text field next to the Search option.
5. If you are replacing, enter the new text in the Replace With text field.
6. Select any options desired: Match Case, Ignore Whitespace, or Use Regular Expression.
7. Choose your Find/Replace option: Find Next, Find All, Replace, or Replace All. If you are in Design view, the Code inspector opens.
8. If Dreamweaver hasn't automatically closed the Find and Replace dialog box (it closes automatically for the Find All and Replace All commands), click Close when you are finished.

CAUTION

As with all Find and Replace operations—especially those in which you decide to Replace All—you need to exercise extreme caution when replacing text throughout your code. If you're unsure about what's going to be affected, choose Find All first and, with Code view or the Code inspector open, step through all the selections. You do this to be positive that no unwanted surprises occur. Should you replace some code in error, you can always undo the operation—but only if the document is open. Replacing text or code in a closed file—as is done when the operation is performed on a folder, the current site, or selected files in the Files panel—is not undoable. Therefore, it is wise to back up your site before performing a Replace All operation.

Using advanced text options in Find and Replace

In Find and Replace operations, the global Replace All isn't appropriate for every situation; sometimes you need a more precise approach. Dreamweaver enables you to fine-tune your searches to pinpoint accuracy. You can look for text within particular tags—and even within particular tags with specific attributes. Moreover, you can find (and replace) text that is outside of particular tags with specific attributes.

Dreamweaver assists you by providing a drop-down list of standard tags. The tags shown depend on the type of document you are viewing, as determined by the filename extension of the open file. For example, although most document types see HTML tags, a document with the `.cfm` extension would also see ColdFusion tags. You can also search for your own custom tags. In addition, you don't have to try to remember which attributes go with which tag; Dreamweaver supplies you with a context-sensitive list of attributes that changes according to the tag selected.

In addition to using the tag's attributes as a search filter, Dreamweaver can also search within the tag for text or another tag. Most HTML tags are so-called *container tags* that consist of an opening tag and a closing tag, such as <em> and </em>. You can set up a filter to look for text surrounded by a specific tag pair—or text outside of a specific set of tags. For example, if you are searching for the word `big`

```
The big, red boat was a <em>big</em> waste of money.
```

you can build a Find and Replace operation that changes one instance of the word (big, red) but not the other (<em>big</em>)—or vice versa.

To look for text in or out of specific tags and attributes, follow these steps:

1. Choose Edit ➪ Find and Replace to open the Find and Replace dialog box.

2. Select the parameters of your search from the Find In option: Current Document, Current Site, Folder, or Selected Files In Site.
3. From the Search drop-down list, select the Text (Advanced) option. The Add (+) and Remove (–) tag options are made available, as shown in Figure 7-7.

FIGURE 7-7

The advanced text features of Find and Replace enable you to manipulate text and code simultaneously.

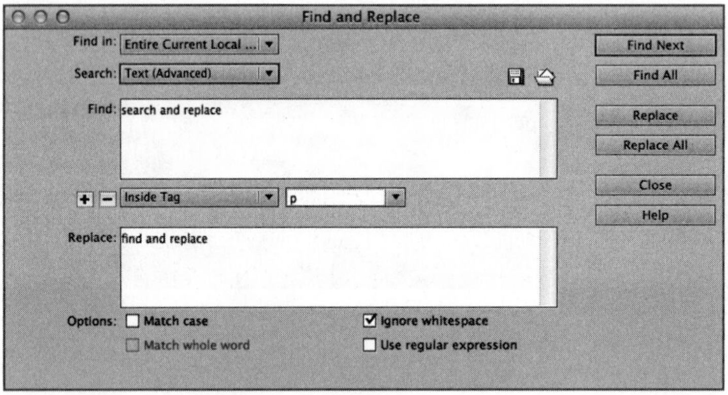

4. Enter the text you're searching for in the Find field next to the Search drop-down list.
5. Select either Inside Tag or Not Inside Tag from the drop-down list. Remember that Inside Tag refers to text that is enclosed within a beginning and ending tag pair, such as <h2></h2>.
6. Select the tag to include or exclude from the adjacent drop-down list or type your own tag.
7. To add a further restriction on the search, click the Add (+) button. Another line of search options is added to the dialog box.
8. Select the additional search filter. The available options are listed in Table 7-1.

TABLE 7-1 Search Filters

Filter	Description
With Attribute	Enables you to select any attribute from the adjacent drop-down list. You can set this attribute to be equal to, less than, greater than, or not equal to any given value by choosing from the available drop-down lists.
Without Attribute	Finds text within a particular tag that does not include a specific attribute. Choose the attribute from the adjacent drop-down list.
Containing	Searches the tag for either specified text or another user-selectable tag found within the initial tag pair.

Filter	Description
Not Containing	Searches the tag for either text or a tag not found within the initial tag pair.
Inside Tag	Enables you to look for text that is within two (or more) sets of specific tags.
Not Inside Tag	Enables you to look for text that is in one tag, but not in another tag, or vice versa.

9. To continue adding filter conditions, click the Add (+) button and repeat Step 8.
10. To remove a filter condition, click the Remove (–) button.
11. If you are replacing text, enter the new text in the Replace text field.
12. Select any options you want: Match Case, Ignore Whitespace, or Use Regular Expression.
13. Choose your Find/Replace option: Find Next, Find All, Replace, or Replace All.

TIP

You can continue to add conditions by clicking the Add (+) button. In fact, I was able to add so many conditions that the Find and Replace dialog box began to disappear off the screen (although I wouldn't recommend this in practice). To quickly erase all conditions, change the Search option to Text or Source Code and then change it back to Text (Advanced).

Replacing HTML tags and attributes

Imagine a new edict has come down from the HTML gurus of your company: No longer is the `<b>` tag to be used to indicate emphasis; from now on, use only the `<strong>` tag. Oh, and by the way, change all the existing pages—all 3,000+ web and intranet pages—so that they're compliant. Dreamweaver makes short work out of nightmare situations such as this by giving you the power to search and replace HTML tags and their attributes.

But Dreamweaver doesn't stop there. Not only can you replace one tag with another; you can also perform the following:

- Change or delete the tag (with or without its contents).
- Set an attribute in the tag to another value.
- Remove any or all attributes.
- Add text and/or code before or after the starting or the ending tag.

To alter your code using Dreamweaver's Find and Replace feature, follow these steps:

1. As with other Find and Replace operations, choose Edit ⇨ Find and Replace to open the dialog box.
2. Select the parameters of your search from the Find In drop-down list: Current Document, Entire Current Local Site, Folder, or Selected Files In Site.
3. From the Search drop-down list, select the Specific Tag option.

   The dialog box changes to include the tag functions.

4. Select the desired tag from the option list next to the Search drop-down list.

TIP

You can either scroll down the list box to find the tag or, once the list has focus, type the first letter of the tag in the box. Dreamweaver scrolls to the group of tags that begin with that letter when the list is visible. To scroll further in the list, type the second and subsequent letters, or use the down or up arrow keys.

5. You can limit the search by specifying an attribute and value with other conditions, as discussed in detail in the previous section.

NOTE

If you want to search for just a tag, click the Remove (-) button to eliminate the additional condition.

6. Make a selection from the Action list shown in Figure 7-8.

   The Action list options are described in Table 7-2.

FIGURE 7-8

The Action list enables you to replace tags or modify them by setting the existing attributes or adding new ones.

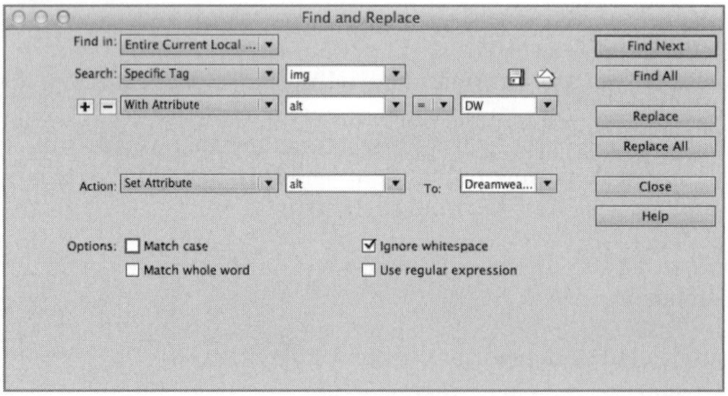

TABLE 7-2 Action List Options

Action	Description
Replace Tag & Contents	Substitutes the selected tag and all included content with a text string; the text string can include HTML code
Replace Contents Only	Changes the content between the specified tags to a given text string, which can also include HTML code
Remove Tag & Contents	Deletes the tag and all contents

Action	Description
Strip Tag	Removes the tag but leaves the previously enclosed content
Change Tag	Substitutes one tag for another
Set Attribute	Sets an existing attribute to a new value or inserts a new attribute set to a specific value
Remove Attribute	Deletes a specified attribute
Add Before Start Tag	Inserts a text string (with or without HTML) before the opening tag
Add After End Tag	Inserts a text string (with or without HTML) after the ending tag
Add After Start Tag	Inserts a text string (with or without HTML) after the opening tag
Add Before End Tag	Inserts a text string (with or without HTML) before the end tag

NOTE

Not all the options in Table 7-2 are available for all tags. Some so-called empty tags, such as `<img>`, consist of a single tag, not tag pairs. Empty tags have only the Replace Tag and Remove Tag options (instead of Replace Tag & Contents, Replace Contents Only, and Remove Tag & Contents) and the Change Tag, Remove Attribute, Add Before, and Add After options (instead of Add Before Start Tag, Add After Start Tag, Add Before End Tag, and Add After End Tag).

7. Select any options desired: Match Case, Ignore Whitespace, or Use Regular Expression.
8. Choose your Find/Replace option: Find Next, Find All, Replace, or Replace All.

Concentrating your search with regular expressions

As powerful as all the other Find and Replace features are, they are boosted to a higher level of flexibility with the addition of regular expressions. I've referred to regular expressions as being similar to wildcards in other programs, but their capabilities are actually far more extensive.

Regular expressions are best described as a *text pattern matching system*. If you can identify any pattern in your text, you can manipulate it with regular expressions. What kind of pattern? Imagine you have a spreadsheet-like table with lots of numbers, showing both dollars and cents, mixed with explanatory text. With regular expressions, you can match the pattern formed by the dollar sign and the decimal point and reformat the entire table, turning all the figures deep blue with a new font—all in one Find and Replace operation.

You can apply regular expressions to any of the types of Find and Replace operations previously discussed by just clicking the Use Regular Expressions checkbox. Note that when you select Use Regular Expression, the Ignore Whitespace option is deselected because the two options are mutually exclusive.

The most basic regular expression is the text itself. If you enable the feature and then enter `th` in the Find text field, Dreamweaver locates every example of *th* in the text and/or source. Although this capability by itself has little use beyond what you can also achieve with standard Find and Replace operations, it's important to remember this functionality as you begin to build your patterns.

CAUTION

When entering text in the Find field of the Find and Replace dialog box, do not include any extra spaces after your search string. Dreamweaver interprets the spaces as part of your search string, and the search only finds your text when it is followed by a space.

Wildcard characters

Initially, it's helpful to be able to use what are traditionally known as *wildcards*—characters that match certain different types of characters. The wildcards in regular expressions represent single characters and are described in Table 7-3. In other words, no single regular expression represents all the characters, as the asterisk does when used in PC file searches (such as *.*). However, such a condition can be represented with a slightly more complex regular expression (described later in this section).

TIP

The backslash character (\) is used to escape special characters so that they can be included in a search. For example, if you want to look for an asterisk, you need to specify it as follows: *. Likewise, when trying to find the backslash character, precede it with another backslash character: \\.

TABLE 7-3 Regular Expression Wildcard Characters

Character	Matches	Example
.	Any single character, including letters, numbers, spaces, punctuation, control characters (like line feed), and so on	**w.c** matches wacky and *How could you?* but not *watch.*
\w	Any single alphanumeric character, including the underscore	**w\wc** matches wacky and *W3C* but not *How could you?*
\W	Any single non-alphanumeric character	**jboy\Widest.com** matches **jboy@idest.com**.
\d	Any single numeric character 0–9	**y\dk** matches *Y2K.*
\D	Any single nonnumeric character	**\D2\D** matches *Y2K* and *H2O.*
\s	Any single whitespace character, including space, nonbreaking space, tab, form feed, or line feed	**\smedia** matches media but not *flashbangmedia.*
\S	Any single non-whitespace character	**\Smedia** matches *media* but not *the media.*
\t	A tab character	Matches any single tab character in the HTML source.

Character	Matches	Example
\•	Form feed	Matches any single form-feed character in the HTML source. A form feed is a control character used to force a page break when printing. Although unlikely, it is possible for this character to appear in your HTML document if you converted a print document to HTML. Most browsers ignore the form-feed character, but you might want to search for and remove the form feed using the `\f` regular expression. A form feed is more likely to occur in a text document.
\n	Line feed	Matches any single line-feed character in the HTML source.
\r	Carriage return	Matches any single carriage-return character in the HTML source.

Matching character positions and repeating characters

With regular expressions, not only can you match the type of character, but you can also match its position in the text. This feature enables you to perform operations on characters at the beginning, end, or middle of the word or line. Regular expressions also enable you to find instances in which a character is repeated an unspecified number of times or a specific number of times. Combined, these features broaden the scope of the patterns that can be found. Table 7-4 details the options available for matching by text placement and character repetition.

TABLE 7-4 Regular Expression Character Positions and Repeating Characters

Character	Matches	Example
^	If searching text in the current document, this finds the search string only if it immediately follows the cursor. If searching source code or searching text in multiple documents, this regular expression finds the search string only if it is at the beginning of the document.	If searching text in the current document, **^l** matches the first **l** in *Call me Ishmael* only if the cursor is positioned after the *a* in the word *Call.* Clicking Find Next would find the second **l** in *Call*, but clicking Next again would not find the **l** in *Ishmael* because the character immediately following the cursor is not an **l**. If searching source code, ^< matches the opening < in the *HTML* <!DOCTYPE...> statement, assuming the < is the first character in the document.
$	End of a document.	**d$** matches the final **d** in *Be afraid. Be very afraid* if that is the last character in the document.
\b	A word boundary, such as a space or carriage return.	**\btext** matches *textbook* but not *SimpleText.*

Continues

TABLE 7-4 *(continued)*

Character	Matches	Example
\B	A non-word boundary inside a word.	**\Btext** matches *SimpleText* but not *textbook.*
*	The preceding character zero or more times.	**b*c** matches *BBC* and *the cold.* In the first example, both instances of **B** and **C** match because the expression **b*c** causes Dreamweaver to look for any number of **b** instances followed by a **c**. In the second example, only the **c** matches because **b*** means to search for zero or more instances of the **b**.
+	The preceding character one or more times.	**b+c** matches *BBC* but not *cold.*
?	The preceding character zero or one time.	**ac?e** matches *ace* and *aerie* but not *axiomatic.*
{n}	Exactly *n* instances of the preceding character.	**e{2}** matches reed and each pair of two **e** instances in *Aieeeeeeee!*; but nothing in *Dreamweaver.*
{n,m}	A minimum of *n* and a maximum of *m* instances of the preceding character.	**C{2,4}** matches *#CC00FF* and *#CCCC00*, but not the full string *#CCCCCC*. If you searched with the regular expression **C{2,4}**, it would first locate the first four instances of **C** in the string *#CCCCCC*. If you clicked Find Next, the search would locate the last two **C**s in the string because the search is looking for two, three, or four **C**s in a row.

Matching character ranges

Beyond single characters, or repetitions of single characters, regular expressions incorporate the capability of finding or excluding ranges of characters. This feature is particularly useful when you're working with groups of names or titles. Ranges are specified in set brackets. A match is made when any one of the characters within the set brackets, not necessarily all the characters, is found. Table 7-5 provides descriptions of how to match character ranges with regular expressions.

TABLE 7-5 **Regular Expression Character Ranges**

Character	Matches	Example
[abc]	Any one of the characters *a*, *b*, or *c*	**[lmrt]** matches the individual *l* and each instance of an *m* in *lemmings*, and the *r* and *t* in *roadtrip*.
[^abc]	Any character except *a*, *b*, or *c*	**[^etc]** matches each character in *GIFs*, but not *etc* in the phrase *GIFs etc*.

Character	Matches	Example
[a-z]	Any character in the range from *a* to *z*	**[l-p]** matches *l* and *o* in *lowery*, and *m*, *n*, *o*, and *p* in *pointman*.
x|y	Either *x* or *y*	**boy|girl** matches both *boy* and *girl*.

Using grouping with regular expressions

All the regular expressions described previously relate to finding a certain string of text within your documents. But after you've located a particular string using regular expressions, how can you use that particular string in the Replace With field? For example, the following list of names:

- John Jacob Jingleheimer Schmidt
- James T. Kirk
- Cara Fishman

can be rearranged so that the last name is first, separated by a comma, like this:

- Schmidt, John Jacob Jingleheimer
- Kirk, James T.
- Fishman, Cara

Dreamweaver enables replacement of regular expressions through grouping expressions. Grouping is perhaps the single most powerful concept in regular expressions. With it, any matched text pattern is easily manipulated. To group a text pattern, enclose it in parentheses in the Find text field. Regular expressions can manage up to nine grouped patterns. In the Replace text field, each grouped pattern is designated by a dollar sign ($) in front of a number (1–9) that indicates the position of the group. For example, enter **$3** in the Replace With box to represent the third grouped pattern in the Find box.

CAUTION

Remember that the dollar sign is also used after a character or pattern to indicate the last character in a line in a Find expression.

Table 7-6 shows how regular expressions use grouping.

TABLE 7-6 Regular Expressions Grouping

Character	Matches	Example
(p) (entered in the Find field)	Any pattern *p*	**(\b\w*)\.(\w*\b)** matches two patterns, the first before a period and the second, after, such as in a filename with an extension. The backslash before the period escapes it so that it is not interpreted as a regular expression.

Continues

TABLE 7-4 *(continued)*

Character	Matches	Example
$1, $2 . . . $9 (entered in the Replace field)	The *nth pattern noted with parentheses*	If the Search field contains the pattern **(\b\w*)\.(\w*\b)**, and the Replace field contains the pattern **$1's extension is ".$2"**, *Chapter09.txt* would be replaced with *Chapter09's extension is ".txt".*

Controlling Whitespace

Whitespace refers to any portion of the page that doesn't contain text, images, or other objects. It includes the space between words and the space above and below paragraphs. This section introduces ways to adjust paragraph margins and the spacing between paragraphs, both with and without CSS.

Indenting text

In Dreamweaver, you cannot indent text as you do with a word processor. Tabs normally have no effect in HTML. Cascading Style Sheets offer the preferred method for indenting the first line of a paragraph. You can set an existing HTML tag, such as <p>, to any indent amount using the Text Indent option found on the Block panel of the Style Sheet dialog box.

TIP
You'll find a full discussion of text indent and other style sheet controls in Chapter 6.

While it's better to use CSS, you can optionally configure Dreamweaver to insert nonbreaking spaces in situations where it would normally ignore the spaces that you type. For example, whenever you type more than one space in a row or when you enter a space at the beginning of a paragraph, HTML, and therefore Dreamweaver, ignores the space. However, if you choose Edit ➪ Preferences (Dreamweaver ➪ Preferences) and select the Allow Multiple Consecutive Spaces option in the General category, Dreamweaver inserts nonbreaking spaces automatically as you type. If you find yourself inserting nonbreaking spaces frequently, enabling this option speeds up your work. Use care when enabling this feature, however. If you are used to having extra spaces ignored, you may inadvertently add undesired spaces within your text.

TIP
If you normally create paper documentation, you may be used to adding two spaces between sentences. For online documentation, use only a single space after a period. Adding two spaces not only goes against the norm, it's more work and can increase your file size by inserting all those extra nonbreaking spaces!

Dreamweaver offers other methods for inserting a nonbreaking space. You can enter its character code—` `—directly into the HTML code or you can use the Nonbreaking Space button in the Characters menu in the Text category of the Insert panel. You can also style your text as preformatted; this technique is discussed later in this chapter.

Working with preformatted text

Browsers ignore formatting niceties considered irrelevant to page content: tabs, extra line feeds, indents, and added whitespace. You can force browsers to read all the text, including whitespace, exactly as you have entered it by applying the preformatted tag pair `<pre>... </pre>`. This tag pair directs the browser to keep any additional whitespace encountered within the text. By default, the `<pre>... </pre>` tag pair also renders its content with a monospace font such as Courier. For these reasons, the `<pre> ... </pre>` tag pair was used to lay out text in columns in the early days of HTML before tables were widely available and before CSS then made table-based layouts obsolete.

You can apply the preformatted tag through the Property inspector, the Insert panel, or the menus. Regardless of the technique for inserting preformatted text, it is easiest to work in Code and Design views—applying changes in Code view and seeing the result in Design view. Select the text, or position the cursor where you want the preformatted text to begin; then use one of these methods to insert the `<pre> ... </pre>` tags:

- In the Property inspector HTML tab, open the Format list box and choose Preformatted.
- On the Insert panel, choose the Text category and click the Preformatted Text button.
- Choose Format ➪ Paragraph Format ➪ Preformatted Text.
- Choose Insert ➪ HTML ➪ Text Objects ➪ Preformatted Text.

The `<pre>` tag is a block element format, like the paragraph or the headings tags, rather than a style. This designation as a block element format has two important implications. First, you can't apply the `<pre> ... </pre>` tag pair to part of a line; when you use this tag pair, the entire paragraph is altered. Second, you can apply styles to preformatted text—this enables you to increase the size or alter the font, but at the same time maintain the whitespace feature made possible with the `<pre>` tag. All text in Figure 7-9 uses the `<pre>` tag; the column on the left is the standard output with a monospace font; the column on the right uses a different font in a larger size.

FIGURE 7-9

Preformatted text gives you full control over the line breaks, tabs, and other whitespace in your web page.

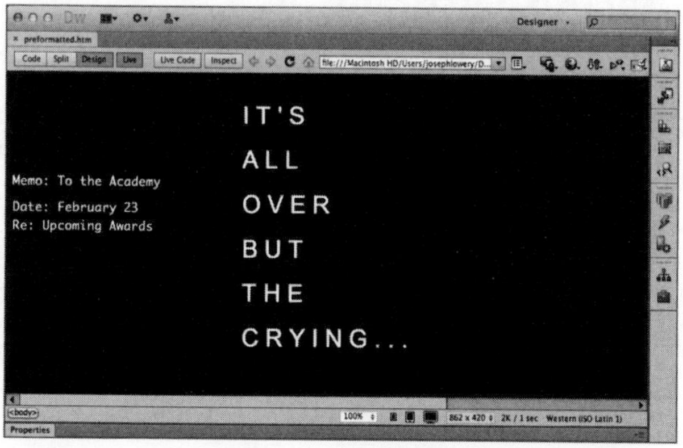

TIP

The CSS equivalent of the <pre> tag is the white-space property, applied with the pre value, like this:

```
white-space: pre;
```

The <br> tag

Just like headings, the paragraph tag falls into the class of HTML objects called *block elements*. As such, any text marked with the <p> . . . </p> tag pair is always rendered with an extra line above and below the text.

NOTE

In XHTML documents, the break tag is coded as <br />. Dreamweaver inserts the correct tag based on the document type.

Break tags are used within block elements, such as headings and paragraphs, to provide a line break where the <br> is inserted. Dreamweaver provides two ways to insert a <br> tag: Choose the Line Break button from the Characters menu in the Text category of the Insert panel, or use the keyboard shortcut Shift+Enter (Shift+Return).

Figure 7-10 demonstrates the effect of the <br> tag. The menu items in Column A on the left are the result of using the <br> tag within a paragraph. In Column B on the right, paragraph tags alone are used. The <h1> heading is also split at the top with a break tag to avoid the insertion of an unwanted line.

You can enable Dreamweaver to mark <br> tags with a symbol: a gold shield with the letters BR and the standard Enter (Return) symbol. To make the break symbol visible, you must first choose Edit ⇨ Preferences (Dreamweaver ⇨ Preferences) and select the Line Breaks checkbox in the Invisible Elements category. Then show invisible elements by choosing View ⇨ Visual Aids ⇨ Invisible Elements.

Overcoming Line-Spacing Difficulties

Line spacing is a major issue and a common problem for web designers. A design often calls for lines to be tightly spaced, but also to be of various sizes. If you use the break tag to separate your lines, you get the tight spacing required, but you won't be able to make each line a different heading size. As far as HTML and your browser are concerned, the text is still one block element, no matter how many line breaks are inserted. If, on the other hand, you make each line a separate paragraph or heading, the line spacing is unattractively *open*.

The best solution for controlling spacing within a text block is to use the CSS line-height property. The majority of browsers now in use support line spacing through CSS, and you can set the line height in pixels, ems, percentages, or multiple.

Often I like to fit my heading and initial following paragraph tightly together. To accomplish this, you need to adjust both the `margin-bottom` of the heading and the `margin-top` of the paragraph. If you want all your headings to work this way, you can set that up in a single CSS rule:

```
h1, h2, h3, h4, h5, h6 { margin-bottom: 0 }
```

It's not a good idea to apply a corresponding zero margin-top to the `p` tag because that would affect all paragraphs. A better approach is to create a class with the right property and use as needed:

```
.firstParagraph { margin-top: 0 }
```


FIGURE 7-10

Break tags, denoted by shield symbols, wrap your lines without the additional line spacing created by <p> tags.

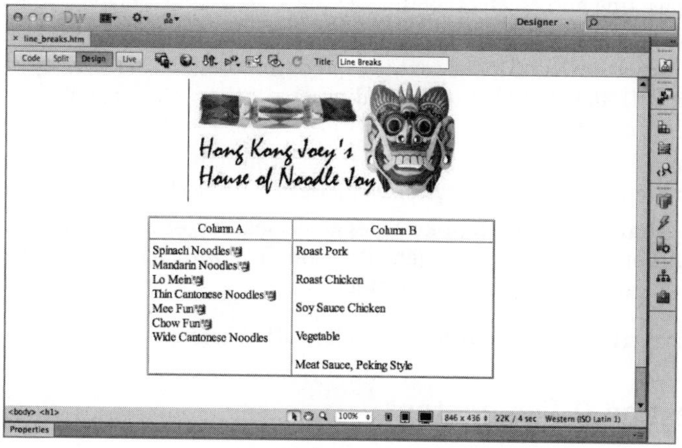

Working with Microsoft Office Documents

The ubiquitous nature of Microsoft Office has intricately tied Word and Excel to the web. Quite often, content stored in documents from these programs must be integrated into a web page. Putting a meeting agenda drafted in Word or a production schedule laid out in Excel on the web is just one of the tasks faced—and dreaded—by office personnel every day. Dreamweaver provides a number of methods to ease the transition from offline Office documents to online content. No matter the path you take, you'll have a range of options to paste your content how you want it to appear.

Importing Office documents

Existing Word or Excel files can be imported directly into Dreamweaver in a single operation. Dreamweaver automatically converts the content from the Office format to HTML. To begin an import operation, choose File ➪ Import and then either Word Document or Excel Document from the submenu.

NOTE
The Import Word Document and Import Excel Document commands are available only on Windows systems.

The content is pasted according to the option chosen at import time. The available options are selected from a list at the bottom of the Import Word Document and Import Excel Document dialog boxes and echo those found in the Copy/Paste category of Preferences.

- **Text Only:** Pastes completely unformatted text; even line breaks or paragraphs are removed.
- **Text With Structure:** Pastes unstyled text while retaining structured elements such as lists, paragraphs, line breaks, and tables.
- **Text, Structure, Basic Formatting:** Adds simple formatting, such as bold, italic, and underline, to structured text. If the text is copied from an HTML document, the pasted text retains any HTML text style tags, including `<b>`, `<i>`, `<u>`, `<strong>`, `<em>`, `<abbr>`, and `<acronym>`.
- **Text, Structure, Full Formatting:** Pasted text keeps all structure and formatting. If the copied text retains inline CSS styles, Dreamweaver pastes them as well.
- **Clean Up Word Paragraph Spacing:** Removes additional spaces between copied Word paragraphs; this option is available when either the Text With Structure or the Text, Structure, Basic Formatting option is selected.

Excel documents are converted to tables with content formatted according to the options.

Copying and pasting Office content

Dreamweaver automatically converts material copied from Word and Excel into clean HTML. The procedure is quite straightforward: Simply copy your content in either Word or Excel using the standard copy or cut commands, switch to Dreamweaver, and paste by choosing Edit ➪ Paste or using the standard keyboard shortcut Ctrl+V (Command+V). The content is pasted according to the settings chosen in the Copy/Paste category of Preferences. These options are the same as those found in the Paste Special dialog box covered earlier in this chapter, shown in Figure 7-11.

Because Dreamweaver is actually converting material from one format to another, you may experience a short delay after pasting. If a great deal of conversion is needed—the more heavily the original content is formatted, the more conversion is required—Dreamweaver displays an alert to let you know that the operation might take some time and gives you the option to cancel.

Dragging and dropping Word and Excel files

Not all Office documents are appropriate for converting to HTML. In some situations, it's best to leave the document in the original format and link to it from the web page. Intranets—where access to Word or Excel is practically guaranteed and lengthy documents are the norm—are prime candidates for this type of design decision. Dreamweaver offers an easy way to make Office files web accessible and gives you the option to use it as you see fit.

FIGURE 7-11

Choose the degree of formatting you want to apply when copying from Microsoft Word through the Paste Special command.

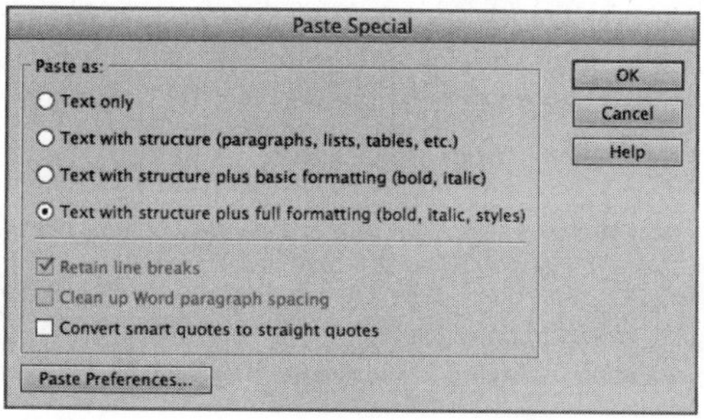

You've seen how a copy and paste operation from Word and/or Excel is relatively seamless. That's fine for material on the clipboard, but what about entire documents? Dreamweaver permits such Microsoft Office documents to be dragged and dropped right onto the page. What happens next for Windows users depends on the settings in Preferences. In the Office Copy/Paste category, you have two basic options: insert the content (formatted according to the standard options) or create a link to the document. On the Mac, a link is always created.

When an Office document is dragged onto the web page (whether from the Files panel or the desktop), the Insert Document dialog box appears, as shown in Figure 7-12. If you opt to insert the file, Dreamweaver automatically converts the document according to the options selected. When you choose to create a link, a text link to the file is inserted.

FIGURE 7-12

Drag-and-drop Office files wherever you'd like the converted document or link to appear.

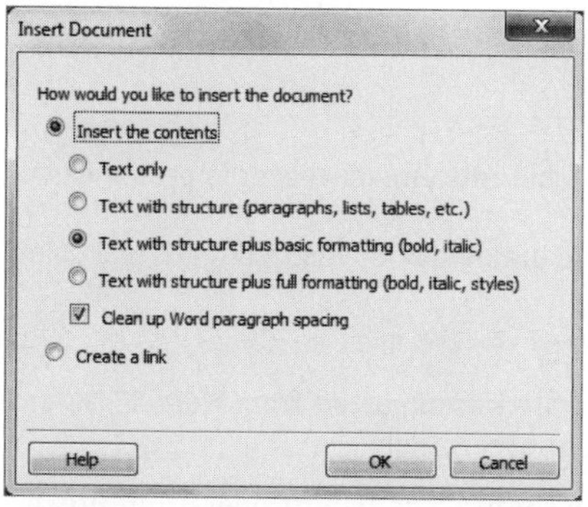

TIP

Dreamweaver will remember the option chosen from one import operation to the other; these settings are independent of the choices made in the Copy/Paste category of Preferences.

Importing Word HTML

Microsoft Word has offered an option to save its documents as HTML since the release of Word 97. Unfortunately, Microsoft's version of HTML output is, at best, highly idiosyncratic. Although you could always open a Word HTML file in Dreamweaver, if you ever had to modify the page—which you almost always do—it took so long to find your way through the convoluted code that you were almost better off building the page from scratch. Fortunately, that's no longer the case with Dreamweaver.

TIP

Another reason to import an HTML file exported from Word, rather than just directly opening and editing it in Dreamweaver, is file size. Results vary, but importing a Word HTML document can reduce its size by half, or even more.

The capability to open and clean up Word HTML documents is a key workflow enhancement for Dreamweaver. Dreamweaver can successfully open and clean up files from most versions of Microsoft Word. You can even apply the current Code Format profile from Preferences so that the HTML is styled to look like native Dreamweaver code.

Naturally, before you can import a Word HTML file, you must create one. To export a document in HTML format in Word 97/98, you choose File ➪ Save as HTML; in Word 2000 and later, the command changed to File ➪ Save As Web Page. Although the wording change may seem to be a move toward less jargon, it's significant what Word actually exports. Starting with Word 2000 (and all the Office 2000 products), Microsoft heartily embraced the XML standard and uses a combination of standard HTML and custom XML code throughout its exported web pages. For example, here's the opening tag from a Microsoft Word 2008 for Mac document, saved as a web page:

```
<html xmlns:v="urn:schemas-microsoft-com:vml"xmlns:o="urn:schemas-
microsoft-com:office:office"xmlns:w="urn:schemas-microsoft-
com:office:word"xmlns:m="http://schemas.microsoft.com/office/2004/
12/omml" xmlns:css="http://macVmlSchemaUri" xmlns="http://www.w3.org/
TR/REC-html40">
```

Dreamweaver alters the preceding code to

```
<html>
```

If you accept the defaults, bringing a Word HTML file into Dreamweaver is pretty easy:

1. Choose File ➪ Open. When the Select File dialog box opens, navigate and select the file that you exported from Word.
2. Choose Commands ➪ Clean Up Word HTML.

   Dreamweaver detects whether the HTML file was exported from Word 97/98 or Word 2000 or later and changes the interface options accordingly.
3. Select options as desired and click OK to confirm the import operation. Dreamweaver cleans up the code according to the options you've selected; for large documents, you may have to wait a noticeable amount of time for this operation to complete. If the Show Log On Completion option is selected, Dreamweaver informs you of the modifications made.

CAUTION
If Dreamweaver can't determine what version of Word generated the file, an alert appears. Although Dreamweaver still tries to clean up the code, it may not function correctly. The same alert appears if you inadvertently select a standard non-HTML Word document.

For most purposes, accepting the defaults is the best way to quickly bring in your Word HTML files. However, because web designers have a wide range of code requirements, Dreamweaver provides a full set of options for tailoring the Word-to-Dreamweaver transformation to your liking. Two different sets of options exist: one for documents saved from Word 97/98 and one for those saved from Word 2000 or newer. The different sets of options can be seen on the Detailed tab of the Clean Up Word HTML dialog box; the Basic tab is the same for both file types. Table 7-7 details the Basic tab options, the Word 97/98 options, and the Word 2000 or newer options.

TABLE 7-7 Import Word HTML Options

Option	Description
Basic	
Remove all Word-specific markup	Deletes all Word-specific tags, including Word XML, conditional tags, empty paragraphs, and margins in <style> tags.
Clean up CSS	Deletes Word-specific CSS code, including inline CSS styles where styles are nested, Microsoft Office (mso) designated styles, non-CSS style declarations, CSS style attributes from tables, and orphaned (unused) style definitions.
Clean up <font> tags	Deletes <font> tags that set the default body text to an absolute font size.
Fix invalidly nested tags	Deletes tags surrounding paragraph and block-level tags.
Apply source formatting	Formats the imported code according to the guidelines of the current Code Format profile set in Preferences.
Show log on completion	Displays a dialog box that lists all alterations when the process is complete.
Detailed options for Word 97/98	
Remove Word-specific markup	Enables the general cleanup of Word-inserted tags.
Word meta and link tags from <head>	Specifically enables Dreamweaver to remove Word-specific <meta> and <link> tags from the <head> section of a document.
Clean up <font> tags	Enables the general cleanup of <font> tags.
Convert size [7-1] to	Specifies which tag, if any, is substituted for a <font size=n> tag. Options are: <h1> through <h6>, <font size=1> through <font size=7>, default size, and don't change.
Detailed options for Word 2000 and newer	
Remove Word-specific markup	Enables the general cleanup of Word-inserted tags.

Continues

TABLE 7-4 *(continued)*

Option	Description
XML from <html> tag	Deletes the Word-generated XML from the <html> tag.
Word meta and link tags from <head>	Specifically enables Dreamweaver to remove Word-specific <meta> and <link> tags from the <head> section of a document.
Word XML markup	Enables the general cleanup of Word-inserted XML tags.
<![if...]><![endif]> conditional tags and their contents	Removes all conditional statements and their contents.
Remove empty paragraphs and margins from styles	Deletes <p> tags without a closing </p>, empty <p></p> pairs, and styles tags including margin attributes—for example, style='margin-top:0in'.
Clean up CSS	Enables the general cleanup of Word-inserted CSS tags.
Remove inline CSS styles when possible	Deletes redundant information in nested styles.
Remove any style property that starts with "mso"	Eliminates Microsoft Office (mso)–specific attributes.
Remove any non-CSS style declaration	Deletes nonstandard style declarations.
Remove all CSS styles from table rows and cells	Eliminates style information from <table>, <tr>, and <td> tags.

Styling Your Text

For the most part, web designers today use CSS to style their text. Text styles can be applied to heading or paragraph tags to achieve a sitewide change of appearance, such as making all h1 headings red and 200 percent high, or to specific sections of a page through class or ID selectors. All the techniques covered in this section can be applied to dynamically inserted text.

Depicting various styles

HTML contains two types of style tags that are philosophically different from each other: logical tags and physical tags. The physical tags describe what text looks like; these include tags for bold, italic, and underlined text. HTML's logical styles denote what the text represents (such as code, a citation, or something typed from the keyboard) rather than what the text will actually look like. The eventual displayed appearance of logical styles is up to the viewer's browser.

Logical styles can be described as structural. They are useful when you are working with documents from different sources—reports from different research laboratories around the country, for instance—and you want a certain conformity of style. If you are trying to achieve a particular look using logical styles, you should consider using the Cascading Style Sheets feature instead of, or in addition to, logical styles. You can apply logical style tags and then use Cascading Style Sheets to define how that style will look when viewed in a browser.

CAUTION

By default, Dreamweaver, in recognition of current web standards, no longer supports certain physical tags. If you highlight a section of text and choose the Bold button from the HTML tab of the Property inspector, Dreamweaver wraps the selection with a `<strong>` tag. If you choose the Bold button while on the CSS tab of the Property inspector, Dreamweaver adds a `font-weight: bold` property to the currently applied style rule. The only way to get the Bold button is by changing an option in Dreamweaver Preferences, as described shortly.

In Dreamweaver, logical style tags can be accessed by choosing Format ➪ Style and selecting from the available style name options. A checkmark appears next to the selected tags. Style tags can be nested (put inside one another), and you can mix such tags within a word, line, or document. You can have a bold, strikethrough, variable style, or you can have an underlined, cited style. (Both variable and cite are particular logical styles covered later in this section.)

NOTE

You can also add the most commonly used styles—bold, italic, strong, and emphasis—by clicking the appropriate button in the Text category of the Insert panel. Dreamweaver will insert `<strong>` and `<em>` for bold and italic, respectively, by default.

Figure 7-13 compares how styles are rendered in Dreamweaver's Live View, Mozilla Firefox, and Google Chrome. Although the various renderings are mostly the same, notice the difference between how the Code, Sample, and Keyboard styles are rendered in Dreamweaver (far left) and in either browser. The various styles may be rendered quite a bit differently in other browsers and other browser versions.

Two of the physical style tags—bold and italic—are controlled by a Preferences setting. Although you can use the `<b>` and `<i>` tags to style text, it is considered better practice to use the equivalent logical tags, `<strong>` and `<em>`. Dreamweaver enables you to specify which tags to use via the Use <strong> And <em> In Place Of <b> And <i> option in the General category of Preferences. If this option is selected (the default), `<strong>` and `<em>` tags are used to code bold or italic text, respectively; if the option is clear, `<b>` and `<i>` tags are used.

To actually apply bold or italic formatting, select the text and click the Bold or Italic button on the Property inspector's HTML tab, or use the keyboard shortcuts (Ctrl+B [Command+B] and Ctrl+I [Command+I], respectively). Buttons for bold, italic, strong, and emphasis are also available in the Text category of the Insert panel.

CAUTION

One physical style, the underline tag, `<u>`, is available only through the Format ➪ Style menu. Use this tag with caution. By default, browsers use underlining to designate links; if you style text with an underline, users expect that text to link somewhere. It's good practice to restrict use of underlining to hotspots, and to avoid underlining as a way to highlight text, even for headings.

FIGURE 7-13

In this comparison chart, the various renderings of style tags are from Dreamweaver's Live View, Firefox 10, and Chrome 17 (from left to right, respectively).

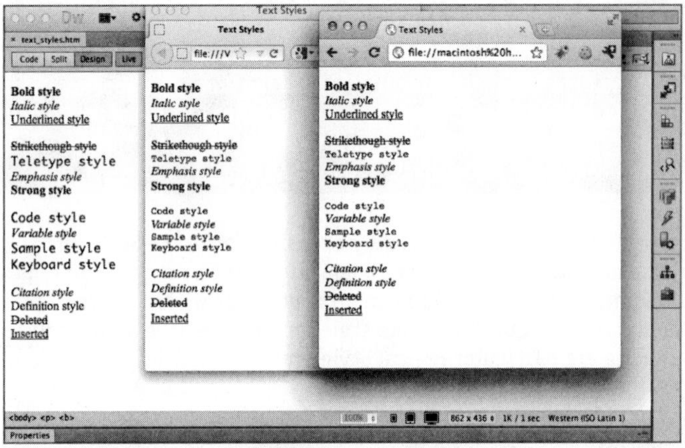

Both physical and logical style tags are described in Table 7-8.

TABLE 7-8 **Text Style Tags**

Style	Tag	Description
Bold	<strong>	Text is rendered with a bold style.
Italic	<em>	Text is rendered with an italic style.
Underline	<u>	Text is rendered underlined.
Strikethrough	<s>	Used primarily in edited documents to depict edited text. Usually rendered with a line through the text.
Teletype	<tt>	Used to represent an old-style typewriter. Rendered in a monospace font such as Courier.
Emphasis	<em>	Used to accentuate certain words relative to the surrounding text. Most often rendered in italic.
Strong	<strong>	Used to strongly accentuate certain words relative to the surrounding text. Most often rendered in boldface.
Code	<code>	Used to depict programming code, usually in a monospace font.
Variable	<var>	Used to mark variables in programming code. Most often displayed in italic.
Sample	<samp>	Used to display characters in a literal sequence, usually in a monospace font.

Style	Tag	Description
Keyboard	<kbd>	Used to indicate what the user should input. Often shown in a monospace font, sometimes in boldface.
Citation	<cite>	Used to mark citations, references, and titles. Most often displayed in italic.
Definition	<dfn>	Used to denote the first, defining instance of a term. Usually displayed in italic.
Deleted	<del>	Used to denote deleted text, to aid in document authoring and editing. You can often find these tags in documents imported from Word HTML files that used the Track Changes feature. Although not fully supported in some browser versions, this style is typically depicted as a line through the text.
Inserted	<ins>	Used to denote inserted text. Like the Deleted style, this is used during the authoring process to keep track of changes. You can often find these tags in documents imported from Word HTML files that used the Track Changes feature. The style is usually depicted as underlined text.

Using the <address> tag

Currently, Dreamweaver does not support one useful style tag: the `<address>` tag. Rendered as italic text by browsers, the `<address> ... </address>` tag pair often marks the signature and e-mail address of a web page's creator.

NOTE

An easy way to do this in Dreamweaver is to use the Quick Tag Editor. Select your text and then press Ctrl+T (Command+T) to automatically enter Wrap Tag mode. If Tag Hints is enabled, all you have to do is start typing the address and press Enter (Return) twice to accept the hint and confirm the tag. In Code view and the Code inspector, the <address> ... </address> tag pair is also available as a Code Hint.

If you're applying the <address> tag to multiple lines, use <br> tags to form line breaks. The following example shows the proper use of the <address> tags:

```
<address><p>The President<br>
 1600 Pennsylvania Avenue NW<br>
 Washington, DC 20500</p></address>
```

This code is shown in a web browser as follows:

The President

1600 Pennsylvania Avenue NW

Washington, DC 20500

TIP

To remove a standard style, highlight the styled text, choose Format ⇨ Style, and select the name of the style you want to remove. The checkmark disappears from the style name. To remove a nonstandard tag such as `<address>`, choose the tag in the Tag Selector and right-click (Control+click) to open the context menu; then select Remove Tag.

Adding abbreviations and acronyms

Two other tags worth noting designate abbreviations, `<abbr> ...</abbr>`, and acronyms, `<acronym> ... </acronym>`. The abbreviation or acronym is enclosed within the tag pair. Both tags may include a `title` attribute, which is used to specify the full text of the abbreviation or acronym. The following code shows examples of both tags:

```
<abbr title="Incorporated">Inc.</abbr>
<acronym title="Object-oriented Programming">OOP</acronym>
```

The `<abbr>` and `<acronym>` tags are widely supported by modern browsers. These tags are not intended to actually change the visual style of the text in a browser, but instead they enable programs that process the document to clearly identify acronyms and abbreviations. For example, in the future, words marked as abbreviations could allow non-visual browsers to read the expanded word, rather than sounding out the abbreviation. If designated as an abbreviation, the letters *PA* could be read as *Pennsylvania* rather than as the word *pa*. In the future, this tag could also be used to provide alternate text for search engines, spell checkers, and translation programs.

In Dreamweaver, you can insert acronyms or abbreviations by clicking the Acronym or Abbreviation button on the Text category of the Insert panel. You can also choose the appropriate command from the Insert ⇨ HTML ⇨ Text Objects menu. These commands open a dialog box where you can enter the expanded text for the acronym or abbreviation.

Modifying Text Format

As a web designer, you easily spend at least as much time adjusting your text as you do getting it into your web pages. Luckily, Dreamweaver puts most of the tools you need for this task right at your fingertips through the Property inspector or the Tag inspector.

On the web today, designers have moved to using Cascading Style Sheets and away from hard-coding text with `<font>` and other tags. All versions of the major web browsers support Cascading Style Sheets, and text formatting enjoys the most widespread browser support of all the CSS rules.

If you're new to CSS and looking for a little background on how to create and apply styles, see Chapter 6.

Adjusting font size

The best-practice route for setting font size with CSS is to apply an existing style—declared in either an internal or an external style sheet—to a tag or selection of text and then to select the new size from the CSS tab of the Property inspector, as shown in Figure 7-14. If no style has been previously attached to the selection, Dreamweaver displays the New CSS Rule dialog box for you to identify the new styles selector, name it, and decide where to store it. After the style is created, it is automatically applied to the current selection.

FIGURE 7-14

Change the size of a CSS style directly through the Size list on the CSS tab of the Property inspector.

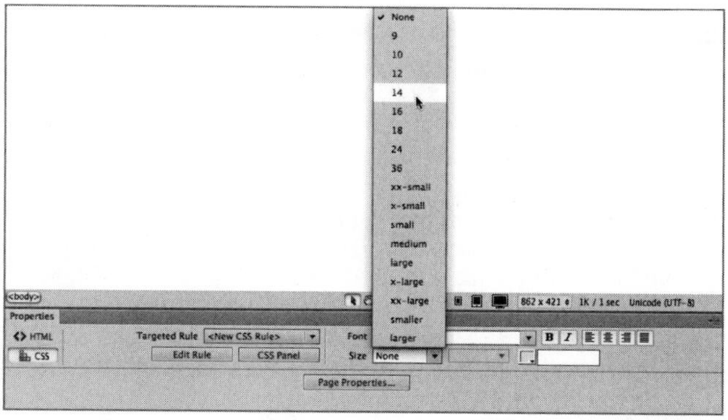

In CSS, the aptly named `font-size` property controls the size of the text. When declared in a selector, `font-size` is used like this:

```
h1 { font-size: 36px; }
```

or like this:

```
#mainsidebar { font-size: 1.2em; }
```

or this:

```
.legal { font-size: xx-small; }
```

As you can see, the `font-size` value may be a precise value (36px), a percentage (1.2em), or an absolute-size keyword (xx-small). In addition to pixels—abbreviated as px—CSS supports other measurement systems: points (pt), inches (in), centimeters (cm), millimeters (mm), and picas (pc), but these systems should be used only for print style sheets.

TIP

Many designers advocate using pixel measurements as a way to achieve a consistent look and feel across browsers.

CSS provides three different relative-based measurement systems for sizing text: `em`, `ex`, and percentage (`%`). All three assume that a specific font size has been declared for the parent or containing tag; if no specific font size is defined, the default setting of the parent's font size is used for comparison. A font size of `1em` is equivalent to whatever the containing tag's font size is; for example, if the containing `<div>` tag has a font size of `20px`, a selector with a font size set to `1.2em` is rendered as `24px`—because 20 times 1.2 is equal to 24. Percentage measurements work exactly the same way as `em` measurements; `1.2%` is the same as `1.2em`.

The `ex` measurement, however, is quite different. Short for x-height, the `ex` measurement system is based on the height of a lowercase *x* in the current font. Character heights vary quite substantially from one font to another: At 72 pixels, an *x* in Times is about 32px high whereas in Arial, it's almost 40px. Because of the widely varying differences, the `ex` measurement system is rarely used.

There are seven `font-size` keywords. The values rely on the browser for final size interpretation, and the sizes for both are relative to each other, as shown in Figure 7-15.

CSS specifications include two additional keywords: `larger` and `smaller`. These relative-based keywords are obviously intended to be used in relation to the current font size. For example, in a `<div>` where the `font-size` value is 10px, any text whose font-size value is `larger` would be rendered at about 12px, whereas a `smaller` value would display text at 8px.

FIGURE 7-15

The font-size property keywords parallel the <font> tag's size attribute values.

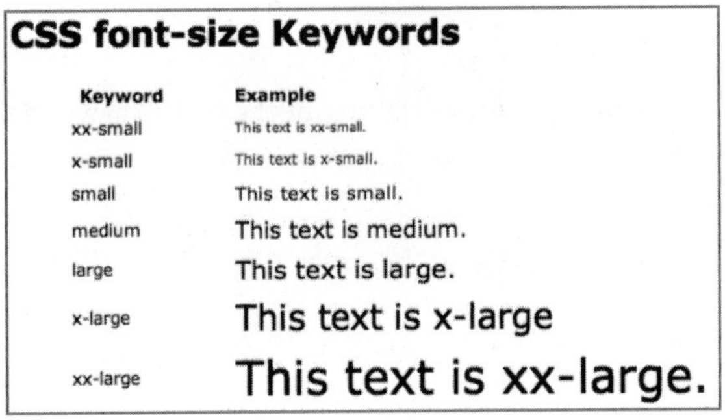
CSS font-size Keywords
Keyword
Example
xx-small
This text is xx-small.
x-small
This text is x-small.
small
This text is small.
medium
This text is medium.
large
This text is large.
x-large
This text is x-large
xx-large
This text is xx-large.

Adding font color

Unless you assign a color to text on your web page, the browser uses its own default, typically black. To change the font color for the entire page, choose Modify ⇨ Page Properties and select a new color from the Text Color swatch in the Appearances (CSS) category. When you're done, the style is written into an internal style sheet for `body`, `td`, and `th` selectors.

You can also apply color to individual headings, words, or paragraphs that you have selected in Dreamweaver. As with text size, when working with CSS the best way to set a color for a selected tag or text range is to apply an existing style that includes the desired color. Font color is defined through the Type category of the CSS Rule Definition dialog box.

Text color is expressed in either a hexadecimal color number or a color name. The hexadecimal color number is based on the color's red-green-blue value and is written like this:

```
#FFFFFF
```

The preceding represents the color white. You can also use standard color names instead of the hexadecimal color numbers. In CSS, the same `color` attribute is used, but written somewhat differently:

```
.pure {color:#FFFFFF;}
.envy {color:green;}
```

TIP

If you want to apply the same color that you've already used elsewhere in your site to your text, you can display the Color category on the Assets panel (choose Window ⇨ Assets). Just select the text in the Document window, select the color swatch in the Assets panel, and click the Apply button in the Assets panel.

Again, you have several ways to add color to your text in Dreamweaver. Click the color box in the Property inspector to open the color picker, displaying a limited palette of colors. Clicking the System Color Picker button in the color picker enables you to choose from a full-spectrum Color dialog box. With either method, Dreamweaver will either add the new color to the current style or open the New CSS Rule dialog box to allow you to create a new one.

TIP

If you're fluent in hexadecimal color values, you're free to enter the hex number directly in the Property inspector Color field, preceded by the number sign or hash mark, like this: `#FF00FF`. Dreamweaver also accepts the abbreviated format where each of the hexadecimal pairs are the same, so that `#FF00FF` is the same as `#F0F`. But what if you come from a different discipline such as print or graphic design? Dreamweaver can also translate RGB function notation. So you could also use `rgb(255,0,255)` or `rgb(100%,0%,100%)`, or even Hue Saturation Lightness values like this: `hsl(30,100%,40%)`. And, if you're not mathematically inclined at all, you can use standard color names, such as `magenta`.

If you approach your coloring task via the menus, the Format ⇨ Color command takes you immediately to the Color dialog box. To use the Property inspector to color a range of text, follow these steps:

1. Select the text you want to color, or position the cursor where you want the new text color to begin.
2. From the Property inspector, you can
   - Type a hexadecimal color number directly into the Text Color text field (make sure that the CSS tab is selected)
   - Type a color name directly into the Text Color text field
   - Select the color box to open the color picker
3. If you chose to type a color name or number directly into the Text Color text field, press Tab or click in the Document window to see the color applied.

4. If you clicked the color box, select your color from the palette of colors available. As you move your pointer over the color swatches, Dreamweaver displays the color and the color's hexadecimal number above.
5. For a wider color selection, open the Color dialog box by selecting the System Color Picker icon in the upper-right corner of the color picker.

   The New CSS Rule dialog box is displayed so you can assign your new color to a new CSS rule.

To access the full-spectrum color picker in Windows, follow these steps:

1. Select your text or position your cursor where you want the new text color to begin.
2. Choose Format ➪ Color to open the Color dialog box, shown on the left in Figure 7-16.

FIGURE 7-16

Use the Color (Colors) dialog box to choose a color for your font outside of the browser-safe palette in both Windows (left) and Mac (right).

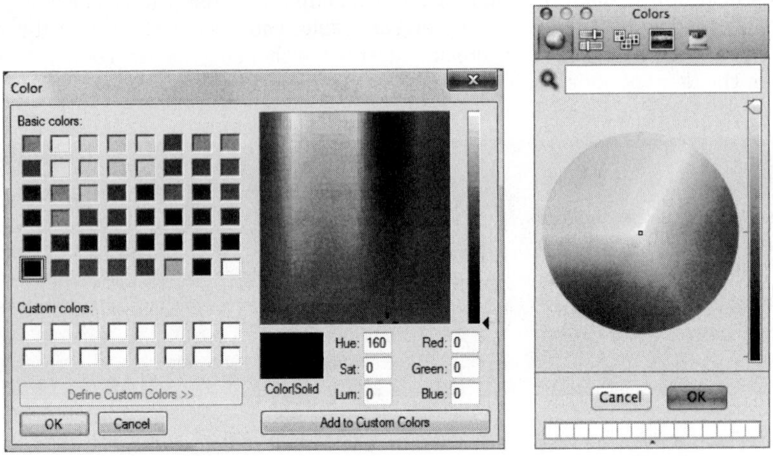

3. Select one of the 48 preset standard colors from the color swatches on the left of the Color dialog box, or use either of the following methods:
   - Select a color by moving the Hue/Saturation pointer and the Luminance pointer.
   - Enter decimal values directly into either the Red, Green, and Blue boxes or the Hue, Saturation, and Luminance boxes.
4. If you create a custom color, you can add it to your palette by clicking Add To Custom Colors. You can add up to 16 custom colors.
5. Click OK when you are finished.

CAUTION

When you add a custom color to your palette in Windows, the new color swatch goes into the currently selected swatch or, if no swatch is selected, the next available swatch. Make sure you have selected an empty or replaceable swatch before clicking the Add To Custom Colors button. To clear the custom colors, first set the palette to white by bringing the Luminance slider all the way to the top. Then, click the Add To Custom Colors button until all the color swatch text fields are empty.

Dreamweaver's Color Pickers

Dreamweaver includes a color picker for selecting colors for all manner of HTML elements: text, table cells, and page background. Dreamweaver's color picker—in keeping with the Adobe common user interface—offers a number of palettes from the context menu from which to choose your colors: Color Cubes, Continuous Tone, Windows OS, Mac OS, and Grayscale. The most common choices for web designers are Color Cubes and Continuous Tone, both of which display the 216 web-safe colors originally common to the Mac and Windows palettes.

After you've opened the text color picker by selecting the color box on the Property inspector, the cursor changes shape into an eyedropper that can sample colors from any of the displayed swatches or from any color onscreen. Simply click the color box and drag the eyedropper over any graphic to choose a color.

Virtually all computers are capable of showing far more than 216 colors now, so the concept of web-safe colors is no longer a necessity. You're free to choose colors outside the 216 range through the color picker.

Mac Users: Bring up the system color picker by clicking the System Color Picker button on the Dreamweaver color picker. The system color picker for the Mac is far more elaborate than the one available for Windows. The Mac version has several color schemes to use: CMYK (for print-related colors), RGB (for screen-based colors), HTML (for web-based colors), and Crayon (for kid-like colors). The CMYK, HTML, and RGB systems offer you color swatches and three or four sliders with text-entry boxes; they accept percentage values for RGB and CMYK, and hex values for HTML. Depending on your OS version, one or more of the color systems also have a Snap-To-Web color option for matching your chosen color to the closest browser-safe color. The Hue, Saturation, and Brightness sliders also have color wheels.

To access the full-spectrum color picker on a Mac (see Figure 7-16), follow these steps:

1. Select the text or position your cursor where you want the new text color to begin.
2. Choose Format ➪ Color to open the Colors dialog box.
3. In the Mac color picker, the list of available pickers is displayed across the top of the dialog box like a toolbar, and each particular interface's options are shown below as they are selected. Choose a color picker by clicking on its icon in the top toolbar, and create the color you want in the rest of the dialog box below. (The number and type of color pickers vary slightly depending on the version of the operating system and whether you've added any third-party color pickers.)
4. When you've found the desired color, click OK.

Assigning a specific font

Along with size and color, you can also specify the typeface in which you want particular text to be rendered. Because of HTML's unique way of handling fonts, Dreamweaver uses a special method for choosing font names for a range of selected text. Before you learn how to change a typeface in Dreamweaver, you should more fully examine how fonts in HTML work.

About HTML fonts

Page layout designers can incorporate as many different fonts as available to their own systems. Web layout designers, on the other hand, can use only those fonts on their viewers' systems. If you designate a paragraph to be in Bodoni Bold Condensed, for instance, and put it on the web, the paragraph is displayed with that font only if that exact font is on the user's system. Otherwise, the browser uses the default system font, which is often Times or Times New Roman.

Fonts are specified in CSS with the `font-family` property. Because a designer can never be certain which fonts are on visitors' computers, HTML enables you to offer a number of options to the browser, as follows:

```
body {font-family: Arial, Helvetica, sans-serif;}
```

The browser encountering the preceding property first looks for the Arial font to render the enclosed text. If Arial isn't there, the browser looks for the next font in the list, which in this case is Helvetica. If it fails to find any of the specified fonts listed, the browser uses whichever font has been assigned to the category for the font—sans serif in this case.

Font Categories

The W3C and some web browsers recognize five main categories of fonts. Although serif and sans serif are most commonly used, all modern browsers support all five generic font categories. In some browsers, the user can control which fonts display for each category.

As illustrated in the following figure, the generic font categories include:

- **Serif:** These fonts are distinguished by serifs, small cross-strokes that appear at the ends of the main strokes of each character. Serif fonts tend to be slightly easier to read on paper, but more difficult to read when viewed on a screen. You may want to limit use of serif fonts to headings or small blocks of text, unless your document is meant to be printed. Examples of serif fonts include Times New Roman, MS Georgia, and Garamond.
- **Sans serif:** These fonts are without serifs, meaning that the letters do not have finishing strokes at the tops and bottoms. Sans serif fonts are easier to read on a screen, and so they are a good choice for large blocks of text within a web page. Sans serif fonts found on many computers include Arial, Helvetica, and Verdana.
- **Monospace:** The distinguishing characteristic of monospace fonts is that all their characters are the same width. These fonts are typically used to depict code samples or in other circumstances that require characters to be precisely aligned. Commonly used monospace fonts include Courier and Courier New.
- **Fantasy:** The characters in these fonts are highly decorative, but still represent letters and numbers (as opposed to pictures or symbols). As with Cursive fonts, you may not want to use these for large blocks of text, but rather employ them to lend emphasis or to set the tone for a page. Examples of Fantasy fonts include Curlz MT, Critter, and Jokerman.

- **Cursive:** These fonts simulate writing in longhand, with strokes joining adjacent letters in a word. Because they can be difficult to read onscreen, you should avoid using large blocks of cursive text. These fonts are more appropriate for page banners or headings, to provide an elegant tone for a web page. Examples of cursive fonts are Zapf-Chancery and Lucida Handwriting.

Selecting a font

The process for assigning a font name to a range of text is similar to that of assigning a font size or color. Instead of selecting one font name, however, you're usually selecting one font series (aka "font stack"). That series could contain three or more fonts as previously explained. Font series are chosen from the Font list in the CSS Rule Definition dialog box's Text category, from the Property inspector CSS tab, or through a menu item. Dreamweaver enables you to assign any font on your system—or even any font you can name—to a font series, as covered in the next section, "Editing the Font List."

To assign a specific font series to your text, follow these steps:

1. Select the text or position your cursor where you want the new text font to begin.
2. From the Property inspector CSS tab, open the drop-down list of font names. You can also display the list of fonts by choosing Format ⇨ Font from the menu bar.
3. Select a font from the Font List. To return to the system font, choose Default Font from the list.

It's also possible to enter the font name or font series directly in the Property inspector's Font drop-down list box.

Editing the font list

With the Edit Font List dialog box, Dreamweaver gives you a point-and-click interface for building your font lists. After the Edit Font List dialog box is open, you can delete an existing font series, add a new one, or change the order of the list so your favorite ones are on top. Figure 7-17 shows the sections of the Edit Font List dialog box: the current font list, the available fonts on your system, and the chosen fonts. The chosen fonts are the individual fonts that you've selected to be incorporated into a font series.

FIGURE 7-17

Dreamweaver's Edit Font List dialog box gives you considerable control over the fonts that you can add to your web page.

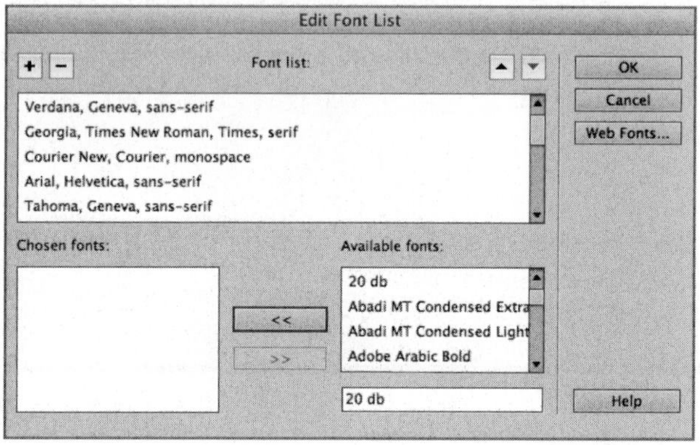

Follow these steps to construct a new font series and add it to the font list:

1. To open the Edit Font List dialog box, expand the Font drop-down list in the Property inspector and select Edit Font List.
2. If the Chosen Fonts box is not empty, clear the Chosen Fonts box by clicking the Add (+) button at the top of the dialog box. You can also scroll down to the bottom of the current Font List and select (Add Fonts In List Below).
3. Select a font from the Available Fonts list. The font categories, such as sans serif and cursive, appear at the end of the Available Fonts list.
4. Click the << button to transfer the selected font to the Chosen Fonts list.
5. To remove a font you no longer want or have chosen in error, highlight it in the Chosen Fonts list and click the >> button.
6. Repeat Steps 3 through 5 until the Chosen Fonts list contains the alternative fonts you want.
7. If you want to add another, separate font series, repeat Steps 2 through 6.
8. Click OK when you are finished adding fonts.

To change the order in which font series are listed in the Font List, follow these steps:

1. In the Edit Font List dialog box, select the font series that you want to move.
2. If you want to move the series higher up the list, click the up arrow button at the top right of the Font List. If you want to move the series lower down the list, click the down arrow button.

To remove a font series from the current Font List, highlight it and click the Remove (–) button at the top left of the list.

Remember that the fonts must be on your system to make them a part of your font list. To add a font that is unavailable on your computer, type the name of the font into the text field below the Available Fonts list and press Enter (Return).

Aligning text

You can easily align text in Dreamweaver, just as you can in a traditional word processing program. CSS supports the alignment of text to the left or right margin, in the center of the containing element, or justified, which causes text to be flush against both left and right margins, creating a block-like appearance.

Like a word processing program, Dreamweaver aligns text one paragraph at a time. You can't left-align one word, center the next, and then right-align the third word in the same paragraph.

When declaring an alignment while defining a CSS rule, select a value from the Text Align list found in the Block category of the CSS Rule Definition dialog box.

To use the Property inspector, switch to the CSS tab and choose any of the Alignment buttons, as shown in Figure 7-18. If a CSS rule is currently selected, the appropriate property for the text-align property is applied to the rule; if not, the New CSS Rule dialog box appears and you'll need to specify the type and name of selector.

FIGURE 7-18

The CSS tab of the Property inspector includes buttons to left-align, center, right-align, and justify your text.

The alignment keyboard shortcuts are as follows:

Alignment	Windows Shortcut	Mac Shortcut
Left	Ctrl+Alt+Shift+L	Command+Option+Shift+L
Center	Ctrl+Alt+Shift+C	Command+Option+Shift+C
Right	Ctrl+Alt+Shift+R	Command+Option+Shift+R
Justify	Ctrl+Alt+Shift+J	Command+Option+Shift+J

Quoting entire paragraphs

HTML offers a tag that enables you to quote whole paragraphs, such as inset quotations or name-and-address blocks. Not too surprisingly, the tag used is called the `<blockquote>` tag. Dreamweaver gives you instant access to the `<blockquote>` tag through the Indent and Outdent buttons located on the HTML tab of the Property inspector, as shown in Figure 7-19.

FIGURE 7-19

Indent and adjust the indentation of paragraphs and blocks of text by using the Indent and Outdent buttons on the HTML tab of the Property inspector.

To blockquote one or more paragraphs, select them and click the Indent button in the Property inspector. Paragraphs can be indented multiple times; each time you click the Indent button, another `<blockquote> . . . </blockquote>` tag pair is added. Note that you can't control how much space a single `<blockquote>` indents a paragraph—that characteristic is determined by the browser.

You also have the option of indenting your paragraphs through the menus by choosing Format ➪ Indent. You can also add the `<blockquote>` tag by clicking the Block Quote button in the Text category of the Insert panel.

If you find that you have gone too far, use the Outdent button, also located on the Property inspector. The Outdent button has no effect if your text is already at the left edge. Alternatively, you can choose Format ➪ Outdent.

TIP

You can tell how many `<blockquote>` tags are being used to create a particular look by placing your cursor in the text and looking at the Tag Selector.

Implementing Web Fonts

Hear that enormous sigh of relief, coupled with shouts of "Hallelujah!"? That's the sound of web designers all over the world celebrating the possibilities of web fonts. As noted earlier, browsers typically only render fonts that are available on the user's system—which means web designers have been stuck using an extremely limited set of common fonts. However, with the increased support of a CSS statement known as `@font-face`, an entire new galaxy of fonts (like that shown in Figure 7-20) has been discovered—and Dreamweaver makes "going there" as straightforward as possible.

FIGURE 7-20

While the logo on this web page is pulled from a graphic program, the headline is live text, rendered with a web font.

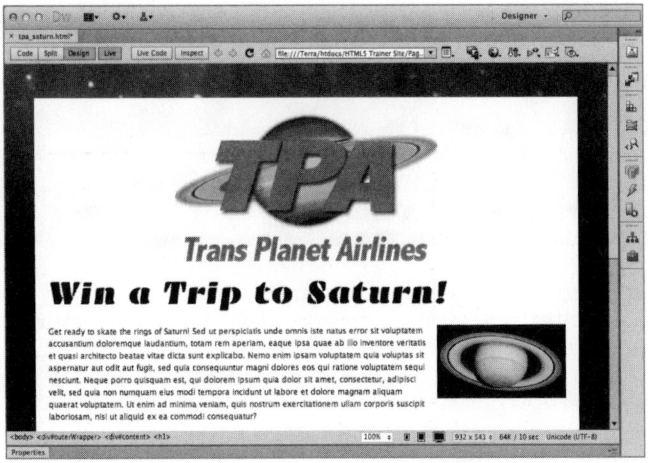

About @font-face

The `@font-face` statement allows the browser to render text in non-native fonts. The fonts can be stored on the web host or in a repository, like Google. Depending on which path you choose, there are trade-offs on speed and affordability, but both are quickly becoming negligible factors so that it's almost a matter of designer preference. Personally, I prefer to maintain control over my assets, so I prefer storing fonts I use on the web server that hosts the site.

In some ways, `@font-face` is similar to the HTML5 `<video>` and `<audio>` tags. All reflect the reality of a range of different formats supported. With `@font-face`, the emerging standard technique requires five different formats:

- **Embedded OpenType (EOT):** Supported by Internet Explorer
- **OpenType (OTF):** Supported by Firefox, Safari, Chrome, and Opera
- **TrueType (TTF):** Supported by Firefox, Safari, Safari Mobile (in iOS 4.2+), Chrome, and Opera
- **Web Open Font Format (WOFF):** Supported by Firefox, Chrome, and Internet Explorer (version 9)
- **Scalable Vector Graphics (SVG):** Supported by Safari (Mobile)

How does the `@font-face` statement bring all these formats together? Here's a look at a typical declaration:

```
@font-face {
    font-family: 'CarbonTypeRegular';
    src: url('carbontype-webfont.eot');
```

```
        src: url('carbontype-webfont.eot?#iefix') format('embedded-
       opentype'),
             url('carbontype-webfont.woff') format('woff'),
             url('carbontype-webfont.ttf') format('truetype'),
             url('carbontype-webfont.svg#CarbonTypeRegular') format('svg');
}
```

TIP

You may be wondering where you can get web fonts from—and how you go about wrangling all these different formats. Numerous type foundries and services have emerged to fill this need. One of the most popular is the jauntily named Font Squirrel (`www.fontsquirrel.com`). Many free fonts are available on the site—and, best of all, you can download a single compressed folder that contains all the necessary formats and the required CSS code.

Once you've included the `@font-face` statement into your CSS, you're ready to apply it to a selector using the value declared for the `font-family` property. Here's the code for setting the `<h1>` tag to be rendered in the web font set up in the `@font-face` statement, `CarbonTypeRegular`.

```
h1 {   font-family: CarbonTypeRegular; }
```

Applying web fonts in Dreamweaver

As the previous section attests, there are a good number of moving parts to properly implement web fonts. Luckily, Dreamweaver is capable of pulling all the components together with only a small bit of help from the designer. All you need to do is put the fonts you want to use—along with a CSS stylesheet containing the `@font-face` statement—in a specific folder and you're good to go.

The folder in question is one that is specified in the Site Setup dialog box. By default, the folder is called webfonts and is located in the site root. To modify this folder setting, follow these steps:

1. Choose Site ➪ Manage Sites and then click Edit once the Manage Sites dialog box opens. Alternatively, you can double-click the site name in the Files panel.
2. When the Site Setup dialog box appears, expand the Advanced Settings category.
3. Select the Web Fonts category.
4. Choose the Browse For Folder icon to select the folder you want to contain your web fonts (see Figure 7-21).
5. Close the Site Setup dialog box, as well as the Manage Sites dialog box if necessary.

WARNING

Although Dreamweaver defines the default web font folder as webfonts in your site root, it doesn't actually create the folder. You'll need to handle that chore yourself.

Once you have your web fonts folder defined, all you need to do is fill it up with your desired fonts. Perhaps the easiest path is to visit the aforementioned Font Squirrel site (`http://www.fontsquirrel.com`) and download one of the font kits. Unzip the download and save the folder in your web fonts folder. Dreamweaver will automatically recognize the fonts contained within the downloaded folder and make them available in the standard font lists found throughout the user interface. As shown in Figure 7-22, web fonts are initially placed at the bottom of the list.

FIGURE 7-21

Change your default web fonts folder through the Site Setup dialog box.

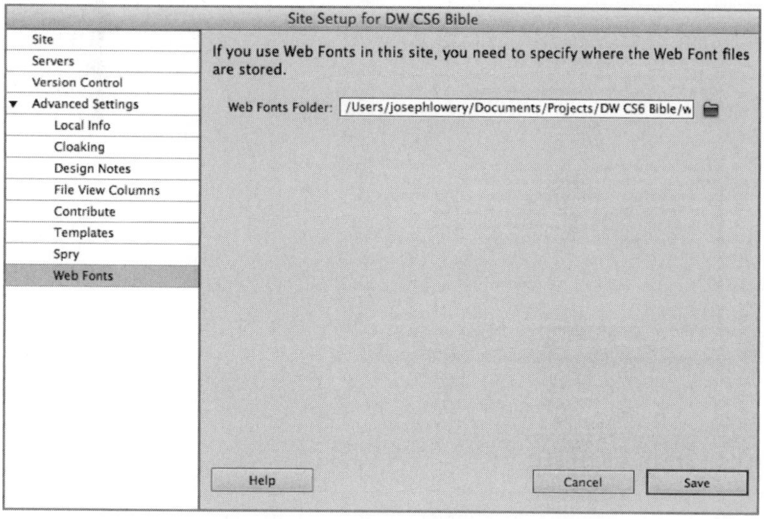

FIGURE 7-22

Web fonts are automatically added to the bottom of every font list in Dreamweaver's interface, including the one on the Property inspector.

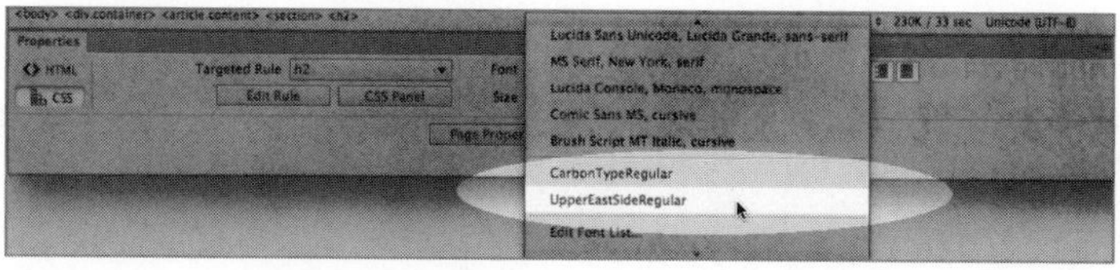

TIP

If your list of fonts is extremely long, you can make any selected one—including a web font—a favorite and move it to the top of the list. In the CSS Definition dialog box, select your font from the Font-family list by clicking the star next to Font-family list in the Type category.

To see the new web font in action, you'll need to enter into Live View (see Figure 7-23) or preview your page in the browser.

FIGURE 7-23

You're free to use as many web fonts on a page as your sense of style permits. Here one font is used for the single <h1> tag and another for the multiple <h2> tags.

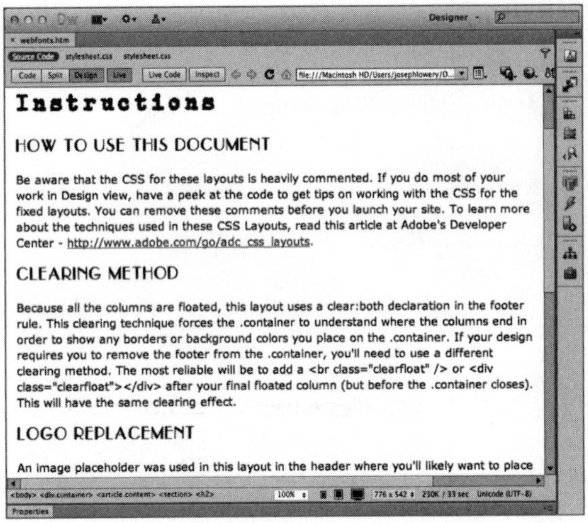

Incorporating Dates

With the web constantly changing, keeping track of when information is updated is important. Dreamweaver includes a command that enables you to insert today's date in your page, in almost any format imaginable. Moreover, you can set the inserted date to be automatically updated every time the page is saved. This means that every time you make a modification to a page and save it, the current date is added.

The Insert Date command uses your system clock to get the current date. In addition, you can elect to add a day name (for example, Thursday) and the time to the basic date information. After the date text is inserted, it can be formatted like any other text—adding color or a specific font type or changing the date's size.

To insert the current date, follow these steps:

1. Choose Insert ➪ Date or select the Date object from the Common category of the Insert panel. The Insert Date dialog box, shown in Figure 7-24, is displayed.
2. If desired, select a Day Format to include in the date from the drop-down list. The options are as follows:

[No Day]	Thu
Thursday,	thu,
Thursday	thu
Thu,	

FIGURE 7-24

Keep track of when a file is updated, using the Date command by checking the Update Automatically On Save option.

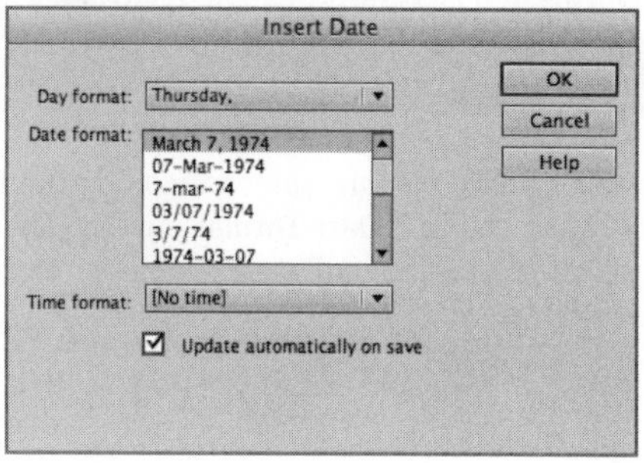

3. Select the desired date format from the drop-down list. The example formats are as follows:

March 7, 1974	7/03/74
07-Mar-1974	07.03.1974
7-mar-74	07.03.74
03/07/1974	7-03-1974
3/7/74	7 March, 1974
1974-03-07	74-03-07
7/3/74	

TIP

If you are creating web pages for the global market, consider using the format designated by the 1974-03-07 example. This year-month-day format is an ISO (International Organization for Standardization) standard and is computer-sortable.

4. Select the desired time format, if any, from the drop-down list. The example formats are as follows:
   - [No Time]
   - 10:18 PM
   - 22:18
5. To modify the date to include the current date every time the file is saved, select the Update Automatically On Save option.
6. Click OK when you're finished.

TIP

It's easy to format an inserted date when the Update Automatically On Save option is *not* selected—it's just plain text, and the formatting can be added easily through the Text Property inspector. However, if the date is to be automatically updated, it's inserted as a special Adobe data type with its own Property inspector. You can style it, however, by applying a CSS style to the containing tag.

If your date object includes the Automatic Update option, you can modify the format. Select the date and, in the Property inspector, click the Edit Date Format button. The Edit Date Format dialog box opens, which is nearly identical to the Insert Date dialog box, except the Update Automatically On Save option is not available.

Commenting Your Code

How do you know when to begin inserting comments into your HTML code? You know the first time you go back to an earlier web page, look at the code, and say, "What on earth was I thinking?" Plan ahead and develop the habit of commenting your code now.

Browsers run fine without your comments, but for any continued development—of the web page or of yourself as a webmaster—commenting your code is extremely beneficial. Sometimes, as in a corporate setting, web pages are co-developed by teams of designers and programmers. In this situation, commenting your code may not just be a good idea; it may be required. An HTML comment looks like the following:

```
<!-- Created by Hummer Associates, Inc. -->
```

You're not restricted to any particular line length or number of lines for comments. The text included between the opening of the comment, `<!--`, and the closing, `-->`, can span regular paragraphs or HTML code. In fact, one of the most common uses for comments during the testing and debugging phase of page design is to *comment out* sections of code as a means of tracking down an elusive bug.

To insert a comment in Dreamweaver, first place your cursor where you want the comment to appear in either the Document window or the Code inspector. Then click the Comment button in the Common category of the Insert panel. This sequence opens the Comment dialog box, where you can type the desired text; click OK when you've finished. Figure 7-25 shows a completed comment in Design and Code views, with the corresponding Property inspector open.

If enabled in Preferences, Dreamweaver inserts a Comment symbol in the Document window. You can hide the Comment symbol by choosing Edit ➪ Preferences (Dreamweaver ➪ Preferences) and then clearing the Comments checkbox in the Invisible Elements category. You can also hide any displayed Invisibles by choosing View ➪ Visual Aids ➪ Invisible Elements or using the keyboard shortcut, Ctrl+Shift+I (Command+Shift+I).

You can also add a comment using the Snippets panel. To use this method, choose Window ➪ Snippets to open the panel and then expand the Comments folder. In the Document window, position the cursor where you want the comment to go. In the Snippets panel, double-click the type of comment you want to add or select the comment, and click the Insert button. If you are working in Code view, type your comment between the inserted tags. If you are working in

Design view, select the Comment symbol; then, in the Comment Property inspector, replace any default text that Dreamweaver may have added with your comment.

The final technique for incorporating a comment is in Code view. The Coding toolbar, initially docked on the left side of the Document window, contains an Apply Comment menu button. The Apply Comment options are:

- **Apply HTML Comment**—Inserts an HTML comment: `<!-- -->`.
- **Apply /* */ Comment**—Inserts a multiline JavaScript/CSS comment: `/* */`.
- **Apply // Comment**—Inserts a single-line JavaScript/CSS comment at the start of a code line: `//`.
- **Apply ' Comment**—Inserts a single-line ASP comment at the start of a code line: `'`.
- **Apply Server Comment**—Inserts a comment applicable to the current server model.

FIGURE 7-25

Comments are extremely useful for inserting into the code information not visible on the rendered web page.

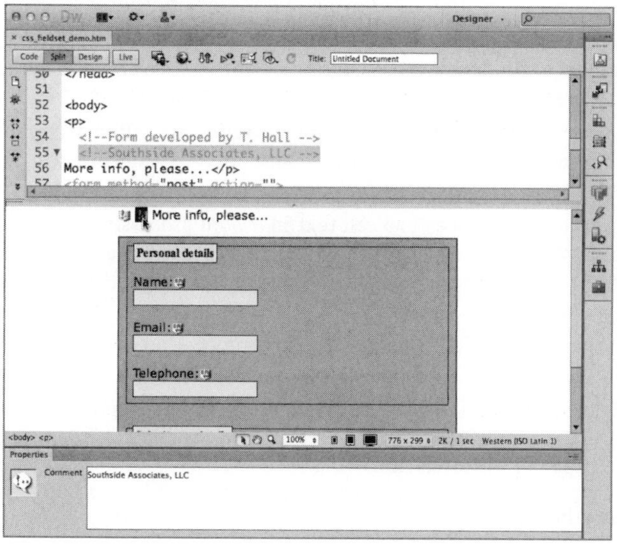

To remove a comment in Code view, select all the code that contains the beginning and ending comment indicators and choose Remove Comment from the Coding toolbar.

> **TIP**
>
> The Snippets panel is really good for commenting out a section of code or text already on the page. With your code or text selected, choose the desired comment style and drop it right on your selection. Prest-O Change-O—instant comments!

To edit a comment in Design view, double-click the Comment symbol to display the current comment in the Property inspector. A comment can be moved or duplicated by selecting its symbol and then using the Cut, Copy, and Paste commands under the Edit menu. You can also right-click (Control+click) the Comment symbol to display the context menu. Finally, you can click and drag Comment symbols to move the corresponding comment to a new location.

Summary

Learning to manipulate text is an essential design skill for creating web pages. Dreamweaver gives you all the tools you need to insert and modify the full range of HTML text quickly and easily. As you work with text on your web pages, keep these points in mind:

- HTML headings are available in six different levels of importance: `<h1>` through `<h6>`. Headings are used primarily as headlines and subheads to separate divisions of the web page.
- Blocks of text are formatted with the paragraph tag `<p>`. Each paragraph is separated from the other paragraphs by a line of whitespace above and below. Use the line break tag, `<br>`, to make lines appear directly above or below one another.
- Dreamweaver offers a full complement of text-editing tools—everything from Cut and Paste to Find and Replace. Dreamweaver's separate Design and Code views make short work of switching between text and code.
- Dreamweaver's Find and Replace feature goes a long way toward automating your work on the current page and throughout the website. Both content and code can be searched in a basic or very advanced fashion.
- You can format web page text much as you can text in a word processing program through CSS. You can select a font's size and color, as well as the font face, through the CSS tab of the Property inspector, and the chosen properties are applied directly to the current rule.
- Dreamweaver supports the use of web fonts by placing a font folder containing all font formats and a CSS stylesheet with the appropriate `@font-face` code in the designated web fonts folder.
- HTML comments are a useful (and often requisite) vehicle, which remains unseen by the casual viewer, for embedding information into a web page. Comments can annotate program code or insert copyright information.

In the next chapter, you learn how to insert and work with graphics.

CHAPTER

8

Inserting Images

IN THIS CHAPTER

Working with foreground and background images

Inserting images from the Assets panel

Dreamweaver Technique: Including Images

Revising graphics

Dreamweaver Technique: Changing Graphics

Modifying image height, width, and margins

Aligning and wrapping text around images

Dividing your page with HTML lines

Putting graphics into motion

Adding rollovers

Dreamweaver's power is evident as you use its visual layout tools to incorporate background and foreground images in your web page designs. This chapter gives you a quick introduction to inserting images that covers techniques for incorporating both background and foreground images—and modifying them using the methods available in Dreamweaver. You also learn about animation graphics and how you can use them in your web pages, along with techniques for creating rollover buttons.

Dreamweaver QUICKSTART

Adding an image to Dreamweaver is very straightforward. Here are the basic steps for inserting a graphic into your web page:

1. Place your cursor where you'd like it to appear on the page.
2. From the Common category of the Insert panel, click the Images: Image button.

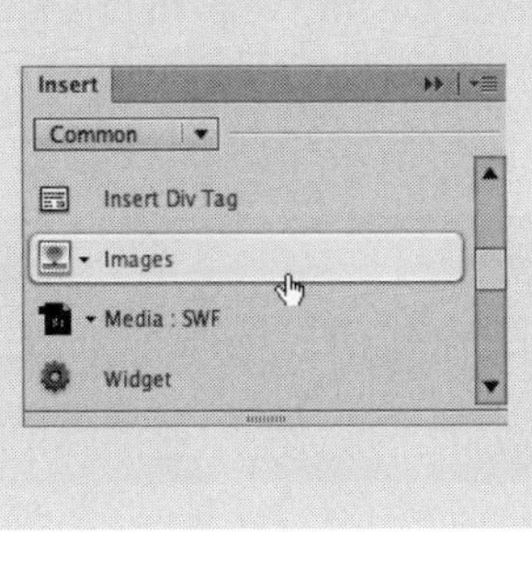

Continues

continued

3. When the Select Image Source dialog box opens, navigate to your image and select it.
4. If you have the Images Accessibility option enabled, enter a short description in the Alternative Text field.

As you'll see in the remainder of this chapter, there's a lot more you can do with images—but this should get you started!

Using Images Inline

Inline images can appear directly next to text—literally in the same line—or they can appear all by themselves in a `<div>` or `<p>` tag. The capability to render images inline and out was one of the major innovations in the evolution of the World Wide Web and opened the door to a flood of design innovation. This section covers all the basics of inserting inline images and modifying their attributes using Dreamweaver.

Inserting images

You can open and preview any graphic in a GIF, JPEG, or PNG format in Dreamweaver. You have many options for placing a graphic on your web page:

- Position your cursor in the document, and from the Common category of the Insert panel, click the Image button.
- Position your cursor in the document, and from the menu bar, choose Insert ➪ Image.
- Position your cursor in the document and press Ctrl+Alt+I (Command+Option+I).
- Drag the Image button from the Images menu of the Insert panel's Common category onto your page.
- Drag an icon from your file manager (Explorer on Windows or from the Finder or the Desktop on a Mac) or from the Files panel onto your page.
- Drag a thumbnail or filename from the Image category of the Assets panel onto your page. This capability is covered in detail in a subsequent section, "Dragging images from the Assets panel."

For all methods except those using the Assets panel or the file manager, Dreamweaver opens the Select Image Source dialog box (shown in Figure 8-1) and asks you for the path or address to your image file. Remember that in HTML, all graphics are stored in separate files linked from your web page.

NOTE

Dreamweaver's Select Image Source dialog box includes an option to select the filename from data sources. This chapter covers inserting static images from the file system. For a brief overview about including dynamic images from data sources, see the "Making Images Dynamic" sidebar later in this chapter; for a more in-depth look, see Chapter 19.

FIGURE 8-1

In the Select Image Source dialog box, you can keep track of your image's location relative to your current web page.

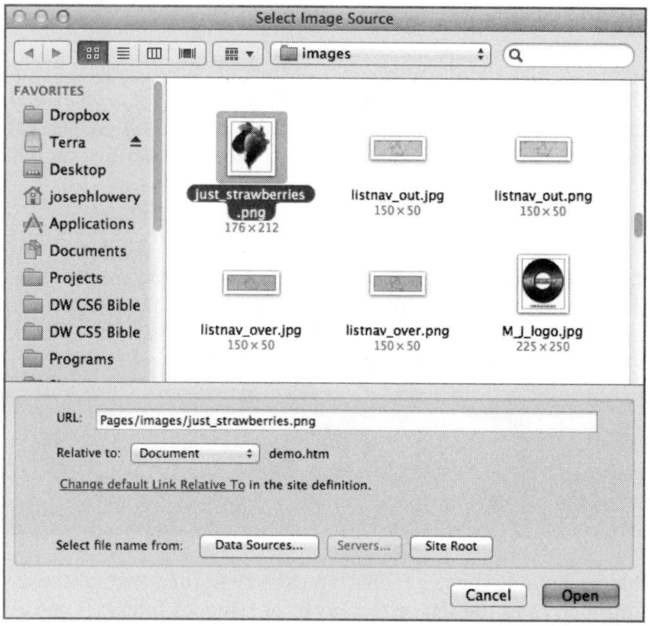

Whether you are choosing from the file system or a data source, the image's address can be a filename, a directory path and filename on your system, a directory path and filename on your remote system, or a full URL to a graphic on a completely separate web server. The file doesn't need to be immediately available for the code to be inserted into your HTML.

TIP

If you have an always-on Internet connection such as cable or DSL, Dreamweaver displays images referenced by absolute URLs right in Design view. Dreamweaver automatically reads and includes the width and height dimensions in the generated source code.

In the lower portion of the dialog box, the URL text box displays the format of the address that Dreamweaver inserts into your code. Below the URL text box is the Relative To list box. Use it to declare an image relative to the document you're working on (the default) or relative to the site root. (After you've saved your document, you can see its name displayed beside the Relative To list box.)

When you insert an image, you may also see the Image Tag Accessibility Attributes dialog box, depending on your preference settings. See the section "Adding image descriptions" for more information about this dialog box.

To take full advantage of Dreamweaver's site management features, you must define a site and save the current web page before beginning to insert images. Chapter 4 has more information about how to begin a Dreamweaver project.

Relative to Document

After you've saved your web page and chosen Relative to Document, Dreamweaver displays the address in the URL text box. If the image is located in a folder on the same level as or within your current site root folder, the address is formatted with just a path and filename. For instance, if you're inserting a graphic from the subfolder named Images, Dreamweaver inserts an address like the following:

```
images/logo.jpg
```

If you try to insert an image currently stored outside of the local site root folder, Dreamweaver automatically copies the image file to your Default Images folder, specified when you first created the site.

TIP

To change the setting for your Default Images folder, choose Site ➪ Manage Sites, and in the Manage Sites dialog box, select the current site and click Edit. In the Local Info category of the Advanced tab of the Site Definition dialog box, you can specify the Default Images folder.

If your site does not include a Default Images folder, you see the prompt window shown in Figure 8-2, asking if you want to copy the image to your local site root folder. If you click Yes, Dreamweaver gives you an opportunity to specify where the image should be saved within the local site. Whenever possible, keep all your images within the local site root folder so that Dreamweaver can handle site management efficiently.

FIGURE 8-2

Dreamweaver reminds you to keep all your graphics within the local site root folder for easy site management.

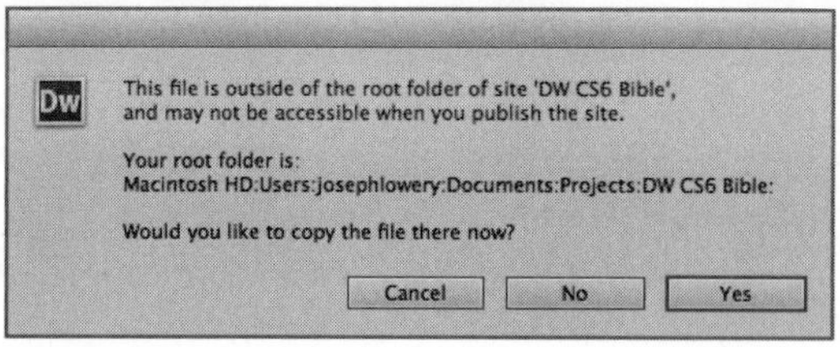

If you attempt to drag an out-of-site image file from the Files panel or from your file manager, and you click No to the prompt asking to copy the file to your site, the file is not inserted. If you attempt to insert the file using the Select Image Source dialog box and answer No, the file is inserted with the `src` attribute pointing to the path of the file. In this case, Dreamweaver appends a prefix that tells the browser to look on your local system for the file. For instance, in Windows, the file listing looks like the following:

```
file:///C|/Dreamweaver/images/logo.jpg
```

whereas on the Mac, the same file is listed as follows:

```
file:///Macintosh HD/Dreamweaver/images/logo.jpg
```

CAUTION

If you upload web pages with this `file:///C|` (`file:///Macintosh HD`) prefix in place, the links to your images are broken. It is easy to miss this error during your testing. Because your local browser can find the referenced image on your system, even when you are browsing the remote site, the web page appears perfect. However, anyone else browsing your website sees only placeholders for broken links. To avoid this error, always save your images within your local site.

Dreamweaver also appends the `file:///C|` prefix (or `file:///Macintosh HD` on a Mac) if you haven't ever saved the document in which you are inserting the image. However, when you save the document, Dreamweaver automatically updates the image addresses to be document-relative.

NOTE

You can choose whether you want your links to images (as well as other dependent files) to be relative to the document or site root through the Local Info category of the Site Setup dialog box.

Relative to Site Root

If you select Site Root in the Relative To field of the Select Image Source dialog box and you are within your site root folder, Dreamweaver appends a leading forward slash to the directory in the path. The addition of this slash enables the browser to correctly read the address. Thus, the same `logo.jpg` file appears in both the URL text box and the HTML code as follows:

```
/images/logo.jpg
```

When you use site root–relative addressing and you select a file outside of the site root, the image file is automatically copied to your Default Images folder, if one exists. If your site does not have a Default Images folder, you get a reminder from Dreamweaver about copying the file into your local site root folder—just as with document-relative addressing.

Making Images Dynamic

Once you're familiar with creating data source connections and establishing recordsets in Dreamweaver, you can display images dynamically. Dreamweaver doesn't actually insert images from a database but rather inserts the path and filenames of the images—right into the `src` attribute of the `<img>` tag.

Continues

continued

The data contained in the field can consist of just a filename, like `logo.gif`, or a path and filename, like `/images/logo.gif`. Under most circumstances, it's better to have just the filename; this structure provides the most flexibility because the path to the file can be added by Dreamweaver.

Follow these steps to include an image dynamically:

1. Make sure you have defined a recordset with at least one field consisting of paths to graphics.
2. Position your cursor where you want your dynamic image to appear.
3. From the Common category of the Insert panel, click Image. Alternatively, you can drag the Image button to the proper place on the page. In either case, the Select Image Source dialog box appears.
4. Navigate to any folder within your Local Root directory. Dreamweaver mishandles the insertion of the image from a data source if the dialog box attempts to reference an image outside the site.
5. From the Select Image Source dialog box, Windows users should choose the Select File Name From Data Sources option at the top of the page. Macintosh users should click the Data Source button found just above the URL field.
6. If necessary, expand the data source to locate and select the appropriate image field. Dreamweaver places the code for inserting the dynamic image into the URL field.
7. If your image data (the paths to the images) contains spaces, tildes, or other nonstandard characters, the data must be encoded to be read properly by the server. From the Format list, select one of the following:
   - Encode – Server.HTMLEncode (ASP JavaScript or Visual Basic)
   - Encode – HTMLEncodedFormat (ASP C#)
   - Encode – URLEncoded Format (ColdFusion)
   - Encode – Response.EncodeURL (JSP)
8. If your data is stored as filenames only, enter any required path in the URL field before the existing code. The path information may be document-relative, site root–relative, or absolute.
9. Click OK when you're finished.

For more details about using dynamic sources for your images, see Chapter 19.

Dragging images from the Assets panel

Web designers often work from a collection of images, much as a painter uses a palette of colors. Reusing images builds consistency in the site, making it easier for a visitor to navigate through it. However, trying to remember the differences between two versions of a logo—one named `logo03.gif` and another named `logo03b.gif`—used to require inserting them both to find the desired image. Dreamweaver eliminates the visual guesswork and simplifies the reuse of graphics with the Assets panel.

The Images category is key to the Assets panel. Not only does the Assets panel list all the GIF, JPEG, and PNG files found in your site—whether or not they are embedded in a web page—selecting any graphic from the list instantly displays a thumbnail. Previewing the images makes it easy to select the proper one, and then all you need to do is drag it from the Assets panel onto the page.

Before you can use graphics from the Assets panel, you must inventory the site by choosing the Refresh Site List button, as shown in Figure 8-3. When you click the Refresh button (or choose Refresh Site List from the context menu on the Assets panel), Dreamweaver examines the current site and creates a list of the graphics, including their sizes, file types, and full paths. To see an image, just click its name, and a thumbnail appears in the preview area of the panel.

TIP

To increase the size of the thumbnail, make the preview area larger by dragging open the border between the preview and the list areas and/or increasing the size of the entire panel. Dreamweaver enlarges the size of the thumbnail while maintaining the width:height ratio, so if you just move the border or resize the panel a little bit, you may not see a significant change. Thumbnails are never displayed larger than their actual size.

FIGURE 8-3

Reuse any graphic in your site or from your Favorites collection by dragging it from the Assets panel.

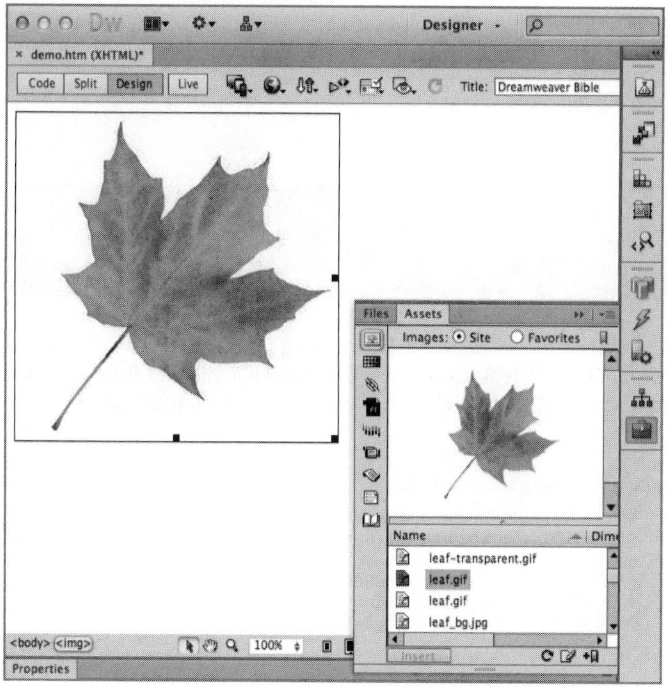

You can insert an image from the Assets panel onto your web page in two ways:

- Drag the image or the file listing onto the page.
- Place your cursor where you'd like the image to appear. Select the image in the Assets panel and click the Insert button.

CAUTION

Do not double-click the image or listing in the Assets panel to insert it onto the page; double-clicking invokes the designated graphics editor, be it Adobe Fireworks, Adobe Photoshop, or another program, and opens that graphic for editing. From the Document window, Ctrl+double-clicking (Command+double-clicking) accomplishes the same thing.

The Dreamweaver Assets panel is designed to help you work efficiently with sites that contain many images. For example, in large sites, it's often difficult to scroll through all the graphics' filenames looking for a particular image. To aid your search, Dreamweaver enables you to sort the Images category by any of the columns displayed in the Assets panel: Name, Size, Type, or Full Path. Clicking the column heading once sorts the assets in an ascending order by that criterion; click the column heading again to sort by that same criterion in a descending order.

You can also use the Favorites list to separately display your most frequently used images, giving you quicker access to them. To add an image to the Favorites list, select the image in the Assets panel, and then click the Add to Favorites button or select Add to Favorites from the Assets panel context menu. To retrieve an image from Favorites, first select the Favorites option at the top of the Assets panel. To switch back to the current site, choose the Site option.

Dreamweaver makes it easy to organize your favorite images by enabling you to create folders in the Favorites list. To create a folder, click the New Favorites Folder button in the Assets panel with the Favorites list displayed. Add images to the folder by dragging the image names in the Favorites list to the folder.

NOTE

Moving an image to a folder in your Favorites list does not change the physical location of the image file in your site. You can organize your Favorites list however you choose without disrupting the organization of files in your site.

If one or more objects are selected on the page, the inserted image is placed after the selection; Dreamweaver does not permit you to replace a selected image with another from the Assets panel. To change one image into another, double-click the graphic on the page to display the Select Image Source dialog box.

One final point about adding images from the Assets panel: If you reference a graphic from a location outside of the site, Dreamweaver asks that you copy the file from its current location. You must click the Refresh Site Files button to display this new image in the Assets panel.

TIP

When you click the Refresh button, Dreamweaver adds new images (and other assets) to the cache of current assets. If you add assets from outside of Dreamweaver—using, for example, a file manager—you might need to completely reload the Assets panel by Ctrl+clicking (Command+clicking) the Refresh button or by selecting Recreate Site List from the Assets panel context menu.

Dreamweaver TECHNIQUE

Including Images

Dreamweaver offers a number of ways to insert images. In this Dreamweaver Technique, you practice a number of common methods.

1. From the Techniques site, expand the 08_Images folder and open the `images_start` file.
2. Place your cursor in front of the first heading: Coming attractions.
3. From the Insert panel's Common category, choose Images: Image.
4. When the Select File dialog box opens, navigate to the images folder in the root of the Techniques site and locate `blueprint.jpg`; click OK when you're ready.
5. If the Image Tag Accessibility Attributes dialog box appears, enter **Blueprint** in the Alternative Text field.
6. In the Property inspector, choose imageLeft from the Class drop-down list.

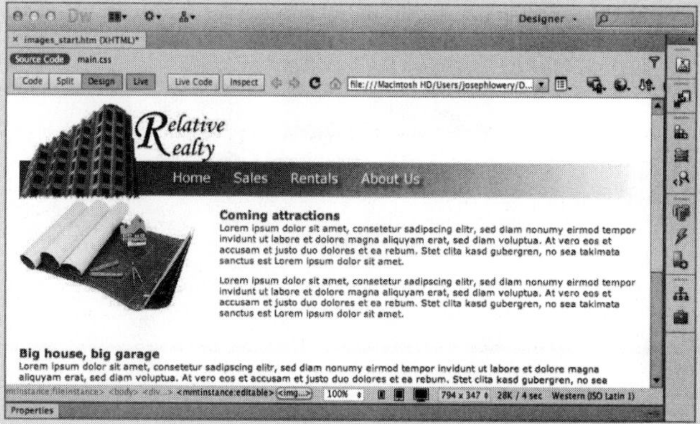

7. You can also use the Assets panel to insert images from your site. Place your cursor in front of the second heading: Big house, big garage.
8. Choose Window ⇨ Assets to bring the Assets panel to the front.

Continues

continued

9. Select the Images category, the first icon on the left of the Assets panel.
10. Locate `under_construction_01.jpg` and click Insert.
11. If the Image Tag Accessibility Attributes dialog box appears, enter **Under construction** in the Alternative Text field.
12. In the Property inspector, choose imageLeft from the Class drop-down list.
13. You can also simply drag images directly onto the page from the Files panel. In the panel, expand the images folder and drag `under_construction_02.jpg` to the left of the third heading, Room to grow.
14. If the Image Tag Accessibility Attributes dialog box appears, enter **Under construction** in the Alternative Text field.
15. In the Property inspector, choose imageRight from the Style drop-down list.

Each of the methods demonstrated works well; use the one you're most comfortable with when adding graphics to a page.

Optimizing and altering images

It's the rare graphic that integrates into the web page design unaltered. Digital photographs often need to be cropped and almost always need to be reduced—either in dimensions, file size, or both. Other images may need to be sharpened to achieve an immediate effect or lightened to fit better into the page palette. Dreamweaver provides several pathways to the perfect web image:

- **Graphic editing within Dreamweaver:** Without even leaving Dreamweaver, you can crop, resample, sharpen, and alter brightness and contrast of any selected GIF or JPG graphic. You don't even have to have a graphics editor such as Adobe Photoshop or Fireworks installed. You'll see how shortly.

- **Image optimization within Dreamweaver:** For more sophisticated image operations—without full-scale editing—choose Optimize from the image context menu. A dialog box opens within Dreamweaver where you can change the settings for the current format or switch to a new format altogether. You explore this option a little later in the "Employing the Optimize Image command" section.
- **Round-trip editing from Dreamweaver to your graphics editor:** For the most complex image modifications, use an external graphics editor such as Adobe Photoshop or Fireworks. Dreamweaver sends files to the editor of your choosing.

If you've inserted a Photoshop PSD file as your image, changes made in Photoshop are automatically updated in Dreamweaver. For more details, see Chapter 24.

The route you take depends on the depth of the modifications required. A key difference among these three different types of operations (one that you'll want to factor into your image-editing decision) is that the tools within Dreamweaver work on the actual graphic exported for web use. After the page containing the image is saved, changes cannot be reversed. If Fireworks is your graphics editor, both the Optimize and the Graphics Editor options can utilize the source files and create the exported file. If you do most of your graphics work in Photoshop, you can make changes to the source files and update the associated exported files. The main advantage to using source graphics is that you have much greater control and flexibility; many types of changes can be done and undone as many times as needed. The primary disadvantage is that not all web designers have the option to alter the source graphics.

Regardless of which route you choose, you'll find it's easy to get there. Dreamweaver has centralized access to all of the graphic tools in the most appropriate place—the Image Property inspector (see Figure 8-4).

FIGURE 8-4

Dreamweaver includes a range of image-editing tools right on the Image Property inspector.

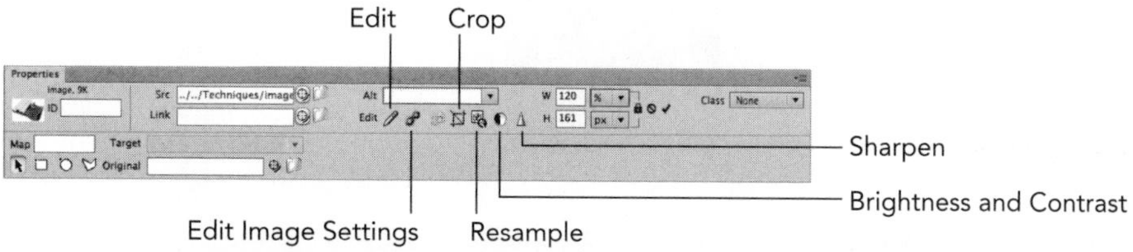

Let's begin your tour of Dreamweaver image-altering options by looking at the built-in tools first.

Cropping graphics

If you want to show only part of a photograph in the real world, you'd use a pair of scissors to crop off what you don't want. With digital graphic tools, no scissors are needed. Images are cropped for two main reasons: to focus attention on a particular area or to reduce file size. Often these reasons work hand in glove because a cropped image is always smaller than the original in both physical dimensions and file size.

Dreamweaver's cropping tool is both powerful and easy to use. When you choose to crop a graphic, a shaded border appears within the graphic. The edges of the border can be dragged to determine how the image should be trimmed. The region outside the border is darkened, but you can still see the full image so you can be sure a vital part of the graphic is not inadvertently cut.

To crop an image, follow these steps:

1. Select the image you want to crop.
2. In the Property inspector, click the Crop button.
3. Dreamweaver displays an alert to warn you that the cropping operation changes the selected image; click OK to clear the dialog box. A shaded border appears within the selected image (see Figure 8-5).
4. Drag the selection handles that appear in the middle of each side to crop the image in a single direction; the cursor changes to a two-headed arrow when in the correct position to crop a side.
5. To move the entire cropping area, drag the highlighted rectangle into the desired position; you can move the cropping area when the cursor is shown as a four-headed arrow, also known as the Grabber hand.

FIGURE 8-5

A repositionable, shaded border appears so that you can crop your images onscreen.

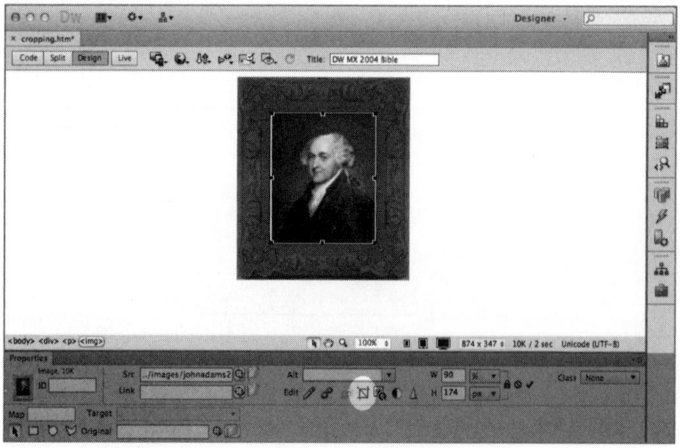

6. To cancel the cropping operation, click anywhere outside the graphic.
7. Complete the crop by double-clicking within the image.

After cropping, you can reverse the effect by choosing Edit ➪ Undo—but only until the page is saved or sent to an external graphics editor.

Resampling after resizing

Finding the perfect size for an image is often a matter of trial and error: It's important that a graphic work together with the entire page layout for maximum effect. Dreamweaver makes it easy to resize an image—just drag the sizing handles to the desired location. (You can find a complete discussion of Dreamweaver's resizing features later in this chapter in the "Adjusting height and width" section.) However, resizing an image in Dreamweaver is not the same as rescaling it in a graphics program; Dreamweaver merely draws the image to fit the chosen dimensions, much as a browser would. It doesn't actually recreate the graphic.

To get the cleanest, clearest representation of a resized graphic, you must resample the image. Resampling refers to the process of adding or subtracting pixels when the image is resized. If a graphic's dimensions are increased, pixels are formulaically added; make the image small and pixels are removed or blended according to a similar algorithm. Dreamweaver includes a resampling option, which becomes available when an image is resized, by either dragging the sizing handles or changing the values in the Width and Height fields of the Property inspector.

Resampling in Dreamweaver is a one-click affair—no parameters are set. Just choose the resized image and click the Resample button on the Property inspector. As with the other built-in tools, an alert informs you that the graphics file is being changed (unless you've selected the Don't Show Me This Message Again option).

How the image resamples really depends on the image itself and the difference between the original image size and the new size. Sometimes, resampling in either direction results in satisfactory images (see Figure 8-6). Typically, I find that small differences work far better than large ones; if you're making a major change in image size, it's often better to use a dedicated graphics editor such as Fireworks or Photoshop.

FIGURE 8-6

These three images demonstrate how an image can be resampled after it has been reduced or increased in size.

Affecting brightness and contrast

Digital photography has opened the floodgates for posting images on the web. Unfortunately, not all images look as good as they might. If you want to make the graphic lighter or darker or perhaps use a little more contrast, Dreamweaver has just the tool you need. The Brightness and Contrast command offers independent control over the two interlinked aspects of an image. Best of all, the Brightness/Contrast dialog box offers a Preview option, as shown in Figure 8-7, so that you can see the changes to the image in real time.

FIGURE 8-7

Preview the changes when using the Brightness and Contrast control to make sure you're getting the effect you want.

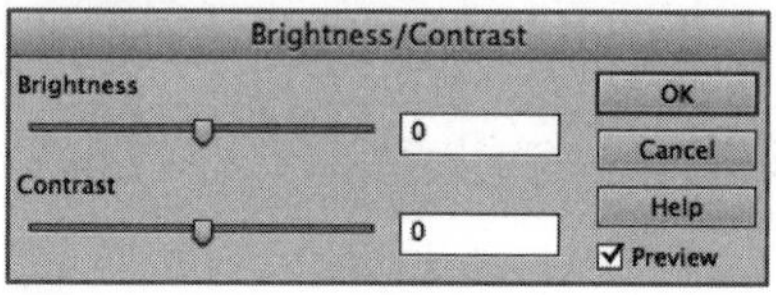

To alter the brightness and/or contrast of an image, follow these steps:

1. Select the image you want to modify.
2. Click the Brightness and Contrast button on the Property inspector. Dreamweaver displays the Brightness/Contrast dialog box.
3. Make sure the Preview box is selected to see the changes applied as you move the controls.
4. Drag the Brightness slider to the left or right. Dragging the slider to the left lowers the brightness; dragging it to the right increases brightness. Alternatively, you can enter a value directly in the Brightness field. Acceptable values are from –100 to 100, with 0 being the default.
5. Move the Contrast slider to the right to increase the contrast or to the left to decrease it. Alternatively, you can enter a value between –100 and 100 in the Contrast field.
6. When you're finished, click OK.

Although Brightness and Contrast is most frequently associated with photographic JPEG images, it can also be used for GIFs. However, be careful if your GIF has a transparent area; altering the brightness and/or contrast too much could make the transparent area visible.

Sharpening graphic lines

In web applications, fuzzy logic is generally sought after, but fuzzy photos are not. You can clear up blurry images with Dreamweaver's Sharpen command found on the Property inspector.

The Sharpen command examines the edges found within a graphic and programmatically increases the contrast of the related pixels. Flat areas of color are left unaffected. The Sharpen dialog box (see Figure 8-8) offers a sliding scale from 0 to 10 where 10 represents the maximum amount of sharpening available in one operation. As with the Brightness/Contrast dialog box, you can select the preview option.

FIGURE 8-8

Bring your images into focus with Dreamweaver's Sharpen feature.

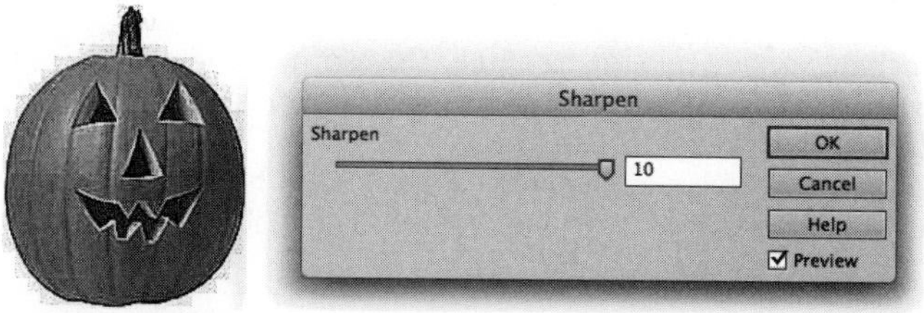

> **NOTE**
>
> If you're using Fireworks or Photoshop and need more sharpening power than Dreamweaver offers, try applying the filter called Unsharp Mask. Despite the name, this filter is terrific for sharpening blurry images.

Employing the Optimize Image command

Not all images are web-ready—especially those that are used in other media such as printing. To provide the best online experience, web graphics must balance appearance and file size. You want your images to look as good as possible at the lowest possible file size because a small file is quicker to download. The process of achieving the balance between the image quality and file size is called optimizing. You can optimize your images without leaving Dreamweaver by running the Optimize command.

The Optimize command actually opens a dialog box (see Figure 8-9) that allows you to change the settings for a specific format or even change formats—all while previewing the image changes in the Document window. Here's what you can do with the Optimize command:

- Switch formats from GIF to JPEG or vice versa. Other formats include animated GIF and PNG.
- Alter the palette depth (the number of colors) or transparency in GIF images.
- Change the JPEG compression quality.

FIGURE 8-9

Get the best web image possible at the lowest file size through the Optimize Image command.

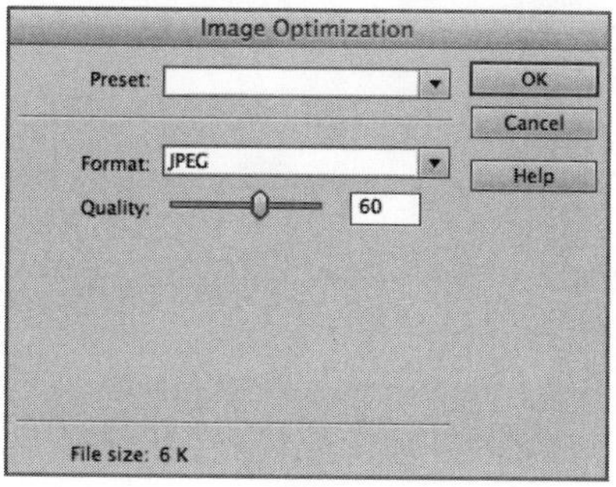

For a full explanation of all that's possible through the Optimize Image command, see Chapter 24.

Editing images

Although Dreamweaver includes some tools for cropping, sharpening, and otherwise revising images in your web pages, it is not a full-featured graphics editor. Certain tasks—such as slicing a larger graphic into sections or adding text to an image—are beyond Dreamweaver's scope. You can, however, set up your graphics editor of choice to work hand in hand with Dreamweaver. Specify your primary graphics editor for each type of graphic in the File Types/Editors category of Preferences.

Dreamweaver TECHNIQUE

Changing Graphics

Dreamweaver's built-in graphics functions are perfect for low-level quick fixes when an image needs to be cropped or resampled. In this Dreamweaver Technique, you have an opportunity to adjust one picture in a number of ways.

1. Open the `images_start.htm` file that you worked on in the last Dreamweaver Technique.
2. Select the second image on the page, next to the "Big house, big garage" heading. As you see, this image has a few problems in the outer part of the picture; with Dreamweaver, you can crop those problem areas right out of view.

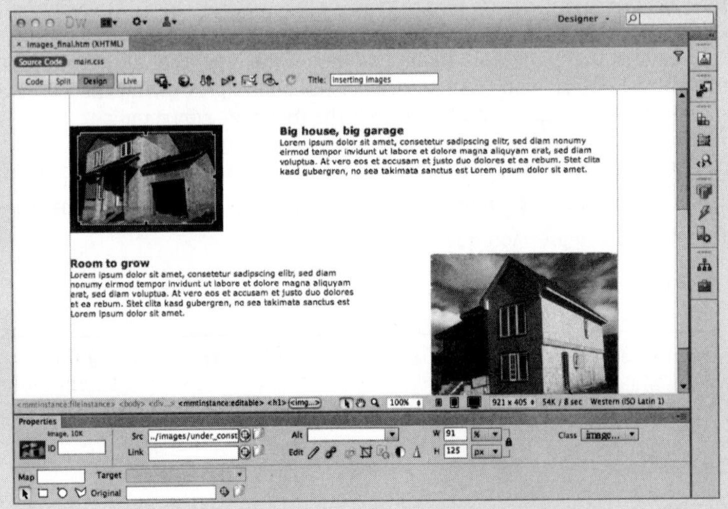

3. On the Property inspector, click Crop.
4. Dreamweaver alerts you that taking this action will affect the selected image; click OK to continue.

5. Move the cropping handles on the top and left to exclude the white patches; move the cropping handles on the right and bottom to the outer edge of the images.
6. When you've moved the cropping handles to the correct position, double-click in the center of the image to confirm your changes. The image is still a bit too big; you can use the built-in Rescale tool to make a simple adjustment.
7. Select the image again and drag the lower-right sizing handle inward to reduce the image size; press the Shift key while dragging to constrain the width/height ratio.
8. Stop resizing the image when the Width attribute in the Property inspector is 215 pixels. While the image appears to be resized, it now needs to be resampled so that it is actually reduced in file size.
9. On the Property inspector, click Resample. You'll notice that the image file size shown in the Property inspector is reduced from 14K to 10K.

   Alternatively, you could click Commit, the check mark next to the width and height dimensions.
10. Dreamweaver again alerts you that taking this action will affect the selected image; click OK to continue.
11. When you're done, save your page.

Although you will always need to work with a graphics editor such as Photoshop or Fireworks for major image modifications, Dreamweaver does a great job on last-minute fixes all by itself.

After you've picked an image editor, clicking the Edit button in the Property inspector opens the application with the current image. When you've made the modifications, just save the file in your image editor and switch back to Dreamweaver. The new, modified graphic has already been included in the web page. If you change the image size, you can click the Reset to Original Size button on the Image Property inspector to see your changes.

If you are using either Photoshop or Fireworks as your image editor, here is some good news: Dreamweaver works very closely with both Photoshop and Fireworks, enabling you to create and modify images with roundtrip ease. Find out more in Chapter 24.

Modifying image attributes

When you insert an image in Dreamweaver, the image tag, `<img>`, is inserted into your HTML code. The `<img>` tag takes several attributes; the most commonly used can be entered through the Property inspector. Code for a basic image looks like the following:

```
<img src="images/myimage.gif" width="172" height="180">
```

Dreamweaver centralizes all its image functions in the Property inspector. The Image Property inspector, shown in Figure 8-10, displays a small thumbnail of the image as well as its file size. Dreamweaver automatically inserts the image filename and path in the Src text box (as the `src` attribute). To replace a currently selected image with another, click the folder icon next to the Src text box, or double-click the image itself. Either sequence opens the Select Image Source dialog box. When you've selected the file, Dreamweaver automatically refreshes the page and corrects the code.

FIGURE 8-10

The Image Property inspector gives you total control over the HTML code for every image.

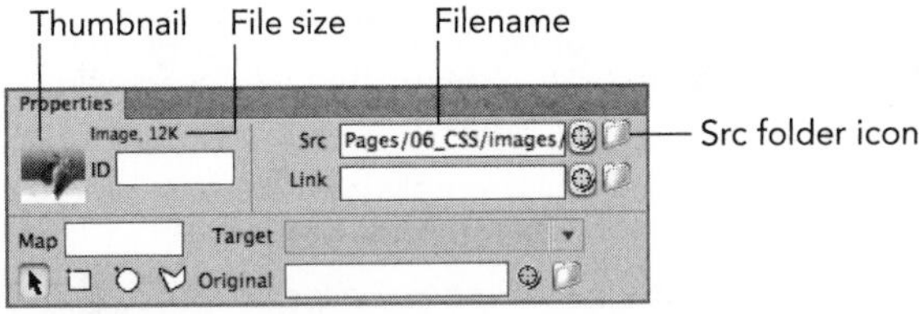

If the Image Property inspector is open when you insert your image, you can begin to modify the image attributes immediately.

Naming your image

When you first insert a graphic into the page, the Image Property inspector displays a blank text box next to the thumbnail and file size. Fill in this box with a unique name for the image, to be used in JavaScript and other applications.

Adjusting height and width

The `width` and `height` attributes are important because browsers build web pages faster when they know the size and shape of the included images. Dreamweaver reads these attributes when the image is first loaded. The width and height values are initially expressed in pixels and are automatically inserted as attributes in the HTML code.

NOTE

Resizing an image just means changing its appearance onscreen; the file size stays exactly the same. To reduce a file size for an image, you need to scale it down in a graphics program such as Fireworks or, once you've resized it in Dreamweaver with the control handles or with the W/H (Width/Height) options, click Resample or Commit in the Property inspector.

Browsers can dynamically resize an image if its height and width on the page are different from the original image's dimensions. For example, you can load your primary logo on the home page and then use a smaller version of it on subsequent pages by inserting the same image with reduced height and width values. Because you're loading the image only once and the browser is resizing it, download time for your web page can be significantly reduced.

NEW FEATURE

To resize an image by a specific value in Dreamweaver, select the image and type the desired number of pixels or the percentage in the Property inspector's H (height) and W (width) fields. You can maintain the width-to-height ratio by clicking Toggle Size Constrain (the padlock icon) adjacent to the size fields.

With Dreamweaver, you can also visually resize your graphics by using the click-and-drag method. A selected image has three sizing handles located on the right, bottom, and lower-right corners of its bounding box. Click any of these handles and drag it out to a new location—when you release the mouse, Dreamweaver resizes the image. To maintain the current height/width aspect ratio, hold down the Shift key after starting to drag the corner sizing handle.

If you alter either the height or the width of an image, Dreamweaver displays a set of new controls next to the size fields. Click Commit (the checkmark icon) to confirm your new dimensions; click Restore to Original Size (the universal "no" symbol) to cancel the resizing operation.

CAUTION

If you elect to enable your viewer's browser to resize your image on the fly using the height/width values you specify, keep in mind that the browser is not a graphics-editing program and that its resizing algorithms are not sophisticated. View your resized images through several browsers to ensure acceptable results.

Adding image descriptions

It's easy for web designers to get caught up in the visual design of their web pages; after all, designers can devote hours to creating a single graphic or to perfectly positioning a graphic on the page relative to other information. Remember, however, that graphics aren't the most effective communication method in every circumstance. Luckily, the `<img>` tag includes two attributes that enable you to describe your image using plain text: `alt` and `longdesc`.

The `alt` attribute gives you a means to include a short description of a graphic. It is used in many ways:

- As a page is loading over the web, the image is first displayed as an empty rectangle if the `<img>` tag contains width and height information. Some browsers display the `alt` description in this rectangle while the image is loading, offering the waiting user a written preview of the forthcoming image.
- In many browsers, the `alt` text displays as a tooltip when the user's pointer passes over the graphic.
- A real benefit of `alt` text is providing input for browsers that don't show graphics. Remember that text-only browsers are still in use, and some users, interested only in content, turn off the graphics to speed up the text display.
- The W3C is working toward standards for browsers for the visually impaired, and the `alt` text can be used to describe the image.

For all these reasons, it's good coding practice (and a validation requirement) to associate an `alt` description with all your graphics. In Dreamweaver, you can enter this alternative text in the Alt text box of the Image Property inspector.

TIP

If the `<img>` tag does not contain an `alt` attribute, some screen readers read the filename when they encounter the image, which slows down how quickly visually impaired users can get to the real information on your page. For images that are purely visual and don't contribute to the meaning of your content, such as bullets or spacer images, include a blank `alt` attribute. To do this, open the Image Property inspector and select `<empty>` from the Alt drop-down list.

Currently, the `alt` attribute is the most valuable tool you have for providing a textual description of your images. However, some images are just too complicated to describe in a few words and are too important to gloss over. For these situations, the HTML 4.0 specification included the `longdesc` attribute. Although none of the major browsers currently support this attribute, Dreamweaver enables you to specify a `longdesc` for your images.

In Dreamweaver, choose Edit ⇨ Preferences (Dreamweaver ⇨ Preferences), and, in the Accessibility category, select the Images checkbox. When you add a new image to your page, the Image Tag Accessibility Attributes dialog box appears, as shown in Figure 8-11. In the Long Description text box, click the folder icon to navigate to an HTML file that contains a textual description of the image.

FIGURE 8-11

The Image Tag Accessibility Attributes dialog box appears when you select the Images option in the Accessibility Preferences.

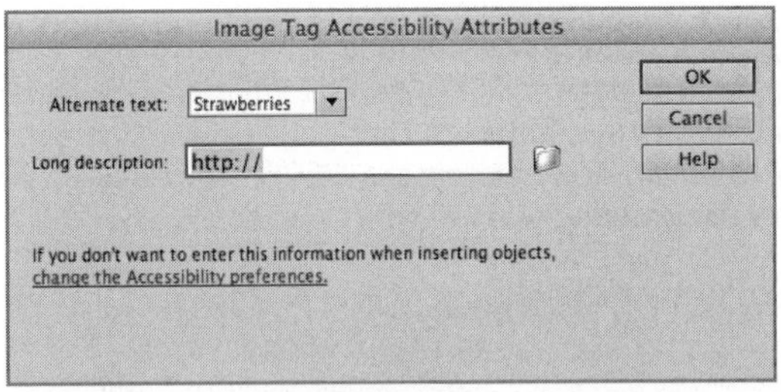

CAUTION

The Image Tag Accessibility Attributes dialog box appears if you drag the image from the Assets panel or use the Insert panel or Insert menu to add the image.

Bordering a graphic

When you're working with thumbnails (small versions of images) on your web page, you may need a quick way to distinguish one from another. The preferred method for adding a border to an image is to use Cascading Style Sheets, as described in Chapter 6.

One of the most frequent cries for help among beginning web designers results from the sudden appearance of a bright blue border around an image. Whenever you assign a link to an image, HTML automatically places a border around that image; the color is determined by the Page Properties Link color, where the default is bright blue. To avoid this border, create a CSS rule that sets the border to 0, like this:

```
img { border: 0; }
```

Working with alignment options

Using CSS, images can be aligned to the left, right, or center—or rather, the line the images are on can be so adjusted. In fact, images have much more flexibility than text in terms of alignment. In addition to the same horizontal alignment options, you can align your images vertically in nine different ways. You can even turn a picture into a floating image type, enabling text to wrap around it.

Horizontal alignment

When you change the horizontal alignment of a line—from left to center or from center to right—the entire paragraph moves. Any inline images that are part of that paragraph also move. Likewise, selecting one of a series of inline images in a row and realigning it horizontally causes all the images in the row to shift.

In Dreamweaver, the horizontal alignment of an inline image is changed in exactly the same way that you realign text—with CSS. To change the alignment of an image, select it and then, through the CSS Styles panel, change the `text-align` property to `left`, `right`, `center`, or `justify`. The `text-align` property aligns the entire line that the image is on and not just the image.

Vertical alignment

Because you can place text next to an image—and images vary so greatly in size—CSS includes a variety of options for specifying just how image and text line up. As you can see from the chart shown in Figure 8-12, a wide range of possibilities is available.

To change the vertical alignment of any graphic in Dreamweaver, set the CSS property `vertical-align` to one of its available values. The various vertical-alignment options are listed in Table 8-1, and you can refer to Figure 8-12 for examples of each type of alignment.

FIGURE 8-12

You can align text and images in a great number of different ways.

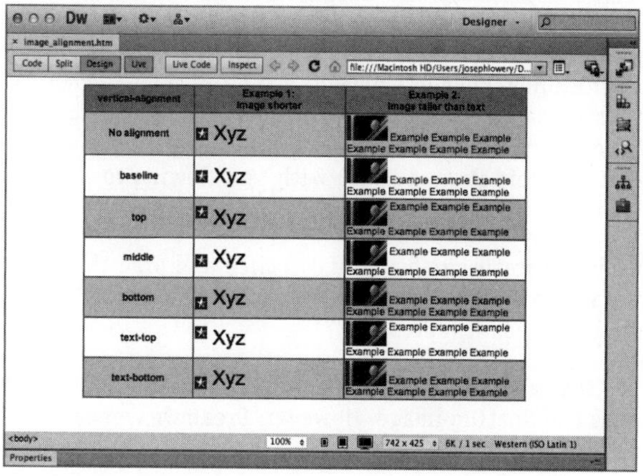

TABLE 8-1 Vertical-Alignment Options

Option	Result
`baseline`	The bottom of the image is aligned with the baseline of the surrounding text.
`Top`	The top of the image is aligned with the top of the tallest object in the current line.
`Middle`	The middle of the image is aligned with the baseline of the current line.
`Bottom`	The bottom of the image is aligned with the baseline of the surrounding text.
`text-top`	The top of the image is aligned with the tallest letter or object in the current line.
`text-bottom`	The bottom of the image is aligned with the descenders (as in y, g, p, and so forth) that fall below the current baseline.
`Sub`	Places the styled text below the adjacent text at a reduced font size.
`Super`	Places the styled text above the adjacent text at a reduced font size.

The last two alignment options, sub and super, are not generally used in connection with images and are not depicted in Figure 8-12.

Wrapping text

Most browsers support wrapping text around an image on a web page—long a popular design option in conventional publishing. On the web, text wrapping is handled in CSS via the `float` property. When applied to a graphic, the image is said to be *floated*.

> **TIP**
>
> Using two float propeties (`left` and `right`) in combination, you can actually position images flush-left and flush-right, with text in the middle. Insert both images side by side and then set the leftmost image to float left and the rightmost one to float right. Insert your text immediately following the second image.

Your text wraps around the image depending on where the floated image is placed (or anchored). If you enable the Anchor Points For Aligned Elements option in the Invisible Elements category of Preferences, Dreamweaver inserts a Floating Image Anchor symbol to mark the floating image's place. Note that the image itself may overlap the anchor, hiding the anchor from view. Figure 8-13 shows two examples of text wrapping: a left-aligned image with text flowing to the right, and a right-aligned image with text flowing to the left.

The Floating Image Anchor is not just a static symbol. You can click and drag the anchor to a new location and cause the paragraph to wrap in a different fashion. Be careful, however. If you delete the anchor, you also delete the image it represents.

You can also wrap a portion of the text around your left- or right-aligned picture and then force the remaining text to appear below the floating image. However, Dreamweaver cannot currently insert the HTML code necessary to do this task through the Image Property inspector. You have to force an opening to appear by inserting a break tag, with the CSS property `clear`, where you want the text to break. The `clear` property has three forms:

- `clear: left`—Causes the line to break and the following text to move down vertically until no floating images are on the left
- `clear: right`—Causes the line to break and the following text to move down vertically until no floating images are on the right
- `clear: both`—Moves the text following the image down until no floating images are on either the left or the right

The `clear` property is generally associated with a selector that is applied to the last element of the parent tag that contains a floated element. For example, if the `<div>` tag contains an image with a `float:left` CSS declaration, a final line break might include a class with a `clear` property.

FIGURE 8-13

Aligning an image left or right enables text to wrap around your images.

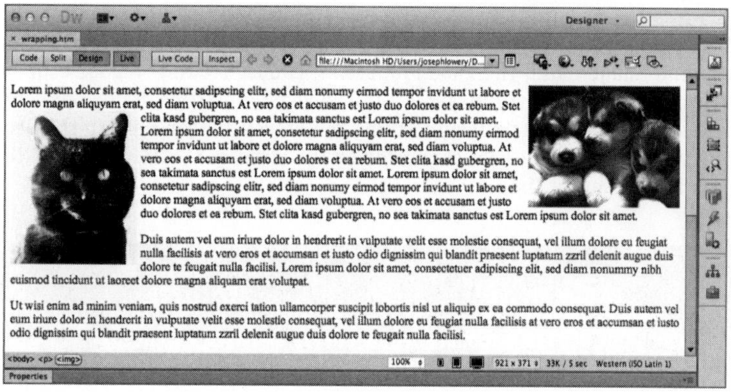

Adding Background Images

In this chapter, you've learned about working with the surface graphics on a web page. You can also place an image in the background of an HTML page. This section covers some of the basic techniques for incorporating a background image in your Dreamweaver page.

Add an image to your background either by using the CSS Styles panel or by modifying the Appearance (CSS) category of the Page Properties. Either technique adds a `background-image` property to a CSS rule.

If you aren't familiar with Cascading Style Sheets, you may want to read Chapter 6 before trying the following procedure. That chapter gets you started with general CSS concepts and outlines specific options for implementing background images.

To implement a background image using the CSS Styles panel, follow these steps:

1. Choose Window ⇨ CSS Styles.
2. On the CSS Styles panel, click Edit Styles and then click the New CSS Rule button.
3. In the New CSS Rule dialog box, choose Tag from the Selector Type list, and in the Selector name drop-down list, select Body. These selections create a background image for the entire document. You can also select a different tag or choose the Make A Custom Style option to assign a background image to a single element on the page, such as a table cell or paragraph.
4. Specify whether you want to save the style definition in an external style sheet or in the current document, and then click OK.
5. In the CSS Style Definition dialog box, select the Background category.
6. In the Background Image field, type the path and filename for the image file, or click Browse to navigate to the file.
7. Designate any other background options, and then click OK.

To specify a background image using the Page Properties, choose Modify ⇨ Page Properties or select Page Properties from the Property inspector. In the Page Properties dialog box, choose the Appearance (CSS) category. Select a graphic by clicking the Browse button next to the Background Image text box. You can use any file format supported by Dreamweaver—GIF, JPEG, or PNG. Choose your tiling options from the Repeat list.

NOTE

Although you can set background images (and colors) as a property of an HTML tag through the Appearance (HTML) category of the Page Properties dialog box, it's not recommended for standards-based web design.

Two key differences exist between background images and the foreground inline images discussed in the preceding sections of this chapter. First and most obvious, all other text and graphics on the web page are superimposed over your chosen background image. This capability can bring extra depth and texture to your work; unfortunately, you have to make sure the foreground text and images work well with the background.

Basically, you want to ascertain that enough contrast exists between foreground and background. You can set the default text and the various link colors using Cascading Style Sheets or through the Page Properties dialog box, shown in Figure 8-14. When trying out a new background pattern, you should set up some dummy text and links. Then click the Apply button on the Page Properties dialog box to test different color combinations.

FIGURE 8-14

If you're using a background image, be sure to check the default colors for text and links to make sure enough contrast exists between background and foreground.

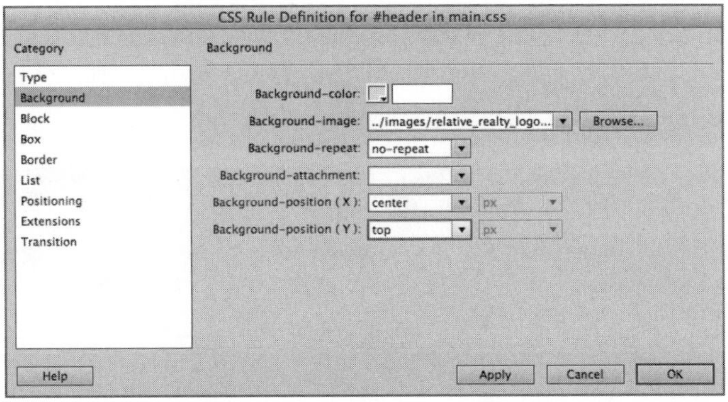

Tiling Images

Web designers use the tiling property of background images to create a variety of effects with very low file-size overhead. The columns typically found on one side of web pages are a good example of tiling. Columns are popular because they enable the designer to place navigational buttons in a visual context. An easy way to create a column that runs the full length of your web page is to use a long, narrow background image.

In the following figure, the background image is 45 pixels high, 1,200 pixels wide, and only 6KB in size. The image is tiled down the page to create the vertical column effect.

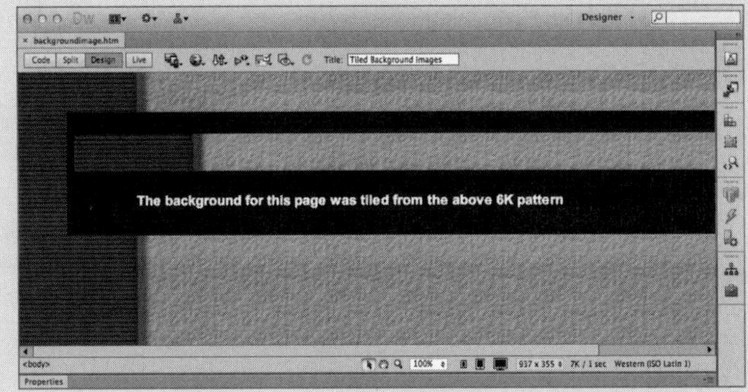

When using Cascading Style Sheets to implement your background image, you can control whether the image tiles horizontally, vertically, in both directions, or not at all.

8

The second distinguishing feature of background images is that the viewing browser completely fills either the browser window or the area behind the content of your web page—whichever is larger. Suppose you have created a page with only a 200 × 200 foreground logo, and you've incorporated an amazing 1,024 × 768 background that took you weeks to compose. A user can't see the fruits of your labor in the background—unless he resizes his browser window to 1,024 × 768. On the other hand, if your background image is smaller than either the browser window or what the web page content needs to display, the browser and Dreamweaver repeat (tile) your image to make up the difference.

TIP

With Cascading Style Sheets, you not only can attach a background image to a page but can also attach a background image to an individual element on a page, such as a single paragraph. Cascading Style Sheets also enable you to designate whether the background image should scroll with the foreground text or if it should remain stationary while the foreground text scrolls over the background.

Dividing the Web Page with Horizontal Rules

HTML includes a standard horizontal line that can divide your web page into specific sections. The horizontal rule tag, `<hr>`, is a good tool for adding a little diversion to your page without adding download time. You can use CSS to control the width (either absolutely or relative to the browser window), the height, the alignment, and the shading of the rule. These horizontal rules appear on a line by themselves; you cannot place text or images on the same line as a horizontal rule.

To insert a horizontal rule in your web page in Dreamweaver (see Figure 8-15), follow these steps:

1. Place your cursor where you want the horizontal rule to appear.
2. From the Common category of the Insert panel, click the Horizontal Rule button or choose Insert ➪ HTML ➪ Horizontal Rule. Dreamweaver inserts the horizontal rule, and the Property inspector, if visible, shows the attributes that you can change for a horizontal rule.

NOTE

While Dreamweaver allows you the option of changing the properties of a horizontal rule in the Property inspector, it's best to use CSS to handle any styling. The various properties for the horizontal rule have been deprecated and are likely not to be supported in future browsers.

As a general practice, size your horizontal rules using the percentage option if you are using them to separate items on a full screen. If you are using the horizontal rules to divide items in a specifically sized table column or cell, use the pixel method.

Many designers prefer to create elaborate horizontal rules; in fact, custom rules are an active area of clip art design. These types of horizontal rules are regular graphics and are inserted and modified as such.

FIGURE 8-15

Although the Horizontal Rule Property inspector includs width, height, and alignment properties, it's better to use CSS to style these HTML lines.

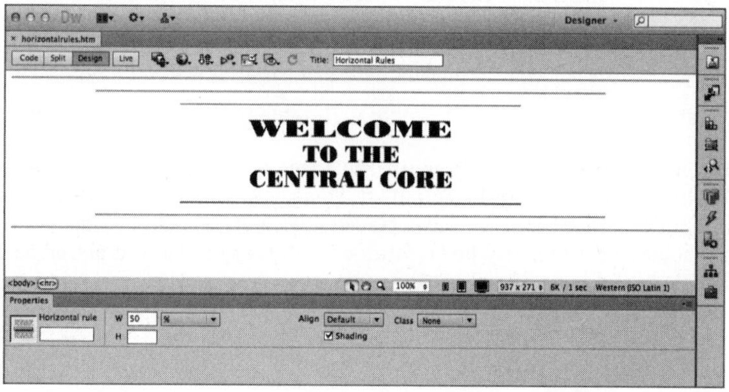

Including Banner Ads

Banner ads have become an essential aspect of the World Wide Web; for the web to remain, for the most part, freely accessible, advertising is needed to support the costs. Banner ads have evolved into the de facto standard. Although numerous variations exist, a banner ad is typically a Flash movie of a particular width and height, within a specified file size.

The Standards and Practices Committee of the Interactive Advertising Bureau (IAB) established a series of standard sizes for banner ads. Although no law dictates that these guidelines have to be followed, the vast majority of commercial sites adhere to the suggested dimensions. The most common banner sizes and other guidelines are available at the IAB website (`http://www.iab.net`).

Acceptable file size for a banner ad is not as clearly specified, but it's just as important. The last thing a hosting site wants is for a large, too-heavy banner to slow down the loading of its page. Most commercial sites have an established maximum file size for any given banner ad. Generally, banner ads are around 30–40KB. The lighter your banner ad, the faster it loads and—as a direct result—the more likely web page visitors stick around to see it.

NOTE

Major sites often have additional criteria for using rich media in banner ads, such as Flash animations or JavaScript. These may include file size, length of animation, behavior when the ad is clicked, and so on.

Inserting a banner ad on a web page is very straightforward. As with any other GIF file, animated or not, all you have to do is insert the image and assign the link. As any advertiser can tell you, the link is as important as the image itself, and you should take special care to ensure that it is correct when inserted. Advertising links are often quite complex because they not only link to a specific page but may also carry information about the referring site. Several companies monitor how many times an ad is selected—the clickthru rate—and often a CGI program is used to communicate with these companies and handle the link. Here's a sample URL from CNet's `News.com` site:

```
http://home.cnet.com/cgi-acc/clickthru.acc? ;
clickid=00001e145ea7d80f00000000&adt=003:10:100&edt=cnet&cat=1:1002:&site=CN
```

Obviously, copying and pasting such URLs is highly preferable to entering them by hand.

Advertisements often come from an outside source, so a web page designer may have to allow space for the ad without incorporating the actual ad. Some web designers create a plain rectangular image of the appropriate size to serve as a placeholder, until the actual image is ready. In Dreamweaver, placeholder ads can easily be maintained as Library items and placed as needed from the Assets panel, as shown in Figure 8-16.

See Chapter 29 for information on creating and using Dreamweaver Library items.

FIGURE 8-16

Use the Library to store standard banner ad images for use as placeholders.

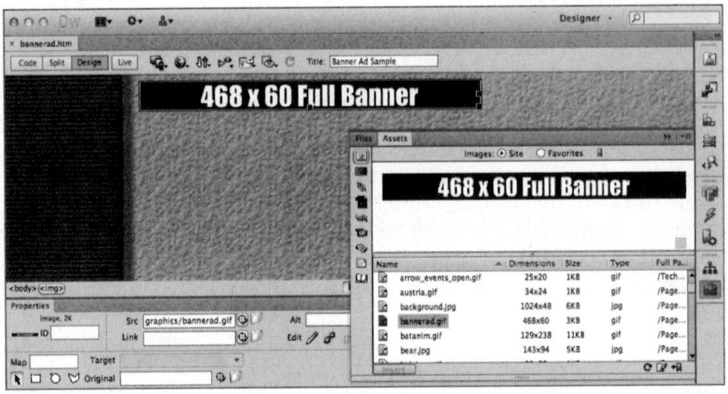

If you'd prefer not to use placeholder graphics as just described, you can instead insert a plain `<img>` tag—with no `src` parameter. When an `<img>` tag without an `src` attribute is in the code, Dreamweaver displays a plain rectangle that can be resized to the proper banner ad dimensions in the Property inspector.

You can insert a placeholder image by clicking the Image Placeholder button on the Insert panel or by choosing Insert ➪ Image Objects ➪ Image Placeholder. In the resulting Image Placeholder dialog box, you can enter an image name, dimensions, color, and alternate text. When the real graphics file is ready, use the Src text box on the Property inspector to specify the new file. The image name and alternate text remain unchanged when you assign the new file, but the dimensions automatically change to match those of the actual image.

Inserting Rollover Images

Rollovers are among the most popular of all web page effects. A *rollover* (also known as a mouseover) occurs when the user's pointer passes over an image and the image changes in some way. It may appear to glow or change color and/or shape. When the pointer moves away from the graphic, the image returns to its original form. The rollover indicates interactivity and attempts to engage the user with a little bit of flair.

Rollovers are usually accomplished with a combination of HTML and JavaScript. Dreamweaver was among the first web authoring tools to automate the production of rollovers through its Swap Image and Swap Image Restore behaviors. Later versions of Dreamweaver make rollovers even easier with the Rollover Image object. With the Rollover Image object, you just pick two images to make a rollover.

If you use Fireworks as your image-editing tool, refer to Chapter 24 to learn another method for creating rollover images.

Technically speaking, a rollover is accomplished by manipulating an `<img>` tag's `src` attribute. Recall that the `src` attribute is responsible for providing the actual filename of the graphic to be displayed; it is, quite literally, the source of the image. A rollover changes the value of `src` from one image file to another. Swapping the `src` value is analogous to having a picture within a frame and changing the picture while keeping the frame.

NOTE

The picture frame analogy is appropriate on one other level: It serves as a reminder of the size barrier inherent in rollovers. A rollover changes only one property of an `<img>` tag, the source—it cannot change any other property, such as height or width. For this reason, both your original image and the image displayed during the rollover should be the same size. If they are not, the alternate image is resized to match the dimensions of the original image.

Dreamweaver's Rollover Image object automatically changes the image back to its original source when the user moves the pointer off the image. Optionally, you can elect to preload the images with the selection of a checkbox. Preloading is a web page technique that reads the intended file or files into the browser's memory before they are displayed. With preloading, the images appear on demand, without any download delay.

Rollovers are typically used for buttons that, when clicked, open another web page. In fact, JavaScript requires that an image include a link before it can detect when a user's pointer moves over it. Dreamweaver automatically includes the minimum link necessary: the # link. Although JavaScript recognizes this symbol as indicating a link, no action is taken if the image is clicked by the user; the #, by itself, is an empty link. You can supply whatever link you want in the Rollover Image object.

TIP

Some browsers link to the top of the page when they encounter a # link. If you want to create a rollover image that doesn't link anywhere, change the # to the following:

```
javascript:;
```

You can change this directly in Code view or in the Link field of the Property inspector for the button.

To include a Rollover Image object in your web page, follow these steps:

1. Place your cursor where you want the rollover image to appear and choose Insert ➪ Image Objects ➪ Rollover Image, or select Rollover Image from the Images menu on the Insert panel's Common category. You can also drag the Rollover Image button to any existing location on the web page. Dreamweaver opens the Insert Rollover Image dialog box shown in Figure 8-17.

FIGURE 8-17

The Rollover Image object makes rollover graphics quick and easy.

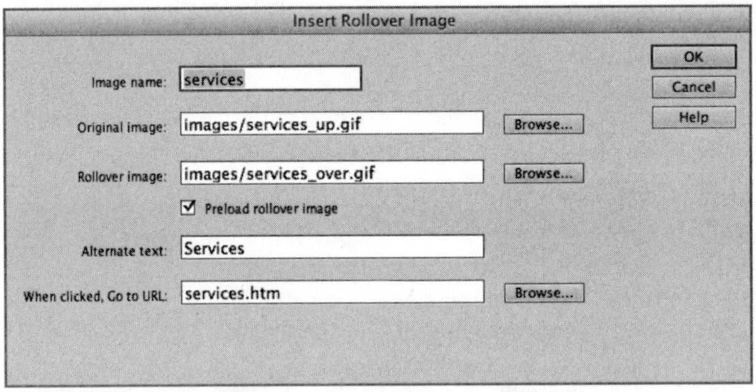

2. You can enter a unique name for the image in the Image Name text box, or you can use the name automatically generated by Dreamweaver.
3. In the Original Image text box, enter the path and name of the graphic you want displayed when the user's mouse is not over the graphic. You can also click the Browse button to select the file. Press Tab when you're done.
4. In the Rollover Image text box, enter the path and name of the graphic file you want displayed when the user's pointer is over the image. You can also click the Browse button to select the file.
5. In the Alternate Text field, type a brief description of the graphic button.
6. If desired, specify a link for the image by entering it in the When Clicked, Go To URL text box or by clicking the Browse button to select the file.
7. To enable images to load only when they are required, deselect the Preload Images option. Generally, it is best to leave this option selected (the default) so that the appearance of the rollover is not delayed.
8. Click OK when you're finished.

TIP

Keep in mind that the Rollover Image object inserts both the original image and its alternate, whereas the Swap Image technique is applied to an existing image in the web page. If you prefer to use the Rollover Image object rather than the Swap Image behavior, nothing prevents you from deleting an existing image from the web page and inserting it again through the Rollover Image object. Just make sure that you note the path and name of the image before you delete it, so you can find it again.

Summary

In this chapter, you learned how to include both foreground and background images in Dreamweaver. Understanding how images are handled in HTML is an absolute necessity for the web designer. As you're inserting images into your web pages, keep these key points in mind:

- Web pages are restricted to using specific graphic formats. Virtually all current browsers support GIF, JPEG, and PNG files. Dreamweaver can preview all three image types.
- Images are inserted in the foreground in Dreamweaver through the Image button on the Insert panel or from the Assets panel. After the graphic is inserted, almost all modifications can be handled through the Property inspector.
- You can use HTML's background image function to lay a full-frame image or a tiled series of the same image underneath your text and graphics. Tiled images can be employed to create columns and other designs with small files.
- Simple graphic editing chores—including cropping and resampling—are available right from Dreamweaver's Property inspector; for finer control, you'll need a graphics editor installed and then you can use either the Optimize Image or Edit options.
- The simplest HTML graphic is the built-in horizontal rule. It is useful for dividing your web page into separate sections. You can size the horizontal rule either absolutely or relatively with CSS.
- Animated images can be inserted alongside and in the same manner as still graphics. The individual frames of a GIF animation must be created in a graphics program and then combined in an animation program.
- With the Rollover Image object, you can easily insert simple rollovers that use two different images. To build a rollover that uses more than two images, you have to use the Swap Image behavior.

In the next chapter, you learn how to use hyperlinks in Dreamweaver.

Summary

CHAPTER 9

Establishing Web Links

IN THIS CHAPTER

Learning about Internet addresses

Linking web pages

Dreamweaver Technique: Linking to Files

Pointing to a file

Creating anchors within web pages

Dreamweaver Technique: Inserting Named Anchors

Targeting URLs

Links *are* the web. Everything else about the medium can be replicated in another form, but without links, there would be no World Wide Web. As your web design work becomes more sophisticated, you'll find additional uses for links: sending mail, connecting to an FTP site—even downloading software.

In this chapter, you learn how Dreamweaver helps you manage various types of links, as well as how to set anchors within documents to get smooth and accurate navigation, and establish targets for your links. To give you a full picture of the possibilities, this chapter begins with an overview of Internet addresses, called URLs.

Understanding URLs

URL stands for Uniform Resource Locator. An awkward phrase, it is one that, nonetheless, describes itself well—the URL's function is to provide a standard method for finding anything on the Internet. From web pages to newsgroups to the smallest graphic on the most esoteric of pages, everything can be referenced through the URL mechanism.

A typical URL for a web page can have up to six different parts. Each part is separated by some combination of a slash, colon, and hash-mark delimiter. When entered as an attribute's value, the entire URL is generally enclosed within quotation marks to ensure that the address is read as one unit. A generic URL using all the parts looks like this:

```
scheme://server:port/path/file#anchor
```

Here's an example that uses every section:

```
http://www.idest.com:80/Dreamweaver/index.htm#bible
```

From left to right, the parts are as follows:

- http—The URL scheme used to access the resource. A scheme is an agreed-upon mechanism for communication, typically between a client and a server. The scheme to reference web servers uses the Hypertext Transfer Protocol (HTTP). Other schemes and their related protocols are discussed later in this section.
- www.idest.com—The name of the server providing the resource. The server can be either a domain name (with or without the www prefix) or an Internet Protocol (IP) address, such as 199.227.52.143.
- :80—The port number to be used on the server. Most URLs do not include a port number, which is analogous to a telephone extension number on the server, because most servers use the defaults.
- /Dreamweaver—The directory path to the resource. Depending on where the resource (for example, the web page) is located on the server, the following paths can be specified: no path (indicating that the resource is in the public root of the server), a single folder name, or a number of folders and subfolders.
- /index.htm—The filename of the resource. If the filename is omitted, the web browser looks for a default page, often named index.html or index.htm. The browser reacts differently depending on the type of file. For example, GIFs and JPEGs are displayed by themselves; executable files and archives (Zip, StuffIt, and so on) are downloaded.
- #bible—The named anchor in the HTML document. This part is another optional section. The named anchor enables the web designer to send the viewer to a particular section of an HTML page.

Although http is one of the most prevalent communication schemes used on the Internet, other schemes are also available. Whereas HTTP is used for accessing web pages, the other schemes are used for such things as transferring files between servers and clients or for sending e-mail. Table 9-1 describes the most common schemes used in URLs.

TABLE 9-1 Common URL Schemes and Associated Protocols

Scheme Syntax	Protocol	Usage
ftp://	File Transfer Protocol (FTP)	Links to an FTP server that is typically used for uploading and downloading files. The server may be accessed anonymously, or it may require a username and password.
http://	Hypertext Transfer Protocol (HTTP)	Used for connecting to a document available on a World Wide Web server.
javascript:	JavaScript	Although it is not part of a true URL, some browsers support a scheme of javascript:, indicating that the browser should execute JavaScript code. This provides an easy way to execute JavaScript code when a user clicks a link.

Scheme Syntax	Protocol	Usage
`mailto:`	Simple Mail Transfer Protocol (SMTP)	Opens an e-mail form with the recipient's address already filled in. These links are useful when embedded in your web pages to provide visitors with an easy feedback method.
`news://`	Network News Transfer Protocol (NNTP)	Connects to the specified Usenet newsgroup. Newsgroups are public, theme-oriented message boards on which anyone can post or reply to a message.
`telnet://`	Telnet	Enables users to log on directly to remote host computers and interact directly with the operating system software.

Part of the richness of today's web browsers stems from their capability to connect to all the preceding (and additional) services.

NOTE

The `mailto:` scheme enables you not only to open up a preaddressed e-mail form but also, with a little extra work, to specify the topic. For example, if Joe Lowery wants to include a link to his e-mail address with the subject heading "Book Feedback," he can insert a link such as the following:

```
mailto:jlowery@idest.com?subject=Book%20Feedback
```

The question mark acts as a delimiter that enables a variable and a value to be passed to the browser; the %20 is the decimal representation for a space that must be read by various servers. When you're trying to encourage feedback from your web page visitors, every little bit helps.

9

Surfing the Web with Hypertext

Often, you assign a link to a word or phrase on your page, an image such as a navigational button, or a section of graphic for an image map (a large graphic in which various parts are links). To test the link, you preview the page in a browser; links are not active in Dreamweaver's Document window.

Designate links in HTML through the anchor tag pair: `<a>` and `</a>`. The anchor tag generally takes one main attribute—the hypertext reference, which is written as follows:

```
href="link name"
```

When you create a link, the anchor pair surrounds the text or object that is being linked. For example, if you link the phrase `Back to Home Page`, it may look like the following:

```
<a href="index.html">Back to Home Page</a>
```

If you attach a link to the image `logo.gif`, your code looks as follows:

```
<a href="home.html"><img src="images/logo.gif"></a>
```

Creating a basic link in Dreamweaver is easy. Simply follow these steps:

1. Select the text, image, or object you want to establish as a link.
2. In the Property inspector, enter the URL in the Link text box, as shown in Figure 9-1. You can use one of the following methods to do so:
   - Type the URL directly into the Link text box.
   - Click the Browse for File folder icon to the right of the Link text box to open the Select File dialog box, where you can browse for the file.
   - Click the Point to File icon and drag your mouse to an existing page in the Files panel or anchor on the current page. This feature is explained later in this section.

You can also create a link by dragging a URL from the Assets panel onto a text or image selection—a procedure covered more fully later in this chapter.

Finally, you can create a link using the Insert menu or Insert panel. Without selecting any text, choose Insert ➪ Hyperlink, or in the Common category of the Insert panel, click the Hyperlink button. The Hyperlink dialog box opens, and you can specify the link text, the URL for the link, and a link target (described later). This method also enables you to specify the following:

- **Tab index:** A number specifying the order in which a user can tab through the page. Links with lower numbers are given focus first, and links with no tab index defined appear last in the tab order.
- **Title field:** A description of the link. In Internet Explorer 6.0, the text appears as a tooltip when the user holds the cursor over the link.
- **Access key:** A single letter that serves as the keyboard equivalent for the hyperlink. Access keys work only in the most recent browser versions, and they do not work consistently. Pressing the Alt (Option) key plus the access key may just select the link, or it may actually execute the link.

NOTE

If you don't see the Hyperlink dialog box when you insert a hyperlink, choose Edit ➪ Preferences (Dreamweaver ➪ Preferences) and, in the General category, select the Show Dialog When Inserting Objects option.

Regardless of how you create a link in Dreamweaver, a few restrictions exist for specifying URLs. Dreamweaver does not support any letters from the extended character set (also known as High ASCII), such as ¡, à, or ñ. Complete URLs must have fewer than a total of 255 characters. You should be cautious about using spaces in pathnames and, therefore, in URLs. Although most browsers can interpret the address, spaces are changed to a `%20` symbol for proper UNIX usage. This change can make your URLs difficult to read.

Text links are, for almost all browsers, rendered with a blue color and underlined. Depending on the background color for your page, you may want to change the color of text links to improve readability. You can specify the document-link color by choosing Modify ➪ Page Properties and selecting the Links color box. In Page Properties, you can also alter the color to which the links change after being selected (the Visited Links color), and the color flashed when the link is clicked (the Active Links color). All of these changes are written as CSS statements in the <head> of the current document.

FIGURE 9-1

You can enter your link directly into the Link text box, click the folder icon to browse for a file, or point to the file directly with the Point to File icon.

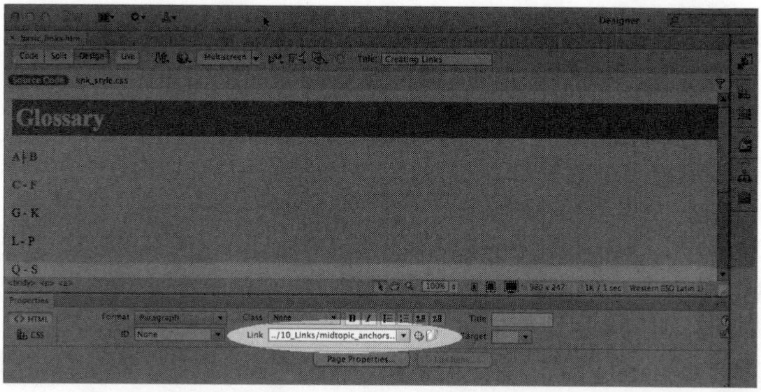

Eliminating underlines from links

Disabling the underline for the anchor tag, <a>, which is normally associated with hyperlinked text, is one modification commonly included in style sheets.

> **CAUTION**
> Be careful when using this technique. Underlined text is a standard method of indicating a hyperlink on the web, and some clients or users may find your pages not as intuitive if the underline indicator is no longer visible.

To disable the underline on the anchor tag, follow these steps:

1. Open the CSS Styles panel by choosing Window ➪ CSS Styles. The CSS Styles panel, shown in Figure 9-2, displays existing styles and provides controls for creating and managing styles.
2. At the bottom of the CSS Styles panel, click the New CSS Rule button. This action opens the New CSS Rule dialog box.
3. Select the Tag option and choose the anchor tag, a, from the drop-down list. Finally, select Define In This Document Only to create an internal CSS style sheet or choose an external style sheet from the drop-down list. Click OK, and the CSS Style Definition dialog box opens.

FIGURE 9-2

The Dreamweaver CSS Styles panel helps you apply consistent styles to a web page.

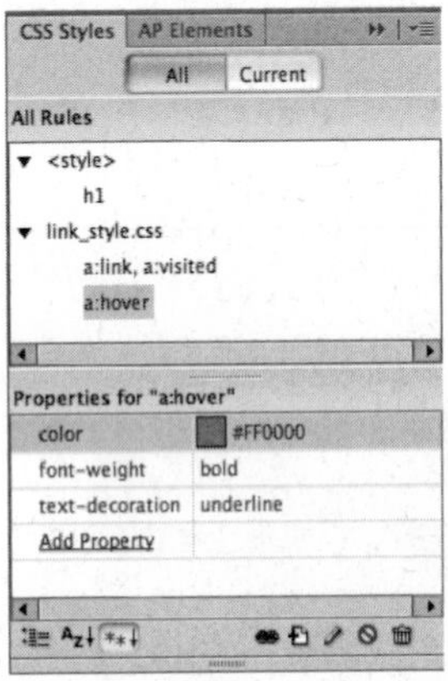

TIP

You can also select the "Compound (based on your selection)" option rather than Tag and choose `a:link` from the drop-down list. You can even employ the `a:hover` style, which enables text to change color or style on rollover. You must, however, define the four CSS Selector styles in a particular order for them to work correctly. Start by defining the `a:link` class and then proceed to define `a:visited`, `a:hover`, and `a:active`, in that order. Note that in Dreamweaver's Design view you can preview only the `a:link` altered style; to see the other styles, use Dreamweaver's Live View or preview the page in a browser.

4. In the CSS Rule Definition window, make sure that the correct category is displayed by selecting Type from the list of categories.
5. In the Text-decoration section of the Type category, select the None option. You can also make any other modifications to the anchor tag style, such as color or font size. Click OK when you're finished.

TIP

Many designers, myself included, like to make the link apparent by styling it bold and putting it in a different color.

The CSS Rule Definition window closes, and any style changes instantly take effect on your page. If you have any previously defined links, the underline disappears from them.

Now, when viewed through a browser, any links that you insert on your page still function as links—the user's pointer still changes into a pointing hand, and the links are active—but no underline appears.

One variation on this technique is to make the underline appear only when the mouse rolls over the link. To accomplish this variation, define a CSS rule for the `a:hover` selector and set the Decoration to Underline.

To eliminate the border around an image designated as a link, create a rule like this:

```
a img { border: none; }
```

This CSS rule looks for any image within an anchor tag and removes the border.

Inserting URLs from the Assets panel

Internet addresses get more complicated every day. Trying to remember them all and avoid typos can make the web designer's job unnecessarily difficult. You can use the Dreamweaver Assets panel's URLs category to drag-and-drop the trickiest URLs with ease.

The Assets panel lists URLs that are already referenced somewhere within your site. If you want to link to the same URL again, just drag it from the Assets panel.

TIP

To avoid rework, after you have typed a URL for a link in a document, test that link in a browser to be sure it's correct. Then, when you assign the same URL to other links using the Assets panel, you can be confident that the link works as expected.

The Assets panel lists only full Internet addresses—whether to files (such as `http://www.idest.com/dreamweaver/`) or to e-mail addresses (such as `mailto:jlowery@idest.com`). Document- or site-relative links are not listed as Assets. To assign a link to a document- or site-relative page, use one of the other linking methods discussed in this chapter, such as pointing to a file.

To assign a URL from the Assets panel, follow these steps:

1. If the Assets panel is not already visible, choose Window ➪ Assets to display it.
2. Click the URLs icon on the side of the Assets panel to display that category (see Figure 9-3).

FIGURE 9-3

Banish typos from your absolute URLs by dragging a link from the Assets panel to any selected text or graphic.

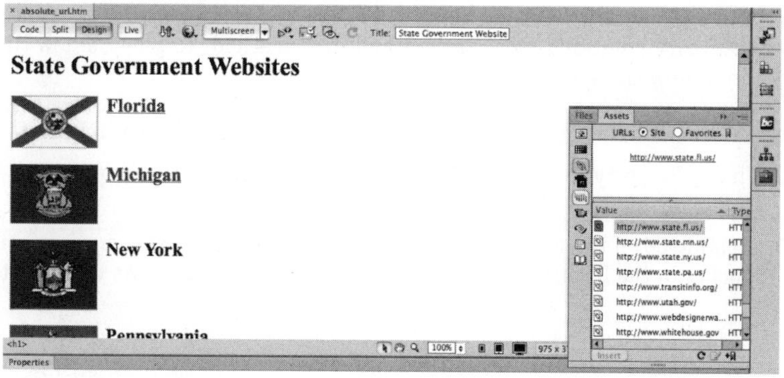

3. If necessary, click the Refresh Site List button on the Assets panel to list the most current links found in the site.

NOTE

As with other Assets panel categories, you need to click the Refresh Site List button to make available all the possible URLs in a site. Alternatively, you could choose Refresh Site List from the context menu on the panel. Either action causes Dreamweaver to scan all the web pages within the site and extract all of the complete Internet addresses it finds.

4. In the Document window, select the text or image you want the link assigned to.
5. Drag the desired link from the Assets panel onto the selected text or image; alternatively, highlight the link in the panel and click the Insert button.

If you don't select text or an image before dragging the URL from the Assets panel, a link is still created in your document. In this situation, Dreamweaver uses the URL name as the hotspot.

The Edit button on the Assets panel is unavailable for the URLs category. Links cannot be edited; they can only be applied as shown in the preview area.

Pointing to a file

Dreamweaver provides an alternative method of identifying a link—pointing to it. By using the Point to File icon on the Property inspector, you can quickly fill in the Link text box by dragging your mouse to any existing named anchor or file visible in the Dreamweaver environment. With the Point to File feature, you can avoid browsing through folder after folder as you search for a file you can clearly see onscreen.

You can point to another open document, to a document in another frame in the same window, or to any named anchor visible on the screen. If your desired link is a named anchor located farther down the page, Dreamweaver automatically scrolls to find it. You can even point to a named anchor in another document, and Dreamweaver will enter the full syntax correctly. Named anchors are covered in detail later in this chapter.

Perhaps one of the slickest ways to apply the Point to File feature is to use it in tandem with the Files panel. The Files panel lists all the existing files in any given website, and when both it and the Document window are onscreen, you can quickly point to any file.

You point to a file with what could be called a drag-and-release mouse technique, as opposed to the more ordinary point-and-click or drag-and-drop method. To select a new link using the Point to File icon, follow these steps:

1. Select the text or the graphic that you'd like to make into a link.
2. In the Property inspector, click and hold the Point to File icon located to the right of the Link text box.
3. Holding down the mouse button, drag the mouse until it is over an existing link or named anchor in the Document window or a file in the Files panel. As you drag the mouse, a line

extends from the Point to File icon, and the reminder `Drag to a file to make a link` appears in the Link text box.

4. When you locate the file you want to link to, release the mouse button. The filename with the accompanying path information is written into the Link text box, as shown in Figure 9-4.

FIGURE 9-4

The Point to File icon enables you to quickly insert a link to any onscreen file.

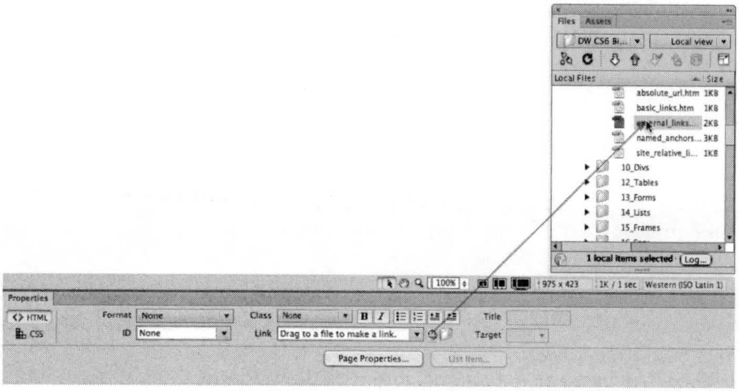

Addressing types

Three types of URLs are used as links: absolute addresses, document-relative addresses, and site-root–relative addresses. The following list briefly looks at these address types:

- Absolute addresses require the full URL, as follows:

  `http://www.adobe.com/products/dreamweaver/`

  This type of address is most often used for referencing links on another web server.

- Document-relative addresses know the scheme, server, and path aspects of the URL. These include additional path information only if the link is outside the current web page's folder. Links in the current document's folder can be addressed with their file-names only. To reference an item in a subfolder, just name the folder, enter a forward slash, and then enter the item's filename, as follows:

  `images/background.gif`

- Site-root–relative addresses are indicated with a leading forward slash:

  `/navigation/upndown.html`

  This example links to a file named `upndown.html` stored in the navigation directory at the current site root. Dreamweaver translates site-relative links to document-relative links when the Preview in Browser feature is used.

TIP

You can set your preference for document- or site-root-relative links on a site-by-site basis. Open your Site Definition dialog box by double-clicking the displayed site name in the Files panel drop-down list. In the Advanced Settings ➪ Local Info category of the Site Definition dialog box, choose the Links Relative To option you'd prefer.

Checking links

A Webmaster must often perform the tedious but necessary task of verifying the links on all the web pages in a site. Because of the web's fluid nature, links can work one day and break the next. Dreamweaver includes powerful link-checking and link-updating capabilities.

Dreamweaver can generate reports for broken links, for external links (links to files outside your site), and for orphaned files (files in your site with no links to them). You can check links for an open document, for all documents in a site, or for selected documents in the Files panel.

WARNING

When Dreamweaver checks your external links, it verifies that the links are well formed and not that they link to an actual page or other file. Be sure to verify your links actually go where they're supposed to before pushing the site live.

To check links in the current document, choose File ➪ Check Page ➪ Links, or press Shift+F8. To generate a link report for the entire site, open the Files panel (Window ➪ Files), and, from the Site menu, choose Check Links Sitewide. To report on links for certain files, select the files or folders in the Files panel, right-click (Control+click) and choose Check Links ➪ Selected Files. If the Link Checker panel is open, you can also click the Check Links button and then select the scope of your check: current document, entire site, or selected files in the site.

TIP

To stop an in-progress link check, click the Stop button in the Link Checker panel.

All these methods open the Link Checker panel, displaying the results of the link check. In the Show drop-down list at the top of the Link Checker panel, select the report you want to see: Broken Links, External Links, or Orphaned Files. The Orphaned Files report is available only if you check the entire site. The Broken Links report verifies not only clickable hotspots to other HTML files but also references to graphics and other external files.

Dreamweaver TECHNIQUE

Linking to Files

Linking to files properly is an essential task in building websites. In this Dreamweaver Technique, you practice linking to other files from text phrases and images.

1. From the Techniques site, expand the 09_Links folder and open the `links_start` file.
2. Select the phrase at the end of the first paragraph of placeholder text, Learn more . . .

3. In the Property inspector next to the Link field, click Browse for File (the folder icon) to open the Select File dialog box.
4. When the Select File dialog box opens, navigate to the 09_Links folder and choose `split_level_details.htm`; click OK when you're done.

The proper path is entered into the Link field by Dreamweaver. Assigning a link to a graphic is just as easy.

5. Select the image next to the Ranch style 2 bedroom label.
6. From the Property inspector, drag the Point to File icon to the Files panel and hover over the new_properties subfolder within the 09_Links folder. The new_properties subfolder expands.
7. Select `ranch_style.htm` and release your left mouse button.
8. Repeat Steps 5–7, selecting the image next to the Multi-level gardener's delight label and selecting `multi_level.htm` in the new_properties folder.
9. Save your page.
10. Press F12 (Option+F12) to test your links in the primary browser.

It's especially important to let Dreamweaver write your links for you when target files are located in a different folder. Get into the habit of using the Browse for File and Point to File icons, and you'll save yourself from linking errors.

You can save the link report by clicking the Save Report button on the Link Checker panel or by right-clicking (Control+clicking) in the panel and choosing Save Results from the pop-up menu. To clear the Link Checker panel, right-click (Control+click) in the Link Checker panel and choose Clear Results.

Double-clicking an entry in the Link Checker panel opens the document where the error occurred, with the broken link selected. You can quickly correct the link using the Property inspector or by choosing Modify ➪ Change Link. To remove the link but leave the hotspot text, clear the Link field in the Property inspector, or choose Modify ➪ Remove Link. If the same URL is referenced in more than one place in your site, you can change all occurrences of it at once. To do this, choose Site ➪ Change Link Sitewide from the main menus, and enter the URL to be changed and then the new URL. Finally, click OK.

Adding an E-mail Link

E-mail links are very common on the web. When a user clicks an e-mail link, it displays a window for sending a new e-mail message (rather than opening a new web page as a regular link does). The message window is convenient because it is preaddressed to the recipient. All the user has to do is add a subject, enter a message, and click Send.

Dreamweaver includes an object that streamlines the process of adding e-mail links. Just enter the text of the link and the e-mail address, and the link is ready. E-mail links, like other links, do not work when clicked in Dreamweaver; they must be previewed in a browser.

To enter an e-mail link, follow these steps:

1. Position your cursor where you want the e-mail link to appear.
2. From the Common category on the Insert panel, click the Email Link button. The Email Link dialog box, shown in Figure 9-5, appears.

FIGURE 9-5

The Email Link dialog box helps you create links that make it simple for your web page visitors to send e-mail messages.

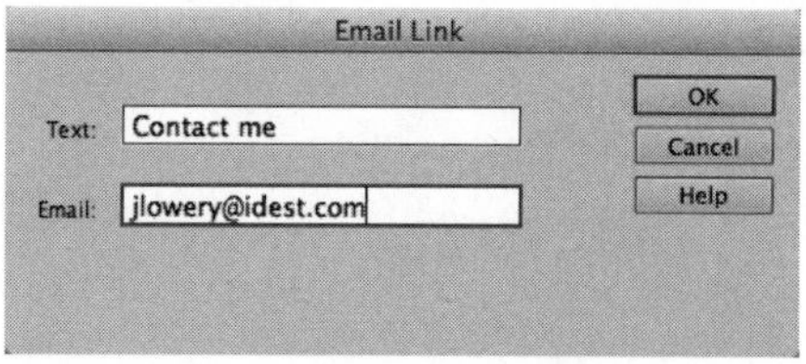

3. Enter the visible text for the link in the Text field.
4. Enter the e-mail address in the Email field.

CAUTION

The e-mail address must be in the format `name@company.com`. Dreamweaver does not check to ensure that you've entered the address in the proper format.

5. Click OK when you're finished.

E-mail Warnings

Here's a bit of the frustration that web designers sometimes face: On some browsers, notably Internet Explorer, users may see a dialog box when the e-mail link is first selected. The dialog box informs them that they are about to send an e-mail message over the Internet. The user has the option not to see these warnings, but there's no way for the web designer to prevent them from appearing when an e-mail link is used. However, another method of collecting data from users—HTML forms—doesn't require the users to have e-mail software installed on their computer, and it allows users to send information to the server without receiving the warning message. Chapter 13 explains how to create HTML forms.

NOTE

If you already have the text for the e-mail link in the document, you can use the Property inspector to insert an e-mail link. Just highlight the text, and in the Link field of the Property inspector, enter the URL in the following format:

```
mailto:name@company.com
```

Make sure that the URL is a valid e-mail address with the `@` sign properly placed.

Navigating with Anchors

Whenever you normally link to an HTML page, through absolute or relative addressing, the browser displays the page from the top. Your web visitors must scroll to any information rendered below the current screen. One HTML technique, however, links to a specific point anywhere on the page regardless of the display window's contents. This technique uses named anchors. A named anchor is simply an HTML anchor tag pair (`<a> . . . </a>`) that includes a `name` attribute. The named anchor serves as a target for links, allowing links to the middle of a page or wherever the named anchor is located within the document. One of the most common uses for named anchors is a Frequently Asked Questions page or FAQ. This allows you to post all of the most common questions together at the top of the page, and when users click on a particular question, they're automatically taken further down the page, sometimes dozens of screens down, to where the question is usually rewritten, followed by the specific answer they were looking for.

Using named anchors is a two-step process, although you usually find this two-step process repeated, in reverse, afterward for convenience (see the Technique later in the chapter). First, you place a named anchor somewhere on your web page. This placement is coded in HTML as an anchor tag using the `name` and `id` attributes, with nothing between the opening and the closing tags. In HTML, named anchors look like the following:

```
<a name="bible" id="bible"></a>
```

NOTE

If an HTML5 doctype is declared, the name attribute is not used, and anchor tags use the ID value.

The second step includes a link to that named anchor from somewhere else on your web page. If used, a named anchor is referenced in the final portion of an Internet address, designated by the hash mark (#), as follows:

```
<a href="http://www.idest.com/Dreamweaver/index.htm#bible">
```

You can include any number of named anchors on a page and any number of links to named anchors on the current page or different pages. Named anchors are commonly used with a table of contents or index.

To insert a named anchor, follow these steps:

1. Place the cursor where you want the named anchor to appear.
2. Choose Insert ➪ Named Anchor. You can also click the Named Anchor button in the Common category of the Insert panel or use the keyboard shortcut Ctrl+Alt+A (Command+Option+A).
3. The Named Anchor dialog box opens. Type the anchor name in the text box.

CAUTION

Named anchors are case-sensitive and must be unique within the page.

When you click OK, Dreamweaver places a named anchor symbol in the current cursor location and opens the Named Anchor Property inspector (shown in Figure 9-6).

FIGURE 9-6

The Named Anchor tag enables you to link to specific areas of a web page.

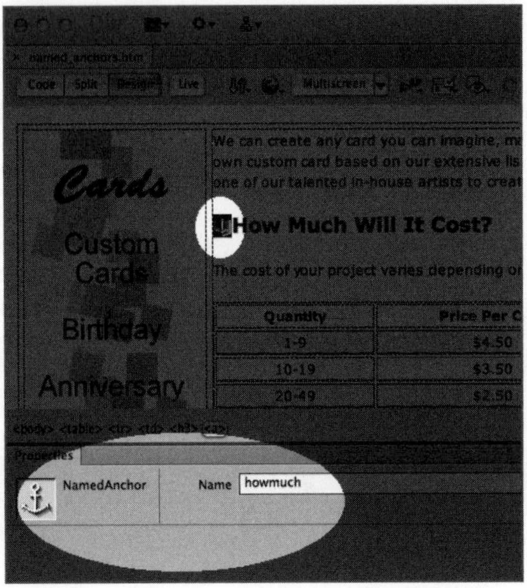

TIP

In Design view, named anchors are represented by a small yellow icon with—surprise!—an anchor image on it in the page. If you can't see the named anchor symbol, choose View ➪ Visual Aids ➪ Invisible Elements; if the symbol is still not visible, update your Preference settings for the Invisible Elements category.

4. To change an anchor's name, click the named anchor symbol within the page and alter the text in the Property inspector.

As with other invisible symbols, the named anchor symbol can be cut and pasted or moved using the drag-and-drop method.

Moving within the same document

One of the major advantages of using named anchors is the almost instantaneous response viewers receive when they link to named anchors from the same page. The browser just scrolls to the particular place in the document because the entire page is already loaded. For long text documents, this capability is an invaluable time-saver.

After you have placed a named anchor in your document, you can link to the anchor. You can create more than one named anchor in your document before adding links to the anchors. To create a link to a named anchor in the same document, follow these steps:

1. Select the text or image that you want to designate as a link.
2. In the Link text box of the Property inspector, type a hash mark (#) followed by the exact anchor name:

   ```
   #start
   ```

   Remember that anchor names are case-sensitive and must be unique in each document.

TIP

Place the named anchor one line above the heading or image to which you want to link the viewer. Browsers tend to be quite literal. If you place the named anchor on the same line, the browser renders it against the top of the window. Placing your named anchor up one line gives your topic a bit of breathing room in the display.

9

In Dreamweaver, you can also use the Point to File icon to choose a named anchor link. If your named anchor is in the same document, just drag the Point to File icon to the named anchor symbol. When you release the mouse, the address for the named anchor is inserted into the Link text box. If the named anchor is on the same page, but off-screen, Dreamweaver automatically scrolls the Document window as you drag toward the edge. In Windows, the closer you move to the edge, the faster Dreamweaver scrolls. Dreamweaver returns the screen to your original location, with the new link at the top of the screen after you release the mouse button.

In long documents with a table of contents or index linking to a number of named anchors, it's common practice—and a good idea—to place a link back to the top of the page after every screen or every topic. This technique enables your users to return to the menu quickly and pick another topic without having to manually scroll all the way back.

Using named anchors in a different page

If your table of contents is on a separate page from the topics of your site, you can use named anchors to send the viewer anywhere on a new page. The technique is the same as that already explained for placing named anchors, but with one minor difference when it comes to linking. Instead of placing a hash mark and name to denote the named anchor, you must first include the URL of the linked page.

Suppose you want to call the disclaimer section of a legal page from your table of contents. You could insert something like the following in the Link text box of the Property inspector:

```
legal.htm#disclaimer
```

This link, when activated, first loads the referenced web page (`legal.htm`) and then goes directly to the named anchor place (`#disclaimer`). Figure 9-7 shows how you enter this in the Property inspector. Keep in mind that you can use any form of addressing prior to the hash mark and named anchor.

FIGURE 9-7

You can link to any part of a separate web page by using named anchors.

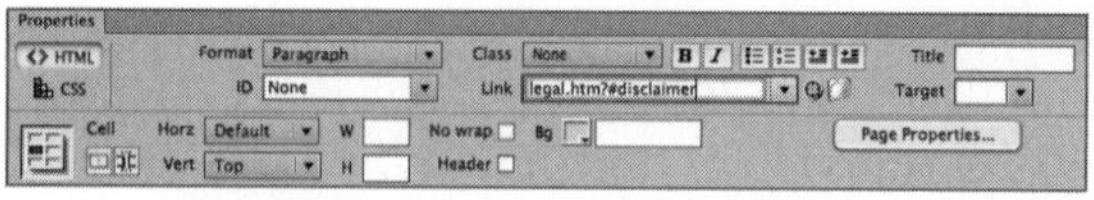

Creating null links

One of the more obscure uses for named anchors comes into play when you are trying to use Dreamweaver's JavaScript Behavior feature. Because JavaScript needs to work with a particular type of tag to perform `onMouseOver` and other events, a useful trick is to create a null link—a link that doesn't actually link to anywhere.

You create a null link by marking some text or an image with a link to #nowhere. You can use any name for the nonexistent named anchor. In fact, you don't even have to use a name—you can just use a hash mark (#) by itself.

There's one problem to note, however: Some earlier browsers had a tendency to send the page to the top if a link of this type is used. Many programmers have begun to substitute an empty call to a JavaScript function instead, such as `javascript:;`. Dreamweaver itself now uses `javascript:;` instead of # when a new behavior is attached to an image.

Dreamweaver TECHNIQUE

Inserting Named Anchors

Named anchors are an excellent way to navigate within a page. In this Dreamweaver Technique, you add links and named anchors to a page to allow the user to move about the page more easily. To save time, three of the five named anchors have been done for you.

1. From the Techniques site, expand the 09_Links folder and open the `anchors_start` file.
2. Scroll down the page and place your cursor in front of the Queens heading.
3. Choose Insert ➪ Named Anchor.
4. When the Named Anchor dialog box appears, enter **queens** in the Anchor Name field.
5. Near the top of the page, select the Queens entry in the list.
6. In the Property inspector's Link field, enter **#queens** and press Tab.

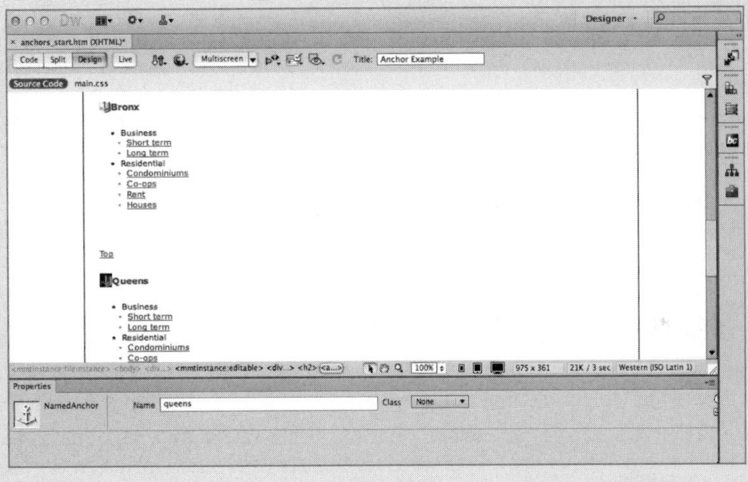

7. Repeat Steps 2–6 to create a named anchor named **statenIsland** and a link for the Staten Island entry, **#statenIsland**.

   It's good practice on a long page to include a link to the top of the page for every named anchor section. Again, most of the work has been done for you; you'll just need to add anchor links for the last two sections and a named anchor at the top of the page.

8. Scroll to the Queens section and select the word Top at the bottom of that section.
9. In the Property inspector's Link field, enter **#top** and press Tab.
10. Repeat Steps 8 and 9 to add a link named **#top** to the word Top following the Staten Island section.

continues

continued

11. The last action is to insert a named anchor named top. Place your cursor at the top of the page and select Insert ➪ Named Anchor.
12. When the Named Anchor dialog box opens, enter **top**.
13. Save your page and press F12 (Option+F12) to test it in your primary browser.

When you test the links, notice that the page moves up and down with each anchor link selected.

Targeting Your Links

Thus far, all the links discussed in this chapter have had a similar effect: They open another web page or section in your browser's window. What if you want to force the browser to open another window and load that new URL in the new window? HTML enables you to specify the target for your links.

Targets are most often used in conjunction with frames—that is, you can make a link in one frame open a file in another. For more information about this technique, see Chapter 15.

Targets do more than just display a page in a certain frame. Take a look at one of the HTML predefined targets used in a situation where you want to load another URL into a new window.

To specify a new browser window as the target for a link, follow these steps:

1. Select the text or image you want to designate as your new link.
2. In the Property inspector, enter the URL into the Link text box. After you've entered a link, the target option becomes active.
3. In the Target drop-down list, select _blank, as shown in Figure 9-8. You can also type it in the list box. Either way, Dreamweaver inserts a `_blank` option in the Target list box. Now, when your link is activated, the browser spawns a new window and loads the referenced link into it. The user has both windows available.

FIGURE 9-8

With the Target attribute, you can force a user's browser to open a separate window to display a specific link.

The _blank target is most often used when the originating web page is acting as a jump station and has numerous links available. By keeping the original web page open, the user can view another page without losing the origin point. You can even use a _blank target with links to named anchors in the same document.

Three other system-wide targets exist: _top, _parent, and _self. Both _top and _parent are primarily used with framesets: The _top target replaces the outermost frameset, and _parent replaces the frameset containing the current page. These two have the same effect, except in the case of nested framesets. The _self target is the default behavior, and only the current page is replaced.

NOTE
Many modern browsers allow windows to be grouped as a series of tabs. If the user has his or her browser preferences set to open new windows in tabs, the _blank target opens in a tab rather than a completely new window.

Summary

Whether they are links for website navigation or jumps to other related sites, hypertext links are an essential part of any web page. Dreamweaver gives you full control over your inserted links. Keep in mind the following points about links:

- Through a unique URL, you can access virtually any web page, graphic, or other item available on the Internet.
- The Hypertext Transfer Protocol (HTTP) is one of the most common methods of Internet connection, but web pages can link to other formats, including FTP, e-mail, and newsgroups.
- Any of the three basic address formats—absolute, document relative, or site-root relative—can be inserted in the Link text box of Dreamweaver's Property inspector to create a link.
- Dreamweaver has several quick linking capabilities in the Assets panel and Point to File feature.
- Named anchors give you the power to jump to specific parts of any web page, whether the page is the current one or one that is located on another server.
- With the _blank target attribute, you can force a link to open in a new browser window, leaving your original window available to the user.

In the next chapter, you learn how to work with AP elements and <div> tags in Dreamweaver.

Part III

Adding Advanced Design Features

IN THIS PART

Chapter 10
Working with Layouts

Chapter 11
Using Behaviors

Chapter 12
Setting Up Tables

Chapter 13
Interactive Forms

Chapter 14
Creating Lists

Chapter 15
Using Frames and Framesets

Chapter 16
Powering Ajax Pages with Spry

Chapter 17
Working with JavaScript Frameworks

CHAPTER

10

Working with Layouts

IN THIS CHAPTER

Understanding how divs and AP elements work in Dreamweaver

Inserting <div> tags

Dreamweaver Technique: Applying a CSS Layout

Working with fluid grids for multiple screens

Modifying AP elements: Resizing, moving, and altering properties

Dreamweaver Technique: Inserting an AP Element

Creating interactive AP elements with Dreamweaver behaviors

For many years, page designers have taken for granted the capability to place text and graphics anywhere on a printed page—even enabling graphics, type, and other elements to bleed off a page. This flexibility in design has eluded web designers until recently. Lack of absolute control over layout has been a high price to pay for the universality of HTML, which makes any web page viewable by any system, regardless of the computer or the screen resolution.

Now, however, the integration of absolutely positioned elements (AP elements) within the Cascading Style Sheets specification has brought both relative and absolute positioning to the web. Page designers with a yen for more control welcome the precision offered with Cascading Style Sheets positioning. Positioning styles are frequently applied to <div> tags, which are used to separate a page into different areas or divisions.

The increase in the number of screen sizes found in mobile devices has brought another challenge to the web designer's door. How is a layout to be seen optimally under the wide range of conditions? One technique with a good deal of support among modern designers is called *fluid grids*. The fluid grid layout combines CSS media queries with a percentage-based layout for the ultimate in flexibility. As you'll see in this chapter, Dreamweaver makes it possible to build a fluid grid layout that adapts to phone, tablet, and desktop screens.

This chapter explores every aspect of how various layout elements work in web pages. With the fundamentals under your belt, you learn how to create, modify, and populate <div> tags, AP elements, and fluid grid layouts in your designs.

Dreamweaver QUICKSTART

If you're already familiar with <div> tags and absolutely positioned elements, here's a quick overview of how to add each to the page.

To insert a <div> tag to your page, follow these steps:

1. From the Common category of the Insert panel, click Insert Div Tag.

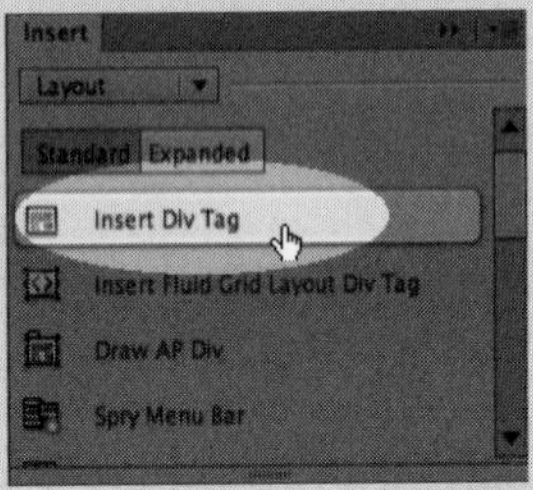

2. When the Insert Div Tag dialog box opens, choose where you'd like the tag to be inserted: at the current cursor position or before—or after—a particular tag.
3. Choose an already-defined class or ID to assign to the <div> tag. Alternatively, you can define a new CSS rule and use it.
4. Click OK to add the <div> tag and placeholder text to the page.

To draw an absolutely positioned element on the page, do this:

1. From the Layout category of the Insert panel, click Draw AP Div.

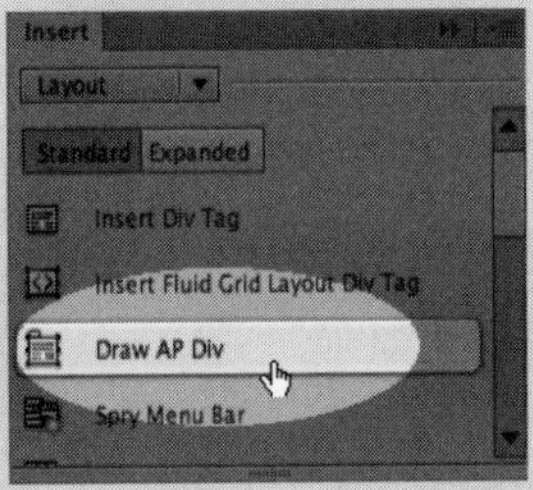

2. Drag out a rectangle the approximate size and shape of the desired AP div.
3. To reposition the AP div, drag its selection handle in the top-left corner to a new screen location.
4. For precise placement or dimensions, change the values in the Property inspector.

Divs and AP Elements 101

When the World Wide Web first made its debut in 1989, few people were concerned about the aesthetic layout of a page. In fact, because the web was a descendant of Standard Generalized Markup Language (SGML)—a multiplatform text document and information markup specification—layout was trivialized. Content and the capability to use hypertext to jump from one page to another were emphasized. After the first graphical web-browser software (Mosaic) was released, it quickly became clear that a page's graphics and layout could enhance a website's accessibility and marketability. Content was still king, but design was moving up quickly.

To relieve the woes of web designers everywhere, the W3C included a feature within the new Cascading Style Sheets specifications that allowed for absolute positioning of an element upon a page. Absolute positioning enables an element, such as an image or block of text, to be placed anywhere on the web page. Browser support for Cascading Style Sheets-Positioning (CSS-P) specification began with fourth-generation browsers and has grown steadily ever since.

The addition of the third dimension, depth, truly turned the positioning specs into AP elements. Now objects can be positioned side by side, and they have a z-index property as well. The z-index gets its name from the practice in geometry of describing three-dimensional space with x, y, and z coordinates; the z-index is also called the stacking order because objects can be stacked upon one another.

All these attributes, and others such as background color, can be assigned to a CSS style, as shown in the following code:

```
#header {
   position: absolute;
   z-index: 1;
   height: 115px;
   width: 400px;
   left: 100px;
   top: 50px;
   background: #FFCC33;
}
```

The CSS style is then applied to a `<div>` tag to represent an area on the page, like this:

```
<div id="header">Header content goes here.</div>
```

Dreamweaver calls `<div>` tags that are drawn with your mouse AP elements; the CSS style is automatically created and embedded in the page for you. Drawing out the same AP element results in the same CSS code, except the selector ID is automatically created for you (apDiv1, apDiv2, and so on) and the code is embedded in the page, like this:

```
<style type="text/css">
<!--
#apDiv11 {
   position: absolute;
   z-index: 1;
```

10

```
    height: 115px;
    width: 400px;
    left: 100px;
    top: 50px;
    background: #FFCC33;
}
-->
</style>
```

The <div> code is also added for you, *sans content*, like this:

```
<div id="apDiv11"></div>
```

Although both approaches are valid, many designers prefer to keep the CSS information in an external style sheet rather than embedded. As you see in this chapter, Dreamweaver supports both methods fully.

If you don't define a unit of measurement for AP element positioning, Dreamweaver defaults to pixels. If you edit out the unit of measurement, the web browser defaults to pixels.

Positioning Measurement

The positioning of AP elements is determined by aligning elements on an x-axis and a y-axis. In CSS, the x-axis (defined as Left in CSS syntax) begins at the left side of the page, and the y-axis (defined as Top in CSS syntax) is measured from the top of the page down. As with many of the other CSS features, you have your choice of measurement systems for Left and Top positioning. All measurements are given in Dreamweaver as a number followed by the abbreviation of the measurement system (without any intervening spaces). The measurement system options are as follows:

Unit	Abbreviation	Measurement
Pixels	px	Relative to the screen
Points	pt	1 pt = 1⁄72 in
Inches	in	1 in = 2.54 cm
Centimeters	cm	1 cm = 0.3937 in
Millimeters	mm	1 mm = 0.03937 in
Picas	pc	1 pc = 12 pt
EMS	em	The height of the element's font
Percentage	%	Relative to the browser window

For the screen-oriented style sheets prevalent on the web, it's best to use pixels, ems, or percentage. You can, however, use points or other measurement units for print style sheets.

Placing <div> Tags

As noted earlier, CSS-P information can be defined in a style sheet or embedded. Defining the CSS rule in a style sheet (either external or internal) has the benefit of truly separating content from presentation, which, in turn, makes it easier to reshape the content via another style sheet for another medium. A block of text, for example, can be positioned on the right when viewed in a monitor and left when printed out. Moreover, many designers find that centralizing the layout information in a style sheet is a far more effective way to work. Often, the same layout is used on multiple pages of a site; with CSS-P rules in an external style sheet, you can modify the layout of all the related pages simply by altering the CSS in the style sheet. To accomplish the same change when the CSS is embedded would require extensive search-and-replace and the re-uploading of every altered file.

Dreamweaver recognizes the importance of the `<div>` tag in modern website design with the integration of the `<div>` object. Not only is the insertion of the `<div>` tag now possible in Design view, but Dreamweaver also provides visual feedback indicating placement and easy modification through the Property and Tag inspectors.

Defining a CSS rule for a <div> tag

When you are using a `<div>` object, the typical workflow is to first create the required CSS rules. For layouts, I prefer to use the ID selector because it is applied to only one `<div>` tag. It's a good idea to give your CSS rules descriptive IDs, such as `#header`, `#footer`, `#mainContent`, and `#navigation`.

If you're not familiar with creating CSS style rules, see Chapter 6 for more information.

To create a CSS rule for use with `<div>` tags, follow these steps:

1. Choose Window ⇨ CSS Styles to open the CSS Styles panel.
2. From the CSS Styles panel, click the New CSS Rule button. This action opens the New CSS Rule dialog box.
3. From the New CSS Rule dialog box, set the Type option to ID.
4. Enter a name for your new style in the Selector field. It's a good idea to create the style for your layout `<div>` tag as an ID. To create an ID, preface the style name with a pound sign, as in `#mainContent`.
5. If you want to create your style in an external style sheet, use the Browse button to locate an existing style sheet.
6. If you want to add the style to the `<head>` region of the current document, select This Document Only from the Rule Definition list.
7. Click OK when you're finished to open the CSS Rule Definition dialog box.
8. Select the Positioning category.

9. From the Positioning category (see Figure 10-1), enter desired values for the following attributes: Position, Width, Height, Visibility, Z-Index, Overflow, Placement (Top, Right, Bottom, and Left), and Clip settings (Top, Right, Bottom, Left). Overflow and Clip settings are optional.

FIGURE 10-1

Use the Positioning category of the CSS Rule Definition dialog box to set AP element attributes in an internal or external style sheet.

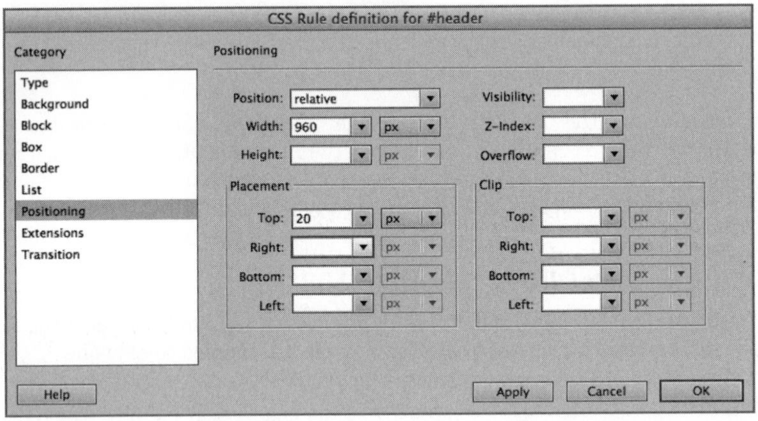

The Position attribute offers four options: Absolute, Fixed, Relative, and Static. An Absolute `<div>` uses the upper-left corner of its nearest positioned ancestor as the origin for the Left and Top measurements, whereas a box with Relative `<div>` tags originates from its current location in the normal document flow. Use Static when you don't want to place the `<div>` in a certain position but you still want to specify a rectangular block. Static `<div>` types ignore the Left and Top attributes.

10. If appropriate, select other categories and enter any additional style sheet attributes. Click OK when you're finished.

Inserting the <div> tag

After you have defined your CSS rule, follow these steps to add a `<div>` tag to the page:

1. Place your cursor where you want the `<div>` tag to appear. You can also select content on a page you'd like to wrap a `<div>` tag around.
2. From the Layout category of the Insert panel, click the Insert Div Tag button. Alternatively, you can choose Insert ➪ Layout Objects ➪ Div Tag. Dreamweaver displays the Insert Div Tag dialog box, as shown in Figure 10-2.
3. Choose the CSS rule from either the Class or the ID list. Dreamweaver shows only those IDs that have not been previously applied.

FIGURE 10-2

Dreamweaver lists all the available CSS rules that can be applied to a new <div> tag, as either as a Class or an ID.

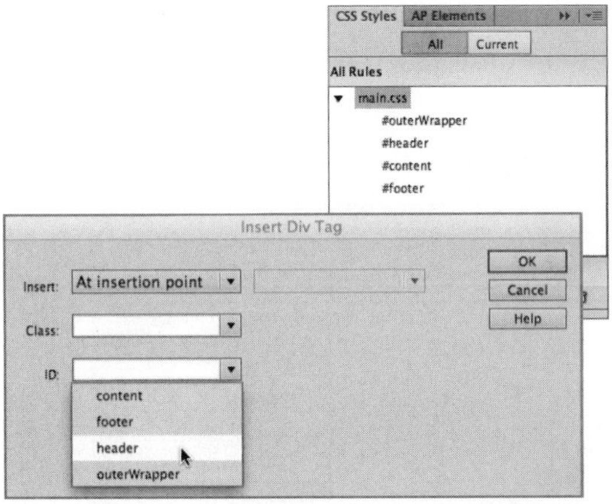

TIP

If the CSS rule is not available from either of the lists—perhaps because the style sheet is dynamically applied—you can enter the name directly into either the Class or the ID field. However, unless Design Time Style Sheets are used to show the styles, the layout won't render properly in Dreamweaver.

4. Select where you'd like the tag placed from the Insert list. Dreamweaver provides different options depending on the makeup of the page and whether content is already selected. Only tags with assigned IDs are listed, along with the <body> tag. Here are the Insert options you can choose from:
   - **At Insertion Point:** Inserts the <div> tag at the current cursor position. This option is available only if no content is selected.
   - **Wrap Around Selection:** Wraps the <div> tag around the currently selected content. Available only if a selection was made prior to inserting the <div> tag.
   - **Before Tag:** Puts the tag before the tag selected in the adjacent field.
   - **After Tag:** Inserts the <div> tag after the tag selected in the adjacent field.
   - **After Start Of Tag:** Places the <div> tag immediately following the opening tag in a tag pair, before any content within the tag.
   - **Before End Of Tag:** Inserts the tag right before the closing tag in a tag pair, after any content within the tag.
5. Click OK when you're finished to insert the tag.

CAUTION

Be sure not to insert the <div> tag in the middle of an empty element. Empty elements, you may remember, are elements that have no corresponding closing tag and contain no content, such as <img> or <br>.

If the <div> tag was not wrapped around previously selected content, Dreamweaver adds placeholder text to help identify the tag and its class or ID. As another helpful aid to identification, a red outline appears when your cursor crosses the outer boundary of the <div>. This highlight is controlled by the Mouse-Over option found in the Highlighting category of the Preferences. The red outline is replaced by a thick blue one when the <div> tag is selected, as shown in Figure 10-3.

FIGURE 10-3

A thick, blue outline appears around the div when selected.

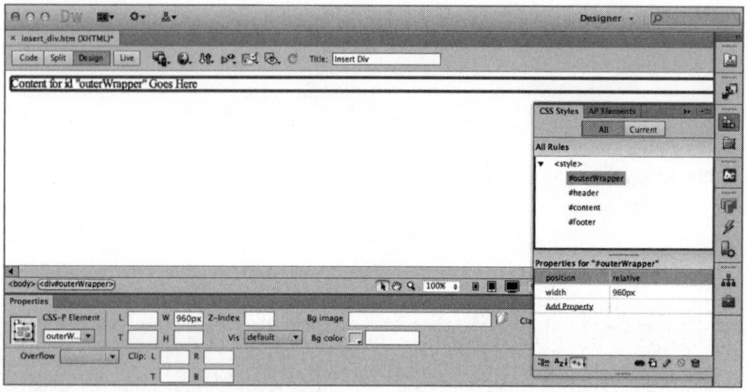

Select the <div> in Design view and the Property inspector displays all the current attributes. If you make any changes in the Property inspector, such as adding or altering the background color, the change is written into the associated CSS style rule. If the <div> tag's position property is set to absolute, the outline is supplemented with positioning and sizing handles. The interaction among object, Property inspector, and style sheet holds true if you drag the selected <div> around the page or resize it using the sizing handles; see the later section "Modifying an AP Element" for more details. You can also modify <div> tag properties by editing the style rule directly or by altering its properties on the Tag inspector panel.

CAUTION

If your layout is controlled by an external style sheet that also controls the layout of other pages in your site, be careful when adjusting the properties of a <div> tag. When you make changes, Dreamweaver modifies the CSS style rule in the external style sheet, potentially altering the layout of other pages using the same style sheet.

Visualizing <div> tags

The <div> tag is a structural element, not intended to be apparent when viewed through the browser at runtime. Design time, however, is another matter. Designers often need to be able to see the underlying structure to craft their layouts; they also need to be able to hide the structure at any point so they can see a browser-like view while designing.

Dreamweaver provides a full slate of visualization options for CSS layouts. Each of the options, found under the Visual Aids menu button on the Document toolbar or the View ➪ Visual Aids menu item, can be toggled in and out of view at will. There are three different visualizations that can be used singly or in combination: CSS Layout Backgrounds, CSS Layout Box Model, and CSS Layout Outlines. The three CSS layout visualization options apply to other page elements in addition to `<div>` tags. Any page element with the CSS declaration of `display:block`, `position:absolute`, or `position:relative` is considered a block layout element and is affected as well. For example, if an `<a>` tag style was set to `display:block`—a common method used when developing CSS navigation buttons—it would be rendered with the same visualizations as `<div>` tags, including sizing handles, and so on.

CSS Inspect

Live View makes it easy for the Dreamweaver designer to accurately preview the current web page as it appears in a modern browser. Unfortunately, by itself, Live View obscures the underlying CSS structure: There's no easy way to see how the various elements fit together. However, Dreamweaver includes an option called Inspect that exposes certain properties of any CSS block-level elements on the page.

NOTE

With Inspect mode enabled, you can quickly view the margins, paddings, border, and content area of any block-level element in Live View. Just click Inspect and hover over any `<div>`, `<p>`, `<span>`, or other tag to display these properties as solid color blocks (see Figure 10-4). In addition, Inspect can highlight the targeted area in both Code view and the CSS Styles panel.

FIGURE 10-4

When Inspect mode is toggled on in Live View, you can reveal the margins, padding, and border of any element by hovering over it.

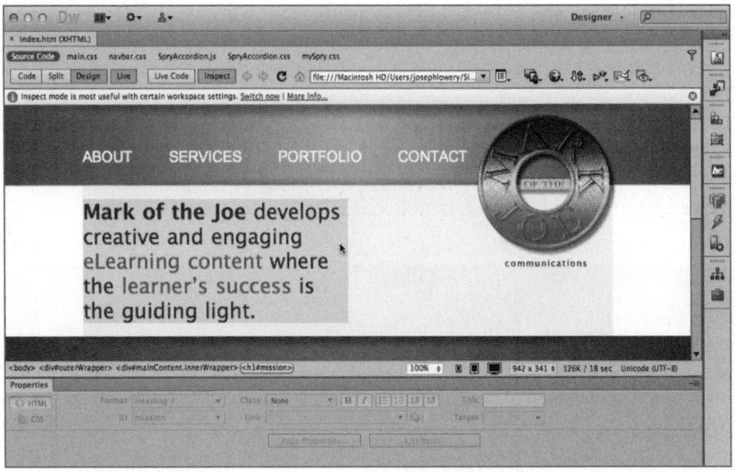

Inspect mode is also available in other Dreamweaver views of the document. If you have Code view or Live Code enabled, the code for the element under the cursor in Live View is highlighted. When the CSS Styles panel is open and Current mode engaged, the CSS rule that applies to the targeted element is shown. You can see both of these effects at once—as well as the box model color highlights in Live View—in Figure 10-5. Better still, any changes made to the CSS Styles panel are instantly reflected in Live View and Inspect mode.

FIGURE 10-5

Inspect mode can also reveal the code and CSS related to a targeted element.

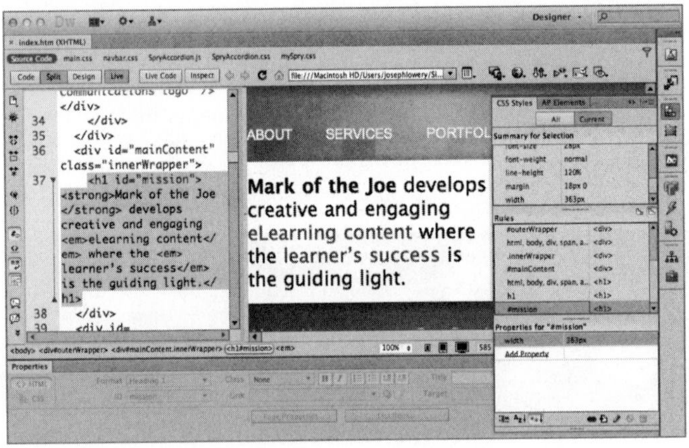

Inspect mode is great for getting a clearer picture of how your page is structured and very useful when debugging a CSS issue.

CSS layout backgrounds

In the early stages of laying out a page, it's often helpful to see your basic building blocks clearly depicted. When you invoke the CSS Layout Background options from the Visual Aids menu, Dreamweaver clears any background image or color previously defined in the CSS styles and replaces them with a different solid color for each `<div>` tag. The resulting patchwork shows at a glance how the page is structured (see Figure 10-6). This option is also useful when debugging layouts because it clearly shows which `<div>` tags—if any—overlap.

TIP

The colors assigned to each of the `<div>` backgrounds are random and can't be predefined. A new set of colors is used every time you toggle CSS Layout Backgrounds into view.

CSS Layout Box Model

All CSS block elements are rendered in the browser according to the CSS box model. The box model, established by the W3C CSS standards body, determines how much room a block element actually takes up on the page. The amount of space required for a block element, such as a <div> tag, is a combination of the declared width, plus the padding, border, and margin settings. For example, say a <div> tag has the following style declared:

```
#myBox {
  width:200px;
  padding:10px;
  border:5px;
  margin:10px;
}
```

FIGURE 10-6

Turn on CSS Layout Backgrounds when first creating your CSS layout or debugging it.

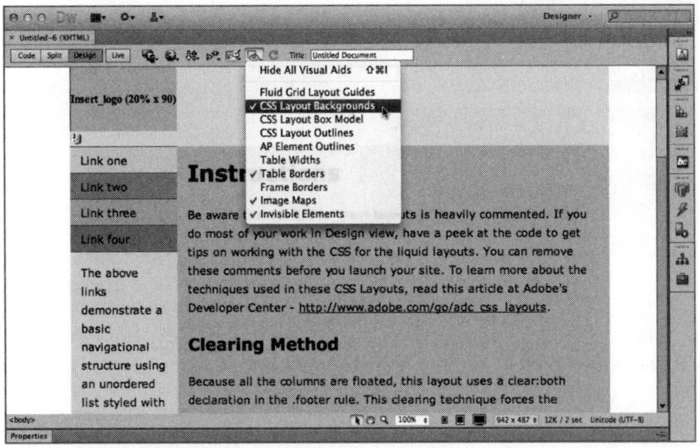

Although nominally, the myBox style appears to be 200 pixels wide, CSS specifications indicate that it will actually take up 250 pixels of space horizontally. Here's how the space requirement is figured:

```
200 pixels content area width
 10 pixels padding-left
 10 pixels padding-right
  5 pixels border-left
  5 pixels border-right
 10 pixels margin-left
 10 pixels margin-right
250 pixels width total
```

To make it easy for you to design with the box model in mind, Dreamweaver provides the CSS Layout Box Model visual aid. When enabled, any selected <div> tag or otherwise affected block element depicts all the contributing elements: content area (the width), padding, borders, and margins. Both the padding and the margins are shown with colored diagonal lines, although in opposing directions, as shown in Figure 10-7.

FIGURE 10-7

The CSS Layout Box Model visual aid reveals the unseen reserved space around layout elements.

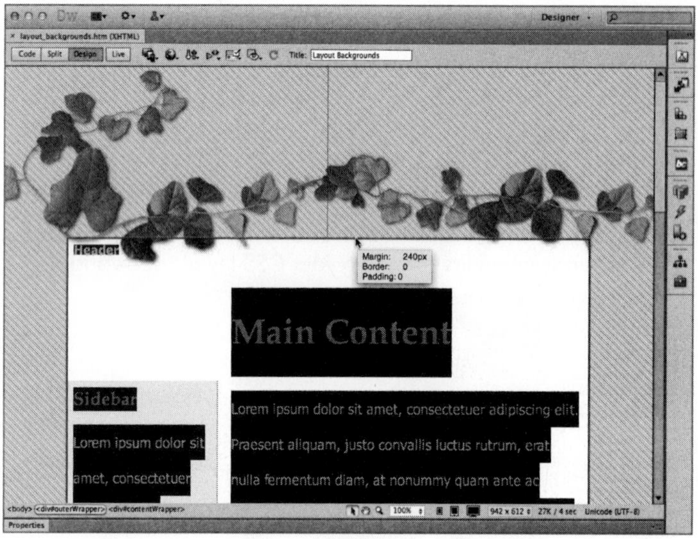

Dreamweaver not only reveals how the layout element is constructed visually but also provides you a wealth of information from tooltips that appear as you move your cursor around the element. The information in the tooltip varies according to cursor's position:

- Hover over the content area to see all the CSS properties, including those related to the box model.
- Move your cursor over the padding or margin areas to see their respective values—for example, `Margin: 10px`.
- With the cursor over the border, the tooltip reveals the current values for the margin, border, and padding properties.

I recommend turning on the CSS Layout Box Model feature in the fine-tuning and debugging stages of your web page development; it's a great tool for understanding exactly why elements on your page are positioned the way they are.

CSS Layout Outlines

CSS Layout Outlines, when enabled, place a border around `<div>` tags and other block layout elements (see Figure 10-8). The outline is a dashed style for inserted `<div>` tags and a solid border for drawn Dreamweaver AP elements.

I tend to keep CSS Layout Outlines enabled during most of my design process; I find having the outlines visible allows me to quickly insert content in just the right places and, more important, select the `<div>` tags for quick refinement.

FIGURE 10-8

Highlight your <div> tags at design time with CSS Layout Outlines.

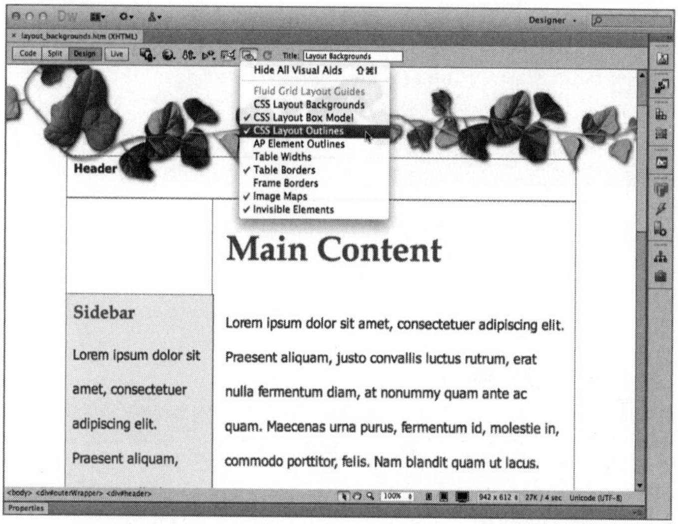

Applying a CSS Layout

In this Technique, you apply previously defined CSS styles to a variety of `<div>` tags to create a basic layout.

1. From the Techniques site, expand the 10_Divs folder and open `div_start.htm`.

   The first style to apply acts as a container for the entire page; to apply this properly, you'll need to position the cursor properly.
2. Place your cursor in the series of links on the page and click the `<p>` tag in the Tag Selector.
3. From the Insert panel's Layout category, click Insert Div Tag.
4. When the Insert Div Tag dialog box opens, make sure the Insert list is set to Wrap Around Selection.
5. From the ID list, choose Wrapper and click OK.

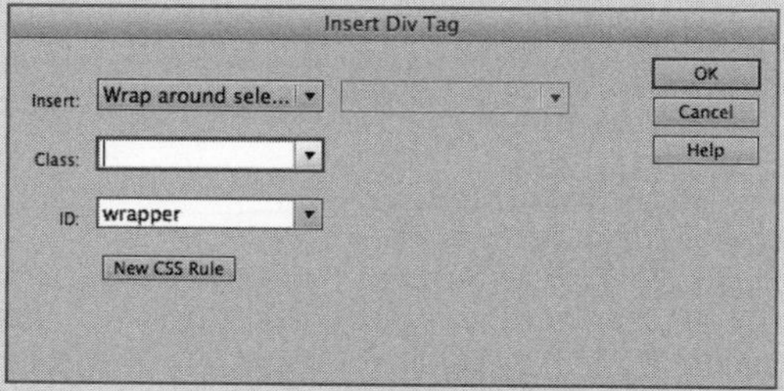

Continues

continued

Next, add the first of three <div> tags, the header, so that it appears with the `wrapper` <div> tag:

1. From the Insert panel's Layout category, click Insert Div Tag.
2. From the Insert list, choose After Start Of Tag and then, when the adjacent list appears, select `<div id="wrapper">`.
3. From the ID list, choose Header and click OK.
4. Click Delete to remove the selected placeholder text.

Now you're ready to insert the `middle` <div> tag after the `header` <div> tag:

1. From the Insert panel's Layout category, click Insert Div Tag.
2. From the Insert list, choose After Tag and then, when the adjacent list appears, select `<div id="header">`.
3. From the ID list, choose Middle and click OK.

The final <div> wraps around navigation links and forms the bottom area, the footer:

1. Place your cursor in the series of links on the page and click the <p> tag in the Tag Selector.
2. From the Insert panel's Layout category, click Insert Div Tag.
3. When the Insert Div Tag dialog box opens, make sure the Insert list is set to Wrap Around Selection and, from the ID list, choose Footer; click OK when you're done.

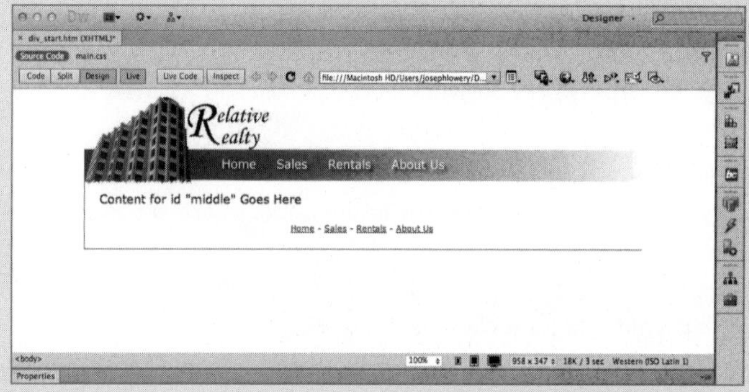

4. Save your page.

Your new CSS-based layout is now ready to be filled out with content.

Designing fluid layouts with a grid

Anyone who has walked into a phone or electronics store recently will agree: Web-enabled screens now come in every size imaginable. While it's possible to keep the same design for all devices—whether desktop, tablet, phone, or whatever—that choice will typically result in a great deal of zooming and scrolling. A far better approach is to optimize the layout for a select number of devices and then switch from one layout to another using CSS media queries. What's even better is building those separate designs with a fluid grid that provides the best fit to myriad screen sizes while maintaining a uniform structure.

NEW FEATURE

Setting up a fluid grid involves determining the number of columns in a particular layout and the amount of space between each column—all in precise percentages of the overall screen target width. While it's entirely doable (given an industrial-grade calculator), it can be a little overwhelming. Dreamweaver now offers to take that chore off your hands with its support for fluid grid layouts. You can create a new fluid grid layout right from the New Document dialog box (see Figure 10-9) and immediately start designing for multiple screens: All your media queries and additional code are set up for you. As you build up your layout, you can easily switch between the three major screen sizes with just a click. When the design is finished, you can preview your work in Live View or a browser, where you'll notice that resizing the screen smoothly adjusts the design, but the relative layout is kept.

FIGURE 10-9

The Fluid Grid Layout dialog box defines three different screen sizes.

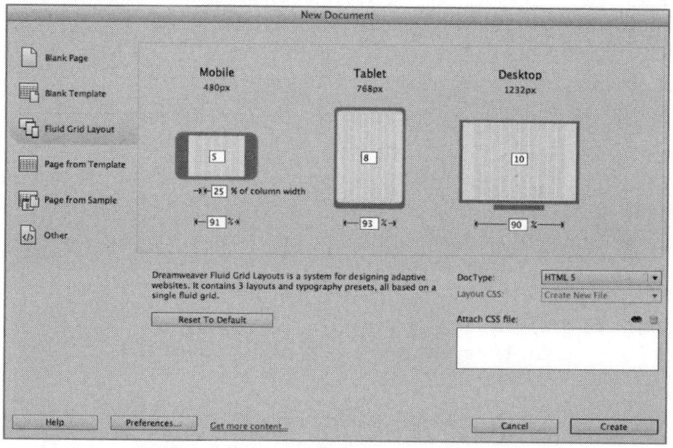

Working with a fluid grid layout

When the page is first created, you'll notice its distinct difference from the standard Document window: A series of columns each separated from the other by a uniform width are displayed in the document's background (see Figure 10-10).

The idea of the fluid grid layout is to use these columns as guides to determine the width of page elements such as `<div>` tags. The accompanying CSS allows these elements to then expand and contract gracefully when the browser window is within one set of media query conditions; this allows the web design to look its best on a large number of similar devices. When a fluid grid layout page is rendered on a different device, the media query statements apply a different, more suitable, set of CSS rules.

FIGURE 10-10

The number of layout columns displayed depends on the screen width; the mobile phone screen shows five columns.

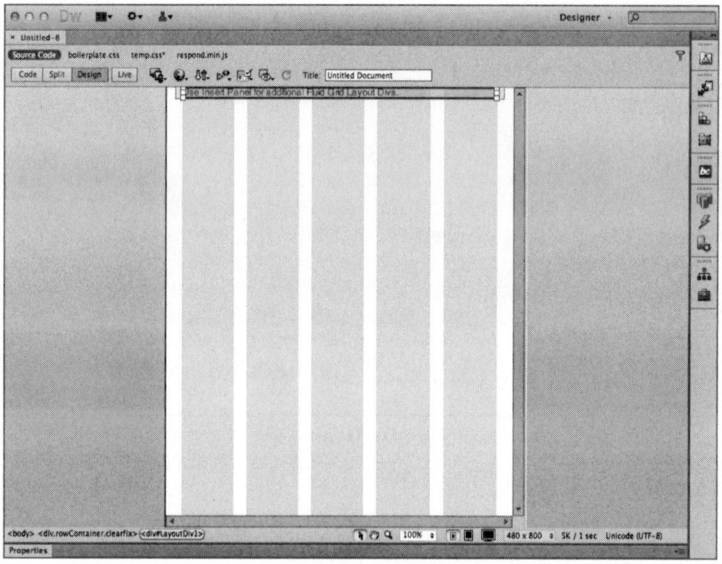

The initial fluid grid layout document, by default, includes one <div> tag within another; the outer <div> tag has `.rowcontainer` and `.clearfix` classes for containing floats. The Document window size is automatically set to mobile phone dimensions. Here's what the starting code in the <body> tag looks like:

```
<div class="rowContainer clearfix">
  <div id="LayoutDiv1">Use Insert Panel for additional Fluid Grid
Layout Divs.</div>
</div>
```

When either <div> is selected, you'll notice a series of handles surrounding it (see Figure 10-11). To resize a <div> tag, drag any of the handles on the right; to reposition the <div> tag, drag any handle on the left.

Dreamweaver provides an easy way to add new <div> tags to a fluid grid layout. To include a new element, expand the Layout category of the Insert panel and click Insert Fluid Grid Layout Div Tag. Dreamweaver will present a dialog box that allows you to specify an ID for the tag with an option to start a new row (see Figure 10-12). If you leave the Start New Row checkbox selected, the CSS rule for the new <div> tag will include a `clear: both` declaration; if the checkbox is not selected, `clear: none` is inserted instead.

FIGURE 10-11

Use the handles to resize and reposition the fluid grid <div> tags.

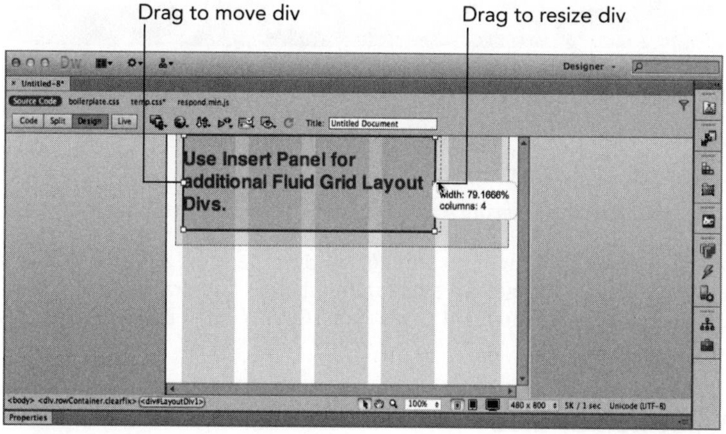

FIGURE 10-12

Add a new <div> tag to your fluid grid layout through the Insert panel object.

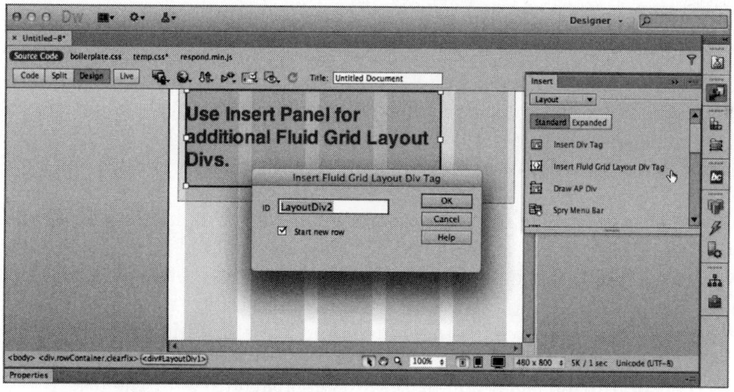

Let's walk through a typical fluid grid workflow so you can understand how to make the most of this new feature:

1. Create a new document by choosing File ➪ New Fluid Grid Layout or, alternatively, File ➪ New and then selecting the Fluid Grid Layout category.
2. Once the new page is created, save it and confirm Dreamweaver's request to copy the helper files to your site.
3. Use the Insert Fluid Grid Layout Div Tag object from the Layout category of the Insert panel to create the page structure.

TIP

If you want to place two or more columns on the same row (not recommended for mobile phone layouts), add `.rowcontainer` and `.clearfix` classes in a surrounding <div> tag.

4. Click Tablet Size in the Status bar.
5. Resize and reposition the existing <div> tags for an optimum tablet layout.
6. Click Desktop Size in the Status bar.
7. Resize and reposition the existing <div> tags for the best desktop layout.

Unlike most layout features in Dreamweaver, fluid grid <div> tags are editable in Live View and Design view. Select any <div> to reveal the surrounding border and draggable handles. To turn off the background grid, toggle off the Fluid Grid Layout Guides entry under the Visual Aids menu button.

Fluid grid layout helper files

When you first save your fluid grid layout page, Dreamweaver asks you to confirm copying two files—`boilerplate.css` and `respond.js`—to your site and then links to those pages from your source code. Let's take a quick look at what these helper files actually do and how you can use them to create better, more responsive sites.

Let's first look at the JavaScript file, `respond.js`. One of the major components of the fluid grid layout is the CSS3 media query statement. Because media queries are a relatively recent development, older browsers, like Internet Explorer 6 through 8, do not support them. The code in `respond.js` changes all that and makes it possible for those browsers to apply the styles found in a CSS style sheet conditionally chosen by a media query. The backwards compatibility brought by `respond.js` goes a long way toward robust cross-browser support for fluid grid layouts.

The CSS helper file, `boilerplate.css`, is much more broad based. This file is a part of a larger effort hosted at `http://html5boilerplate.com/` that has created a full starting point for HTML5 sites to work with the full spectrum of browsers, from Internet Explorer 6 to the most recent mobile-ready programs. The `boilerplate.css` copied by Dreamweaver to your site is well documented, so it's easy to see what's included. Here are a few highlights:

- HTML5 displays definitions that add backwards compatibility for the latest web language version.
- Numerous tweaks for improving readability in the browser.
- Many CSS rules that promote uniformity across browsers in tables, form elements, media tags.
- Helper classes to hide page elements from both screenreaders and browsers (`.hidden`) or just browsers (`.visuallyhidden`).

The fluid grid layout source code integrates one of the HTML5 Boilerplate methods throughout, but notably right up front, as a replacement for the standard technique for using conditional comments. Rather than include a range of style corrections, the fluid grid layout uses conditional comments to set up a series of conditional classes, such as `.ie6`, `.ie7`, and `.oldie`, right in the opening <html> tag. This method allows designers to create targeted CSS rules within their standard style sheets, like this:

```
.ie6 aside { width: 120px; } //standard aside width 123px;
```

All in all, the fluid grid layout helper files make it far easier for the modern web designer to work efficiently and effectively.

Creating AP Elements with Dreamweaver

Dreamweaver enables you to drag out absolutely positioned <div> tags, also known as AP elements, creatively and precisely—and without coding. You can drag out an AP element, placing and sizing it by eye, or choose to do it by the numbers—it's up to you. Moreover, you can combine the methods, quickly eyeballing and roughing out an AP element layout and then aligning the edges precisely. For web design that approaches conventional page layout, Dreamweaver even includes rulers and a grid to which you can snap your AP elements. Creating AP elements in Dreamweaver can be handled in one of three ways:

- You can drag out an AP element after clicking the Draw AP Div button on the Insert panel.
- You can add an AP element in a predetermined size by choosing Insert ➪ Layout Objects ➪ AP Div.
- You can create an AP element with mathematical precision through the CSS Styles panel.

The first two methods are quite intuitive and are explained in the following section. The CSS Styles panel method is examined later.

Inserting an AP element object

When you want to draw out your AP element quickly, use the object approach. If you come from a traditional page-designer background and are accustomed to using a program such as QuarkXPress or InDesign, you're already familiar with drawing out frames or text boxes with the click-and-drag technique. Dreamweaver uses the same method for placing and sizing new AP element objects. To draw out an AP element as an object, follow these steps:

1. From the Layout category of the Insert panel, click the Draw AP Div button. Your pointer becomes a crosshairs cursor. (If you decide not to draw out an AP element, you can press Esc at this point or just click once without dragging to abort the process.)
2. Click anywhere in your document to position the AP element and drag out a rectangle. Release the mouse button when you have an approximate size and shape that is satisfactory (see Figure 10-13).

After you've dragged out your AP element, notice several changes to the screen. First, the AP element now has a small box on the outside of the upper-left corner. This box, shown in Figure 10-14, is the Selection handle, which you can use to move an existing AP element around the web page. When you click the selection handle, eight resize handles appear around the perimeter of the AP element.

FIGURE 10-13

After selecting the Draw AP Div object in the Insert panel (Layout category), the pointer becomes crosshairs when you are working on the page. Click and drag to create the AP element.

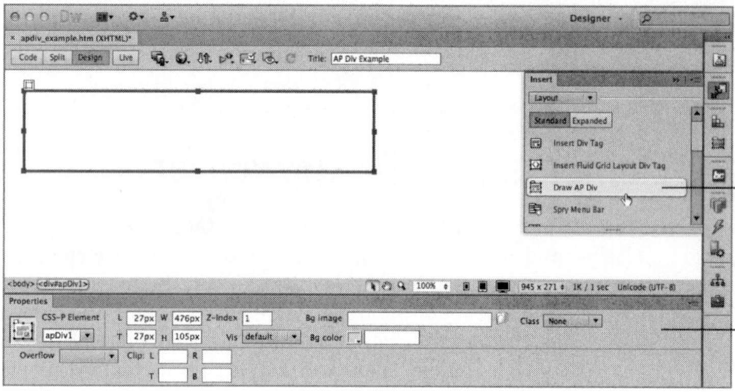

FIGURE 10-14

After an AP element is created, you can move it by dragging the selection handle and size it with the resize handles.

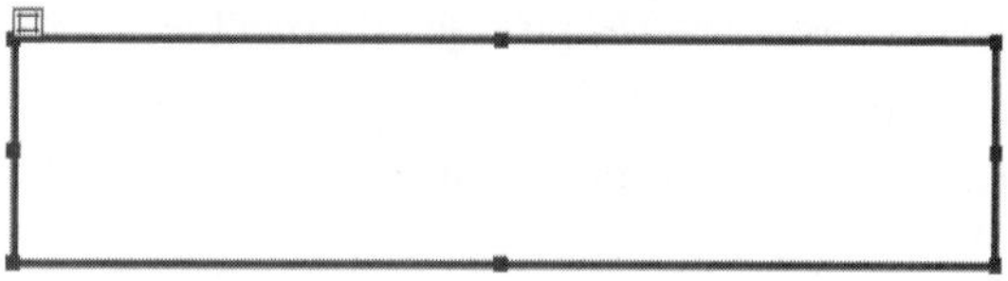

Another subtle but important addition to the screen is the AP element icon. Like the other Invisible Element icons, the AP element icon (when enabled in Preferences) can be cut, copied, pasted, and repositioned. When you move the AP element icon, however, its corresponding AP element does not move—you are actually only moving the code for the AP element to a different place in the HTML source. Generally, the location of the actual AP element code in the HTML is immaterial—however, you may want to locate your AP element source in a specific area to be appropriately placed for accessibility purposes. Dragging and positioning AP element icons one after another is a quick way to achieve this task.

Using the Insert ➪ Layout Objects ➪ AP Div option

The second method for creating an AP element is to use the menus. Instead of selecting an object from the Insert panel, choose Insert ➪ Layout Objects ➪ AP Div. Unlike the click-and-drag method, inserting an AP element through the menu automatically creates an AP element in the upper-left corner; the default size is 200 pixels wide by 115 pixels high.

Although the AP element is by default positioned in the upper-left corner of the Document window, it does not have any coordinates listed in the Property inspector. The position coordinates are added when you drag the AP element into a new position. If you repeatedly add new AP elements through the menus without moving them to new positions, each AP element stacks directly on top of the previous one, with no offset.

> **CAUTION**
> It's important to assign a specific position (left and top) to every AP element. Otherwise, the browser displays all AP elements directly on top of one another. To give an AP element measurements, after you've inserted it through the menu, be sure to drag the AP element, even slightly, or manually type coordinates in the Property inspector.

Setting default characteristics of an AP element

You can designate the default size—as well as other features—of the inserted AP element with Insert ➪ Layout Objects ➪ AP Div. Choose Edit ➪ Preferences (Dreamweaver ➪ Preferences) or use the keyboard shortcut Ctrl+U (Command+U) to open the Preferences dialog box. Select the AP Elements category. The AP Elements Preferences category (see Figure 10-15) helps you set the AP element attributes described in Table 10-1.

FIGURE 10-15

If you're building AP elements to a certain specification, use the AP Elements Preferences category to designate your options.

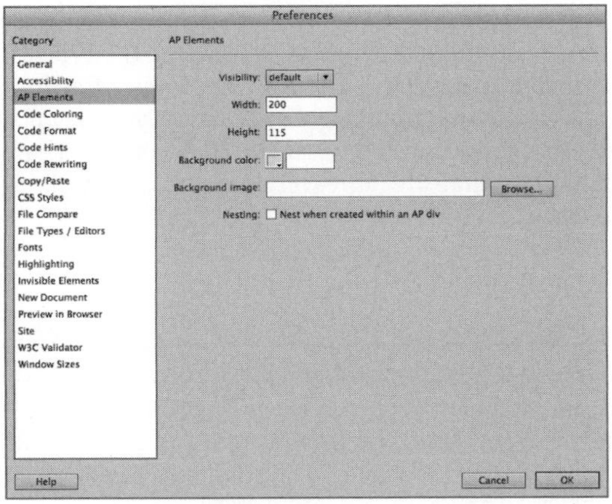

TABLE 10-1 AP Elements Preferences

AP Element Attribute	Description
Visibility	Determines the initial state of visibility for an AP element. The options are Default, Inherit, Visible, and Hidden.
Width	Sets the width of the AP element in the measurement system of your choice. The default is 200 pixels.

Continues

TABLE 10-1 *(continued)*

AP Element Attribute	Description
Height	Sets the height of the AP element in the measurement system of your choice. The default is 115 pixels.
Background Color	Sets a color for the AP element background. Select the color from the color palette of web-safe colors.
Background Image	Sets an image for the AP element background. In the text box, enter the path to the graphics file or click the Browse button to locate the file.
Nesting	If you want to nest AP elements when one AP element is placed in the other automatically, check the Nest When Created Within An AP Div checkbox.

Choosing relative instead of absolute positioning

In many cases, absolute positioning uses the top-left corner of the web page—the position at which the <body> tag begins—as the point of origin for positioning the AP elements. You can also specify measurements relative to other objects, such as <divs>. Dreamweaver offers several methods to accomplish relative positioning.

Using the Relative attribute

In the first method for handling relative positioning, you select Relative as the Type attribute in the Style Sheet Positioning category. Relative positioning does not force a fixed position; instead, the positioning is guided by the HTML tags around it. For example, you may place a list of some items within a <div> tag and set the positioning relative to the table. You can see the effect of this sequence in Figure 10-16. Notice that Dreamweaver does not display sizing handles or a selection handle for relative AP elements.

FIGURE 10-16

The selected AP element is positioned relative to the bottom of the surrounding <div> tag.

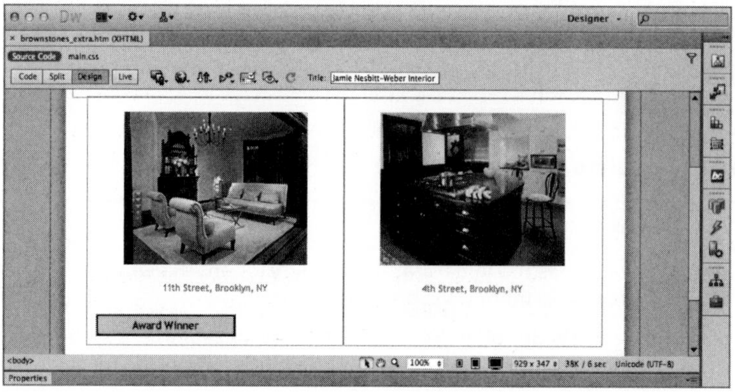

Relative attributes can be useful, particularly if you want to place the positioned objects within free-flowing HTML. Free-flowing HTML repositions itself based on the size of the browser. When you're using this technique, remember to place your relative AP elements within AP elements. Otherwise, when the end user resizes the browser, the relative AP elements position themselves relative to the browser and not to the AP elements. This situation can produce messy results—use relative positioning with caution when mixed with absolute AP elements.

Using nested AP elements

The second technique for positioning AP elements relatively uses nested AP elements. After you nest one AP element inside another, the inner AP element uses the upper-left corner of the outer AP element as its orientation point. One approach for creating a nested AP element is to position your cursor in the outer AP element and press Alt (Option) after you start to drag out your AP element. For more details about nesting layers, refer to the section "Nesting with the AP Elements panel" later in this chapter.

Modifying an AP Element

Dreamweaver helps you deftly alter AP elements after you have created them. Because of the complexity of managing AP elements, Dreamweaver offers a tool in addition to the usual Property inspector: the AP Elements panel. This tool enables you to select any of the AP elements on the current page quickly, change AP element relationships, modify their visibility, and adjust their stacking order. You can also alter the visibility and stacking order of a selected AP element in the Property inspector, along with many other attributes. Before any modifications can be accomplished, however, you have to select the AP element.

Selecting an AP element

You can choose from several methods to select an AP element for alteration (see Figure 10-17). The selection method you choose generally depends on the complexity of your page layout:

- When you have only a few AP elements that are not overlapping, just click the selection handle of an AP element to select it.
- When you have AP elements placed in specific places in the HTML code (for example, an AP element embedded in a table using relative positioning), click the AP Element icon.
- When you have many overlapping AP elements that are being addressed by one or more JavaScript functions, use the AP Elements panel to choose an AP element by ID.
- When you're working with invisible AP elements, click the `<div>` (or `<span>`) tag in the Tag Selector to reveal the outline of the AP element.

Resizing an AP element

To resize an AP element, position the pointer over one of the eight resize handles surrounding the selected AP element. When over the handles, the pointer changes shape to a two- or four-headed arrow. Now click and drag the AP element to a new size and shape.

10

You can also use the arrow keys to resize your AP element with more precision. The following keyboard shortcuts change the width and height dimensions while the AP element remains anchored by the upper-left corner:

- When the AP element is selected, press Ctrl+arrow (Command+arrow) to expand or contract the AP element by 1 pixel.
- Press Ctrl+Shift+arrow (Command+Shift+arrow) to increase or decrease the selected AP element by 10 pixels.

FIGURE 10-17

There are a number of different methods for selecting an AP element to modify.

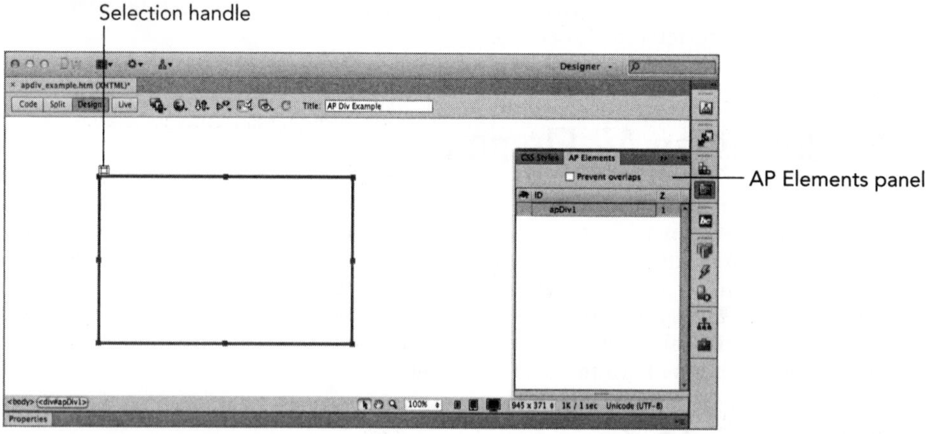

> **TIP**
>
> You can quickly preview the position of an AP element on a web page without leaving Dreamweaver in a couple of ways. One technique is to switch to Live View. Another method would be to deselect the View ➪ Visual Aids ➪ AP Element Borders option. This leaves the AP element outline displayed only when the AP element is selected; otherwise, it is not shown.

Moving an AP element

The easiest way to reposition an AP element is to drag the selection handle. If you don't see the handle on an AP element, click anywhere in the AP element. You can drag the AP element anywhere on the screen—or off the bottom or right side of the screen. To move the AP element off the left side or top of the screen, enter a negative value in the left and top (L and T) text boxes of the CSS-P Property inspector; whenever an AP element is selected, the CSS-P Property inspector is available.

TIP

To hide the AP element completely, match the negative value with the width or height of the AP element. For example, if your AP element is 220 pixels wide and you want to position it off-screen to the left (so that the AP element can slide onto the page at the click of a mouse), set the Left position at -220 pixels.

As with resizing AP elements, you can also use the arrow keys to move the AP element more precisely:

- Press any arrow key to move the selected AP element 1 pixel in any direction.
- Use Shift+arrow to move the selected AP element by 10 pixels.

Using the CSS-P Property inspector

You can modify almost all the CSS-P attributes for your AP element right from the CSS-P Property inspector, shown in Figure 10-18. Certain attributes, such as width, height, and background image and color are self-explanatory or recognizable from other objects. Other AP elements-only attributes, such as visibility and inheritance, require further explanation. Table 10-2 describes all the CSS-P properties, and the following sections discuss the features unique to AP elements.

FIGURE 10-18

The CSS-P Property inspector makes it easy to move, resize, hide, and manipulate all the visual elements of an AP element.

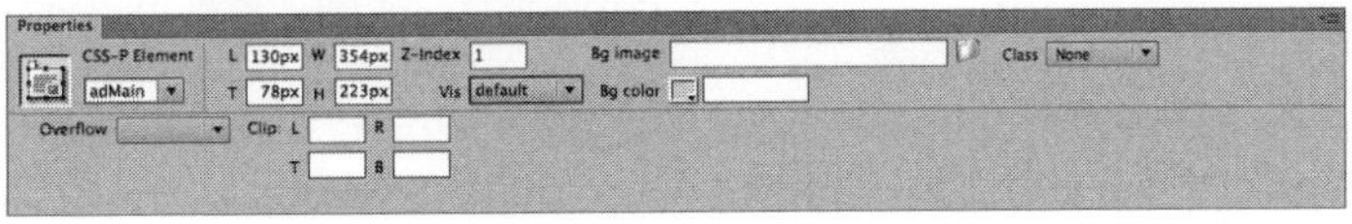

TABLE 10-2 CSS-P Property Inspector Options

CSS-P Attribute	Possible Values	Description
BgColor	Any hexadecimal or valid color name	Background color for the AP element.
BgImage	Any valid graphic file	Background image for the AP element.
Clip (Top, Bottom, Left, Right)	Any positive integer	Measurements for the displayable region of the AP element. If the values are not specified, the entire AP element is visible.

Continues

TABLE 10-2 *(continued)*

CSS-P Attribute	Possible Values	Description
H (Height)	Any positive integer measurement in pixels, centimeters, millimeters, inches, points, percentage, ems, or picas	Vertical measurement of the AP element.
ID	A unique ID without spaces or special characters	A label for the AP element so that it can be addressed by style sheets or JavaScript functions.
L (Left)	Any integer measurement in pixels, centimeters, millimeters, inches, points, percentage, ems, or picas	Distance measured from the origin point on the left.
Overflow	`visible`, `scroll`, `hidden`, or `auto`	An indication of how text or images larger than the AP element should be handled.
T (Top)	Any integer measurement in pixels, centimeters, millimeters, inches, points, percentage, ems, or picas	The distance measured from the origin point on the top.
Tag	span or div	Type of HTML tag to use for the AP element.
Vis (Visibility)	default, inherit, visible, or hidden	An indication of whether an AP element is displayed. If visibility is set to inherit, the AP element takes on the characteristic of the parent AP element.
W (Width)	Any positive integer measurement in pixels, centimeters, millimeters, inches, points, percentage, ems, or picas	The horizontal measurement of the AP element.
Z-Index	Any integer	Stacking order of the AP element relative to other AP elements on the web page. Higher numbers are closer to the top.

ID

IDs are important when working with AP elements. So you can refer to them properly for both CSS and JavaScript purposes, each AP element must have a unique ID attribute, unique among the AP elements and unique among every other object on the web page. Dreamweaver automatically names each AP element as it is created in sequence: apDiv1, apDiv2, and so forth. You can enter an ID that is easier for you to remember by replacing the provided ID in the text box on the far left of the Property inspector.

Dreamweaver TECHNIQUE

Inserting an AP Element

In this Technique, you add a Dreamweaver AP element to a CSS layout. The AP element is absolutely positioned within a relatively positioned <div> tag so that if the centered layout moves, the AP element stays in the proper place.

1. From the 10_Div folder, open `apDiv_start.htm`.
2. Place your cursor in the header <div>.
3. From the Insert panel's Layout category, click Draw AP Div.
4. Begin dragging out a rectangle on the right side of the header div and, while dragging, press and hold Alt (Option). When your rectangle is approximately 150 pixels wide by 50 pixels high, release the mouse and then Alt (Option). By pressing Alt (Option) while drawing the AP element, Dreamweaver puts the code for the AP element at the cursor position, inside the header <div>, effectively nesting the AP element.

CAUTION

As of this writing, there is a bug in the Windows implementation for nesting AP <div> tags: Pressing the Alt key while drawing an AP div does not insert a <div> tag and instead displays the Code Navigator. To work around this issue, first open Preferences and switch to the AP Element category. Then, enable the Nesting option. When the Nesting option is enabled, you won't need to press Alt while drawing an AP div to nest it. As long as your cursor is in another <div> tag, such as the header, it will nest automatically.

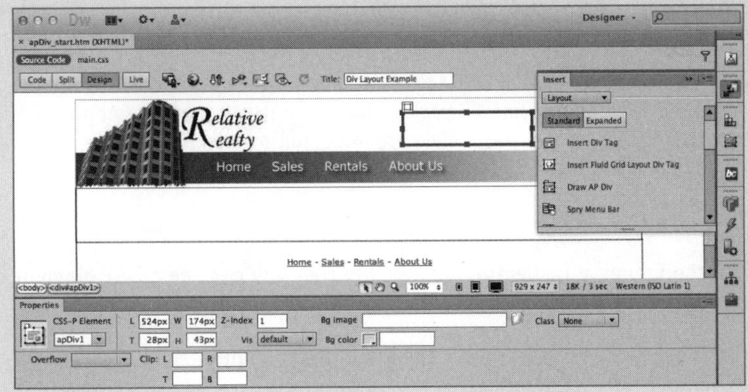

5. With your cursor inside the newly drawn AP element, switch to the Insert panel's Common category and click Images: Image.
6. In the Select Image Source dialog box, navigate to the images folder and select `new_properties.jpg`. Note that the Property inspector shows the image's dimensions as 166 × 55 pixels.
7. Select the AP element handle, and in its Property inspector, change the Width value to `166px` and Height to `55px`.

Continues

continued

8. Precisely position the AP element by setting the Left value to `533px` and Top to `50px`.
9. The last step is to rename the AP element and its accompanying style from the generic apDiv1 to something more precise. In the Property inspector's Name field, enter `new_properties`.

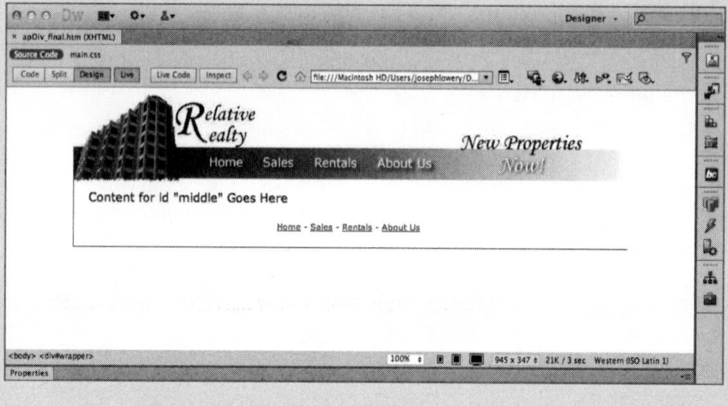

10. Save your page.

If you test your page by previewing in the browser, you'll notice that the absolutely positioned AP element stays in the correct place even if the window is resized.

Tag attribute

The Tag drop-down list contains the HTML tags that can be associated with the AP element. By default, the positioned AP element has `<div>` as the tag, but you can also choose `<span>`. As previously noted, the `<div>` and `<span>` tags are endorsed by the World Wide Web Consortium group as part of its CSS standards.

Visibility

Visibility (`Vis` in the Property inspector) defines whether you can see an AP element on a web page. Four values are available:

- **Default:** Enables the browser to set the visibility attribute. Most browsers use the `inherit` value as their default.
- **Inherit:** Sets the visibility to the same value as that of the parent positioned element, which enables a series of elements to be hidden or made visible by changing only one parent element.
- **Visible:** Causes the AP element and all its contents to be displayed.
- **Hidden:** Makes the current AP element and all its contents invisible.

Remember the following when you're specifying visibility:

- Whether or not you can see an AP element, remember that the AP element is still part of the page and demands some of the page-loading time. Hiding an AP element does not affect the layout of the page, and invisible graphics take just as long to download as visible graphics.
- When you are defining the visibility of a positioned object or AP element, do not use `default` as the visibility value. A designer does not necessarily know whether the site's end user has set the default visibility to `visible` or `hidden`. Designing an effective web page can be difficult without this knowledge. The common browser default is for visibility to be inherited, if not specifically shown or hidden.

Overflow

Typically, an AP element expands to fit the text or graphics inserted into it. You can, however, restrict the size of an AP element by changing the height and width values in the Property inspector. What happens when you define an AP element to be too small for an image, or when an amount of text depends on the setting of the AP element's `overflow` attribute? AP elements (the `<div>` and `<span>` tags) support four different overflow settings:

- **Visible (Default):** All the overflowing text or image is displayed, and the height and width settings established for the AP element are ignored. It's possible for overflowing content to overlap other content on the page.
- **Hidden:** The portion of the text or graphic that overflows the dimensions is not visible.
- **Scroll:** Horizontal and vertical scroll bars are added to the AP element regardless of the content size or amount, and regardless of the AP element's measurements.
- **Auto:** When the content of the AP element exceeds the width and/or height values, horizontal and vertical scroll bars appear.

Most modern browsers render the `overflow` attribute correctly, as shown in Figure 10-19.

<div> Versus <span>

The major difference between `<div>` and `<span>` is that the `<div>` is a block-level element and the `<span>` is inline.

When you are positioning relatively (the elements are in the normal flow of the document), a `<div>` always causes the next element to appear on a new line. Block-level elements, such as `<h1>` and `<p>`, always create a new line unless the display property is set to inline using CSS.

The reverse is true of `<span>` tags. The `<span>` tag is an inline element and displays just like an image or link, without altering the text around it.

Generally, `<div>` tags are used for block-level elements that require positioning, and `<span>` tags are more commonly used to apply inline formatting over positioning.

FIGURE 10-19

When your contents are larger than the dimensions of your AP element, you can regulate the results with the overflow attribute.

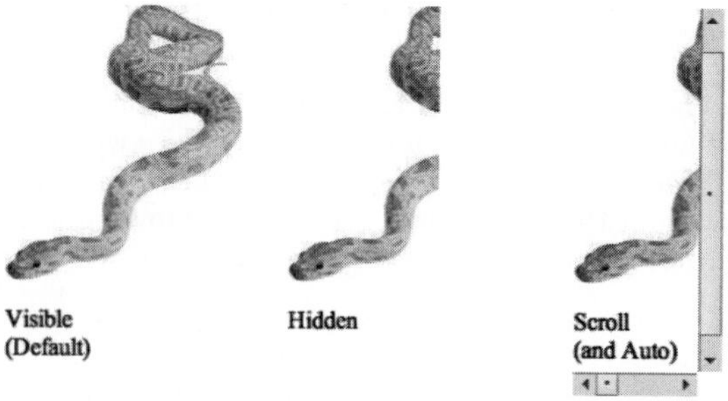

Clipping

If you're familiar with the process of cropping an image, you'll quickly grasp the concept of clipping AP elements. Just as desktop publishing software hides, but doesn't delete, the portion of the picture outside the crop marks, AP elements can mask the area outside the clipping region defined by the Left, Top, Right, and Bottom values in the Clip section of the CSS-P Property inspector.

All clipping values are measured from the upper-left corner of the AP element. You can use any CSS standard measurement system such as pixels (the default) or ems.

The current implementation of CSS supports only rectangular clipping. When you look at the code for a clipped AP element, you see the values you inserted in the CSS-P Property inspector in parentheses following the `clip` attribute, with the `rect` (for rectangular) keyword, as follows:

```
<div id="apDiv1" style="position:absolute; left:54px; top:24px; ;
width:400px; height:115px; z-index:1; visibility:inherit; ;
clip:rect(10px 100px 100px 10px)">
```

Generally, you specify values for all four criteria: Left, Top, Right, and Bottom. You can also leave the Left and Top values empty or use the keyword `auto`—which causes the Left and Top values to be set at the origin point: 0,0. If you leave any of the clipping values blank, the blank attributes are set to `auto`.

Z-index

One of an AP element's most powerful features is its capability to appear above or below other AP elements. You can change this order, known as the z-index, dynamically. Whenever a new AP element is added, Dreamweaver automatically increments the z-index—AP elements with higher z-index values are positioned above AP elements with lower z-index values. The z-index can be adjusted manually in either the CSS-P Property inspector or the AP Elements panel. The z-index must be an integer, either negative or positive.

TIP

Although some web designers use high values for the z-index, such as 3,000, the z-index is completely relative. The only reason to increase a z-index to an extremely high number is to ensure that a particular AP element remains on top.

Certain types of objects—including Java applets, plugins, and ActiveX controls—ignore the z-index setting when included in an AP element and appear as the uppermost AP element. However, certain plugin controls—most notably Flash—can be made to respect the z-index. If you need HTML content on top of active content, you can always hide the AP element containing the ActiveX control when necessary.

CAUTION

Working with the `above` and `below` attributes can be confusing. Notice that they determine which AP element is to appear on top of or underneath the current AP element, and not which AP element the present AP element is above or below.

Background image or color

Inserting a background image or color with the CSS-P Property inspector works like changing the background image or color for a table (as explained in Chapter 12). To insert an image, enter the path to the file in the Bg Image text box or select the folder icon to locate the image file on your system or network. If the AP element is larger than the image, the image is tiled, just as it would be in the background of a web page or table, unless you modify the CSS background property for the element.

To give an AP element a background color, enter the color name (in either its hexadecimal or its nominal form) in the Bg Color text box. You can also select the color box to pick your color from the color palette.

The AP Elements panel

Dreamweaver offers another tool to help manage the AP elements in your web page: the AP Elements panel. Although this tool doesn't display as many properties about each element as the Property inspector, the AP Elements panel gives you a good overview of all the AP elements on your page. It also provides a quick method of selecting an AP element—even when it's off-screen—and enables you to change the z-index and the nesting order.

The AP Elements panel, shown in Figure 10-20, can be opened either through the Window menu (Window ➪ AP Elements) or by pressing the keyboard shortcut F2.

Modifying properties with the AP Elements panel

The AP Elements panel lists the visibility, name, and z-index settings for each AP element. You can modify all these properties directly through the AP Elements panel.

FIGURE 10-20

Use the AP Elements panel to quickly select—or alter the visibility or relationships of—all the AP elements on your page.

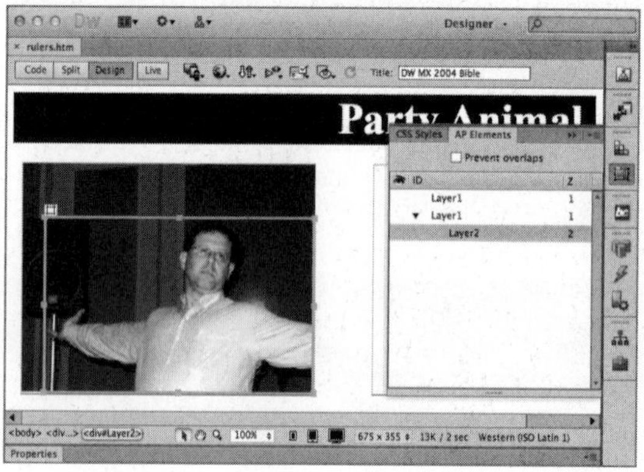

The visibility of a particular AP element is noted by the eye symbol in the first column of the inspector. Clicking the eye symbol cycles you through three different visibility states:

- **Eye closed:** Indicates that the AP element is hidden
- **Eye open:** Indicates that the AP element is visible
- **No eye:** Indicates that the visibility attribute is set to the default (which, for both Navigator and Internet Explorer, means inherit)

TIP

To change all your AP elements to a single state simultaneously, click the eye symbol in the column header. Unlike the individual eyes in front of each AP element name, the overall eye toggles between open and shut.

You can also change an AP element's name (in the second column of the AP Elements panel). Just double-click the current AP element name in the inspector; the name is highlighted. Type in the new name and press Enter (Return) to complete the change.

You can alter the z-index (stacking order) in the third column in the same manner. Double-click the z-index value, and then type in the new value and press Enter (Return). You can enter any positive or negative integer.

Nesting with the AP Elements panel

Another task managed by the AP Elements panel is nesting or unnesting AP elements. This process is also referred to as creating parent-child AP elements. To nest one AP element inside another through the AP Elements panel, follow these steps:

1. Choose Window ➪ AP Elements or press F2 to open the AP Elements panel.
2. Press the Ctrl (Command) key, click the name of the AP element to be nested (the child), and drag it on top of the other AP element (the parent).

3. When you see a rectangle around the parent AP element's name, release the mouse. The child AP element is indented underneath the parent AP element, and the parent AP element has a minus sign (a downward-pointing triangle on the Mac) attached to the front of its name.
4. To hide the child AP element from view, click the minus sign (a downward-pointing triangle on the Mac) in front of the parent AP element's name. After the child AP element is hidden, the minus sign turns into a plus sign (a right-pointing triangle on the Mac).
5. To reveal the child AP element, click the plus sign (a right-pointing triangle on the Mac).
6. To undo a nested AP element, select the child AP element and drag it to a new position in the AP Elements panel.

You can use the nesting features of the AP Elements panel to hide many AP elements quickly. If the visibility of all child AP elements is set to the default—with no eye displayed—then by hiding the parent AP element, you cause all the child AP elements to inherit that visibility setting and also disappear from view.

TIP

You can also delete an AP element from the AP Elements panel. Just highlight the AP element to be removed and press the Delete key. Dreamweaver also enables you to delete nested AP elements as a group by selecting the parent AP element and pressing Delete. To remove a parent AP element but keep all children, use the Tag Selector. Select the parent tag, right-click (Control+click), and then choose Remove Tag.

Aligning AP elements

With the capability to position AP elements anywhere on a page comes additional responsibility and potential problems. In anything that involves animation, correct alignment of moving parts is crucial. As you begin to set up your AP elements, their exact placement and alignment become critical. Dreamweaver includes two tools to simplify layered web page design: the ruler and the grid.

Rulers and grids are familiar concepts in traditional desktop publishing. Dreamweaver's ruler shows the x-axis and y-axis in pixels, inches, or centimeters along the outer edge of the Document window. The grid crisscrosses the page with lines to support a visual guideline when you're placing objects. You can even enable a snap-to-grid feature to ensure easy, absolute alignment.

Using the ruler

With traditional web design, "eyeballing it" was the only option available for web page layout. The absolute positioning capability of AP elements remedied this deficiency. Now online designers have a more precise and familiar system of alignment: the ruler. Dreamweaver's ruler can be displayed in several different measurement units and with your choice of origin point.

To toggle the ruler in Dreamweaver, choose View ➪ Rulers ➪ Show or use the keyboard shortcut Ctrl+Alt+R (Command+Option+R). Horizontal and vertical rulers appear along the top and the left sides of the Document window, as shown in Figure 10-21. As you move the pointer, a light-gray line indicates the position on both rulers.

FIGURE 10-21

Use the horizontal and vertical rulers to assist your AP element placement and overall web page layout.

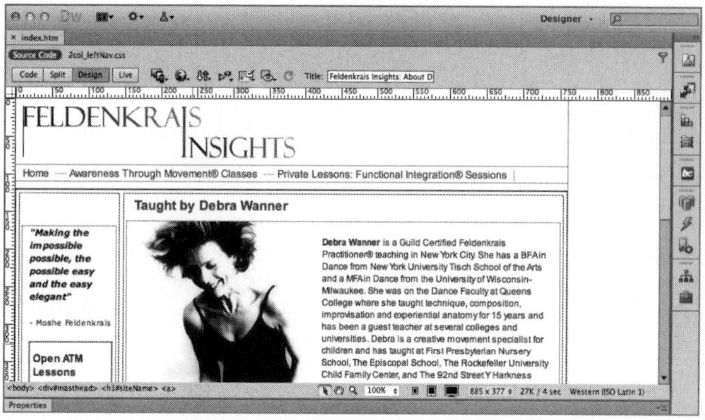

By default, the ruler uses pixels as its measurement system. You can change the default by choosing View ➪ Rulers and selecting either inches or centimeters.

Dreamweaver also enables you to move the ruler origin to a new position. Normally, the upper-left corner of the page acts as the origin point for the ruler. On some occasions, it's helpful to start the measurement at a different location—at the bottom-right edge of an advertisement, for example. To move the origin point, select the intersection of the horizontal and vertical rulers and drag the crosshairs to a new location. When you release the mouse button, both rulers are adjusted to show negative values above and to the right of the new origin point. To return the origin point to its default setting, choose View ➪ Rulers ➪ Reset Origin, or you can simply double-click the intersection of the rulers.

TIP

You can access a ruler context menu by right-clicking (Control+clicking) the ruler itself. The context menu enables you to change the system of measurement, reset the origin point, or hide the rulers.

Working with guides

With the advent of CSS layouts, web designers found themselves needing a toolset more traditionally associated with graphic programs: guides. A guide is a single, thin, positionable line used at design time to align elements on a page. Guides are either horizontal or vertical and stretch from one edge of the browser window to the other.

Dreamweaver guides are wonderfully powerful and incorporate standard features found in graphics programs like Photoshop and Fireworks, as well as some unique web-centric options. Guides can be shown or hidden, set precisely, or varied in color. You can snap guides to the grid and/or objects; you can even do the reverse and have objects snap to guides. Dreamweaver designers will find guides a welcome addition to their working toolbox.

Before you can display a guide, you have to meet two conditions: The View ➪ Guides ➪ Show Guides option must be enabled along with View ➪ Rulers ➪ Show Rulers. The standard method for deploying a guide in Dreamweaver is the same as in those other programs: with rulers displayed, the user drags a guide onto the document (see Figure 10-22). Horizontal guides are dragged from the ruler on the top edge, and vertical guides are dragged from the left edge ruler. You can have as many guides on your page as you want.

Positioning and removing guides

To place a guide on the page, follow these steps:

1. Choose View ➪ Rulers ➪ Show to toggle the rulers into view.
2. Select View ➪ Guides ➪ Show Guides so that the option is checked.
3. To place a horizontal guide on the page, drag a guide from the ruler at the top of the page.
4. To place a vertical guide on the page, drag a guide from the ruler at the left of the page.

Once positioned, guides can be moved at any time. You can visually position guides by dragging them to a new location on the page; when your cursor is over the guide, you'll see a tooltip with the precise horizontal or vertical coordinate of the guide in pixels from the top or left of the page, respectively.

To remove a single guide, drag it back into the horizontal or vertical ruler. You can remove all guides on the page by selecting View ➪ Guides ➪ Clear Guides. If you just want to hide the guides, choose View ➪ Guides ➪ Show Guides again or use the keyboard shortcut Ctrl+; (Command+;).

FIGURE 10-22

Guides work well in a CSS-P layout design environment.

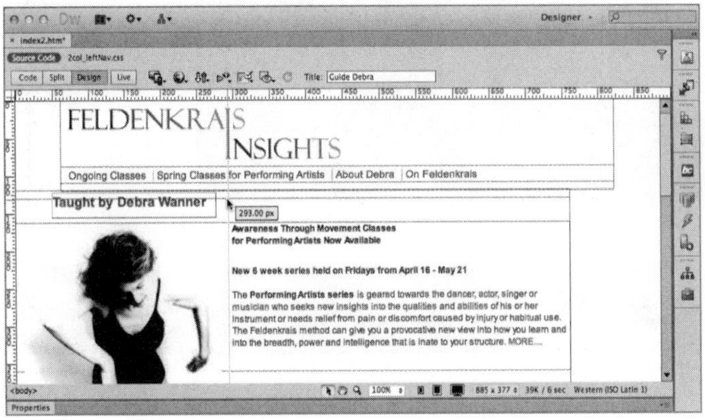

Displaying guide measurements

One of the slicker guide features implemented in Dreamweaver is the display of distance measurement. If you have a single horizontal or vertical guide onscreen and press Ctrl (Command),

Dreamweaver will show you the distance from the guide to the window's edge in your cursor area. Place your cursor between two guides of the same type (either horizontal or vertical) and press Ctrl (Command), and you'll see the distance that separates them, as shown in Figure 10-23.

Locking and snapping guides

Dreamweaver gives you complete control over guides and positionable page elements. You can lock your guides so that they are not accidentally moved when repositioning elements. You can also snap your elements to your guides or guides to your elements—or both. Here's how it's all done:

- Prevent your guides from being moved by choosing View ➪ Guides ➪ Lock Guides or using the keyboard shortcut, Ctrl+Alt+; (Command+Option+;).
- Align your layout blocks to existing guides by enabling View ➪ Guides ➪ Snap Guides or using the keyboard shortcut, Ctrl+Shift+; (Command+Shift+;).
- Snap guides to the edges of layout blocks by selecting View ➪ Guides ➪ Guides Snap to Elements or using the keyboard shortcut, Ctrl+Shift+/ (Command+Shift+/).

FIGURE 10-23

Bring up the distance between two guides in pixels by holding Ctrl on Windows or Command on a Mac.

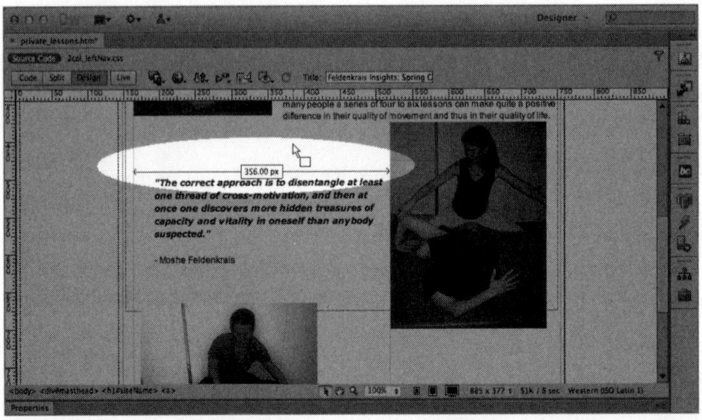

TIP

Guides are retained when you save the page and restored when the page is re-opened.

Precise guide placement

Guides can be positioned precisely as well as by dragging. To set a guide's horizontal or vertical placement to a specific value, follow these steps:

1. Double-click the guide you want to move.
2. When the Move Guide dialog box opens, enter the desired position in the Location field.

3. Select the measurement system (pixels, centimeters, inches, or percentages) from the list.

   To use the percentage measurement, enter a value between 0.00 and 100.00; Dreamweaver will reposition the guide according to the width or height of your Document window.

4. Click OK.

Editing guide settings

By default, the guides are colored a bright green, and the distance indicators are a dark blue. If these colors don't contrast enough with your layout to be seen clearly, you can adjust the colors through the Edit Guides dialog box. The Edit Guides dialog box also provides all-in-place access to basic guide controls: Show Guides, Snap To Guides, Lock Guides, Guides Snap To Elements, and Clear All (see Figure 10-24). To access the Edit Guides dialog box, choose View ➪ Guides ➪ Edit Guides.

FIGURE 10-24

Alter the color of your guides for maximum visibility.

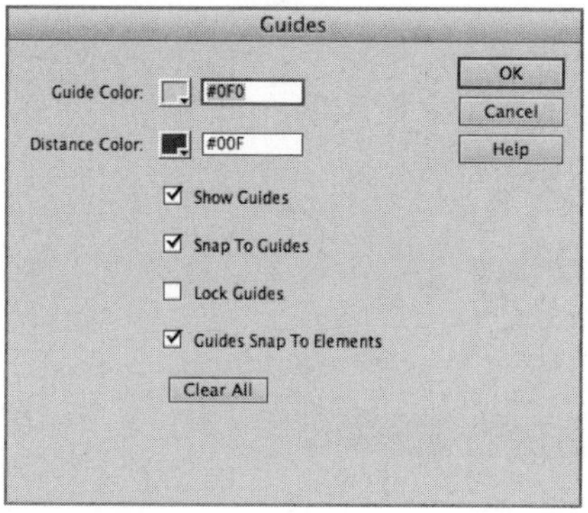

Showing the browser window fold

One application in the guide feature set unique to Dreamweaver is especially useful for web designers: showing the browser window fold. When a browser displays a web page, the portion initially visible is said to be "above the fold." The concept of a fold comes from the world of newspaper journalism where papers are divided into a top and bottom portion by the way they are folded. Dreamweaver can quickly display the fold of a browser window—that is, the viewable area—through guides.

Five of the most common browser window configurations are available through the Guides submenu:

- 640 × 480, Default
- 640 × 480, Maximized
- 800 × 600, Maximized
- 832 × 624, Maximized
- 1,024 × 768, Maximized

10

You'll recognize the dimensions from the Window Size selector on the Status bar. When you select any of these options from the View ➪ Guides menu, Dreamweaver inserts two guides—one horizontal and another vertical—to form the right and bottom edge of the browser window (see Figure 10-25). With these guides onscreen, designers can place their key content so that it will be visible immediately in the chosen screen resolution.

FIGURE 10-25

Make sure your most important content is above the fold with guides.

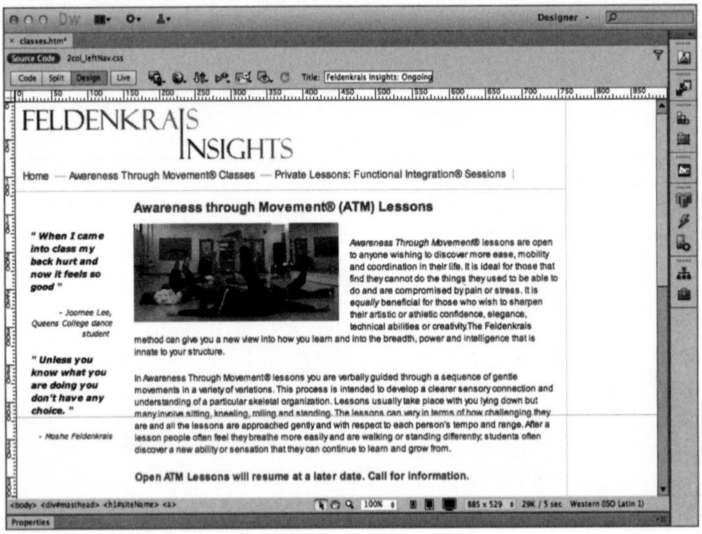

Aligning objects with the grid

Rulers and guides are generally good for positioning single objects, but a grid is extremely helpful when aligning one object to another. With Dreamweaver's grid facility, you can align elements visually or snap them to the grid. You can set many of the grid's other features, including grid spacing, color, and type.

To turn on the grid, choose View ➪ Grid ➪ Show or press Ctrl+Alt+G (Command+Option+G). By default, the grid is displayed with tan lines set at 50-pixel increments.

The snap-to-grid feature is enabled by choosing View ➪ Grid ➪ Snap To or with the keyboard shortcut Ctrl+Alt+Shift+G (Command+Option+Shift+G). When activated, snap-to-grid causes the upper-left corner of an AP element to be placed at the nearest grid intersection when the AP element is moved.

Like most of Dreamweaver's tools, you can customize the grid. To alter the grid settings, choose View ➪ Grid ➪ Settings, and the Grid Settings dialog box opens. In the Grid Settings dialog box, shown in Figure 10-26, you can change any of the settings shown in Table 10-3 (just click OK when you've finished adjusting the settings).

FIGURE 10-26

Dreamweaver's grid feature is extremely handy for aligning a series of objects.

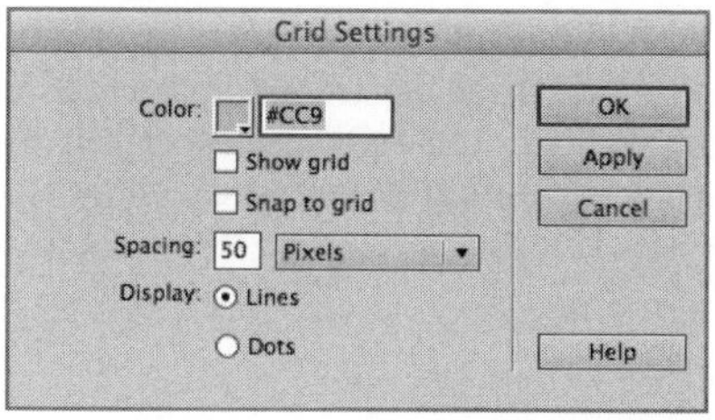

TABLE 10-3 Grid Settings Dialog Box Options

Grid Setting	Description
Color	Change the default color (tan) by selecting the color box (which brings up color palette) or by typing a new value in the text box.
Show Grid	Show or hide the grid with this checkbox toggle.
Snap To Grid	Toggle the checkbox to enable or disable the snap-to-grid feature.
Spacing	Adjust the distance between grid points by entering a numeric value in the text box.
Spacing Unit of Measure	Select pixels, inches, or centimeters from the Spacing drop-down list.
Display	Choose either solid lines or dots for the gridlines.

Adding elements to an AP element

After you have created and initially positioned your AP elements, you can begin to fill them with content. Inserting objects in an AP element is just like inserting objects in a web page. The same insertion methods are available to you:

- Position the cursor inside an AP element, choose Insert in the menu bar, and select an object to insert.
- With the cursor inside an AP element, select any object from the Insert panel. Note that you cannot select the Draw AP Div object.
- Drag an object from the Insert panel and drop it inside the AP element.

Forms and AP elements

When you're mixing forms and AP elements, follow only one rule: Always put the form completely inside the AP element. If you place the AP element within the form, all form elements after the AP element tags are ignored. With the form completely enclosed in the AP element, the form can safely be positioned anywhere on the page and all form elements still remain completely active.

Although this rule means that you can't split one form onto separate AP elements, you can set up multiple forms on multiple AP elements—and still have them all communicate to one final CGI or other program. This technique uses JavaScript to send the user-input values in the separate forms to hidden fields in the form with the Submit button. Suppose, for example, that you have three separate forms gathering information in three separate AP elements on a web page. Call them formA, formB, and formC on apDiv1, apDiv2, and apDiv3, respectively. When the Submit button in formC on layer3 is selected, a JavaScript function is first called by means of an `onClick` event in the button's `<input>` tag. The function, in part, looks like the following:

```
function gatherData() {
  document.formC.hidden1.value = document.formA.text1.value
  document.formC.hidden2.value = document.formB.text2.value
}
```

Notice how every value from the various forms is sent to a hidden field in formC, the form with the Submit button. Now, when the form is submitted, all the hidden information gathered from the various forms is submitted along with formC's own information.

NOTE

To make the code cross-browser compatible, you can use an initialization function that allows for the differences, or you can build the code into the `onClick` function. (For more information about building cross-browser-compatible code, see Chapter 30.)

Using the Tracing Image Feature with AP Elements

Page-layout artists are often confronted with webpage designs that have been comped in a graphics program. Dreamweaver's Tracing Image function enables you to use such images to guide the precise placement of graphics, text, tables, and forms in your web page, enabling you to match the original design as closely as possible.

To use a Tracing Image, the graphic must be saved in JPEG, GIF, or PNG format. After the Tracing Image has been placed in your page, it is viewable only in Dreamweaver—it will never appear in a browser. A placed Tracing Image hides any background color or background graphic in your web page. Preview your page in a browser or hide the Tracing Image to view your page without it.

CAUTION

If you're concerned about your page validating, be sure to remove the Tracing Image after you've completed the page. The Tracing Image uses a number of attributes, such as `tracingsrc` and `tracingopacity`, none of which validate, inside the `<body>` tag.

Adding the Tracing Image to your page

To add a Tracing Image to your Dreamweaver page, choose View ➪ Tracing Image ➪ Load. This brings up a Select Image Source dialog box that enables you to select the graphic to use as a Tracing Image.

Clicking Select brings up the Page Properties dialog box, shown in Figure 10-27, in which you can specify the opacity of the Tracing Image in a range from Transparent (0%) to Opaque (100%). You can change the Tracing Image or its transparency at any point by choosing Modify ➪ Page Properties to bring up the Page Properties dialog box. You can toggle between hiding and showing the Tracing Image by choosing View ➪ Tracing Image ➪ Show. You can also enter the Tracing Image directly in the Page Properties dialog box by entering its path in the Tracing Image text box or by clicking the Browse button to locate the image.

NOTE

Even though the Browse dialog box for the Tracing Image enables you to choose from a data source, the image is not displayed on the page.

FIGURE 10-27

Setting the transparency of the Tracing Image to a setting such as 50 percent can help you differentiate between it and the content AP elements you are positioning.

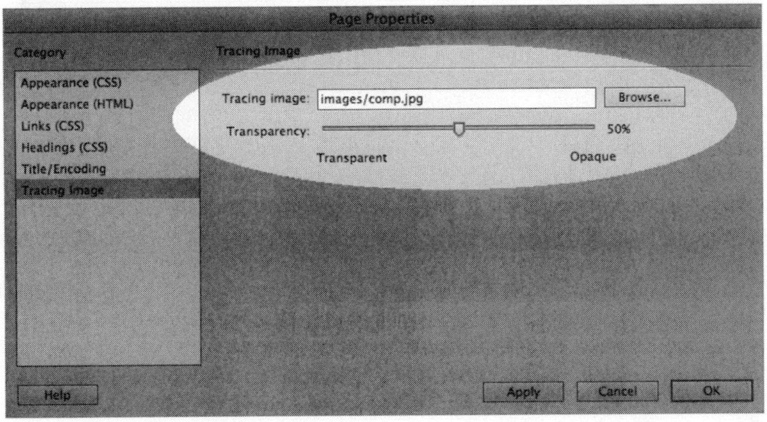

Moving the Tracing Image

The Tracing Image cannot be selected and moved the same way as other objects on your page. Instead, you must move the Tracing Image using menu commands. You have several options for adjusting the Tracing Image's position to better fit your design. First, you can align the Tracing Image with any object on your page by selecting the object and then choosing View ➪ Tracing Image ➪ Align with Selection. This procedure lines up the upper-left corner of the Tracing Image with the upper-left corner of the bounding box of the AP element you've selected.

To precisely or visually move the Tracing Image to a specific location, choose View ➪ Tracing Image ➪ Adjust Position. Enter the x and y coordinates into their respective boxes in the Adjust Tracing Image Position dialog box, as shown in Figure 10-28. For more hands-on positioning, click in the position fields and use the arrow keys to nudge the tracing AP element up, down, left, or right, one pixel at a time. Holding down the Shift key while pressing the arrow keys moves the Tracing Image in 5-pixel increments. Finally, you can return the Tracing Image to its default location of 0 pixels down from the top and 0 pixels in from the left by choosing View ➪ Tracing Image ➪ Reset Position.

FIGURE 10-28

Use the Adjust Tracing Image Position dialog box to precisely place your graphic template.

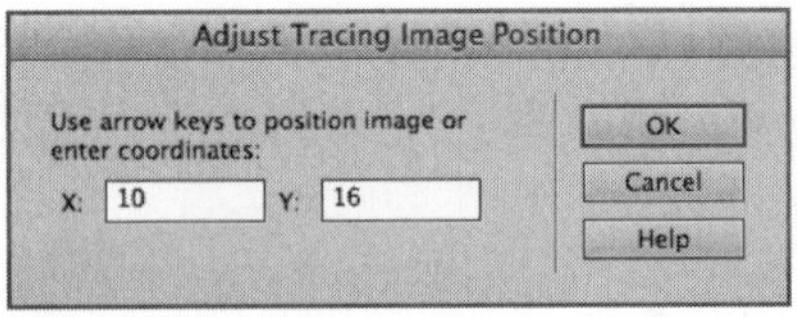

Activating AP Elements with Behaviors

Although absolute positioning is a major reason to use AP elements, you may have other motives for using this capability. All the properties of an AP element—the coordinates, size and shape, depth, visibility, and clipping—can be altered dynamically and interactively. Normally, dynamically resetting an AP element's properties entails some fairly daunting JavaScript programming. Now, with one of Dreamweaver's core features—behaviors—activating AP elements is possible for nonprogrammers as well.

If you want to learn more about behaviors, Chapter 11 describes Dreamweaver's rich behaviors feature.

Behaviors consist of two parts: the event and the action. In Dreamweaver, three standard actions are designed specifically for working with AP elements:

- **Drag AP Element:** Enables the user to move the AP element and get a response to that movement.
- **Set Text of Container:** Enables the interactive alteration of the content of any AP element to include any HTML, not just text.
- **Show-Hide Elements:** Controls the visibility of AP elements, either interactively or through some preprogrammed action on the page.

You can find detailed information about these actions in their respective sections in Chapter 11. The following sections outline how to use these behaviors to activate your AP elements.

Drag AP Element

For the web designer, positioning an AP element is easy: Click the selection handle and drag the AP element to a new location. For the readers of your pages, moving an AP element is next to impossible—unless you incorporate the Drag AP Element action into the page's design.

With the Drag AP Element action, you can set up interactive pages in which the user can rearrange elements of the design to achieve an effect or make a selection. The Drag AP Element action includes an option that enables your application to execute a JavaScript command if the user drops the AP element on a specific target. In the example shown in Figure 10-29, each pair of shoes is in its own AP element. When the user drops a pair in the bag, a one-line JavaScript command opens the desired catalog page and order form.

After you've created all your AP elements, you're ready to attach the behavior. Because Drag AP Element initializes the script to make the interaction possible, you should always associate this behavior with the `<body>` tag and the `onLoad` event. Follow these steps to use the Drag AP Element action and to designate the settings for the drag operation:

1. Choose the `<body>` tag from the Tag Selector in the status bar.
2. Choose Window ➪ Behaviors or press Shift+F4. The Behaviors panel opens.
3. Click the Add (+) button and choose Drag AP Element from the Add Action drop-down list.
4. In the Drag AP Element dialog box, select the AP element you want to make available for dragging.
5. To limit the movement of the dragged AP element, select Constrained from the Movement drop-down list. Enter the coordinates needed to specify the direction to which you want to limit the movement in the Up, Down, Left, and/or Right text boxes.
6. To establish a location for a target, enter coordinates in the Drop Target: Left and Top text boxes. You can fill these text boxes with the selected AP element's present location by clicking the Get Current Position button.
7. You can also set a snap-to area around the target's coordinates. When released in the target's location, the dragged AP element snaps to this area. Enter a pixel value in the Snap If Within text box.
8. Click the Advanced tab.
9. Designate the drag handle:
   - To enable the entire AP element to act as a drag handle, select Entire Element from the drop-down menu.
   - To limit the area to be used as a drag handle, select Area Within Element from the drop-down menu. Enter the Left and Top coordinates and the Width and Height dimensions in the appropriate text boxes.
10. To keep the AP element in its current depth and not bring it to the front, clear the checkbox for While Dragging: Bring Element To The Front. To change the stacking order of the AP element when it is released after dragging, select either Leave On Top or Restore Z-Index from the drop-down list.
11. To execute a JavaScript command when the AP element is dropped on the target, enter the code in the Call JavaScript text box. If you want the script to execute every time the AP element is dropped, enter the code in the When Dropped: Call JavaScript text box. If the code should execute only when the AP element is dropped on the target, make sure the Only If Snapped checkbox is selected.
12. To change the event that triggers the action (the default is `onLoad`), select an event from the drop-down list in the Events column.

FIGURE 10-29

On this interactive page, visitors can drop merchandise into the shopping bag; this feature is made possible with the Drag AP Element action.

Set Text of Container

You've seen how AP elements can dynamically move, and change their visibility and their depth—but did you know that you can also change an AP element's content dynamically? With Dreamweaver, you can do it easily (and you're not restricted to AP elements; any containing element will do). A standard behavior, Set Text Of Container, enables you to swap the entire contents of one AP element for whatever you'd like. You're not limited to exchanging just text, either. Anything you can put into HTML, you can swap—which is pretty much everything!

Targeted JavaScript Commands

You can enter the following simple yet useful JavaScript commands in the Snap JavaScript text box of the Drag AP Element dialog box:

- To display a brief message to the user after the AP element is dropped, use the `alert()` function:

  ```
  alert("You hit the target")
  ```

- To send the user to another web page when the AP element is dropped in the right location, use the JavaScript location object:

  ```
  location = "http://www.yourdomain.com/yourpage.html"
  ```

The location object can also be used with relative URLs.

This behavior is extremely useful for putting up context-sensitive help and other information. Rather than construct a series of AP elements that you show and hide, a single AP element is used, and just the contents change. To use Set Text Of Container, follow these steps:

1. Insert and name your AP elements as desired.
2. Select the graphic, button, or text link you'd like to act as the trigger for changing the content of the AP element.
3. Choose Window ➪ Behaviors or press Shift+F4 to open the Behaviors panel.
4. Choose Set Text ➪ Set Text of Container from the Add (+) drop-down list. The Set Text of Container dialog box (shown in Figure 10-30) shows a list of the available elements with an ID in the current web page and provides a space for the new content.
5. Select the ID element you want to alter from the Container drop-down list.
6. Enter the text or code in the New HTML text area. You can enter either plain text, which is rendered in the default paragraph style, or any amount of HTML code, including `<img>`, `<table>`, or other tags.

TIP

If you're entering a large amount of HTML, don't bother doing so by hand—Dreamweaver can do it for you. On a blank page, create your HTML content and then select it and switch to Code view to copy it. Then, in the Set Text of Container dialog box, paste the code using Ctrl+V (Command+V).

7. Click OK when you're finished.

FIGURE 10-30

Swap out all the contents of an ID element using the Set Text Of Container behavior.

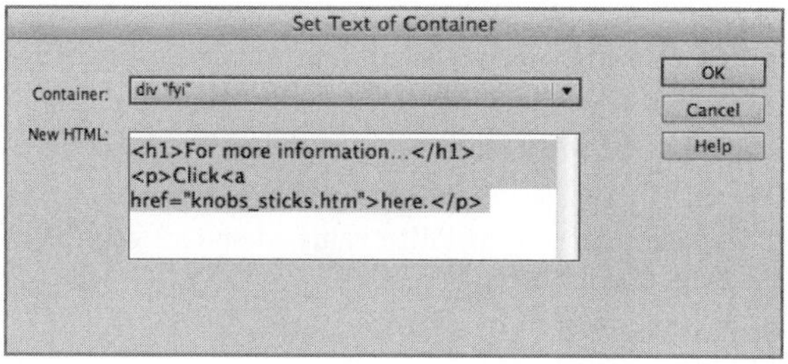

If you want several ID elements to change when a single event is triggered, just add more Set Text Of Container behaviors to the same object.

NOTE

You may need to change the behavior event from its default; to do so, click the down arrow in between the Event and the Action columns on the Behaviors panel and choose a new event from the list.

Show-Hide Elements

The capability to implement interactive control of an element's visibility offers tremendous potential to the web designer. The Show-Hide Elements action makes this implementation straightforward and simple to set up. With the Show-Hide Elements action, you can simultaneously show one or more elements while hiding as many other elements as necessary. Create your elements and give them a unique ID before invoking the Show-Hide Elements action. To use Show-Hide Elements, follow these steps:

1. Select an image, link, or other HTML tag to which to attach the behavior.
2. Choose Window ➪ Behaviors or press Shift+F4 to open the Behaviors panel.
3. Choose Show-Hide Elements from the Add (+) drop-down list. The Show-Hide Elements dialog box (see Figure 10-31) shows a list of the available AP elements in the open web page.

FIGURE 10-31

With the Show-Hide Elements behavior attached, you can easily program the visibility of all the AP elements in your web page.

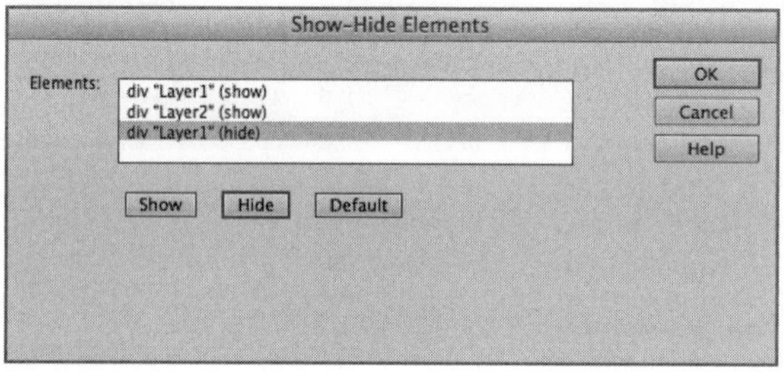

4. To cause a hidden AP element to be revealed when this event is fired, select the AP element from the list and click the Show button.
5. To hide a visible AP element when this event is fired, select its ID from the list and click the Hide button.
6. To restore an AP element's default visibility value when this event is fired, select the AP element and click the Default button.
7. Click OK when you are finished.
8. If the default event is not suitable, use the drop-down list in the Events column to select a different one.

Summary

AP elements are effective placement tools for developing the layout of a page. Anyone used to designing with desktop publishing tools can quickly learn to work with <div> tags and AP elements effectively. Keep these points in mind:

- A <div> tag can be styled for layout purposes using CSS.
- Dreamweaver calls a drawn out <div> tag with embedded CSS styling an AP element.
- AP elements are visible only on fourth-generation and later browsers.
- Dreamweaver includes a number of visual aids to help you create a <div>-based layout.
- The fluid grid layout makes it possible to design for multiple screens simultaneously.
- AP elements can be used to place HTML content anywhere on a web page.
- You can stack AP elements on top of one another. This depth control is referred to as the stacking order or the z-index.
- AP elements can be constructed so that the end user can display or hide them interactively, or alter their position, size, and depth dynamically.
- Dreamweaver provides guides, rulers, and grids to help with AP element placement and alignment.
- You can easily activate AP elements by using Dreamweaver's built-in JavaScript behaviors.

In the next chapter, you learn how to use Dreamweaver behaviors to enhance the interactivity of your sites.

CHAPTER

11

Using Behaviors

IN THIS CHAPTER

Behavior basics

Dreamweaver Technique: Incorporating Behaviors

Adding a behavior's event and action

Dreamweaver Technique: Modifying Behaviors

Looking at the standard behaviors

Behaviors are truly one of the power tools in Dreamweaver. With Dreamweaver behaviors, any web designer can make AP elements appear and disappear, execute any number of rollovers, and even apply an advanced JavaScript effect—all without knowing even a snippet of JavaScript. In the hands of an accomplished JavaScript programmer, Dreamweaver behaviors can be customized or created from scratch to automate the most difficult web effect.

Creating behaviors is one of the more challenging Dreamweaver features to master. Implementing these gems, however, is a piece of cake. This chapter examines the concepts behind behaviors and the reality of using them. It details the use of all the behaviors included with Dreamweaver, as well as some from notable third-party sources. This chapter also contains tips for managing your ever-increasing library of behaviors.

Understanding Behaviors, Events, and Actions

A behavior, in Adobe parlance, is the combination of an event and an action. In the electronic age, you push a button (the event) and something (the action) occurs—such as changing the channel on the TV with your remote.

In Dreamweaver, events can be something as interactive as a user's click of a link or as automatic as the loading of a web page. Behaviors are said to be attached to a specific element on your page, whether it's a text link, an image, or even the `<body>` tag.

Dreamweaver has simplified the process of working with behaviors by including default events in every object on the web page. Instead of having to think about both *how you want to do something and what you want to do, you only have to focus on the what—the action.*

To understand the concept of behaviors and how they are structured, examine the three essential steps for adding a behavior to your web page:

1. **Pick a tag.** All behaviors are connected to a specific HTML element (tag). You can attach a behavior to everything from the `<body>`, to an `<a>` tag, to the `<textarea>` of a form, and so on. If a certain behavior is unavailable, it's because the necessary element isn't present on the page.
2. **Select an action.** Dreamweaver enables only those actions available to the specific elements on your page. You can't, for instance, choose the Show-Hide Elements action until you insert one or more AP elements. Behaviors guide you to the workable options.
3. **Enter the parameters.** Behaviors get their power from their flexibility. Each action comes with its own dialog box that contains parameters you can use to customize the JavaScript code output. Depending on the action, you can choose source files, set attributes, and enable/disable features. The parameter dialog box can even dynamically update to reflect your current web page.

Dreamweaver CS6 comes with 25 cross-browser compatible actions, and both Adobe and third-party developers have made many additional actions available. Behaviors greatly extend the range of possibilities for the modern web designer—with no requirement to learn JavaScript programming. All you need to know about attaching behaviors is presented in the following section.

Another approach to behaviors is to incorporate functionality from JavaScript frameworks such as jQuery or YUI. You can learn more about adding these types of enhancements in Chapter 17.

Attaching a Behavior

When you see the code generated by Dreamweaver, you understand why setting up a behavior is also referred to as attaching a behavior. As previously noted, Dreamweaver needs a specific HTML tag to assign the behavior (Step 1). The anchor tag `<a>` is often used because, in JavaScript, links can respond to several different events, including `onClick`. Here's an example:

```
<a href="#" onClick="MM_popupMsg('Thanks for coming!')">Exit Here</a>
```

You're not restricted to one event per tag or even one action per event. Multiple events can be associated with a tag to handle various user actions. For example, you may have an image that does all the following things:

- Highlights when the user's pointer moves over the image
- Reveals a hidden AP element in another area of the page when the user clicks the mouse button on the image
- Shakes when the user releases the mouse button on the image

Likewise, a single event can trigger several actions. Updating multiple frames through a single link used to be difficult—but no more. Dreamweaver makes it easy by enabling you to attach several Go To URL actions to the same event, `onClick`. In addition, you are not restricted to attaching multiple instances of the same action to a single event. For example, in a site that uses a lot of multimedia, you can tie all the following actions to a single `onClick` event:

- Fade in an element across the screen (with the Fade action)
- Display a second graphic in place of the first (with the Swap Image action)
- Show the copyright information for the audio piece in the status bar (with the Set Text of Status Bar action)

You can even determine the order of execution for the actions connected to a single event.

With Dreamweaver behaviors, hours of complex JavaScript coding are reduced to a handful of mouse clicks and a minimum of data entry. All behavior assigning and modifications are handled through the Behaviors panel.

Using the Behaviors panel

The Behaviors panel provides two columns (see Figure 11-1) that neatly sum up the behaviors concept in general: events and actions. After you attach a behavior, the triggering event (`onClick`, `onMouseOver`, and so on) is shown on the left, and its associated action—what exactly is triggered—is on the right. A down arrow between the event and the action, when clicked, displays other available events for the current browser model. Double-click the action to open its parameter dialog box, where you can modify the action's attributes.

As usual in Dreamweaver, you have your choice of methods for opening the Behaviors panel:

- Choose Window ➪ Behaviors.
- Select the Behaviors tab from the Tag Inspector panel, if visible.
- Use the keyboard shortcut Shift+F4 (an on/off toggle).

FIGURE 11-1

You can handle everything about a behavior through the Behaviors panel.

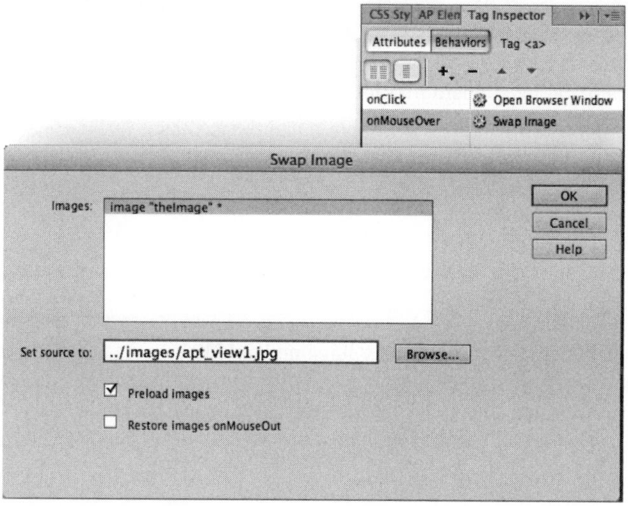

TIP

The Behaviors panel can be closed by toggling it off with Shift+F4 or hidden along with all the other panels by pressing F4.

After you have attached a behavior to a tag and closed the associated action's parameter dialog box, Dreamweaver writes the necessary HTML and JavaScript code into your document. Because it contains functions that must be callable from anywhere in the document, the bulk of the JavaScript code is placed in the `<head>` section of the page; the code that links selected tags to these functions is written in the `<body>` section. A few actions place HTML code at the bottom of the `<body>`. However, most of the code—there can be a lot of code to handle all the cross-browser contingencies—is placed between `<script> ... </script>` tags in the `<head>`.

Adding a behavior

The procedure for adding (or attaching) a behavior is simple. As noted earlier, you can assign only certain events to particular tags, and these options are further limited by the type of browser used.

NOTE

Even in the latest browsers, key events such as `onMouseDown`, `onMouseOver`, and `onMouseOut` work only with anchor tags. To circumvent this limitation, Dreamweaver can enclose an element, such as `<img>`, with an anchor tag that links to nowhere: `src="javascript:;"`. Events that use the anchor tag in this fashion appear in parentheses in the drop-down list of events—for example, `<A> onMouseOver`.

To add a behavior to an element in your web page, follow these steps:

1. Select an object (element) in the Document window.

TIP

To assign a behavior to the entire page, select the `<body>` tag from the Tag Selector (below the Document window).

2. Open the Behaviors panel by choosing Window ➪ Behaviors or by pressing Shift+F4.
3. Click the Add (+) button to reveal the available options, as shown in Figure 11-2. Select one from the drop-down list.
4. Enter the desired values in the action's parameter dialog box.
5. Click OK to close the dialog box when you're finished.

   Dreamweaver adds a line to the Behaviors panel displaying the attached event and its associated action.

A trigger—whether it's an image or a text link—may have multiple behaviors attached to it. One graphical navigation element can, for instance, perform a Swap Image when the user's mouse moves over it and a Swap Image Restore when the mouse moves away, and, when clicked, can show another web page in an additional, smaller window with the Open Browser Window behavior.

FIGURE 11-2

The enabled options on the Add (+) drop-down list change according to what's on the current page and which tag is selected.

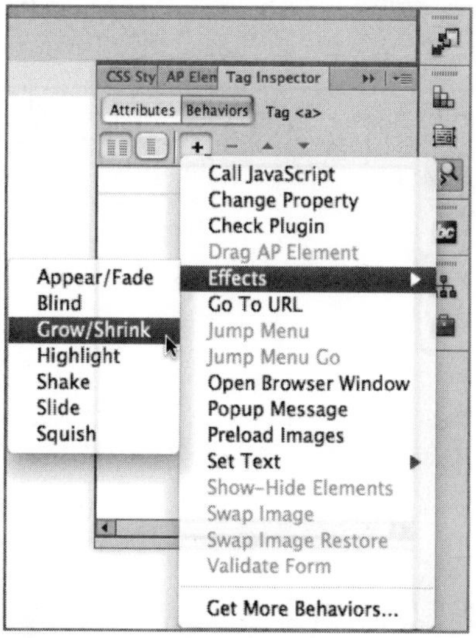

TIP

Dreamweaver includes a Get More Behaviors menu option at the bottom of the Add (+) drop-down list. To use this feature, connect to the Internet and select Get More Behaviors in Dreamweaver. You are whisked away to the Adobe Marketplace & Exchange, a service from Adobe with a huge selection of extensions of all flavors, including behaviors.

Managing events

Every time Dreamweaver attaches a behavior to a tag, it inserts an event for you. The default event that is chosen is based on the selected tag. A single file, `HTML 401.htm` found in the Configuration\Behaviors\Events\ folder, lists all tags and their events. The entries look like this:

```
<INPUT TYPE="Text" onBlur="*" onChange="" onFocus="" onSelect="">
```

The default event for each tag is marked with an asterisk; in the preceding example, `onBlur` is the default event. After you've selected an action and completed its parameter dialog box, the default event appears in the Events column of the Behaviors panel alongside the action in the Actions column.

TIP

If you find yourself changing a particular tag's default event over and over again to some other event, you might want to modify the appropriate Event file to pick your alternative as the default. To do this, open the `HTML 4.01.htm` file found in the Dreamweaver CS6\Configuration\Behaviors\Events folder, switch to Code view, and move the asterisk to a different event for that particular tag. Resave the file and restart Dreamweaver to try out your new default behavior.

If you don't want to select the default event in a certain instance, you can easily choose another. To do so, click the down arrow next to the displayed event in the Behaviors panel and select the event you want in the drop-down list (see Figure 11-3).

FIGURE 11-3

You can change the event by selecting a different one from the drop-down list.

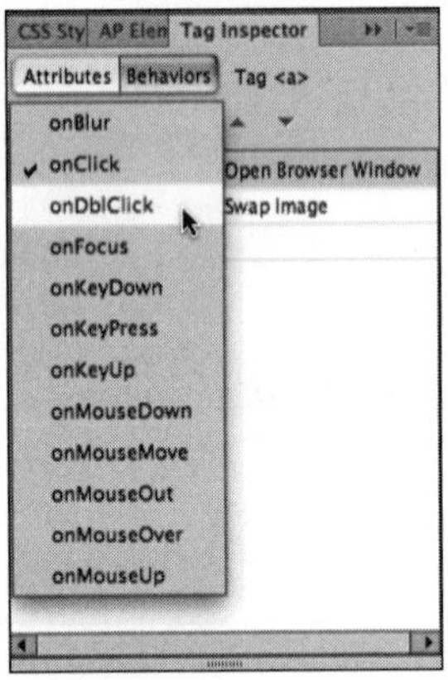

Dreamweaver TECHNIQUE

Incorporating Behaviors

In this Technique, you add a series of Dreamweaver standard behaviors that display a different image whenever a link is moused over.

1. In the Files panel, switch to the Dreamweaver Bible working site previously created.
2. Go to Techniques\11_Behaviors and open the file `behaviors_start.htm`.
3. Select the text "Living Room" beneath the picture.
4. In the Link field of the Properties panel, enter `javascript:;` to create a link.
5. Choose Window ⇨ Behaviors to open the Behaviors panel.
6. In the Behaviors panel, click Add (+) and select Swap Image.
7. When the Swap Image dialog box opens, set the following parameters:
   - Select Browse and choose `apt_view1.jpg` from the Techniques/images folder.
   - Clear the Restore Images onMouseOut option.
8. Click OK when you're done. Note that the behavior has been added to the Behaviors panel with the default event, `onMouseOver`.

9. Select the text Kitchen North and repeat Steps 4–8, selecting `apt_view2.jpg` as the file to show in the Swap Image behavior dialog box.
10. Select the text Kitchen South and repeat Steps 4–8, selecting `apt_view3.jpg` as the file to show in the Swap Image behavior dialog box.
11. Save your page.

When you're done, each of the three links underneath the picture will have its own behavior; test the page in a browser to verify that the images change when your mouse rolls over the different links.

NOTE

Although any HTML tag could potentially be used to attach a behavior, the most commonly used by far are the `<body>` tag (for entire-page events such as `onLoad`), the `<img>` tag (used as a button), and the link tag, `<a>`.

Triggering Custom Functions

Although the standard behaviors can accomplish a great deal—and extensions available from the Adobe Marketplace & Exchange can do even more—sometimes a developer needs to trigger a custom function. Dreamweaver provides a way to link an event to a function quickly, right in the Behaviors panel. The action column of the Behaviors panel not only displays behaviors applied in the usual manner but is also editable. In other words, you can enter your own function call directly into the Behaviors panel, and Dreamweaver writes the code into the tag.

Here's how it works. Suppose you want to trigger a custom JavaScript function called `showTotal()` whenever the user clicks a special graphic:

1. Select the image, and in the Link field of the Properties panel, enter **javascript:;**.
2. In the Behaviors panel, click the Event column and choose an event from the drop-down list. In this case, select `onClick`.
3. Enter the custom function call and any arguments in the Action column. The function might be entered like this: `showTotal('checkout','USD')`, where the two arguments are presented in a comma-separated list, using single quotes.
4. Press Tab to confirm the code entry.

If you check the <a> surrounding the image, you find that Dreamweaver has now added the following to the tag: `onClick="showTotal('checkout','USD')"`.

The function call or arguments can include dynamic components; a lightning bolt symbol that opens the Dynamic Data dialog box is available from the Action column. Moreover, you can combine your custom function call with other standard behaviors. To remove the code, select the custom entry and click Remove (–), just as you would for a regular behavior.

Standard actions

As of this writing, 25 standard actions ship with Dreamweaver CS6. Each action operates independently of and is different from the others, although many share common functions. Each action is associated with a different parameter dialog box to enable easy attribute entry.

The following sections describe the standard actions: what the actions do, what requirements must be met for them to be activated, what options are available, and, most important of all, how to use the actions. Dreamweaver CS6 behaviors are designed to work exclusively in modern browsers.

Call JavaScript

With Call JavaScript, you can execute any JavaScript function—standard or custom—with a single mouse click or other event. As your JavaScript savvy grows, you'll find yourself using this behavior again and again.

Call JavaScript is straightforward to use; simply type the JavaScript code or the name of the function you want to trigger into the dialog box. If, for example, you want to get some input from a visitor, you can use JavaScript's built-in `prompt()` method like this:

```
result = prompt('Whom shall I say is calling?','')
```

When this code is triggered, a small dialog box appears with your query (here, `'Whom shall I say is calling?'`) and a blank space for an input string. The second argument in the `prompt()` method enables you to include a default answer—to leave it blank, just use an empty string (two single quotes with nothing in between), as shown in the preceding code snippet.

NOTE

You can use either single or double quotes in your Call JavaScript behavior; Dreamweaver automatically adjusts for whichever you choose. I find it easier to use single quotes because Dreamweaver translates double quotes into character entities; that is, " becomes `"`.

Naturally, you can use Call JavaScript to handle more complex chores as well. To call a specific custom function that is already in the <head> section of your page, just enter its name—along with any necessary arguments—in the Call JavaScript dialog box, shown in Figure 11-4.

FIGURE 11-4

Trigger any JavaScript function by attaching a Call JavaScript behavior to an image or text.

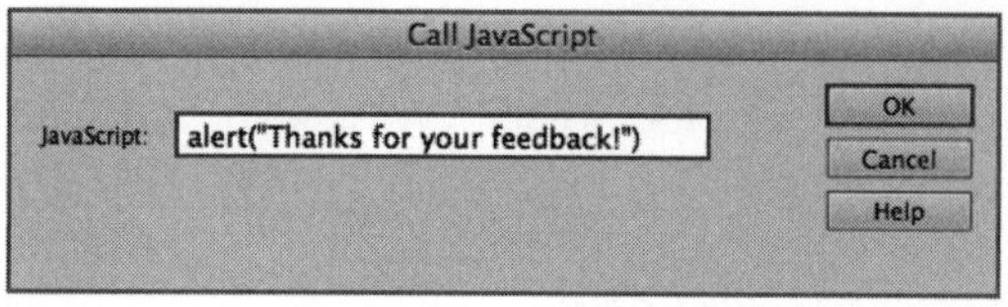

To use the Call JavaScript behavior, follow these steps:

1. Select the object to trigger the action.
2. From the Behaviors panel, click the Add (+) button and select Call JavaScript.
3. In the Call JavaScript dialog box, enter your code in the JavaScript text box.
4. Click OK when you're finished.

Change Property

The Change Property action enables you to dynamically alter properties of each of the following tags:

- `<div>`
- `<span>`
- `<p>`
- `<tr>`
- `<td>`
- `<img>`
- `<form>`
- `<textarea>`
- `<select>`

You can also alter the following `<input>` types:

- `checkbox`
- `radio`
- `text`
- `password`

The tags, as well as the browser being targeted, determine exactly which properties can be altered. The Change Property dialog box (see Figure 11-5) offers a list of the selected tags in the current page.

FIGURE 11-5

The Change Property dialog box enables you to dynamically alter attributes of certain tags.

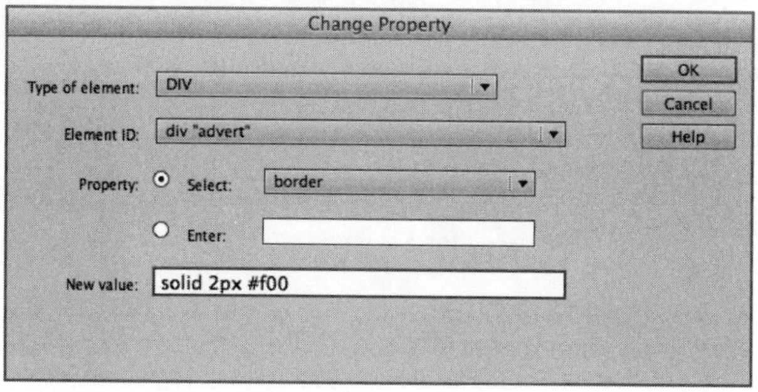

CAUTION

It's important that you name the objects you want to alter so that Dreamweaver can properly identify them. Remember to use unique names that begin with a letter and contain no spaces or special characters (such as `@`, `?`, and `&`).

This behavior is especially useful for changing the properties of forms and form elements. Be sure to name the form if you want to use Change Property in this manner. To use the Change Property action, follow these steps:

1. Select the object to trigger the action.
2. From the Behaviors panel, click the Add (+) button and select Change Property.
3. In the Change Property dialog box, choose the type of object whose property you want to change—FORM, DIV, INPUT/TEXT, and so on—from the Type Of Element drop-down list.
4. In the Element ID drop-down list, select the name of the object whose property you want to change.
5. Click the Select radio button and choose the property to change. If you don't find the property in the drop-down list box, you can type it yourself in the Enter text box.

NOTE

Many properties in the various browsers are read-only and cannot be dynamically altered. Those properties listed in the option list are always dynamic.

6. In the New Value text box, type the property's new value to be inserted when the event is fired.
7. Click OK when you're finished.

Check Plugin

If certain pages on your website require the use of one or more plugins, you can use the Check Plugin action to see if a visitor has the necessary plugin installed. After Check Plugin has examined this, it can route users with the appropriate plugin to one URL and users without it to another URL. You can look for only one plugin at a time, but you can use multiple instances of the Check Plugin action, if needed.

WARNING

Test heavily before committing to using this technique as it is not fully supported in modern browsers.

By default, the parameter dialog box for Check Plugin (see Figure 11-6) offers five plugins: Flash, Shockwave, LiveAudio, QuickTime, and Windows Media Player. You can check for any other plugin by entering its name in the Enter text box. Use the name exactly as it appears in bold (without the version number) in Netscape's About Plug-ins area—for example, `Nullsoft Winamp Plug-in for Gecko`.

FIGURE 11-6

Running a media-intensive site? Use the Check Plugin action to divert visitors without plugins to alternative pages.

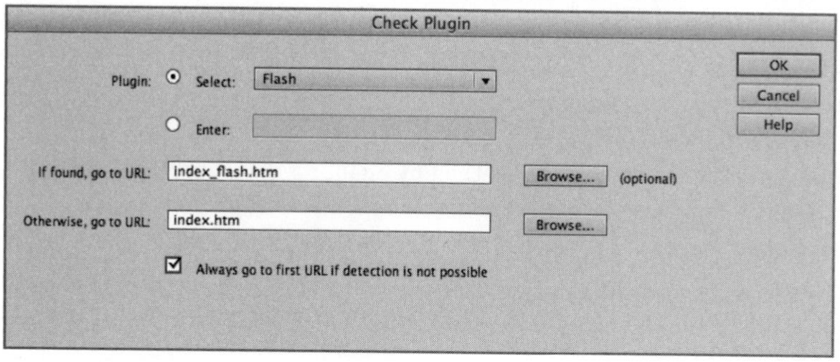

To use the Check Plugin action, follow these steps:

1. Select the object to trigger the action.
2. From the Behaviors panel, click the Add (+) button and select Check Plugin.
3. Select a plugin from the drop-down list or type another plugin name in the Enter text box.

NOTE

The names presented in the drop-down list are abbreviated—more recognizable names—and not the formal names inserted into the code. For example, when you select Shockwave, Shockwave for Director is actually input into the code. On the other hand, any plugin name you enter manually into the Enter field is inserted verbatim.

4. If you want to send users who are confirmed to have the plugin to a different page, enter that URL (absolute or relative) in the If Found, Go To URL text box or use the Browse button to locate the file. If you want these users to stay on the current page, leave the text box empty.
5. In the Otherwise, Go To URL text box, enter the URL for users who do not have the required plugin.
6. Should the plugin detection fail—which, as explained earlier, happens regularly in Internet Explorer, whether or not the plugin is actually present—you can keep the user on the initial page. To do so, enable the Always Go To First URL If Detection Is Not Possible option. Otherwise, if the detection fails for any reason, users are sent to the URL listed in the Otherwise field.
7. Click OK when you're finished.

Drag AP Element

The Drag AP Element action provides some spectacular—and interactive—effects with little effort on the part of the designer. Drag AP Element enables your web page visitors to move AP elements—and all that they contain—around the screen with the drag-and-drop technique. With the Drag AP Element action, you can easily set up the following capabilities for the user:

- Enabling AP elements to be dragged anywhere on the screen
- Restricting the dragging to a particular direction or combination of directions—a horizontal sliding AP element can be restricted to left and right movement, for instance
- Limiting the drag handle to a portion of the AP element such as the upper bar or enabling the whole AP element to be used
- Providing an alternative clipping method by enabling only a portion of the AP element to be dragged
- Enabling changing of the AP elements' stacking order while dragging or on mouse release
- Setting a snap-to target area on your web page for AP elements that the user releases within a defined radius
- Programming a JavaScript command to be executed when the snap-to target is hit or every time the AP element is released

AP elements are some of the more powerful features in Dreamweaver. To get the most out of the AP element-oriented behaviors, familiarize yourself with AP elements by examining Chapter 10.

One or more AP elements must reside in your web page before the Drag AP Element action becomes available for selection from the Add (+) drop-down list. You must attach the action to the <body>—you can, however, attach separate Drag AP Element behaviors to different AP elements to get different AP element-dragging effects.

Drag AP Element's parameter dialog box (see Figure 11-7) includes a Get Current Position button that puts the left and top coordinates of the selected AP element into the Drop Target Left/Top boxes. If you plan on using targeting, make sure to place your AP element at the target location before attaching the behavior.

FIGURE 11-7

With the Drag AP Element action, you can set up your AP elements to be repositioned by the user.

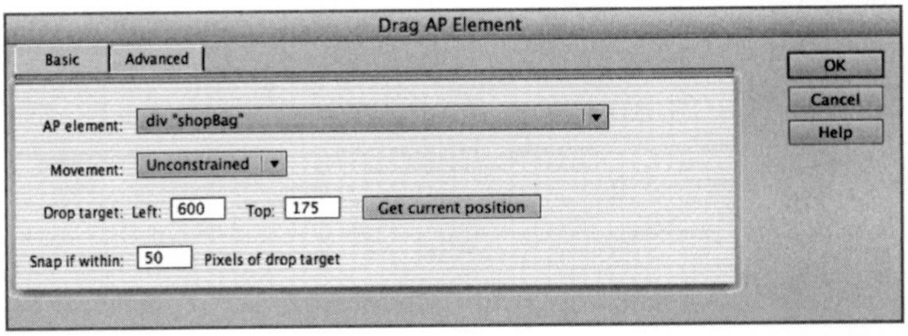

To use the Drag AP Element action, follow these steps:

1. Make sure that you have one or more AP elements on your page; then select the `<body>` tag.
2. From the Behaviors panel, click the Add (+) button and select Drag AP Element.
3. If the Basic tab of the parameter dialog box is not selected, select it now.
4. In the AP Element drop-down list, select the AP element you want to make draggable.
5. To limit the movement of the AP element, change the Movement option from Unconstrained to Constrained. Text boxes for Up, Down, Left, and Right appear. Enter pixel values in the text boxes to control the range of motion:
   - To constrain movement vertically, enter positive numbers in the Up and Down text boxes and zeros in the Left and Right text boxes.
   - To constrain movement horizontally, enter positive numbers in the Left and Right text boxes and zeros in the Up and Down text boxes.
   - To enable movement in a rectangular region, enter positive values in all four text boxes.
6. To establish a location for a target for the dragged AP element, enter coordinates in the Drop Target: Left and Top text boxes. Click the Get Current Position button to fill these text boxes with the AP element's current location.
7. To set a snap-to area around the target coordinates where the AP element falls if released in the target location, enter a pixel value in the Snap If Within text box.
8. For additional options, select the Advanced tab of the parameter dialog box.
9. If you want the whole AP element to act as a drag handle, select Entire AP Element from the Drag Handle drop-down list. If, instead, you want to limit the area to be used as a drag handle, select Area Within AP Element from the Drag Handle drop-down list. L(eft), T(op), W(idth), and H(eight) text boxes appear. In the appropriate boxes, enter the left and top coordinates of the drag handle in pixels, as well as the dimensions for the width and height.
10. To control the positioning of the dragged AP element, set the following While Dragging options:
    - To keep the AP element in its current depth (that is, to avoid bringing it to the front when it is dragged), clear the checkbox for While Dragging: Bring AP Element To The Front.
    - To change the stacking order of the AP element when it is released, select the checkbox and pick either Leave On Top or Restore Z-index from the drop-down list.
11. To execute a JavaScript command while the AP element is being dragged, enter the command or function in the Call JavaScript text box.
12. To execute a JavaScript command when the AP element is dropped on the target, enter the code in the When Dropped: Call JavaScript text box. If you want the JavaScript to execute only when the AP element is snapped to its target, select the Only If Snapped option. This option requires that a value be entered in the Snap If Within text box in the Basic tab.
13. Click OK when you're finished.

NOTE

If you—or others on your team—have the requisite JavaScript programming skills, you can gather information output from the Drag AP Element behavior to enhance your pages. Dreamweaver declares three variables for each draggable AP element: `MM_UPDOWN` (the y coordinate), `MM_LEFTRIGHT` (the x coordinate), and `MM_SNAPPED` (true, if the AP element has reached the specified target). Before you can get any of these properties, you must get an object reference for the proper AP element. Another function, `MM_findObj(AP elementname)`, handles that chore.

Go to URL

Dreamweaver brings the same power of links—with a lot more flexibility—to any event with the Go to URL action. Although frames have largely fallen out of use, one of the trickier tasks in using them on legacy sites is updating two or more frames simultaneously with a single button click. The Go to URL action handily streamlines this process for the web designer. Go to URL can also be used as a preload router that sends the user to another web page after the `onLoad` event has finished. The Go To URL dialog box (see Figure 11-8) displays any existing frames in the current page or frameset. To load multiple URLs at the same time, select the first frame from the Open In list and enter the desired page or location in the URL text box. Next, select the second frame from the list and enter its URL, and so on. If you select a frame to which a URL is already assigned, that address appears in the URL text box.

FIGURE 11-8

You can update two or more frames at the same time with the Go to URL action.

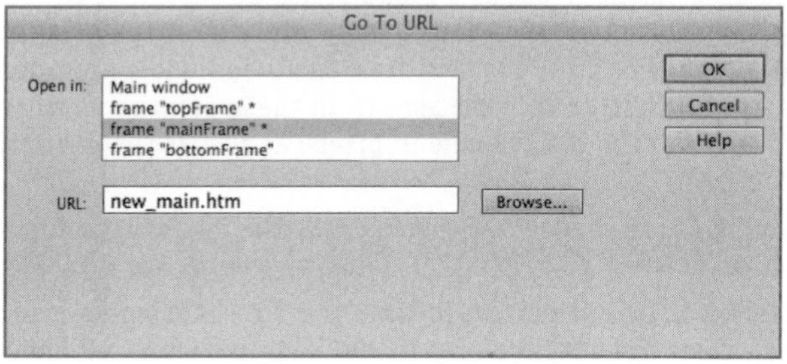

To use the Go to URL action, follow these steps:

1. Select the object to trigger the action.
2. From the Behaviors panel, click the Add (+) button and select Go to URL.
3. From the Go To URL dialog box, select the target for your link from the list in the Open In window.
4. Enter the path of the file to open in the URL text box or click the Browse button to locate a file. An asterisk appears next to the frame name to indicate that a URL has been chosen.
5. To select another target to load a different URL, repeat Steps 3 and 4.
6. Click OK when you're finished.

Jump Menu and Jump Menu Go

Although most behaviors insert original code to activate an element of the web page, several behaviors are included to edit code inserted by a Dreamweaver object. The Jump Menu and Jump Menu Go behaviors both require a previously inserted Jump Menu object before they become active. The Jump Menu behavior is used to edit an existing Jump Menu object, and the Jump Menu Go behavior adds a graphic image as a Go button.

To find out more about the Jump Menu object, see Chapter 13.

To use the Jump Menu behavior to edit an existing Jump Menu object, follow these steps:

1. Select the Jump Menu object previously inserted into the page.
2. In the Behaviors panel, double-click the listed Jump Menu behavior.
3. Make your modifications in the Jump Menu dialog box, as shown in Figure 11-9. You can alter the existing menu item names or their associated URLs, add new menu items, or reorder the list through the Jump Menu dialog box.
4. Click OK when you're finished.

FIGURE 11-9

Use the Jump Menu behavior to modify a previously inserted Jump Menu object.

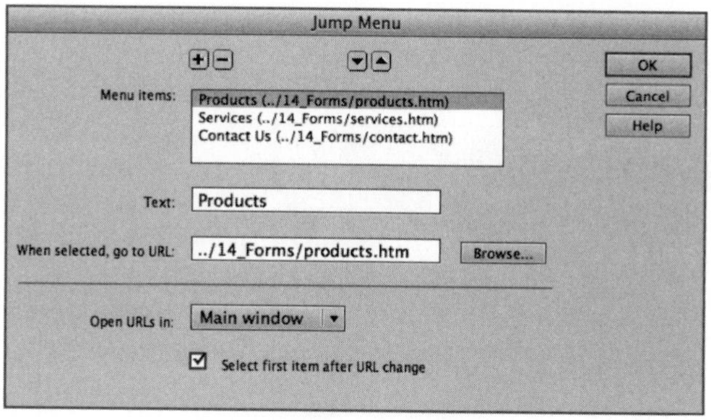

To add a button to activate the Jump Menu object, follow these steps:

1. Select the image or form button you'd like to make into a Go button. A Jump Menu object must be on the current page for the Jump Menu Go behavior to be available.
2. From the Behaviors panel, select Jump Menu Go from the Add (+) drop-down list. The Jump Menu Go dialog box, shown in Figure 11-10, is displayed.
3. Select the name of the Jump Menu object you want to activate from the option list.
4. Click OK when you're finished.

FIGURE 11-10

Add a graphic or standard button as a Go button with the Jump Menu Go behavior.

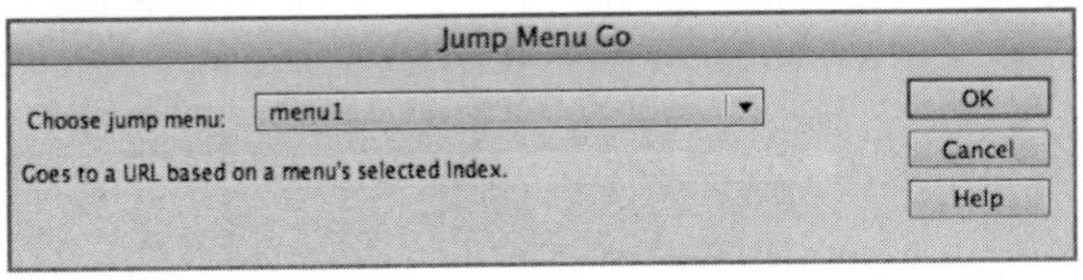

Open Browser Window

With the Open Browser Window action, you can open a new browser window and specify its exact size and attributes. You can even set it up to receive JavaScript events.

You can also open a new browser window with a regular link by specifying `target="_blank"`, but you can't control any of the window's attributes with this method. You do get this control with the parameter dialog box of the Open Browser Window action (see Figure 11-11). This dialog box enables you to set the window width and height and select whether to display the Navigation Toolbar, Location Toolbar, Status Bar, Menu Bar, Scrollbars As Needed, and/or Resize Handles. You can also name your new window, a necessary step for advanced JavaScript control.

FIGURE 11-11

Use the Open Browser Window action to program a pop-up advertisement or remote control.

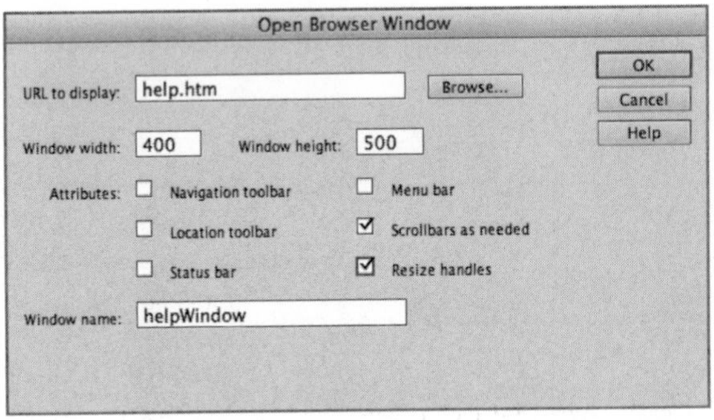

You have to explicitly select any of the attributes that you want to appear in your new window. Your new browser window contains only the attributes you've checked, plus basic window elements such as a title bar and a Close button.

CAUTION

Most modern browsers have pop-up blockers that will stop the Open Browser Window action from functioning. Although there is nothing you, as a page designer, can do to override the pop-up blocker, you might consider adding a note to your page indicating that pop-up windows are in use on your page.

To use the Open Browser Window action, follow these steps:

1. Select the object to trigger the action.
2. From the Behaviors panel, click the Add (+) button, and select Open Browser Window.
3. In the URL To Display text box, enter the address of the web page you want to display in the new window. You can also click the Browse button to locate the file.
4. To specify the window's size, enter the width and height values in the appropriate text boxes. You must enter both a width and height measurement, or the new browser window opens to its default size.
5. Check the appropriate Attributes checkboxes to show the desired window features.
6. If you plan on using JavaScript to address or control the window, type a unique name in the Window Name text box. This name cannot contain spaces or special characters. Dreamweaver alerts you if the name you've entered is unacceptable.
7. Click OK when you're finished.

Popup Message

You can send a quick message to your users with the Popup Message behavior. When triggered, this action opens a JavaScript alert box that displays your specified message. You enter your message in the Message text box on the action's parameter dialog box (see Figure 11-12).

To use the Popup Message action, follow these steps:

1. Select the object to trigger the action.
2. From the Behaviors panel, click the Add (+) button and select Popup Message.
3. Enter your text in the Message text box.
4. Click OK when you're finished.

TIP

You can include JavaScript functions or references in your text messages by surrounding the JavaScript with curly braces. For example, you can incorporate today's date in a message like this:

```
Welcome to our site on {new Date()}!
```

You could also pull data from a form into your alert-box message, as in this example:

```
Thanks for filling out our survey,i {document.surveyForm.firstname.value}.
```

If you need to display a curly brace in a message, you must precede it with a backslash character, as in `\{` or `\}`.

Preload Images

Designs commonly require a particular image or several images to be displayed immediately when called by an action or a timeline. Because of the nature of HTML, all graphics are separate files that are normally downloaded when needed. To get the snappy response required for certain designs, graphics need to be preloaded or cached so that they are available. The Preload Images action performs this important service. You designate the images you want to cache for later use through the Preload Images parameter dialog box (see Figure 11-13).

FIGURE 11-12

Send a message to your users with the Popup Message action.

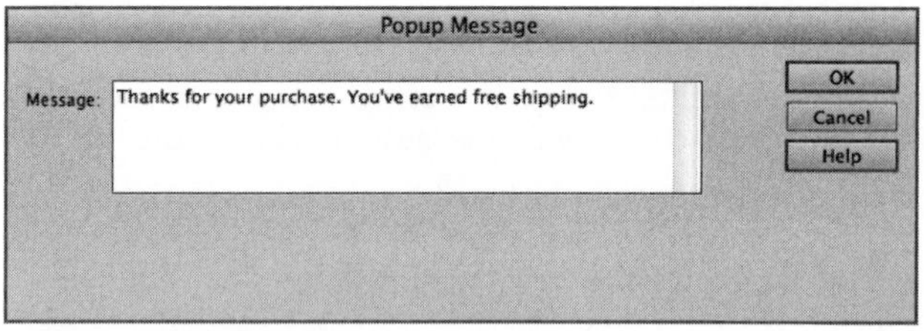

FIGURE 11-13

Media-rich websites respond much faster when images have been cached with the Preload Images action.

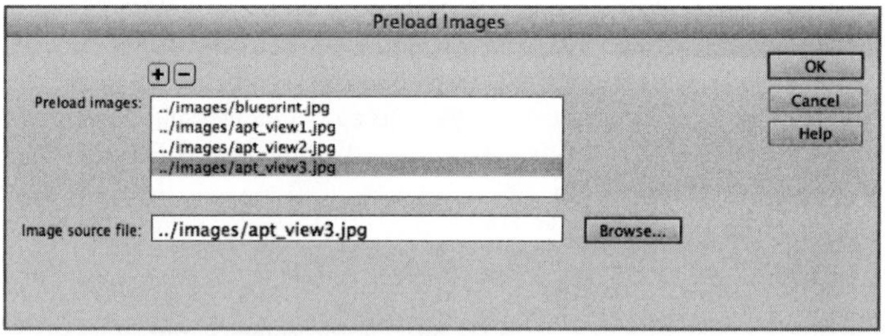

NOTE

You don't need to use the Preload Images action if you're creating rollovers. Both the Rollover object and the Swap Image action enable you to preload images from their dialog boxes.

To use the Preload Images action, follow these steps:

1. Select the object to trigger the action.
2. From the Behaviors panel, click the Add (+) button and select Preload Images.
3. In the Preload Images parameter dialog box, enter the path to the image file in the Image Source File text box, or click the Browse button to locate the file.
4. To add another file, click the Add (+) button and repeat Step 3.

CAUTION

After you've specified your first file to be preloaded, be sure to click the Add (+) button for each successive file you want to add to the list. Otherwise, the highlighted file is replaced by the next entry.

5. To remove a file from the Preload Images list, select it and click the Remove (–) button.
6. Click OK when you're finished.

Set Text of Container

Dreamweaver has grouped together four similar behaviors under the Set Text heading. The first, Set Text of Container, enables you to do much more than change a word or two—you can dynamically rewrite the entire code for any containing element. You can even incorporate JavaScript functions or interactive information into the new content. The Set Text of Container behavior replaces the entire HTML contents of the target—and the target can be any tag with an ID.

> **TIP**
>
> Unlike another behavior in this group, Set Text of Frame, the Set Text of Container dialog box provides no button for getting the current HTML. Here's a workaround. Before invoking the behavior, switch to Code view and copy all the elements inside the desired element. Then you can paste your clipboard into the New HTML text area using the keyboard shortcut Ctrl+V (Cmd+V). Be careful not to select the surrounding element tag, such as the `<div>`; if you do, you are pasting one surrounding element in another.

To set the text of an AP element dynamically, follow these steps:

1. Make sure that the AP element you want to change has been created and named properly.
2. Select the object to trigger the action.
3. From the Behaviors panel, click the Add (+) button and choose Set Text ➪ Set Text of Container from the option list. The Set Text of Container dialog box opens, as shown in Figure 11-14.
4. Select the element to modify from the Container drop-down list.

FIGURE 11-14

Use the Set Text of Container behavior to replace all of the HTML in any element with an ID.

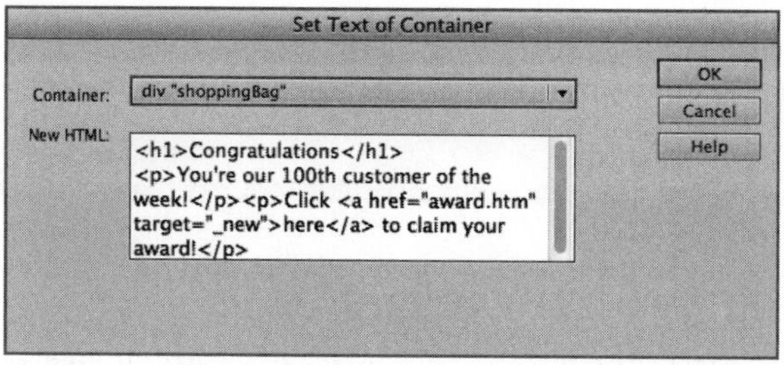

5. Enter the replacement code in the New HTML text area.
6. Click OK when you're finished.

Set Text of Frame

The Set Text of Frame action replaces all the contents of the <body> tag of a frame. Dreamweaver supplies a handy Get Current HTML button that enables you to easily keep everything you want to retain and change only a heading or other element. Naturally, you must be within a frameset to use this behavior, and the frames must be named correctly—that is, uniquely without special characters or spaces.

To change the content of a frame dynamically, follow these steps:

1. Select the triggering object.
2. From the Behaviors panel, click the Add (+) button and choose Set Text ➪ Set Text of Frame. The Set Text of Frame dialog box opens, as shown in Figure 11-15.

FIGURE 11-15

The Set Text of Frame behavior enables you to interactively update the contents of any frame in the current frameset.

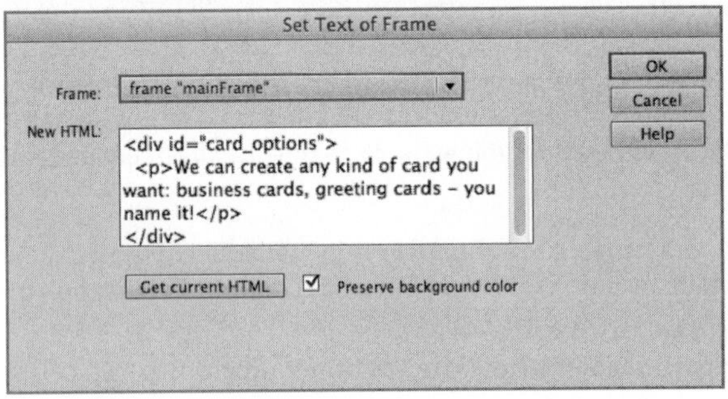

3. Choose the frame you want to alter from the Frame drop-down list.
4. Enter the code for the changing frame in the New HTML text area. Keep in mind that you're changing not just a word or phrase but all the HTML contained in the <body> section of the frame.

TIP

With all four Set Text behaviors, you can include JavaScript code by enclosing it in curly braces: { . . . }.

5. If you want to keep the majority of the code, click the Get Current HTML button and change only those portions necessary.
6. To maintain the frame's <body> attributes, such as the background and text colors, select the Preserve Background Color option. If this option is not selected, the frame's background and text colors are replaced by the default values (a white background and black text).
7. Click OK when you're finished.

Set Text of Status Bar

Use the Set Text of Status Bar action to display a text message in the browser's status bar based on a user's action, such as moving the pointer over an image. The message stays displayed in the status bar until another message replaces it. System messages, such as URLs, tend to be temporary and visible only when the user's mouse is over a link.

> **NOTE**
>
> Some browsers, including Internet Explorer 6 and 7, will not display the change of status bar text without changing user preferences. Moreover, many modern browsers do not show a status bar by default.

The only limit to the length of the message is the size of the browser's status bar; you should test your message in various browsers to make sure that it is completely visible.

> **TIP**
>
> To display a message only when a user's pointer is over an image or link, use one Set Text of Status Bar action, attached to an `onMouseOver` event, with your desired status bar message. Use another Set Text of Status Bar action, attached to an `onMouseOut` event, that has a null string (" ") as the text.

You enter all text in the Message field of the Set Text of Status Bar parameter dialog box (see Figure 11-16).

FIGURE 11-16

Use the Set Text of Status Bar action to guide your users with instructions in the browser window's status bar.

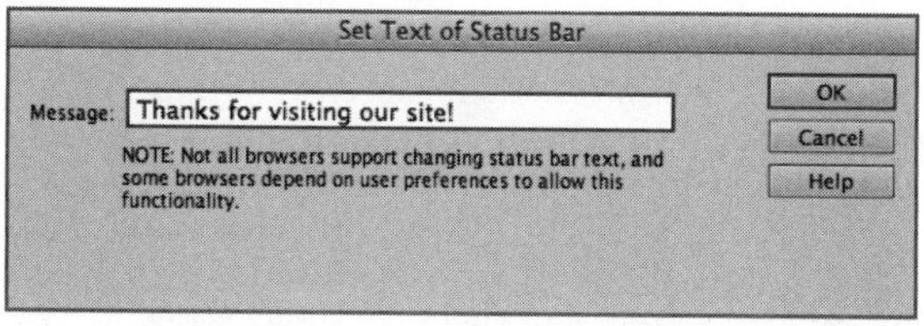

To use the Set Text of Status Bar action, follow these steps:

1. Select the object to trigger the action.
2. From the Behaviors panel, click the Add (+) button and select Set Text of Status Bar.
3. Enter your text in the Message text box.
4. Click OK when you're finished.

Set Text of Text Field

Set Text of Text Field, the final Set Text behavior, enables you to dynamically update any text or text area field. A text field must be present on the page for the behavior to be available. To change the displayed text of a text or text area field, follow these steps:

1. From the Behaviors panel, click the Add (+) button and choose Set Text ➪ Set Text of Text Field from the Add Action list. The Set Text of Text Field dialog box is displayed, as shown in Figure 11-17.
2. Select the desired text field from the drop-down list.
3. Enter the new text and/or JavaScript in the New Text area.
4. Click OK when you're finished.

FIGURE 11-17

Dynamically update text/text area form elements with the Set Text of Text Field behavior.

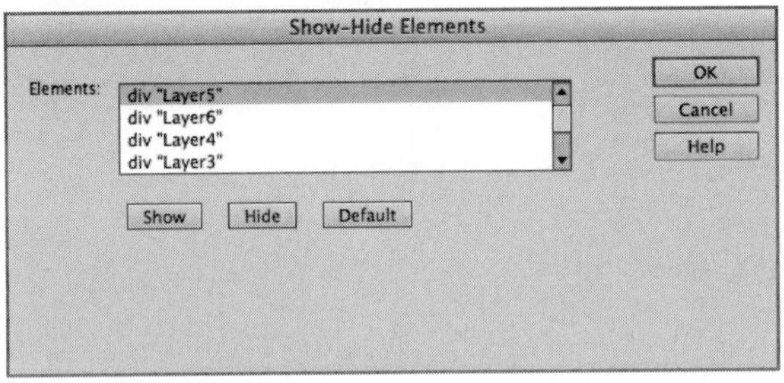

Show-Hide Elements

One of the key features of Dynamic HTML AP elements is their capability to appear and disappear on command. The Show-Hide Elements action gives you easy control over the visibility attribute for all elements with an ID in the current web page. In addition to explicitly showing or hiding elements, this action can also restore elements to the default visibility setting.

The Show-Hide Elements action is often used to reveal or conceal a single element; however, you are not restricted to hiding or showing just one element at a time. The action's parameter dialog box (see Figure 11-18) shows you a list of all the elements with an ID in the current web page from which you can choose as many as you want to show or hide.

To use the Show-Hide Elements action, follow these steps:

1. Select the object to trigger the action.
2. From the Behaviors panel, click the Add (+) button and select Show-Hide Elements. The Show-Hide Elements parameter dialog box displays a list of the available elements in the current web page.

FIGURE 11-18

The Show-Hide Elements action can make any number of hidden elements visible, hide any number of visible elements, or both.

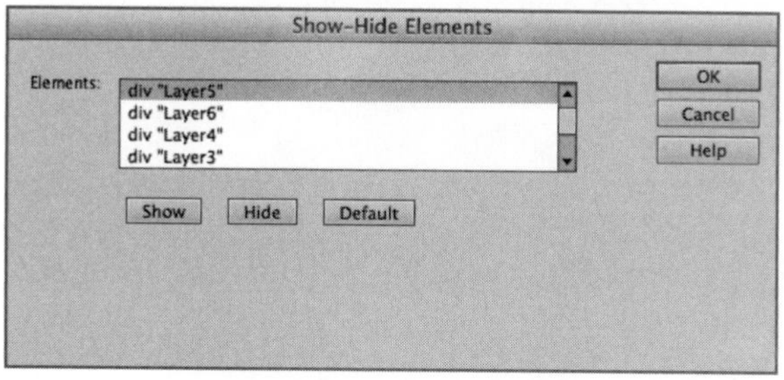

3. To show a hidden element, select the element from the Elements list and click the Show button.
4. To hide a shown element, select its name from the list and click the Hide button.
5. To restore an element's default visibility value, select the element and click the Default button.
6. Click OK when you're finished.

Swap Image and Swap Image Restore

Button rollovers are one of the most frequently used techniques in web design today. In a typical button rollover, a user's pointer moves over one image, and the graphic appears to change in some way, seeming to glow or change color. Actually, the `onMouseOver` event triggers the almost instantaneous swapping of one image for another. Dreamweaver automates this difficult coding task with the Swap Image action and its companion, the Swap Image Restore action.

In recognition of how rollovers commonly work in the real world, Dreamweaver makes it possible to combine Swap Image and Swap Image Restore in one easy operation—as well as to preload all the images. Moreover, you can use a link in one frame to trigger a rollover in another frame without having to tweak the code as you did in earlier Dreamweaver versions.

When the dialog box for the Swap Image action opens (see Figure 11-19), it automatically loads a list of all the image names it finds in the current web page. The names are taken from IDs applied to the image; the phrase "unnamed <img>" appears in the dialog box for each image that does not have an ID assigned. You select the image you want to change—which could be the same image to which you are attaching the behavior—and specify the image file you want to replace with the rolled-over image. You can swap more than one image with each Swap Image action. For example, if you want an entire submenu to change when a user rolls over a particular option, you can use a single Swap Image action to switch all the submenu button images.

NOTE

If the Restore Images `onMouseOut` option was selected in the Swap Image parameter dialog box, Dreamweaver adds two lines to the Behaviors panel: Swap Image and Swap Image Restore.

FIGURE 11-19

The Swap Image action is used primarily for handling button image rollovers.

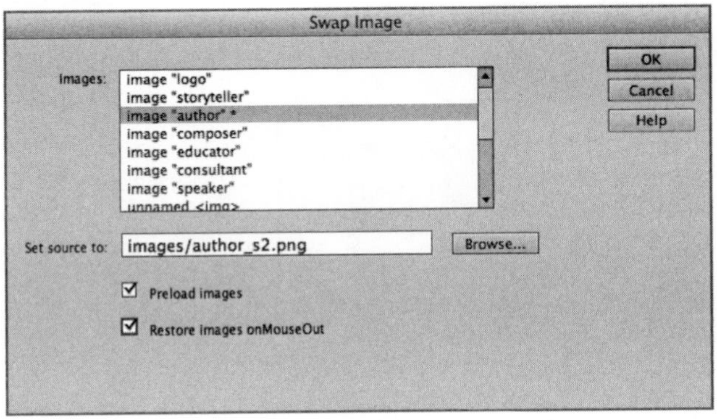

If you choose not to enable the Restore Images onMouseOut option, which changes the image back to the original, you attach the Swap Image Restore action to another event. The Swap Image Restore action can be used only after a Swap Image action. No parameter dialog box exists for the Swap Image Restore action—just a dialog box confirming your selection.

CAUTION

If the swapped-in image has different dimensions than the image it replaces, the swapped-in image is resized to the height and width of the first image.

To use the Swap Image action, follow these steps:

1. Select the object to trigger the action.
2. From the Behaviors panel, click the Add (+) button and select Swap Image.
3. In the Swap Image parameter dialog box, choose an available image from the Images list.
4. In the Set Source To text box, enter the path to the image that you want to swap. You can also click the Browse button to locate the file. An asterisk appears at the end of the selected image name to indicate an alternative image has been selected.
5. To swap additional images using the same event, repeat Steps 3 and 4.
6. To preload all images involved in the Swap Image action when the page loads, make sure the Preload Images option is checked.
7. To cause the selected images to revert to their original source when the user mouses away from the selected object, make sure that the Restore Images onMouseOut option is selected.
8. Click OK when you're finished.

Validate Form

When you set up a form for user input, you establish each field with a purpose. The name field, the e-mail address field, and the ZIP code field all have their own requirements for input. Unless you are using a CGI program specifically designed to check the user's input, form fields usually accept input of any type. Even if the CGI program can handle it, this server-side method ties up server time and is relatively slow. The Dreamweaver Validate Form action checks any text field's input and returns the form to the user if any of the entries are unacceptable. You can also use this action to designate any text field as a required field.

Validate Form can be used to check either single or multiple text fields in a form. If you attach a Validate Form action to a single text box, you alert the user to any errors as he or she is filling out this field. To check multiple form fields, the Validate Form action must be attached to the form's `<form>` tag.

The Validate Form dialog box (see Figure 11-20) enables you to designate any text field as required, and you can evaluate its contents. You can require the input of a text field to be a number, an e-mail address (for instance, `jdoe@anywhere.com`), or a number within a range. The number range you specify can include positive whole numbers, negative numbers, or decimals.

FIGURE 11-20

The Validate Form action checks your form's entries client-side, without CGI programming.

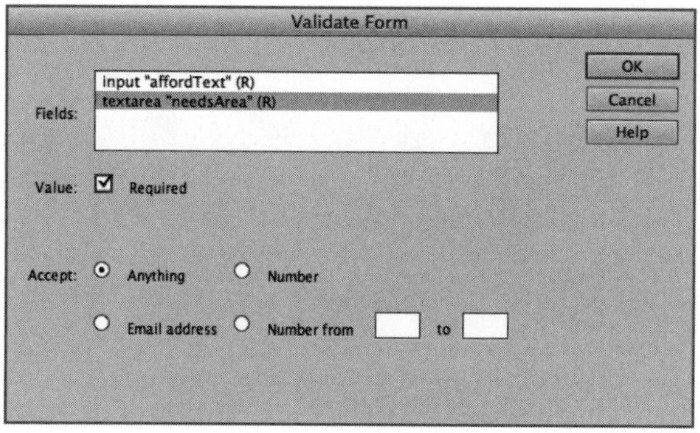

To use the Validate Form action, follow these steps:

1. Select the form object to trigger the action: a single text field, the `<form>` tag (use the Tag Selector), or the Submit button for multiple text fields.
2. From the Behaviors panel, click the Add (+) button and select Validate Form.
3. If you are validating an entire form, select a text field from the Fields list. If you are validating a single field, the selected form object is chosen for you and appears in the Fields list.
4. To make the field required, select the Value: Required checkbox.
5. To set the kind of input expected, select one of the following Accept options:
   - **Anything:** Accepts any input.
   - **Number:** Enables any sort of numeric input in the range of zeros through nines. You cannot mix text such as parentheses or hyphens and numbers, however, as in a telephone number such as (212) 555-1212.

- **Email Address:** Looks for an e-mail address with the @ sign. (This is not a foolproof e-mail address check because it validates illegal addresses such as human@somewhere, @somewhere.com, human@somewhere.overtherainbow, and so on.)
- **Number From:** Enables you to enter two numbers, one in each text box, to define the number range.

6. Click OK when you're finished.

Spry effects in Dreamweaver

As part of the Spry framework, Adobe has included a series of seven effects in Dreamweaver's standard behaviors. These behaviors add a whole new level of interactivity to the web designer's palette without requiring any additional hand-coding. Now designers can easily fade text in or out, make an image for a photo album appear to grow out of the page, smoothly slide a submenu in, and much, much more.

Each of the effects depends on an external JavaScript file, `SpryEffects.js`. The needed reference for this file is automatically added to the page and the file is placed in the SpryAssets folder in your site root the first time an effect is added. You'll need to publish the JavaScript file to your site along with your page for the effects to work properly. The seven effects, detailed in the following sections, are:

- Appear/Fade
- Blind
- Grow/Shrink
- Highlight
- Shake
- Slide
- Squish

Appear/Fade

As you might expect, the Appear/Fade effect causes a targeted page element to appear or fade over a set period of time. You could, for example, fade in an AP element with additional information when a user clicks a Help icon. Likewise, because the behavior allows the effect to be toggled, the AP element could fade out with another click of the same icon.

Appear/Fade requires a tag with an assigned ID as the target element; any HTML tag except `applet`, `body`, `iframe`, `object`, `tr`, `tbody`, or `th` can be used. You'll be able to control the duration of the fade, as well as its percentage; you could, for example, fade an image from 100 percent to 40 percent over 3,000 milliseconds (3 seconds).

To use the Appear/Fade effect, follow these steps:

1. Make sure that the element you want to affect is contained within a tag with an ID on your page.
2. Select the object to trigger the effect.
3. From the Behaviors panel, click the Add (+) button and select Effect ➪ Appear/Fade.

4. In the Appear/Fade dialog box (see Figure 11-21), select the tag with an ID you want to appear or fade.
5. Enter the length of the effect (in milliseconds) in the Effect Duration field (1,000 milliseconds equals 1 second).
6. Choose whether you'd like the targeted element to Appear or Fade from the Effect list.
7. If you chose Appear:
   a. Set the starting opacity percentage in the Appear From field.
   b. Set the ending opacity percentage in the Appear To field.
8. If you chose Fade:
   a. Set the starting opacity percentage in the Fade From field.
   b. Set the ending opacity percentage in the Fade To field.

FIGURE 11-21

Fade page elements in and out at the click of a link or when the page loads with the Appear/Fade effect.

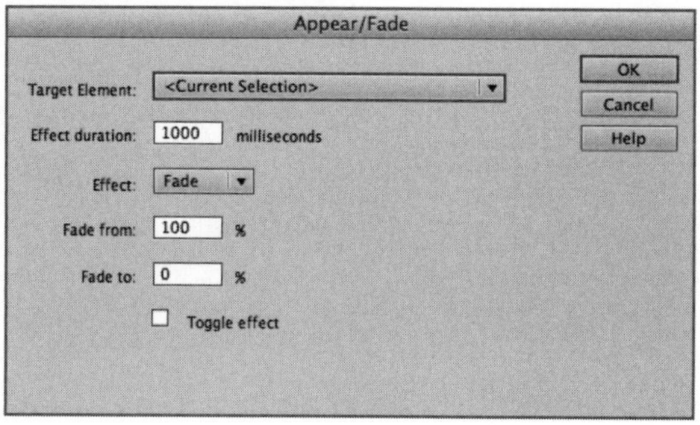

9. If you'd like the reverse effect to occur the next time the trigger is selected, click the Toggle Effect checkbox.
10. Click OK when you're done.

Blind

The Blind effect emulates window blinds raising and lowering. However, these particular types of blinds are attached to the bottom of the windowsill, not the top, so the content is hidden when the blinds go up and revealed when the blinds go down.

To use the Blind effect, follow these steps:

1. Make sure that the element you want to affect is contained within an acceptable tag with an ID on your page.

   Only the following tags can be used for the Blind effect: `address`, `dd`, `div`, `dl`, `dt`, `form`, `h1`, `h2`, `h3`, `h4`, `h5`, `h6`, `p`, `ol`, `ul`, `li`, `applet`, `center`, `dir`, `menu`, or `pre`.

2. Select the object to trigger the effect.
3. From the Behaviors panel, click the Add (+) button and select Effect ➪ Blind.
4. In the Blind dialog box (see Figure 11-22), select the tag with an ID you want to hide or reveal.

FIGURE 11-22

Imagine window blinds going up to hide the targeted content and down to reveal it with the Blind effect.

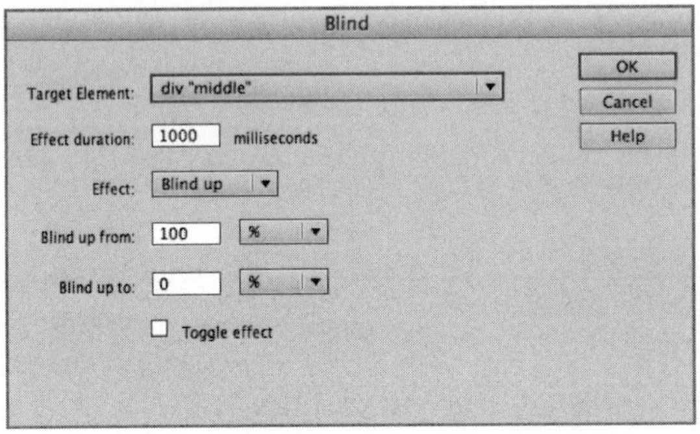

5. Enter the length of the effect (in milliseconds) in the Effect Duration field (1,000 milliseconds equals 1 second).
6. If you'd like the targeted element to be hidden, choose Blind Up from the Effect list; to reveal a previously hidden element, choose Blind Down.
7. If you chose Blind Up:
   a. Set the starting percentage in the Blind Up From field.
   b. Set the ending percentage in the Blind Up To field.
8. If you chose Blind Down:
   a. Set the starting percentage in the Blind Down From field.
   b. Set the ending percentage in the Blind Down To field.
9. If you'd like the reverse effect to occur the next time the trigger is selected, click the Toggle Effect checkbox.
10. Click OK when you're done.

Grow/Shrink

The Grow/Shrink effect reduces or enlarges the targeted content. This effect can be used to temporarily make an image bigger when the page visitor mouses over a thumbnail and smaller when the visitor moves the mouse off the thumbnail. In addition to controlling the duration of the effect, you also have the option of growing or shrinking from the center of the target or from the upper-left corner.

TIP

To achieve the aforementioned effect of the thumbnail growing and shrinking according to the mouse position, apply the Grow/Shrink effect twice: First, grow the image slightly with an `onMouseOver` event, and then second, shrink it back to its original dimensions with an `onMouseOut` event.

To use the Grow/Shrink effect, follow these steps:

1. Make sure that the element you want to affect is contained within an acceptable tag with an ID on your page.

   Only one of the following tags can be used with the Grow/Shrink effect: `address`, `dd`, `div`, `dl`, `dt`, `form`, `p`, `ol`, `ul`, `applet`, `center`, `dir`, `menu`, `img`, or `pre`.
2. Select the object to trigger the effect.
3. From the Behaviors panel, click the Add (+) button and select Effect ➪ Grow/Shrink.
4. In the Grow/Shrink dialog box (see Figure 11-23), select the tag with an ID you want to grow or shrink.
5. Enter the length of the effect (in milliseconds) in the Effect Duration field (1,000 milliseconds equals 1 second).
6. From the Effect list, choose whether you'd like the targeted element to Grow or Shrink.

FIGURE 11-23

Enlarge or reduce the size of an image interactively with the Grow/Shrink effect.

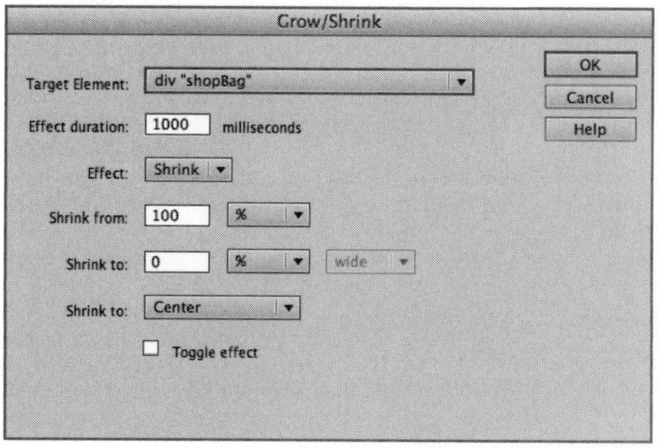

7. If you chose Grow:
   a. Set the starting opacity percentage in the Grow From field.
   b. Set the ending opacity percentage in the Grow To field.
   c. Choose the desired direction (Center or Top Left Corner) from the Grow From list.
8. If you chose Shrink:
   a. Set the starting opacity percentage in the Shrink From field.
   b. Set the ending opacity percentage in the Shrink To field.
   c. Choose the desired direction (Center or Top Left Corner) from the Shrink To list.

9. If you'd like the reverse effect to occur the next time the trigger is selected, click the Toggle Effect checkbox.
10. Click OK when you're done.

Highlight

The fading highlight, one of the earliest Web 2.0 techniques, was first implemented by web application developers 37Signals (`www.37signals.com`). In this technique, a certain event (such as a page loading or a user tabbing into a form element) triggers a sudden burst of color behind a section of text, which quickly fades away. The effect works well to momentarily bring the page visitor's attention to a particular page element without disrupting the final layout. You can accomplish this same result—with many variations—by applying the Highlight effect.

To use the Highlight effect, follow these steps:

1. Make sure that the element you want to affect is contained within an appropriate tag with an ID on your page.

   Any HTML tag can be used with a Highlight effect, except for the following: `applet`, `body`, `frame`, `frameset`, or `noframes`.
2. Select the object to trigger the effect.
3. From the Behaviors panel, click the Add (+) button and select Effect ➪ Highlight.
4. In the Highlight dialog box (see Figure 11-24), select the tag with an ID you want to highlight.

FIGURE 11-24

Assign the Highlight effect to the body tag's onLoad effect to add to a page area an initial burst of color that quickly disappears.

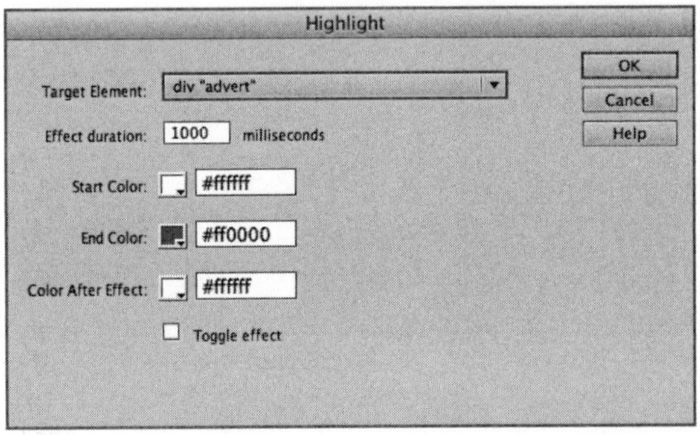

5. Enter the length of the effect (in milliseconds) in the Effect Duration field (1,000 milliseconds equals 1 second).
6. Choose the initial background color from the Start Color swatch.
7. Choose the background color the initial color fades to from the End Color swatch.
8. Choose the background color displayed after the fade is completed from the Color After Effect swatch.

9. If you'd like the reverse effect to occur the next time the trigger is selected, click the Toggle Effect checkbox.
10. Click OK when you're done.

Shake

If you've ever mistyped your password on the login screen on Mac OS X, you've experienced the Shake effect. Shake moves the targeted element back and forth several times in a side-to-side manner. This effect is a sure attention grabber when used sparingly. The Dreamweaver implementation does not offer any user-selectable parameters such as duration or distance; you can select only the targeted tag.

To use the Shake effect, follow these steps:

1. Make sure that the element you want to affect is contained within an appropriate tag with an ID on your page.

   Apply the Shake effect to any of the following tags: `address`, `blockquote`, `dd`, `div`, `dl`, `dt`, `fieldset`, `form`, `h1`, `h2`, `h3`, `h4`, `h5`, `h6`, `iframe`, `img`, `object`, `p`, `ol`, `ul`, `li`, `applet`, `dir`, `hr`, `menu`, `pre`, or `table`.
2. Select the object to trigger the effect.
3. From the Behaviors panel, click the Add (+) button and select Effect ➪ Shake.
4. In the Shake dialog box (see Figure 11-25), select the tag with an ID you want to shake.
5. Click OK when you're done.

FIGURE 11-25

The Shake effect moves the targeted element 20 pixels to the left and right for a few seconds.

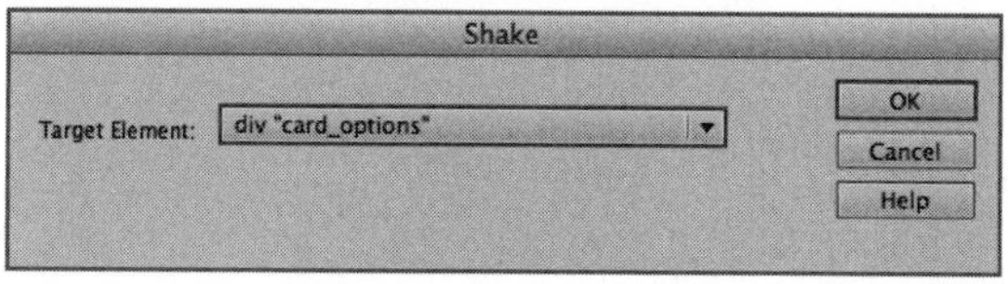

Slide

The Slide effect is similar to the Blind effect in that the content in both is either hidden or revealed. However, with Slide, the content itself appears to move in or out of view. Slide is different from all the other effects in another way: Slide requires an outer `<div>` tag with an ID that surrounds another tag with an ID. For example, the relevant code might look like this:

```
<div id="wrapper">
  <div id="content">
    <p>Content to slide</p>
  </div>
</div>
```

The Slide effect targets the surrounding `<div>` tag; in this example, the targeted tag would be `<div id="wrapper">`.

To use the Slide effect, follow these steps:

1. Make sure that the element you want to affect is contained within an appropriate tag with an ID on your page.

   Use the Slide effect with any of the following tags: `blockquote`, `dd`, `div`, `form`, `center`, `table`, `span`, `input`, `textarea`, `select`, or `image`.
2. Select the object to trigger the effect.
3. From the Behaviors panel, click the Add (+) button and select Effect ➪ Slide.
4. In the Slide dialog box (see Figure 11-26), select the tag with an ID you want to hide or reveal.

FIGURE 11-26

Make sure you target the content's surrounding div when applying the Slide effect.

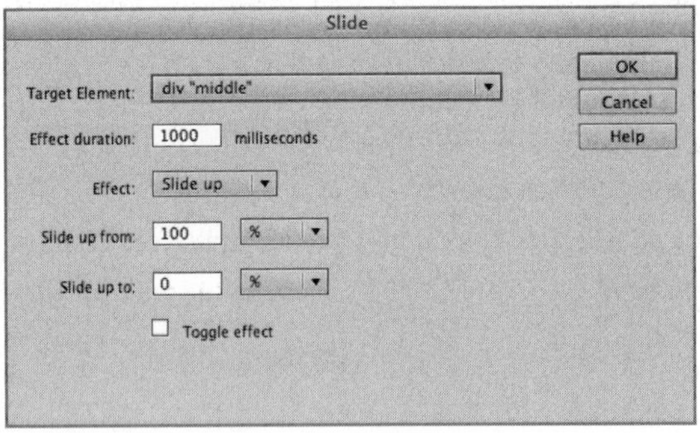

5. Enter the length of the effect (in milliseconds) in the Effect Duration field.
6. If you'd like the targeted element to be hidden, choose Slide Up from the Effect list; to reveal a previously hidden element, choose Slide Down.
7. If you chose Slide Up:
   a. Set the starting percentage in the Slide Up From field.
   b. Set the ending percentage in the Slide Up To field.
8. If you chose Slide Down:
   a. Set the starting percentage in the Slide Down From field.
   b. Set the ending percentage in the Slide Down To field.
9. If you'd like the reverse effect to occur the next time the trigger is selected, click the Toggle Effect checkbox.
10. Click OK when you're done.

Squish

The Squish effect is similar to a specialized use of the Grow/Shrink effect. When a Squish effect is triggered, the targeted page element shrinks from 100 percent to 0 percent in the element's upper-left corner; trigger the effect again and the element grows to 100 percent in the opposite direction. Like Shake, the only user-defined parameter is the choice of the target element.

To use the Squish effect, follow these steps:

1. Make sure that the element you want to affect is contained within an appropriate tag with an ID on your page.

   Only the following tags can be used with the Squish effect: `address`, `dd`, `div`, `dl`, `dt`, `form`, `img`, `p`, `ol`, `ul`, `applet`, `center`, `dir`, `menu`, or `pre`.
2. Select the object to trigger the effect.
3. From the Behaviors panel, click the Add (+) button and select Effect ➪ Squish.
4. In the Squish dialog box (see Figure 11-27), select the tag with an ID you want to squish.
5. Click OK when you're done.

FIGURE 11-27

The Squish effect automatically toggles, shrinking and growing the targeted page element.

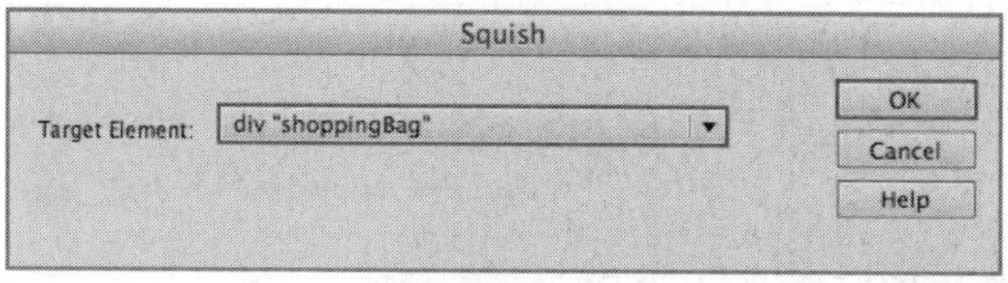

Installing, Managing, and Modifying Behaviors

The standard behaviors that come with Dreamweaver are indeed impressive, but they're really just the beginning. Because existing behaviors can be modified and new ones created from scratch, you can continue to add behaviors as you need them.

To install a new Dreamweaver behavior, follow these steps:

1. Locate the behavior, which must be packaged as an MXP extension file; for example: `alignLayer.mxp`, `cleanupPage.mxp`, and so on.

CAUTION

The website for this book (`www.wiley.com/go/dreamweavercs6bible`) contains several useful MXP behavior extension files. In addition, you can find a large selection of MXP extension files on the Adobe Marketplace & Exchange site, which you can reach by choosing Help ➪ Dreamweaver Exchange.

2. To install the extension in Dreamweaver (or in Fireworks or Flash, for that matter), either double-click the MXP extension file or choose Help ➪ Manage Extensions to open the Extension Manager (shown in Figure 11-28) and choose File ➪ Install Extension to select the file. Some extensions remain inaccessible until you've quit and restarted Dreamweaver; in most cases, you will be prompted to do so.

NOTE

Depending on your browser, you might be given the choice of installing a Dreamweaver Exchange extension file directly from the Exchange site or to save it first to disk and install it from there. If you choose to install the extension file directly from the Exchange site, the Extension Manager handles the installation automatically. If you choose to save the extension file to disk, a good place to save it is the Downloaded Extensions folder within your Dreamweaver CS6 folder.

FIGURE 11-28

Use the Extension Manager to install, remove, and temporarily enable/disable MXP extension files from Dreamweaver, Fireworks, or Flash.

Altering the parameters of a behavior

You can alter any of the attributes for your inserted behaviors at any time. To modify a behavior you have already attached, follow these steps:

1. Open the Behaviors panel.
2. Select the object in the Document window or the tag in the Tag Selector to which your behavior is attached.
3. Double-click the action that you want to alter. The appropriate dialog box opens, with the previously selected parameters.
4. Make any modifications to the existing settings for the action.
5. Click OK when you are finished.

Sequencing behaviors

When you have more than one action attached to a particular event, the order of the actions is often important. For example, you might want to apply the Change Text action to a section of the page before you attract attention to it with the Highlight effect. To specify the sequence in which Dreamweaver triggers the actions, reposition them as necessary in the Actions column. To do this, simply select an action and use the up and down arrow buttons (refer to Figure 11-1) to reposition it in the list.

Deleting behaviors

To remove a behavior from a list of behaviors attached to a particular event, simply highlight the behavior and click the Remove (–) button.

Dreamweaver TECHNIQUE

Modifying Behaviors

To further reveal the power of Dreamweaver's standard behaviors, add another series of behaviors to your practice page. In the process, you'll get a chance to adjust attributes of an applied behavior.

1. From the Files panel, re-open the `behaviors_start.htm` file you previously worked on.
2. Place your cursor anywhere in the Living Room link.
3. From the Behaviors panel, click Add (+) and select Open Browser Window.
4. In the Open Browser Window dialog box, set the following parameters:
   - Click the Browse button and choose `living_room.htm` from the dialog box.
   - In the Window Width field, enter **200**.
   - In the Window Height field, enter **100**.
   - Select the Resize Handles option.
5. Click OK when you're done.

   A second behavior is added to the link in the Behaviors panel, with the default event of onClick.
6. Save your file and press F12 (Option+F12) to preview the page in your primary browser.
7. Click the Living Room link to test the behavior.
8. You'll notice that the window height is too small for the text; you can easily make the adjustment. In Dreamweaver's Behaviors panel, double-click the Open Browser Window event to re-open the dialog box.
9. Change the Window Height value to 150; click OK when you're done.

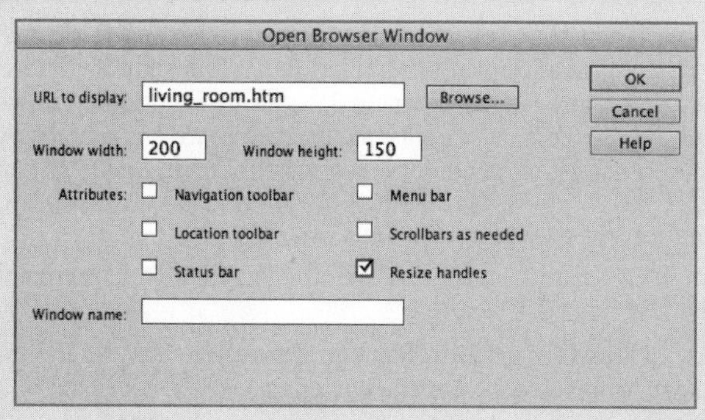

Continues

continued

10. To verify that the change is sufficient, test the page in the browser as before.
11. In Dreamweaver, repeat Steps 2–5 for the Kitchen North link and set the Browser Window behavior to open `kitchen.htm` with a width of 200 pixels and height of 150 pixels.
12. Repeat Steps 2–5 for the Kitchen South link and again set the Browser Window behavior to open `kitchen.htm` with a width of 200 pixels and height of 150 pixels.

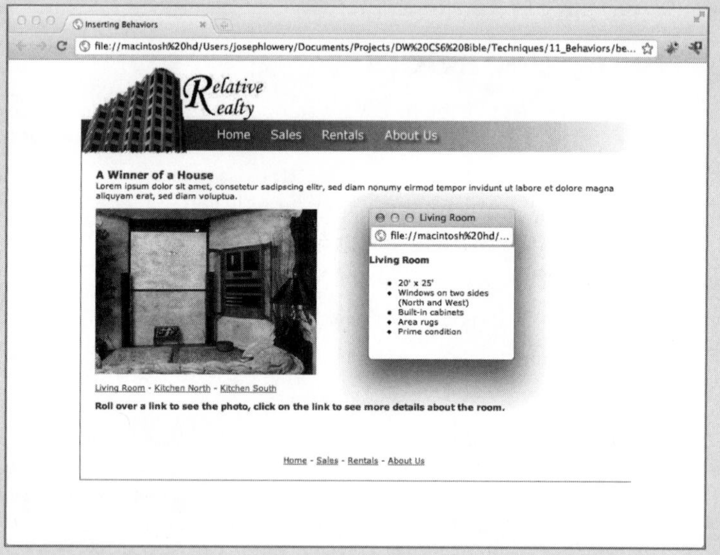

13. Save your page.

Test your page in the browser to verify that all the windows open as expected.

Summary

Dreamweaver behaviors can greatly extend the web designer's palette of possibilities—even if the web designer is an accomplished JavaScript programmer. Behaviors simplify and automate the process of incorporating common and not-so-common JavaScript functions. The versatility of the behavior format enables anyone proficient in JavaScript to create custom actions that can be attached to any event. When considering behaviors, keep the following points in mind:

- Behaviors are combinations of events and actions.
- Behaviors are written in HTML and JavaScript and are completely customizable from within Dreamweaver.
- Dreamweaver includes 25 standard actions. Some actions are not available unless a particular object is included, and selected, on the current page.

In the next chapter, you learn how to work with tables and structured data.

CHAPTER

12

Setting Up Tables

IN THIS CHAPTER

Learning about tables in HTML

Setting up a table in Dreamweaver

Dreamweaver Technique: Adding a Table to the Page

Customizing tables

Sorting table contents

Dreamweaver Technique: Inserting Table Content

Dreamweaver Technique: Adjusting Table Properties

Importing tabular data

Tables bring structure to a web page, and they are especially important when displaying data for web applications. Whether it is used to align numbers in a spreadsheet or arrange columns of information on a page, an HTML table brings a bit of order to otherwise free-flowing content. Tables are the preferred method for presenting structured information and, because of the backward capabilities of many e-mail clients, design HTML e-mails.

Dreamweaver's implementation of tables reflects this trend in web page design. Drag-and-drop table sizing, easy organization of rows and columns, and instant table reformatting all help get the job done in the shortest time possible. Table editing features enable you to select and modify anything in a table—from a single cell to multiple columns. Moreover, using Dreamweaver's commands, you can sort static table data in a variety of ways or completely reformat it.

This chapter covers everything you need to know to get started creating HTML tables in Dreamweaver. You can also dynamically add data to tables from an external data source using server-side processing. Using dynamic data is covered in Chapter 19.

HTML Table Fundamentals

A table is basically a grid that expands as you add text or images. Tables consist of three main components: rows, columns, and cells. Rows extend across a table from left to right, and columns run up and down. A cell is the area within the intersection of a row and a column; it's where you enter your information. Cells expand to fit whatever they hold. If you have enabled the table border, your browser shows the outline of the entire table and each cell.

Adding a Table

If you're familiar with HTML tables and just want to know how to add a table in Dreamweaver, follow these steps:

1. Place your cursor on the page where you'd like the table to appear.

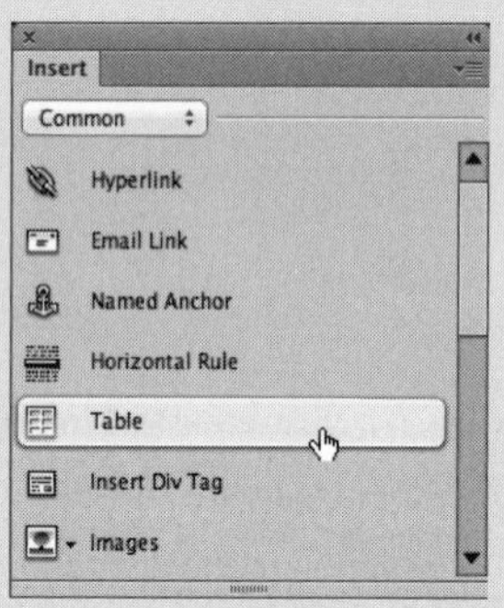

2. From the Common category of the Insert panel, click Table.
3. When the Table dialog box appears, enter the number of rows and columns you want to start within the appropriate fields.
4. Set the width of the table in pixels or percentage.
5. Specify any of the other parameters you want, such as border width, cell padding, cell spacing, header placement, and caption.
6. Click OK.

Add content to the table by clicking into any cell and typing or inserting images or other media. As you'll learn in the rest of this chapter, there's a lot you can do with tables, but this should get you started.

In HTML, the structure and all the data of a table are contained between the table tag pair, `<table>` and `</table>`. The `<table>` tag can take numerous attributes, determining a table's width (which can be given in absolute pixel measurement or as a percentage of the screen), as well as the border, alignment on the page, and background color. You can also control the size of the spacing between cells and the amount of padding within cells.

NOTE

You can insert a `<table> . . . </table>` pair directly in your code by choosing Insert ⇨ Table Objects ⇨ Table or by clicking the Table Tag button in the Common category of the Insert panel. You must do this in Code view, where you can see the exact location of your cursor before inserting the tag pair.

HTML uses a strict hierarchy when describing a table. You can see this clearly in Listing 12-1, which shows the HTML generated from a simple table in Dreamweaver.

LISTING 12-1 Code for an HTML Table

```
<table border="1" width="75%">
  <tr>
    <td> </td>
    <td> </td>
    <td> </td>
  </tr>
  <tr>
    <td> </td>
    <td> </td>
    <td> </td>
  </tr>
  <tr>
    <td> </td>
    <td> </td>
    <td> </td>
  </tr>
</table>
```

12

NOTE

The ` ` in the table code is HTML for a non-breaking space. Dreamweaver inserts this code in each empty table cell because some browsers collapse the cell without it. Enter any text or image in the cell, and Dreamweaver automatically removes the ` ` code.

Rows

After the opening `<table>` tag comes the first row tag `<tr> ... </tr>` pair. Within the current row, you can specify attributes for horizontal alignment or vertical alignment. In addition, browsers recognize row color as an added option.

If you are working directly in Code view, you can insert a `<tr> ... </tr>` pair by choosing Insert ➪ Table Objects ➪ TR. See "Inserting rows and columns" later in this chapter for methods of inserting rows in Design view.

Cells

Cells are marked in HTML with the `<td> ... </td>` tag pair. No specific code exists for a column; rather, the number of columns is determined by the maximum number of cells within a single table row. For example, in Listing 12-1, notice the three sets of `<td>` tags between each `<tr>` pair. This means the table has three columns.

NOTE

Most `<table>`, `<tr>`, and `<td>` attributes are better set up using CSS; attributes such as `bgcolor` were deprecated under HTML 4.0 and XHTML 1.0 specifications and have been removed from XHTML 1.1 and HTML5 entirely.

A cell can span more than one row or column—in these cases, you see a `rowspan=value` or `colspan=value` attribute in the <td> tag, as illustrated in Listing 12-2. This code is also for a table with three rows and three columns, but the second cell in the first row spans two columns.

LISTING 12-2 HTML Table with Column Spanning

```
<table width="75%"  border="0">
  <tr>
    <td> </td>
    <td colspan="2"> </td>
  </tr>
  <tr>
    <td> </td>
    <td> </td>
    <td> </td>
  </tr>
  <tr>
    <td> </td>
    <td> </td>
    <td> </td>
  </tr>
</table>
```

Cells can also be given horizontal or vertical alignment attributes, which override any similar attributes specified by the table row. When you give a cell a particular width, all the cells in that column are affected. Width can be specified either in an absolute pixel measurement or as a percentage of the overall table.

NOTE

Again, modern web designers prefer to use CSS rather than HTML attributes to format and style table cells and entire tables. Both the `align` and `bgcolor` attributes have been deprecated, and recent browsers don't support other attributes such as height.

In Code view, you can insert a <td> . . . </td> pair to define a single table cell by choosing Insert ➪ Table Objects ➪ TD.

Column and row headings

HTML uses a special type of cell called a *table header* for column and row headings. Information in these cells is marked with a <th> tag and is generally rendered in boldface, horizontally centered within the cell.

To insert a <th> . . . </th> pair for a table heading cell, choose Insert ➪ Table Objects ➪ TH. See the section "Setting cell, column, and row properties" later in this chapter for another way to designate table header cells.

TIP

After the initial `<table>` tag, you can place an optional caption for the table. In Dreamweaver, you can enter the `<caption>` tag in the Code view or Code inspector by choosing Insert ➪ Table Objects ➪ Caption. From Code view, you can also click the Table Caption button in the Tables category of the Insert panel.

The following example shows how the tag works:

```
<caption valign="bottom">Table of Periodic Elements</caption>
```

12

Inserting Tables in Dreamweaver

You can control almost all of a table's HTML features through Dreamweaver's point-and-click interface. To insert a table in the current cursor position, use one of the following methods:

- Choose Insert ➪ Table.
- Click the Table button in either the Common or the Layout categories of the Insert panel.
- Use the keyboard shortcut: Ctrl+Alt+T (Command+Option+T).

Depending on your preference settings, any one of these methods either immediately inserts a table into your page or opens the Table dialog box. The dialog box is bypassed—and the previous settings used—if the Show Dialog When Inserting Objects option in Preferences is not enabled. The Table dialog box, shown in Figure 12-1, contains the values shown in Table 12-1 when it is first displayed.

TABLE 12-1 Default Values for the Table Dialog Box

Attribute	Default	Description
Rows	3	Sets the number of horizontal rows.
Columns	3	Sets the number of vertical columns.
Width	200 pixels	Sets the preset width of the table. This can be specified as a percentage of the containing element (screen, AP element, or another table) or an absolute pixel size.
Border	1 pixel	Sets the width of the border around each cell and the entire table.
Cell Padding	0	Sets the space between a cell's border and its contents, measured in pixels. A value of 0 indicates no margin space within the cell.
Cell Spacing	0	Sets the number of pixels between each cell. A value of 0 indicates no space between cells.

Continues

TABLE 12-1 *(continued)*

Attribute	Default	Description
Header	None	Determines whether the top row and/or column is designated as a header cell. In addition to simply creating the header cell with `<th>` tags instead of the usual `<td>`, this attribute adds the `scope` attribute to the cell. The `scope` attribute helps nonvisual browsers interpret and present the structure of the table, by indicating whether the cell is a column heading or a row heading. In visual browsers, text in header rows or columns is typically displayed as bold and centered.
Caption	Blank	Sets a brief description for the table.
Align Caption	default	Enables you to specify whether the table caption appears at the top, bottom, left, or right of the table. Choosing default does not add an `align` attribute to the `<caption>` tag and uses the browser's default alignment instead. Note that the `align` attribute on the `<caption>` tag is deprecated in HTML 4.0. This means that, although the attribute is still currently supported, the preferred method to achieve the same effect in newer browsers is to use CSS.
Summary	Blank	Enables you to add the summary attribute to your `<table>` tag. The summary is a verbal description of the table layout, so that people who are having the page read to them (for example, through a nonvisual browser) can understand it. For example, your summary could say, "This table compares the number of students and teachers in each Minnesota secondary school for the years 1997 through 2002. It lists each school in Minnesota, grouped by school district. For each of the years 1997 through 2002, there are columns for the number of students and number of teachers in each school." This is particularly important for complex tables. The text you enter for the summary is not displayed in visual browsers.

If you aren't sure of the number of rows and/or columns you need, put in your best guess—you can add or delete rows or columns later as necessary.

The default table is sized to take up 200 percent of the browser window. You can alter this percentage by changing the value in the Width text box. The table maintains this proportion as you add text or images, except in the following situations:

- When an image is larger than the specified percentage
- When the `nowrap` attribute is used for the cell or table row and there is too much text to fit

In either case, the percentage set for the table is ignored, and the cell and table expand to accommodate the text or image. (For further information on the nowrap attribute, see the "Cell wrap" section later in this chapter.)

FIGURE 12-1

The Table dialog box starts out with a default table of three columns and three rows; you can adjust it as needed, and Dreamweaver will remember your last choices.

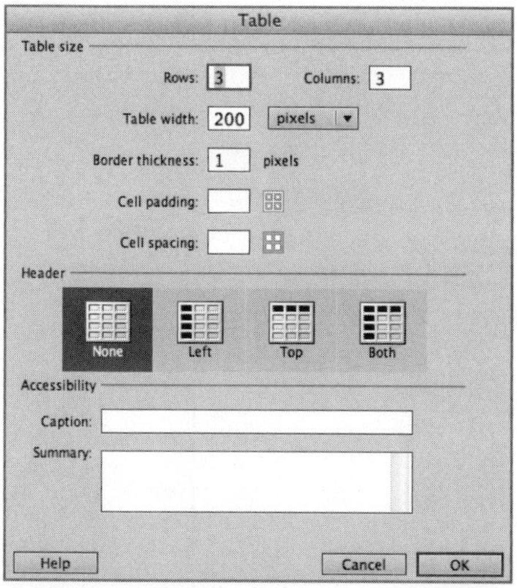

NOTE

The Table dialog box uses what are called *sticky settings*, displaying your previously used settings the next time you open the dialog box. This handy feature enables you to set the border width to 0, for example, and forget about resetting it each time.

If you prefer to enter the table width as an absolute pixel value, instead of the relative percentage, type the number of pixels in the Width text box and select Pixels in the drop-down list of width options.

With Dreamweaver's Table Widths feature, you can tell at a glance whether your table and cells are set to percentages or pixels—and exactly what these values are. The Table Widths feature is a design-time visual aid that appears above or below (depending on its position in the window) a table when one or more table cells are active. The widths are presented in two lines: The outermost line shows the width of the entire table, and the innermost line displays cell-width measurements.

With the Table Widths feature enabled, tables or cells using percentages actually display two values. The first value shown is the actual percentage; it is followed by a second value in parentheses that indicates the current size in pixels. For example, if a table is set to 75% and placed in a browser window where the interior screen width is 970 pixels, the actual width of the table is 693 pixels. Dreamweaver displays 75% (693), as shown in Figure 12-2. The same figure shows two other tables: one at 100%, which takes up the full width of the browser window, minus any margins. The third table is fixed at 400 pixels—approximately half of an 800 × 600 window.

FIGURE 12-2

In addition to displaying overall table and column widths, the Table Width visual aid provides a quick method for working with columns.

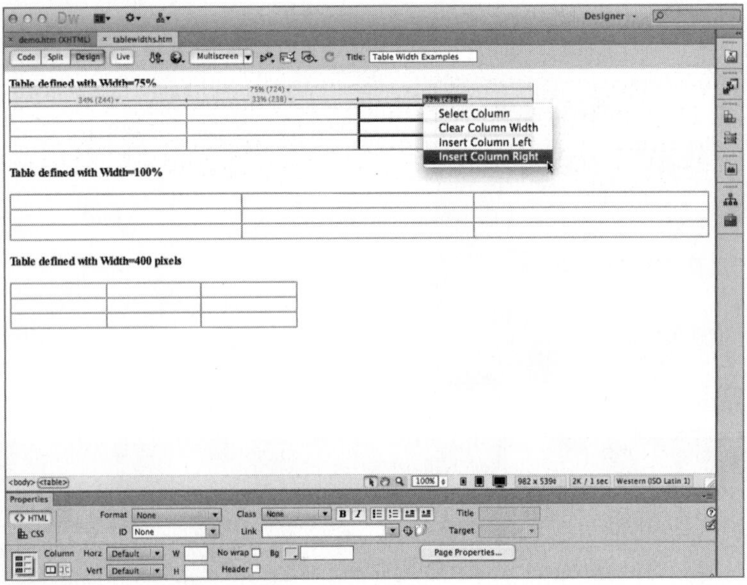

Although viewing Table Widths definitely helps with certain stages of the design process, it can impede others. To turn off the dimensioning, deselect View ➪ Visual Aids ➪ Table Widths; the same option exists under the View Options menu of the Document toolbar.

TIP

You don't have to declare a width for your table at all. If you delete the value in the Width text box of the Table dialog box, your table starts out as small as possible and only expands to accommodate inserted text or images. However, this can make it difficult to position your cursor inside a cell to enter content—a situation Expanded Tables mode (covered later in this chapter) is intended to alleviate.

The Table Widths feature also offers a number of context menus to make table operations even easier. Click the down arrow next to the table width measurement to select the table, clear all heights and/or widths, make all widths consistent, or hide the table widths. Choose the down arrow over a column to select that column, clear the column width, or insert columns to either side.

Dreamweaver TECHNIQUE

Adding a Table to the Page

In this first Technique of the chapter, you practice inserting two tables and setting their initial values.

1. In the Files panel, switch to the Dreamweaver Bible working site previously created.
2. Expand the 12_Tables folder and open the file `table_start.htm`.
3. Place your cursor at the end of the first paragraph under the About Us heading and press Enter (Return) to create a new line.
4. From the Insert panel's Common category, click the Table object.
5. When the Insert Table dialog box opens, set the following parameters:

   Rows: **4**

   Columns: **2**

   Table Width: **500 pixels**

   Border Thickness: **0**

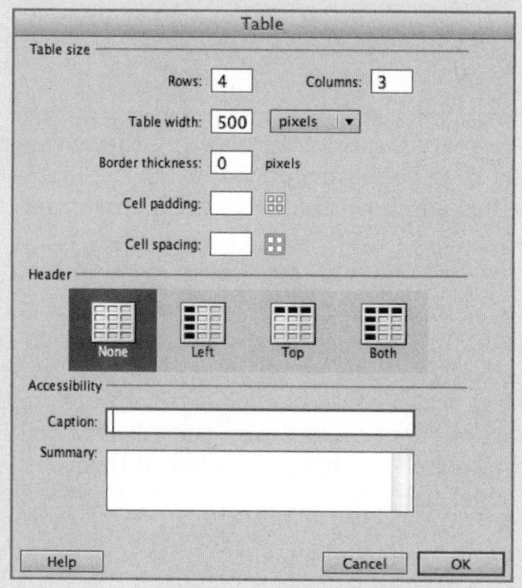

6. Leave both the Cell Padding and Cell Spacing fields blank.
7. In the Header area, select Left.
8. Leave all the fields in the Accessibility area at their defaults and click OK.

continues

continued

The first table is inserted at the cursor position, ready for data. Now, add a second table near the bottom of the page.

1. Place your cursor at the end of the paragraph under the Our Top Staff heading and press Enter (Return).
2. Click the Table object on the Insert panel.
3. When the Insert Table dialog box opens, set the following parameters:

   Rows: **4**

   Columns: **4**

   Table width: **75 percent**

   Border Thickness: **0**
4. Leave both the Cell Padding and the Cell Spacing fields blank.
5. In the Header area, select Top.
6. Leave all the fields in the Accessibility area at their defaults and click OK.
7. Save your page.

In the next Techniques, you continue working with these practice tables, adding content and changing their structure.

Modifying Tables

Most modifications to tables start in the Property inspector. Dreamweaver helps you manage the basic table parameters—width, border, and alignment—and provides attributes for other useful but more arcane features of a table. These include converting table width from pixels to percentage of the screen, and vice versa.

Selecting table elements

As with text or images, the first step in altering a table (or any of its elements) is selection. Dreamweaver simplifies the selection process, making it easy to change both the properties and the contents of entire tables, selected rows or columns, and even non-adjacent cells. You can change the vertical alignment of a row, for example, with a click or two of the mouse—instead of highlighting and modifying each individual cell.

In Dreamweaver, you can select the following elements of a table:

- The entire table
- A single row
- Multiple rows, either adjacent or separate
- A single column

- Multiple columns, either adjacent or separate
- A single cell
- Multiple cells, either adjacent or separate

After you select a table element, you can modify its properties.

Selecting in Expanded Tables mode

It's fairly easy to select table elements when the table is fully expanded—but tables aren't always set to a 100% width. In fact, designers often remove all table width values for their layouts, thus collapsing the table to fit the content. Although this is often necessary, you may have difficulty placing your cursor in the right cell in a collapsed table. You can speed up the selection and design process considerably by temporarily entering into Expanded Tables mode.

To enable Expanded Tables mode, choose View ➪ Table Mode ➪ Expanded Tables Mode or use the keyboard shortcut F6 (Option+F6). An indicator bar appears on top of the document window when you enter Expanded Tables mode.

Expanded Tables mode makes cell selection easier by temporarily adding a border (if there is none) and increasing the cell padding and spacing. These visual changes effectively make the table and its cells view much more apparent and selection far easier. All changes in Dreamweaver's Design view are temporary and strictly visual—no code is ever rewritten. While you are in Expanded Tables mode, an outline (red, by default) appears around the table or any cells your cursor moves over. The outline color is controlled by the Mouse-Over option found on the Highlighting category of the Preferences. Ctrl+click (Command+click) an outlined cell or table to select it.

TIP

You don't need to be in Expanded Tables mode to see the table outlines. If the Mouse-Over option is enabled, the outlines appear when you're in Standard mode when you hold down the Ctrl (Command) key and move over the table.

Expanded Tables mode is best used on an as-needed basis, and you can quickly toggle between it and Standard mode by pressing F6 (Option+F6).

Selecting an entire table

Several methods are available for selecting the entire table, whether you're a menu- or mouse-oriented designer. To select the table via a menu, do one of the following:

- With the cursor positioned in the tables, choose Modify ➪ Table ➪ Select Table.
- With any table row already selected, choose Edit ➪ Select Parent Tag or use the keyboard shortcut, Ctrl+[(Command+[).
- Right-click (Control+click) inside a table to display the context menu and choose Table ➪ Select Table.

To select an entire table with the mouse, use one of the following techniques:

- Click the bottom or right border of the table. You can also click anywhere along the table border when the pointer becomes a four-sided arrow.

- Select the `<table>` tag in the Tag Selector.
- Click immediately to one side of the table and drag the mouse over the table.

The selected table is surrounded by a black border, with sizing handles on the right, bottom, and bottom-right corner (as shown in Figure 12-3), just like a selected graphic.

Selecting a row or column

Altering rows or columns of table text without Dreamweaver is a major, time-consuming chore. Each cell has to be individually selected and the changes applied. Dreamweaver has an intuitive method for selecting single or multiple columns and rows, comparable—and in some ways, superior—to major word processing programs.

FIGURE 12-3

A selected table can be identified by the black border outlining the table and the three sizing handles.

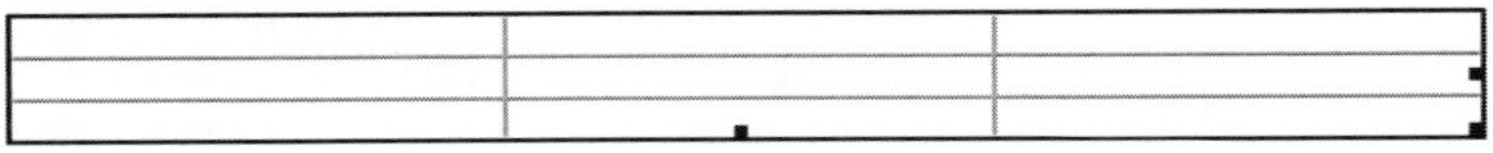

As with entire tables, you have several methods for selecting columns or rows. None of the techniques, however, uses the main menus; row and column selections are handled primarily with the mouse. In fact, you can select an entire row or column with one click.

The one-click method for selecting a single column or row requires that you position your pointer directly above the column or to the left of the row you want to choose. This is similar to the way you select a row or column in a Microsoft Word table. Move the pointer slowly toward the table—when the pointer becomes a single arrow, with the arrowhead pointing down for columns and to the right for rows, click the mouse. All the cells in the selected column or row are bounded with a black border. Any changes now made in the Property inspector affect all of the cells in the selected column or row.

You can select multiple, contiguous columns or rows by dragging the single-arrow pointer across several columns or rows. To select a number of columns or rows that are not next to one another, press the Ctrl (Command) key while selecting each individual column, using the one-click method.

TIP

If you have trouble positioning the mouse so that the single-arrow pointer appears, you can use two other methods to select cells in columns or rows. In the first method, you click and drag across all the cells in a column or row. The second method uses another keyboard modifier, the Shift key. With this technique, click once in the first cell of the column or row. Then, hold down the Shift key while you click in the final cell of the column or row (in Mac OS X, you must perform two single-clicks in the final cell). You can also use this technique to select cells in multiple adjacent columns or rows; just click in the last cell of another column or row.

Selecting cells

Sometimes you need to change an attribute of just a few cells in a table, but not the entire row—or you might need to merge several cells to form one wide column span. In these situations, and many others, you can use Dreamweaver's cell selection capabilities. As with columns and rows, you can select multiple cells, whether or not they are adjacent.

Individual cells are generally selected by dragging the mouse across one or more cell boundaries. To select a single cell, click anywhere in the cell and drag the mouse into another cell. As you pass the border between the two cells, the initial cell is highlighted. If you continue dragging the mouse across another cell boundary, the second cell is selected, and so on. Note that you have to drag the mouse into another cell and not cross the table border onto the page. For example, to highlight the lower-right cell of a table, you drag the mouse up or to the left.

TIP

You can also select a single cell by pressing the Ctrl (Command) key and clicking once in the cell, or you can select the rightmost `<td>` tag in the Tag Selector.

Extended cell selection in Dreamweaver is handled identically to extended text selection in most word processing programs. To select adjacent cells, click in the first desired cell, press and hold the Shift key, and click in the final desired cell. Dreamweaver selects everything in a rectangular area, using the first cell as the upper-left corner of the rectangle and the last cell as the lower-right corner. You could, for instance, select all the cells in an entire table by clicking in the upper-left cell and then Shift+clicking the lower-right cell.

Just as the Shift key is used to make adjacent cell selections, the Ctrl (Command) key is used for all non-adjacent cell selections. You can highlight any number of individual cells—whether or not they are next to one another—by pressing the Ctrl (Command) key while you click in each cell.

TIP

If you Ctrl+click (Command+click) a cell that is already selected, that cell is deselected—regardless of the method you used to select the cell initially.

Editing a table's contents

Before you learn how to change a table's attributes, let's look at basic editing techniques. Editing table text in Dreamweaver is slightly different from editing text outside of tables. When you begin to enter text into a table cell, the table borders expand to accommodate your new data, assuming no width has been set. The other cells appear to shrink, but they, too, expand after you start typing in text or inserting an image. Unless a cell's width is specified, the cell currently being edited expands or contracts, and the other cells are forced to adjust their width. Figure 12-4 shows a table (with one row and three columns) in three different states. In the top table, only the first cell contains text; notice how the other cells have contracted. In the middle table, text has been entered into the second cell as well, and you can see how the first cell is now smaller. Finally, in the bottom table, all three cells contain text, and the other two cells have adjusted their width to compensate for the expanding third cell.

FIGURE 12-4

As text is entered into a cell, the cell expands and other cells contract, even if they already contain text.

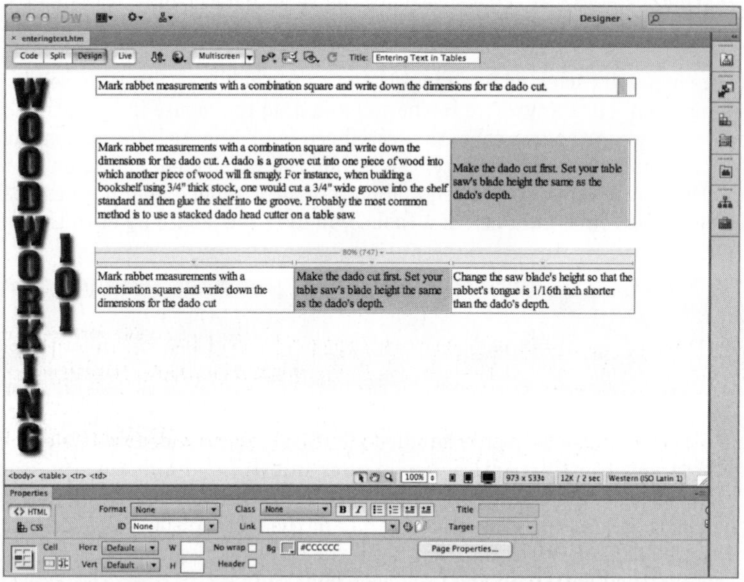

TIP

You can control whether a table expands and contracts with text or if it keeps a set width by using the table-layout CSS property. Define `table-layout: fixed` for the `table` selector to rely on the widths of the table and columns for table rendering. If you have a large table of data, the `table-layout: fixed` declaration can speed up the browser display significantly. Use `table-layout: auto` if you want the table to change size according to the amount of content in each cell.

If you look closely at the middle table in Figure 12-4, you can see that the text doesn't line up vertically. That's because the default vertical alignment in Dreamweaver, as in most browsers, provides for entries to be positioned in the vertical middle of the cell. (Later in this section, you learn how to adjust the vertical alignment.)

The expandability of table cells is very significant when you are inserting information from a data source because the data is often of varying length. See Chapter 21 for details about how to use Dreamweaver's Live Data view to check your layout.

Moving through a table

When you've finished entering your text in the first cell, you can move to the next cell in the row by pressing the Tab key. When you reach the end of a row, pressing Tab takes your cursor to the first cell of the next row. To go backward, cell to cell, press Shift+Tab.

TIP

Pressing Tab has a special function when you're in the last cell of a table—it adds a new row, with the same column configuration as the current one.

The Home and End keys take you to the beginning and end, respectively, of the cursor's current line. If a cell's contents are large enough for the text to wrap in the cell, move to the top of the current cell by pressing Ctrl+Home (Command+Home). To get to the bottom of the current cell in such a circumstance, press Ctrl+End (Command+End).

When you're at the beginning or end of the contents in a cell, you can also use the arrow keys to navigate from cell to cell. Use the left and right arrows to move from cell to cell in a row, and the up and down arrows to move from cell to cell in a column. When you come to the end of a row or column, the arrow keys move to the first cell in the next row or column. If you're moving left to right, the cursor goes from the end of one row to the beginning of the next row—and vice versa if you move from right to left. When moving from top to bottom, the cursor goes from the end of one column to the start of the next, and vice versa when moving bottom to top.

TIP

To enter a table without using the mouse, position the cursor directly before the table, press Shift+right arrow to select the table, and then press the down arrow key to move into the first cell. To move out of a table without using the mouse, press Ctrl+A (Command+A) twice to select the entire table and then use either the left or the right arrow to exit the table.

Cutting, copying, and pasting in tables

In the early days of web design, woe to you if you accidentally left out a cell of information. It was often almost faster to redo the entire table than to make room by meticulously cutting and pasting everything, one cell at a time. Dreamweaver ends that painstaking work forever with its advanced cutting and pasting features. You can copy a range of cells from one table to another and maintain all the attributes (such as color and alignment, as well as the content—text or images). You can also copy just the contents and ignore the attributes.

Dreamweaver has one basic restriction to table cut-and-paste operations: Your selected cells must form a rectangle. In other words, although you can select non-adjacent cells, columns, or rows and modify their properties, you can't cut or copy them. Should you try, you get a message from Dreamweaver like the one shown in Figure 12-5; the table above the notification in this figure illustrates an incorrect cell selection.

Copying attributes and contents

When you copy or cut a cell using the regular commands, Dreamweaver automatically copies everything—content, formatting, and cell format—in the selected cell. Then, pasting the cell reproduces it; however, you can get different results depending on where the cell (or column or row) is pasted.

FIGURE 12-5

Dreamweaver enables you to cut or copy selected cells only when they form a rectangle.

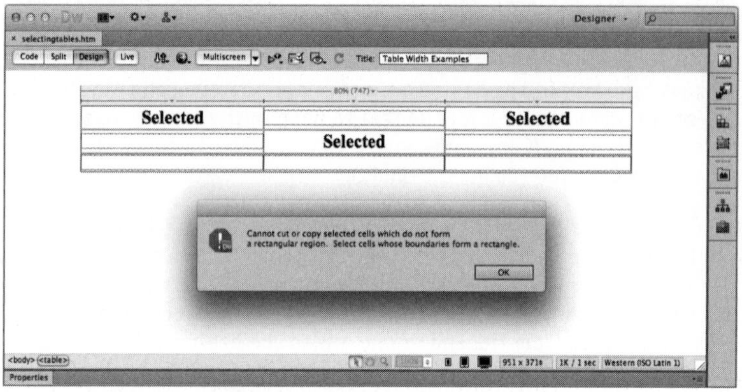

To cut or copy both the contents and the attributes of any cell, row, or column, follow these steps:

1. Select the cells you want to cut or copy. Remember that to cut or copy a range of cells in Dreamweaver, you must select cells that form a solid rectangular region.
2. To copy cells, choose Edit ➪ Copy or use the keyboard shortcut, Ctrl+C (Command+C).
3. To cut cells, choose Edit ➪ Cut or use the keyboard shortcut, Ctrl+X (Command+X). If you cut an individual cell, the contents are removed, but the cell remains. If, however, you cut an entire row or column, the cells are removed.
4. Position your cursor to paste the cells in the desired location:
   - To replace a cell with a cell on the clipboard, click anywhere in the cell to be replaced. If you cut or copy multiple cells that do not make up a full column or row, click in the upper-left corner of the cells you want to replace. For example, a range of six cells in a 2 × 3 configuration replaces the same configuration when pasted. Dreamweaver alerts you if you try to paste one configuration of cells into a different cell configuration.
   - To insert a new row with the row on the clipboard, click anywhere in the row immediately below where you'd like the new row to appear.
   - To insert a new column with the column on the clipboard, click anywhere in the column immediately to the right of where you'd like the new column to appear.
   - To replace an existing row or column in a table, select the row or column. If you've cut or copied multiple rows or columns, you must select an equivalent configuration of cells to replace.
   - To insert a new table based on the copied or cut cells, click anywhere outside of the table.
5. Paste the copied or cut cells by choosing Edit ➪ Paste or pressing Ctrl+V (Command+V).

TIP

To move a row or column that you've cut from the interior of a table to the exterior (the right or bottom), you have to first expand the number of cells in the table. To do this, first select the table by choosing Modify ➪ Table ➪ Select Table or by using one of the other techniques previously described. Next, in the Table Property inspector, increase the number of rows or columns by altering the values in the Rows or Cols text boxes. Finally, select the newly added rows or columns and choose Edit ➪ Paste.

Copying contents only

You often need to move data from one cell to another, while keeping the destination cell's attributes, such as its background color or border, intact. For this, use Dreamweaver's facility for copying just the contents of a cell.

To copy only the contents, select a cell and copy as previously described; then, instead of choosing Edit ➪ Paste, choose Edit ➪ Paste Special or use the keyboard shortcut Ctrl+Shift+V (Command+Shift+V). Once the Paste Special dialog box opens, choose the Text Only option and click OK. Unlike copying both contents and attributes, as described in the previous section, content-only copying has a couple of limitations:

- You can copy the contents of only one cell at a time, and you can paste those contents into only one cell at a time.
- You can't replace the entire contents of one cell with another and maintain all the text attributes (font, color, and size) of the destination cell in Design view. If you select all the text to be replaced, Dreamweaver also selects the CSS that holds the attributes and replaces those as well; instead of applying the CSS style to the `<td>` tag, however, it wraps the text in a similarly styled `<span>` tag. With CSS, cut and paste the entire text and then right-click (Control+click) the `<span>` tag in the Tag Selector and choose Remove Tag.

Dreamweaver TECHNIQUE

Inserting Table Content

In this Technique, you begin inserting content into the table so you can see first hand how table cells react to text and images.

1. From the Files panel, open the previously saved `table_start.htm` file.
2. Enter the following content in the top table:

Founded	1995
Headquarters	New York, NY
Agents	35

Notice that as you enter content, the width of the table cells changes to accommodate the text; you can refresh the table at any time by clicking outside of it. The entries in the first column are automatically bolded and centered because they are table header or <th> tags.

Continues

continued

3. Enter the following content in the bottom table, leaving the first column blank:

Leading Agents	Specialty	Contact
Paul Thrasher	Rentals	paul@rrealty.com
Lydia Catch	Houses	lydia@rrealty.com
Frank Gordon	Co-ops	frank@rrealty.com

4. Place your cursor in the blank cell of the first column, second row and choose Image from the Common category of the Insert panel.
5. When the Select Image Source dialog box opens, navigate to the images folder in the root of the Techniques site and select `paul_thrasher.jpg`.
6. Repeat Steps 4 and 5 for the next two cells, inserting `lydia_catch.jpg` and `frank_gordon.jpg`, respectively.
7. Save your page.

The table grows to compensate for the size of the images. In the next Technique, you adjust the table's properties to achieve a different look and feel.

Working with table properties

The `<table>` tag has a large number of attributes, and most of them can be modified through Dreamweaver's Property inspector. As with all objects, you must select the table before it can be altered. Choose Modify ➪ Table ➪ Select Table or use one of the other selection techniques previously described.

After you've selected the table, the Property inspector presents the table properties, as shown in Figure 12-6. If the inspector isn't open, choose Window ➪ Properties.

FIGURE 12-6

The expanded Table Property inspector gives you control over all the table-wide attributes.

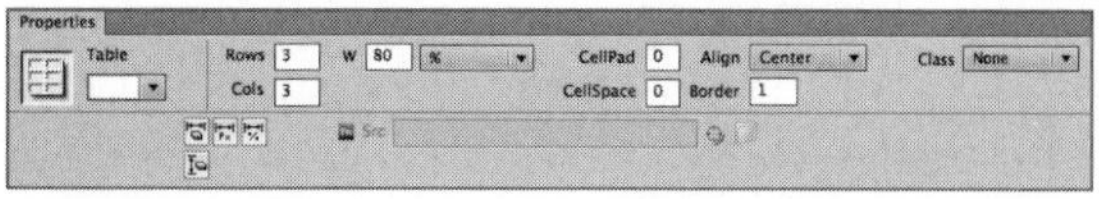

Setting alignment

Aligning a table in Dreamweaver goes beyond the expected left, right, and center options. You can also make a table into a free-floating object, around which you can wrap text—to the left or right.

Figure 12-7 illustrates some of the different results you can get from aligning your table.

FIGURE 12-7

Tables can be centered, as well as aligned left or right—with or without text wrapping.

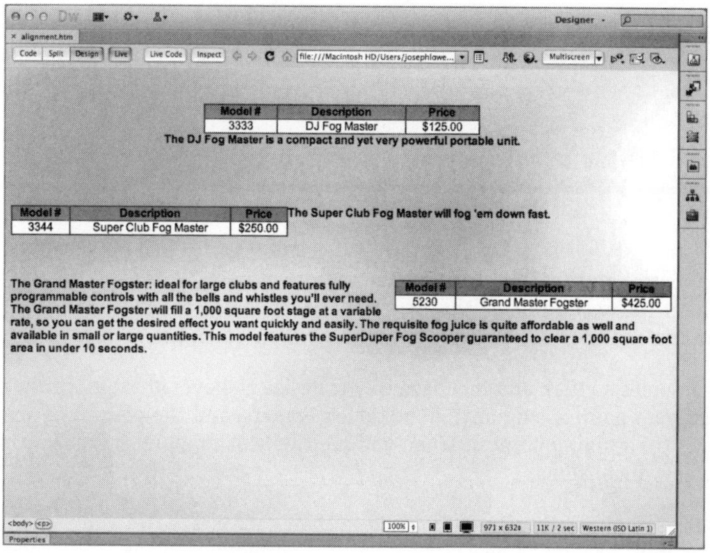

Because the <table> tag is a block element, CSS can be used to float the table on the page to the left or right. Subsequent text wraps around the table to one side or the other. Although Dreamweaver lets you align the table left or right from the Property inspector to achieve a similar effect in older browsers, the `align` attribute in tables has been deprecated.

To align the table without allowing text to wrap, you need to put the table within a <div> tag and set the <div> tag's align style to `left`, `right`, or `center` values with CSS. Although you may be tempted to use the <div> tag's align attribute, that attribute also has been deprecated.

Centering a Table in CSS

The align attribute in the <table> tag is deprecated in HTML 4.0, which means a newer, preferred method of achieving the same effect is available. In this case, CSS, covered in Chapter 6, provide the preferred method of setting an object's alignment. To center a table using CSS and be compatible with older browsers like Internet Explorer 6, you need two CSS rules: one for the table itself and one for a <div> surrounding the table. If, for example, the `class` of the `div` is `centerDiv`, the CSS rules look like this:

```
.centerDiv {
   text-align: center;
}
```

Continues

continued

```
.centerDiv table {
   margin-right: auto;
   margin-left: auto;
   text-align: left;
}
```

An alternative to writing the `margin-right` and `margin-left` property separately is to combine them like this: `margin: 0 auto`. Without the `text-align: left` attribute in the `.centerDiv table` rule, the text in the table is centered.

This CSS code is used later in this chapter in a Dreamweaver Technique.

Resizing a table

The primary sizing control on the Table Property inspector is the W (Width) text box. You can assign a new width for the entire table either in a screen percentage or pixels. Just enter your value in the W text box and then select % or Pixels in the drop-down list of options.

Dreamweaver also provides a quick and intuitive way to resize the overall table width, and the column widths. Pass your pointer over any of the table's borders, and the pointer becomes a two-headed arrow; this is the resizing pointer. When you see the resizing pointer, you can click and drag any border to new dimensions.

As noted earlier, tables are initially sized according to their contents. After you move a table border in Dreamweaver, however, the new sizes are written directly into the HTML code, and the column width is adjusted—unless the contents cannot fit. If, for example, an inserted image is 115 pixels wide and the cell has a width of only 90 pixels, the cell expands to fit the image. The same is true if you try to fit an extremely long, unbroken text string, such as a complex URL, into a cell that's too narrow to hold it.

NOTE

What about height? The height attribute for the `<table>` tag has been removed in HTML 4.0 and later by the W3C, and its further use is highly discouraged. Although rendered in Dreamweaver, the attribute no longer functions properly in most modern browsers, including Firefox, Safari, and Netscape 6.x. You'll need to use CSS (described in Chapter 6) to set the height and, preferably, the width.

Changes to the width of a cell or column are shown in the <td> tags, as are changes to a row's width, through the use of the `width` attribute. You can see these changes by selecting the table, cell, column, or row affected and looking at the W text box values.

For a clearer view of what happens when you resize a cell, row, or column, it's best to look at the HTML. Here's the HTML for an empty table, resized:

```
<table border="1" width="70%">
  <tr>
    <td width="21%"> </td>
    <td width="34%"> </td>
```

```
    <td width="45%"> </td>
  </tr>
  <tr>
    <td width="21%"> </td>
    <td width="34%"> </td>
    <td width="45%"> </td>
  </tr>
  <tr>
    <td width="21%"> </td>
    <td width="34%"> </td>
    <td width="45%"> </td>
  </tr>
</table>
```

Notice how the width for both the cells and the entire table are expressed as percentages. If the table width were initially set at a pixel value, the cell widths would have been, too.

You can switch from percentages to pixels in all the table measurements, and even clear all the values at once, with the click of a button. Several measurement controls appear in the lower-left portion of the expanded Table Property inspector, as shown in Figure 12-8.

12

FIGURE 12-8

You can make table-wide changes with the control buttons in the Table Property inspector.

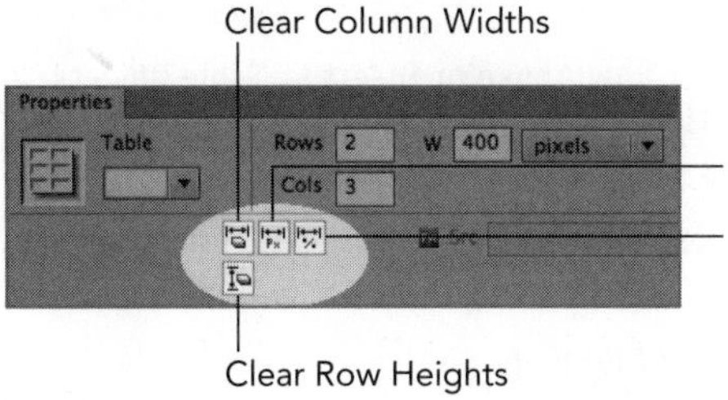

Table 12-2 shows the measurement controls provided in the Table Property inspector.

TABLE 12-2 Table Property Inspector Measurement Controls

Measurement Control Button	Description
Clear Column Widths	Deletes all the `width` attributes found in the `<td>` tags
Convert Table Widths To Pixels	Translates the current width of all cells and the entire table from percentages to pixels
Convert Table Widths To Percent	Translates the current width of all cells and the entire table from pixels to percentages
Clear Row Heights	Erases all the `height` attributes in the current table

NOTE

Selecting Clear Row Heights doesn't affect the table height value.

If you clear both row heights and column widths, the table goes back to its "grow as needed" format and, if empty, shrinks to its smallest possible size.

NOTE

When converting width percentages to pixels, and vice versa, keep in mind that the percentages are relative to the size of the browser window—and in the development phase that browser window is Dreamweaver. Use the Window Size option on the status bar to expand Dreamweaver's Document window to the size you expect your website to be seen at in various browser settings.

Inserting rows and columns

You can change the number of rows and columns in a table at any time. Dreamweaver provides a variety of methods for adding and removing rows and columns; you can add them either directly or by invoking a dialog box.

You have several options for adding a single row directly:

- Position the cursor in the last cell of the last row and press Tab to add a new row below the present one.
- Choose Insert ➪ Table Objects ➪ Insert Row Above or Insert ➪ Table Objects ➪ Insert Row Below to add a new row in a particular spot.
- Choose Modify ➪ Table ➪ Insert Row to insert a new row above the current row.
- Right-click (Control+click) in the table to open the context menu and choose Table ➪ Insert Row. Rows added in this way are inserted above the current row.

You have three ways to add a new column to your table directly:

- Choose Insert ➪ Table Objects ➪ Insert Column to the Left or Insert ➪ Table Objects ➪ Insert Column to the Right to add a new column in a specific place.
- Choose Modify ➪ Table ➪ Insert Column to insert a new column to the left of the current column.
- Right-click (Control+click) to open the context menu and choose Table ➪ Insert Column from the context menu. The column is inserted to the left of the current column.

You can add multiple rows and columns in either of the following ways:

- Increase the number of rows indicated in the Rows text box of the Table Property inspector. All new rows added in this manner appear below the last table row. Similarly, you can increase the number of columns indicated in the Cols text box of the Table Property inspector. Columns added in this way appear to the right of the last column.
- Use the Insert Rows or Columns dialog box.

The Insert Rows or Columns feature enables you to include any number of rows or columns anywhere relative to your current cursor position.

To add multiple columns using the Insert Rows or Columns dialog box, follow these steps:

1. Position the cursor anywhere in the row or column next to where the new row or column will be inserted.
2. Open the Insert Rows or Columns dialog box (shown in Figure 12-9) by choosing Modify ➪ Table ➪ Insert Rows or Columns or by choosing Table ➪ Insert Rows or Columns from the context menu.
3. Select either Rows or Columns.
4. Enter the number of rows or columns you want to insert—you can either type in a value or use the arrows to increase or decrease the number.

FIGURE 12-9

Use the Insert Rows or Columns feature to add several columns or rows simultaneously.

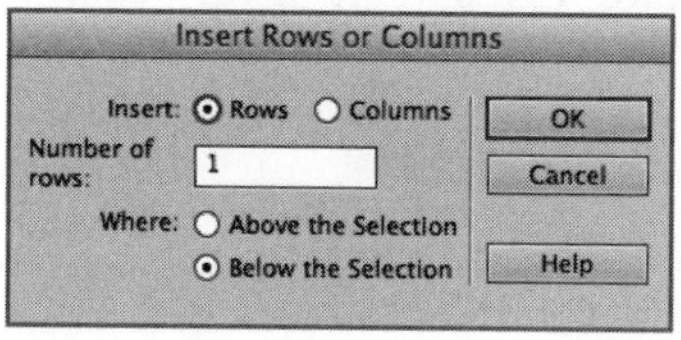

5. Select where you want the rows or columns to be inserted.
   - If you have selected the Rows option, you can insert the rows either above or below the selection (the current row).
   - If you have selected the Columns option, you can insert the columns either before or after the current column.
6. Click OK when you're finished.

Deleting rows and columns

The easiest way to delete a row or column is to select it and press the Delete key. You can also use the context menu to remove the current column or row by choosing Delete Column or Delete Row, respectively.

Alternatively, you can use the Table Property inspector to delete multiple columns and rows by reducing the numbers in the Cols or Rows text boxes. Columns are deleted from the right side of the table, and rows are removed from the bottom.

CAUTION

Exercise extreme caution when deleting columns or rows. Dreamweaver does not ask for confirmation, and it removes these columns and/or rows whether or not they contain data.

Setting table borders and backgrounds

Borders are the solid outlines of the table itself. A border's width is measured in pixels; the default width is 1 pixel. You can alter this width in the Border field of the Table Property inspector. Again, it's better to do this in CSS unless you're creating an HTML e-mail.

To make the border invisible, specify a border of 0 width. You can still resize your table by clicking and dragging the borders, even when the border is set to 0. When the View ➪ Visual Aids ➪ Table Borders option is selected, Dreamweaver displays a thin dashed line to represent the border; this line is not visible when the page is viewed in a browser.

When the border is visible, you can also see each cell outlined. The width of the outline around the cells stays constant, regardless of the border's width. However, you can control the amount of space between each cell with the CellSpace value in the Table Property inspector, covered in the section "Working with cell spacing and cell padding" later in this chapter.

To change the width of a border in Dreamweaver, select your table and enter a new value in the Border text box. With a wider border, you can see the default shading: The top and left sides are a light shade, and the bottom and right sides are darker, giving the table border a pseudo-3D appearance. Figure 12-10 shows single-cell tables with borders of various widths, contrasting `background` attribute and CSS style usage as rendered in Live View.

FIGURE 12-10

Borders are far more flexible when applied with CSS.

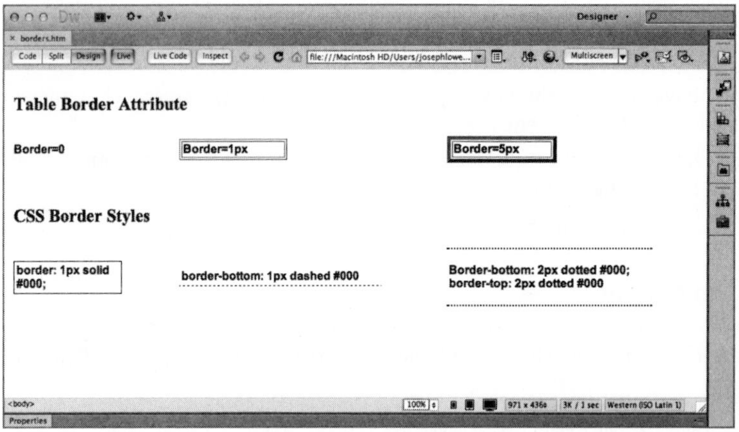

In Dreamweaver, you can directly assign colors to the border. Again, you get much greater control and standards compliance if you use CSS.

In addition to colored borders, a table can also have a colored background. (By default, the table is initially transparent.)

Working with cell spacing and cell padding

HTML gives you two methods to add whitespace in tables. Cell spacing controls the width between each cell, and cell padding controls the margins within each cell. You can set these values independently through the Table Property inspector.

> **TIP**
>
> If no cell spacing or padding value is indicated in the Table Property inspector, most browsers use a default value of 2 pixels for cell spacing and 1 pixel for cell padding. If your web page design calls for a close arrangement of cells, change either (or both) the CellSpace or the CellPad values to 1 or 0. A preferred alternative technique is to set a CSS declaration using the `border-collapse` property, like this: `border-collapse: collapse`.

To change the amount of whitespace between each cell in a table, enter a new value in the CellSpace text box of the Table Property inspector. If you want to adjust the amount of whitespace between the inside borders of the cell and the actual cell data, alter the value in the CellPad text box of the Table Property inspector. Figure 12-11 shows an example of tables with wide (10 pixels) cell spacing and cell padding values (the shaded space is the actual cell size).

FIGURE 12-11

You can add additional whitespace between each cell (cell spacing) or within each cell (cell padding).

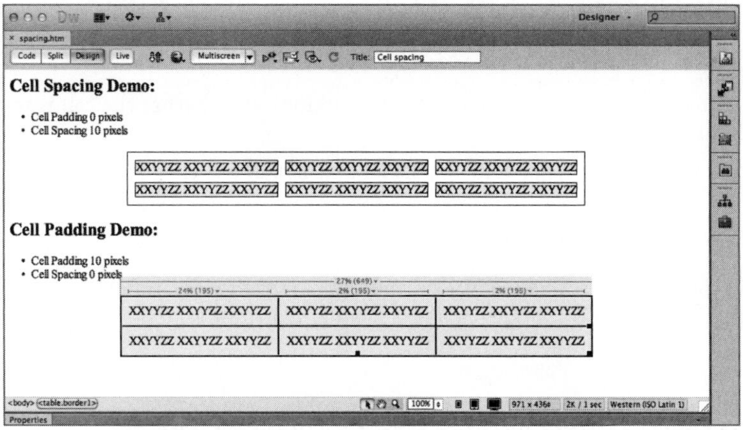

Merging and splitting cells

You have seen how cells in HTML tables can extend across (span) multiple columns or rows. By default, a cell spans one column or one row. Increasing a cell's span enables you to group any number of topics under one heading. You are effectively merging one cell with another to create a larger cell. Likewise, a cell can be split into multiple rows or columns.

Dreamweaver enables you to combine and divide cells in two different ways. If you're more comfortable with the concept of merging and splitting cells, you can use two handy buttons on the Property inspector. If, on the other hand, you prefer the older method of increasing and decreasing row or column span, you can still access these commands through the main menu and the context menus.

To combine two or more cells, first select the cells you want to merge. Then, from the Property inspector, click the Merge Cells button or press the keyboard shortcut, M. If the Merge button is not available, multiple cells have not been selected.

To divide a cell, follow these steps:

1. Position your cursor in the cell to be split.
2. From the Property inspector, click the Split Cell button or press the keyboard shortcut, Ctrl+Alt+S (Command+Option+S). The Split Cell dialog box (shown in Figure 12-12) appears.

FIGURE 12-12

Use the Split Cell dialog box to divide cells horizontally or vertically.

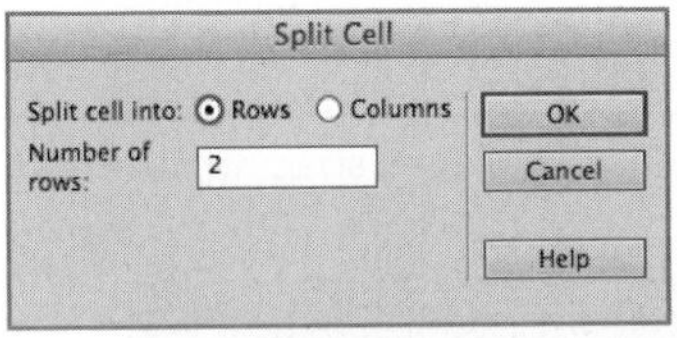

3. Select either the Rows or the Columns option to indicate whether the cell is to be split horizontally or vertically.
4. Enter the number of rows or columns in the text box or use the arrows to change the value.
5. Click OK when you're finished.

You can achieve the same effect by using the menus. To do so, first position the cursor in the cell to be affected and then choose one of the commands shown in Table 12-3 from the Modify ➪ Table menu.

TABLE 12-3 Commands for Merging and Splitting Cells

Command	Description
Increase Row Span	Joins the current cell with the cell below it
Increase Column Span	Joins the current cell with the cell immediately to its right
Decrease Row Span	Separates two or more previously spanned cells from the bottom cell
Decrease Column Span	Separates two or more previously spanned cells from the right edge

Existing text or images are put in the same cell if the cells containing them are joined to span rows or columns. Figure 12-13 shows a table containing both row and column spanning.

FIGURE 12-13

This spreadsheet-like report was built using Dreamweaver's row- and column-spanning features.

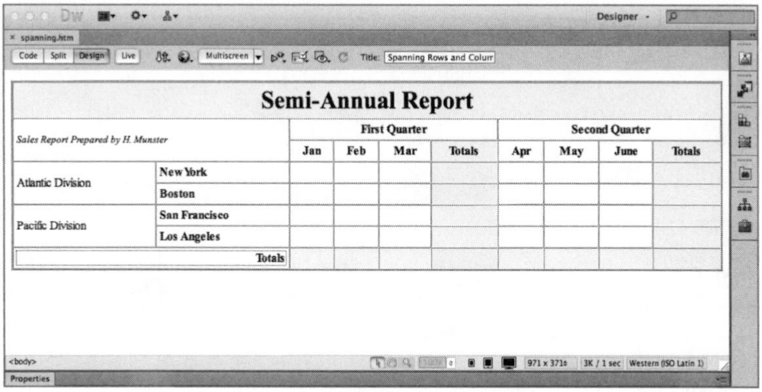

TIP

Show restraint when splitting and merging cells, or your table will be difficult to maintain. When you are building a complex table such as the one in Figure 12-13, it's best to map out your table before you begin constructing it and to complete it prior to entering your data.

Dreamweaver TECHNIQUE

Adjusting Table Properties

In this Technique, you practice aligning tables to achieve two different effects, as well as merging cells and clearing column widths.

1. Open the `table_start.htm` file that you worked on earlier in this chapter.
2. From the CSS Styles panel, click New CSS Rule.
3. In the New CSS Rule dialog box, choose the Class option and enter **.rightTable** in the Name field; click OK when you're done.
4. Switch to the Box category and, from the Float list, choose Right and click OK.
5. Select the first table by dragging your mouse across the right border into the table.
6. From the Property inspector's Class list, choose rightTable.

Continues

continued

Notice that the table is instantly positioned to the right, and the following paragraph flows to the left. Now position the bottom table in the center without wrapping.

1. Select the bottom table.
2. From the Layout category of the Insert panel, choose Insert Div Tag.

   The necessary CSS rules (discussed earlier in the "Centering a Table in CSS" sidebar) are already in the attached CSS style sheet.
3. When the Insert Div Tag dialog box opens, leave the Insert list entry set to Wrap Around Selection.
4. Choose centerDiv from the Class list and click OK when you're done.

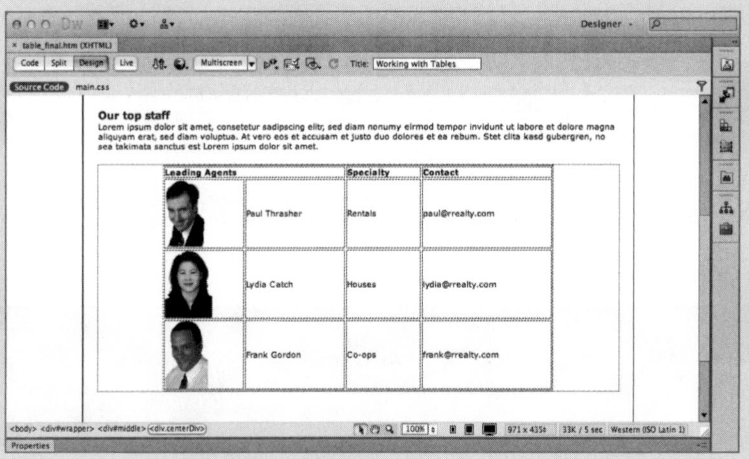

Dreamweaver creates a surrounding <div> tag and centers the table within it.

Your final task is to remove the widths from the lower table columns so that they tightly fit the data.

1. Select the bottom table again, if necessary.
2. From the lower portion of the Property inspector, click Clear Column Widths.
3. Save your page.

The table columns collapse to just the widths needed.

Setting cell, column, and row properties

In addition to the overall table controls, Dreamweaver helps you set numerous properties for individual cells one at a time, by the column or by the row. When attributes overlap or conflict, such as different background colors for a cell in the same row and column, the more specific target has precedence. The hierarchy, from most general to most specific, is as follows: tables, rows, columns, and cells.

You can call up the specific Property inspector by selecting the cell, row, or column you want to modify. The Cell, Row, and Column Property inspectors each affect similar attributes. The following sections explain how the attributes work, both in general and—if any differences exist—specifically (in regard to the cell, row, or column).

Horizontal alignment

You can set the horizontal alignment attribute, `align`, to specify the default alignment, or left, right, or center alignment, for the contents of a cell, row, or column. This attribute can be overridden by setting the alignment for the individual line or image. Generally, left is the default horizontal alignment for cells.

Vertical alignment

The HTML `valign` attribute specifies whether the cell's contents are vertically aligned to the cell's top, middle, or bottom, or along the baseline. Typically, browsers align cells vertically in the middle by default. Select the Vertical Alignment list in the Property inspector to specify a different alignment.

Top, middle, and bottom vertical alignments work pretty much as you would expect. A baseline vertical alignment displays text near the top of the cell and positions the text—regardless of font size—so that the baselines of all the text in the affected row, column, or cell are the same. Figure 12-14 illustrates how images and text of various sizes are displayed under the different vertical alignment options.

FIGURE 12-14

You can vertically align text and images in several arrangements in a table cell, row, or column.

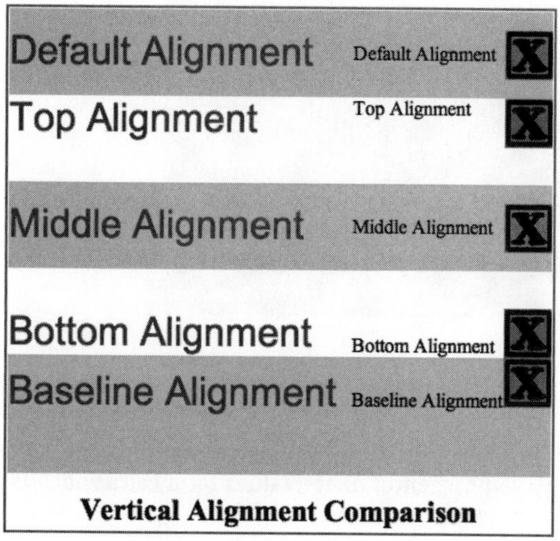

Cell wrap

Normal behavior for any cell is to automatically wrap text or a series of images within the cell's borders. You can turn off this automatic feature by selecting the No Wrap option in the Property inspector for the cell, row, or column.

You might use this option, for example, if you need three images to appear side by side in one cell. In analyzing the results, however, you might find that on some smaller size screens or browser windows that the last image wraps to the next line.

NOTE

A preferred method of preventing the contents of a cell from wrapping is to use Cascading Style Sheets to define a style with the `white-space` attribute set to `nowrap` (for example, `.foo {white-space:nowrap;}`. The `nowrap` attribute has been deprecated for `<td>` tags.

Table header cells

Quite often in tables, a column or row functions as the heading for that section of the table, labeling all the information in that particular section. Dreamweaver has an option for designating these cells: the Header option. Table header cells are usually rendered in boldface and horizontally centered in each cell. Figure 12-15 shows an example of a table in which both the first row and the first column are marked as table header cells.

FIGURE 12-15

Table header cells are a good way to note a category's labels—for a row, column, or both.

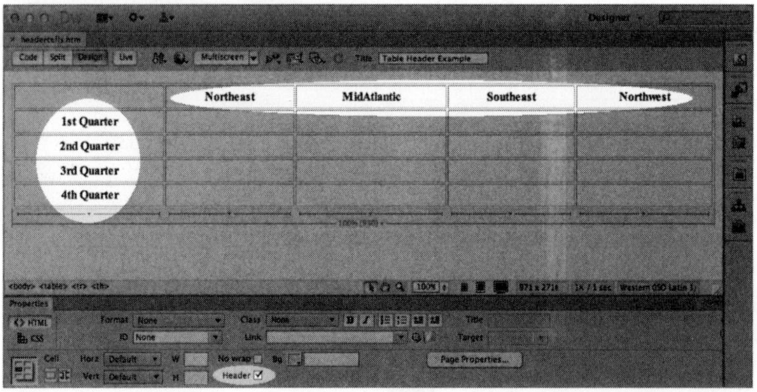

Cell width and height

The gridlike structure of a table makes it impossible to resize only one cell in a multicolumn/multirow table. Therefore, the only way you can enter exact values for a cell's width is through the W text box available in the Property inspector. You can enter values in pixels or as a percentage of the table. The default enables cells to automatically resize with no restrictions outside of the overall dimensions of the table.

Similarly, whenever you change a cell's height, the entire row is altered. If you drag the row to a new height, the value is written into the H text box for all cells in the row. On the other hand, if you specify a single cell's height, the row resizes, but you can see the value only in the cell you've changed. If different cells in the same row are assigned different heights, the row is sized to the tallest height.

Color elements

Just as you can specify color backgrounds for the overall table, you can do the same for columns, rows, or individual cells. Corresponding color swatches and text boxes are available in the Property inspector for `Bg`, the background color, which specifies the color for the selected cell, row, or column. Selecting the color box opens the standard color picker. This tag has been deprecated for all table elements—including `<table>`, `<tr>`, and `<td>`—and it is strongly advised that CSS be used to apply coloring.

As with all Dreamweaver color pickers, you can use the Eyedropper tool to select a color from the web-safe palette or from any item on a page. You can also click the Default color button to delete any previously selected color. Finally, click the System Color Picker button to open the Color dialog box and select any available color.

Sorting Tables

Have you ever painstakingly built a table, alphabetizing every last entry by last name and first name, only to have the client call with a list of 13 additional names? "Oh, and could you sort them by ZIP code instead of last name?" Dreamweaver contains a Table Sort command designed to make short work of such requests. All you do is select your table, and you're ready to do a two-level-deep sort, either alphabetically or numerically.

The Sort Table command can rearrange a table of any size; more important, it's HTML-savvy, and gives you the option of keeping the formatting of your table rows. This capability enables you to maintain a table with alternating row colors and still sort the data—something not even the most powerful word processors can handle. The Sort Table command is useful for generating different views of the same data without having to use a database.

The Sort Table command is straightforward to use; just follow these steps:

1. Position the cursor inside the table.
2. Choose Commands ➪ Sort Table. The Sort Table dialog box (shown in Figure 12-16) opens.
3. Select the primary sort column from the Sort By option list. Dreamweaver automatically lists every column in the selected table in the option list.
4. Set the type of the primary sort by picking either Alphabetically or Numerically from the first Order option list.
5. Select the direction of the sort by selecting either Ascending or Descending from the second Order option list.

FIGURE 12-16

Sort your tables numerically or alphabetically with the Sort Table command.

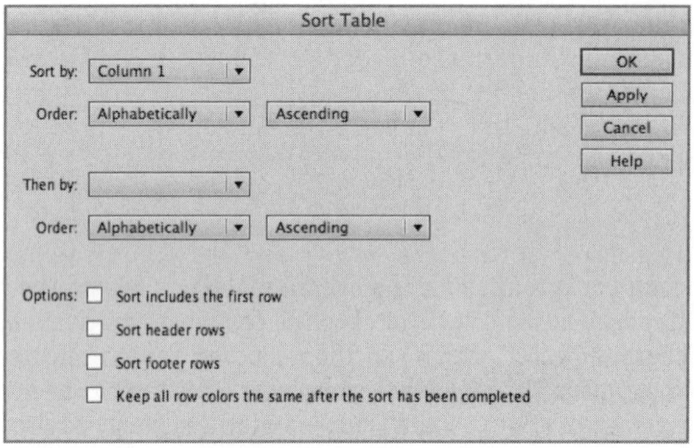

6. If you want to add a second level of sorting, repeat Steps 3 through 5 in the Then By section.
7. If your selected table does not include a header row, select the Sort Includes The First Row option.
8. If your selected table includes one or more rows coded within `<thead> . . . </thead>` or `<tfoot> . . . </tfoot>` tags, and you want those rows to be included in the sort, select the appropriate option.

NOTE

The <thead> and <tfoot> HTML tags designate one or more table rows as forming a table heading or footer. The footer displays at the bottom of the table. It is typically used to duplicate the heading for long tables. These tags are not supported on all browsers.

9. If you have formatted your table with alternating row colors, choose the Keep All Row Colors The Same After The Sort Has Been Completed option.
10. Click OK when you're finished.

TIP

As with any sorting program, if you leave blank cells in the column on which you're basing the sort, those rows appear as a group on top of the table for an ascending sort and at the end for a descending sort. Make sure that all the cells in your sort criteria column are filled correctly.

Importing Tabular Data

In the computer age, there's nothing more frustrating than having information in a digital format and still having to enter it manually—either by typing it in or by cutting and pasting—to get it on the web. This frustration is multiplied when it comes to table data, whether created in a spreadsheet or database program. You have to transfer numerous small pieces of data, and it all has to be properly related and positioned.

Dreamweaver's Import Tabular Data command goes a long way toward alleviating the tedium—not to mention the frustration—of dealing with tabular information. The Import Tabular Data command reads any delimited text file and inserts the information in a series of rows and columns. You can even set most characteristics for the table to be created, including the width, cell padding, cell spacing, and border.

Quite often, the first step in the process of importing table data into Dreamweaver is exporting it from another program. Most spreadsheet and database programs have some capability to output information to a text file. Each bit of data (whether it's from a cell of a spreadsheet or a field of a database) is separated—or *delimited*—from every other bit of data by a special character, typically a tab or comma. In Dreamweaver, you can use the Import Tabular Data dialog box to choose which delimiter is used, ensuring a clean transfer with no loss of data.

TIP

Although you have many types of delimiters to choose from, you might want to default to exporting tab-delimited files. With a tab-delimited file, you usually don't have to worry if any of your data contains the delimiter–which would throw off the import. However, testing has shown that Dreamweaver correctly handles comma-delimited files with and without quotes, so you can also use that format safely.

To import a tabular data file, follow these steps:

1. Be sure the data you want to import has been saved or exported in the proper format: a delimited text file.
2. Open the Import Tabular Data dialog box, shown in Figure 12-17, in one of the following ways:
   - Choose File ➪ Import ➪ Tabular Data.
   - Choose Insert ➪ Table Objects ➪ Import Tabular Data.
   - Click the Tabular Data button in the Data category of the Insert panel.
3. Click the Browse button to find the desired file.
4. Select the delimiter used to separate the fields or cells of data from the Delimiter option list. The options are Tab, Comma, Semicolon, Colon, and Other.

TIP

If you select a file with a `.csv` extension, the comma delimiter is automatically chosen, although you can change the option if necessary. CSV is short for Comma-Separated Values.

5. If you choose Other from the Delimiter list, a blank field appears to the right of the list. Enter the special character, such as the pipe (|), used as the delimiter in the exported file. Now that the imported file characteristics are set, you can predefine the table into which the information will be imported.

FIGURE 12-17

Any external data saved in a delimited text file can be brought into Dreamweaver with the Import Tabular Data command.

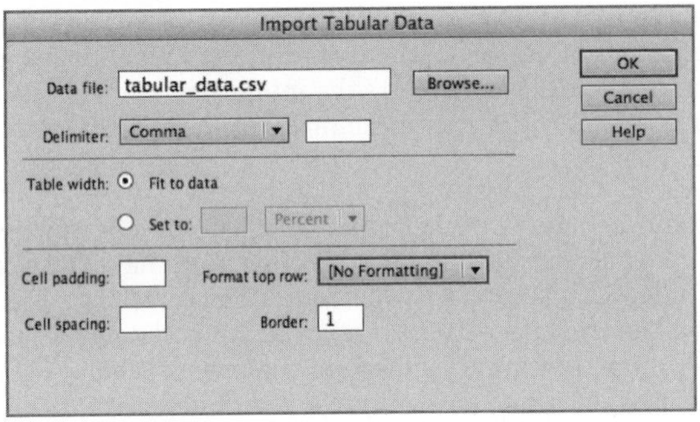

6. If you want to set a particular table width, enter a value in the Set To field and select either Pixels or Percent from the option list. If you want the imported file to determine the size of the table, keep the Fit To Data option selected.
7. Enter any Cell Padding or Cell Spacing values desired in their respective fields. As with standard tables, if you don't enter a value, most browsers render Cell Padding as 2 pixels and Cell Spacing as 1 pixel.
8. If you'd like to style the first row, pick Bold, Italic, or Bold Italic from the Format Top Row option list. This option is typically used when the imported file contains a header row.
9. Set the Border field to the desired width, if any. If you don't want a border displayed at all, set the Border field to 0.
10. Click OK when you're finished.

Although the Import Table Data option is under the File menu, it doesn't open a new file—the new table is created at the current cursor position.

CAUTION

If your data is imported incorrectly, double-check the delimiter used (by opening the file in a text editor). If Dreamweaver is expecting a comma delimiter and your file uses tabs, data is not formatted properly.

Summary

Tables are extremely powerful web page design tools. Dreamweaver enables you to modify both the appearance and the structure of your HTML tables through a combination of Property inspectors, dialog boxes, and click-and-drag mouse movements. Mastering tables is an essential skill for any modern web designer and worth the somewhat challenging learning curve. When working with tables, here are the key points to keep in mind:

- An HTML table consists of a series of rows and columns presented in a gridlike arrangement. Tables can be sized absolutely, in pixels, or as a percentage, relative to the width of the browser's window.
- Dreamweaver inserts a table whose dimensions can be altered through the Insert panel or the Insert ➪ Table menu. After it is placed in the page, the table must be selected before any of its properties can be modified through the Table Property inspector.
- Table editing is greatly simplified in Dreamweaver. You can select multiple cells, columns, or rows—and modify all their contents in one fell swoop.
- You can assign certain properties—such as background color and alignment—for a table's columns, rows, or cells through their respective Property inspectors. The properties of a cell override those set for its column or row.
- CSS can, and should, be used for specifying the visual properties of the table.
- Dreamweaver brings power to table-building with the Sort Table command, as well as a connection to the outside world with its Import Tabular Data option.

In the next chapter, you learn how to create and use forms in your web pages.

CHAPTER

13

Enabling User Interaction with Forms

IN THIS CHAPTER

Forms overview

Including forms in your web page

Using text fields and text areas

Enabling options with radio buttons, checkboxes, and drop-down lists

Dreamweaver Technique: Building a Form, Part 1

Dreamweaver Technique: Building a Form, Part 2

Building a jump menu

Incorporating buttons in forms

Adding hidden fields and password fields

Making forms accessible

Working with HTML5 form elements

Combining CSS with forms

A form, in the everyday world and on the web, is a type of structured communication. When you apply for a driver's license, you're not told to randomly write down personal information; you're asked to fill out a form that asks for specific information, one piece at a time, in a specific manner. Web-based forms are just as precise, if not more so.

Dreamweaver has a robust and superior implementation of HTML forms—from the dedicated Forms category in the Insert panel to various form-specific Property inspectors. In addition to their importance as communication tools connecting the browsing public to web server applications, forms are an integral part of building some of Dreamweaver's own objects. Forms also serve as major tools for web developers because they can be altered on the fly; it's possible, for example, for a selection in one drop-down list to determine the contents of another. The dynamic aspects of forms are covered in Chapter 22.

Dreamweaver also includes another robust method of implementing forms: Spry. Once you understand how to set up a form and how the various form elements are applied, you learn in Chapter 16 how Spry form widgets are put to use.

In this chapter, you learn how forms are structured and then created within Dreamweaver. Each form object is explored in detail—text fields, radio buttons, checkboxes, menus, list boxes, command buttons, hidden fields, file fields, image fields, and password fields.

Dreamweaver QUICKSTART

Forms are a pretty complex, but essential, part of the web. If you're already familiar with the ins and outs of forms and just want to get going in Dreamweaver, here's how you get started:

1. Place your cursor where you want your form to appear on your page.
2. In the Insert panel, switch to the Forms category and click Form.

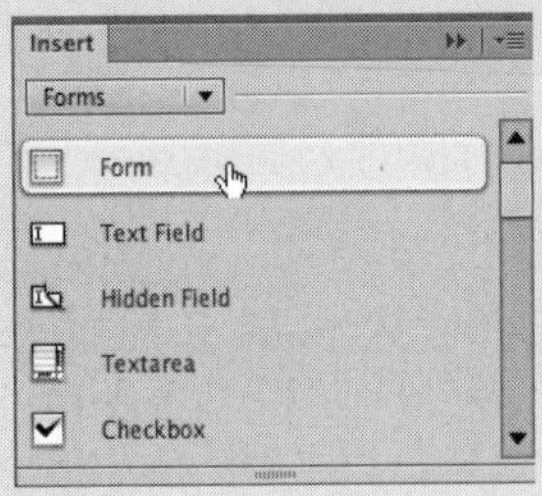

3. Insert whatever form elements you need—text field, checkbox, radio buttons, and so on—within the `<form>` tag.
4. Add validation, either through the Spry Validation form elements or via Dreamweaver behaviors.
5. Select the `<form>` tag and add the Action, Method, and Enctype in the Property inspector.
6. Make sure your server-side coding, such as ColdFusion, PHP, ASP, or CGI, is in place to process the submitted form.

Feel free to use the rest of the chapter as a reference guide as you build forms to gather information from your web visitors.

How HTML Forms Work

Forms have a special function in HTML: They support interaction. Virtually all HTML elements apart from forms are concerned with structure—delivering the content to the user, if you will. Forms, on the other hand, enable the user to read information passively from the screen and to send information back. Without forms, the web would be a one-way street.

Forms have numerous uses on the web, such as for surveys, electronic commerce, guest books, polls, and even real-time custom graphics creation. For such feedback to be possible, forms require an additional component beyond what is seen onscreen so that each form can complete its function. Every form needs some type of connection to a web server, whether it is through one of the Dreamweaver server models or a common gateway interface (CGI) script.

Forms, like HTML tables, are self-contained units within a web page. All the elements of a form are contained within the form tag pair `<form>` and `</form>`. You cannot nest forms as you do tables, although there's nothing to stop you from having multiple forms on a page.

The most commonly used attributes of the `<form>` tag include the following:

- `method`: Tells the browser and the web server how to present the form contents to the application that will process the form. The two possible `method` values are `get` and `post`. The `get` method passes the attached information with a URL; this method places limitations on the amount and format of data that can be passed to the application. The `post` method enables the application program to receive the information as standard input and imposes no limits on the passed data.
- `action`: Determines what should be done with the form content. Most commonly, `action` is set to a URL for running a specific web application or for sending e-mail.

Typical HTML for a `<form>` tag looks something like the following:

```
<form method="post" action="http://www.idest.com/_cgi-bin/mailcall.pl">
```

NOTE

The `.pl` extension in the preceding example form tag stands for Perl, a scripting language often used to create CGI programs. Perl can be edited in any regular text editor. You can also use other server models like PHP.

13

Within each form is a series of input controls—text fields, radio buttons, checkboxes, and so on. Each type handles a particular sort of input; in fact, the main tag for these elements is the `<input>` tag. With one exception, the `<textarea>` tag, all form input types are implemented by specifying the `type` attribute. The text box tag, for example, is written as follows:

```
<input type="text" name="lastname">
```

All form input tags must have a `name` attribute, which identifies the control. In the preceding example, `name` is assigned a value of `"lastname"`. Information input by the user in a control, such as a text field, is sent to the server along with the value of that control's `name` attribute. Thus, if I were to fill out a form with a text box asking for my last name, such as the one produced by the preceding tag, part of the message sent to the server would include the following string:

```
lastname=Lowery
```

NOTE

Form fields can also contain an ID or class attribute that permits them to be styled by CSS. See the "Styling Forms with CSS" section of this chapter to learn more.

Servers send all the information from a form in one long text string to whatever program or address is specified in the `action` attribute. It's up to the program or the recipient of the form message to parse the string. For instance, if I were to fill out a small form—with my name, e-mail address, and a short comment such as "Good work!"—the server would send a text string similar to the following:

```
lastname=Lowery&address=jlowery@idest.com&comment=Good+work%21
```

As you can see, the various fields are separated by ampersands (&) and the individual words within the responses are separated by plus signs (+). Most non-alphanumeric characters—such as the exclamation mark in the example—are represented by their hexadecimal values. Decoding this text string is called *parsing* the response.

TIP

To ease maintenance of your code, choose a name that is descriptive but that is not a reserved word. For example, it is better to name a text field `lastname` than just `name`.

Inserting a Form in Dreamweaver

A form is inserted just like any other object in Dreamweaver. Place the cursor where you want your form to start and then either click the Form button in the Forms category of the Insert panel (see Figure 13-1) or choose Insert ➪ Form ➪ Form from the menu. Dreamweaver inserts a red outline stretching across the Document window to indicate the form.

NOTE

If you can't see the outline of the form, choose View ➪ Visual Aids ➪ Invisible Elements. If you still can't see the form, choose Edit ➪ Preferences (Dreamweaver ➪ Preferences) and click the Form Delimiter checkbox in the Invisible Elements category. Clear the checkbox if you don't want to see the form outline.

If you have the Property inspector open, the Form Property inspector appears when you insert a form. As Figure 13-1 shows, you can specify several values regarding forms; in addition to the Action and the Method, which correspond to the attributes previously discussed, you can also specify a Form ID, Enctype value, and Target.

FIGURE 13-1

Inserting a form creates a red outline of the form and, if the Property inspector is open, displays the Form Property inspector with form-specific properties.

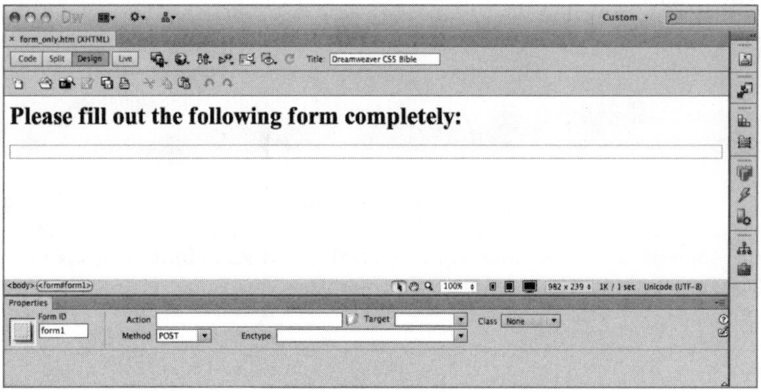

Because of the interactive nature of forms, web programmers often use them to gather information from the user. To do this, programmers must specify a form ID, which enables them to reference a form using JavaScript or other languages.

In the Action text box, you can directly enter a URL or mailto address, or you can select the folder icon and browse for a file.

NOTE

Sending your form data via a mailto address is doable but is highly problematic. Some browsers, most notably Internet Explorer, are set to warn the user initially whenever a form button using mailto is selected. Although many users let the mail go through, they do have the option to stop it from being sent. However, there is no way to detect whether users have an e-mail client such as Outlook or Thunderbird installed on their systems, which is a necessary element for the mailto technique to work.

The method defaults to `post`, the most commonly used option. You can also choose `get` or `default`, which leaves the method up to the browser. In most cases, you should leave the method set to `post`.

Enctype stands for encoding type; this value tells the server in what format the data is being sent. For more information, refer to the "Declaring the Encoding Type (Enctype)" sidebar in this chapter.

Finally, the Target field tells the server which frame or window to use when displaying a response to the form. If you don't specify a target, any response displays in the current frame or window.

Forms cannot be placed inline with any other element such as text or graphics. Keep in mind the following additional considerations when it comes to mixing forms and other web page elements:

- Forms expand as objects are inserted into them; you can't resize a form by dragging its boundaries.
- The outline of a form is invisible in a browser; there is no border to turn on or off. You can, however, use CSS to set a border or background color for the entire form.
- Forms and tables can be used together only if the form either completely encloses the table or is completely enclosed inside the table. In other words, you can't have a form spanning part of a table.
- Forms can be inserted within AP elements, and multiple forms can be in multiple AP elements. However, the AP element must completely enclose the form. As with forms spanning tables, you can't have a form spanning two or more AP elements. (A workaround for this limitation is discussed in Chapter 10.)

Declaring the Encoding Type (Enctype)

The `<form>` attribute enctype is helpful in formatting material returned via a form. It specifies how the information is being sent, so the server software knows how to interpret the input.

By default, enctype is set to `application/x-www-form-urlencoded`, which is responsible for encoding the form response with ampersands between entries, equal signs linking form element names to their values, spaces as plus signs, and all non-alphanumeric characters in hexadecimal format, such as `%3F` (a question mark).

Continues

continued

A second enctype value, `text/plain`, is useful for e-mail replies. Instead of one long string, your form data is transmitted in a more readable format, with each form element and its value on a separate line, as shown in the following example:

```
fname=Joseph
lname=Lowery
email=jlowery@idest.com
comment=Please send me the information on your new products!
```

Another enctype value, `multipart/form-data`, is used only when a file is being uploaded as part of the form. There's a further restriction: The method must be set to `post` instead of `get`.

Dreamweaver includes an Enctype list box on the Form Property inspector so you can easily specify the encoding type. You can choose a value from the drop-down list or manually enter a value in the Enctype list box.

Using Text Fields

Anytime you use a form to gather text information typed in by a user, you use a form object called a text field. Text fields can hold any number of alphanumeric and punctuation characters. The web designer can decide whether the text field is displayed in one line or several. When the HTML is written, a multiple-line text field uses a `<textarea>` tag, and a single-line text field is coded with `<input type="text">`.

Inserting text fields

To insert a single-line text field in Dreamweaver, you can use any of the following methods:

- From the Forms category of the Insert panel, click the Text Field button to place a text field at your current cursor position.
- Choose Insert ➪ Form ➪ Text Field from the menu, which inserts a text field at the current cursor position.
- Drag the Text Field button from the Insert panel to any existing location in the Document window and release the mouse button to position the text field.

TIP

You can use any of these methods to insert text fields in either Design view or Code view. When you insert a text field or most other form controls in Code view, the Tag Editor for the `<input>` tag opens automatically, enabling you to specify any attributes for the tag.

When you insert a text field, the Property inspector, when displayed, shows you the available attributes (see Figure 13-2). You measure the size of a text field by the number of characters it can display at one time. You can change the length of a text field by inserting a value in the Char Width text box or by declaring a width value for an applied CSS style; the latter is, by far, the recommended approach. By default, Dreamweaver inserts a text field approximately 20 characters wide. The "approximately" is important here because the final size of the text field is ultimately controlled by the browser used to view the page. Unless you limit the number of possible characters by entering a value in the Max Chars text box, the user can enter as many characters as desired, but not all the characters will necessarily be visible at one time; the text scrolls horizontally in the box as the user types.

FIGURE 13-2

The text field of a form enables the user to type any required information.

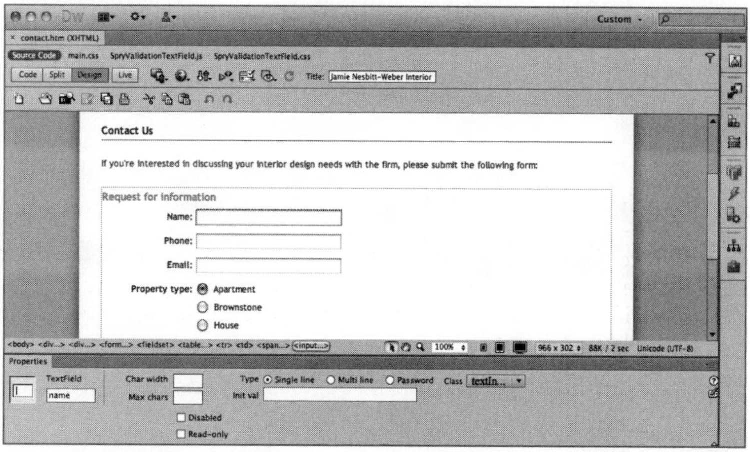

NOTE

The value in Char Width determines the visible width of the field; the value in Max Chars actually determines the number of characters that can be entered.

The Init Value text box on the Text Field Property inspector is used to insert a default text string. The user can overwrite this value, if desired. Should you need to display some text but not allow users to enter their own text, choose the Read-Only option. This property will most likely come into play only when you're displaying dynamic data already recorded that you don't want to change.

You can also, with the check of the Disabled option, lock your text field from entry and change its appearance. Browsers interpret the disabled property differently: Internet Explorer grays out the text by reducing the opacity, whereas Firefox adds a light-blue background color. To control the appearance, use a style rule with a CSS attribute selector—set in square brackets—like this:

```
input[disabled] {
  background-color: white;
```

```
    color: #ccc;
    border: solid 1px #ccc;
}
```

Creating password fields

Typically, any text entered into text fields is displayed as you expect—programmers refer to this process as *echoing*. You can turn off echoing by selecting the Password option in the Text Field Property inspector. When a text field is designated as a password field, all text entered by the user shows up as asterisks or dots.

Use the password field when you want to protect the user's input from prying eyes (just as your PIN is hidden when you enter it at an ATM, for instance). The information entered in a password field is not encrypted or scrambled in any way, and when sent to the web application, it is received as regular text.

Only single-line text fields can be set as password fields. You cannot make a multiline `<textarea>` tag act as a password field without employing JavaScript or some other programming language.

NOTE
Making sure that your user fills out the form properly is called *validating the input*. Dreamweaver includes a standard form validation behavior, covered in Chapter 11.

Inserting multiline text areas

When you want to give your users a generous amount of room to write, you can expand not just the width of the text area but also its height. Dreamweaver gives you the following options for creating a multiline text area:

- Insert a single-line text field on the page as previously described and convert the field to multiple lines by choosing the Multi line option in the Text Field Property inspector.
- Directly insert the Textarea form element using the Insert panel or Insert menu. To do this, position your cursor where you want to insert the text area and choose Insert ⇨ Form ⇨ Textarea or click the Textarea button in the Forms category of the Insert panel.

Figure 13-3 shows a typical multiline text field embedded in a form.

The text area that is initially created is approximately 45 characters wide and 5 lines high, with horizontal and vertical scroll bars. You control the width of a multiline text area by entering a value in the Char Width text box of the Text Field Property inspector, just as you do for single-line text fields. The height of the text area is set equal to the value in the Num Lines text box. As with the default single-line text field, the user can enter any amount of text. Unlike the single-line text field, in which you can restrict the number of characters that can be input through the Max Chars text box, you cannot restrict the number of characters the user enters into a multiline text area.

FIGURE 13-3

The Multiline option of the Text Field Property inspector opens up a text area for more user information.

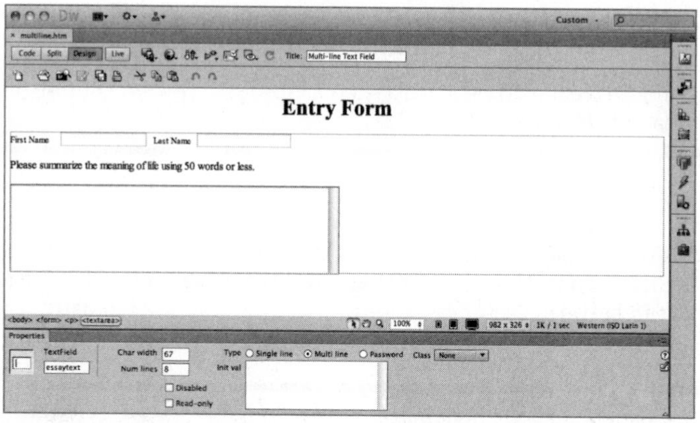

Constructing Neat Forms

Although they are especially good when you are working on a larger, complex form, I find that tables and forms are made for each other—even in this age of CSS. Besides the speed of layout, another advantage that tables offer is the capability to right-align text labels next to your text fields; it's worth noting that the align attribute for the <td> tag is still valid HTML as of version 4; however, it's obsolete in HTML5. The top form in the following figure uses preformatted text to get different-sized form fields to line up properly, whereas the bottom form in the figure uses a table.

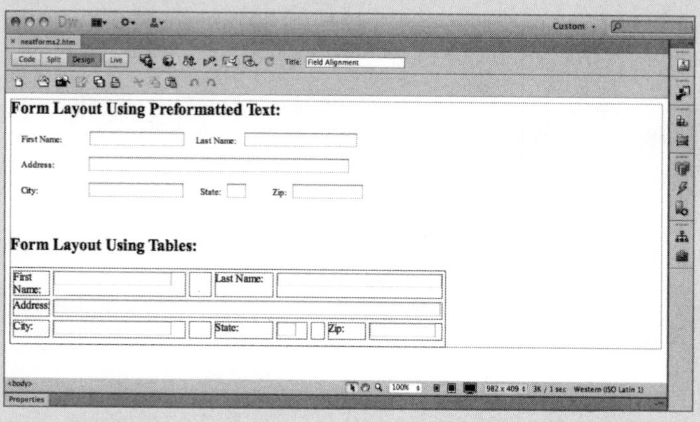

Continues

continued

Combining different-sized text fields on a single row—for example, when you're asking for a city, state, and ZIP code combination—can make the task of lining up your form even more difficult. Most often, you spend a fair amount of time in a trial-and-error effort to make the text fields match. Be sure to check your results in the various browsers as you build your form.

Tables are just the beginning stage in creating a clean, easy-to-read form. For greater control, be sure to read "Styling Forms with CSS" later in this chapter.

Another option when creating multiline text fields is to preload the text area with any default text you like. Enter this text in the Init Val text box of the Text Field Property inspector. When Dreamweaver writes the HTML code, this text is not entered as a value, as it is for the single-line text field, but rather put in between the `<textarea> . . . </textarea>` tag pair.

Grouping Form Controls

In desktop applications, you may be used to seeing related controls grouped together, with a thin border around them. You can achieve a similar effect in your HTML forms by enclosing the related form elements within the `<fieldset>` ... `</fieldset>` tag pair, as shown in the following code:

```
<fieldset>
  <legend>Address</legend>
    <label>Street <input type="text" name="street" ></label>
    <label>City <input type="text" name="city" ></label>
    <label>State <input type="text" name="state" ></label>
    <label>Zip <input type="text" name="zip"></label>
</fieldset>
```

In this example, the `<fieldset>` tags group the text fields, and the `<legend>` tag creates a label describing the group of controls. In the most recent browsers, the legend appears as a label above the control group, as shown in the following figure.

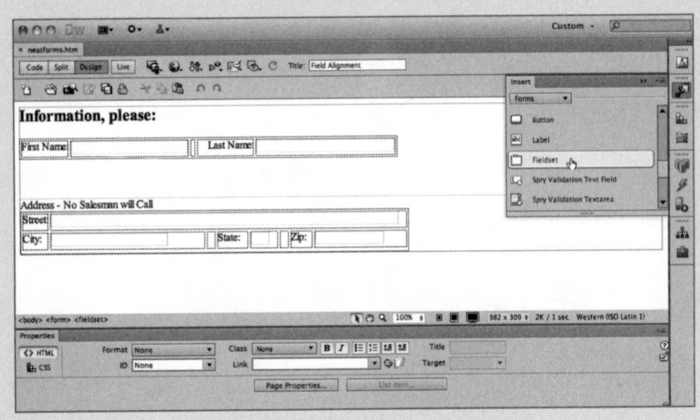

In Dreamweaver's Code view, you can add the <fieldset> and <legend> tags by selecting a set of existing controls that you'd like to group and then clicking the Fieldset button in the Forms category of the Insert panel. If you are in Design view when you click the Fieldset button, Dreamweaver automatically switches to the split view and makes Code view active. However, it is best to apply the <fieldset> tag in Code view so you can be sure you have correctly selected all the HTML tags to be grouped.

Note that the <fieldset> tag is not supported in all browsers, but Dreamweaver renders it just fine.

Providing Checkboxes and Radio Buttons

When you want your web page user to choose between a specific set of options in your form, you can use either checkboxes or radio buttons. Checkboxes enable you to offer a series of options from which the user can pick as many as he or she wants. Radio buttons, on the other hand, restrict your user to only one selection from a number of options.

NOTE

You can achieve the same functionality as checkboxes and radio buttons with a different look by using drop-down lists and menu boxes. These methods for presenting options to the user are described shortly.

Checkboxes

Checkboxes are often used in a "Select All That Apply" type of section, when you want to enable the user to choose as many of the listed options as desired (see Figure 13-4). You insert a checkbox in much the same way you do a text field: Select or drag the CheckBox object from the Insert panel or choose Insert ⇨ Form ⇨ CheckBox.

Like other form objects, checkboxes can be given a unique name in the Checkbox Property inspector. If you don't provide a name, Dreamweaver inserts a generic one, such as checkbox4.

FIGURE 13-4

Checkboxes are one way of offering the web page visitor any number of options to choose from.

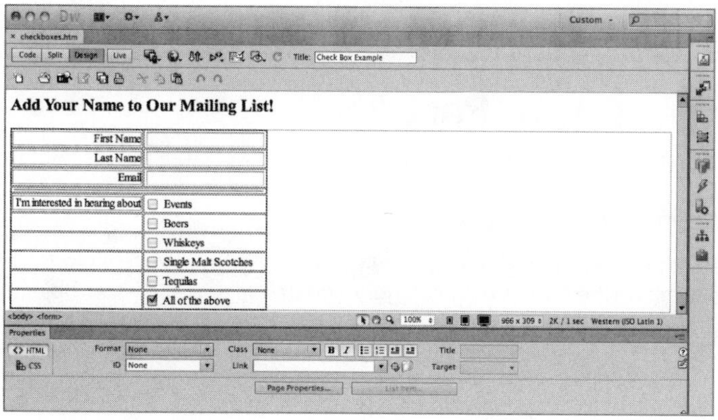

In the Checked Value text box, fill in the information you want passed to a program when the user selects the checkbox. By default, a checkbox starts out unchecked, but you can change that by changing the Initial State option to Checked.

If you need to put in a bunch of checkboxes quickly, use the Checkbox Group object. You'll have an opportunity to add as many checkboxes as desired, each with their own label and value. You can also choose to separate the checkboxes with line breaks or put them in a table.

Radio buttons

You can use radio buttons to offer users a set of options from which they can choose only one. If a user changes his or her mind after choosing one radio button, selecting another one automatically deselects the first choice. Dreamweaver gives you the following options for inserting radio buttons:

- To insert radio buttons one at a time, select or drag the Radio Button button from the Forms category of the Insert panel, or choose Insert ➪ Form ➪ Radio Button.
- To insert several related radio buttons at one time, select or drag the Radio Group button from the Forms category of the Insert panel, or choose Insert ➪ Form ➪ Radio Group.

Unlike checkboxes and text fields, each radio button in the set does not have a unique name—instead, each group of radio buttons has a name. If you give the entire set of radio buttons the same name, browsers can assign one value to the radio button set. That value is determined by the contents of the Checked Value text box in the Property inspector. Figure 13-5 shows two different sets of radio buttons. The figure shows the Property inspector for one of the radio buttons in the osRadio group, on the right. In this example, each button in the group is assigned the name osRadio.

To designate the default selection for each radio button group, you select the particular radio button and make the Initial State option Checked instead of Unchecked. In the form shown in Figure 13-5, the default selection for the osRadio group is Mac OS X.

TIP

Because you must give all radio buttons in the same set the same name, you can speed up your work a bit by creating one button, copying it, and then pasting the others. Don't forget to change the Checked Value for each button, however.

Dreamweaver TECHNIQUE

Building a Form, Part 1

In this Technique, you create a form that eventually incorporates most of the form elements. You add the form to the page, the table to hold the form elements, and the first of the form objects: text fields and radio buttons.

For this Technique, make sure the Accessibility options are disabled by opening Edit ➪ Preferences (Dreamweaver ➪ Preferences), selecting the Accessibility category, and deselecting the Form Objects option.

1. In the Files panel, switch to the Dreamweaver Bible working site that you created previously.

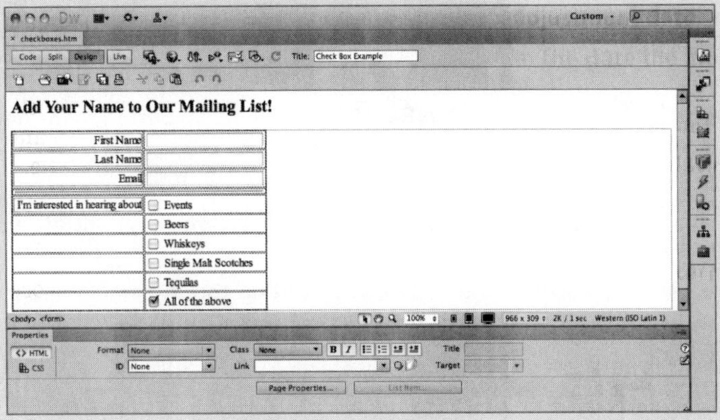

2. Go to Techniques\13_Forms and open the file `forms_start.htm`.
3. Place your cursor at the end of the first paragraph under the Tell Us What You're Looking For heading and press Enter (Return) to create a new line.
4. In the Insert panel, switch to the Forms category and click the Form object.
5. With your cursor inside the red form outline, change to the Common category and choose Table.
6. When the Insert Table dialog box opens, insert a 6-row, 2-column table that is 400 pixels wide with 0 for border thickness.

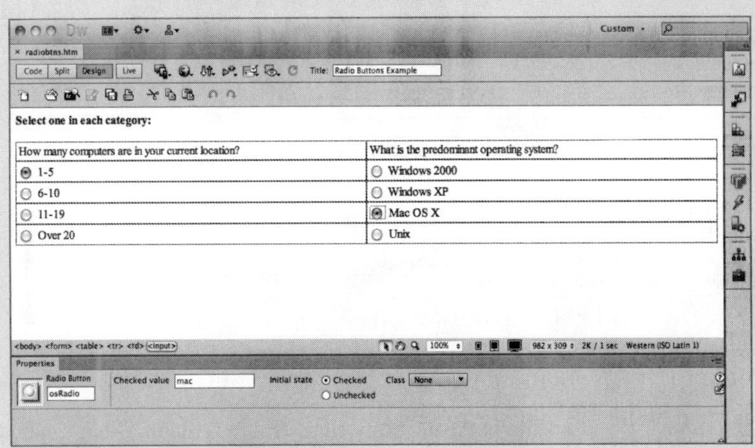

7. Select all the cells in the first column and, from the Property inspector's Class list, choose formLabel. The formLabel CSS rule makes the content in the designated cells bold and right-aligned.
8. Place your cursor in the first cell, first column and enter **I want to:** . Be sure to leave a space after the colon to add separation between the label and the form elements.

Continues

continued

9. Switch back to the Forms category in the Insert panel and drag a Radio Button into the first row, second column.
10. With the radio button still selected, enter **buyRentRB** into the Radio Button Name field of the Property inspector and **buy** in the Checked Value field.
11. Move your cursor to the right of the radio button and add the text **Buy**.
12. Repeat Steps 9–11 to add a second radio button. Use the same name (**buyRentRB**), a different value (**rent**), and a corresponding label (**Rent**).
13. In the second row, first column, enter the text **I can afford up to:** . Again, be sure to leave a space after the colon to add separation between the label and the form elements.
14. From the Insert panel's Forms category, drag a Text Field into the adjacent cell.
15. With the text field selected, enter **affordText** in the Property inspector's TextField Name field.
16. Save your page.

In the next Technique, you complete the form, adding the remaining form elements.

FIGURE 13-5

Radio buttons enable a user to make just one selection from a group of options.

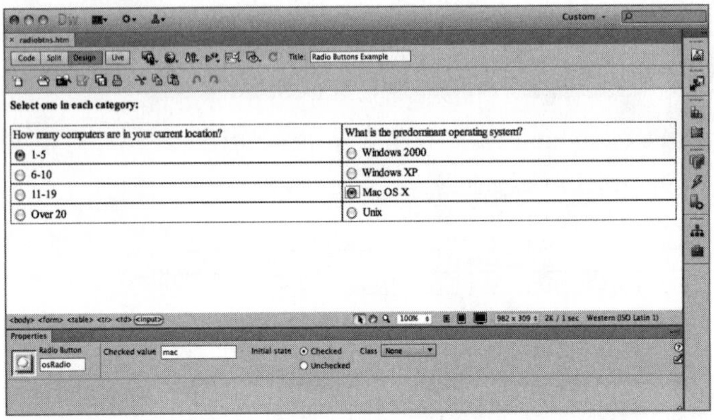

You can create an entire set of radio buttons at one time using the Radio Group command. When you select the Radio Group button from the Forms category of the Insert panel, or choose Insert ➪ Form ➪ Radio Group, the Radio Group dialog box appears, as shown in Figure 13-6. This dialog box not only lets you define multiple radio buttons at once but automatically formats them either in a table or using line breaks, at your discretion.

Follow these steps to set up your radio button group in the Radio Group dialog box:

1. In the Name text box, replace the default name with a meaningful name for your new set of radio buttons.
2. Each entry in the list represents a separate radio button in the group; the dialog box opens with two filler buttons as an example. Click the first entry in the Label list and replace the word Radio with the label for the first button in your group. Press Tab to move to the Value column, and replace the default with the appropriate value for your button; this is the data that is sent to the server when the radio button is selected.

   Repeat this step for the second radio button in your set.
3. If you have more than two radio buttons in your set, click the Add (+) button to add another item to the list and fill out the appropriate value, as explained in Step 2.
4. Specify whether you want your radio buttons inserted on separate lines using the `<br>` tag or automatically formatted in a table.
5. Click OK.

FIGURE 13-6

Use the Radio Group dialog box to create an entire set of radio buttons at one time.

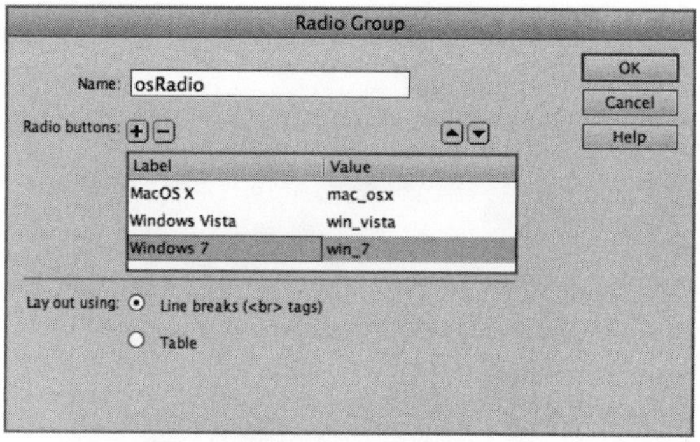

Creating Form Lists and Menus

Another way to offer your user options, in a more compact form than radio buttons and checkboxes, is with form lists and menus. Both objects can create single-line entries in your form that expand or scroll to reveal all the available options. You can also determine how deep you want the scrolling list to be—that is, how many options you want displayed at one time.

Drop-down menus

A drop-down menu should be familiar to everyday users of computers: The menu is initially displayed as a single-line text box with an arrow button at the right end; when the button is clicked, the other options are revealed in a list or menu. (Whether the list pops up or drops down depends on its position on the screen at the time it is selected. Normally, the list drops down, unless it is close to the bottom of the screen.) After the user selects one of the listed options and the mouse is released, the list closes, and the selected value remains displayed in the text box.

Insert a drop-down menu in Dreamweaver as you would any other form object, with one of the following actions:

- From the Forms category of the Insert panel, select the List/Menu button to place a drop-down menu at the current cursor position.
- Choose Insert ➪ Form ➪ List/Menu to insert a drop-down menu at the current cursor position.
- Drag the List/Menu button from the Insert panel to any location in the Document window and release the mouse button to position the drop-down menu.

With the List/Menu object inserted, make sure the Menu option (not the List option) is selected in the Property inspector, as shown in Figure 13-7. You can also name the drop-down menu by typing a name in the Select Name text box; if you don't, Dreamweaver supplies a generic "select" name.

FIGURE 13-7

Create a drop-down menu by inserting a List/Menu object and then selecting the Menu option in the List/Menu Property inspector.

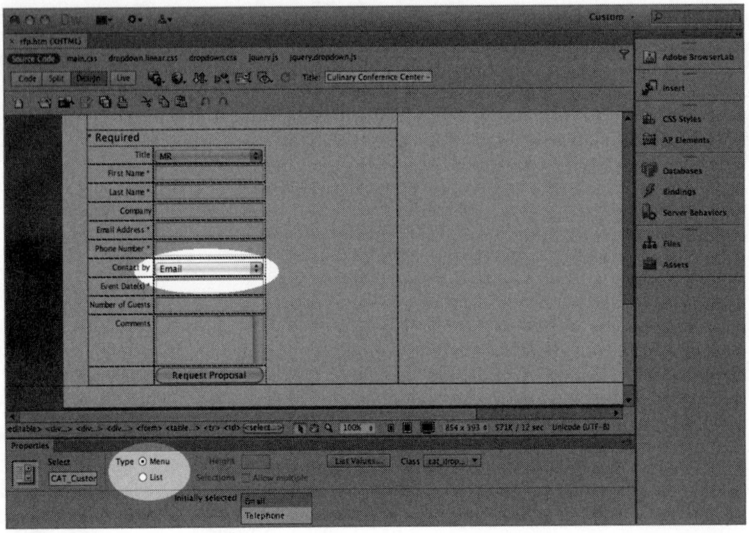

Menu values

The HTML code for a drop-down menu uses the <select> ... </select> tag pair surrounding a number of <option> ... </option> tag pairs. Dreamweaver gives you a straightforward user interface for entering labels and values for the options on your menu. The menu item's label is what is displayed on the drop-down list; its value is what is sent to the server-side processor when this particular option is selected.

To enter the labels and values for a drop-down menu—or for a scrolling list—follow these steps:

1. Select the menu for which you want to enter values.
2. From the List/Menu Property inspector, click the List Values button. The List Values dialog box appears (see Figure 13-8).

FIGURE 13-8

Use the List Values dialog box to enter and modify the items in a drop-down menu or scrolling list.

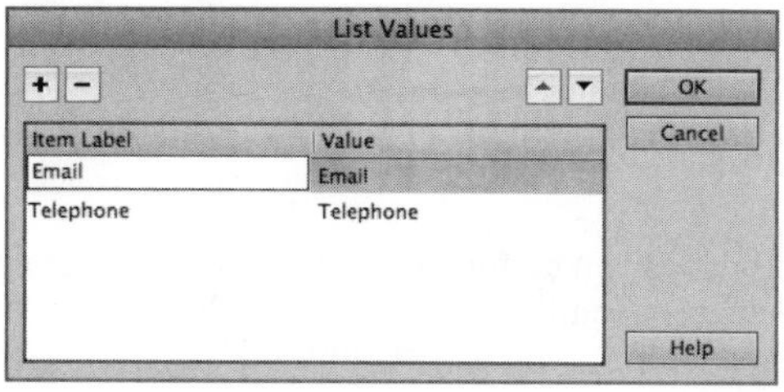

3. In the Item Label column, enter the label for the first item. Press the Tab key to move to the Value column.
4. Enter the value to be associated with this item. Press the Tab key.
5. Continue entering items and values by repeating Steps 3 and 4.
6. To delete an item's label and value in the List Values dialog box, highlight it and click the Delete (–) button at the top of the list. To delete either the item's label or its value, but not both, highlight either the label or the value and press the Delete or Backspace key.
7. To continue adding items, click the Add (+) button or continue using the Tab key.
8. To rearrange the order of items in the list, select an item and press the up or down arrow button to reposition it.
9. Click OK when you're finished.

If you haven't entered a value for every item, the server-side application receives the label instead. Generally, however, it is a good idea to specify a value for all items.

You can preselect any item in a drop-down menu so that it appears in the list box initially and is highlighted when the full list is displayed. Dreamweaver enables you to make your selection from the Initially Selected menu in the Property inspector. The Initially Selected menu is empty until you enter items through the List Values dialog box. You can preselect only one item for a drop-down menu.

TIP

To clear the selection in the Initially Selected list, hold down the Ctrl (Command) key as you click the highlighted item.

Scrolling lists

A scrolling list differs from a drop-down menu in three respects. First, and most obvious, the scrolling list field has up and down arrow buttons, rather than an option arrow button; the user can scroll the list, showing as little as one item at a time, instead of the entire list. Second, you can control the height of the scrolling list, enabling it to display more than one item—or all available items—simultaneously. Third, you can enable the user to select more than one item at a time, as with checkboxes.

A scrolling list is inserted in the same manner as a drop-down menu—through the Insert panel by choosing Insert ➪ Form ➪ Form. After the object is inserted, select the List option in the List/Menu Property inspector.

Enter items for your scrolling list just as you do for a drop-down menu, by starting with the List Values button in the Property inspector and filling in the List Values dialog box. Figure 13-9 shows a sample list box, as it appears in the Document window.

FIGURE 13-9

Unlike menus, scrolling lists can show more than one item on the screen at a time.

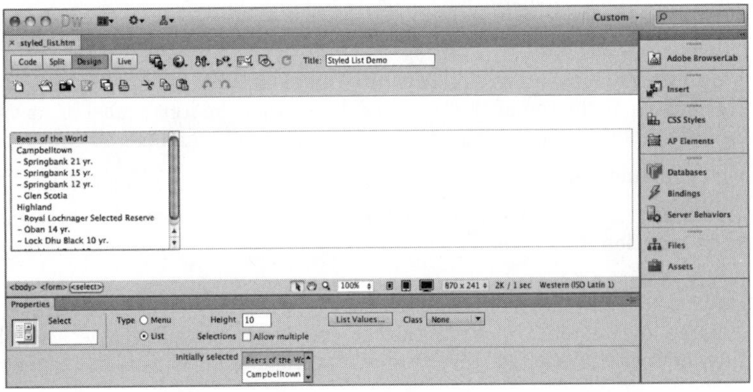

By default, the Selections checkbox for Allow Multiple is cleared in the List/Menu Property inspector. When you enable multiple selections (by selecting the Allow Multiple checkbox), the user can select more than one item in the list by using two keyboard modifiers, the Shift and Ctrl (Command) keys:

- To select several adjacent items in the list, the user must click the first item in the list, press the Shift key, and select the last item in the list.
- To select several nonadjacent items, the user must hold down the Ctrl (Command) key while selecting the items.

Other than the highlighted text, no acknowledgment (such as a checkmark) appears in the list. As with drop-down menus, the web designer can preselect options by highlighting them in the Initially Selected menu. Use the same techniques with the Shift and Ctrl (Command) modifier keys as a user would.

Keep the following in mind as you are working with scrolling lists:

- If you disable the Allow Multiple Selections box and set a Height value of 1 or clear the Height field entirely, the list appears as a drop-down menu.
- With Allow Multiple Selections enabled, if you do not set a Height value at all, the browser determines how many items appear onscreen. In the Dreamweaver Document window, only one item is displayed. To exercise control over your scrolling list, it is best to insert a Height value.
- The number of characters in the longest label determines the width of both the scrolling list and the drop-down menu. To widen the List/Menu object, you must directly enter additional spaces (` `) in the HTML code; Dreamweaver does not recognize additional spaces entered through the List Values dialog box. For example, to expand the example Favorite Beer List/Menu object, use the Code inspector or another editor to change

  ```
  <option value="oatmeal">Oatmeal Stout</option>
  ```

  to the following:

  ```
  <option value="oatmeal">Oatmeal Stout
     </option>
  ```

13

Dreamweaver TECHNIQUE

Building a Form, Part 2

Now you're ready to complete the form started earlier in this chapter.

For this Technique, make sure the Accessibility options are disabled by opening Edit ➪ Preferences (Dreamweaver ➪ Preferences), selecting the Accessibility category, and deselecting the Form Objects option.

1. In the Files panel, re-open the `forms_start.htm` file you previously worked on.
2. In the first column of the third row, enter this label: **I need this many bedrooms:** . Be sure to leave a space after the colon to match the other labels.
3. From the Insert panel's Forms category, drag a List/Menu object into the second column of the third row.
4. In the Property inspector's Select Name field, enter **roomList**.
5. Click List Values in the Property inspector.

Continues

continued

6. When the List Values dialog box opens, enter the following Item Label/Value pairs:

Item Label	Value
1	1
2	2
3	3
4	4
5+	5+

   Click OK when you're done to close the dialog box.

7. From the Initially Selected list in the Property inspector, choose the first value, 1.

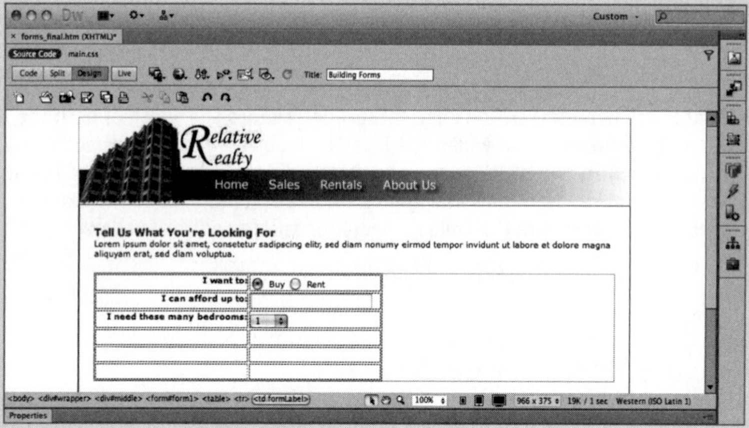

8. Place your cursor in the first column of the next row and enter the label **I need:** .
9. From the Insert panel, drag a checkbox object into the second column of the same row.
10. In the Property inspector name field, enter **laundryCB**.
11. Move to the right of the checkbox, add a space and enter the label **Laundry Room**; press Shift+Enter (Shift+Return) to create a line break.
12. Repeat Steps 9–11 twice more to insert one checkbox with the name **garageCB** and labeled **Garage** and another named **viewsCB** and labeled **Views**.
13. In the second-to-last row, first cell, enter the label **My special needs are:** .
14. From the Insert panel, drag a Textarea object into the second column of the same row.
15. In the Property inspector's Name field, enter **needsArea**.
16. Drag a Button object from the Insert panel to the second column in the last row.

17. In the Property inspector's Value field, enter **Send Info**.

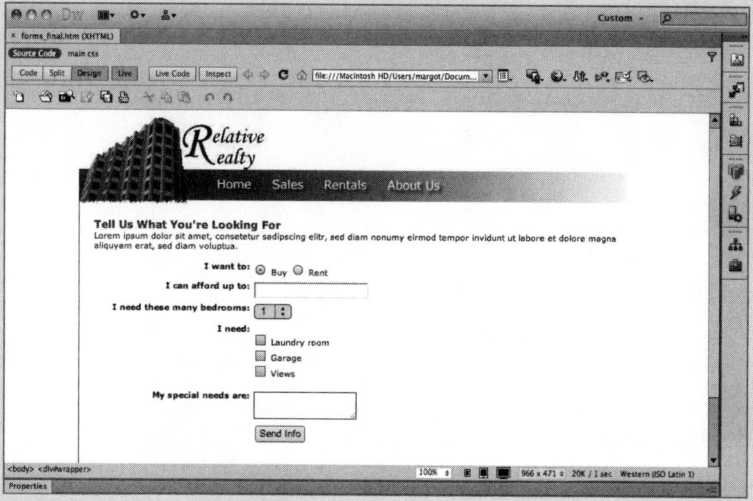

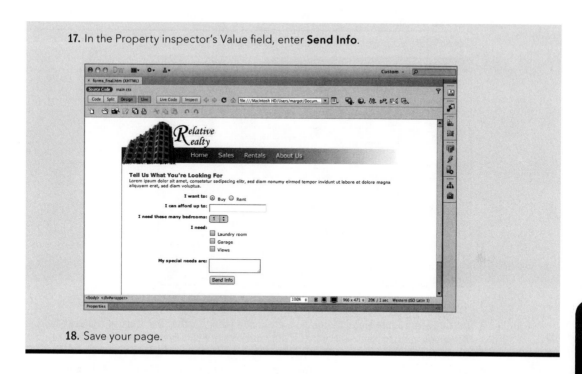

18. Save your page.

Navigating with a Jump Menu

It's not always practical to use a series of buttons as the primary navigation tool on a website. For sites that want to offer access to a great number of pages, a jump menu can be a better way to go. A jump menu uses the menu form element to list the various options; when one of the options is chosen, the browser loads—or jumps to—a new page. In addition to providing a single mechanism for navigation, a jump menu is easy to update because it doesn't require that you lay out the page again. Because they are JavaScript-driven, jump menus can even be updated dynamically.

Dreamweaver includes a Jump Menu object that handles all the JavaScript coding for you—all you have to provide is a list of item names and associated URLs. Dreamweaver even drops in a Go button for you, if you choose. The Jump Menu object is easily used in a legacy frame-based layout for targeting specific frames. After the object is inserted, you can modify the Jump Menu object like any other list object, through the List/Menu Property inspector. To insert a jump menu, follow these steps:

1. Position your cursor in the current form (if one exists), where you'd like the jump menu to appear. If you haven't already inserted a form, don't worry—Dreamweaver automatically inserts one for you.
2. From the Forms category of the Insert panel, click the Jump Menu button. The Insert Jump Menu dialog box, shown in Figure 13-10, is displayed.

FIGURE 13-10

Consolidate your website navigation through a jump menu.

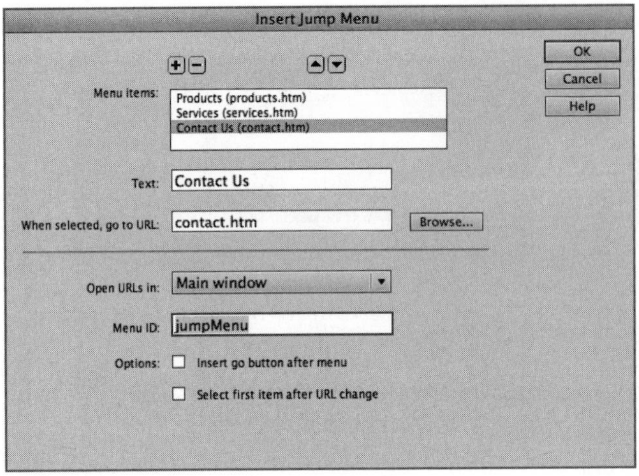

3. In the Insert Jump Menu dialog box, enter the label for the first item in the Text field. When you confirm your entry by tabbing out of the field, Dreamweaver updates the Menu Items list.
4. Enter the path and filename of the page you want opened for the current item in the When Selected, Go To URL field; alternatively, you can click the Browse button to select your file.
5. To add additional jump menu items, click the Add (+) button and repeat Steps 3 and 4.
6. You can adjust the positioning of the items in the jump menu by selecting an item in the Menu Items list and using the up and down arrows to move it higher or lower.
7. From the Open URLs In list, pick the destination target for the page. Unless you're working in a frameset, you have only one option—Main Window. When a Jump Menu object is added in a frameset, Dreamweaver displays all frame names, as well as Main Window, as options.
8. To reset the menu selection to the top item after every jump, choose Select First Item After URL Change.
9. Click OK when you're finished.

Dreamweaver inserts the new jump menu with the appropriate linking code.

Modifying a jump menu

After you've inserted your Jump Menu object, you can modify it in one of two ways: through the standard List/Menu Property inspector or through the Jump Menu behavior. Whereas the List

Property inspector uses a List Value dialog box, editing the Jump Menu behavior opens a dialog box similar to the one used to insert the Jump Menu object.

To alter the items in an existing jump menu via the List/Menu Property inspector, select the jump menu and click the List Values button. In the List Values dialog box, the jump menu labels are on the left and the URLs are on the right. You can add, move, or delete items as you would with any other list.

NOTE

One caveat for adding new URLs to the jump menu through the Property inspector: Any filenames with spaces or special characters should be URL-encoded. In other words, if one of your filenames is `about us.htm`, it should be entered using the hexadecimal equivalent for a space (`%20`): `about%20us.htm`. Also, if you enter a filename or URL that contains special characters in the List Values dialog box, the resulting code translates the special characters into their HTML codes, thus breaking the URL. Most notably, an ampersand (&) entered in the List Values dialog box is encoded as `&`.

If you'd prefer to work in the same environment as you did when creating the Jump Menu object, go the Behaviors panel route. Select the jump menu. Then, from the Behaviors panel, double-click the Jump Menu action. The Jump Menu dialog box opens—it's identical to the Insert Jump Menu dialog box except that the Go button option is not available.

Wrapping Graphics Around a Jump Menu

Jump menus are useful in many circumstances, but as a raw form element they often stick out of a web page design like a sore thumb. Some designers solve this dilemma by including their jump menu within a specially constructed graphic. The easiest way to create such a graphic is to use a program such as Fireworks, which enables a single image to be sliced into separate parts. The slices are then exported to an HTML file and reassembled in a table.

When you create your graphic, leave room for the jump menu to be inserted in Dreamweaver. Reserving space for a jump menu usually entails designating one slice as a nongraphic or text-only slice in your graphics program. After you bring the HTML into Dreamweaver, insert the Jump Menu object in the empty table cell.

Here are a few pointers for wrapping a graphic around a jump menu:

- Use a flat color—not a gradient—as the background for the menu.
- Work with web-safe colors in the graphics program; they're far easier to match in Dreamweaver.
- Set the background color of the graphic to be the background color of the cell of the table holding your jump menu.
- Make sure you leave enough height in your graphic to accommodate the jump menu in all browsers.

Continues

continued

- Form elements are drawn by the user's operating system and are vastly different on each platform. Test your designs extensively.
- Integrate your Go button, if you're using one, right in the graphic. Be sure to set it as its own slice so that it comes in as a separate image and can be activated with a Jump Menu Go behavior. In the following figure, a graphical Go button appears to the right of the jump menu.

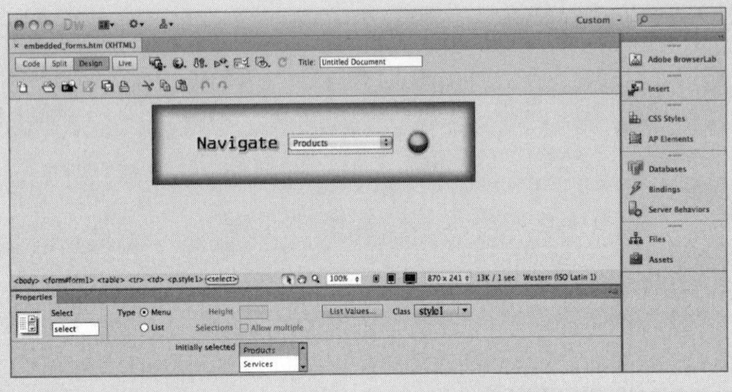

Activating Go buttons

The Dreamweaver jump menu is activated immediately whenever a user makes a selection from the list. So why would you want a Go button? The Go button, as implemented in Dreamweaver, is useful for selecting the first item in a jump menu list. To ensure that the Go button is the sole means for activating a jump selection, you need to remove an attached behavior. Select the jump menu item, open the Behaviors panel, and delete the Jump Menu event.

TIP

Some web designers prefer to use a non-URL option for the first item, such as Please Select A Department. When entering such a non-URL option, set the Go To URL (or the value in the List Value Properties) to `javascript:;` to create a null link.

The generic Go button is a nice convenience, but it's a little, well, generic. To switch from a standard Go button to a graphical Go button of your choosing, follow these steps:

1. Insert the image that you want to use as your new Go button next to the jump menu.
2. With the new graphic selected, open the Behaviors panel.
3. Select Jump Menu Go from the Add Event drop-down list. Dreamweaver displays a dialog box showing all available jump menus.
4. Choose the name of the current jump menu from the Jump Menu Go dialog box list and click OK when you're finished.
5. If necessary, delete the Dreamweaver-inserted Go button.

Activating Your Form with Buttons

Buttons are essential to HTML forms. You can place all the form objects you want on a page, but until your user clicks that Submit button, there's no interaction between the client and the server. HTML provides three basic types of buttons: Submit, Reset, and Command.

Submit, Reset, and Command buttons

A Submit button sends the form to the specified action (generally the URL of a server-side program or a mailto address) using the noted method (generally `post`). A Reset button clears all the fields in the form. Submit and Reset are both reserved HTML terms used to invoke specific actions.

A Command button permits the execution of functions defined by the web designer, as programmed in JavaScript or other languages.

To insert a button in Dreamweaver, follow these steps:

1. Position the cursor where you want the button to appear. Then either select Button in the Forms category of the Insert panel or choose Insert ➪ Form ➪ Button from the menu. Alternatively, you can simply drag the Button control from the Insert panel and drop it into place on an existing form.
2. In the Button Property inspector, select the button action type. In Figure 13-11, the Property inspector indicates that the Submit Form button action is selected (this is the default). To make a Reset button, select the Reset Form option. To make a Command button, select the None option.
3. To rename a button as you want it to appear on the web page, enter the new name in the Label text box.

When working with Command buttons, it's not enough to just insert the button and give it a name. You have to link the button to a specific function. A common technique is to use JavaScript's `onClick` event to call a function detailed in the `<script>` section of the document:

```
<input type="BUTTON" name="submit2" value="yes"
onClick="doFunction()">
```

FIGURE 13-11

You can choose an action and a label for a button through the Button Property inspector.

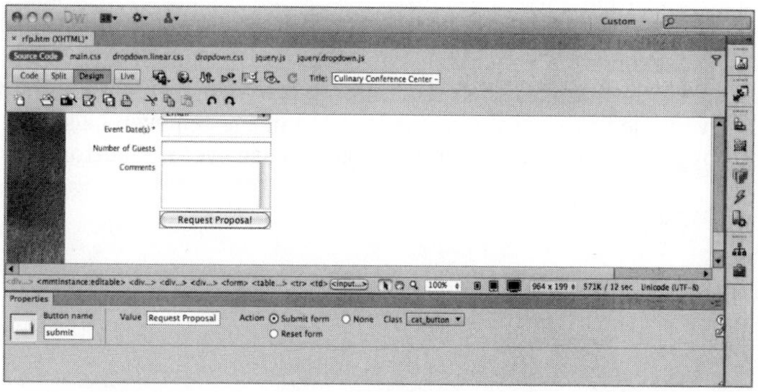

Graphical buttons

HTML doesn't limit you to the browser-style default buttons. You can also use an image as a Submit, Reset, or Command button. Dreamweaver has the capability to add an image field just like other form elements: Place the cursor in the desired position and choose Insert ➪ Form ➪ Image Field, or select the Image Field button from the Forms category of the Insert panel. You can use multiple image fields in a form to give users graphical options, as shown in Figure 13-12.

When the user clicks the picture that you've designated as an image field for a Submit button, the form is submitted. Any other functionality, such as resetting the fields, must be coded in JavaScript or another language and triggered by attaching an `onClick` event to the button. This can be handled through the Dreamweaver behaviors, covered in Chapter 11, or by hand-coding the script and adding code for the `onClick` event to the button.

FIGURE 13-12

Each flag in this page is more than an image; it's an image field that also acts as a Submit button.

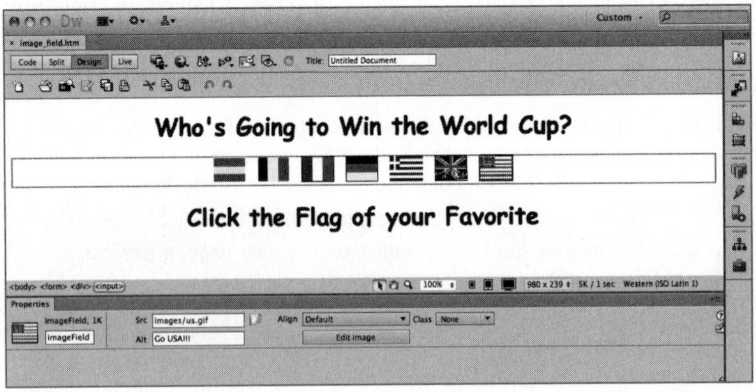

In fact, when the user clicks a graphical button, not only does it submit your form, but it passes along the x, y coordinates of the image. The x coordinate is submitted using the name of the field with an `.x` attached; likewise, the y coordinate is submitted with the name of the field with a `.y` attached. Although this latter feature isn't often used, it's always good to know all the capabilities of your HTML tools.

Another technique is involved if you want to include more graphical buttons than a single Submit button on your form. Because only one image field can be used as a Submit button, a standard image is inserted, and JavaScript handles the programming chores required for submitting or resetting the form. An advantage to this technique is that the image can even be set up as a roll-over, meaning that the image changes as the user moves the mouse over the button.

To use an image for a Submit or Reset button, follow these steps:

1. Choose Insert ➪ Image or click the Image button in the Common category of the Insert panel.
2. In the Insert Image dialog box, enter the path to your image or select the folder icon to locate the file. The image can be in GIF, JPEG, or PNG format.
3. Give the image an ID and alternative text using the appropriate text boxes in the Property inspector.
4. In the Link field of the Property inspector, enter the following code for a graphical Submit button:

   ```
   javascript:document.form1.submit()
   ```

   Similarly, enter this code for a Reset button:

   ```
   javascript:document.form1.reset()
   ```

NOTE
Be sure to change the code to reflect your specifics: the name of your form and the name of your images.

Using Hidden and File Fields

13

You should also be aware of two other special-purpose form fields, the hidden field and the file field, which are supported by all major browsers. The hidden field is extremely useful for passing variables to your web application programs, and the file field enables users to attach a file to the form being submitted.

The hidden input type

When passing information from a form to a CGI program or other server applications like PHP, the programmer often needs to send data that should not be made visible to the user. The data could be a variable needed by the CGI program to set information on the recipient of the form, or it could be a URL to which the server program redirects the user after the form is submitted. To send this sort of information unseen by the form user, you can use a hidden form object.

The hidden field is inserted in a form much like the other form elements. Place your cursor in the desired position and choose Insert ➪ Form ➪ Hidden Field or click the Hidden Field button in the Forms category of the Insert panel.

The hidden object is another input type, just like the text, radio button, and checkbox types. A hidden variable looks like the following in HTML:

```
<input type="hidden" name="recipient" value="jlowery@idest.com">
```

As you would expect, this tag has no representation when it's viewed through a browser. However, Dreamweaver does display a Hidden Form Element symbol in the Document window. You can turn off the display of this symbol by deselecting the Hidden Form Field option from the Invisible Elements category of Preferences.

The file input type

The file input type is typically used to browse for files to be uploaded in an application. You'll need to include server-side processing via PHP or another language to complete the file upload.

The file field is inserted in a form much like the other form elements. Place your cursor in the desired position and choose Insert ➪ Form ➪ File Field or click the File Field button in the Forms category of the Insert panel. Dreamweaver automatically inserts what appears to be a text box with a Browse button. In a browser, the user's selection of the Browse button displays a standard Open File dialog box from which a file can be selected to go with the form.

Improving Accessibility

You can do several things to make your HTML forms more accessible to people with visual impairments who may be using a nonvisual browser or a screen reader. Many of these options are also useful for users accessing the page visually.

Dreamweaver makes it easy for web page authors to improve the accessibility of their web forms by setting an option in the Accessibility category of the Preferences dialog box.

To turn on the accessibility controls for forms, choose Edit ➪ Preferences (Dreamweaver ➪ Preferences) and then, in the Accessibility category, select the Form Objects checkbox. With this option enabled, every time you insert a form object, the Input Tag Accessibility Attributes dialog box, shown in Figure 13-13, is displayed. A friendly reminder that this dialog box is controlled by Preferences is included in the dialog box.

NOTE
The Input Tag Accessibility Attributes dialog box does not appear when you insert jump menus or radio groups. However, it does appear when you insert individual radio buttons.

In the Input Tag Accessibility Attributes dialog box, you first have an option to enter an ID; the ID is referenced by the `<label>` tag `for` attribute, described later in this section. Next, the Label field associates a textual label with the form object you are inserting. It does this by inserting `<label> . . . </label>` tags in your form. This label is visible in the browser window. By using the `<label>` tag, you can explicitly associate the text with a particular control. You have two options for achieving this association:

- **Wrap with label tag:** This option encloses the form element within the `<label> . . . </label>` pair. Here's an example:

```
<label>First Name
  <input type="text" name="mytextfield">
</label>
```

- **Attach label tag using `for` attribute:** This option adds an attribute to the `<label>` tag that matches the `id` attribute of the form element. Choose this option, for example, when you use a table to align form elements and the label and control appear in separate table cells. The following example illustrates the use of the `for` attribute:

```
<label for="mytextfield">First Name</label>
  <input type="text" name="textfield2" id="mytextfield">
```

FIGURE 13-13

The Input Tag Accessibility Attributes dialog box is displayed only when you have enabled the Form Objects option in the Accessibility category of Preferences.

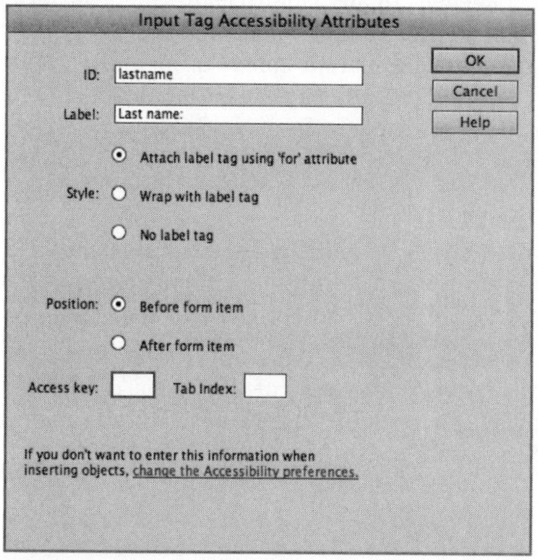

TIP

You can also insert a `<label> . . . </label>` pair by clicking the Label button in the Forms category of the Insert panel. This button is best used in Code view.

Although you may visually achieve the same effect by simply typing the text in the Document window, a nonvisual browser cannot associate plain text with any particular object. This is also the effect if you choose the No Label Tag option.

The final option you have when inserting a label is whether it should appear before or after the form element you are inserting.

In the Access Key field of the Input Tag Accessibility Attributes dialog box, type a single letter that serves as a shortcut to the form element. When users press the shortcut key for a given control, focus goes to that form element. Depending on their browsers and operating systems, users may have to hold down an additional key, referred to as a modifier key, such as Ctrl, Alt, or Command, for the shortcut to work.

The final control in the Input Tag Accessibility Attributes dialog box is the Tab Index. It adds the `tabindex` attribute to the `<input>` HTML tag. In this field, type a positive number indicating the order in which the control should receive focus when the user is tabbing through the form. Lower numbers receive focus first in the tabbing order; if items have the same number, the form element that appears first in the page receives focus first. Form elements with a `tabindex` of zero or with no `tabindex` specified appear last in the tab order.

Exploring HTML5 Form Elements

Form-related elements are more impacted by the HTML5 specifications than other tag categories —and their introduction was sorely needed. In addition to codifying a variety of more specific input types for text fields—such as `email` and `url`—adding a host of new attributes, HTML5 also standardized the code for a number of different controls, including sliders and calendars. While Dreamweaver CS6 does not yet include full drag-and-drop object support for these tags, it has integrated complete code hinting for the new form elements, so you can begin inserting them into your web pages.

To be fair to Dreamweaver, while the HTML5 specs are good to go, browser support is spotty at best. As of this writing, only Opera renders all of the new form elements and attributes as designed. For example, let's say you add the following code to your page:

```
<input type="date" name="eventDate" id="eventDate" />
```

If you look at it in any browser except a recent version of Opera, you'd see a standard text field that accepts a manually entered date. However, in Opera, you see a text field that, when clicked, displays a calendar capable of picking a date with a click, as shown in Figure 13-14.

FIGURE 13-14

Set an <input> tag type to one of the numerous HTML5 date-related values and Opera renders a fully functioning date picker.

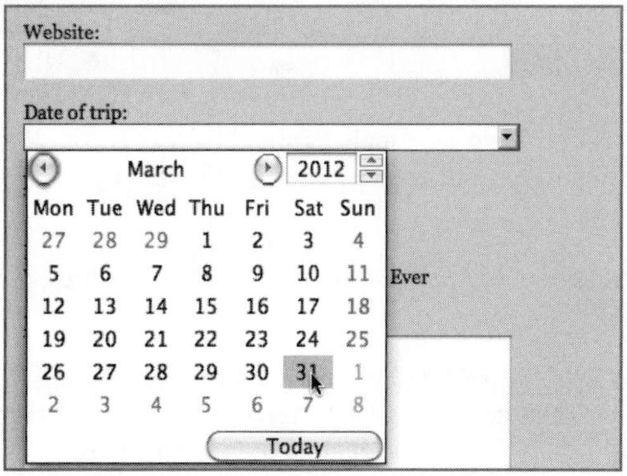

The good news is that all the HTML5 form-related tags and attributes are future-proof. Unsupported attributes are ignored, and if a browser doesn't recognize the input type, it simply depicts a text field. So feel free to use Dreamweaver to include the new HTML5 elements with the knowledge that, for once, you're ahead of the curve.

Enhanced HTML5 attributes

HTML5 proffers a very useful set of new attributes to the `<input>` tag. Unfortunately, the majority is not supported widely across browsers as of this writing. Here's a list of the most valuable ones:

- `autocomplete`: When set to `on`, this attribute forces browsers to remember earlier entries and displays them in a drop-down list when the first couple of letters are entered; a press of the Enter (Return) key completes the entry in the text field. When the `autocomplete` value is set to `off`, earlier entries are not stored.
- `autofocus`: When included, this parameter puts focus (and the user's cursor) in the associated form control when the page loads. You can use `autofocus="autofocus"` if you're following an XHTML syntax or just `autofocus` if you're not.
- `max`: Defines the maximum number of characters permitted.
- `min`: Determines the minimum number of characters allowed.
- `placeholder`: Displays the value of this attribute initially in the text field typically as a hint for the associated form element's use. The value is removed when the form field is given focus.
- `required`: Ensures that the form field has an entry when the form is submitted.

13

As of this writing, support for these attributes is most complete in Opera 11.*x* and Safari 5.*x* browsers.

HTML5-specific input types

The text input field is pretty much the universal bucket of the form elements, used to gather names, addresses, phone numbers, e-mail addresses, and other bits of information. HTML5 has moved toward giving many of those kinds of data their own type, including `email`, `tel` (phone numbers), and `url` (web addresses).

The new input types are dirt-simple to use: You just insert the desired category as the `type` attribute value. Here, for example, is the code for a text field used to hold an e-mail address:

```
<input type="email" name="email" id="email">
```

Dreamweaver makes it even easier by providing a custom Property inspector for input tags where you can enter the type directly, as shown in Figure 13-15.

What are the advantages of using more specific input types? The pluses are mostly seen in mobile browsers now. For example, when a user tabs into an e-mail type field in a mobile device that uses Apple's WebKit engine, special characters are presented—including `@`—to make completing the e-mail address field easy. Similarly, a phone number in a `tel` type field is displayed ready to be dialed. As noted earlier, there's no real downside to using HTML5 types. If a browser doesn't recognize the specific type, it renders the default: a text field.

FIGURE 13-15

Use Dreamweaver's Property inspector to change the type of an input field.

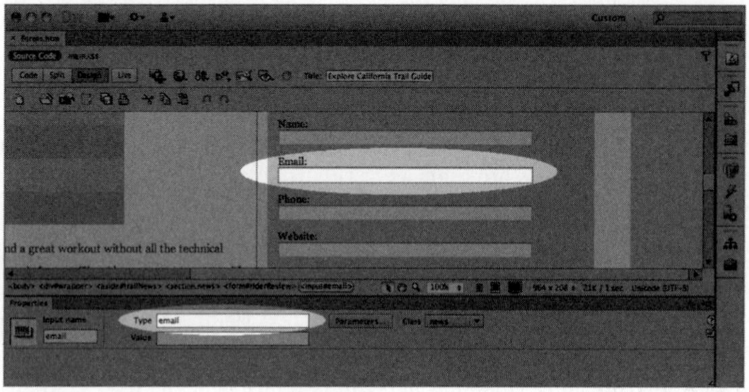

Next-gen form controls

For many years, web designers restricted to using nothing but standard HTML looked longingly at their snazzy Flash or Flex cousins. But envy no more! HTML5 has added its own zippy new form controls for selecting numbers and dates. Again, browser support is limited, but the promise is tantalizing.

The new number type, when rendered properly, displays what is referred to as a spinner control, where the user can click up or down arrows to increment or decrement the initial value. Designers can set minimum, maximum, and initial values with the following attributes, respectively: `min`, `max`, and `value`, as shown in the following code:

```
<input type="number" name="riders" id="riders" tabindex="60" min="1"
max="10" value="1">
```

An example of the spinner control, rendered in the latest Opera browser, is shown at the top of Figure 13-16.

Sometimes it's easier to pick a number within a specific range by sliding an indicator along a scale. When the HTML5 `range` type is properly rendered, you get a slider control like that shown in the bottom of Figure 13-16. Again, designers can define minimum, maximum, and initial values, as well as step values to control the number increments.

FIGURE 13-16

Use Dreamweaver's Property inspector to change the type of an input field.

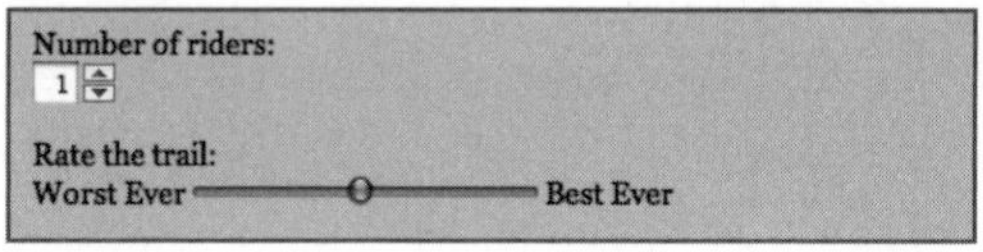

The datepicker, shown earlier in Figure 13-14, is the final new form control offering from the HTML5 specification. The use of different input types display different types of calendars:

- `date`: Shows a full month and allows the user to pick a single day
- `datetime`: Displays a month with a user-selected day, next to a spinner control for the time
- `month`: Shows a full month and allows the user to pick the desired month
- `week`: Shows a full month and allows the user to pick the week of the year
- `time`: Shows an initial time in a spinner control

While all of these values need to be entered in Dreamweaver by hand, code hinting for them is fully supported.

Styling Forms with CSS

In many ways, forms are the real workhorses of the web—but that doesn't mean they have to be plain. Until CSS use became prevalent, little could be done to alter the way forms and form elements looked on the web. Standardizing text field sizes between PC and Macintosh was a problem because the different operating systems interpreted character width differently; moreover, the field sizes may vary from browser to browser.

CSS gives the form designer much more flexibility, both to integrate and to isolate the form and form elements. Text fields, for example, can take on a shade of a site's background color or adopt the same typeface used on the page. Similarly, you can draw attention to the form itself by giving it a contrasting background; this enables you to format lengthy drop-down lists for easy reading.

If you're not familiar with CSS in general or, specifically, how it is applied in Dreamweaver, see Chapter 6.

Highlighting the form

The `<form>` tag is a containing element that, like the `<div>` tag, is not rendered by default. Both tags, in fact, can be styled with CSS—you can even position a form on the page via CSS declarations. Browser support varies for some of the more esoteric CSS properties applied to the form tag, but more common attributes such as background color and border are rendered properly in most cases. Best of all, if CSS does not support certain attributes, these attributes are just ignored and the form renders plainly.

Frequently, a web page contains only a single form. In these situations, styling the `<form>` tag itself will have the desired results. For example, the following CSS rule gives the entire form a bright orange background and a blue border:

```
form {
    background: #FF9900;
    border: thin solid #0000FF;
    padding: 10px;
}
```

Padding is added to move the form elements in from the edges, as shown in Figure 13-17.

FIGURE 13-17

Apply CSS coloring to the form to make it stand out on the page.

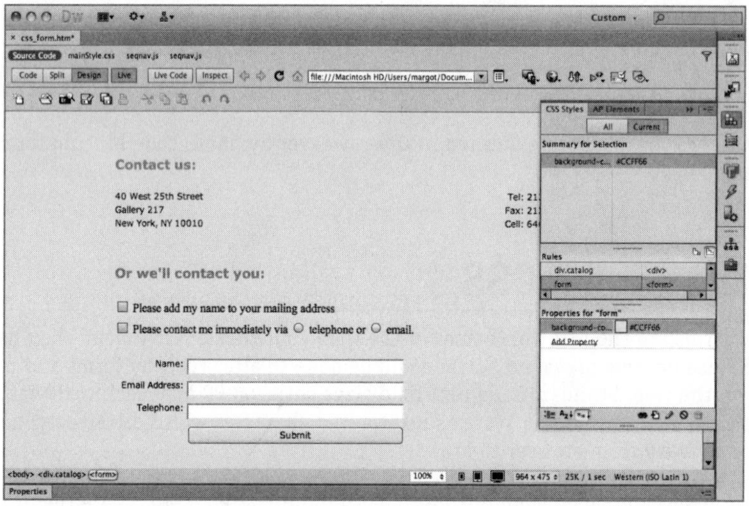

Should your page contain more than one form and you want to style each one differently, create a CSS ID or class selector for each form. In this situation, choose the ID or Class selector in the New CSS Rule dialog box and enter a unique ID or class—such as form#topform or form.bottom-form—in the Selector field. Also set the ID or class of the form tag when using this method.

Altering input fields

The `<form>` and `<div>` tags differ in terms of how they handle inheritance. Elements within a form do not inherit the CSS properties of the form, but elements within a `<div>` tag do inherit the `div`'s CSS attributes. You must, therefore, take another route for styling all the text fields in a given form. The best way to affect multiple form elements all at once is to style the `<input>` tag. You may recall that the `<input>` tag is used to create text fields, radio buttons, check-boxes, and Submit buttons.

For example, this CSS rule gives all the input elements a uniform background color, as well as a specific color, font, and size for the text fields:

```
input {
    background-color: #F5F5F5;
    color: #660099;
    font: 10px Verdana, Arial, Helvetica, sans-serif;
}
```

CSS styles the text fields for initial text and text entered by the user, as shown in Figure 13-18, as previewed in Dreamweaver's Live View.

FIGURE 13-18

Keep the text in your text fields looking like the rest of your page through CSS styling of the input tag.

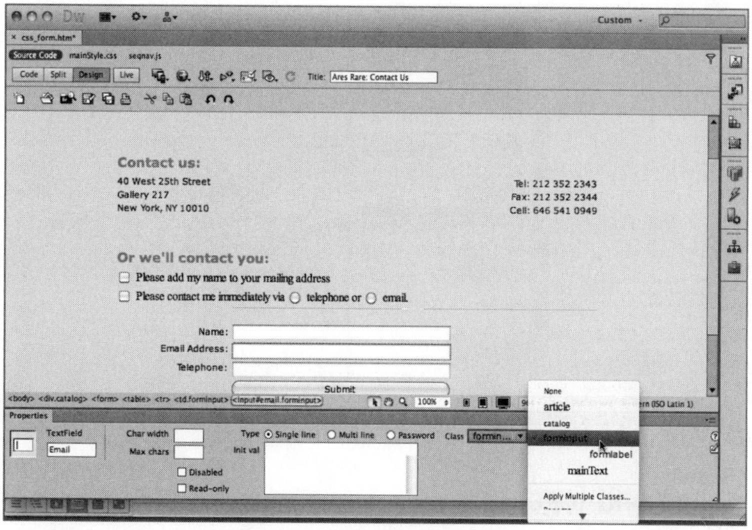

NOTE

Remember that a multiline text field is really a different tag—`<textarea>`—than the single-line text field. You have to create a CSS rule for both `<input>` and `<textarea>` tags.

One of the best uses for CSS and text fields is to set the width of the field. This method is far more flexible and responsive than using the Char Width field on the Property inspector for each individual text field. It is best to set the width on a CSS class rather than alter it directly in the CSS rule for the input tag. Why? The width setting not only affects all the single-line text fields but also alters checkboxes and radio buttons—which are also input tags. After the CSS rule is defined, set the class of a selected text field from the Property inspector.

Distinguishing lists and menus

The Select (List/Menu) object is composed of two tags: `<select>` and `<option>`. The `<select>` tag is the overall container for the list items; use `<select>` to style the width, typeface, and font size of all drop-down lists on the page uniformly. Individual list items can be styled by setting a class on the separate option tags. Although this operation must be performed by hand and is somewhat tedious, it does open the door to many possibilities.

If you have a very long drop-down list that includes a wide range of items organized by category, with judicious CSS styling, main category headings can be in one color and subitems in another, as shown in Figure 13-19.

FIGURE 13-19

CSS classes for menu items must be applied by hand to separate <option> tags.

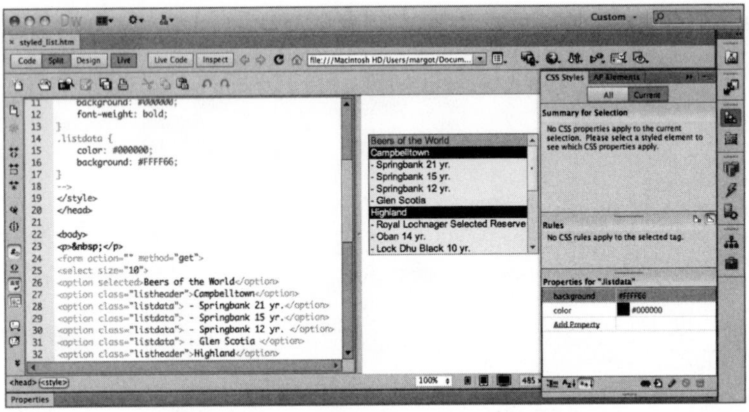

Changing labels and legends

A form is more than a collection of text fields and checkboxes; labels play an equally important role in form organization and usability. Form labels are often applied in one of two ways. The standard technique is to place most of the labels in a single column of a table, with the form elements in another. Designers are also increasingly using the `<label>` tag as a means of enhancing accessibility. A Dreamweaver CSS methodology is available for whichever route you take when labeling your forms.

In a situation where all the labels are arranged in a table column, it's best to create a CSS class for your labels and apply it to the `<td>` tags. The most efficient way to do this is to first select the column containing the labels and then choose the desired class from the Style list on the Property inspector. Dreamweaver applies the selected class to each of the `<td>` cells in the column.

If your layout uses `<label>` tags, CSS control is even easier. Add a specific CSS style for the `<label>` tag to create a uniform appearance for all your labels. Note that you may still need to adjust the dimensions of the label column separately because setting the width in CSS for the `<label>` tag has no effect.

Two other form-related tags—`<fieldset>` and `<legend>`—are available for CSS styling. As described earlier in this chapter in the sidebar "Grouping Form Controls," the two are used together to visually associate related form elements. Style the `<fieldset>` tag to alter the outlining border or add padding from the edge of the border. Change the `<legend>` style when you want to give it a separate background color and/or border, as shown in Figure 13-20.

FIGURE 13-20

Style the <fieldset> and <legend> tags to really make them stand out from a form with a colored background.

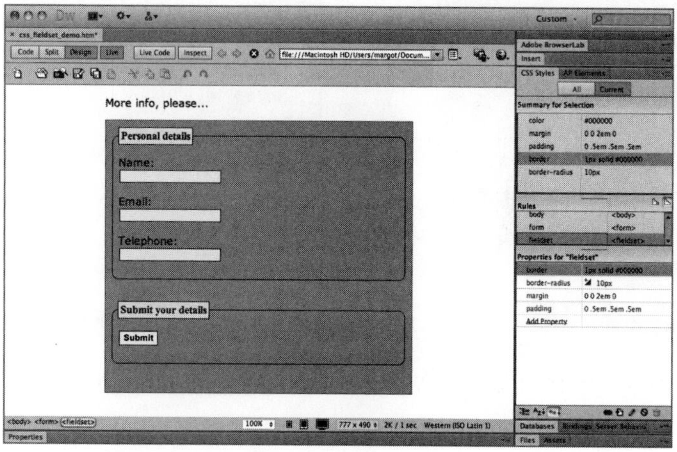

Highlighting focus

Want to spotlight the interactivity of a form? CSS includes a pseudo-element selector (so called because it is valid only when an element is in a particular state) that takes effect when a form element is selected. The CSS selector is `:focus` and it works with `<input>`, `<select>`, and `<textarea>` tags.

To create a `:focus` selector, follow these steps:

1. Select New CSS Rule from the CSS Styles panel.
2. In the New CSS Rule dialog box, select the Compound selector option.
3. Enter the name of the tag you want to affect followed by **:focus** in the Selector field. For example, if you wanted to alter all the text fields, radio buttons, checkboxes, and buttons when they receive focus, enter **input:focus**.
4. Click OK to close the New CSS Rule dialog box and open the CSS Rule Definition dialog box.
5. Choose the desired styles from the various categories and click OK when you're finished.

Preview the page in a compatible browser such as Mozilla Firefox, Internet Explorer 7 or better, Safari, and so on to experience the CSS changes (see Figure 13-21).

FIGURE 13-21

Text in a selected field is shown in bright red and bold, thanks to the :focus selector.

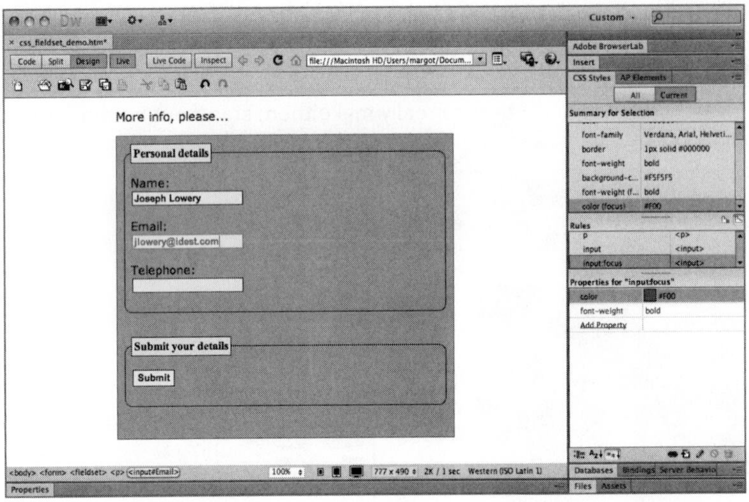

Summary

HTML forms provide a basic line of communication from web page visitor to website applications. With Dreamweaver, you can enter and modify most varieties of form inputs, including text fields and checkboxes. When adding forms to your web pages, keep these points in mind:

- For the most part, a complete form requires two working parts: the form object inserted in your web page and a CGI program or PHP code stored on your web server.
- To avoid using a server-side script, you can use a mailto address, rather than a URL pointing to a program in a form's `action` attribute. However, you still have to parse the form reply to convert it to a usable format.
- The basic types of form input are text fields, text areas, radio buttons, checkboxes, drop-down menus, and scrolling lists.
- Dreamweaver includes a Jump Menu object, which uses a drop-down list as a navigational system.
- After a user completes a form, it has to be sent to the server-side application, usually through a Submit button on the form. Dreamweaver also supports Reset and user-definable Command buttons.
- Dreamweaver includes code-hinting level support for HTML5 form elements and attributes.
- You can gain a lot more control of how your form integrates into your web page by applying CSS styles to the form elements—including the form itself.

In the next chapter, you learn how to use Dreamweaver to create bulleted and numbered lists.

CHAPTER

14

Creating Lists

IN THIS CHAPTER

Bulleting your points

Dreamweaver Technique: Adding Unordered Lists

Using a numbered list

Dreamweaver Technique: Inserting Ordered Lists

Applying CSS to lists

Dreamweaver Technique: Applying Definition Lists

Building a glossary

Inserting menu and directory lists

Lists serve several different functions in all publications, including web pages. A bulleted list can itemize a topic's points or catalog the properties of an object. A numbered list is helpful for giving step-by-step instructions. From a page designer's point of view, a list can break up the page and simultaneously draw the viewer's eye to key details.

Lists are an important alternative to the basic textual tools of paragraphs and headings. In this chapter, you study Dreamweaver's tools for designing and working with each of the three basic types of lists available in HTML:

- Unordered lists
- Ordered lists
- Definition lists

The various list types can also be combined to create outlines. Dreamweaver supplies a straightforward method for building these nested lists.

Creating Unordered (Bulleted) Lists

What word processing programs and layout artists refer to as *bulleted lists* are known in HTML as *unordered lists*. An unordered list is used when the sequence of the listed items is unimportant, as in a recipe's list of ingredients. Each unordered list item is set off by a leading character, and the remainder of the line is indented. By default, the leading character is the bullet—a small, filled-in circle; however, you can create a custom bullet through Cascading Style Sheets.

Dreamweaver QUICKSTART

Need to add lists to your page and can't wait? Here's how you insert an unordered (bulleted) or ordered (numbered) list:

1. Place your cursor where you'd like the list to appear.
2. In the HTML tab of the Property inspector, click either Unordered List or Ordered List.

3. Type your list item and press Enter (Return) to create another list item.
4. When you're finished with your list, press Enter (Return) one last time and deselect Unordered List or Ordered List on the Property inspector.

In the rest of the chapter, you'll see that there's much more that you can do with the various kinds of lists available to you.

You can either create the unordered list from scratch or convert existing text into the bulleted format. To begin an unordered list from scratch, position the cursor where you want to start the list. Then click the Unordered List button, supplied conveniently on the Text Property inspector, or use the Format ➪ List ➪ Unordered List command. You can also click the Unordered List button in the Text category of the Insert panel. Figure 14-1 shows an unordered list and the associated Text Property inspector.

FIGURE 14-1

Formulate an itemized list of items where the sequence isn't important as an unordered list.

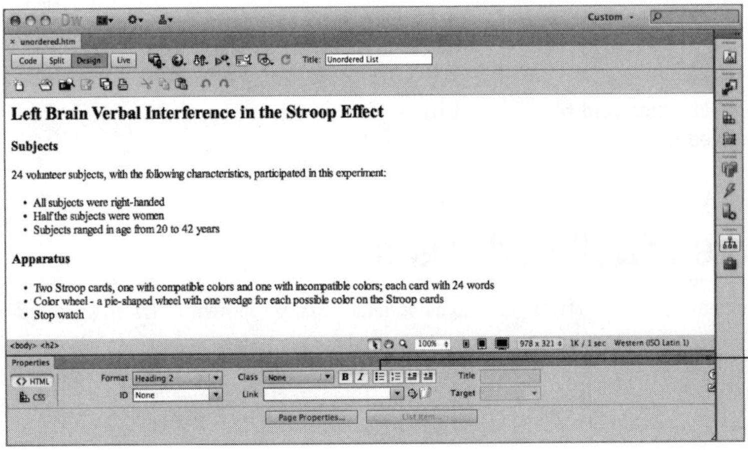

If you are changing existing text into a list, select the paragraphs first and then use the menu command or the Unordered List button on the HTML tab of the Property inspector or the Text category of the Insert panel.

Dreamweaver creates one list item for every paragraph. As you can see from Figure 14-1, list items are generally rendered closer together than regular paragraphs. A list, unlike other block elements such as paragraphs or headings, is not formatted with additional space above and below each line.

NOTE

In Dreamweaver, the word "paragraph" is used literally to mean any text designated with a paragraph tag. Certainly, you can apply a heading format to an HTML list, but you probably won't like the results: The heading format reinserts that additional space below and above each list item—the ones generally not used by the list format. If you want your list items to appear larger, change the font size through Cascading Style Sheets.

Editing unordered lists

After a series of paragraphs is formatted as an unordered list, you can easily add additional bulleted items. The basic editing techniques are the same for all types of lists:

- To continue adding items at the end of a list, simply press Enter (Return) to create each new list item. Another bullet is inserted, as long as the preceding item is not empty.
- To insert an item within an unordered list, place your cursor at the end of the item above the desired position for the added item and press Enter (Return).
- List items can be copied or cut and pasted to a different place on the list. When selecting a list item, use the Tag Selector in the status bar to be sure you select the tags enclosing the list item, not just the list item text. Position your cursor at the start of the list item that will follow the pasted entry and choose Edit ➪ Paste.
- To end a bulleted list, you can press Enter (Return) twice or deselect the Unordered List button on the Text Property inspector.

List tags

You may occasionally need to tweak your list code by hand. Two HTML tags are used in creating an unordered list. The first is the outer tag, which defines the type of list; the second is the item delimiter. Unordered lists are designated with the `<ul> . . . </ul>` tag pair, and the delimiter is the `<li> . . . </li>` pair. The unordered list code in Code view looks like the following:

```
<ul>
  <li>All subjects were right-handed</li>
  <li>Half the subjects were women</li>
  <li>Subjects ranged in age from 20 to 42 years</li>
</ul>
```

TIP

If you are working in Code view, you can click the List Item button in the Text category of the Insert panel to insert a <li> . . . </li> pair. Insert the tags <ul> . . . </ul> by clicking the Unordered List button on the Insert panel.

If a list item is too long to fit in a single line, the browser indents the text that wraps. By inserting a line break code, you can emulate this behavior even when you're working with lines that aren't long enough to need wrapping. To insert a line break, click the Line Break button in the Characters category of the Insert panel or choose Insert ➪ HTML ➪ Special Characters ➪ Line Break. Alternatively, use the key combination Shift+Enter (Shift+Return), or just type **
** in your code. Figure 14-2 shows examples of both approaches: inserted line breaks to force wrapping and the long paragraph that wraps naturally.

TIP

If you are not creating an XHTML document, use `<br>` instead of `<br />`. When you press Shift+Enter (Shift+Return), Dreamweaver automatically determines the correct format to use for the break tag based on the `DOCTYPE` statement, visible at the top of the document in Code view.

FIGURE 14-2

A list is indented if the text wraps around the screen (as with the second bullet point) or if you insert a line break, as shown in the first bullet point.

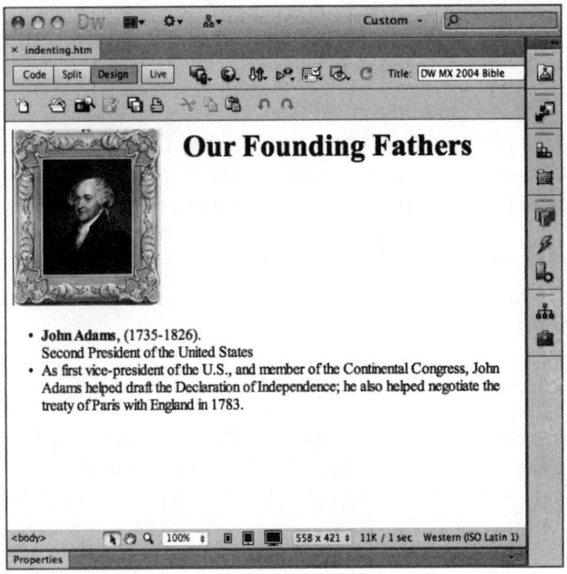

Dreamweaver TECHNIQUE

Adding Unordered Lists

In this Technique, you practice adding an unordered list to a web page.

1. In the Files panel, switch to the Dreamweaver Bible working site previously created.

2. Go to Techniques\14_Lists and open the file `lists_start.htm`.
3. Place your cursor below the paragraph following the Relative Realty Benefits heading.
4. In the Property inspector, click Unordered List. A bullet symbol appears, indicating the first list item.
5. Enter the following text: **Local realtor team**.
6. Press Enter (Return) and enter the next bullet point: **Highly qualified personnel**.
7. Press Enter (Return) and enter the next bullet point: **A-Z assistance**.

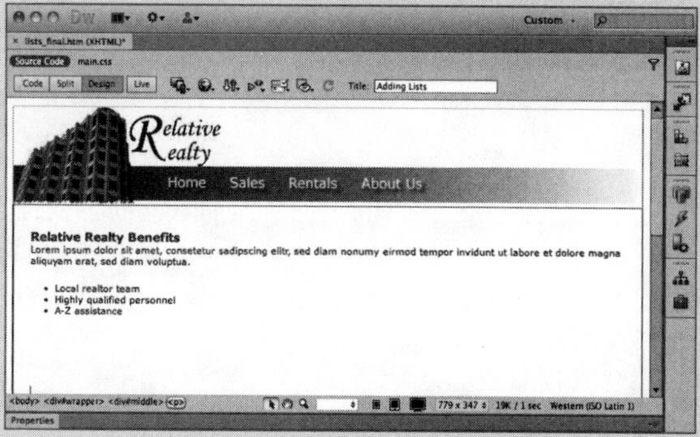

8. You can nest one unordered list inside another to create sublists. Place your cursor after the second bullet point and press Enter (Return).
9. In the Property inspector, click Text Indent.
10. You can also create a sublist by pressing Tab. Enter the text for the first item in the sublist: **#1 Local Firm**.
11. Press Enter (Return) and enter the next bullet point: **Top Ten state sales agents**.

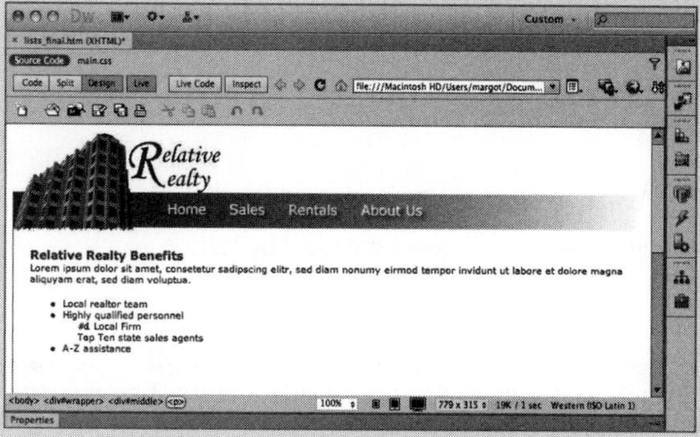

12. Save your page.

In the next Dreamweaver Technique, you add ordered (numbered) lists to the page.

Using other bullet symbols

Most browsers depict the default bullet as a small filled-in circle. In HTML, you can use any of the Dreamweaver-supported strategies to change the shape of your bullets. Your choices are to:

- Add an attribute to the `<ul>` or `<li>` tag to specify one of several other bullet shapes.
- Use Cascading Style Sheets to define a new bullet shape.

In HTML, the `<ul>` and `<li>` tags can include a `type` attribute that defines the shape of the bullet. Although the `type` attribute doesn't include a wide range of different bullet symbols, you have a few options. Dreamweaver offers two bullet styles: bullet, a small filled-in circle (the default), and square.

NOTE

In the HTML 4.0 specification, the `type` attribute is deprecated. This means that although still supported by current browsers, the attribute has been replaced by a newer or more desirable method of achieving the same thing. In this case, the `type` attribute has been replaced by newer Cascading Style Sheet attributes. Because the `type` attribute is deprecated, it may not be supported at all in future versions of HTML. On a practical level, however, major browsers tend to continue supporting deprecated tags and elements so that older web pages continue to display correctly. According to the HTML specification, if a browser stops supporting the attribute, the browser should simply ignore the attribute when encountered in a page.

Dreamweaver gives you access to the `type` attribute in Code view. To change the bullet style for the entire unordered list, follow these steps:

1. In Design view, place your cursor anywhere in the list, but don't select an entire `<li>` tag.
2. In the HTML tab of the Property inspector, click List Item.
3. When the List Properties dialog box appears, make sure List Type is set to Bulleted List.
4. From the Style list choose one of the following:
   - **[Default]:** No style is listed, and the browser applies its default, usually a solid circle.
   - **Bullet:** A solid circle.
   - **Square:** A solid square.
5. Click OK.

The previous steps change the bullet style for all items within the list.

Styling lists with CSS

A more modern technique for installing bullet styles uses style sheets. Using Cascading Style Sheets (CSS), you can switch a list or list item's bullet style to the same shapes that the `<ul>` and `<li>` type attribute can. With a style sheet, however, you can perform one additional task. You can assign the bullet style type to a specific file—in other words, you can customize your bullet image. Internet Explorer, Firefox, Safari, and other standards-compliant browsers support this feature fully.

NOTE

If you're totally unfamiliar with CSS, you'll be happy to know that Cascading Style Sheets are covered in depth in Chapter 6.

Here is a brief version of the steps for using a style sheet to assign a new bullet symbol:

1. Choose Window ➪ CSS Styles or press Shift+F11.
2. In the CSS Styles panel, click the New CSS Rule button.
3. In the New CSS Rule dialog box, select the Tag menu option from the Selector Type menu to redefine the HTML tag.
4. From the Selector name list, select the `ul` tag.
5. From the Rule Definition menu, select an option to determine whether the style definition is saved in the current document or in a separate style sheet file. Refer to Chapter 6 for more information about making this decision.
6. Click OK.
7. In the CSS Rule Definition dialog box that appears, select List in the Category list (see Figure 14-3).
8. Find your graphics file by clicking the Browse button next to the List-style-image text box. Click OK when you're finished.

FIGURE 14-3

You can use Cascading Style Sheets to specify a bullet image for your web page.

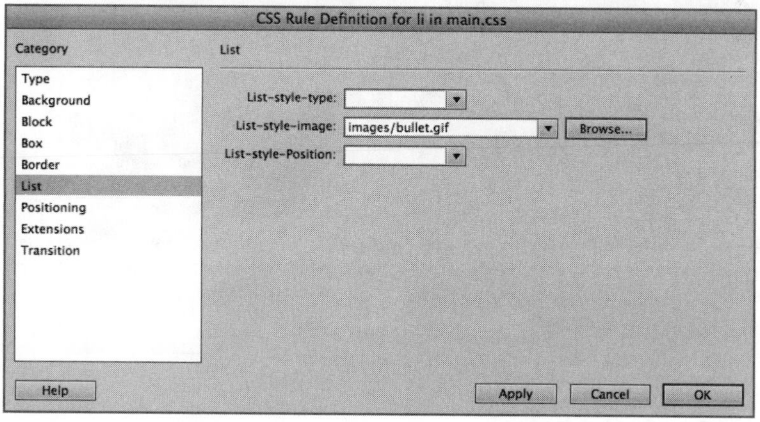

Mastering Ordered (Numbered) Lists

Unlike a bulleted list, in which sequence is not vital, order is important in the *ordered* (or numbered) list. The major advantage of an ordered list is the automatic generation of list item numbers and automatic renumbering when you're editing. If you've ever had to renumber a legal document because paragraph 14.b became paragraph 2.a, you recognize the time-saving benefits of this feature.

Ordered lists offer a slightly wider variety of built-in styles than unordered lists, but you cannot customize the leading character further. For instance, you cannot surround a character with parentheses or offset it with a dash. Once again, the browser is the final arbiter of how your list is viewed.

Many of the same techniques used with unordered lists work with ordered lists. To start a new numbered list in Dreamweaver, place your cursor where you want the new list to begin. Then, in the Text Property inspector, click the Ordered List button or choose Format ➪ List ➪ Ordered List. You can also click the Ordered List button in the Text category of the Insert panel.

As with unordered lists, you can also convert existing paragraphs into a numbered list. First, select your text; then click the Ordered List button on the Property inspector or choose Format ➪ List ➪ Ordered List.

The default numbering system is Arabic numerals: 1, 2, 3, and so forth (see Figure 14-4). In a following section, you learn how to alter this default to use other numbering formats or to create an alphabetic list.

FIGURE 14-4

An ordered list is used on this page to create a numbered sequence.

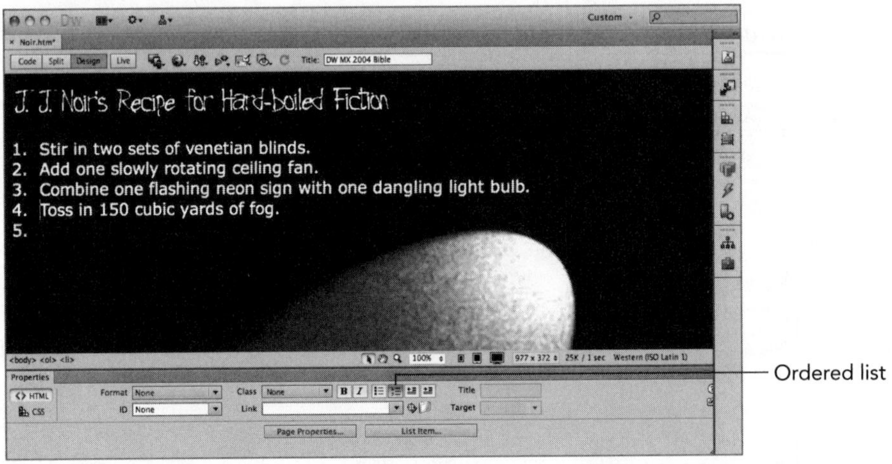

Editing ordered lists

The HTML code for an ordered list is `<ol>`. Both `<ol>` and `<ul>` use the list item tag, `<li>`, to mark individual entries, and Dreamweaver handles the formatting identically:

```
<ol>
  <li>Stir in two sets of Venetian blinds.</li>
```

```
    <li>Add one slowly rotating ceiling fan.</li>
    <li>Combine one flashing neon sign with one dangling light bulb.</li>
    <li>Toss in 150 cubic yards of fog.</li>
    <li></li>
  </ol>
```

The empty list item pair, `<li> ... </li>`, is displayed on the page as the next number in sequence.

Dreamweaver TECHNIQUE

Inserting Ordered Lists

Ordered lists are inserted in a similar fashion to unordered ones but have the advantage of automatically being renumbered when moved.

1. In the Files panel, reopen the `lists_start.htm` file.
2. Place your cursor below the paragraph following the Top Three Reasons to Buy Now heading.
3. In the Property inspector, click Ordered List.

   The number 1 appears, indicating the first list item.
4. Enter the following text: **Lower interest rates**.
5. Press Enter (Return) and enter the next item: **Best investment going**.
6. Press Enter (Return) and enter the final item: **Owning your home means security**.
7. You can re-order a numbered list easily. With your cursor still in the final list item, choose the `<li>` tag from the Tag Selector.
8. Drag the selected list item and drop it in front of the first list item.

   The items are automatically renumbered.

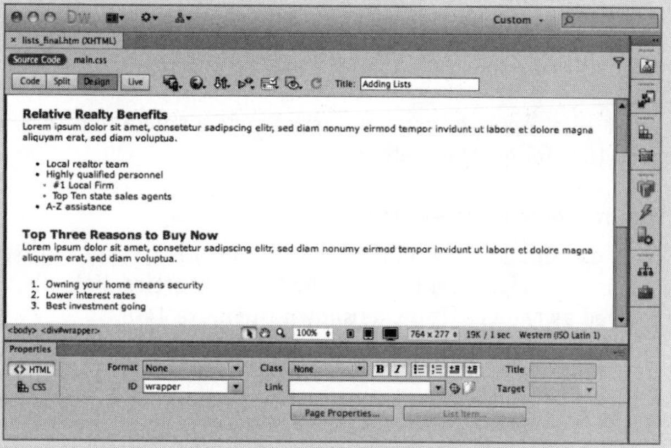

9. Save your page.

In the next Dreamweaver Technique, you work with a special kind of list, the definition list.

Modifications to an ordered list are handled in the same manner as those to an unordered list. The results are far more dramatic, however:

- To continue adding to the sequence of numbers, position your cursor at the end of what is currently the last item and press Enter (Return). The next number in sequence is generated, and any styles in use (such as font size) are applied to the new list item.
- To insert a new item within the list, put your cursor at the end of the item you want to precede the new item and press Enter (Return). Dreamweaver inserts a new number in sequence and automatically renumbers the following numbers.
- To rearrange a numbered list, highlight the entire list item you want to move. Using the drag-and-drop method, release the mouse when your cursor is in front of the item immediately below the new location for the item you are moving. Again, Dreamweaver automatically renumbers the list items in order.
- To end an item in a numbered list, press Enter (Return) twice, or press Enter (Return) and deselect the Ordered List button on the Text Property inspector.

Using other numbering styles

You can apply these different numbering styles to your numbered lists:

CAUTION

Although this technique is still supported by browsers, the use of the type attribute in list tags has been deprecated; as with unordered lists, it's a better practice to style your ordered lists with CSS.

- **Arabic Numerals:** 1, 2, 3, and so forth (this is the default style)
- **Roman Small:** i, ii, iii, and so forth
- **Roman Large:** I, II, III, and so forth
- **Alphabet Small:** a, b, c, and so forth
- **Alphabet Large:** A, B, C, and so forth

You can restyle your entire list all at once, or you can just change a single list item. To change the style of the entire ordered list, follow these steps:

1. Position your cursor anywhere in an existing list.
2. If necessary, click the expander arrow on the Text Property inspector to display the additional options. Click the List Item button. The List Properties dialog box opens with Numbered List displayed as the List Type, as shown in Figure 14-5.
3. Open the drop-down list of Style options and choose any of the numbering types.
4. Click OK.

NOTE

If the List Item button is inactive in your Text Property inspector, make sure that you have only one list item selected. Selecting more than one list item deactivates the List Item button.

FIGURE 14-5

Use the List Properties dialog box to alter the numbering style in an ordered list.

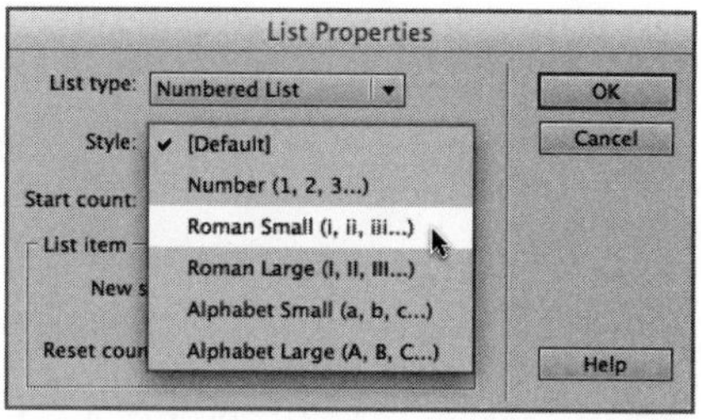

As with unordered lists, when you modify the style of one ordered list item, all the other items in the same list adopt that style. To alter the style of a single item, follow these steps:

1. Select the item you want to change.
2. In the expanded portion of the Text Property inspector, click the List Item button.
3. From the List Item section of the List Properties dialog box, open the New Style list of options.
4. Select one of the numbering options.

Although you can't automatically generate an outline with a different numbering system for each level, you can simulate this kind of outline with nested lists. See the section "Using Nested Lists" later in this chapter.

Creating Navigation Buttons from Lists

CSS has made many innovations possible in web design. One of them is styled navigation buttons that look and act like sliced-bitmapped graphics with JavaScript rollover capability. CSS navigation bars, however, take up much less bandwidth, are instantly accessible, and are far easier to modify than bitmapped graphics. Although the same technique discussed in this section could be applied to a series of paragraph tags, the unordered list is a more natural fit. Of course, you don't want the bulleted list to look like a bulleted list, and CSS makes such a transformation possible with ease.

Here's an overview of the process:

1. Create background graphics for both the standard and the mouse-over views.
2. Put a list of links in a `<div>` tag. Each link serves as a separate button.
3. Build the CSS file that combines the background graphics and the links.
4. Apply the appropriate CSS ID to the `<div>` tag—and let CSS do the rest.

In addition to standard rollover behavior, this technique makes it possible to style an individual list item as the current page indicator, as shown in Figure 14-6.

FIGURE 14-6

Turn a bulleted list into a navbar with CSS and just two low-bandwidth images.

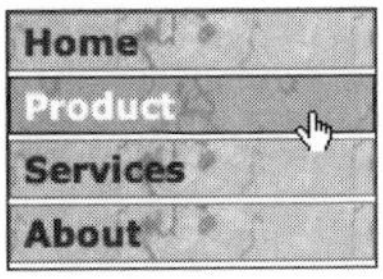

Step 1: Preparing background graphics

A little bit of prep work is needed before you can begin applying CSS to your list. The first step is to use a graphics program, such as Fireworks or Photoshop, to make the button images. Two separate but similar images are needed: one for the initial button look and another for the rollover view.

Here's the process I used to create my graphic images with Fireworks:

1. In Fireworks, create a new document larger than you expect your button to be. My initial document was 300 × 200. You can, of course, create a document the same size as your button image, but the Fit Canvas feature of Fireworks makes trimming the excess canvas area a one-click operation.
2. Using the Rectangle tool, draw an object slightly larger than the expected width and height of a single button; my image is 150 pixels wide by 50 pixels high. The image is to be used in the background of your navigation element and should be large enough so that it does not tile.
3. Style your rectangle however you choose. I used an orange solid fill (#FF9900) and applied a Vein texture at 80 percent. It's a good idea to create your graphics with the dual states in mind. I'll be able to create a darker version of my image for the rollover just by altering the texture percentage.
4. Select outside of the image and then choose Fit To Canvas from the Property inspector to trim the excess canvas from your background image.
5. Export in either JPG or GIF format. This serves as the background for my initial button (also referred to as mouse-out), so I've named this image `listnav_out.jpg` and stored it in my Dreamweaver site.
6. Alter the graphic to represent the rollover state. I simply lowered the Vein texture setting to 60 percent, which darkens the image significantly. Figure 14-7 shows a comparison between the two figures.
7. Export the image with an appropriate name; my second image is called `listnav_over.jpg`.

Be sure to save your source file so that you can easily make alterations as needed. With your images created, you're ready to move into Dreamweaver to create the list and encompassing `<div>` tag.

FIGURE 14-7

These two images were exported from the same source file; the only difference is the texture setting.

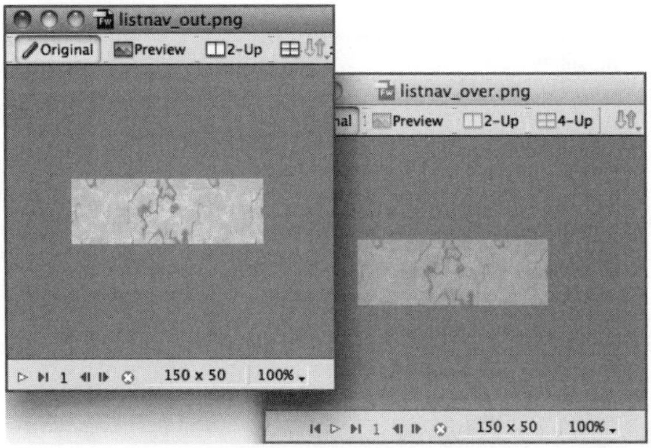

Step 2: Creating the list and containing <div>

Next, create the basic HTML and text elements for the CSS navigation bar. Because one of the elements you need is an absolutely positioned `<div>` tag, you can set up your CSS file and enter the first of the CSS definitions.

> **TIP**
>
> It's not absolutely necessary for you to create the CSS before you insert the tags, but because Dreamweaver renders each new style as it is applied, this approach gives you a better sense of what the CSS styles are doing.

To set up the CSS file with the first of the CSS definitions, follow these steps:

1. Create a new CSS file by choosing File ➪ New and selecting CSS from the General category. I named my file `listnav.css`.
2. Open the HTML or dynamic page to which you want to add the navigation.
3. From the CSS Styles panel, select Attach Style Sheet; when the dialog box opens, link or import your previously created style sheet. Click OK to close the dialog box when you're done.
4. Now define the first of your CSS, which positions and gives the basic shape to the navigation bar. From the CSS Styles panel, select New CSS Rule.
5. In the New CSS Rule dialog box, select ID from the Selector Type list and enter the name for the element to contain the list navigation; I called mine `#listnav`. You'll recall that the opening hash mark designates an ID selector in CSS.

6. Click OK to open the CSS Rule Definition dialog box and switch to the Positioning category.
7. Set these values in the Positioning category, as shown in Figure 14-8:

Position	Absolute
Width	151 pixels
Top	50 pixels
Left	25 pixels

FIGURE 14-8

Determine where the navigation element is to appear by setting values in the Positioning category.

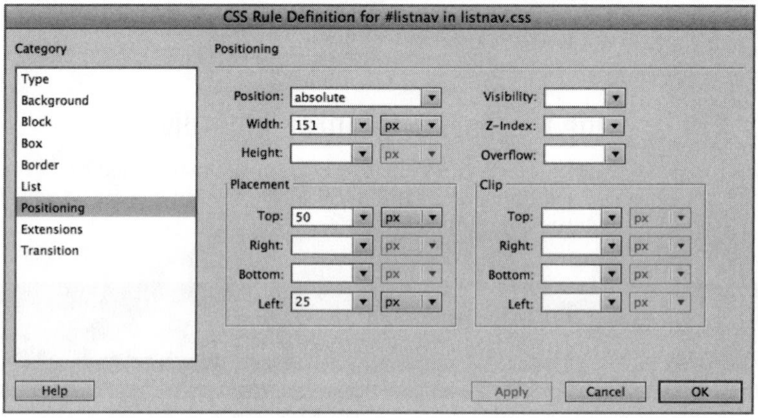

8. When you're finished, click OK to close the CSS Rule Definition dialog box. The next step combines two actions into one: inserting a `<div>` tag and assigning the CSS style you just created.
9. From the Layout category of the Insert panel, select Insert Div Tag.
10. In the dialog box, choose the just-defined CSS style from the ID list. When you click OK, your `<div>` is added to the page with some placeholder text. Now you're ready to add your list items.
11. Delete the placeholder text in the `<div>` and, from the Property inspector, select Unordered List.
12. Enter the text for your button labels, one button per bullet. I've got four list items:
    - Home
    - Products
    - Services
    - About

13. Be sure to avoid placing any unnecessary paragraph returns following the list. Only the list items you want to appear as buttons should be in the <div> tag.
14. Add a link to each list item by selecting the text and entering a filename in the Link field of the Property inspector. Alternatively, you can click the folder icon and choose a file from the Select File dialog box.

At this point, you have a plain bullet list of links in an absolutely positioned <div> tag on your page, as shown in Figure 14-9. Now you're ready to start styling!

FIGURE 14-9

Making each list item a link is a major step toward converting them into CSS buttons.

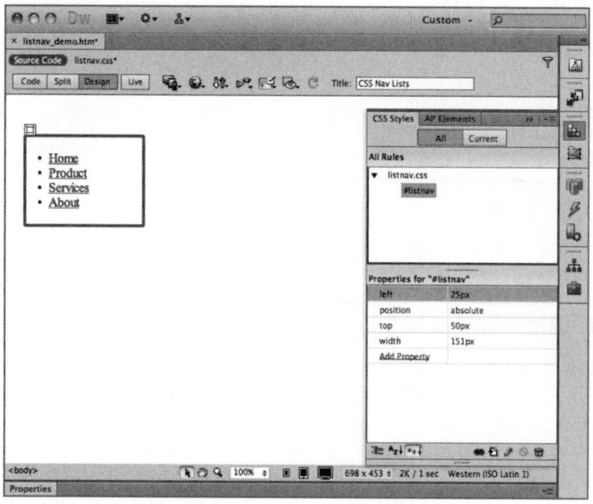

Step 3: Building the CSS styles

The definition of the CSS styles is at the heart of this technique. In all, six different styles are needed:

- `#listnav ul`—Defines the font face and size for all the list items, removes the standard bullet, and clears the margin and padding.
- `#listnav li`—Ensures a bottom margin is present to separate each list item.
- `#listnav a`—Extends the active area of the link to the block-level and adds a background image, width, and border.
- `#listnav a:link`, `#listnav a:visited`—Defines the look of the text when the buttons are in their standard and already-visited states, giving a specific color and removing the underline from the link.
- `#listnav a:hover`—Swaps the background image and alters the text color in the rollover state.
- `#sellistnav a:link`, `#sellistnav a:visited`, `#sellistnav a:hover`—Sets the look and feel of the selected button, indicating the current page in a navigation bar.

Because I've already laid the foundation with a list of links inside a `<div>` with a defined CSS ID, the changes are immediately evident in Dreamweaver.

The process is the same for defining each CSS rule. Each rule is named with the Compound selector type chosen in the New CSS Rule dialog box, which enables the user to enter any type of selector.

To get started with `#listnav ul`, follow these steps:

1. From the CSS Styles panel, select New CSS Rule.
2. In the New CSS Rule dialog box, with Selector Type set to Compound, enter **#listnav ul** in the Selector field and click OK to open the CSS Rule Definition dialog box.
3. Set these values in the Type category:

Font	Verdana, Geneva, sans-serif
Size	14 pixels
Weight	Bold

4. Set these values in the Box category:

Margin	0 pixels (for all)
Padding	0 pixels (for all)

5. Set these values in the Border category:

Style	Solid (for all)
Width	1 pixel (for all)
Color	#990000 (for all)

6. Set this value in the List category:

Type	None

7. When you're finished, click OK to close the CSS Rule Definition dialog box.

You should notice an immediate difference in Dreamweaver. The bulleted list is already starting to look much more button-like (see Figure 14-10).

The next style, `#listnav li`, affects each list item individually. Follow these steps:

1. From the CSS Styles panel, select New CSS Rule.

FIGURE 14-10

After you define the #listnav ul style, the bullets disappear from the unordered list.

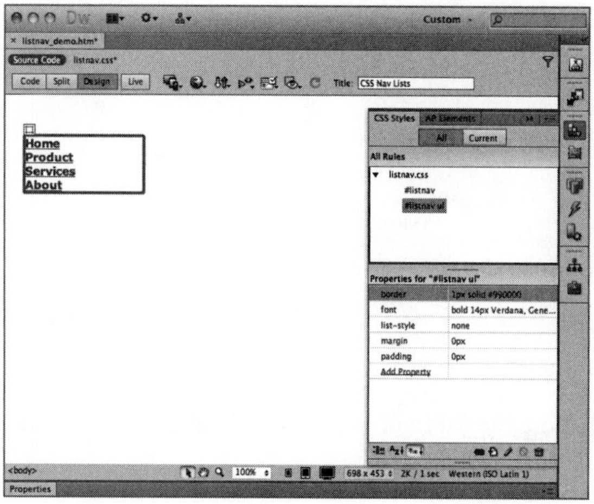

2. In the New CSS Rule dialog box, with Selector Type set to Compound, enter **#listnav li** in the Selector field and click OK to open the CSS Rule Definition dialog box.
3. Set this value in the Box category:

Margin-Bottom	2 pixels

   The `Margin-Bottom` value determines the distance between each of the navigation buttons; increase the value to make the buttons farther apart.
4. When you're finished, click OK to close the CSS Rule definition dialog box.

Now, to build up the `#listnav a:` style, follow these steps:

1. From the CSS Styles panel, select New CSS Rule.
2. In the New CSS Rule dialog box, with Selector Type set to Compound, enter **#listnav a** in the Selector field and click OK to open the CSS Rule Definition dialog box.
3. In the Background category, click Browse and choose the exported image to represent the mouse-out. For my navigation bar, the file is `listnav_out.jpg`. Set these remaining values in the Background category:

Repeat	no-repeat
Background-position (x)	center
Background-position (y)	center

14

4. Set this value in the Block category:

Display	Block

5. Set these values in the Box category:

Width	140 pixels
Padding-Top	2 pixels
Padding-Right	2 pixels
Padding-Bottom	2 pixels
Padding-Left	5 pixels

These values determine the width of the block and set the position of the text within it.

6. Set these values in the Border category:

Style	Solid (for all)
Width	1 pixel (for all)
Color	#CC9900 (for all)

7. When you're finished, click OK to close the CSS Rule Definition dialog box.

With the background image in place, the buttons are really beginning to take shape (see Figure 14-11).

FIGURE 14-11

Adding a background image completely transforms an unordered list item into a navigation button.

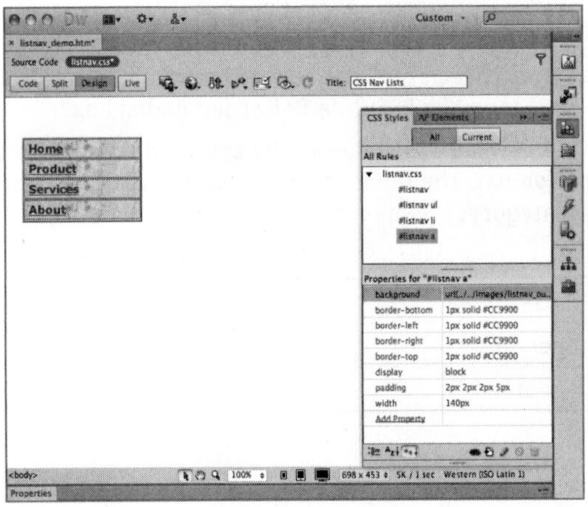

Next, to define two CSS rules—`#listnav a:link` and `#listnav a:visited`—at once, follow these steps:

1. From the CSS Styles panel, select New CSS Rule.
2. In the New CSS Rule dialog box, with Selector Type set to Compound, enter **#listnav a:link, #listnav a:visited** in the Selector field and click OK to open the CSS Rule Definition dialog box.
3. Set these values in the Type category:

Color	#993300
Decoration	none

   Setting Decoration to none turns off a link's underline.

4. When you're finished, click OK to close the CSS Rule Definition dialog box.

Next, you want to define the `#listnav a:hover` style. Follow these steps:

1. From the CSS Styles panel, select New CSS Rule.
2. In the New CSS Rule dialog box, with Selector Type set to Compound, enter **#listnav a:hover** in the Selector field and click OK to open the CSS Rule Definition dialog box.
3. Set this value in the Type category:

Color	#FFFFFF

4. In the Background category, click Browse and choose the exported image to represent the mouse-out. For my navigation bar, the file is `listnav_over.jpg`.
5. Set these values in the Border category:

Style	Solid (for all)
Width	1 pixel (for all)
Color	#990000 (for all)

6. When you're finished, click OK to close the CSS Rule Definition dialog box.

14

The last style won't appear to have any effect until you preview the page in a browser or switch to Live View, as shown in Figure 14-12.

The final style is applied to whatever link represents the current page. As such, it's an exact duplicate of the style just created for `#listnav a:hover`, which makes it a breeze to create. Follow these steps:

1. In the CSS Styles panel, right-click (Control+click) the `#listnav a:hover` style and choose Duplicate from the context menu.

2. In the Duplicate CSS Rule dialog box, enter **#sellistnav a:link, #sellistnav a:visited, #sellistnav a:hover** in the Selector field.
3. When you're finished, click OK to close the dialog box.

The style you just created is really the only one that you must apply, and you take care of that last detail in the following section.

FIGURE 14-12

The #listnav a:hover style governs the rollover appearance.

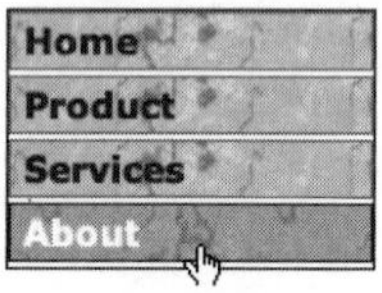

Step 4: Applying the CSS

Because of the way the CSS is written—and the fact that the containing <div> tag was assigned a CSS ID from the beginning—almost all the styles are automatically applied. The only one left is the style that makes the current link appear selected.

To apply the selected link style, follow these steps:

1. Place your cursor in the list item that represents the current page. For demonstration purposes, I'll use Home.
2. In the Tag Selector, right-click (Control+click) the <li> tag for the selected item. From the menu that opens, choose Set ID ➪ sellistnav, as shown in Figure 14-13.

FIGURE 14-13

Changing the ID of a list item's link tag creates a down state.

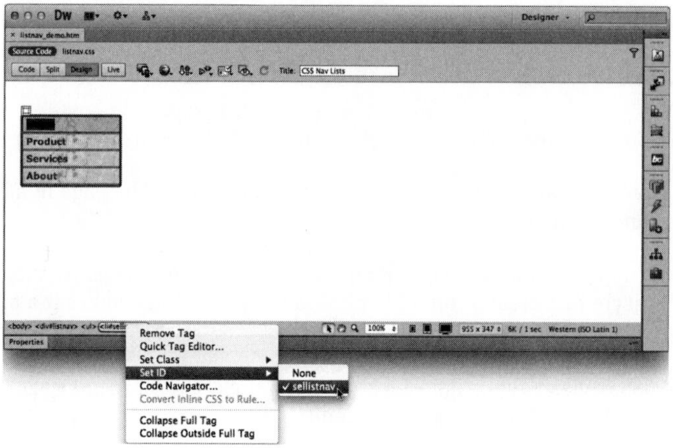

That's it—your unordered list is now a fully functioning navigation bar. To modify any of the labels on the buttons, just modify the text directly. To add a new button, create a new list item by adding a paragraph return after any existing list item. Your new list item turns into a button the second you add a link to it.

Making Definition Lists

A *definition* list is another type of list in HTML. Unlike ordered and unordered lists, definition lists don't use leading characters such as bullets or numbers in the list items. Definition lists are commonly used in glossaries or other types of documents in which you have a list of terms followed by descriptions or explanations.

Browsers generally render a definition list with the definition term flush left and the definition data indented, as shown in Figure 14-14. As you can see, no additional styling is added. You can, however, format either the item or the definition with the Format ➪ Style options or, preferably, by using Cascading Style Sheets.

FIGURE 14-14

Definition lists are ideal for glossaries or other situations in which you have a list of terms followed by their definitions.

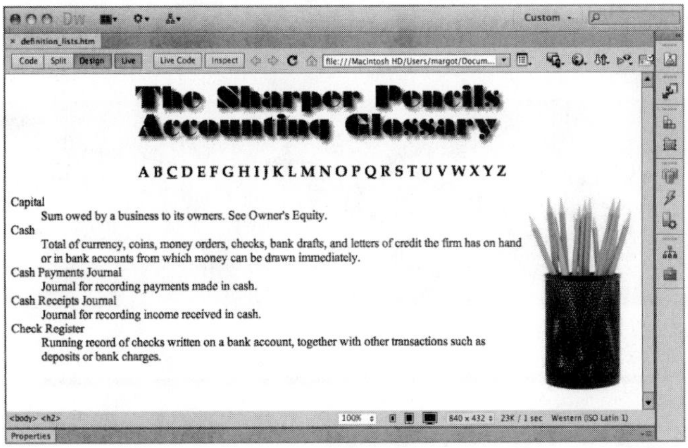

To begin your definition list in Dreamweaver, follow these steps:

1. Choose Format ➪ List ➪ Definition List or click the Definition List button in the Text category of the Insert panel.
2. Type the definition term and press Enter (Return) when you are finished. Dreamweaver indents the next line.
3. Type the definition data and press Enter (Return) when you are finished.

4. Repeat Steps 2 and 3 until you have finished your definition list.
5. Press Enter (Return) twice to stop entering definition list items.

TIP

If you have an extended definition, you may want to format it in more than one paragraph. Because definition lists are formatted with the terms and their definition data in alternating sequence, you have to use the line break tag, `<br>` (or `<br />` for XHTML documents), to create blank space under the definition if you want to separate it into paragraphs. Press Shift+Enter (Shift+Return) or click the Line Break button on the Insert panel to enter one or two `<br>` tags to separate paragraphs with one or two blank lines. Alternatively, you could add paragraphs within the `<dd>` tag and apply additional padding to the `dd p` selector with CSS.

When you insert a definition list, Dreamweaver denotes it in code using the `<dl> . . . </dl>` tag pair. Definition terms are marked with a `<dt>` tag, and definition data uses the `<dd>` tag. A complete definition list looks like the following in HTML:

```
<dl>
  <dt>Capital</dt>
  <dd>Sum owed by a business to its owners. See Owner's Equity.</dd>
  <dt>Cash</dt>
  <dd>Total of currency, coins, money orders, checks, bank
    drafts, and letters of credit the firm has on hand or in bank
    accounts from which money can be drawn immediately.</dd>
  <dt>Cash Payments Journal</dt>
  <dd>Journal for recording payments made in cash.</dd>
</dl>
```

TIP

You can vary the structure of a definition list from the standard definition term followed by the definition data format, but you have to code this variation by hand. For instance, if you want a series of consecutive terms with no definition in between, you need to insert the `<dt> . . . </dt>` pairs directly in Code view or in the Code inspector. To facilitate the insertion of these tags, you can click the Definition Term and Definition Description buttons in the Text category of the Insert panel to insert the appropriate tags in Code view.

Dreamweaver TECHNIQUE

Applying Definition Lists

Although definition lists are not used as frequently as unordered or ordered lists on the web, they're perfect under specific circumstances.

1. In the Files panel, reopen the file `lists_start.htm`, which you worked on in the previous Dreamweaver Technique.
2. Place your cursor below the paragraph following the Real Estate Terms heading.
3. Select Format ➪ Lists ➪ Definition Lists.

   Unlike the other list types, no special indicator is displayed.

4. Enter the following text for the definition term: **adjustment date**.
5. Press Enter (Return) and enter the definition data: **The date the interest rate changes on an adjustable-rate mortgage.**
6. Press Enter (Return) again and enter the second term: **assessment**.
7. Press Enter (Return) again and enter the second definition: **The placing of a value on property for the purpose of taxation.**
8. Press Enter (Return) again and enter the final term: **assumption**.
9. Press Enter (Return) again and enter the final definition: **The term applied when a buyer assumes the seller's mortgage.**

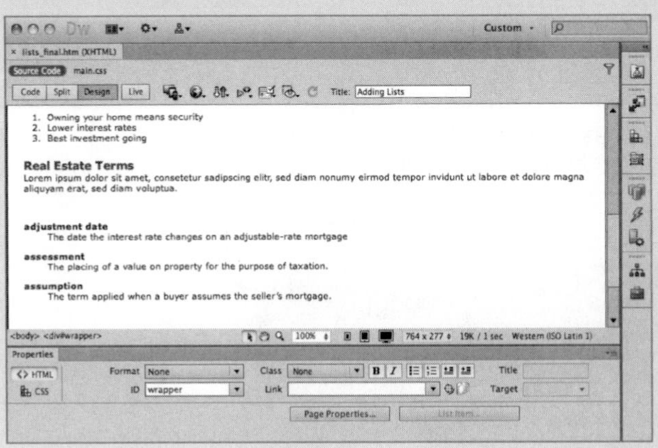

10. Save your page.

Using Nested Lists

You can combine, or nest, lists in almost any fashion. For instance, you can mix an ordered and unordered list to create a numbered list with bulleted points. You can have one numbered list inside another numbered list. You can also start with one numbering style such as Roman Large, switch to another style such as Alphabet Small, and return to Roman Large to continue the sequence (like an outline).

Dreamweaver offers an easy route for making nested lists. The Indent button in the Text Property inspector—when used within a list—automatically creates a nested list. The ordered list in Figure 14-15, for example, has a couple of bulleted points (unordered list items) inserted within it. Notice how the new items are indented one level.

Follow these steps to create a nested list in Dreamweaver:

1. In an existing list, select the text that you want to indent and reformat with a different style.

2. In the Text Property inspector, click the Indent button. Alternatively, you can choose the Format ➪ Indent command. Dreamweaver indents the selected text and creates a separate list in the HTML code with the original list's properties.
3. Go to the List Properties dialog box and select another list type or style, as described in preceding sections.

NOTE

Nested unordered lists exhibit a cool feature in most browsers—they automatically change the list style for each level. In many browsers, the outermost level is displayed with a bullet, the second level with a circle, and the third level with a square. This feature provides automatic outlining from an unexpected source! For ordered lists, the style of indented items does not change automatically.

FIGURE 14-15

Dreamweaver automatically generates the code necessary to build nested lists when you use the Indent button on the Text Property inspector.

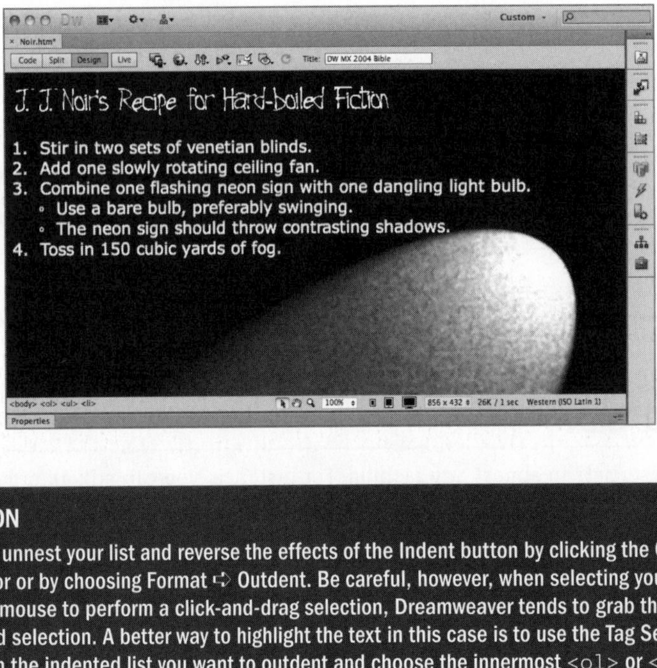

CAUTION

You can unnest your list and reverse the effects of the Indent button by clicking the Outdent button in the Text Property inspector or by choosing Format ➪ Outdent. Be careful, however, when selecting your text for this operation. When you use the mouse to perform a click-and-drag selection, Dreamweaver tends to grab the closing list item tag above your intended selection. A better way to highlight the text in this case is to use the Tag Selector on the status bar. Place the cursor in the indented list you want to outdent and choose the innermost `<ol>` or `<ul>` tag from the Tag Selector.

To see why one list contained inside another list is considered to be nested, look at the code created by Dreamweaver for the following list type:

```
<ol>
  <li>Stir in two sets of Venetian blinds.</li>
  <li>Add one slowly rotating ceiling fan.</li>
  <li>Combine one flashing neon sign with one dangling light bulb.
```

```
    <ul>
      <li>Use a bare bulb, preferably swinging.</li>
      <li>The neon sign should throw contrasting shadows.</li>
    </ul>
  </li>
  <li>Toss in 150 cubic yards of fog.</li>
</ol>
```

Notice how the unordered tag pair, `<ul> ... </ul>`, is completely contained between the ordered list items.

CAUTION

If you don't indent your list items before you change the list format, Dreamweaver breaks the current list into three separate lists: one for the original list above the selected text, another for the selected text itself, and a third list for the items following the selected text. If you don't want this arrangement, use the Tag Selector to select the entire list you want to indent, and then click the Indent button in the Text Property inspector. Dreamweaver nests the list as described previously.

Accessing Special List Types

Dreamweaver gives you access to a couple of special-use list types: menu lists and directory lists. When the tags for these lists—<menu> and <dir>, respectively—were included in the HTML 2.0 specification, they were intended to offer several ways to present lists of short items. Unfortunately, browsers tend to render both tags as unordered lists. You can use Cascading Style Sheets to restyle these built-in tags for use in 4.0 and later browsers.

NOTE

Both the <menu> and the <dir> tags are deprecated in HTML 4.0. Because most browsers format these lists like unordered lists, you should typically just use ordered lists instead of either of these list types. Ordered lists are supported in older browsers and will continue to be supported for the foreseeable future.

14

Menu lists

A menu list generally comprises single items with each item on its own individual line. To apply a menu list style, follow these steps:

CAUTION

The <menu> tag has been deprecated in HTML 4.01 and is used infrequently. A better choice would be to use an unordered list.

1. In an existing list, select one item.
2. In the expanded Text Property inspector, click the List Item button.

3. In the List Properties dialog box, open the List Type drop-down list and choose Menu List, as shown in Figure 14-16.
4. Click OK.

FIGURE 14-16

Choose a menu list when you need to make a simple list of items in an unordered fashion.

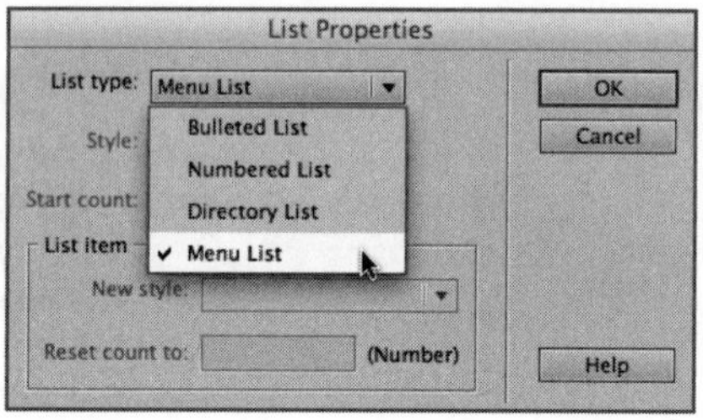

Directory lists

The directory list was originally intended to provide web designers with an easy way to create multiple-column lists of short items. Unfortunately, the most current browsers present the directory list's items in one long list, rather than in columns.

The directory list format is applied in the same way as the menu list, and here as well, most browsers render the format as an unordered list with bullets. To create a directory list, follow these steps:

1. In the current list, select one item.
2. In the expanded Text Property inspector, click the List Item button.
3. In the List Properties dialog box, from the List Type drop-down list (refer to Figure 14-16) choose Directory List.
4. Click OK.

Summary

Lists are extremely useful to the website designer from the perspectives of both content and layout. Dreamweaver offers point-and-click control over the full range of list capabilities. Keep these points about lists in mind:

- The primary list types in HTML are unordered, ordered, and definition lists.
- Use unordered lists when you want to itemize your text in no particular order. Dreamweaver can apply any of the built-in styles to unordered lists, or you can customize your own list style through Cascading Style Sheets.

- An ordered list is a numbered list. Items are automatically numbered when added, and the entire list is renumbered when items are rearranged or deleted. Dreamweaver gives you access to different styles of numbering—including regular Arabic, Roman numerals, and uppercase or lowercase letters.
- CSS styles can significantly adjust the look and feel of your lists, both unordered and ordered, even to the point of converting them into a navigation bar.
- Definition lists are designed to display glossaries and other documents in which terms are followed by definitions. A definition list is generally rendered without leading characters such as bullets or numbers; instead, the list terms are displayed flush left, and the definitions are indented.
- Dreamweaver gives you the power to nest your lists at the touch of a button—the Indent button on the Text Property inspector. Nested lists enable you to show different outline levels and to mix ordered and unordered lists.
- Although deprecated, menu and directory lists are also supported by Dreamweaver. These special lists are rendered in a similar fashion, but they can be adapted through style sheets' different uses.

In the next chapter, you learn how to work with frames and framesets in Dreamweaver.

CHAPTER

15

Using Frames and Framesets

IN THIS CHAPTER

Examining the fundamentals of HTML frames and framesets

Creating frames in a new document, visually and with frame objects

Selecting, saving, and closing framesets

Dreamweaver Technique: Establishing a Frameset

Altering frame and frameset properties

Opening links in specific frames

Targeting multiple frames with a single click

Dreamweaver Technique: Setting Frame Targets

Inserting frameless content

Understanding iframes

The first time I fully appreciated the power of frames, I was visiting a site that displayed examples of what the webmaster considered "bad" web pages. The site was essentially a jump-station with a series of links. The author used a frameset with three frames: one that ran all the way across the top of the page, displaying a logo and other basic information; one narrow panel on the left with a scrolling set of links to the sites themselves; and the main viewing area, which took up two-thirds of the center screen. Selecting any of the links caused the site to appear in the main viewing frame.

I was astounded when I finally realized that each frame was truly an independent web page and that you didn't have to use only web pages on your own site—you could link to any page on the Internet. That was when I also realized the amount of work involved in establishing a frame website: Every page displayed on that site used multiple HTML pages.

Be aware that the use of frames is controversial. Designers opposed to their use give a number of reasons. One argument is that dealing with frames often confuses users, especially as they navigate through a site. Another reason cited by designers is that search engines have difficulty indexing a frame-based site. Other areas of concern include the fact that the pages can't be bookmarked, that they're inaccessible to users with screen readers, that there is little visual support in modern browsers, and, with the exception of iframes, that frames are not supported at all in HTML5. Moreover, mobile browsers are considering dropping future support for frames. Nonetheless, frames are valid in versions of HTML prior to HTML5, and Dreamweaver does support their use.

CAUTION

Although the technology enables you to include any page on the web within your own frameset, Internet etiquette and, in some cases, copyright law dictate that you obtain permission to display another site's pages within your own site and that you clearly credit work that is not your own.

Dreamweaver takes the head-pounding complexity out of coding and managing frames with a point-and-click interface. You get easy access to the commands for modifying the properties of the overall frame structure, as well as each individual frame. This chapter gives you an overview of frames, as well as all the specifics you need for inserting and modifying frames and framesets. Special attention is given to defining the unique look of frames through borders, scroll bars, and margins.

Dreamweaver QUICKSTART

If you're familiar with frames and just want to know how to create one in Dreamweaver, here's one quick technique:

1. Choose File ➪ New.
2. When the New Document dialog opens, choose Page from Sample.
3. In the Sample Folder category, choose Framesets.

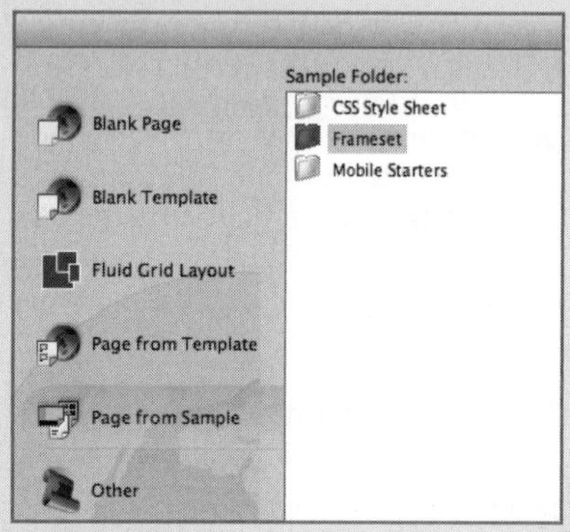

4. From the Sample Folder category, select the type of frameset you want.
5. Click Create.

There are a couple of other ways to create framesets and many ways you can fine-tune them—all covered in this chapter.

Frames and Framesets: The Basics

It's best to think of frames in two major parts: the frameset and the frames. The frameset is the HTML document that defines the framing structure—the number of individual frames that make up a page, their initial size, and the attributes shared among all the frames. A frameset is never displayed by itself. Frames, on the other hand, are complete HTML documents that can be viewed and edited separately or together in the organization described by the frameset.

A frameset performs the function of the <body> tags that contain the content of a web page in an HTML document. Here's what the HTML for a basic frameset looks like:

```
<frameset rows="50%,50%">
  <frame src="top.html">
  <frame src="bottom.html">
</frameset>
```

Notice that the content of a <frameset> tag consists entirely of <frame> tags, each one referring to a different web page. The only other element that can be used inside of a <frameset> tag is another <frameset> tag.

In Dreamweaver's Code view, you can directly add a <frameset> ... </frameset> tag pair and common frame layouts by clicking the Frameset button on the Layout menu of the Insert panel's HTML category. Of course, Dreamweaver gives you other ways to create framesets in Design view; see the next section for more information.

Creating a Frameset and Frames

Dreamweaver offers you two strategies for creating a frameset. You can explicitly create a frameset file and add content to each of the frames, or you can start with existing content and create a frameset around it. You can achieve the same results using either method. Within Dreamweaver, you can create a frameset in any of the following ways:

- Create a new, empty frameset using the File ➪ New command, and then add content to the frames.
- Start with an existing document and use drag-and-drop to draw frames around the document.
- Start with an existing document and apply one of several common frameset layouts to it, using menu commands or the Insert panel.

NOTE
The Insert panel's Layout category contains the Frames menu.

Creating a new frameset file

Most of the framesets still employed on the web today use two or three frames, albeit in different configurations. For example, a common setup is to have one narrow frame spanning the top of the page to hold a banner and some site navigation; below it is a left frame to hold a table of contents or additional navigation, and a large right frame to hold the content of the site (see Figure 15-1).

Dreamweaver gives you quick access to a full array of the most common setups when you create a frameset document from scratch using the File ➪ New command. Of course, you can customize any of these initial frameset setups by resizing the frames or adding new frames, as described in the sections "Working with the Frameset Property Inspector" and "Adding More Frames," later in this chapter.

FIGURE 15-1

The most common designs using framesets call for only two or three frames.

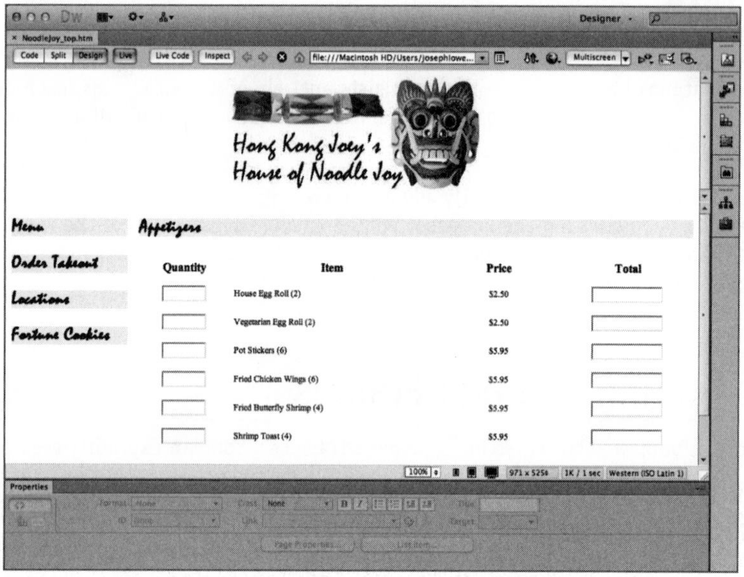

To explicitly create a new frameset file, follow these steps:

1. Choose File ➪ New or press Ctrl+N (Command+N).
2. In the New Document dialog box, choose the Page From Sample category.
3. From the Sample Folder list, choose Frameset. A list of possible framesets appears, as shown in Figure 15-2.
4. Select the desired entry from the Framesets list. A description and abstract preview of that frameset display.
5. Click Create to create the frameset and display it in the Document window. The Frame Tag Accessibility Attributes dialog may appear, depending on your preferences.

After you've created a new frameset, you can enter text, images, and other content in each of the frames, as you would for any other HTML document. Alternatively, you can change individual frames to contain previously created documents by clicking in a frame and choosing the File ➪ Open in Frame command. As explained later in this chapter, you can also add more frames to the frameset, resize the frames, and change other frame properties (such as the capability to scroll).

FIGURE 15-2

In the New Document dialog box, you can choose from many pre-formed framesets.

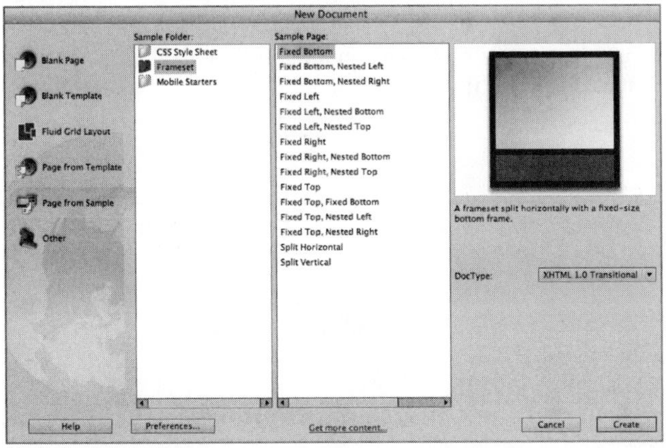

NOTE

For almost all the frame objects, Dreamweaver creates one or more frames with a set size. Although, by default, the set width or height is 80 pixels, you can easily resize the frame by dragging the frame border. The only framesets that do not have at least one set frame are the Split Horizontal and Split Vertical framesets (for these, the two frames are divided equally). Dreamweaver also sets the Scroll option to No for frames with absolute sizes.

Creating a frameset visually

Another way of creating a frameset is to start with an existing document and use the mouse to drag-and-drop the frame borders into position. When you do this, Dreamweaver creates all the new files necessary for your frameset. To create a frameset visually, using the mouse, follow these steps:

1. If necessary, switch to Design view by clicking the Show Design View button on the Document toolbar or by choosing View ➪ Design. (You can also work in the Split view, but these steps do not apply to Code view.)
2. Turn on the frame borders in Design view by choosing View ➪ Visual Aids ➪ Frame Borders. A 3-pixel-wide inner border appears along the edges of your Design view. These borders indicate the boundaries of your frames so that you can edit them easily; these borders do not

appear when the frameset is viewed in a browser window. See "Working with the Frameset Property Inspector," later in this chapter, to learn how to make the borders visible in a browser.

3. Position the cursor over any of the frame borders. If your pointer is over any side of a frame border, it changes into a two-headed arrow; it changes into a four-headed arrow (or a drag-hand on the Mac) when it's over a corner.
4. Drag the frame border into the middle of the Document window. Figure 15-3 shows a four-frame frameset.

Dreamweaver initially assigns a temporary filename and an absolute pixel value to your HTML frameset code. Both can be modified later if you want.

FIGURE 15-3

After you've enabled the frame borders, you can drag out your frameset structure with the mouse.

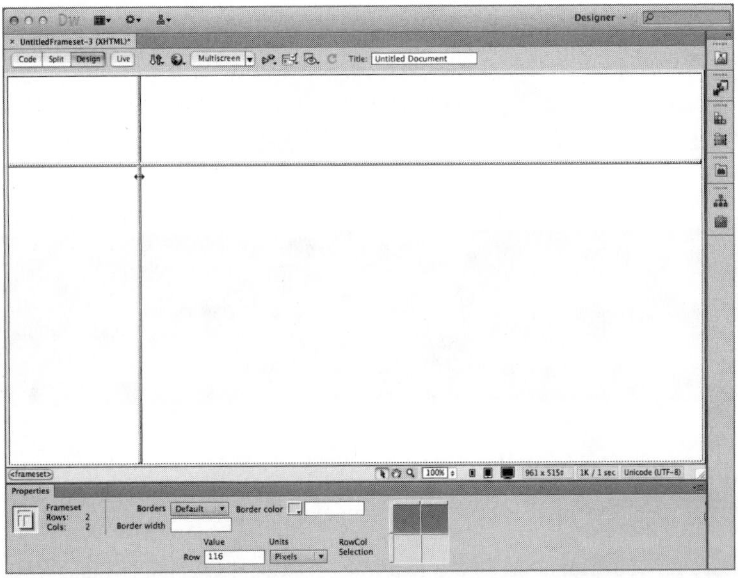

TIP

With the other methods of frameset creation, you can initially create a frameset with only two or three frames. Although you can further split these into additional frames, the fastest way to create a frameset with four frames is by Alt+dragging (Option+dragging) the corner of the frame border.

When the frameset is selected, Dreamweaver displays a black, dotted line along all the frame borders and within every frame. You can easily reposition any frameset border by clicking and dragging it. If you just want to move the border, make sure you don't press the Alt (Option) key while dragging the border because that action creates additional frames.

NOTE

Another method of creating a frameset by splitting the page into frames uses the menus. Open a document that you want to appear in one of the frames. Then choose Modify ➪ Frameset and, from the submenu, select the direction in which you would like to split the frame: left, right, up, or down. Left or right splits the frame in half vertically; up or down splits it horizontally in half. The direction indicates where the content will go; for example, the Split Frame ➪ Left command splits the page into columns and places the existing document into the left frame.

Creating framesets quickly with frame objects

Dragging out your frameset in Dreamweaver is a clear-cut method of setting up the various frames. However, despite the ease of this procedure, it can still be a bit of a chore to create even simple framesets by clicking and dragging. To hasten the development workflow, Dreamweaver uses frame objects, which can build a frameset with a single click.

As previously mentioned, most websites using frames follow a simple, general pattern. Dreamweaver includes frame objects for the most common frameset configurations. The frame objects are available through the Frames menu found in the Layout category of the Insert panel shown in Figure 15-4. Choose one of the basic designs, and you're ready to tweak the frame sizes and begin filling in the content. This method gives you a great combination: ease of use with design flexibility.

The frame objects are roughly organized from simplest framesets to most complex. On the Insert panel, notice that each of the icons shows a sample frameset with one blue section. The placement of the color is significant. The blue indicates in which frame the current page will appear when the frameset is constructed. For example, if you begin to construct your main content page, and then decide to turn it into a frameset with separate navigation strip frames to the left and above it, you choose the Top and Nested Left Frame button. Figure 15-5 provides a before-and-after example, first with the preframe content and then with the same content after a Top and Left Bottom Frame object has been applied.

The framesets available from the Frames category of the Insert panel are as follows:

- **Left:** Inserts a blank frame to the left of the current page.
- **Right:** Inserts a blank frame to the right of the current page.
- **Top:** Inserts a blank frame above the current page.
- **Bottom:** Inserts a blank frame below the current page.
- **Bottom and Nested Left:** Makes a nested frameset with three frames; the bottom frame spans the width of the other frames. The current page is placed in the upper-right frame.
- **Bottom and Nested Right:** Makes a nested frameset with three frames, with the bottom frame spanning the other frames. The current page appears in the upper-left frame.
- **Left and Nested Bottom:** Opens a nested frameset with three frames. The left frame spans the other frames, and Dreamweaver places the current page in the upper-right frame.
- **Right and Nested Bottom:** Makes a nested frameset with three frames, with the right frame spanning the other frames. The current page is placed in the upper-left frame.

FIGURE 15-4

The Frames category of the Insert panel holds the most commonly used frameset configurations.

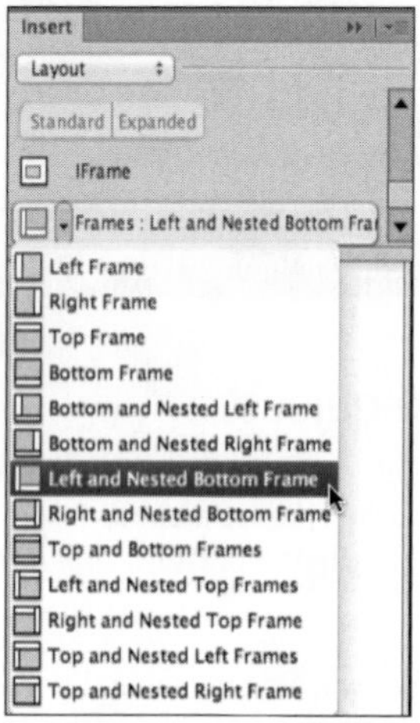

- **Top and Bottom:** Inserts a three-frame frameset, with all frames spanning the width of the entire window. Dreamweaver places the current page in the center frame.
- **Left and Nested Top:** Creates a nested frameset with three frames, with the left frame spanning the height of the other frames. Dreamweaver puts the current page in the lower-right frame.
- **Right and Nested Top:** Inserts a nested frameset with three frames, with the right frame spanning the height of the other frames. The current page is placed in the lower-left frame.
- **Top and Nested Left:** Creates a nested frameset with three frames, with the upper frame spanning the width of the other frames. The current page is put in the lower-right frame.
- **Top and Nested Right:** Inserts a nested frameset with three frames, with the top frame spanning the other frames. Dreamweaver inserts the current page in the lower-left frame.

Using the frame object can be, quite literally, a one-click operation. Just select the desired frameset from the Frames menu of the Insert panel, and Dreamweaver automatically turns on Frame Borders, if necessary, and creates and names the required frames. For all frame objects, the existing page is moved to a frame in which the scrolling option is set at Default, and the size is relative to the rest of the frameset. In other words, the existing page can be scrolled, and it expands to fill the content.

TIP

Because Dreamweaver automatically puts the existing document into an expandable frame with scroll bars, it's most efficient to apply a frame object to an existing page only if that page is intended to be the primary content frame. Otherwise, it's better to select the frame object while a blank page is open and then use the File ➪ Open in Frame command to load any existing pages into individual frames.

FIGURE 15-5

Existing content is incorporated into a new frameset when a frame object is chosen. *Top: Before. Bottom: After.*

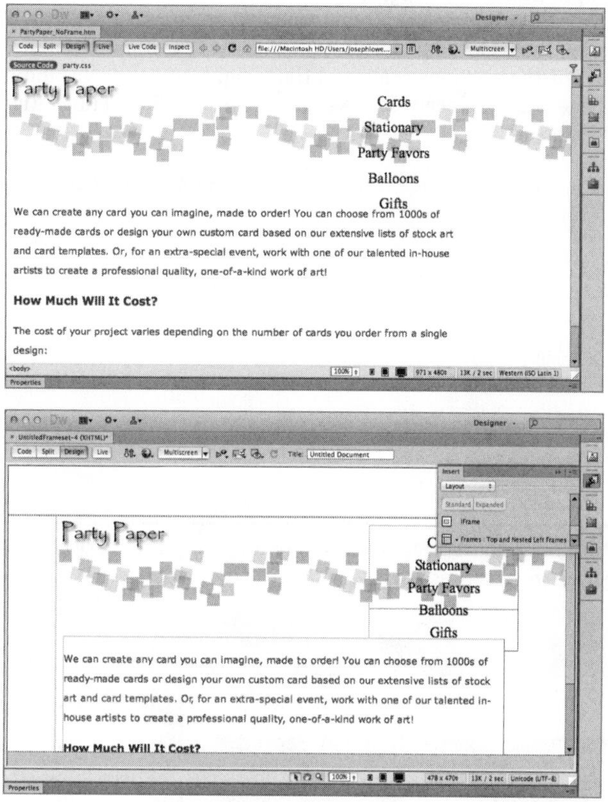

Adding More Frames

Regardless of how you create your initial frameset, you're not limited to your initial frame choices. In addition to being able to drag frame borders into position and place them visually, you can also set the size through the Frameset Property inspector, as described in the next section. Furthermore, you can continue to split either the entire frame or each column or row as needed—using either menu commands or the mouse. When you divide a column or row into one or more frames, you are actually nesting one frameset inside another.

TIP

After you've created the basic frame structure, you can choose View ➪ Visual Aids ➪ Frame Borders again (it's a toggle) to turn off the borders and create a more accurate preview of your page.

Using the menus

To split an existing frame using the menus, position the cursor in the frame you want to alter and choose Modify ➪ Frameset ➪ Split Frame Left, Right, Up, or Down. Figure 15-6 shows a two-row frameset in which the bottom row is split into two columns and then repositioned. The Frameset Property inspector would indicate that the inner frameset (2 columns, 1 row) is selected. The direction you choose in the last part of the previous command (left, right, up, or down) indicates the frame in which the existing page will be placed. For example, selecting Split Frame Right places the current page in the right frame.

You can clearly see the nested nature of the code in the following HTML fragment for the frameset in Figure 15-6:

```
<frameset rows="80,*">
  <frame src="ExistingTop.htm" name="topFrame">
  <frameset rows="*" cols="130,614">
    <frame src="UntitledFrame-12">
    <frame src="ExistingLower.htm" name="mainFrame">
  </frameset>
</frameset>
```

FIGURE 15-6

Use the Modify ➪ Frameset menu command to split an existing frame into additional columns or rows and create a nested frameset.

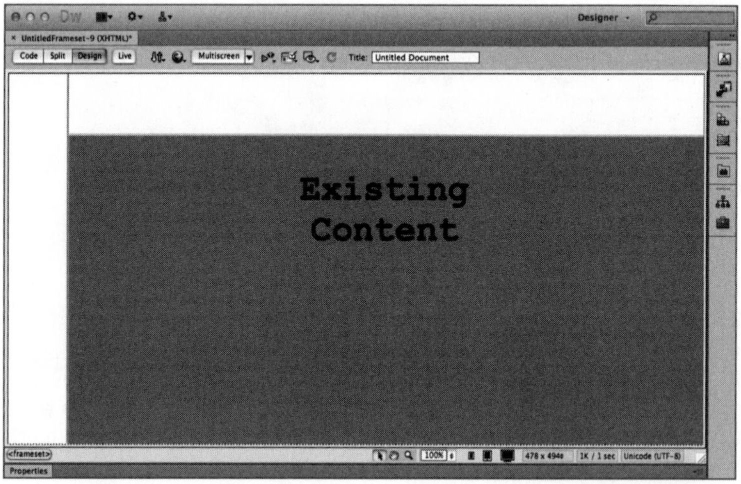

Using the mouse

When you use the menus to split a frame, only the currently selected frame is split. To create additional columns or rows that span the entire web page, use the mouse method instead. Select the specific frameset to which you want to add rows or columns and then Alt+drag (Option+drag) any of the frame's borders that span the entire page, such as one of the outer borders. Figure 15-7 shows a new row added along the bottom of the previous frame structure.

FIGURE 15-7

An additional frame row was added using the Alt+drag (Option+drag) method.

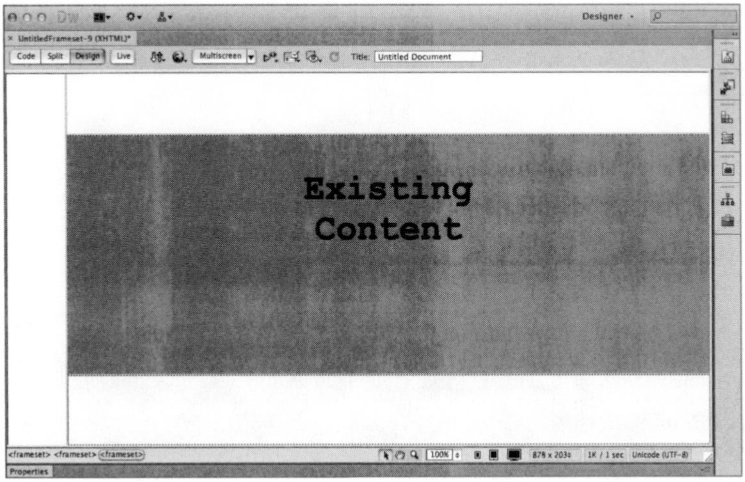

Selecting, Saving, and Closing Framesets

After you've initially created your frameset in Dreamweaver, you need to learn some basics before modifying the frameset or individual frames. For example, it's very easy to select framesets or individual frames if you know how. In addition, before changing your framesets, you must save your changes and close the frameset files.

Selecting framesets and frames

To change or view the properties of a frameset or a specific frame, you first select the frameset or frame. You can choose either the frameset itself or one of the frames within it from Design view or from the Frames panel.

The Frames panel shows an accurate representation of all the frames in your web page. Open the Frames panel by selecting Window ➪ Frames or using the keyboard shortcut Shift+F2. As you can see on the right in Figure 15-8, the Frames panel displays the names, if assigned, of the individual frames and no name if none is assigned. Nested framesets are shown with a heavier border.

To select a frameset, click an outside border of the frameset in the Frames panel. You can also select a frameset by clicking any border of the frameset in Design view. If you can't see the frame borders, choose View ➪ Visual Aids ➪ Frame Borders.

15

FIGURE 15-8

Use the Frames panel to visually select a frame to modify.

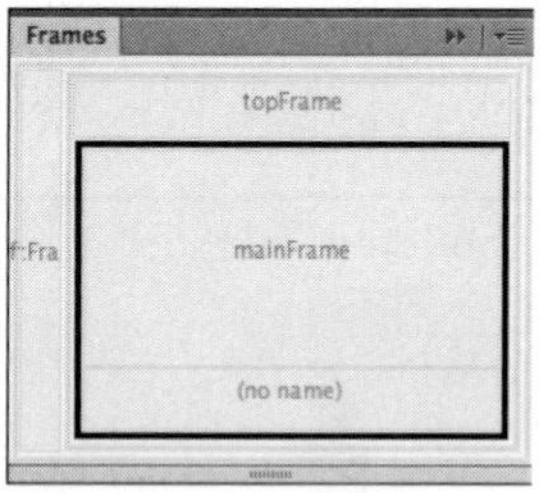

To select a specific frame, click inside the represented image of the frame in the Frames panel. You can resize the Frames panel to get a better sense of the page layout, especially for complex pages. You can also select a frame by pressing Alt (Option+Shift) and clicking in the desired frame in the Document window.

TIP

When you are working with multiple framesets, use the Tag Selector together with the Frames panel to identify the correct nested frameset. Selecting a frameset in the Tag Selector causes it to be identified in the Frames panel with a heavy black border.

After a frame is selected, you can move from one frame to another within the same frameset by pressing Alt (Command) and then using the right and left arrow keys. You can move from a nested frameset to its parent frame by using the keyboard shortcut Alt+↑ (Command+↑). Likewise, you can move from a parent frameset to its child frame by pressing Alt+↓ (Command+↓).

Saving framesets and frames

Remember that when you're working with frames, you're working with multiple HTML files. You must be careful to save not only all the individual frames that make up your web page but also the frameset itself.

Dreamweaver makes it easy to save framesets and included frames by providing several special commands. To save a frameset, select the frameset as previously described and choose File ➪ Save Frameset to open the standard Save File dialog box. You can also save a copy of the current frameset by choosing File ➪ Save Frameset As and then specifying a filename and location for the new copy.

You can save a single frame by clicking in the frame and then choosing File ➪ Save Frame. You can also make a copy of a document within a frame by choosing File ➪ Save Frame As and then entering a filename and location.

Although you can save each frame separately in the frameset, it can be a chore unless you choose File ➪ Save All. The first time this command is invoked, Dreamweaver cycles through each of the open frames and displays the Save File dialog box. Each subsequent time you choose File ➪ Save All, Dreamweaver automatically saves every updated file in the frameset.

TIP

As you are saving all the files in the frameset for the first time, you see a separate Save As dialog box for each previously unsaved file. You can tell which file you are currently saving by looking in Design view—a dotted, black line borders the frame currently being saved.

Closing framesets

There's no real trick to closing a Dreamweaver frameset: Just choose File ➪ Close, as you would for any other file. If you have made changes to any of the frames or to the frameset itself since the last time you've saved, Dreamweaver asks if you want to save your changes before it closes the files. When you are asked to save a file, in Design view, a dotted black border appears around the frame or frameset that needs to be saved.

Dreamweaver TECHNIQUE

Establishing a Frameset

This Technique creates a frameset from scratch and brings in existing content for each of the frames.

1. Within the Dreamweaver Technique site, choose File ➪ New.
2. When the New Document dialog box opens, select the Blank Page category.
3. From the Page Type list, choose HTML.
4. From the Layout list, choose <none>.
5. Click Create.
6. Choose Insert ➪ HTML Frames Top and Bottom.

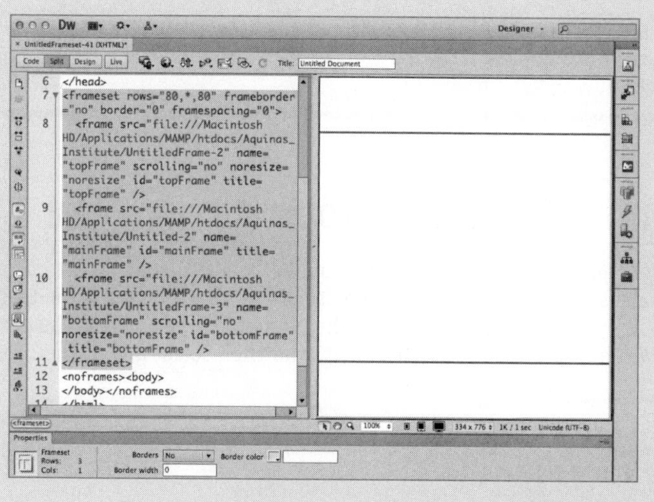

Continues

continued

Dreamweaver creates the new frameset; the Frame Tag Accessibility Attributes dialog may appear requesting that you name each of the framesets (or accept the default names), depending on your preferences.

7. In the Title field of the Document toolbar, type **Relative Realty** and press Enter (Return). It's best to name the frameset when it's first created because the frameset is currently selected; novices often make the mistake of applying a title to one of the frame pages rather than the frameset.
8. Choose File ➪ Save Frameset As and, when the Save As dialog box appears, store the file in the 15_Frames folder as **frames_start.htm**.
9. Shift+Alt+click (Shift+Option+click) in the top frame.
10. From the Property inspector, drag the Src target icon to the Files panel and point to `header_fr.htm` in the 15_Frames folder.

TIP

I find it helpful to add an `_fr` suffix to all my individual frame files to identify them as part of a frameset.

11. Click the frame border between the top and middle frames to select the frameset.
12. In the Property inspector, make sure the top frame is selected in the representation and enter **115 pixels** for the Row value.
13. Shift+Alt+click (Shift+Option+click) in the middle frame and, in the Property inspector, drag the Src point-to-file icon to the Files panel and point to `home_fr.htm`. Depending on your screen resolution and size of your Dreamweaver window, you may see scroll bars appear.
14. Shift+Alt+click (Shift+Option+click) in the bottom frame and, in the Property inspector, drag the Src point-to-file icon to the Files panel and point to `footer_fr.htm`.
15. Leave the default Row values for middle and bottom frames and choose File ➪ Save Frameset.

If you investigate the individual frame pages, you'll see that they all connect to a different CSS file than other pages in the Dreamweaver Techniques site. For the `main_fr.css` file, the outside border attributes have been removed to work better within the frameset.

Working with the Frameset Property Inspector

The Frameset Property inspector manages elements, such as the borders, that are common to all the frames within a frameset. It also offers more precise sizing control over individual rows and columns than you can achieve visually by dragging the borders. If the Property inspector is not already open, choose Window ➪ Properties to access it, and then select any of the frame borders in Design view.

Resizing frames in a frameset

With HTML, when you want to specify the size of a frame, you work with the row or column in which the frame resides. Dreamweaver gives you two ways to alter a frame's size: by dragging the border or, for more precision, by specifying a value in the Property inspector.

> **TIP**
> When a browser visits a web page that uses frames, it displays the title found in the frameset HTML document for the entire frame. The easiest way to set that title is to select the frameset and enter the name directly in the Title field of the Document toolbar, if visible. You can also set the title by selecting the frameset and choosing Modify ⇨ Page Properties. In the Page Properties dialog box, select the Title/Encoding category and enter your choice of title in the Title text box, as you would for any other web page. All the other options in the Page Properties dialog box—including background color and text color—apply to the `<noframes>` content, covered in the section "Handling Frameless Browsers" later in this chapter.

As shown in Figure 15-9, Dreamweaver's Frameset Property inspector contains a Row/Column selector to display the structure of the selected frameset. For each frameset, click the tab along the top or left side of the Row/Column selector to choose the column or row you want to modify.

FIGURE 15-9

In the Frameset Property inspector, you use the Row/Column selector tabs to choose which frame you are going to resize.

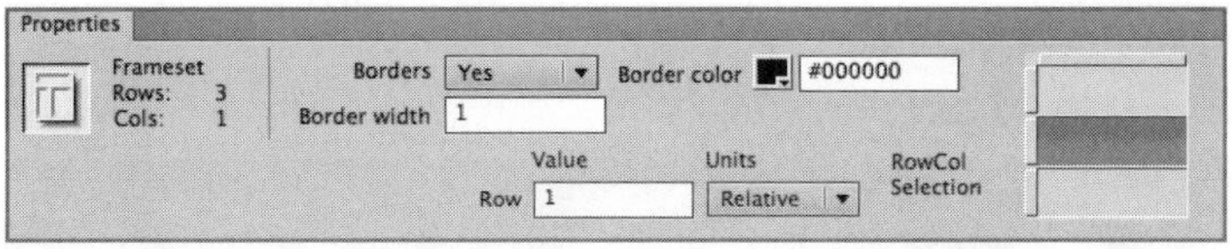

> **TIP**
> The Row/Column selector shows only the rows and columns for one frameset at a time. Therefore, if your design uses nested framesets, you won't see an exact duplicate of your entire web page in the Row/Column selector.

Whether you need to modify just a row, a column, or both a row and a column depends on the location of the frame:

- If the frame spans the width or height of an entire page, like the first column shown in Figure 15-7, select the corresponding tab on the left side of the Row/Column selector.
- If the frame spans the height of an entire page, select the equivalent tab along the top of the Row/Column selector.
- If the frame does not span either the entire height or the entire width (refer to the middle row in Figure 15-7), select both its column and its row and modify the size of each in turn.

After you have selected the row or column, you can specify its size in several ways:

- To specify the size in pixels, enter a number in the Frameset Property inspector's Value text box and select Pixels as the Units option.
- To specify the size as a percentage of the screen, enter a number from 1 to 100 in the Value text box and select Percent as the Units option.
- To specify a size relative to the other columns or rows, first select Relative as the Units option. Now you have two choices:
  - To set the size to occupy the remainder of the screen, delete any number that may be entered in the Value text box; optionally, you can enter **1**.
  - To scale the frame relative to the other rows or columns, type the scale factor in the Value text box. For example, if you want the frame to be twice the size of another relative frame, put a **2** in the Value text box.

NOTE

The Relative size operator is generally used to indicate that you want the current frame to take up the balance of the frameset column or row. This operator makes it easy to specify a size without having to calculate pixel widths and ensures that the frame has the largest possible size.

Manipulating frameset borders

By default, Dreamweaver sets up your framesets so that all the frames have borders that are invisible when viewed in a browser. You can, however, set borders to be visible, alter the border color, and change the border width. All the border controls are handled through the Frameset Property inspector.

TIP

Dreamweaver also provides border controls for individual frames. Just as table cell settings override options set for the entire table, the individual frame options override those determined for the entire frameset, as described in the section "Working with the Frame Property Inspector," later in this chapter. Use the frameset border controls when you want to make a global change to the borders, such as turning them all off.

If you are working with nested framesets, select the outermost frameset before you begin making any modifications to the borders. You can tell that you've selected the outermost frameset by looking at the Dreamweaver Tag Selector; it shows only one `<frameset>` in bold. If you select an inner nested frameset, you see more than one `<frameset>` in the Tag Selector.

Enabling borders

When a frameset is first created, Dreamweaver sets borders to be invisible in all browsers. You can expressly turn the frameset borders on or off through the Property inspector.

Unfortunately, different browsers control frame borders differently. Some browsers base the presence of borders on the value in the Borders drop-down list, whereas others use the Border Width text box. To enable borders for all browsers, enter a non-zero number in the Border Width text box; and in the Borders drop-down list of options, choose Yes.

The opposite is also true; if you want borders to be invisible for all browsers, set the Borders drop-down list to No, and specify **0** for the Border Width. If you turn off the borders for your frameset, you can still work in Dreamweaver with View ➪ Visual Aids ➪ Frame Borders enabled. This option gives you quick access to modifying the frameset. The borders are not displayed, however, when your web page is previewed in a browser.

Border color options

To change the frameset border color, select the Border Color text box and enter either a color name or a hexadecimal color value. You can also select the color box and choose a new border color from the color picker. If you click the small painter's palette in the upper-right corner of the color picker, the Color dialog box opens, just as with other color pickers in Dreamweaver.

CAUTION

If you have nested framesets on your web page, make sure that you've selected the correct frameset before you make any modifications through the Property inspector.

Modifying a Frame

What makes the whole concept of a web page frameset work so well is the flexibility of each frame:

- You can design your page so that some frames are fixed in size and others are expandable.
- You can attach scroll bars to some frames and not others.
- Any frame can have its own background image, and yet all frames can appear as one seamless picture.
- Borders can be enabled—and colored—for one set of frames but left off for another set.

Dreamweaver uses a Frame Property inspector to specify most of a frame's attributes. Others are handled through devices already familiar to you, such as the Page Properties dialog box.

Page properties

Each frame is its own HTML document and, as such, each frame can have independent page properties. To alter the page properties of a frame, position the cursor in the frame and choose Modify ➪ Page Properties. You can also use the keyboard shortcut, Ctrl+J (Command+J). Alternatively, you can select Page Properties from the context menu by right-clicking (Control+clicking) any open space on the frame's page.

From the Page Properties dialog box, you can assign a title, although it is not visible to the user unless the frame is viewed as a separate page. If you plan to use the individual frames as separate pages in your `<noframes>` content (see "Handling Frameless Browsers" at the end of this chapter), it's a good practice to title every page. You can also assign a background and the various link colors to the nonframe content by selecting the desired color box or entering a color name into the appropriate text box in either the Appearance (CSS) or the Appearance (HTML) category of the Page Properties dialog box.

The Page Properties dialog box respects the Dreamweaver preference for CSS or HTML when working in frames, just as it does with a standard page. For more details on setting the Page Properties, see the section "Establishing Page Properties" in Chapter 5.

Joining Background Images in Frames

One popular technique inserts background images into separate frames so that they blend into a seamless, single image. This takes careful planning and coordination between the designer of the graphic and the author of the web page.

To accomplish this image consolidation operation, you must first slice the image in an image-processing program, such as Adobe Fireworks or Adobe Photoshop. Then you save each part as a separate graphic, ensuring that no border is around these image sections—each cut-up piece becomes the background image for a particular frame. Next, set the background image of each frame to the matching graphic using a CSS rule for the body selector. Be sure to turn off the borders for the frameset and set the border width to zero.

Correctly size each piece to ensure that no gaps appear in your joined background. A good practice is to use absolute pixel measurements for images that fill the frame; if the background images tile, set the frame spacing to Relative.

Working with the Frame Property inspector

Using the Frame Property inspector, you can assign names to each of your frames, specify what document should display within each frame, add or remove scroll bars, specify whether the user can resize the frame, and more. To view the Property inspector for a frame, first select the frame by using the Frames panel or by holding down the Alt+Shift (Option+Shift) key as you click within the frame.

Naming your frames

Naming each frame is essential to getting the most power from a frame-structured web page. The frame's name is used to make the content inserted from a hyperlink appear in that particular frame. For more information about targeting a link, see the section "Targeting Frame Content," later in this chapter.

Frame names must follow specific guidelines, as explained in the following steps:

1. Select the frame you want to name in the Frames panel.
2. If necessary, open the Property inspector by choosing Window ➪ Properties.

3. In the Frame Property inspector, shown in Figure 15-10, add the frame's name in the text box under the Frame Name label. Frame names have the following restrictions:
   - You must use one word, with no spaces, but you can camelCase a word to make it easier to write two words as one.
   - You may not use special characters such as quotation marks and question marks. You may use the underscore (_) or hyphen (-) characters.
   - You may not use certain reserved frame names: `_blank`, `_parent`, `_self`, and `_top`.

FIGURE 15-10

The Frame Property inspector enables you to name the frame and control all the frame's attributes.

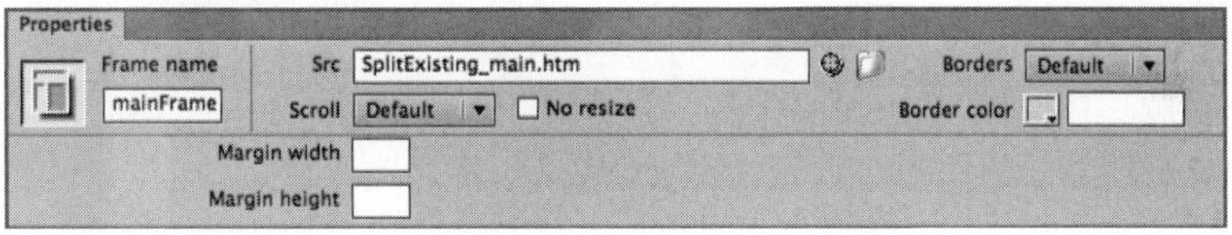

Opening a web page into a frame

You don't have to build all web pages in frames from scratch. You can load an existing web page into any frame. If you've selected a frame and the Frame Property inspector is open, just type the link directly into the Src text box or click the folder icon to browse for your file. Alternatively, you can position your cursor in a frame (without selecting the frame) and choose File ➪ Open in Frame.

Setting borders

You can typically set most border options adequately in the Frameset Property inspector, yet you can override some of the options, such as color, for each individual frame. These possibilities have practical limitations, however.

From the Frame Property inspector for a selected frame, you can make the borders visible by choosing Yes in the Borders drop-down list or make them invisible by choosing No. Leaving the Borders option at Default gives control to the frameset settings. You can also change a frame's border color by choosing the Border Color swatch in a selected frame's Property inspector.

CAUTION

Different browser versions on different operating systems treat the border settings for individual frames differently. To complicate the situation, sometimes the settings on the outmost frameset control how the individual frame border settings act. For example, if the frameset border is set to Default, and the individual frame border is set to No, the border still appears in Internet Explorer 6.0 running on Windows—but as flat, rather than three-dimensional. If you elect to set the border property for an individual frame, be sure to test on as many browsers and platforms as possible.

Additional limitations come into play when you try to implement one of your border modifications. Because frames share common borders, it is difficult to isolate an individual frame and have the change affect only the selected frame. As an example, Figure 15-11 shows a frameset in which the borders are set to No for all frames except the one on the lower right. Notice how the left border of the lower-right frame extends to the top, including the left border of the upper-right frame. You have two possible workarounds for this problem. First, you can design your frames so that their borders do not touch, as in a multi-row frameset. Second, you can create a background image for a frame that includes a border design, or you can apply the CSS border property.

FIGURE 15-11

If you want to use isolated frame borders, you have to carefully plan your web page frameset to avoid overlapping borders.

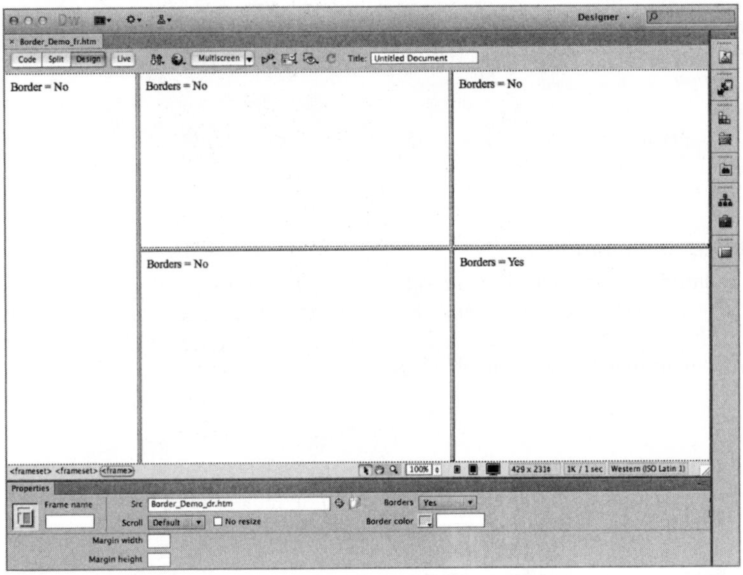

Adding scroll bars

Frames are commonly used because users can enable or disable scroll bars for each frame. Scroll bars are used when the browser window is too small to display all the information in the web page frame. The browser window's size is completely controlled by the user, so the web designer must apply the various scroll bar options on a frame-by-frame basis, depending on the look desired and the frame's content.

Four options are available from the Scroll drop-down list on the Frame Property inspector:

- **Default:** Leaves the use of scroll bars up to the browser.
- **Yes:** Forces scroll bars to appear regardless of the amount of content.

- **No:** Disables scroll bars.
- **Auto:** Turns scroll bars on if the content of the frame extends horizontally or vertically beyond what the browser window can display.

The page shown in Figure 15-12 uses automatic scroll bars in the lower-right frame; you can see one on the far right.

FIGURE 15-12

The top frame of this web page has the scroll bars turned off, and the bottom frame has the scroll bars enabled.

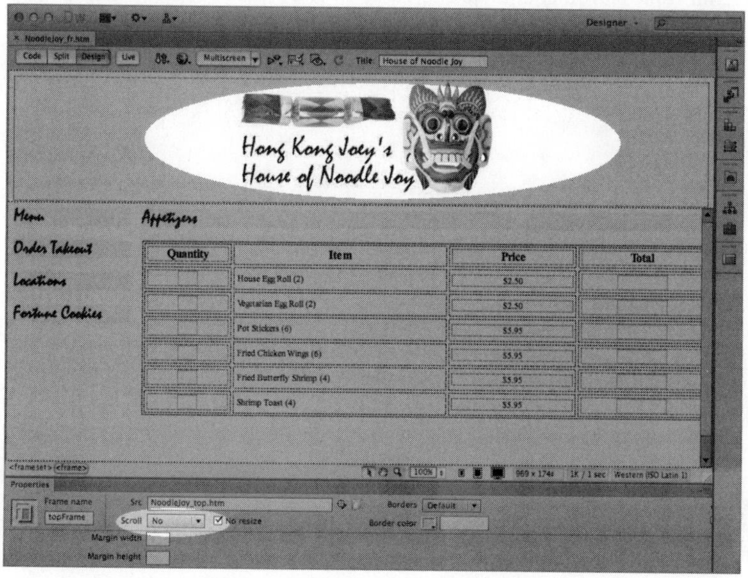

Resizing

For some browsers, unless otherwise specified, frames are resizable by the user; that is, a visitor to your website can widen, narrow, lengthen, or shorten a frame by dragging the border to a new position. You can disable this resizing capability, however, on a frame-by-frame basis. In the Frame Property inspector, select the No Resize option to turn off the resizing feature.

TIP

Although it might be tempting to select No Resize for every frame, it's best to enable resizing to allow users to expand the frame if necessary, except in frames that require a set size to maintain their functionality (frames containing navigational controls, for example).

When you first create a frameset using the Frames menu on the Insert panel, or by selecting an item in the Framesets category when you choose File ⇨ New, the frame designated as containing the body of the page is resizable, and all other frames are fixed. Frames added by Alt+dragging (Option+dragging) the frame borders with the mouse or by choosing the Modify ➪ Frameset menu commands are resizable by default.

Setting margins

Just as you can pad table cells with additional space to separate text and graphics, you can offset content in frames. Dreamweaver enables you to control the left/right margins and the top/bottom margins independently. If no margin values are specified, about 6 pixels of space are between the content and the left or right frame borders, and about 15 pixels of space are between the content and the top or bottom frame borders.

To alter the left and right margins, change the value in the Frame Property inspector's Margin Width text box; to change the top and bottom margins, enter a new value in the Margin Height text box. (If you don't see the Margin Width and Margin Height text boxes, select the expander arrow in the lower-right corner of the Property inspector.)

Modifying content

You can update a frame's content in any way you see fit. Sometimes, it's necessary to keep an eye on how altering a single frame's content affects the entire frameset. Other times, it is easier—and faster—to work on each frame individually and later load the frames into the frameset to see the final result.

With Dreamweaver's multiple-document structure, you can have it both ways. Work on the individual frame files in one or more Document windows and the frameset in yet another. If you use File ➪ Save All to save your changes in an individual frame document, switching back to the frameset window automatically shows your changed frames.

CAUTION
To preview changes made to a web page using frames, you must first save the changed files.

Deleting frames

As you're building your web page frameset, you inevitably try a frame design that does not work. How do you delete a frame once you've created it? Click the frame border and drag it into the border of the enclosing (or parent) frame. When no parent frame is present, drag the frame border to the edge of the page. If the frame being deleted contains any unsaved content, Dreamweaver asks if you'd like to save the file before closing it.

TIP
Because the enclosing frameset and each individual frame are all discrete HTML pages, each keeps track of its own edits and other changes. Therefore, each has its own undo memory. If you are in a particular frame and try to undo a frameset alteration, such as adding a new frame to the set, it won't work. To reverse an edit to the frameset, you have to select the frameset and choose Edit ➪ Undo, or use one of the keyboard shortcuts (Ctrl+Z or Command+Z). To reverse the creation of a frameset, you must select Undo twice.

Targeting Frame Content

One of the major uses of frames is for navigational control. One frame acts as the navigation center, offering links to various web pages in a site. When the user selects one of the links, the web page appears in another frame on the page, and that frame, if necessary, can scroll independently of the navigation frame. This technique keeps the navigation links always visible and accessible.

When you assign a link to appear in a particular frame of your web page, you are said to be assigning a *target* for the link. You can target specific frames in your web page, and you can target structural parts of a frameset. In Dreamweaver, targets for typical text or image links are assigned through the Text and Image Property inspectors. You also encounter frame target options elsewhere in the Dreamweaver interface, such as when you use behaviors that create links, like the jump menu behavior (see Chapter 11).

Targeting sections of your frameset

In the section "Naming your frames," you learned that certain names are reserved. The following four special names are reserved by HTML for the parts of a frameset that are used in targeting: `_blank`, `_parent`, `_self`, and `_top`. With them, you can cause content from a link to overwrite the current frame or to appear in an entirely new browser window.

To target a link to a section of your frameset, follow these steps:

1. Select the text or image you want to use as your link.
2. In the Text (or Image) Property inspector, enter the URL and/or named anchor in the Link text box. Alternatively, you can click the folder icon to browse for the file.
3. Select the Target text box. (You may need to expand the Property inspector to see the Target text box.)
4. Select one of the following reserved target names from the drop-down list of Target options (see Figure 15-13) or type an entry into the text box:
   - `_blank`: Opens the link into a new browser window and keeps the current window available.
   - `_parent`: Opens the link into the parent frameset of the current frame, if any.
   - `_self`: Opens the link into the current frame, replacing its contents (the default).
   - `_top`: Opens the link into the outermost frameset of the current web page, replacing all frames.

FIGURE 15-13

Choose your frame target from the Property inspector's Target drop-down list.

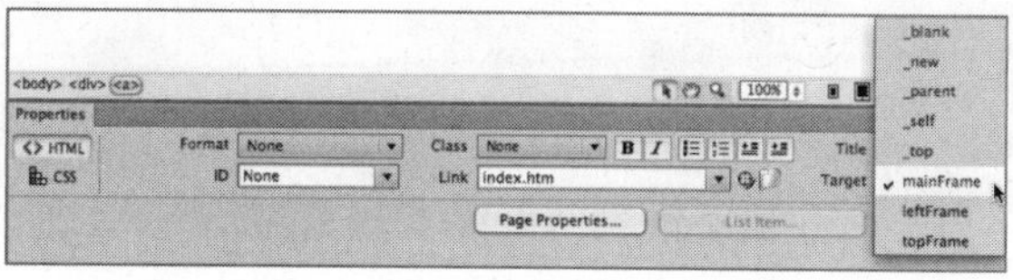

The generic nature of these reserved target names enables you to use them repeatedly on different web pages, without having to code a particular reference each time.

CAUTION

A phenomenon known as *recursive frames* can be dangerous to your site setup. For example, say you have a frameset named `index_frame.html`. If you include a link to `index_frame.html` in any frame on your current page and leave the target empty or set the target as `_self`, when the user selects that link, the entire frameset loads into the current frame—including another link to `index_frame.html`. Browsers can handle about three or four iterations of this recursion before they crash. To avoid the problem, set your frameset target to `_top`.

Targeting specific frames in your frameset

Recall the importance of naming each frame in your frameset. After you have entered a name in the Name text box of the Frame Property inspector, Dreamweaver dynamically updates the Target list to include that name. This feature enables you to target specific frames in your frameset in the same manner that you target the reserved names noted previously.

Although you can always type the frame name directly in the Target text box, the drop-down list comes in handy for this task. Not only can you avoid keeping track of the various frame names in your web page, but you prevent typing errors as well. Targets are case-sensitive, and names must match exactly or the browser won't be able to find the target.

Updating two or more frames at once

Sooner or later, most web designers using frames need to update more than one frame with a single click. The problem is, you can't group two or more URLs together in an anchor tag. Here is an easy-to-implement solution, thanks to Dreamweaver's behaviors.

If you're not familiar with Dreamweaver's JavaScript behaviors, you might want to look at Chapter 11 before continuing.

To update more than one frame target from a single link, follow these steps:

1. Select your link text or image in the frame.
2. If you selected text for your link, type **`javascript:;`** in the Link field of the Text Property inspector.

   The behavior cannot be attached directly to the text; instead, it must be associated with an anchor or an image. Typing `javascript:;` in the Link field creates the necessary anchor tag.

TIP

If one of the multiple links targets the frame that contains the hotspot, instead of typing `javascript:;` in the Link field, you can enter the path to the file that will load in that frame.

3. Open the Behaviors panel by choosing Window ➪ Behaviors.

4. Click the Add (+) button at the top of the Behaviors panel to display the list of available behaviors and choose Go To URL.
5. Dreamweaver displays the Go To URL dialog box (see Figure 15-14) and scans your document for all named frames. Select a target frame from the list of windows or frames.

FIGURE 15-14

You can cause two or more frames, marked by the trailing asterisk, to update from a single link by using Dreamweaver's Go To URL behavior.

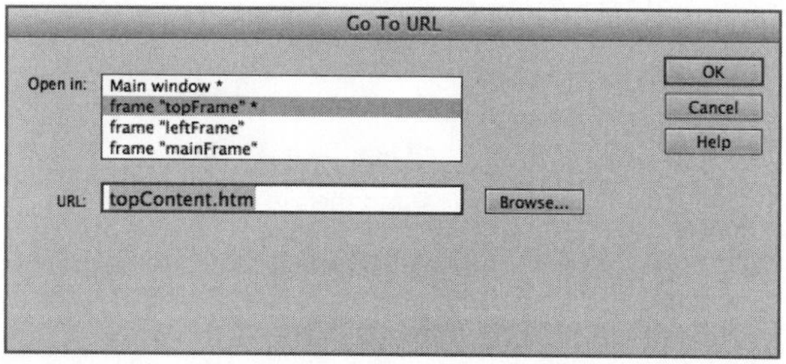

CAUTION

You won't be able to use this behavior until you name your frames as detailed in the section "Naming your frames" earlier in this chapter.

6. Enter a URL or click the Browse button to select one. Dreamweaver places an asterisk after the targeted frame to indicate that a URL has been selected for it. You can see this in Figure 15-14.
7. Repeat Steps 5 and 6 for any additional frames you want to target.
8. Click OK when you're finished.
9. If `onClick` is not already listed in the Events column of the Behaviors panel, click the arrow button next to the event and choose `(onClick)` from the event list.

Now, whenever you click your one link, the browser opens the URLs in the targeted frames in the order specified.

Dreamweaver TECHNIQUE

Setting Frame Targets

In this Technique, you set the text navigation links to work properly with the frameset. Three links open pages within the frameset and a fourth opens a page outside the frameset.

1. Re-open the frameset previously saved, `frames_start.htm`.
2. In the bottom frame, select the text `Home`.

Continues

continued

3. From the Property inspector, drag the Link point-to-file icon to the `home_fr.htm` file.
4. Select mainFrame from the Target list.

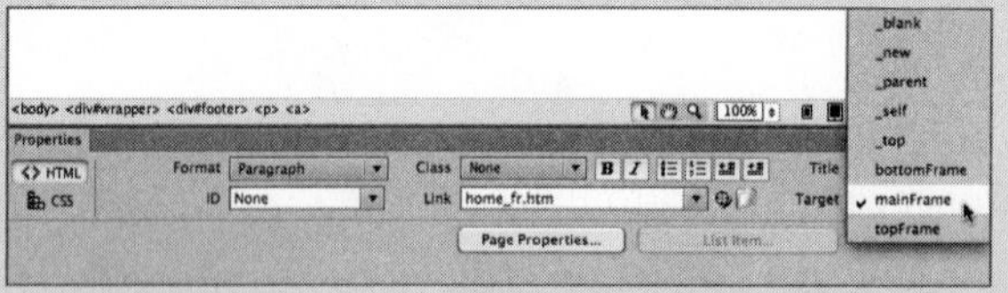

Dreamweaver automatically adds the names of frames in the current frameset to the Target list.

5. Repeat Steps 2–4, with the text `Sales` and the file `sales_fr.htm`.
6. Repeat Steps 2–4 again, with the text `Rentals` and the file `rentals_fr.htm`. Make sure that you set the Target list to mainFrame for both the previous links.
7. Select the final text phrase, `About Us`, and drag the Link point-to-file icon to the `about.htm` file. Because `about.htm` is a standard HTML file and not part of the frameset, you'll choose a different target.
8. From the Target list, choose `_top`.
9. Save your page and press F12 (Option+F12) to preview the frameset in your primary browser.

When you try the navigation links, notice that the first three links open their pages within the frameset as expected, whereas the fourth link, `about.htm`, replaces the frameset with a single page. If you click the Home link at the bottom of this page, the frameset re-opens.

Handling Frameless Browsers

Some older browser versions, still in use to a small degree today, do not support frames. HTML has a built-in mechanism for working with browsers that are not frame-enabled: the `<noframes> ... </noframes>` tag pair.

A more vital reason to use the `<noframes>` tag than to support older browsers is that most of the search engine indexing systems (called *spiders*) don't work with frames. If your frameset is `index.html` and you want the spider to find the rest of your site, the `<noframes>` content must include descriptive text and navigational links to other pages in your site.

When you begin to construct any frameset, Dreamweaver automatically inserts a `<noframes>` area just below the closing `</frameset>` tag. If a browser is not frames-capable, it ignores the frameset and frame information and renders what is found in the `<noframes>` section.

What should you put into the `<noframes>` section? To ensure the widest possible audience, webmasters typically insert links to a nonframe version of the site. The links can be as obvious or as discreet as you care to make them and, if used, are placed on the site's home page.

Dreamweaver includes a facility for easily adding and modifying the <noframes> content. Choose Modify ➪ Frameset ➪ Edit NoFrames Content to open the NoFrames Content window. As you can see in Figure 15-15, this window is identical to the regular Dreamweaver Document window, with the exception of the text "NoFrames Content" in a label at the top of the editing area.

In this window, you have access to all the same objects and panels that you normally do. When you have finished editing your <noframes> content, choose Modify ➪ Frameset ➪ Edit NoFrames Content again to deselect the option and return to the frameset.

Keep the following pointers in mind when working in the NoFrames Content window:

- The page properties of the <noframes> content are the same as the page properties of the frameset. You can select the frameset and then choose Modify ➪ Page Properties to open the Page Properties dialog box. While in the NoFrames Content window, you can also right-click (Control+click) in any open space to access the Page Properties command.
- Dreamweaver disables the File ➪ Open commands when the NoFrames Content window is onscreen. To move existing content into the <noframes> section, use Dreamweaver's Copy and Paste features.
- The <noframes> section is located in the frameset page, which is the primary page examined by search engine spiders. It's a good idea to enter <meta> tag information detailing the site in the frameset page. While you're in the NoFrames Content window, you can insert the <meta> tags using the Head category of the Common Insert panel.

FIGURE 15-15

Through the Edit NoFrames Content command, Dreamweaver enables you to specify what's seen by visitors whose browsers are not frame-capable.

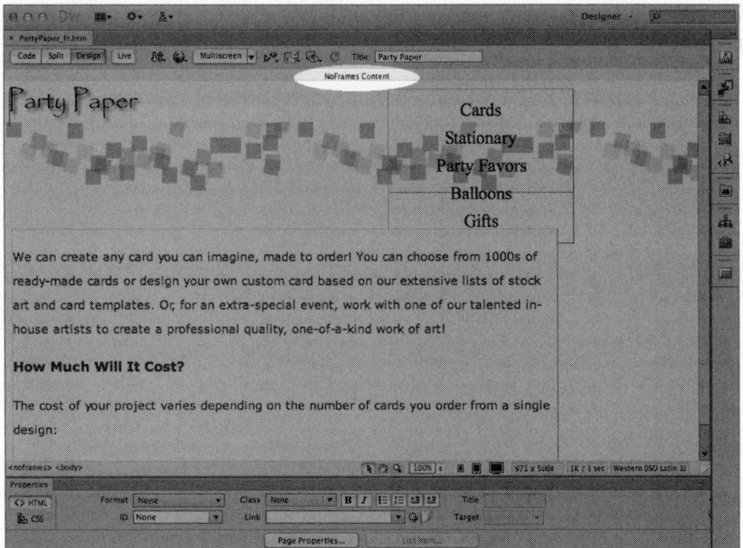

Investigating iframes

The <iframe> tag (short for inline frames) is an HTML 4.0 specification and is the only kind of frame supported in HTML5. An iframe is used to include one HTML document inside another—without building a frameset. What makes iframes visually arresting and extremely useful is their capability to display scroll bars automatically, as shown in Figure 15-16. iframes are supported by all current major desktop browsers, but support is variable in mobile browsers and in assistive devices.

FIGURE 15-16

The iframe—also known as an inline frame—is a technique for including one HTML page within another visible in Live View or when previewed in a browser.

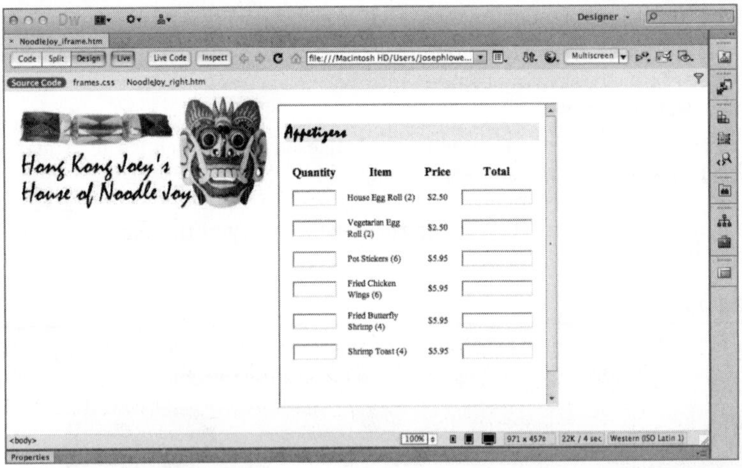

The <iframe> tag uses the src attribute to specify which HTML file is to be included. Any content—text, images, or whatever—found between the opening and the closing <iframe> tags is displayed only if the browser does *not* support iframes. In other words, it's the no-iframe content. Here's an iframe code example:

```
<iframe src="/includes/salespromo.htm" name="promoFrame" i
style="position:absolute; width:200px; height:300px; top:139px; i
left:530px">Iframes are not supported by this browser.</iframe>
```

If you're familiar with Cascading Style Sheet AP elements, you may notice that the style attribute is identical in iframes. This has an interesting effect in Dreamweaver: iframe code with the style attribute set to position:absolute is displayed like an AP element, as shown in Figure 15-17. This makes positioning and resizing the iframe straightforward. To see the actual iframe content, preview the page in Live View or in a compatible browser.

FIGURE 15-17

When you view an absolutely positioned iframe tag in Dreamweaver, it appears like an AP element, complete with resizing handles.

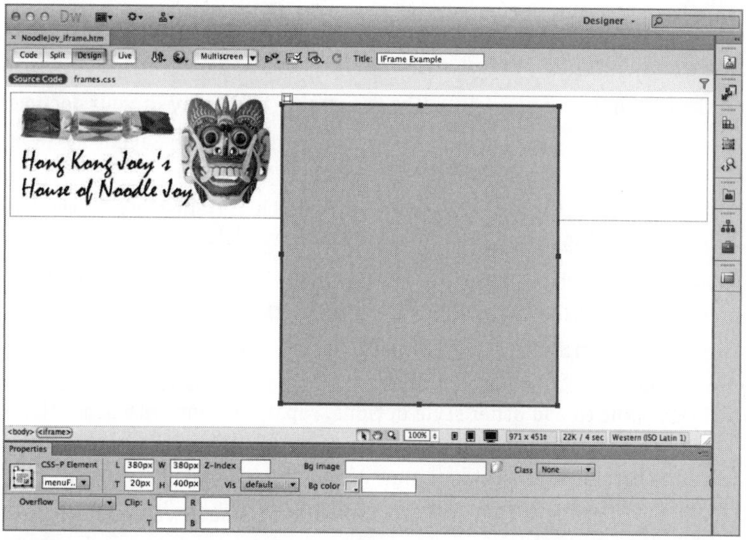

NOTE

An iframe is depicted in Design view as a solid rectangle, even if absolute positioning is not used. Although you can't see the content at design time in Dreamweaver without switching to Live View or previewing the page in a browser, the iframe dimensions are rendered correctly to preserve the layout. You can also edit the contents of an iframe by using Dreamweaver's Related Files toolbar.

CAUTION

Specifying `position:absolute` in the `style` attribute enables you to exactly position a floating frame on the page. However, if you specify `position:absolute` and your other content is not contained within AP elements, your floating frame may overlap the other content on your page. For this reason, it is best to use floating frames in combination with a CSS-based layout.

You can also specify a style of `position:relative`. In this case, browsers display the floating frame on the page relative to the other page content, even if that content is not contained within AP elements. Note, however, that Design view does not always correctly display floating frames that are positioned relatively, and sometimes the floating frame overlaps existing content, making it difficult to edit. Again, it is best to lay out your content using CSS positioning and specify `position:absolute` for your `<iframe>` if you are using floating frames.

15

In Dreamweaver, iframes are referred to as *floating frames*. Dreamweaver facilitates the inclusion of iframes in your documents with the iFrame button in the Layout category of the Insert panel or in the Frames submenu of Dreamweaver's HTML menu.

To insert a floating frame in your document, follow these steps:

1. If you are working in Design view, switch to Code view by choosing View ➪ Code.
2. Position the cursor where you would like the iframe to display in your document.
3. Insert the `<iframe>` tag by clicking the iframe button on the Layout menu of the Insert panel.
4. Specify the attributes for the `<iframe>` tag. To do this, right-click (Control+click) the tag and choose Edit Tag <iframe> from the drop-down list.
5. The Tag Editor for iframes opens. In this dialog box, specify at least the following:
   - **Source:** This is the file that will be displayed within the floating frame.
   - **Scrolling:** This attribute specifies whether scroll bars will appear in the frame.
   - **Style:** In the Style Sheet/Accessibility category, type **position:absolute** in the Style box. If you want to add other style options, separate them with semicolons.
   - **Alternate Content:** Select the Alternate Content category and then specify the text that will be displayed in browsers that don't support floating frames.
6. In Design view, you can size and position the floating frame as you would any AP element.

Refer to Chapter 10 for more information about positioning and sizing AP elements.

Summary

Frames were, at one point, a significant tool for web designers; however, they are not used very much today. Dreamweaver gives web designers working on older websites that still contain frames a quick and easy access to frame design through its drag-and-drop interface. When you're working with frames and framesets, keep these points in mind:

- A framed web page consists of a separate HTML document for each frame and one additional file that describes the frame structure, called the *frameset.*
- A frameset comprises columns and rows, which can be sized absolutely in pixels as a percentage of the browser window or relative to the other columns or rows.
- Dreamweaver enables you to reposition frame borders by dragging them to a new location. You can also add new frames by Alt+clicking (Option+clicking) as you drag any existing frame border.
- Framesets can be nested to create more complex column and row arrangements. Selecting the frame border displays the Frameset Property inspector.
- Select any individual frame through the Frames panel. After you select the frame, you can display the Frame Property inspector.

- Make your links appear in a specific frame by assigning targets to the links. Dreamweaver supports both structured and named targets. You can update two or more frames with one link by using the Dreamweaver Go To URL behavior.
- You should include information and/or links for browsers that are not frame-capable through Dreamweaver's Edit NoFrames Content feature.
- Floating frames (better known as iframes), as defined in HTML 4.0 and later, can be implemented in Dreamweaver by initially hand-editing the `<iframe>` tag in Code view. After inserting the tag, the floating frame can be sized and positioned in Design view.

In the next chapter, you learn how to work with Ajax technologies, which combine XML, JavaScript, and CSS, in general, and Adobe's own Ajax implementation, Spry, in particular.

CHAPTER

16

Powering Ajax Pages with Spry

IN THIS CHAPTER

- Understanding Ajax
- Learning about Spry
- Incorporating Spry XML data
- Dreamweaver Technique: Adding Spry Data
- Validating with Spry form widgets
- Advancing layouts with Spry widgets
- Applying Spry effects

Remember the first time you saw Google Maps? If you're like me, after you'd spent a good amount of time clicking and dragging the map around or zooming in on a satellite view, you did a right-click to confirm your suspicion that it was done with Flash. Wrong! The magic of Google Maps (`http://maps.google.com`), as well as other sophisticated sites such as Flickr (`http://www.flickr.com`) and Yahoo! Tech (`http://news.yahoo.com/tech/`), is that they all rely on a relatively new technology known as Ajax. Ajax combines advanced JavaScript coding, Document Object Model (DOM) manipulation, and, optionally, XML data to allow partial page refreshes without long waits for a new page of HTML to arrive from the server.

Ajax is highly touted as a key component of the next-generation Internet, known when it was introduced as Web 2.0. To make it possible for more and more people to integrate Ajax techniques into their sites, numerous implementations have been developed. One such implementation, Spry, was developed by Adobe and released for use by the general public. The Dreamweaver engineers took Spry to the next level and developed a series of objects and features to make it easy for designers to incorporate the advanced functionality of Ajax into their sites.

This chapter explores the relationship between Ajax, Spry, and the Spry tools in Dreamweaver. After an overview that provides the background you'll need on Ajax and Spry, you learn how to use the Spry data tools to create interactive page regions that update instantly, without requiring a full page refresh. You also get a look at a series of Spry widgets, which bring sophisticated JavaScript functionality to both layout and form validation. The chapter closes with an in-depth look at Spry effects—client-side behaviors guaranteed to spice up your sites and have your page visitors wondering how you did it.

Understanding Ajax and Spry

Ajax and Spry are two complementary technologies. The first, Ajax, is the name given to an overall technique for seamlessly updating portions of a page. The second, Spry, is a specific implementation of Ajax, developed and released by Adobe on its Labs mini-site (`http://labs.adobe.com/technologies/spry`).

In this section, you dive a bit deeper into both Ajax and Spry to better help you understand how the technologies work and what their uses are.

What is Ajax?

By now, you've probably heard that Ajax is short for Asynchronous JavaScript and XML—and the key, least understood, word is *asynchronous*. An asynchronous action is one that occurs out of the normal sequence. On the web, the typical sequence is something like this:

1. The user's browser loads a web page.
2. The user clicks a link on the page.
3. The browser sends the request for the linked page to the host computer.
4. The host computer sends the HTML and dependent files to the user's browser.
5. The browser displays the page to the user.

This series of steps occurs regardless of whether an entirely new page or just a section of the page is requested in what is referred to as a *full-page refresh*. One of the key benefits of Ajax is that it enables a *partial-page refresh*. Ajax acts as a middleman between the browser and the host computer, requesting only the data needed, out of the normal sequence. Here's a similar sequence with an Ajax-driven page:

1. The user's browser loads the web page, along with the associated data.
2. The user clicks the link on the page, requesting new data.
3. The Ajax engine intercepts the link and sends the data to the browser.
4. The browser displays the page to the user.

In addition to having fewer steps, it's also important to realize that no long-distance fetching is involved; all the data is already loaded into the Ajax engine, ready for delivery. This makes page updates very fast and also reduces the server load.

Ajax is not without its limitations, however. Because the implementation depends on JavaScript, site visitors with JavaScript turned off will not have the same experience. Moreover, some browser functionality, such as the Back button and bookmarking, does not work as might be expected with Ajax-driven pages; you cannot, for example, use the browser Back button to review previous Ajax data selections, nor can you bookmark them. Perhaps most important, accessibility suffers significantly under standard Ajax implementations; only a handful of screen readers are equipped to handle partial page updates. Designers need to carefully weigh Ajax's pros against its cons before incorporating the technologies into their sites.

What is Spry?

Ajax is a big hit in the web community, and many, many developers have begun to look for ways to make it easier to integrate into their sites. Adobe jumped on the Ajax bandwagon with Spry in early 2006 through a public release of the technology on the Adobe Labs site (see Figure 16-1). Spry is officially known as a *framework* for Ajax: A framework is a set of JavaScript libraries combined with methods for applying the JavaScript functions in standard web pages.

FIGURE 16-1

Investigate the Spry framework at the Adobe Labs site.

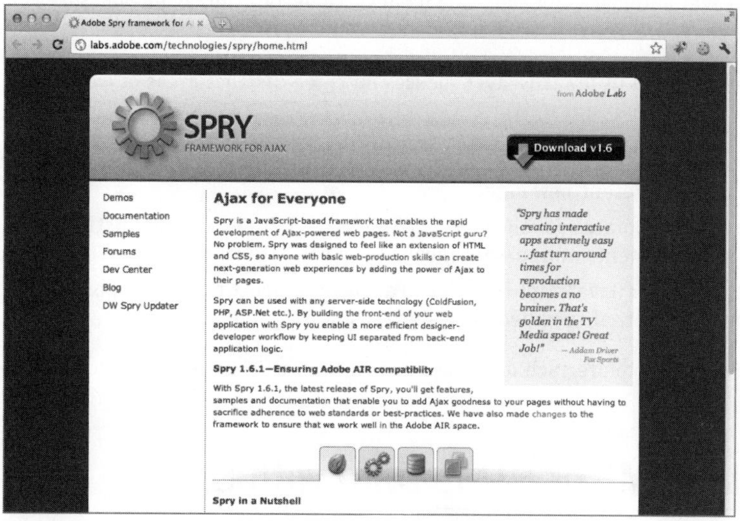

NOTE

As of this writing, the version available on the Adobe Labs site and the one available in Dreamweaver CS6 are the same, version 1.6.1. It is possible that a new version of Spry will be released on Labs before the next major release of Dreamweaver. If that is the case, the Dreamweaver team will likely provide an updated extension to bring both in sync.

The initial step to working with Spry is to include links to the necessary JavaScript files in your document. When you begin to work with Spry data objects, two key files, `xpath.js` and `SpryData.js`, are required. Dreamweaver automatically transfers the files you need to your site root and links to these files:

```
<script src="SpryAssets/xpath.js" type="text/javascript"></script>
<script src="SpryAssets/SpryData.js" type="text/javascript"></script>
```

Applying other Spry functionality, such as widgets or effects, requires other JavaScript files to be included.

One of the unique approaches of the Spry framework is that it is tag-based. Many other Ajax frameworks rely solely on JavaScript function calls embedded in links. Spry uses tag attributes like `spry:region` to indicate Ajax functionality, like this:

```
<div spry:region="ds1">
```

To ensure that such nonstandard coding still passes validation, Adobe maintains an XML document online that exposes the proprietary code. Such a document is called an *XML namespace* and is defined in the opening `<html>` tag of each document, like this (bolded for emphasis):

```
<html xmlns="http://www.w3.org/1999/xhtml" xmlns:spry=i
"http://ns.adobe.com/spry">
```

Again, Dreamweaver automatically adds this namespace declaration whenever Spry functionality is added to the page.

The Spry implementation in Dreamweaver focuses on three distinct areas of web page development:

- **Data:** Combines XML or HTML data with HTML pages, updating only the required portions of the page to present new data.
- **Widgets:** Incorporates advanced JavaScript and CSS to enable sophisticated, interactive page layout elements and instantaneous form validation.
- **Effects:** Provides JavaScript libraries to achieve complex movements or interactions, like fading in and out, of specified page elements.

The following sections explore each of these separate Spry uses in detail.

Integrating XML or HTML Data with Spry

One of the most compelling uses of Spry is to incorporate static data into a standard web page. A typical use case includes a standard XML file and two separate, but connected, areas on a single page. One area, called the master region, lists the main data topics, such as movie titles. The second area, the detail region, displays related aspects of the selected main topic, that is, the movie's plot, director, cast, and poster. Whenever a user selects a different main topic, the details—and only the details—change; the rest of the page is not reloaded. You can find a good example of this type of Spry-driven interaction on Adobe Labs (`http://labs.adobe.com/technologies/spry/demos/rssreader/index.html`), shown in Figure 16-2.

When working with Spry, designers can choose between XML or HTML structured data. As you see over the next two sections, the Spry Data Set Wizard adapts to your initial choice of the type of data you want to integrate.

Merging HTML data into web pages

XML is, without a doubt, a powerful tool in bringing data to the web. However, sometimes it can be difficult, if not overwhelming, to implement. If you find yourself shying away from XML, Dreamweaver has a simpler path for your data to travel: good old HTML.

FIGURE 16-2

Choose any Adobe product from the master region on the left to see related info in the detail region on the right.

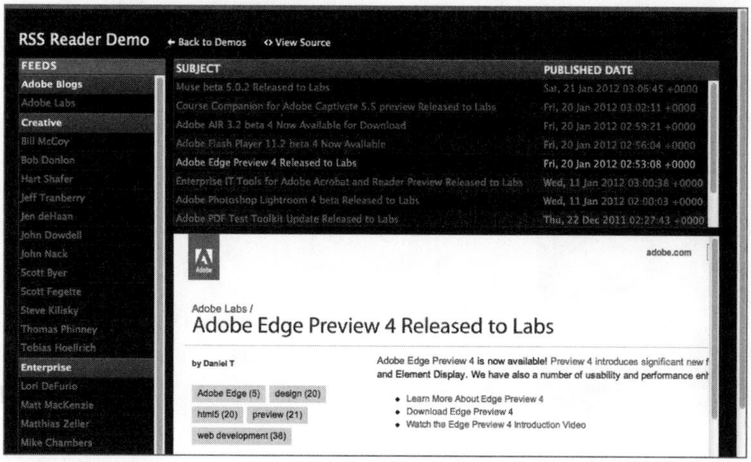

The Spry Data Set Wizard reads HTML pages containing text and images in tables, lists, `<div>` tags, or paragraphs. Tables are the default choice and very easy to set up. Once a table or other HTML structure with data has been identified, you can include or exclude data columns just as you can with XML. The final step of the Spry Data Set Wizard for either data source choice provides the same range of output options.

NOTE

If you're creating an HTML data source, tables are definitely the way to go. Although Dreamweaver supports other HTML elements, such as lists and divs, tables are the easiest to set up and use—you can even have multiple data tables on the same page. You'll have to give each table tag a unique ID so that it can be read properly.

The data in an HTML table looks like the table shown in Figure 16-3, with the header cells (Type, Photo, Address, City, and so on) acting as data column names. The data records themselves are located in the subsequent rows.

To establish a Spry Data Set with HTML data, follow these steps:

1. From the Spry or Data category of the Insert panel, choose Spry Data Set. Alternatively, you can choose Insert ➪ Spry ➪ Spry Data Set. Another option is available from the Bindings panel where you can choose Add (+) and select Spry Data Set from the list. The Spry Data Set dialog box opens.

   The Spry Data Set dialog box is divided into three steps. The first, Select Data Source, gives you an opportunity to specify your data.

2. From the Select Data Type list, choose HTML.

FIGURE 16-3

Data in a table can be read into a Spry Data Set just as easily as XML data can.

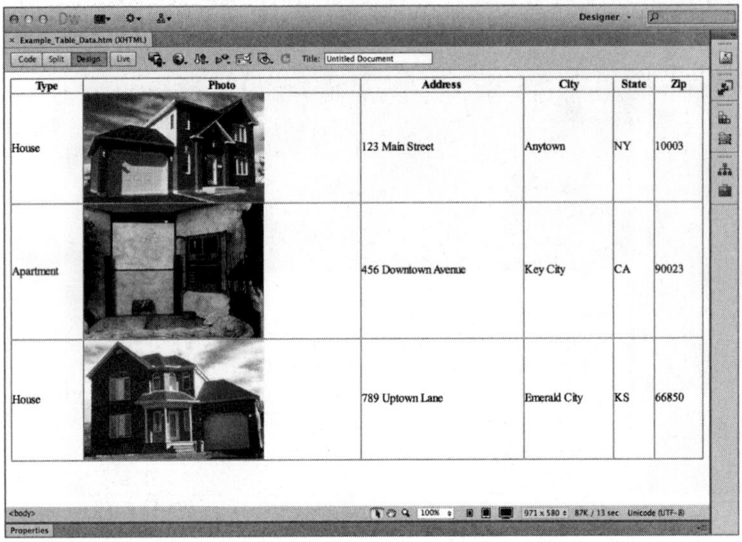

3. Enter a name for your data set in the Data Set Name field or keep the default suggestion, typically ds1.
4. Choose the tag to look for from the Detect list. The default is Tables, but you can also choose Divs, Lists, and Custom. If you select Custom, you can enter the name of any tag in the editable list.
5. Click Browse to locate your data file. Either a local HTML file in the site or an online file with an absolute URL can be used. However, the file must be located within the same domain as the current page for security reasons.
6. If you're working with a web application that creates your data file dynamically, choose Design Time Feed to select an example data file to use in page development.

   The Spry Data Set Wizard displays the information found in the Data Selection window. Dreamweaver identifies data containers with yellow arrows, as shown in Figure 16-4.
7. Click the yellow arrow pointing to the data you want to use. You can also choose the ID from the Data Containers list. When the data is selected, the yellow arrow turns green and the data structure is highlighted and previewed below.
8. If you want to narrow your data options, choose the Advanced Data Selection option and then enter CSS classes in either the Row Selectors or the Column Selectors fields.
9. Click Next to proceed.

   In the second step of the wizard, Set Data Options, you define data column types and other settings, such as the column by which you want the data sorted, if at all (see Figure 16-5).

FIGURE 16-4

Dreamweaver detects all the available HTML data sources on a page and asks that you specify the one you want.

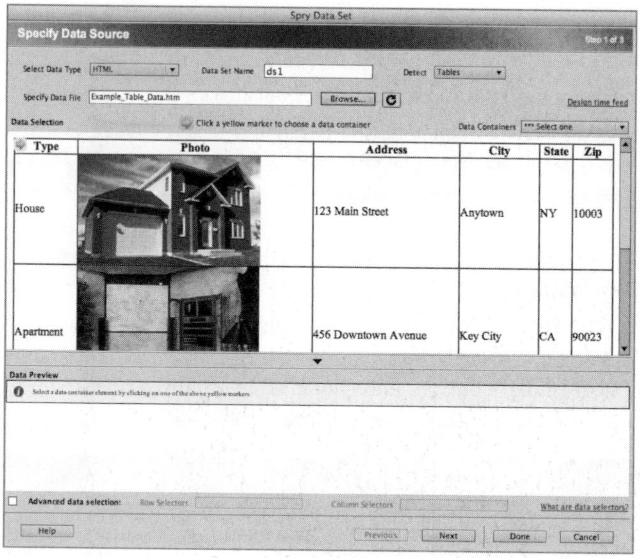

FIGURE 16-5

Assigning a data type to a column makes it possible to correctly sort text, date, numeric, and even HTML content.

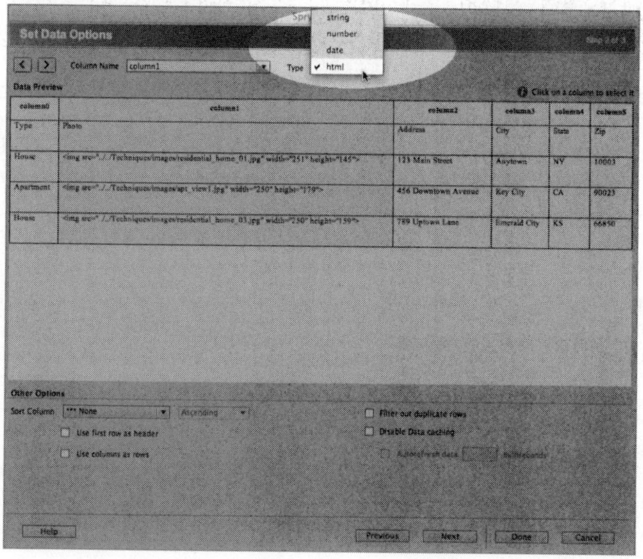

10. Select each column in turn and set its type: string, number, date, or HTML. You can select a column in several ways:
    - Click the right and left arrows to move from one column to another.
    - Choose the column from the Column Name list.
    - Select a column header with your mouse.
11. Next, you have an opportunity to set a number of options:
    - If you want your data to be displayed in a particular order, choose the column from the Sort Column list and set the adjacent list to either Ascending or Descending.
    - If your table includes a header row, make sure the Use First Row As Header option is selected.
    - If your table is set up with the header cells in the first column, choose the Use Columns As Rows option.
    - If your data is repeated, choose the Filter Out Duplicate Rows option.
    - If your data is dynamically refreshed, choose the Disable Data Caching option and select the Autorefresh Data option, entering a value in milliseconds where 1,000 is equal to 1 second.

NOTE

If the Autorefresh option is not enabled, the data is loaded just once, when the page is first requested.

12. Click Next to proceed.

    On the final step of the wizard, Choose Insert Options, you select one of five options for outputting your data (see Figure 16-6). Four of the options provide different layout possibilities, whereas the fifth option sets up the data for insertion but doesn't actually insert any HTML. Each of the four layout options has its own Set Up dialog box. These options are the same as those offered for XML data.
13. Choose the desired display option for your Spry data:
    - **Insert Table:** Adds a standard table to the page, enhanced to include sortable columns. Click Set Up to choose which columns, in which order, are included. You can also choose to make any column not sortable; all are, by default. In addition, you'll have the option of assigning CSS classes to style odd and even rows, as well as classes for hover and selected states. A final option allows detail regions to be updated when a row is clicked; this option is automatically added in the master/detail layout.
    - **Insert Master/Detail Layout:** Adds a repeating series of master items on the left of the page and a linked detail section on the right. When a master item is selected, the columns in the detail area are updated. Click Set Up to choose the columns and their order for both the master and detail the sections; you can also determine the type of container (div, p, span, or heading tag) for any detail column.
    - **Insert Stacked Containers:** Adds chosen data in a series of block elements, one after the other. Click Set Up to choose data columns and order and to set the type of container. Options for containers include div, p, span, or any heading tag.

- **Insert Stacked Containers With Spotlight Area:** Inserts two data areas, side-by-side. Typically, the left area is for one or two featured elements, such as an image or primary category, and the right is for the remaining data. Click Set Up to choose data for each section and the type of container (div, p, span, or heading tag) for any data column.
- **Do Not Insert HTML:** Populates the Bindings panel with the data set and columns for manual layout.

14. Click Finish.

    If one of the four layout options was chosen, the HTML is added to the page.

15. Save your page. When you save your page the first time a Spry XML Data Set is created, Dreamweaver informs you that supporting files have been copied to your site and must be uploaded to your remote site for final implementation. The Spry support files in this case are `SpryData.js` and `SpryHTMLDataSet.js`; both are placed in a SpryAssets folder at the root of the local site.

FIGURE 16-6

Dreamweaver provides a range of layout options, including a completely custom one.

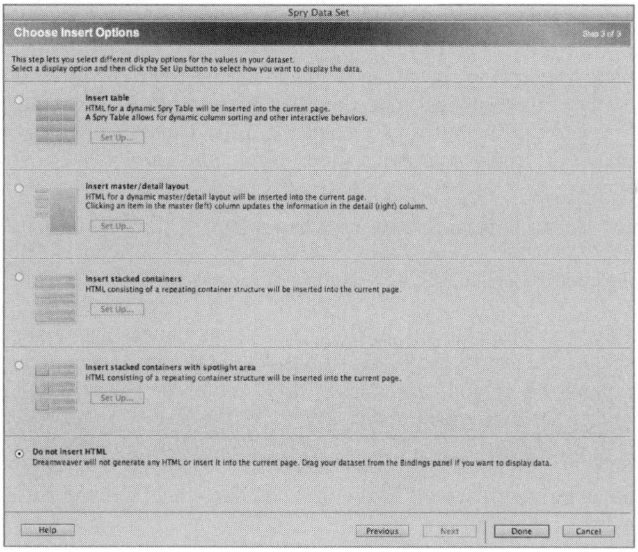

Once your Spry Data Set layout is added to the page, you can test it easily by entering into Live View.

NOTE

If you opted to choose Do Not Insert HTML as the layout option, you'll need to add both a Spry Region and a Spry Repeat object to the page, along with the data inserted from the Bindings panel.

Connecting to XML data

Dreamweaver refers to every connection to an XML file as a data set. Each data set connects to a specific tag or *node* within a single XML file. You'll recall that an XML file is structured to allow repeated data, like this:

```
<?xml version="1.0" encoding="ISO-8859-1"?>
<properties>
  <property>
    <type>House</type>
    <address>123 Main Street</address>
    <city>Anytown</city>
    <state>NY</state>
    <zip>10003</zip>
  </property>
  <property>
    <type>Apartment</type>
    <address>456 Downtown Avenue</address>
    <city>Key City</city>
    <state>CA</state>
    <zip>90023</zip>
  </property>
</properties>
```

In this example code, the `<property>` tag is the node that repeats; the XML data file could contain as many `<property>` nodes as needed. Once the data set has been established and the node identified, you can include any of the subordinate nodes (in this example, `<type>`, `<address>`, `<city>`, `<state>`, and `<zip>`) as data in your page.

To learn more about the structure of XML, see Chapter 32.

To establish a Spry Data Set with XML data, follow these steps:

1. From the Spry or Data category of the Insert panel, choose Spry Data Set. Alternatively, you can choose Insert ➪ Spry ➪ Spry Data Set. Another option is available from the Bindings panel where you can choose Add (+) and select Spry Data Set from the list. The Spry Data Set dialog box opens.
2. From the Select Data Type list, choose XML.
3. Enter a name for your data set in the Data Set Name field or keep the default suggestion, typically ds1.
4. Click Browse to locate your data file. Either a local XML file in the site or an online file with an absolute URL can be used. However, the file must be located within the same domain as the current page for security reasons.
5. If you're working with a web application that creates your data file dynamically, choose Design Time Feed to select an example data file to use in page development.
6. Select the desired node. In most cases, you'll want to select a repeating node, identified with a plus sign, shown in Figure 16-7. There are, however, circumstances in which a non-repeating node is desired. You might, for example, need to establish a data set to get the overall or meta information. Both repeating and non-repeating nodes should contain children or subordinate nodes.

FIGURE 16-7

Choose the repeating node to get all your XML data.

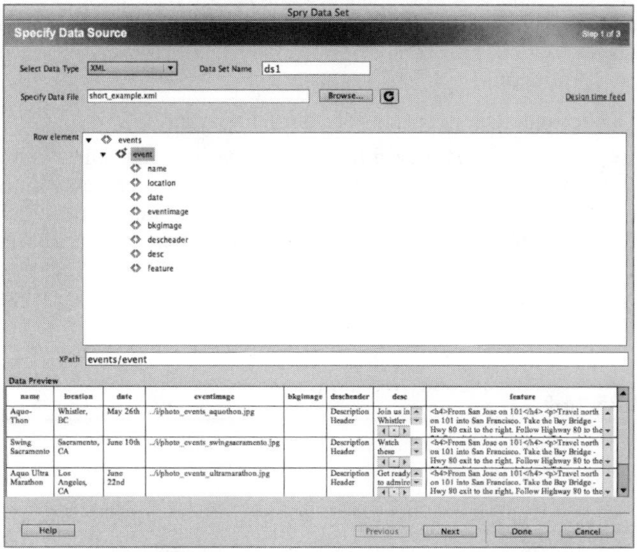

When the data structure is selected, the data is displayed in the Data Preview area.

7. Click Next to proceed.

   The second step of the wizard, Set Data Options, is where you define data column types and other settings, such as the column by which you want the data sorted, if at all.

8. Select each column in turn and set its type: string, number, date, or HTML. You can select a column in several ways:
   - Click the right and left arrows to move from one column to another.
   - Choose the column from the Column Name list.
   - Select a column header with your mouse.

9. Next, you have an opportunity to set a number of options:
   - If you want your data to be displayed in a particular order, choose the column from the Sort Column list and set the adjacent list to either Ascending or Descending.
   - If your data is repeated, choose the Filter Out Duplicate Rows option.
   - If your data is dynamically refreshed, choose the Disable Data Caching option and select the Autorefresh Data option, entering a value in milliseconds where 1,000 is equal to 1 second.

NOTE

If the Autorefresh option is not enabled, the data is loaded just once, when the page is first requested.

10. Click Next to proceed.

    On the final screen of the wizard, Choose Insert Options, you'll select one of five options for outputting your data. Four of the options provide different layout possibilities, whereas the fifth option sets up the data for insertion, but doesn't actually insert any HTML. Each of the four layout options has its own Set Up dialog box. These options are the same as those offered for HTML data.

11. Choose the desired display option for your Spry data:

    - **Insert Table:** Adds a standard table to the page, enhanced to include sortable columns. Click Set Up (see Figure 16-8) to choose which columns, in which order, are included. You can also choose to make any column not sortable; all are, by default. In addition, you'll have the option of assigning CSS classes to style odd and even rows, as well as classes for hover and selected states. A final option allows detail regions to be updated when a row is clicked; this option is automatically added in the master/detail layout.

FIGURE 16-8

With the Insert Table layout, you can set a variety of classes to control the static and interactive data design.

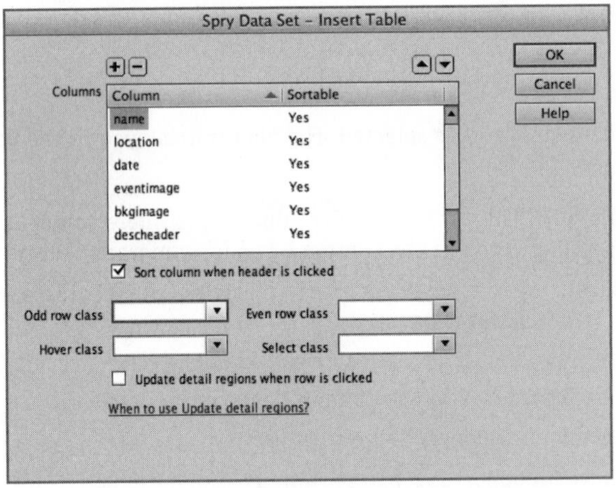

- **Insert Master/Detail Layout:** Adds a repeating series of master items on the left of the page and a linked detail section on the right. When a master item is selected, the columns in the detail area are updated. Click Set Up to choose the columns and their order for both the master the and detail sections; you can also determine the type of container (div, p, span, or heading tag) for any detail column.
- **Insert Stacked Containers:** Adds chosen data in a series of block elements, one after the other. Click Set Up to choose data columns and order and to set the type of container. Options for containers include div, p, span, or any heading tag.
- **Insert Stacked Containers With Spotlight Area:** Inserts two data areas, side by side. Typically, the left area is for one or two featured elements, such as an image or primary

category, and the right is for the remaining data. Click Set Up to choose data for each section and the type of container (div, p, span, or heading tag) for any data column.

- **Do Not Insert HTML:** Populates the Bindings panel with the data set and columns for manual layout.

12. Click Finish.

    If one of the four layout options was chosen, the HTML is added to the page.

13. Save your page. When you save your page the first time a Spry XML Data Set is created, Dreamweaver informs you that supporting files have been copied to your site and must be uploaded to your remote site for final implementation. The Spry support files in this case are `SpryData.js` and `xpath.js`; both are placed in a SpryAssets folder at the root of the local site.

After you've completed the Spry XML Data Set dialog box, the data set is listed in the Bindings panel; expand the entry to view the included columns, as shown in Figure 16-9.

In Code view, the data set object is declared through the JavaScript keyword `new`:

```
var ds1 = new Spry.Data.XMLDataSet("example.xml",
"events/event",{sortOnLoad:"name",sortOrderOnLoad:"ascending"});
```

Next, you learn how to identify specific areas of the page as Spry regions.

FIGURE 16-9

You can always add new instances of your Spry data from the Bindings panel.

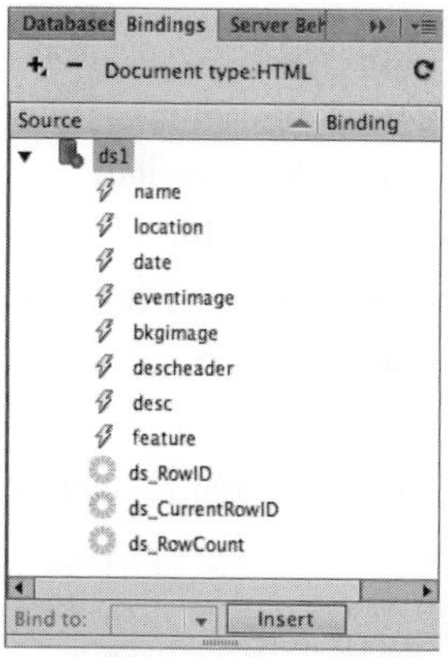

Defining Spry regions

A Spry region is an area on the page where Spry data can be used. A Spry region is identified by a proprietary attribute, typically added to either `<div>` or `<span>` tags, like this:

```
<div spry:region = "ds1">
```

This code is automatically entered for you when the Spry Data Set Wizard is completed.

There are two types of Spry regions: master and detail. The master region uses the `spry:region` attribute, whereas the detail region uses `spry:detailregion`. If the data is not in a master/detail layout, the `spry:region` attribute is applied to the data area. A detail region is one that depends on a selection from a master region. For example, you could have a master region that includes the addresses of various properties, whereas the detail region might show an image and a description of the user-selected property.

Dreamweaver includes a Spry Region object that inserts code that can be used in three different ways:

- Insert a new `<div>` or `<span>` tag at the current cursor location.
- Wrap a `<div>` or `<span>` tag around the current selection.
- Replace the selection with a new `<div>` or `<span>` tag.

TIP

To identify an existing tag as a Spry region, use the Quick Tag Editor or Code view to add a `spry:region` or `spry:detailregion` attribute manually. To make the task as easy as possible, code hinting is available for this—and, in fact, all—Spry attributes. Set the Spry region attribute equal to the defined data set you want to appear in the region. Spry regions can be added to tags other than `<div>` and `<span>`; however, they cannot be added to the following tags: `<col>`, `<colgroup>`, `<frameset>`, `<html>`, `<iframe>`, `<style>`, `<table>`, `<tbody>`, `<tfoot>`, `<thead>`, `<title>`, and `<tr>`.

To add a Spry region to your page, follow these steps:

1. To add an empty Spry region, place your cursor where you'd like the region code to appear; to place a Spry region around existing content, select the desired content.
2. From the Spry or Data categories of the Insert panel, choose Spry Region.
   The Insert Spry Region dialog box appears, as shown in Figure 16-10.
3. Select the type of tag you'd like to use—either DIV or SPAN—from the Container options.
4. Choose the type of tag—standard Region or Detail Region—from the Type options.
5. Select the desired data set from the Spry Data Set list.
6. If you have a current selection, choose either the Wrap Selection or the Replace Selection option.

CAUTION

Replace Selection completely removes your selection, including all content contained within it, and substitutes either a `<div>` or a `<span>` tag with the chosen attributes.

7. Click OK when you're done.

If you've chosen to insert a new <div> or <span> tag, Dreamweaver inserts it with a bit of placeholder content, as shown in Figure 16-11. Spry regions are further identified in the Tag Selector with a reddish-orange background color.

FIGURE 16-10

Identify where you'd like your Spry data to appear by inserting a Spry region.

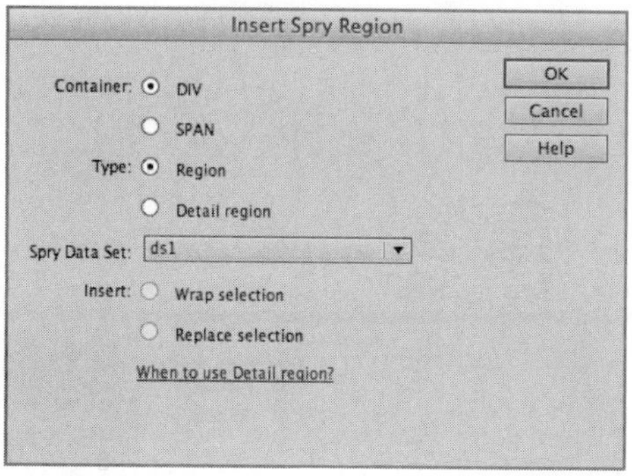

FIGURE 16-11

Inserted Spry regions are identified by their placeholder content and highlighted tag in the Tag Selector.

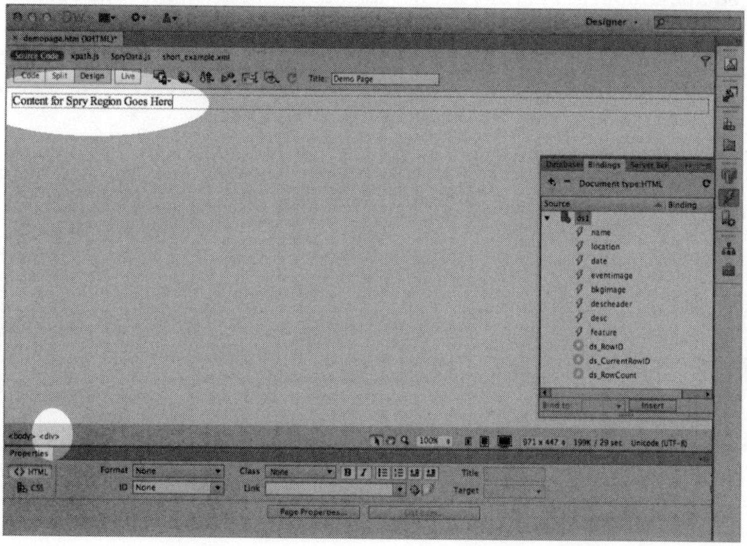

Associating Master and Detail Regions

In this section, you've learned how to create two different types of Spry regions: master and detail. But how do you link the two? The standard method is to use an `onClick` event within the master region. Let's say that you have a master Spry region contained in a series of `<div>` tags with a couple of data columns, like this:

```
<div spry:region="ds1" class="MasterContainer">
<div class="MasterColumn" spry:repeat="ds1" spry:setrow="ds1" spry:hover=
  "MasterColumnHover" spry:select="MasterColumnSelected">{name}<br />
  {location}<br />
  {date}</div>
</div>
```

The key code line here is the `spry:setrow` attribute:

```
spry:setrow="ds1"
```

Binding data to the page

After a Spry XML Data Set has been defined, Spry data columns are shown in the Bindings panel. Inserted data columns are contained within curly braces, such as `{address}`, and must be placed within Spry regions to work properly.

These data columns can easily be inserted into Spry regions in several ways:

- **Dragged and dropped:** Drag any data column to any position with the Spry region. If the data column is dropped on a selection, the selection will be replaced.
- **Inserted:** Place your cursor where you'd like the selected data column to appear, and click Insert. As with the drag-and-drop method, any selected text or element will be replaced by the inserted data column.
- **Manually entered:** The proper code (the data column name surrounded by curly braces) can be entered by hand in either Design or Code view as long as it is entered within a Spry region.

TIP

For more complex pages involving multiple data sets, binding data requires a different syntax, like this: `{ds1::name}`. In the more complete syntax, the data set name precedes the data column name with double colons between the two elements.

A typical workflow might be to convert an existing layout with static, placeholder text to one that displays Spry data. In this workflow, you would attach the Spry XML Data Set, surround your intended data areas with Spry regions, and then begin replacing the placeholder text with Spry data columns.

Dragging or inserting works well when the data column is a text, number, or data type, but what if it is the path to an image file? If you've set the data column type to Image Link in the XML Spry Data Set dialog box, the data column is inserted within an <img>, like this:

```
<img src="{eventimage}"/>
```

To set the image src attribute for a Spry data column that has *not* been set as an Image Link type, follow these steps:

1. Place your cursor within the Spry region where you'd like your image to appear.
2. From the Common category of the Insert panel, choose Images: Image.
3. When the Select Image Source dialog box appears, change the Select File Name From option to Data Sources.
4. If necessary, expand the desired data set node.
5. Select the data column that contains the filename of the image, as shown in Figure 16-12.
6. If the images are stored in a folder different from the current page, enter the path to the folder in the URL field before the inserted code.
7. When you're done, click OK.

FIGURE 16-12

Any connected Spry Data Set can be accessed through the Select Image Source dialog box.

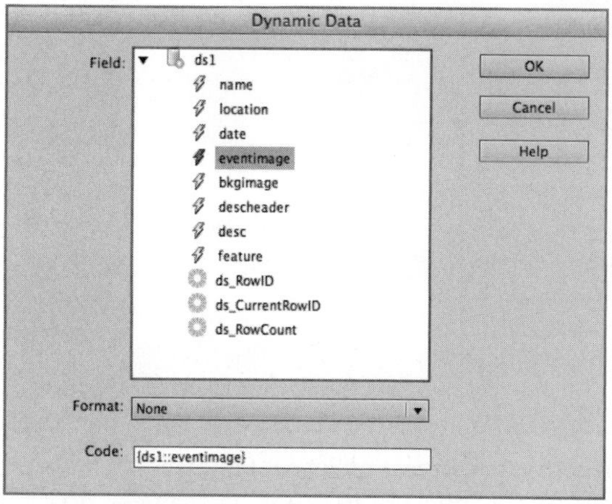

The methods covered so far will allow you to display a single set of data on the page. In the next section, you discover how to display all the data by setting up repeating Spry regions.

Repeating Spry regions

For Spry data regions to be truly effective, all the instances of the chosen data have to be displayed. Spry offers a number of methods for easily setting up your data to be repeated, including the Spry Repeat and Spry Repeat List objects. Both of these objects use either the `spry:repeat` or the `spry:repeatchildren` attribute, like this:

```
<div spry:repeat="ds1">
```

As with the `spry:region`, the `spry:repeat` attributes require the name of the data set to work with.

The Spry Repeat object is similar to Spry Region and is used when you want to insert a new `<div>` or `<span>` tag or wrap the current selection with either of these tags. To apply a Spry repeat region with the Spry Repeat object, follow these steps:

1. To add an empty Spry repeat tag, place your cursor where you'd like the region code to appear; to place a Spry repeat tag around existing content, select the desired content.
2. From the Spry or Data categories of the Insert panel, choose Spry Repeat. The Insert Spry Repeat dialog box appears, as shown in Figure 16-13.

FIGURE 16-13

To display all the data in an XML file, insert a Spry Repeat object.

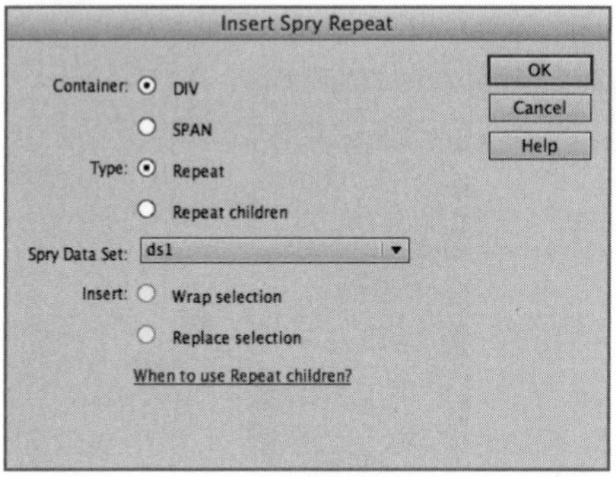

3. Select the type of tag you'd like to use—either DIV or SPAN—from the Container options.
4. Choose the type of attribute—Repeat or Repeat Children—from the Type options.

   When should you use Repeat and when Repeat Children? In most typical cases, they both display the same results. However, the `spry:repeatchildren` attribute is more flexible and robust and is recommended for situations where the data might be filtered or conditionally displayed. For more details on these scenarios, see the sidebar "Restricting Repeated Spry Data" later in this section.
5. Select the desired data set from the Spry Data Set list.
6. If you have a current selection, choose either the Wrap Selection or the Replace Selection option.
7. Click OK when you're done.

Like Spry Region, placeholder text is inserted if a new <div> or <span> tag is chosen. You'll need to delete the placeholder text and add any Spry data from the Binding panel and/or HTML tags you want repeated.

To repeat a table row, you'll need to add the `spry:repeat` or `spry:repeatchildren` attribute to the <tr> tag manually in Code view or through the Quick Tag Editor, like this:

```
<tr spry:repeatchildren = "ds1">
```

TIP

The Spry Repeat object works well to repeat enclosed <p> tags or data inline.

The Spry Repeat List object allows you to apply Spry repeat attributes to four different tag options: <ol>, <ul>, <dl>, and <select>. Unlike the Spry Repeat object, the Spry Repeat List object includes an option to select the data column you want to repeat; with the <dl> and <select> tags, you have the ability to select two separate data columns.

For those new to HTML, an <ol> tag is an ordered or numbered list; a <ul> tag is an unordered or bulleted list; a <dl> tag is a definition list; and a <select> tag is a drop-down form element. To learn more about the list tags, see Chapter 14, and for form tags, see Chapter 13.

To insert an <ol>, <ul>, <dl>, or <select> tag with a Spry repeat attribute, follow these steps:

1. Place your cursor where you'd like the tag to appear.
2. From the Spry or Data categories of the Insert panel, choose Spry Repeat List.

   The Insert Spry Repeat List object, showing the default options, appears (see Figure 16-14).

FIGURE 16-14

Choose from any of four different HTML tags to repeat in the Insert Spry Repeat List dialog box.

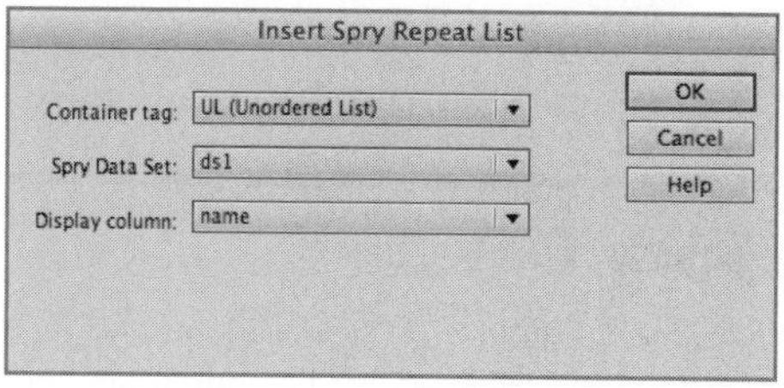

3. Select the desired tag from the Container Tag list.

   The available options change depending on the tag selected.
4. Choose your data set from the Spry Data Set list.

5. Select the options for your chosen tag:
   - If you chose a <ul> or <ol> tag, select the desired Spry data column from the Display Column list.
   - If you chose a <dl> tag, select the desired Spry data columns for both the <dt> and the <dd> tags from the DT Column and DD Column lists, respectively.
   - If you chose a <select> tag, select the desired Spry data columns for the labels and values from the Display Column and Value Column, respectively.
6. Click OK when you're done.

Dreamweaver inserts both the HTML tags and the Spry attributes. Although it's highly unlikely that you would include multiple tags in a single Spry region, it's entirely possible, as shown in Figure 16-15.

FIGURE 16-15

The same data can be presented in a multitude of ways through the Spry Repeat List object.

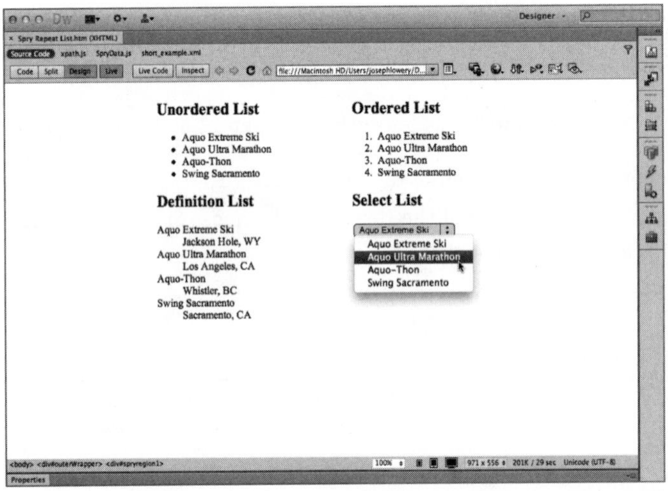

Restricting Repeated Spry Data

Use of either Spry repeat attribute returns all of the data in the associated XML data source. There are times you might want to limit or filter the data returned. Spry includes a couple of conditional attributes that you can use to restrict the data displayed: `spry:if` and `spry:choose`.

The `spry:if` attribute evaluates a JavaScript expression, which can include the Spry data column. If the expression evaluates to zero, the data is not shown. Here's an example that uses regular expressions to display only those data entries in the Spry name data column that start with an "A":

```
<li spry:if="'{name}'.search(/^a/) != -1;">{name}</li>
```

The `spry:if` attribute either displays the data or doesn't. To provide multiple responses—similar to an if/then clause—you can use the `spry:choose` attribute, like this:

```
<div spry:choose="spry:choose">
  <div spry:when="'{city}' == 'New York'">{name}</div>
  <div spry:when="'{city}' != 'New York'">No New York entries were found.
  </div>
</div>
```

For more details on Spry conditional coding, see `http://labs.adobe.com/technologies/spry/articles/data_set_overview/#ConditionalConstructsSection`.

Enhanced CSS for Spry

Because Spry uses JavaScript rather than standard links to make entire rows or columns clickable, the user's pointer does not automatically change to a hand to indicate a link. You can, however, add a `cursor:pointer` property to your CSS applied classes to compensate. This changes the user's mouse pointer to the hand symbol. To be backward compatible with earlier browsers, you'll need to include another `cursor` property with the value of `hand`, like this:

```
th {
  cursor: pointer;
  cursor: hand;
}
```

Dreamweaver TECHNIQUE

Adding Spry Data

The simplest way to incorporate Spry data into your web pages is to create an HTML data page and apply a Spry Data Set. This Dreamweaver Technique takes you through the necessary steps for adding Spry data to your page.

1. From the Techniques site, expand the 16_Spry folder and open the `spry_data_start` file.

   Click your cursor in the area below the opening paragraph.

2. From the Insert panel's Spry category, choose Spry Data Set.

Continues

continued

3. Leave the default data type (HTML) and data set name, ds1, and click Browse. In the Select XML Source dialog box, navigate to the 16_Spry folder and locate `properties_table.html`; click OK when you're ready.
4. Click the yellow arrow in the Data Selection area to choose the data on the page. Click Next.
5. In the Data Set Columns area, select Photo and choose html from the Data Type list. Select Bed and choose Number from the Data Type list. Repeat the same operation for Bath.
6. From the Sort list, choose Type.

   Now that the HTML data connection is established, let's set up the layout.

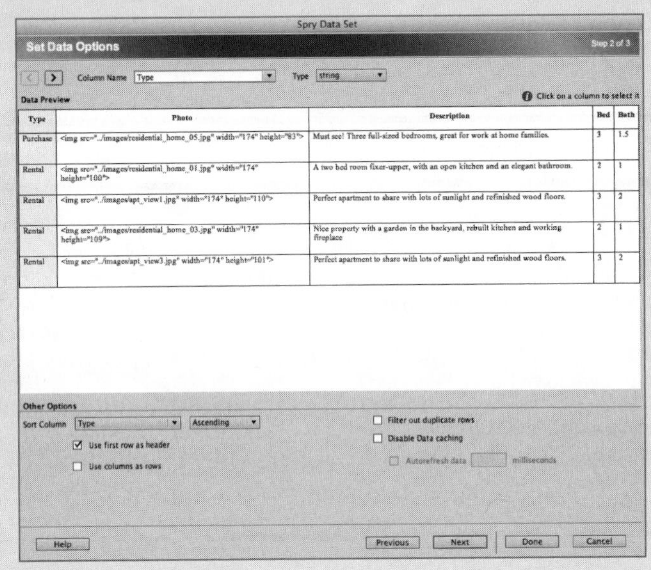

7. Click Next.
8. From the Choose Insert Options page, choose the Insert Stacked Containers With Spotlight Area option.
9. Click Set Up. When the Insert Spry Spotlight Layout dialog box appears, choose Add (+) in the Spotlight Columns area and select Photo from the Add Columns dialog box; click OK. With Photo selected, click Up to move this data column above Type. Select Type and change the Container Type to H2.
10. In the Stacked Columns section, select Photo and click Remove (–). Set the Container Type for Description to H2. For both Bed and Bath, set the Container Type to P.
11. Click OK to close the Insert Spry Spotlight Layout dialog box.
12. Click Done.

13. Place your cursor before the `{Bed}` variable and enter **Beds:**, followed by a space. Repeat the step to add **Baths:** (and a space) before the `{Bath}` variable.
14. Select Live View to preview your page.

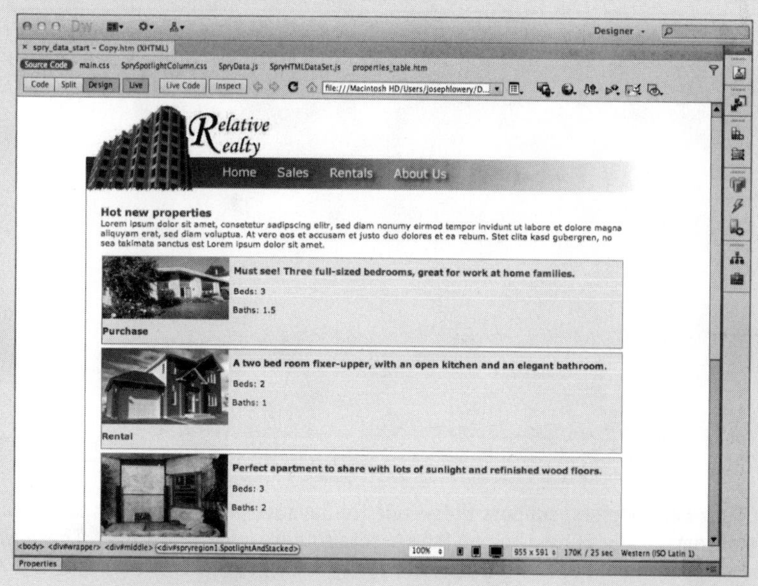

When the page is previewed, you'll see the HTML data displayed, complete with state-changing effects.

Enhancing Your Site with Spry Widgets

Spry is not limited to data manipulation. Another Spry implementation, called *widgets*, combines HTML, JavaScript, and CSS to produce advanced interactive layouts and form controls. Spry layout widgets bring sophisticated design options—such as pure CSS menus and tabbed panels—to the web professional's palette, whereas Spry form widgets solve one of the web's most persistent problems, form validation, brilliantly.

All Spry widgets share certain common characteristics. First, they are extremely easy to implement: typically, only a dragged-and-dropped object is required. Second, all widgets rely on a customized Property inspector to make Design view modifications a snap. Finally, each widget is completely customizable through associated CSS rules—it's easy to integrate widgets into the look and feel of any CSS-based site.

Another commonality that Spry widgets share is their representation in Design view: Each is contained by a blue border with an identifying tab, as shown in Figure 16-16, much like editable regions for Dreamweaver templates. To select any widget to modify the values of its Property inspector, click the blue tab.

FIGURE 16-16

Select a widget's blue tab to invoke its Property inspector.

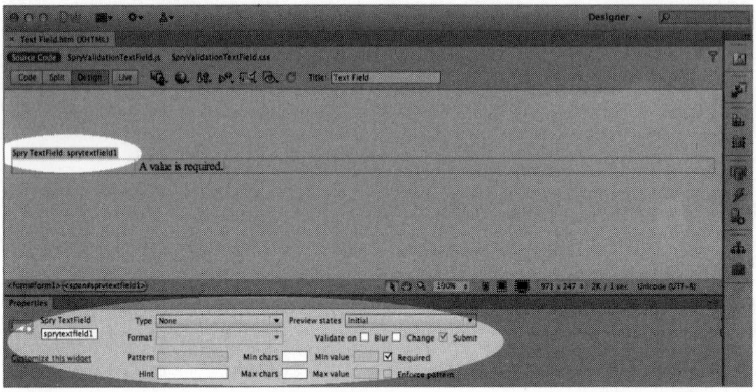

As with the Spry Data objects, support files—one for JavaScript and one for CSS for each Spry widget—are automatically copied to the SpryAssets folder in your site root. These files are required and must be uploaded to your live site along with your other web pages and assets.

For all their similarities, each of the Spry widgets offers a great deal of individual functionality. The following sections show you how you can maximize that functionality to get the most out of your pages, starting with the Spry form validation widgets.

Validating form fields

Validating form fields is like visiting the dentist: Everybody knows they've got to do it, but the experience is so stressful that avoidance comes easily. Form validations ensure that your site visitors are entering the right kind of data into your forms—an often critical requirement, especially if the data is being stored in a spreadsheet or database. The typical form validation method requires multiple steps for each form element: First, the form element must be added to the page, a client-side or server-side behavior added, and finally error messages applied. With the Spry form validation widgets, all of these tasks are included in a single step.

Because filling out a form is an interactive process, each of the Spry form widgets is capable of displaying different states; the number of states depends on the type of form element and the options chosen at design time. The custom Property inspector for each widget gives you the flexibility to switch between the various states at design time. For example, you could choose the Spry Validation Text Field widget's Invalid Format state to modify the error message and then switch to the Valid state to fine-tune the background-color property for a successful entry.

Another common feature among the Spry form widgets is the ability to apply the validation at multiple points in the process. By default, all the widgets automatically perform the requested validation when the user submits the form. Designers can also opt to perform the validation when the user clicks or tabs outside of a form field (`onBlur`) or when the value in the form field is altered (`onChange`).

CAUTION

It's important to understand that the name that appears in the Property inspector when the Spry validation widget is selected is not the name of the form element. The name of a form element is often a critical part of a web application. To name a form element within a Spry widget, click anywhere on the page outside of the widget and then click the form element itself; the Property inspector for the form element is now available and the name can be entered in the upper-left corner.

In all, there are seven different Spry widgets for various form elements: text field, textarea, checkbox, select, password, confirm, and radio group. Let's start our tour of them by taking a look at the Spry Validation Text Field first.

Spry Validation Text Field

The text field is arguably the most common form element because it can be used for so many different purposes. Whether you're gathering names, e-mail addresses, phone numbers, or even Social Security numbers, the text field is the perfect choice. Because of the wide range of types of information it is possible to enter into the text field, it requires the most varied range of validation. The Spry Validation Text Field offers 14 different types:

- None
- Integer
- Email Address
- Date
- Time
- Credit Card
- Zip Code
- Phone Number
- Social Security Number
- Currency
- Real Number/Scientific Notation
- IP Address
- URL
- Custom

Some of the validation types—date, time, credit card, ZIP code, phone number, currency, and IP address—include a range of formats to choose from as well, expanding the validation possibilities. Moreover, the custom validation option opens the door for web designers to specify any pattern of letters, numbers, and special characters.

To insert a Spry Validation Text Field widget, follow these steps:

1. Place your cursor where you'd like your text field to appear.

2. From the Spry or Forms categories of the Insert panel, choose Spry Validation Text Field.
3. If your Dreamweaver Preferences are set to display the accessibility attributes for form fields, the Input Form Accessibility Attributes dialog is displayed; click OK after you've completed the desired fields.
4. If your cursor is not within a <form> tag, Dreamweaver asks if you'd like to add one; click Yes.
5. From the Spry TextField Property inspector (see Figure 16-17), select the kind of validation to apply from the Type list.

FIGURE 16-17

Choose the kind of validation you'd like from the Type list.

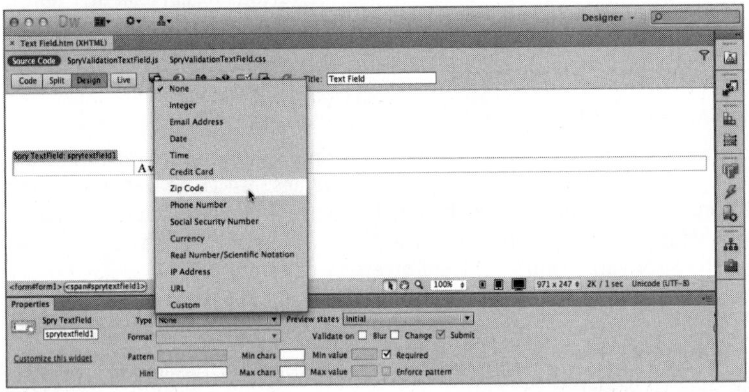

If you just want to make sure a text value of some kind is entered, leave the Type set to None and verify that the Required option is selected.

6. If you've chosen a validation type with a number of formats, choose the one you want from the Format list.
7. If you want the form field to check the validation prior to submitting the form, select the Validate On Blur or Change options. You can select both options but for text fields, validating on blur—after the user has tabbed or clicked away from the field—covers all possibilities, including whether or not the user has changed the entry.
8. Enter any text you want to appear as the default entry in the Hint field. When the user selects a text field with a hint in it, the hint is removed. This functionality allows you to prompt your user for the desired information.
9. Set any other available options for the chosen validation. Depending on the validation type chosen, you may be able to set the minimum and maximum number of characters, as well as the minimum and maximum value.
10. If you'd like the user to be able to enter only the desired characters, select the Enforce Pattern option. When the Enforce Pattern option is enabled, the user cannot enter invalid characters; the characters in the form field briefly flash red and the invalid character is discarded.

Creating Custom Validation Patterns

A number of the validation types or formats allow you to specify your own validation pattern. The Spry framework provides a range of special characters to establish a custom pattern, as detailed in the following table.

Character	Represents
0	Digits between 0 and 9
A or a	Case-sensitive upper- or lowercase alphabetic characters
B or b	Case-insensitive upper- or lowercase alphabetic characters
X or x	Case-sensitive upper- or lowercase alphanumeric characters
Y or y	Case-insensitive upper- or lowercase alphanumeric characters
?	Any character

For example, if you wanted to specify a telephone number with a format like (212) 555-1212, you would enter (000) 000-0000 in the Pattern field of the Property inspector with the Format set to Custom Pattern. If the Enforce Pattern option is selected, the open parenthesis appears after the first number is entered and the other non-numeric characters appear as the user enters the numbers; non-numbers are not accepted.

NOTE

When a Spry Validation Text Field is on the page, when the user saves the file, a notice appears regarding the supporting files as with the Spry data objects. Here, the files copied to the local root that need to be posted online are `SpryValidationTextField.css` and `SpryValidationTextField.js`.

After you've set the validation options for the text field, you can customize the various states. The Spry Validation Text Field widget offers up to four different states:

- **Initial:** The default state of the text field; if a Hint has been specified, it is shown within the text field in the Initial state.
- **Required:** Displays an error message if no value has been entered into the field when validated.
- **Invalid Format:** Displays an error message if an invalid value has been entered into the field when validated.
- **Valid:** Shown when the entry has passed validation.

To switch from one state to another, choose a different entry from the Preview States list in the Property inspector. When you do, Design view changes to reveal or hide the possible error messages and CSS styling. You can easily modify any displayed message, as shown in Figure 16-18.

FIGURE 16-18

Customize your error messages by first changing the Preview state.

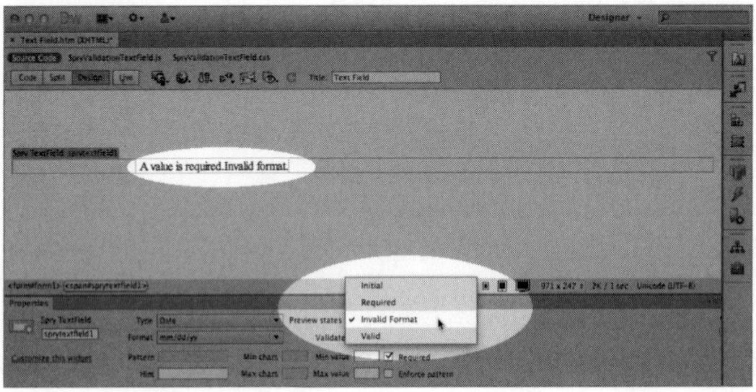

It's just as easy to customize the CSS for any portion of the validated form field such as the border around the error message or the background color of the valid entry. Simply switch to the desired state, place your cursor in the text you want to re-style, and choose the CSS button in the Property inspector. The first time you select the CSS button, the CSS Styles panel opens in Current mode, with all the properties of the currently selected element available. Make any desired updates and save the external CSS file to store your changes.

Using Validation Widgets with Tables

Many designers use two- or three-column tables to keep their forms neat and tidy—and you'll need to do a little code manipulation to get Spry Validation widgets to fit within that structure. Say that you have a three-column table, with the first column intended for labels, the second for the form field, and the third for validation error messages. The best technique that I have discovered for integrating Spry Validation widgets into such a table is to begin by placing the widget in the middle cell of the row. Assuming you have a label in the first column, your code will look like this:

```
<tr>
  <td>Name:</td>
  <td><span id="sprytextfield1">
    <input type="text" name="text1" id="text1" />
  <span class="textfieldRequiredMsg">A value is required.</span></span></td>
  <td> </td>
</tr>
```

Next, move the `id` attribute, here `id="sprytextfield1"`, from the outer <span> tag to the <tr> tag. Then, delete the outer <span> tags; because you've identified the entire row with the Spry ID, these are no longer necessary. Finally, move the <span> tag with the required message to the third column. Your final code will look like this:

```
<tr id="sprytextfield1">
  <td>Name:</td>
```

```
    <td><input type="text" name="text1" id="text1" /></td>
    <td><span class="textfieldRequiredMsg">A value is required.</span></td>
</tr>
```

Unfortunately, this rearrangement of the code causes the Spry Property inspector not to be shown, so I recommended that all adjustments to the widget take place prior to moving the code.

Spry Validation Textarea

The textarea form element is used to gather any amount of text, from a couple of words to several paragraphs. Because the textarea is open to accept any type of input, there is no validation type as with the text field. However, it is not uncommon for the number of characters to be limited in some fashion, either with a minimum, a maximum, or both. The Spry Validation Textarea widget easily handles these requirements—and with a great deal of flair.

The Spry Validation Textarea widget can easily make the textarea field required through a Property inspector option. You can specify the number of characters desired: minimum, maximum, or both. Any attempt to enter text beyond the maximum characters can be blocked. To help the user keep track, you can add a counter to show either the number of characters entered or the number remaining.

To insert a Spry Validation Textarea widget, follow these steps:

1. Place your cursor where you'd like your textarea to appear.
2. From the Spry or Forms categories of the Insert panel, choose Spry Validation Textarea.
3. If your Dreamweaver Preferences are set to display the accessibility attributes for form fields, the Input Form Accessibility Attributes dialog is displayed; click OK after you've completed the appropriate fields.
4. If your cursor is not within a `<form>` tag, Dreamweaver asks if you'd like to add one; click Yes.
5. In the Spry Textarea Property inspector (see Figure 16-19), choose whether the field should be required by setting or clearing the Required checkbox.
6. If you want the form field to check the validation prior to submitting the form, select the Validate On Blur or Change options.
7. To restrict the number of characters entered, set the minimum and/or maximum number of characters in the Min Chars and Max Chars fields, respectively.
8. To add a counter showing the number of characters entered into the field, select the Counter: Chars Count option; to add a counter showing the number of characters that can still be entered, select the Counter: Chars Remaining option. You need to enter a value in the Max Chars field to enable the Counter: Chars Remaining option.
9. If you've set a maximum number of characters and want to prohibit the user from entering any additional characters, select the Block Extra Characters option.

NOTE

When you save your file the first time after adding a Spry Validation Textfield widget, Dreamweaver will notify you of the supporting files: `SpryValidationTextarea.css` **and** `SpryValidationTextarea.js`.

FIGURE 16-19

Limit the number of characters—minimum, maximum, or both—with the Spry Validation Textarea widget.

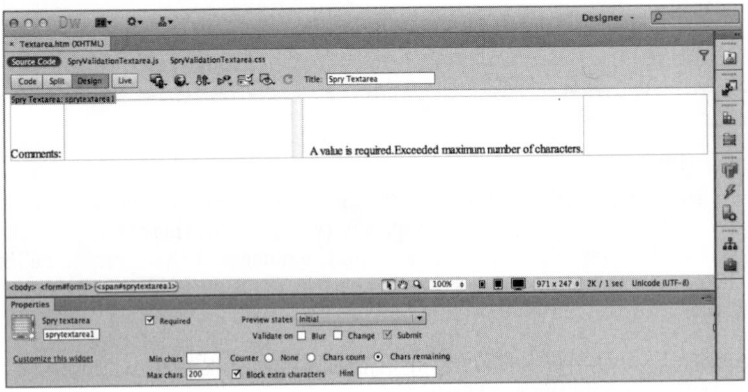

Depending on your Property inspector settings, the Spry Validation Textarea widget provides up to five different states:

- **Initial:** The default state of the text field; if a Hint has been specified, it is shown within the textarea field in the Initial state.
- **Required:** Displays an error message if no value has been entered into the field when validated.
- **Min. # Of Chars Not Met:** Available if a value is entered in the Min Chars field of the Property inspector, and displays an error message if the current character count is less than the minimum.
- **Exceeded Max. # Of Chars:** Available if a value is entered in the Max Chars field of the Property inspector, and displays an error message if the current character count is greater than the minimum.
- **Valid:** Shown when the entry has passed validation.

As with the other form validation widgets, you can switch from one state to another by selecting a different entry from the Preview States list in the Property inspector. This action exposes the possible error messages and CSS styling for each state so you can modify them if desired, as shown in Figure 16-20.

TIP

The counter feature of the Spry Validation Textarea widget really helps with usability. However, both the Chars Count and the Chars Remaining options simply add a number without any identifying text. To add a label to the counter, switch to Code view and search for `<span id="countsprytextarea1">`. Place a label, such as **Characters used:**, before this span tag, not within it.

FIGURE 16-20

Set a countdown counter so that your visitors will know exactly how many more characters they can add to a Spry Validation Textarea widget.

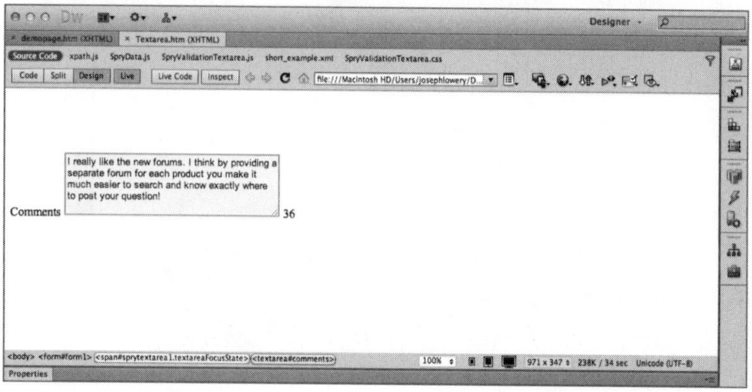

Spry Validation Select

Select lists, also known as drop-down menus, provide the user with a number of choices to choose from. Validating a select list typically means ensuring that the user makes a choice—and the Spry Validation Select widget handles this chore well. Additionally, you can even make sure the user does not select a separator or other invalid choice.

> **TIP**
>
> The Spry Validation Select widget does not provide a field in the Property inspector for adding a hint, but you can set up your first option with a blank value to achieve the same effect.

To insert a Spry Validation Select widget, follow these steps:

1. Place your cursor where you'd like your select list to appear.
2. From the Spry or Forms categories of the Insert panel, choose Spry Validation Select.
3. If your Dreamweaver Preferences are set to display the accessibility attributes for form fields, the Input Form Accessibility Attributes dialog box is displayed; click OK after you've completed the desired fields.
4. If your cursor is not within a `<form>` tag, Dreamweaver asks if you'd like to add one; click Yes.
5. From the Spry Select Property inspector (see Figure 16-21), choose whether a choice should be required by setting or clearing the Blank Value checkbox.

   For the Blank Value option to work properly, you'll need to include one option, typically the top one, with no value, like this:

   ```
   <option value="" selected="selected">Make a choice</option>
   ```

FIGURE 16-21

Force the user to make a choice with the Spry Validation Select widget.

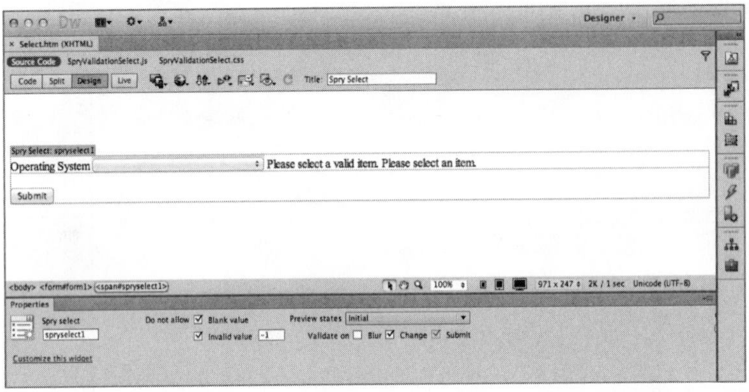

6. If you want the form field to check the validation prior to submitting the form, select the Validate On Blur or Change options.
7. If your form includes separators or other non-meaningful choices, select the Invalid Value option and set the value to restrict in the adjacent field.

   The Invalid Value option is intended to prohibit users from selecting options like this one:

```
<option value="-1">-----------------------------</option>
```

NOTE

When you save your file the first time after adding a Spry Validation Select widget, Dreamweaver will notify you of the supporting files: `SpryValidationSelect.css` **and** `SpryValidationSelect.js`.

Depending on your Property inspector settings, the Spry Validation Select widget provides up to four different states:

- **Initial:** The default state of the text field.
- **Required:** Displays an error message if the Blank Value option has been selected and no choice has been made.
- **Invalid:** Displays an error message if the Invalid Value option has been selected and the user has selected an entry with the designated improper value.
- **Valid:** Shown when the entry has passed validation.

As with the other form validation widgets, you switch from one state to another by selecting a different entry from the Preview States list in the Property inspector. This action exposes the possible error messages and CSS stylings for each state so you can modify them if desired.

Spry Validation Checkbox

Spry Validation Checkbox can be used with a single checkbox if it is required or with multiple checkboxes to control the number selected. An individual required checkbox is often used to certify that the site visitor has read and agrees to a statement, typically legal in nature, like the terms of use. Multiple checkbox validation comes into play when the application requires that the visitor select a number of options within a certain range.

To insert a Spry Validation Checkbox widget, follow these steps:

1. Place your cursor where you'd like your validation checkbox to appear.
2. From the Spry or Forms categories of the Insert panel, choose Spry Validation Checkbox.
3. If your Dreamweaver Preferences are set to display the accessibility attributes for form fields, the Input Form Accessibility Attributes dialog box is displayed; click OK after you've completed the appropriate fields.
4. If your cursor is not within a `<form>` tag, Dreamweaver asks if you'd like to add one; click Yes.
5. From the Spry Checkbox Property inspector (see Figure 16-22), choose whether you want to validate a single checkbox or multiple checkboxes by selecting the Required or Enforce Range option, respectively.

FIGURE 16-22

Single checkboxes can be required with the Spry Validation Checkbox widget.

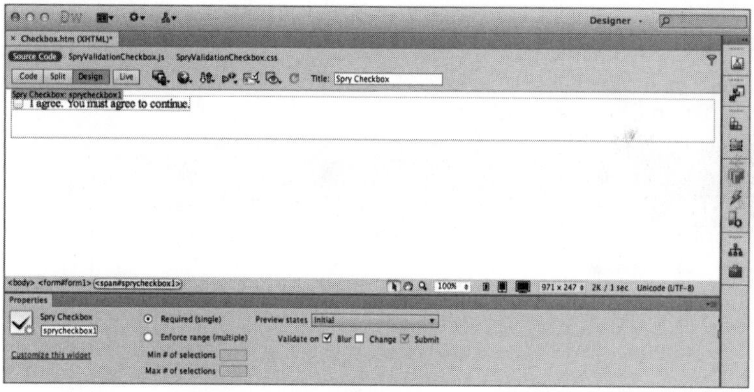

6. If you want the form field to check the validation prior to submitting the form, select the Validate On Blur or Change options.
7. If you chose the Enforce Range option, enter either the minimum number of choices in the Min. # Of Selections field or the maximum number in the Max. # Of Selections field, or both.

NOTE

When you save your file the first time after adding a Spry Validation Checkbox widget, Dreamweaver will notify you of the supporting files: `SpryValidationCheckbox.css` and `SpryValidationCheckbox.js`.

Depending on your Property inspector settings, the Spry Validation Checkbox widget provides up to four different states:

- **Initial:** The default state of the text field.
- **Required:** Displays an error message if the Required option has been selected and the checkbox is unchecked.
- **Min. # Of Selections Not Met:** Displays an error message if the Enforce Range option has been selected and the current number of selected checkboxes is less than the minimum specified.
- **Max. # Of Selections Exceeded:** Displays an error message if the Enforce Range option has been selected and the current number of selected checkboxes is more than the maximum specified.

As with the other form validation widgets, you switch from one state to another by selecting a different entry from the Preview States list in the Property inspector. This action exposes the possible error messages and CSS stylings for each state so you can modify them if desired.

If you're working with multiple checkboxes, once you've inserted the Spry Validation Checkbox widget, all the other checkboxes entered should be standard ones, as shown in Figure 16-23. Also, you'll want to make sure that all inserted checkboxes are within the `<span id="sprycheckbox">` tag.

FIGURE 16-23

To validate multiple checkboxes, use standard Dreamweaver checkboxes after the inserted Spry Validation Checkbox widget.

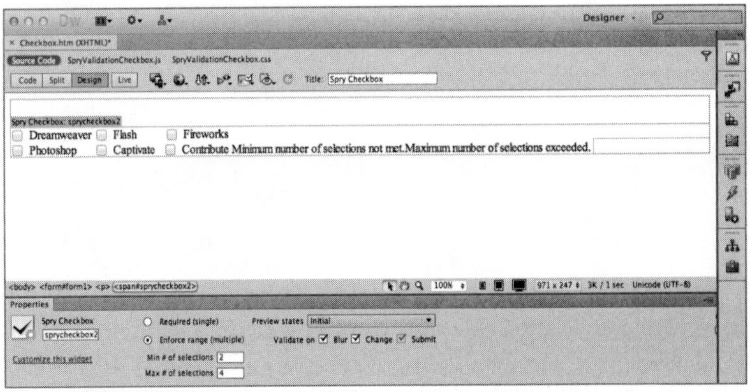

Spry Validation Password

A password form field is a special type of text field where the entered characters are hidden with asterisks or bullets. A Spry Validation Password widget allows you to specify the degree or strength of the accepted password. You can, for example, set a minimum number of characters that must contain a certain number of letters (a defined number of them uppercase), numbers, and special characters. Error messages are available to indicate whether a minimum has been reached or a maximum has been exceeded. The degree of control available in the Spry Validation Password widget makes it the perfect entry for forms initially establishing a password; if the password is just being entered, you can simply use the required option and check your password as you would normally.

To insert a Spry Validation Password widget, follow these steps:

1. Place your cursor where you'd like your password field to appear.
2. From the Spry or Forms categories of the Insert panel, choose Spry Validation Password.
3. If your Dreamweaver Preferences are set to display the accessibility attributes for form fields, the Input Form Accessibility Attributes dialog box is displayed; click OK after you've completed the appropriate fields.
4. If your cursor is not within a <form> tag, Dreamweaver asks if you'd like to add one; click Yes.
5. From the Spry Password Property inspector (see Figure 16-24), choose whether the field should be required by setting or clearing the Required checkbox.

FIGURE 16-24

Set the required strength of a new password with the Spry Validation Password widget.

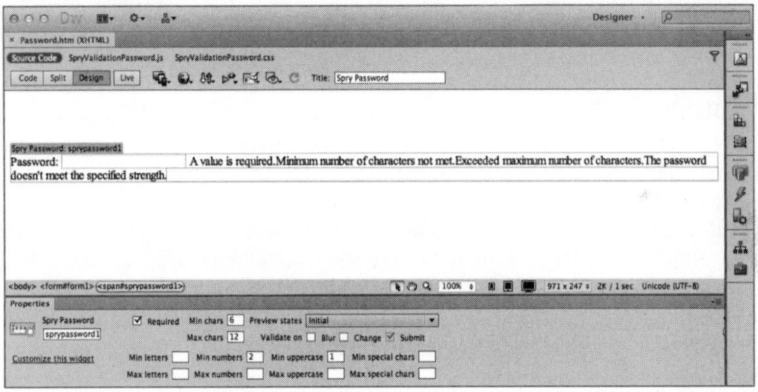

6. If you want the form field to check the validation prior to submitting the form, select the Validate On Blur or Change options.
7. If you want to restrict the number of characters entered, set the minimum and/or maximum number of characters in the Min Chars and Max Chars fields, respectively.
8. Optionally, set minimum and maximum values for letters, numbers, uppercase, and special characters.

Depending on your Property inspector settings, the Spry Validation password widget provides up to six different states:

- **Initial:** The default state of the text field; if a Hint has been specified, it is shown within the text field in the Initial state.
- **Required:** Displays an error message if no value has been entered into the field when validated.

- **Invalid Strength:** Available if a value is entered in any of the optional fields for minimum and maximum letters, numbers, uppercase, and special characters.
- **Min. # Of Chars Not Met:** Available if a value is entered in the Min Chars field of the Property inspector, and displays an error message if the current character count is less than the minimum.
- **Exceeded Max. # Of Chars:** Available if a value is entered in the Max Chars field of the Property inspector, and displays an error message if the current character count is greater than the minimum.
- **Valid:** Shown when the entry has passed validation.

As with the other form validation widgets, you can switch from one state to another by selecting a different entry from the Preview States list in the Property inspector. This action exposes the possible error messages and CSS stylings for each state so you can modify them if desired. If you've activated the Invalid Strength error message, it's a good idea to be as specific as possible in your error message to make sure visitors know what is required.

NOTE

When you save your file the first time after adding a Spry Validation Password widget, Dreamweaver will notify you of the supporting files: `SpryValidationPassword.css` **and** `SpryValidationPassword.js`.

Spry Validation Confirm

Some data is absolutely essential to get right, like a password or an e-mail address being entered for the first time. The Spry Validation Confirm widget is perfect for such a task. Best of all, it's extremely easy to set up. Just drop it on the page and point to the form field already on the page you'd like the entry in the Spry Validation Confirm field compared to. If the fields match, it passes validation, otherwise an error message is displayed. You can use the Spry Validation Confirm widget in combination with regular or Spry text or password fields.

To insert a Spry Validation Confirm widget, follow these steps:

1. Place your cursor where you'd like your confirm field to appear.
2. From the Spry or Forms categories of the Insert panel, choose Spry Validation Confirm.
3. If your Dreamweaver Preferences are set to display the accessibility attributes for form fields, the Input Form Accessibility Attributes dialog box is displayed; click OK after you've completed the appropriate fields.
4. If your cursor is not within a `<form>` tag, Dreamweaver asks if you'd like to add one; click Yes.
5. From the Spry Confirm Property inspector (see Figure 16-25), choose whether the field should be required by setting or clearing the Required checkbox.
6. If you want the form field to check the validation prior to submitting the form, select the Validate On Blur or Change options.
7. From the Validate Against list, choose the field you want to compare.

   Dreamweaver displays a list of currently available fields in the order they appear on the page and initially selects the field directly above the confirm field. This follows the typical use case for a confirmation field.

FIGURE 16-25

Compare one field to another with the Spry Validation Confirm widget.

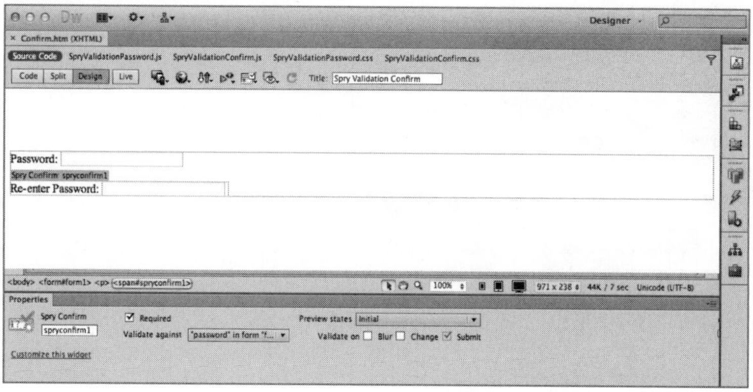

Depending on your Property inspector settings, the Spry Validation Confirm widget provides up to four different states:

- **Initial:** The default state of the text field; if a Hint has been specified, it is shown within the textarea field in the Initial state.
- **Required:** Displays an error message if no value has been entered into the field when validated.
- **Invalid:** Displays an error message if the values entered in the two designated fields do not match.
- **Valid:** Shown when the entry has passed validation.

> **NOTE**
> When you save your file the first time after adding a Spry Validation Confirm widget, Dreamweaver will notify you of the supporting files: `SpryValidationConfirm.css` and `SpryValidationConfirm.js`.

Spry Validation Radio Group

The Spry Validation Radio Group is very similar to the standard Dreamweaver radio group. The same dialog box is used to define new radio buttons, and they can be grouped in similar ways, either separated by a line break or inserted in a table. Unlike the standard radio group, however, the Spry Validation Radio Group displays an error message if no choice or the incorrect choice is made. Radio groups are used to get a mutually exclusive choice in a form and are often established with no preference displayed. The Spry Validation Radio Group allows the designer to include an invalid response, like None, initially chosen, which would throw an error if left selected.

To insert a Spry Validation Radio Group widget, follow these steps:

1. Place your cursor where you'd like your radio group field to appear.
2. From the Spry or Forms categories of the Insert panel, choose Spry Validation Radio Group.

   The Spry Validation Radio Group dialog box appears (see Figure 16-26).

FIGURE 16-26

Add as many radio buttons as needed in the Spry Validation Radio Group.

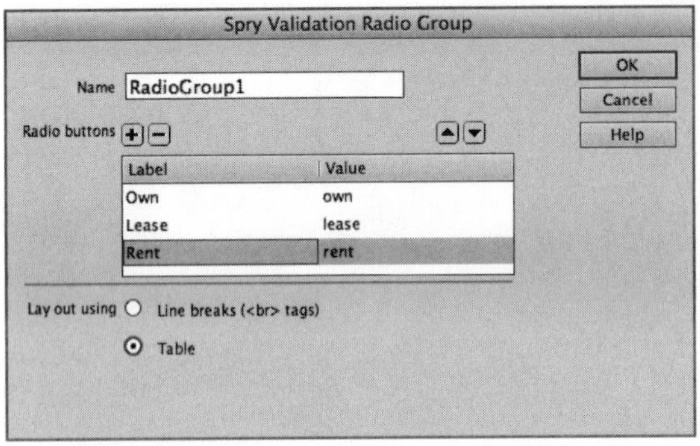

3. In the Name text box, replace the default name with a meaningful name for your new set of radio buttons.
4. Each entry in the list represents a separate radio button in the group; the dialog box opens with two filler buttons as an example. Click the first entry in the Label list and replace the word Radio with the label for the first button in your group. Press Tab to move to the Value column, and replace the default with the appropriate value for your button; this is the data that is sent to the server when the radio button is selected.

   Repeat this step for the second radio button in your set.
5. If you have more than two radio buttons in your set, click the Add (+) button to add another item to the list and fill out the appropriate value, as explained in Step 3.
6. Specify whether you want your radio buttons inserted on separate lines using the `<br>` tag, or automatically formatted in a table.
7. Click OK.
8. From the Spry Confirm Property inspector, choose whether the field should be required by setting or clearing the Required checkbox.
9. If you want the form field to check the validation prior to submitting the form, select the Validate On Blur or Change options.
10. If you want an error message to appear when an empty value has been chosen, enter the value of the radio button in the Empty field.
11. If you want an error message to appear when an invalid value has been chosen, enter the value of the radio button in the Invalid field.

For both Empty and Invalid validation to work properly, you need to make sure that the radio button and the corresponding field in the Property inspector match. For example, if you have a radio button with the label Please Make A Choice and give it a value of 0, you might enter a 0 in the Invalid field of the Spry Radio Group Property inspector.

NOTE

When you save your file the first time after adding a Spry Validation Radio widget, Dreamweaver will notify you of the supporting files: `SpryValidationRadio.css` and `SpryValidationRadio.js`.

Extending layout options

Designers are always on the hunt for an innovative way to improve the layout of their web pages—and the Spry layout widgets are ready to be put to work. These five widgets—Spry Menu Bar, Spry Tabbed Panel, Spry Accordion, Spry Collapsible Panel, and Spry Tooltip—greatly expand the designer's layout palette. Take a look at the kind of flexibility now built into Dreamweaver:

- Standards-based navigation bars capable of supporting multiple levels in either vertical or horizontal orientation.
- A series of interconnected tabs, each with their own content area, easy to switch from one to the other.
- Multiple sliding panels that interact with one another: Slide one area open and the other areas close.
- Individual pods in which the content can be hidden or revealed under user control.
- Fully customizable tooltips can appear—with fade or other effects—wherever additional, optional content is needed, not just on links.

All of the Spry layout widgets use advanced JavaScript and CSS techniques; like the form widgets, each requires a pair of external files that must be placed online. The layout widgets are just as easy to implement and configure, too. Once dropped on the page, any layout widget can be quickly modified through the custom Property inspector. Better still, for those widgets that involve multiple content areas, Dreamweaver is capable of showing tabs or panels individually in Design view. Layout widgets are fully customizable as well, so designers can totally make these sophisticated layout options their own.

Spry Menu Bar

Standards-based navigation bars have a number of advantages: They load very quickly, they're more accessible than graphics-based navigation, and they're very easy to label. However, they have one major disadvantage: They're very difficult to code correctly. The Spry Menu Bar in Dreamweaver dispenses with the downside with its instantaneous drag-and-drop application, while keeping all the upsides—and even adding some more.

A standards-based menu bar typically uses unordered list tags (a.k.a. bullets) that have been heavily styled with CSS to achieve multilevel navigation. The Spry Menu Bar widget can be applied horizontally or vertically and offers a main navigation level with up to two levels of drop-down or fly-out submenus. Once the widget is placed on the page, the custom Property inspector provides an intuitive way to adjust the menu in any way you'd desire. You can add more main or submenu items, re-label them, add appropriate links, restyle, and even add tooltips.

To add a Spry Menu Bar to your page, follow these steps:

1. Place your cursor where you'd like your menu bar to appear.

2. From the Spry or Layout categories of the Insert panel, choose Spry Menu Bar.
3. When the Spry Menu Bar dialog box opens, choose either Horizontal or Vertical to set the orientation of your navigation bar; click OK. Dreamweaver inserts the initial navigation bar and displays the custom Property inspector. The default horizontal menu bar is shown in Figure 16-27.

FIGURE 16-27

After you choose your navigation bar's orientation, the default Spry Menu Bar is added to the page.

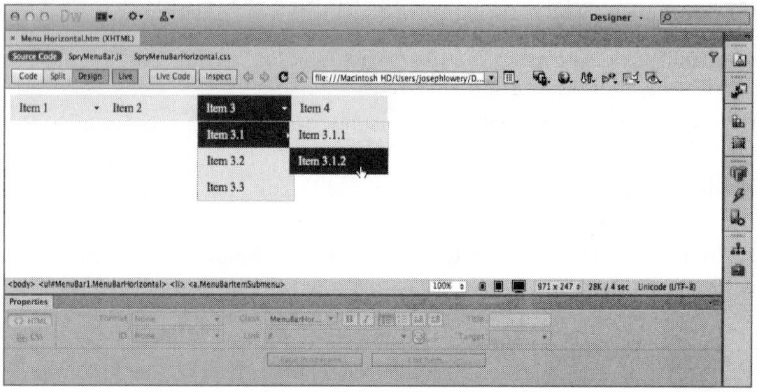

4. To change the label for any menu item, select the Spry Menu Bar and then in the Property inspector enter a new value in the Text field. You can also modify the displayed text directly in Design view. To reveal other menu items, select their entry in the Property inspector.
5. To create a link, select the menu item in the Property inspector and enter the path in the Link field or use the Browse folder to select the file.
6. To add a tooltip to a menu item, select it and enter the text for the tooltip in the Title field.
7. To specify a target for a menu item link, select the menu item and enter the target keyword or name in the Target field. Standard keywords for targets include `_blank`, `_parent`, `_top`, and `_self`. You can also enter a frame name.

TIP

A great way to quickly modify your menu labels, links, and structure in Design view is to select the Turn Styles Off button in the Spry Menu Bar widget Property inspector. With the styles off, you'll see just the unordered list and can make any necessary edits very simply.

To adjust a main menu or submenu item, follow these steps:

1. To add a new main menu item, choose Add (+) above the first column in the Property inspector.

New menu items are added with the label Untitled Item; modify the label in the Text field.

2. To add a submenu item, select the parent menu item and choose Add (+) above the second or third column.
3. To remove a menu item, select it in the Property inspector and choose Remove (–). If the menu item has any associated submenus, Dreamweaver asks for a confirmation before deleting; click OK to remove the menu item and its children.
4. To change the order of a menu item, select it and choose the up or down arrow in the current column.

NOTE

As with the form widgets, the first time you save a file with a Spry Menu Bar widget, Dreamweaver lets you know which supporting files have been copied to your site and will need to be posted online. There are different support files for the horizontal and vertical menus bars.

Vertical menus (see Figure 16-28) are just as simple to create and modify. Once they are inserted, you can easily change the labels and links, either through the Spry Menu Bar widget Property inspector or, once the menu item is visible, directly in Design view.

FIGURE 16-28

Put a menu on the side of any page with the Spry Menu Bar widget.

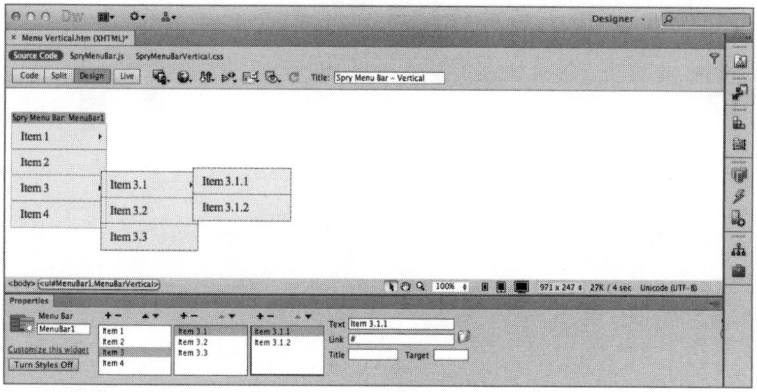

Modifying the CSS of a Spry layout widget is somewhat more involved than changing a form widget's style, but still is quite possible. The key is knowing which styles to adjust. One technique that works for me is to select the text in the menu item you want to adjust and then open the CSS Styles panel in Current mode. If the CSS property you want to modify is not found in the Summary panel, select the next tag to the left of the current one in the Tag Selector. This action effectively walks up the DOM. Continue moving up the DOM until you find the desired property in the CSS Styles panel and make your modification.

TIP

Spry also includes a number of pseudo-classes to handle various link states, like `:hover` and `:visited`. If defined, you'll find these listed in the Rules pane.

Spry Tabbed Panel

The Spry Tabbed Panels are a terrific way to pack a lot of content into a small amount of space. With a tabbed panel, the site visitor sees a series of tabs when the page first loads, with one of the tab's contents displayed; a single click allows the user to switch to any other tab. The Spry Tabbed Panel widget is just as easy to set up and customize as the previous widgets.

To add a Spry Tabbed Panel widget to your page, follow these steps:

1. Place your cursor where you'd like your tabbed panel to appear.
2. From the Spry or Layout categories of the Insert panel, choose Spry Tabbed Panel Bar.

   The default tabbed panel, with two tabs, is inserted into the page, and the custom Property inspector (see Figure 16-29) is displayed.

FIGURE 16-29

A Spry Tabbed Panel widget expands to the width of its container.

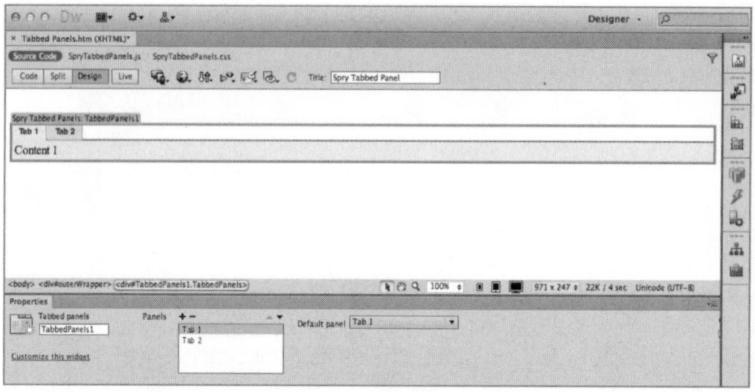

3. To increase the number of tabs, select the Spry widget and from the Property inspector choose Add (+).

   The new tab is inserted below the currently selected entry.
4. To remove a previously inserted tab, choose Remove (–).
5. To change the order of the tabs, select any tab and use the Up and Down buttons to adjust the tab position.

   Tabs nearer to the top in the Property inspector are, in Design view, positioned to the left of the tabs beneath them.
6. To set the tab initially shown when the page loads, select the tab name from the Default list.

NOTE

As expected, the first time you save a file with a Spry Tabbed Panel widget, Dreamweaver lets you know of the supporting files that have been copied to your site and will need to be posted online. The Spry Tabbed Panel widget relies on two supporting files: `SpryTabbedPanels.js` and `SpryTabbedPanels.css`.

All modifications to the tab labels and content areas are performed directly in Design view. If you want to change the label on a tab, simply select the text and replace it; the custom Property inspector recognizes your new name. To add content, replace the placeholder phrase with your own material. Anything you can put on a web page, you can put in a tab.

To switch to a different tab, you can select the tab entry in the Property inspector. For a more design-centric focus, move your mouse over the currently unexposed tab. When the eye icon appears on the right of the tab (see Figure 16-30), click the tab to bring it forward for styling or adding content.

FIGURE 16-30

The eye icon indicates that Dreamweaver is ready to switch to hidden content areas in Spry widgets such as the Tabbed Panel.

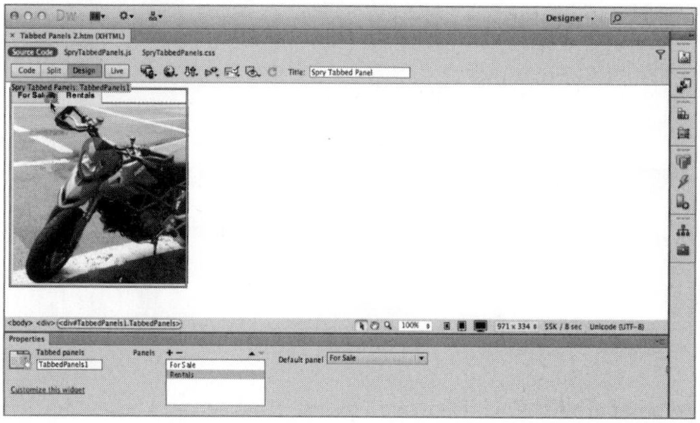

Spry Accordion Panel

If tabbed panels were a popular television show, the spin-off could be called "Spry Accordion: The Next Generation." Like tabbed panels, an accordion panel layout is great for containing a good deal of information in a tighter space. Unlike tabbed panels, however, the label portion for an accordion panel runs the full width of the panel and, when selected, smoothly slides open to reveal the content. Spry Accordion Panel widgets, for all their slickness, are extremely easy to incorporate into a page and just as easy to customize.

TIP

Unlike with the Spry Tabbed Panel, there's no way to change the default panel in the Property inspector. The top panel is always open by default.

To add a Spry Accordion Panel widget to your page, follow these steps:

1. Place your cursor where you'd like your accordion panel to appear.
2. From the Spry or Layout categories of the Insert panel, choose Spry Accordion Panel Bar.

   The default accordion panel, with two tabs, is inserted into the page and the custom Property inspector (see Figure 16-31) displays.

FIGURE 16-31

When a Spry Accordion Panel is selected, it smoothly glides open.

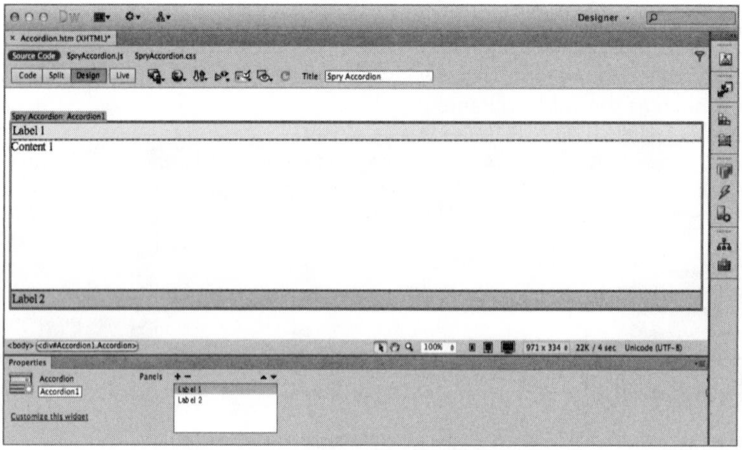

3. To increase the number of panels, from the Property inspector choose Add (+).

   The new tab is inserted below the currently selected entry.
4. To remove a previously inserted panel, choose Remove (–).
5. To change the order of the panel, select any tab and use the Up and Down buttons to adjust the panel position.

   Panels nearer to the top in the Property inspector are, in Design view, positioned to the left of the panels beneath them.

NOTE

Like the other widgets, the first time you save a file with a Spry Accordion Panel widget, Dreamweaver tells you of the supporting files that have been copied to your site and will need to be posted online. The Spry Accordion Panel widget relies on two supporting files: `SpryAccordion.js` and `SpryAccordion.css`.

If you take a look at the HTML code for the Spry Accordion Panel, you'll see that it is essentially a series of nested <div> tags:

```
<div id="Accordion1" class="Accordion" tabindex="0">
  <div class="AccordionPanel">
    <div class="AccordionPanelTab">Label 1</div>
    <div class="AccordionPanelContent">Content 1</div>
  </div>
  <div class="AccordionPanel">
    <div class="AccordionPanelTab">Label 2</div>
    <div class="AccordionPanelContent">Content 2</div>
  </div>
</div>
```

The real magic comes from the attached JavaScript script and the script tag at the bottom of the page that initializes the accordion object:

```
<script type="text/javascript">
<!--
var Accordion1 = new Spry.Widget.Accordion("Accordion1");
//-->
</script>
```

Modifications to the accordion panel labels and content areas are, like the tabbed panels, performed directly in Design view. To change the label on a panel, select the text and replace it. To add any content, remove the placeholder phrase and insert your material. Again, you can switch from one panel to another via the Property inspector or by choosing the eye icon in Design view.

Spry Collapsible Panel

A Spry Collapsible Panel is, in a sense, a single accordion panel. The same style of layout is used with the label placed in the full-width top tab and, when clicked, it collapses or expands. Because there is no other associated panel, only the tab remains when the panel collapses. The panel can be either open or closed when the page is initially displayed.

To add a Spry Collapsible Panel widget to your page, follow these steps:

1. Place your cursor where you'd like your collapsible panel to appear.
2. From the Insert panel's Spry or Layout category, choose Spry Collapsible Panel Bar. The default collapsible panel is inserted into the page and the custom Property inspector (see Figure 16-32) displays.
3. To set the panel to be open when the page loads, choose Open from the Default State list; to set the panel to be collapsed, choose Closed.

NOTE

As with the other widgets, the first time you save a file with a Spry Collapsible Panel widget, Dreamweaver tells you of the supporting files that have been copied to your site and will need to be posted online. The Spry Collapsible Panel widget relies on two supporting files: `SpryCollapsiblePanel.js` and `SpryCollapsiblePanel.css`.

Because the Spry Collapsible Panel widget can be either open or closed when the web page loads, Dreamweaver lets you control that condition. From the Collapsible Panel Property inspector, you can choose either Open or Closed from the Display list. This feature also makes it easy to edit or style content. As with Tabbed and Accordion Panel widgets, you also have the option to select the eye icon that appears when your cursor moves over the Collapsible Panel tab; with the Collapsible Panel widget, the eye icon toggles between open and closed to reflect the state of the panel.

One additional control on the Property inspector allows you to turn the animation on or off. If the animation is disabled, the panel collapses or expands immediately.

FIGURE 16-32

The Spry Collapsible Panel can be set to either open or closed by default.

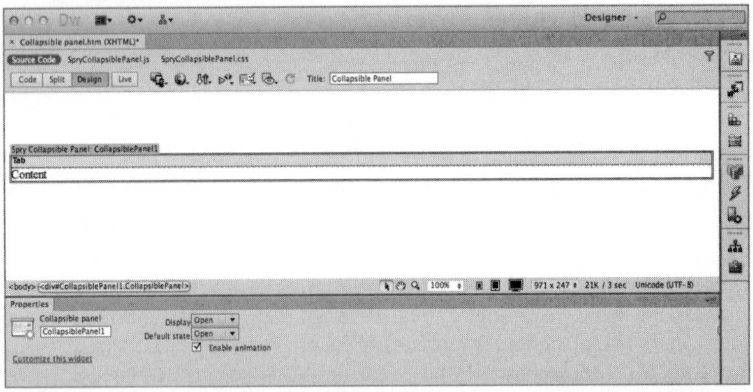

> **TIP**
>
> **Like other panels, this widget expands to the width of the container—a perfect layout device for a sidebar. Even better, it's possible to stack them within a single container, as shown in Figure 16-33. When the top Spry Collapsible Panel is expanded, the panels below it are pushed down; when collapsed, they move up to fill the space. All in all, a very nice effect.**

FIGURE 16-33

Stack two or more Spry Collapsible Panel widgets on top of each other with ease.

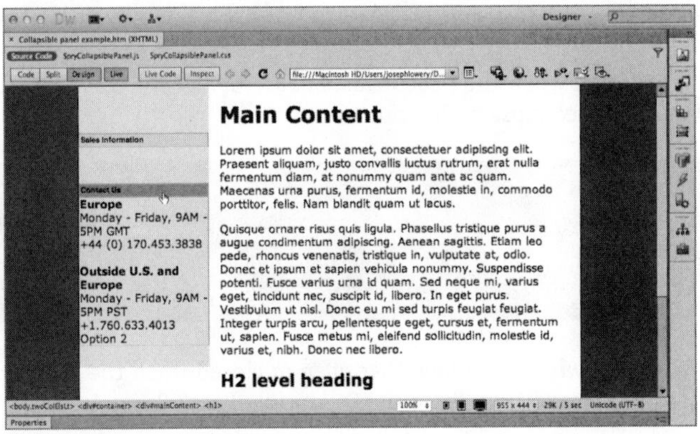

Spry Tooltip

Pretty much all browsers support alt and title text that appears when you hover your mouse over a link. Unfortunately, the messaging capabilities are extremely limited: plain text, in a single line, with no possible style variations. Spry Tooltip to the rescue!

> **NOTE**
>
> The Spry Tooltip widget has many benefits. First and foremost, you can insert any type or amount of content and format it to your heart's content. You're free to insert images, paragraphs, short articles—really anything you want. The Spry Tooltip widget can be attached to any page element, not just a link, including a word or phrase, an image, or form element. Once it is implemented, you can apply effects to the Spry Tooltip so that it fades in and out of view or is revealed and hidden with a wipe. You can even cause the tooltip to follow the mouse for more interactivity.

The Spry Tooltip widget is, like all other Spry layout components, very easy to add to the page and customize. Once inserted, a region, highlighted by the familiar blue Spry tab and border, is placed on the bottom of the page where you can personalize and customize your tooltip. When you're ready to test, just switch to Live View and move your mouse over the selected text, as shown in Figure 16-34.

FIGURE 16-34

The Spry Tooltip widget can include images, text, or any other content.

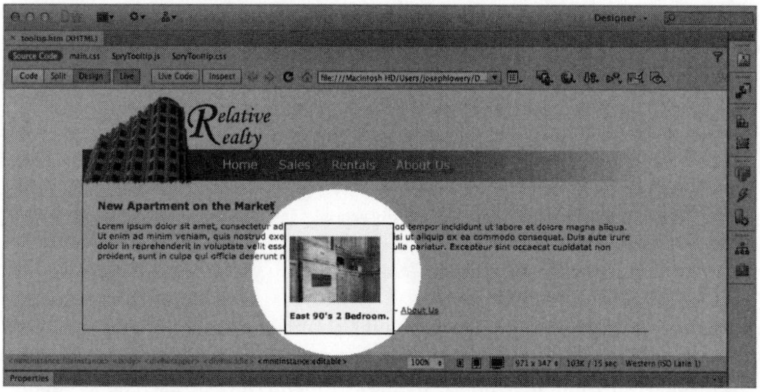

Use Spry Tooltips wherever you want to display additional, optional information.

To add a Spry Tooltip widget to your page, follow these steps:

1. Select the page element where you'd like your tooltip to display when the user hovers his mouse over it.
2. From the Insert panel's Spry or Layout category, choose Spry Tooltip Bar. The default tooltip panel is inserted into the page and the custom Property inspector displays (refer back to Figure 16-34).
3. To define the tooltip, modify the contents of the Spry Tooltip region.

4. If you want the tooltip to appear to be attached to the visitor's mouse, choose the Follow Mouse option.
5. To keep the tooltip open whether the mouse is above the triggering element or the tooltip itself, choose the Hide On Mouse Out option. Without this option selected, the tooltip closes when the mouse moves away from the triggering element only.
6. To add an effect when the tooltip appears and disappears, choose either Fade or Blind. The Fade option dims the tooltip in and out, and Blind reveals and hides the tooltip like a window blind.
7. To reposition the tooltip, add a value to the Horizontal Offset field, the Vertical Offset field, or both.

   The initial placement of the tooltip is 20 pixels to the right and below the cursor.
8. To change the amount of time it takes for the tooltip to appear, add a value (in milliseconds) to the Show Delay field.
9. To change the amount of time it takes for the tooltip to disappear, add a value (in milliseconds) to the Hide Delay field.

TIP

Like the other widgets, the first time you save a file with a Spry Tooltop widget, Dreamweaver tells you of the two supporting files that have been copied to your site and will need to be posted online: `SpryTooltip.js` and `SpryTooltip.css`.

You can style the tooltip div directly or add another div within it. I've found that it is often a good idea to wrap your tooltip content in a border and add a bit of padding.

Spry Effects

The third category of the Spry framework in Dreamweaver is Spry effects. Spry effects rely on next-generation JavaScript techniques just as Spry data and Spry widgets do. And, like the other Web 2.0 implementations, Spry effects are very simple to implement and adjust.

Essentially, Spry effects are a group of Dreamweaver client-side behaviors. Behaviors are typically applied to a text or image link, although some are appropriate for the `<body>` tag. Once you have selected the triggering element, choose Window ➪ Behaviors or use the keyboard shortcut Shift+F4 to open the Behaviors panel. Then choose Add (+) and select your desired behavior from the list; all of the Spry effects are grouped in the Effects submenu. A dialog box for the behavior will appear, like the one for the Highlight effect shown in Figure 16-35. Once completed, the behavior's event and action are listed in the Behaviors panel. To modify the settings, just double-click the name of the applied behavior.

All of the Spry effects are covered in detail in the "Spry Effects in Dreamweaver" section of Chapter 11.

FIGURE 16-35

Spry effects, such as Highlight, offer a range of options in their dialog boxes.

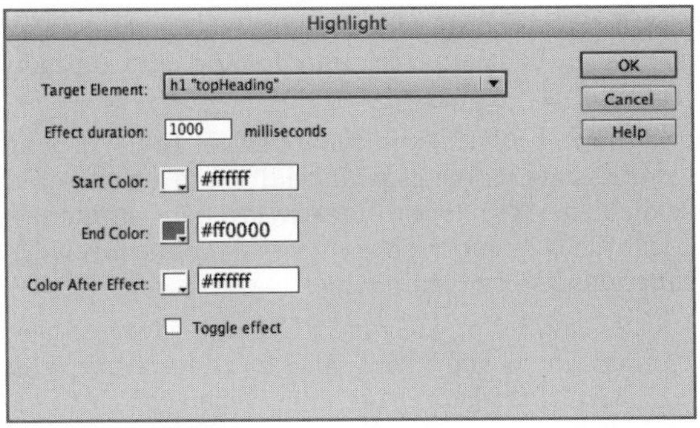

Collectively, the Spry effects provide a new level of visual effects for the Dreamweaver designer. In all, there are seven different effects:

- **Appear/Fade:** Interactively triggers a targeted page element, such as a `<div>` tag, to appear or fade over a set period of time.
- **Blind:** Simulates window blinds closing to hide specified content and opening to reveal it.
- **Grow/Shrink:** Reduces or enlarges the targeted content for a set duration; you also have the option of growing or shrinking from the center of the target or from the upper-left corner.
- **Highlight:** Displays a sudden burst of background color behind a page element, which then fades away for a set period of time.
- **Shake:** Moves the targeted element left and right quickly, shaking it from side to side.
- **Slide:** Similar to the Blind effect in that it hides or reveals targeted content; however, with Slide, it is the content itself that appears to move in or out of view. This effect requires an outer `<div>` tag with an ID that surrounds another tag with an ID.
- **Squish:** Shrinks from 100 percent to 0 percent in the targeted element's upper-left corner; the effect can be applied again to grow the element to 100 percent in the opposite direction.

NOTE

The JavaScript engine for all the effects is contained in a single file, `SpryEffects.js`. This file is included in your page automatically whenever you apply a Spry effect.

Summary

Without a doubt, Ajax has significantly increased the options a web designer has to choose from. Adobe's implementation of the Spry framework provides a greatly simplified road map to help the web professional incorporate these options. Dreamweaver takes the final step by providing a set of tools designers can use to take their sites to the next level:

- Ajax combines advanced JavaScript methods with DOM manipulation to seamlessly integrate XML data into web pages. The Spry framework for Ajax, developed by Adobe, greatly simplifies implementing this technology.
- The Spry data tools are used to establish a connection to either an HTML or an XML data source and then expose the data on the page. In addition to a series of lower-level objects such as the Spry Region and Spry Repeat, Dreamweaver also offers the Spry Data Set Wizard, which supplies all the code for displaying Spry data in a diverse number of ways along with special functions like column sorting.
- Spry Widgets are an amalgam of JavaScript, CSS, and HTML that advances the web designer's art in two major areas: forms and layout. All Spry widgets can be straightforwardly added to a page and modified through the custom Property inspector and Design view.
- The Spry form widgets make it possible to quickly and easily add form validation to text fields, textareas, select lists, radio button groups, passwords, confirm fields, and checkboxes. Complete customizable error messages to guide the user appear whenever validation fails.
- Five different Spry layout widgets are available: Menu Bars, Tabbed Panels, Accordion Panels, Collapsible Panels, and Tooltips. Each of these widgets can be extended via the Property inspector and personalized through attached CSS style sheets.
- The seven Spry Effects in Dreamweaver are next-generation behaviors that control the appearance of targeted page elements, such as particular `<div>` tags. All Spry effects can be found in the Behaviors panel, under the Effects menu entry.

In the next chapter, you learn how to take advantage of the numerous JavaScript frameworks such as jQuery and MooTools and the wide range of widgets and effects freely available on the web.

CHAPTER

17

Working with JavaScript Frameworks

IN THIS CHAPTER

- Working with JavaScript
- Using Code Hints
- Working with jQuery framework functions
- Implementing web widgets
- Crafting mobile apps in jQuery
- Compiling mobile app builds

In recent years, JavaScript has moved to the forefront of web technologies and is now a key tool in developing engaging online experiences. Driving this widespread adoption of JavaScript is the development and proliferation of numerous JavaScript frameworks. "Framework" is another term for code library or collection of useful functions, maintained in one or more external files.

A great number of frameworks are available today—some estimates place the number well over 200. Among the most popular JavaScript frameworks are the Yahoo! User Interface Library (better known as YUI), jQuery, MooTools, and Prototype. As noted throughout this book, Adobe has developed its own framework, Spry, from which many components (or widgets) and effects are integrated into Dreamweaver.

All of the frameworks have their followers and even advocates. Dreamweaver, rather than become married to a single framework—even one from its own company—has evolved into a mutually supportive platform. Now advanced coding functionality, such as code hinting and code completion previously available to the most broad-based technologies such as HTML, ColdFusion, and PHP, is automatically implemented for a referenced framework. Even custom coding can benefit from the on-the-fly code hinting available in Dreamweaver.

Although this enhanced JavaScript support is great news for coders, what about designers and those who are not as proficient in scripting? The Dreamweaver team has broadened its open framework support to embrace a new type of extension: the web widget. A web widget is a layout element that relies on an accepted JavaScript framework for its functionality. Drop a web widget like the YUI Calendar on your page and not only do you get a working utility, but the necessary external JavaScript files are automatically attached to your source code.

Even better, the newly released Widget Browser—an extension to Dreamweaver—allows you to configure widgets from other frameworks, specifying parameter values for styles and other properties, without coding. Once you've customized your web widget, the Widget Browser inserts the code directly into your current page, complete with links to all necessary libraries and related files.

This chapter covers the implication of the JavaScript evolution in Dreamweaver from start to finish. Here, you learn how to take the most advantage of core JavaScript coding capabilities when working with frameworks in Dreamweaver. You also learn how to get, install, and integrate web widgets into your sites. Finally, this chapter covers the development and packaging of web widgets so you too can play your part in spreading the JavaScript revolution.

Using JavaScript Frameworks

To the novice coder, integrating JavaScript framework functionality can be quickly overwhelming. Although Dreamweaver doesn't eliminate the need to have a certain level of familiarity with JavaScript coding practices, it does make it significantly easier to get up to speed when using a particular framework.

CAUTION

Whenever you link to an external JavaScript file, such as those used in JavaScript frameworks, Dreamweaver automatically introspects the code and enables a wide range of helper functions. Automatic code hinting is the primary aid to hand-coders now available in Dreamweaver. If you're familiar with the standard HTML code hinting that has long been a part of Dreamweaver, you'll appreciate how valuable this feature is when applied to unfamiliar JavaScript territory. Code hinting in Dreamweaver is quite robust and exposes JavaScript primitives, functions, parameters, classes, class properties, methods, and variables.

For example, let's say you're coding a function that opens a JavaScript window and, in your `<script>` tag, you type the word `window` and then a period. Dreamweaver will immediately present a complete list of JavaScript methods and properties available to the window object, shown in Figure 17-1. Note that in addition to the methods and properties listed on the left, the relevant object is shown in the second column and the organizing system or framework in the third. Here, because window is a document-level object, most of the methods and properties are listed as belonging to DOM 0. Look closely, however, and you will see one property, `childSandboxBridge`, which is part of the AIR framework. Dreamweaver displays Code Hints for all available frameworks, whether built-in, as with DOM and AIR, or attached through a link on the page.

Code hinting, however, goes much deeper than displaying the initial method or property. Let's continue with the example and say that, after entering `window.open`, you enter an opening parenthesis. Now, Dreamweaver shows you in a tooltip the method and all of its arguments in a comma-separated list, like this:

```
window.open(url, name, features, replace)
```

FIGURE 17-1

Robust code hinting opens the door to working with new frameworks.

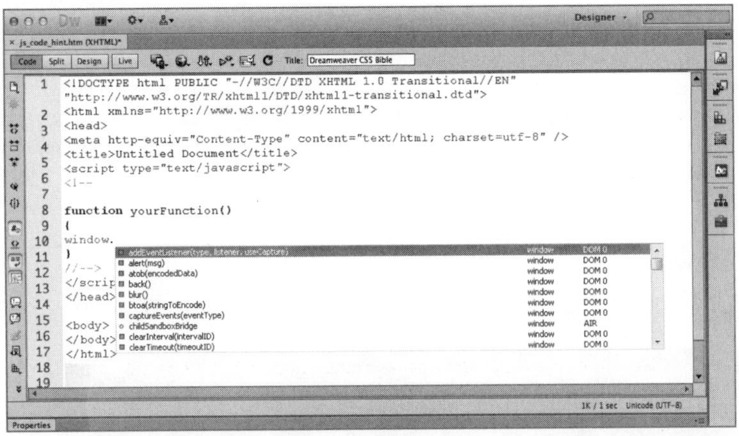

TIP

If you've mistyped and have to backspace, code hinting may not appear at first. You can always bring your Code Hints up by pressing Ctrl+space (Command+space).

You'll notice that the initial argument, `url`, is bolded to indicate that this is the next one to be completed. After you enter a filename in quotes for the URL, followed by a comma, Dreamweaver prompts you for the parameter:

```
window.open(url, name, features, replace)
```

And so on, until all the arguments are entered or you close the parentheses. The same granular level of assistance is provided for any referenced framework.

You'll want to make sure code hinting is enabled and set up to your liking through Dreamweaver preferences. For more details, see the "Code Hints Preferences" section in Chapter 3.

Integrating Framework Functions

Starting to work with a JavaScript framework is very straightforward—the difficulty comes in writing your code properly. As noted, however, Dreamweaver helps the process as much as possible. This section takes a look at how one might begin working with one of the more popular frameworks, jQuery.

The jQuery framework was initially developed by John Resig in early 2006. As a robust, freely available open source framework, jQuery grew in popularity rapidly and attracted numerous programmers to the ongoing development team. jQuery is most widely known for its compelling, easy-to-use effects.

To download a copy of jQuery, follow these steps:

1. Visit the site at `http://www.jquery.com`.
2. Above the Download (jQuery) button, choose the Development option and click the Download button (see Figure 17-2).

FIGURE 17-2

jQuery is freely downloadable and contained within a single file.

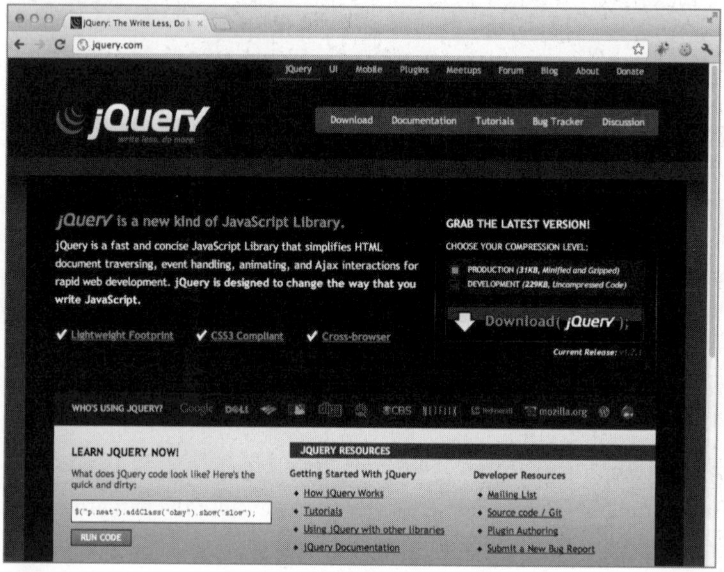

jQuery is available in two compression levels: Production, which has all whitespace removed and weighs only 15KB, and Development, which is formatted in a readable fashion with a file weight of 94KB. If you're just starting out, the Development version is a better choice so you can actually see how the code works. When you're ready to deploy your page, switch to the lighter Production version by changing the `<script>` `src` attribute.

3. Click the link to the current version of jQuery and save the file into your site root, preferably in a scripts folder.

With the jQuery file available locally, you're ready to integrate it into your page.

To add a simple jQuery function to your page, follow these steps:

1. In Dreamweaver, switch to Code view.
2. Place your cursor above the closing `</head>` tag and press Enter (Return).

3. Enter the following code:

```
<script type="text/javascript" scr="[path to jQuery file]"></script>
```

where the path to the jQuery file is the folder and filename for the downloaded jQuery JavaScript document. You can use Code Hints to help you locate the file quickly and enter the path correctly. After you enter the src attribute, a Browse option will appear; highlight it and press Enter (Return). The Select File dialog box will appear, and you can navigate to the jQuery file and click OK.

4. Press Enter (Return) and enter the following code:

```
<script type="text/javascript">
<!--

-->
</script>
```


TIP

Dreamweaver has a good number of handy coding snippets you can use, especially for JavaScript. To insert an initial `<script>` block, open the Snippets panel and expand the JavaScript node. Then select Starter Script and click Insert or drag it onto the page.

Now your page is ready for your first jQuery function, the traditional "Hello world" greeting. Whereas older-style JavaScript implementation used triggering events as attributes in the HTML markup, such as `onClick` and `onLoad`, the modern style of JavaScript coding—as employed by jQuery—is to be unobtrusive and keep the interactive functions separate from the markup and presentation. Therefore, instead of an `onLoad` event added to the `<body>` tag, jQuery uses a `ready()` function applied to the document object.

5. Within the `<script>` tag, enter the following code:

```
$(document).ready(function(){

})
```

Dreamweaver's code hinting should kick in after you type the period following `(document)` and you can press Enter (Return) once `ready(handler)(e)` is displayed in the Code Hint list. When inserted, this code resolves to:

```
$(document).ready(function(e) {

});
```

The included `(e)` is an instance of the JavaScript Event object; you can, if you aren't specifically working with the Event object, remove it. Let's complete the function by adding some standard JavaScript.

6. In the blank line within the `ready()` function, enter this code:

```
alert("Hello World!");
```

7. Test your code by entering Live View.

Dreamweaver goes into Split view and then, once the document has loaded, displays the alert, shown in Figure 17-3.

FIGURE 17-3

jQuery uses a ready() function to know when to begin processing.

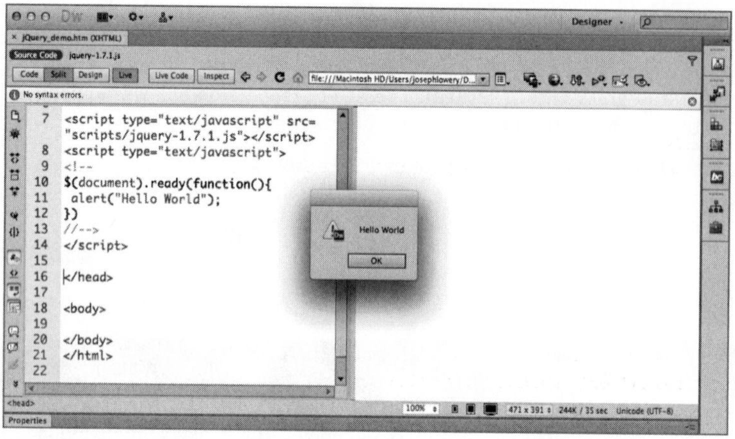

Actual jQuery coding typically follows a specific pattern—one that Dreamweaver can easily follow. The code usually starts off by identifying the object by ID, class name, tag, or other CSS selector, as in these examples:

```
$("a")
$("#header")
$(".pullQuote")
$("ul a")
```

Once you've identified what's to be affected, you provide an action or function. For example, if you wanted to add a CSS class called `.highlight` to all the <a> tags in your page, you would use code like this:

```
$("a").addClass("highlight");
```

Note that the class name that is added does not include a leading period, so the attribute would be written properly—that is, `class="highlight"` and not `class=".highlight"`.

jQuery allows you to chain functions, one after the other. So, if you wanted to only add the `.highlight` class to an <a> tag with a class of `.current`, you could write your code this way:

```
$("a").filter(".current").addClass("highlight");
```

Of course, jQuery can handle much more sophisticated effects. Let's take a look at creating a stylized animated tooltip.

NOTE

This technique of displaying a stylized, animated tooltip was created by Nick La, creator of Web Designer Wall (`http://www.webdesignerwall.com`) as part of his "jQuery Tutorials for Designer" series.

The HTML markup here combines an unordered list, links, and <em> tags. Each list item comprises an <a> tag, followed by an <em> tag, like this:

```
<li>
  <a href="http://www.feldenkraisinsights.com">Debra Wanner</a>
  <em>Choreographer, Dancer and Feldenkrais Practioner</em>
</li>
```

CSS is used to display the list items as buttons in a horizontal bar with a graphic image background. The <em> tag is also given a background image, but is absolutely positioned to appear above the navigation button.

The jQuery code uses a built-in `animate()` function to make the content of the <em> tag appear like a tooltip (see Figure 17-4):

```
$(document).ready(function(){
  $(".menu a").hover(function() {
    $(this).next("em").animate({opacity: "show",top: "-75"},"slow");
  }, function() {
    $(this).next("em").animate({opacity: "hide", top: "-85"}, "fast");
  });
})
```

What's not apparent in the printed image is the animated effect of the tooltip simultaneously fading in and moving into position.

FIGURE 17-4

With jQuery, stylish tooltips can be made to fade in above menu items.

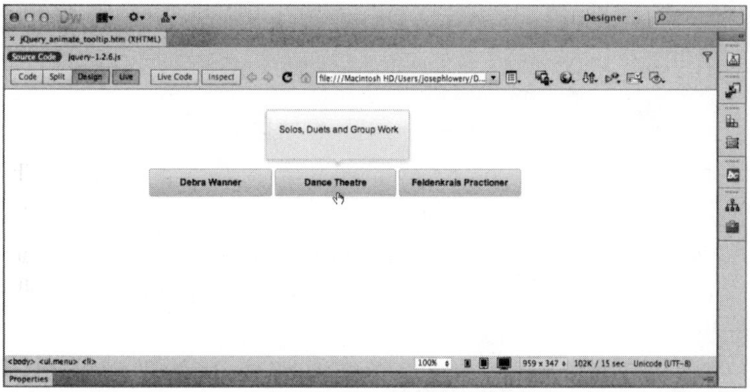

Implementing a Web Widget

A great many JavaScript frameworks are on the web, many with a large collection of user interfaces and other layout objects available. To take advantage of this wealth of functionality, Dreamweaver supports a new type of extension, the web widget, in two ways.

The legacy web widget, introduced in Dreamweaver CS4, is installed like any other extension, through the Adobe Extension Manager. Once incorporated into Dreamweaver, these web widgets are available through the Insert panel and can be added to a page with ease. Dragging a web widget onto your page not only adds the necessary HTML markup but also links to any necessary JavaScript and CSS files. When you save your page, these files are automatically copied to your site.

NOTE

Newer web widgets don't need to be installed to be used. The Adobe AIR-powered Widget Browser allows you to specify any necessary parameters for the widget, such as the skin background color, in a dynamic user interface. When you're ready, the code for the widget is inserted in the Dreamweaver page, with HTML in the `<body>` and links to external JavaScript and CSS files in the `<head>` area. Any required files are also copied to your site.

Techniques for inserting both types of widgets are described in the following pages.

Installing and using legacy web widgets

Legacy web widgets are hosted in a special section of the Adobe Exchange, which can be reached directly from within Dreamweaver. Let's run through the steps to locate one such web widget, install it, and incorporate it into a page:

1. From the Dreamweaver Application bar Extend Dreamweaver menu button, choose Browse for Other Dreamweaver Extensions (see Figure 17-5).

FIGURE 17-5

Looking for new web widgets? They're just a click away on the Application bar.

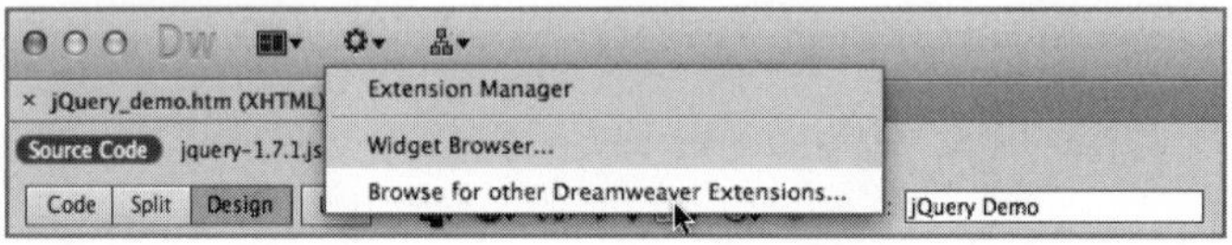

2. In the Adobe Exchange, click Web Widgets from the category list.
3. When the Web Widget catalog opens, locate the YUI Calendar and click Download.

   You'll need to be logged in with your Adobe ID before you can download anything from the Exchange.
4. Save the file on your desktop, and when the download is complete, double-click it to install with the Adobe Extension Manager.
5. When the Extension Manager asks if you would accept the license agreement, click OK to continue.
6. After the installation is complete, return to Dreamweaver. Quit and re-start the program.

   As with many extensions, you'll need to quit and relaunch Dreamweaver when installing most web widgets.
7. In the Insert panel, switch to the newly added YUI category.

8. Drag the Calendar object onto the page.

   Dreamweaver inserts an empty <div> tag on the page, which is identified with a blue tab and border. When selected, the YUI Calendar Property inspector is displayed, as shown in Figure 17-6.

9. Enter Live View to display the calendar (see Figure 17-7).

FIGURE 17-6

The YUI Calendar inserts an empty <div> that is replaced with a calendar widget at runtime.

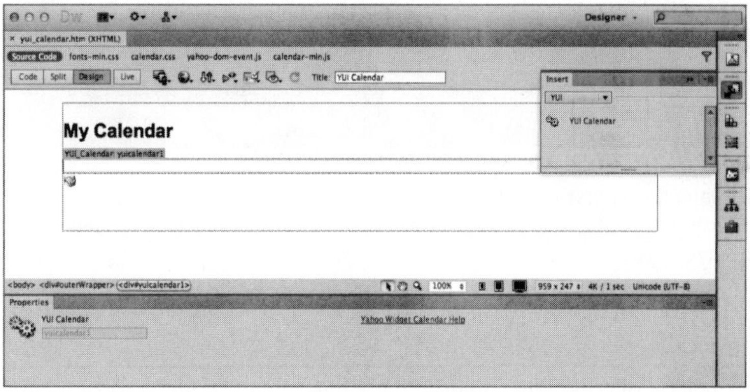

FIGURE 17-7

In Live View or when previewed in the browser, the YUI Calendar is active.

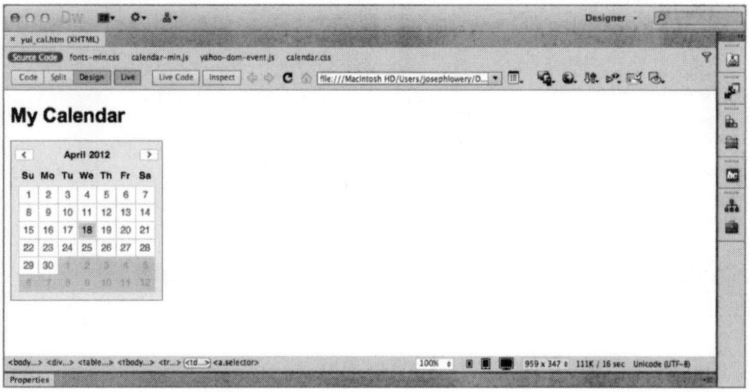

A calendar like the YUI one has many uses. It could be used as a date picker for form fields, to select a range of dates, or to indicate events, just to name a few. Moreover, the calendar is extremely configurable. To give you an idea of how it can be changed, let's add a bit of code that makes the calendar start on Monday, rather than Sunday:

10. Switch to Code view and place your cursor in front of this line:

```
yuicalendar1.render();
```

The `render()` function draws the specific instance of the calendar object, which is named yuicalendar1.

11. Press Enter (Return) and enter the following code:

```
yuicalendar1.cfg.setProperty("start_weekday","1");
```

12. Click Refresh and switch to Live View to see the updated calendar (see Figure 17-8).
13. Save your file. Dreamweaver will remind you of the files you'll need to publish when your site goes live.

TIP

To learn more about the YUI Calendar, visit `http://developer.yahoo.com/yui/calendar/`, which you also can reach by clicking the YUI Widget Calendar Help link in the Property inspector.

The YUI Calendar is just one of the web widgets available on the Adobe Exchange. Widgets from jQuery, MooTools, and YUI frameworks are ready to bring advanced functionality to your Dreamweaver pages.

FIGURE 17-8

With a small bit of code, the calendar can be reconfigured to start on a different day of the week.

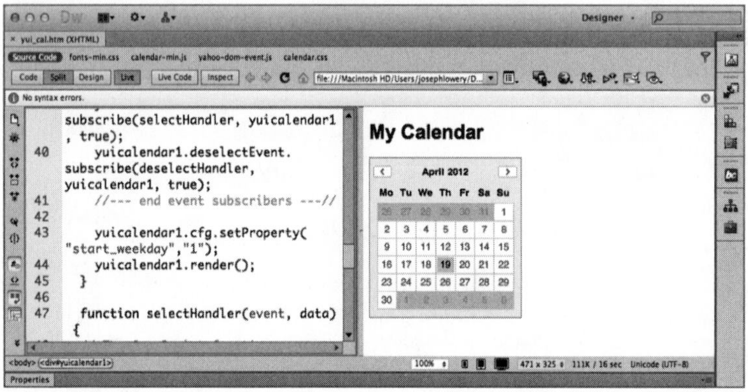

Working with the Widget Browser

While the legacy web widget approach offers a good deal of flexibility and makes it easy to insert the same widget repeatedly, added widgets can be difficult to customize. Each framework has its own coding standards, and they all employ a specific syntax to change available attributes. Many of the attributes are concerned with the look and feel of the widget and may need to be customized to blend into the design of the site. The Widget Browser exposes the vast majority of these parameters in an adaptive user interface that changes according to the attributes available. Once the widget has been personalized, Dreamweaver inserts the code directly into the page and copies any required files to your site. Moreover, you can create and store your own custom configurations to re-use whenever you'd like.

The Widget Browser does not come preinstalled in Dreamweaver—it's an Adobe AIR application you'll need to download and install. Luckily, Dreamweaver detects whether it is already installed or not and takes you right to the download page to make the process as smooth as possible.

To install the Widget Browser, follow these steps:

1. Choose Extend Dreamweaver ➪ Widget Browser from the Application bar; Extend Dreamweaver is the gear icon shown in Figure 17-9.

FIGURE 17-9

Choose Widget Browser from the Extend Dreamweaver menu in the Application bar.

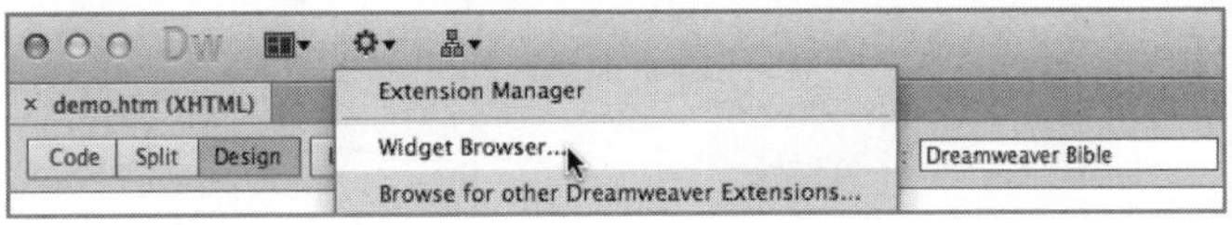

2. If the Widget Browser is not installed, Dreamweaver displays an alert that asks if you'd like to download and install the application. Click OK to proceed.
3. Dreamweaver opens your primary browser, if necessary, and goes directly to the web address on the Adobe site for downloading the application.
4. Sign in with your Adobe ID.
5. Click Download.

   As noted earlier, the Widget Browser is an AIR application and, once downloaded to your system, will install itself, with your permission.
6. When asked if it's okay if the Widget Browser is installed, click OK.

After the Widget Browser installation is complete, it's ready to go to work. Because it is an AIR application and not installed via the Extension Manager, there's no need to reboot Dreamweaver before you use the Widget Browser. Ready to see how it works?

To insert a customized web widget with the Widget Browser, follow these steps:

1. Place your cursor where you'd like a widget to appear on your page.
2. Choose Dreamweaver Extensions ➪ Widget Browser from the Application bar.
3. When the Widget Browser opens, choose Adobe Exchange to locate the desired widget (see Figure 17-10).

   Dreamweaver displays a list of available widgets. Choose any widget to learn more about it.

4. When you've found the widget you want to add to your page, click Add to My Widgets.
5. Once the license screen appears, click I Agree to continue.

   When the widget has been added to your collection, you'll have an opportunity to customize your widget and create a new preset or insert the widget from Dreamweaver. If you're ready to use the widget as it is, click Close. Then, in Dreamweaver, choose Insert ➪ Widget to add to the page; you'll have an opportunity to choose any of the widgets in your collection and select any of their presets.
6. To customize the widget, click Go to My Widgets.

FIGURE 17-10

Use the Widget Browser to quickly insert customized widgets.

7. From the My Widgets screen, select the newly added widget.
8. Choose the configuration from the Developer Preset list that most closely resembles the configuration you desire.
9. Click Configure.
10. In the Configure screen, change any of the available properties.

    The preview area updates with every configuration change, as shown in Figure 17-11.
11. Specify values from their default settings for any properties you want to change.

    The number of properties available for customization and their structure in the Widget Browser varies. Some widgets include multiple categories of properties organized in accordion panels, which you can expand to modify the properties contained within. For example, the widget in Figure 17-11 has three categories: Binding & Behavior, View, and Slideshow Controls.

12. Enter a unique name for your preset in the Name field and a description, if desired, in the Description field.
13. When you're done, click Save Preset.

FIGURE 17-11

The Widget Browser maintains a list of Developer Presets from which you can create your own presets.

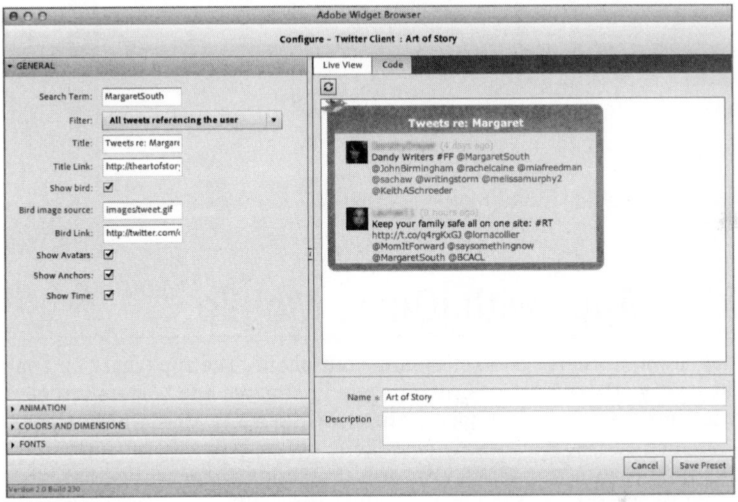

14. You're ready to add the custom widget to your Dreamweaver page.
15. In Dreamweaver, choose Insert ➪ Widget.
16. When the Widget dialog box appears, choose the desired widget and preset from their respective lists and then click OK.
17. Dreamweaver adds the widget to the page (see Figure 17-12) and notifies you of any files you'll have to publish to your remote site.

Although it varies from widget to widget, typically two code blocks will be added: one, to the current cursor location to represent where the widget will be displayed and a second, consisting of a series of links to external JavaScript and CSS files, in the `<head>`.

Most widgets will not be correctly visible (if at all) in Design view; you'll need to switch to Live View to get the full effect. Unfortunately, the Widget Browser is not reentrant—which means you can't re-open it to modify your personalized attributes. You're free to make changes to the code itself or delete the inserted widget and reapply by running the Widget Browser again.

FIGURE 17-12

Once your widget code is inserted, it's best to preview the results in Live View.

Building Apps with jQuery Mobile

Don't look now, but there's an explosion in your phone. The app (short for application) market has blown away all expectations with no end in site. An app is more targeted than a website and typically strives to meet a specific need. While many apps are developed with lower-level languages such as C++, it's entirely possible to create a successful app using the standard tools of today's website designer: HTML, CSS, and JavaScript. Dreamweaver has ratcheted "possible" to "doable" by tightly integrating jQuery Mobile support.

Just as jQuery is a superlative framework for standard websites, jQuery Mobile is a parallel framework for mobile devices. As such, it delivers a common user experience across devices as it supports an amazing spectrum of platforms, listed as of this writing at `http://jquerymobile.com/blog/2012/01/26/jquery-mobile-1-0-1-released/#platforms`. jQuery Mobile offers a robust API and complete theme support to ensure an easily updateable, uniform look and feel across all pages in the app.

Dreamweaver has embraced jQuery Mobile fully. You can hit the ground running with any of the Mobile Starters offering links to support files remotely or locally, your choice. To fill out your content, there's a complete slate of compatible objects for drag-and-drop implementation and integrated support for styling—or, as the jQuery Mobile folks say, *theming*—the application. With a nod to the reality of developing on a fast-moving platform, Dreamweaver makes it very easy to link to the latest versions of the support files, or, if you're just dipping your toe in the water, you can tell Dreamweaver to use locally stored files. No matter which route you take, you'll soon find that developing mobile apps with Dreamweaver and jQuery Mobile to be fast, fun, and ever so addicting.

Creating a jQuery Mobile page

There are two basic approaches to creating a jQuery Mobile app in Dreamweaver. You can create a series of linked pages in one step using Dreamweaver's Mobile Starters or you can build the app from the ground up. Let's take a look at the Mobile Starters method first with the following steps:

1. Choose File ➪ New (see Figure 17-13).

FIGURE 17-13

Get a jump on building a jQuery Mobile app with the Mobile Starters.

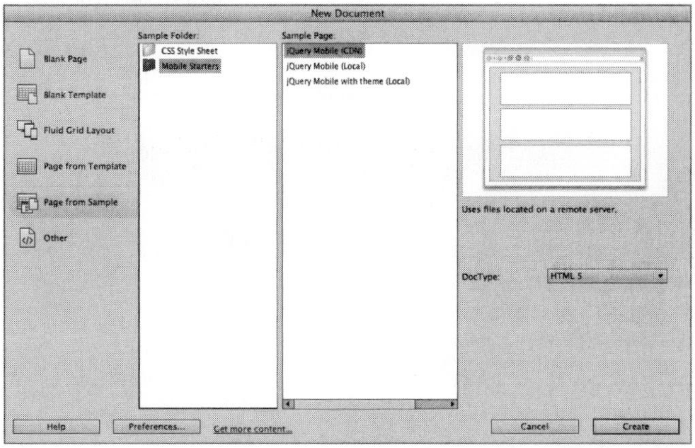

2. From the first column, choose Page from Sample.
3. From the Sample Folder column, choose Mobile Starters.
4. From the Sample Page column, choose one of the three options:
   - **jQuery Mobile (CDN):** Links to files stored on a content delivery network (CDN).
   - **jQuery Mobile (Local):** Copies jQuery Mobile files to your local site root.
   - **jQuery Mobile with theme (Local):** Copies jQuery Mobile files, with a separate CSS theme file, to your local site root.
5. For optimal performance, leave the DocType list set to HTML 5.
6. Click Create.

In Design or Code view, you'll see a series of `<div>` tags, each with a header defining the page number, a content area, and a footer (see Figure 17-14). To facilitate quick Ajax-driven transitions from one page to another, the typical jQuery Mobile app consists of one or more HTML pages containing several `<div>` tags, each of which represents a separate application page. The HTML valid attribute `data-role` is used to specify what is a page and what is a header, content area, footer, or other division. Figure 17-14 shows what a single page looks like in jQuery Mobile.

FIGURE 17-14

jQuery Mobile pages are composed of <div> tags defining a series of pages.

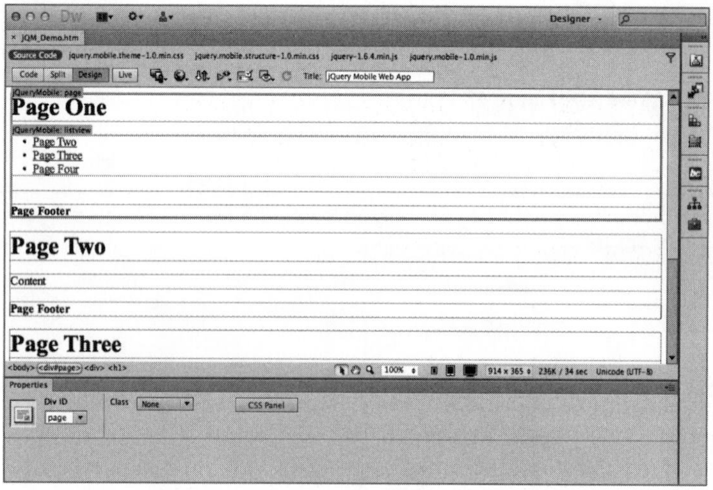


```
<div data-role="page" id="page2">
  <div data-role="header">
    <h1>Page Two</h1>
  </div>
  <div data-role="content">
    Content
  </div>
  <div data-role="footer">
    <h4>Page Footer</h4>
  </div>
</div>
```

TIP

jQuery Mobile has a very rich, well-documented API. To begin exploring it, go to `http://jquerymobile.com/demos/`.

While it's not obvious from Design view, the Mobile Starter pages all come with professional-grade styling. Enter Live View and switch the window size to a smart phone size like 320 × 480 to experience how the jQuery Mobile app works right out of the box (see Figure 17-15).

Once in Live View, Ctrl+click (Command+click) any of the page links (Page Two, Page Three, and so on) or the angle bracket icons to move to another page. Note the smooth sliding transition as the next page appears. Transitions are built into jQuery Mobile and can easily be modified in the code. To move back to the home page, click Refresh and then Back in the Document toolbar.

FIGURE 17-15

jQuery Mobile pages are composed of <div> tags defining a series of pages.

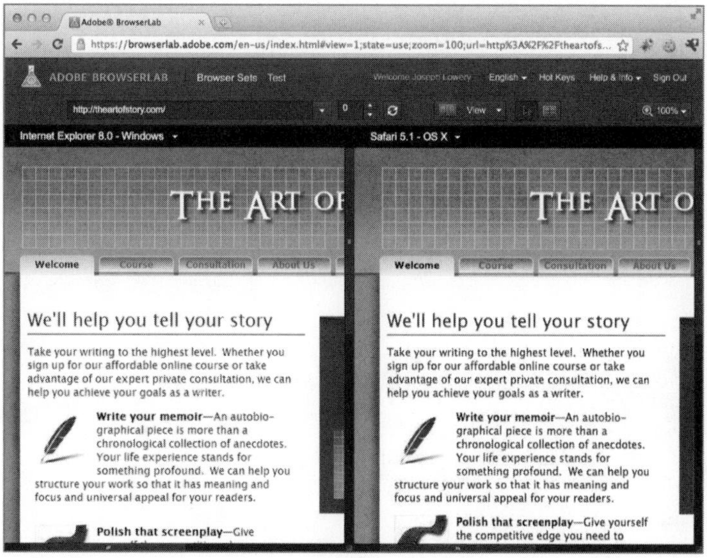

NOTE

Although the Mobile Starter samples come with links from the home page to the three other pre-built pages, there is no built-in link back to the home page. You can easily add a link within the content area of each page with code like this:

```
<p> <a href="#page" data-direction="reverse" data-role="button">Home</a>
</p>
```

Both the `data-direction` and `data-role` attributes are optional but will give your link a more unified look and feel.

You can continue to build out your jQuery Mobile app by adding more "pages" and customizing the content with standard Dreamweaver tools. Additionally, you can insert any of the items found in the jQuery Mobile category of the Insert panel—described in detail in the next section.

Inserting jQuery objects

Not only do the jQuery Mobile objects allow you to extend the functionality of your app, but they're also the gateway to creating a jQuery Mobile app from the ground up.

To start building a jQuery Mobile app from scratch, all you need is a standard saved HTML file. From that very low entry point, you add a Page object from the jQuery Mobile category of the Insert panel (see Figure 17-16).

FIGURE 17-16

The jQuery Mobile objects deliver a great deal of advanced functionality in consistently styled packages.

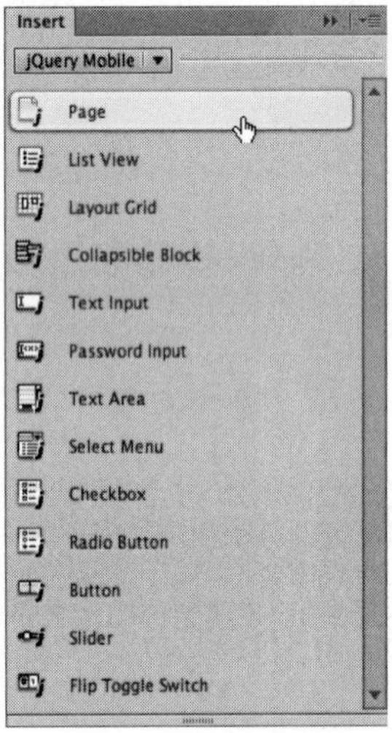

When you insert your first Page object, you'll be presented with the jQuery Mobile Files dialog box, where you decide whether you'd prefer to link to remote (CDN) or local files (see Figure 17-17). If you choose any of the local options when you save your HTML file, Dreamweaver will copy the pages to your local site.

FIGURE 17-17

Dreamweaver gives you the option to choose between remote or locally hosted jQuery Mobile files.

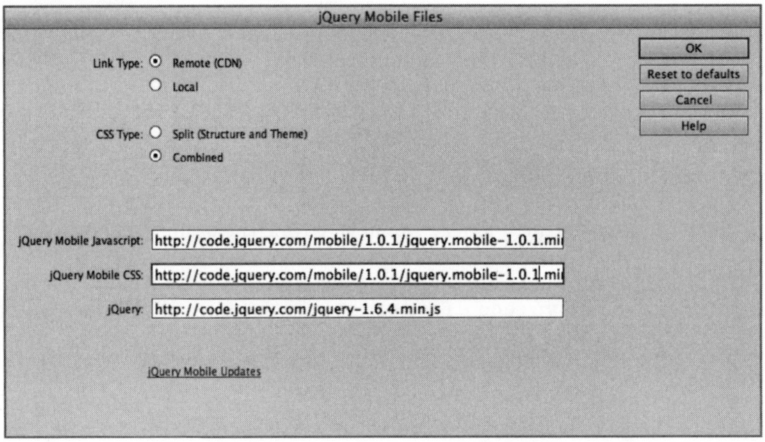

> **TIP**
>
> In the jQuery Mobile Files dialog box, you can also link to different versions of the support files by changing the default paths. This facility allows you to use the latest versions of the jQuery Mobile and jQuery files, either remotely or locally.

Once the initial page is set up, you can begin filling out the application by dropping in standard text, images, or other content. New jQuery Mobile pages are created by inserting additional `<div>` tags with unique IDs and a `data-role="page"` attribute.

The jQuery Mobile category of the Insert panel contains 13 different objects, targeted for mobile apps. Some are devoted to layout (Page, List View, Layout Grid, and Collapsible Block) while the rest are intended to be used in forms or for general user interaction. Table 17-1 details each of the objects in turn.

TABLE 17-1 jQuery Mobile Objects

Icon	Name	Description
	Page	Inserts code for a <div> tag with a data-role attribute of page. With optional header and footer sections.
	List View	Adds code for an unordered or ordered list with a data-role attribute of listview and a variety of options.
	Layout Grid	Inserts code for a user-definable grid of layout <div> tags.
	Collapsible Block	Includes code for creating a jQuery-driven collapsing and expanding area.
	Text Input	Adds a <label> tag and <input> text field within a <div> tag with a data-role attribute of fieldcontain.
	Password Input	Same as Text Input, but the <input> tag is set to type=password.
	Text Area	Same as Text Input, with a <textarea> instead of <input> tag.
	Select Menu	Same as Text Input, with a <select> instead of <input> tag.
	Checkbox	Same as Text Input, but the <input> tag is set to type=checkbox.
	Radio Button	Same as Text Input, but the <input> tag is set to type=radio.
	Button	Inserts code for one or more links, <button> or <input> tags that act as buttons.

Continues

TABLE 17-1 *(continued)*

Icon	Name	Description
	Slider	Same as Text Input, but the <input> tag is set to type=range.
	Flip Toggle Switch	Same as Select Menu with two options specified (Off and On) and data-role=slider.

The jQuery Mobile objects are extremely powerful and, when previewed in Live View or a browser, terrific looking. With relative ease, you can build apps that include a graphic table of contents (see Figure 17-18, left), collapsible panels (see Figure 17-18, middle), or text and images (see Figure 17-18, right).

FIGURE 17-18

Three views of a jQuery Mobile created with the Dreamweaver objects and standard tools.

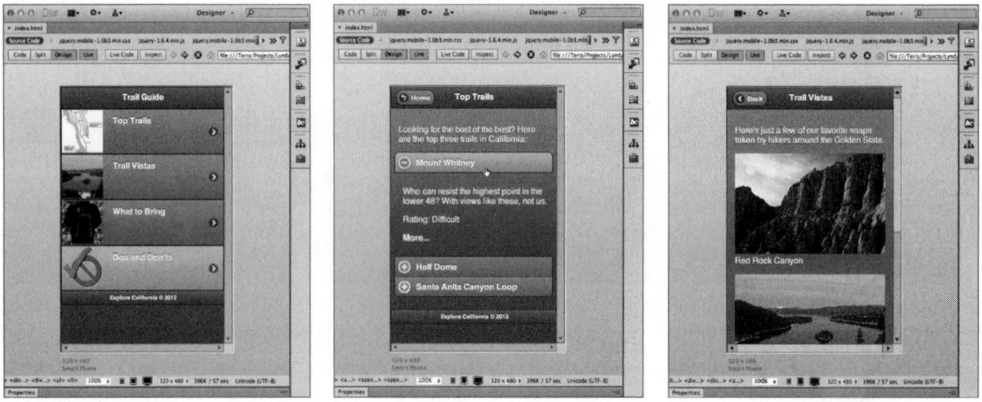

Styling with jQuery themes

As noted several times in the first part of this section, one of the key features of jQuery Mobile is theming. A theme is a consistent series of styles that can be quickly applied and adjusted app-wide. jQuery Mobile organizes its themes alphabetically, from *a* to *z*; initially, there are five themes available in the Dreamweaver Mobile Starter pages: a, b, c, d, and e. Theoretically, one application could have up to 26 different themes applied to various user interface elements. More realistically, most designers will mix and match two or three themes. What's more, each of the 26 available themes can be completely customized—a process made far simpler with the introduction of a visual interface known as the jQuery Mobile ThemeRoller.

By default, the Dreamweaver Mobile Starter pages are rendered with theme "a," a dark gray style seen in Figure 17-19 on the left. On the right, the same page with theme "e" (a bright yellow style) is shown. To make the change, the same attribute was added to the page, header, and footer <div> tags: `data-theme="e"`. A slightly different attribute, `data-theme="e"`, was applied to the <div> tag used to hold the content. While it may appear to be needlessly onerous to have to add the same attribute repeatedly, it actually makes the layout far more flexible than it would be otherwise. You can, for example, mix and match the themes as desired. For example, the page, header, and footer could be one theme and the content another.

FIGURE 17-19

Quickly shift your app from one theme to another with the addition of a simple code attribute.

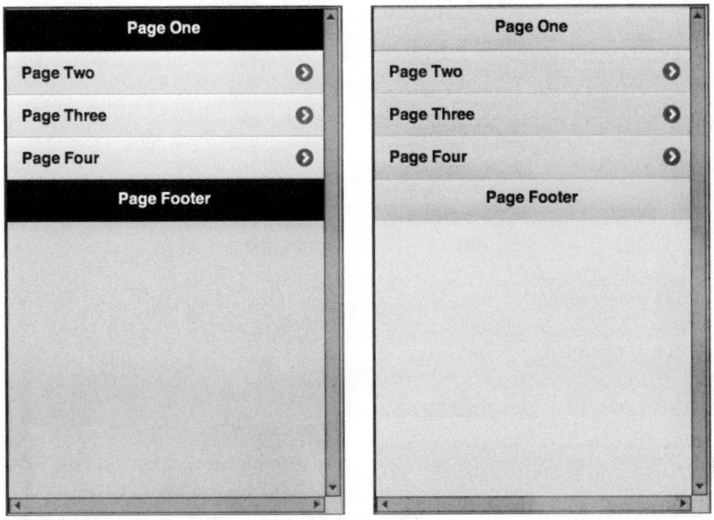

In addition to supporting the `data-theme` attribute in Code view with full code-hinting support, Dreamweaver supplies a point-and-click method for applying themes with the jQuery Mobile Swatches panel. To use this panel, choose Window ➪ jQuery Mobile Swatches and enter Live View. Click any page element in the Document window and then select a theme swatch from the panel (see Figure 17-20).

So, I can hear those among you muttering, "Great, but there are only the default five themes to choose from?" Absolutely not! Any theme can be customized as much as desired by modifying the CSS. While this level of control is welcome, it can be time-consuming to re-style all the moving parts of a jQuery Mobile app by hand. Luckily, there's an alternative: the jQuery Mobile ThemeRoller (see Figure 17-21).

The jQuery Mobile ThemeRoller can be found online at `http://jquerymobile.com/themeroller/` and quickly reached by clicking the Get More Themes link found on the jQuery Mobile Swatches panel. Once you arrive at the site (see Figure 17-22), you can quickly create your custom themes by dragging and dropping fully customizable colors from the bar above to the various interface elements. You can also fine-tune the values and change other properties, such as the global font-family, through the sidebar labeled Theme Settings. You're free to define up to 26 different themes; the site recommends that you create at least 3. Once you're done, you can download the theme. You'll need to uncompress the files and store them in your local site root.

The final step is to link your jQuery Mobile source files to the new CSS style sheet. It is recommended that the new `<link>` tag be placed after the default CSS files for the cascade to work properly.

FIGURE 17-20

Pick a theme visually from the jQuery Mobile Swatches panel.

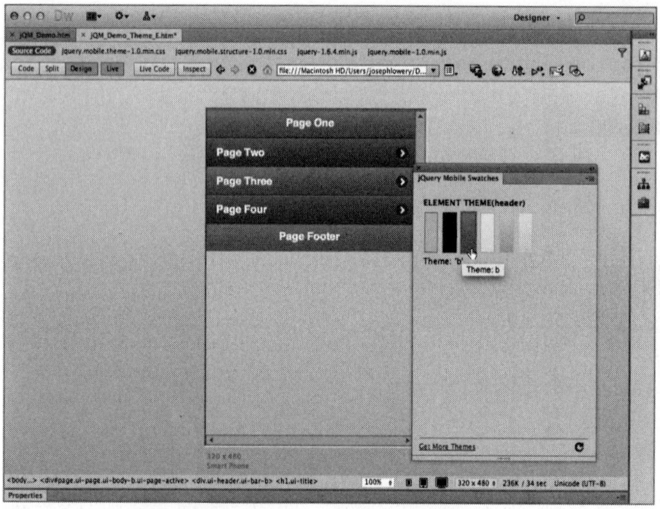

FIGURE 17-21

Additional theme options become available for certain page elements, such as buttons.

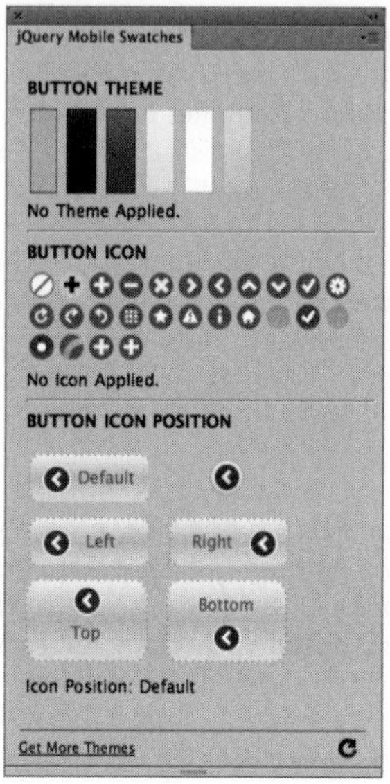

FIGURE 17-22

Create custom themes with drag-and-drop ease via the jQuery Mobile ThemeRoller.

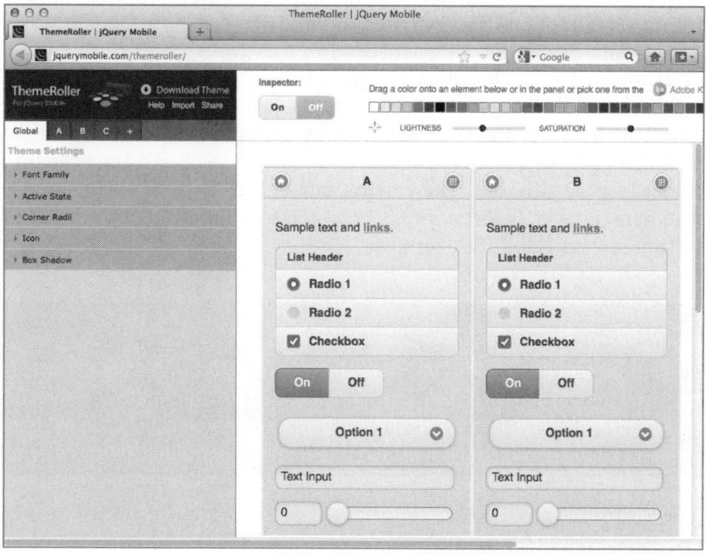

TIP

If you're like me, you'll find yourself spending an inordinate amount of time with the jQuery Mobile ThemeRoller. One of my favorite tools is the built-in connection to Adobe Kuler, a great way to find inspiring and beautiful color combinations.

Working with PhoneGap

If you read through the previous section, you may be wondering if jQuery Mobile is all you can do with mobile apps in Dreamweaver. In fact, it's just the start. Dreamweaver also includes a direct connection to a technology called PhoneGap. PhoneGap is a cross-platform framework for developing native mobile applications with HTML, CSS, and JavaScript. It includes hooks into many core functions that allow you to integrate advanced features such as file storage, database access, camera, compass, and many others. Once the application is developed, it can be compiled and deployed on a wide range of mobile devices, including iOS, Android, Windows 7, Blackberry, and more.

TIP

To learn more about all you can do with PhoneGap, visit the source itself: `http://phonegap.com/`.

The company that created PhoneGap, Nitobi, was acquired by Adobe, and the source code for PhoneGap was contributed to the Apache Software Foundation where it is slated to become a fully open-source project. To avoid confusion between the contributed code and the PhoneGap code that Nitobi continues to work on, the contributed code was renamed Cordova.

The easiest way to start working with PhoneGap is, again, through the Mobile Starter sample pages. Once you've created your basic starter, you'll need to add a JavaScript file to drive the PhoneGap functions. You can get this file from the PhoneGap site by clicking the download button. Once it is downloaded, unzip the package and copy the file `cordova-1.6.0.js` from the lib/android folder to a scripts folder in your site root. The version number in the filename may be different from the one described here. Finally, insert a `<script>` tag to link to the newly copied JavaScript file in the <head> section of your Mobile Starter page.

NEW FEATURE

Developing a PhoneGap application is beyond the scope of this book, but you can start with a basic jQuery Mobile app and then take the next step . . . all the way to your phone. Dreamweaver CS6 includes a direct connection to a key PhoneGap service, PhoneGap Build. With PhoneGap Build, you can upload your project files and get back a series of URLs so you can download different builds for your app for all supported mobile platforms. Pretty amazing, eh?

Here's how it works:

1. Choose Site ➪ PhoneGap Build.
2. When the dialog box opens, click Start PhoneGap Build Service (see Figure 17-23).
3. The log-in screen for PhoneGap Build service appears; log-in or register if necessary.
4. Select the project files to upload from the site.

FIGURE 17-23

Make the connection to the PhoneGap Build service right from within Dreamweaver.

5. Click Upload Project.

   Once the files have been uploaded, PhoneGap Build begins generating your application for a variety of platforms.

6. To install a build of your application on your mobile device, take a picture of the Quick Response (QR) code with the camera of your mobile device and follow the prompts, as shown in Figure 17-24.

7. To store a copy of the project files locally, click Download for each desired platform.

FIGURE 17-24

You'll need a QR code reader app to install a PhoneGap build on your mobile device.

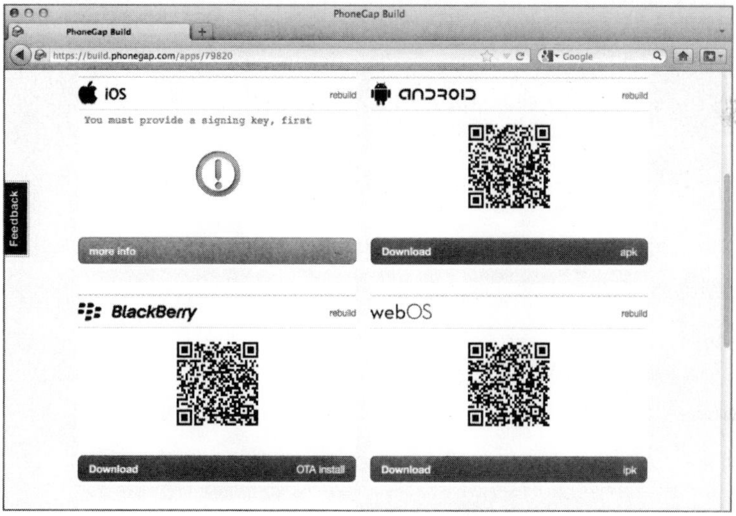

The PhoneGap service is free for the development of an unlimited number of public apps (available to anyone) and one private app. Additional private apps can be developed under a sliding scale pricing plan. For more information, see `https://build.phonegap.com/`.

Summary

Dreamweaver has opened itself to the world of advanced JavaScript frameworks. Now visual designers and hard-core coders alike can take advantage of the rich tapestry of enhanced, interactive layout devices such as accordion panels and sophisticated user interfaces such as multi-month calendars. The enhancements that make this possible in Dreamweaver include:

- An advanced JavaScript engine that provides automatic code hinting to core JavaScript objects, as well as linked JavaScript frameworks to make sure your coding syntax is correct.

- Easy implementation of JavaScript web widgets, which allow drag-and-drop implementation and immediate gratification through Live View.
- An easy-to-use tool that converts JavaScript framework components into Dreamweaver installable web widgets.
- The Widget Browser allows you to customize widget properties before adding the required code to your page.
- The jQuery Mobile framework is fully integrated into Dreamweaver and provides a quick route to developing mobile apps with HTML, CSS, and JavaScript.
- Integration with the PhoneGap Build service, accessible through the Site menu, which allows you to compile a mobile app, ready for activation and use.

In the next chapter, you begin to learn about the dynamic side of Dreamweaver in an exploration of database connections and recordsets.

Part IV

Incorporating Dynamic Data

IN THIS PART

Chapter 18
Establishing Connections and Recordsets

Chapter 19
Making Data Dynamic

Chapter 20
Managing Data

Chapter 21
Working with Dynamic Live View

Chapter 22
Crafting Multi-Page Applications

Chapter 23
Using Web Content Management Systems

CHAPTER

18

Establishing Connections and Recordsets

IN THIS CHAPTER

Examining the structured world of databases

Dreamweaver Technique: Setting Up a Dynamic Site

Making a basic connection

Dreamweaver Technique: Declaring an ODBC Data Source

Dreamweaver Technique: Creating an ASP Connection

Dreamweaver Technique: Defining a ColdFusion Connection

Dreamweaver Technique: Setting Up a PHP Connection

Crafting custom connection strings

Pinpointing data with recordsets

Dreamweaver Technique: Defining a Recordset

Writing SQL queries

Although Dreamweaver can be used to build any sort of web application, one of its biggest strengths is its capability to present and manage dynamically accessed data. In other words, many designers use Dreamweaver to display and alter information from a database on the web. But to handle that information, you must first establish a connection between the web page and the desired data source and then you must define a selection of records from that data source.

Dreamweaver is adept at handling both of these pieces. You can connect to virtually any data source—databases, spreadsheets, and even standard text files—in a number of different ways. Dreamweaver offers a variety of connection types, ranging from the simplest with the highest overhead, DSN (Data Source Name), to the more complex, but most efficient, OLE DB. This chapter explains how the connections are made in Dreamweaver and why some are more robust than others.

After you have established a connection and your web page is ready to communicate with your data source, you must create a *recordset*. You can think of a recordset as the key topic of conversation in a dialogue between a web application and a data source. It is the result of a query made to the database based on your specifications.

For most basic recordsets, Dreamweaver provides a point-and-click interface. You can also construct more advanced recordsets that make extensive use of Structured Query Language (SQL) within Dreamweaver. Both methods are detailed in this chapter; if you are a beginner unfamiliar with database concepts, be sure to read the following section.

Data Source Basics

Data sources store information systematically. Here, the crucial word is *systematically*. Many other technologies, both low end and high end, store information—a shelf of books, a shoebox full of receipts, even a collection of web pages. Few methods, however, store information in a way that facilitates structured and uniform retrieval. The precise nature of the structure varies from one type of database to another, but fundamentally, they are all the same.

NOTE
The term "data source" is a more generic name for a database. In this book, the two terms are used interchangeably.

The two different types of data sources are *system-based* and *file-based*. File-based data sources store their data in physical files; Access, Excel, and dBase are all examples of file-based data sources. A system-based data source works with data stored in its own dedicated server where the database system resides. MS SQL Server, Oracle, PostgreSQL, and MySQL are system-based. Both types of data sources are structured in fundamentally the same way.

A database is made up of a series of *records*. Each record can be thought of as a snapshot of a particular set of details. The details are known as *fields*, and each field contains pertinent information or data. A single database record can be made up of any number of fields of varying types—some fields hold only numbers or only dates, whereas others are open-ended and can hold any type of information. A series of database records that have the same fields is commonly referred to as a *table*; a simple table is also known as a *flat-file database*. Like a word-processing or HTML table, a database table has rows and columns. Each column represents a field, and each row represents a record. For example, the following table called BookTitles describes a series of books.

Title	Author	Pages	Published
JavaScript Bible	Danny Goodman	1,248	2007
CSS Hacks and Filters	Joseph Lowery	266	2005
HTML5 24-Hour Trainer	Joseph Lowery	1,016	2011

The first row in the table contains the field names Title, Author, Pages, and Published. Each subsequent row contains a complete record. This table is in no particular order; however, one of the reasons why databases are so powerful is their sorting capability. If you were to sort the

BookTitles table by page count, listing the books with the fewest pages first, it would look like the following table.

Title	Author	Pages	Published
CSS Hacks and Filters	Joseph Lowery	266	2005
HTML5 24-Hour Trainer	Joseph Lowery	1,016	2011
JavaScript Bible	Danny Goodman	1,248	2007

To simplify data manipulation, many databases require that a table have an *index field* in which each entry is unique. In the preceding table, the Title field could serve as an index field because each title is unique. Not all tables can use a regular field as an index, however, because of duplicate titles or names. For example, you may not be able to use a CustomerName field as an index because you may have more than one "John Smith" in your database. If that's the case, you need to create a separate ID field using an AutoNumber type if you're working in Microsoft Access. If you're working in SQL Server, create an integer field and mark it as an Identity type. Either method guarantees a unique ID for each record by assigning an incrementing number to each entry in the database.

Index fields, also called *key fields*, become an absolute necessity when two or more tables—or flat-file databases—are combined to create a *relational database*. As the name implies, a relational database presents related information. For example, suppose that you create another table called BookSales to accompany the previous book database example:

Region	Sales	Title
East	10,000	*JavaScript Bible*
South	20,500	*JavaScript Bible*
West	42,000	*JavaScript Bible*
North	25,000	*JavaScript Bible*
East	15,000	*HTML5 24-Hour Trainer*
South	12,000	*HTML5 24-Hour Trainer*
West	8,000	*HTML5 24-Hour Trainer*
North	21,000	*HTML5 24-Hour Trainer*
East	8,330	*CSS Hacks and Filters*
South	6,500	*CSS Hacks and Filters*
West	8,000	*CSS Hacks and Filters*
North	7,400	*CSS Hacks and Filters*

To get a list of authors sorted according to sales figures, you have to combine the two databases. A field common to both tables is used to create the juncture, or *join*. Here, the common field is the index field Title. Although flat-file databases can be used in many situations, most industrial-strength applications use relational databases to access information.

In addition to changing the sort order of a table, database information can also be selectively retrieved by using a *filter*. A filter is often represented by a `WHERE` statement, as in "Show me the books where regional sales were at least 10,000 and less than 20,000." Applying this filter to the BookSales table results in the following table:

Region	Sales	Title
East	10,000	*JavaScript Bible*
East	15,000	*HTML5 24-Hour Trainer*
South	12,000	*HTML5 24-Hour Trainer*

The common language understood by many web-available databases is *Structured Query Language*, or SQL. A SQL statement tells the database precisely what information you're looking for and in what form you want it. Although SQL statements can become quite complex, a relatively simple SQL statement has just four parts:

- `SELECT`: Picks the fields to display
- `FROM`: Chooses the tables from which to gather the information
- `WHERE`: Describes the filter criteria and/or the joins
- `ORDER`: Specifies the sorting criteria

A sample SQL statement translation of the instruction "Show me the books where regional sales were more than 10,000 but less than 20,000" looks like the following:

```
SELECT Title
FROM BookSales
WHERE (Sales > 10000) AND (Sales < 20000)
ORDER by Sales
```

Joins between two or more tables are depicted in SQL with an equals sign and are considered part of the filter in the `WHERE` statement. To show the sales by author's name, you could revise the SQL statement to read as follows:

```
SELECT Title, Author
FROM BookTitles, BookSales
WHERE BookTitles = BookSales AND ((Sales > 10000) AND (Sales < 20000))
ORDER by Author
```

TIP

The quick way to display all the fields in a table is to use a SQL statement with a wildcard, like this:

```
SELECT * FROM BookTitles
```

The asterisk indicates that you want to choose every field. From a server-resources standpoint, however, this is an inefficient way to retrieve all records. If possible, select all your fields individually. Using the asterisk forces the database to determine what all the field names are, instead of defining exactly what fields to retrieve.

Understanding How Active Content Pages Work

The journey for a static web page from user to server is straightforward, even for the most complex, graphics-laden, JavaScript-laden page. The user clicks a link that sends a signal to the server to send that page. An active content page—with full database connectivity—travels a much different route.

NOTE

Although a good number of applications were developed using ASP during the early history of the web, Microsoft stopped development in 2001. The successor to ASP is ASP.NET, which is not supported by Dreamweaver. The information in this section is offered to those developers who need to work with legacy ASP sites and in the interest of covering all of Dreamweaver's features.

An active content page is a blend of traditional HTML and a database server language such as PHP, Active Server Pages (ASP), or ColdFusion Markup Language (CFML). When a user accesses an active content page, the requested page is passed through the web and database servers where the code is processed, and a new HTML page is generated. That page is then sent on to the user. Figure 18-1 illustrates this process.

FIGURE 18-1

An active content page is processed by a database server prior to being sent to the user.

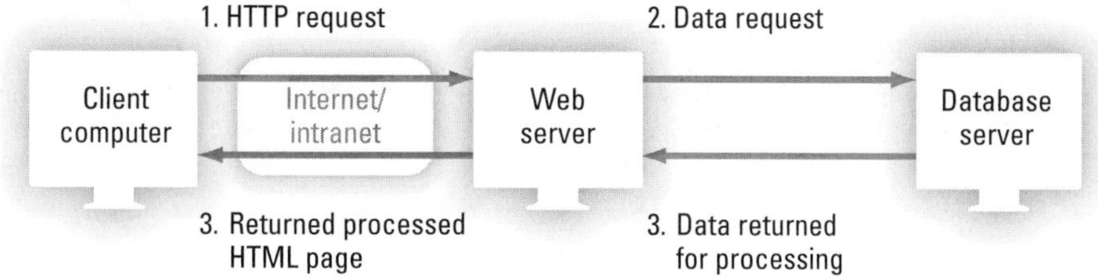

Active content servers can connect to more than databases. Other possibilities include the following:

- **Directory servers:** Directory servers control the permissions for large corporations and determine who is granted access to what group of files. With a directory server, two people—with different clearances—can see two different pages when clicking the same link.
- **Mail servers:** E-mail communication can be fully automated through a mail server. Responses to forms are categorized and forwarded to the proper parties. Mass mailings can go out at the click of a button. Messages can be automatically incorporated into web pages.
- **File servers:** By and large, HTML by itself has no file manipulation capabilities. However, with a file server, files can be uploaded, copied, renamed, moved, deleted, and more.

The primary HTML vehicle for interfacing with a database server is the form.

Dreamweaver TECHNIQUE

Setting Up a Dynamic Site

Before you can use Dreamweaver to create dynamic pages, you have to make sure your site is defined properly. All the Dreamweaver Techniques in this chapter, as well as those in the other chapters in Part IV of this book, rely on a dynamic site.

NOTE

Although it is possible to use the same site previously created for the Dreamweaver Techniques, it's easier to create a second site specifically for dynamic applications.

1. Copy the Techniques folder from the website to your web server root. On Windows, the web server root is located at `C:\Inetpub\wwwroot`; on Macintosh, you'll find it at `/Users/`*`your_user_name`*`/Sites`.
2. Choose Site ➪ New Site.
3. When the Site Setup dialog box appears, enter the name of your site, which in this case is **Techniques - Dynamic,** and browse to the folder previously created in the local web server root.

   Because Dreamweaver will need a local web address to render the pages in Live View, let's enter that now.
4. Expand the Advanced Settings section and choose the Local Info category.
5. In the web URL field, enter the same address used in the browser to enter the site. In my example, it's `http://localhost/Techniques/`.

   The final step is to set up a staging server with the proper server model chosen.
6. Choose the Servers category.
7. Click Add A New Server (+).
8. In the Basics tab, enter a name for your server in the Server Name field. A standard choice would be Testing.
9. Choose Local/Network from the Connect Using list.

10. Click the Server Folder Browse icon and navigate to the local site root folder.
11. Switch to the Advanced tab.
12. From the Server Model list in the Testing Server area, choose your server model and click Save.
13. Confirm that the Testing checkbox is selected in the Servers category and click Save.

Any new pages you now create for your site will be configured for your server model. If, for example, you've opted for an ASP site, your new page will include ASP code at the top of the file, as well as an `.asp` extension, whereas files for a PHP site will have a `.php` extension.

Opening a Connection to a Data Source

If you're a *Star Trek* fan (of any generation), you're likely to remember the phrase "Open a channel, Lieutenant." With these words, the Captain was asking to establish a communication link between the Enterprise and whatever alien vessel was hovering nearby. Not only are the technical lines of communication enabled, but any necessary translation services are also put into play. When you connect to a data source in Dreamweaver, you're opening a channel between your web pages and a designated data source. (Notice that I'm referring to lowercase data, not Data, the android; I'll save that extended metaphor for another time.)

18

As noted earlier, you have numerous ways to connect to a data source. The simplest, DSN, requires some administrative setup and has a negative impact on server performance. Alternatives, such as DSN-less and OLE DB connections, require the developer to have more information on hand—such as the exact location of the data source on the server—but are less server-intensive.

Regardless of the connection method you use, Dreamweaver handles the connection in basically the same fashion. ColdFusion is the only language that's handled differently, by linking to the data source directly either through the DSN in the `CFQUERY` tag or through a Data Source Name variable in the `Application.cfm` file. After you define a connection, as detailed in the following sections, a server-side include is inserted into your document above the opening `<html>` tag, like this one for ASP:

```
<!--#include file="Connections/connDBA.asp" -->
```

or this one in PHP:

```
<?php require_once('Connections/connDBA.php'); ?>
```

In each case, Dreamweaver creates a folder called Connections at the site root for the server-side include files. The same file is referenced on every page that uses the defined data source connection. By using a server-side include, Dreamweaver provides a one-step method for updating all the pages using the same connection in the site. To define, edit, and manage your connections, open the Databases panel in the Application panel group (see Figure 18-2).

The first thing you see in your Databases panel is a short checklist of what to do before you can start adding connections. Basically, you must:

1. Define a site.

2. Define a default dynamic document type for your site.
3. Set up the site's testing server.

FIGURE 18-2

Data source connections are managed on a site-by-site basis through the Databases panel.

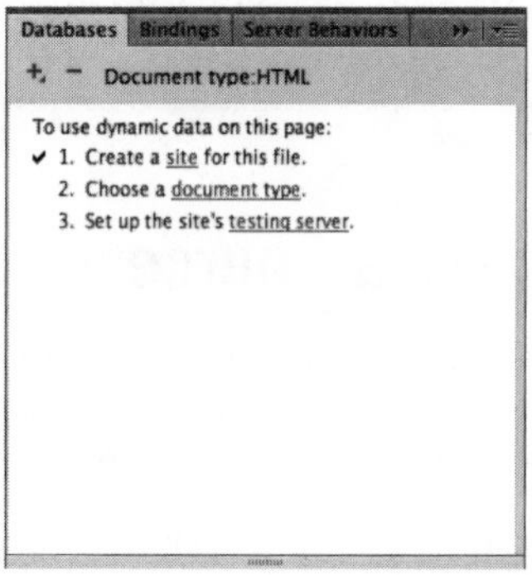

Some server languages may have additional requirements. Each criterion contains a link that opens the appropriate dialog box for changing these settings. Once all the criteria have checkmarks next to them, you're ready to add connections. After you create your first connection, you have access to all the database information in the panel (see Figure 18-3).

FIGURE 18-3

Connecting to a database gives you access to all the tables, views, and stored procedures for that database.

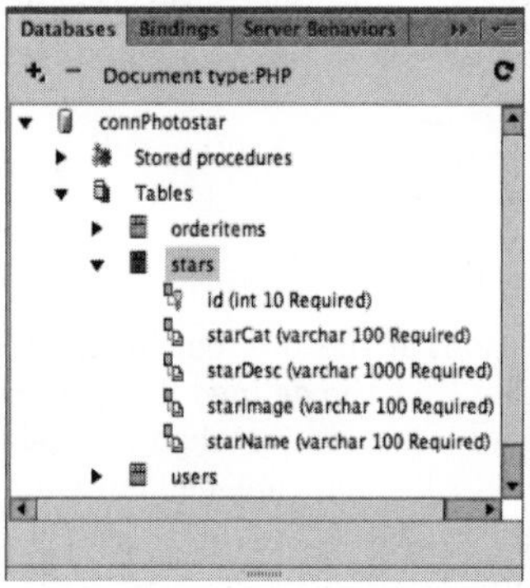

When you've finished defining your connections, upload the files in the Connection folder so they work on your remote server. If you upload a file containing a connection and opt to include dependent files when you upload it, the connection files are uploaded automatically.

Using data source names

Data sources, like graphic files, come in different formats. Databases developed in Access are different from those developed in Oracle or MySQL. To enable applications to access a variety of data sources, the Open Database Connectivity (ODBC) standard was developed. ODBC is a type of universal translator that enables web (and other) applications to read from and write to databases by using a specific driver for a particular database type. Windows systems include drivers for data sources created in Microsoft Access, SQL Server, dBase, Oracle, FoxPro, Excel, and Paradox. There's even a driver for reading straight text files, which usually contain comma-separated values. Macintosh users should connect to the ODBC drivers on their testing servers.

The Data Source Name (DSN) protocol was established to simplify the process of connecting via ODBC. Just as a domain name such as `www.idest.com` is an alias for an Internet Protocol number (for example, `64.70.242.110`), a DSN is an alias for the actual location of a data source. Locally, on Windows systems, DSNs are managed through the ODBC Data Source Administrator. Remotely, DSNs are set up by system administrators on the testing server.

Even if you ultimately decide to use a more efficient method of connecting to the data source, DSNs are very useful during the development phase. Every server model, except for PHP and .NET, supports DSNs. To set up a local DSN on a Windows system, follow these steps:

1. Windows 7, Windows Vista, and Windows XP users should select Data Sources (ODBC) from the Administrative Tools folder in the Control Panel. The ODBC Data Source Administrator opens.

NOTE

If you're working with a Macintosh and want to use an ODBC DSN connection—or just prefer to work with the actual data on the server—the DSN must be established on your testing server by the system administrator. All database communication is then handled online.

2. From the ODBC Data Source Administrator, select the System DSN tab. The System DSN tab lists all the DSNs previously defined for your system.
3. From the System DSN tab, click Add. The Create New Data Source dialog box opens.
4. Choose the appropriate driver for your data source from the list. The driver for Access databases is listed as Microsoft Access Driver (`*.mdb`); the driver for Oracle databases is shown as Microsoft ODBC for Oracle. Click Finish when you're ready. A setup dialog box for the driver selected appears next. Each setup dialog box is somewhat different.

NOTE

If you don't see a driver for your database listed here, get one from the manufacturer or database sponsor. If you are working with MySQL databases, you can get an ODBC driver from `http://dev.mysql.com/downloads/connector/odbc/`.

5. In the setup dialog box, enter the Data Source Name and select the data source. Following are examples of the most commonly used data sources:
   - For Access databases, click Select to locate the database (see Figure 18-4). If a username and password are required, click Advanced to enter that information.
   - For Excel spreadsheets, choose Select Workbook to locate the proper file. Select Options to limit the number of rows accessed.
   - For SQL Server, select a name from the Server drop-down list. Choose (local) if your system also acts as the SQL Server. Click Finish when you are done.
   - For MySQL databases, enter the MySQL host name or IP address and the full path to the MySQL database. You can enter a username and password on the same screen. The MySQL ODBC driver also offers a wide range of options you can enable.

FIGURE 18-4

To use an existing Access database, click the Select button from the ODBC Microsoft Access Setup dialog box.

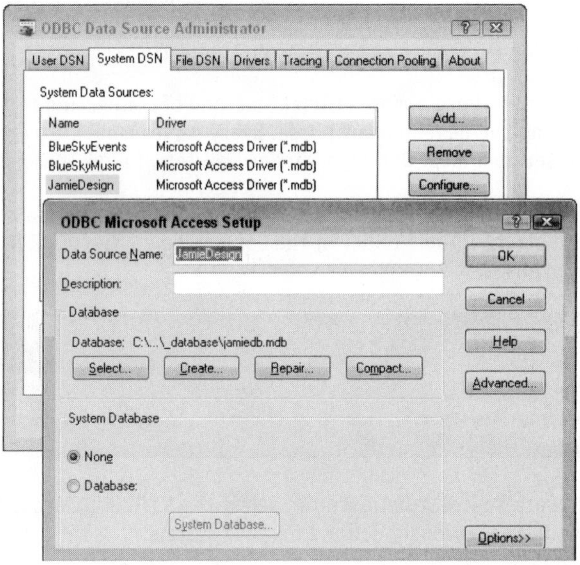

6. When you've closed the setup dialog box, click OK to close the ODBC Data Source Administrator.

After you've created a DSN for your data source, you're ready to create an ODBC DSN connection in Dreamweaver. Although the basic procedure is the same for all five server models, the specific steps are different enough to warrant the individual descriptions presented in the following sections.

Dreamweaver TECHNIQUE

Declaring an ODBC Data Source

A first step for ASP and ColdFusion users on Windows is to establish an ODBC data source. Although this operation is not strictly necessary for ColdFusion, it does make setting up a connection easier.

1. In Windows, choose Start ➪ Administrative Tools ➪ Data Sources (ODBC).
2. From the ODBC Data Source Administrator, select the System DSN tab.
3. Click Add to open the Create New Data Source dialog box.
4. Select the Microsoft Access Driver (`*.mdb`) entry from the list and click Finish.
5. In the setup dialog box, enter **RelativeRealty** in the Data Source Name field.
6. Click Select and navigate to `Relative_Realty.mdb` in the `Techniques\Database\ASP_CF` folder.

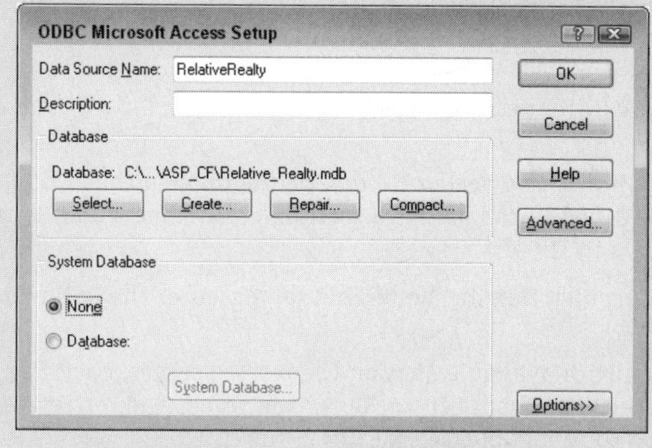

7. Click OK once to close the ODBC Microsoft Access dialog box and again to close the ODBC Data Source Administrator dialog box.

Now when you create a connection in Dreamweaver, your new DSN is waiting for you.

ASP

A DSN connection is often an ASP developer's first choice for rapid development because of its easy setup. To establish a DSN connection in Dreamweaver, follow these steps:

1. Choose Window ➪ Databases to display the Databases panel, as shown in Figure 18-5.
2. Click the Add (+) button and select Data Source Name (DSN) from the drop-down list.
3. The Data Source Name (DSN) dialog box displays. If you're creating a connection on a testing server, choose the Dreamweaver Should Connect Using DSN On Testing Server option; otherwise, choose the Using Local DSN option. These options are not available on the Mac; you must always use the testing server.

FIGURE 18-5

A drop-down list appears when you click the Add (+) button, enabling you to select a DSN-type connection.

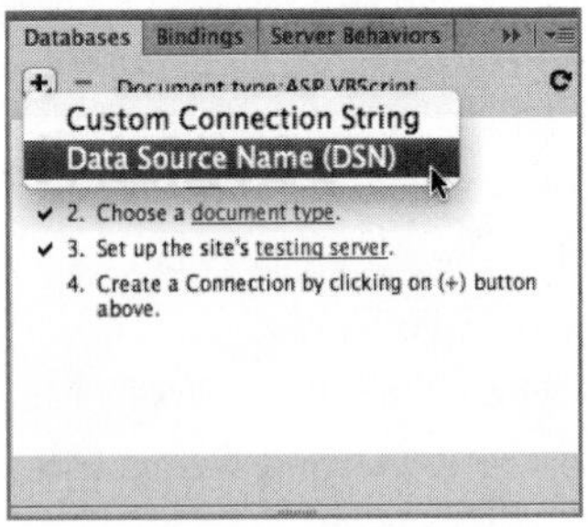

4. Enter a label for your new connection in the Connection Name field. It's a good habit to identify your connections with the prefix `conn`; for example, you might label your connection `connDBA`.
5. If you're defining a local DSN connection, select an entry from the Data Source Name (DSN) drop-down list.

   If your DSN has not been previously declared, click Define to open the ODBC Data Source Administrator and, as outlined in the previous section, create a new DSN. When you're done, the new DSN appears in the list.
6. If you are defining a DSN connection on the testing server, enter the DSN name in the field.

   To select the DSN from a list of available ones on the testing server, click the DSN button. Dreamweaver attempts to connect to the testing server and retrieve a list of assigned DSNs. If your DSN is available, select it from the list.
7. If necessary, enter a username and password in the appropriate fields.
8. Certain databases, such as those from Oracle, enable you to restrict the number of database items available from a connection. To limit the available tables, click Advanced and enter the desired Schema and/or Catalog.
9. To ensure that your connection is properly set up, click Test on the Data Source Name (DSN) dialog box. If the connection is established, Dreamweaver tells you the connection was successful.
10. When you're finished, click OK to close the Data Source Name (DSN) dialog box. The new connection is listed in the Databases tab of the Application panel.

ColdFusion

ColdFusion seamlessly integrates with the ODBC Data Source Administrator to use the DSNs already established on the system. Furthermore, new DSNs may be set up from within the ColdFusion Administrator. This compatibility makes establishing standard DSN connections very straightforward in Dreamweaver. Best of all, you can download and install a free version of ColdFusion for developing and testing web applications. Visit `www.adobe.com/go/coldfusion` for more details.

Dreamweaver TECHNIQUE

Creating an ASP Connection

In this Dreamweaver Technique, you establish your connection to the DSN previously created. Work through this technique if you're using either the ASP-VBScript server model or a local development system.

1. In the Databases panel, click the Add (+) button and select Data Source Name (DSN) from the drop-down list.
2. In the Data Source Name dialog box, enter **connRelative** in the Connection field.
3. From the Data Source Name (DSN) list, choose RelativeRealty.
4. Leave both the User Name and the Password fields blank.
5. Make sure that the Using Local DSN option is selected and click Test.

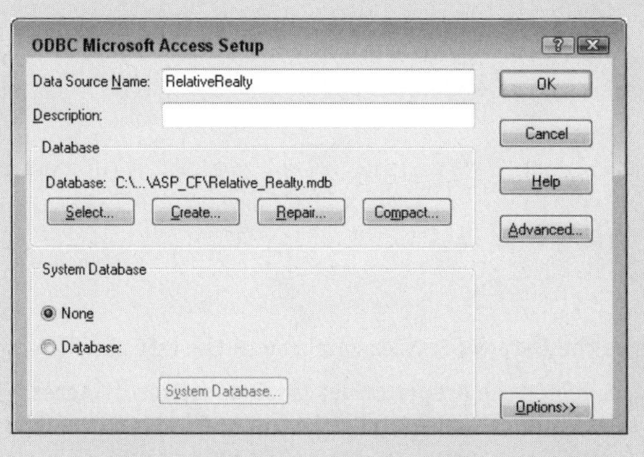

6. If Dreamweaver tells you the connection was successful, click OK to close the dialog box; otherwise, double-check your settings and test again.
7. When you're finished, click OK to close the Data Source Name (DSN) dialog box. The new connection is listed in the Databases tab of the Application panel.

After the dialog box closes, you'll see connRelative listed in the Databases panel.

NOTE

In Dreamweaver, DSN connections in ColdFusion have a limitation. Dreamweaver only supports the use of stored procedures, a type of encapsulated SQL statement, for SQL Server databases with the standard DSN connection. To use stored procedures with databases other than SQL Server, you must connect via a JDBC (Java Database Connectivity) driver available through the Data Source Name—Advanced option, covered later in this section. The JDBC driver also enables Macintosh users to connect to a local database without going through ColdFusion.

You can enter new DSNs for ColdFusion through the ODBC Data Source Administrator as detailed previously, or you can use the ColdFusion Administrator. To make a standard DSN connection for ColdFusion server models, follow these steps:

1. Choose Window ⇨ Databases to display the Databases panel.
2. Click the Modify Data Sources button (see Figure 18-6) to open the ColdFusion Administrator home page.

FIGURE 18-6

Use the Modify Data Sources button in the Databases panel to get to the ColdFusion Administrator.

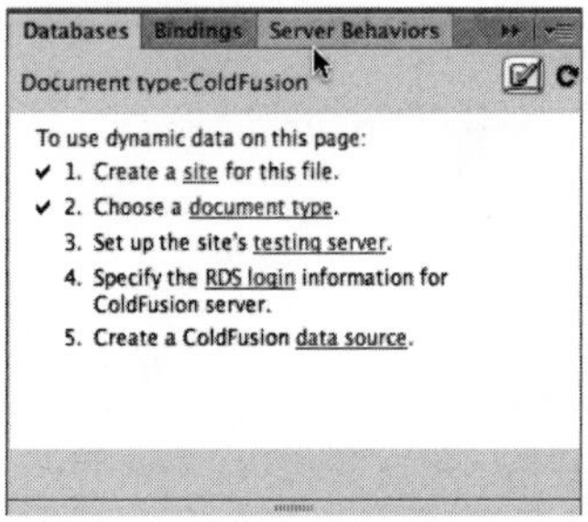

3. Choose Data Sources from the Data & Services category in the left panel.
4. On the Data Sources page, select the proper driver (such as Microsoft Access) from the drop-down list, enter a Data Source Name, and click the Add button (see Figure 18-7).
5. On the Create ODBC Data Source page, enter the path to the database in the Database File or System Database field. Alternatively, you can click the appropriate Browser Server button to locate the file. If needed, enter a username and password.
6. When you're finished, click Submit. ColdFusion creates and verifies the DSN, displaying it in the ODBC Data Sources page.

Dreamweaver TECHNIQUE

Defining a ColdFusion Connection

Although you can define a ColdFusion connection to an Access database within Dreamweaver, it's actually easier to accomplish in the ColdFusion Administrator.

1. From the Databases panel, click Modify Data Sources to open the ColdFusion Administrator home page.
2. In the ColdFusion Administrator home page, choose Data Sources from the Data & Services category.
3. On the Data Sources page, enter **RelativeRealty** in the Data Source Name field.
4. Select the Microsoft Access entry from the Driver list.

5. Click Add. The Create ODBC Data Source page opens and displays the information established when the ODBC data source was created in the previous Technique.
6. Verify the name and the path to the database in the Database File field.
7. Click Submit.

   ColdFusion creates and verifies the ODBC data source.
8. Return to Dreamweaver and, in the Databases panel, click Refresh.

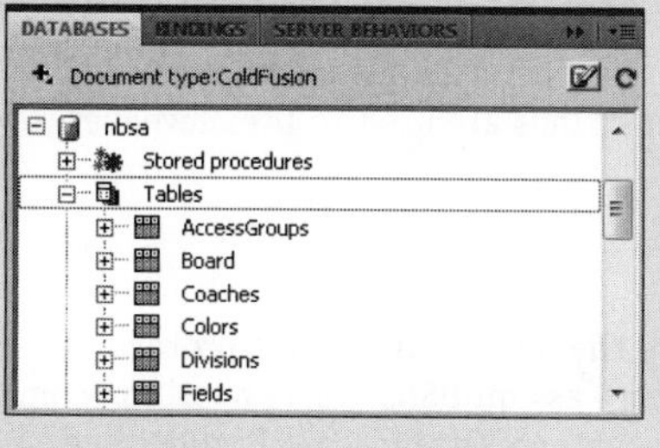

Dreamweaver does not automatically scan the ColdFusion Administrator for new connections, so a refresh is required. Feel free to expand the new entry and explore the database structure.

FIGURE 18-7

The ColdFusion Administrator includes an application for creating new DSNs.

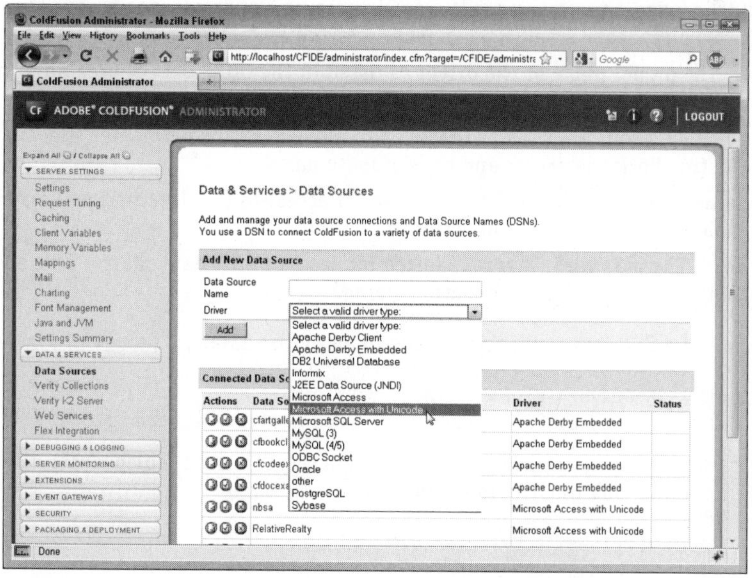

PHP

PHP doesn't support DSN connections. Dreamweaver's PHP server model supports only MySQL connections through its own ODBC drivers. See the "DSN-less Connections for ASP" section later in this chapter for more information about making connections with this server model.

Specifying connection strings

Although a DSN connection may be the easiest to set up, it's not the most robust type of connection. In Dreamweaver, you can explicitly declare the details implied by a DSN connection by specifying a connection string. The connection string states the name of the driver, the path to the data source, and any additional information needed, such as username and password—all in one long string of text. Two types of connection strings are used in Dreamweaver: DSN-less connections and OLE DB connections.

DSN-less connections for ASP

In the real world, ASP developers wanting to use the Data Source Name protocol often face a problem: They cannot get system administrators to assign DSNs. Some hosting companies limit the number of DSNs per site or charge a fee for each one. Often, it's difficult to get a hosting company to respond in a timely fashion. ASP developers can bypass all these potential headaches in Dreamweaver by using a DSN-less connection.

A DSN-less connection uses the same driver as a DSN connection, but without relying on the definition of a Data Source Name. The syntax of a DSN-less connection varies for each type of database but basically has five parts:

- **Provider:** The underlying mechanism that connects the ODBC driver to the application. For ODBC drivers, the provider is MSDASQL; because the provider is always the same for ODBC, the entry is optional in a connection string and understood if omitted.
- **Driver:** The proper name of the driver as listed in the ODBC Data Source Administrator.
- **Path to data source:** Typically, this full path to a database is called the `DBQ`; however, with some data sources, such as Oracle and SQL Server, this parameter appears in two parts, listing both the server and the database name.
- **Username:** The username, if any, required for access to the data source. This element is often abbreviated `UID` in a connection string.
- **Password:** The password, if any, required for access to the data source. This element is often abbreviated `PWD` in a connection string.

Here's an example of a DSN-less connection string to an Access database named `dbaEvents.mdb`:

```
Provider=MSDASQL;Driver={Microsoft Access Driver i
(*.mdb)};DBQ=c:\clients\dba\data\dbaEvents.mdb;UID=jlowery;PWD=hoosier7;
```

If the same data source were in SQL Server format (on a server named "euripedes"), the DSN-less connection string would look like the following:

```
Provider=MSDASQL;Driver={SQL Server};i
Server=euripedes;Database=dbaEvents.mdb;i
UID=jlowery;PWD=hoosier7;
```

To enter a DSN-less connection in Dreamweaver, follow these steps:

1. Choose Window ➪ Databases to display the Databases panel.
2. Click the Add (+) button and choose Custom Connection String from the drop-down list. The Custom Connection String dialog box is displayed (see Figure 18-8).
3. Enter a label for your new connection in the Connection Name field.
4. Enter the complete connection string in the Connection String field.

TIP

It's often easier to type your connection string into a text editor first—making sure that your syntax and parameters are correct—and then cut and paste it into the dialog box field.

5. If you're creating a connection on a testing server, choose the Using Driver On Testing Server option; otherwise, choose the Using Driver On This Machine option.

FIGURE 18-8

For a DSN-less connection, all your data source connectivity information—the driver, the path to the database, and even the username and password—is entered in one long text string.

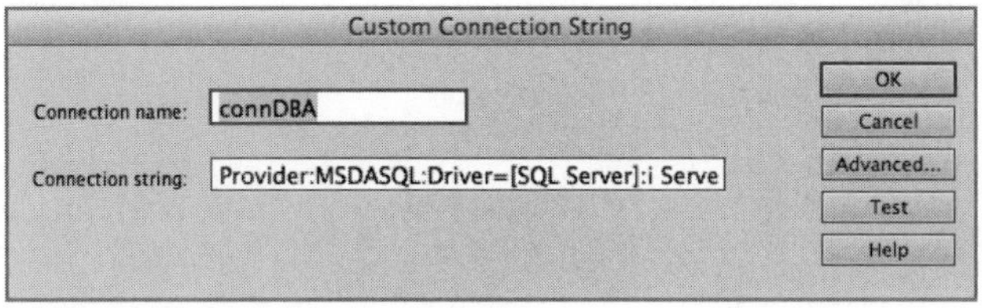

6. Certain databases, such as those from Oracle, enable you to restrict the number of database items available from a connection. To limit the available tables, click Advanced and enter the desired Schema and/or Catalog.
7. To make sure that your connection is properly set up, click the Test button in the Custom Connection String dialog box. If the connection is established, Dreamweaver reports the success.
8. Click OK to close the Custom Connection String dialog box. The new connection is now listed in the Databases panel.

Finding the Path with Server.MapPath

Right up there with the importance of getting your ASP hosting company to set up a DSN quickly is getting the company to tell you exactly where your virtual site is set up on its server. You must have this information if you're going to successfully use a DSN-less connection. Luckily, ASP includes a server-side command that you can use to find the path to your data source. The `Server.MapPath()` command returns the full path of the server when given the relative path to your data source.

Continues

continued

For example, I have a site called `myway.com`. Within my site, I have a database, `thehighway.mdb`, located in the data folder off my site root. On my system, the relative path to the database is `\myway\data\thehighway.mdb`. When I issue the following command on my host's server:

```
Server.MapPath("/myway/data/thehighway.mdb")
```

I get back the full path, which might be something like the following:

```
E:\HTDOCS\jlowery\myway\data\thehighway.mdb
```

The `Server.MapPath()` function can be used in an ASP page or within the Custom Connection String dialog box to find the location of a file. Use the following code syntax for an ASP page:

```
<%@ LANGUAGE="VBSCRIPT" %>
<%
Dim ThatPath
ThatPath = Server.MapPath("\myway\data\thehighway.mdb")
Response.Write "Path to database: " & ThatPath
%>
```

After saving the ASP page and uploading it to your server, execute the page by typing in its URL. The full path to your data source appears in the browser.

Although this is adequate, your pages could break if your site is moved on the server or to another server altogether. A better method is to include the `Server.MapPath()` function as part of the custom connection string. Here's an example of such a string:

```
"Driver={Microsoft Access Driver (*.mdb)};DBQ=" & i
Server.MapPath("/myway/data/thehighway.mdb")
```

Note the use of quotes and the ampersand before the `Server.MapPath()` function. Essentially, you are concatenating two text strings to make one long one.

The `Server.MapPath()` function can be used only when the Using Driver On Testing Server option in the Custom Connection String dialog box is selected.

OLE DB

Although DSN-less connections don't require an actual Data Source Name to be registered, they still rely on the same ODBC drivers. ODBC itself is a type of translator that relies on an OLE (Object Linking and Embedding) DB provider to make the connection. The most efficient way to connect to a data source is to use an OLE DB provider directly. Dreamweaver enables direct OLE DB connections through the Custom Connection String option.

OLE DB connection strings are similar to DSN-less connections except that only the provider parameter (not the driver parameter) is included. The following is an OLE DB connection string to an Access database:

```
Provider=Microsoft.Jet.OLE DB.4.0;
Data Source=d:\clients\dba\data\dbaEvents.mdb;
```

Different data sources require different providers. SQL Server uses `SQLOLE DB`, whereas Oracle needs `OraOLE DB`. Follow these steps to create an OLE DB connection string:

1. Choose Window ➪ Databases to display the Databases panel.
2. Click the Add (+) button and select Custom Connection String from the drop-down list. The Custom Connection String dialog box is displayed.
3. Enter a label for your new connection in the Connection Name field.
4. Enter the complete connection string in the Connection String field.
5. If you're creating a connection on a testing server, choose the Using Driver On Testing Server option; otherwise, choose the Using Driver On This Machine option. This option is not available on the Mac.
6. To limit the available tables, click Advanced and enter the desired Schema and/or Catalog.
7. To ensure that your connection is properly set up, click Test in the Custom Connection String dialog box. Dreamweaver tells you if the connection was established successfully.
8. When you're finished, click OK to close the Custom Connection String dialog box. The new connection is listed in the Connections dialog box.

TIP

Create a blank .NET document and use the OLE DB Connection builders to create your DSN-less strings; then, copy and paste the strings into your ASP connection dialog box.

PHP

Dreamweaver's PHP model supports MySQL connections only. Both PHP and MySQL enjoy a very wide userbase, partly because of their open-source nature.

TIP

If you're just starting out in dynamic web development and want to work with PHP and MySQL, there's a number of freely available packages that can help you set up your development environment. Windows users should look at WampServer (`www.wampserver.com/en/`) and Mac users, MAMP (`www.mamp.info/en/`).

To set up your MySQL connections, follow these steps:

1. Choose Window ➪ Databases to display the Databases panel.
2. Click the Add (+) button and choose MySQL Connection from the drop-down list. The MySQL Connection dialog box is displayed, as shown in Figure 18-9.
3. Enter a label for your new connection in the Connection Name field.
4. Enter the IP or domain address of your MySQL server in the MySQL Server field.
5. Enter your database username in the User Name field.

FIGURE 18-9

Just complete a few steps to set up your MySQL connections in PHP.

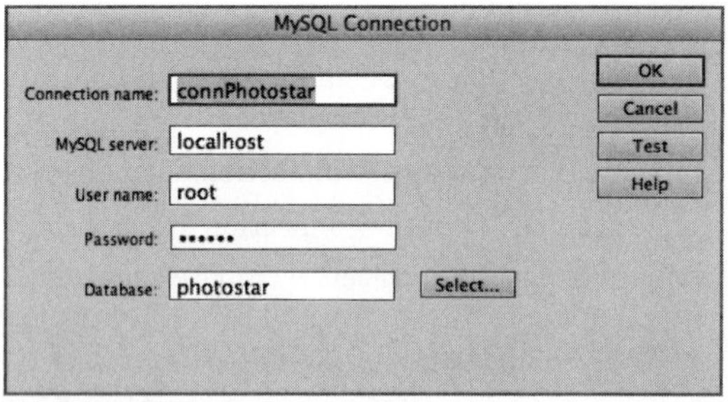

6. Enter your database password in the Password field.
7. Enter the database name in the Database field, or click Select and choose from a list of all the databases to which you have access.
8. To ensure that your connection is properly set up, click Test in the Custom Connection String dialog box. Dreamweaver lets you know whether the test failed or succeeded.
9. When you're finished, click OK to close the Custom Connection String dialog box. The new connection is listed in the Connections dialog box.

Dreamweaver TECHNIQUE

Setting Up a PHP Connection

Once your MySQL data source has been established, you can create a connection to use with PHP.

You'll need to have already created and installed the Relative_Realty data source in MySQL located in the Techniques\Databases\PHP folder. See the Readme file in the folder for setup instructions.

1. In the Databases panel, click Add (+) and select MySQL Connection from the drop-down list.
2. When the MySQL Connection dialog box opens, enter **RelativeRealty** in the Connection Name field.
3. Enter the IP or domain address of your MySQL server in the MySQL Server field. If you're using a local development system, enter **localhost**.
4. Enter your database username in the User Name field.
5. Enter your database password in the Password field.
6. Click Select to display the available databases and choose Relative_Realty.
7. Click Test to verify the connection.
8. If Dreamweaver indicates success, click OK to close the dialog box; otherwise, re-check your entered values and test again.

You'll find your new connection listed in the Databases panel.

Managing Connections

In general, you create connections as needed and forget about them. All you have to do is include them in a page, and Dreamweaver handles the rest. On occasion, however, you must alter existing connections or remove outdated connections. All management of connections is handled inside the Databases panel.

To change the parameters of an existing connection, open the Databases panel, right-click (Control+click) the connection, and select Edit Connection. The type of connection determines which dialog box opens; a DSN connection, for example, opens the Data Source Name (DSN) dialog box.

Although you can alter any of the existing parameters during an editing session, you cannot switch from a DSN-type connection to a DSN-less–type connection via the Edit option. In addition, Dreamweaver does not allow you to rename an existing connection. With a bit of sleight of hand, however, you can make the conversion and keep all of your connections valid. To convert a connection from DSN to a DSN-less or OLE DB–type connection, follow these steps:

1. Create a new connection of the desired type using one of the procedures described previously. This is a temporary connection that will be removed in the final step.
2. Right-click (Control+click) the old DSN connection from the Databases panel and choose Delete Connection. It's a good idea to jot down the name of the original connection before deleting it; you use the same name later in this procedure.
3. Dreamweaver warns you that this action cannot be undone. Choose OK to proceed.
4. Right-click (Control+click) the new connection and select Duplicate Connection. The appropriate dialog box is displayed depending on the type of connection being duplicated.
5. In the dialog box for the duplicated connection, enter the name of the original connection. Click OK when you're finished.
6. In the Databases panel, delete the first, temporary connection by right-clicking (Control+clicking) and choosing Delete Connection.

Although this procedure is somewhat convoluted, after you've completed it, you have effectively upgraded your connection from a DSN to an OLE DB–type connection. The next time you put any of your web pages on the remote server, be sure to include the dependent files for that page. Alternatively, you could put the file (now found in the Connections folder of the site) directly on the server.

Maintaining Design and Runtime Connections

The first step is to create the connection you'd like to use on the server and then put it on the site in the Connections folder. Next, create a local connection of a different type, named the same as the remote connection. Because Dreamweaver uses a server-side include referencing only the name of the file, your different connections are the same on both locations.

WARNING

One caveat when uploading your local files to your remote site: You must not use Dreamweaver's Put Dependent Files option. If you do, Dreamweaver overwrites the remote connection file with the local one.

Extracting Recordsets

Establishing a connection with a data source is not enough to begin working with that data—you must explicitly state what part of the data you want, whether it's all of it or just one record. This defined collection of data is called a *recordset.*

Within the code, you use a query written in SQL to define a recordset. Dreamweaver provides two methods for building recordsets:

- The simple Recordset dialog box, which uses a subset of SQL to enable point-and-click recordset building
- The advanced Recordset dialog box, which exposes the SQL format and enables you to write your SQL statement directly

After you define a recordset, Dreamweaver displays the available columns in the Bindings panel for use in web applications, as well as a few generic data items such as first record and last record. The columns can then be placed on the page wherever needed, much like an image from the Assets panel.

Building simple recordsets

Many recordsets are straightforward and can be expressed in a simple sentence:

- "Show me all the salesmen in the Eastern region."
- "Tell me which beers are currently on tap."
- "Give me a list of all the CDs in my collection by Elvis Costello."

Dreamweaver provides a point-and-click interface (see Figure 18-10) for creating simple recordsets that do not require the developer to know or write SQL. You can think of working with the simple Recordset dialog box as drilling down to the required information. You start by selecting a previously defined connection. Within that connection there may be many tables of data—in the simple Recordset dialog box, you can work with only one table. Choose the table you want and then select the columns you need. You can use all the columns, some of them, or just one. Because servers maintain a recordset in memory during their use, it's always best to select only the data you need.

Next, you filter the selected columns to a particular set of data. If you leave the filter wide open, all the records are available. In the simple recordset, you may use one column as a filter; in the previous examples, the filters would be something like:

- `Region = Eastern;`
- `On Tap = Yes`
- `Artist = Elvis Costello`

Finally, after you have defined a recordset, you can sort it by one field in either an ascending or a descending order.

To create a simple recordset, follow these steps:

1. From either the Bindings panel or the Server Behaviors panel, click the Add (+) button and choose Recordset (Query) from the drop-down list.
2. In the Recordset dialog box, enter an identifying label for your recordset in the Name field.

TIP

It's good practice to prefix your recordset name with `rs`—as in `rsDBA`. This prefix quickly identifies the recordset in the code.

FIGURE 18-10

Although it is limited in power, the Recordset dialog box enables developers to construct a recordset without knowing SQL.

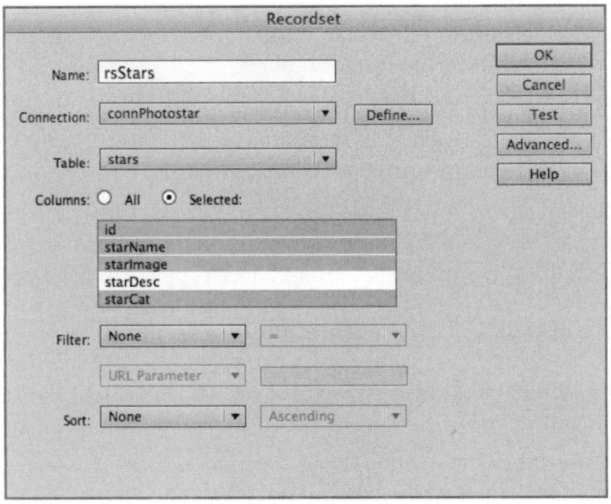

3. Select a connection from the Connection drop-down list.
4. If the desired connection has not been declared, click the Define button to open the Connections dialog box. After a connection has been selected, the available tables are shown.
5. From the Tables drop-down list, select a table to work with. The chosen table's fields are displayed in the Columns list.
6. By default, all the columns are included in the recordset. To specify certain columns, choose the Selected option and then any desired field. Press Shift+click to select contiguous columns and Ctrl+click (Command+click) to select columns not next to one another.

7. All the records in the selected columns are available by default. To limit the recordset further, use the four Filter drop-down lists as follows:
   - From the first drop-down list, choose the field on which you want to base your filter. This list changes dynamically according to which table you've selected.
   - From the second drop-down list, choose the expression you want to compare with the data from the selected column in the first drop-down list. Available expressions are `=`, `>`, `<`, `>=`, `<=`, `<>`, `begins with`, `ends with`, and `contains`. Most of these are obvious except for <>, which means *not* equal to.
   - From the third drop-down list, choose the type of value to compare to the selected field. Available types are as follows: URL parameter, Form variable, Cookie, Session variable, Server variable, or Entered value. (These types are explained in the following bulleted list.)
   - Enter the value to compare to the selected field in the fourth input field. Values entered are not case-sensitive.
8. To sort the data, select a column from the first drop-down list under Sort, and then select either Ascending or Descending from the second list.
9. You can see what results are returned for the recordset at any time by clicking Test.
10. Click OK when you're finished.

TIP

To see how your simple recordset translates into SQL, click the Advanced button. You can return to the original dialog box by selecting Simple on the advanced Recordset dialog box.

Perhaps the most challenging aspect to building a recordset is selecting the proper filter. Many web applications rely on the filter mechanism of recordset queries to display the proper data. The following list describes how each of the different filter types is used:

- **URL parameter:** URL parameters are arguments added onto the address of a page, typically by a form using the `GET` method. For example, the URL `http://www.idest.com/mail_list.asp?email=jblow@anyhoo.com` indicates that the e-mail field would be set to `jblow@anyhoo.com`. URL parameters are encoded so that no spaces or high ASCII characters are transmitted directly.
- **Form variable:** Form variables are passed by forms using the `POST` method. For example, a form is submitted that contains a text field named `emailText`. Using the Form variable type, you can derive a recordset based on the domain of the e-mail address submitted.
- **Cookie:** A cookie is a small text file placed on the client's machine that may be read or written to by a web application. Cookies are often used for authentication. After a user has been verified, the stored cookie value may be examined to permit—or deny—entrance to particular sections of the website.
- **Session variable:** A session variable is similar to a cookie, but it is maintained on the server side. Session variables are often used to track a visitor's progress through the site.

- **Server variable:** Server variables are maintained throughout the life of an application. Page counters are good examples of server variables. The life of an application lasts from the time the website starts (because the server was turned on or the site started) to the time the website stops (a server reboot or shutting down the site service).
- **Entered value:** The entered value is an absolute value to which the selected field is compared. If, for example, I wanted to display only the DVDs in my database whose title started with the letter *D*, I would choose `begins with` as an operator and `D` as my entered value.

Writing advanced SQL statements

The simple Recordset dialog box is perfectly suited for building recordsets derived from one table and determined by one parameter. Many web applications, however, require data to be supplied from multiple, related tables based on numerous factors. The SQL language is flexible enough to handle the most complex query—and Dreamweaver provides the advanced Recordset dialog box for this very purpose. To get a better idea of what is meant by the phrase *advanced recordset*, compare the following SQL for the plain language query "Show me all the salesmen in the Eastern region":

```
SELECT salesmen FROM employees WHERE region = "east"
```

to the SQL necessary for the query "Show me all the salesmen booking over $200,000 in sales in the Eastern and Southern regions":

```
SELECT salesmen FROM employees WHERE sales > 200000 AND (region = "east"
OR region = "south")
```


In Dreamweaver, the rule of thumb is as follows: Whenever any portion of your SQL query uses more than one element of any piece of SQL (two `ORDER BY` statements, two `WHERE` statements, or even two tables), you must use the advanced Recordset dialog box (see Figure 18-11). It comprises four main areas:

- The topmost section includes fields for entering the recordset's name and data source connection.
- The SQL section comprises a large text area, which contains the code executed to create the recordset. You can enter your SQL directly, copy and paste from a query in Access, or use the Database Items section to create your queries via point and click.

TIP

To write advanced SQL queries, you can create your queries using the Query Builder in Microsoft Access, the View Builder in Microsoft SQL, or MySQL Workbench (`http://dev.mysql.com/downloads/workbench/`). These tools make it easy to create complex joins and filtering in a visual environment. You can then copy and paste the generated SQL directly into the SQL window in Dreamweaver.

- The third area is used for defining variables to be included in the SQL query. These variables must be entered into the SQL area manually.
- The area marked Database Items contains an expandable tree of all the data items available through the currently selected connection, including all tables (and their

associated columns), views (also known as *queries* in Access), and stored procedures. Next to the tree is a button for three of the major clauses of a SQL statement: `SELECT`, `WHERE`, and `ORDER BY`.

To create an advanced recordset, follow these steps:

1. From either the Bindings or the Server Behaviors panel, click the Add (+) button and choose Recordset (Query) from the drop-down list.
2. If the simple Recordset dialog box displays, click Advanced. Dreamweaver remembers the last mode used to build a recordset, so the next time you create a recordset, the advanced Recordset dialog box will display.
3. In the advanced Recordset dialog box, enter an identifying label for your recordset in the Name field.
4. Select a connection from the drop-down list of that name.
5. If the desired connection has not been declared, click Define to open the Connections dialog box. Select a connection, and the available tables are shown in the Database Items tree. You can enter your SQL query by hand or by using the Database Items tree.
6. To create your SQL statement manually, enter it directly into the SQL text area.

FIGURE 18-11

To work with more than one table or to filter against more than one field, use Dreamweaver's advanced Recordset dialog box.

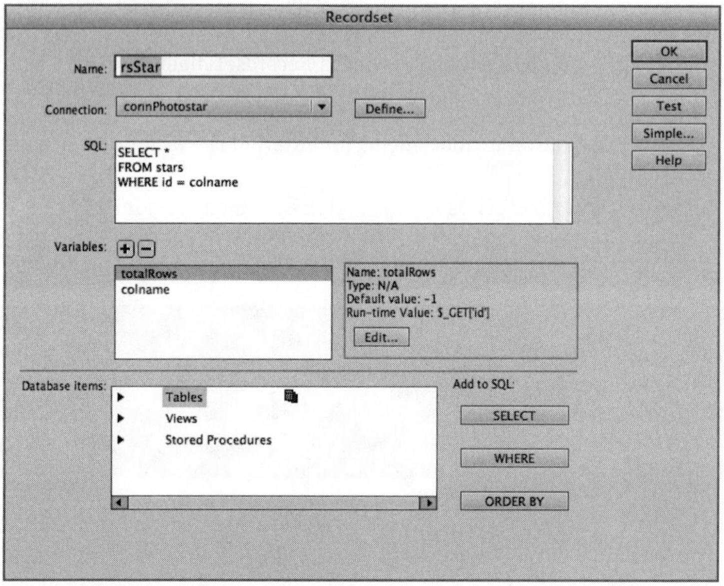

TIP

If you're using Microsoft Access for your database, you can create your query using the Access Query Builder, switch to SQL view, copy the code, and paste the code directly into the SQL text area. This is a fast way to create complex join statements, and it can save a lot of troubleshooting time.

7. Select from the following to use the Database Items point-and-click method:
   - For the `SELECT` clause of the SQL query, expand the Tables section of the tree to pick the desired table and, under that table, the desired column. With the column selected, click the SELECT button.
   - You can add only one column at a time; repeat this step to include additional columns.
   - For the `WHERE` clause of the SQL query, choose the desired column and click the WHERE button. Complete the clause by entering an operator (such as =, <, >, or `LIKE`) and a comparative value. The value may be a constant or a variable defined in the Variables area.
   - For the `ORDER BY` clause of the SQL query, choose the desired column and click the ORDER BY button. Add the keyword `ASC` for an ascending sort or `DESC` for a descending sort.
8. To include a variable in the SQL statement, click the Add (+) button in the Variables section. Enter a name for the variable and its default and runtime values in the appropriate columns.
9. Click Test to see what results are returned by your SQL query.
10. Click OK when you're finished.

After you complete your advanced recordset, you can click the Simple button to switch to the simple Recordset dialog box *only if* the defined recordset references one table that is filtered and ordered by one column using basic operators. In other words, the simple Recordset dialog box has to be able to build the SQL statement. If this is not the case, Dreamweaver alerts you to this and returns you to the advanced Recordset dialog box.

For a better idea of how the advanced Recordset dialog box is used, look at a step-by-step procedure used to create the SQL query that returns the results of a user-run search. For this example, suppose you want to search the `LOCATIONS` table of `dbadata.mdb` (an Access database). The search criteria come from a form element on another page, a text field named `searchText`; the search criteria are incorporated into the SQL query as a variable named `varSearch`. The final query reads as follows:

```
SELECT ADDRESS, CITY, STATE_COUNTRY
FROM LOCATIONS
WHERE LOCATION_NAME LIKE '%varsearch%'
ORDER BY LOCATION_NAME
```

The following is one approach to building this SQL query in the advanced Recordset dialog box:

1. Open the advanced Recordset dialog box by clicking the Add (+) button on the Bindings panel and choosing Recordset (Query) from the drop-down list.
2. Select the appropriate connection, connDBA.

3. Begin building the SQL query by expanding the Tables tree in the Database Items section, and then selecting `LOCATIONS`. Select `LOCATION_NAME` as the column under `LOCATIONS`.
4. With `LOCATION_NAME` highlighted, click SELECT.

   Dreamweaver puts the initial part of the query, `SELECT LOCATION_NAME FROM LOCATIONS`, in the SQL field.
5. While `LOCATION_NAME` is still selected, click WHERE. Dreamweaver adds the `WHERE` clause. The SQL query now reads as follows: `SELECT TRIPNAME FROM LOCATIONS WHERE LOCATION_NAME`.
6. With `CITY` selected, click ORDER BY.

   After Dreamweaver adds the `ORDER BY` clause, the SQL query reads as follows: `SELECT LOCATION_NAME FROM LOCATIONS WHERE LOCATION_NAME ORDER BY CITY`. You've done as much as you can with the Database Items section, and it's time to add the variables and keywords.
7. In the Variables section, click the Add button and enter the following values (shown in parentheses):
   - **Name (**`varSearch`**):** This is the name that appears in the SQL query.
   - **Default Value (**`%`**):** The percent sign acts as a wildcard character for most databases. The default value is inserted into the variable if no other value is entered. With a wildcard character as a default value, if you submit the search with no criteria, all the locations in the database are returned.
   - **Runtime Value (**`Request.Form("searchText")`**):** The runtime value is submitted to the application server and returns with whatever was entered in the form from the input field named `searchText`.

   That does it for the variable.
8. In the SQL text field, add the phrase **LIKE '%varSearch%'** to the `WHERE LOCATION_NAME` clause, as shown in Figure 18-12. The `LIKE` operator compares two text values, and the variable is put in quotes with wildcard characters, the percent sign, on either side. This use of wildcards ensures that the entire data string is compared against the search criteria. Without them, only exact matches would return results. Click OK to add the recordset to your page.

NOTE

Keywords in SQL, such as `SELECT`, `FROM`, and `LIKE`, are often uppercased to distinguish them from field names and other code, although you are not required to do so.

An alternative approach to the method just described is to work out the SQL in advance and enter it directly into the SQL area without using the Database Items area at all. The only other element that you include is the variable. Which approach should you use? If you need to include complicated field names, I recommend using the point-and-click method to avoid typos. This method is also useful when you are using columns from different tables that have the same name; in this situation, Dreamweaver prepends the table name followed by a period, as follows: `LOCATIONS.LOCATION_NAME`.

Working with recordsets

Recordsets need to be modified from time to time. To alter an existing recordset, double-click its name in the Bindings panel. The Recordset dialog box opens with the existing values. Which Recordset dialog box opens—simple or advanced—depends on two things: whether the recordset can be displayed only in the advanced dialog box and which dialog box was open last. If, for example, you are working with a simple recordset but had the advanced Recordset dialog box open last, the advanced Recordset dialog box opens.

FIGURE 18-12

The LIKE operator, not available in the simple Recordset dialog box, is essential for constructing database searches.

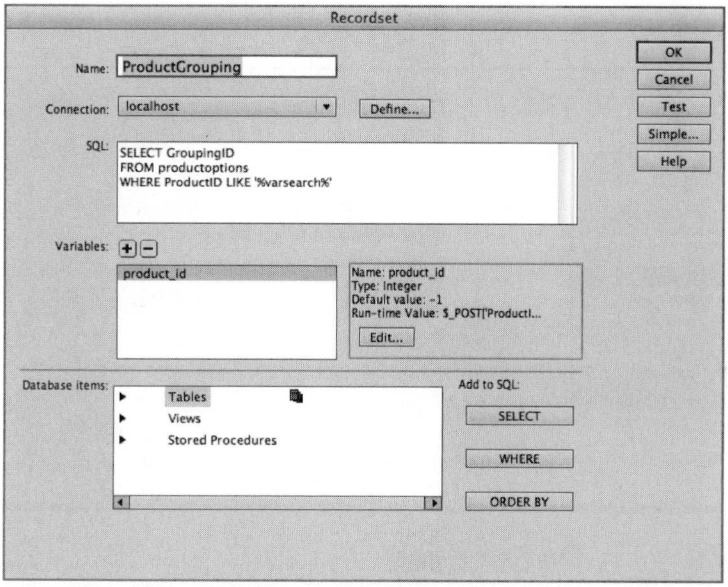

WARNING

When you're editing the recordset, be sure you're double-clicking its name rather than the plus or minus sign or the rotating triangle symbol in front of the name. Double-clicking the symbols only expands and collapses the recordset tree.

It's not unusual for the same recordsets to be used on different pages—and it's even more likely that similar recordsets will be needed. Dreamweaver enables you to copy a recordset from one page to another. Although this is good for those few times you use exactly the same recordset on multiple pages, it's also great for the many times when recordsets are only slightly different. To copy a recordset from one page to another, follow these steps:

1. In the Bindings panel, select the recordset you'd like to copy.
2. Right-click (Control+click) the recordset and choose Copy, as shown in Figure 18-13.
3. Open the page to which you want to copy the recordset.
4. Right-click in the Bindings panel and choose Paste from the context menu. You can also choose Edit ➪ Paste or use the keyboard shortcut, Ctrl+V (Command+V). However, you can only use the Copy command from the context menu of the Bindings panel.

Deleting a recordset from a page is very straightforward. Simply select the recordset from the Bindings panel and click the Remove (–) button.

FIGURE 18-13

Copying a recordset from one page to another and then modifying the copy is a quick way to build similar recordsets.

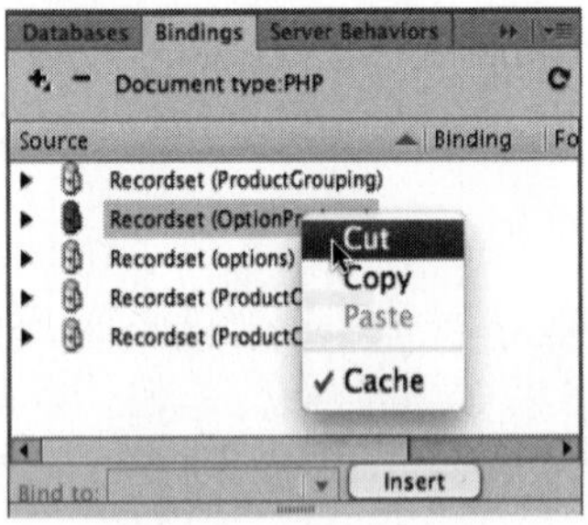

Dreamweaver TECHNIQUE

Defining a Recordset

Once you've created a connection in one of the other Dreamweaver Techniques in this chapter, you're ready to put it to use. In this Technique, you build your first recordset and view the data chosen.

1. From the Files panel, open the recordset file for your server model in the `18_Dynamic_Connections` folder. If you're working with ASP, open `recordset.asp`; for ColdFusion, choose `recordset.cfm`, and PHP users should select `recordset.php`.
2. Although you won't actually be placing any recordset-derived data on the page, you need to have a dynamic page open to make the Application panels accessible. From the Bindings panel, click Add (+) and select Recordset (Query) from the list.
3. When the Recordset dialog box opens, make sure you're in Simple and not Advanced mode; if necessary, click Simple.

4. In the Name field, enter **rsAgents**.
5. From the Connection list, choose RelativeRealty.
6. From the Table list, choose Agents (agents in PHP).
7. Leave the Columns option set to All.

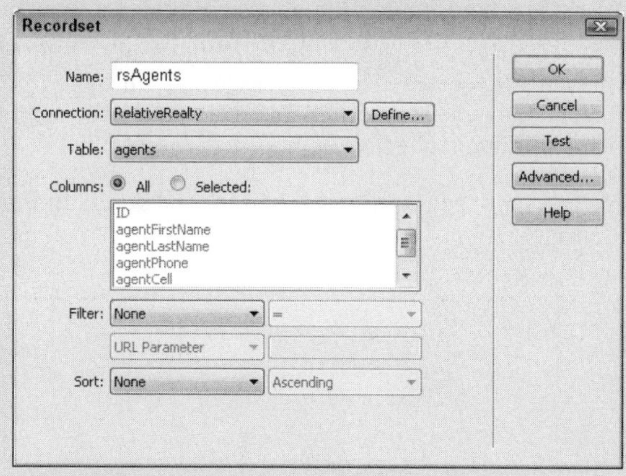

8. From the Sort list, choose agentLastName and Ascending.
9. Click Test to view the chosen data. You should see three records, each with a several columns of data in alphabetical order by last name.
10. When you're done viewing the data, click OK once to close the Test SQL Statement dialog box and again to close the Recordset dialog box.

Although this Technique did not result in any dynamic data being placed on the page, recordset creation is crucial to the development of dynamic applications.

Summary

Although some web applications don't use a data source, the vast majority do. Dreamweaver enables you to connect to any data source for which you have a driver through a variety of methods, ranging from the simplest to the most robust. With a connection established, setting up a recordset is the essential next step. Only after a recordset has been created can you place data on a Dreamweaver page. Mastering these two skills gives your Dreamweaver web applications the access they require and the data they need. As you are laying the foundation for your Dreamweaver pages, keep the following points in mind:

- A Dreamweaver connection—after it is defined—is available site-wide. Dreamweaver uses one server-side include per page for each connection, but the connection file itself needs to be uploaded to the site only once.

- Although DSN connections are the most straightforward, they also carry the greatest overhead. Whenever possible, use OLE DB connections for the runtime connection.
- ASP developers may use the `Server.MapPath()` function to determine the physical location of their database on a remote system. Dreamweaver allows `Server.MapPath()` to be used in a custom connection string as well.
- Dreamweaver offers two entirely different interfaces for creating recordsets. The simple Recordset dialog box can create recordsets relying on a single table and a single criterion, whereas the advanced Recordset dialog box offers unlimited options, permitting you to write your own SQL query.
- Recordsets can be copied from one page to another. You can modify the copy to receive a different set of data with a minimum of effort.

In the next chapter, you learn how dynamic text is inserted, edited, and styled in Dreamweaver, as well as how to link to dynamic images.

CHAPTER

19

Making Data Dynamic

IN THIS CHAPTER

Integrating text from a data source

Dreamweaver Technique: Adding Dynamic Data

Formatting dynamic text

Inserting graphics dynamically

Dreamweaver Technique: Making Dynamic Images

Working with Flash dynamically

By the time a visitor sees an active web page in his or her browser, its data should blend seamlessly into the rest of the page. As with a well-crafted form letter, the reader shouldn't be able to tell where the basic structure starts and the dynamically generated data begins. Much of the work in Dreamweaver consists of properly placing and formatting data into a page layout.

You're not limited to dynamically integrating basic text into your web applications with Dreamweaver. After text is included, you can format its look and feel on both the client-and the server-sides. Additionally, you can include images, form elements such as checkboxes, drop-down lists, and even multimedia elements such as Flash movies on the fly. Finally, Dreamweaver permits almost any HTML attribute to be dynamically altered. This chapter explores all the fundamentals necessary for integrating dynamic data into your web page.

Working with Dynamic Text

The Bindings panel is the key tool for accessing dynamic text. With a recordset expanded, any or all of the available fields within it are ready to be placed on the page. Moreover, after a field is inserted into the page and selected, the Bindings panel reflects its current data format.

Before you begin including dynamic data, you need to establish a data source connection and recordset, so be sure you're familiar with the techniques described in Chapter 18 before proceeding.

Inserting dynamic text

After you have a recordset or other data source declared, adding dynamic text is as simple as dragging a field name onto the page. After the field is inserted, Dreamweaver displays it with the syntax `{recordset_name.field_name}`. For example, the column named CITY located in a recordset named rsLocations is displayed as `{rsLocations.CITY}`. If you choose View ⇨ Visual Aids and enable the Invisible Elements option, the inserted data is highlighted (according to the color selected in Preferences), as shown in Figure 19-1.

FIGURE 19-1

Placeholders for dynamic data are considered invisible elements in Dreamweaver and are highlighted accordingly.

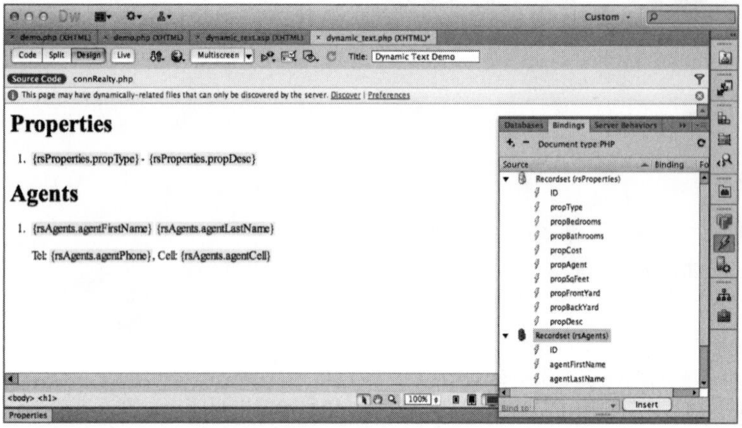

Dynamic pages are a combination of standard HTML and dynamic elements. It's possible to build the page in any order. You can insert your dynamic elements first, followed by HTML objects, or you can build the HTML page before adding your data. Many designers, whether they're working by themselves or on a team, find the latter method more productive. One common technique is to use static placeholders to mark where the dynamic data should go, as shown in Figure 19-2.

FIGURE 19-2

You can use plain HTML placeholders to indicate where the dynamic data should be dropped from the Bindings panel.

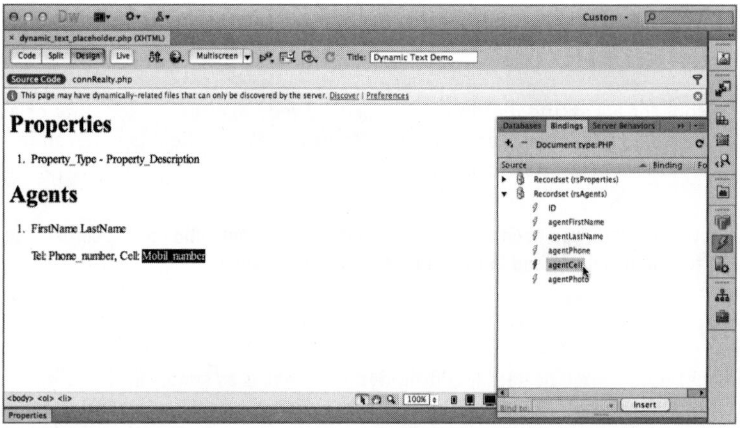

Perhaps the quickest way to bring dynamic data onto the page is to use the drag-and-drop capability, as detailed in the following steps:

1. In the Document window, select the static placeholder text to be replaced by the dynamic data.
2. From the Bindings panel, expand your recordset or other data source until the desired field or dynamic element is displayed.
3. Drag the dynamic data from the Bindings panel and drop it on the selected text.

   If you are not using placeholder text, you can drop the dynamic data wherever you'd like it to appear.

In some situations—when a table has many dynamic data fields, for example—the Insert method is easier than the drag-and-drop technique. For those cases, first select the placeholder text or position your cursor if no placeholders are used. Then highlight the desired dynamic data and click the Insert button on the bottom of the Bindings panel.

TIP

Occasionally, the dot notation syntax leads to extremely long names, which can make the layout process more difficult. You can switch from using the curly braces and full data name to just using the curly braces—and then switch back again—by choosing the desired option from the Show Dynamic Text As drop-down list. (This list is found under the Invisible Elements category of Preferences.)

Viewing dynamic data

You have three basic ways to see your page with the data extracted from the data source and fully integrated into the HTML:

- Upload the page to your remote testing server and view it through a web browser.
- Use Dreamweaver's Preview in Browser feature to test your page on the testing server. Dreamweaver takes care of uploading the files for you.
- Switch to Live View within Dreamweaver.

19

Which should you use? Uploading or previewing your page is great for giving an accurate browser rendering of your dynamic (or static) page, but you can't edit the elements or styles. The final method—Live View—is handiest when you want to display your dynamic data and still retain CSS editability. The other methods are important to keep in mind and should be included in a regular routine of web application development.

To see your data within the page quickly in Live Data view, choose View ⇨ Live View or click Live View in the Document toolbar. Alternatively, you can use the keyboard shortcut, Alt+F11 (Option+F11). However you choose to enter Live View, you see the same actions take place. The Live View toolbar appears in the Document window as Dreamweaver processes your page with the testing server declared in your site definition. If Dreamweaver is able to connect to the application server and encounters no errors, your data is displayed within the page, as shown in Figure 19-3.

Without any additional server behaviors—most notably Repeat Region—all data displayed is from the first record of the chosen recordset.

FIGURE 19-3

Live View uses your designated testing server to display actual data from your data source in design time.

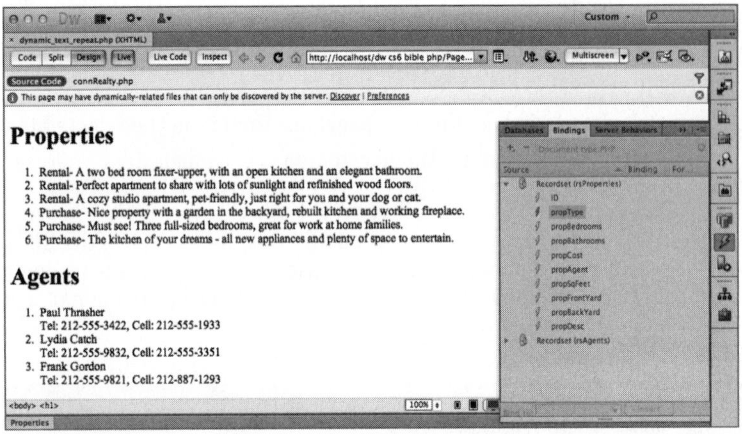

Live View has more features regarding data than are noted here—all of which are covered in Chapter 21.

Dreamweaver TECHNIQUE

Adding Dynamic Data

In this Technique, you begin to familiarize yourself with binding dynamic data to the page.

1. From the Techniques - Dynamic site (established in Chapter 18), expand the 19_Dynamic_Data folder and open the `dyn_data_start` file for your server model.
2. From the Bindings panel, click Add (+) and select Recordset (Query) from the list.
3. When the Recordset dialog box opens, make sure that you're in Simple, not Advanced, mode; if necessary, click Simple.
4. In the Name field, enter **rsAgents**.
5. From the Connection list, choose RelativeRealty.
6. From the Table list, choose Agents (agents in PHP).
7. Leave the Columns option set to All.
8. From the Sort list, choose agentLastName and Ascending.
9. Click OK to close the dialog box.
10. Now that the recordset has been created, you can begin to bind the data to the page. You'll find it easier to work with the table if you enable Visual Aids ➪ Table Borders and disable CSS Layout Outlines from the Document toolbar.

11. Place your cursor in the second cell from the left, in the second row under the middle of the phrase, Leading Agents.
12. In the Bindings panel, expand the rsAgents recordset.

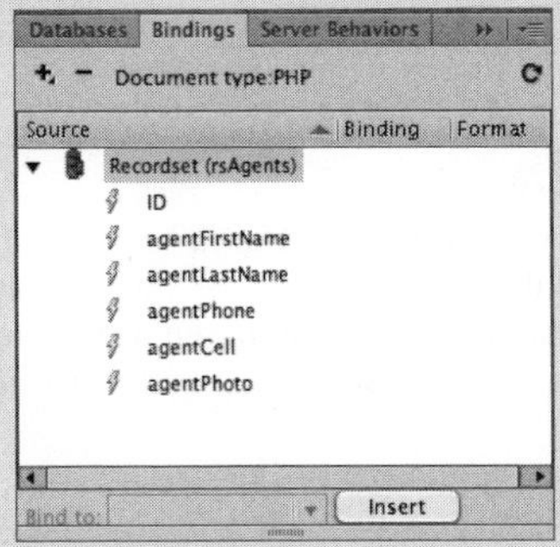

13. Select the agentFirstName entry from the Bindings panel and click Insert.

NOTE

Although you're using the Insert method here, you could have dragged the dynamic entries from the Bindings panel onto the page.

14. Move your cursor to the right of the dynamic data just inserted and add a space.
15. From the Bindings panel, choose agentLastName and click Insert.
16. Place your cursor in the cell under the Office Phone label, choose agentPhone from the Bindings panel, and click Insert.
17. Place your cursor in the cell under the Cell Phone label, choose agentCell from the Bindings panel, and click Insert.
18. Choose View ➪ Live View to test your operation.
19. Choose View ➪ Live View again to disable it, and save your page.

In the next Technique, you add a dynamic image to the page along with some server-side formatting.

Formatting Dynamic Data

After a field has been incorporated into a page, it acts just like any other text within a tag. Dynamic text can be either formatted with HTML tags—such as `<h2>`, `<strong>`, or `<span>`—or styled with Cascading Style Sheets (CSS). The easiest method is simply to replace the static placeholder text, styled as your layout demands, with the dynamic text. The tags and CSS surrounding any dynamic text can be altered at any time.

TIP

It's also possible to include HTML tags in the stored data. When the data is included in the page, the browser interprets the HTML normally. For example, you can have a memo field in an Access database (for data containing more than 255 characters) with italic tags (`<i>`) surrounding key phrases. This is perfectly acceptable to Access—which sees the tags as just text—and also perfectly acceptable to Dreamweaver.

Data formatting

Dreamweaver not only supports client-side formatting of your dynamic data but also offers a wide range of server-side formats, and it gives you the capability to create your own. Information is stored in databases according to a particular type. Some fields are designated as text, others are numbers, and still others fall under the date/time category. The same data type within a specific category may be formatted in numerous ways.

Dates are a good example of why data formatting is important. In the United States, dates are typically presented in a month-day-year format—such as March 31, 2008. In much of the rest of the world, however, dates are presented in a day-month-year format, as in 31 March 2008. By default, servers are generally set to display dates appropriate to their regions. The same holds true for currency: U.S. currency figures are presented with a dollar sign, for example, and UK currency is shown as euros or English pounds.

When initially inserted onto the page from the Bindings panel, dynamic data does not have a specific format applied. Data from currency and time/date use the default formats for their data types. Different formats are chosen from the Bindings panel, as outlined in the following steps:

1. Select the dynamic data that you want to format from the Document window. The corresponding field in the Bindings panel is highlighted.
2. From the Bindings panel, click the down arrow under the Format column to reveal the format list, as shown in Figure 19-4.

TIP

The Bindings panel is usually pretty narrow. The Format column may be hidden off the right side of the screen. Use the scrollbar to move to the right and resize the Source column to make it narrower, or simply make the Bindings panel wider to get access to the right-hand columns.

3. From the Format List, select the appropriate category for your data.
4. If more than one format is available, choose a specific format from the category's submenu.

To see the newly applied format, choose View ➪ Live View or click the Live View button on the Document toolbar.

Each of Dreamweaver's server models offers slightly different data formats through the Bindings panel. A complete list of all the standard data formats, with relevant examples, is shown in Tables 19-1 (ASP), 19-2 (ColdFusion), and 19-3 (PHP).

FIGURE 19-4

The format list, which is different for each server model, lets you specify your data's format according to its type.

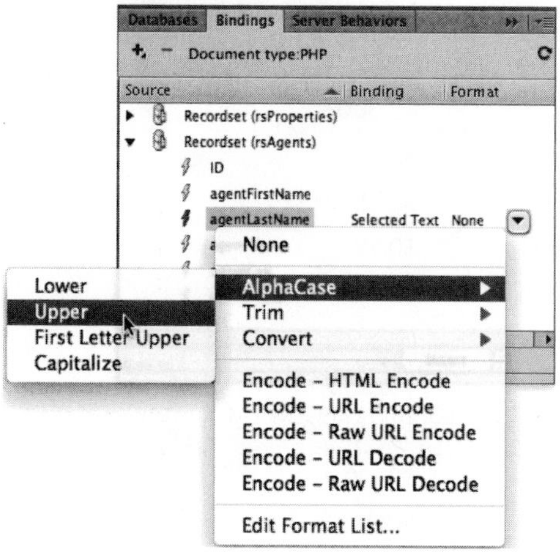

TABLE 19-1 ASP Data Formats

Format	Option	Example
Date/Time	General Format	3/31/2008
	Long Format	Monday, March 31, 2008
	Short Format	3/31/2008
	Weekday, Month Date, Year	Monday, March 31, 2008
	Date Month Year	31 March 2008
	Month Date, Year	March 31, 2008
	YY-M-DD	08-3-31
	YY-MM-DD	08-03-31
	DD-MM-YYYY	31-03-2008
	M/D/YY	3/31/08
	DD/MM/YY	31/03/08
	YY/MM/DD	08/03/31
	Long Time Format	9:15:00 PM
	Short Time Format	21:15
	h:MM:SS AM/PM	9:15:00 PM
	HH:MM:SS	21:15:00

Continues

TABLE 19-1 *(continued)*

Format	Option	Example
	hh:MM:SS a.m./p.m.	09:15:00 p.m.
	HH:MM	21:15
Currency	Default	$2,300.99
	2 Decimal Places	$23.99
	Rounded to Integer	$23.51 = $24
	Leading 0 If Fractional	$0.99
	No Leading 0 If Fractional	$.99
	() If Negative	($23.99)
	Minus If Negative	–$23.99
	Group Digits	$2,300.99
	Do Not Group Digits	$2300.99
Number	Default	2,300
	2 Decimal Places	23.00
	Rounded to Integer	23.51 = 24
	Leading 0 If Fractional	0.99
	No Leading 0 If Fractional	.99
	() If Negative	(23)
	Minus If Negative	–23
	Group Digits	2,300
	Do Not Group Digits	2300
Percent	Default	2,300%
	2 Decimal Places	23.00%
	Rounded to Integer	23.51% = 24%
	Leading 0 If Fractional	0.99%
	No Leading 0 If Fractional	.99%
	() If Negative	(23%)
	Minus If Negative	–23%
	Group Digits	2,300%
	Do Not Group Digits	2300%
AlphaCase	Upper	Mixed Case = MIXED CASE
	Lower	Mixed Case = mixed case
Trim	Left	" Widgets " = "Widgets "
	Right	" Widgets " = " Widgets"
	Both	" Widgets " = "Widgets"

Format	Option	Example
Absolute Value	N/A	+23 or –23 = 23
Round Integer	N/A	23.51 = 24
Encode—Server .HTMLEncode	N/A	I'm <b>bold</b> =I'm <b>bold</b>
Encode—Server .URLEncode	N/A	www.idest.com/Party Time = www.idest .com/Party%20Time
Path—Server .MapPath	N/A	Server.MapPath(/myDocs) = D:/HTDOCS/ lowery/myDocs

TABLE 19-2 ColdFusion Data Formats

Format	Option	Example
Date/Time	General Date Format	31-Mar-08
	Weekday, Month Date, Year	Monday, March 31, 2008
	Date Month Year	31 March 2008
	Month Date, Year	March 31, 2008
	DD-MM-YY	31-03-08
	YY-M-DD	08-3-31
	YY-MM-DD	08-03-31
	DD-MM-YYYY	31-03-2008
	M/D/YY	3/31/08
	DD/MM/YY	31/03/08
	YY/MM/DD	08/03/31
	General Time Format	9:15 PM
	h:MM:SS AM/PM	9:15:00 PM
	HH:MM:SS	21:15:00
	hh:MM:SS A/P	09:15:00 P
	HH:MM	21:15
Currency	General Format	2,300.99
	Dollar Format	$2,300.99
	Local Format	$2,300.99
	International Format	USD2,300.00
Number	Default	2,300.99
	2 Decimal Places	23.99
	Rounded to Integer	23.51 = $24

Continues

TABLE 19-2 *(continued)*

Format	Option	Example
	() If Negative	(23.99)
	Minus If Negative	–23.99
	Do Not Group Digits	2300.99
AlphaCase	Upper	Mixed Case = MIXED CASE
	Lower	Mixed Case = mixed case
Trim	Left	" Widgets " = "Widgets "
	Right	" Widgets " = " Widgets"
	Both	" Widgets " = "Widgets"
	StripCR	"The End" = "The End"
Math	Abs	Returns the absolute value
	Atn	Returns the arctangent
	Ceiling	Returns the next highest integer
	Cos	Returns the cosine
	DecrementValue	Lowers the number by 1
	Exp	Returns the exponent
	Fix	Rounds the number toward zero
	IncrementValue	Increases the number by 1
	Int	Returns an integer
	Log	Returns the natural logarithm
	Log10	Returns the logarithm to base 10
	Randomize	Seeds the random number generator
	Round	Rounds to the closest integer
	Sgn	Returns 1 for positive numbers, –1 for negative numbers
	Sin	Returns the sine
	Sqr	Returns the square root
	Tan	Returns the tangent
Encode—URLEncoded Format	N/A	www.idest.com/Party Time = www.idest.com/Party%20Time
Encode—PreserveSingleQuotes	N/A	'The Answer' = 'The Answer'
String—Reverse	N/A	'The Answer' = 'rewsnA ehT'

TABLE 19-3 PHP Data Formats

Format	Option	Example
AlphaCase	Lower	My Widgets = my widgets
	Upper	My Widgets = MY WIDGETS
	First Letter Upper	My Widgets = My widgets
	Capitalize	My Widgets = My Widgets
Trim	Left	" Widgets " = "Widgets "
	Right	" Widgets " = " Widgets"
	Both	" Widgets " = "Widgets"
Encode	HTML Encode	I'm <b>bold</b> = I'm <b>bold</b>
	URL Encode	www.idest.com/Party Time = www.idest.com/Party+Time
	Raw URL Encode	www.idest.com/Party Time = www.idest.com/Party%20Time
	URL Decode	www.idest.com/Party+Time = www.idest.com/Party Time
	Raw URL Decode	www.idest.com/Party%20Time = www.idest.com/Party Time

Editing and creating new data formats

Although Dreamweaver includes a wide variety of format selections, sometimes only a custom format will do. In Dreamweaver Code view, you can edit existing currency, number, or percent formats, or you can create your own version of any of these types from scratch. After a new format has been defined—or an old one has been altered—that format is available for any sites using the same server model under which it was created. To edit or create a new data format, follow these steps:

1. Select the inserted dynamic data in the Document window that requires the custom format. The corresponding field is highlighted in the Bindings panel.
2. In the Bindings panel, click the down arrow in the Format column and choose Edit Format List from the drop-down menu. The Edit Format List dialog box, shown in Figure 19-5, is displayed.

FIGURE 19-5

Only currency, number, and percent format types can be edited or created through the Edit Format List dialog box.

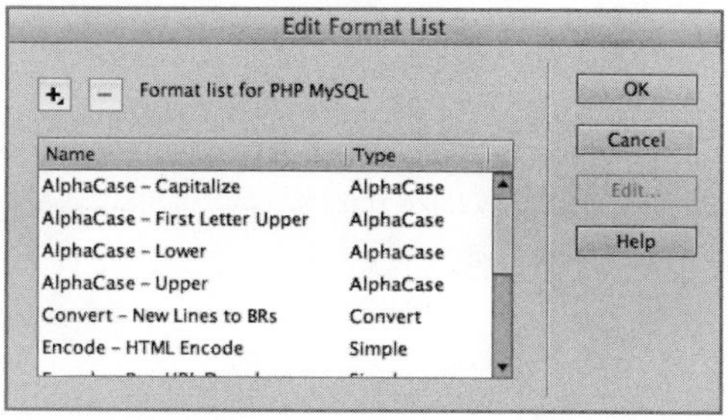

3. To alter an existing currency, number, or percent format, select the format and click the Edit button. If you prefer to create an entirely new format, click the Add (+) button and from the pop-up list select Number, Currency, or Percent. The appropriate dialog box opens. If you attempt to edit a format other than the three types allowed, Dreamweaver notes that the format has no parameters to customize.

NOTE

You can't edit any of the built-in formats or add additional formats in the .NET server model without manually editing the format configuration files in the Dreamweaver Configuration folder.

4. In the Number, Currency, or Percent dialog box, design your format by adjusting the four available drop-down lists:
   - **# Digits after Decimal Point:** Choose a value from 0 to 20.
   - **Leading Zero (if Fraction):** Select Yes, No, or Default for locale.
   - **Negative:** Select Parentheses, Minus sign, or Default for locale.
   - **Group Digits:** Select Yes, No, or Default for locale.

NOTE

Although each of the dialog boxes offers different options, they work exactly the same. You can also choose Get More Formats from the drop-down list to go directly to Adobe Marketplace & Exchange.

5. When you're finished, click OK to close the specific format dialog box.
6. Give the format a name to be displayed in the Format column in the Bindings panel.
7. To edit or create another format, repeat Steps 3 through 6.
8. To delete a format, select it from the list and click Remove.
9. When you're finished, click OK.

Dreamweaver applies your newly created format to the selected dynamic data. Use Live View to preview your new format.

Additional Time/Date Formatting

The Edit Format List option works well for currency, number, and percent formats, but it does not permit new time and/or date formats. I recently built a site for which the client wanted the time to be shown in a particular way—for example, 9 PM. The closest format in Dreamweaver displays that time as 9:00:00 PM. To show the time as desired, I needed to do some hand-coding.

The site I built for the client uses an ASP server model with VBScript as its scripting language. My first task was to show only the hour portion of time. VBScript has a function that does exactly this, aptly named `Hour()`. When applied to my dynamic data code, it looks like this:

```
<%=Hour(rsEvents.Fields.Item("showTime").Value) %>
```

Unfortunately, the `Hour()` function returns values according to a 24-hour clock (also known as military time), so 9 PM becomes 21. The second problem is that the `Hour()` function returns only a number and does not include an AM or PM designation. To solve these problems, I wrote a small ASP routine that incorporated the Dreamweaver-generated code:

```
<%
Dim myTime, myShift
myShift = "AM"
myTime = Hour(rsEvents.Fields.Item("showTime").Value)
If (myTime > 12) Then
    myTime = myTime-12
    myShift = "PM"
End If
Response.write myTime & myShift
%>
```

This routine works well for the site, but it would have to be modified to handle 12 noon and 12 midnight. In addition to the `Hour()` function, VBScript has similar functions to extract other time elements: `Minute()` and `Second()`. For dates, use the comparable `Month()`, `Day()`, and `Year()` functions. All of these functions return number values, which you can convert to names with further use of the `MonthName()` function. The `Weekday()` and `WeekdayName()` functions are used together to display either full or abbreviated day names. For example, to get the date to appear as Sunday, February 11, without the year imposed by Dreamweaver's standard formats, I would use code like this:

```
<%= WeekdayName(Weekday((rsEvents.Fields.Item("showDate").Value)))
& ", "
MonthName(Month((rsEvents.Fields.Item("showDate").Value)))
& " "
Day((rsEvents.Fields.Item("showDate").Value))
%>
```

There are commercial solutions to the problem of limited Date/Time formats in ASP. The DWfaq Date/Time Server Formats extension from `www.dwfaq.com/store` contains more than 100 date formats and allows you to customize each one using the Edit Format steps in the previous section.

ColdFusion developers have a much easier way of manipulating times and dates with the `TimeFormat()` and `DateFormat()` functions. For example, here's the ColdFusion code for displaying a date in my example format (such as Sunday, February 11):

```
#DateFormat("#rsEvents.showDate#", "dddd, mmmm d")#
```


Making Images Dynamic

The web is both a textual and a visual medium. You've seen how Dreamweaver replaces static text with dynamic text from a database. But how does it handle images? Dreamweaver dynamically inserts images by using the path to the image rather than the image itself. Proper database setup is critical for Dreamweaver to correctly deliver dynamic images. For example, a product database might have the following records:

SKU#	Name	Cost	Image
10101	Widget-O-Wonder	$99.99	/images/products/w_wonder.gif
10102	WidgetMatic	$49.99	/images/products/w_matic.gif
10103	Widget-Ultimo	$999.99	/images/products/w_ultimo.gif

In this example, Dreamweaver extracts the data from the Image field and plugs that data into an attribute of the `<img>` tag's `src` attribute. Because site-root–relative links are used in the data source, the images can be inserted dynamically from any page in the site. If your dynamic images are located on a remote server, you must enter a full URL—with the `http://` prefix—in a text field in the data source.

CAUTION

Some databases, including Access, allow fields to be set up as hyperlink types. Although it may not seem logical, fields containing paths to images should be a text type, not a hyperlink type. Hyperlink type fields are used only inside Microsoft Access applications and are never used for live sites. Hyperlink-type images already include the HTML code for a link. That won't work in Dreamweaver.

It is also possible to use document-relative pathnames in image fields of the database. However, you have to be careful which pages the dynamic images are inserted into; the pages must be stored in the proper location relative to the path of the images.

Perhaps the best course of action is to store just the filenames of the images themselves in the data source. When the dynamic image is inserted into Dreamweaver, additional path information can be added as needed. For example, suppose the image field contained only filenames with no path information, such as `w_wonder.gif` in a field named `images` of a recordset `rsProducts`. Here's an example of how that code would be generated by Dreamweaver for ASP:

```
<%=(rsProducts.Fields.Item("images").Value)%>
```

In Dreamweaver, you can preface that code—either when it is inserted or through the Property inspector—with any necessary path information. If my document is at the site root and the images are stored in the /images/products folder, I adjust the code like this:

```
images/products/<%=(rsProducts.Fields.Item("images").Value)%>
```

After your data source is correctly set up for images, inserting them in Dreamweaver is very straightforward, as shown in the following steps:

1. Make sure that you define a recordset with at least one field consisting of paths to graphics.
2. Position your cursor where you want your dynamic image to appear.
3. From the Common category of the Insert panel, select Insert Image.

Alternatively, you can drag the Insert Image button to the proper place on the page. In either case, the Select Image Source dialog box appears.

4. From the Select Image Source dialog box, Windows users should choose the Select File Name From Data Sources option at the top of the page. Macintosh users should click the Data Sources button found just below the URL field.

   If necessary, expand the data source to locate and select the desired image field, as shown in Figure 19-6. Dreamweaver places the code for inserting the dynamic image into the URL field.
5. If your image data (the paths to the images) contains spaces, tildes, or other nonstandard characters, the data must be encoded properly to be read by the server. From the Format List, select Encode—HTML Encode (PHP); Encode—Server.HTMLEncode (ASP); or Encode—URLEncoded Format (ColdFusion).
6. If your data is stored as filenames only, enter any required path in the URL field before the existing code. The path information may be document-relative, site-root–relative, or absolute.
7. When you're finished, click OK.

You can get a quick view of your work by choosing View ➪ Live View or by clicking the Live View button on the Document toolbar. The placeholder icon for the dynamic image initially appears in its default size of 32 × 32 pixels, but it expands to full size after you enable Live Data or you view the page through the testing server.

TIP

If possible, store the height and width of your images in separate fields in the database. This prevents images from resizing in the browser and causing the page to jump as the browser determines each image's size. You also need the height and width for each image if you're validating against an XHTML `DOCTYPE`.

FIGURE 19-6

When inserting a dynamic image, you specify only the data source and field. Dreamweaver automatically inserts the image with the correct dimensions.

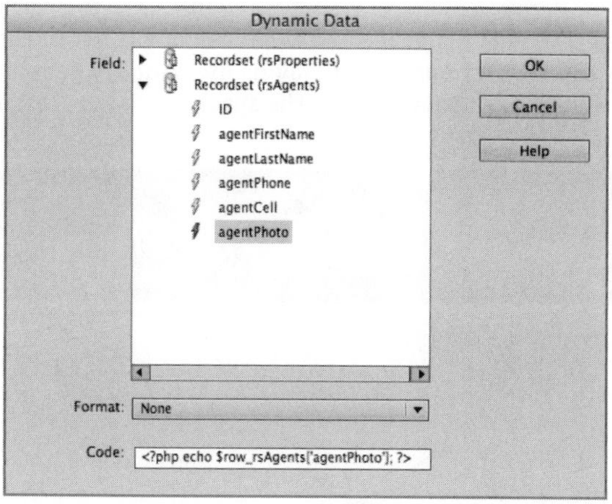

19

If you use static graphic placeholders in your design, you can use an alternative technique. From the Bindings panel, drag the field containing the image names onto the static graphic. If your data is just filenames without path information, you have to add the required path to the beginning of the `src` attribute in the Property inspector or the Tag inspector.

NOTE
Some databases support storing the actual images as a Binary Large Object (BLOB). The BLOB protocol is not supported directly in Dreamweaver.

Just as you can assign a dynamic value to the `<img>` tag's `src` attribute, you can assign any data-source–derived value to any other attribute by *binding* (attaching) the field to the attribute. Attributes are generally assigned dynamic values through the Bindings panel or the Property inspector, after which the Bindings panel displays the attribute attached to each field in the Binding column. A data field used for dynamic images, for instance, shows `img.src` in its Binding column.

I recently used Dreamweaver to create a content-management system for a client. The page uses a standard template with areas for the heading, bylines, content, and images, served dynamically according to the topic. The images each have a specific alignment—some are set to the browser default, whereas others are aligned left or right. To handle this correctly, you create a separate field for image alignment in the data source.

With the database properly prepared, the attributes are set dynamically by following these steps:

1. Select the placeholder for the dynamic image, which is already inserted on the page.
2. From the Bindings panel, select the field that contains the data for the attribute you'd like to dynamically generate.
3. At the bottom of the Bindings panel, choose the desired attribute from the Bind To list, as shown in Figure 19-7, or click the down arrow in the Binding column if you've already bound an attribute to the image.

   The Bind To list changes according to the object selected. To change the alignment on an `<img>` tag, choose `img.align` from the list.
4. Select Bind. The selected attribute is displayed in the Binding column of the chosen field.

To get an idea of what's possible, select a dynamic image and then look at the list in the Binding column. The `<img>` tag offers 23 different attributes that may be dynamically generated—everything from the heavily recommended `alt` parameter to the special case `vrml` attribute.

NOTE
To find the details on any or all of these attributes, choose Help ➪ Reference, choose O'Reilly HTML Reference from the Book list, and then pick IMG from the list of tags.

FIGURE 19-7

Change more than just the image dynamically by using the Bind To feature to link any tag attribute to a data source.

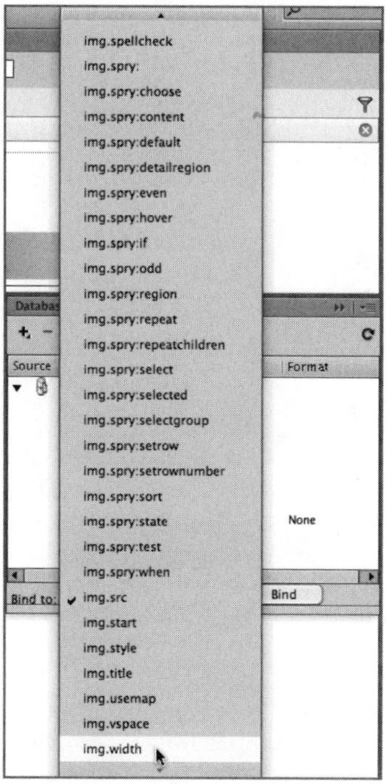

Dreamweaver TECHNIQUE

Making Dynamic Images

The next phase in developing this dynamic page is to add thumbnail images and server-side formatting.

1. Open the `dyn_data_start` file for your server model previously worked upon.
2. Select the rsAgents.agentFirstName dynamic text on the page.
3. Press Shift+Tab to move to the previous cell.

   An alternative approach to make sure your cursor is properly placed is to enter Expanded Table mode by pressing F6.
4. From the Common category of the Insert toolbar, choose Images: Image.
5. When the Select Image Source dialog box opens, choose the Select File Name From Data Sources option.
6. Expand the rsAgents recordset, and select agentPhoto.

Continues

19

continued

7. In the URL field, place your cursor at the beginning of the inserted code and enter the path to the images folder: `../images/`.

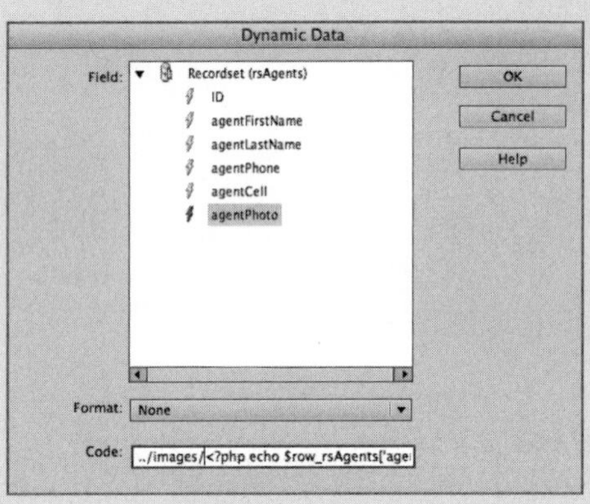

8. Click OK when you're done.
9. Test your page by switching to Live View (View ➪ Live View). CSS formatting can be added while in Live View. When you're done, turn off Live View.
10. From the Bindings panel, select the agentFirstName entry.
11. Select the Format list on the far right of the entry and, from the list, choose AlphaCase ➪ Upper.

    You may need to scroll the Bindings panel to the left to see the drop-down arrow in the Format column. After you make the format change, the agent's first name will automatically be uppercased.

12. Choose View ➪ Live View again to re-enter the mode and preview the revised data. Save your page.

You'll revisit this page in the next chapter when you learn how to show additional data from a recordset on the page using a Dreamweaver server behavior.

Integrating Flash and Other Dynamic Media

Just as text and images can be inserted into documents on the fly, all manner of multimedia—including Flash and files requiring ActiveX controls or applets—can also be dynamically incorporated. The core technique of attaching a data source is the same for multimedia files as it is for images; when you insert a multimedia object, choose the desired data source from Dreamweaver's dialog box. The linking code is automatically written into the proper parameter for the object.

Most multimedia objects are inserted into HTML by using an `<object>` tag, an `<embed>` tag, or a combination of the two; Java applets use the `<applet>` tag. Dreamweaver handles the basic file assignments for specific programs with its own icon in the Insert panel: Examples are Flash and Shockwave. If you examine the code, you can see that even these objects use the `<param>` tag (short for *parameter*) to declare the source of the media file. ActiveX and applet files rely on `<param>` tags to specify needed attributes. Dreamweaver enables you to choose either static or dynamic values for any `<param>` tag.

NOTE

When you insert a Flash or Shockwave movie, Dreamweaver now includes a JavaScript file and references a function from that file. All parameters (dynamic and otherwise) inserted through the Property inspector and associated dialog boxes are correctly written into the JavaScript code automatically.

You enter the `<param>` values through the Parameters dialog box, which is displayed when you click the Parameters button on the Property inspector. As shown in Figure 19-8, the Dreamweaver Parameters dialog box consists of two columns, one for the name of the parameter and one for the corresponding value. Entries in either column can be assigned dynamic content by clicking the lightning bolt icon. When this icon is selected, the Dynamic Data dialog box opens and an appropriate data source—from those already declared in the Bindings panel—can be assigned.

FIGURE 19-8

Dynamically alter parameters for any multimedia object by clicking the lightning bolt icon and picking a proper data source.

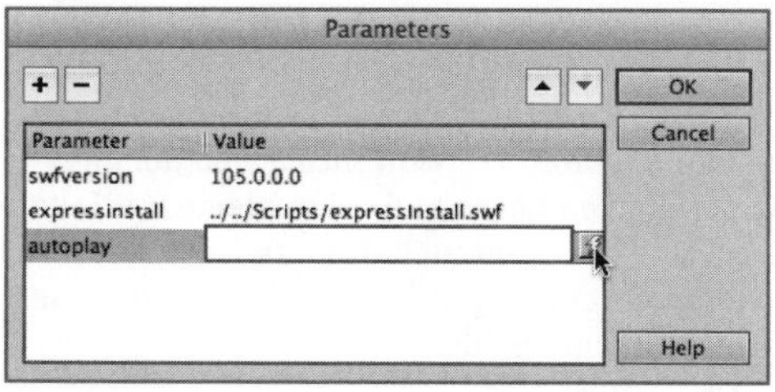

How you store the path to the movie is critical if you're dynamically switching Flash movies. As with images, perhaps the best tactic is to use only the filename in the database field and supply additional path information as needed. Here are the steps to display different Flash movies dynamically:

1. Position your cursor where you'd like your dynamic content to appear, and click Insert SWF from the Common category of the Insert panel.

   Alternatively, you can drag the Insert SWF button to the proper place on the page. In either case, the Select File dialog box appears.
2. Windows users choose the Select File Name From Data Sources option at the top of the page. Macintosh users select the Data Sources button found just below the URL field.
3. Expand the data source to locate and select the desired field with the Flash movie filenames.
4. If your Flash data (the paths to the movies) contains spaces, tildes, or other nonstandard characters, the data must be encoded to be read properly by the server. From the Format List, select Encode—Server.HTMLEncode (ASP); Encode—HTMLEncodedFormat (.NET); Encode—URLEncoded Format (ColdFusion); or Encode—Response.EncodeURL (JSP).
5. If your data is stored as filenames only, enter any required path in the URL field before the existing code.
6. You can also link any Flash attributes to a dynamic source by clicking the Parameters button to open the Parameters dialog box, entering a dynamic value by clicking the lightning bolt symbol under the Name or Value column, and choosing an appropriate data source from the Dynamic Data dialog box.
7. Click OK when you're finished.

For more details on integrating Flash movies in your web pages, see Chapter 25.

Summary

Incorporating dynamic data into your standard web pages is a core skill for building data-driven web applications, along with establishing a data source connection and defining a recordset. After you have these three components in place, you can begin combining HTML pages with text, images, and even multimedia data. Dreamweaver combines sophisticated connectivity with drag-and-drop simplicity for quick insertion of dynamic content. Keep the following items in mind as you begin to integrate data-driven and static content:

- The Bindings panel displays fields available for insertion into a web document, much like the Assets panel, which shows available images and other elements. Like the Assets panel, data is inserted from the Bindings panel through drag-and-drop. Alternatively, or for complex layouts, you can position your cursor precisely and click the Insert button instead of dragging and dropping the dynamic fields.
- Dynamic text accepts two types of formatting: client-side and server-side. Client-side formatting is another term for standard HTML and CSS formatting; dynamic text may be styled with the same tags and attributes as regular text. The final look for these tags and attributes is interpreted by the browser. Server-side formatting, on the other hand, reshapes the data from the data source before it passes it on to the browser.

- If you encounter trouble inserting dynamic images into your web applications, chances are you're not doing anything wrong in Dreamweaver. The error may lie in your database setup. It's key to store the path and/or filename of the images in the data source as a text field rather than as a hyperlink.
- Dreamweaver does not support loading images as binary images from data sources, otherwise known as Binary Large Objects (BLOBs).
- SWF files—in fact, any multimedia file—can be dynamically inserted into a Dreamweaver page. Again, storing just the filename or the filename and path in the database field is the best approach.
- Any attribute, whether of a multimedia object or regular image, can be dynamically derived. The Parameters dialog box offers options for inputting either dynamic or static attributes and values on multimedia objects, and the Bindings panel allows you to bind dynamic data to attributes.

In the next chapter, you see how to begin managing your data in Dreamweaver.

CHAPTER

20

Managing Data

IN THIS CHAPTER

- Repeating data on a page
- Dreamweaver Technique: Applying a Repeat Region
- Selectively showing and hiding areas
- Moving from record group to record group
- Using Data objects for instant recordset navigation
- Dreamweaver Technique: Establishing Recordset Navigation

With the power to access the data of the world—or at least your part of it—comes great responsibility. As a web page designer, you determine how best to present that information. This includes not only the surrounding look and feel but also how the data itself is structured. How many records should you show at once? One? Ten? All? How should the user navigate from one group of records to another? What should the user see when there are no more records to display? Obviously, there are no definitive answers to these questions; each response must take into account the intent of the page, the type of data involved, and the audience for that data. This chapter can't give you precise solutions for every web application, but it does give you the tools to devise your own solutions.

Displaying Data Conditionally

What makes a web page into a web application? Connectivity to a data source by itself does not make a web application—after all, you're merely setting up the possibility for data integration, not actually utilizing it. Some would say that it is the power to programmatically control the display of the data that is at the heart of an application. Dreamweaver handles this conditional display of data primarily through its Server Behaviors panel. You can, for example, opt to display the data—or any other page element—only if certain conditions are met, such as an empty recordset. Before you look at the options for showing and hiding data conditionally, let's first examine what is perhaps the most commonly used Dreamweaver server behavior: Repeat Region.

Repeating data

After establishing a data source connection and defining a recordset, Dreamweaver displays all the available fields in the Bindings panel. Regardless of how many records are contained in the declared recordset, you see only one record when you drag one or more fields onto your page and preview the file. To see multiple records from the same recordset on a single page, you can apply the Repeat Region server behavior.

The Repeat Region server behavior is very straightforward and extremely flexible. After selecting the dynamic data and any surrounding code you'd like to repeat, you specify the number of repetitions—you also have an option to display all the records in the recordset. The key phrase in the previous sentence is "and any surrounding code." If you select only the dynamic data itself, the data is repeated one record after another. You have to include some HTML element to enable the repeated data to appear separately, as on a different line. Some of the most commonly used separation elements and their HTML tags are:

- **Line break:** `<br>`
- **Paragraph:** `<p> . . . </p>`
- **Table row:** `<tr> . . . </tr>`
- **Table data:** `<td> . . . </td>`
- **Unordered or ordered list item:** `<li> . . . </li>`

For the Repeat Region to work correctly, you must select both the opening and the closing tags that surround the dynamic data, as shown in Design view in Figure 20-1. The surest way to do this is to place your cursor on the dynamic data and choose the surrounding element from the Tag Selector.

FIGURE 20-1

To automatically number your data, apply a Repeat Region to the <li> tag within an ordered (or numbered) list. Here PHP adds a do loop to repeat the elements.

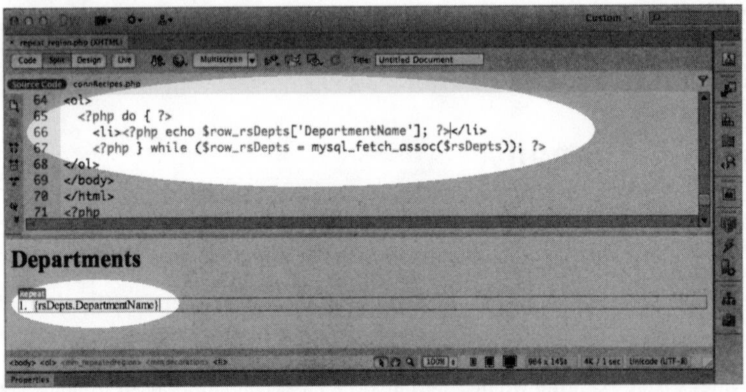

To implement a Repeat Region, follow these steps:

1. Select the dynamic data and surrounding code that you would like to repeat.
2. From the Server Behaviors panel, click Add (+) and select Repeat Region from the list. The Repeat Region dialog box, shown in Figure 20-2, appears.
3. Choose the recordset you want to work with from the Recordset drop-down list.

FIGURE 20-2

With the Repeat Region server behavior, you can show some or all the records in the chosen recordset.

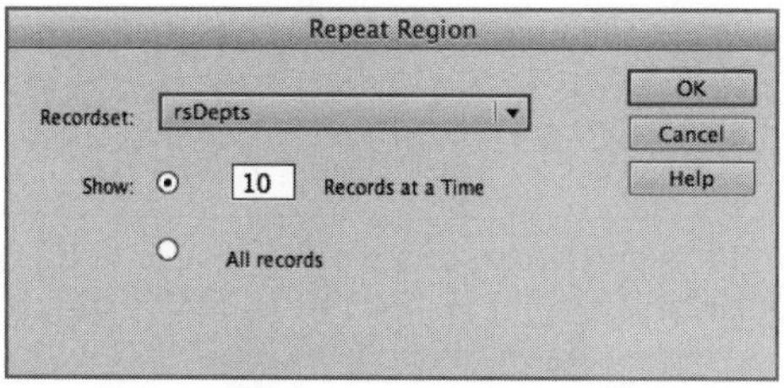

4. If you want to present a subset of the recordset, enter the number of records you want to display in the Show: Records field.

   The default is to show 10 records at a time. You can change that value to anything you like if you select the Show: Records option.
5. If you want to display every record in the recordset, choose the Show: All Records option.
6. Click OK when you're finished.

TIP

To test your implementation, make sure that the View ⇨ Visual Aids ⇨ Invisible Elements option is enabled. Then click the Live View button on the Document toolbar. Dreamweaver displays each repeated selection with a highlight.

Although all the repeated elements are displayed on the screen, only the initial element within a Repeat Region can be altered. If you change the initial element's formatting, you must click the Refresh button from the Live View toolbar to apply those changes to the other elements; this holds true even if you have Auto Refresh enabled.

Multiple Repeat Region server behaviors may coexist on the same page, extracting data from either the same recordset or a different one. However, if you use the same recordset again, you need to reset it so that Dreamweaver is extracting from the beginning. To do this, locate the second Repeat Region server behavior in the code by selecting its entry from the Server Behaviors panel and switching to Code view. Above the first line of server code, add the code appropriate to your server model (substitute the name of your recordset for *rsMine*):

```
ASP          <% rsMine.MoveFirst() %>
PHP          <? mysql_data_seek($rsMine, 0) ?>
```

NOTE

ColdFusion handles this for you. If you start a new ColdFusion `<cfoutput>` block based on your recordsets, it starts from the beginning again.

If you do not insert the resetting code, the second Repeat Region picks up where the first one left off. For example, if 10 records are displayed in the initial Repeat Region, the second Repeat Region starts with the 11th record. If you chose all records for the first Repeat Region, nothing is shown in the second Repeat Region.

Now that you know how to do this by hand, it's time to show you the quick way. (I know it's cruel, but everyone has to learn the hard way first.) Dreamweaver offers a fast and simple way to add a table of records with a Repeat Region in just one step. Choose Insert ⇨ Data Objects ⇨ Dynamic Data ⇨ Dynamic Table or click the Dynamic Table icon in the Data category ⇨ Dynamic Data of the Insert panel. The Dynamic Table dialog box, shown in Figure 20-3, is now active.

FIGURE 20-3

Use the Dynamic Table Data object to add dynamic lists of tabular data quickly. You can save lots of time by skipping the tedious task of adding all your dynamic text manually.

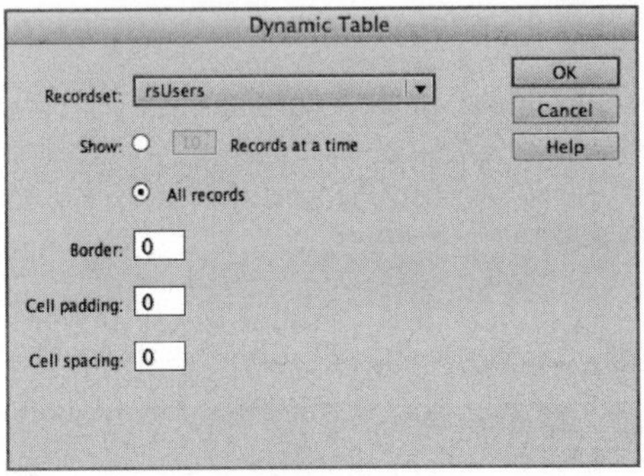

This dialog box has just a few options:

- **Recordset:** Choose the recordset you want displayed in your table.
- **Show:** Choose whether to show a limited number of records or all records. This adds a regular Repeat Region to your field, just as you did earlier in this section.
- **Table attributes:** Specify your table border, cell padding, and cell spacing.

After you click OK, the table contains the field names in the first row, the data items in the second row, and a Repeat Region wrapped around the second row, as shown in Figure 20-4.

Dreamweaver TECHNIQUE

Applying a Repeat Region

Repeat Region is one of the most frequently used server behaviors. In this Technique, you apply a Repeat Region server behavior to a previously created table row so that multiple data records can be displayed.

1. From the Techniques - Dynamic site (established in Chapter 18), expand the 20_Managing_Data folder and open the `managing_data_start` file for your server model.

   If you followed the Technique in the previous chapter, you'll recognize this page. There is, however, one small difference: An additional recordset has been added to illustrate an important concept.

2. Place your cursor in the row of dynamic data by selecting any of the inserted fields, such as rsAgents.agentPhone.
3. From the Tag Selector, choose the <tr> tag.

   Choosing the <tr> tag ensures that the entire row of data will be repeated.
4. From the Server Behaviors panel, click Add (+) and select Repeat Region from the list.
5. When the Repeat Region dialog box opens, choose rsAgents from the Recordset list.

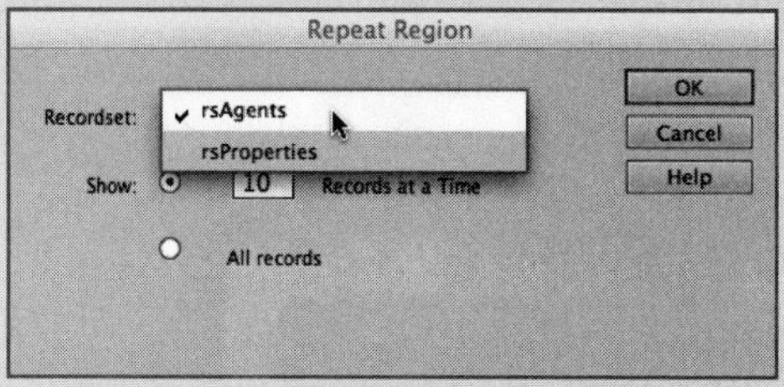

   You must be sure to select the recordset you want to repeat; if you were to leave the default choice, rsProperties, no additional data would be displayed because there is no dynamic data from that recordset in the table row.
6. Leave the default Show 10 Records at a Time option, and click OK.

   In Dreamweaver's Design view, a thin border appears around the row along with a tab indicating the Repeat Region.
7. Test your newly applied server behavior by choosing View ➪ Live View.

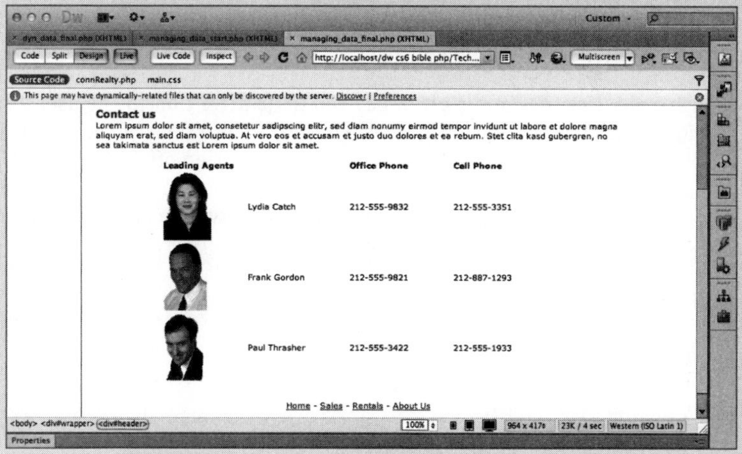

Continues

continued

8. Choose View ➪ Live View again to exit the mode.
9. Save your page.

In the next Technique, you see how to add elements to the page to indicate which records are currently displayed and to navigate through a larger recordset.

FIGURE 20-4

With the results from the Dynamic Table Data object, you simply change the basic table formatting and the table headings, and you're done.

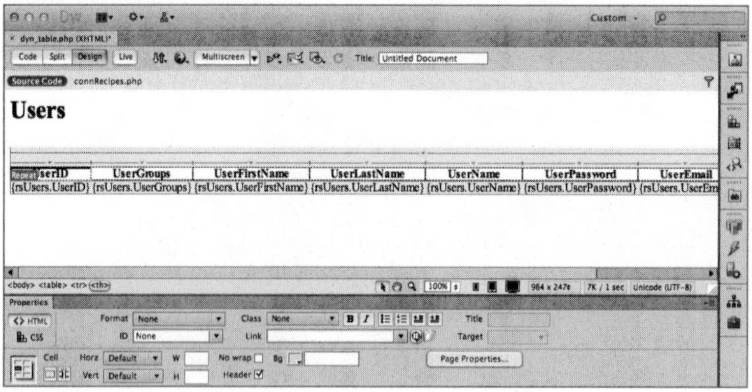

Showing and hiding page elements

In the rush to push a site live, designers often pay too little attention to the user experience. When you are designing static web pages, it's especially easy to lose sight of the importance of the user interface. However, with dynamic pages—where user interaction often determines what's on the page—an intuitive, reactive design helps to focus the audience on the content, rather than the engine driving the content. Dreamweaver provides a set of server behaviors that enable you to show or hide any area of the page dynamically: the Show Region server behaviors.

The six Show Region server behaviors are as follows:

- Show Region If Recordset Is Empty
- Show Region If Recordset Is Not Empty
- Show Region If First Page
- Show Region If Not First Page
- Show Region If Last Page
- Show Region If Not Last Page

TIP

Don't let the terminology throw you: Although they are all called Show Region server behaviors, you can just as easily use them to hide an area.

Dreamweaver's capability to conditionally hide or reveal areas of the page is extremely helpful for smoothing the user experience. For example, suppose you have a web application that shows all 23 items in a particular recordset, 5 at a time, with Next and Previous links (see Figure 20-5). The record navigation controls enable users to page through the recordset, forward and backward. When they reach the final record, the Next and Last buttons should be hidden; when they're on the first record, the Previous and First buttons should be hidden. I've used Show Region If Not Last Page to hide the Next button and Show Region If Not First Page to hide the Previous button.

FIGURE 20-5

Use Dreamweaver's Show Region server behavior to display or hide navigation buttons, depending on the dynamic data shown.

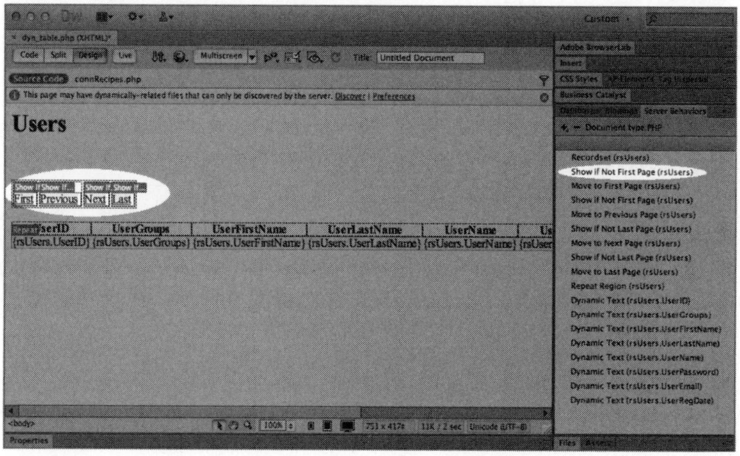

To apply a Show Region server behavior, follow these steps:

1. Select the page area you would like to conditionally show.
2. From the Server Behaviors panel, click Add (+) and select one of the server behaviors from the Show Record submenu. The dialog box for the specific Show Record server behavior you chose is displayed, like the one shown in Figure 20-6. The dialog boxes for all the Show Record server behaviors are identical.
3. From the Recordset list, select the recordset on which to base the Show Page condition.
4. Click OK when you're done.

20

FIGURE 20-6

To use a Show Record server behavior, simply choose a region to show/hide and a recordset.

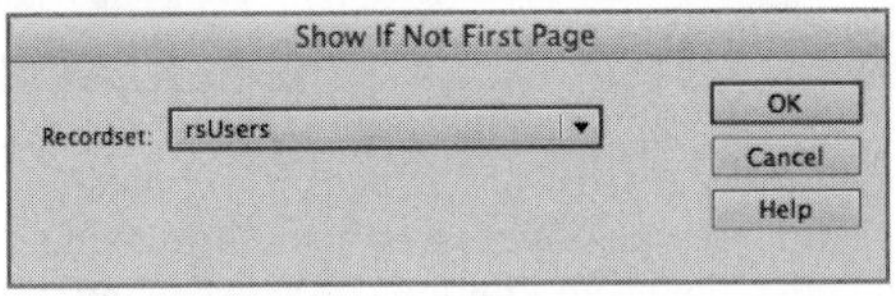

Typically, the Show Region server behaviors are used in pairs. Apply a Show Region If Not First Page server behavior to a Previous Page link—it hides the link when the user is on the first record. Similarly, apply a Show Region If Not Last Page server behavior to the Next Page link to cause the link to disappear when the last record is called.

Only the first two Show Region server behaviors—Show Region If Recordset Is Empty and Show Region If Recordset Is Not Empty—can be applied to a page without any preconditions. The other four Show Region server behaviors require that one other type of server behavior be present on the page: the Recordset Paging server behavior. The Recordset Paging server behaviors act like VCR controls, adding a link that, when selected, displays the first, last, next, or previous set of records. The Recordset Paging server behaviors are covered in more detail in the next section.

Handling Record Navigation

So far in this chapter, you've seen how to repeat dynamic data and how to hide and display data and other page elements programmatically. Now it's time to put some real interactive controls into the hands of your web application users. Dreamweaver includes a set of server behaviors that enable users to page through your recordset much as if they were flipping the pages of a catalog.

You can approach Dreamweaver's record navigation through two avenues: One is a do-it-yourself route where you assemble the navigation piece by piece, and the other lets Dreamweaver do most of the work for you. To better understand how record navigation works, examine the piece-by-piece approach first.

Building record navigation links

As mentioned earlier, Dreamweaver includes a set of Recordset Paging server behaviors to control navigation within a recordset. Again, the application is straightforward: Select the text or image you'd like to serve as a trigger and attach the appropriate server behavior. When selected, the trigger fires the server-side code that retrieves the chosen record. If a Repeat Region is inserted on the page, the next or previous group of records is displayed.

You can find five server behaviors under the Recordset Paging submenu:

- Move To First Page
- Move To Previous Page
- Move To Next Page

- Move To Last Page
- Move To Specific Page

NOTE

Move To Specific Page is most often used in conjunction with a search routine or a master-detail application.

As noted, you can use either text or images as your controls. Navigation links, such as those shown in Figure 20-7, may include rollovers or other client-side behaviors.

FIGURE 20-7

You can use images—with or without rollovers—to navigate through a recordset with Dreamweaver's Recordset Paging server behaviors.

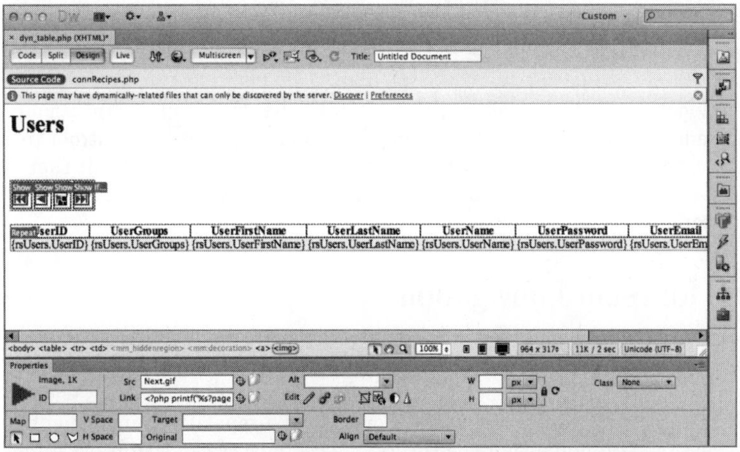

TIP

You don't need to add an initial or placeholder link to your image or text. When the Recordset Paging server behavior is applied, the link is written for you.

To create recordset navigation links, follow these steps:

1. Select the text or image to which you'd like to attach the server behavior.
2. From the Server Behaviors panel, click Add (+). Choose the desired behavior from the Recordset Paging submenu. The appropriate Recordset Paging dialog box appears. If you've made a selection, as suggested in Step 1, it's highlighted in the Link list, as shown in Figure 20-8; otherwise, a new text link is created.
3. Make sure that the selection in the Link list is the link you want.
4. Choose the recordset you want to work with from the Recordset drop-down list.
5. Click OK when you're finished.
6. Repeat Steps 1 through 5 to add more recordset navigation elements.

20

FIGURE 20-8

The Recordset Paging server behaviors identify your selected target, whether it is an image or text.

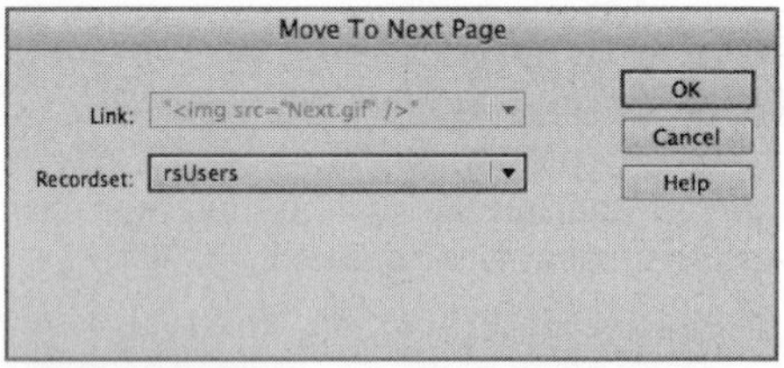

NOTE

Record navigation is done within a particular recordset; you can't link one recordset to another using the Dreamweaver server behaviors or Data objects.

After you've added your navigation controls, you may want to take the next step toward a more complete user interface by adding Show Region server behaviors to ensure that the controls are displayed only when they serve a purpose. For example, if you have a navigation element that moves to the last record of a recordset, you probably want to attach a Show If Not Last Page server behavior to the trigger.

Using Data objects for record navigation

Although the process for setting up a single navigation control is fairly simple, you'd have to perform that process four times (as well as attach four additional server behaviors) to accomplish what the Recordset Navigation Bar does in one operation. The Recordset Navigation Bar is one of Dreamweaver's Data objects—one that can take the drudgery out of a repetitious implementation. These objects are accessible through either the Insert ⇨ Data Objects ⇨ Recordset Paging menu or the Data ⇨ Recordset Paging category in the Insert panel.

The Recordset Navigation Bar Data object serves the following purposes:

- Adds four links to the page in a borderless, single-row table: First, Previous, Next, and Last. The links may be either text or graphics.
- Attaches the appropriate Recordset Paging server behavior to the four links.
- Adds a Show Region server behavior to each of the links:
  - Show If Not First Page is added to the First and Previous record links.
  - Show If Not Last Page is added to the Next and Last record links.
- Centers the table on the page or containing element and sets the width to 50%.

What's even more impressive about this list of functions is that they are implemented with a single command, which in turn, references a very simple dialog box, as shown in Figure 20-9.

FIGURE 20-9

The Recordset Navigation Bar dialog box offers a choice between text links and graphics.

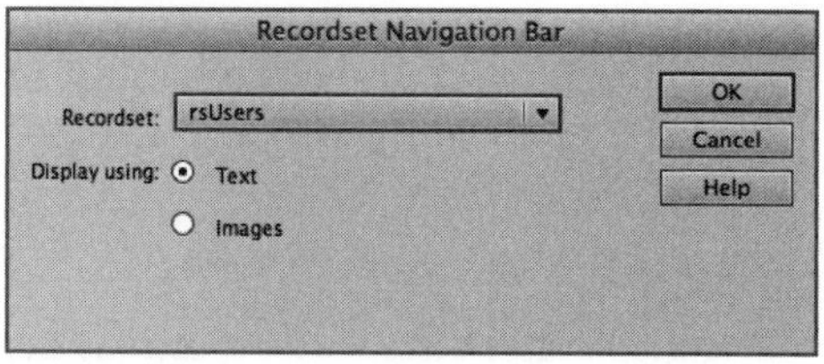

Here's how it works:

1. Choose Insert ➪ Data Objects ➪ Recordset Paging ➪ Recordset Navigation Bar, or choose Recordset Paging ➪ Insert Recordset Navigation Bar from the Data category of the Insert panel. The Recordset Navigation Bar dialog box is displayed.
2. Select the data you want to control from the Recordset list.
3. To create a series of text links, choose the Display Using Text option.
4. To use graphics to trigger the navigation, choose the Display Using Images option.
5. Click OK.

CAUTION

You must save the page if you select the Display Using Images option. Dreamweaver copies images from the Shared/Dreamweaver/Images folder when you choose this option, and the page into which they are being inserted must be saved to store the images properly in the site. They are stored in the same folder as the page containing them.

After the recordset navigation bar has been inserted, you can adjust the text or images in any way you see fit. The text may be styled or modified, and you can even swap out the images—by changing the `src` attribute—for other graphics.

Tracking record status

Another Data object inserts the text and all the server behaviors necessary to identify the records currently being viewed. By default, the syntax used by the Recordset Navigation Status Data object is:

```
Records First_Record_Shown to Last_Record_Shown of Total_Records
```

This syntax works perfectly for web applications that use a Repeat Region server behavior to show multiple records. When viewed through the browser, the recordset navigation status output looks like this:

```
Records 5 to 10 of 37
```

If you're displaying one record at a time, you can adjust the Data object code inserted so that it is similar to the following:

```
Record First_Record_Shown of Total_Records
```

Like the recordset navigation bar, the recordset navigation status Data object works with only one recordset at a time:

1. Choose Insert ➪ Data Objects ➪ Display Record Count ➪ Recordset Navigation Status, or click the Display Record Count ➪ Recordset Navigation Status icon on the Data category of the Insert panel. The Recordset Navigation Status dialog box appears, as shown in Figure 20-10.
2. Select the data you want to control from the Recordset list.
3. Click OK when you're finished.

FIGURE 20-10

The Recordset Navigation Status Data object inserts three different server behaviors in one operation.

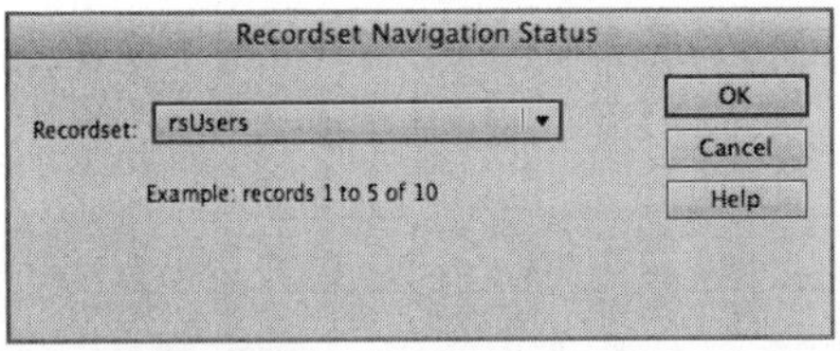

Dreamweaver TECHNIQUE

Establishing Recordset Navigation

In this Technique, you make sure your site visitors get a complete picture of the data you're displaying by adding the two Dreamweaver Data objects you've just learned: Recordset Navigation Status and Recordset Navigation Bar.

1. Open the `managing_data_start` file for the server model you worked on in the previous Technique.

   The first task is to extend the table to accompany the objects.
2. Place your cursor in the first row of the table next to any of the header labels, such as Leading Agent.
3. Press Ctrl+M (Command+M) to insert a new row above the current row.
4. You need to merge the second and third cells of the top table row to make room for the Data objects. Select the two cells above Office Phone and Cell Phone and, from the Property inspector, click Merge Cells.

5. To insert the first Data object, place your cursor in the first cell of the top row and, from the Data category of the Insert panel, click Display Record Count ➪ Recordset Navigation Status.

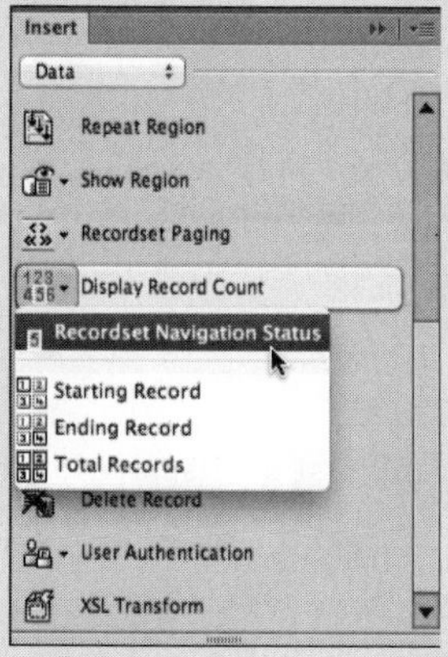

6. When the Recordset Navigation Status object opens, choose rsAgents from the Recordset list and click OK.

   Dreamweaver inserts the dynamic code for your server model, which, at runtime, will specify which records are currently being viewed.

7. Now add the capability to move through a recordset. Place your cursor in the second cell of the top row and, from the Insert panel's Data category, choose Recordset Paging: Recordset Navigation Bar.

8. In the Recordset Navigation Bar dialog box, choose rsAgent from the Recordset list, leave the default Display Using Text option, and click OK. The Recordset Navigation Bar table, along with all the necessary server behaviors, is added to the page.

9. Test your page by choosing View ➪ Live View or clicking the Live View button.

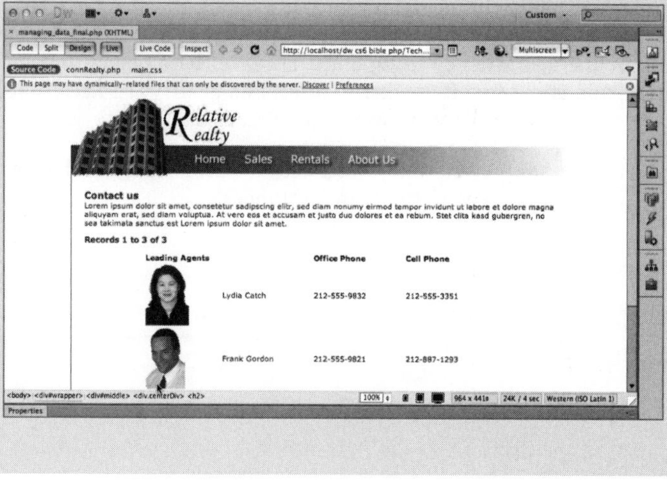

Continues

20

continued

You'll see one of the results from inserting one of the objects—the Recordset Navigation Status—but not the other. Because the returned recordset contains fewer than the number of records set to be displayed by the Repeat Region server behavior (10), the automatically applied conditional server behaviors hide the recordset navigation bar. It is, however, ready to be displayed should the recordset ever expand beyond the set value.

10. When you're done, exit Live View by choosing View ➪ Live View again and save your page.

Summary

To be part of an effective web application, dynamic data can't just be displayed; it has to be designed. Dreamweaver, through a variety of server behaviors, gives you the power to selectively repeat page elements, as well as show them programmatically. Data design is an important aspect of integrating the server-side with the client-side. As you look for ways to manage the data in your web applications more effectively, remember the following points:

- Dreamweaver's Repeat Region server behavior can help you to show as much of the data on a single page as you desire. Repeat Region server behaviors are usually applied to table rows, but they can also be used with line breaks, paragraphs, list items, or any other HTML element.
- It's often necessary to show data only if a certain condition is met. Dreamweaver handles these operations through a variety of Show Region server behaviors. With these tools, you can also selectively display any element—text, graphic, or dynamic data—on the current page.
- After you have the capability to display a portion of your data, you must navigate the recordset. Dreamweaver's Recordset Paging server behaviors can show the next or previous record (or group of records, if the Repeat Region server behavior is used), as well as enable you to quickly navigate to the first or last record of your data.
- Recordset navigation can be integrated in several ways. You can add each building block (the graphics or the text, the server behaviors, and so on) by itself, or you can accomplish the same task in one operation by using a Dreamweaver Data object. Depending on the web application, you might find it quicker to insert and modify the Recordset Navigation Bar Data object rather than build your own step-by-step.

In the next chapter, you learn how you can use Dreamweaver's Live View to enhance your workflow and test your application under a variety of circumstances.

CHAPTER

21

Working with Dynamic Live View

IN THIS CHAPTER

Understanding the Live View process

Designing in Live View

Testing different variable values

Dreamweaver Technique: Changing HTTP Request Settings

Previewing with a testing server

When I first started with print and design layout (back in the pre-computer dinosaur age), I would drive all over the city to finish a job. After receiving the client's go-ahead, I had to pick up my type from a phototypesetter and my images from a stat house. Then, back at my studio, I'd cut and paste—and I mean literally, with scissors and glue—the text and images into place, hoping against hope that I had specified the type and image sizes correctly. If not, it was back in the car for another trip or two around town. Ah, the good old days.

Now designers (especially those who design for the web) have the luxury of developing their creations right in their own studio. Until Dreamweaver, however, the development of a web application often undertook a faster, albeit parallel, course to my inner-city travels. After a basic page was designed, complete with server-side code, the document had to be uploaded to a testing server and then viewed in a browser over the Internet. If—make that *when*—changes were needed, the pages were revamped back in the studio. Because the designer was not able to lay out the page with the actual data in place, modifications were a trial-and-error process that often required many, many trips to the server and back.

Dreamweaver's Live View eliminates the tedium and the lengthy time required for the upload-preview-modify-upload cycle. It enables developers to work with the layout while the actual data is live on the page. If a table width needs to be adjusted because one of the records is too long, you can make the change immediately with no guesswork.

Live View processes the page in the chosen server model. If the page requires variables, such as search criteria, to run properly, the Live View feature enables you to set such values as needed. Although a preliminary discussion of Live View was presented in Chapter 20, this chapter covers all the necessary details for using both basic and advanced Live View capabilities.

Live View is a terrific time-saving feature, but you can't rely on it totally for testing your web application. You still need to preview the page in various browsers to ensure cross-browser compatibility. The final section of this chapter is dedicated to Dreamweaver's Preview In Browser feature and its relationship to your testing server.

Engaging Live View

After your site is properly set up, entering Live View is just a click away. Click the Live View button on the toolbar to refresh Dreamweaver's Document window and to replace all the dynamic data placeholders with information from the declared data source.

To get the most out of Live View—and to avoid problems—you need a firm grasp of how Dreamweaver is able to present your data, live. The following sections can help you understand this time-saving feature.

How Live View works

Once you enter Live View, there's a lot going on under the hood:

1. The developer inserts dynamic data elements into a standard HTML page. The dynamic data is represented by placeholders that combine the recordset and field names in a set of curly braces, such as `{rsEmployees.FirstName}`.
2. When the Live View is enabled, Dreamweaver creates a hidden, temporary copy of the current page.
3. The temporary page is stored in the folder designated in the Testing Server category of the Site Definition dialog box.
4. Dreamweaver instructs the defined testing server to execute the server-side code within the page and passes along any variables that have been specified. The URL prefix designated in the Site Definition Testing Server category is used to invoke the page.
5. When the code is executed, Dreamweaver reads the resulting HTML code.
6. Dreamweaver displays the page with its built-in rendering engine.

If all goes well, a page with dynamic data placeholders (shown in Figure 21-1) is replaced with the actual data integrated into Live View (shown in Figure 21-2).

If Dreamweaver encounters an error, it displays a message that explains where the process failed and suggests some possible remedies.

Setting up for Live View

As noted in the summary of how Live View works, several values found in the Testing Server category of the Site Definition dialog are key to this feature's operation. Live View must know the location of the site root for the temporary page and how that location may be reached with an HTTP request. If either of these values is not found, the attempt to switch to Live View is aborted and an error message appears.

Two different methods exist for accessing the testing server: locally through a network, or remotely via FTP. If a testing server is to be accessed locally, the location of the folder storing the pages is entered when setting up a testing server in the Server Folder field, shown in Figure 21-3. If you're using a local web server such as Internet Information Services (IIS) on your local testing machine, this entry is likely to be the same as your Local Root Folder, as defined in the Local Info category of the Site Definition dialog box. The other field essential to proper Live View operation is the URL Prefix field. When Live View sends the HTTP request to the testing server, the address contained in this field prefaces the name of the temporary page. For example, if my page is named `about.php` and the URL prefix is `http://localhost/dba`, the URL used is `http://localhost/dba/about.php`.

FIGURE 21-1

This table contains a row with four dynamic data fields, surrounded by a Repeat Region server behavior.

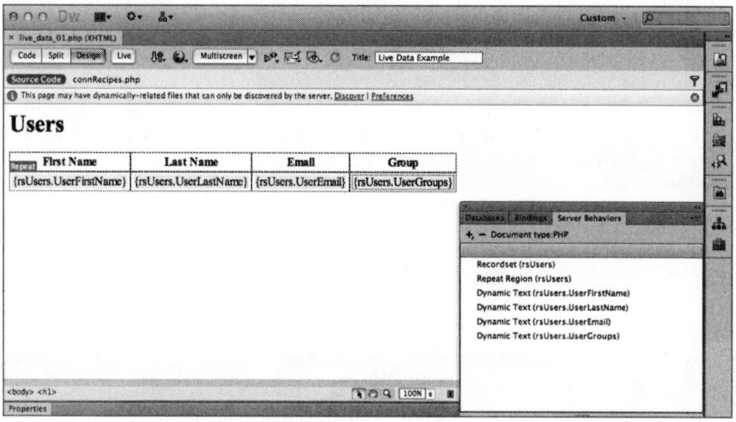

FIGURE 21-2

After Live View is enabled, the full number of records allowed by the Repeat Region is displayed and provides an accurate representation of the data.

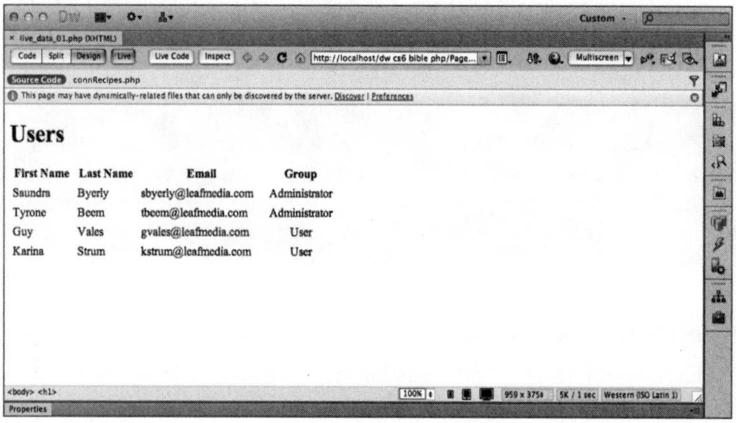

FIGURE 21-3

Enter the path to your testing server in the Server Folder field.

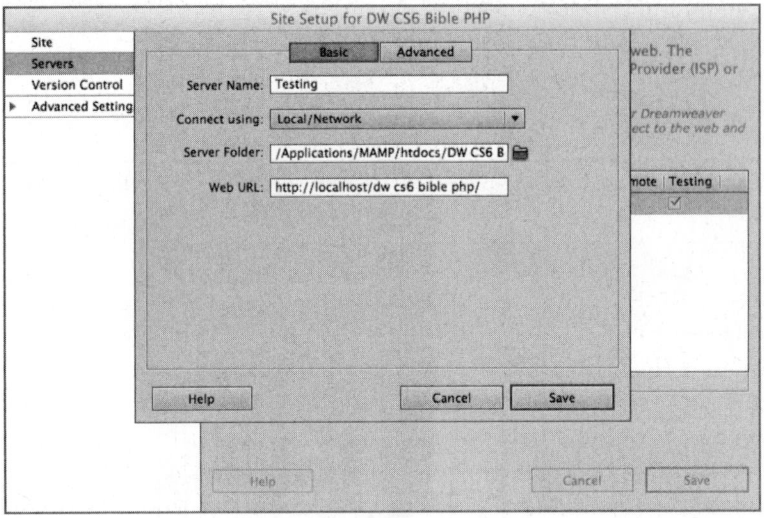

TIP

Localhost is common shorthand for addressing a local web server; generally, you can also use the Internet Protocol (IP) address 127.0.0.1.

Initially, Dreamweaver inserts only the `http://localhost/` address into the URL Prefix field. This works if your local site root corresponds to the local web server root. On Windows, under a Internet Information Services (IIS) web server, the local web server root is typically `c:/Inetpub/wwwroot/`; if you're using Mac's included web server, the [username]:Sites folder is the local web server.

TIP

There are a number of all-in-one systems to help with your development needs, which include a web server, MySQL, and PHP. By default, each of these programs specifies a folder to act as your site root. MAMP (`http://www.mamp.info`), for the Mac, uses `[username]:Applications:MAMP:htdocs`, whereas WampServer (`http://www.wampserver.com`), for Windows, uses `c:\wamp\www\`.

Entering and exiting Live View

Dreamweaver provides several different methods for invoking Live View, as shown in Figure 21-4. Use the one that best suits your work style:

FIGURE 21-4

Live View renders the current page through the testing server and displays any dynamic data.

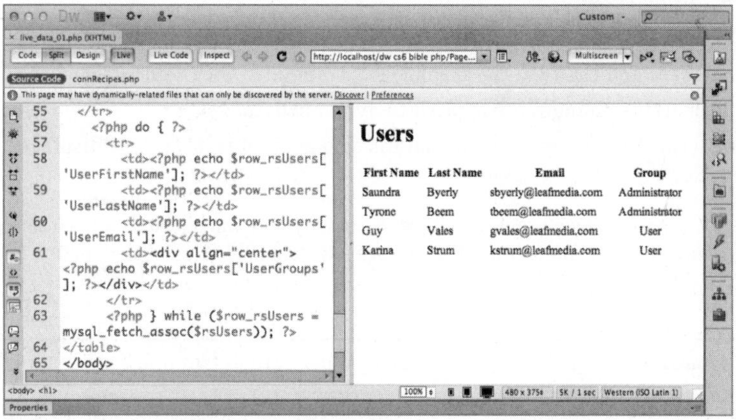

- Click Live View in the Document toolbar.
- Choose View ➪ Live View from the main menu.
- Use the keyboard shortcut Alt+F11 (Option+F11).

Regardless of the method used, Dreamweaver initially displays an alert that asks if you'd like to update the copy on the testing server. To preview the most recent changes, click Yes.

Once you're in Live View, executing any of these actions returns you to Standard mode, where you see dynamic data placeholders.

TIP

If, for any reason, you need to interrupt the Live View connection process, click the Stop button on the Live View toolbar. The Stop button remains active only while Dreamweaver is transitioning into Live View.

Making changes in Live View

If a feature in a software program can be said to have a *raison d'être*, then modifying the layout must surely be the *raison d'être* of *Live View*. When in Live View, new elements—dynamic or static—can be formatted or styled using HTML or CSS.

Live View solves the thorny challenge of laying out a table without resorting to a time-consuming trial-and-error approach. For instance, varying lengths of data in the same column often complicate designing a table layout with dynamic data. If, for example, the sample data includes a last name field that is 12 characters long and the real data contains a hyphenated name that is 25 characters long, you have a problem. When working in Live View, you can see the entire page as it would be generated on the server, including dynamic elements and repeating table rows, with all the styling applied.

The Live View toolbar includes a Refresh button (see Figure 21-5), which, when clicked, resends your application to the server for processing and then redisplays the page in the Document window. The Refresh option is valuable in the following circumstances:

- Information from the data source is reassessed. This feature enables you to make changes in the database and then see those changes incorporated into your page.
- Server formatting changes are applied to dynamic data.
- CSS formatting applied to dynamic data is also applied to Live View displayed through a Repeat Region server behavior.

Repeat Region server behaviors enable multiple records from the same recordset to be incorporated into a page. For details on how to insert and manage a Repeat Region, see Chapter 20.

FIGURE 21-5

Use Live View to make sure your layout works well with the actual data that appears on the page.

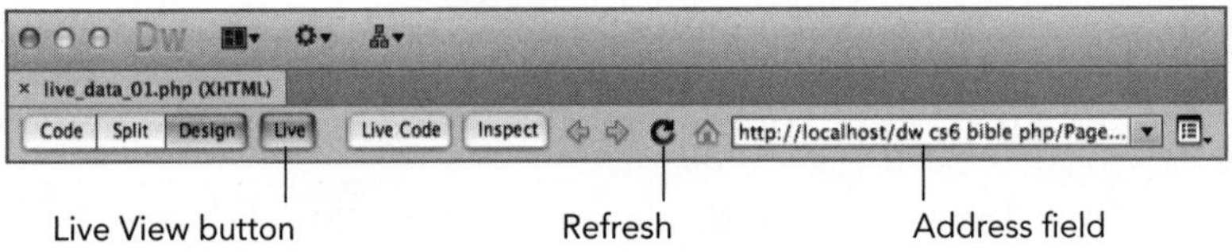

HTTP Request Settings

Although the capability to work with data from the current recordset is impressive, it's really only half the story of Live View. Many web applications depend on variables used when the page is processed by the testing server. Users may intentionally submit these variables when they fill out a form or they may submit variables unintentionally when they navigate from a particular page. Session or application variables, from authentication routines or simple counters, may also be integrated into a page. Dreamweaver permits developers to interactively alter all such variables and preview the resulting web page. This facility not only enables the designer to work with a wide range of real-life conditions but also facilitates testing of the application under a variety of circumstances. Dreamweaver offers two avenues of approach to variable handling: through the Address field and through the Settings dialog box.

Getting the query string

Remember the first time you noticed that the link you clicked was carrying quite a bit of additional baggage? Where you might have selected a link that took you to a specific product page with a URL such as `http://www.idest.com/products/widgets.htm`, the link in the Location field of your browser looked more like the following:

```
http://www.idest.com/products/products.asp?prod=widget&sessionID=2343215&
login=no&visited=gadgets%20%r%20us
```

The text following the question mark is called a *query string*, or the *URL parameters*. Query strings are used by web applications to pass information from one page to the next. Frequently, you see a query string after submitting a form. Forms using the `Get` method pass their variables by appending a question mark and the form information to the URL of the requested page. The form information is in a series of name/value pairs, and each name/value pair is linked by an equal sign, as follows:

```
Firstname=Joseph
```

Query strings may include any number of name/value pairs, separated by an ampersand. Thus, for a form that passes the data entered into a first name field and a last name field, the query string may look like this:

```
?firstname=Joseph&lastname=Lowery
```

Neither single nor double quotation marks are used because they are HTML attributes. Quotation marks and other characters—including spaces, apostrophes, and tildes—are represented by hexadecimal values so that they are properly understood by servers. Such strings are said to be *URL encoded*, and they are designated by an initial percent sign, followed by the ASCII value of the character in hexadecimal. The following table offers some commonly used encoding values:

TABLE 21-1 Commonly Used Encoding Values

Character	Symbol	ASCII Value
Space		%20
Apostrophe or single quotation mark	'	%27
Double quotation mark	"	%22
Tilde	~	%7E
Less than	<	%3C
Greater than	>	%3E

The query string field appears in the Live View toolbar by default, prefaced by the URL path used by Live View plus a question mark. The URL path, question mark, and text entered into the field constitute the complete URL submitted to the testing server when you invoke or refresh Live View.

NOTE

Depending on the length of the pathname, some elements, such as folders, may be represented by an ellipsis (three dots) so that Dreamweaver can display the filename and question mark.

Consider an example that uses the query string. Suppose that you've developed a page for an organization that displays employees and whether they're under contract. The contract status shown depends on the link selected by the user; the links are identical except for the query string portion. For non-contracted employees, the link reads `employees.cfm?contract=no`, whereas for contracted employees, the link reads `employees.cfm?contract=yes`. The recordset on the `employees.cfm` page uses a filter that sets the Contract field equal to the URL parameter called `contract`.

NOTE

Although the query string field is present by default, you can disable it by switching the Method option in the HTTP Request Settings dialog box from `Get` to `Post`. To re-enable the query string field, choose View ⇨ Live View Options ⇨ HTTP Request Settings and select `Get` as the Method option.

After entering Live View by any of the methods described previously, you can switch back and forth between the two sets of returned data by changing the value in the query string `name=value` pair. In this instance, the two accepted values—as defined in the data source—are `no` for employees not under contract and `yes` for employees under contract. After changing the value and pressing Enter (Return), Live View is refreshed, as shown in Figure 21-6.

FIGURE 21-6

You can use the query string field of the Live View toolbar, seen in the tooltip, to test different scenarios for your web application.

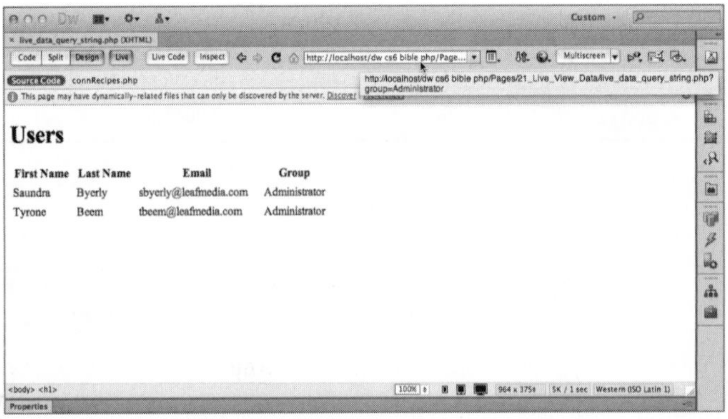

CAUTION

If you encounter a Live View error indicating that the page cannot be displayed because the current record could not be found, you're probably including values in the query string that do not match any records in a recordset on the page. You have a couple of options for proceeding. Press the Esc key to dismiss the error dialog box and enter a new value in the query string field. (Don't click the Close button on the dialog box, or you'll close the Live View and the Live View toolbar.) Alternatively, you can enter a name/value pair through the HTTP Request Settings dialog box as outlined in the following section.

Posting responses with HTTP Request Settings

Although the query string is handy for changing one or two simple variables, the more complex the variables, the less convenient it becomes. Dreamweaver offers another route to controlling Live View variables: Live View settings. The HTTP Request Settings dialog box, shown in Figure 21-7, offers several important advantages over the query string:

- The name/value pairs are easier to enter and maintain in a straightforward two-column table.

- URL encoding is handled automatically by Dreamweaver: with query strings.
- Variables may be sent to the application by either the Get or the Post method. The query string uses only the Get method.
- Variable settings may be optionally stored. If you select this option, Dreamweaver uses its Design Notes facility to maintain the variables.

FIGURE 21-7

Invoke the HTTP Request Settings command to simulate forms using either the GET or the POST method.

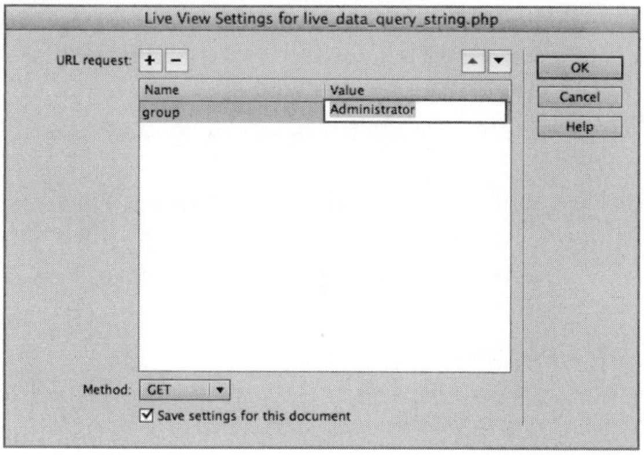

To establish variables using the HTTP Request Settings feature, follow these steps:

1. Choose View ➪ Live View Options ➪ HTTP Request Settings, or enter Live View and select Settings from the Live View toolbar. The HTTP Request Settings dialog box for the current page is displayed, with the title Live View Settings.
2. To create a new variable, click the Add (+) button.
3. In the Name column, enter the name of the variable.
4. In the corresponding field under the Value column, enter a value for the variable.
5. Repeat Steps 2 through 4 to add additional variables.
6. To delete a name/value pair, select it and click the Remove (–) button.
7. You can adjust the sequence in which the variables are presented to the page by using the Up and Down buttons to move name/value pairs higher or lower in the list.
8. By default, Dreamweaver sends variables to a page using the GET method, which appends URL-encoded name/value pairs in a query string. To simulate a form passing variables in an encapsulated, hidden manner, choose POST from the Method list.
9. To store your variable settings, select the Save Settings For This Document option. Dreamweaver requires that Design Notes be enabled in order to save the Live View settings. If Design Notes is disabled when you select this option, you get an opportunity to enable it.

TIP

If you choose the GET method, enter the variables and their values without encoding them for the URL. Dreamweaver translates any necessary characters into their hexadecimal equivalents when the Live View page is processed.

Dreamweaver TECHNIQUE

Changing HTTP Request Settings

In this Technique, you practice working with Live View settings, both in the dialog box and in the Live View query string field.

1. From the Techniques - Dynamic site (established in Chapter 18), expand the 21_Live_Data folder and open the `live_data_start` file for your server model.

   Before you can use the Live View settings to alter the preview, you need to know how the recordset is being filtered.

2. In the Bindings panel, double-click the Recordset (rsProperties) entry to reopen the associated dialog box.
3. Take note of the Filter section and you'll see that the recordset is filtered by the URL parameter `type`.
4. Click Cancel to close the Recordset dialog box.
5. Now that you know what variable the recordset is filtered on, you can specify it in the Live View settings. Choose View ➪ Live View Options ➪ HTTP Request Settings.
6. When the HTTP Request Settings dialog box opens, click Add (+) and in the Name column enter **type** and press Tab.
7. In the Value column, enter **rental** and click OK.

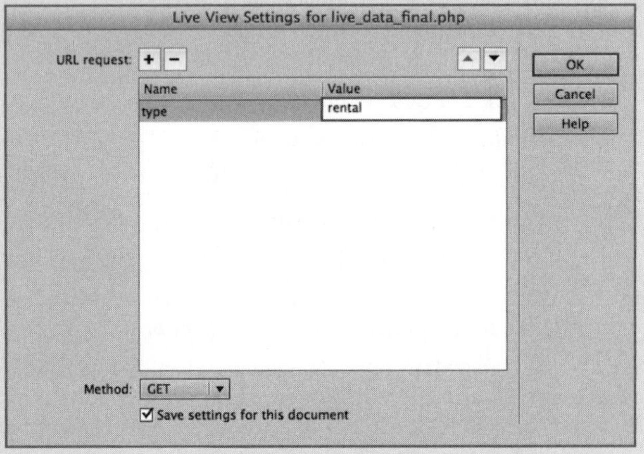

8. Choose View ➪ Live View.

   Only the rental type records are displayed. Now, switch to a different set of records.

9. In the Live View Query String field, change the type value from **rental** to **purchase** so that the entire query string reads `type=purchase`, and press Enter (Return).

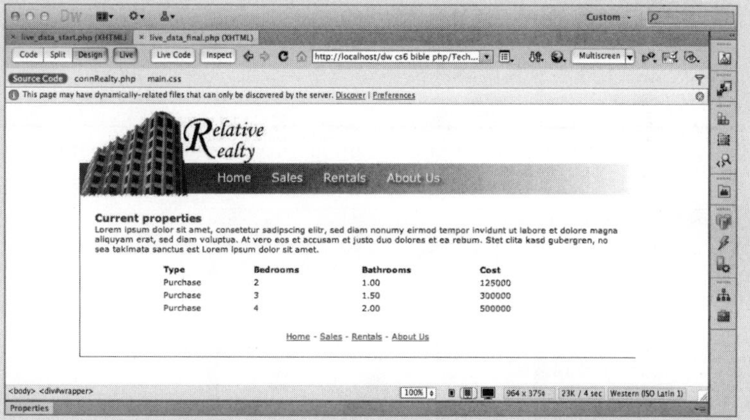

10. Choose View ➪ Live View again to return to standard Design view.

Although you can discover which parameters are used to filter the recordset, you can't uncover the expected values from within Dreamweaver. If they weren't provided for you as in this Technique, you'd need to examine the data source to see what values were expected and stored.

Previewing an Application in the Browser

Live View saves a tremendous amount of time in the early design phase, yet when it comes time to test your application in various browsers—a necessary step for virtually all web developers—there is no substitute for previewing in the browser. Dreamweaver does a decent job of approximating a browser's-eye view of your page. However, with so many variations between the major browsers—not to mention the versions within each major browser—you must test your page in as many browsers as possible. Dreamweaver's Preview In Browser feature enables you to specify up to 13 different browsers in Preferences. After this feature is defined, you can test your page by choosing File ➪ Preview In Browser ➪ Browser Name at any point. If the toolbar is open, you can also choose a browser under the Preview/Debug in Browser option.

To view web applications properly, Dreamweaver must process the pages with a testing server. To use this facility, you must satisfy two requirements:

- Specify the route to the testing server, either via a local (or networked) folder or through FTP in the Servers category of the Site Definition dialog box.
- Transfer any dependent or related files to the testing server. Although you don't have to include dependent files such as graphics on the current page, you must transfer server-side includes, such as the connection script. Related files are other pages referenced in the web application; Dreamweaver only uploads a copy of the current page during the Preview In Browser operation.

After the testing server is properly set up (as described in Chapter 5), you can transfer any necessary files quickly in the Files window. On the Files window toolbar, click the Testing Server button. The files on the testing server are displayed in the Testing Server pane of the Site window, as shown in Figure 21-8. Transfer files from the local site by dragging them from the local pane to the Testing Server pane or by selecting the files and then clicking the Put or the Check In button.

FIGURE 21-8

The Dreamweaver Site window enables you to connect to the testing server or the remote server.

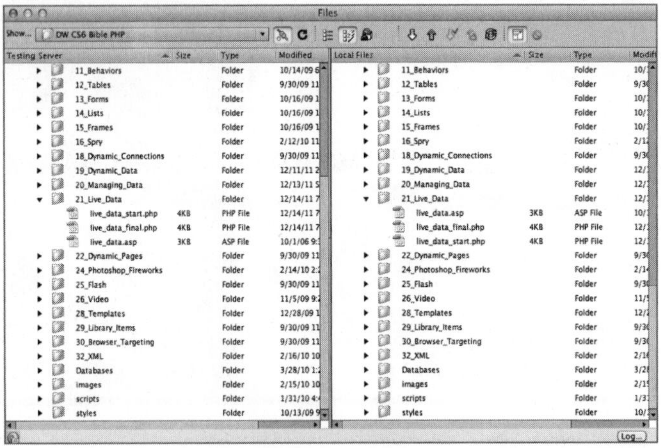

> **TIP**
>
> When you begin to test a new page, let Dreamweaver transfer the dependent files for you. Simply transfer a saved copy of the current page to the testing server and okay the request to transfer the dependent files as well. To take advantage of this feature, make sure that you select the Dependent Files: Prompt On Put/Check In option found in the Site category of Preferences.

Using the Server Debug Panel with ColdFusion (Windows Only)

The Server Debug panel, a Windows-only feature, offers you an integrated view of all errors and server variables on your ColdFusion pages. The Server Debug view also gives you the capability to browse your site inside the Dreamweaver interface, testing values as you go.

To enable debugging directly inside Dreamweaver, follow these simple steps:

1. Enable server debugging by choosing Debugging & Logging ➪ Debug Output Settings in the left-hand pane of the ColdFusion Administrator (see Figure 21-9). The Debug Output Settings page opens in the right-hand pane. Select the Enable Robust Exception Information and Enable Request Debugging Output options and click Submit Changes.

   FIGURE 21-9

   Enable the server debugging options in ColdFusion before using the Server Debug panel in Dreamweaver.

   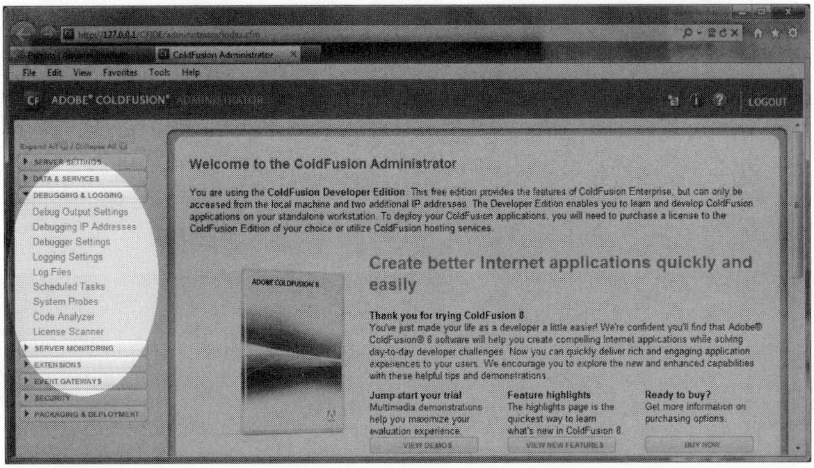

2. In Dreamweaver, choose View ➪ Server Debug, and an additional toolbar with the following buttons appears directly above your document window:
   - **Backward:** Emulates the browser Back button and takes you to the previous page in your history.
   - **Forward:** Emulates the browser Forward button and takes you to the next page in your history.
   - **Stop:** Emulates the browser Stop button and stops the current page from processing.
   - **Refresh:** Emulates the browser Refresh button and reloads the current page.

   It also includes an Address bar for passing query string values to your page and enabling you to see where you are in your site.

   When you preview Live View, you can see all the Server Debug output (see Figure 21-10), and you can browse through your pages just as you would in a regular web browser.

3. Open the Server Debug panel (see Figure 21-11) by choosing Window ➪ Results or pressing F7 and selecting the Server Debug tab. The Server Debug panel should now be shown below the Property inspector.

After you open the Server Debug panel, you can see all your variables, as well as any errors. Any exceptions provide a link to the page that is throwing the error. If that error was contained inside a <CFINCLUDE>, the URL for the page is a clickable link next to the error.

FIGURE 21-10

The Server Debug view gives you additional options on the toolbar for browsing your ColdFusion documents.

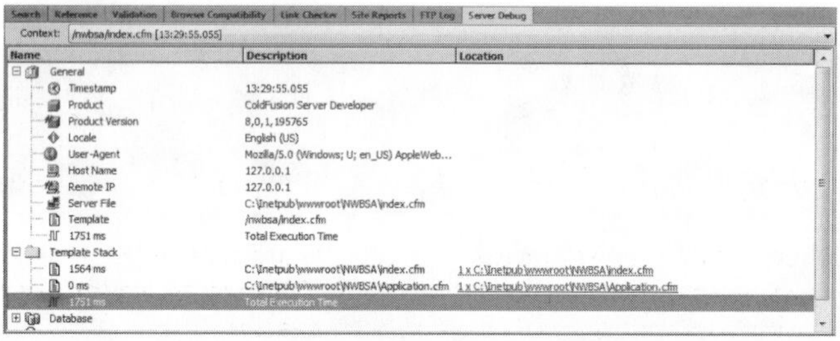

> **TIP**
>
> If you right-click inside the Server Debug panel, you can choose Select All and copy the contents of the panel by choosing Copy from the context menu. You can then paste it inside a new document—in Dreamweaver or another text editor—for future reference or to send to another ColdFusion developer for further debugging.

FIGURE 21-11

The Server Debug panel gives you a quick overview of all the returned variables from the ColdFusion server.

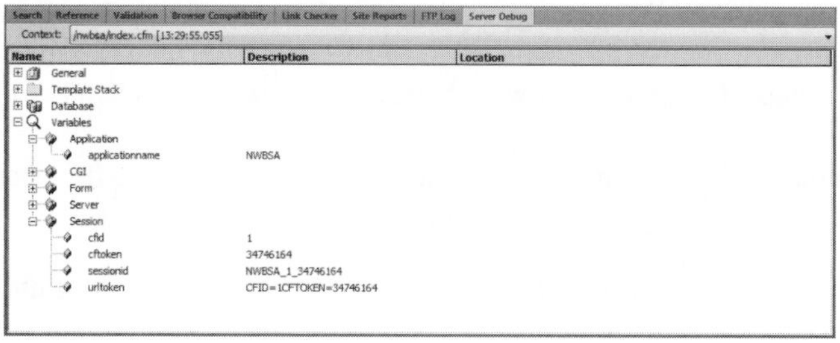

Summary

Sometimes, when an unusual idea appears in a software program, it's hard to separate the merely glitzy from the truly grand. As implemented in Dreamweaver, Live View proves to be very functional and, thus, more than a flash in the pan—although I have to admit, it's pretty darn cool as well. To make the most of Live View, remember the following points:

- Live View depends on proper setup of the testing server to run dynamic pages smoothly. If any of the information entered into the Servers category of the Site Definition dialog box is incomplete or incorrect, Dreamweaver won't be able to process your web application and display the results successfully.
- Both the query string field and the Settings button in the Live View toolbar offer developers a way to test their web application with different variables. Use the query string field to emulate the passing of URL parameters and the Settings dialog box for `Post`-enabled forms.
- To try different server environments, enter the appropriate code in the Initialization Script field of the Settings dialog box. This facility enables you to test different application variables, session variables, and other variables easily.
- Be sure to use Dreamweaver's Preview In Browser feature to give your web application a real-world tryout before going live. To test your page, transfer dependent and related files using the Site window from the local site to the testing server pane.
- Use Dreamweaver's tight ColdFusion integration and the Server Debug panel (Windows only) to quickly debug your ColdFusion applications.

In the next chapter, you learn how to create multiple page applications.

CHAPTER

22

Crafting Multi-Page Applications

IN THIS CHAPTER

Forwarding parameters via a URL

Automating application object production

Getting values from a form

Dreamweaver Technique: Building a Search Page

Making form elements dynamic

Administering data sources with web applications

Dreamweaver Technique: Creating the Results Page

Displaying variables

Authenticating site visitors

In a website composed of static HTML pages, each page generally stands on its own and is developed individually. In a dynamic website, however, applications often require multiple pages to be effective. A prime example is the master-detail web application where a search box on one page leads to a master list of results on a second page, each of which, in turn, is linked to a third dynamically generated detail page. To execute the application, variables and other information must be passed from one page to the next. The dynamic website developer has a variety of tools capable of handling this task, including forms and session variables. All these methods for creating multiple-page web applications are available in Dreamweaver and are covered in this chapter. I also show you a one-step procedure for developing a master-detail web application.

Additionally, this chapter covers the use of form elements such as text fields, checkboxes, and drop-down lists for dynamic data display. Form elements are extremely useful to the web application developer because they let the developer update objects on the fly. By making a choice in one drop-down list, the developer can determine which options are available in another list. This chapter also describes how to put your new knowledge of form elements to work in creating a search field. Finally, you learn how to protect your site by authenticating your site visitors and permitting access only to authorized visitors.

Using the URL to Pass Parameters

In a static website, links are used to navigate from one page to another. In a dynamic website, links can have an additional function: passing parameters to an application server so that it can determine the dynamic content on the linked page. The added parameters are known as a *query string* and follow the standard URL after a question mark, like this:

```
dvd_details.php?movie=Serenity
```

Every parameter is composed of a name/value pair separated by an equal sign. If more than one parameter is sent, each pair is separated by an ampersand, as in the following example:

```
dvd_details.php?movie=Serenity&genre=scifi
```

Unlike in HTML or other languages, quotation marks are not used to set off the values. Quotation marks and other non-alphanumeric characters including spaces, single quotes, and tildes must be translated into encoded characters so that the server interprets them correctly. Spaces, for instance, are rendered as `%20`, as shown here:

```
dvd_details.php?movie=Serenity&genre=scifi&director=Joss%20Whedon
```

Dreamweaver provides all the tools necessary for constructing query strings within its point-and-click interface. However, if you understand the required syntax, you can quickly test your page using the Address field found on the Live View toolbar.

Sending parameters

With a master-detail web application—explained below—typically only a single parameter is used. The parameter uniquely identifies the record selected on the master page and is appended to the link for the detail page. For example, suppose the detail page is `details.php`, the identifying variable is called `tripID`, and the specific item is `Conquering K2`. The full link, with the query string, reads:

```
details.php?tripID=Conquering%20K2
```

NOTE

Master pages are one of two types: The master list is defined either by the designer or by the search criteria submitted by the user. The examples in this section are designer-based and rely on a specific recordset being declared. Details on how to create a search field are covered later in this chapter in the Dreamweaver Technique "Building a Search Page."

To insert the proper code within Dreamweaver, you'll need to add the name/value pair parameters to the linking text, image, or dynamic data. When you create a link, you'll have the option to click the Parameters button, shown in Figure 22-1, to start the process.

To add dynamic parameters, follow these steps:

1. Select the page element—text, graphic, or dynamic data—to use as the link to the detail page.
2. From the Property inspector, click the Browse For File icon next to the Link field.
3. When the Select File dialog box opens, choose the file you want to link to.
4. Once the file has been selected, click Parameters.

FIGURE 22-1

The Parameters button in the Select File dialog box allows you to add URL parameters to any link.

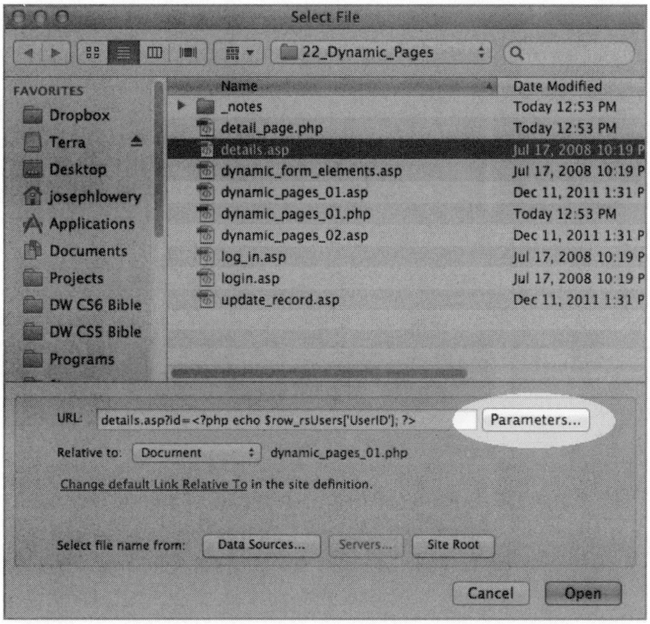

5. In the Parameters dialog box, click Add (+).
6. In the Name column, enter the variable name.
7. Press Tab and, in the Value column, click the dynamic data (lightning bolt) icon (see Figure 22-2).
8. In the Dynamic Data dialog box, expand the Recordset entry and select the desired dynamic value.
9. Click OK once to close the Dynamic Data dialog box, again to close the Parameters dialog box, and a third time to the close Select Files dialog box.

TIP

It's a good idea to prototype all the pages in your application before you begin adding content, especially server-side code. Existing pages are easy to link to through a Select File dialog box, and doing so reduces the chance of typographical errors.

Now that the link is passing parameters successfully, it's time to make sure that the detail page is set up to receive them properly.

FIGURE 22-2

Select the dynamic data for the URL parameter from any available recordset.

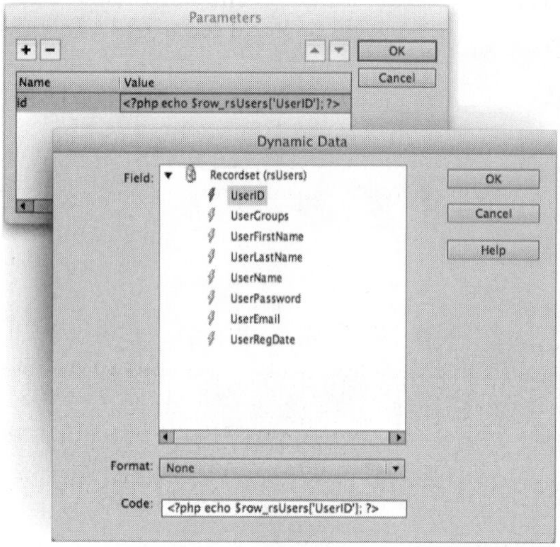

Receiving parameters

Dreamweaver provides two routes for your detail page to use the parameter passed to it by the master page: a filtered recordset or a Dreamweaver server behavior. In general, the first method is less processor-intensive and thus the better choice of the two. The filtered recordset technique returns a recordset of one record—the one used in the detail. If you use the server behavior technique, the entire recordset from the master page is made available, and only the specific record is displayed. You should use the entire recordset method if you want to do recordset paging from one record to the next.

To learn more about recordset paging, see Chapter 20.

Regardless of which technique you use, the detail page should include whatever dynamic data is appropriate. This, of course, requires a recordset. If you're using the server behavior technique, the recordset is generally left unfiltered; in many situations, you can copy the recordset used in the master page and paste it in the detail page using the context-sensitive menus on the Bindings panel. After the recordset is pasted onto the page, you can modify it to include additional fields by double-clicking the recordset entry in the Bindings panel.

Filtering a detail page recordset in Simple mode

You can create the filtered recordset in either the simple Recordset or the advanced Recordset dialog box. To use the simple Recordset dialog box, follow these steps:

See Chapter 18 for more on the simple and advanced Recordset dialog boxes.

1. From the Bindings panel, click the Add (+) button and choose Recordset from the list.

2. After you've chosen the name, connection, and table, select the fields required by your details page from the Columns list.
3. From the first Filter list, select the field that coincides with the value passed by the URL parameter, as shown in Figure 22-3. This field should contain unique values that can be used to identify each record.
4. From the second Filter list, select the equals operator (=).

FIGURE 22-3

Setting a filter in the simple Recordset dialog box requires that you complete four fields under the Filter heading.

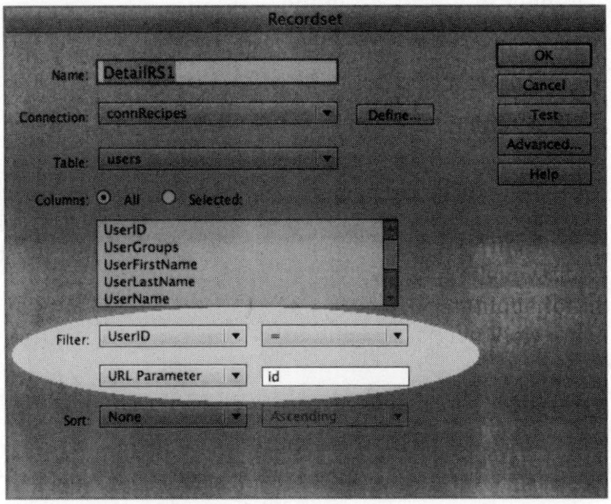

5. From the third Filter list, ASP, PHP, and ColdFusion users should choose the URL Parameter.
6. In the fourth Filter field, enter the variable name passed by the master page in the Go To Detail Page server behavior. Avoid names with spaces or other special characters; these names must be URL-encoded and may be difficult to manage.
7. Click OK when you're finished.

You can preview the results of your detail page in Live View, but be sure to set up the HTTP request settings first. Choose View ➪ Live View Options ➪ HTTP Request Settings to begin. When the HTTP Request Settings dialog box is open, enter the URL parameter name in the Name column and the value you'd like to test in the Value column. Make sure the Method option is set to `Get`, and click OK. Your Live View preview should now include the specified record, just as if the user had chosen it.

TIP

After entering Live View, you can test a variety of different records without reopening the HTTP Request Settings dialog box. In the Address field found on the Live Data toolbar, change the URL parameter's current value and press Enter (Return). If you enter a value not found in the data source, Dreamweaver displays an error indicating that it cannot display the page.

To test your master-detail application, save both pages and then preview the master page in the browser. When you select the link to the detail page, you should see your chosen record.

Filtering a detail page recordset in Advanced mode

Sometimes you need to define a more complex recordset than is possible in the Simple Recordset dialog box. You can effectively add the same filter-by-URL-parameter argument for such recordsets in the Advanced Recordset dialog box by altering the SQL statement. Filtering in a SQL statement is handled by the `WHERE` clause.

To create a detail page filter, declare a variable and add a `WHERE` clause referencing that variable. The runtime value portion of the variable is different for each server model. Assume that you want to declare a variable called `theBrand`, and the field is named `Brand`. In the Variables section of the Advanced Recordset dialog box, click the Add (+) button and then enter the values in the table that follows, according to your server model.

Server Model	Name	Default Value	Runtime Value
ASP	theBrand	%	Request.QueryString("Brand")
ColdFusion	theBrand	%	#URL.Brand#
PHP	theBrand	%	<?php echo $HTTP_GET_VARS['Brand']; ?>

In this example, the `WHERE` clause would read:

```
WHERE Brand = 'theBrand'
```

If you have already created a URL-parameter filtered recordset in the Simple Recordset dialog box and then switch to the Advanced mode, you will notice that Dreamweaver uses the variable name `MMColParam`. You can continue to use this variable name or change it to something more meaningful if you prefer.

Using a server behavior to filter a recordset

As noted earlier, the other method for connecting a master page with a detail page involves using a Dreamweaver server behavior. The Move To Specific Record server behavior is applied on the detail page itself and may be attached at any time. Unlike the filtered recordset approach, which uses a single record in the recordset, Move To Specific Record requires a recordset that includes all the possible records and their data. This gives you the capability to move through the recordset using the Recordset Paging server behaviors. The record specified by the URL parameter, as interpreted by the server behavior, is extracted from the overall recordset and its data displayed. To use the Move To Specific Record server behavior to create a detail page, follow these steps:

NOTE
The Move To Specific Record server behavior is not available for PHP or ColdFusion.

1. Establish a recordset that contains all the possible records that could be requested by the master page.
2. From the Server Behaviors panel, choose Move To Specific Record from the Move To Record submenu. The Move To Specific Record dialog box is displayed, as shown in Figure 22-4.

FIGURE 22-4

An alternative method for creating a detail page uses the Move To Specific Record server behavior.

3. Select the desired recordset from the list labeled Move To Record In.
4. Choose the field referenced in the URL parameter from the Where Column field.
5. Enter the variable in the URL parameter in the Matches URL Parameter field.
6. Click OK when you're finished.

CAUTION
Although Dreamweaver provides this method for creating a detail page—and I've covered it here for the sake of completeness—it's really not the recommended method. Because this technique relies on the use of a full recordset, it is far more resource-intensive than the filtered recordset method. However, this method is required if you are going to use Recordset Paging.

Automating Master-Detail Page production

Although Dreamweaver has made crafting master-detail web applications by hand extremely accessible, it can be a tedious series of steps, especially if you have to produce a number of applications for a site. To ease the monotony—and enhance your production efforts—Dreamweaver includes the Master-Detail Page Set application object that, after a single dialog box is completed, creates all the elements for a linked master-detail web application.

The master page elements are inserted in the current document, which must contain a recordset. The inserted elements and code, shown in Figure 22-5, are as follows:

- A two-row table with a column for each field
- A header row composed of all the field names selected in the dialog box
- Dynamic text for all selected fields, placed into the second row
- A Repeat Region server behavior surrounding the second row
- A Go To Detail Page server behavior linking to the newly created detail page
- A recordset navigation bar with text links and appropriate Show Region server behaviors in place
- A recordset status bar showing the current record count

FIGURE 22-5

The Master-Detail Page Set application object adds all the designated fields and the required server behaviors to the current page.

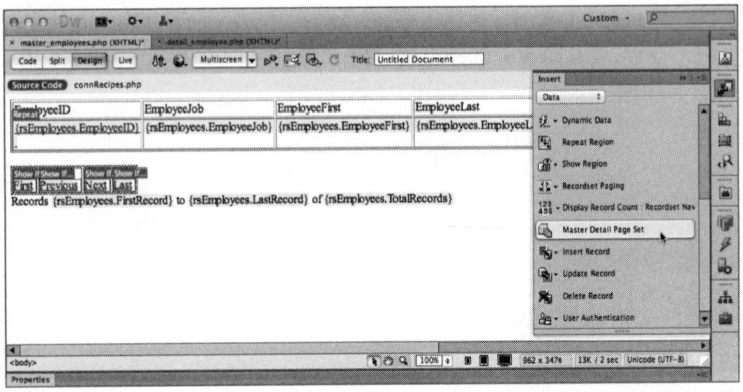

The detail page is created when the Master-Detail Page Set object is executed. As shown in Figure 22-6, the detail page is blank except for a two-column table, which contains a row for each field. The first column displays all the field names in the designated order, and the second column holds Dynamic Text elements, one for each of the fields.

To create a web application using the Master-Detail Page Set application object, follow these steps:

1. Be sure that the current page, which will become the master page, includes the desired recordset and has been saved. The recordset must contain all the fields you want to display on the detail page, as well as the fields for the master page.

TIP

When creating master-detail pages, I generally create my initial recordset and choose all records. After I've created my page set, I trim down the recordset on the master page by selecting only those fields necessary for the master page.

FIGURE 22-6

Only the fields, data, and necessary server behaviors are included in the newly created detail page.

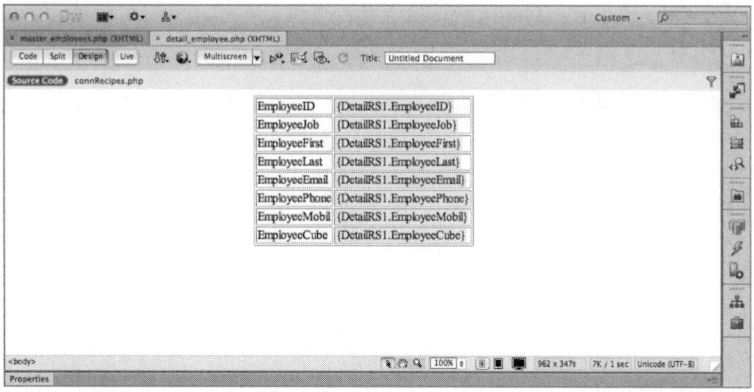

2. Place your cursor where you'd like the table, Recordset Navigation Bar, and Recordset Navigation Status element to appear.
3. Choose Insert ➪ Data Objects ➪ Master-Detail Page Set. You can also drag the Master-Detail Page Set icon from the Data category of the Insert panel to the desired location on the page. The Insert Master-Detail Page Set dialog box is shown in Figure 22-7.

FIGURE 22-7

Select the fields and their relative positions to lay out the columns for both the master and the detail pages.

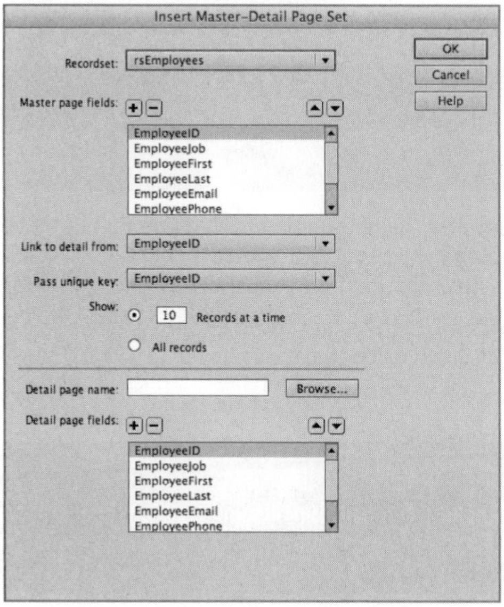

4. Select the recordset you'd like to use from the Recordset list.
5. In the Master Page Fields area, choose any fields you do not want to appear on the master and click the Remove (-) button.

   Dreamweaver, by default, includes all the available fields in a selected recordset. If you'd like to include any fields that are not in the current recordset, you must click Cancel and modify the recordset.

   If you change your mind after you remove a field from the list of fields to be inserted into the master page, click the Add (+) button and reinsert the field.
6. Alter the positioning of the fields in the master page table by selecting the field and using the up and down arrows above the Master Page Fields area. The master page table is horizontal with the topmost fields in the Master Page Fields area appearing on the left and the bottommost fields on the right. Clicking the up arrow moves a field to the left; clicking the down arrow moves it to the right.
7. Choose a field from the Link To Detail From list that serves as a link to the detail page. Only the fields remaining in the Master Page Fields area are available in the Link To Detail From list.
8. From the Pass Unique Key list, select the field that identifies each record for use in the URL parameter. The field in the Link To Detail From list and the one in the Pass Unique Key list do not have to be the same. You can, for example, use an employee's last name as the link and the employee ID number—not displayed in the master page fields—as the unique key. The Pass Unique Key list includes all the fields in the chosen recordset whether or not they are displayed onscreen.
9. Select the number of records you'd like displayed in the Repeat Region. Choose All to display every record in the recordset. Now that you have defined the master page portion of your application, define the elements for the detail page.
10. Enter the path to the detail page in the Detail Page Name field or click Browse to locate the file, if it exists.

WARNING

The master and detail pages must be in the same folder for the Master-Detail Page Set application object to function properly.

11. From the Detail Page Fields area, select any fields that you do not want to display on the detail page and click the Remove (-) button. Again, by default, Dreamweaver displays all the available fields in the recordset, and you must delete those you don't want to show.
12. To change the order in which the fields are inserted into the detail page table, select the field and use the up or down arrow buttons above the Detail Page Fields area.
13. Click OK when you're done.

NOTE

After the application object has finished inserting master page elements and creating the detail page, be sure to save the master page. Dreamweaver saves the detail page automatically, but it does not save the master page as part of the creation process.

The Master-Detail Page Set application object—especially the detail page—works well with Dreamweaver templates. After the master and detail pages are created, you can apply any Dreamweaver template to integrate the results into your site. To prepare the template, just make sure that at least one editable region exists for all the visual elements inserted into the master and detail pages. The Server-Object–generated detail page is especially well suited to template use because the created page contains only the table and its dynamic elements. After applying such a template, as shown in Figure 22-8, you may still need to tweak the design by altering the table properties.

To find out more about Dreamweaver templates, see Chapter 28.

FIGURE 22-8

Drag a template from the Assets panel onto a detail page to quickly change the look and feel of a generated document.

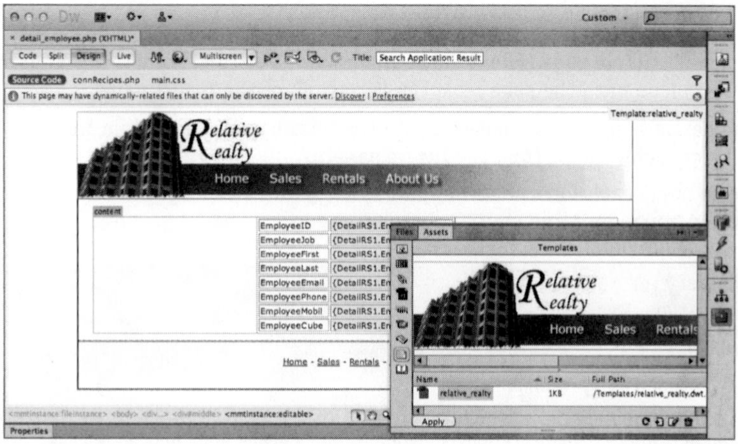

Getting Values from a Form

Next to clicking on links, a user's prime interaction with a web page is through the form. Forms are used in almost every web application in one form (minor pun intended) or another. A web page that is gathering information from a user always contains a form that uses a variety of elements, such as text fields, checkboxes, radio buttons, and drop-down lists. Although forms are important to web applications, not every page containing a form needs to be executed by an application server. You can, however, pass information from a form to a dynamic page.

In the earlier discussions of master-detail web applications, the master page was always generated by the developer's recordset selection without any user input. This section examines how you can develop user-driven master pages in Dreamweaver.

There are four key elements:

- A static HTML page containing a form. (Although it's possible to use a dynamic page, none of what the search page accomplishes requires server-side code.)
- One or more uniquely named form elements. (The naming of the form element is vital to getting the correct value into the application.)
- A link from the static page to the dynamic page inserted as a relative or an absolute URL in the `action` parameter of the form.
- A filter on the recordset of the dynamic page that reads the value passed from the form.

Passing single values from a form

The recordset filter, if it relates to a single form element, can be set in the simple Recordset dialog box. More sophisticated filters, which depend on values received from multiple form elements, must be created in the advanced Recordset dialog box. To set up a form to send user selections to a master page or other web application, follow these steps:

1. Create a static HTML page (File ➪ New) and choose Insert ➪ Form ➪ Form, or drag an Insert Form icon onto the page from the Forms tab of the Insert panel.
2. Add the desired input form elements into the form by selecting them from the Insert ➪ Form Objects submenu or from the Insert panel.

   Be sure to name each form element appropriately and uniquely. You need to recall this name when you're building your application page.

> **TIP**
>
> It's best to adopt a naming strategy that you can use over and over again. My preference is to name each form element with two parts: context and type. The first part of the name describes its context or how it is used on the page; the second part indicates which kind of form element is used. For example, a text field that holds the last name of a visitor is called `lastnameText`, whereas a drop-down list that lists office locations is `locationsList`. After a while, your naming convention becomes second nature to you, and you can easily remember what each form element has been named.

3. Select the `<form>` tag on the Tag Selector and, in the Action field of the Property inspector, enter the path to the dynamic page containing the application. Alternatively, you can click the folder icon to locate the file.
4. Also in the Property inspector, set the `Method` property of the form to `Post`.

   When you're passing variables and values via the URL query-string technique, described previously in the section "Using the URL to Pass Parameters," use the `Get` method. To pass the values of the form without exposing them in the URL, use `Post`.
5. Save your page.

> **NOTE**
>
> When you're deciding whether to use `Post` or `Get` to pass your parameters, also decide whether you want to be able to pass those variables easily to other pages. `Get` is the easier method to use when passing variables. If you're going to use them for only this single page, use `Post` to keep the query string clean.

Now you're ready to implement the receiving portion of your form-value passing application. To do so, follow these steps:

1. Create a new dynamic page for your master page application.
2. Insert a recordset by clicking the Add (+) button on the Bindings panel and selecting Recordset from the list.
3. In the Simple Recordset dialog box, choose your recordset name, connection, table, and columns.
4. In the Filter area, from the first Filter list, select the field that matches the value passed by the form element. For example, if you are filtering a recordset based on the location specified in a form's drop-down list, choose the field—called location, perhaps—that contains the specified value.
5. From the second Filter list, select the equals operator (=).
6. From the third Filter list, choose Form Variable from the list.
7. In the fourth Filter field, enter the name of the form element. In this example, the form element is named `locationList`.
8. Click OK when you're finished.
9. Apply the Master-Detail Page application object to create the master page.

22

Test your application by saving the master page and previewing the initial page with the form. You can also use View ➪ Live View Options ➪ HTTP Request Settings to try different values for your form variable; be sure to change the Method to `Post` in the HTTP Request Settings dialog box.

Passing multiple values from a form

For more complex recordsets, you have to write the SQL statement in Dreamweaver's Advanced Recordset dialog box. The same technique described earlier in the "Filtering a Detail Page Recordset in Advanced Mode" section applies here. Declare a variable that uses one of the runtime values in the following table:

Server Model	Name	Default Value	Runtime Value
ASP	theVariable	%	Request.Form("Fieldname")
ColdFusion	theVariable	%	#Form.Fieldname#
PHP	theVariable	%	<?php echo $HTTP_POST_VARS['Fieldname']; ?>

The `WHERE` clause of the SQL sets the fieldname to the variable that acts as a filter, as in this example:

```
WHERE dbadata.Location = theLocation
```

Multiple form variables can also be set up in the Advanced Recordset dialog box. Assume that you want your master page to display a list of employees in a particular department at a specific office. The form might include a drop-down list that displays a number of departments, as well as a radio button group for the different offices. If `theDept` is the variable for the department form list value and `theLocation` is the variable for the office radio button value, the SQL statement looks like this:

```
SELECT * FROM Employees WHERE Department = theDept ;
AND Location = theLocation
```

Passing form and URL values to a related page

Master-detail web applications aren't the only applications that can benefit from information entered on a form. Other applications sometimes offer a link to a related page—such as a special note pertinent to only a user-specified selection. To implement such pages, the application page needs the same form information passed to the master page. For ColdFusion and ASP server models, Dreamweaver includes a Go To Related Page server behavior, which delivers the form values to the linked page; the behavior can also pass URL values by themselves or in conjunction with values from forms.

As with other server behaviors in the Go To category, Go To Related Page can be applied to text, images, or dynamic page elements. In a master page with a Repeat Region, you can attach Go To Related Page to an element within the repeating region and have it be available for every entry. To attach a Go To Related Page server behavior, follow these steps:

1. On a page that has had form or URL values passed to it, select the page element—text, image, or dynamic data—to use as the trigger for your behavior.
2. From the Server Behaviors panel, click the Add (+) button and select Go To Related Page from the list. The Go To Related Page server behavior dialog box appears, as shown in Figure 22-9.
3. In the dialog box, verify that the text or code for the selected element displayed in the Link field is correct.
4. Enter the path to the target page in the Related Page field or click Browse to locate an existing dynamic page.
5. If you want to carry over values received from a query string, select the URL Parameters option.
6. If you want to pass values received from a form, select the Form Parameters option.
7. Click OK when you're finished.

The Go To Related Page server behavior can also be used to carry results of a form within a series of pages. In other words, if the first Go To Related Page server behavior passed the form or URL values from the master page to the first related page, you can include another Go To Related Page server behavior linked to a second related page.

CAUTION
You cannot use the Go To Related Page server behavior to link to a dynamic page that uses the Move To Specific Record server behavior. The Move To Specific Record server behavior overwrites the form or URL values passed by the Go To Related Page server behavior with its own. Instead of a Move To Specific Record server behavior on the target page, create a recordset filtered from the passed form/URL values.

FIGURE 22-9

The Go To Related Page server behavior can convey form values, URL values, or both to another dynamic page.

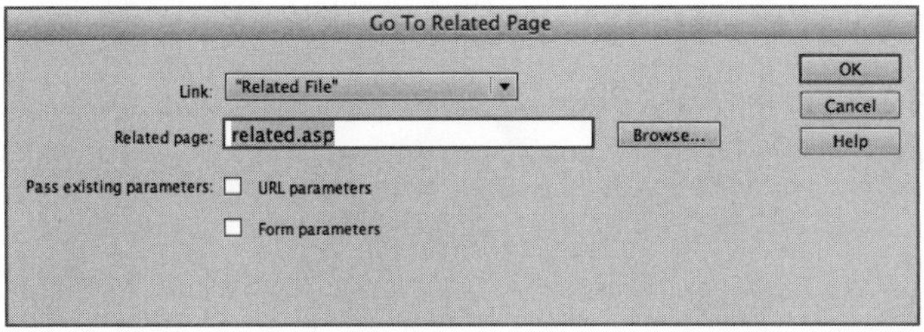

Dreamweaver TECHNIQUE

Building a Search Page

A dynamic application that searches a database uses two pages: one to specify the search parameters and another to display the results page. In this Technique, you create the search page.

> **NOTE**
>
> This Technique assumes that in Dreamweaver Preferences, under the Accessibility category, Form Objects is checked (as it is by default).

1. From the Techniques - Dynamic site (established in Chapter 18), expand the 22_Dynamic_Pages folder and open the `search_start` file for your server model.
2. Place your cursor below the opening paragraph of placeholder text, in the `<div>` tag with the class of `.centered`.
3. From the Forms category of the Insert panel, click Form.
4. In the Property inspector, click the Action field's Browse For File folder icon and select the `results_start` file for your server model in the current folder.
5. Make sure your cursor is inside the form and, from the Insert panel's Common category, choose Table.
6. In the Table dialog box, specify these settings:

Setting	Value
Rows	2
Columns	2
Width	300 pixels
Border thickness	0 pixels

Continues

continued

7. When you're done, click OK.
8. Place your cursor in the second cell of the top row and, from the Forms category of the Insert panel, choose Text Field.
9. When the Input Tag Accessibility Attributes dialog box opens, enter **searchField** in the ID field and **Keywords** in the Label field.
10. Make sure that Style: Attach label tag using "for" attributes and Position: Before form element are selected and click OK.
11. Place your cursor in the text Keywords and, from the Tag Selector, choose `<label>`.
12. Cut the selected `<label>` tag by pressing Ctrl+X (Command+X).
13. Move your cursor to the first cell of the top row and paste the copied tag by pressing Ctrl+V (Command+V).
14. Select the `<td>` tag from the Tag Selector and then, from the Property inspector's Class list, choose `formLabel`.
15. Place your cursor in the second row (directly beneath the text field) and, from the Insert panel, choose Button to add code for a button to the page.

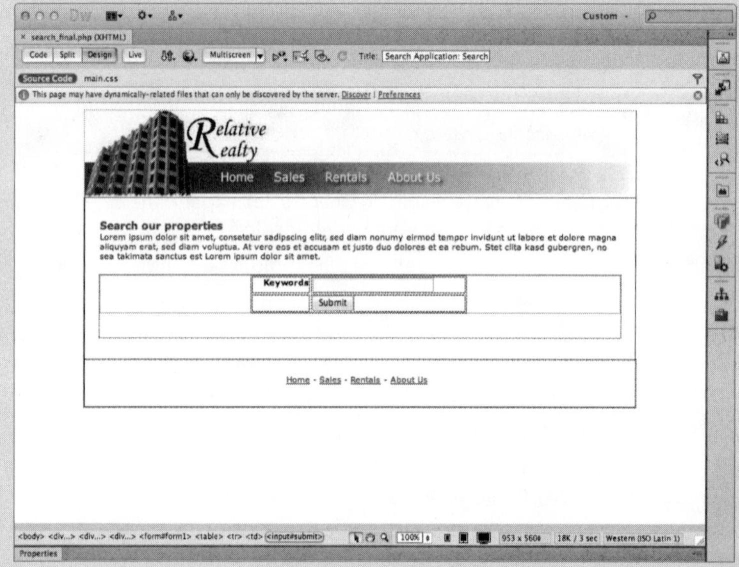

16. When the Input Tag Accessibility Attributes dialog box opens, enter **submit** in the ID field and ensure that the Style: No label tag is selected. Click OK.
17. Save your page.

In the next Technique, you build the results page to accompany this search page.

Establishing Dynamic Form Elements

Forms and form elements play a much larger role in web applications than just filtering recordsets. Forms are also necessary for inserting new records in a data source and for updating existing records. Dreamweaver lets you convert standard form elements into dynamic ones so that they can reflect and modify a record's data.

Although the general conversion from a static to a dynamic form element is handled in the same fashion for all elements—by applying a Dynamic Form Elements server behavior to an existing form element—almost every element has different dialog boxes with varying parameters.

Text fields

Text fields are extremely flexible and essential for inputting freeform text into data sources. To create a dynamic text field, follow these steps:

1. Insert a text field into a form on a page with a recordset or other data source. It's a good idea to name the text field and form at this point. Although you can always change the names later, I find that naming the elements early avoids problems later.
2. Select the text field.
3. From the Server Behaviors panel, choose Dynamic Form Elements ⇨ Dynamic Text Field.
4. In the Dynamic Text Field dialog box that appears (see Figure 22-10), verify that the correct form element is chosen in the Text Field list. If necessary, choose a different text field.
5. Click the Set Value To lightning bolt icon to display the available data sources.
6. Choose a field from the Dynamic Data dialog box.
7. If you want, you can apply a server format to the data by choosing an entry in the Format list.
8. Click OK to close the Dynamic Data dialog box and, after reviewing your choices, click OK again to close the Dynamic Text Field dialog box.

FIGURE 22-10

Use a dynamically linked text field to display data in an editable format.

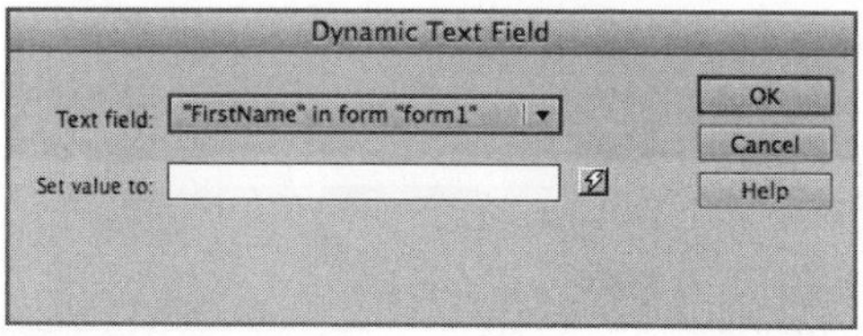

The dynamic data is inserted into what is called the *initial value* of the form field. You can see the data of the current recordset by selecting View ⇨ Live View. Switch out of Live View to adjust the width of the text field to accommodate your dynamic data—and all the other standard parameters of a text field—through the Property inspector.

> **TIP**
> Unless you're working with a legacy site, it's far better to create a custom CSS class for the text field than use an attribute to control the width. Not only is the measurement standard more precise in CSS than in standard HTML, but it can be updated for all applicable text fields in one operation rather than in a tag-by-tag fashion.

After you become familiar with Dreamweaver's workings, you can use the Bindings panel to skip most of the previous steps. To use the Bindings panel, follow these steps:

1. Insert a text field into a form on a page with a recordset or other data source.
2. Select the text field.
3. Open the Bindings panel and select the dynamic data to bind to your text field.
4. Click Bind at the bottom of the Bindings panel.

Checkboxes

When you attach a checkbox to dynamic data, the checked and unchecked state reflects the true or false state of a Yes/No (also known as a boolean) type of database field. Not only is this visual method easily understood at a glance, but checkboxes are extremely easy to update. To convert a static checkbox to a dynamic one, follow these steps:

1. Select a checkbox in a form on a page with a recordset.
2. From the Server Behaviors panel, choose Dynamic Form Elements ⇨ Dynamic CheckBox. The Dynamic CheckBox dialog box appears, as shown in Figure 22-11.

FIGURE 22-11

Checkboxes can depict whether a particular field of a record is noted as True in the data source.

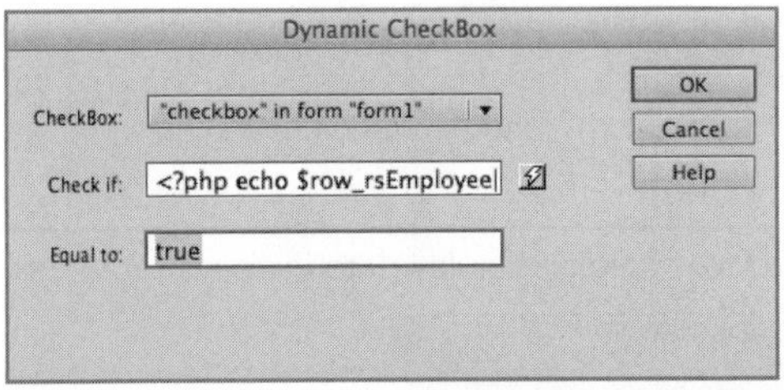

> **TIP**
> Click the Dynamic button in the Property inspector to go straight to this dialog box.

3. Verify that your selected checkbox is correctly named in the CheckBox list.
4. Click the Check If lightning bolt icon to display the available data sources.
5. Choose a field from the Dynamic Data dialog box.

6. If desired, you can apply a server format to the data by choosing an entry in the Format list. Click OK when you're finished to close the Dynamic Data dialog box.
7. Enter the value expected for a selected checkbox in the Equal To field. This value is data source dependent. For many data sources, `1` is used to represent true; for others, a `-1` is used. When working with Yes/No fields from Access databases, enter **True.**

WARNING

Be sure to capitalize the letter *T*; lowercase true does not work properly.

8. Click OK when you're finished.

TIP

Although checkboxes are typically used to show the state of Yes/No data fields, they can also be tied to text data fields and selected if the field is equal to a given value. When applying the Dynamic CheckBox server behavior, choose the text field and enter the exact text string you want to match in the Equal To field.

22

Radio buttons

Radio buttons provide a good way to represent a field that has a limited number of options. Suppose your data source includes a Comment Type field that offers three possible choices: Positive (Pos), Negative (Neg), and Other (Other). To illustrate which type of comment a user submits, your web application might display a series of three radio buttons, one for each type. If the radio buttons are dynamically tied to the Comment Type field, they show the correct type for each comment. As with checkboxes, radio buttons are very easy to modify—one click and you're done. To link radio buttons to dynamic data, follow these steps:

1. Select a group of radio buttons on a dynamic page with an available data source.
2. From the Server Behaviors panel, choose Dynamic Form Elements ➪ Dynamic Radio Buttons. The Dynamic Radio Group dialog box appears, as shown in Figure 22-12.
3. Verify that your selected form element is displayed in the Radio Button Group list.
4. In the Radio Button Values area, choose the first entry shown and, if necessary, change the Value field to reflect the expected data.
5. Repeat Step 4 for every radio button in the group.
6. Click the Select Value Equal To lightning bolt icon to display the available data sources.

FIGURE 22-12

Radio buttons can reflect a limited number of choices within a data source field.

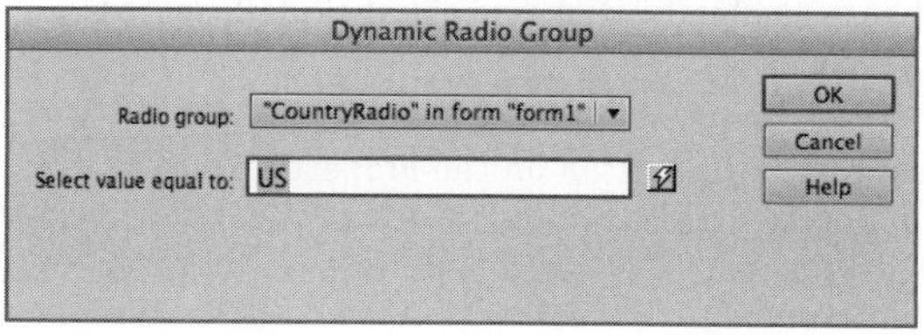

7. Choose a field from the Dynamic Data dialog box. Be sure to select a data source field with values parallel to those entered in the radio button group.
8. If desired, you can apply a server format to the data by choosing an entry in the Format list. Click OK when you're done to close the Dynamic Data dialog box.
9. Click OK when you're finished to close the Dynamic Radio Group dialog box.

List/menus

Typographical errors are the bane of data entry. Regardless of how careful users are, whenever they must enter an exact phrase of any length, typos are inevitable. If the set of desired responses from a user is limited, the list/menu form element provides a good alternative to a text field. An e-commerce site, for instance, might use a list/menu form element (also called a drop-down list or select list) to enable the user to navigate from one product line to another. With Dreamweaver, the drop-down list may be filled (populated) with dynamic data so that the navigation tool can keep track of the products entered in the data source.

A drop-down list is composed of two parts: the label and the value. The *label* is what the user sees when he or she selects the list; the value is what the user submits by selecting a particular list choice. In many situations, both the label and the value may be the same; in these cases, you can use the same data source field for both. Otherwise, you need data source fields available—this is how the product navigation example works. One data source field contains an entry for every product line (the label), and another field contains a URL to that product line's page on the website (the value). To link a drop-down list to dynamic data, follow these steps:

1. Insert a list/menu form element on a dynamic page with a recordset.
2. If you have more than one list/menu on the page, select the one you want to convert.
3. From the Server Behaviors panel, choose Dynamic Form Elements ➪ Dynamic List/Menu. The Dynamic List/Menu dialog box (see Figure 22-13) is displayed.
4. In the Static Options box, add any nondynamic items to the top of the list menu. This could be something as simple as a label for the list menu or as complicated as a full URL with query strings for search pages.
5. Choose the recordset you want to work with from the Options From Recordset list.
6. Verify that the desired drop-down list is displayed in the Menu list.
7. Choose the field from your data source containing the items you want submitted by the user from the Values list.
8. Choose the field you want displayed to the user from your data source containing the items from the Labels list.
9. To preselect an item, enter its value in the Select Value Equal To field or use the lightning bolt icon to choose a value from the established data sources.
10. Click OK when you're finished.

You should also notice the new Dynamic button on the Property inspector. Click the button to open the corresponding dialog box. This is another quick way to get to the options without going through the Server Behaviors panel.

FIGURE 22-13

Dynamic lists give the user a distinct series of items pulled from a database, from which to choose.

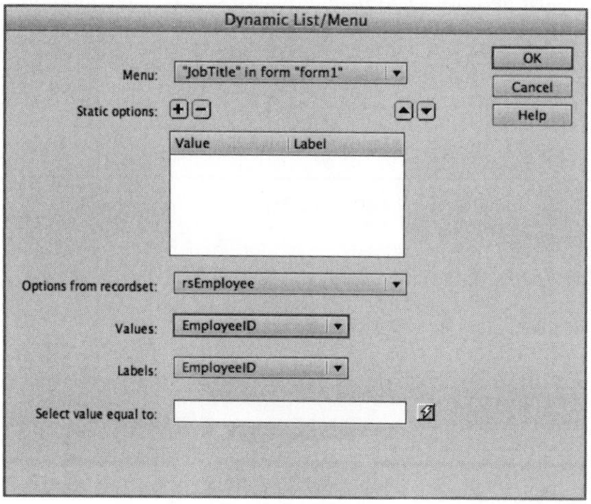

Managing Data Sources Online

Data source connectivity is a two-way street. Not only can data be extracted and displayed over the web, but web applications can also manage records found in data sources. With the power to add, modify, and remove data comes a terrific opportunity. From a web application builder's perspective, I find that almost half of my client work is concerned with data source management.

Like the common master-detail application, Dreamweaver offers both a manual and an automatic method of performing the most common management tasks. There are data objects for inserting and for updating records. Both methods are detailed in the following sections.

Inserting data

To insert records into a data source, you need the following:

- An active page
- A form placed on the page
- One form element per data source field
- A Submit button
- An Insert Record server behavior

No recordset or other data source is necessary, nor are there any special requirements for the form itself—you don't even have to specify an action or a method. The Insert Record server behavior handles most of the coding chores.

Inserting data manually

Form elements are typically arranged in a table with labels for each field, as shown in Figure 22-14. Naturally, you can format the table however you like; I generally prefer a two-column table with the labels in the first column, right-aligned, and the form elements in the second column, left-aligned. It's best to name the form elements so that you can identify them easily and ensure that each element is unique. A reset button is optional—but recommended if the form has many fields.

FIGURE 22-14

You don't need to define a recordset for an insert record page.

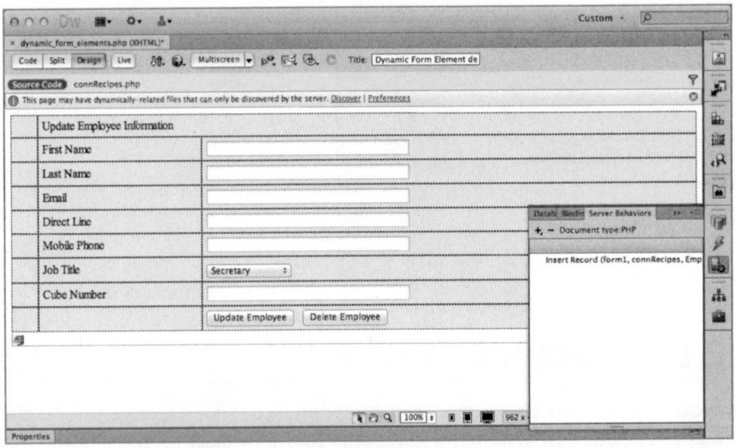

> **TIP**
>
> **You can save a step in the Insert Record server behavior setup by giving your form elements the same names as their relevant data source fields. Dreamweaver automatically assigns the form elements to any data fields with matching names. Unfortunately, this process could expose the field names in your database and give hackers more information about your database than you'd like them to know.**

After you've constructed your table inside the form and placed the form elements, follow these steps to add the Insert Record server behavior:

1. From the Server Behaviors panel, choose Insert Record. The Insert Record dialog box appears.
2. From the Insert Record dialog box, choose a connection from the Connection drop-down list. If you need to establish a new connection, click Define.
3. Select the data table you want to use from the Insert Into Table list.
4. Enter the path to the destination page in the After Inserting, Go To field, or click the Browse button to locate the file. It's important to select a confirmation or other page for users to go to after the form is submitted. If you don't, there is no feedback to the user and no change is apparent.

5. Select the name of the form to be used from the Get Values From list. If there is only one form on the page, the form is preselected.
6. Do the following for each object listed in the Form Elements area:
   - From the Column list, select the data source field into which you want to insert the value of the form object.
   - From the Submit As list, choose the data source type for the data. The options are:
     - Text
     - Numeric
     - Date
     - Date MS Access
     - Checkbox Y, N
     - Checkbox 1,0
     - Check -1,0
     - Checkbox MS Access
7. Click OK when you're finished.

Inserting data with the Record Insertion Form

With the Record Insertion Form application object, you create a new dynamic page (ASP, ColdFusion, or PHP) and apply the object. Dreamweaver creates the HTML table, includes the form elements and their labels, makes the connection to the data source, and adds the appropriate server-side code. Moreover, this application object is flexible enough to include seven different form element types—Text Field, Text Area, Menu, Hidden Field, CheckBox, Radio Group, and Password Field—as well as Text.

The Menu and Radio Group options are interesting because they enable you to enter the labels and values either manually or dynamically. To take advantage of Dreamweaver's capability to generate dynamic menus and radio buttons, you must have a recordset or other data source on the page. To insert the Record Insertion Form application object, follow these steps:

1. Place your cursor where you'd like the form to appear and choose Insert ➪ Data Objects ➪ Insert Record ➪ Record Insertion Form. Alternatively, you can drag the Record Insertion Form object, located within the Insert Record options, from the Data category of the Insert panel onto your page. The Record Insertion Form dialog box appears, as shown in Figure 22-15.
2. From the Record Insertion Form dialog box, choose a connection from the Connection drop-down list. If you need to establish a new connection, click Define.
3. Select the data table from the Table list.
4. Enter the path to the destination page in the After Inserting, Go To field or click the Browse button to locate the file. At this point, Dreamweaver has added an entry in the Form Fields area for every field in the data source.
5. Delete any unwanted fields by selecting their entries in the Form Fields area and clicking the Remove (–) button.

TIP

It's best to remove any fields that use auto-incrementing numbers. Such fields are commonly used to generate unique identification numbers for each record and are automatically incremented when a new record is added.

6. Select the first entry in the Form Fields area.
7. If desired, modify the text in the Label field to a more descriptive term than the name of the data source column automatically supplied by Dreamweaver.

FIGURE 22-15

The Record Insertion Form application object automatically creates a label and form element for every field in the selected data table.

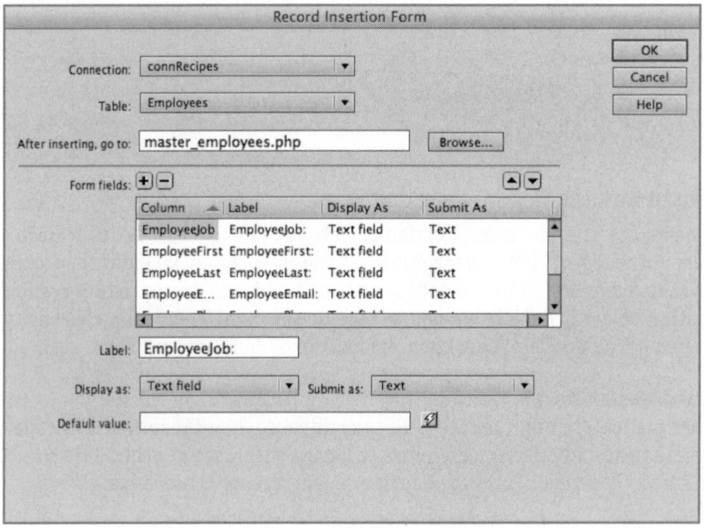

8. Choose the form element type from the Display As list. (By default, Dreamweaver uses Text Field.)
   - If you choose either Menu or Radio Group, click the Properties button that appears to further define the form element.
   - With text fields, text areas, and text you can set an initial value in the Default Value field.
   - For checkboxes, select whether the element should be Checked or Unchecked.
9. Choose the data format from the Submit As list.
10. Click OK when you're done.

Updating data

In the day-to-day operations of most websites, you update records more often than you insert new records. The process in Dreamweaver for creating an update records page is similar to the one for the insert records application, with one important difference—you must have a recordset defined.

Creating an update page

Detail pages are good candidates to transform into update applications. They already have the features necessary for an update application; namely, they have a recordset or other method for specifying a single record, and they are often generated from master-type pages. The major difference between a detail and an update page is that an update records application also requires specific server-side code—which is supplied in Dreamweaver by the Update Record server behavior.

As with the insert record application, you can choose either to create all the components of an update record page yourself or to use the application object to build them for you. To prepare the page for adding the Update Record server behavior, make sure you include a form element for every data field you want to update as well as a Submit button. Neither the action nor method attributes of the form need to be set—the Update Record server behavior handles that chore. To insert an Update Record server behavior, follow these steps:

1. From the Server Behaviors panel, choose Update Record. The Update Record dialog box appears, as shown in Figure 22-16.

FIGURE 22-16

With an Update Record web application, your data source can be modified remotely.

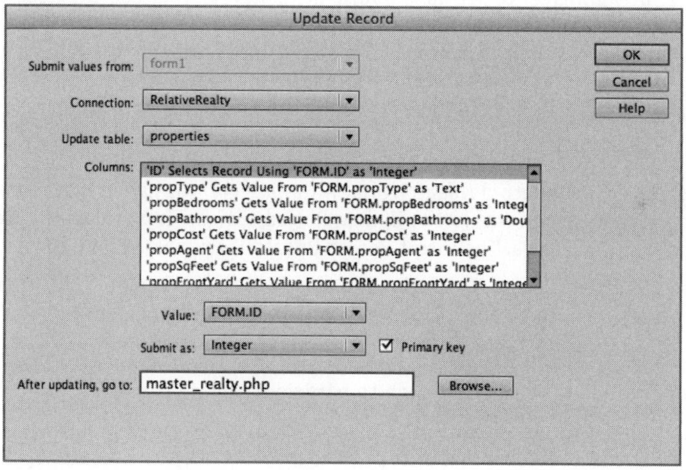

2. From the Update Record dialog box, choose a connection from the Connection drop-down list. If you need to establish a new connection, click Define.
3. Select the data table from the Table To Update list.
4. Choose the data source on which to base your update from the Select Record From list.
5. Select the key field from the Unique Key Column list. Dreamweaver attempts to detect whether the field is a number type and, if so, it selects the Numeric option.
6. Enter the path to the destination page in the After Updating, Go To field, or click the Browse button to locate the file.
7. Select the name of the form to be used from the Get Values From list. If there is only one form on the page, the form is preselected.

8. For each object listed in the Form Elements area:
   - In the Column list, select the data source field into which you can insert the value of the form object.
   - Choose the data source type for the data from the Submit As list. The options are:
     - Text
     - Numeric
     - Date
     - Date MS Access
     - Checkbox Y, N
     - Checkbox 1,0
     - Check -1,0
     - Checkbox MS Access
9. Click OK when you're done.

Using the Record Update Form object

If you'd prefer Dreamweaver to set up the form elements for you, use the Record Update Form application object. Before you can insert this application object, you must define a recordset or other data source from which to extract the data. The advantage of using Dreamweaver is sheer speed: Instead of manually creating the form, let Dreamweaver do the grunt work for you. To create an update record application using the application object, follow these steps:

1. Place your cursor where you'd like the form to appear and choose Insert ➪ Data Objects ➪ Update Record ➪ Record Update Form. Alternatively, you can drag the Insert Record Update Form object, located within the Update Record options, from the Data category of the Insert panel onto your page. The Insert Record Update Form dialog box is displayed.
2. From the Insert Record Update Form dialog box, choose a connection from the Connection drop-down list. To establish a new connection, click Define.
3. Select the data table to modify from the Table To Update list.
4. Choose the data source on which to base your update from the Select Record From list.
5. Select the key field from the Unique Key Column list. Dreamweaver attempts to detect whether the field is a number type and, if so, selects the Numeric option.
6. Enter the path to the destination page in the After Updating, Go To field, or click the Browse button to locate the file. At this point, Dreamweaver has added an entry in the Form Fields area for every field in the data source.
7. Delete any unwanted fields by selecting the field's entry in the Form Fields area and clicking the Remove (–) button.
8. Select the first entry in the Form Fields area.
9. If desired, modify the text in the Label field to a more descriptive term than the name of the data source column automatically supplied by Dreamweaver.

10. Choose the desired form element type from the Display As list. (By default, Dreamweaver uses Text Field.)
    - If you choose either Menu or Radio Group, click the Properties button that appears to further define the form element.
    - With text fields, text areas, and text you can set an initial value in the Default Value field.
    - For checkboxes, select whether the element should be Checked or Unchecked.

TIP

For fields that you want to display but that don't want users to alter—such as a unique key field—choose Text.

11. Choose the data format from the Submit As list.
12. Click OK when you're finished.

When these steps are completed, Dreamweaver inserts a borderless two-column table with the requested form elements and labels, similar to the one shown in Figure 22-17. As with other data objects, you can easily apply a template and include the generated elements in an editable region.

FIGURE 22-17

The Record Update Form application object creates all the elements and code necessary for modifying data source records online.

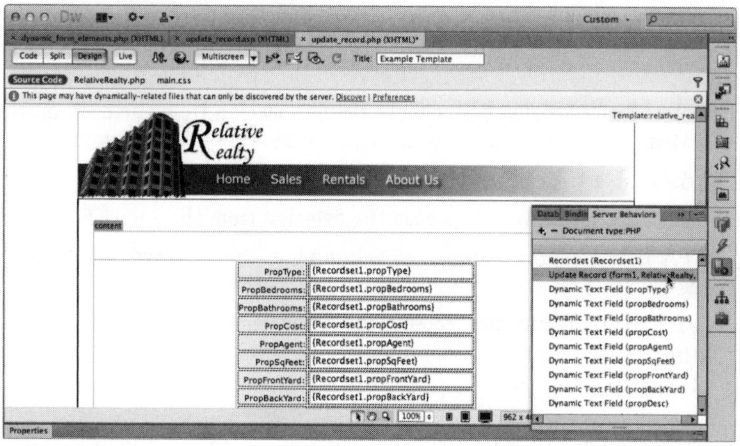

Deleting data

Eliminating outdated or otherwise unneeded records is a key task in properly maintaining a data source. The Delete Record server behavior greatly simplifies this chore. All that the Delete Record server behavior requires is a recordset and a form with a Submit button.

TIP
Although it's not mandatory, it's good practice to provide enough detail—displayed in a read-only format—so that the user can be sure he is removing the correct record. A confirmation message on the Submit button (with something akin to, "Are you sure you want to do this?") is nice also.

To attach a Delete Record server behavior to a form, follow these steps:

1. Make sure that a form exists on a dynamic page that includes at least one recordset.
2. From the Server Behaviors panel, choose Delete Record. The Delete Record dialog box is displayed, as shown in Figure 22-18.

FIGURE 22-18

Maintain an up-to-date data source with the Delete Record server behavior.

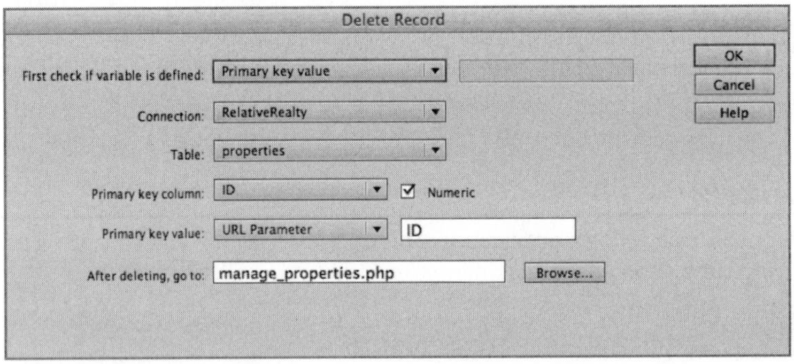

3. From the Delete Record dialog box, choose the Connection from the drop-down list. If you need to establish a new connection, click Define.
4. Select the data table to delete from the Delete From Table list.
5. Choose the data source on which to base the deletion from the Select Record From list.
6. Select the key field from the Unique Key Column list. Dreamweaver attempts to detect whether the field is a number type and, if so, selects the Numeric option.
7. Enter the path to the destination page in the After Deleting, Go To field, or click the Browse button to locate the file.
8. Choose the form that contains the Delete Submit button.

The Delete Record server behavior is executed when the user clicks the Submit button in the form. It's a good idea to confirm the deletion with your user on the destination page.

Inserting Variables

Variables are essential to any programming, and assorted variables are available depending on the server model. Although you must set all variables by hand or with a custom server behavior, Dreamweaver provides a method for reading or displaying almost every kind of variable.

All variables are made available through the Add list of the Bindings panel. After a variable has been added as a data source, it can be dragged and dropped anywhere on the page or included via the Insert button. Which variables are available depends upon the server model. The vast majority of dialog boxes for variables are single-entry fields that are requesting the name of the specific variable, like the one shown in Figure 22-19.

FIGURE 22-19

After you establish a session variable, it is made available for use in the Bindings panel.

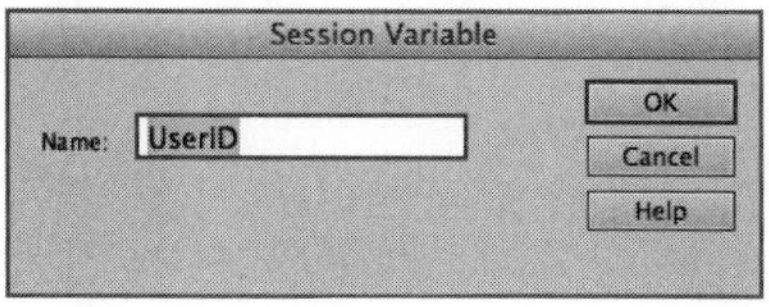

Application and session variables

Both application and session variables are used throughout web applications. An *application variable* is one that continues to exist as long as the application is active; in this situation, the application is the website itself. Application variables are available to all users of a site. A hit counter often uses an application variable to track the number of visitors to a site.

Although all users can see the results of a calculation involving application variables, *session variables* are user-specific. A session starts when a user first visits a site and ends shortly after the user leaves. Session variables are often used for user authentication and to maintain information about users as they travel through the site; shopping carts often employ session variables. Both application and session variables are available in ASP, PHP, and ColdFusion.

Request and other variables

Each of the server models has a range of variables available aside from application and server variables. All are accessible through the Add (+) button of the Bindings panel, and all, except for ASP Request variables, use a one-field dialog box for the name of the variable. In the case of the ASP Request variables, all five types of variables are available through a drop-down list on the Request Variable dialog box. After you've chosen your variable, enter it into the Name field. Table 22-1 provides a breakdown of the available variables for each of the Dreamweaver server models.

TABLE 22-1 Variables for Dreamweaver Server Models

Server Model	Variables
ASP	Request, Session, Application
ColdFusion	Form, URL, Session, Client, Application, Cookie, CGI, Server Variable, Local Variable
PHP	Form, URL, Session, Cookie, Server, Environment

Dreamweaver TECHNIQUE

Creating the Results Page

To complete the search application begun in the previous Technique, you need to create a results page. Unlike the search page, the results page contains server-side code easily inserted through Dreamweaver.

1. From the 22_Dynamic_Pages folder in the Techniques - Dynamic site, open the `results_start` file for your server model.

   To save time, a table has already been added to the page to hold your search results. The first task is to add a recordset to the page.
2. From the Bindings panel, click Add (+) and select Recordset (Query) from the list.
3. In the Recordset dialog box's Simple mode, enter **rsResults** in the Name field.
4. From the Connection list, choose RelativeRealty.
5. From the Table list, select properties.

   To return the proper results for the search, you need to limit the recordset to records in which the database's description field contains the keyword searched for. You'll recall that text field in the search page was named searchField.
6. Set the Filter options like this:

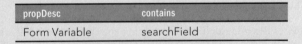

propDesc	contains
Form Variable	searchField

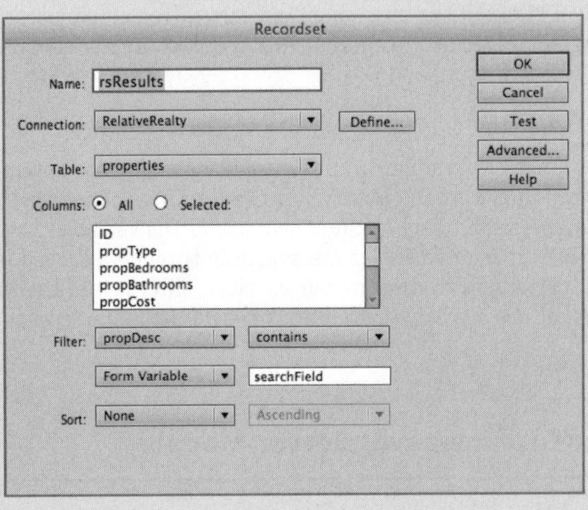

7. Leave the Sort list at its default setting and click OK.

   With the recordset defined, you're ready to begin binding data to the page.

8. In the Bindings panel, expand the Recordset (rsResults) entry.
9. Place the proper dynamic data in position:
   - Drag `propType` to the cell under the Type label.
   - Drag `propDesc` to the cell under the Description label.
   - Drag `propBedrooms` to the cell under the Bedrooms label.
   - Drag `propBathrooms` to the cell under the Bathrooms label.
   - Drag `propAgent` to the cell under the Agent label.
10. Select the `<td>` tag surrounding the propBedrooms dynamic text and, from the Class list of the Property inspector, choose `.centerDiv`. Repeat for the `<td>` tags containing propBathrooms and propAgent.
11. Select any of the dynamic elements just added to the page such as `rsResults.propType` and, from the Tag Selector, choose the `<tr>` tag.
12. From the Server Behaviors panel, click Add (+) and select Repeat Region from the list.
13. In the Repeat Region server behavior, make sure that rsResults is the chosen recordset and set the option Show All Records; click OK when you're ready.
14. Save your page.
15. In the Files panel, select both the pages of the search application—`search_start` and `results_start`—for your server model and choose Put to publish the files to the Testing server.

To test your search application, preview the previously built `search_start` page in a browser. Enter a keyword (such as "kitchen") in the text field and click Search; the results page will display any matching entries.

You can also test your Results page in Dreamweaver by choosing HTTP Request Settings from the Live View Options button on the Document toolbar. Once opened, enter **searchField** in the Name column and your search criteria, for example, **kitchen**, in the Value column; choose Post from the Method list and click OK. Enter Live View to see the results of your search.

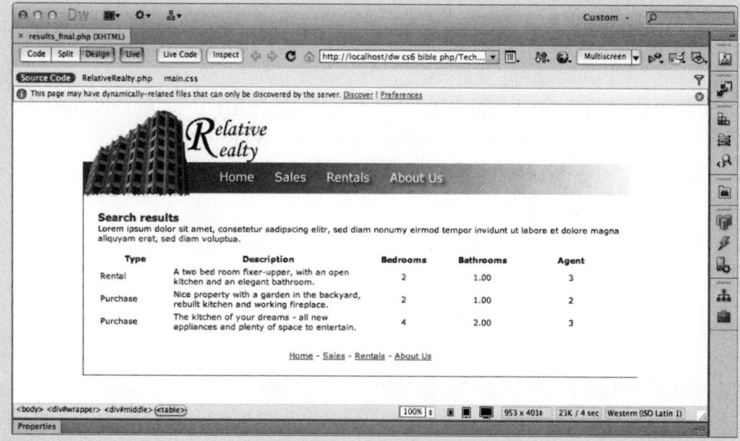

Connecting to the Customer

Fundamentally, you have two types of customers: new customers and returning customers. The goal of almost every enterprise is to turn the former into the latter. To that end, e-commerce sites try to make the customer experience as pleasant as possible. What makes for an enjoyable customer visit? Volumes have been written on that subject, but I'll concentrate here on just one facet: the customer's account.

Early on in the history of web stores, it wasn't uncommon to require returning customers to re-enter all their pertinent billing and shipping information. The e-commerce sites had no way of tracking all that data. Now, the vast majority of online stores—particularly the successful ones—offer a way for customers to open an account to store their basic information. Just as important, customers can easily identify themselves on their return, thus accessing their account information and enabling it to be applied to a new order.

You may want to restrict certain areas of your site to registered users or those who have paid for a subscription. Various levels of sophistication are possible here, but the most fundamental requirements are a way to identify returning customers and a way to add new ones.

Logging in existing customers

The most common way to identify returning customers is to allow them to log in. A login page can be as simple as a three-element form: two text fields—one for the username and one for the password—and a Submit button. The form connects to a data source containing a list of users and their passwords, among other information, and verifies that the submitted username corresponds to the submitted password. Dreamweaver accomplishes this task with the appropriately named Log In User server behavior.

The Log In User server behavior redirects authorized users to one page and unauthorized users to another. In addition, it creates a session variable containing the username. This session variable can then be employed on other pages as required.

To apply the Log In User server behavior, make sure your page has, at a minimum, a form with text fields for the username and password and a Submit button. You're now ready to follow these steps:

1. From the Server Behaviors panel, click the Add (+) button and choose User Authentication ➪ Log In User. The Log In User dialog box is displayed, as shown in Figure 22-20.
2. If there is more than one form on the page, select the form containing the username and password fields from the Get Input From Form list.
3. Select the form element used to gather the username from the Username Field list.
4. Select the form element used to gather the password from the Password Field list.
5. Choose a connection to the data source containing the table of registered users from the Validate Using Connection list.
6. Select the table of registered users from the Table list.
7. Choose the field containing the username from the Username Column list.
8. Choose the field containing the password from the Password Column list.

FIGURE 22-20

The Log In User server behavior can be used to gather information about a returning customer.

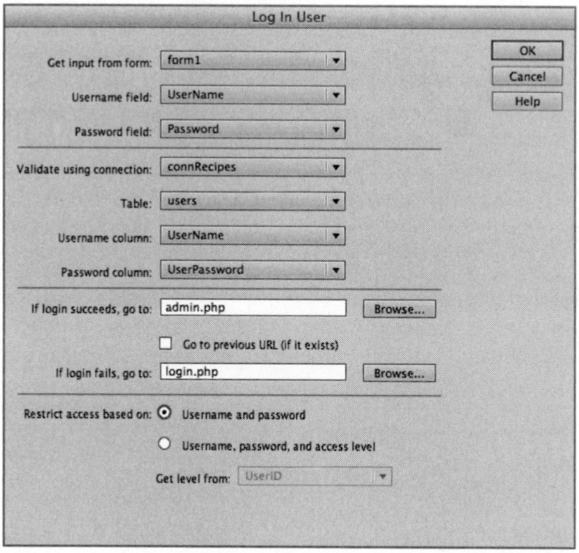

9. Enter the path to the page for the authorized user in the If Log In Succeeds, Go To field.
10. If you want the user to proceed to the previously selected link, rather than the page entered in Step 9, select the Go To Previous URL option.
11. Enter the path to the page for the unauthorized user in the If Log In Fails, Go To field.
12. If access levels should be evaluated as part of the authentication, choose the following:
    - Restrict Access Based On Username, Password, and Access Level
    - The data source field containing the access level data from the Get Level From list
13. Click OK when you're finished.

Restricting access

Now that you've got your users added and logging in, you need to protect those pages that require authorized access. Such pages could be user profile information or perhaps information that a user has paid a subscription to access. Dreamweaver provides two different types of access restriction. The first method just determines if a user is logged in or not. The second includes restriction based on access levels defined in your database.

To restrict access based on whether a user has logged in, follow these steps:

1. Open a dynamic page that you want to restrict access to.
2. In the Server Behaviors panel, click the Add (+) button and select User Authentication ➪ Restrict Access To Page. The Restrict Access To Page dialog box, shown in Figure 22-21, is displayed.

FIGURE 22-21

Dreamweaver's Restrict Access To Page server behaviors enable you to restrict access to sensitive parts of your site.

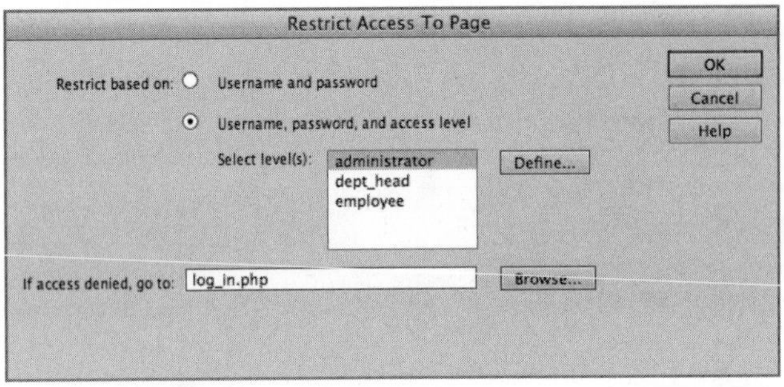

3. Choose the Username And Password radio button to restrict access to those users already logged in.
4. In the If Access Denied, Go To box, browse to the URL you want to send users to if they're not authorized to view the page. This page should have a sentence or two telling users why they're at this page, as well as a form for them to log in.

To restrict pages based on access level, add a login page, as described in the previous section. This is handy if you want to have one login for both your administrators and your regular customers. One access level may allow a user to change user details, whereas another only allows a user to view those details. First you choose the Restrict Access Based On Username, Password, and Access Level option (Step 12 of creating the login form in the previous section). Next, choose the field from your table that contains the access levels, as shown in Figure 22-22.

To restrict use based on access levels, follow these steps:

1. Open a dynamic page that you want access restricted to.
2. In the Server Behaviors panel, click the Add (+) button and select User Authentication ➪ Restrict Access To Page. The Restrict Access To Page dialog box, shown in Figure 22-23, is displayed.
3. Choose the Username, Password, and Access Level radio button.
4. Choose one or more groups from the Select Level(s) area.
5. To add new groups to the Select Level(s) list:
   - Click Define to open the Define Access Levels dialog box.
   - Enter the name for the access level in the Name field. The name must match a value stored in your data source in whichever column is designated for the group access levels.
   - To add additional levels, click the Add (+) button and enter another name.
   - To delete any levels, choose the level in the list area and click the Remove (–) button.
   - Click OK to close the Define Access Levels dialog box.

6. Enter the path to the file to which you are redirecting unauthorized users in the If Access Denied, Go To field. Alternatively, click the Browse button to locate the file.
7. Click OK when you're finished.

FIGURE 22-22

Use the Get Level From list menu in the Log In User dialog box to restrict a page's access to a specific group of users. This gives you more granular control over your site.

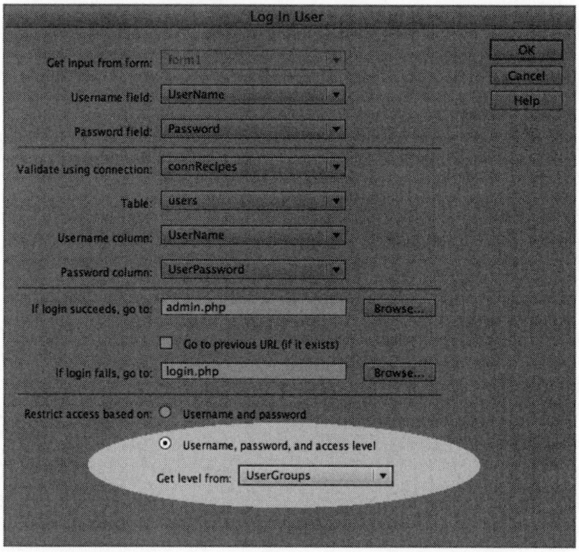

FIGURE 22-23

Define as many access levels as you want to restrict certain sections of your site to a subset of your members.

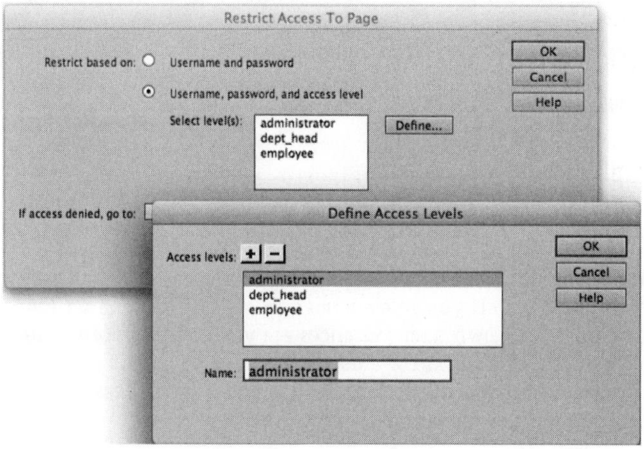

Helping users log out

It's always a good idea to give your customer an easy way to log out of your site—a way that also destroys all the session variables associated with his login and ensures that his coworkers can't jump on his computer (right after he leaves for some coffee) and gain access to information they shouldn't have. Logging a user out in Dreamweaver is just a matter of one simple server behavior.

To use the Log Out User server behavior, follow these steps:

1. To apply the server behavior to a specific link on the page, select that link.
2. From the Server Behaviors panel, click the Add (+) button and choose User Authentication ➪ Log Out User. The Log Out User dialog box, shown in Figure 22-24, opens.

FIGURE 22-24

You can log a user out automatically by choosing the Log Out When Page Loads option on an order confirmation page.

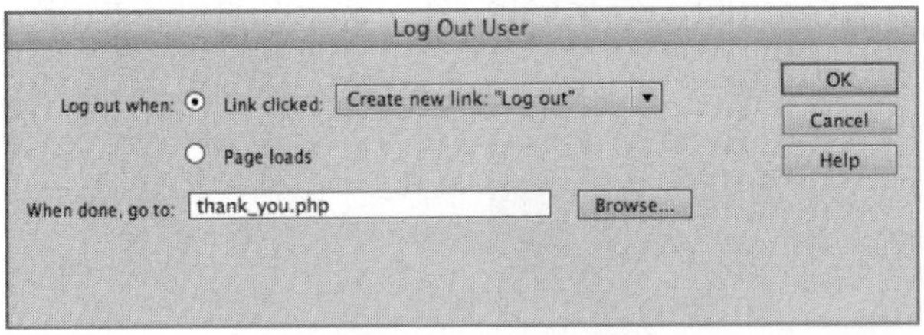

3. To trigger the server behavior with a link, choose the Log Out When Link Clicked option and make sure your selected link is chosen in the list. If no link is preselected, Dreamweaver offers to apply the server behavior to a new link, Log Out.
4. To automatically log out users when the current page is viewed, select the Log Out When Page Loads option.
5. If you're using a link as a trigger, enter the path to the destination page in the When Done, Go To field. Alternatively, click the Browse button to locate the file.

CAUTION

Do not use the When Done, Go To option if you are automatically logging out a user when the page loads. If you do, the user never sees the current page.

6. Click OK when you're finished.

Adding new customers

An application that adds new customers is essentially the same as an insert record application, with one additional function. If you've ever tried to get a username on America Online that even remotely resembles your own name, chances are you've encountered the function I'm talking about—just ask bobsmith01234x. For a username to be useful, it must be unique; therefore, the web application must check a submitted username for uniqueness. Dreamweaver's Check New Username server behavior does just this.

Before you can apply the Check New Username server behavior, however, you must create a page with the proper form elements for all the data necessary. Moreover, you need a Dreamweaver Insert Record server behavior (refer to Figure 22-15 earlier in this chapter). As the name implies, the Insert Record server behavior creates a new record and adds it to the specified data source.

The one difference between a standard Insert Record server behavior and the one used in this circumstance is that you leave the destination page field (After Inserting, Go To) blank. Leaving this field empty enables the Check New Username server behavior to control the redirection.

The Check New Username server behavior verifies that the requested username is not already in the data source and redirects the user if it is. To add a Check New Username server behavior to your page, follow these steps:

1. From the Server Behaviors panel, click the Add (+) button and choose User Authentication ➪ Check New Username. The Check New Username dialog box is displayed.
2. Select the form element that contains the requested username from the Username list. If a form element is called `username`, Dreamweaver automatically selects that entry.
3. Enter the path to the file you want a user to see if the requested name is already stored in the data source in the If Already Exists, Go To field, or click Browse to locate the file.
4. Click OK when you're finished.

Summary

Although numerous web applications use only a single dynamic page, crafting multipage applications gives you more opportunity to build a robust user experience for your visitors. It's key for every web developer to master the various methods for passing information from one page to another. When building your first multiple-page web applications, keep these points in mind:

- Dreamweaver can send and receive parameters from one page to another by appending them in an encoded fashion to the linked URL. The additional text is known as a query string.
- You can send values from a form either by way of the query string or, in a hidden manner, in a separate object seen only by the server. The first technique uses the `Get` method and the second technique uses the `Post` method.
- Dreamweaver includes several data objects that reduce the building of common dynamic components—or even whole applications—to one step. Data objects can be combined with Dreamweaver templates for rapid application development.
- To craft applications that update records in a data source, you must know how to tie the various form elements to dynamic data. In Dreamweaver, the basic procedure is to include a standard form element, and then choose the appropriate server behavior from the Dynamic Form Elements submenu of the Server Behaviors panel.
- Many web applications are concerned not with publicly viewed sites on the web but rather with administratively oriented pages designed to manage data sources remotely. Dreamweaver includes a full complement of tools for inserting new records, updating existing ones, and deleting data that is no longer required.

- After you've declared a variable in Dreamweaver, it is available for display through the Bindings panel. Each server model has its own set of variables.
- Dreamweaver enables you to create a user authentication system quickly to protect valuable customer information or paid subscription sites. You can even set different access levels for administrators and regular customers.

In the next chapter, you learn how to work with content management system-based sites in Dreamweaver.

CHAPTER

23

Using Web Content Management Systems

IN THIS CHAPTER

- All about web content management systems
- Working with WordPress in Dreamweaver
- Discovering dynamically related files
- Updating existing images
- Inserting new WordPress images in Dreamweaver

The seemingly infinite capacity of the Internet to store and display content has contributed to a seismic shift in web design and development. More and more organizations, companies, and even individuals are relying on web content management systems (CMS) to maintain and grow their sites. But what tool can web professionals use to design and customize these sites? Dreamweaver, of course.

Dreamweaver has been architecturally extended to pull together and expose the myriad files that typically make up a CMS site. With the Dynamic Related Files feature, Dreamweaver discovers files nested deep inside other included files, whether they are explicitly or programmatically linked. A built-in filtering mechanism helps you to pinpoint just the files you need, and the efficient Code Navigator can take you directly to the code for easy modification. Moreover, Dreamweaver's Live View not only renders the page with web-standards efficiency but allows you to follow links from page to page—even those that lead offsite.

In this chapter, you'll get a chance to explore the rich and compelling world of web CMS and dive deep into one of its leading citizens—WordPress—and its integration with Dreamweaver. You learn how to set up each as a Dreamweaver site and how to customize the look and feel of CMS-driven output. Best of all, you'll open the door to a robust and potentially lucrative area of web design and development where you can leverage your Dreamweaver skills to achieve great results.

Understanding Web Content Management Systems

A web content management system is a web application that makes it possible for non-technical users to add and update content to a site, without knowing HTML or CSS. There are a great many web CMS systems (as opposed to enterprise CMS or those used for document management) available. To date, Wikipedia lists 60 that use PHP with a database (almost all MySQL); amazingly very few of those are commercial—the vast majority are open source and freely available. No doubt, the high degree of accessibility has played a major factor in the popularity of these applications.

Once installed, many web CMS applications work basically the same way. They all allow their site owners to update their sites via a web-based interface, typically offering WYSIWYG controls. New content, including complete pages, can easily be added through a web-based interface, such as the WordPress Dashboard (see Figure 23-1). Multiple users can contribute under a variety of roles—ranging from writers to copy editors to publishers—for a consistent and secure workflow. Most CMS apps offer blogging features that provide a high degree of social interactivity and simple syndication.

FIGURE 23-1

The WordPress Dashboard offers word processing–like features for creating and editing posts.

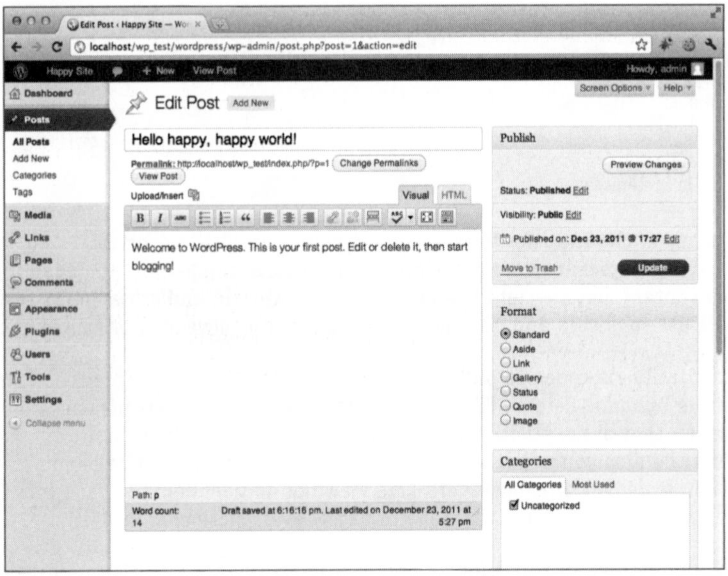

The open source nature of the majority of web CMS applications has greatly enhanced their popularity and usefulness. Not only do the top web CMS apps—WordPress, Joomla, and Drupal—all enjoy their own vast supportive community, a full spectrum of designs and extensions has emerged as a result. Cross-pollination from one platform to another is quite common; a plugin developed for WordPress frequently inspires a Joomla extension and a Drupal module—and vice versa.

These main web CMS apps share a structural similarity as well. They are all PHP applications that integrate with a MySQL database. Web development environments are also alike: Designers can use the same combination of Apache, PHP language, and MySQL database servers to work in WordPress, Joomla, or Drupal sites. Ultimately, all combine a great many files—a mix of HTML, CSS, JavaScript, and PHP—to dynamically construct their pages, rendered by the browser and presented to the user.

It is this consistent architecture that allows Dreamweaver to work efficiently with a range of CMS applications. The same mechanism is used to discover dynamically related files and navigate directly to styling code regardless of the CMS app. It's important to realize that the primary goal of CMS applications is to provide user-driven site maintenance, not site creation. The savvy web designer has a vital role to play in the initial design and ongoing customization of any CMS-based site.

Working with WordPress

WordPress is best known as one of the leading tools for creating and maintaining blogs. Blogs are, of course, composed of a number of individual posts combined with static content to display about the author information and contact details. It's an easy leap from displaying a series of blog posts on a personal interest to rendering a series of articles in a university's newspaper (`http://news.harvard.edu/gazette/`) or news items concerning the workings of a diplomatic post (`http://geneva.usmission.gov/`)—all of which is possible, and has been done, with WordPress.

NOTE

Although the balance of this chapter is specific to WordPress, the same essential techniques apply to other PHP-driven CMS applications such as Drupal and Joomla for installing, integrating with a site, and modifying in Dreamweaver.

A WordPress site comprises content pulled from a MySQL database and presented in a series of templated pages that, overall, are referred to as a *theme*. A WordPress theme, in turn, is made up of PHP files styled with HTML and CSS, frequently combined with JavaScript widgets for expanded functionality. One of the hallmarks of WordPress is the large number of themes available and how easy it is to change from one theme to another. Modifying a specific theme in WordPress alone can be challenging; luckily this task is made far easier with Dreamweaver.

WordPress, like the two other web CMS applications covered in this chapter, may seem overwhelming in its capabilities and complexity, so it's important to keep in mind that, at its heart, it's just another PHP application. And, as such, WordPress can be hosted on a site-by-site basis, which makes it an ideal platform for web designers and developers to share with their clients.

The overall WordPress structure will look very familiar to the modern web designer, while the individual page structure might take some time to understand. The initially displayed page, `index.php`, combines a header, sidebar, and footer with the main content area. WordPress code often combines standard HTML with PHP code to pull together the required elements. For example, here's how the default WordPress theme (as of this writing), Twenty-Eleven, defines the opening header:

```
<header id="branding" role="banner">
  <hgroup>
    <h1 id="site-title"><span><a href="<?php echo esc_url( home_url
( '/' ) ); ?>" title="<?php echo esc_attr( get_bloginfo
( 'name', 'display' ) ); ?>" rel="home"><?php bloginfo
( 'name' ); ?></a></span></h1>
    <h2 id="site-description"><?php bloginfo( 'description' ); ?>
</h2>
  </hgroup>
<?php
  // Check to see if the header image has been removed
  $header_image = get_header_image();
  if ( ! empty( $header_image ) ) :
?>
```

Here, an HTML5 `<header>` tag with an ID of `branding` encloses an `<hgroup>` tag, which holds the title and subtitle of the site. The `<hgroup>` tag is followed by PHP code to add the header image to the page. Put it all together, and a site with the name "Happy Site" and description "The Happiest Site on Earth" renders, as in Figure 23-2.

FIGURE 23-2

A combination of HTML and custom PHP function calls are used to render the site pages.

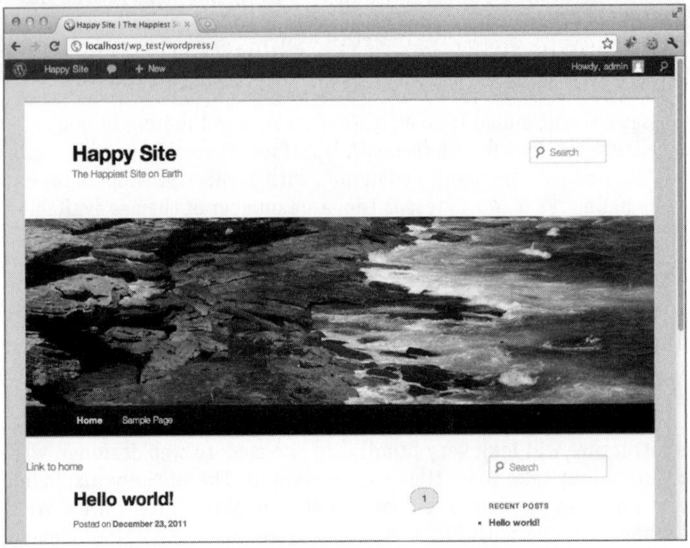

You can use IDs, tags, and classes to style the WordPress elements however you like. For example, to change the look of the site name in the header, you would use Dreamweaver to change properties for the `#site-title` ID selector.

In the next section, you'll see how to set up and install WordPress on a local development system such as a Dreamweaver site.

Installing WordPress

One of the features that places WordPress among the most frequently used web CMS apps is its quick and easy installation. Integrating WordPress into Dreamweaver is just as straightforward. Both procedures, however, require that PHP and MySQL servers be in place and up and running.

> **TIP**
>
> **Many developers find that all-in-one development packages such as XAMPP for Windows and MAMP for Macs provide a simple route to follow. Both products install and set up an Apache web server, PHP language server, and MySQL database server. Additional, necessary tools, such as phpMyAdmin, are also included and easily accessible. You can find XAMPP at `http://www.apachefriends.org/en/xampp.html` and MAMP at `http://www.mamp.info/en/index.html`.**

Once your development environment is working properly, follow these steps to install WordPress and set up a WordPress site in Dreamweaver:

1. Open your browser and go to `http://wordpress.org/download/` (see Figure 23-3).

FIGURE 23-3

The WordPress site provides the latest download at no charge.

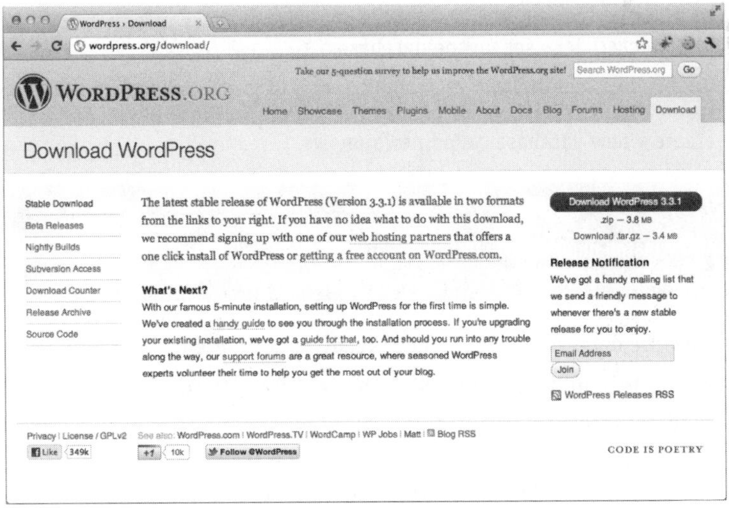

2. Click the Download WordPress (version number) button.

   As of this writing, the current version is WordPress 3.3.1.

3. When the download is finished, double-click to unzip the files.

4. Open the newly generated folder and copy all the files.

   Now you're ready to create the folder that will contain your local site.

5. Make a new folder in the root of your web server. On PCs, the web server is located at `C:\inetpub\wwwroot`; on Macs it is located at `[Main Drive]:Users:[username]:Sites`.

TIP

The all-in-one web server packages typically have their own site root folders. For MAMP, it is `Applications:MAMP:htdocs` while for XAMPP it is `C:\Program Files\xampp\htdocs`.

6. Paste all the files you copied in Step 4 into the new site folder.

The next series of steps will configure your WordPress installation using the local web server.

1. In your browser, enter the web address to your new site folder. For example, if the site folder name was happy_site, the web address for a MAMP installation would be `http://localhost:8888/happy_site/`. The numbers following localhost refer to the port used by MAMP.

2. WordPress detects that this is a new installation and notes that a configuration file named `wp-config.php` file is needed. Click the Create A Configuration File button.

   On the next screen, WordPress tells you the database information you'll need. Before you proceed, let's set up the database.

3. On a MySQL administrative program, such as phpMyAdmin, create a new database corresponding to the name of your site or client. In Figure 23-4, I've used phpMyAdmin to create a new database called newbienews.

TIP

Both MAMP and XAMPP install phpMyAdmin by default. If you set up your development system using another method, you can download phpMyAdmin at `http://www.phpmyadmin.net/home_page/index.php`.

   With the database created, you're ready to complete the WordPress configuration.

4. Return to your browser and click the Let's Go button.

   WordPress requests needed information for making the proper database connection.

5. On the next screen, enter the name of the database you just created, the username and password, and the host (typically localhost). Leave the other values as is and click Submit.

6. If WordPress can communicate with your database, you'll get a message saying so (or what to do if it can't), and you're ready to complete the operation—click Run The Install.
7. On the next screen, enter the name of your site or blog in the Blog Title field, your username and password, and your e-mail address where indicated. If you want to list your blog with search engines, keep that option selected. Click Install WordPress.

   If all goes well, WordPress presents you with a username (admin) and program-generated password.

FIGURE 23-4

Setting up an empty database is the first key step when creating a WordPress site.

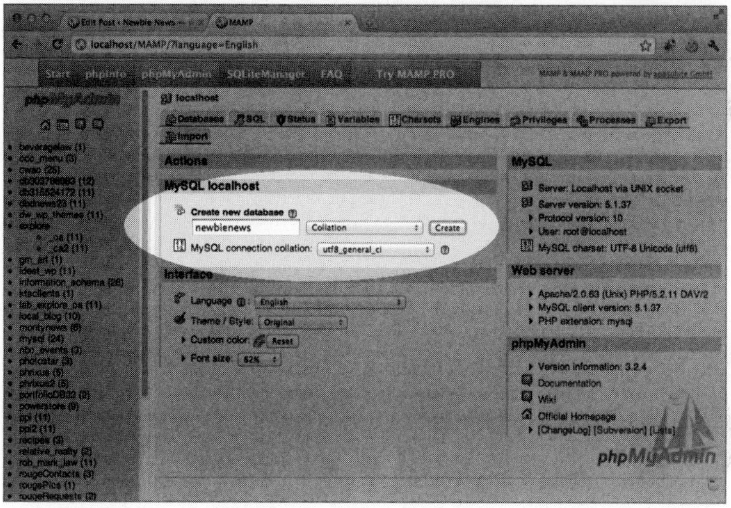

8. Copy the password—you'll be able to change it to a more memorable one shortly—and click Log In.
9. Enter `admin` in the User Name field and paste the copied password in the Password field; click Log In.

   The WordPress Dashboard is now displayed. It's best to change your password right away.
10. Click the Yes, Take Me To My Profile Page link found in the highlighted box at the top of the page.
11. On the bottom of the Profile page, enter a new entry in the New Password field. Repeat the password in the next field to confirm and click Update Profile.
12. Click the Visit Site link, located on the upper left of the Dashboard, to view your WordPress site with the default template (see Figure 23-5).

FIGURE 23-5

The default WordPress site integrates your site name in a default template with an example post.

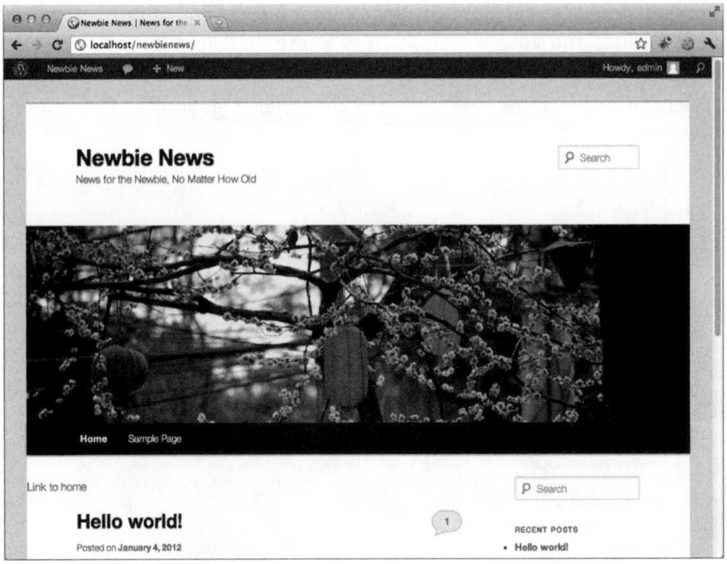

Your WordPress configuration is complete; now it's time to make the Dreamweaver connection!

1. In Dreamweaver, choose Site ➪ New Site.
2. When the Site Setup dialog box appears, enter the name of your site and browse to the folder previously created in the local web server root.

   Because Dreamweaver will need a local web address to render the pages in Live View, let's enter that now.
3. Expand the Advanced Settings section and choose the Local Info category.
4. In the web address field, enter the same address used in the browser to enter the WordPress site. In my example, it's `http://localhost/newbienews/` (see Figure 23-6).

   The final phase is to set up a staging server with the proper server model chosen.
5. Choose the Servers category.
6. Click Add A New Server (+).
7. In the Basics tab, enter a name for your server in the Server Name field. A standard choice would be **Staging**.
8. Choose Local/Network from the Connect Using list.
9. Click the Remote Folder Browse icon and navigate to the site root folder containing all the WordPress files.
10. Switch to the Advanced tab.

11. From the Server Model list in the Staging Server area, choose PHP MySQL and click Save (see Figure 23-7).
12. Confirm that the Testing checkbox is selected in the Servers category and click Save.

FIGURE 23-6

Specifying the localhost web address allows Dreamweaver to render pages properly in Live View and when previewing in the browser.

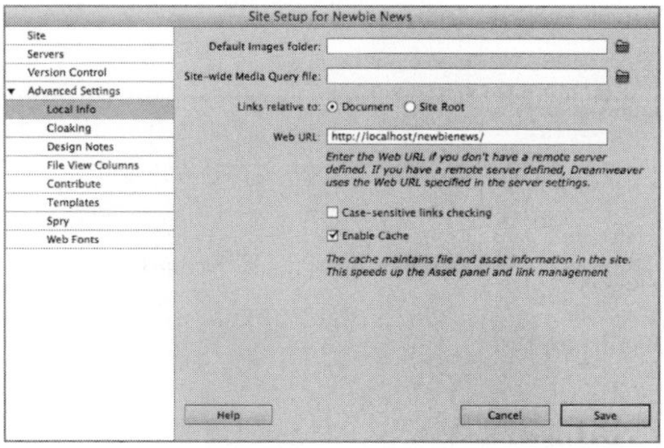

FIGURE 23-7

Only the PHP MySQL server model is supported for working with dynamically related files such as those found in CMS apps.

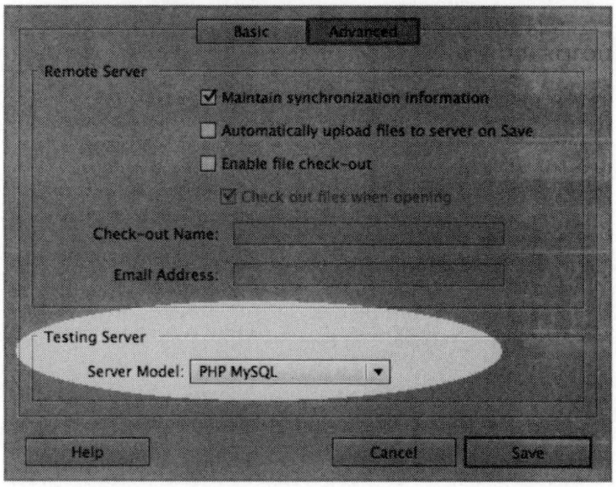

More congratulations are in order! You've successfully connected Dreamweaver to your WordPress site. Now, let's verify the connection by opening the home page for the site.

1. From the Files panel, open `index.php`.

   When the page loads, it appears to be empty in Design view with very little code displayed in Code view. This is to be expected in CMS-based sites. Because the pages are pieced together from myriad related files, you won't see anything until they are processed by a properly set up server and application—which in Dreamweaver you can do with the click of a button.

2. Click Live View.

The same page displayed in the browser as the home page for your WordPress site is now rendered in Dreamweaver, as shown in Figure 23-8. You're now ready to begin exploring your CMS application in the next section.

FIGURE 23-8

Live View brings together all the dynamically related files in one completed page.

Discovering dynamically related files

Related files are external files linked to the HTML source code either directly or indirectly through another linked file. For example, you might link to an external style sheet, which, in turn, imports another external style sheet. Both CSS files would appear automatically in the Related Files bar located just under the document tab, as would any associated JavaScript file or server-side includes.

Open any PHP page and the Info bar appears at the top of Document Window with a message reading, "This page may have dynamically related files that can only be discovered by the server" followed by two links, Discover and Preferences (see Figure 23-9). If you click Discover, Dreamweaver initially warns you that to complete the operation, it will run all the included server-side scripts and asks if you'd like to continue. Once you're comfortable with the procedure, feel free to select the Do Not Show Again option. After Dreamweaver has processed the page, it displays any associated files it finds in the Related Files bar. Click on any named file to display it in Code view (or the code side of Split view if you are in Display view).

FIGURE 23-9

The Info bar appears, glowing to attract your attention, to help you discover dynamically related files.

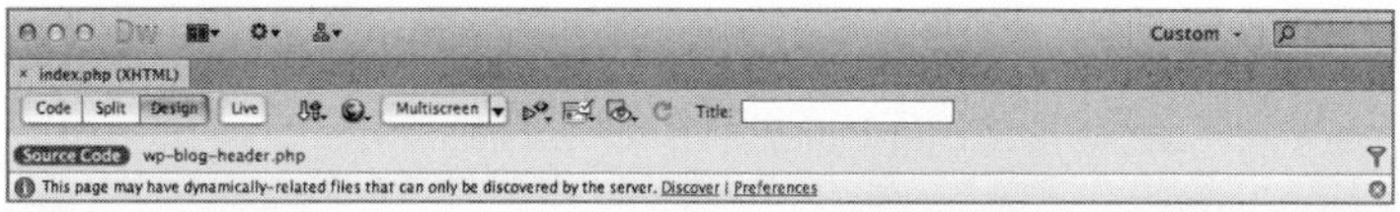

TIP

If you select a related file that has been checked out, a Checkout link is shown in the Info bar; click the link to check out the file and display it. Likewise, if you select a related file that is not stored locally, a Get link is shown; click the link to retrieve the file. You can only get files that are stored on a server to which you have access.

If you click the Preferences link in the Info bar, you'll have an opportunity to automatically discover dynamically related files. I prefer to keep this option at the default manual settings so I get the related files only when I need them.

To keep you from being overwhelmed with related files, Dreamweaver includes a powerful filtering mechanism. To access the Filter Related Files options, click the funnel icon on the far right of the Related Files bar (see Figure 23-10). A drop-down list of file types—each selected with a checkmark—is displayed. This list is generated on the fly by Dreamweaver and represents all of the editable file types associated with the source code. To exclude a file type from the related files list, clear the checkmark; to include it, re-check the file type. For example, if I wanted to just see the external style sheets associated with a page, I would toggle the checkmark off all file types except `.css`. To access all the files again, I would choose Show All File Types.

FIGURE 23-10

The Filter Related Files list of available file types is dynamically generated according to the related files discovered.

Quite often, you'll need to be more specific in your filtering. If you're looking for a PHP file dealing with the header, you might limit the filter to display only PHP documents and still have 60 or so files to wade through. The Custom Filter option makes it possible to filter by full or partial filename. If you know the filename is `header.php`, you can enter that directly in the Custom Filter dialog box. If, on the other hand, you know only that the filename includes the word "header," you can use asterisks as wildcards to locate the file; in this situation, you would enter `*header*.php`

(see Figure 23-11). If Dreamweaver cannot find any files that match your custom filter, you'll see an alert box informing you that Dreamweaver cannot apply a filter that results in no related files.

FIGURE 23-11

Set up a custom filter to pinpoint files that include specified filenames.

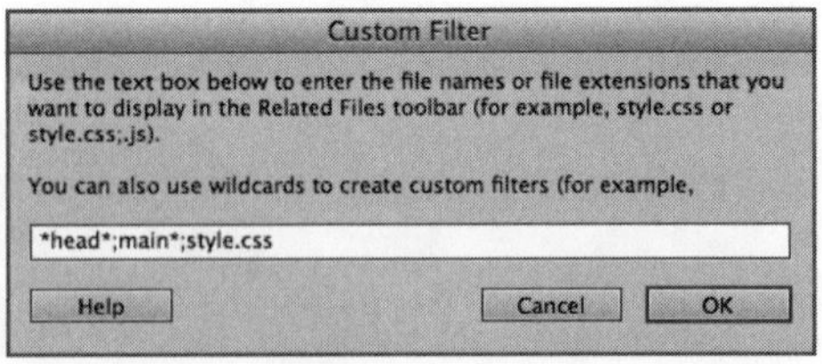

TIP

Multiple custom filters can be applied at once by separating each filter with a semicolon, like this: `*head*;main*;style.css`.

Customizing your WordPress site

Now that you've set up your WordPress site in Dreamweaver and understand how to use the Related Files feature, you're ready to begin customizing your site. Modifying the CSS within WordPress without Dreamweaver is a code-based task and requires a seemingly endless series of trial-and-error attempts. Once the WordPress site has been integrated in Dreamweaver, however, you can customize the CSS quickly and easily through the CSS Styles panel. Of course, if you'd prefer to edit the CSS style sheet by hand, you also have that option.

To show you how it works, let's change a number of CSS properties from their settings in the default WordPress template.

1. With `index.php` from the WordPress site open, click Discover in the Info bar to display the dynamically related files.
2. When Dreamweaver informs you that it will execute all scripts contained in the pages, click Yes.

   Dreamweaver quickly processes the pages on your local server and displays the results in the Related Files bar. As there are more files than can fit on the screen, scroll bars appear on either side, as well as a Show More button (see Figure 23-12). Click Show More to list all the related files in a drop-down list.
3. To see the rendered page, click Live View.

   The home page of the WordPress site is displayed. The CSS Styles panel is accessible in Live View so you can change rules and properties and have an immediate effect. To demonstrate this, let's change the page's font-family.

FIGURE 23-12

When there are too many dynamically related filenames to show, scroll bars and a Show More button are displayed in the Related Files bar.

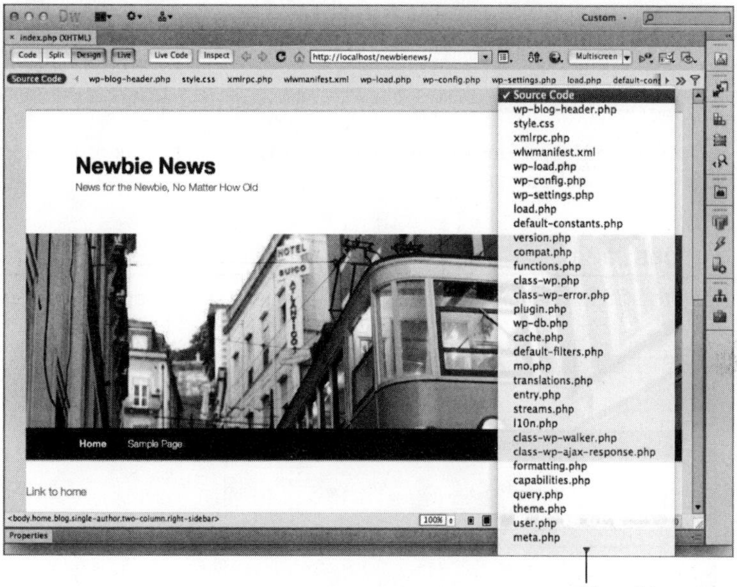

4. In the CSS Styles panel, switch to Current mode and click into the text of the first paragraph.

   Current mode will display whatever CSS rules and properties apply to the currently selected element(s) on the page.

5. From the Summary pane, choose the font property.

   When you select the Font property, the CSS rule that governs that particular property is selected in the Rules pane. In this case, the selector is `body, input, textarea`.

6. At the bottom of the CSS panel, click Edit Rule.

   In many cases, it is easy to change the value of a CSS property directly in the Properties pane. Here, because the Font property values are presented in their shorthand format, it is much simpler to use Dreamweaver's dedicated dialog box for making changes.

7. When the CSS Rule Definition dialog box opens, make sure you're in the Type category and then choose "Palatino Linotype, Book Antiqua, Palatino, serif" from the Font-family list (see Figure 23-13). Click OK when you're done.

   Notice that the font-family change takes place in Live View immediately. This change takes place not only on this page but on all associated pages in the site that use the same style sheet. To verify this, you can use Dreamweaver's Follow Link capabilities.

8. Press Ctrl (Command) and click Sample Page in the main navigation menu.

   The Sample Page is loaded with the modified Font-family (see Figure 23-14).

TIP

If you'd prefer to navigate more naturally through your site, choose Follow Links Continuously from the Live View Options menu button on the Browser Navigation toolbar.

9. To return to the previous page, click either the Back button or the Home button in the Browser Navigation bar.

FIGURE 23-13

Use the CSS Styles panel in Live View to effect style changes to your WordPress page instantly.

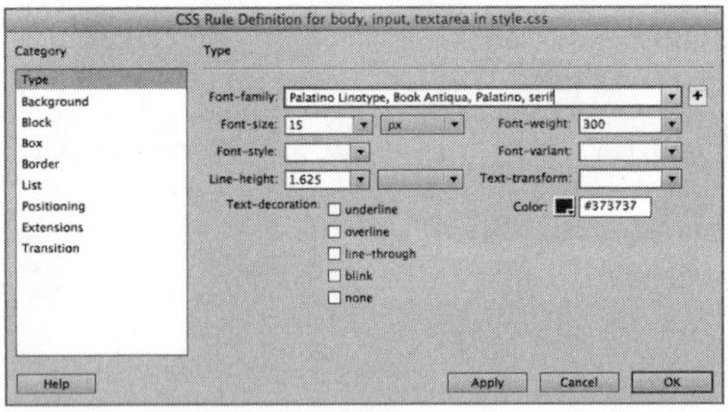

FIGURE 23-14

Navigate to linked pages, like the Sample Page, in your WordPress site quickly and easily.

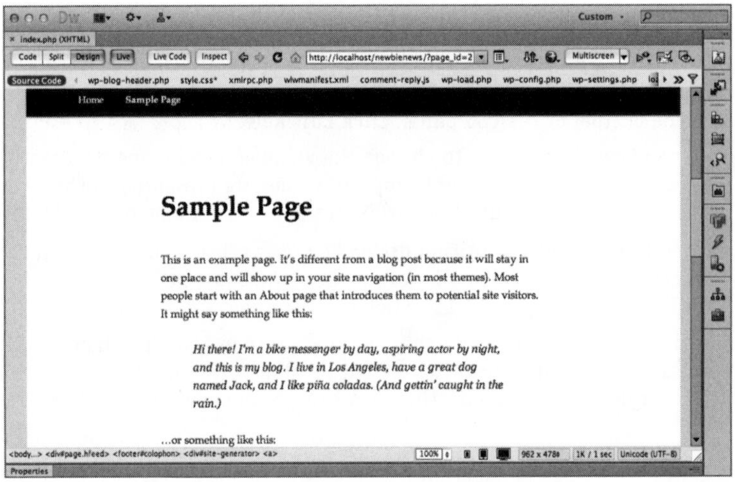

If (or, should you be like me, *when*) you make a CSS change you don't want to keep, you need to open the style sheet containing the modified rule and press Ctrl+Z (Command+Z) or choose Edit ➪ Undo.

CSS styles are just the beginning of what can be modified in a WordPress site. In the next section, I show you how to change existing graphics and insert new images.

Adjusting graphics in a WordPress site

Adding images to a WordPress blog post is very straightforward: Simply choose Insert Image in the WYSIWYG editor, select a local file to upload, and set any desired properties. WordPress handles all the coding and file transfer to the server. Should you need to incorporate graphics for your layout, however, you'll need to take special steps beyond the standard Dreamweaver procedure.

Before we cover adding new images, however, a couple of more common techniques for doing so need to be addressed. A good many designers working on WordPress sites start with an existing template and modify it to fit their needs. Part of the modification process is customizing or replacing existing images.

The CSS Styles panel is an excellent tool for discovering which images or colors are being used and where they are located. Let's say, for example, you wanted to change the background color in the default theme, Twenty-Eleven. The best technique for identifying which color or image is used to create the background is to enter into Live View, open the CSS Styles panel in Current mode, click into the page, and then choose `<body>` from the Tag Selector. The applicable CSS rules are displayed in the CSS Styles panel, including one for the background property. If you select the background property, you'll see that the color is set to `#e2e2e2` in Figure 23-15. You can easily change that color directly in the CSS Properties pane.

You can also create a background image in a graphics program such as Photoshop or Fireworks and change the page background as you see fit. Save the file in the images folder of your current theme (newbienews ➪ wp-content ➪ themes ➪ current theme ➪ Images), modify the background property, and refresh the Live View page to display the revised background, as shown in Figure 23-16.

But what about entirely new images? To add a new image in a WordPress theme, you'll need to incorporate some custom PHP coding. For example, let's say you want to replace the site name and description used in the default template header with a company logo, linked to the home page. The first task is to locate the code that generates this text. As you might expect, this code can be found in the `header.php` file. Use the Related Files Custom Filter feature to quickly locate that file.

Once you've found and opened `header.php`, you'll see the code for the header section right after the opening `<body>` tag:

```
<div id="page" class="hfeed">
  <header id="branding" role="banner">
      <hgroup>
        <h1 id="site-title"><span><a href="<?php echo esc_url( home_url( '/' ) )
; ?>" title="<?php echo esc_attr( get_bloginfo( 'name', 'display' ) ); ?>"
 rel="home"><?php bloginfo( 'name' ); ?></a></span></h1>
        <h2 id="site-description"><?php bloginfo( 'description' ); ?></h2>
      </hgroup>
```

FIGURE 23-15

The default header background image includes the border around the page, as well as the blue center background.

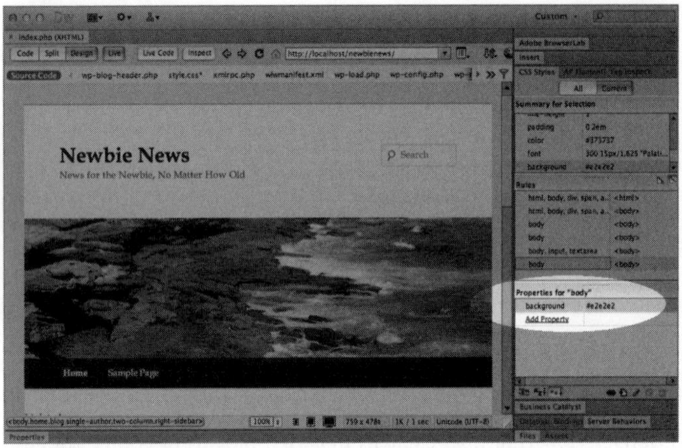

FIGURE 23-16

A modified file with the same filename is a quick and easy way to customize graphics in a WordPress design.

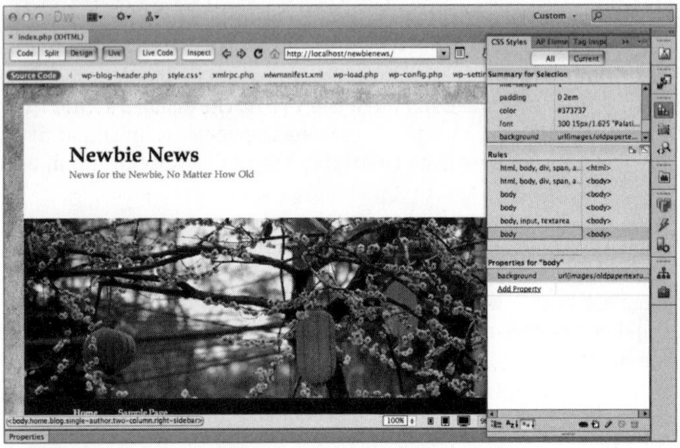

The PHP function on the third line inserts the name of the blog in an <h1>, surrounded by a link to the home page, which is also called by a PHP function:

```
<h1 id="site-title"><span><a href="<?php echo esc_url( home_url( '/' ) ); ?>"
 title="<?php echo esc_attr( get_bloginfo( 'name', 'display' ) ); ?>"
 rel="home"><?php bloginfo( 'name' ); ?></a></span></h1>
```

To replace the name of the blog with a logo image, you would delete the <h1> tag pair and the following PHP function call:

```
<? php bloginfo('name'); ?>
```

Within the <a> tag pair, insert a standard <img> tag that references your logo:

```
<img src="images/logo.png" width="215" height="120" alt="Newbie News" />
```

In order to find an image in a given theme, you'll need to add a bit of PHP code in the `src` attribute that calls the URL of the currently applied template or theme. Your image tag will now look like this:

```
<img src="<?php bloginfo('template_url'); ?>/images/logo.png" width="215"
 height="120" alt="Newbie News" />
```

The additional code has been bolded so you can quickly see what was added. Finally, the fourth line, which sets up an <h2> tag that holds the description text, should be left alone:

```
<h2 id="site-description"><?php bloginfo( 'description' ); ?></h2>
```

When you're done, the revised header code will look like this:

```
<header id="branding" role="banner">
  <hgroup>
    <a href="<?php echo esc_url( home_url( '/' ) ); ?>" title="
<?php echo esc_attr( get_bloginfo( 'name', 'display' ) ); ?>" rel="home">
<img src="<?php bloginfo('template_url); ?>/images/logo.png" width="215"
 height="120" alt="Newbie News" /></a>
    <h2 id="site-description"><?php bloginfo( 'description' ); ?></h2>
  </hgroup>
```

To dismiss the header image, you'll need to go into your WordPress Dashboard and, from the Appearance ➪ Headers section, choose the option not to show any graphics. Then, in Dreamweaver, turn on Live View once more to review the results of your combined graphic and coding efforts. I've added a bit of CSS styling to move the description text over, as shown in Figure 23-17.

Summary

Dreamweaver can render complex documents comprising hundreds of external files. This capability makes it a great tool for working with sites created for web content management systems such as WordPress. You can use Dreamweaver to discover dynamically related files so you can modify CSS styles, change existing images, or insert new ones, and supply the necessary code to customize CMS themes. Here are key points to remember when working with web CMS applications in Dreamweaver:

- Web content management systems are among the fastest-growing web design techniques because of the ease of site maintenance and open source nature of the leading applications, such as WordPress, Joomla, and Drupal.

FIGURE 23-17

Inserting a new image requires a combination of HTML and PHP coding.

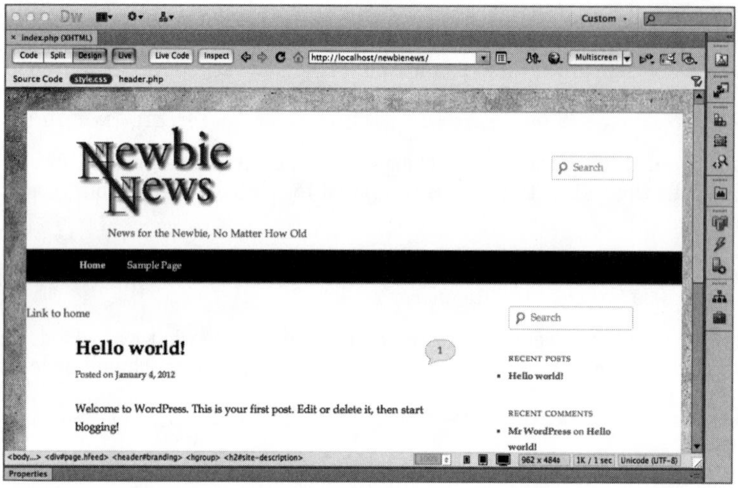

Once you have a proper development environment established with a web server, PHP language server, and MySQL database server, WordPress is fairly easy to install—and even easier to integrate into a Dreamweaver site.

- CMS apps such as WordPress are highly structured and use numerous external files to construct a page. Dreamweaver can discover these files and make them available in the Related Files bar for your inspection or modification.
- When viewing a CMS page in Dreamweaver's Live View, you can modify any CSS rule or property; all changes are applied to the `styles.css` file.
- Existing images can be modified and then re-saved with the original filename for a quick transformation. Another technique to update the current theme is to replace one background image URL in the CSS Styles panel with another.
- Inserting a new image requires a combination of HTML and PHP coding. In addition to the standard `<img>` tag, the `src` attribute must include PHP code pointing to the current theme file location.

In the next chapter, you learn how to integrate graphics created by Photoshop and Fireworks into your Dreamweaver site.

Part V

Including Multimedia Elements

IN THIS PART

Chapter 24
Adobe Photoshop, Fireworks, and Bridge Integration

Chapter 25
Inserting Flash Elements

Chapter 26
Adding Video to Your Web Page

Chapter 27
Using Audio on Your Web Page

CHAPTER

24

Adobe Photoshop, Fireworks, and Bridge Integration

IN THIS CHAPTER

Investigating the Photoshop and Dreamweaver workflow

Dreamweaver Technique: Keeping Photoshop Smart Objects in Sync

Exploring the Fireworks/Dreamweaver connection

Using Fireworks from within Dreamweaver

Dreamweaver Technique: Optimizing Graphics

Working with image placeholders

Dreamweaver Technique: Combining Images in Fireworks

Sending a graphic to Fireworks

Embedding Fireworks code

Managing files with Bridge

Adobe has a wide array of market-leading tools under its roof, and several are of special interest to web designers: Adobe Photoshop and Adobe Fireworks in graphics and Dreamweaver in web authoring. Web designers, especially those new to the field, often pair Photoshop and Dreamweaver in their workflow. In a recent release of both products, as part of the Creative Suite bundle, their integration was further tightened. Now, you can modify a source file in Photoshop for an image placed into a Dreamweaver page—and then update it in Dreamweaver with a single click. In this chapter, you learn the various ways that you can effortlessly tie Photoshop and Dreamweaver together.

Websites—particularly the images—are constantly being tweaked and modified. This fact of web life explains why Fireworks, Adobe's premier web graphics tool, is popular among many web designers. One of Fireworks' main claims to fame is that everything is editable all the time. If that were all that Fireworks did, the program would already have earned a place on every web designer's shelf just for its sheer expediency. Fireworks has many other extraordinary graphic capabilities, however, and Dreamweaver can tap that power directly.

Adobe's Dreamweaver and Fireworks products are tightly integrated. You can optimize your images—reduce the file size, crop the graphic, make colors transparent—within Dreamweaver, using the Fireworks engine (and without opening Fireworks). Moreover, you can edit an image in any fashion in Fireworks and, with one click of the Done button, automatically export the graphic with its updated settings. Perhaps most important of all, Dreamweaver can control Fireworks—creating graphics on the fly—and then insert the results in Dreamweaver.

A key Fireworks feature is the capability to output HTML and JavaScript for easy creation of rollovers, sliced images, and image maps with behaviors. You can even opt to create pop-up menus with standards-compliant CSS. With Fireworks, you can specify Dreamweaver-style code so that all your web pages are consistent. After Fireworks generates the HTML, Dreamweaver's Insert Fireworks HTML object makes code insertion effortless. Dreamweaver recognizes images—whether whole or sliced—as coming from Fireworks, and displays a special Property inspector.

The Adobe integration doesn't stop there. Adobe Bridge is a highly evolved visual browser and panel, which is now accessible directly from within Dreamweaver. In the final section of this chapter, you learn how to take advantage of Bridge's advanced image cataloging. Web pages and web graphics are closely tied to each other. With the tight integration between Dreamweaver and the other Adobe products—Photoshop, Fireworks, and Bridge—the web designer's world is moving toward a single design environment.

Dreamweaver QUICKSTART

This chapter covers a lot of territory in various Adobe graphics programs, but one of the key operations is opening a Photoshop PSD file in Dreamweaver. Here's how it's done:

1. Place your cursor where you'd like your image to appear.
2. From the Common category of the Insert panel, choose Images: Image.

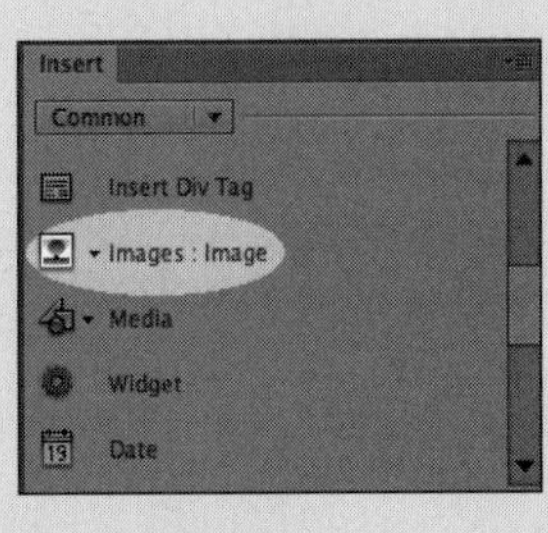

3. In the Select Images dialog box, navigate to your Photoshop source files and choose the one you want; click OK (Choose).
4. When the Image Optimization dialog box appears, select one of the Preset options or choose JPEG, GIF, or PNG from the Format list and adjust the settings to optimize the graphic for best image at the smallest size; click OK when you're done.

Every Photoshop file added to your Dreamweaver page is inserted as a Smart Object—which you learn more about (and lots more) in the chapter that follows.

Bringing in Photoshop Images

Adobe Photoshop, the graphics program powerhouse, was primarily developed to work with print. Although it has long included the capability to export web-compatible formats such as JPEG, GIF, and PNG, the path from Photoshop to Dreamweaver has been an arduous one. Moreover, the reverse direction—necessary for fine-tuning graphics—was just as time-consuming. For years, web designers everywhere put up with repetitive, tedious steps just to use two of their favorite programs together.

Happily, the workflow between the two industry leaders has been smoothed. Now, Dreamweaver not only recognizes the Photoshop native file format (PSD), and offers an in-product conversion to a web-compatible format, but also inserts those graphics as Smart Objects. A Smart Object image keeps track of the original source and lets you know whether the two—Photoshop source and web image—are in sync. If they're not, you can update the web image quickly and easily.

Moreover, designers can copy any selection in Photoshop and paste it into Dreamweaver—and get the same immediate conversion option as if they opened a PSD file.

Inserting Photoshop files

Like all native formats from major graphics programs, Photoshop's PSD format is proprietary and not suitable for viewing on the web. Each file contains a great deal of non-graphical information, such as layer structure, color palettes, and typography details. Consequently, PSD files are typically many times larger than their web counterparts—for example, one PSD file of a single image against a background is 578KB, whereas the same file in JPEG format, with light compression, might be only 23KB. Clearly, for a Photoshop file to be used online, it has to undergo a significant conversion—a conversion Dreamweaver is quite able to handle.

TIP
Users of previous versions of Dreamweaver should note that this workflow has changed significantly for the Dreamweaver CS6 release.

When you insert a PSD file into Dreamweaver, the Image Optimization dialog box appears, as shown in Figure 24-1. Designers choose the desired web format and can further optimize the image to achieve the maximum quality with the minimum file size through a series of format-specific controls. For example, if you choose JPEG format, a slider control that affects the Quality (or compression) setting is available. Similarly, GIF format offers the ability to limit the number of colors. Optimization settings are applied in real time to the inserted image, so you can judge what works best.

If you're not sure where to start, check out the possibilities in the Preset list. There are six commonly chosen options:

- PNG24 for Photos (Sharp Details)
- JPEG for Photos (Continuous Tones)

- PNG8 for Logos and Text
- JPEG High for Maximum Compatibility
- GIF for Background Images (Patterns)
- PNG32 for Background Images (Gradients)

FIGURE 24-1

Opening a Photoshop file in Dreamweaver automatically allows you to optimize the image for the web.

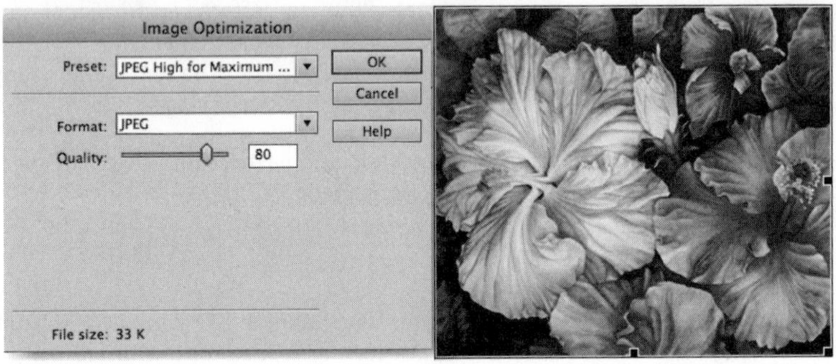

To insert an image in Photoshop format into Dreamweaver, follow these steps:

1. Place your cursor where you'd like the image to appear.
2. Click the Image button from the Common category of the Insert panel or choose Insert ⇨ Image. Alternatively, you can drag the Image button from the Insert panel to the desired location.
3. When the Select Image Source dialog box opens, navigate to and select a Photoshop native file (with a PSD extension), and click Open. The Image Optimization dialog box opens, with the chosen image displayed.
4. Choose the desired web format from the Format list or select a predefined option that combines a format and setting from the Preset list.

   Dreamweaver can convert a PSD file to GIF, JPEG, and PNG formats.
5. Choose your settings for the selected format.
6. When you're done, click OK. The Save Web Image dialog box is displayed.
7. In the Save Web Image dialog box, navigate to the location within your site to store your image and, if desired, enter a new filename.
8. When you're ready, click Save.

After the graphic is inserted, the Property inspector identifies it as a Photoshop-derived image, displays the PSD source, and offers an Edit in Photoshop option, as shown in Figure 24-2, in addition to the standard image properties. To return to the Image Optimization dialog box, click Edit Image Settings, also in the Property inspector and identified in Figure 24-2.

FIGURE 24-2

Photoshop images are easily identified in the Property inspector.

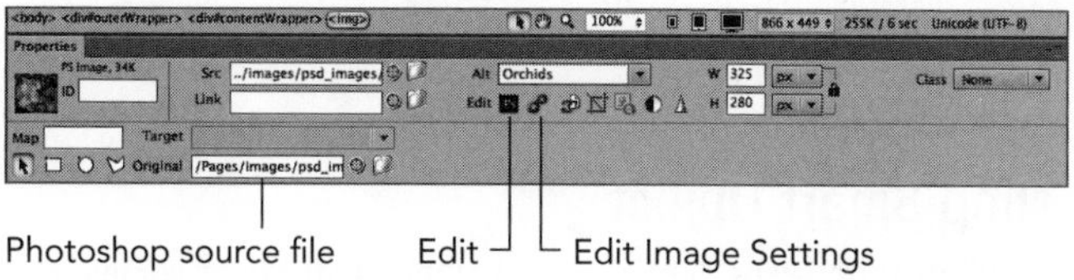

You'll also notice an overlaid symbol in the upper-left corner. This symbol indicates that this is a Photoshop Smart Object, which is covered in the upcoming section, "Updating a Photoshop Smart Object."

Copying and pasting from Photoshop

Many designers use their graphics program to create the layout and then use parts of the design in Dreamweaver. Although these individual elements could be saved as separate files and then inserted using the procedure outlined in the previous section, it's much faster to simply copy what you need from one program, Photoshop, and paste it into another, Dreamweaver.

The same conversion mechanism used for inserting a PSD file into Dreamweaver—the Image Optimization dialog box—is used when copying and pasting an image.

To copy a selection from Photoshop to Dreamweaver, follow these steps:

1. In Photoshop, make your selection.
2. To copy the selection in the currently selected layer, choose Edit ⇨ Copy or press Ctrl+C (Command+C); to copy all the layers contained within the selection, choose Edit ⇨ Copy Merged.

> **TIP**
> You're not limited to copies of simple selections or merged layers: You can also copy slices. In Photoshop, after you've made your slices with the Slice tool, use the Slice Select tool to choose them. Then copy the selected slice with either the menu or the keyboard shortcut.

3. In Dreamweaver, place your cursor where you'd like the image to appear.
4. Choose Edit ⇨ Paste or press Ctrl+V (Command+V). The Image Optimization dialog box opens, with the copied image displayed.
5. In the Options tab, choose the desired web format from the Format list.
6. Choose your settings for the selected format.
7. When you're done, click OK. The Save Web Image dialog box is displayed.
8. In the Save Web Image dialog box, navigate to the location within your site to store your image and enter a new filename.
9. When you're ready, click Save.

The same Property inspector is used for converted PSD files and for those images pasted from Photoshop. Again, a Smart Object symbol is displayed on top of the image in the upper-left corner. Whether the images come from a Photoshop file or the Photoshop clipboard, they are inserted as Smart Object images and, as you'll see in the next section, this means you can easily modify the source and reapply your changes.

Updating a Photoshop Smart Object

Any image originating from Photoshop—whether imported from a PSD file or copied and pasted—can be modified in Photoshop and easily updated in Dreamweaver. Because these Dreamweaver images keep track of their Photoshop source images, they are referred to as Smart Objects. As noted earlier, a Smart Object is identified by a symbol overlaid on the upper-left corner of the image; the symbol tells the sync status at a glance. When the Photoshop image is first inserted, the Smart Object is in sync with the source and the symbol is completely green; if the source is changed, the symbol turns half red. Tooltips further help clarify the sync status when you roll over the symbol. Out-of-sync Smart Objects can be updated and brought into sync with the click of the Update from Original button on the Property inspector, as shown in Figure 24-3.

FIGURE 24-3

Update Photoshop Smart Objects with the click of a Property inspector button.

Once the image has been inserted into Dreamweaver, there are two files you can modify: the original source graphic and the converted web-compatible file. The process is different for changing each of the two file types; each procedure is detailed next.

TIP

You can use any version from Photoshop CS4 and later to take advantage of the integration of Smart Object technology in Dreamweaver.

To modify the source image from Photoshop via the Smart Object connection, follow these steps:

1. Select the image in Design view.
2. From the Property inspector, choose the PS icon to the right of Edit. Alternatively, you can press Ctrl (Command) and double-click the image to launch the original source graphic in Photoshop.

   You're also free to modify the source graphic directly in Photoshop, without initiating the process in Dreamweaver.
3. When the source image appears in Photoshop, make any desired changes.
4. Return to Dreamweaver and, with the original image selected, choose Update from Original in the Property inspector or from the context menu.

The updated image is optimized according to the previous conversion settings and inserted in the page. Smart Objects are smart enough to retain any scaling done in Dreamweaver, as well as the optimized settings.

If you resize a Smart Object image, a warning indicator is added to the sync symbol; you can resample the source for optimum rescaling by selecting the Update from Original option on the Property inspector.

TIP

What if you have multiple Smart Object images inserted into your web pages from a single Photoshop source? If the source is updated, all the related Smart Objects will be marked as out of sync and you have the option to update them individually or all at once. To update multiple Smart Objects, open the Assets panel and select all the images you want to modify; all of the images will display the out-of-sync indicator in the Assets panel preview window. Then, right-click (Windows) or Ctrl-click (Mac) and choose Update from Original.

If you don't have the source image available or you'd prefer to change the web-compatible file, you'll need to send the image to Photoshop in a slightly different way.

To modify the web-compatible image converted from Photoshop, follow these steps:

1. Select the image in Design view.
2. Choose Modify ➪ Image ➪ Edit With ➪ Adobe Photoshop CS5 or right-click the image and choose Edit With ➪ Adobe Photoshop CS6.

TIP

If you prefer to use keyboard shortcuts, you'll need to make sure that Photoshop is set up as your primary editor for JPEG, GIF, and PNG formats in the File Types / Editors category of Preferences. Once you've made that assignment, you can press the Alt (Option) key while double-clicking an image to open the file in Photoshop.

3. When the source image appears in Photoshop, make any desired changes.
4. Select the modified image.

5. Choose Edit ➪ Copy or press Ctrl+C (Command+C) to copy the selection to the clipboard.
6. In Dreamweaver, with the original image selected, choose Edit ➪ Paste or press Ctrl+V (Command+V).

Naturally, any changes made to the web-ready image will not be reflected in the original PSD file.

Dreamweaver TECHNIQUE

Keeping Photoshop Smart Objects in Sync

Dreamweaver and Photoshop's Smart Object connection makes it possible to quickly update a web-based image in Dreamweaver if the source of that image has been modified in Photoshop.

Note: This Dreamweaver Technique requires Photoshop CS4 or later, as well as Dreamweaver CS6.

1. From the Techniques site, expand the 24_Photoshop_Fireworks folder and open the `photoshop_start` file.
2. Select the top image on the page, `residential_home_01ps.jpg`.

   Note the Smart Object symbol in the upper-left corner of the image. The green symbol indicates that the image is in sync with the Photoshop source.

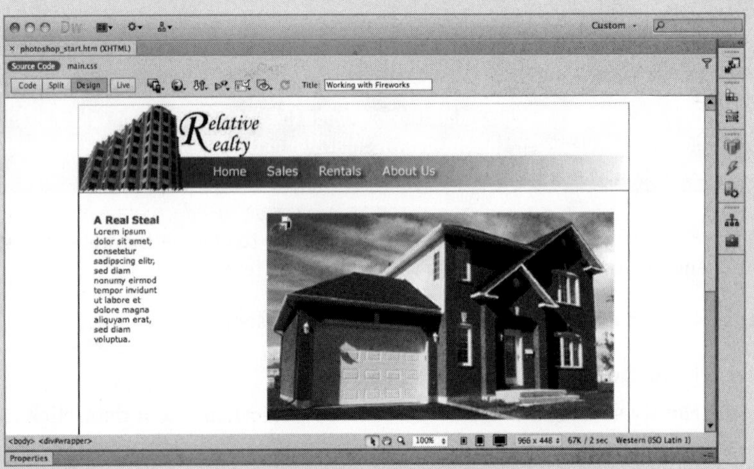

3. From the Property inspector, click the Edit icon.

   Photoshop launches and displays the selected image.
4. Now select a second image to blend with the first by choosing from the Photoshop menu File ➪ Place.
5. In the Import dialog box, navigate to the Techniques\Images folder and choose `sold_sign.png`.
6. Place the bounding box in the center of the image, and double-click to confirm the placement.

   The imported file is in standard PSD format with a transparent background, so it can blend into the other image seamlessly.

7. Choose File ➪ Save.
8. Switch back to Dreamweaver and note that the Smart Objects symbol is half red and half green.
9. Select the image and, from the Property inspector, click Update from Original.

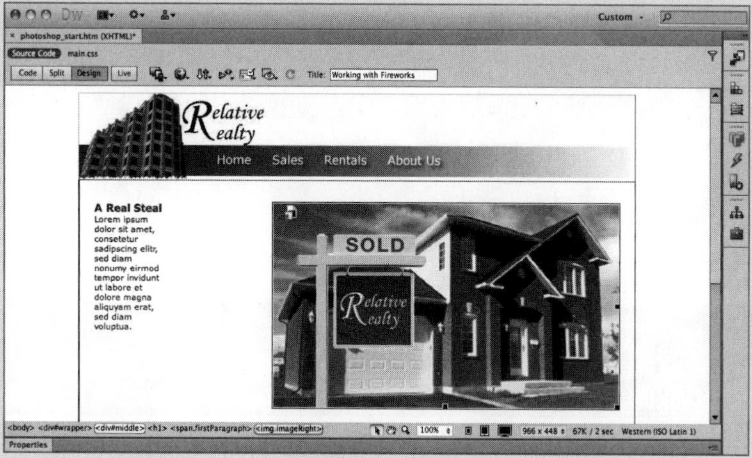

Smart Objects greatly smooth the workflow between Photoshop and Dreamweaver.

Integrating Fireworks

Adobe Fireworks combines the best of both vector and bitmap technologies and is one of the first graphics programs to use PNG as its native format. Exceptional export capabilities are available in Fireworks so you can optimize images for file size, color, and scale. Moreover, Fireworks is terrific at generating GIF animations, rollovers, image maps, and sliced images.

Dreamweaver has a few graphics tricks of its own now. Even without Fireworks, you can crop, resample, and brighten images—and more. For a discussion of Dreamweaver's built-in graphics capabilities, see Chapter 8.

With Dreamweaver and Fireworks, you have two ways to alter inserted graphics: the Modify ➪ Image ➪ Optimize command and the Edit button in the Image Property inspector.

Modifying a Fireworks image

Although you can design the most beautiful, compelling image possible in your graphics program, if it's intended for the Internet, it must be viewed in a web page. Not only must the graphic work in the context of the entire page, but you also have to take the file size of the web graphic into account. All these factors mean that most, if not all, images require some degree of modification after they're included in a web page. Dreamweaver's Modify ➪ Image ➪ Optimize command facilitates these changes via the Image Optimization dialog box, shown in Figure 24-4.

FIGURE 24-4

You can optimize images from within Dreamweaver, with or without Fireworks installed.

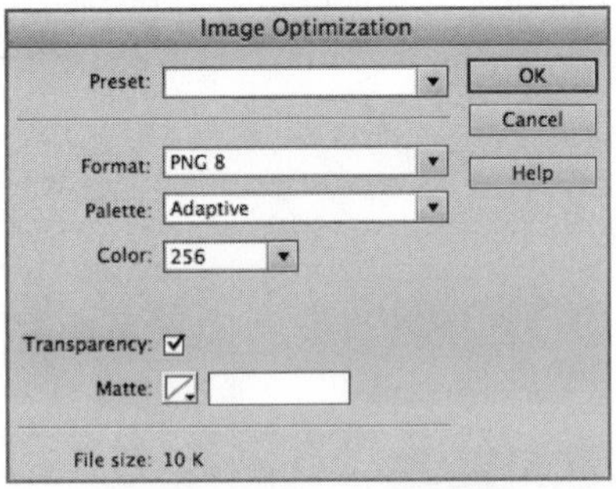

NOTE

If you crop or rescale an inserted image in Fireworks, you must update its height and width in Dreamweaver. The easiest way to accomplish this is to click the Reset Size button in the Image Property inspector.

Fireworks saves its source files in an expanded PNG format to maintain full editability of the images. Graphics for the web must be exported from Fireworks in GIF, JPEG, or standard PNG format. Dreamweaver's Optimize command modifies the exported file only in Dreamweaver, while the Edit command in the Property inspector can make changes to either the source file or the exported file in Fireworks. In many situations, better results are achieved by using the source file, especially when optimizing includes rescaling or resampling. Some situations, however, require that you leave the source file as-is and modify only the exported files. Suppose, for example, that one source file is used to generate several different export files, each with different backgrounds (or *canvases*, as they are called in Fireworks). In that case, you are better off modifying the specific exported file, rather than the general source image.

TIP

You can open the Image Optimization dialog box with the currently selected image by choosing Edit Image Settings from the Property inspector.

Dreamweaver enables you to choose which type of image you want to modify.

If you want to change the source file of a graphic, select the image and then choose one of the following alternatives:

- Choose Modify ⇨ Image ⇨ Edit Original With ⇨ Adobe Fireworks CS6 (or other listed program).
- Click Edit in the Property inspector and when the Open File dialog appears in Fireworks, locate the Fireworks source file.

NOTE

If you're working with a Fireworks source file, the changes are saved to both your source file and the exported file; otherwise, only the exported file is altered.

If you want to change the exported file of a graphic, select the image and then choose one of the following alternatives:

- Choose Modify ➪ Image ➪ Edit With ➪ Adobe Fireworks CS6 (or other listed program) or Browse to select an editor.
- Click Edit in the Property inspector, and when the Open File dialog box appears in Fireworks, click Cancel.
- Click Edit Image Settings or Commands ➪ Optimize Image to change the format and format-related options in the Image Optimization dialog box in Dreamweaver.

NOTE

The current page must have been saved at least once before the Optimize command can be run. The current state of the page doesn't have to be previously saved, but a valid file must exist for the command to work properly. If you haven't saved the file, Dreamweaver alerts you to this fact when you call the command.

If you've sent a file from Dreamweaver to Fireworks for modification, you'll see an indication of the roundtrip editing in progress just above the Document Window in Fireworks, as shown in Figure 24-5. When you've completed your changes, click Done.

FIGURE 24-5

When you're finished editing an image placed in a Dreamweaver page in Fireworks, click the Done button to save the file and send it back to Dreamweaver.

24

Exploring Fireworks Source and Export Files

The separate source file is an important concept in Fireworks, and I strongly advise you to use it. Generally, when working in Fireworks, you have a minimum of two files for every image output to the web: your source file and your exported web image. Whenever you make major alterations, it's best to make them to the source file and then update the export files. Not only is it easier to work this way, but you also get a better image.

Source files are always Fireworks-style PNG files. Fireworks-style PNG files differ slightly from the regular PNG format because they include additional information, such as paths and effects used, that can be read only by Fireworks. The exported file is usually in GIF or JPEG format, although it can be in standard PNG format. Many web designers keep their source files in a separate folder from their exported web images so that the two don't get confused. Fireworks CS6 now offers an option to identify source file PNGs from flattened or exported PNGs by appending a `.fw` suffix to the filename, before the file extension. So, for example, a Fireworks source file would have the name `orchids.fw.png`, while the exported file would be `orchids.png`. This source-and-export file combination also prevents you from inadvertently re-editing a lossy compressed file, such as a JPEG image, and reapplying the compression (thus exacerbating the lossiness).

Because of server capacity limitations, most web designers upload the exported GIF/JPEG image files (the files that actually appear in the web page) to their servers, but they do not upload the source PNG image files from which these GIFs/JPEGs are derived. If you use this approach, you can take advantage of Dreamweaver's Cloaking feature to cloak your PNG files, thus automatically preventing them from being uploaded, as discussed in Chapter 4.

TIP

You can also invoke the Optimize Image command from the Property inspector. With the image selected, click Optimize—it's the second button from the left in the Edit area and looks like a pair of gears.

Dreamweaver TECHNIQUE

Optimizing Graphics

Dreamweaver and Fireworks' tight integration makes it possible to resize your graphics visually in Dreamweaver and use the Fireworks engine to optimize it to your chosen physical size, as well as a reduced file size.

1. From the Techniques site, expand the 24_Photoshop_Fireworks folder and open the `fireworks_start` file.

   The top image on the page is too big and needs to be reduced in both file size and dimensions.

2. Select the image of the two-story house, `residential_home_01.jpg`, so that the sizing handles appear.
3. Begin dragging the size handle in the lower-right corner and then press and hold the Shift key to constrain the resizing. If you don't constrain the resizing, the width-to-height proportion may not be consistent with the original image.

4. Resize the picture until it's approximately two-thirds of its original size.
5. When the image size is more appropriate to the page, select Commit Image Size, the checkmark next to the width and height in the Property inspector.
6. With the image still selected, click Edit Settings from the Property inspector.
7. In the Image Optimization dialog box, drag the Quality slider down around 60 until you find a suitable image quality and file size. Keep an eye on the image as you move the slider. At 70 percent, the file size drops from the original size of 29KB to 11KB—a significant reduction, without a noticeable image quality change.
8. When you're ready, click OK. The image is optimized.

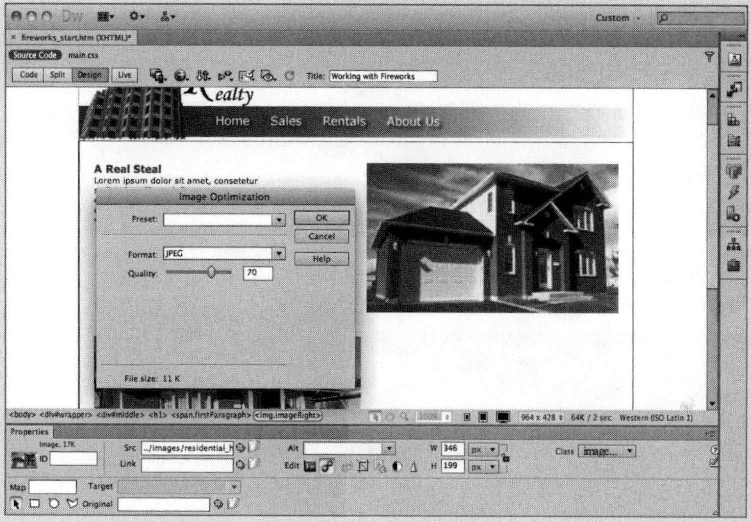

9. Save your page.

The Optimize Image command is great for adjusting the file size of an image; in the next Dreamweaver Technique, you see how to send images from Dreamweaver to Fireworks for more elaborate editing.

Editing an image in Fireworks

Optimizing an image is great when all you need to do is tweak the file size or rescale the image. Other images require more detailed modification—such as when a client requests that the wording or order of a series of navigational buttons be changed. Dreamweaver enables you to specify Fireworks as your graphics editor. If you've done so, you can take advantage of Fireworks' capability to keep every element of your graphic always editable. Believe me—this is a major advantage.

In Dreamweaver, external editors can be set for any file format; you can even assign more than one editor to a file type. When you install the Adobe Creative Suite, Fireworks is preset as the primary external editor for GIF, JPEG, and PNG files. If you install Fireworks outside the Suite's setup, Dreamweaver Preferences handles the external editor assignment. To assign Fireworks to an existing file type, follow these steps:

1. Choose Edit ➪ Preferences (Dreamweaver ➪ Preferences) to open the Preferences dialog box.
2. Select the File Types/Editors category.
3. Select the file type (GIF, JPEG, or PNG) from the Extensions list (see Figure 24-6).
4. Click the Add (+) button above the Editors list. The Select External Editor dialog box opens.
5. Locate the editor application and click Open when you're ready.
6. Click the Make Primary button while the editor you want is highlighted in the Editors list.

Now, whenever you want to edit a graphic, select the image and click the Edit in Fireworks button in the Property inspector. You can also right-click (Control+click) the image and select Edit With Fireworks to start editing it. Fireworks starts up if it's not already open. As with the Optimize Image command, if the inserted image is a GIF or a JPEG and not a PNG, Fireworks asks if you'd like to work with a separate source file, if that option in Fireworks Preferences is set. If you choose to do so, Fireworks automatically loads the source file.

FIGURE 24-6

Define Fireworks as your external editor for GIF, JPEG, and PNG files to enable the back-and-forth interaction between Dreamweaver and Fireworks.

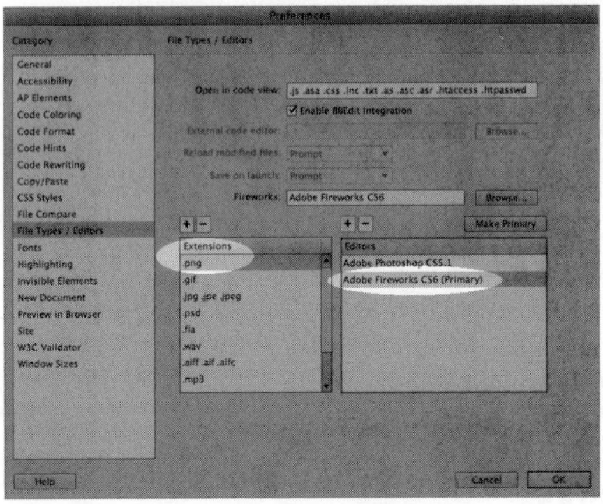

When the image opens in Fireworks, the document window indicates that the image is being edited from Dreamweaver in Fireworks, as shown in Figure 24-5. A Done button is also available in the Document window for completing the operation after you've made the alterations to your file in Fireworks. Alternatively, you can choose File ➪ Update or use the keyboard shortcut Ctrl+S (Command+S). If you're working with a Fireworks source file (PNG), both the source file and the exported file are updated and saved.

Replacing an image placeholder using Fireworks

As discussed in Chapter 8, when designing a page, you can defer the task of inserting final artwork by using image placeholders instead of actual images; then, at the appropriate time, you can replace these image placeholders with the actual images. Working this way can facilitate smooth, trouble-free interaction between your website design and your graphics departments.

To use Fireworks to replace your Dreamweaver image placeholders, follow these steps:

1. In Dreamweaver, open the page that contains the image placeholder you want to replace.
2. Select the image placeholder and click the Create button in the Property inspector. Or simply Ctrl+double-click (Command+double-click) the image placeholder.

   Fireworks launches and creates a new, blank PNG file whose canvas size is set to the width/height of the placeholder image, as shown in Figure 24-7.

FIGURE 24-7

You can use Fireworks to replace your Dreamweaver image placeholders with actual images.

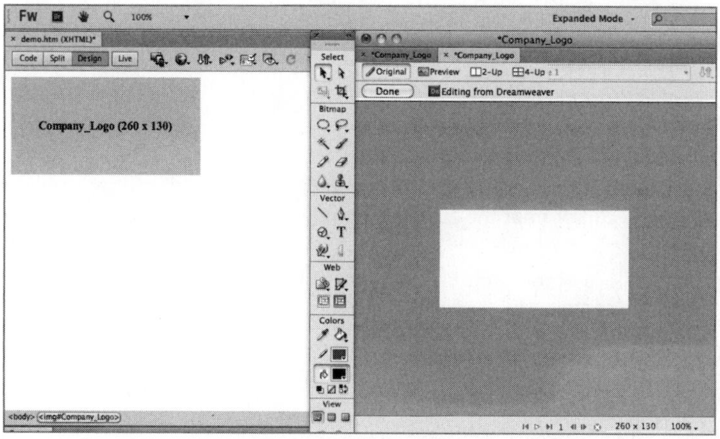

3. In Fireworks, create the desired image.
4. When you are finished, click Done.

   Fireworks first prompts you to save the image as a PNG (source) file. It then prompts you to export the file in a suitable web format: GIF or JPEG. Dreamweaver automatically replaces the selected image placeholder with this exported image.

After you've used this procedure to replace a Dreamweaver image placeholder, you can easily edit the image in Fireworks by using the techniques described in the previous section of this chapter (the Edit button in the Property inspector and the Edit With Fireworks command).

Applying Sprites

For many years, web designers relied on JavaScript to swap separate images when a user hovered her mouse over a graphical element, like a navigation item. While this technique is still in use (and covered in the following section, "Inserting Rollovers"), many designers have begun to rely on CSS to handle the state-driven changes in an image. As in the next section, it's possible to accomplish CSS image manipulation with a series of separate images, but the trend is to use a single image, called a *sprite*, to achieve the same effect. The use of one image instead of several reduces the use of bandwidth and processor time while making it easier for the designer to keep track of and manage the site's assets.

Dreamweaver TECHNIQUE

Combining Images in Fireworks

In this Dreamweaver Technique, you use Dreamweaver's Edit capability to combine an image on the page with another.

1. Open the `fireworks_start.htm` file previously worked on.
2. Select the bottom image on the page, `residential_home_02.jpg`.
3. From the Property inspector, click the Edit icon.

   Fireworks launches and displays the selected image in a special editing window.
4. Now select a second image to blend with the first by opening the Fireworks menu and choosing File ➪ Import.
5. In the Import dialog box, navigate to the Techniques\images folder and choose `sold_sign.png`.
6. Place the angle cursor near the top left of the image, and click once to place the imported graphic.

   The imported file is in standard PNG format with transparency enabled, so it can blend into the other image seamlessly.

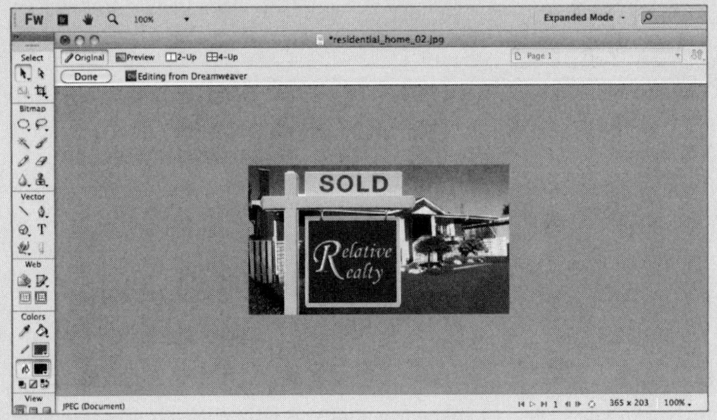

7. Reposition the imported image to your liking; when you're satisfied, click Done.
8. Fireworks closes and Dreamweaver is brought to the forefront; when your revised image appears, save your page.

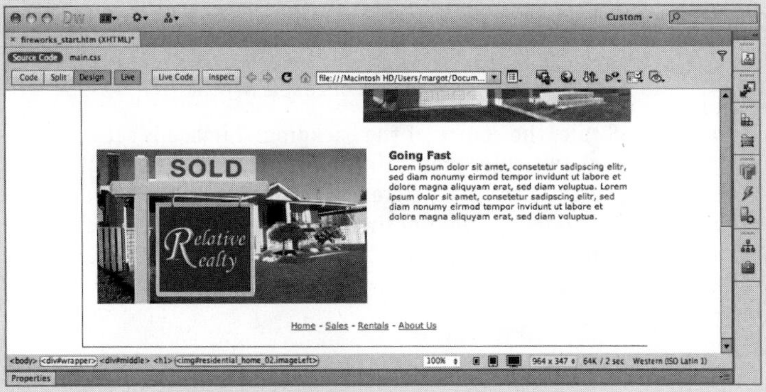

Combining images is just one of the ways you can use Dreamweaver and Fireworks together.

With a sprite image, changes to the CSS `background-image` property's `position` parameter make a different image appear in the browser. Typically, a sprite image shows two to four similar, but distinct images, as shown in Figure 24-8.

FIGURE 24-8

Images created in Fireworks CS6 can easily be output as sprite images, complete with CSS.

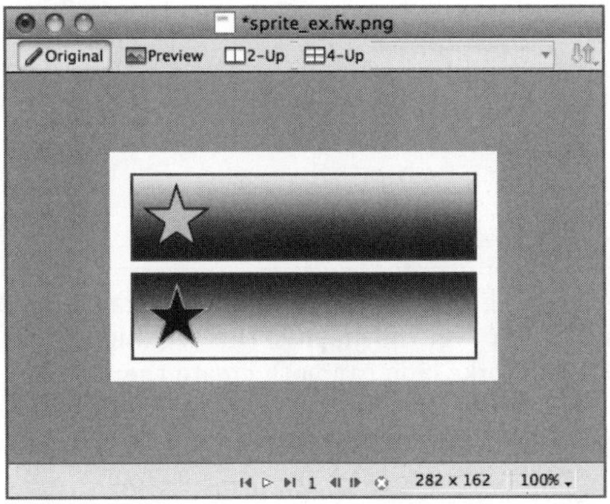

Once you've create a base image, it's very straightforward to clone and change a few key aspects, such as gradient direction or symbol colors to distinguish one image from another. Then, you can create slices of each image and opt to export them as CSS Sprites. The export operation stores a single image that combines the two sprite elements in a web-ready format and a CSS file. Here's the code from an example CSS Sprite export:

```
.sprite_ex{ background:url("sprite_ex.jpg") top left no-repeat; }
.spritehover_s1{ width:252px; height:62px; background-position:-10px -10px; }
.spritelink_s1{ width:252px; height:62px; background-position:-272px -10px; }
```

As you can see, in the first CSS rule, the source of the background image is set using the exported file, `sprite_ex.jpg`. The next two rules maintain the same width and height and shift the `background-position` property to show a different, selected view of the overall sprite image. Once you change those two rules to reflect your desired interaction (using, for example, `a:link` and `a:hover` selectors), your resulting output could easily be applied to a navigation bar, as shown in Figure 24-9.

FIGURE 24-9

Combine the exported CSS sprite image and code with your own HTML to create an interactive navigation bar.

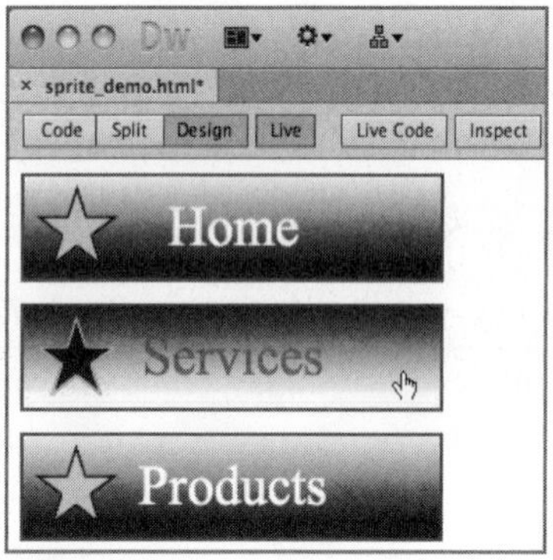

Inserting Rollovers

The rollover is a fairly common but effective web technique to indicate interactivity. Named after the user action of rolling the mouse pointer over the graphic, this technique uses from two to four different images per button. With Fireworks, you can both create the graphics and output the necessary HTML and JavaScript code from the same program. Moreover, Fireworks adds some sophisticated twists to the standard on/off rollovers to enable you to easily enhance your web page.

Rollovers created in Fireworks can be inserted into Dreamweaver using several methods. First, you can use Fireworks to build the images, and then you just export them and attach the behaviors in Dreamweaver. This technique works well for graphics going into AP elements or images with other attached behaviors. The second method of integrating Fireworks-created rollovers involves transferring the actual code generated by Fireworks into Dreamweaver—a procedure that can be handled with one command, Insert Fireworks HTML: Insert ➪ Image Objects ➪ Fireworks HTML.

Using Dreamweaver's behaviors

With its full-spectrum editability, Fireworks excels at building consistent rollover graphics simply. The possible states of an image in a rollover—up, over, down, and over while down—are handled in Fireworks as separate states, formerly called frames. As in an animated GIF, each state has the same dimensions, but the content is slightly altered to indicate the separate user actions. For example, Figure 24-10 shows the different states of a rollover button, side by side.

FIGURE 24-10

A Fireworks-created rollover can be made of four separate states.

Image	Home	Home	Home	Home
User's Pointer	Up	Over	Down	Over Down
Fireworks State	1	2	3	4

NOTE

Many web designers use just the initial two states—up and over—in their rollover buttons. The third state, down, takes place when the user clicks the button, and it is useful if you want to indicate that moment to the user. The down state also indicates which button has been clicked (which is down) when a new page appears, but the same navigation bar is used, notably with states. The fourth state (over while down) is called when the user's pointer rolls over the previously selected button.

You can attach the rollover behaviors to your images in several ways in Dreamweaver. The following technique uses Dreamweaver's Rollover object. To create a rollover by attaching Dreamweaver behaviors to Fireworks-created graphics, follow these steps:

1. Create your graphics in Fireworks, using a different state for each rollover state.

CAUTION

You cannot use Fireworks' Edit ➪ Insert ➪ New Button command to build your button for this technique because the separate states are not stored as states.

2. In Fireworks, choose File ➪ Export. The Export dialog box opens (see Figure 24-11).
3. If you want, type a new name in the File Name text box. In this operation, the File Name text is used as a base name by Fireworks to identify multiple images exported from a single file. When you are exporting states, the default settings append `_sn`, where `n` is the number of the state. State numbers 1–9 are listed with a leading zero (for example, `MainButton_s01`).

FIGURE 24-11

From Fireworks, you can export each state as a separate file to be used in Dreamweaver rollovers.

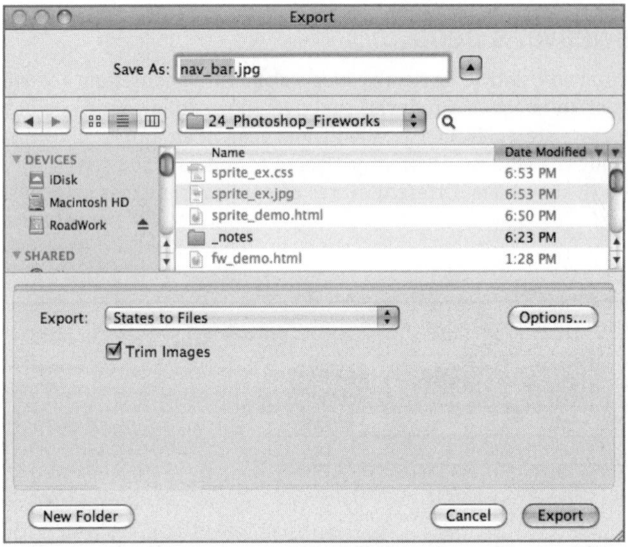

4. In the Save As Type list box, select States To Files.
5. If desired, select the Trim Images option. When Trim Images is on, Fireworks automatically crops the exported images to fit the objects on each state. This procedure makes for smaller, more flexible image files.

CAUTION

I recommend that, in most situations, you opt to trim your images when exporting states as files. But here's an exception to watch out for: If a button in one state has a drop shadow, its trimmed size will be slightly larger than the non-drop-shadow buttons. Swapping it forces it to fit the smaller button's image space, which causes a jagged, amateurish swap display.

6. Click the Save button to store your states as separate files.
7. From the Common category of the Insert panel, choose the Rollover Image object.
8. In the Insert Rollover Image dialog box, click the Original Image Browse button to locate the image stored with the first state designation: `_s01`.
9. If you want, give your image a unique name different from the one automatically assigned in the Image Name text box.
10. Click the Rollover Image Browse button to locate the image stored with the second state designation: `_s02`.

11. When you're finished, click OK.
12. If you'd like to use the down (_s03) and over while down (_s04) images, attach additional Swap Image behaviors to the image files. For help, see Chapter 11.

Another approach is to build the entire navigation bar—complete with rollovers—in Fireworks. Rather than create and export one button at a time, all the navigation buttons are created as one graphic, and slices or hotspots are used to make the different objects or areas interact differently. You learn more about slices and hotspots later in this chapter.

Using Fireworks' code

In some ways, Fireworks is a hybrid program, capable of simultaneously outputting terrific graphics and sophisticated code. You can even select the type of code you want generated in Fireworks: Dreamweaver HTML, Dreamweaver XHTML, Dreamweaver Library, CSS and Images, or code compatible with other web authoring programs. You can also find a more general Generic code option. All these options can be chosen during the Export procedure.

CAUTION
Fireworks has the capability to convert graphics to CSS-based layouts, complete with sliced images, background graphics, and external style sheets. For graphics thus converted using their CSS and Images export, you don't need to do anything special in Dreamweaver—just open the page as you would any other web page. Unlike other Fireworks exported code, there are no roundtrip capabilities with this export option, however.

For rollovers, Fireworks generally outputs to two different sections of the HTML document, the `<head>` and the `<body>`; only the FrontPage style keeps all the code together. The `<head>` section contains the JavaScript code for activating the rollovers and preloading the images; `<body>` contains the HTML references to the images themselves, their links, and the event triggers used (`onClick` or `onMouseOver`).

The general procedure is to first create your graphics in Fireworks and then export them, simultaneously generating a page of code. Now, the just-generated Fireworks HTML page can be incorporated in Dreamweaver. Dreamweaver includes two slick methods for including your Fireworks output code and images. The Insert Fireworks HTML object places the code—and the linked images—right at your current cursor position. You also have the option to export your Fireworks HTML directly to the clipboard and paste it, verbatim, into Dreamweaver.

CAUTION
If you paste the Fireworks rollover code manually into a Dreamweaver HTML document, take care to merge the existing `<head>` and `<body>` code with the Fireworks rollover code. And remember: An HTML document can have only one `<head>` and one `<body>` tag!

Just as an image requires a link to create a rollover in Dreamweaver, a Fireworks image needs to be designated as either a *slice* or a *hotspot*. The Fireworks program describes slices and hotspots as being part of the graphic's web layer. The web layer can be hidden or locked, but not deleted. Figure 24-12 shows the same button with both a slice and a hotspot attached.

FIGURE 24-12

The Fireworks image on the left uses a slice object, whereas the image on the right uses a polygon hotspot.

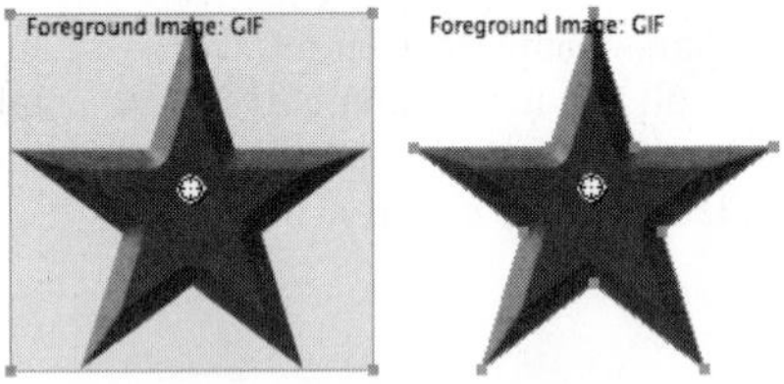

Slices are rectangular areas that permit different parts of the same graphic to be saved as separate formats—the entire graphic is formatted as an HTML table. Each slice can also be given its own URL and have one or more behaviors attached to it.

A Fireworks *hotspot* is an area defined for an image map. Hotspots can be rectangular, elliptical, or polygonal—just like those created by Dreamweaver with the Image Map tools. Because Fireworks is an object-oriented graphics program, any selected image (or part of an image) can be automatically converted to a hotspot. Like slices, hotspots can have both URLs and behaviors assigned to them.

NOTE

In addition to the technique outlined in the text that follows, you can also use Fireworks' Button Editor (available by choosing Edit ➪ Insert ➪ New Button) to create your rollover images and behaviors.

To include Fireworks-generated code in your Dreamweaver document, follow these steps in Fireworks:

1. Create your graphics in Fireworks, placing the image for each interactive rollover state—up, over, down (optional), and over while down (optional)—in its own state.
2. With the object in its first state selected, create the hotspot(s) or slice(s).

   To do so automatically, choose Edit ➪ Insert ➪ Hotspot or Edit ➪ Insert ➪ Rectangular Slice. To do so manually, use the Hotspot or Slice tools in the Fireworks toolbox.
3. Where appropriate, use Fireworks' Property inspector to assign URLs to hotspots or slices.
4. Click the target symbol displayed in the center of the hotspot or slice to display a menu of available behaviors.

   Alternatively, you can open Fireworks' Behavior inspector and click the Add Behavior (+) button.
5. If you are working on a slice, select the Simple Rollover or Swap Image behavior. If you are working on a hotspot, choose the Swap Image behavior (Simple Rollover is not available for hotspots).
6. Export the object by choosing File ➪ Export to open the Export dialog box.
7. Enter a name in the File Name text box and make sure that the HTML and Images option is displayed in the Save As Type drop-down list.

TIP

The Simple Rollover behavior is used to create single- or multiple-button rollovers in which one image is replaced by another image in the same location; only two states are used for a Simple Rollover. Use the Swap Image behavior to create more complex rollovers, such as those in which the rollover triggers an image change in another location. A third alternative, the Nav Bar, should be used in situations where the navigation system is to be placed in a stateset. The Nav Bar behavior can display all four states (up, over, down, and over while down).

If you intend to use the graphics in several places on your site, choose Dreamweaver Library (`.lbi`) from the Save As Type drop-down list.

8. To change the type of HTML/XHTML code generated, click the Options button and make a selection from the Style drop-down list.

   Dreamweaver HTML code is the default style; other options include Dreamweaver XHTML, Air HTML and XHTML, GoLive HTML and XHTML, Generic HTML and XHTML, and JQuery HTML.

9. Select the location in which to store your HTML code by navigating to the appropriate folder. Note that Dreamweaver Library code must be saved in a site's Library folder.

   If you prefer to not save your HTML, select Copy To Clipboard from the HTML drop-down list.

10. To save your graphics in a separate folder, select the Put Images In Subfolder option.

CAUTION

Fireworks defaults to placing the graphics in a subfolder called Images, even if one does not exist. To specify a different folder, click the Browse button.

11. When you're finished, click Save.

When Fireworks completes the exporting, you have one HTML file (unless you've chosen the Copy To Clipboard option) and multiple image files—one for each slice and state. Now you're ready to integrate these images and code into your Dreamweaver page. Which method you use depends on the HTML style you selected when the graphics were exported from Fireworks:

24

- If you chose Dreamweaver HTML, use the Insert Fireworks HTML object.
- If you chose Dreamweaver Library, open the Library panel in Dreamweaver and insert the corresponding Library item.
- If you chose Copy To Clipboard, position your cursor where you'd like the graphics to appear and choose Edit ➪ Paste or press Ctrl+V (Command+V).

Both the Library and the Clipboard methods are one-step, self-explanatory techniques—and using the Insert Fireworks HTML object is only a bit more complex. To insert the Fireworks code and images into your Dreamweaver page using the Insert Fireworks HTML object, follow these steps:

1. Make sure that you've exported your graphics and HTML from Fireworks with the Dreamweaver HTML style selected.

2. Select the Fireworks HTML object from the Images menu of the Insert panel's Common category or choose Insert ➪ Image Objects ➪ Fireworks HTML. The Insert Fireworks HTML dialog box, shown in Figure 24-13, appears.

FIGURE 24-13

Import Fireworks code directly into Dreamweaver with the Insert Fireworks HTML object.

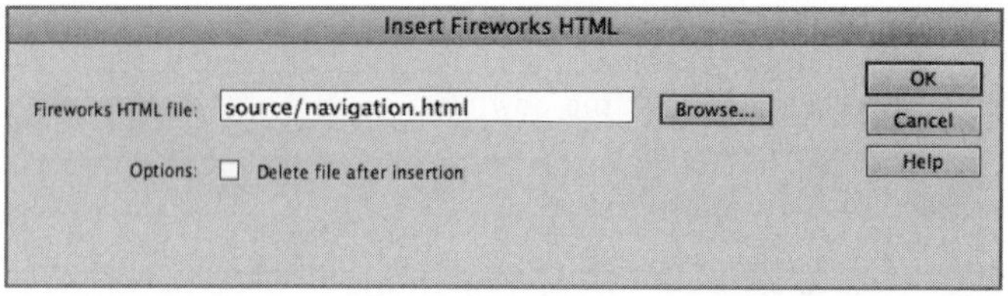

3. If you want to delete the Fireworks-generated HTML file after the code is inserted, select the Delete File After Insertion option. This can help keep your site folder tidy.
4. Enter the path to the Fireworks HTML file or click the Browse button to locate the file.
5. When you're finished, click OK. Dreamweaver inserts the Fireworks HTML and graphics at the current cursor location.

NOTE
If you're a hands-on web designer, you can also use the Code inspector to copy and paste the JavaScript and HTML code.

All the methods for inserting Fireworks HTML work with images that have either hotspots or sliced objects (or both), whether or not behaviors are attached.

Modifying sliced images

Placing sliced images on your web page couldn't be simpler, thanks to the Insert Fireworks HTML command. However, like standard non-sliced graphics, sliced images often need to be modified. One technique that many designers use is to create a framing graphic that contains HTML text; in Fireworks, a sliced area designated as an HTML slice can hold any HTML content. Text often has to be modified. If it is in a framing graphic, the image may need to be changed so that the table cells remain the same size as in the original design. This prevents the separate slices from becoming apparent.

In Dreamweaver, sliced images from Fireworks are recognized as a Fireworks table and can be modified through a dedicated Property inspector, as shown in Figure 24-14. The Fireworks Table Property inspector displays the PNG source file and an Edit button for sending the entire table back to Fireworks for alterations. As with non-sliced graphics, click Done on the document title bar in Fireworks when your modifications are complete to update the source and exported files. The newly exported images are then reloaded into Dreamweaver.

FIGURE 24-14

Modify sliced graphics by first selecting the surrounding table and then clicking the Edit button in the Fireworks Table Property inspector.

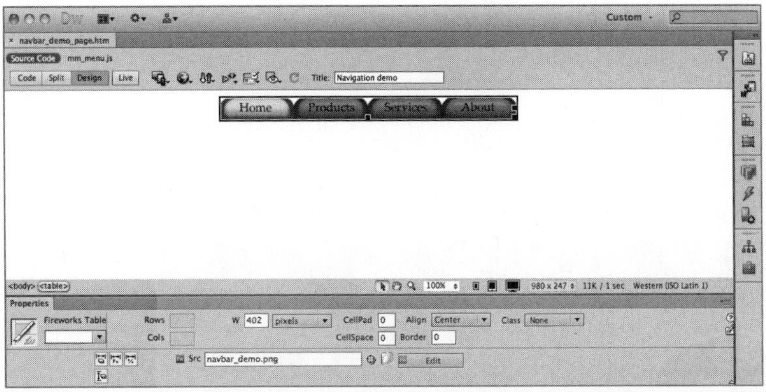

> **CAUTION**
>
> Although Fireworks attempts to honor any changes you make to the HTML table in Dreamweaver, certain changes may cause Fireworks to modify your Dreamweaver table code. If, for example, you add or remove cells to or from the table in Dreamweaver and then go to edit the table in Fireworks, Fireworks displays an alert that it will replace the table in Dreamweaver. To avoid having your original table modified inappropriately by Fireworks, simply click Done right away when you get such an alert (before making any changes). Doing so keeps the original table as-is in Dreamweaver. At this point, make a backup of the entire current page; then go ahead and try out your Fireworks table edit.

Working with Bridge

Few software programs are named more aptly than Adobe Bridge. As a visual browser of images, Flash movies, and documents, Bridge establishes a connection to these assets from the Adobe program. Bridge is installed with every Adobe Creative Suite variation and is available to all programs within those bundles, including Dreamweaver.

Although Bridge displays files, it is far more than an Adobe-built replacement for Windows Explorer on the PC or the Finder on the Mac. With Bridge, you can apply keywords, labels, and ratings to any image or file. Furthermore, Bridge offers powerful sorting capabilities that can filter the displayed thumbnails by date, file type, and keyword. These two key features easily work together. You could, for example, set up a keyword using a client's name and apply that keyword to a set of assets. Then, to locate all the JPEG images associated with the client's keyword with a rating of 3–5 stars, it would take just a few clicks of the mouse.

Dreamweaver offers two methods of launching Bridge. From the menus, choose File ➪ Browse in Bridge to open the program or, from the Standard toolbar, click the Browse in Bridge button (see Figure 24-15). Naturally, there is a keyboard shortcut as well: Ctrl+Alt+O (Command+Option+O).

Once you've located your assets, it's easy to bring them into Dreamweaver. Perhaps the simplest method is to just drag them from Bridge and drop them into Dreamweaver. Bridge has a Compact mode that reduces its window to a quarter size and places it in the bottom left of the screen, always on top (see Figure 24-16). From Bridge, you can also choose the File ➪ Place ➪ In Dreamweaver, and the selected asset will be inserted in the current cursor location in Dreamweaver. If the asset is stored outside of the current site root, you are asked to copy it to the site. Once saved locally, the image is incorporated into the page.

FIGURE 24-15

Launch Bridge right from within Dreamweaver by using the menu, toolbar, or keyboard shortcut.

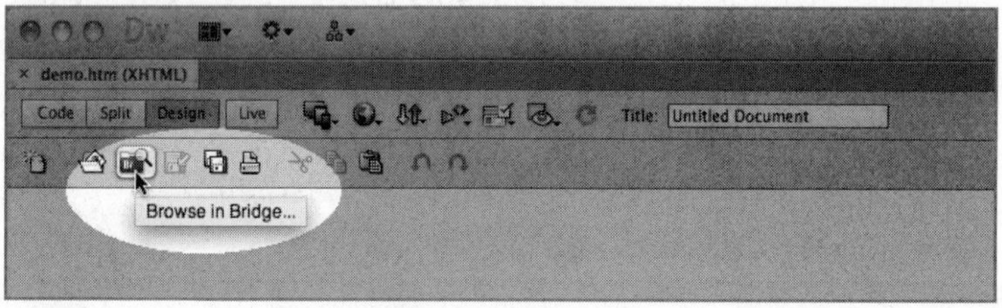

FIGURE 24-16

Working in Bridge's Compact mode allows you to browse your assets and drag them directly into Dreamweaver.

To bring a file shown in Bridge into Dreamweaver, follow these steps:

1. Choose File ➪ Browse in Bridge or, from the Standard toolbar, click Browse in Bridge.
2. When Bridge opens, locate the desired asset.
3. Drag the asset from Bridge to Dreamweaver or, alternatively, choose File ➪ Place ➪ In Dreamweaver.
4. If the asset is located outside of the current site root, a dialog appears to ask if you'd like to copy the file to the site; click Yes and choose a location for the file in the Copy File As dialog box.
5. The asset is placed in the Dreamweaver document.

Because of the ease in which graphic thumbnails are presented, Bridge is most likely to be used in conjunction with graphic assets, but you can access other types of files as well. PDF files, HTML pages, Flash movies, Microsoft Office documents, MP3 files, and more are all displayed in Bridge. All of these file types, with the exception of Flash movies and Microsoft Office documents, are added to the page as a text link. Any SWF file inserts the required code for playing in the web page. If you have Microsoft Office installed, you'll be given an opportunity to insert the document content (Windows only) or the document name as a link (both Windows and Mac).

Summary

Creating web pages is almost never done with a single application: In addition to a web layout program, you need a program capable of outputting web graphics—and both Photoshop and Fireworks provide world-class graphics generators and optimizers. Adobe has integrated several functions with Dreamweaver and its other programs to streamline production and simplify modification. The following are some of the key features:

- Photoshop images can be incorporated into Dreamweaver by opening the PSD file, by copying and pasting it, or by dragging a file into Dreamweaver. In any event, Dreamweaver converts it to a web-ready format of the designer's choosing as a Smart Object. An onscreen symbol indicates whether or not the Smart Object is in sync with its Photoshop source. If not, the Dreamweaver image can be updated with a single click.
- You can update images placed in Dreamweaver with Photoshop or Fireworks in two ways: Optimize or Edit. With the Optimize Image command, just the Image Preview portion of Fireworks opens; with the Edit command, the full versions of Photoshop or Fireworks are run.
- Graphics and HTML exported from Fireworks can be incorporated into a Dreamweaver page in numerous ways: as a Library item, as an HTML file (complete with behavior code), or as an item pasted from the clipboard.
- Adobe's asset manager, Bridge, can be launched and accessed from within Dreamweaver. Files located in Bridge can be dragged directly into Dreamweaver.

In the next chapter, you learn how to incorporate Flash and Shockwave movies into your Dreamweaver web pages.

CHAPTER

25

Inserting Flash Elements

IN THIS CHAPTER

Getting to know Flash

Using Flash in Dreamweaver

Editing Flash movies

Inserting a Shockwave movie

Animated splash screens, sound-enabled banners, button bars with special fonts, and other exciting web elements are often built with Adobe's Flash. Flash combines vector graphics and streaming into great-looking, very-low-bandwidth files that can be viewed in a browser using the Flash Player plugin. Flash's vector graphics have also turned out to be just the thing for web-based animations. Over a number of versions, Flash morphed into a solid application platform, with player implementations in cell phones, handheld devices, and even billboards. Although Flash has taken its knocks in the mobile arena, a huge base of installed web-based players remains, and Flash is still a popular way to liven up a web page, particularly for a non-mobile website.

As you might expect, Adobe makes it easy to incorporate Flash files into your Dreamweaver projects. All these formats have special objects that provide control over nearly all their parameters through the Property inspector—and each format is cross-browser compatible by default. To take full advantage of the enhanced graphics potential of Flash, you need to understand the various parameters available to each format. In addition to covering this material, this chapter shows you how to use independent controls—both inline and with frames—for your Flash movies.

This chapter also covers related Adobe technologies, including Shockwave.

One of the most exciting options in Dreamweaver is the inclusion of Flash video. This topic is covered in Chapter 26.

Including SWF Files in Dreamweaver Projects

Dreamweaver makes it easy to bring Flash files—also known as SWF files—into your web pages. The Insert panel provides an object for each type of movie, located in the Media menu of the Common category. Dreamweaver enables you to play the SWF in the Document window when in Live View. When not playing, Dreamweaver displays a plugin placeholder icon (see Figure 25-1). The inserted code is valid HTML and works cross-browser.

FIGURE 25-1

Dreamweaver includes many interface elements for working with Flash.

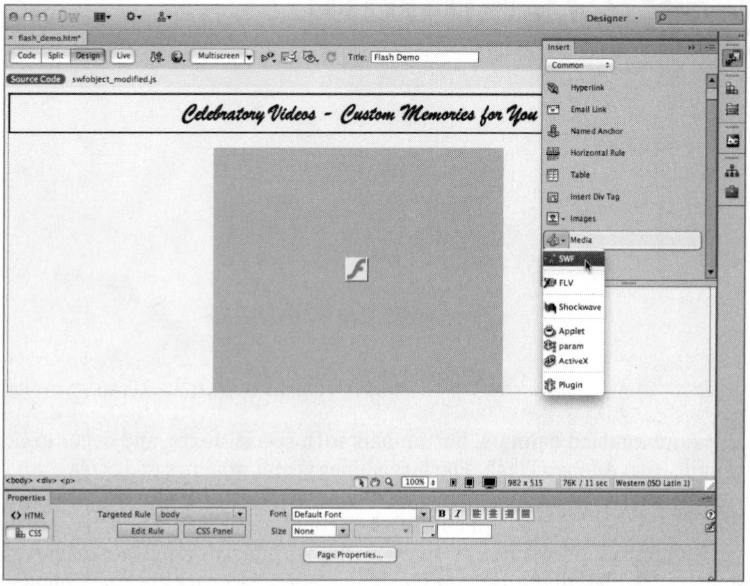

To include an SWF file in your web page, follow these steps:

1. Position the cursor in the Document window where you'd like the movie to appear.
2. Insert the movie using any of the following methods:
   - Choose Insert ➪ Media ➪ SWF from the main Dreamweaver menu.
   - From the Media menu of the Insert panel's Common category, choose SWF.
   - Drag the movie object from the SWF category of the Assets panel to the Document window.
3. In the Select File dialog box, enter the path and the filename in the File Name text box or click the Browse button to locate the file. Click OK.

NOTE

If you drag the movie from the Assets panel, Step 3 is not applicable because Dreamweaver automatically sets the File attribute to that of your movie file.

4. If you clicked OK in the Select File dialog box, and if Media is selected in your Accessibility preferences (Edit ➪ Preferences ➪ Accessibility or Dreamweaver ➪ Preferences ➪ Accessibility on a Mac), the Object Tag Accessibility Attributes dialog box appears, as shown in Figure 25-2. In the Title field, enter a title for your media object.

FIGURE 25-2

Use the Object Tag Accessibility Attributes dialog box to specify a title, access key, and tab index for your inserted media objects.

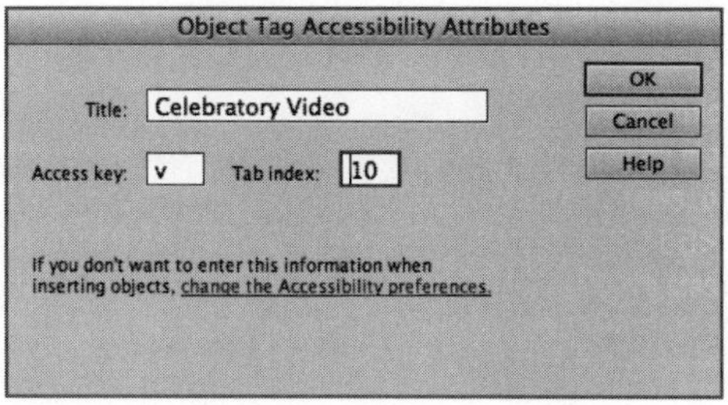

5. In the Access Key field, enter a one-letter access key for your object to select the object in the browser with the proper key combination, which varies by browser—and even browser version. For example, for Internet Explorer, you'd press Alt (Option) + access key; with Safari 3, it's Alt (Ctrl) + access key, but for Safari 4 and later, it's Alt (Ctrl+Option) plus the access key.

NOTE

Entering an Access Key value only places the accesskey attribute in the <object> tag; it's up to the browser to properly interpret what action, if any, should be taken when the access key combination is pressed.

6. In the Tab Index field, enter a number for the tab index of your object. By entering a number, you can specify the order in which users tab through objects and links on your page. Pressing Tab successively jumps from the object or link whose tab index is set to 1, to the object or link whose tab index is set to 2, and so on. For this to work correctly, you must specify the tabindex attribute for all the page's objects and links.

   Dreamweaver inserts a small plugin placeholder in the current cursor position, and the Property inspector displays the appropriate information for an SWF file, with the correct width and height dimensions.
7. Preview the SWF file in the Document window by choosing Live View.
8. End the preview of your file by toggling off Live View.

The code inserted is an evolved technique designed to work across browsers while remaining web-standards compliant. This Flash embedding method uses the SWFObject.js file developed by Geoff Stearns, Michael Williams, and Bobby van der Sluis of SWFFix and modified by the Dreamweaver engineering team. Whenever you insert a Flash file, Dreamweaver includes two external files (swfobject_modified.js and expressinstall.swf) along with the standardized <object> tag.

The inserted code accomplishes a number of goals:

- Plays SWF files in a wide variety of browsers including Internet Explorer 5 and greater, Netscape 7, Opera 7.5 and greater, and all versions of Firefox, Safari, and Mozilla.

- Sets up Flash Player version detection.
- Includes in-place Flash Player installation.
- Auto-activates the Flash content in Internet Explorer browsers.
- Validates as standard HTML/XHTML.

CAUTION

You must be sure to upload the two dependent files when you publish your site to the web. Failure to do so will result in your SWF file not playing or even being visible. Although Dreamweaver reminds you to transfer the files the first time you save your page after inserting an SWF file, it's easy to forget to do so. Failure to upload these files is the number one problem users have when working with Flash content: The Dreamweaver forums are littered with folks falling into this trap.

Designating SWF Attributes

SWF files require some basic parameters to play correctly and also offer a number of optional parameters as well. Dreamweaver allows you to set almost all the attributes for Flash movies through the Property inspector.

To set or modify the attributes for an SWF file, follow these steps:

1. After your Flash movie has been inserted in the Document window, make sure that it is selected. Dreamweaver automatically inserts the correct dimensions for your Flash movie.
2. Set any attributes in the Property inspector as needed for your Flash movie. In addition, you can also set the parameters described in Table 25-1.

TABLE 25-1 Additional Property Inspector Options for Flash Objects

Flash Parameter	Possible Values	Description
Autoplay	Checked (default)	Enables the Flash movie to begin playing as soon as possible.
Loop	Checked (default)	Plays movie continuously if checked; otherwise, movie plays once.
Quality		Controls anti-aliasing during playback.
	High (default)	Anti-aliasing is turned on. This can slow the playback frame rate considerably on slower computers.
	Low	No anti-aliasing is used; this setting is best for animations that must be played quickly.
	Auto High	The animation begins in High (with anti-aliasing) and switches to Low if the host computer is too slow.

Flash Parameter	Possible Values	Description
	Auto Low	Starts the animation in Low (no anti-aliasing) and then switches to High if the host machine is fast enough.
Src		Specifies the .fla Flash source file. To edit an .swf Flash movie file, you must modify the movie's .fla source file.
Scale		Determines how the movie fits into the dimensions as specified in the Width and Height text boxes.
	Show All (default)	Displays the entire movie in the given dimensions while maintaining the file's original aspect ratio. Some of the background may be visible with this setting.
	Exact Fit	Scales the movie precisely into the dimensions without regard for the aspect ratio. It is possible that the image could be distorted with this setting.
	No Border	Fits the movie into the given dimensions so that no borders are showing and maintains the original aspect ratio. Some of the movie may be cut off with this setting.
Wmode		Determines how the movie is rendered in regard to the background.
	Window (default)	Displays the movie in its own window on top of other content.
	Opaque	Renders the movie in accordance to z-index values.
	Transparent	Allows elements under the movie to show through the background of the movie if the background is transparent.

Setting Scale in Flash movies

To avoid unexpected results, be careful when setting the Scale parameter. If you have to size a Flash movie out of its aspect ratio, the Flash Player must know what to do with any extra room it has to fill. Figure 25-3 demonstrates the different results that the Scale attribute can provide. Only the picture on the left is at its proper dimensions.

TIP

Dreamweaver makes it easy to rescale a Flash movie. First, in the Property inspector, make sure the original width and height of your file are displayed in the W and H text boxes. Then, while holding down the Shift key, click and drag the corner resizing handle of the Flash placeholder icon to the new size for the movie. By Shift+dragging, you retain the aspect ratio set in the Property inspector, which enables you to quickly enlarge or reduce your movie without distortion.

FIGURE 25-3

Your setting for the Scale attribute determines how your movie is viewed when resized with the plugin width and height measurements.

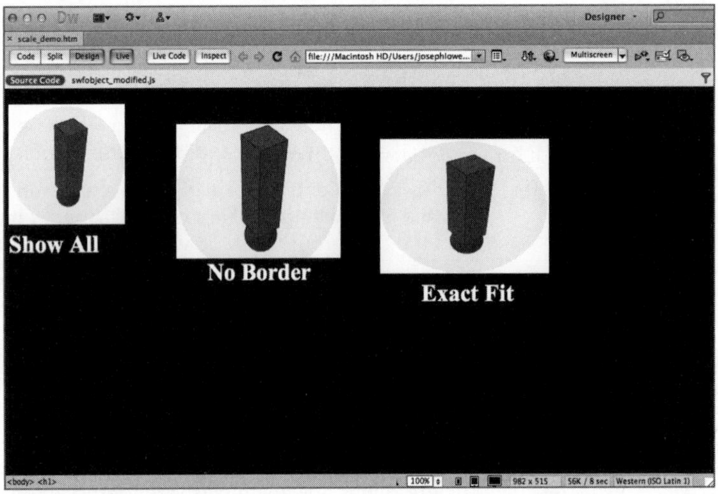

Additional parameters for Flash

Flash has two additional attributes that can be entered through the Parameters dialog box (click the Parameters button on the Property inspector): `salign` and `swliveconnect`. The `salign` attribute determines how the movie aligns itself to the surrounding frame when the Scale attribute is set to Show All. In addition, `salign` determines which portion of the image is cut off when the Scale attribute is set to No Border. The alignment can be set to L (left), R (right), T (top), or B (bottom). You can also use these values in combination. For example, if you set `salign` to `RB`, the movie aligns with the bottom-right edge or the lower-right corner of the frame.

The `swliveconnect` attribute comes into play when you're using FSCommands or JavaScript in your Flash movies. FSCommands are interactive commands, such as Go To URL, issued from inside the Flash movie. The Netscape browser initializes Java when first called—and if your Flash movie uses FSCommands or JavaScript, it uses Java to communicate with the Netscape Plugin interface, LiveConnect. Because not all Flash movies need the LiveConnect connection, you can prevent Java from being initialized by entering the `swliveconnect` attribute in the Parameters dialog box and setting its value to `false`. When the `swliveconnect=false` parameter is found by the browser, the Java is not initialized as part of the loading process—and your movie loads more quickly.

Configuring MIME Types

As with any plugin, your web server has to have the correct MIME types set before Shockwave files can be properly served to your users. If your web page plays Shockwave and Flash movies locally, but not remotely, chances are good that the correct MIME types need to be added. The system administrator generally handles configuring MIME types.

The system administrator needs to know the following information to correctly configure the MIME types:

- **Flash:** `application/x-shockwave-flash` (`.swf`)
- **Shockwave:** `application/x-director` (`.dcr, .dir, .dxr`)

Both Shockwave and Flash are popular plugins, and it's likely that the web server is already configured to recognize the appropriate file types.

Editing SWF Files from Within Dreamweaver

You can modify Flash movies only so much within Dreamweaver—certain changes require that the movie source be altered in Flash itself. Dreamweaver provides a direct connection to Flash: Flash Edit. You can edit your Flash movies from within Dreamweaver (provided, of course, that you have Flash installed on your system and the FLA source file). Dreamweaver doesn't do the actual movie editing work, of course. Here's how it works.

When you click the Flash Edit button, Dreamweaver launches Flash; you edit your movie in Flash, save your update, exit Flash, and end up back in Dreamweaver. It makes for a seamless Dreamweaver/Flash collaboration.

To edit a Flash movie from within Dreamweaver, follow these steps:

1. In Dreamweaver, open the document that contains the Flash movie.
2. Do one of the following to begin editing your movie in Flash:
   - Select the Flash movie placeholder, and in the Flash Property inspector, click the Edit button.
   - Ctrl+double-click (Command+double-click) the Flash movie placeholder.
   - Right-click (Control+click) the movie placeholder, and choose Edit with Flash from the shortcut menu.
3. Dreamweaver launches Flash and automatically opens the selected movie's source FLA file or prompts you to open it manually. (To enable Flash to open the FLA file automatically, you must assign it to the Flash object's Src field in Dreamweaver.)
4. In Flash, make changes to your movie. The Flash Document window indicates that you are editing a movie from Dreamweaver, as shown in Figure 25-4.
5. When you are finished editing in Flash, click the Done button. Flash saves your changes to the source FLA file, updates the SWF file, and then whisks you back to Dreamweaver.

FIGURE 25-4

Using Dreamweaver's Flash Edit button, you can edit your Flash movies without having to exit/restart the Dreamweaver program.

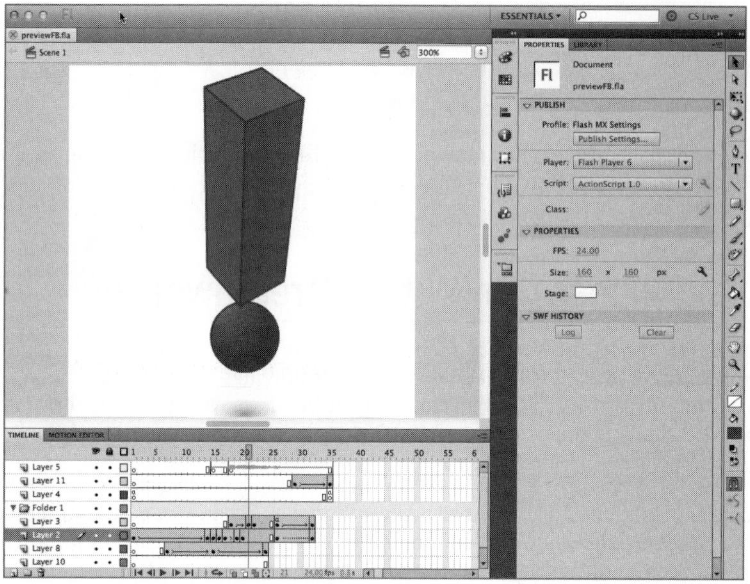

Adding Shockwave Files

Flash is not Adobe's only solution for building interactive presentations for the web. For many web designers, Shockwave was their first introduction to web interactivity. With Shockwave, multimedia files created in Adobe's flagship CD-ROM authoring package, Director, can be compiled to run in a browser window. This functionality gives web designers the capability to build just about anything—including arcade-style games and multimedia web front-ends—bringing a CD-ROM look and feel to the web.

Before you can successfully include a Shockwave file, you need to know one small bit of information—the dimensions of your movie. Dreamweaver automatically reads the dimensions of your Flash file when you insert the Flash movie object. Unfortunately, if you're incorporating a Shockwave movie, you must enter the dimensions in the Property inspector. To find the width and height of a Shockwave movie, load it into Director and then choose Modify ➪ Movie ➪ Properties to open the Property inspector. The dimensions are located on the Movie category of the inspector.

To add a Shockwave file to your web page, follow these steps:

1. Place your cursor where you'd like to insert the Shockwave movie.
2. Insert the movie using any of the following methods:

- Choose Insert ⇨ Media ⇨ Shockwave from the main Dreamweaver menu.
- From the Media menu of the Insert panel's Common category, choose Shockwave.
- Drag the movie object from the Assets panel to the Document window. Remember to choose the appropriate category in the Assets panel: Shockwave or Flash.

3. In the Select File dialog box, enter the path and the filename in the File Name text box or click the Browse button to locate the file. Click OK.

   Shockwave files use a `.dcr` extension.

NOTE
As with Flash, if you drag the Shockwave movie from the Assets panel, Step 3 is not needed.

Dreamweaver displays a placeholder for the Shockwave file. You'll need to preview the file in a browser with the Shockwave plugin to see your movie in action.

You can apply a number of attributes to fine-tune your Shockwave file; they're described in Table 25-2.

TABLE 25-2 Property Inspector Parameters for Shockwave Objects

Shockwave Parameters	Description
Align	Enables you to choose an option to alter the alignment of the movie. In addition to the browser default, your options include Baseline, Top, Middle, Bottom, Texttop, Absolute Middle, Absolute Bottom, Left, and Right.
Bg	Enables you to specify a background color for the movie area. Note that this color also appears while the movie is loading and after it is done playing.
V Space	Enables you to increase the amount of space between other elements on the page and the top and bottom of the movie plugin by entering a pixel value in the V (Vertical) Space text box. Again, the default is zero.
H Space	Enables you to increase the space to the left and right of the movie by entering a value in the H (Horizontal) Space text box. The default is zero.
Name	Enables you to enter a unique name in the unlabeled field on the far left of the Property inspector. The name is used by JavaScript and other languages to identify the movie.
W	Sets the width of the movie.
H	Sets the height of the movie.
Class	Applies the CSS class to the movie.

Summary

Together, the interactive power of Shockwave and the speedy glitz of Flash can enliven web content like nothing else. Dreamweaver is extremely well suited for integrating and displaying Shockwave and Flash movies. Here are some key points to keep in mind:

- Flash movies are a way to enhance your web pages with vector animations, interactivity, and streaming audio. Flash movies require the Flash Player plugin or ActiveX control.
- Dreamweaver has built-in objects for Flash movies, also called SWF files. All the important parameters are accessible directly through the Property inspector.
- Dreamweaver automatically writes code to handle a full range of browsers; however, you must be sure to upload the generated JavaScript file found in the Scripts folder along with `expressInstall.swf`.
- Saving your Director movies as Shockwave movies enables them to be played on the web with the help of a plugin or ActiveX control.
- You can launch Flash to edit Flash movies right from within Dreamweaver.
- You need only three parameters to incorporate a Shockwave movie: the file's location, height, and width. Dreamweaver automatically imports a Flash movie's dimensions. You can get the exact measurements of a Shockwave movie from within Director.

In the next chapter, you learn how to add video to your web pages.

CHAPTER

26

Adding Video to Your Web Page

IN THIS CHAPTER

Creating video for the web

Dreamweaver Technique: Adding Flash Video

Including video clips in your web pages

Inserting QuickTime Player movies

Using streaming videos

Coding HTML5 Video

There's no doubt that video on the web has truly come into its own. From online video's humble beginnings as a grainy, jerky, quarter-screen-sized moving image to the full-screen, high-fidelity movie-like imagery of today, video is an essential element for many websites.

There are numerous plugins for video playback including Adobe Flash video, QuickTime, RealVideo, and Windows Media Player. With all of these players, video can be downloaded to the user and then automatically played with a helper application, or it can be streamed to the user so that it plays while it's downloading. However, there is no single plugin that can play on all desktops and mobile devices.

With the introduction of the HTML5 `<video>` tag, plugin free video is not only an option, it could very well be the future. Dreamweaver CS6 offers full code-hinting support to this new (but growing) kid on the block.

This chapter describes the many different methods for incorporating video—whether you're downloading an MPEG file or streaming a movie—into your web pages through Dreamweaver.

Dreamweaver QUICKSTART

While there are several different ways to add video to your Dreamweaver pages, by far the most popular is Flash video, specifically Flash progressive video, which doesn't require a special server. Here's the quickest way to get this type of video up and running:

1. Make sure your page is saved, and place your cursor where you'd like Flash video to appear.

Continues

continued

2. From the Common category of the Insert panel, click Media: FLV.

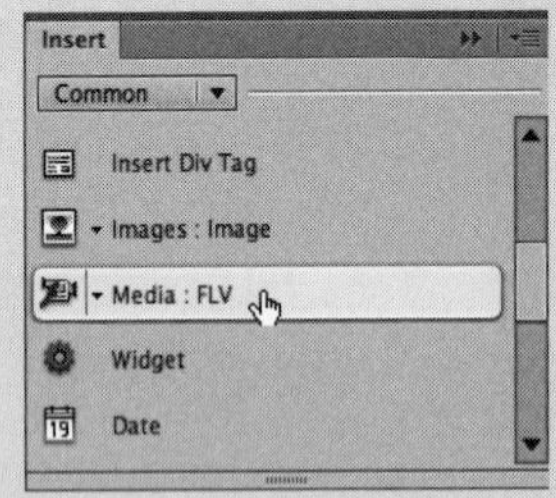

3. When the Insert FLV dialog box appears, make sure Video Type is set to Progressive Download Video and click Browse to locate the FLV file.
4. Choose the types of player controls you'd like from the Skin list, the size of the movie, and the desired options. Click OK.
5. When you publish your files online, be sure to upload the JavaScript files necessary to display the Flash video and the associated FLV and SWF files.

Web video in general and Flash video in particular constitute a very rich field to explore as you'll learn as you move ahead in this chapter.

The Flash Video Revolution

With the introduction of video in Flash MX, Adobe planted the seeds of a revolution. Suddenly, video on the web was easy. Although early Flash video did not have the same quality as the more established players such as QuickTime, it had one major advantage: ubiquity. With a cross-platform player proliferation of more than 90 percent, Flash video's accessibility outweighed its drawbacks. Adobe built on the intense interest generated by the early player's capabilities and improved the video output and experience with each subsequent release. Video output by the current version, Flash Professional CS6, is certainly as good as video displayed by any other web method. It must be noted, however, that Flash video is unable to play on iOS devices (such as the iPhone and iPad) and will likely be restricted from Android devices as well in the near future.

Any Dreamweaver web designer or developer has the power to easily incorporate high-quality video into any site. Ease of entry is a key factor, and Dreamweaver makes it drop-in simple; designers can even gain the majority of benefits of Flash video without incurring the additional expense of a specialized server. For those clients and projects that require a higher-end experience, Flash offers a streaming alternative. As you learn later in this chapter, Dreamweaver's Insert Flash Video feature handles either option easily.

Encoding video

To incorporate Flash video on your site, you'll need to first acquire the video, either by importing it directly from a digital camera or by retrieving a file in a video format, such as `.avi`, `.mpg`,

`.mov`, or `.wmv`. After you have a video file, you'll need to convert it to a Flash video file (FLV) in a process called *encoding*. Encoding a video compresses it using a specific algorithm or codec. FLV files encoded with Sorenson Spark can be played in Flash Player 6 and higher, whereas On2 VP6-encoded FLV files require Flash Player 8 or higher. High-definition video must be encoded in FLV format with the H.264 codec and needs Flash Player 9 or higher.

Numerous paths to encoding FLV files are available, including the following:

- **Flash Video Import Wizard:** A feature of Flash Professional, the Flash Video Import Wizard works with all popular video formats, including QuickTime movies, Video for Windows (`.avi`), Windows Media (`.wmv`), and video directly retrieved from your camera (`.dv` or `.dvi`). The Flash Video Import Wizard works with one video file at a time.
- **Adobe Media Encoder:** The Adobe Media Encoder is a separate program included with Flash Professional (see Figure 26-1). The key advantage to the Media Encoder is that it allows you to encode many video files (again, from all formats) to an FLV-compatible codec. Encoding a video file can be time-intensive: a 35-second video took 23 minutes to encode in On2 VP6 format at medium quality.
- **Third-party applications:** A number of third-party batch encoding tools now support the FLV format as well. For example, you can convert video to FLV format with Telestream Agility 2G.

When encoding, you'll need to decide which type of video output to use: *streaming* or *progressive*. The relative pros and cons are discussed in the next section.

TIP

There is a third type of Flash video output to use: *embedding*. When you embed video in a Flash movie (which would then be inserted into the web page), you're combining both video and Flash animation in a single movie. This process results in a much larger file and is only really useful for videos lasting 5 seconds or less. It is strongly recommended by Adobe and others that your video remain an external file and not be embedded.

Progressive download versus streaming

One of the first questions you'll need to address when adding Flash video to your web page is: How will the video be delivered? The two core methods available are *progressive download* and *streaming*. Both methods are alike in that they use external video files in FLV format in conjunction with an `.swf` file that acts as a video player.

Progressive download begins playing as soon as the first segment has been received by the site visitor and continues to download while the video is playing. Typically, the delay is relatively short, but there it may be longer depending on download speed. There is, however, a major plus for progressive download over streaming: You can host the files on any kind of server. Because progressive download does not require a specialized server, such as Flash Media Server (formerly Flash Communication Server), it is much less expensive to display.

TIP

You'll need at least Flash Player 7 if you use the progressive download method; streaming video can use Flash Player 6 or better.

FIGURE 26-1

Open the Adobe Media Encoder settings to choose the optimal delivery quality for your Flash video.

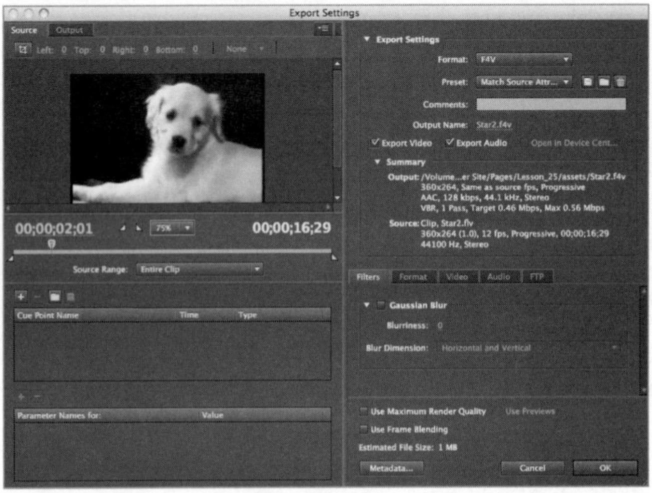

Streaming video, however, can definitely be worth the cost. Video begins playing almost immediately and is more efficient for both the network in general and the viewer's computer specifically. Streaming video is also fully *seekable*—in other words, the video playhead can be moved anywhere to instantly view video from that point. With progressive download, you can only seek portions of the video that have already been downloaded. The truly advanced features of web video—live feed, interactive control, video messaging, and so on—are only possible with streaming video.

NOTE

A couple of hosted streaming services are available for Flash video. Adobe has partnered with a number of content delivery providers under their Flash Video Streaming Service umbrella aimed at enterprise customers; learn more by visiting `www.adobe.com/products/flashmediaserver/fvss`.

Inserting Flash video

The FLV object makes it as easy to add Flash video to your web page as it is to add any other Flash movie—with even greater flexibility and control. Not only is your video added to the page, but it's accompanied by your choice of built-in controller. Flash detection code is automatically added to your page so that users are alerted if they don't have the required version.

As noted before, your choice of delivery method for your video—either progressive download or streaming—is a key one. The importance of this choice is reflected in the Insert FLV dialog box; depending on your choice, different options appear, and the steps for including a video object vary. For this reason, instructions for including an FLV object of each type are presented separately.

Including a progressive download FLV file

To add a progressive download FLV object to your page, follow these steps:

1. Place your cursor where you'd like the FLV object to appear.
2. From the Insert panel's Common category, choose Media: FLV.

   The Insert FLV dialog box appears, as shown in Figure 26-2.
3. Make sure that Progressive Download Video is selected in the Video Type list.
4. Click Browse to locate the desired FLV video file or enter the path directly into the URL field.

FIGURE 26-2

Progressive download video can be hosted on any standard web server.

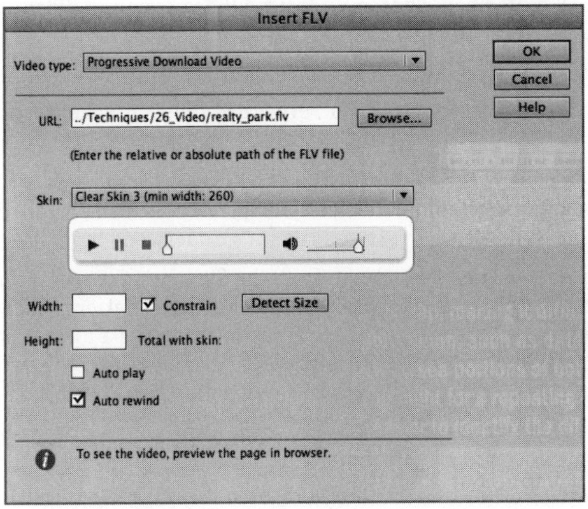

5. Choose the type of controller you'd like from the Skin list.

   You have three basic choices (Clear Skin, Corona Skin, and Halo Skin), each in three variations. Each variation within a given style offers a different set of controls and requires a different minimum width. The preview area gives you a clear idea of what to expect, and the minimum widths are listed for each entry.
6. Enter the dimensions of the movie (including controller) by either clicking Detect Size or entering the values directly into the Width and Height fields.
7. If you'd like the movie to begin as soon as possible when the page loads, select the Auto Play option.
8. If you'd like the movie to rewind to the beginning after it has played, enable the Auto Rewind option.
9. Click OK when you're done.

You can see your video in action by previewing the page in a browser.

TIP

To see the message displayed for a site visitor without the proper Flash Player version installed, click the Eye icon on the tab above the inserted FLV object. The default message is: "Content on this page requires a newer version of Adobe Flash Player." You're free to change it if you like, although it's a good idea to keep the Get Adobe Flash Player graphic and corresponding link so folks can see your video properly.

Adding a streaming FLV file

To add a streaming FLV object to your page, follow these steps:

1. Place your cursor where you'd like the FLV object to appear.
2. From the Insert panel's Common category, choose Media: FLV.
3. In the Insert FLV dialog box, choose Streaming Video from the Video Type list. The options in the dialog box change, as shown in Figure 26-3.
4. Enter the path to the streaming server, application, and instance in the URI field.

   Streaming servers like the Flash Media Server use the Real Time Messaging Protocol, designated by `rtmp://`. An example of a full URI is `rtmp://123.45.678.90/bigVid/bv`.
5. Enter the name of the FLV file you'd like to display in the Stream Name field. (You can leave off the `.flv` file extension if you like; it's understood by the server.)
6. Choose the type of controller you'd like from the Skin list. There are three basic choices (Clear Skin, Corona Skin, and Halo Skin), each in three variations. Each variation within a given style offers a different set of controls and requires a different minimum width. The preview area gives you a clear idea of what to expect, and the minimum widths are listed for each entry.
7. Enter the dimensions of the movie (including controller) by either clicking Detect Size or entering the values directly into the Width and Height fields.
8. If you're broadcasting live video, click the Live Video Feed option.
9. If you'd like the movie to begin as soon as possible when the page loads, select the Auto Play option.
10. If you'd like the movie to rewind to the beginning after it has played, enable the Auto Rewind option.
11. Enter the number of seconds of video you'd like to buffer before it begins playing. The default buffer value is `0`, which means the video will be available for playing immediately after the page loads. Extend the buffer value if your video is encoded at a higher bit rate than the site visitor's connection speed or if connectivity problems persist.
12. Click OK when you're done.

You'll need to publish your files to the server, as described in the next section, before you can view the streaming video in your web page.

FIGURE 26-3

Streaming video requires a specialized Flash video server, such as Flash Media Server.

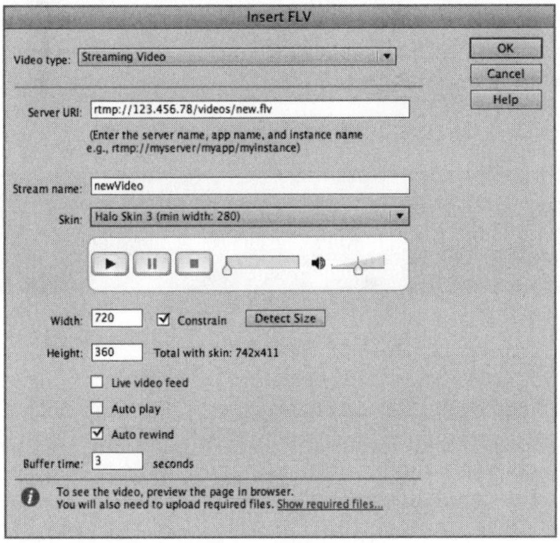

Publishing Flash video files

An FLV object actually requires a number of files to be viewed on the HTML page. In addition to the encoded video file with the `.flv` extension, it requires a container file called either `FLVPlayer_Progressive.swf` or `FLVPlayer_Streaming.swf`, depending on your choice of delivery method; this container file is the actual Flash movie called by the Flash Player. A file holding the video controls or skin is also used—for example, `Clear_Skin_1.swf`. Both of these support files are created for you by the Insert Flash Video object in the same folder as the HTML page the video is inserted in. Streaming video also requires that another generated file, `main.asc`, be placed in the Application folder of your Flash Media Server or Flash Communications Server. Finally, because Dreamweaver automatically writes the Flash code to web standards and makes an express install available if the page visitor doesn't have the right version of Flash installed, you'll also need to upload the `swfobject_modified.js` and `expressInstall.swf` files found in the Scripts folder of your site root.

Publishing the files to the server for either type of Flash video delivery can be accomplished in a simplified operation. If you are publishing a progressive download video, make sure that Dreamweaver Preferences are set to prompt you to upload dependent files when your page is put or checked in. Both `.swf` support files and the FLV video file are considered dependent files by Dreamweaver and will be published to their correct locations when you click OK to upload dependent files.

CAUTION

If you don't rely on Dreamweaver's capability to publish dependent files, make sure that you publish all the associated files or your video will not be visible to your site visitors.

A similar publishing capability is available for streaming Flash videos, with significant differences. When you select the inserted streaming video object, a custom Property inspector is displayed. In addition to permitting the modification of most Flash Video object attributes, the Property inspector also contains an Upload Media button. When you click Upload Media, the two created `.swf` files for the container and the skin are uploaded to the specified web server; as noted by a Dreamweaver alert, you will be required to publish the `main.asc` and the FLV file to your streaming server Applications folder.

TIP

Should you choose not to take advantage of the Upload Media feature, you can select the Show Required Files link in the Property inspector to see what files need to go where for your streaming video.

Modifying Flash video parameters

Each of the different types of Flash Video object has its own Property inspector. Both allow easy modification of most previously set attributes; only the type of delivery, progressive video or streaming, is omitted. If you need to change a movie from one delivery type to another, you'll need to delete the inserted object and re-select Insert Flash Video to choose a different type.

With a streaming Flash Video object, you have the option of altering the dimensions, the skin, the options to Auto Play or Auto Rewind, and, most important, the video source (see Figure 26-4). Because the FLV video source file is external to the video container, database-driven applications can even set the source dynamically.

FIGURE 26-4

Once a progressive download video object has been inserted into the page, you can alter almost all the parameters through the custom Property inspector.

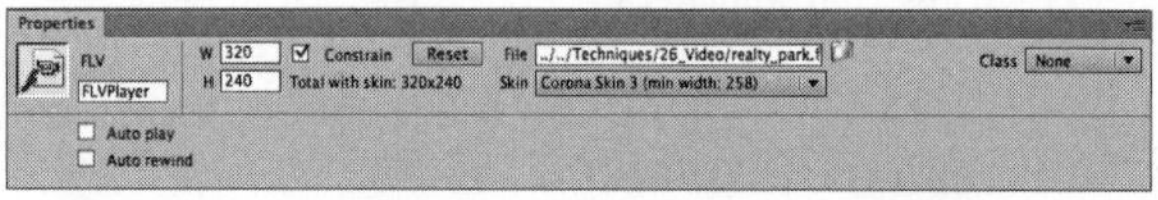

CAUTION

As noted earlier, the Insert Flash Video object stores the additional dependent files it creates in the same location at the current web page. If you want to move either the skin `.swf` or the source FLV to a more appropriate folder, you'll have to adjust the inserted code. Although Dreamweaver will ask if you want to update the `.swf` and web page, the `<object>` tags that compose the Flash movie are not changed. If you move the skin `.swf` file, change the Skin value in the `FlashVars param` statement of the `<object>` tags. Likewise, if you move the source FLV file, change the `streamName` value in both object tags.

Dreamweaver TECHNIQUE

Adding Flash Video

In this Dreamweaver Technique, you insert a progressive download video into a web page, complete with overlaid video controls.

1. From the Techniques site, expand the 26_Video folder and open the `video_start` file.
2. Place your cursor at the start of the placeholder paragraph, below the Explore the Neighborhood headline.
3. From the Common category of the Insert panel, choose Media: FLV.
4. When the Insert FLV dialog box opens, make sure that Video Type is set to Progressive Download Video.
5. Click Browse and locate the `realty_park.flv` file in the 26_Video folder.
6. From the Skin list, choose Corona Skin 2 (min width: 141).
7. Click Detect Size to retrieve the original video dimensions.
8. Select the Auto Rewind option and click OK to close the dialog box.
9. From the Property inspector Class list, choose imageRight.
10. Save the file and then press F12 (Option+F12) to preview the file in your primary browser.

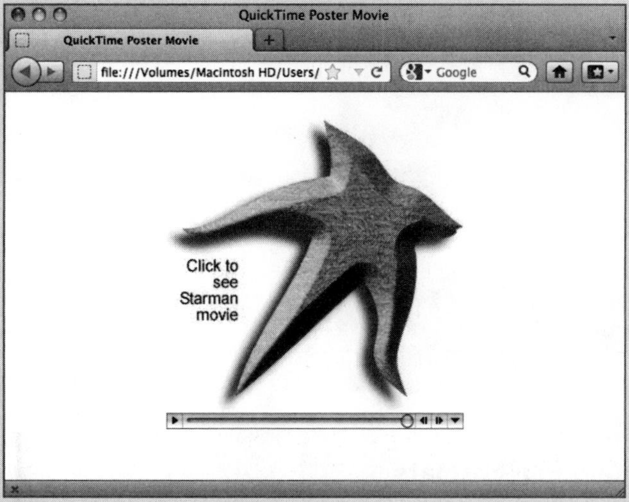

The video controls are displayed on the initial image until you click Play. After the movie begins playing, if you move your cursor off the video, the controls disappear; they reappear whenever your mouse pointer hovers over the video.

Working with Video Clips

If you have short video clips you'd like to put on the web, you may not need the industrial strength—or the hassle and expense—of a streaming media solution. Short video clips can be included in a web page just by linking to them or embedding them.

Depending on the viewer's software setup, video clips either download completely and then start playing right away or start playing as soon as enough of the video has arrived to make uninterrupted playback possible, as shown in Figure 26-5.

Video clips come in a few common formats, described in Table 26-1. In addition to the video format itself, what *codec* (encoder/decoder) a particular video clip uses is also important. A codec provides video compression, and it is required for decompression at playback time. Many codecs are included with Windows and with QuickTime, so codecs are not usually a problem unless you're authoring for platforms other than Windows and Macintosh.

FIGURE 26-5

QuickTime Player starts playing video clips when it has downloaded enough to ensure that playback is uninterrupted.

TABLE 26-1 Video Clip File Formats

Video Format	Typical Filename Extension	Description
MPEG	.mpg, .mpeg, .mpe, mp4	The MPEG video format is the work of the Motion Picture Experts Group. Windows computers usually play MPEG video clips with Windows Media Player or another, older Microsoft player. Macintosh systems play MPEG clips with QuickTime.

Video Format	Typical Filename Extension	Description
OGG Theora	.ogg	A format developed by the Xigh open source foundation used in the HTML5 <video> tag.
QuickTime	.mov	QuickTime movies can contain a multitude of media types and usually require QuickTime for playback.
QuickTime Video	.mov	A QuickTime movie that contains plain video only and can be played by almost any video player on a machine that doesn't have QuickTime installed, as long as the right codec is available.
Video for Windows (AVI)	.avi	The popular (but now officially unsupported) format used by Microsoft's Video for Windows (also known as ActiveMovie or NetShow). As with QuickTime Video, clips can be played in almost any player, as long as the right codec is installed.
WebM	.webm	A royalty-free high-quality video container pioneered by Google for use in HTML5 <video> tag.

MPEG, QuickTime Video, or AVI clips are good candidates for linking or embedding because a wide variety of players on multiple platforms can play them. QuickTime movies are best aimed squarely at the QuickTime Player because of the multiple media types that they contain. If you're using the HTML5 <video> tag, you'll need to make available .mp4, .ogg, and .webm formats to achieve cross-browser compatibilty.

Linking to video

To keep twenty-first century TV/movie-addicted users interested in your site, you might want to spice things up by including a (low-bandwidth!) video or two. To add a video clip to your Dreamweaver web page, follow these steps:

1. Select the text, image, or dynamic element that you want to serve as the link to the video file.

TIP

If you use an image as a link, you might want to use a frame from the video clip in order to provide a preview.

2. In the Property inspector, enter the name of the video file in the Link text field or click the Folder icon to browse for the file, as shown in Figure 26-6. To choose a dynamic source, choose the Select File Name From Data Sources option in the Select File dialog box. Be sure your selected data source contains either relative or absolute links to a video file.
3. Because video files can be quite large, it's also good practice to note the file size next to the link name or enter it in the Alt text field.

FIGURE 26-6

You can insert any video file for user-download by creating a link to it, as if it were a simple web page.

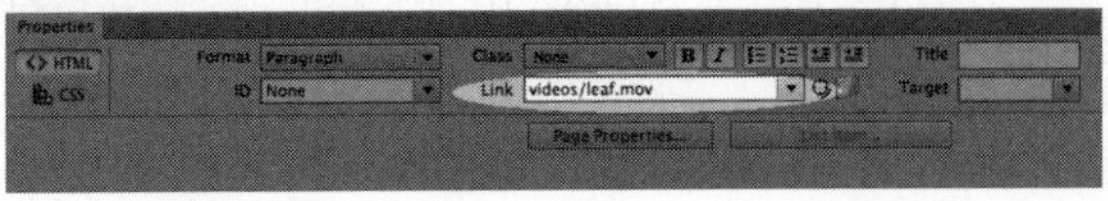

Embedding video

You can gain more control over the way your video clip plays by embedding it in the web page with the `<embed>` tag. Modifying the attributes of the `<embed>` tag enables you to modify how the video is presented. Video clips inserted this way play back in whatever players are available, just as linked video clips do.

The Assets panel includes a Movies category that holds QuickTime movies and MPEG videos. As with all the other Assets panel categories, you must click the Refresh Site List button (the curved arrow at the bottom of the Assets panel) to initially populate the panel with all the movies in the current site.

To embed a simple video clip in a web page, follow these steps:

1. Choose Insert ➪ Media ➪ Plugin. Alternatively, you can select the Plugin object from the Media menu of the Insert panel found in the Common category or drag the file from the Movie category of the Assets panel to your web page.
2. If you inserted a Plugin object, select the video file in the Select File dialog box. Movies dragged onto the page from the Assets panel already include the source path. The Plugin placeholder is displayed as a 32 pixel × 32 pixel icon.
3. In the Plugin Property inspector, enter the dimensions of your video clip in the width and height boxes, marked W and H, respectively, or size the Plugin object directly by dragging one of its selection handles.

Playing Videos in Dreamweaver

Dreamweaver can access and use Firefox (or, more generally, Mozilla) plugins to display video right in the Document window at design time. These plugins can be installed in Firefox's Plugins folder, in Internet Explorer's Plugins folder, or in Dreamweaver's own Plug-ins folder. Dreamweaver checks all three every time it starts up. Many plugins come with browser-specific installation programs.

To play a particular video in Dreamweaver's Document window for a supported plugin, all you have to do is enter into Live View and, if necessary, click Play on the video controls. To stop playback, switch out of Live View or click the video controller Stop button.

CAUTION

Unsupported plugins are listed in the `UnsupportedPlugins.txt` file in Dreamweaver's Configuration/Plugins folder. As of this writing, only the DirectorShockwave plugin is listed in this file. If you continue to have problems playing plugins in Dreamweaver, check the file for compatibility.

Inserting QuickTime Movies

The HTML command for incorporating a QuickTime movie (or any other medium that requires a plugin) is the `<embed>` tag. Because so many different types of plugins exist, Dreamweaver uses a generic Plugin inspector that enables an unlimited number of parameters to be specified.

Only three `<embed>` tag parameters are absolutely required for a QuickTime movie: the source of the file, the movie's width, and the movie's height. The QuickTime Plugin, however, also offers an amazing array of additional `<embed>` tag attributes to enable you to fine-tune the way content is presented.

NOTE

The QuickTime Plugin is used by both Netscape and Internet Explorer on both Windows and Macintosh to enable the browser to interface with QuickTime.

To insert a QuickTime movie in your web page, follow these steps:

1. Choose Insert ➪ Media ➪ Plugin. Alternatively, you can select the Plugin object from the Media group of the Insert panel found in the Common category or drag the file from the Movie category of the Assets panel to your web page.
2. If you insert a Plugin object, select the QuickTime movie file in the Select File dialog box. If you drag the movie file from the Assets panel, the Plugin's `src` attribute is automatically set to the QuickTime movie file pathname.

TIP

If you're working on a Macintosh and your QuickTime movie doesn't have a filename extension, add `.mov` to the end of its name before embedding it or placing it on the web.

3. In the Plugin Property inspector (shown in Figure 26-7), enter the dimensions of your QuickTime movie in the width (W) and height (H) fields, or size the Plugin object directly by dragging one of its selection handles.

TIP

If you don't know the dimensions of your QuickTime movie, open it in the QuickTime Player, choose Movie ➪ Get Movie Properties, and select Size from the options list on the right of the dialog box that appears.

FIGURE 26-7

When inserting a QuickTime movie, specify the properties and values in the Plugin Property inspector.

4. In the Plg URL text field, enter **http://www.apple.com/quicktime/**. This is the web address to which users who don't have QuickTime are directed by their browser.
5. Click the Parameters button in the Plugin Property inspector panel to open the Parameters dialog box (see Figure 26-8), where you can enter additional <embed> tag attributes: the name in the left column and the value in the right column. Use Tab to move between the columns. Table 26-2 lists the most commonly used <embed> tag parameters for QuickTime movies. Use this list to add any parameters, and click OK when you're done.

FIGURE 26-8

Use the Parameters dialog box to enter attributes for any plugin. Dynamic values can be entered by clicking the lightning bolt icon and choosing a field from a defined recordset.

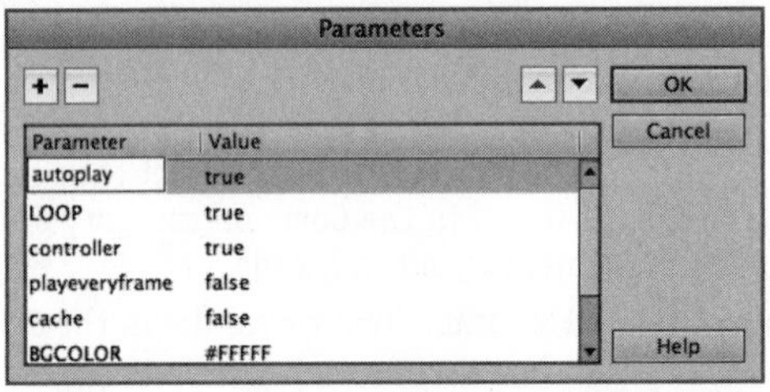

NOTE

Any of the parameters or their values can be linked to a data source by clicking the lightning bolt icon in the value field and choosing an appropriate data field from the Dynamic Data dialog box that opens.

TABLE 26-2 QuickTime Plugin Parameters

QuickTime Plugin Parameter	Possible Values	Description
Autoplay	True or false; default set by user in QuickTime Plugin Settings	When this is set to false, a movie won't play until the user clicks Play in the controller. Otherwise, it starts playing as soon as enough data is downloaded to ensure uninterrupted playback.

QuickTime Plugin Parameter	Possible Values	Description
Bgcolor	RGB colors in hexadecimal, such as #FFFFFF; or valid HTML color names, such as "red"	Specifies the color of the space set aside by the width and height attributes but not taken up by the QuickTime movie. Add a border to a QuickTime movie by setting the appropriate bgcolor and increasing the width and height attributes by a few pixels.
Cache	True or false; default set by user in QuickTime Plugin Settings	Specifies whether the browser should store the movie in its cache for later retrieval. Doesn't work in IE.
Controller	True (default for most movies) or false (default for QuickTime VR, Flash, and image files)	Displays the controller panel attached to the bottom of the movie.
Dontflatten whensaving	(Does not take a value)	When included, using the Save As QuickTime option on the QuickTime Plugin's controller menu saves the movie without resolving references (not self-contained).
endtime	30-frame SMPTE time-code—hours:minutes:seconds:frames (30ths of a second)	Indicates the point in the movie where playback should stop.
Height	A value in pixels; usually the height of the movie	Reserves a space in the page for the QuickTime movie.
Hidden	(Does not take a value)	Tells the QuickTime Plugin not to show the movie. Audio is played, however.
Href	URL	A link to go to when the movie is clicked. You can supply either an absolute or a relative URL. QuickTime movies replace the current movie in-place; web pages open in the browser.
kioskmode	True or false (default)	Eliminates the QuickTime Plugin's controller menu when set to true.
Loop	True, false (default), or palindrome	Causes the movie to loop continuously when set to true. The palindrome value causes the QuickTime Player to play alternately forward and backward.
Movieid	A number	A number identifying the movie so that another wired sprite movie can control it.
Moviename	A name	A name identifying the movie so that another wired sprite movie can control it.
Playeveryframe	True or false (default)	When set to true, forces the movie to play every frame, even if it must do so at a slower rate than real time. Disables audio and QuickTime Music tracks.
Pluginspage	`www.apple.com/quicktime`	Where users who don't have QuickTime should be sent to get it.

Continues

TABLE 26-2 *(continued)*

QuickTime Plugin Parameter	Possible Values	Description
Qtnextn	URL	Specifies a movie as being *n* in a sequence of movies. The movie specified in the src attribute is movie 0 (zero).
Qtnext	goto*n*	Tells the QuickTime Plugin to open movie *n* in an already specified sequence of movies.
Qtsrc	URL	Tells the QuickTime Plugin to open this URL instead of the one specified by the src attribute. This is a way to open files that don't have a .mov filename extension—such as MP3 files—with the QuickTime Plugin, regardless of how the user's system is set up. Use a dummy movie in the src attribute.
qtsrcchoke speed	Movie-rate, or a number in bytes per second	Downloads the movie specified in the qtsrc attribute in chunks; movie-rate indicates to use the movie's data rate.
scale	to fit, aspect, or a number (default is 1)	Resizes the QuickTime Player movie. By setting scale to fit, you can scale the movie to the dimensions of the embedded box as specified by the height and width values. Setting scale to aspect resizes the movie to either the height or the width, while maintaining the proper aspect ratio of the movie. Set to a number; the size of the movie is multiplied by that number.
starttime	30-frame SMPTE time-code—hours:minutes:seconds:frames (30ths of a second)	Indicates the point in the movie where playback should start.
Target	Name of a valid frame or window (_self, _parent, _top, _blank, or an explicit frame/window name) or QuickTimePlayer	Enables the link specified in the href attribute to be targeted to a specific frame or window. The value QuickTimePlayer causes the movie specified in the href attribute to be opened in the QuickTime Player.
Targetcache	True or false (default)	Same as the cache attribute but for the movie called by a poster movie using the href attribute.
Volume	0 to 100 (default)	Controls the volume of the audio track(s). 0 is softest; 100 is loudest.
Width	A value in pixels; usually the width of the movie	Reserves a space in the page for the QuickTime movie.

TIP

Dreamweaver's Plugin Property inspector enables you to enter several additional attributes generally used with other objects, such as images. These include `Align` (alignment), `V Space` (vertical space), `H Space` (horizontal space), and `Border` (border). You can also enter a name in the Plugin text field if you plan to refer to your QuickTime movie in JavaScript or another programming language.

Before inserting a QuickTime movie into a web page, it's helpful to know what version of QuickTime your movie requires. Because QuickTime movies can contain a variety of track types, each with a different type of medium, some movies may play back with QuickTime 6 or earlier, whereas others require QuickTime 7 or higher.

Integrating HTML5 Video Code

Perhaps the single tag that kicked HTML5 into high gear acceptance-wise is the `<video>` tag. The `<video>` tag brings video player functionality directly to the browser, without the use of a plugin. This became a very big deal when Apple decided to exclude the use of Flash in the iPhone and iPad and, more recently, when Adobe announced that it was discontinuing future development of the Flash player for mobile devices.

Here's the most basic use of the `<video>` tag:

```
<video src="assets/vesta.mp4" controls="controls"></video>
```

Although there is no Video object to be found yet in the Insert panel, Dreamweaver does offer complete code hinting support for the `<video>` tag. For the time being, use of this tag requires hand-coding.

The `src` attribute identifies the video file to play, and the `controls` attribute displays the play, pause, seek bar, and volume controls, as shown in Figure 26-9. Other optional attributes include `autoplay`, `loop`, and `preload`.

Another set of essential attributes defines the dimensions of the video player: `width` and `height`. It's best to make note of the dimensions of your video when encoding, as not all browsers can detect the video size automatically.

TIP

The `poster` attribute is another helpful attribute for the `<video>` tag. Set the poster value to the path of a static image in a web-compatible format—GIF, JPEG, or PNG—and the image is displayed before the user clicks the play button. Be sure not to include the `autoplay` attribute.

Unfortunately, browser support for the `<video>` tag is not uniform. No single video format can be played across all browsers. Table 26-3 shows which browsers support which video formats as of this writing.

FIGURE 26-9

In a compatible browser, the <video> tag displays a functioning video player with a complete set of controls.

TABLE 26-3 HTML5 Browser Support for Video Formats

Browser	MP4 Support	WebM Support
Internet Explorer	Yes	No
Google Chrome	Yes	Yes
Firefox	No	Yes
Safari	Yes	No
Opera	Partial	Yes

To achieve full cross-browser video playback, you must include multiple `<source>` tags within the `<video>` tag pair, like this:

```
<video width="320" height="240" controls="controls">
  <source src="assets/vesta.mp4"  type='video/mp4; codecs="avc1.42E01E,
mp4a.40.2"' />
  <source src="assets/vesta.webm" type="video/webm; codecs='vp8, vorbis"' />
</video>
```

Within each `<source>` tag is a rather robust `type` attribute that details both the video format—such as `video/mp4`—and the codecs used in the encoding of the video. The `codecs` portion of the `type` attribute lists the video codec first, followed by the audio one—for example, `codecs='vp8, vorbis'`. Note the careful use of double and single quotation marks within the attribute.

Note

A bug in the iPad and iPhone implementation of the <video> tag only allows those systems to recognize the first <source> tag. Because they use a Safari-based browser, be sure to put your .mp4 format first.

You can take the <video> tag implementation one step further by including a Flash fallback for the ultimate in cross-browser compatibility. If your site visitor uses an older browser that does not recognize the <video> tag, it will be ignored and the Flash Player, invoked through the <object> and <embed> tag methods, will be used. Here's how that code might look:

```
<video width="320" height="240" controls="controls">
  <source src="assets/vesta.mp4"  type='video/mp4; codecs="avc1.42E01E,
mp4a.40.2"' />
  <source src="assets/vesta.webm" type="video/webm; codecs='vp8, vorbis"' />
<object id="player1" classid="clsid:D27CDB6E-AE6D-11cf-96B8-444553540000"
\width="480" height="270">
    <param name="movie" value="player.swf" />
    <param name="quality" value="high" />
    <param name="wmode" value="opaque" />
    <param name="swfversion" value="6.0.65.0" />
    <param name="flashvars" value="file=assets/vesta2.flv&autostart=true" />
    <param name="allowfullscreen" value="true" />
    <param name="allowscriptaccess" value="always" />
    <embed flashvars="file=assets/vesta.flv&autostart=true" allowfullscreen=
"true" allowscriptaccess="always" id="player1" name="player1" src=
"player.swf" width="480" height="270" />
  </object>
</video>
```

Note

Video codec support is a rapidly shifting landscape that you'll have to keep up on. For example, Google announced in January 2011 that it would drop support for MP4 but, as of this writing, still has not. A good place to keep track of what's happening with HTML5 video is http://www.longtailvideo.com/html5/.

Summary

Digital video on the web is everywhere. If you're considering adding video to your web pages, keep these points in mind:

- Even with compression, digital video has steep storage and download requirements.
- Flash video is an easy-to-use, comprehensive solution now immediately available in Dreamweaver in either progressive download or streaming delivery modes.
- You can include a digital video movie to be downloaded in your web page by linking to it as if it were a web page.

- Use Dreamweaver's Plugin object when you want your video to be presented inline on your web page. The Plugin Property inspector then enables you to alter the video's parameters for any video architecture.
- QuickTime is a cross-platform, multimedia architecture that offers much more than just video.
- To enable your visitors to view your digital video clips as soon as possible, use a streaming video technology such as HTTP Live Streaming, Flash, RealMedia, QuickTime, or Windows Media. Streaming video files can be displayed in a separate player or embedded in the web page.
- The HTML5 `<video>` tag is gaining a great deal of momentum, especially on mobile devices. Dreamweaver supports the `<video>` tag through Code view.

In the next chapter, you learn how Dreamweaver helps you incorporate sound and music into your web pages.

CHAPTER

27

Using Audio on Your Web Page

IN THIS CHAPTER

- Digital audio fundamentals
- Music files overview
- MP3 mini-primer
- Linking and embedding sound
- Streaming audio
- Incorporating podcasts

Websites tend to be divided into two categories: those totally without sound, and those that use a lot of it. There's not much middle ground. Many music and entertainment sites rely heavily on both streaming audio and downloadable audio files, such as MP3.

In this chapter, you learn how to use audio in the web pages you design with Dreamweaver. You look at traditional digital audio formats, such as AIFF and WAV, and how you can turn these into files suitable for publishing on the web, in formats such as MP3. Finally, you learn how to link to an individual podcast and a podcast feed.

Lest you forget that you're dreamweaving here, you also look at some Dreamweaver extensions you can use to get audio-enabled sites up and running in no time. But before you leap into those deep waters, it's a good idea to get an overview of digital audio and its place on the web.

Dreamweaver QUICKSTART

Essentially, there are three ways you can work with sound on the web: You can link to an audio file, embed a plugin, or insert an audio-based SWF file. The following is the quick approach to all three methods. Let's first look at the steps to link to a sound file:

1. Select the text or image you want to use as a link.

Continues

continued

2. From the Property inspector, click the Browse for File icon to locate the audio format file.

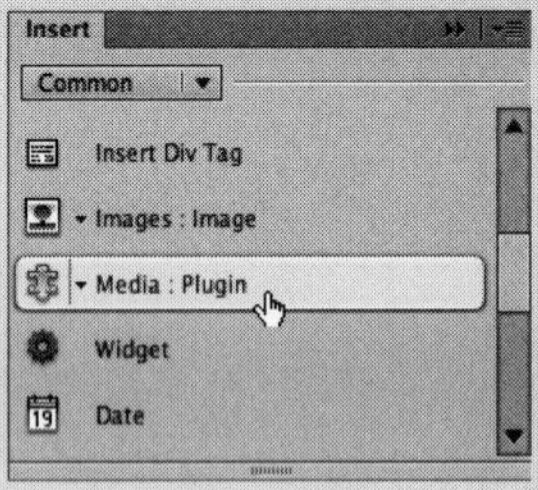

To embed a plugin for WAV or MP3 files, follow these steps:

1. Put your cursor where you want the plugin to appear.
2. From the Common category of the Insert panel, click Media: Plugin.
3. When the Select File dialog box opens, choose your audio source file.
4. Resize the plugin placeholder to match the dimensions of the plugin's player controls.

To insert an SWF file, follow these steps:

1. Put your cursor where you want the plugin to appear.
2. From the Common category of the Insert panel, click Media: SWF.
3. When the Select File dialog box opens, choose your SWF file.

There's a lot more to know about working with sound with Dreamweaver—all detailed in this chapter—but that should get you started.

Linking to Audio Files

The simplest way to add sound to a web page is to create a link to an audio file by specifying the file path in the Link text box of the Text or Image Property inspector. When the user clicks that link, the sound file downloads, and whatever program has been designated to handle that type of file opens in a separate window. The link can be text or, as shown in Figure 27-1, an image. An exception to this is the QuickTime Plugin. Instead of opening linked audio files in the QuickTime Player, it opens them within the browser window as if they were a new web page. To get back to your web page, the user clicks the browser's Back button.

To create a link to an audio file in Dreamweaver, follow these steps:

1. Select the text or image that you want to serve as the link to the audio file.
2. In the Property inspector, enter the name of the audio file in the Link text box, or click the Folder icon to browse for the file. To link to a dynamic source, choose Select File Name from Data Sources and select an appropriate field from the available recordset(s).
3. Because audio files can be large, it's good practice to note the file size in the status bar or to enter it as part of the information in the Alt text box for your image.

FIGURE 27-1

When the HotFlash logo link is clicked, the browser downloads the sample hotflash.mp3 file, which then opens the associated player and plays it.

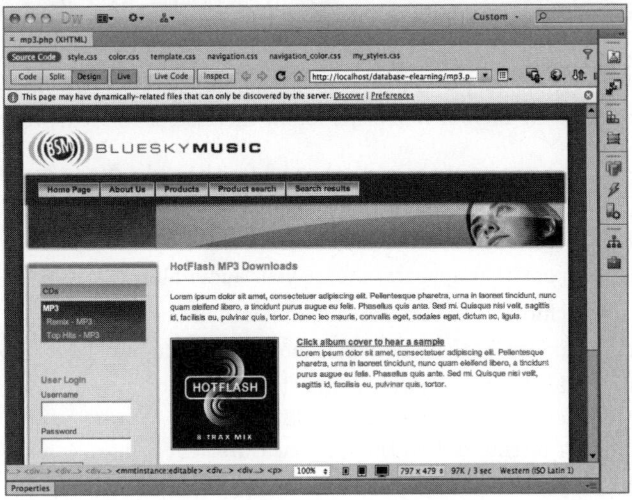

When you use the link technique for incorporating sound, you have no control over the position or appearance of the player. However, you can control these factors and more by embedding your audio.

Embedding Sounds and Music

Embedding a sound file truly integrates the audio into your web page. Embedding the sound file also gives you a much greater degree of control over the presentation of the audio player itself, including the following:

- The clip's play volume
- Which part, if any, of the player's controls is visible
- The starting and ending points of the music clip

As with any other embedded object, you can present the visual display inline with other text elements—aligned to the top, middle, or bottom of the text, or blocked left or right to enable text to flow around it. Dreamweaver controls all these parameters through two different objects: the Plugin object and the ActiveX object. Each type of object calls a specific type of player. With the Plugin object, you get whatever is currently set in the user's system to handle the type of music file you've referenced: You might get the QuickTime Player in one instance and Winamp in another. Calling the Windows Media Player as an ActiveX object explicitly enables you to modify a great number of parameters for Internet Explorer. You learn about all your embedding options, including techniques for cross-browser audio, in the next few sections.

CAUTION

The <embed> tag used by the Plugin object is not included in the HTML 4.*x* specifications and will not validate. If validation is important to you, use an <object> tag or Flash method described later in this section.

As with video, Dreamweaver uses the generic Plugin object to embed audio in your web page. The object requires only three parameters: the source of the audio file and the width and height of the object. To embed an audio file in your web page, follow these steps in Dreamweaver:

1. Position the cursor where you want the control panel for the audio file to appear.
2. Insert the Plugin object by choosing Insert ➪ Media ➪ Plugin or by clicking the Plugin button from the Media menu from the Insert panel's Common category.
3. In the Select File dialog box that appears, choose your audio file.
4. Use one of these two techniques to size the Plugin placeholder:
   - Click the resizing handles on the Plugin placeholder and drag it out to a new size.
   - Enter the desired values in the W (Width) and the H (Height) text boxes of the Property inspector.

   You'll need to do a bit of testing to find the ideal measurement values. Many systems, including mine, default to the QuickTime plugin for playing WAV or MP3 files. For this plugin, you can start with a width of 100 pixels and a height of 18 pixels, as shown in Figure 27-2; a wider width displays more audio controls. For systems that use Windows Media Player, you'll need a width of approximately 144 pixels and height of 50 to display all controls. You may need to adjust the width and/or height after further testing.

FIGURE 27-2

The QuickTime player for MP3 and WAV files takes up only a small amount of space.

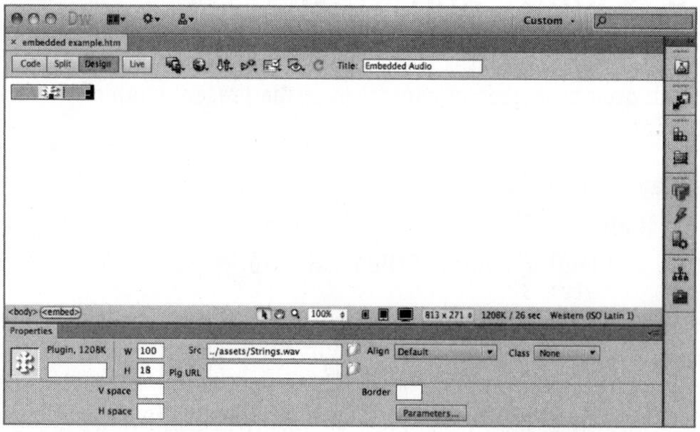

When the Plugin object is inserted, Dreamweaver displays the generic Plugin placeholder.

Playing Background Music

Background music, played while the user is viewing online material, is one of the web's hidden treasures. When used tastefully, background music can enhance the overall impact of the page. Conversely, when abused, it can drive users away in droves.

Playing Sound with Flash

Flash is a solid alternative for playing MP3 audio, whether in the background or through an in-page controller—you can even control it through JavaScript in Dreamweaver. Flash has supported sound from early on and in recent years has strengthened its MP3 playback mechanism. If you're working with a Flash designer, creating an MP3 playback movie is relatively straightforward.

One robust solution for incorporating Flash audio is provided by Scott Schiller with his SoundManager API project (`http://www.schillmania.com/projects/soundmanager2/`). The SoundManager API is an open source JavaScript library, freely available. The site contains a range of tutorials and full documentation.

If you're looking for a drop-in solution, a series of low-cost commercial players is available from WimpyPlayer (`http://www.wimpyplayer.com`). These Flash MP3 players support both PHP and ASP., as well as XML playlists.

An embedded player is best inserted using Dreamweaver's ActiveX object—the embedded player consists of two ActiveX objects, one for the player control (or controls) and one for the audio file itself. The separation of content and player makes it easy to link the content to a data source while maintaining the same control panel.

Making a regular embedded sound into a background sound is as simple as adding a few parameters to the `<embed>` tag: `hidden` tells the browser not to display any controls, `autostart` tells it to start playback automatically, and `loop` tells it to play the audio continuously. Although you can add these attributes to the `<embed>` tag manually in the HTML Code window, it's easier to add them using the Property inspector. Follow these steps to embed background music in a web page:

1. Position the cursor near the top of your web page. Choose Insert ➪ Media ➪ Plugin, or click the Plugin button from the Media group in the Common category of the Insert panel.
2. Choose your audio file in the Select File dialog box.

   Dreamweaver inserts a 32 pixel × 32 pixel placeholder to indicate where the Plugin code is located. You can resize the placeholder so your layout won't be affected.
3. In the Property inspector, enter **2** in both the H (Height) and W (Width) text boxes.

NOTE

Entering a width and height attribute is necessary for compatibility with older browsers.

4. If your Property inspector is not already expanded, expand it now (by clicking the arrow icon in the lower-right corner of the inspector). Click the Parameters button to open the Parameters dialog box.

5. In the Parameters dialog box, click the Add (+) button and enter **hidden** in the Parameter column. Click in the Parameter column and type in the first parameter. Use Tab to move to the Value column and enter **true**, as shown in Figure 27-3. Use Tab again to move to the next parameter.

   The following list of tips can help you navigate and use this dialog box:

   - Use Shift+Tab if you need to move backward through the list.
   - To delete a parameter/value pair, highlight it and click the Delete (–) button at the top of the Parameter column.
   - To add a new parameter, click the Add (+) button to move to the first blank line, and use Tab to move to the next parameter.
   - To move a parameter from one position in the list to another, highlight it and click the up or down arrow buttons at the top of the Parameter column.

6. Enter **autostart** as the next parameter, and give it the value **true**.

FIGURE 27-3

Dreamweaver inserts a 32 pixel × 32 pixel placeholder denoting a Plugin object for playing a MIDI file as background music, controllable via the Parameters dialog box.

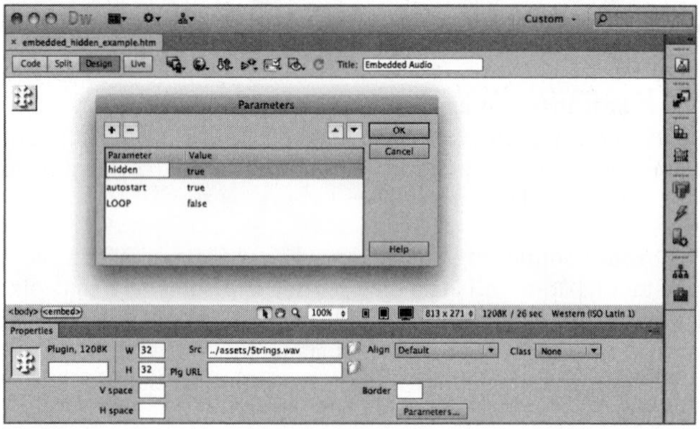

7. To make the audio clip repeat, enter **loop** as the next parameter; in the Value column, enter the number of times you want the sound to repeat. To make the audio repeat indefinitely, enter **true** as the value.

8. Click OK to finish.

Targeting Specific Plugins

You can exercise a much finer degree of control over the audio in your pages by calling specific plugins. The trade-off, unfortunately, is that by designating a plugin, you reduce the size of your potential audience. Some plugins are specific to a browser or browser version. Moreover, plugins that aren't distributed with the major browsers face an uphill battle in terms of market penetration. If you use a plugin, you can always expect some users to be resistant to downloading the necessary software. Before you incorporate any plugin, you must weigh these issues against your overall design plan.

Windows Media Player audio

The Windows Media Player is Internet Explorer's default multimedia player. You can use it to play the standard audio formats, including MP3, WAV, AIFF, AU, and MIDI files. Calling Windows Media Player directly as an ActiveX control, however, gives you far more flexibility over the player's appearance and functionality: You can also control its width, height, control panel display, volume, number of loops, and so on.

To incorporate the Windows Media Player ActiveX control, follow these steps:

1. Position the cursor where you would like the Windows Media Player control panel to appear. Choose Insert ⇨ Media ⇨ ActiveX or click the ActiveX button from the Media category of the Insert panel. The Property inspector displays the ActiveX object options.
2. In the ClassID text box, enter the ID for the Windows Media Player control: **CLSID:6BF52A52-394A-11D3-B153-00C04F79FAA6**.

TIP

If you've entered this long Windows Media Player class ID previously, you can click the arrow button and choose the ID from the drop-down list.

3. Change the width and height values in the W and H text boxes to match the desired control display. The Windows Media Player display resizes to match your dimensions as closely as possible.
4. Click the Parameters button.
5. Click the Add (+) button and enter the first parameter: **FileName**. Use Tab to move to the Value column.
6. Enter the path and filename for your audio file. Unfortunately, there is no Browse button in the Parameters dialog box so you must enter the pathname by hand. If the audio file resides in your site, be sure to specify a relative URL rather than an absolute one.
7. Continue entering the desired parameters and values for your audio file, as shown in Figure 27-4.
8. Click OK when you're finished.

The Windows Media Player ActiveX control has many parameters to choose from—well over 80. Explaining all these parameters is beyond the scope of this book, but Table 27-1 describes the key parameters.

NOTE

As with plugins, all the parameters and/or values of an ActiveX control may be linked to a dynamic source. From the Parameters dialog box, click the lightning bolt icon in either the Parameter or the Value column to expose the available recordset fields.

CAUTION

Windows Media Player's default volume setting is 0, but this is the highest setting, not the lowest setting. Specifying a higher number for the volume parameter lowers the volume of the sound.

FIGURE 27-4

Inserting a Windows Media Player ActiveX control object into a web page.

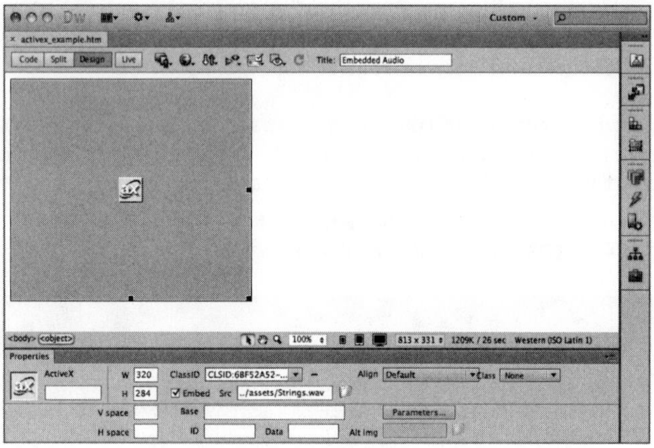

TABLE 27-1 Windows Media Player Parameters

WMP Parameter	Possible Values	Description
AutoStart	True (default) or false	Determines if the sound begins playing when the download is complete.
FileName	Any valid sound-file URL	Specifies the sound file to be played.
PlayCount	Any integer	Sets the number of times the file should repeat. If the value is 0, the sound loops continuously. The default is 1.
SelectionStart	Number of seconds	Determines the beginning point for the audio clip, relative to the start of the file.
SelectionEnd	Number of seconds	Determines the ending point for the audio clip, relative to the start of the file.
ShowControls	True (default) or false	Shows the control panel if set to true.
ShowDisplay	True or false (default)	Shows the display panel if set to true.
Volume	Any integer, from 0 (loudest, default) to 10,000 (softest)	Sets the volume of the audio.

Using embed with ActiveX

All ActiveX controls are included in HTML's <object> ... </object> tag pair. Dreamweaver codes this for you when you insert any ActiveX control. Some older browsers don't recognize the <object> tag, and Internet Explorer doesn't recognize the <embed> tag when it's within an <object> tag, so it's possible to target both browsers with one <object> and <embed> pair.

After you've entered the FileName parameter and value for the Windows Media Player ActiveX control, select the Embed checkbox in the Property inspector. The same name that you specified as the FileName now appears in the Embed text box. Dreamweaver takes advantage of the fact that Netscape doesn't recognize the <object> tag by inserting the <embed> tag inside the <object> ... </object> tag pair. The resulting HTML looks like the following:

```
<object classid="CLSID:6BF52A52-394A-11D3-B153-00C04F79FAA6"
 width="193" height="270">
  <param name="FileName" value="sounds/Fantasy.mid">
  <param name="PlayCount" value="0">
  <param name="ShowDisplay" value="true">
  <embed src="sounds/Fantasy.mid" width="193" height="270"
   filename="sounds/Fantasy.mid" playcount="0" showdisplay="true">
  </embed>
</object>
```

Note that Dreamweaver picks up the attributes and parameters from the ActiveX control to use in the <embed> tag. You often have to adjust these, especially the width and height values, which differ markedly for Internet Explorer and Netscape audio player displays.

Integrating Podcasts

A podcast is, in essence, a digital multimedia file, suitable for playback on computers or portable media devices. Although there are an increasing number of video podcasts, audio podcasts make up the great majority of available content. A podcast is, like many other audio files, often stored in an MP3 format. What makes a podcast different is that the content is typically syndicated via XML files called *feeds*. The syndication makes it possible for someone to subscribe to a particular podcast feed and automatically receive the latest audio program.

One reason podcasts are popular is that they are easy to create. Anyone with a relatively recent computer, a microphone (even one built into a laptop), and audio recording software can create one. Once the audio recording has been saved as an MP3 file, it's a good idea to add identifying tags called *ID3 tags*. ID3 tags are like <meta> tags and typically contain details about the podcast, such as the title, the name of the creator, and, where pertinent, keywords that describe the content. When the file is played, the MP3 player extracts the ID3 tags and displays the info.

TIP

One popular program for adding ID3 tags to an MP3 file is Apple's iTunes, available for free on both Macintosh and Windows platforms. To assign ID3 tags, select a file imported in the iTunes Library. Choose File ➪ Get Info. You can add or modify the details as needed in the Info tab of the displayed dialog box. When you're done, you can use the Advanced menu to convert your selected iTunes file to MP3 format and drag it into a folder for use on the web.

Podcast XML feeds

Most syndicated podcasts rely on a special form of an XML file format known as RSS. There's a bit of dispute over what RSS actually stands for—Really Simple Syndication, Rich Site Summary, or RDF Site Summary are among the contenders—but, bottom line, they all mean the same thing: a consistent format for publishing content.

If you're completely new to XML and want to know more, check out Chapter 32, "Integrating XML and XSLT," before continuing.

The key containing elements of an RSS feed are the opening XML indicator, an `<rss>` tag, and a `<channel>` tag, like this:

```
<?xml version="1.0" encoding="utf-8"?>
  <rss version="2.0">
    <channel>
    </channel>
  </rss>
```

Within the `<channel>` tag, you'll find a series of meta-like tags including the title, description, language, and copyright details, as well as a link to the HTML page that hosts the main content:

```
<channel>
  <title>My Podcasts</title>
  <link>http://www.idest.com/</link>
  <description>The latest Dreamweaver news</description>
  <language>en-us</language>
  <copyright>Copyright 2012 idest</copyright>
</channel>
```

Following these tags, but still within the `<channel>` tags, are the individual `<item>` tags that describe and provide links to each podcast. A typical `<item>` might look like this:

```
<item>
  <title>New York, New York</title>
  <link>http://www.idest.com/pod/121507.htm</link>
  <description>
    How to add podcasts to your Web pages.
  </description>
  <enclosure url="http://www.idest.com/media/pd01.mp3"
length="640561" type="audio/mpeg"/>
</item>
```

Within each `<item>` tag, the `<enclosure>` tag links to the actual MP3 podcast file. You'll note that the `<enclosure>` tag is referred to as an empty tag because, like `<img>`, it does not have both opening and ending tag pairs—it's just a single tag. You can have as many `<item>` tags in your channel as you'd like, each representing a single podcast.

A completed RSS feed XML file might look like this:

```
<?xml version="1.0" encoding="utf-8"?>
  <rss version="2.0">
```

```
    <channel>
      <title>My Podcasts</title>
      <link>http://www.idest.com/</link>
      <description>The latest Dreamweaver news</description>
      <language>en-us</language>
      <copyright>Copyright 2009 idest</copyright>
      <item>
        <title>New York, New York</title>
        <link>http://www.idest.com/pod/091507.htm</link>
        <description>How to add podcasts to your Web
pages.</description>
        <enclosure url="http://www.idest.com/media/pd01.mp3"
length="640561" type="audio/mpeg"/>
      </item>
    </channel>
  </rss>
```


Linking to podcasts and feeds

It's up to the web designer whether a separate link to an individual podcast is provided along with the link to the podcast RSS feed. As noted earlier, linking to an MP3 file is just like linking to any other file: Simply select the text or graphic and, in the Property inspector, enter the path to the MP3 file.

RSS feeds are linked in a similar manner, but the link goes to an XML file rather than an MP3 file. To help identify RSS feeds, a common symbol has been widely adopted. The orange and white feed icon (see Figure 27-5) was initially approved for use by both the Mozilla and the Microsoft browser teams in 2005 and later by the other major browser producers, and you can find it at `http://feedicons.com` in a variety of formats.

FIGURE 27-5

Link to your RSS podcast feed with the popularly recognized orange and white icon.

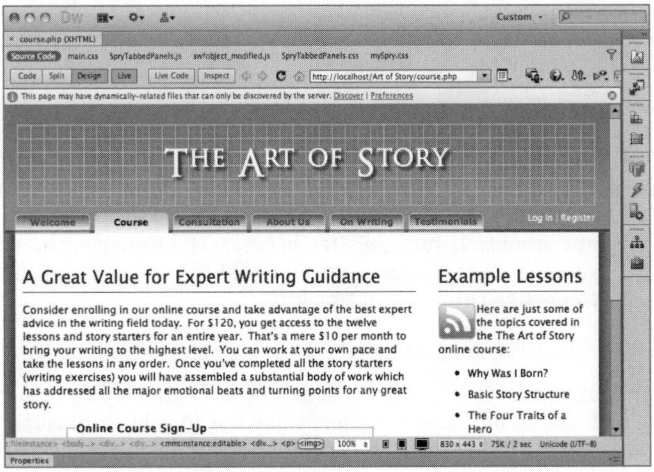

Coding an HTML5 Player for Audio

Although it didn't make as big a splash as the corresponding tag for video, the HTML5 <audio> tag still has made an impact. Now, the primary audio formats can be played natively, without an additional plugin.

As with the <video> tag, the basic <audio> tag is very straightforward:

```
<audio src="assets/fb_demo_song.mp3" controls="controls"></audio>
```

The src attribute defines the path to an appropriate sound file, either relative or absolute. The controls attribute tells the compliant browser to display basic play/pause volume controls and a seek bar, as shown in Figure 27-6.

FIGURE 27-6

Plugin-free audio playback is now possible with the HTML5 <audio> tag.

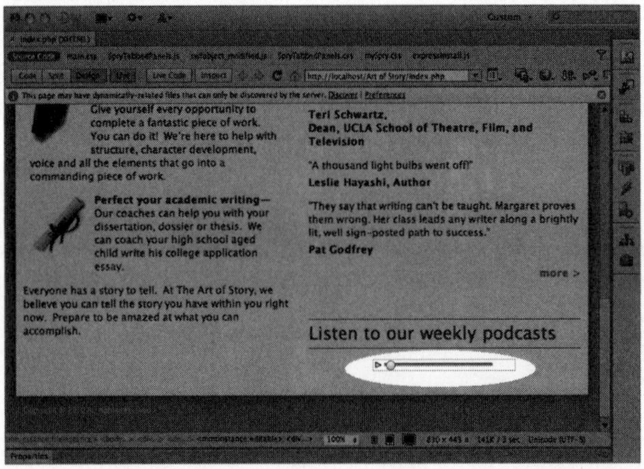

> **NOTE**
>
> **If you're not using XHTML syntax, the code would read:**
>
> ```
> <audio src="assets/fb_demo_song.mp3" controls></audio>
> ```
>
> **The controls attribute is what is known as a boolean; its presence, even without a value, enables the attribute.**

Why wouldn't you always want the controls to show? In some cases, for example, you might want to just play music in the background. In this situation, you would delete the controls attribute and insert an autoplay one, like this:

```
<audio src="assets/fb_demo_song.mp3" autoplay="autoplay"></audio>
```

This combination of attributes would cause the designated song to begin playing immediately when the browser is ready. Of course, not all web visitors enjoy a sudden burst of music when visiting a site. Luckily, the <audio> tag supports a variety of JavaScript functions that can also be used to create custom buttons.

To pause the music with custom controls, create a button with JavaScript attached, like this:

```
<audio id="mySong" src="../assets/fb_demo_song.mp3" autoplay="autoplay"></audio>
<button onclick="javascript:document.getElementById('mySong').volume=0;" >Mute
Music</button>
```

In this code, the <audio> tag now has an id attribute, so the JavaScript function can properly target the tag. The onclick event handler in the <button> tag pinpoints the <audio> tag and sets the volume to zero when clicked.

As with the <video> tag, different browsers support different file formats. Table 27-2 shows the current state of audio format support.

TABLE 27-2 HTML5 Browser Support for Audio Formats

Browser	MP3 Support	WAV Support	Ogg Vorbis Support
Internet Explorer	Yes	Yes	No
Firefox	No	Yes	Yes
Google Chrome	Yes	No	Yes
Safari	Yes	Yes	No
Opera	No	Yes	Yes

The <audio> tag handles the lack of universal single-format support with the <source> tag. To support all of the major browsers, you'd need to offer at least two of the formats, such as MP3 and Ogg Vorbis, with code like this:

```
<audio controls="controls">
  <source src="assets/mySong.ogg" type="audio/ogg" />
  <source src="assets/mySong.mp3" type="audio/mpeg" />
</audio>
```

When the browser encounters this code, it displays the controls and tries to play the first source file in the Ogg Vorbis format. If that format is not supported, it moves to the second format, MP3. You can include as many <source> tags as needed to cover your desired browser range. The type attribute assists the browser by identifying the proper MIME type for each format. Should the browser not support any of the formats, you can even include a link so the user can download the song:

```
<audio controls="controls">
  <source src="assets/mySong.ogg" type="audio/ogg" />
  <source src="assets/mySong.mp3" type="audio/mpeg" />
  <a href="assets/mySong.mp3">Download</a>
</audio>
```

NOTE

Converting audio files from one format requires dedicated software such as the open source Audacity or an online application like the one found at http://media.io/. The Media.IO converter allows you to set the quality (which also determines file size) and recreate files in the major audio formats. Both Audacity and Media.IO are free.

Two other <audio> tag attributes are worth mentioning: loop and preload. As the name implies, the loop attribute causes the audio file to begin again after it is completed:

```
<audio id="mySong" src="../assets/fb_demo_song.mp3" autoplay="autoplay"
loop="loop"></audio>
```

The loop attribute creates an all-or-none situation. Once it is set, the audio continues to loop forever. Naturally, you'd want to be careful about setting up a web page where music loops continuously in the background with no way to stop it.

The preload attribute determines whether the browser fully loads the audio before the page is displayed. There are three possible values:

- auto: When set to auto, the entire audio is downloaded before the page is displayed.
- meta: If the meta value is used, only the metadata (such as author, date created, and so on) is loaded on page load.
- none: Neither audio or metadata is preloaded.

You need to be careful if you have many <audio> tags on your page. Excessive use of the preload attribute set to auto (which is the default) could result in a long delay before your page is displayed.

Summary

Adding sound to a web page brings it into the realm of multimedia. Dreamweaver gives you numerous methods to handle the various audio formats, both static and streaming. When you use custom Dreamweaver objects and actions, enhancing your website with audio is a snap. When adding audio to your web pages, keep these points in mind:

- The common downloadable audio file formats are MP3, AIFF, and WAV.
- The common downloadable music file formats are MP3 and MIDI.
- You can either link to a sound or embed it in your web page. With standard audio, the linking technique calls an independent, free-floating player; the embedding technique incorporates the player into the design of the page. Hiding the player creates background music or sound.
- Third-party plugins offer far greater control over the appearance and functionality of the sound than relying on a browser's default plugin; to use a third-party plugin, however, your user must download it.
- Designers can link to individual podcasts, which are typically in MP3 format, as well as a podcast feed, which is stored as an XML file.
- Dreamweaver supports the HTML5 <audio> tag, which can be used in many current browsers for plugin-free audio playback.

In the next chapter, you learn how to use Dreamweaver templates to enhance your web page creation skills.

Part VI

Enhancing Productivity and Website Management

IN THIS PART

Chapter 28
Using Dreamweaver Templates

Chapter 29
Using Library Items and Server-Side Includes

Chapter 30
Maximizing Cross-Browser Compatibility

Chapter 31
Building Websites with a Team

Chapter 32
Integrating XML and XSLT

CHAPTER

28

Using Dreamweaver Templates

IN THIS CHAPTER

- Working with templates
- Building your own templates
- Working with editable and locked regions
- Dreamweaver Technique: Converting a Page to a Template
- Setting up repeating regions
- Dreamweaver Technique: Applying Additional Editable Regions
- Inserting optional regions
- Creating nested templates
- Evaluating template expressions
- Modifying the default web page
- Managing InContext Editing

Let's face it: Web design is a combination of glory and grunt work. Creating the initial design for a website can be fun and exciting, but when you have to implement your wonderful new design on 200 or more pages, the excitement fades as you try to figure out the quickest way to finish the work. Enter templates. Using templates properly can be a tremendous time-saver. Moreover, a template ensures that your website has a consistent look and feel, which, in turn, generally means that it's easier for users to navigate.

In Dreamweaver, you can produce new documents from a standard design saved as a template, just as you do in a word processing program. Furthermore, you can alter a template and update all the files that were created from it earlier; this capability extends the power of the repeating element Libraries to overall page design. Templates also form the bridge to one of the key technologies shaping the web—Extensible Markup Language (XML).

Dreamweaver now also works with a different kind of template, one that allows your clients to edit their content right in the browser. Adobe InContext Editing is a service that makes it possible for web designers to offload the onerous task of updating site content to the clients while maintaining the overall design of the site.

Dreamweaver makes it easy to access all kinds of templates—everything from your own creations to the default blank page—whether you're updating them yourself or providing them to your client for InContext Editing. This chapter demonstrates the mechanisms behind Dreamweaver templates and shows you a range of strategies for getting the most out of them.

Understanding Templates

Templates exist in many forms. Furniture makers use master patterns as templates to create the same basic design repeatedly, using new wood stains or upholstery to differentiate the final product. A stencil, in which the inside of a letter, word, or design is cut out, is a type of template as well. With computers, templates form the basic document into which specific details are added to create new, distinct documents.

Dreamweaver templates, in terms of functionality, are a combination of traditional templates and updatable Library elements. After a new page is created from a template, the document remains attached to the original template unless specifically separated or detached. The new document maintains a connection to previous pages in a site. If the original template is altered, all the documents created from it can be automatically updated. This relationship is also true of Dreamweaver's repeating element Libraries. In fact, templates can include Library elements.

Library items work hand in hand with templates. See Chapter 29 for a detailed discussion of Library items.

When a template is first created, the entire page is locked; locked sections of a template cannot be changed in a document derived from that template. A key process in defining a template is to designate certain areas as regions that can be changed in some way in a template-derived document. Dreamweaver supports four different regions in a template:

- **Editable regions:** The area, such as all the code, within an editable region may be altered. In a page where all the navigation code is locked, for instance, the content area can be designated as an editable region.
- **Editable attributes:** Within a locked tag, specific attributes can be made editable. For example, you can unlock the class attribute for the `<body>` tag while keeping all other attributes secure.
- **Optional regions:** Content within an optional region may or may not be displayed, depending on certain conditions set by the template designer.
- **Repeating regions:** Certain areas in an otherwise locked object (typically a table) can be repeated as many times as needed in a template-derived document. Repeating regions are great for controlling the overall look and feel of a table but allowing the number of detail rows to vary.

All the various region types require template markup within the document. You can also combine certain template regions—you could, for example, make some of the content within a repeating region editable and keep some of it locked.

Naturally, templates can be altered to mark additional editable areas or to relock editable areas. Moreover, you can detach a document created from a template at any time and edit anything in the document. You cannot, however, reattach the document to the template without losing (or seriously misplacing) inserted content. On the other hand, you can give a document based on one template a completely different look (without changing the content) by applying another template with identical regions.

Let's look at an example template. The layout, background, and navigation controls are identical on every page. One basic template page (shown in Figure 28-1) is created, and all the final pages are created from the template. Notice the highlighting surrounding certain areas in the template. In a template, the specified regions are highlighted, and the locked areas are not. A tab further identifies each region to make it easier to add the right content in the right area.

FIGURE 28-1

In a template, designated regions are clearly marked and distinguished from the rest of the page, which is locked and cannot be changed.

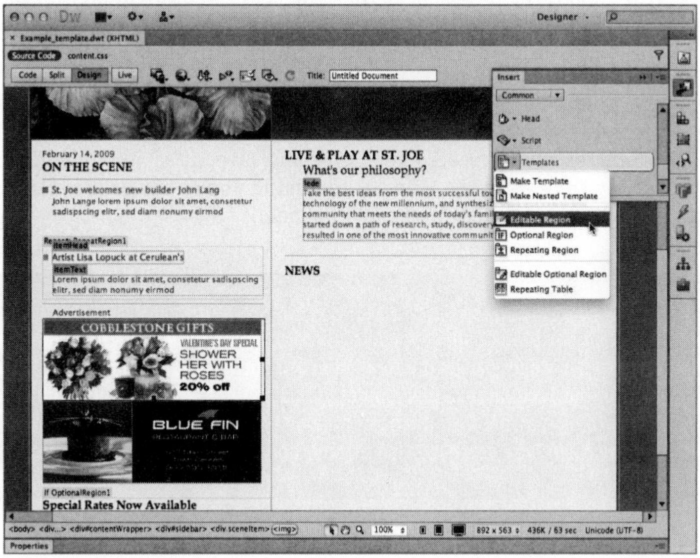

Creating Your Own Templates

You can use any design you like for your own template. Perhaps the best path to take is to finalize a single page that has all the elements that you want to include in your template. Then, convert that document to a template and proceed to mark all the changeable areas—whether text or image—as a type of region. Before saving your file as a template, consider the following points when designing your basic page:

- **Use placeholders where you can.** Whether it's dummy text or a temporary graphic, a placeholder gives shape to your page. Placeholders also make it easier to remember which elements to include. If you are using an image placeholder, set a temporary height and width through the Property inspector or by dragging the image placeholder's sizing handles. Of course, you can also just insert a sample graphic.
- **Finalize and incorporate as much content as possible in the template.** If you find yourself repeatedly adding the same information or objects to a page, add them to your template. The more structured elements you can include, the faster your pages can be produced.
- **Use sample objects on the template.** Often, you have to enter the same basic object, such as a plugin for a digital movie, on every page with only the filename changing.

Enter your repeating object (with as many preset parameters as possible) on your template page. Then, you have only to select a new filename for each page.

- **Include your <meta> information.** Search engines rely on `<meta>` tags to get the overview of a page and then scan the balance of the page to get the details. You can enter a Keyword or Description object from the HTML category of the Insert panel so that all the web pages in your site have the same basic information for cataloging.
- **Set up an external style sheet.** Since you'll be working with multiple pages, it's a good idea to work with an external style sheet from the beginning. Dreamweaver handles all the necessary path changes to make sure that the CSS file you link to in the template is linked properly in your child pages.

You can create a template from a web document with one command: File ➪ Save As Template. Dreamweaver stores all templates in a Templates folder created for each defined site with a special file extension (`.dwt`). After you've created your page and saved it as a template, notice that Dreamweaver inserts `<<Template>>` in the title bar to remind you of the page's status. Now you're ready to begin defining the template's editable regions.

NOTE
You can also create a template from an entirely blank page if you like. To do so, open the Assets panel and select the Templates category. From the Templates category, click the New Template button. You can find more information about how to use the Assets panel of the Templates category later in this chapter. Another approach to achieve the same result is to choose File ➪ New to display the New Document dialog box, select the Blank Page category, and then choose HTML template from the Page Type category. Use this method when you want to build an XHTML-compliant template from scratch.

Using Editable Regions

As noted earlier, when you convert an existing document into a template via the Save As Template command, the entire document is initially locked. If you attempt to create a document from a template at this stage, Dreamweaver alerts you that the template doesn't have any editable regions, and you cannot change anything on the page. Editable regions are a key element in templates.

Marking existing content as editable

Editable regions can either surround existing content or stand alone without any content. As noted earlier, in both cases you must give the region a unique name. Dreamweaver uses the unique name to identify the editable region when entering new content, applying the template, and exporting or importing XML.

NOTE
As I noted previously, each editable region must have a unique name, but the name need only be different from any other editable region on the same page. The same name could be used for objects, JavaScript functions, or editable regions on a different template.

To mark an existing area as an editable region, follow these steps:

1. Select the text, object, or area on the page that you want to convert to an editable region.

TIP

The general rule with editable regions is that you need to select a complete tag pair, such as `<table> . . . </table>`. This strategy has several implications. For instance, although you can mark an entire table, one or more contiguous rows, or a single cell as editable, you can't mark multiple cells, separated rows, or a column. Attempting to do so marks a multiple row region. You have to select each cell individually (`<td> . . . </td>`). In addition, you can select the content of an `<div>` tag to be editable and keep the tag itself locked (so that its class and/or ID cannot be altered). However, if you select the `<div>` tag to be editable, you can't lock the content.

2. Choose Insert ➪ Template Objects ➪ Editable Region. You can also use the keyboard shortcut Ctrl+Alt+V (Command+Option+V), or right-click (Control+click) the selection and choose Templates ➪ New Editable Region from the context menu. Whichever method you choose, Dreamweaver displays the New Editable Region dialog box shown in Figure 28-2.

   Now, editable template regions—as well as the other region types—are just a mouse click away.

   Alternatively, you can choose, from the Common category of the Insert panel, the Templates group and click once on the Editable Region icon. You can also drag the icon over the selected text. Either action brings up the New Editable Region dialog box.

3. Enter a unique name for the selected area. Click OK if you're finished, or click Cancel to abort the operation.

28

FIGURE 28-2

The descriptive name you enter for a new editable region must be unique.

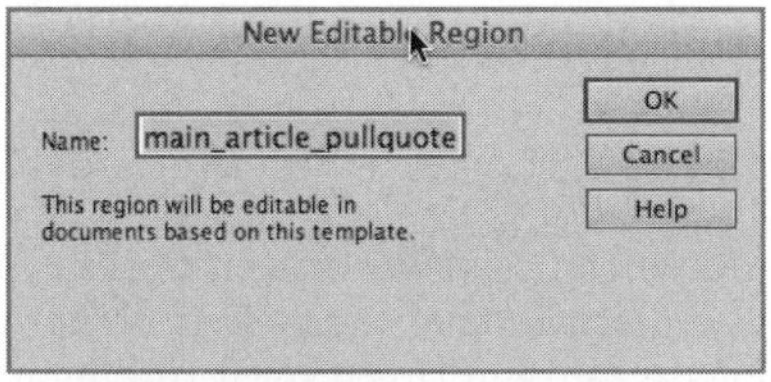

CAUTION

Although you can use spaces in editable region names, some characters are not permitted. The illegal characters are the ampersand (&), double quote ("), single quote ('), and left and right angle brackets (< and >).

Dreamweaver outlines the selection with the color picked in Preferences on the Highlighting panel, shown if View ➪ Visual Aids ➪ Invisible Elements is enabled. The name for your newly designated region is displayed on a tab marking the area; the region is also listed in the Modify ➪ Templates submenu. If still selected, the region name has a checkmark next to it in the Templates submenu. You can jump to any other editable region by selecting its name from this dynamic list.

Inserting a new editable region

Sometimes it's helpful to create a new editable region in which no content currently exists. In these situations, the editable region name doubles as a label identifying the type of content expected, such as `CatalogPrice`. Dreamweaver always highlights the entry in the template in a small tab above the region.

To insert a new editable region, follow these steps:

1. Place your cursor anywhere on the template page without selecting any item in particular.
2. Choose Insert ➪ Template Objects ➪ Editable Region. Alternatively, click the Editable Region icon on the Templates menu of the Insert panel.
3. Enter a unique name for the new region. Click OK when you're finished, or click Cancel to abort the operation.

Dreamweaver inserts the new region name in the document, marks it with a named tab, and adds the name to the dynamic region list (which you can display by choosing Modify ➪ Templates).

Two editable regions, one for the web page's title and one for other `<head>` content, are automatically created when you save a document as a template. The title is stored in a special editable region called `doctitle`, and the `<head>` content region is named `head`. To change the title (which initially takes the same title as the template), enter the new text in the Title field of the Document toolbar. You can also use the keyboard shortcut Ctrl+J (Command+J) to open the Page Properties dialog box. Finally, you can select View ➪ Head Content and click the Title icon—with the visible region outline—to enter the new text in the Property inspector.

The `head` editable region may not appear very useful during the template creation phase, but when you begin creating documents based on a template, it really shines. New `<meta>` tags, CSS style links and rules, and behavior-added JavaScript all take advantage of the `head` editable region.

Creating links in templates

A common problem that designers encounter with Dreamweaver templates centers on links. People often add links to their templates and discover that these links do not work when new pages are derived from the templates. The main cause of this error is linking to a non-existent page or element by hand—that is, typing in the link, rather than using the Select File dialog box to choose it. Designers tend to set the links according to their final site structures, without taking into account how templates are stored in Dreamweaver.

Recommended linking technique

There's an easy way to make sure the links in your template pages are correct. For example, when creating a template, suppose you have links to three pages—`products.htm`, `services.htm`, and `about.htm`—all in the root of your site. Both `products.htm` and `services.htm` have been created, so you click the Folder icon in the Property inspector and select those files. Dreamweaver inserts those links as follows: `../products.htm` and `../services.htm`. The `../` indicates the directory above the current directory—which makes sense only when you remember that all templates are stored in a subfolder of the site root called Templates. These links are correctly resolved when a document is derived from this template to reflect the stored location of the new file.

Let's assume that the third file, `about.htm`, has not yet been created, and so you enter that link by hand. The common mistake is entering the pathname as it should appear when it's used: `about.htm`. However, because the page is saved in the Templates folder, Dreamweaver converts that link to `/Templates/about.htm` for any page derived from the template—and the link will fail. This type of error also applies to dependent files, such as graphics or other media.

The best solution is to always use the Folder or the Point-to-File icon to link to an existing file when building your templates. If the file does not exist, and if you don't want to create a placeholder page for it, link to another existing file in the same folder and modify the link manually.

Handling special template workflows

There is one special circumstance in which you would not use the Folder or Point-to-File icon to do your linking for you. Let's suppose your site design calls for each page to link to a CSS file in the same folder as the file itself; a technique like this is used when you want to vary pages by departments and each department has its own folder. In this circumstance, linking in the standard template manner wouldn't work because you're effectively linking to a number of files and not just one. To accomplish this goal, you'll need to use a special syntax in your `href` attribute, like this:

```
<link href="@@('departmentStyles.css')@@" rel="stylesheet" type="text/css" />
```

As you see later in this chapter, the double @ signs and parentheses characters are generally used to designate template expressions. Here, they're used to tell Dreamweaver not to alter the `href` value. These types of links will obviously need to be coded by hand.

Another variation of the more typical template workflow is to store your dependent files—such as images, includes, and CSS style sheets—in the Templates folder. Dreamweaver novices often take this approach because it makes sense to them to group all their assets in subfolders immediately below the current page. Although this is generally a solid practice when creating sites, it's not the way Templates are intended to work. However, Dreamweaver is flexible enough to be used this way, but only if you make a change to your Site Setup settings. In the Site Setup dialog box, switch to the Advanced Settings ⇨ Templates category (see Figure 28-3) and clear the Template Updating checkbox. This action changes this option from its default state, Don't Rewrite Document Relative Paths, to one that will rewrite such paths in the Templates folder. Failure to turn off the Template Updating option will result in broken links to any dependent files in your Templates folder for any child page.

CAUTION

Just to be absolutely clear: Although the Template Updating option makes it possible to store your dependent files in the Templates folder, it's a bad idea and strongly discouraged. It is a far better practice to maintain such assets in a folder off the site root. Items in the Templates folder are generally not published to the web, and if your images or includes are stored there, they're likely to be forgotten.

FIGURE 28-3

Leave the Don't Rewrite Document Relative Paths option in its default checked state unless you are storing dependent files such as images or includes in your Templates folder (not recommended).

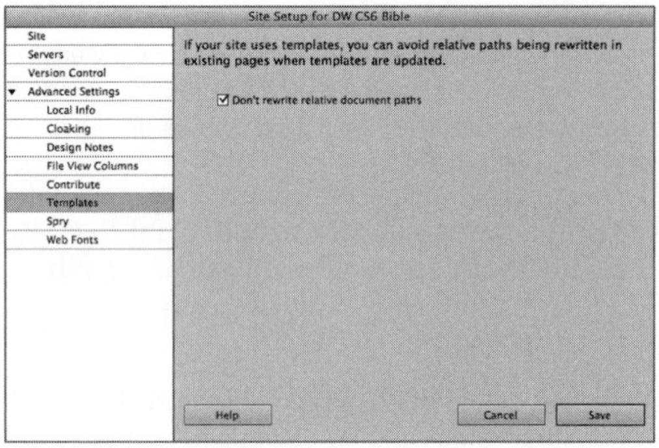

Locking an editable region

Inevitably, you'll sometimes mark as editable a region that you'd prefer to keep locked. Similarly, you may discover that every page constructed to date has required inputting the same content, so it should be entered on the template and locked. In either event, converting an editable region to a locked one is a simple operation.

To lock an editable region, follow these steps:

1. Place your cursor in the editable region you want to lock.
2. Choose Modify ➪ Templates ➪ Remove Template Markup. The same menu selection is available from the context menu.

CAUTION

If you are removing a newly inserted editable region that contains only the region name—which happens when an empty editable region is added—the content is not removed and must be deleted by hand on the template. Otherwise, it appears as part of the document created from a template and won't be accessible.

Adding Content to Template Documents

Constructing a template is only half the job—using it to create new pages is the other half. Because the basic layout is complete and you're only dropping in new images and entering new text, creating pages based on templates takes just a fraction of the time needed to create regular web pages. Dreamweaver makes it easy to enter new content as well—you can even move from one template region to the next, much like filling out a form (which, of course, is exactly what you're doing).

To create a new document based on a template, follow these steps:

1. In the Template category of the Assets panel, select the desired template and choose the New From Template option from the panel's context menu. Alternatively, choose File ⇨ New. Then, from the New Document dialog box, select the Page From Template category and choose the site and desired template, as shown in Figure 28-4.

FIGURE 28-4

A list of all the templates by site is accessible by choosing Page From Template in the New Document dialog box.

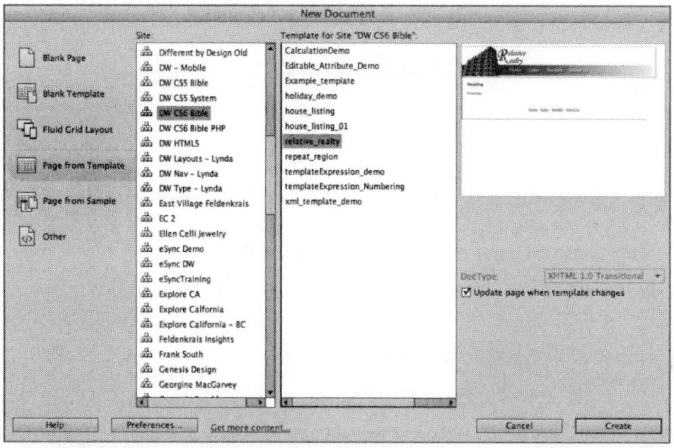

2. If you want to maintain a connection between the template-derived document and the template, leave the Update Page When Template Changes option selected. To detach the template from the newly created document and make the entire page editable, deselect the option.
3. Click OK when you're finished.

When your new page opens, the editable regions are again highlighted, as shown in Figure 28-5; furthermore, the cursor is only active when it is over an unlocked region. If you have the Code view open, you also see that the locked region is highlighted in a different color—by default, gray. Document highlighting makes it easy to differentiate the two types of regions.

NOTE

A document created from a template is known as an *instance of that template.*

28

FIGURE 28-5

In a document based on a template, the template regions are clearly marked.

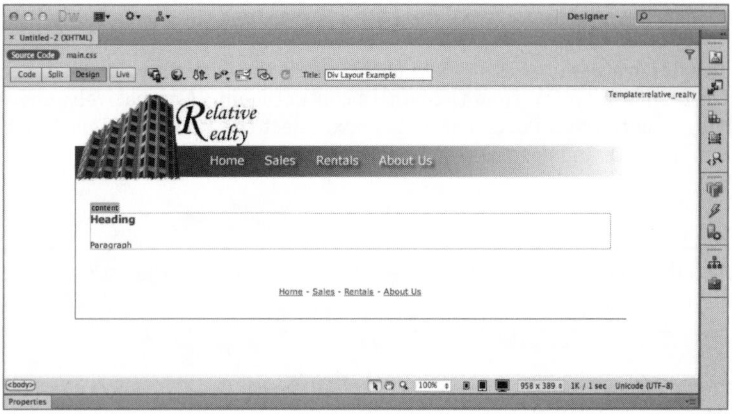

Generally, it is easiest to select the editable region name or placeholder first and then enter the new content. Selecting the editable regions can be handled in several ways:

- Highlight the region name or placeholder with the mouse.
- Position your cursor inside any editable region and select the `<mmtinstance:editable>` tag in the Tag Selector.
- Choose Modify ➪ Templates and select the name of your editable region from the dynamic list.

NOTE

If all your editable regions are separate cells in a table, you can tab forward and Shift+Tab backward through the cells. With each press of the Tab key, all the content in the cell is selected, whether it is an editable region name or a placeholder.

Naturally, you should save your document to retain all the new content that's been added.

TIP

Behaviors can be added without any additional coding or workarounds to links within editable regions. You cannot, however, add a behavior to text or an image in a locked region.

Dreamweaver TECHNIQUE

Converting a Page to a Template

In this Dreamweaver Technique, you convert an existing page to a template and apply editable regions to several page elements.

1. From the Techniques site, expand the 28_Template folder and open the `template_start` file.
2. Choose File ➪ Save as Template.
3. In the Save As Template dialog box, enter **house_listing** in the Save As field and click Save.
4. When the Update Links dialog box appears, click Yes.
5. Dreamweaver stores the new file in the Templates folder as `house_listing.dwt`. The next task is to begin adding editable regions to the template. Select the text "A Real Steal" by dragging across it with your mouse.

   Because you want to make just the text inside the `<h1>` tag an editable region and not the entire element, it's best not to use the Tag Selector in this case.
6. From the Insert panel's Common category, choose Templates: Editable Region.
7. In the New Editable Region dialog box, enter **Headline** in the Name field.
8. If you have Visual Aids ➪ Invisible Elements enabled, you'll see a border appear around the editable region, as well as a tab naming the area. Delete the selected original text and enter the placeholder text **Short Headline**.
9. Place your cursor in the first paragraph of text and choose the `<p.firstParagraph>` tag from the Tag Selector.
10. Repeat Steps 6 and 7 to create a new editable region; name the region **Description**.

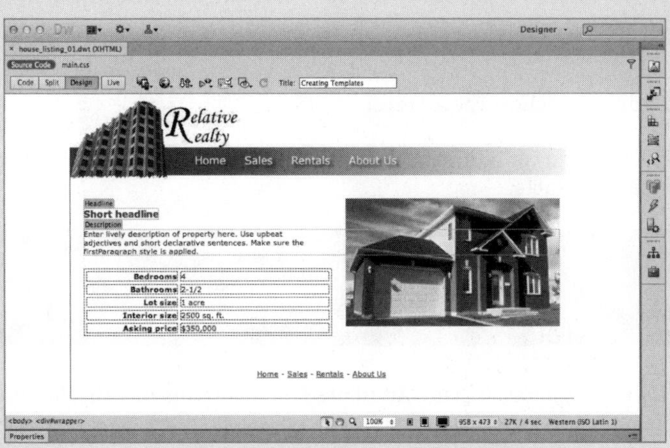

11. Press Delete to remove the selected original text. Press Enter (Return) to create a new paragraph and enter this placeholder text: **Enter lively description of property here. Use upbeat adjectives and short declarative sentences. Make sure the firstParagraph style is applied.**

Continues

28

continued

12. In the Property inspector, choose firstParagraph from the Style list.
13. Select the second paragraph in the Tag Selector and click Delete to remove it.
14. Save your page; Dreamweaver notes that the Headline editable region is within a block tag. Click OK to acknowledge that this is by design.

In the next Technique, you expand on this template.

Making Attributes Editable

Now that you understand the basics of template design and implementation, you can proceed to some of the more advanced features. Editable regions can encompass any portion of the page, from a single tag up to the entire <body>. But what if you want to make just a portion of a tag—an attribute—editable and keep the rest of the tag locked? I once worked on a site where the client wanted to tie the background color of a table's header row to a graphic on the page. Every couple of weeks, I would get an e-mail asking for help to fix the page—broken while the client was trying to change the one attribute, `bgcolor`. It was a frustrating situation for both the client and me.

Dreamweaver gives you control over your editable areas right down to the attribute level. Not only can an attribute be made editable, but you can restrict its type and even provide default values. All the editable attributes on a page are displayed within a single dialog box, centralizing updates. Each of the various types of attributes—text, number, URL, color, boolean—has a specific interface for choosing a value. A color-type attribute, for example, uses a Dreamweaver-style color picker.

To make an attribute editable, follow these steps:

1. With the template open for editing, select the tag or object that contains the attribute you want to make editable.

NOTE

Your selection should be outside an editable region. If you try to change the attribute of a tag within an editable region, Dreamweaver reminds you that this tag is already fully editable.

2. Choose Modify ➪ Templates ➪ Make Attribute Editable to display the Editable Tag Attributes dialog box, as shown in Figure 28-6.
3. Select the desired attribute from the Attribute drop-down list.

TIP

For quicker editing, make sure your selected tag already contains the attribute you'd like to make editable. The Attribute drop-down list shows all the parameters within a selected tag, whether or not they have values.

FIGURE 28-6

With the Editable Tag Attributes dialog box, you can extend access to any attribute—even a custom one—of any tag in a locked area.

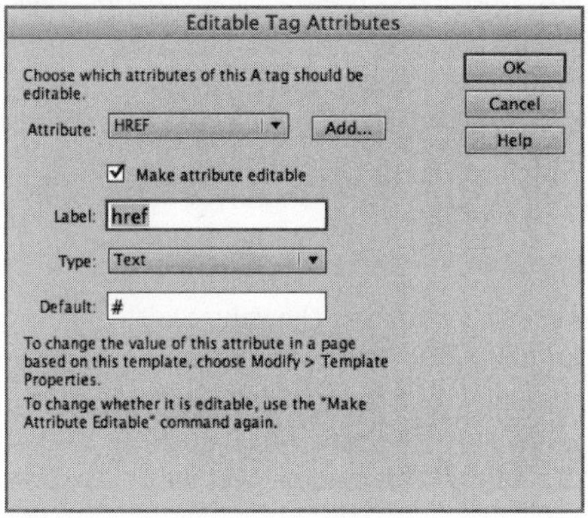

4. If the attribute you want is not available from the drop-down list, click Add and enter the attribute in the pop-up dialog box. After you've confirmed your entry in the pop-up dialog box by clicking OK, your attribute appears in the Attribute drop-down list. New entries are always uppercased in the list, but do not appear uppercased in the code if specified otherwise in the Tag Library Editor.
5. Select the Make Attribute Editable option. The Make Attribute Editable option may seem redundant in this dialog box, but it enables you to make a number of attributes editable in the same tag while leaving others locked.
6. Enter a unique name for the tag's editable attribute in the Label field. The Label is used to identify this specific editable attribute and is displayed in the Template Properties dialog box when the attribute is modified. Pick a name that identifies both the tag and the attribute, like `logoTableBgColor` for the `bgcolor` attribute of a table containing the logo.
7. Select a Type from the drop-down list. Here are the five options:
   - **Select** this type for attributes requiring a text-based value, such as the `<img>` tag's `alt` attribute.
   - **URL:** Choose this type when the attribute value points to a file or requires an Internet address, such as the `href` attribute of the `<a>` tag. Designating an attribute as a URL type enables Dreamweaver to update the link if the file is moved or renamed.
   - **Color:** Use the Color type for those attributes specifying a color value, such as the `<tr>` tag's `bgcolor` attribute. The major benefit of identifying color-related attributes as such is the color picker that is made available in the Template Properties dialog box.
   - **True/False:** Select this type if the attribute is a boolean, meaning it accepts a value of true or false only—for example, the `<object>` tag's `hidden` attribute.
   - **Number:** Choose the Number type when an attribute requires a numeric value, such as the `<img>` tag's `height` and `width` attribute.

CAUTION

If you need to enter a percentage, such as 50%, or another value that contains both numbers and other characters, select the Text type for your editable attribute. Although you might think the Number type is more logical, Dreamweaver generates errors when the template is saved with this type entered.

8. Enter the desired initial value for the attribute in the Default field. If the attribute is already present in the selected tag, the current value is displayed in the Default field. For new attributes, the Default field is initially blank.
9. Click OK when you're finished.

Editable attributes are noted in the code by surrounding the values with double @ signs, like this:

```
<img src="@@(monthlyImageSrc)@@" width="100" height="50"
  align="@@(monthlyImageAlign)@@">
```

In this example, the `<img>` tag has two editable attributes, `src` and `align`, which are set to variable values: `@@(monthlyImageSrc)@@` and `@@(monthlyImageAlign)@@`, respectively.

TIP

You can apply the same editable attribute to different tags. For example, you might want different regions on the page to share the same `class`. Although you can repeat the Make Attribute Editable command for every variable, you might find it more efficient to simply copy and paste the variable value.

When you examine the template file, note two Adobe comments inserted in the <head> section:

```
<!-- TemplateParam name="monthlyImageSrc" type="URL" value=
 "../images/admin.gif" -->
<!-- TemplateParam name="monthlyImageAlign" type="text" value="left" -->
```

These `TemplateParam` tags are used by Dreamweaver to identify the editable attributes and provide their types and default values.

CAUTION

The default values set in editable attributes are not rendered when viewing the template in the Design view, only in the template-derived document. This is a known bug in Dreamweaver.

Setting Editable Attributes

After you've inserted your editable attributes in the template, Dreamweaver provides a straightforward user interface for editing them in template-derived documents. Whether you choose File ➪ New or select the template in the Assets panel to create your new document, you find a new command available under the Modify menu: Template Properties.

The Template Properties dialog box, shown in Figure 28-7, lists all the editable attributes found on a single page. Selecting each property brings up the editing options for that particular attribute type (text, number, color, URL, and true/false) and the current associated value. After modifying any or all of the template properties, Dreamweaver refreshes the page and displays the attributes with their new values.

FIGURE 28-7

How you specify the value for an editable attribute in the Template Properties dialog box depends on the type of attribute.

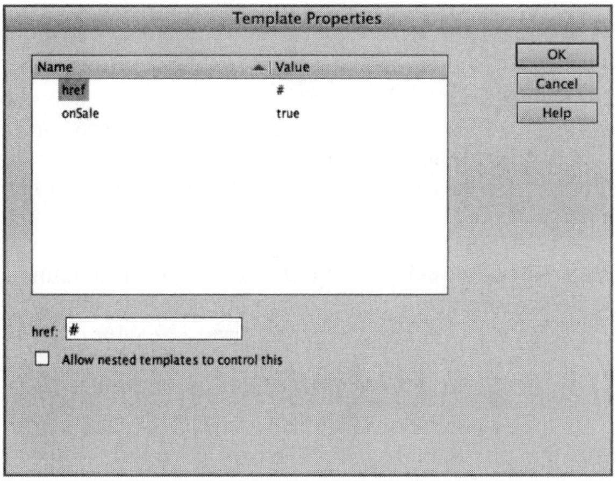

With each of the Template Properties types, you have the option to allow the nested template to control the attribute. Select this option if you intend to save the current document as a template—thus creating a nested template—and if you want documents based on that nested template to set the attribute value. You can also choose this option when editing a nested template. Nested templates are covered in depth later in this chapter.

To set the editable attributes on a template-based document, follow these steps:

1. Choose Modify ➪ Template Properties. The Template Properties dialog box is displayed.
2. Select the attribute to specify its value.
3. If you want to allow the attribute to be modified in a document based on a nested template, choose the Allow Nested Templates To Control This option. If the option is selected, the phrase `pass through` in parentheses replaces the attribute value editing options.
4. Enter the new value for the attribute. Depending on the type of attribute you select, you enter the value differently:
   - For Text, Number, and URL type attributes, enter the new value in the text field next to the editable attribute name.

- For Color type attributes, select the color picker to sample the desired color from the color palette or any area on the screen. You can also enter the hexadecimal color value or color name directly in the associated text field.
- For True/False type attributes, select the Show Attribute Name option to set the value to true and deselect it to set the value to false.

5. To set the value of any other editable attribute on the page, choose the attribute from the list and repeat Steps 3 and 4.
6. Click OK when you're finished.

Enabling Repeating Regions

Data-driven pages handle repeating regions elegantly. A single row of a table is bound to data, and the application server returns as many requested rows as are available. However, not all pages are data-driven—and not all areas of a page that repeat can be bound to a data source. Dreamweaver provides solutions for both the server-side—the Repeat Region server behavior—and the client-side—the template-based repeating region feature.

A repeating region, like an editable region, is applied to a template and may surround any *tag-complete area* (an area containing both a beginning tag and an ending tag) on a page. Typically, repeating regions wrap around the same types of areas as their server behavior cousins, such as table rows. However, unlike the Repeat Region server behavior, template-repeating regions are expanded and manipulated manually in a template-based document. Keep in mind one other important aspect of repeating regions: They aren't automatically editable—you have to include an editable region within a repeating region to make it so. The capability to lock specific portions of repeating regions makes this an extremely powerful feature.

To insert a repeating region, follow these steps:

1. Select the portion of the page that you want to repeat. As noted earlier, a repeating region cannot overlap a tag pair. If you attempt to do this, Dreamweaver automatically extends the selection so that the entire tag is included.
2. Choose Insert ➪ Template Objects ➪ Repeating Region or, from the Templates group of the Insert panel, click the Repeating Region.
3. Enter a unique name in the New Repeating Region dialog box and click OK. Dreamweaver automatically provides a name, but as always, it's best if you supply a meaningful name. Dreamweaver surrounds the repeating region with a blue border and tab with the keyword "Repeat" and the name of the region, as shown in Figure 28-8.

As mentioned earlier, repeating regions are not, by default, editable. To make a repeating region editable, select the content within the repeating region—not the repeating region itself—and then create an editable region by either clicking the Editable Region icon in the Templates menu of the Insert panel or choosing Insert ➪ Template Objects ➪ Editable Region. You must give the editable region a unique name as usual.

FIGURE 28-8

Repeating regions are marked in templates with an outline and named tab, just like editable and optional regions.

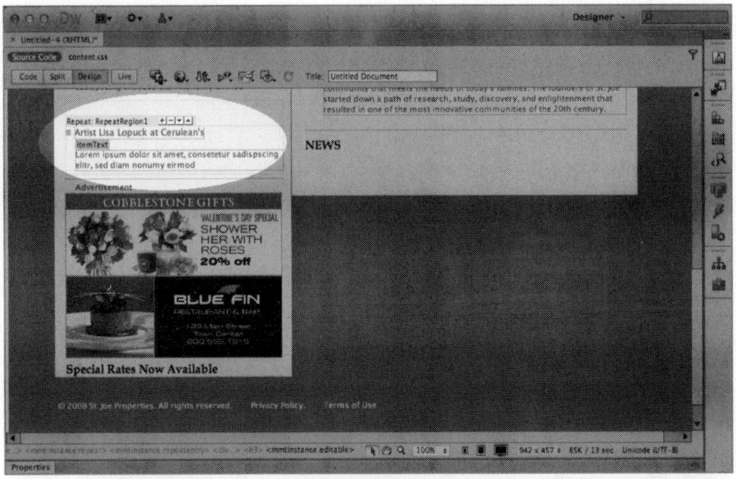

> **CAUTION**
> You may notice that the repeating and editable regions tabs overlap, making it difficult to see the repeating region name. I've found it handy to use fairly long names for the repeating region, such as dataRowRepeating, and relatively short names for the editable region, such as dataRow, to enable me to see portions of both tabs. Also, although all template regions use the same color established in Preferences, the highlight for a repeating region is significantly lighter than that for editable regions. This color variation makes it much easier to identify the different types of regions.

Modifying a repeating region

The power of repeating regions isn't apparent until you open a template-based document containing one. With Invisible Elements enabled, you notice a series of buttons above each repeating region, as shown in Figure 28-9. With these controls, new entries—identical to the content contained within the repeating region—are added, deleted, or moved from one position to another. You can even copy and paste content within a repeating region.

To modify a repeating region in a template-based document, follow these steps:

1. Make sure View ➪ Visual Aids ➪ Invisible Elements is enabled.
2. Locate the four buttons above the repeating region:
   - To add a new entry, click the Add (+) button. New entries are inserted below the current cursor selection. New entries are selected after they are created.
   - To delete an existing entry, position your cursor in the entry and click the Remove (-) button.

- To move an entry down, place your cursor in the entry and click the Down button.
- To move an entry up, place your cursor in the entry and click the Up button.

FIGURE 28-9

Entries can be added and removed in a repeating region; they can also be reordered.

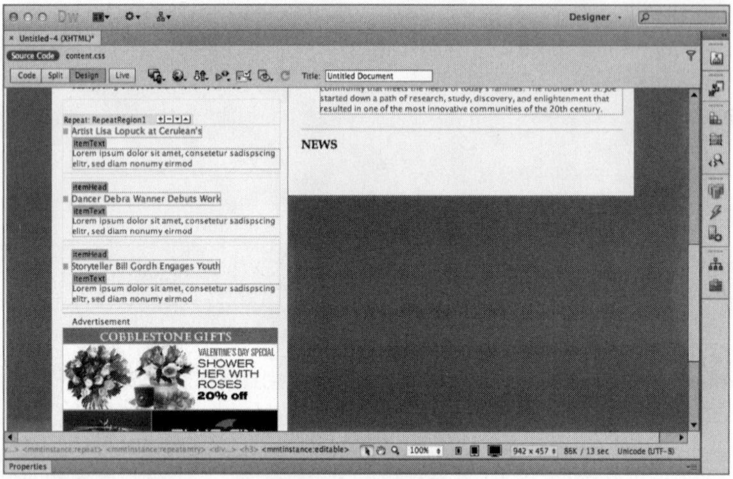

3. To copy and paste an entry, follow these steps:
   a. Position your cursor in the entry.
   b. Choose Edit ➪ Repeating Entries ➪ Copy Repeated Entry.
   c. Choose Edit ➪ Paste or Edit ➪ Repeating Entries ➪ Paste Repeated Entry.

If you prefer to work with Invisible Elements off, Dreamweaver provides corresponding menu options under both the main and the context menus. In fact, the menu options are, in some ways, more powerful and can be immediate time-savers. Look in the main menu under Modify ➪ Templates ➪ Repeating Entries or, in the context menu under Templates, for these commands:

- New Entry Before Selection
- New Entry After Selection
- Move Entry Up
- Move Entry Down

Constructing a repeating table

Repeating regions are used so commonly in tables that Dreamweaver provides a tool to create both a table and a repeating region at the same time. The Repeating Table object opens the standard table dialog box with the added capability to define which rows are within a repeating region. When inserted, the repeating region is all set up—and even includes a separate editable region in each cell, as shown in Figure 28-10.

To insert a Repeating Table, follow these steps:

1. In your template open for editing, position your cursor where you'd like the table to appear and choose Insert ➪ Template Objects ➪ Repeating Table. Alternatively, you can drag the Repeating Table icon from the Templates menu of the Insert panel. The Insert Repeating Table dialog box, shown in Figure 28-11, is displayed.
2. Enter the values desired for the table attributes: Rows, Columns, Cell Padding, Cell Spacing, Width, and Border.

If you're not familiar with setting up a table, see Chapter 12.

FIGURE 28-10

The Repeating Table object also includes editable regions for every cell in the repeating region rows.

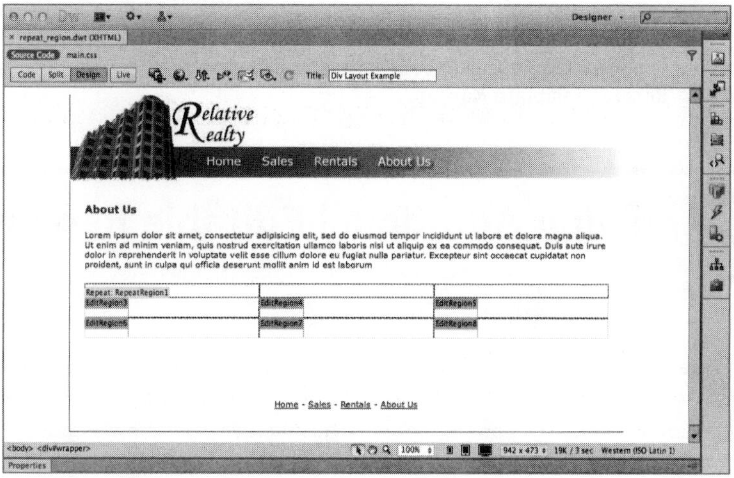

3. Determine which rows of the table are to be repeated by entering the number of the first row in the Starting Row field and the number of the last row in the Ending Row field. For example, if you want only the second row of the table to repeat, your values are Starting Row: 2 and Ending Row: 2. However, if you want three rows to repeat starting with row 2, the values are Starting Row: 2 and Ending Row: 5.
4. Enter a unique name for the repeating region in the Region Name field or leave the Dreamweaver-supplied default name.
5. Click OK when you're finished.

FIGURE 28-11

With the Repeating Table feature, you can define multiple rows to repeat.

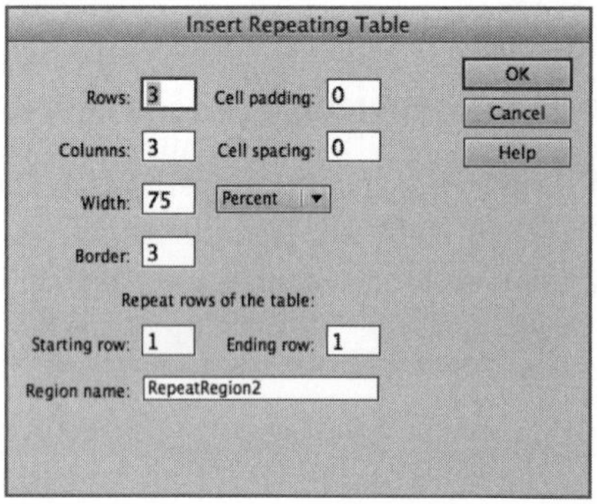

After the table is created, notice that every cell in the designated repeating region is editable. Dreamweaver automatically inserts separate editable regions and names them incrementally EditRegion1, EditRegion2, and so on. By defining each cell as editable, rather than the entire row, Dreamweaver gives you the option to retain the editability on a cell-by-cell basis. If the cell should not be editable, position your cursor anywhere in the cell and choose Modify ➪ Templates ➪ Remove Template Markup.

Dreamweaver TECHNIQUE

Applying Additional Editable Regions

In the previous Dreamweaver Technique, you began the process of converting an existing page into a template. This Technique takes the next step and includes editable regions within a table.

1. Open the file created in the previous Dreamweaver Technique from the Templates folder, `house_listing.dwt`.
2. You can apply editable regions to more than just text. Images are also good candidates, but first, it's a good idea to create a generic image placeholder. Select the image of the house in the page and delete it.
3. From the Insert panel's Common category, choose Images: Image Placeholder.
4. When the Image Placeholder dialog box opens, enter **House** in the Name field, **324** in Width, and **188** in Height; click OK when you're done.
5. Select the image placeholder and, from the Property inspector's Class list, choose imageRight.
6. With the image selected, choose Template: Editable Region.
7. In the New Editable Region dialog box, enter **House Image** in the Name field.
8. Tables are another page element that is easily made template-friendly. Select the value in the table cell next to the Bedrooms label and choose Templates: Editable Region.

9. In the New Editable Region dialog box, enter **Bedrooms** in the Name field and click OK.
10. Repeat Steps 8 and 9 to create editable regions for each of the values in the second column of the table; make your selections and name your editable regions like this:

Selection	Editable Region Name
2½	Bathrooms
1 acre	Acres
2500 sq. ft.	Square Feet
350,000	Price

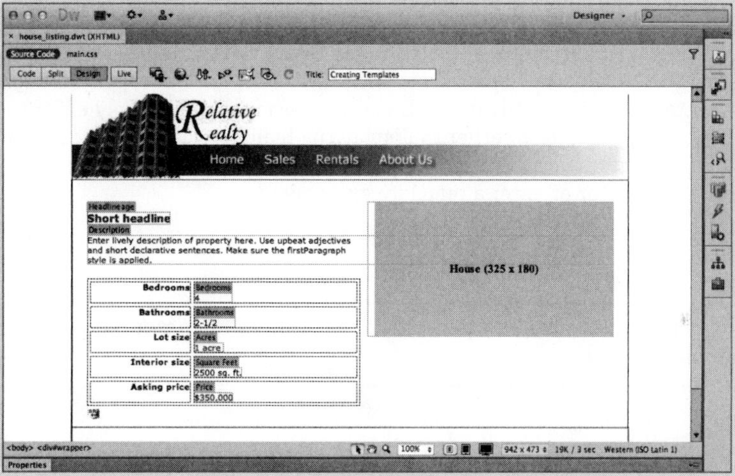

11. Save your page; click OK to acknowledge that some block content is within an editable region—if desired, you can select the Don't Show Me This Message Again option to avoid this alert in the future.

Editable regions are a cornerstone of the template structure and, as you can see, have a great number of uses.

Establishing Optional Regions

One of my clients quite regularly wanted to feature one of his products over the others, so we developed a special logo exactly for that purpose. Whenever a product was to be highlighted, I modified the page to include the special logo rather than the standard one. Typically, this took up to a half hour every time the change was made. Not only did I have to find the catalog page with the to-be-featured item and replace the logo—something else I had to hunt for—I also had to find the previously featured item page and revert the special logo placed there to the standard one. Not difficult work, but certainly tedious.

Dreamweaver's Optional Region feature is intended to reduce, if not eliminate, such tiresome chores. Content placed on a template within an optional region is conditionally shown or not shown on the template-derived page. In the just-described situation, this feature enables me to put both logos in the same template, each in its own optional region. By default, the main logo is shown, but if I decide not to show it, the special logo is shown in its place. Optional regions are extremely powerful.

Optional regions work somewhat like a cross between repeating regions and editable attributes. Like repeating regions, optional regions can surround any portion of a page; also, they are not editable by default, although it's possible to create an editable optional region. After an optional region has been placed on the template page—as with editable attributes—the Template Properties dialog box is used to set the condition that displays or hides the content on a template-derived page.

The conditions that control an optional region range from a basic true/false or boolean statement to more complex, evaluated expressions. Reflecting this, the New Optional Region dialog box contains two tabs, Basic and Advanced. Under the Basic tab, you simply enter the name for the optional region and indicate whether to display the region by default. The Advanced tab, shown in Figure 28-12, gives you the opportunity to set the condition dependent on another existing template parameter or enter a template expression.

FIGURE 28-12

Optional regions can be controlled by the state of another parameter directly or by the evaluation of a template expression.

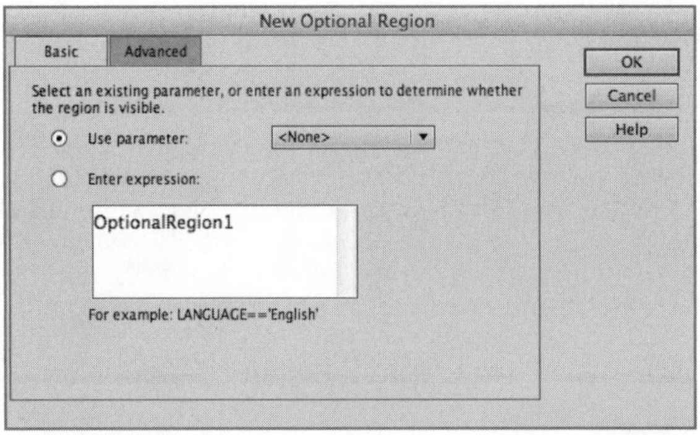

NOTE

The Basic and Advanced tabs are mutually exclusive. The tab showing when OK is selected determines which template parameter is used.

Now, look at an example to see how both the Basic and the Advanced approaches work together. Take the situation, described at the beginning of this section, which requires the use of a special logo every so often. To accomplish this, I create one optional region using the Basic tab of the New Optional Region dialog box. In this region, I just enter a name, mainLogoRegion, and enable the Show By Default option. In this region, I place my standard logo. The Basic tab creates a template parameter with code like this in the <head>:

```
<!-- TemplateParam name="mainLogoRegion" type="boolean" value="true" -->
```

Next, I create a second optional region and select the Advanced tab of the New Optional Region dialog box. I want this region to be displayed only when the other region is not. To achieve this effect, I select the Enter Expression option and enter the following in the text area:

```
mainLogoRegion != true
```

With optional regions, the name is the same as the condition; so translated into English, this expression reads, "Show this region if `mainLogoRegion` is not shown." As shown in Figure 28-13, Dreamweaver uses the condition as the name of the optional region, and this name is represented in the tab above the optional regions.

FIGURE 28-13

Complex expressions can be used to show or hide optional regions.

Dreamweaver template expressions support a subset of JavaScript operators, so I could have also written this expression like this:

```
!mainLogoRegion
```

In a different situation, you might want to tie a number of noncontiguous optional regions together so that if the main region shows, the others would as well. You achieve this by setting Use Parameter to the name of the main region. You'll find a more detailed discussion of template expressions a little later in this chapter.

To insert an optional region, follow these steps:

1. Choose Insert ➪ Template Objects ➪ Optional Region or, from the Templates menu of the Insert panel, click the Optional Region icon.
2. If you want to create a template parameter, from the Basic tab, follow these steps:
   a. Enter a unique name for the optional region in the Name field.
   b. Choose the Show By Default option if you want to make the region initially viewable.
3. If you want to link this optional region to the state of another optional region, from the Advanced tab, follow these steps:
   a. Select the Use Parameter option.
   b. Choose an existing optional region from the drop-down list.
4. If you want to control the optional region display with a template parameter, from the Advanced tab, follow these steps:
   a. Select the Enter Expression option.
   b. Enter the desired expression in the text area.

   Template parameters are explored in depth later in this chapter.
5. Click OK when you're finished.

Combining editable and optional regions

Similar to repeating regions, optional regions by themselves are not editable. Many uses exist for optional regions with the designed content either displayed or not displayed. However, in certain situations, the optional content needs to be editable as well. For such situations, Dreamweaver provides the Editable Optional Region object.

The procedure for adding an editable optional region is exactly the same as for inserting an optional region—Dreamweaver automatically includes an editable region within the optional region. The new editable region is also automatically named.

TIP

You can change the name of the automatically added editable region by selecting the template region tab or its tag in the Tag Selector and then changing the name in the Property inspector.

To add an editable optional region, follow these steps:

1. Choose Insert ➪ Template Objects ➪ Editable Optional Region or, from the Templates menu of the Insert panel, click the Editable Optional Region icon.
2. Follow the procedure outlined for inserting an optional region.
3. Click OK when you're finished.

Of course, if you want to add an editable region to an optional region containing locked content, you can always do so when editing the template.

Setting optional region properties

Although you set up an area of the page to be optionally displayed in the template, you actually choose the display option—whether to show or hide the region—in the document created from the template. As with editable attributes, the Template Properties dialog box handles control of the optional regions. Unlike editable attributes, optional regions only use true/false values to determine whether a selected region is either shown (true) or not shown (false).

Instead of the template parameter statement found in templates, Dreamweaver inserts instance parameters into the <head> section of the template-derived document, like this one:

```
<!-- InstanceParam name="mainLogoRegion" type="boolean" value="true" -->
```

To set the parameters of an optional region in a template-based document, follow these steps:

1. Choose Modify ➪ Template Properties. The Template Properties dialog box is displayed.
2. Select the optional region you want to affect.
3. If you want to allow the optional region to be modified in a document based on a nested template, choose the Allow Nested Templates To Control This option. If the option is selected, the phrase pass through in parentheses replaces the Show Attribute Name option and appears in the list.

Learn about nested templates in a section later in this chapter appropriately named "Nesting Templates."

4. Otherwise, select the *Show Name* option to set the value to true and deselect it to set the value to false.
5. To set the value of any other optional regions on the page, choose the entry from the list and repeat Steps 2 through 4.
6. Click OK when you're finished.

Evaluating template expressions

So far in this chapter, you've seen a little of what template expressions can do. With optional regions, template expressions are either set explicitly or evaluated to true or false. Template expressions can also be used throughout the template to great effect. Here is a short list of what's possible with template expressions:

- Alternate the background color of a row contained in a repeating region.
- Automatically number each row in a repeating region.
- List the total number of rows in a repeating region.
- Show an optional region if a certain number of rows are used, or another region if that number of rows is exceeded.
- Create sequential navigation links, allowing users to page to the next—or previous—document in a series.

- Compute values displayed in a table, displaying items such as basic cost, tax, shipping, and total.
- Display particular content depending on the position of the row—first, second, second-to-last, or last, for example—in the repeating region.

Two types of template expressions exist: template expression statements and inline template expressions. Template expression statements take the form of a specialized HTML comment, like this:

```
<!-- TemplateExpr expr="fileExt" -->
```

Template expression statements are coded by hand. Inline template expressions are surrounded by parentheses and double @ signs, like this:

```
@@(fileExt)@@
```

Inline template expressions can only be entered by hand, but they are very flexible. You can insert an inline template expression as an attribute into any of Dreamweaver's text field interfaces, such as the Link field of the text Property inspector or the Bg (Background Color) field of the row Property inspector. Template expressions not entered as attributes appear as Invisible Elements with a double @ sign symbol, as shown in Figure 28-14. Template expression statements appear with a script icon.

CAUTION
Although you can enter an inline template expression in Code view without a problem, you cannot enter one on the page in Design view.

Template expression language and object model

Template expressions are written in their own language, which uses a subset of JavaScript operators and its own object model. The syntax of template expressions closely resembles that of JavaScript, and both use a similar dot notation to refer to the properties of a specific object. Similar to JavaScript, Dreamweaver template expressions also have their own object model, although the object model for template expressions is much more limited in scope.

The elements supported by Dreamweaver template expressions are detailed in Table 28-1.

TABLE 28-1 Template Expression Features and Operators

Literals	Syntax	Example
Numeric Literal	Double-quoted numbers	`"123"`
String Literal	Double-quoted string	`"Chapter"`
Boolean Literals	true/false	`true`
String Concatenation	string1 + string2	`"Number of rows: " + _numRows`

<table>
<tr><th>Literals</th><th>Syntax</th><th>Example</th></tr>
<tr><td>Ternary Operators</td><td></td><td></td></tr>
<tr><td>Conditional</td><td>condition ? resultA : resultB</td><td><code>(_index & 1) ? #FFFFFF : #CCCCCC</code></td></tr>
<tr><td>Logical Operators</td><td></td><td></td></tr>
<tr><td>Logical NOT</td><td>!operand</td><td><code>!mainLogoRegion</code></td></tr>
<tr><td>Logical AND</td><td>operand1 && operand2</td><td><code>onSale && nowFeatured</code></td></tr>
<tr><td>Logical OR</td><td>operand1 || operand2</td><td><code>onSale || nowFeatured</code></td></tr>
<tr><td>Arithmetic Operators</td><td></td><td></td></tr>
<tr><td>Addition</td><td>operand1 + operand2</td><td><code>_numRows + 1</code></td></tr>
<tr><td>Subtraction</td><td>operand1 – operand2</td><td><code>_index - 1</code></td></tr>
<tr><td>Multiplication</td><td>operand1 * operand2</td><td><code>basePrice * taxBase</code></td></tr>
<tr><td>Division</td><td>operand1 / operand2</td><td><code>numSold / quantityShown</code></td></tr>
<tr><td>Modulo</td><td>operand1 % operand2</td><td><code>_index % 2</code></td></tr>
<tr><td>Comparison Operators</td><td></td><td></td></tr>
<tr><td>Less Than</td><td>operand1 < operand2</td><td><code>inStock < numSold</code></td></tr>
<tr><td>Greater Than</td><td>operand1 > operand2</td><td><code>numSold > numShipped</code></td></tr>
<tr><td>Less Than or Equal</td><td>operand1 <= operand2</td><td><code>_index <= _numRows</code></td></tr>
<tr><td>Greater Than or Equal</td><td>operand1 >= operand2</td><td><code>_numRows >= pageLimit</code></td></tr>
<tr><td>Equal</td><td>operand1 == operand2</td><td><code>_index == 10</code></td></tr>
<tr><td>Not Equal</td><td>operand1 != operand2</td><td><code>_numRows != 1</code></td></tr>
<tr><td>Bitwise Operators</td><td></td><td></td></tr>
<tr><td>Bitwise NOT</td><td>~operand</td><td><code>~4</code></td></tr>
<tr><td>Bitwise AND</td><td>operand1 & operand2</td><td><code>_index & 1</code></td></tr>
<tr><td>Bitwise OR</td><td>operand1 | operand2</td><td><code>4 | 8</code></td></tr>
<tr><td>Bitwise XOR</td><td>operand1 ^ operand2</td><td><code>2 ^ 4</code></td></tr>
<tr><td>Bitwise Signed Right Shift</td><td>operand1 >> n</td><td><code>8 >> 1</code></td></tr>
<tr><td>Bitwise Left Shift</td><td>operand << n</td><td><code>1 << 0</code></td></tr>
</table>

The template expressions document model is made up of two primary objects: `_document` and `_repeat`. The document object contains all the template variables found on the page. For example, if you create an optional region with the name `altImageRegion`, you can refer to it in a document expression with the following statement:

```
<!-- TemplateBeginIf cond="_document.altImageRegion" -->
```

FIGURE 28-14

Template expressions can be entered as either statements or inline code.

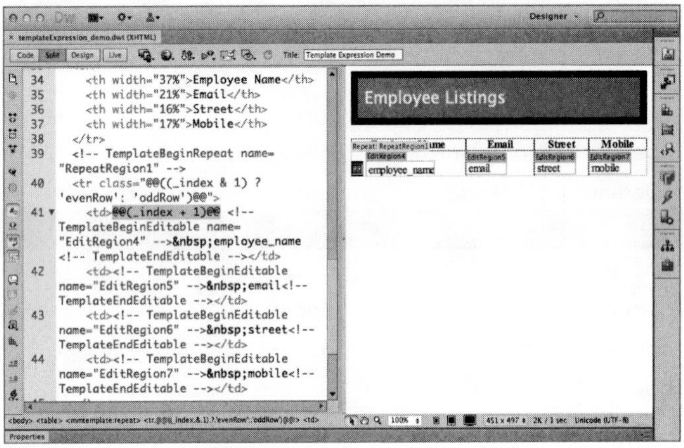

However, the `_document` prefix is implicit, and the same statement can be written like this:

```
<!-- TemplateBeginIf cond="altImageRegion" -->
```

As you may suspect, the `_repeat` object refers to a repeating region. The `_repeat` object has a number of very useful properties, as shown in Table 28-2.

TABLE 28-2 _repeat Object Properties

Property	Description
`_index`	Returns the index number of the current entry. The `_index` property is zero-based, so for the first entry of a repeating region, `_index` equals zero.
`_numRows`	Returns the total number of entries in a repeating region.
`_isFirst`	Returns `True` if the current entry is the first entry of a repeating region, `False` otherwise.
`_isLast`	Returns `True` if the current entry is the last entry of a repeating region, `False` otherwise.
`_prevRecord`	Returns the `_repeat` object for the entry before the current entry. For example, if `_index` = 2, then `_prevRecord._index` = 1. If `_prevRecord` is used in the first entry, an error occurs.
`_nextRecord`	Returns the `_repeat` object for the entry after the current entry. For example, if `_index` = 2, then `_nextRecord._index` = 3.
`_parent`	Returns the `_repeat` object for a repeating region enclosing the current repeating region. For example, use `_parent._numRows` to find the total number of rows of the outer repeating region.

The _repeat object is also implicit, and it is not necessary to reference it specifically in a template expression.

Multiple-if template expressions

Certain template expressions cannot be handled by referencing a single condition—"If A is true, show B" does not cover every possible circumstance. What if you wanted to test against multiple conditions and provide multiple results? Can Dreamweaver handle something like "If A is true, show B; but if C is true, show D—and if neither of them is true, show E"? With the help of multiple-if expressions, you bet it can.

With a multiple-if template expression, you can test for any number of conditions and act accordingly. Multiple-if expressions use two different template expressions: one to close the entire expression and another one for each separate case. Here is an example:

```
<!-- TemplateBeginMultipleIf -->
<!-- checks value of template parameter SKU and shows the desired image-->
  <!-- TemplateBeginIfClause cond = "SKU == 101">
   <img src = "/images/ring101.tif" width="125" height="125">
  <!-- TemplateEndIfClause-->

  <!-- TemplateBeginIfClause cond = "SKU == 102">
   <img src = "/images/bracelet102.gif" width="125" height="125">
  <!-- TemplateEndIfClause-->

  <!-- TemplateBeginIfClause cond = "SKU == 103">
   <img src = "/images/necklace103.gif" width="125" height="125">
  <!-- TemplateEndIfClause-->

  //default display if none of the other conditions are met
  <!-- TemplateBeginIfClause cond = "SKU != 103">
   <img src = "/images/spacer.gif" width="125" height="125">
  <!-- TemplateEndIfClause-->
<!-- TemplateEndMultipleIf -->
```

In this code, if none of the conditions are met, a blank spacer image is displayed. As with other template expressions, multiple-if expressions must be coded by hand.

Template expression examples

Template expressions obviously have a great deal of power built in, but how do you put it to use? Let's look at some specific examples to help you get a better understanding of template expressions in general, as well as to give you some useful tools.

Alternating row background colors

If you have a data-filled table of any significant size, alternating background colors for each row greatly increases the readability of the data. Template expressions provide a technique for specifying the two classes with different background colors—and automatically applying the right color whenever a new row is added in a repeating region. The key to this technique is the conditional operator.

28

The conditional operator has three parts: the condition and the two results. If the condition is evaluated as true, the first result is applied; if it is not, the second is applied. In this case, the condition that is examined involves the `_index` property, which returns the position of the current row. By combining the `_index` property with the bitwise AND operator, `&`, like this:

```
_index & 1
```

`True` is returned every other row, starting with the second row. The full template expression specifies the two classes as hexadecimal values; the second value specified (here, `oddRow`, a CSS class, which has a `background-color` property with a light yellow value) is returned in the first row, the first value (`evenRow`, another CSS class with a white background color) in the following row, and so on:

```
@@((_index & 1) ? 'evenRow' : 'oddRow')@@
```

This template expression is entered as the `class` attribute for the table row containing the data in a template's repeating region. Note the use of the single quotes around the class values; quotes are needed in the conditional operator syntax, and single quotes are used here because Dreamweaver encloses the entire attribute value with double quotes.

Here's the code for the entire table in the template document. The tag containing the alternating row background color is shown in bold:

```
<table width="100%" border="0" cellspacing="0" cellpadding="0">
  <tr>
    <th>Item</th>
    <th>SKU</th>
    <th>Price</th>
  </tr>
  <!-- TemplateBeginRepeat name="repeatRow" -->
 <tr class="@@((_index & 1) ? 'evenRow': 'oddRow')@@">
    <td><!-- TemplateBeginEditable name="itemEdit" -->itemEdit<!--
TemplateEndEditable --></td>
    <td><!-- TemplateBeginEditable name="skuEdit" -->skuEdit<!--
TemplateEndEditable --></td>
    <td><!-- TemplateBeginEditable name="priceEdit" -->priceEdit<!--
TemplateEndEditable -->
    </td>
  </tr>
  <!-- TemplateEndRepeat -->
</table>
```

You won't see any changes in the template itself—for the full effect, you have to open up a document based on the template and add a few rows. As you can see in Figure 28-15, whenever another entry is added to the repeating region in the template-based document, the alternating color is automatically applied.

TIP

As written, the code in this technique alternates color every row. To alternate the color every two rows, change the value in the condition from `1` to `2` so that the template expression reads:

```
@@((_index & 2) ? 'evenRow' : 'oddRow')@@
```

FIGURE 28-15

Using a conditional operator for the class attribute automatically generates alternating row colors in a repeating region.

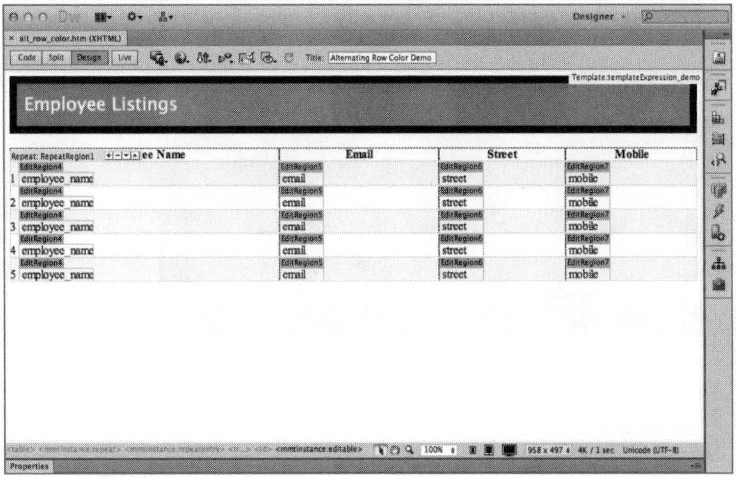

Automatic row numbering

In a template with a repeating region, you often want the flexibility of adding as many rows as required and adding a reference number to each row. The `_index` property of the template object model provides an easy way to number rows automatically. The only trick to this technique is to remember that `_index` is a zero-based property and you add a `1` to have the correct row number displayed.

Here's the template expression by itself:

```
@@(_index + 1)@@
```

This code should be entered directly in Code view within the repeating region. You can combine this with any other text, such as a following period or color or styles. Here's an example, bolded, in a right-aligned table cell with several non-breaking spaces trailing to create a decimal-aligned look:

```
<td align="right">@@(_index + 1)@@     </td>
```

28

The right-align and non-breaking space combination keeps numbering in line no matter how entries are involved, as shown in Figure 28-16.

FIGURE 28-16

The _index property helps to automatically number rows in a repeating region.

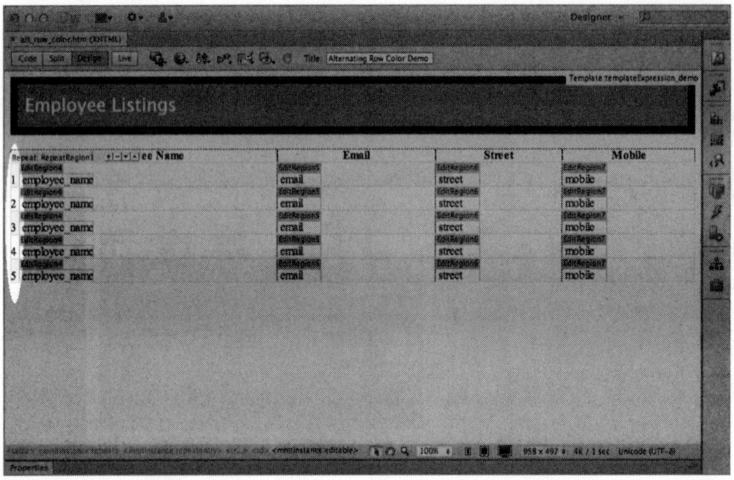

Computing values in a table

After a value has been entered for a template expression variable, it can be used in calculations and can also be used as a deciding factor in a multiple-if statement. For example, each page of a template shows a catalog item and all the relevant information. Included in that relevant information is the price—an element that may fluctuate far more than the description or picture of the item. Should the client want to offer a special discount for higher quantities, template expressions can automatically calculate the new price and the savings.

In this example, I've set up one template parameter, `priceVar`, and given it a default value of `100`:

```
<!-- TemplateParam name="priceVar" type="number" value="100" -->
```

This code goes in the non-editable portion of the template's `<head>`. The example application, shown in Figure 28-17, uses three different template expressions. The first, `@@priceVar@@`, displays the parameter set with the Template Properties dialog box.

The second shows the quantity price—which, here, is the base price times 3:

```
@@(priceVar * 3)@@
```

The third expression displays the savings a buyer could receive by buying in quantity. In this example formula, the price times 3 is subtracted from the price times 5:

```
@@((priceVar * 5) - (priceVar * 3))@@
```

Again, you can add whatever text or styles are necessary. Here, a dollar sign is placed in front of every expression that is followed by a decimal point and two zeros, as you can see in Listing 28-1.

FIGURE 28-17

Template expressions, set in Template Properties, can be used to calculate other values in a template-based document.

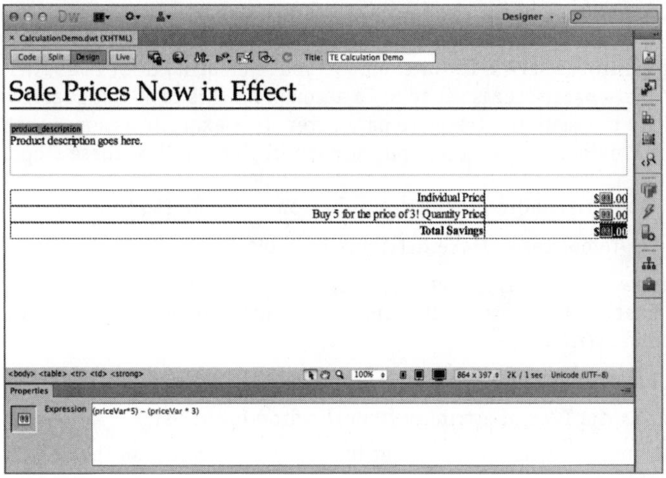

LISTING 28-1 Template Expressions Computing Example

```
<table width="100%"  border="0" cellspacing="0" cellpadding="0">
  <tr>
    <td width="77%" align="right">Individual Price</td>
    <td width="23%" align="right">$@@(priceVar)@@.00</td>
  </tr>
  <tr>
    <td align="right">Buy 5 for the price of 3! Quantity Price</td>
    <td align="right">$@@(priceVar * 3)@@.00</td>
  </tr>
  <tr>
    <td align="right"><strong>Total Savings</strong></td>
    <td align="right"><strong>$@@((priceVar * 5)@@ - (priceVar * i
))@@.00</strong></td>
  </tr>
</table>
```

Now the calculations on this template are ready to be used for any product in the catalog, at any price point, offering the same deal. All you need to do is create a page based on this template and change the template property `priceVar`.

Sequential navigation links

Although much of the web is based on the principle that you can link to any page from any other page, certain situations—such as help or instructional applications—require sequential navigation. Numerous help applications use some form of Previous and Next buttons, for example. If these files are named sequentially—such as docFile10, docFile11, docFile12, and so on—template expressions can be used to automatically code the links to the prior and subsequent pages.

You can rely on template expressions for the capability to handle string concatenation to create these auto-updating links. The first task is to set up a template parameter to be used as the number of the current file in the series. If, for example, you're creating `docFile5.htm` from your template, the template parameter is set to 5. To accomplish this task, use Dreamweaver's editable attribute facility to create the template parameter. This example assumes that you are editing a template with Previous and Next buttons already in place. Follow these steps:

1. Select the `<a>` tag surrounding the Previous button from the Tag Selector.
2. Choose Modify ➪ Templates ➪ Make Attribute Editable.
3. In the Editable Tag Attributes dialog box, click Add (+) and enter a dummy attribute name such as **baseLink**. Choose an attribute name that will be ignored by browsers rather than a real attribute.
4. Make sure that Make Attribute Editable is selected.
5. Choose Number as the Type of attribute from the drop-down list.
6. Enter a default number. This number is set for every file created, so the default value is merely a placeholder.

Now you can use the template parameter set up in a template expression. Follow these steps:

1. Click the Previous button or link on the template page.
2. In the Property inspector, enter code similar to the following in the Link field:

   ```
   @@('docFile' + (baseLink - 1) + '.htm')@@
   ```
   In this example, the sequential files are all within the same folder and named `docFile1.htm`, `docFile2.htm`, and so on. My template parameter, defined in the previous step, is called **baseLink**.
3. Click the Next button to perform a similar operation.
4. In the Link field, enter code like this:

   ```
   @@('docFile' + (baseLink + 1) + '.htm')@@
   ```
   Here, instead of subtracting a number from the base value, as you did for the Previous button link, you add one.

After the template is saved, create a file based on the template. Now you're ready to specify the template parameter. Follow these steps:

1. Choose Modify ➪ Template Properties and select the editable attribute established in the template.

2. Enter the number value corresponding to the filename of the current sequentially named page. For example, if the file is named `docFile5.htm`, enter **5**.
3. Click OK when you're finished.

When you preview your page, notice that the Previous and Next buttons now link the proper pages in the sequence, as shown in Figure 28-18.

FIGURE 28-18

Although it looks like a standard link, this code was generated by Dreamweaver during the design-time construction of this template-based document.

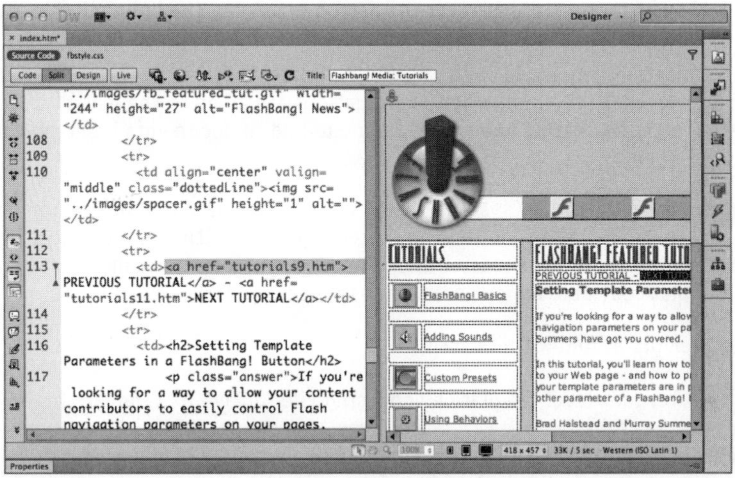

> **TIP**
>
> You can also use optional regions to hide the Previous button when the template-based page is the first in the series and the Next button when a page is the last in the series. It's all in the power of template expressions.

Nesting Templates

The simple template, with its combination of locked and editable regions, truly reflects the reality of many web pages where the overall structure is constant and the details of the content vary. Often, however, a single locked area is too rigid to really be useful in a complex site. Suppose for a moment you're working on a site for a magazine publisher with multiple brands. The client wants a general look and feel for the entire site with separate navigation and content for each magazine. One way to achieve this effect is to use multiple templates—one set for each magazine, all incorporating the parent-company style. The problem here is that to effect changes on the highest level, all the templates need to be changed. Another way—a better way—is to use nested templates.

Nested templates allow template-based documents to have numerous tiers of locked regions. With nested templates, the magazine publisher in our example could make a change to just the master template, and the modifications would ripple through all the other magazine-specific templates and on down to their related pages. Best of all, there's no real limit on nesting templates: Your template-based files can be as deeply nested as you need them to be.

Here's an overview of how nested templates work:

- A new page based on the master template is created and saved as a template; this new document is the nested template.
- Within the editable areas originally set up in the master template, new editable areas are placed. All areas not designated as editable in the nested template are locked.
- A new document is created, based on the nested template. The only editable areas are those inserted in the nested template.
- When modifications are made to the nested template, the changes are reflected in the pages based on that template. When modifications are made to the master template, the changes are applied both to the nested template and to documents based on the nested template.

Dreamweaver employs a color-coding system to help you differentiate editable regions inserted in the master template from those added in the nested template. Although you can't tell it in this black-and-white screenshot, the master template editable regions are shown in orange, whereas nested template editable regions are shown in blue (see Figure 28-19).

To create a nested template, follow these steps:

1. Create a master root-level template by choosing File ➪ Save As Template for an existing page or selecting New Template from the Template category of the Assets panel for new documents. The master template contains all the elements—navigation, logos, footers, and so on—common to all template-based pages in the site.
2. Insert editable regions wherever variable content is desired in the master template and save the template when you're ready.
3. Create a new document based on the master template by following these steps:
   a. Choose File ➪ New to open the New Document dialog box.
   b. Select the Templates category.
   c. Make sure the current site is selected in the Templates For list.
   d. Select the desired master template from the Template list.
   e. Click Create.
4. Save the newly created document as a template. By saving a template-derived document as a template, a nested template is created.
5. In the nested template, make any changes needed within the editable regions. These changes are locked in any document based on the nested template.

FIGURE 28-19

The master template editable region—the region in the center here—is highlighted with an orange outline. The nested template editable regions, the outside regions, are blue.

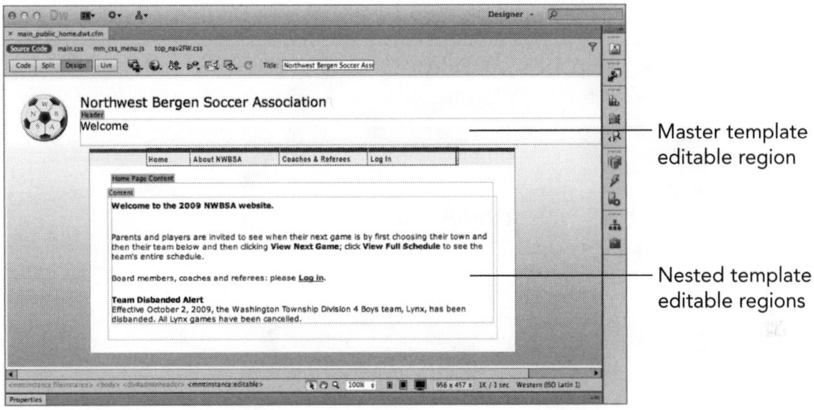

6. Add any desired template regions (editable, repeating, or optional) within the existing editable regions from the master template. When the first editable region is inserted in the nested template, the editable regions from the master template turn orange to differentiate them from the new regions.
7. After you've finished adding the desired template regions to the nested template, save the file.

Now, when creating documents based on the nested template, you are still able to modify content within an editable region—but only those editable regions added in the nested template.

Working with Templates in the Assets Panel

As a site grows, so does the number of templates it employs. Overall management of your templates is conducted through the Templates category of the Assets panel. You can open the Templates category by choosing Window ➪ Assets and clicking the Template icon on the left side of the Assets panel. The Templates category, shown in Figure 28-20, displays a list of the current site's available templates in the lower pane and a preview of the selected template in the upper pane.

The Templates category has these five buttons along the bottom:

- **Apply:** Creates a document derived from the currently selected template if the current document is blank; if the current document is based on a template, this option changes the locked regions of the document to match the selected template.
- **Refresh Site List:** Displays the list of all templates currently in the site.

- **New Template:** Creates a new blank template.
- **Edit:** Loads the selected template for modification.
- **Delete:** Removes the selected template.

FIGURE 28-20

Use the Templates category of the Assets panel to preview, delete, open, create, or apply your current site's templates.

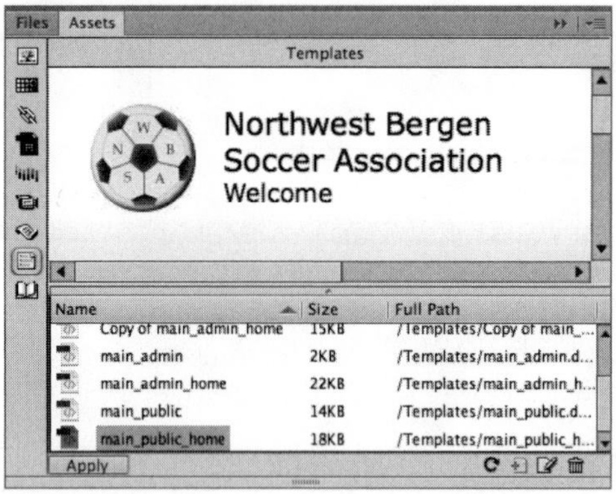

The Assets panel's context menu offers all these options and more, as explained in Table 28-3.

TABLE 28-3 **Template Category Context Menu**

Command	Description
Refresh Site List	Displays the list of all templates currently in the site cache.
Recreate Site List	Reloads the template site list into the cache.
New Template	Starts a new blank template.
New From Template	Creates a new page from the selected template.
Edit	Opens the selected template for modifying.
Apply	Creates a document derived from the currently selected template if the current document is blank. If the current document is based on a template, this option changes the locked regions of the document to match the selected template. The same effects can also be achieved by dragging the template from the Assets panel to the current document.
Rename	Renames the selected template.
Delete	Removes the selected template.

Command	Description
Update Current Page	Applies any changes made in the template to the current page, if the current page is derived from a template.
Update Site	Applies any changes made in any templates to all template-based documents in the site.
Copy to Site	Copies the highlighted template, but none of the dependent files, to the selected site.
Locate in Site	Opens the Site panel and highlights the selected template.

Creating a blank template

Not all templates are created from existing documents. Some web designers prefer to create their templates from scratch. To create a blank template, follow these steps:

1. Open the Templates category of the Assets panel by selecting its symbol.
2. From the Templates category, select New Template. A new, untitled template is created.
3. Enter a title for your new template and press Enter (Return).
4. While the new template is selected, click the Edit button. The blank template opens in a new Dreamweaver document window.
5. Insert your page elements.
6. Mark any elements or areas as editable regions using one of the methods previously described.
7. Save your template.

Opening and deleting templates

You can edit a template—to change the locked or editable regions—in several ways. To use the first method, choose File ⇨ Open and, in the Open dialog box, change the Files Of Type to Template Files (`*.dwt`) on Windows systems, or select Template Files from the Enable drop-down list on Macintosh systems. Then, locate the Templates folder in your defined site to select the template to open.

The second method of opening a template for modification uses the Templates category of the Assets panel. Select a template to modify and click the Edit button. You can also double-click your template to open it for editing. Finally, if you're working in the Site panel, open a template by selecting the Templates folder for your site and opening any of the files found there.

TIP

After you've made your modifications to the template, you don't have to use the Save As Template command to store the file—you can use the regular File ⇨ Save command or the keyboard shortcut Ctrl+S (Command+S). On the other hand, if you want to save your template under a new name, use the Save As command.

As with any set of files, there comes a time to clean house and remove files that are no longer in use. To remove a template, first open the Templates category of the Assets panel. Next, select the file you want to remove and click the Delete button.

CAUTION
Dreamweaver does not alert you if files exist that were created from the template that you're about to delete. Deleting the template, in effect, "orphans" those documents, and they can no longer be updated via a template.

Applying templates

Dreamweaver makes it easy to try a variety of different looks for your document while maintaining the same content. After you've created a document from a template, you can apply any other template to it. The only requirement is that the two templates have editable regions with the same names. When might this feature come in handy? In one scenario, you might develop a number of possible website designs for a client and create templates for each approach, which are then applied to the identical content. Or, in an ongoing site, you could completely change the look of a catalog seasonally but retain all the content.

To apply a template to a document, follow these steps:

1. Open the Templates category of the Assets panel.
2. Make sure the web page to which you want to apply the style is the active document.
3. From the Templates category, select the template you want to use and click the Apply button.

TIP
You can also drag onto the current page the template you'd like to apply or choose Modify ➪ Templates ➪ Apply Template to Page from the menus.

4. If content exists without a matching editable region, Dreamweaver displays the Inconsistent Region Names dialog box. To keep the content, select the listed editable regions from the template being applied in which you want the content to appear and click OK.

The new template is applied to the document, and all the new locked areas replace all the old locked areas.

Mapping inconsistent template regions

When Dreamweaver applies a template to a page, it attempts to map the regions on the two pages to one another. If there is a one-to-one correspondence between the regions on the page and the regions on the template—for every editable region in the template, an editable region exists with the same name on the page—everything goes smoothly, and the template is applied without incident. If, however, the region names do not match—for example, the template's main content area is called `theContent`, whereas the page's main content area is called `mainContent`—Dreamweaver gives you the opportunity to place the content properly with the Inconsistent Region Names dialog box, shown in Figure 28-21.

The Inconsistent Region Names dialog box appears automatically when Dreamweaver finds regions that do not match in a template and the document to which the template is being applied. You can map the content in the document to any region in the template or discard the content. However, you cannot ignore the unmapped content; Dreamweaver does not proceed with the template application until all inconsistently named regions are addressed in some fashion.

FIGURE 28-21

The Inconsistent Region Names dialog box works with the full range of template regions, as well as template properties.

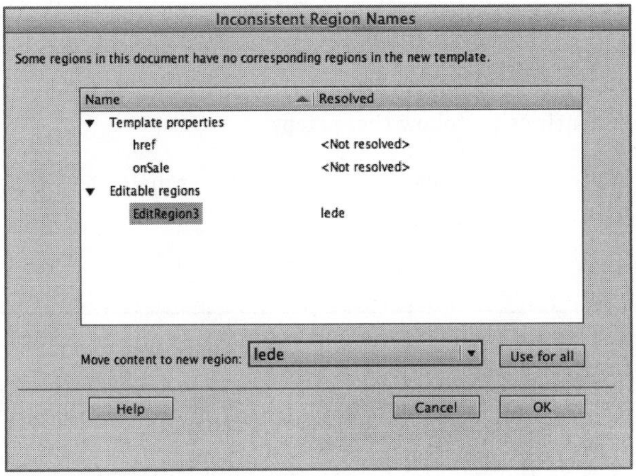

To handle inconsistently named regions, follow these steps:

1. When the Inconsistent Region Names dialog box appears, select the first unresolved region.
2. From the Move Content To New Region drop-down list, select the region you want to assign to the unmapped region.
3. If no region is suitable and you want to discard the content, choose Nowhere from the list.
4. To use the same choice for all regions displayed, choose the Use For All option.
5. To map another region, select its name from the list and repeat Steps 2 through 4.
6. Click OK when you're finished.

You always find certain regions, such as `doctitle` and `head`, listed in the Move Content To New Region list. In general, you would not want to move any body-area content into these regions.

TIP

The region names must match precisely—including the case of the two names—or the Inconsistent Region Names dialog box appears.

Updating Templates

Anytime you save a change to an existing template—whether or not any documents have been created from it—Dreamweaver asks if you'd like to update all the documents in the local site attached to the template. You can also update the current page or the entire site at any time, just as you can update Library elements. Updating documents based on a template can save you an enormous amount of time—especially when numerous changes are involved.

To update a single page, open the page and choose Modify ➪ Templates ➪ Update Current Page or select the same command from the context menu of the Assets panel. Either way, the update is instantly applied.

To update a series of pages or an entire site, follow these steps:

1. Choose Modify ➪ Templates ➪ Update Pages. The Update Pages dialog box, shown in Figure 28-22, appears.

FIGURE 28-22

Any changes made to a template can be applied automatically to the template's associated files by using the Update Pages command.

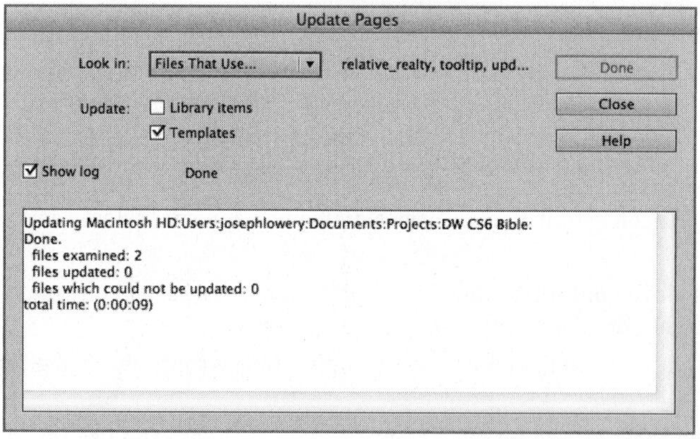

2. To update all the documents using all the templates for an entire site, choose Entire Site from the Look In option; then select the name of the site from the accompanying drop-down list.

3. To update pages using a particular template, choose Files That Use from the Look In option and then select the name of the template.
4. To view a report of the progress of the update, make sure that the Show Log option is enabled.
5. Click Start to begin the update process.

The log window displays a list of the files examined and updated, the total number of files that could not be updated, and the elapsed time.

Removing Template Markup

Mistakes are made, clients change their minds, bosses change directions—for whatever reason, you'll find that you need to remove template markup from time to time. Luckily, Dreamweaver has made it as easy to delete the template indicators as it is to insert them. With a little know-how, you can remove template markup from an editable attribute for an entire site.

Deleting template markup individually

Quite often I find I need to convert an editable region in a template to a locked area. You can accomplish this change in one of two ways—you can delete the surrounding template tags in the code or you can use a Dreamweaver command, Remove Template Markup. Personally, I find the command approach to be much faster and more efficient. Individual template markup can only be removed from the template itself.

To remove any surrounding template code via the command, place your cursor within the template region and choose Modify ➪ Templates ➪ Remove Template Markup. Alternatively, right-click (Control+click) and choose Templates ➪ Remove Template Markup.

The Remove Template Markup command works only on the template markup immediately enclosing the cursor position. If, for example, you need to remove an editable optional region and convert the content to being locked, you issue the Remove Template Markup command twice: once to remove the editable region and again to remove the optional region.

CAUTION
Using the Remove Template Markup command to remove an optional region does not delete the corresponding TemplateParam statement in the `<head>` tag. If no other optional region uses the same TemplateParam statement, you must remove the code manually.

Removing template markup from an entire page

Template-derived documents don't need to stay template-derived documents forever. All you need do is to detach the document from its template, and all template markup in the page is removed. To detach a document from the template, choose Modify ➪ Templates ➪ Detach from Template.

NOTE

If, for any reason, you need to remove all of the markup from a template itself, the fastest way is to create a document from that template and then issue the Detach From Template command.

Exporting a site without template markup

Not all sites are template-based. Dreamweaver gives you the power to strip all of the template markup from template-based documents in an entire site. This command is particularly useful when migrating previously template-based documents to a site that does not use templates. Just to hedge your bets, Dreamweaver optionally exports the data from your template-based documents into XML files so that, if necessary, the data can be applied to a new template.

The Export Without Markup command handles more than just the templates, however. An entire copy of your site is copied to a new folder, *sans* template markup. Even the Template folder itself, with all the site's templates intact, is copied. Best of all, this is not necessarily a one time feature. If repeated, you have the option to extract only the modified files.

To export a site without template markup, follow these steps:

1. Choose Modify ➪ Templates ➪ Export Without Markup. The Export Site Without Template Markup dialog box, shown in Figure 28-23, appears.

FIGURE 28-23

The Export Without Markup command duplicates your entire site in another folder while simultaneously removing all markup from template-derived files.

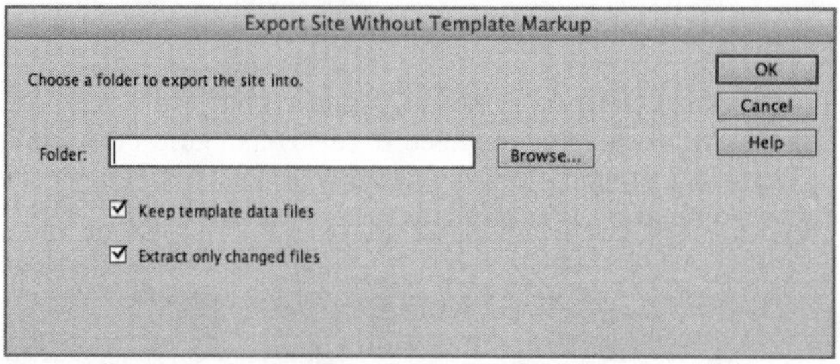

2. Enter the path to the folder to hold the exported site or click the Browse button to locate the folder. Because the entire site is exported, the folder you choose may not be contained in the current site.
3. If you want to maintain the data from the template-based documents, choose the Keep Template Data Files option.

Dreamweaver stores the data in a standard XML file format. For more about Dreamweaver's XML export features, see Chapter 32.

4. If you have previously exported the site with this command and want to update your export, choose the Extract Only Changed Files option.
5. Click OK when you're finished.

After the operation is completed, you'll probably want to define a new site to manage the exported files—Dreamweaver does not do this task for you automatically.

Changing the Default Document

Each time you open a new document in Dreamweaver, a blank page is created. The code that makes up that blank page depends on which document type you choose—HTML, XML, ColdFusion, or ASP.NET, among others. The default documents on which the new pages are based are all stored in the Dreamweaver CS6\Configuration\DocumentTypes\NewDocuments folder. A selected default page works in a similar fashion to the templates in that you can create new documents from it, but no editable or locked regions exist—everything in the page can always be altered. For example, the basic HTML document is a bare-bones structure with only a few properties specified—a document type and a character set:

```
<!DOCTYPE html PUBLIC "-//W3C//DTD XHTML 1.0 Transitional//EN" ~CA
"http://www.w3.org/TR/xhtml1/DTD/xhtml1-transitional.dtd">
<html xmlns="http://www.w3.org/1999/xhtml">
<head>
<meta http-equiv="Content-Type" content="text/html; charset=utf-8" />
<title>Untitled Document</title>
</head>

<body>
</body>
</html>
```

28

Naturally, you can change any of these elements—and add many, many more—after you've opened a page. But what if you want to have a <meta> tag with creator information in every page that comes out of your web design company? You can do it in Dreamweaver manually, but it's a bother, and chances are good that you'll forget. Luckily, Dreamweaver provides a more efficient solution.

In keeping with its overall design philosophy of extensibility, Dreamweaver enables you to modify the default file as you would any other file. Just choose File ➪ Open and select the appropriate file from the Dreamweaver CS6\Configuration\DocumentTypes\NewDocuments folder. After you have made your changes, save the file as you would normally. Now, to test your modifications, choose File ➪ New and select your document type. Your modifications appear in the new document.

Editing Content in the Browser

One of the primary uses of Dreamweaver templates is updating client sites. With primary portions of the design—such as the logo and navigation—locked, targeted editable areas containing web page content can quickly be modified. However, to make any changes on pages derived from Dreamweaver, you'd typically need a desktop tool such as Adobe Contribute or Dreamweaver itself. Many site owners are more business-oriented than web-savvy and don't have the skills or time to devote to mastering a software package. For them, the solution is Adobe InContext Editing.

InContext Editing is an in-browser editing service available in Business Catalyst sites, using web pages with special markup from Dreamweaver. These pages can be modified using any modern browser, starting from Internet Explorer 6, Firefox 3, and Safari 3.1. Clients can change or add text, images, or links. Specially designated sections, such as event listings, can be repeated and modified or reordered. Despite all this access, designers maintain a high degree of control. Not only can they establish which areas are editable and which are not, but they can also control the level of editability—from full stylistic freedom to plain-text editing only.

The workflow for creating, publishing, and editing InContext Editing pages goes like this:

1. The designer creates a page in Dreamweaver.
2. InContext Editing versions of editable and repeating regions are added to the page through Dreamweaver tools.
3. The designer publishes the page to a site that has been registered with the Adobe Business Catalyst service.
4. The client navigates to the InContext Editing–enabled page and presses a keyboard shortcut to log in.
5. Once logged in, the client makes any desired changes to the site, saves the page, and clicks Publish.

Next, you learn how to integrate InContext Editing controls into your web pages.

Setting up InContext Editing templates

Unlike Dreamweaver templates, you don't have to save an InContext Editing–enabled page as a template to make it functional. All you need to do is to add one or more InContext Editing regions to the page and, when you publish the page to your site, put a number of InContext Editing–related files online. From a designer's standpoint, it takes only a few minutes to make an existing page client-editable.

Dreamweaver includes an InContext Editing category in the Insert panel with two entries:

- **Create Editable Region:** Adds a `<div>` tag or tag attribute that allows the enclosed content to be modified through InContext Editing.
- **Create Repeating Region:** Adds code that allows an InContext Editing user to repeat a specific section of code and change it. Users can also reorder code blocks within the repeating region.

Although the objects are very straightforward to apply, they do permit the designers to exercise a fair amount of control. Each object is discussed in turn in the following sections.

NOTE

It's important to realize that InContext Editing pages are not the same as Dreamweaver templates, discussed earlier in this chapter. You cannot, as a designer, create pages based on InContext Editing-enabled pages, and, therefore, you can't update a master template to change derived pages. You (or the client) can, however, duplicate a page once it has been published and add new content through the InContext Editing toolbar in the browser.

Adding an editable region

An InContext Editing editable region can be applied to any portion of the page. Once it is applied, Dreamweaver adds a single attribute to the code, like this:

```
<div ice:editable="*">
```

The value of the `ice:editable` attribute is initially set to an asterisk, which indicates that all editing options are available. If you turn off all the options, so that the content can only be changed but not styled, the `ice:editing` value is empty. Selecting one or more options will cause the available options to be written into the code, like this:

```
<div ice:editable="bold,align_right,align_center,align_left">
```

To add an InContext Editing editable region to the page, follow these steps:

1. Place your cursor in the area you want to make editable.
2. From the Insert panel, choose the InContext Editing category.
3. Select Create Editable Region.
4. In the Create Editable Region dialog box (see Figure 28-24), choose to wrap the current selection with a `<div>` tag or transform the parent tag into an editable region by adding the InContext Editing attribute. Click OK.

   Which option you choose depends on your design. Sometimes wrapping a new `<div>` tag around existing content causes elements to shift, and it is better to take the attribute route by transforming the parent tag.
5. Select the desired options in the Editable Region Property inspector.

FIGURE 28-24

If you have already selected the parent tag for your editable region, the option to Transform The Parent Tag Into An Editable Region is disabled.

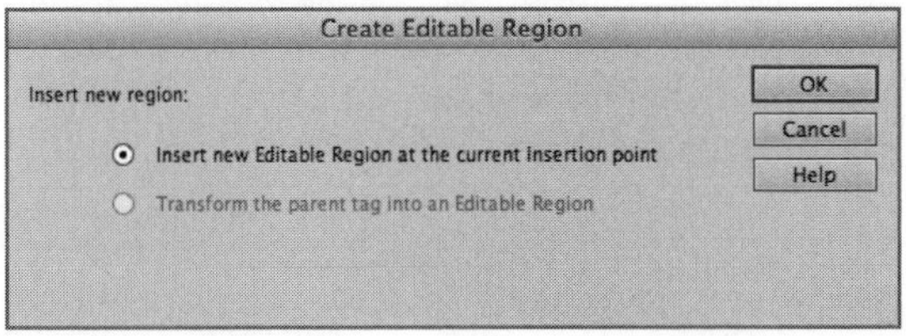

> **NOTE**
> Unlike with standard Dreamweaver templates, you can't add editable regions within `<heading>` or other tags. Therefore, if you don't want clients to modify the format or style of the content, select Uncheck All in the InContext Editing Property inspector to disable all editing options.

InContext Editing gives you a wide variety of options to choose from, as shown in Figure 28-25. You can quickly eliminate all of them by choosing Uncheck All or bring them all back by clicking Check All. The available options are listed in Table 28-4.

FIGURE 28-25

By default, all options are enabled when you insert a new InContext Editing editable region.

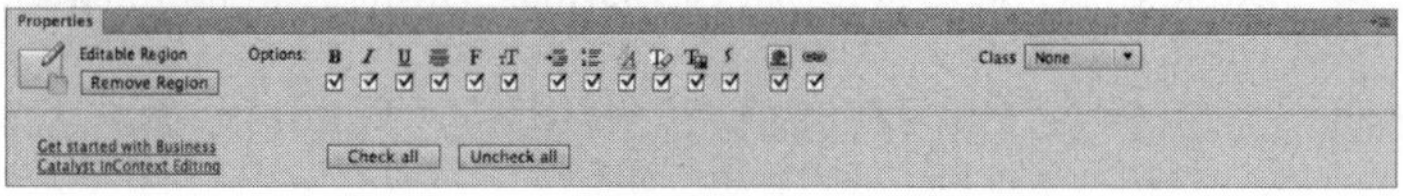

TABLE 28-4 **InContext Editing Property Inspector Options**

Icon	Name	Description
	Bold	Displays a bold button to add a <span> tag with the inline CSS property font-weight: bold.
	Italic	Displays an italic button to add a <span> tag with the inline CSS property font-style: italic.
	Underline	Displays an underline button to insert <u> tags.
	Alignment buttons	Displays left, center, right, and justify buttons.
	Font Face	Displays a drop-down list with a standard selection of web font families.
	Font Size	Displays a drop-down list of seven font sizes, from 10 px to 48 px.
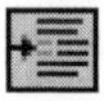	Indent and Outdent buttons	Displays buttons to move the text in by adding a <blockquote> tag or out by removing a <blockquote> tag.
	Numbered List and Bulleted List	Displays buttons for converting paragraphs to an ordered or unordered list.
	Paragraph Styles	Displays a drop-down list of HTML formats, including: paragraph and Heading 1 through Heading 6.
	Background Color	Displays a color picker for adding a background color to a selection.
	Font Color	Displays a color picker for adding a color to a selection.

Icon	Name	Description
	CSS Styles	Displays a drop-down list of CSS classes, as chosen through the Manage Available CSS Classes object.
	Image/Media	Displays controls for adding and managing images and other media.
	Link	Displays controls for adding and managing links.

You can also use the Class drop-down list included in the InContext Editing Property inspector to specify a CSS class for any InContext Editing–added `<div>` tag.

Like standard editable regions and Spry elements, an InContext Editing region is identified by a tab and blue border, as shown in Figure 28-26. Unlike editable regions, you don't need to name them separately.

FIGURE 28-26

To invoke the InContext Editing Property inspector, click the blue tab surrounding the content.

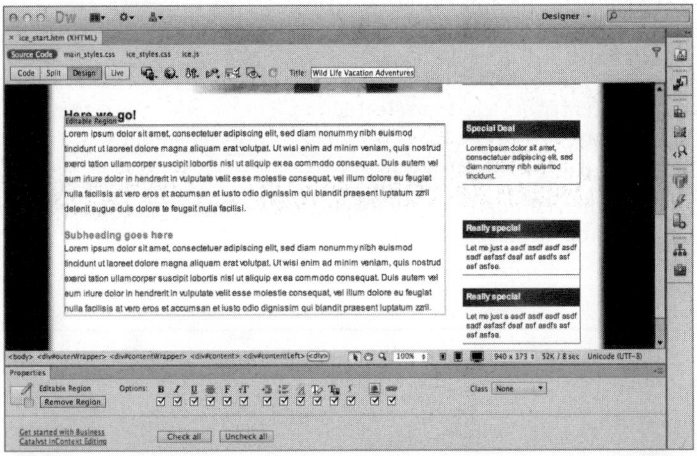

> **NOTE**
> If you'd like to get a jump start on your pages—and incorporate InContext Editing—Dreamweaver has just the feature for you. When you create a new HTML page with one of Dreamweaver's pre-built CSS layouts (available through the New dialog box), you'll see an option to Enable InContext Editing. Click that checkbox and Dreamweaver will generate a CSS standards-compliant page where the main content area is already enclosed in an InContext Editing editable region. Customize the page however you like, save, and you are ready to post to the InContext Editing server.

To remove a selected InContext Editing editable region from your page, choose Remove Region from the Property inspector.

TIP

When you remove an InContext Editing editable region through the Property inspector, only the `ice:editable` region is removed. If code such as `<div ice:editable="*">` is wrapped around the content, the `<div>` tag remains. To remove both tag and attribute, right-click the `<div>` tag in the Tag Selector and choose Remove Tag.

Repeating page sections

The InContext Editing repeating region works in exactly the same way as the Dreamweaver template repeating region. Add a repeating region to a section of the page that includes at least one editable region, and when the page is published, the user can add more instances of the section and change the content, reorder them, or delete them. Repeating regions are excellent for page sections such as blog posts, event listings, and news items.

To add an InContext Editing repeating region to the page, follow these steps:

1. Make sure that you have added InContext Editing editable regions to any section of the page you want to repeat.
2. Select the outermost section of the element you want to repeat in the Tag Selector or in Code view.

   Typically, a `<div>` tag is used as a containing element for a repeating section. You can include as many editable and non-editable sections within the containing `<div>` tag as you like.
3. From the Insert panel's InContext Editing category, choose Create Repeating Region.

   Dreamweaver adds an attribute to the selected tag, `ice:repeating="true"`, and also adds another attribute, `ice:repeatinggroup="*"`, to the parent tag. This parent tag will contain all instances of the repeating region.
4. In the Repeating Regions Group Property inspector, deselect either of the default options: Reorder or Add/Remove, as shown in Figure 28-27.

FIGURE 28-27

Give your client the capability to grow the page content in a controlled fashion through InContext Editing repeating regions.

With the Reorder option enabled, controls that allow the client to move items up and down appear above the repeating region in the browser. This functionality is useful, for example, to place a new item before an existing item. When the Add/Remove option is checked, similar controls for inserting and deleting a repeating section are made available.

5. Save your page. Three new files are copied to your site: `ice.conf.js`, `ice.js`, and `ide.html`.

You can use the InContext Editing repeating region facility in combination with non-editable sections of the page as well. Imagine, for instance, that you have a number of news items that you do not want to allow the client to remove. If you create a dummy news item to which you apply the InContext Editing editable regions and then the repeating region, Dreamweaver will mark the entire news section—with both editable and non-editable items—as the Repeating Regions Group. When the client goes to edit this section in the browser, only the editable item can be deleted or reordered.

Summary

Much of a web designer's responsibility is related to document production, and Dreamweaver offers a comprehensive template solution to reduce the workload. When planning your strategy for building an entire website, remember that templates provide these advantages:

- Templates can be created from any web page.
- Dreamweaver templates combine locked and editable regions. Editable regions must be defined individually.
- After you declare a template, you can create new documents from it.
- With Dreamweaver's repeating regions, you can add or remove data from tables without altering the table structure.
- Show or hide content with each new template-derived document with Dreamweaver optional regions.
- Nested templates can be used to structurally organize locked and editable content.
- If a template is altered, pages built from that template can be automatically updated, but will need to be re-uploaded if already on the site.
- The default template that Dreamweaver uses can be modified so that every time you choose File ➪ New and select a file type, a new version of your customized template is created.
- Adobe offers a service, Business Catalyst InContext Editing, which makes it easy for clients to update their own web page content in any modern browser without affecting the overall design. Dreamweaver designers can set up editable regions and repeating regions.

In the next chapter, you learn how to streamline production and site maintenance by using repeating page elements from the Dreamweaver Library.

CHAPTER

29

Using Library Items and Server-Side Includes

IN THIS CHAPTER

Understanding Dreamweaver Library basics

Making and inserting Library items

Managing your Dreamweaver Library

Dreamweaver Technique: Building a Library Item

Updating your websites with Libraries

Dreamweaver Technique: Applying and Modifying Library Items

Using server-side includes

One of the challenges of designing a website is ensuring that buttons, copyright notices, and other cross-site features always remain consistent. Fortunately, Dreamweaver offers a useful feature called a *Library item* that helps you insert a repeating element, such as a navigation bar or a company logo, into every web page you create. With one command, you can update and maintain Library items efficiently and productively.

In this chapter, you examine the nature and the importance of repeating elements and learn how to effectively use the Dreamweaver Library feature for all your sites. In addition, you see how to use *server-side includes*—generally known as *SSIs*—to integrate code and content at both design time and runtime.

Dreamweaver QUICKSTART

Library items are a Dreamweaver-only concept, but if you think you've got the concept down and just want to put them to use, there are two things you need to know. First, you should know how to create a Library item:

1. Select the part of the page you want to turn into a Library item.
2. Choose Window ➪ Assets.

Continues

continued

3. Click the Library category (bottom icon on left).

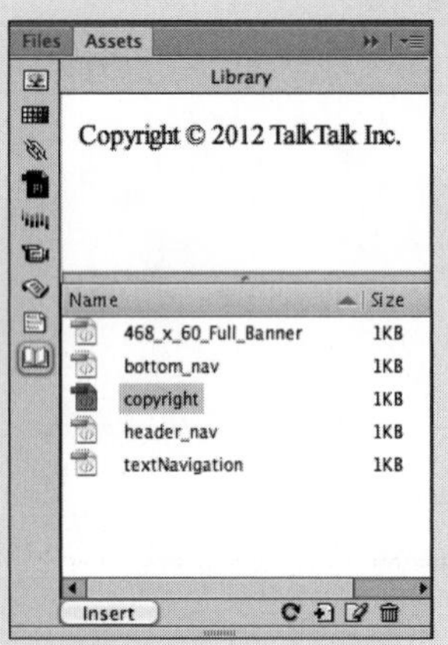

4. Click the New Library Item button at the bottom of the Assets panel.
5. Enter a unique name for the new item.

You'll also need to know one of the ways to insert a Library item. Here's one method:

1. Open the Assets panel and click the Library category.
2. Drag the desired item onto the page and drop it where it is needed.

Dreamweaver Library Items

Library items within Dreamweaver are another means for you, as a designer, to maintain consistency throughout your site. Imagine that you have a navigation bar on every page that contains links to all the other pages on your site. It's highly likely that you'll eventually (probably more than once) need to make changes to that navigation bar. In a traditional web development environment, you must modify every single page. This creates numerous opportunities for making mistakes, missing pages, and adding code in the wrong place. Moreover, the whole process is tedious—ask anyone who has had to modify the copyright notice at the bottom of every web page for a site with more than 1,000 pages.

One traditional method of updating repeating elements is to use *server-side includes*. A server-side include causes the server to place a component, such as a copyright notice, in a specified area of a web page when it's sent to the user. This arrangement, however, increases the strain on your already overworked web server, and many hosting computers do not permit server-side includes for this reason. To add to the designer's frustrations, you can't lay out a web page in a WYSIWYG format and simultaneously see the server-side scripts (unless you're using Dreamweaver). Therefore, either you take the time to calculate the specific amount of space the server-side script takes up on the web page or you cross your fingers and guess.

Dreamweaver offers you a better way. You can use an important innovation called the *Library*. The Library is designed to make repetitive updating quick, easy, and as error-free as possible. The Library's key features include the following:

- Any item—whether text or graphic—that goes into the body of your web page can be designated as a Library item.
- After they are created, Library items can be placed instantly in any web page in your site, without your having to retype, reinsert, or reformat text and graphics.
- Library items can be altered at any time. After the editing is complete, Dreamweaver gives you the option to update the website immediately or postpone the update until later. If you are making a number of alterations to your Library items, you can wait until you're finished with all the updates and then make the changes across the board in one operation.
- You can update one page at a time or you can update the entire site all at once.
- A Library item can be converted back to a regular non-Library element of a web page at any time.
- Library items can be copied from one site to another.
- Library items can combine Dreamweaver behaviors—and their underlying JavaScript code—with onscreen elements, so you don't have to rebuild the same pop-up window every time, reapplying the behaviors repeatedly.

Using the Library Assets Panel

Dreamweaver's Library control center is located on the Assets panel in the Library category. Here you find the tools for creating, modifying, updating, and managing your Library items. Shown in Figure 29-1, the Library category is as flexible and easy to use as Dreamweaver's other primary panels, with straightforward command buttons, a listing of all available Library items, and a handy Preview area.

You have two ways to access the Library items:

- Choose Window ⇨ Assets.
- Click the Library icon on the Assets panel.

Ideally, you save the most time by creating all your Library items before you begin constructing your web pages, but most web designers don't work that way. Feel free to include, modify, and update your Library items as often as necessary as your website evolves—that's part of the power and flexibility you gain through Dreamweaver's Library.

FIGURE 29-1

With the Dreamweaver Library feature, you can easily add and modify objects on an entire website.

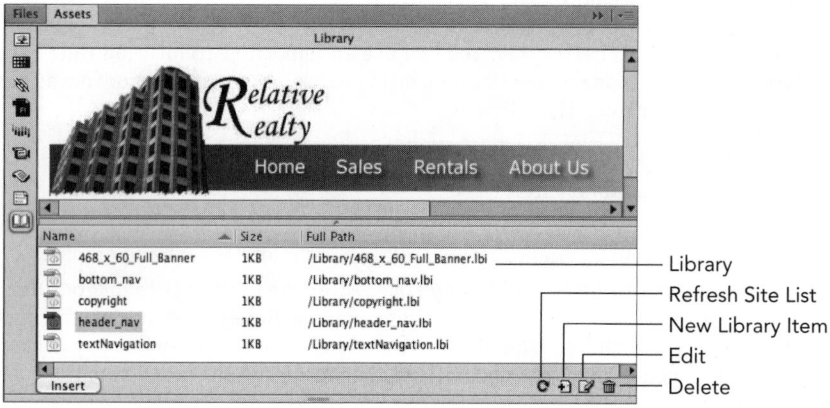

Adding a Library item

Before you can insert or update a Library item, that item must be designated as a Library item within the web page. To add an item to your site's Library, follow these steps:

CAUTION

Dreamweaver can include Library items only in the `<body>` section of an HTML document. You cannot, for instance, create a series of `<meta>` tags for your pages that must go in the `<head>` section.

1. Select any part of the web page that you want to make into a Library item.
2. Open the Library category of the Assets panel.
3. From the Library category (refer again to Figure 29-1), click the New Library Item button.

   The selected page element is displayed in the preview area of the Library category. In the Library item list a new entry is highlighted with the default name Untitled.

NOTE

If the text you've selected has been styled by a CSS rule, Dreamweaver warns you that the appearance may be different because the style rule is not included in the Library item. To ensure that the appearance is the same, include the Library item only on those pages with the appropriate CSS styles.

4. Enter a unique name for your new Library item and press Enter (Return). The Library item list is re-sorted alphabetically, if necessary, and the new item is included.

Drag-and-Drop Creation of Library Items

A second option for creating Library items is the drag-and-drop method. Simply select an object or objects on a page and drag them to the Library category (either the preview area or the Site list pane); release the mouse button to drop them in.

You can drag any object into the Library panel: text, tables, images, Java applets, plugins, and/or ActiveX controls. Essentially, anything in the Document window that can be HTML code can be dragged to the Library. Similarly, as you might suspect, the reverse is true: Library items can be placed in your web page by dragging them from the Library category and dropping them anywhere in the Document window.

When a portion of your web page has been designated as a Library item, yellow highlighting is displayed over the entire item within the Document window. The highlighting helps you to quickly recognize a Library item. If you find the effect distracting, you can disable it. Go to Edit ➪ Preferences (Dreamweaver ➪ Preferences) and, from the Highlighting panel of the Preferences dialog box, clear the checkbox to the right of the Library Items color selection. Alternatively, clearing View ➪ Visual Aids ➪ Invisible Elements hides Library Item highlighting, along with any other invisible items on your page.

Moving Library items to a new site

Although Library items are specific to each site, they can be used in more than one site. When you make your first Library item, Dreamweaver creates a folder called Library in the local root folder for the current site. To move the Library item to a new site, follow these steps:

1. Open the Library category from the Assets panel.
2. Right-click (Control+click) the Library item you want to move.
3. Put your mouse over the Copy To Site section of the context menu, and then choose the site you want to copy the Library item to.

CAUTION
Be sure to move any dependent files or other assets, such as images and media files, associated with Library items yourself. The Copy To Site function does not move dependent files.

29

Inserting a Library item in your web page

When you create a website, you always need to incorporate certain features, including a standard set of link buttons along the top, a consistent banner on various pages, and a copyright notice along the bottom. Adding these items to a page using Library items can be as easy as dragging and dropping them.

You must first create a website and then designate Library items (as explained in the preceding section). After these items exist, you can add the items to any page created within your site. To add Library items to a document, follow these steps:

1. Position the cursor where you want the Library item to appear.
2. From the Library category, select the item you want to use.
3. Click the Insert button. The highlighted Library item appears on the web page.

TIP

As noted earlier, you can also use the drag-and-drop method to place Library items in the Document window.

When you add a Library item to a page, you notice a number of immediate changes. As mentioned, the added Library item is highlighted. If you click anywhere on the item, the entire Library item is selected.

Dreamweaver treats the entire Library item entry as an external object being linked to the current page. You cannot modify Library items directly on a page. For information about editing Library entries, see the section "Editing a Library Item," later in this chapter.

While the Library item is highlighted, notice that the Properties panel also changes. Instead of displaying the properties for the HTML object that is selected, the item is identified as a Library item, as shown in Figure 29-2.

You can also see evidence of Library items in the HTML for the current page. Open the Code inspector, and you can see that several lines of code have been added. The following code example indicates one Library item:

```
<!-- #BeginLibraryItem "/Library/Copyright.lbi" --><span i
class="fineprint">Copyright &copy; 2010</span><!-- #EndLibraryItem -->
```

In this case, the Library item happens to be a phrase: `Copyright © 2012`. (The character entity `©` is used to represent the c-in-a-circle copyright mark in HTML.) In addition to the span wrapping the copyright, notice the text before and after the HTML code. These are commands within the comments (indicated by `<!--` and `-->`) that tell Dreamweaver it is looking at a Library item. One line marks the beginning of the Library item:

```
<!-- #BeginLibraryItem "/Library/Copyright.lbi" -->
```

and another marks the end:

```
<!-- #EndLibraryItem -->
```

Two items are of interest here. First, notice how the Library demarcation surrounds not just the text (`Copyright © 2012`) but all its formatting attributes as well. Library items can do far more than just cut and paste raw text. The second thing to note is that the Library markers are placed discretely within HTML comments. Web browsers ignore the Library markers and render the code in between them.

FIGURE 29-2

The Library Item Properties panel identifies the source file for any selected Library entry.

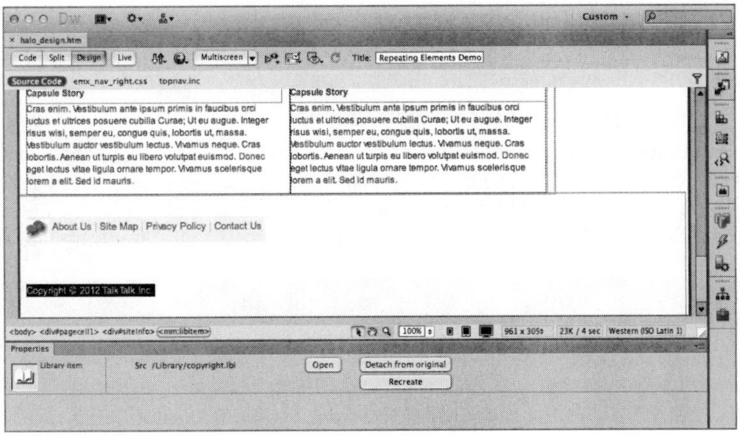

The value in the opening Library code, "/Library/Copyright.lbi", is the source file for the Library entry. This file is located in the Library folder, inside of the current site root folder. Library source (.lbi) files can be opened with a text editor or in Dreamweaver; they consist of plain HTML code without the <html> and <body> tags.

The .lbi file for the title example contains the following:

```
<span class="fineprint">Copyright &copy; 2010</span>
```

The power of repeating elements is that they are simply HTML. You need not learn proprietary languages to customize Library items. Anything, except for information found in the header of a web page, can be included in a Library file.

The importance of the <!-- #BeginLibraryItem> and <!-- #EndLibraryItem> tags becomes evident when you start to update Library items for a site. You examine how Dreamweaver can be used to automatically update your entire website in the section "Updating Your Websites with Libraries," later in this chapter.

29

Deleting an item from the Library

Removing an entry from your site's Library is a two-step process. First, you must delete the item from the Library category. Second, if you want to keep the item on your page, you must make it editable again. Until you complete the second step, Dreamweaver maintains the Library highlighting and, more important, prevents you from modifying the element.

To delete an item from the Library, follow these steps:

1. Open the web page containing the Library item you want to delete.

2. Open the Library category by choosing Window ➪ Assets.
3. Select the Library item in the Site list and click the Delete button.
4. Dreamweaver asks if you are sure you want to delete the item. Click Yes, and the entry is removed from the Library item list. (Or click No to cancel.)
5. In the Document window, select the element you are removing from the Library.
6. In the Properties panel, click Detach From Original.
7. As shown in Figure 29-3, Dreamweaver warns you that if you proceed, the item cannot be automatically updated (as a Library element). Click OK to proceed. The yellow Library highlighting vanishes, and the element can now be modified individually. Select the Don't Warn Me Again box to disable any future warnings about detaching Library items.

NOTE

Should you unintentionally delete a Library item in the Library category, you can restore it if you still have the entry included in a web page. Select the element within the page and, in the Properties panel, click the Recreate button. Dreamweaver restores the item, with the original Library name, to the Library item list.

FIGURE 29-3

When you detach a Library item from its original source, Dreamweaver alerts you that, if you proceed, you won't be able to update the item automatically using the Library function.

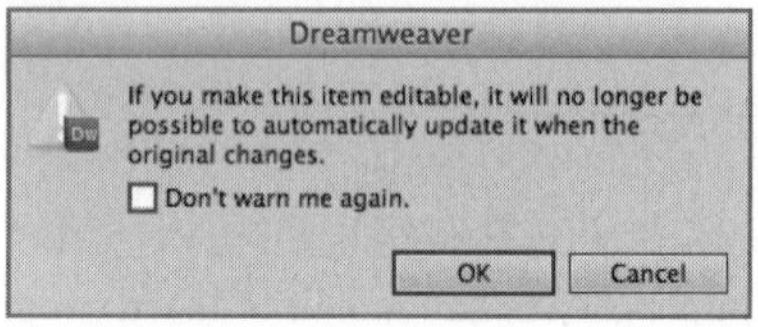

Renaming a Library item

It's easy to rename a Library item, both in the Assets panel and across your site. Dreamweaver automatically updates the name for any embedded Library item. To give an existing Library entry a new name, open the Library category and click the name of the item twice, slowly—do not double-click. Alternatively, you can select Rename from the context menu of the Assets panel. The name is highlighted and a small box appears around it. Enter the new name and press Enter (Return).

Dreamweaver then displays the Update Files dialog box with a list of files that contain the renamed Library item. Select Update to rename the Library item across the site. If you select Don't Update, the Library item is renamed only in the Library category. Furthermore, your embedded Library items are orphaned—that is, no master Library item is associated with them, and they are not updatable.

Dreamweaver TECHNIQUE

Building a Library Item

One of the most common—and useful—applications for a Library item concerns site navigation. In this Dreamweaver Technique, you create a Library item for the bottom, text-based navigation and apply it to a number of pages.

1. From the Techniques site, expand the 29_Library_Items folder and open the `library_items_start1.htm` file.
2. In Design view, move to the bottom of the page and place your cursor in the footer area text navigation.
3. In the Tag Selector, select the <p> tag.

   Although you can create a Library item out of any code fragment, it's generally best to work with a complete tag.
4. From the Files panel group, click the Assets tab.
5. Choose the Library category, the bottom icon on the left side of the Assets panel.
6. Click New Library Item from the bottom row of the Assets panel.
7. Dreamweaver reminds you that the Library item may not look the same when inserted in other pages because of the associated CSS; click OK to acknowledge the reminder.

   Your selection is converted into a Library item and displayed in the Assets panel.
8. Replace the Untitled Library item name with **textNavigation**, and press Enter (Return).

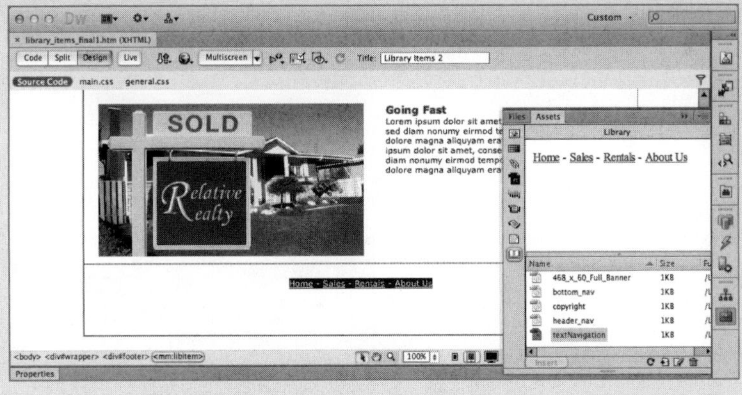

9. Dreamweaver asks if you'd like to update the links in the current `.lbi` file; click Update.
10. Save your page.

If you have Invisible Elements enabled, you might notice a light yellow highlight now around the text navigation; this indicates that it is no longer directly editable and is now a Library item.

Editing a Library Item

Rarely do you create a Library item that is perfect from the beginning and never needs to be changed. Whether because of site redesign or the addition of new sections to a site, you'll find yourself going back to Library items and modifying them, sometimes repeatedly. You can use the full power of Dreamweaver's design capabilities to alter your Library items, within the constraints of Library items in general. In other words, you can modify an image, reformat a body of text, or add new material to a boilerplate paragraph, and the resulting changes are reflected across your website. However, you cannot add anything not contained in the HTML `<body>` tags to a Library item.

To modify Library items, Dreamweaver uses a standard editing window identifiable by the `.lbi` extension in the tab. You access this editing window through the Library category or the Properties panel. Follow these steps to modify an existing Library item:

1. In the Library category of the Assets panel, select the item you want to modify from the list of available entries.
2. Click the Open Library Item button. The Library editing window opens with the selected entry displayed, as shown in Figure 29-4.

FIGURE 29-4

Use the Library editing window to modify existing Library items.

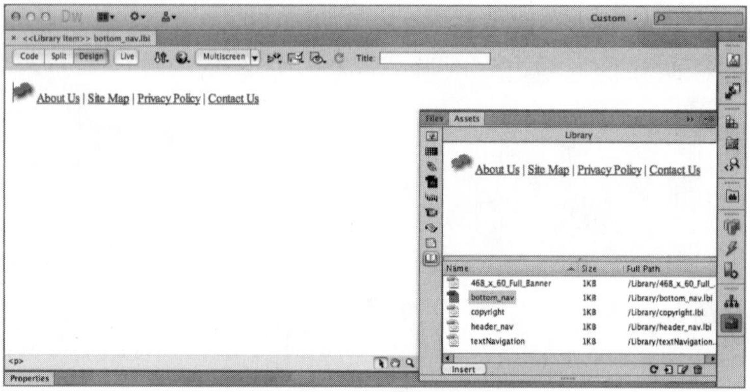

3. Make any necessary modifications to the Library entry.
4. When you are finished with your changes, choose File ➪ Save, or press Ctrl+S (Command+S).
5. Dreamweaver notes that your Library item has been modified and then asks if you would like to update all the pages in your site that contain the item. Click Yes to update all the Library items, including the one just modified, or click No to postpone the update. (See the next section, "Updating Your Websites with Libraries," for a more in-depth explanation of the updating process.)
6. Close the editing window by clicking the Close button or choosing File ➪ Close.

After you've completed the editing operation and closed the editing window, you can open any page containing the modified Library item to view the changes.

TIP

If your Library item is styled with an external style sheet and you'd like to see how it renders while editing, use Dreamweaver's Design Time Style Sheet feature. From the CSS Styles panel Option menu, select Design Time; when the Design Time Style Sheet dialog box opens, select the style sheet from the Show Only At Design Time area.

Dreamweaver now allows you to use native Dreamweaver behaviors inside Library items. That means you can place a navigation bar, a link for a pop-up window, or any other Dreamweaver behavior inside your Library item. When the Library item is added to the page, the accompanying JavaScript is also added.

CAUTION

You cannot use some features, such as custom JavaScript and styles, to the fullest extent when editing Library items. Each of these modifications requires a function or link to be placed in the <head> tags of a page—a task that the Dreamweaver Library function cannot handle for styles and custom JavaScript.

Updating Your Websites with Libraries

The effectiveness of the Dreamweaver Library feature becomes more significant when it comes time to update an entire multipage site. Dreamweaver offers two opportunities for you to update your site:

- You can immediately update every page on your site when you edit a Library item. After you save the alterations, Dreamweaver asks if you'd like to apply the update to the other pages in your site. If you click Yes, Dreamweaver not only applies the current modification to all pages in the site but also applies any other alterations that you have made previously in this Library.
- The second way to modify a Library item is by using the Modify ➪ Library command; when you use this method, you can choose to update the current page or the entire site. To update just the current page, choose Modify ➪ Library ➪ Update Current Page. Dreamweaver quickly checks to see what Library items you are managing on the current page and then compares them to the site's Library items. If any differences exist, Dreamweaver modifies the page accordingly.

To update an entire website, follow these steps:

1. Choose Modify ➪ Library ➪ Update Pages. The Update Pages dialog box opens (see Figure 29-5).
2. If you want Dreamweaver to update all the Library items in all the web pages in your site, select Entire Site from the Look In drop-down list and choose the name of your site in the drop-down list on the right. You can also have Dreamweaver update only the pages in your

site that contain a specific Library item. Select the Files That Use option from the Look In drop-down list and then select the Library item that you would like to have updated across your site from the drop-down list on the right.

FIGURE 29-5

The Update Pages dialog box enables you to apply any changes to your Library items across an entire site and informs you of the progress.

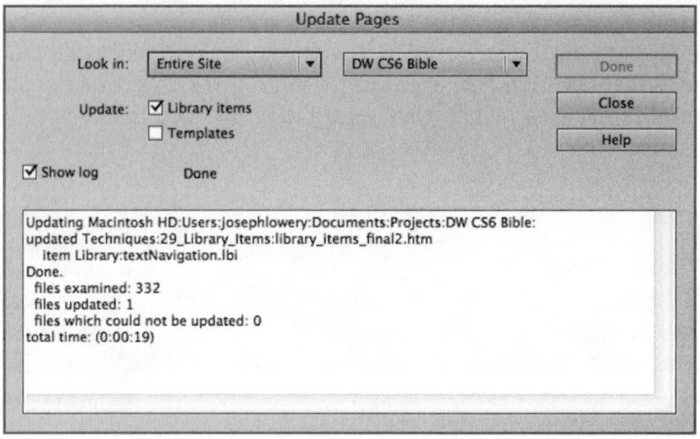

3. If you want to see the results from the update process, leave the Show Log checkbox selected. (Turning off the Show Log option reduces the size of the Site Update dialog box.)
4. Click the Start button. Dreamweaver processes the entire site for Library updates. Any Library items contained are modified to reflect the changes.

NOTE

Although Dreamweaver does modify Library items on currently open pages during an Update Site operation, you have to save the pages to accept the changes.

The Update Pages log displays any errors encountered in the update operation. The following log notation indicates that one web page contains a reference to a Library item that has been removed:

```
item Library\Untitled2.lbi--not updated, library item not found
```

Although this is not a critical error, you might want to use Dreamweaver's Find And Replace feature to search your website for the code and remove it.

NOTE

When Dreamweaver is updating Library items, every page is physically changed with the necessary Library item code. This means that every file containing a Library item must be (re)uploaded to the server.

Dreamweaver TECHNIQUE

Applying and Modifying Library Items

In this Technique, you see how easy it is to add Library items to the page and update them as necessary.

1. From the Techniques site, open the `library_items_start2.htm` file from the 29_Library_Items folder.
2. Place your cursor at the bottom of the page in the `#footer` div.
3. Select the placeholder <p> tag there and remove it by pressing Delete.
4. From the Assets panel, select the Library category if necessary.
5. Choose the textNavigation entry.
6. Click Insert at the bottom of the Assets panel.

   You can also drag Library items onto the page.
7. Save your page.
8. Now that you have the same Library item in a couple of locations, alter it. Double-click the textNavigation Library item.

   Dreamweaver opens the Library item file in its own window.
9. Place your cursor after the About Us link and enter the following: **- Guides**.
10. Select the word Guides and, from the Properties panel's Link field, drag the Point To File icon to the file `guides.htm` in the 29_Library_Items folder.

    It's always best to let Dreamweaver create the links for templates and Library items. Creating links by hand is probably the number one cause for problems with Library items.
11. Choose File ➪ Save.
12. Dreamweaver displays the Update Library Items dialog box with the pages containing the current Library item. Click Update.
13. While Dreamweaver processes the modifications, the Update Pages dialog box is displayed; click Close when it's finished.

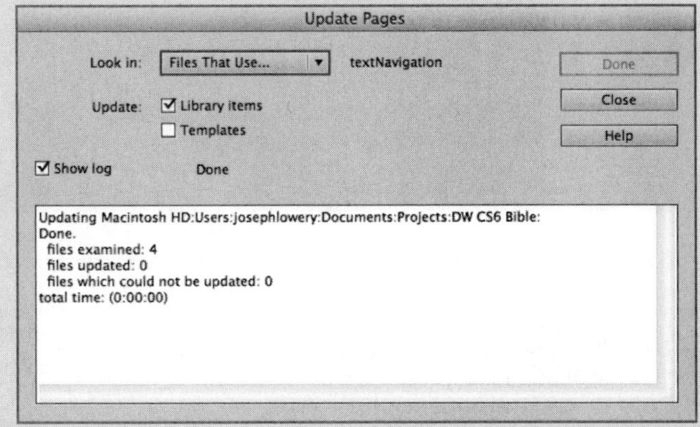

Continues

continued

14. Close the `textNavigation.lbi` file.

    Notice that the `library_items_start2.htm` file has been modified and the new item is now available from the text navigation.

15. Choose File ➪ Save to store the `library_items_start2.htm` file.

If you like, you can open the original file, `library_items_start1.htm`, to verify that it, too, has been updated.

Applying Server-Side Includes

In some ways, the server-side include (SSI) is the predecessor of the Dreamweaver Library item. The difference between them is that Dreamweaver updates the web pages with Library items at design time, whereas the server handles the updating with server-side includes at runtime (when the files are actually served to the user). Server-side includes can also include server variables, such as the current date and time (both local and Greenwich Mean Time) or the date on which the current file was last saved.

CAUTION

The Related Files bar makes it much quicker to modify SSI files. Server-side includes linked in the source automatically appear in the Related Files bar. Just click the link to edit immediately in Code view. Start up Live View to see your modifications take effect instantly.

Because server-side includes are integrated in the standard HTML code, a special file extension identifies pages using them. Pages with server-side includes are most often saved with either the `.shtml` or the `.shtm` extension on UNIX servers and `.asp` or `.aspx` on Windows servers. When a server encounters such a file, the file is read and processed by the server.

CAUTION

Not all servers support server-side includes. Some web-hosting companies disable the function because of potential security risks and performance issues. Each `.shtml` page requires additional processing time, and if a site uses many SSI pages, the server can slow down significantly. Be sure to check with your web host as to its policy before including SSIs in your web pages.

Server-side includes are often used to insert header or footer items into the `<body>` of an HTML page. Typically, the server-side include itself is just a file with HTML. To insert a file, use SSI code like the following:

```
<!-- #include file="footer.html" -->
```

Note how the HTML comment structure is used to wrap around the SSI directive. This ensures that browsers ignore the code but servers do not. The `file` attribute defines the pathname of the file to be included, relative to the current page. To include a file relative to the current site root, use the `virtual` attribute, as follows:

```
<!-- #include virtual= "/main/images/spaceman.jpg" -->
```

As evident in this example, you can use SSIs to include more than just HTML files—you can also include graphics.

With Dreamweaver's translator mechanism, server-side includes are visible in the Document window during the design process. In Dreamweaver, server-side–include translation is now automatic as long as the Show Contents Of Included File option, found in the Invisible Elements category of Preferences, remains enabled.

One of the major benefits of SSIs is that information can be inserted from the server itself, such as the current file size or time. One tag, <!-- #echo -->, is used to define a custom variable that is returned when the SSI is called, as well as numerous *environmental variables*. An environmental variable is information available to the server, such as the date a file was last modified or its URL.

Table 29-1 details the possible server tags and their attributes.

TABLE 29-1 Server-Side Include Variables

Tag	Attribute	Description
<!-- #config -->	errmsg, sizefmt, or timefmt	Used to customize error messages, file size, or time and date displays
<!-- #echo -->	var or environmental variables such as last_modified, document_name, document_url, date_local, or date_gmt	Returns the specified variable
<!-- #exec -->	cmd or cgi	Executes a system command or CGI program
<!-- #flastmod -->	file or virtual	Displays the last modified date of a file other than the current one
<!-- #fsize -->	file or virtual	Displays the size of a file other than the current one
<!-- #include -->	file or virtual	Inserts the contents of the specified file into the current one

Adding server-side includes

Dreamweaver has made inserting a server-side include in your web page straightforward. You can use a Dreamweaver object to easily select and bring in the files to be included. Any other type of SSI, such as declaring a variable, must be entered by hand, but you can use the Comment object to do so without opening the Code view.

WARNING

It's important to understand that server-side includes are not full HTML files but rather a section of HTML code. If you use Dreamweaver to create an HTML file as a starting point, you have to remove all of the non-essential code (including the `<html>`, `<head>`, and `<body>` tag pairs) for the SSI.

To use server-side includes to incorporate a file, follow these steps:

1. In the Document window, place your cursor at the location where you would like to add the server-side include.
2. Choose Insert ➪ Server-Side Include or choose Server-Side Include from the Insert panel's Common category. The standard Select File dialog box appears.
3. In the Select File dialog box, type the URL of the HTML page you would like to include in the File Name text box or use the Browse button to locate the file. Click OK when you're finished.

NOTE

Through the Select File dialog box, you can also select a data source for a dynamically-inserted SSI or link to an SSI already published on a server through the Sites and Servers interface. However, SSIs inserted in this manner can be previewed in Dreamweaver only in the Live Data view.

Dreamweaver displays the contents of the HTML file at the desired location in your page. Should the Properties panel be available, the SSI Properties panel is displayed (see Figure 29-6).

4. In the Properties panel, if the server-side include calls a file-relative document path, select the Type File option. Alternatively, if the SSI calls a site-root–relative file, choose the Type Virtual option.

FIGURE 29-6

The selected text is actually a server-side include automatically translated by Dreamweaver, as evident from the SSI Properties panel.

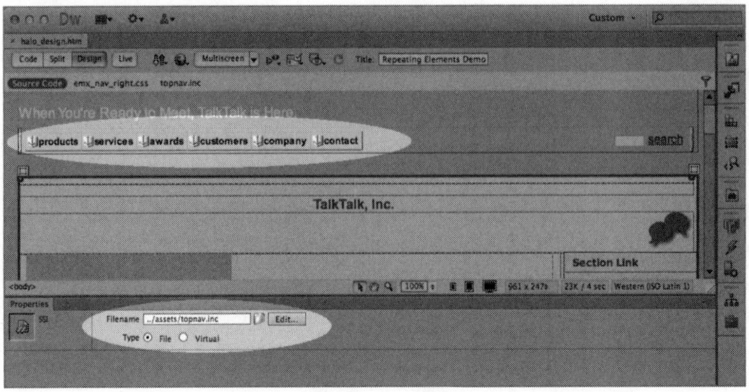

Editing server-side includes

As is the case with Library items, you cannot directly edit files that have been inserted into a web page using server-side includes. In fact, should you try, the entire text block highlights as one. The code for a server-side–included file is quickly accessible through the Related Files bar.

To edit the contents of the server-side–included file, follow these steps:

1. From the Related Files bar, choose the server-side file you want to edit.

   If you want to see changes applied to the design, enter Live View.
2. Make any changes desired to the code.
3. Choose Source from the Related Files bar.

   If you're in Live View, the changes will now be displayed.

Another, older way to edit your SSI is to select it and then click the Edit button in the Properties panel. The file will open in a new Dreamweaver window for editing. Save your file and then switch back to your source file to see the changes. Although this technique still works, using the Related Files bar with Live View is much faster.

Unlike when you are editing Library items, Dreamweaver does not ask if any other linked files should be updated because all blending of regular HTML and SSIs happens at runtime or when the file is open in Dreamweaver and the SSI translator is engaged.

Summary

In this chapter, you learned how you can easily and effectively create Library items that can be repeated throughout an entire site to help maintain consistency. When you work with Library items, keep these points in mind:

- Library items can consist of any text, object, or HTML code contained in the `<body>` of a web page.
- The quickest method to create a Library item is to drag the code from the Dreamweaver Document window into the Library category's list area (or to click the new Library item button).
- Editing Library items is also easy: Just click the Edit button in the Assets panel or choose Open from the Properties panel, and you can swiftly make all your changes in a separate Dreamweaver Library Item window.
- The Modify ➪ Library ➪ Update Pages command enables easy maintenance of your website.
- Server-side includes enable the server to insert files into the final HTML at runtime. Dreamweaver's translation feature enables you to preview these effects, and the Related Files bar gives you immediate access.

In the next chapter, you learn how to ensure cross-browser compatibility with Dreamweaver.

CHAPTER

30

Maximizing Cross-Browser Compatibility

IN THIS CHAPTER

Maintaining different versions of web pages

Validating your code

Testing your page against specific browsers

Handling cross-browser compatibility

Each new release of a browser is a double-edged sword. On one hand, an exciting array of new features becomes possible. On the other, web designers have to cope with yet another browser-compatibility issue. In today's market, you find the following in use:

- A fair number of current browsers, although reasonably standards-compliant, which are still different from one another in implementation
- A vast array of mobile browsers occupying a very fluid space that ranges from the Apple iPhone (with its faithful but Flash-less web page rendering) to tiny cell phone screens that display text and links only

Browser compatibility is one of a web designer's primary concerns (not to mention the source of major headaches), and many strategies are evolving to deal with the issue. Dreamweaver is at the forefront of cross-browser web page design, in terms of both the type of code it routinely outputs and its specialty functions. This chapter examines the browser-targeting techniques available in Dreamweaver. From multi-browser code to W3C and XML validation capabilities, Dreamweaver helps you get your web pages out with the most features to the widest audience.

Converting Pages in Dreamweaver

Websites are constantly upgraded and modified. You'll eventually need to enhance a more traditional site with new features, such as AP elements. Some of the older sites used elaborately nested tables on their pages to create a semblance of absolute positioning; normally, upgrading these web pages takes hours and hours of tedious cutting and pasting. Dreamweaver can bring these older pages up to speed with the Convert Tables To AP Divs command, which you reach via Modify Convert ➪ Tables to AP Divs. Dreamweaver also includes a command to convert tables to AP elements, preserving their location but enabling greater design flexibility and dynamic control. A webmaster's life just got a tad easier.

The Convert Tables To AP Divs command can also be used to convert a page created by another web authoring program that uses nested tables for positioning. After tables have been transformed into AP elements, the layout of the entire page is much easier to modify. It's even possible to make the switch to more modern capabilities, modify your page, and then, with the Convert AP Divs To Tables command, re-create your older page in a newer format.

The name of the Convert Tables To AP Divs command is a little misleading. After you issue this command, *every* HTML element in the new page—not just the tables—is placed in an AP element. Moreover, every cell with content in every table is converted into its own AP element. In other words, if you are working with a 3 × 3 table in which one cell is left empty, Dreamweaver creates eight different AP elements just for the table.

NOTE

If you want to convert an older page to a page with AP elements, but the page has no tables, Dreamweaver places all the content in one AP element, as if the `<body>` tag were one big single-cell table.

To convert an older web page with (or without) tables to a more modern standards-compliant web page with AP elements, follow these steps:

1. Choose Modify ➪ Convert ➪ Tables To AP Divs.
2. Select the desired options from the Convert Tables To AP Divs dialog box that opens (see Figure 30-1):
   - **Prevent Overlaps:** Isolates all AP elements from one another. AP elements need to remain separate if the opposite process (Convert AP Divs To Tables) is invoked.
   - **Show AP Elements Panel:** Displays the AP elements panel for easy selection and renaming of the newly created AP elements.
   - **Show Grid:** Reveals the standard grid, useful for aligning AP elements.
   - **Snap to Grid:** Every new AP element created is positioned to the closed grid point. Exercise caution when choosing this option because your table layout is likely to be highly revised.
3. When you're done, click OK to close the dialog box.

Dreamweaver converts the page immediately. If you need to return to a table-based layout, choose File ➪ Convert ➪ AP Divs To Tables.

To learn how to use Dreamweaver's AP Divs To Tables roundtrip features, see Chapter 10.

FIGURE 30-1

The Convert Tables To AP Divs dialog box

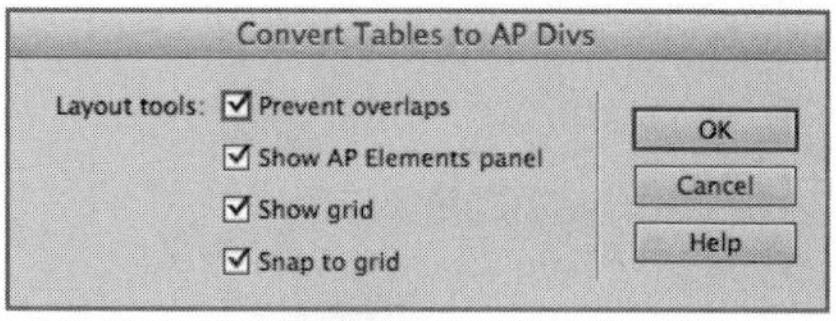

Validating Your Code

Most browsers are very forgiving. They can take a document riddled with HTML infractions and, through "intelligent" interpretation, manage to display the page beautifully, with no indication that anything is awry with the underlying code. As a responsible web author, however, you should never rely on the kindness of your users' browsers! It's far safer to take the extra time to validate the correctness of your code's syntax rather than risk having a browser that's less forgiving than you had hoped.

New Feature

To validate an HTML page, most web professionals find that the W3C service is the most complete service. Until CS5.5, you had to use a browser to validate your HTML (`http://validator.w3.org`) or CSS (`http://jigsaw.w3.org/css-validator`). In Dreamweaver CS6, you now have the option of validating your HTML natively, without leaving the program, although you'll still have to use the browser to check your CSS.

The W3C Validator supports a wide range of tag-based languages, including XHTML, XML, MathML 2.0, SVG, and SMIL 1.0 (Synchronized Multimedia Integrated Language). And you can customize how the W3C Validator works, as discussed in the next section, "Setting W3C Validator Preferences."

To validate a web page, follow these steps:

1. Open the document you want to validate.
2. For HTML files, choose File ➪ Validate ➪ Validate Current Document (W3C). For dynamic files for use with a server model like PHP or ColdFusion, enter into Live View and choose File ➪ Validate ➪ Validate Live Document (W3C). If it is an XML or XHTML file, choose File ➪ Validate ➪ As XML.

   If you opt to validate the current document via the W3C service, Dreamweaver will inform you that it is going to submit your file for validation. Click OK.
3. After the Validator runs, the results—filenames, line numbers, and error descriptions—are listed in the Validation panel, as shown in Figure 30-2.

FIGURE 30-2

It's up to you to decide how to handle errors flagged in Dreamweaver's Validation panel.

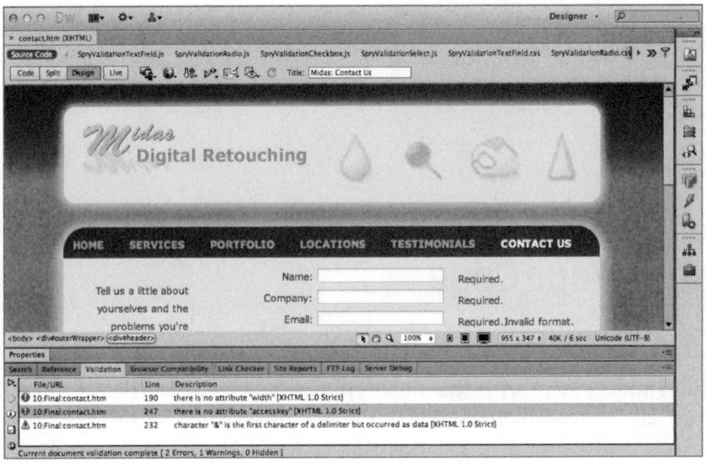

4. Double-click an error in the list to display the offending code in the document.
5. To display the error report in your primary browser, click the Browse Report button. To keep a record of the report, print the browser page or click the Save Report button to generate an XML report file. For specific details regarding the error, click the More Info button.
6. If you regard the error or warning as acceptable and don't want to be alerted to a particular issue, right-click (Control+click) the error or warning and choose Hide Error.

   In a perfect world, you'd want to code your web pages so there would be no errors or warnings. Many designers find that in the fast-evolving world of web coding, perfection isn't always obtainable and certain warnings or even errors must grudgingly be allowed to remain. For example, because HTML5 is not a finished standard as of this writing, you'll always get a warning about coding your pages with an HTML5 doctype. This, I would argue, is an acceptable warning and one that can safely be hidden.

TIP

Right-click (Control+click) in the Validation panel to bring up a context menu that lets you browse the error report, save the report, and more.

Setting W3C Validator preferences

You can customize how the W3C Validator works by changing its preferences. For example, you can specify which document types should be checked against and which errors from the Validator should be hidden from view. To set your W3C Validator preferences:

1. Choose Edit ➪ Preferences (Dreamweaver ➪ Preferences) to open the Preferences dialog box and then click the W3C Validator category to display the options (see Figure 30-3).

2. Select the doctype you want the W3C Validator to check against if no explicit doctype is found in the page.

FIGURE 30-3

You can use the options in the Validator category of the Preferences dialog box to customize the workings of your Dreamweaver W3C Validator.

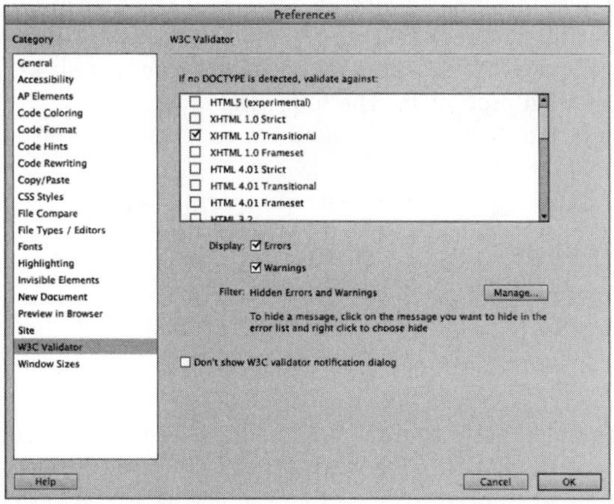

3. Under Display, select whether you want errors and/or warnings to be shown.
4. If you previously have hidden any errors or warnings when the W3C Validator was run and want to show them again, click Manage to open the W3C Validator Hidden Errors And Warnings dialog box (see Figure 30-4). Select any hidden error or warning you want to see and click Remove.
5. Click OK to close the Preferences dialog box.

FIGURE 30-4

You can show any previously hidden validation error or warning by removing the entry from the W3C Validator Hidden Errors And Warnings dialog box.

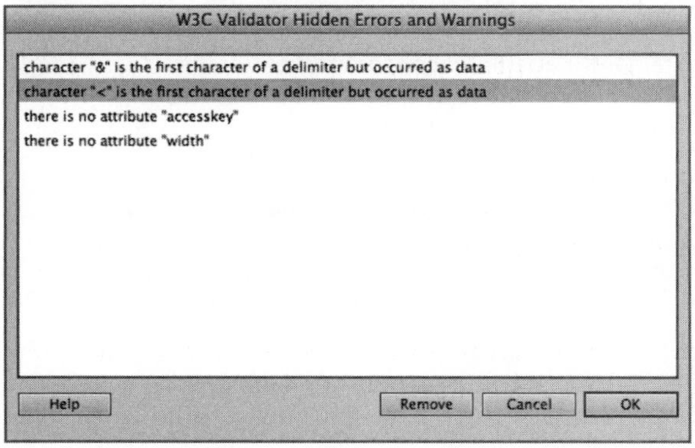

30

Checking Your Page for Compatibility

Testing is an absolute must when you're building a website. It's critical that you view your pages on as many browsers/versions and platforms as possible—especially in the age of CSS design. Variations in layout, color, gamma, page offset, and capabilities must be observed before they can be adjusted.

A more basic, preliminary type of testing can also be done right from within Dreamweaver. Dreamweaver's Browser Compatibility Check feature (File ➪ Check Page ➪ Browser Compatibility) enables you to check a web page against any number of browser profiles for known CSS issues. Currently, Dreamweaver comes with profiles for the following browsers:

- Chrome 7.0–9.0
- Firefox 1.0–4.0
- Internet Explorer 5.0–9.0
- Netscape 7.0–8.0
- Opera 7.0–9.0
- Safari 1.0–5.0

You can choose to check your page or site against a single browser profile, all of them, or anything in between. Although not a substitute for real-world testing, the Browser Compatibility Check feature can help you pinpoint potential issues and problematic code at design time.

Dreamweaver checks for common CSS issues across the full range of browsers. By default, the BCC feature checks against the minimum versions of the following browsers: Chrome 7.0, Firefox 1.5, Internet Explorer (Windows) 6.0, Netscape Navigator 8.0, Opera 8.0, and Safari 2.0. When the issue is detected, a brief description appears in the Browser Compatibility Check category of the Results panel. In addition, a link to a more in-depth discussion of the issue, complete with possible solutions, on the Adobe-hosted CSS Advisor mini-site is made available.

The issues and a brief description are listed in Table 30-1.

TABLE 30-1 Browser Compatibility Errors

CSS Issue	Description	Browsers Affected
Positioned Tables/ AP Elements Bug	A positioned table is not considered a container for absolutely positioned elements. The AP elements are positioned relative to the browser window instead.	Firefox 1.0, 1.5, 2.0, 3.5, 3.6, 4.0 Netscape 7.0, 8.0
Border Chaos Bug	When the second of two consecutive block-level boxes has a negative top margin and that same box or one of its ancestors has a border, the borders will not render correctly.	Internet Explorer 6.0

CSS Issue	Description	Browsers Affected
Col and Colgroup/ Caption Conflict	If the caption tag is placed directly after the opening table tag as required by the HTML 4.01 specification, any styles applied to col and colgroup tags in the same table are ignored.	Safari 2.0
The Disappearing List Background Bug	When list items have background colors or images, and the list is placed within a floated, relatively positioned container, the backgrounds may not render as specified.	Internet Explorer 5.0, 5.5, 6.0
Disappearing Button Background Bug	A floated button will lose its background and borders when floated, leaving only the button text.	Opera 7.0, 8.0
Disappearing Dropdown in Floated List Bug	A drop-down menu (select) inside a floated list (ul, ol, dl) with overflow: auto will disappear when the user changes the menu's value.	Firefox 1.0
Disappearing Dropdown in Floated List Bug	A drop-down menu (select) inside a floated list (ul, ol, dl) with overflow: auto will not be visible unless the menu is inside a form tag.	Internet Explorer for Macintosh 5.2
Disappearing Label/Input Bug	If a group of floated <label>foo</label><input /> pairs is separated by br tags and placed inside any container (including the body) on which the letter-spacing property is set, one of the following problems occurs, depending on whether line breaks or other whitespace occurs between the tags: (1) every other pair disappears. (2) only the first label and input appear. (3) all inputs appear, but all labels except the first disappear.	Internet Explorer 5.0, 5.5, 6.0, 7.0, 8.0, 9.0
Doubled Float Margin Bug	When a margin is applied to a floated box on the same side as the direction of the float, the margin is doubled. This bug affects only the first float in a row of one or more floats.	Internet Explorer 5.0, 5.5, 6.0
Duplicate Indent Bug	When a margin is applied to a floated box on the opposite side as the direction of the float, and the floated box is directly followed by inline content, the first line of inline content will be indented by the same amount as the margin.	Internet Explorer 5.0, 5.5, 6.0
Escaping Floats Bug	If a series of floats followed by a clearing div is placed inside a container with no specified width or height, and the floats' width exceeds the natural width of the container, the container will not expand vertically to fit the floats—and the floats will extend outside the container.	Internet Explorer 5.0, 5.5, 6.0, 7.0

Continues

TABLE 30-1 *(continued)*

CSS Issue	Description	Browsers Affected
Expanding Box Problem	Any content that does not fit in a fixed-width or -height box causes the box to expand to fit the content rather than let the content overflow.	Internet Explorer 5.0, 5.5, 6.0
Extra Whitespace in List Links Bug	If a link with display: block and no explicit dimensions is inside a list item, any spaces or line breaks that follow the list item in the code will cause extra whitespace to appear in the browser.	Internet Explorer 5.0, 5.5, 6.0
First Line/Text Transform Bug	text-transform: uppercase is ignored when applied to the :first-line pseudo-element.	Safari 2.0, 3.0, 4.0, 5.0; Chrome 7.0, 8.0, 9.0
Float Drop Problem	If a container (including the browser window itself) is not wide enough to accommodate both a float with a specified width and any content with a specified width that follows it, the content after the float will drop below the float rather than wrap around it.	Internet Explorer 5.0, 5.5, 6.0, 7.0
Floating Non-Float Bug	If a non-floated element with a specified width directly follows a left-floated element with a specified width, the non-floated container will appear to the right of the floated element instead of allowing the floated element to overlap it.	Internet Explorer 5.0, 5.5, 6.0, 7.0 Internet Explorer for Macintosh 5.2
Overlapping Floats and Headers Bug	If the second or any subsequent float in a document is directly preceded by a header, the first line of text after the float will overlap the float rather than wrap around it.	Firefox 1.0
Font Variant/Text Transform Conflict	text-transform: uppercase and text-transform: lowercase are ignored when combined with font-variant: small-caps.	Internet Explorer 5.0, 5.5, 6.0, 7.0 Internet Explorer for Macintosh 5.2
Full Height Flash Bug	A Flash movie with a height of 100 percent will not fill the browser window unless height: 100 percent is specified for the movie's container.	Firefox 1.0, 1.5, 2.0 Netscape 7.0, 8.0
Guillotine Bug	If an element contains both a float that is not cleared and links that use an a:hover rule to change certain properties in non-floated content after the float, hovering over the links could cause the bottom of the floated content to be chopped off.	Internet Explorer 5.0, 5.5, 6.0

CSS Issue	Description	Browsers Affected
Half Line-Height Bug	If line-height is defined for a block, it will collapse by half for any line that contains an inline replaced element (img, input, textarea, select, or object).	Internet Explorer 5.0, 5.5, 6.0
Magik Creeping Text Bug	Text inside a block element will creep to the left if the block is nested inside another block element that has border-left, padding-bottom, and no specified width or height.	Internet Explorer 5.5, 6.0
Missing First Letter Bug	When a text-containing block element with position: relative and letter-spacing but no specified width or height is inside another block element that has no specified width, height, padding-top, or border-top, the first letter of the text in the inner element might disappear.	Internet Explorer 5.5
Three Pixel Text Jog	When anonymous line boxes (boxes that contain inline content) are adjacent to a float, a 3-pixel gap appears between the line box and the edge of the float. This gap disappears when the content clears the float, causing the content to "jog" 3 pixels in the direction of the float. Note that the gap may be difficult to see when left-aligned text is adjacent to a right float, but it does exist—and it can lead to "float drop" in tight layouts.	Internet Explorer 5.0, 5.5, 6.0
Unscrollable Content Bug	If one or more absolutely positioned elements are placed within a relatively positioned element with no assigned dimensions, either no scroll bar will appear at all or it will not extend far enough to view all of the content. (Note: This bug will not affect your page if the content in the AP element does not extend beyond the height of the viewport.)	Internet Explorer 5.0, 5.5, 6.0
Z-Index Bug	Positioned containers define a new stacking order, even when the computed z-index of the container is auto. This can cause positioned children of the container to appear above other positioned elements on the page when they should not.	Internet Explorer 5.0, 5.5, 6.0, 7.0

Checking your pages

The Check Browser Compatibility command is found under the Document toolbar's Check Page menu button. When this command is selected, Dreamweaver tests the page when it is opened against the browsers selected in the Target Browsers dialog box, as shown in Figure 30-5.

To modify the current settings, follow these steps:

1. Choose Settings from the Browser Compatibility Check menu.
2. In the displayed Target Browsers dialog box, select the browsers you want to verify your pages against.
3. For each selected browser, choose the minimum version for testing from the drop-down list.
4. When you're finished, click OK.

FIGURE 30-5

Use the Target Browsers dialog box to choose the minimum browser versions that you want to work correctly with your pages.

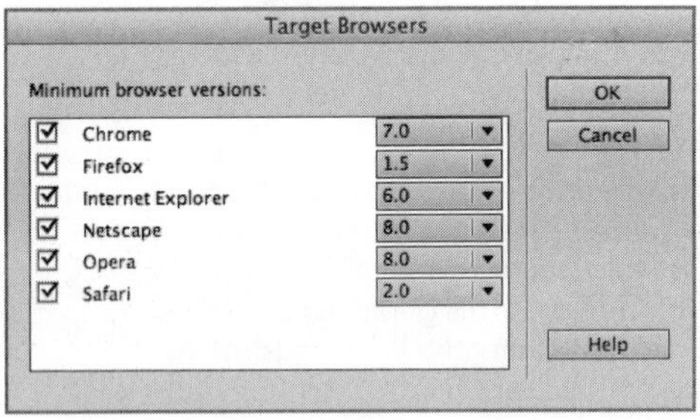

Excluding page elements from issue checking

Dreamweaver includes built-in syntax rules for each browser, which generally are applied to each file checked. However, you have the option to exclude specific tags, attributes, or attribute values from the testing process. This feature is extremely useful when your designs must include an element unsupported by one or more browsers and you don't want to be reminded of the issue each time the page is checked. The list of excluded elements is contained in the `Exceptions.xml` file maintained in the Configuration/BrowserProfiles folder. Dreamweaver gives you quick access to modifying this file when you open the Browser Check menu and choose Edit Ignored Issues List.

To modify the `Exceptions.xml` file, follow these steps:

1. From an HTML file, open the Browser Check menu from the Document toolbar and choose Edit Ignored Issues List.

> **TIP**
> This command is not available from XML files.

Dreamweaver opens the `Exceptions.xml` file.

2. Enter any desired exceptions in the XML file between the `<exceptions> ... </exceptions>` tag pair. As noted in the file comments, the following three types of exceptions are allowed:

Element	Example
Browser Compatibility Issue	<issue id="THREE_PIXEL_JOG" name="Three Pixel Text Jog"/>
CSS Property	<cssProperty property="font-family"/>
CSS Value	<cssValue property="font-family"/>

3. Add the desired exception in the proper format. Make sure that your code is outside the commented section but inside the `<exceptions> ... </exceptions>` tag pair.
4. When you're finished, save the file.

TIP

To quickly add an error to the exceptions list, you can right-click (Control+click) on any displayed error in the Browser Compatibility Check category of the Results panel and choose Ignore Issue to add it to the `Exceptions.xml` file.

Viewing and correcting issues

If Dreamweaver finds any issues on your page, they are listed in the Browser Compatibility Check category of the Results panel. Double-click any issue listing to highlight the problematic section. You can verify your change has eliminated the issue by using any of the methods described in the following steps:

1. Open the Check Page ➪ Browser Compatibility Check menu or choose File ➪ Check Page ➪ Browser Compatibility. Dreamweaver checks the page and lists the results in the Browser Compatibility Check category of the Results panel, as shown in Figure 30-6. This is a handy debugging tool; it lists a relevancy rating, the line number, the issue name, and a short description for each item found.

   The relevancy rating indicates how sure Dreamweaver is that the highlighted selection is affected by the indicated issue. There are four relevancy rating symbols ranging from a quarter-filled circle to a completely filled circle—the more filled the circle, the more sure Dreamweaver is of its assessment.

   For more detailed information, click the View Solutions link to visit a related page in the CSS Advisor section of `http://www.adobe.com/`. See the "Visiting the CSS Advisor" sidebar in this chapter for more details about this informative web resource.

   Double-clicking an item in the list selects the affected element. Dreamweaver displays the results temporarily and deletes them when you check another page or close the program.

30

FIGURE 30-6

The Browser Compatibility Check panel displays a summary of all the issues it finds for the current file.

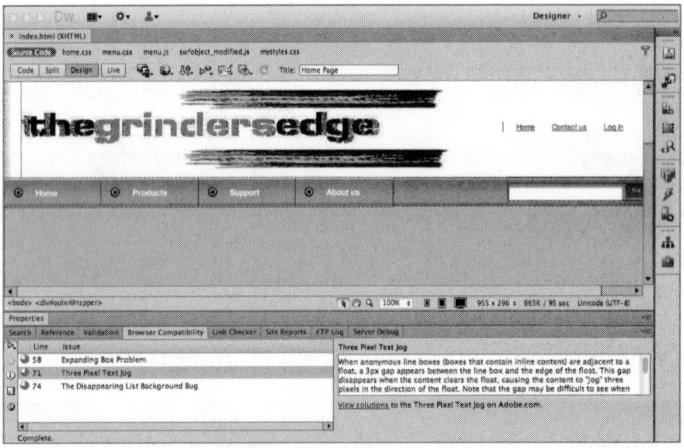

2. To display a report of these results in your primary browser (see Figure 30-7), click the Browse Report button.
3. To keep a hard copy record, print the Dreamweaver Browser Compatibility Check page from your browser. To keep a digital record, click the Save Report button in the Browser Compatibility Check panel to generate an XML report file.

The Dreamweaver Browser Compatibility Check report offers both a summary and a detail section. The summary lists the browser(s) being tested and any errors or warnings. Totals for each category are listed beneath the columns.

The detail section of the browser check report, shown in Figure 30-8, lists the following:

- The file path and name
- The relevancy rating
- A description of the offending issue
- The browsers that do not support the tag or attribute
- The issue name
- Line numbers indicating where the error occurred

Using the results of the Browser Compatibility Check

How you handle the flagged issues in Dreamweaver's Browser Compatibility Check report is entirely dependent on the design goals you have established for your site. If your mission is to be totally accessible to every browser on the market, you need to look at your page and/or site with the earliest browsers and pay special attention to those areas of possible trouble noted by the report. On the other hand, if your standards are a little more relaxed—or more targeted—you can ignore issues related to browsers that rarely visit your site.

FIGURE 30-7

Send the Browser Compatibility Check issue report to your browser for printing or easy viewing.

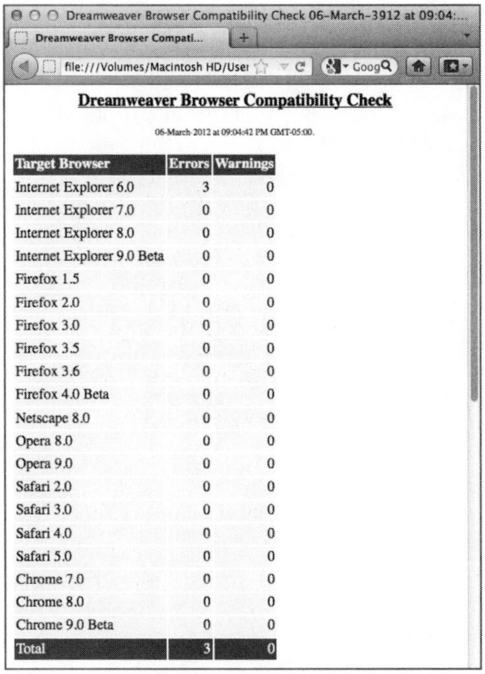

FIGURE 30-8

You can find detailed information on the lower half of the Dreamweaver Browser Compatibility Check report.

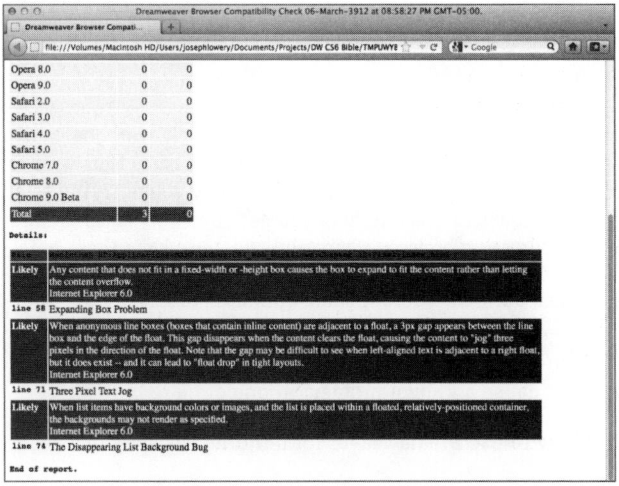

Visiting the CSS Advisor

One of the most difficult CSS-related tasks is debugging—and fixing—browser compatibility issues. Because of the vast number of variations possible with CSS layouts, not every problem is immediately identifiable much less reparable. The CSS Advisor mini-site on Adobe.com (`http://www.adobe.com/go/cssadvisor`) takes a community-based approach to help web developers find their way out of the CSS jungle.

Each time you run Dreamweaver's Browser Compatibility Check and discover a problem, a context-sensitive link to the relevant article in the CSS Advisor site is made available. An issue page succinctly lays out the problem and solution—and, best of all, goes into detailed steps for implementing the solution, complete with sample code.

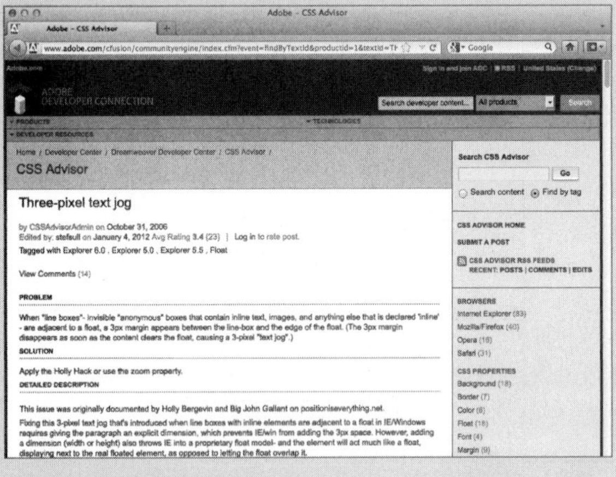

To keep up with the moving-target nature of CSS rendering in browsers, the CSS Advisor relies on a series of community experts, both within and outside of Adobe, to supply the most widely adopted resolutions. Visitors can comment on any CSS Advisor article; these comments, if judged relevant, are incorporated into the site. Moreover, visitors can rate each article according to its usefulness and applicability.

Summary

Unless you're building a website for a strictly controlled intranet (for which everyone is using the same browser), it's critical that you address the browser-compatibility issues that your website is certain to face. Whether it's cross-browser or backward compatibility you're trying to achieve, Dreamweaver has features and techniques in place to help you get your web pages viewed by the maximum number of users. When addressing browser-compatibility issues, keep these points in mind:

- You can use Dreamweaver's built-in, customizable Validator to check your code for tag or syntax errors on HTML, PHP, XML, and XHTML pages.
- Dreamweaver enables you to check your web page against a browser profile to look for CSS implementations that cause a known problem in one or more browsers.

In the next chapter, you learn how to use Dreamweaver for building websites in a team environment.

CHAPTER

31

Building Websites with a Team

IN THIS CHAPTER

- Keeping current with Check In/Check Out
- Storing information with Design Notes
- Assembling interactive reports
- Integrating with Contribute
- Using Visual SourceSafe with Dreamweaver
- Accessing a WebDAV server
- Source control with Subversion

Major websites that are designed, developed, and maintained by one person are increasingly rare. After a site has reached a certain complexity and size, it's far more timely and cost-effective to divide responsibility for different areas among different people. For all its positive aspects, team development has an equal number of shortcomings—as anyone who has had his or her work overwritten by another developer working on the same page will attest.

Dreamweaver includes a number of features that make it easy for teams to work together. In addition to the existing Check In/Check Out facility, version control and collaborative authoring have been enabled in Dreamweaver through the connectivity to the WebDAV (Web-based Distributed Authoring and Versioning) standard. Of special note is Dreamweaver's robust support for Subversion, the open source version-control system.

Another member of the Adobe software family, Contribute, is tightly integrated with Dreamweaver. Contribute-enabled sites can be administered directly from within Dreamweaver with full access to the latest version of Contribute administrative controls.

In addition to providing links to industry-standard protocols used in team development, Dreamweaver also includes a more accessible Design Notes feature. When custom file columns (which rely on Design Notes to store their information) are set up, a project's status is just a glance away. For more detailed feedback, Dreamweaver's Reports command provides an interactive method for uncovering problems and offers a direct link to fixing them. As with many Dreamweaver features, the Reports mechanism is extensible, which means JavaScript-savvy developers can create their own custom reports to further assist their team. This chapter examines the various Dreamweaver tools—both old and new—for developing websites with a team.

Following Check In/Check Out Procedures

Site development can be subdivided in as many different ways as there are site development teams. In one group, all the graphics may be handled by one person or department, whereas layout is handled by another, and JavaScript coding is handled by yet another. Or, one team may be given total responsibility over one section of a website—the products section, for example—whereas another team handles the services division. No matter how the responsibilities are shared, the danger of overlap always exists. Two or more team members might unknowingly work on the same page, graphic, or other web element—and one person's work might replace the other's when the work is transferred to the remote site. Suddenly, the oh-so-efficient division of labor becomes a logistical nightmare.

Dreamweaver's core protection for team website development is its Check In/Check Out system. When properly established and adhered to, the Check In/Check Out system stops files from being overwritten improperly. It also lets everyone on the team know who is working on what file, and it provides a direct method of contacting team members, right from within Dreamweaver.

As with any team effort, to get the most out of the Check In/Check Out system everybody must follow the rules:

- **Rule Number 1:** All team members must have Check In/Check Out set up for their Dreamweaver-defined sites.
- **Rule Number 2:** All team members must have Design Notes enabled in their Site Setup (in order to share Design Notes information).

And, arguably the most important rule:

- **Rule Number 3:** All team members must use Dreamweaver to transfer files to and from the remote server.

If the Check In/Check Out system fails and a file is accidentally overwritten, it is invariably because Rule Number 3 was broken: Someone uploaded or downloaded a file to or from the web server using a tool other than Dreamweaver.

Check In/Check Out overview

Before I discuss the Check In/Check Out setup procedure, examine how the process actually works with two fictional team members, Eric and Bella:

1. Eric receives an e-mail with a note to update the content on the "About Our Company" page with news of a merger that has just occurred.
2. Bella receives a similar note—except Bella is the graphic artist and needs to change the logo to reflect the new organization.
3. Eric connects to the remote site, selects the `about.htm` file, and clicks the Check Out button on Dreamweaver's Files panel toolbar. If Eric had clicked Get instead of Check Out, he would have received a read-only file on his system.
4. Dreamweaver asks Eric if he would like to include dependent files in the transfer. Because he doesn't know that Bella needs to work on the site also, he clicks OK. The file on the

remote system is downloaded to Eric's machine, and a small green checkmark appears next to the name of each file transferred in both the Remote Site and the Local Files views, as shown in Figure 31-1.

FIGURE 31-1

For a checked-out file, a checkmark is placed next to the filename on both the local and the remote sites. The checkmark is green if you checked it out and red if someone else checked it out.

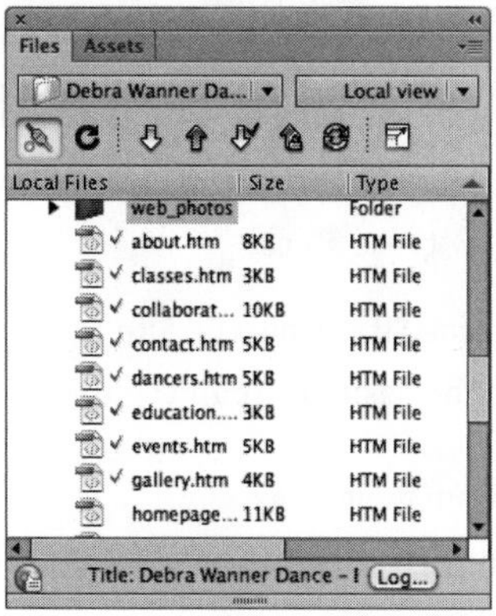

5. Bella connects to the remote site in Dreamweaver and sees a red check next to the file she needs to work on, `about.htm`. Next to the file is the name of the person who currently has the file, Eric, as well as his e-mail address.
6. Bella selects the link to Eric's e-mail address and drops him a note asking him to let her know when he's done.
7. Eric finishes adding the content to the page and clicks the Check In button to transfer the files back to the remote server. The checkmarks are removed from both the Remote and the Local views, and the local version of `about.htm` is marked as read-only by Dreamweaver, indicated with a closed padlock symbol. This feature prevents Eric from working on the file without first checking it out.
8. Bella receives Eric's "I'm done!" e-mail and retrieves the file by clicking the Check Out button in the Files panel toolbar. Now, on Bella's machine, the transferred files have a green checkmark and her name, whereas on Eric's screen, the checkmarks are displayed in red.
9. After she's finished working on the graphics side of the page, ensuring that Eric's new content wraps properly around her new logo, Bella selects the HTML file and then clicks Check In. By opting to transfer the dependent files as well, she ensures that all her new graphics are properly transferred. Again, the checkmarks are removed, and the local files are set to read-only.
10. The work is completed without anyone stepping on anyone else's toes—or files.

CAUTION

Dreamweaver places a small text file with a `.lck` (lock) extension on both the server and the local site for each checked-out document. The `.lck` file stores the Check Out name of the person transferring the files and, if available, his or her e-mail address. These files must not be deleted from the server because their existence signals to Dreamweaver that a file has been checked out. After the file is checked back in, the `.lck` file is deleted from the server.

Enabling Check In/Check Out

Dreamweaver's Check In/Check Out system is activated through the Site Setup dialog box. The Check In/Check Out settings must be input individually for each site; no global option exists for all sites. Although it's generally best to set it up when the site is initially defined, you can enable Check In/Check Out at any time.

To establish the Check In/Check Out feature, follow these steps:

1. Choose Site ➪ Manage Sites or select Manage Sites from the Site list in the Files panel.
2. From the Manage Sites dialog box, select the desired site in the list and choose Edit or click the New button to define a new site.
3. Select the Servers category in the Site Setup dialog box.
4. Choose any previously defined server and then click Edit or click New to create a new server.
5. From the Access list, choose either FTP or Local/Network.
6. From the Servers pop-up panel, click Advanced.
7. Choose the Enable file checkout option.
8. Enter the name you displayed under the Checked Out By column in the Check-out name field. It's a good idea to use a name identifies that not only you but also the system on which you're working. Thus, jlowery-laptop or jlowery-iMac is a better choice than just jlowery.
9. To enable team members to send you a message from within Dreamweaver, enter your full e-mail address in the E-mail Address field, as shown in Figure 31-2.

   Entering an e-mail address converts the Checked Out By name to an active link. If you select the link, the default e-mail program opens a new message form.
10. Make sure that any other information necessary for establishing an FTP or network connection is entered.
11. Click Save to close the Servers panel pop-up.
12. Click Save again to close the Site Setup dialog box.
13. From the Manage Sites dialog box, click Done.

NOTE

The preceding procedure works for both FTP and network-connected remote sites. If you are working within a WebDAV environment, see the "Communicating with WebDAV" section later in this chapter, which discusses enabling Check In and Check Out protocols for that environment.

FIGURE 31-2

Add your name and e-mail address to the Check out file feature so other team members will know whom to contact if you have checked out a needed file.

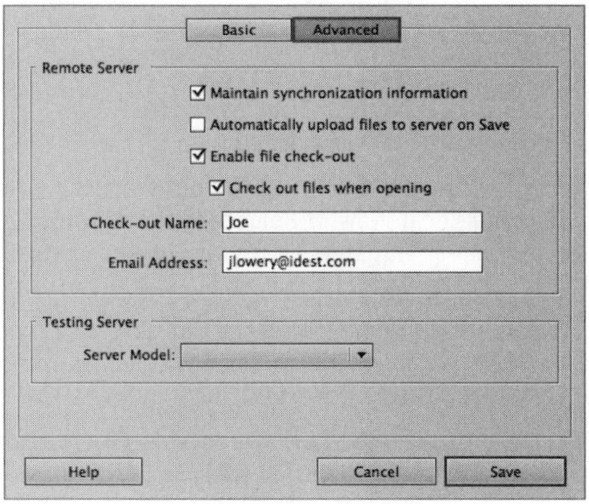

Checking files in and out

After the Check In/Check Out feature is enabled, additional buttons and commands become available. The Files panel toolbar shows both a Check Out File(s) button and a Check In button, as shown in Figure 31-3, and the Site ➪ Check Out and Site ➪ Check In commands become active. The redundancy of these commands makes it feasible to check files in and out from wherever you happen to be working in the Dreamweaver environment.

FIGURE 31-3

The Check In and Check Out buttons do not appear unless Enable Check In/Check Out has been selected in the Site Setup dialog box.

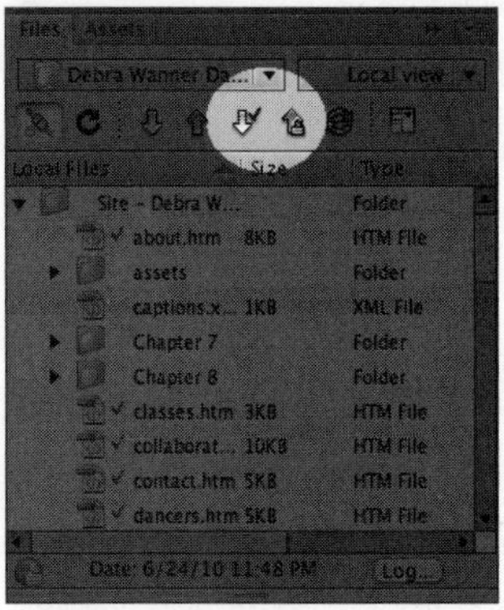

To check out a file or series of files from the Files panel, follow these steps:

1. Choose Window ➪ Files to open the Files panel. If you prefer to use keyboard shortcuts, press F8 (Command+Shift+F).
2. If necessary, select the desired site—where Check In/Check Out has been enabled—from the Site drop-down list.
3. Click the Connect button in the Files panel toolbar. If you've chosen Local/Network as your remote access method, you're connected automatically.
4. Choose the HTML or other web documents you want to check out from the Files panel (it doesn't matter whether you're using Local view or Remote view). It's not necessary to select the dependent files; Dreamweaver transfers those for you automatically.
5. Click Check Out File(s) in the Files panel toolbar or select Site ➪ Check Out. If you *get* the files instead of checking them out, either by clicking the Get button or by dragging the files from the Remote Site listing to the Local Files listing, the local file becomes read-only, but the remote files are not marked as checked out.
6. If the Prompt On Get/Check Out option is selected in Preferences ➪ Site, Dreamweaver asks if you'd like to transfer the dependent files. Click Yes to do so or No to transfer only the selected files. When Dreamweaver has completed the transfer, green checkmarks appear next to each primary file (HTML, ASP, ColdFusion, and so on) in both the Remote Site and the Local Files views; dependent files are made read-only locally, designated by a padlock symbol.

I recommend checking out all the files that you need in a work session right at the start. Although you can check out an open document—by choosing Site ➪ Check Out or by selecting Check Out from the File Management button on the toolbar—Dreamweaver transfers the remote file to your local system, possibly overwriting any changes you've made. Dreamweaver does ask you if you want to replace the local version with the remote file; to abort the procedure, click No.

TIP

To edit a graphic or other dependent file that has been locked as part of the checkout process, you can unlock the file from the Files panel. Right-click (Control+click) the file in the Files panel and, from the context menu, choose Turn Off Read Only. (The Turn Off Read Only option is called Unlock on the Mac.) One related tip: To quickly select the file for an image, choose the image in the Assets panel; and from the context menu, choose Locate In Site.

After you've completed your work on a particular file, you're ready to check it back in. To check in the current file, follow these steps:

1. Choose Site ➪ Check In or click Check In on the Files panel toolbar.
2. If you haven't saved your file, but you've enabled the Save Files Before Putting option from the Site category in Preferences, your file is automatically saved; otherwise, Dreamweaver asks if you want to store the file before transferring it.
3. If Prompt On Put/Check In is enabled, Dreamweaver asks if you want to transfer the dependent files as well. If any changes have been made to the dependent files, click Yes.

   After the files are transferred, Dreamweaver removes the checkmarks from the files and makes the local files read-only.

NOTE

Ever start working on a file only to realize you're working on the wrong one? If you make this or any other mistake that makes you wish you could go back to the original version when working with a checked-out file, don't worry. Even if you've saved your changes locally, you can choose Site ➪ Undo Check Out (or select Undo Check Out from the Site button on the Files panel toolbar) to retransfer the posted file from the remote site. The local file is made read-only, and the file is no longer checked out under your name.

Keeping Track with Design Notes

When several people are working on a site, they can't just rely on the web pages to speak for themselves. In any team collaboration, a great deal of organizational information needs to be communicated behind the scenes: who's working on what areas, the status of any given file, when the project is due, what modifications are needed, and so on. Dreamweaver includes a feature called Design Notes that is designed to facilitate team communication in a very flexible manner.

Dreamweaver Design Notes are small files that, in a sense, attach themselves to the web pages or objects they concern. A Design Note can be attached to any HTML page, graphic, or media file inserted into a page. Design Notes follow their corresponding file whenever that file is moved or renamed using the Dreamweaver Files panel; moreover, a Design Note is deleted if the file to which it is related is deleted. Design Notes have the same base name as the file to which they are attached—including that file's extension—but are designated with an `.mno` extension. For example, the Design Note for the file `index.htm` would be called `index.htm.mno`; Design Notes are stored in the _notes subfolder, which is not displayed in the Dreamweaver Files panel.

Design Notes can be entered and viewed through the Design Notes dialog box, shown in Figure 31-4. This dialog box may optionally be set to appear when a file is opened, thus passing instructions from one team member to another automatically. In addition to the Design Notes dialog box, you can configure File view columns to display Design Note information right in the Files panel; the File view columns feature is covered in the section "Browsing File View Columns" later in this chapter.

Setting up for Design Notes

Design Notes are enabled by default, but they can be turned off on a site-by-site basis. To disable Design Notes, follow these steps:

1. Choose Site ➪ Manage Sites or select Manage Sites from the Site listing to open the Manage Sites dialog box.
2. In the Manage Sites dialog box, select the site you want to alter and choose Edit.
3. In the Site Setup dialog box, expand Advanced Settings and then select the Design Notes category (see Figure 31-5).
4. Clear the Maintain Design Notes option to completely stop Dreamweaver from creating Design Notes. Dreamweaver alerts you to the consequences of disabling Design Notes. Click OK to continue.
5. If you want to work with Design Notes locally, but don't want to automatically transfer them to the remote site, leave Maintain Design Notes checked, and uncheck Upload Design Notes For Sharing.

6. To remove Design Notes that no longer have an associated file—which can happen if a file is deleted or renamed by a program other than Dreamweaver—click the Clean Up button. Dreamweaver gives you an opportunity to confirm the delete operation.
7. Click Save to close the Site Setup dialog box, and then click Done to close the Manage Sites dialog box.

FIGURE 31-4

You can configure a Design Note to pop up whenever a file is opened to alert a fellow team member of work to be done.

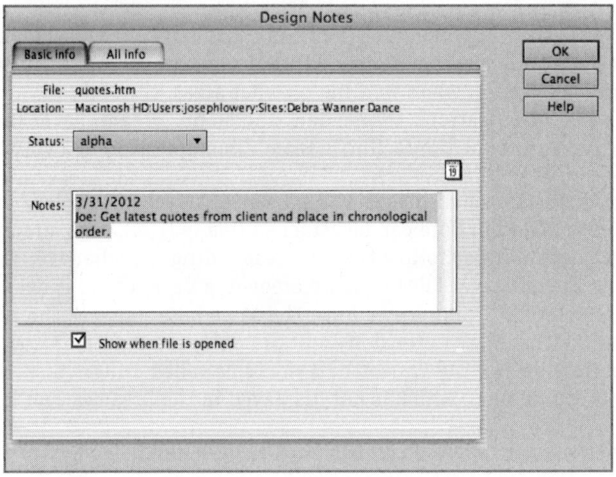

FIGURE 31-5

Design Notes play an important role in cross-product integration when working with Photoshop, Fireworks, Flash, and Contribute.

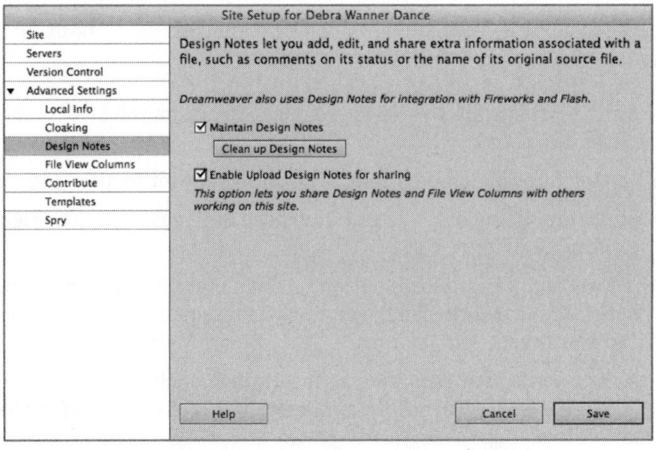

Design Notes serve two different purposes. From a team perspective, they're invaluable for tracking a project's progress and passing information among team members. However, Design Notes are also used by Dreamweaver and other Adobe products, including Fireworks, to pass data between programs and program commands. For example, Fireworks uses Design Notes to store the location of a Fireworks source file that is displayed in the Image Property inspector when you select the exported graphic in Dreamweaver.

Keep in mind the dual nature of Design Notes. I strongly recommend—whether you work with a large team or you're a team of one—that you keep Design Notes enabled and fully functioning.

Setting the status with Design Notes

What is the one thing a website project manager always wants to know? The status of every page under development: what's still in the planning stages, what has been drafted, what has made it to beta, and what's ready to go live? The manager who has an awareness of each page's status can prioritize appropriately and add additional resources to the development of a page if necessary. Individual team members who are working on a page should also know how far along that page is.

Design Notes put the Status category front and center for all files. It's the one standard field that is always available, and it offers eight different values and one custom value. Entries may be date-stamped in the Note's area to show a history of revisions, as shown in Figure 31-6. Optionally, you can elect to display the Design Note the next time the file is opened by anyone.

FIGURE 31-6

Design Notes can maintain a history of revisions for any web page.

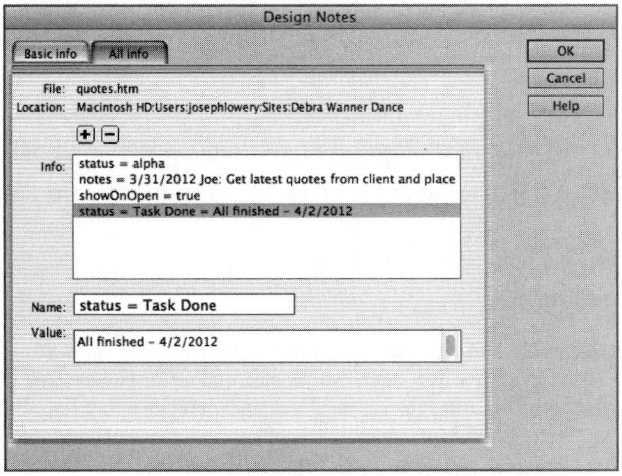

To enter the status of a file, follow these steps:

1. Choose File ➪ Design Notes to open the Design Notes dialog box. To insert a Design Note for an object embedded on a web page, such as a graphic, Flash movie, or other multimedia element, right-click (Control+click) the object and choose Design Notes from the context menu.

2. On the Basic Info tab of the Design Notes dialog box, choose one of the following standard options from the Status drop-down list: draft, revision1, revision2, revision3, alpha, beta, final, or needs attention.
3. To add the current date (mm/dd/yyyy, such as 03/07/2012) to the Notes field, click the Calendar icon.
4. Enter any desired text into the Notes field. The same Notes text is displayed regardless of which Status option you choose.
5. If you'd like the Design Notes dialog box with the current information to appear the next time the page is loaded, select the Show When File Is Opened option. The Show When File Is Opened option is available only for Design Notes attached to pages, not for Design Notes attached to page elements such as images.
6. Click OK when you're finished.

Creating custom Design Notes

Aside from monitoring the status of a project, you can use a Design Note to describe any single item. The All Info tab of the Design Notes dialog box enables you to enter any number of name/value pairs, which can be viewed in the Design Note itself or—more effectively—in the File view columns. This mechanism might be used to indicate which graphic artist in your department has primary responsibility for the page or how many billable hours the page has accrued. You can also use the All Info tab to set a custom value for the Status list on the Basic Info tab.

To enter a new name/value pair, follow these steps:

1. Choose File ➪ Design Notes to open the Design Notes dialog box.
2. Select the All Info tab. If a Status and/or Notes entry has been made on the Basic Info tab, you'll see these values listed in the Info area.
3. Click the Add (+) button to enter a new name/value pair.
4. In the Name field, enter the term you want to use.
5. In the Value field, enter the information you want associated with the current term.
6. To edit an entry, select it from the list in the Info area and alter either the Name or the Value field.
7. To delete an entry, select it and click the Remove (–) button.
8. Click OK when you're finished.

As noted earlier, you can create a custom Status list option in the All Info tab. To do so, just enter **status** (case-sensitive) in the Name field of a new name/value pair and enter the desired listing in the Value field. If you switch to the Basic Info tab, you find your new status entry listed as the last item. You can add only one custom status entry; if you add another, it replaces the previous one.

Viewing Design Notes

To fully view a Design Note, you have several options. You can choose File ➪ Design Notes to open the dialog box; in Windows, this option is available from either the Document window or the Files panel. A second method is to right-click (Control+click) the file in either the File or the Site Map view of the Files panel and select the Design Notes option from the context menu. Finally, if a Design Note is attached to a file, you'll see an icon in the Notes column of the File view, as shown in Figure 31-7. Double-clicking the Notes icon opens the Design Note associated with that file.

FIGURE 31-7

Get immediate access to previously created Design Notes by double-clicking the icon in the Notes column.

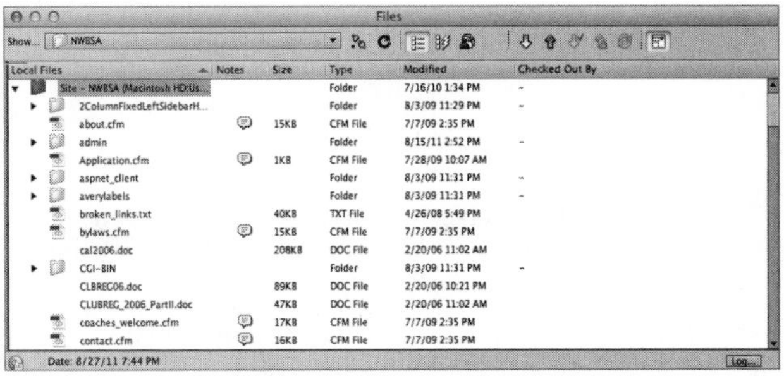

Browsing File View Columns

Although Design Notes can hold a lot of information about a web page or element, the details are kept out of sight. With an eye toward heightening the visibility of Design Notes data—thus making them more useful—the Dreamweaver engineers have tied the columns of the Files panel's File view directly to Design Notes. In the previous section, you saw how the Notes column indicated that a Design Note existed for a particular file; now you learn how to create custom File view columns to display any value stored in a Design Note.

With custom columns in the File view, a quick glance at the Files panel can reveal which files are completed, which are in revision, and which need attention. Moreover, custom columns can be sorted, just as regular columns. You can, for instance, easily group all the files with the same due date, or those coded by the same programmer. File view columns—even the built-in ones such as Type and Modified—can be realigned, re-ordered, or hidden. Only the Local Files column cannot be altered or moved. With this level of customization possible, virtually the entire File view can be reshaped, like the one in Figure 31-8.

The six standard columns—Local Files (which shows the filename), Notes, Size, Type, Modified, and Checked Out By—can be supplemented by any number of custom columns. Modification of the column setup is handled in the File View Columns category of the Site Setup dialog box. File views are managed on a per-site basis; when defining the File views, you can determine if the views are to be seen by anyone accessing the development site. Likewise, any custom column can optionally be shared among team members.

FIGURE 31-8

File view columns can be substantially reorganized to reflect the concerns of your team on a project-by-project basis.

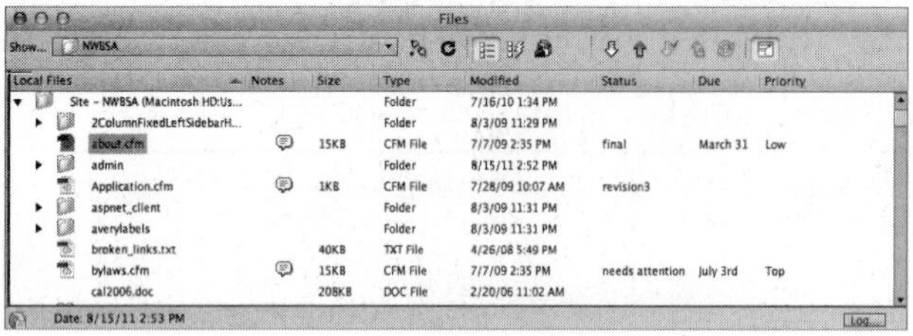

To create a custom File view, follow these steps:

1. Open the File View Columns category by selecting Manage Sites and open the Site Setup for the desired site. Then select the File View Columns option from the Advanced Settings category list.
2. If you'd like team members to see the custom columns you're developing, select Enable Column Sharing. You also need to choose the Share With All Users Of This Site option for each custom column you want to share.
3. To add a custom column, click the Add (+) button. A new entry at the end of the list is created.
4. Enter a unique name for the column in the Column Name field. If you enter an existing name, Dreamweaver warns you and requests a new name before proceeding.
5. Pick a Design Note field to link to the new column from the Associate With Design Note list. You can choose one of the suggested Design Note fields (assigned, due, priority, or status) or you can enter your own. Design Note fields can be uppercase, lowercase, or mixed-case; multiple words are also allowed.
6. Select an Alignment option from the list: Left, Center, or Right. Columns that hold numeric or date values should be aligned to the right.
7. Make sure the Show option is selected.
8. To share this column with fellow team members, choose the Share With All Users Of This Site option. Selecting this option causes Dreamweaver to create a file called `dwSiteColumnsAll.xml` within the _notes folder on the remote site. When another member of your team connects to the site, Dreamweaver reads this file and incorporates it into that person's Site Setup. This enables any other user to see the same column set up on his or her system.
9. Use the up and down arrows to reposition the column.
10. To add additional columns, repeat Steps 3 through 9.
11. Click OK when you're finished.

How might a team benefit from custom File view columns? Some of the possibilities for custom columns include the following:

- Project Manager
- Lead Designer
- Lead Programmer
- Template Used
- Date Created
- Date Due
- Percentage Complete
- Client Contact

CAUTION

File view columns are sorted alphabetically even if the values are numeric. For example, if you have three files with the numeric values 100, 50, and 10 percent, an ascending sort displays 10, 100, 50 percent. As a workaround, use decimal values (.10, .50, and 1.00) to represent percentages, and the files will be sorted correctly. If your columns require date values, use leading zeros in dates, such as 01/03, to ensure that the columns are properly sorted.

Although having the Design Notes information visible in File view columns is extremely helpful for maintaining an overview of a website, Dreamweaver takes the feature a step further. After a custom file column is established, you can handle additions and modifications to the Design Note from the Files panel. Click in the custom column of the file; the existing information, if any, is highlighted and can be altered. If there is no data in the column, the column becomes editable.

NOTE

Although the Design Note is actually a separate file, you cannot change File view columns for a locked file. One solution is to temporarily turn off the read-only feature and then add the File view info and relock the file if necessary.

To turn off the read-only feature, right-click (Control+click) the file in the Files panel and, from the context menu, choose Turn Off Read Only. (The Turn Off Read Only option is called Unlock on the Mac.)

Generating Reports

Although custom File view columns can present a tremendous degree of detail, the data is only viewable from the Files panel. Often, managers and team members need to extract certain bits of information about a site in order to know where they stand and fix problems in an organized, timely fashion. Some webmasters use third-party utilities to comb their sites and generate lists of errors, which can then be assigned for resolution. These utilities can also be used to establish workflow patterns as they gather information, such as which pages are currently incomplete, or who is currently working on what site elements.

Dreamweaver reports give the webmaster and team members a new tool for efficiently building websites. The information from a Dreamweaver report can be instantly used—double-clicking any report detail opens the referenced file—or stored as an XML file for later output. Dreamweaver includes seven standard reports that may be generated individually or combined into one. As with many Dreamweaver features, the Reports command is extensible, enabling users to build custom reports.

How do Dreamweaver reports work? The user must first choose from a variety of scopes: the current document, selected files in the site, all the files in a particular folder, or the entire site. After the scope has been selected, the report elements—what the report actually covers—are selected. The report is then run, and Dreamweaver outputs the results into a floating panel, as shown in Figure 31-9. Each entry in the Results panel is capable of opening the listed file; in the case of reports querying the underlying HTML, the entries lead directly to the referenced code.

Generated reports can also be saved for later use. The reports are saved in an XML file format that can be imported into a web page, database, or spreadsheet program. Although this information can be extracted by hand, the structured format of the XML file makes it a perfect candidate for an automated process handled by an extension or other utility.

Two different types of Dreamweaver reports are available: those concerned with the code in the pages themselves and those accessing workflow details (see Figure 31-10).

To access a Dreamweaver report, follow these steps:

1. Choose Site ➪ Reports, or click the Play icon in the Site Reports panel. Windows users can choose the command from either the Document window or the Files panel menus.
2. Select which reports you'd like to include from either the Workflow or the HTML Reports categories.
3. If you choose an option from the Workflow category, the Report Settings button activates. Click it to define the report search for Workflow reports such as Design Notes, as shown in Figure 31-11.

   Dreamweaver remembers the Report On setting each time you run this command. The Report Settings options are covered in detail later, in the section "Using Workflow Reports."

FIGURE 31-9

Dreamweaver reports return interactive results—just double-click any listed entry to open the related file.

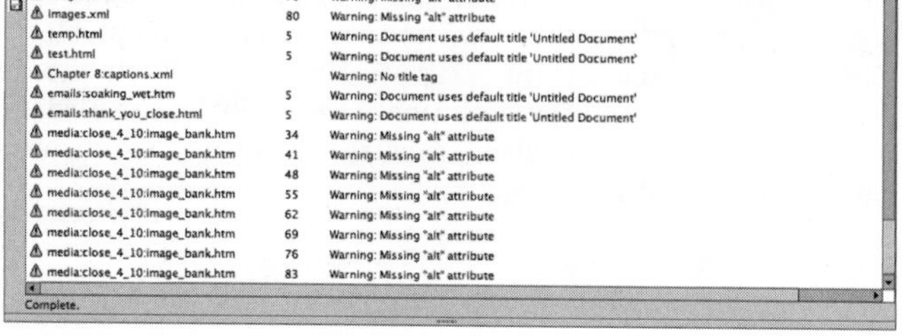

FIGURE 31-10

Generate either code-oriented or workflow reports.

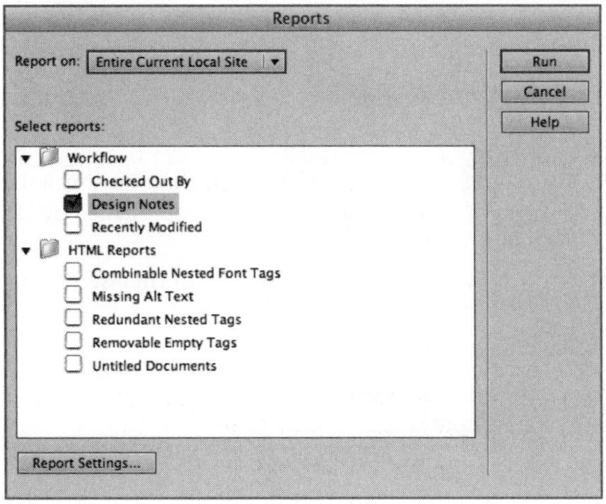

FIGURE 31-11

Fine-tune your Design Notes report by clicking Report Settings.

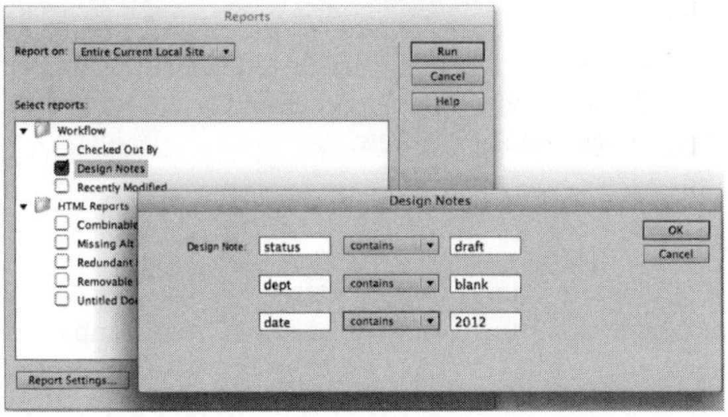

4. Click the Run button. The Site Reports panel appears if it isn't already active. As the report is processed, results are listed in the upper window.
5. From the Site Reports panel, you can click the Stop icon to halt the report.
6. To open any referenced file, double-click the entry or right-click (Control+click) the entry and select Open File from the context menu.
7. To store the report as an XML file, select Save Report and enter a file and path in the Save File dialog box.

Entries in the Site Reports panel are initially sorted by filename in an ascending order; however, selecting any column heading (File, Line, or Description) re-sorts the list accordingly. If many result listings are returned, the Site Reports panel can be resized to display more of them.

Outputting HTML reports

Dreamweaver includes five options under the HTML Reports category:

- **Combinable Nested Font Tags:** Looks for code in which the font tag has been applied to the same text at different times, as shown in the following example:

```
<font color="#000000"><font size=+1>Monday, December 15th @7pm
</font></font>
```

- **Missing Alt Text:** Searches for `<img>` tags in which the `alt` attribute is empty or missing entirely. To comply with accessibility guidelines established by the W3C, all images should have `alt` attributes that describe the graphic.
- **Redundant Nested Tags:** Identifies tags nested within themselves, as shown in the following example:

```
<strong><strong>On Sale!</strong></strong>
```

- **Removable Empty Tags:** Finds non-empty tags (that is, tags with both an opening and a closing element) with no content, as in this code:

```
<div align="center"> </div>
```

- **Untitled Documents:** Looks for pages that have no title or use the default Untitled Document text.

You can run any or all of the HTML reports at the same time—just select the desired report(s) from the Reports dialog box. The Site Reports panel lists the name of the file, the line number where the search condition was found, and an error message for each entry. Selecting a file displays the error message with additional detail, if available, in the Detailed Description area. Select Open File from the context menu or double-click an entry to load the file if it's available. If the file is currently locked, Dreamweaver asks if you'd like to view the read-only file or unlock it. All HTML report files are displayed in the split-screen Code and Design view.

Using Workflow reports

Workflow reports, unlike HTML reports, don't examine the code of web pages. They look at the metadata—the information about the information—of a site. Three standard reports are available under the Workflow heading:

- **Checked Out By:** Displays any file checked out by a particular person as designated in the Report Settings dialog box. If nothing is entered in the Report Settings dialog box, a list of all files in the selected scope that have been checked out by anyone is returned.

NOTE
To run this report, you must be able to connect to your remote site.

- **Recently Modified:** Returns a list of pages modified in a user-definable period along with their modification date; you can, optionally, search for pages modified by a specific user, if the site is being administered by Contribute. All options are shown in Figure 31-12.

In addition to the Results panel listing, this report also automatically opens a print-ready version in your primary browser with links to each page listed. The pages can be viewed either locally—best for static pages—or through the testing server, which is necessary for dynamic pages.

- **Design Notes:** Examines the designated files according to search criteria set up in the Report Settings dialog box. Searches can be conducted on a maximum of three criteria. If no criterion is entered, a list of all files with Design Notes in the selected scope is returned.

FIGURE 31-12

Get a complete printable report on files changed in a given time frame by running the Recently Modified report.

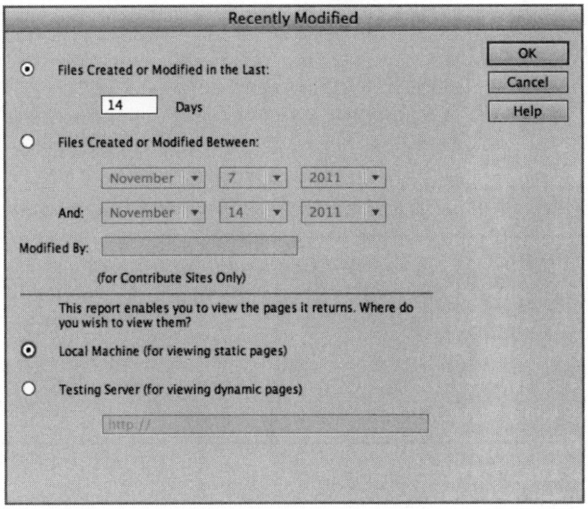

The Report Settings dialog box for the Design Notes reports is relatively flexible because it enables *and*-type searches. To use the Design Notes Report Settings dialog box, follow these steps:

1. In the Reports dialog box, select the Design Notes option under the Workflow category. The Report Settings button is made available.
2. Click Report Settings. The Report Settings dialog box opens; the previous Design Notes Settings are restored.
3. In the Report Settings dialog box, enter the name of the Design Notes field in the first column. The name of the Design Notes field is case-sensitive, so entering **Status** in the Report Settings dialog box will not match **status** in the Design Note.
4. Choose a criteria type from the middle column drop-down list. The options are as follows: contains, does not contain, is, is not, and matches regex.
5. In the third column, enter the value of the Design Notes field being sought. As with the Design Notes field, the value search is case-sensitive.

6. To add a second or third condition to the query, repeat Steps 3 through 5 in the second and third line of the Report Settings dialog box. Additional conditionals are applied in an *and*-type search. For example, a setting where the first line reads:

   ```
   status is revision3
   ```

   and the second line reads:

   ```
   done is 1.00
   ```

   returns all Design Notes for which both conditions are true. Currently, there is no way to perform an *or*-type search.
7. Click OK when you're finished.
8. Click Run to execute the search.

Of all the criteria options—`is`, `is not`, `contains`, and so on—available in the Report Settings dialog box for Design Notes, the most powerful is `matches regex`. Regular Expressions are pattern-matching mechanisms and, as such, are extremely flexible. The syntax, however, is unique and requires a bit of use before it becomes second nature. Here are some examples you might find useful:

Regular Expression	Matches
`.*`	Any text
`[^.]`	An empty string
`\d`	Any single number
`[0-5]`	Any digit from 0 to 5
`graphics|code`	Either the word `graphics` or the word `code`

Administering Adobe Contribute Sites

One of a web designer's greatest challenges is the ongoing maintenance of a site. In many situations, websites thrive on current information and, without continual updates, lose their effectiveness. Site maintenance is a prickly thorn bush for all involved: Web developers find it time-consuming and a distraction from their primary business, design. Website owners want editorial control and immediate access—without the technical administrative headaches.

Adobe Contribute was introduced to solve the thorny problem of website upkeep. Contribute makes it easy for non-technical users to modify and add content to their websites; if your users are familiar with a word processor and a browser, they'll be able to master Contribute with little effort. After a content contributor has an established connection to a site—a process Contribute greatly simplifies—all he does is browse to a page, make his edits, and publish it back to the web. The Contribute interface, shown in Figure 31-13, is designed with the non-technical user in mind.

If you're a designer working with content contributors using Contribute, you can easily set up your site to be compatible. Contribute compatibility relies on key team-oriented features discussed elsewhere in this chapter: Check In/Check Out and Design Notes.

FIGURE 31-13

Contribute packs a lot of power in a simplified interface, allowing the non-technically savvy to modify web pages with ease.

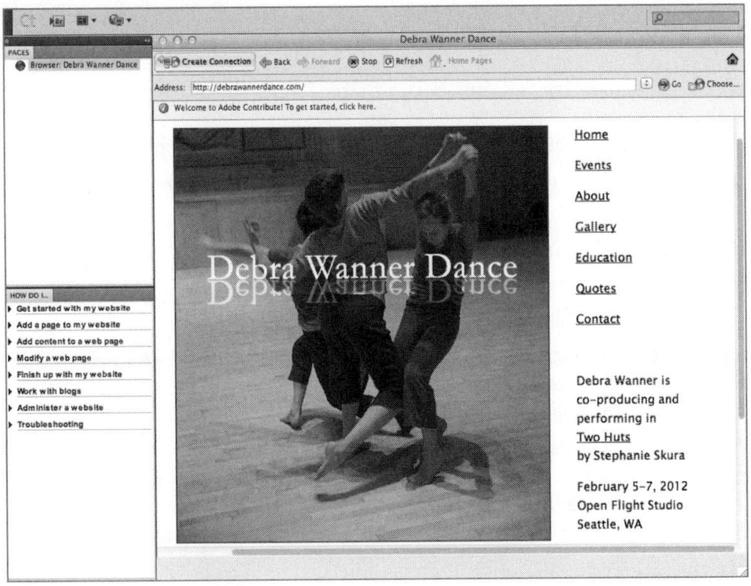

The key to Contribute is controlled access. Although the program makes it easy for anyone to modify pages on the web, it also restricts what changes can be made. Some of the restrictions are inherent in the types of pages that make up the site—Dreamweaver templates, for example, are ideally suited for allowing only designated sections of a document to be edited. However, many basic limitations, such as which pages can be edited, are established by the Contribute administrator. Although Contribute sites can be administered from within Contribute itself, its tight integration with Dreamweaver provides another path: The same administrative options are available within Dreamweaver.

NOTE

To administer Contribute from within Dreamweaver, Contribute 2.0 or better must be installed on the same machine as Dreamweaver; greater functionality comes from working with Contribute 3.1 or higher.

Setting up Contribute compatibility

Like other sitewide settings, Contribute compatibility is managed through the Site Setup dialog box. As noted earlier, Contribute utilizes several optional Dreamweaver features—Design Notes and Check In/Check Out—controlled through the same interface. For your convenience, if you opt to establish Contribute administration, Dreamweaver enables all the necessary options with one click, if you have not previously done so.

NOTE

To make Contribute compatibility available, the site must be configured with the proper form of remote access, such as FTP or SFTP. WebDAV is not compatible with Contribute. RDS-based sites require custom settings for Contribute compatibility.

To set up Contribute compatibility for your current site, follow these steps:

1. Choose Site ➪ Manage Sites. The Manage Sites dialog box is displayed.
2. With the current site selected in the Manage Sites dialog box, click Edit. The Site Setup dialog box appears.
3. From the Advanced Settings view of the Site Setup dialog box, select the Contribute category.
4. Select the Enable Contribute Compatibility option.
5. If you have not previously enabled Design Notes (for both local and remote use) and Check In/Check Out, Dreamweaver displays a dialog box informing you of their necessity and offers to automatically enable these settings; click OK to continue.
6. If Check In/Check Out was not previously set up, the Contribute Site Settings dialog box is displayed. Enter a checkout name and e-mail address in the appropriate fields, and click OK. Dreamweaver displays the Site Root URL for the current site, as shown in Figure 31-14, gathered from the information entered in the Remote Site category.
7. To verify the Site Root URL, click Test.
8. Click OK when you're finished to close the Site Setup dialog box.

FIGURE 31-14

After you've enabled Contribute compatibility, be sure to test the connection.

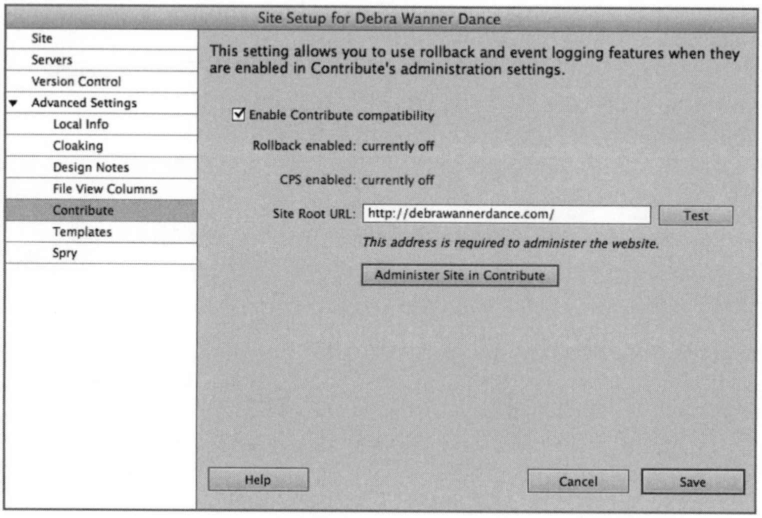

The Contribute category in Preferences updates to reflect the newly set up Contribute administration. In addition to the URL to the site, you'll also see indicators concerning the status of rollback (the ability to reinstate previous versions) and CPS (Contribute Publishing Services).

Entering sitewide administrator settings

Each Contribute site has a single administrator. The administrator is responsible for controlling overall access to the site as well as establishing editing parameters. Among other options, the administrator can allow pages edited by Contribute users to be rolled back to previous versions. When you enable Contribute compatibility, you're establishing yourself as the site administrator.

NOTE

Before you can set up yourself as an administrator, Contribute compatibility must be enabled as described in the previous section, and you must have a network connection.

To begin modifying Contribute settings, click Administer Site In Contribute in the Contribute category of the Site Setup dialog box. The primary administrative interface, shown in Figure 31-15, opens after a connection is established.

FIGURE 31-15

The Administer Website dialog box available through Dreamweaver is the same as the one found in Contribute.

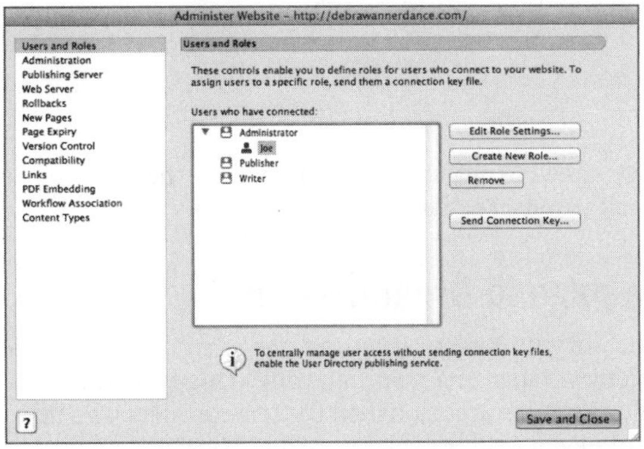

To modify the settings that control administration, follow these steps:

1. From the Administer Website dialog box, select Administration. The Administration dialog box is displayed, as shown in Figure 31-16.
2. To change the administrator's e-mail address, enter a valid e-mail address in the Contact E-mail Address field.

TIP

For administrative duties, it's a good idea to use a special e-mail address that is different from your checkout address, such as administrator@idest.com. Use your e-mail client to sort the incoming administrative queries into a special folder.

3. To alter the current administrator password, click Set Administrator Password and enter the old password and new password where indicated in the Set Administrator Password dialog box; click OK to return to the Sitewide Settings dialog box.
4. To stop administering the Contribute site, click Remove Administration and click Yes when asked to confirm your choice.

FIGURE 31-16

Modify primary administrative settings through the Administration category.

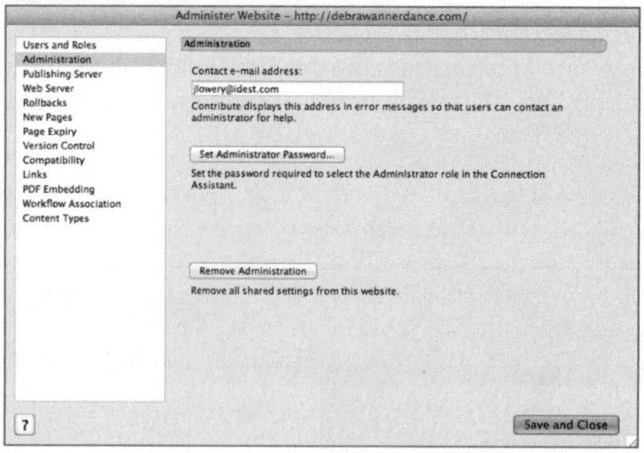

After you've chosen all the necessary sitewide options, click OK to close the Sitewide Settings dialog box and return to the Administer Website dialog box.

Rolling back a Contribute page in Dreamweaver

If you've enabled Contribute compatibility in Dreamweaver and the administrator has enabled rollbacks, you can revert to a previous version of a modified page. This feature can be a lifesaver, especially when you're dealing with less accomplished Contribute users who may just be finding their way. The rollback feature even enables you to see a preview of the page to make sure that you're bringing back the correct version.

CAUTION

Whether rollbacks are allowed—and how many previous versions to make available—is a significant decision. Enabling this option means that all users can store previous versions of all their edited pages and that all users can roll back any page they can access, whether they or someone else made the edits. You also must make sure that adequate server space is available to store the number of files maintained by the rollback option.

Before you can roll back a page in Dreamweaver, however, the capability to do so must be enabled through Contribute administration, as described in the following steps:

1. From the Contribute category in the Site Setup dialog box, select Administer Site.

   Dreamweaver indicates that rollbacks are not enabled.
2. Enter the administrator's password in the provided dialog box.
3. When the Administer Website dialog box appears, select the Rollbacks category.
4. Select the Enable Rollbacks option.
5. Specify the number of versions to be kept by entering a number in the pop-up list; by default, Contribute maintains the previous three versions of every page in a folder on the server called _baks—you can opt to store up to 99 versions.
6. Click Close to verify the changes to the Administer Website dialog box.

   Dreamweaver now shows that rollbacks are enabled.
7. Click OK to dismiss the Site Setup dialog box.

To roll back a page in Dreamweaver, follow these steps:

1. In the Files panel, right-click (Control+click) the page you want to revert and choose Roll Back Page from the contextual menu. The Roll Back Page dialog box is displayed, listing each of the previous versions and when they were published and by whom.

> **NOTE**
> If you edit a page in Dreamweaver or with any other program other than Contribute, you'll see a note that the version was created outside of Contribute in the Published by column, as shown in Figure 31-17, rather than the Contribute user's name.

2. To view a page version, select it from the list and choose Show Preview. The Roll Back Page dialog box opens a preview in your default browser. While the preview is open, you can choose another version from the list to view.
3. When you've found the version you want to use, click Roll Back. Dreamweaver switches the current version of the page with the selected version on the server, and the Roll Back Page dialog box closes.

FIGURE 31-17

Roll back any page in a Contribute-enabled site right from within Dreamweaver—whether editing in Contribute or outside of it.

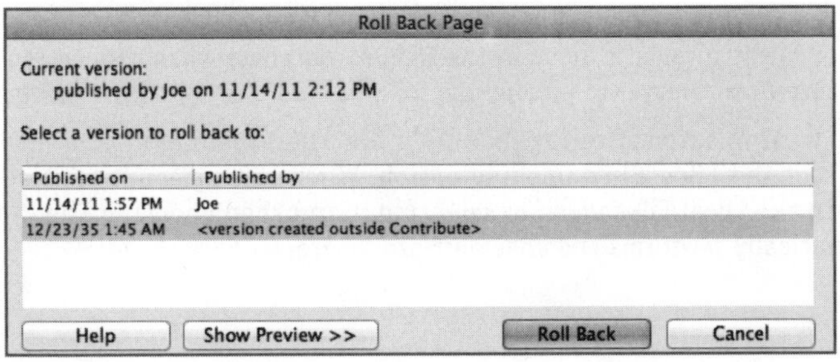

What happens to the page replaced during a rollback operation? It also becomes a rollback version and, if necessary, can be brought back through the same process.

Communicating with WebDAV

Web-based Distributed Authoring and Versioning (WebDAV) is an Internet protocol that enables web developers to collaborate over the web itself. WebDAV enables developers to log in over the web to work on a common set of files. Normally, the HTTP protocol, the basis for most Internet communication, permits files only to be read. With the WebDAV set of extensions installed, you can also write files to the server. More important, you can lock files to prevent multiple, simultaneous edits; in other words, files may be checked out for modification and checked in when the update is complete.

Dreamweaver supports the WebDAV protocol, enabling developers and designers around the world to work together on a single site. The WebDAV setup is, like RDS, handled through the Remote Info category of the Site Setup dialog box. After it is established, the Dreamweaver/WebDAV connection is transparent, and the Check In/Check Out features work as they do on a standard FTP or network connection.

Dreamweaver's implementation of WebDAV connectivity is geared toward Microsoft IIS and Apache servers. Both have been fully tested and are supported. WebDAV implementations on other servers may interact erratically, or not at all, with Dreamweaver. For more in-depth information on WebDAV, including a list of publicly available servers, visit `http://www.webdav.org`.

To establish a WebDAV connection, follow these steps:

1. Choose Site ➪ Manage Sites.
2. From the Manage Sites dialog box, choose the site to be connected to the WebDAV server from the list and click Edit.
3. Select the Remote Info category.
4. From the Access drop-down list, choose WebDAV.

   All the connection information is entered through the displayed settings, shown in Figure 31-18.
5. Enter the absolute URL to the WebDAV server in the URL field.
6. Enter your WebDAV login name in the Login field.
7. Enter your WebDAV password in the Password field.
8. Enter your Check out name and then put your e-mail address in the Email address field. The username and e-mail address are displayed for checked-out files.
9. To circumvent automatic logon to the WebDAV database when connecting in Dreamweaver—and cause Dreamweaver to prompt you for a password every time—deselect the Save option.
10. If you want to automatically check out a file when opening it from the Files panel, select the Check Out Files When Opening option. When this option is enabled, double-clicking a file in the Local Files view (or selecting it and then choosing File ➪ Open Selection) automatically performs the checkout procedure.

11. Click OK to close the Site Setup dialog box.
12. Click Done to close the Manage Sites dialog box.

FIGURE 31-18

After WebDAV is enabled, team members can collaborate over the web itself to develop websites.

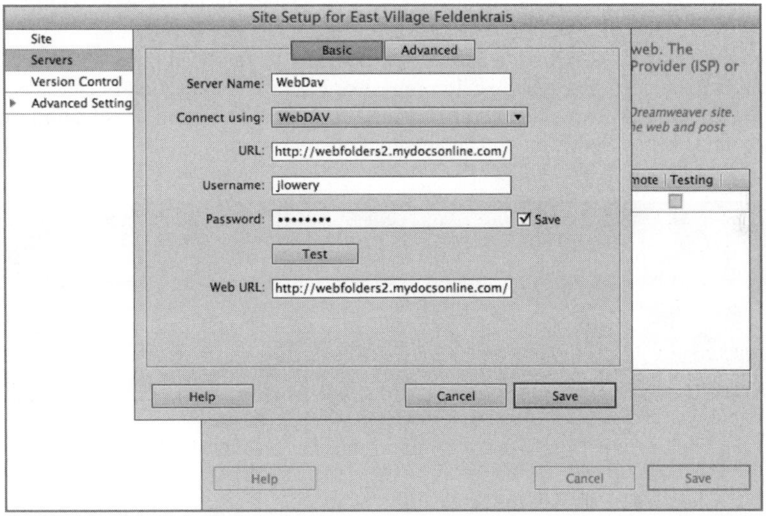

To use the WebDAV server, click the Connect button on the Files panel toolbar or choose Site ➪ Connect.

Version Control with Subversion

Subversion, often abbreviated SVN, is an extremely popular open source version-control system. The goal of Subversion is to allow multiple developers to work on the same site or source code. Subversion is available on Mac and Linux platforms, as well as being freely available. Moreover, Subversion allows multiple developers access, automatically merging changes to different parts of the page and notifies users if a conflict arises. These differences have led to widespread adoption, especially among web developer teams in larger organizations. In recognition of this workflow, Subversion is robustly supported in Dreamweaver.

Developers whose companies relied on Subversion for their version control used to have to perform a kind of Texas two-step for common operations. Getting and putting files from the central Subversion source, called a repository, was usually handled by another client program such as TurtleSVN, which moved the files in and out of a Dreamweaver local site root. From there, developers would make any necessary code changes, save their files, and then return to the third-party client to put—or commit—their modified documents. Dreamweaver now makes it possible to connect directly to the Subversion repository, check out and commit files, and even receive notification of file conflicts.

Dreamweaver has seamlessly integrated its support for Subversion. Common file operations take place through the Files panel where a file's status is clearly represented. Less frequently used commands are available through right-click context menus. And, as you discover in the next section, setup is right where you'd expect it to be: in the Site Setup dialog box.

Connecting to a Subversion server

In order for you to work with a Subversion repository, you need to establish a connection to it. Similar to a remote site, a Subversion repository requires you to log in to a specific server address with a recognized username and password. The declaration of all these details and any other necessary ones is handled through the Version Control category of the Site Setup dialog box.

NOTE

Although you can download and install the Subversion server software on your local development system, a great number of ISPs make it available at little or no cost. For this book, I've been using myVersionControl (`http://www.myversioncontrol.com`), which offers free access for up to 4MB of storage. Additional storage is offered for a small monthly fee. Account setup is very straightforward and, best of all, integrates with Dreamweaver without a hitch.

To establish a connection to a Subversion repository, follow these steps:

1. Choose Site ➪ Manage Sites.
2. When the Manage Sites dialog box is displayed, choose the site you want to work with and then click Edit.

   If you're creating a new site, choose New ➪ Site.
3. In the Site Setup dialog box, switch to the Version Control category.
4. From the Access list, choose Subversion.
5. Choose the protocol from the Protocol list (see Figure 31-19).

   Many ISPs use HTTPS for their Subversion protocol; if you are connecting to a networked server, check with your network administrator for the proper details.
6. Enter the address to the Subversion server in the Server Address field, without the protocol: for example, `idest.myversioncontrol.com` instead of `https://idest.myversioncontrol.com`.
7. Enter the path to your repository in the Repository Path field.

   Generally, the repository path is at least two levels deep, as in `/subversion/cs5`. Be sure to include a leading forward slash and omit the trailing one.
8. If your Subversion server is on a different port than usual, enter the port number in the adjacent field.
9. Enter your username in the Username field and password in the Password field.

10. When you're done, click Test. If the connection is successful, Dreamweaver presents an alert to inform you that both server and project are accessible, as shown in Figure 31-20.
11. Click Save to close the Site Setup dialog box and Done to close the Manage Sites dialog box.

FIGURE 31-19

Make the connection to your Subversion server through the Site Setup dialog box.

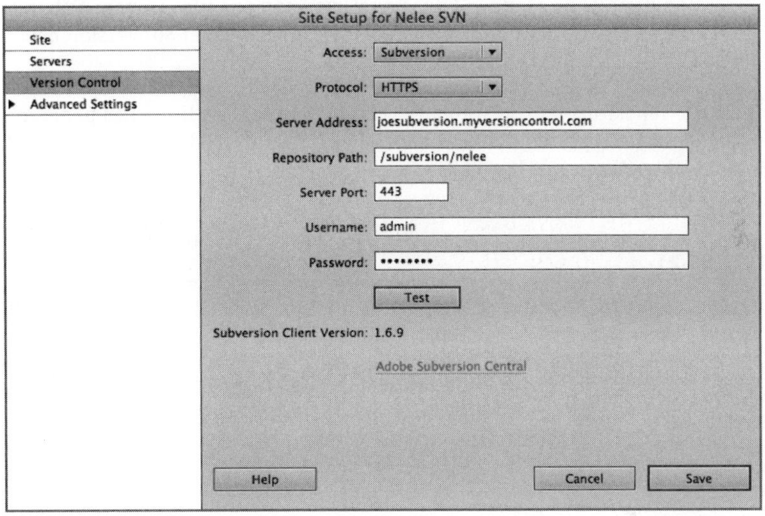

FIGURE 31-20

Your connection to the Subversion server can be tested directly.

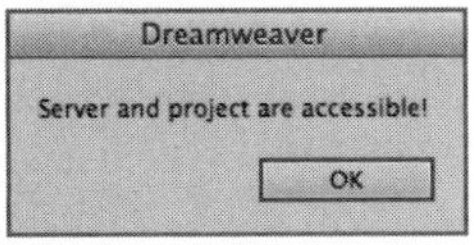

Now that your connection is made, you can begin working with files in the repository.

Managing files in the repository

Communication is the key to any team effort and, in Subversion, the repository is communication central. Checking files in and out of the repository should become second nature for any developer working on a Subversion project—it is how the overall project stays current. Dreamweaver keeps the process straightforward and all the operations easily accessible. Not only does Dreamweaver give you a live view of the repository, but you can also tell local file status—whether a file has been retrieved from the repository and remains unchanged or has been modified and is now ready for check in. Should you encounter a problem and need to revert to a previous version, you can easily do so. Moreover, if you are extensively overhauling a page and require exclusive ownership, locking—and unlocking—a file is just a click away.

Viewing local and repository files

Just as you can view your files on a remote site root in the Files panel or both local and remote files side-by-side in the extended Files panel, you can see files in your Subversion repository. Moreover, because a connection has been established, special Subversion commands are available in both the local and the repository views.

To view your repository in the standard (that is, non-expanded) Files panel, choose Repository View from the View list at the top of the panel (see Figure 31-21). Right-click (Control+click) on any file or folder to reveal the Subversion shortcut menu.

FIGURE 31-21

Switch to the Repository view of the Files panel to see files already committed to the project.

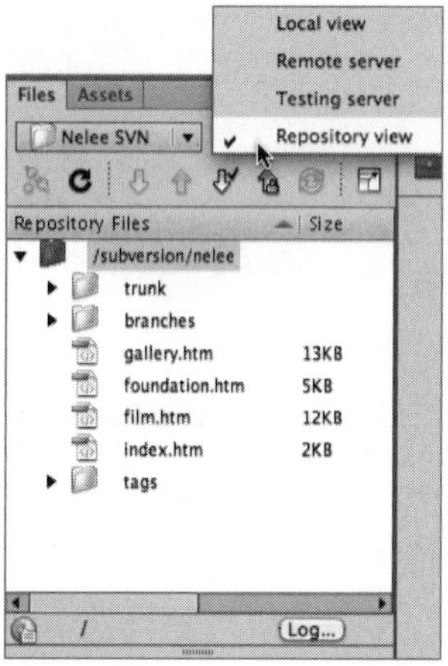

To see both local and repository files, click Expand on the Files panel. When the expanded Site panel appears, if you haven't previously chosen Repository View, click Repository Files to connect to your Subversion server and project (see Figure 31-22).

NOTE

Unlike with remote folders and testing servers, you can't drag-and-drop between the Local Files pane and the Repository Files pane in the extended Files panel. All transfers from one system to the other must be made through the context menus or the icons at the top of the Files panel.

FIGURE 31-22

Quickly check the status of files in both the Repository and the Local Files views through the extended Files panel.

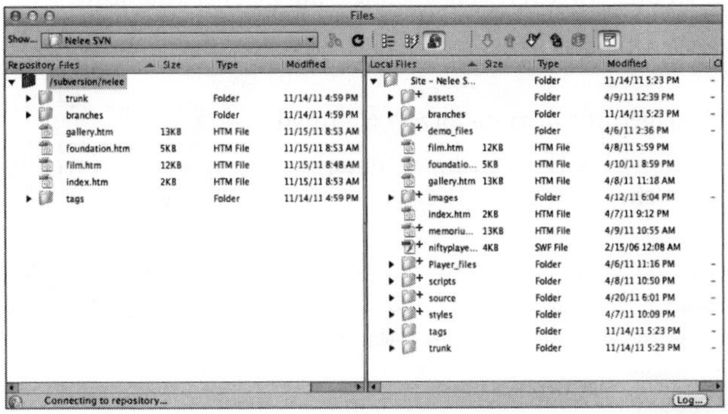

Getting the latest version

Assuming some work has already started on your Subversion project, the first thing you'll want to do is get all the current files. With Dreamweaver and Subversion, you can do this by choosing the Get Latest Version command.

To move work from the Subversion repository to your local site, follow these steps:

1. From the Files panel, click Expand.
2. In the expanded Files panel, choose Repository Files.
3. When the repository files are displayed, right-click (Control+click) on any file or folder you want to copy to your local site and choose Get Latest Version.

   The Background File Activity panel displays the progress and closes automatically when done. If you are copying a great many files, click Hide and continue working in Dreamweaver.

Dreamweaver indicates a file's status in three ways:

- Files that are retrieved from the repository and not yet modified have no identifying icons in the Files panel.
- Files that are found in the local site, but not in the repository, are noted with a plus sign.
- Files that have been modified locally, but not yet checked in to the repository, are indicated with a checkmark.

To make sure you've got the most current status of a file or folder, select it in the Files panel and choose Version Control ➪ Update Status.

Committing files

The process of posting a modified document to the Subversion repository is called *committing a file*. When a file is committed, the Subversion server compares it to the existing version in the repository and merges them. In Dreamweaver, you commit a file by checking it in.

To commit a file, follow these steps:

1. From the Files panel, select one or more locally modified files.

   You can easily identify any file that has been changed since it was retrieved from the repository by the green checkmark on the screen next to its name (see Figure 31-23).

FIGURE 31-23

Files with changes are shown with a green checkmark.

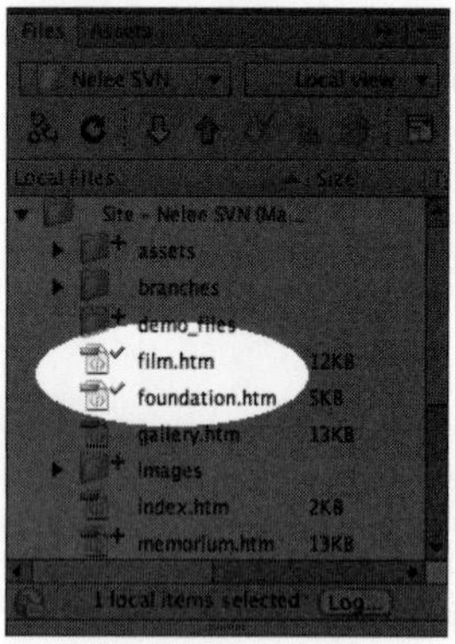

2. Click Check In.

   You can also choose Check In from the context menu or from the File Management menu button in the Document toolbar.

3. When the CheckIn dialog box (see Figure 31-24) appears, select any file you want to transfer and, if desired, enter a comment in the Commit Message field.
4. If a file you're not ready to commit appears in the list, select it and click Ignore.
5. When you're ready, click Commit.

   Dreamweaver displays the Background File Activity dialog box as the files are being transferred.

It's important to keep in mind that until you commit a file, your work has not been integrated into the project.

Getting latest versions

So far you've seen how to post your work to the Subversion project, but how do you integrate another developer's work with your local files? The Get Local Version command does exactly that. When you choose Get Local Version, the selected file does not replace your current version, but rather merges with it. Any code in the repository version that is not in your local file—which does not conflict with any changes you have made—is written into your local file.

FIGURE 31-24

You can commit or ignore individual files in the CheckIn dialog box.

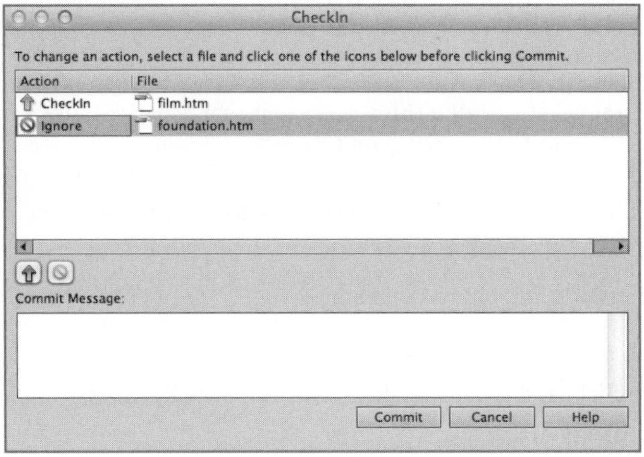

To get the latest version of a file or files, follow these steps:

1. From the Files panel, select one or more files you wish to update.
2. Right-click (Control+click) and choose Version Control ⇨ Get Latest Version.
3. The Background File Activity dialog box displays the progress of the transfer and closes when the operation is complete.

You'll notice that if the file you got the latest version of has been modified locally, the green checkmark remains after the operation. This is because the files have been merged to include your local changes, but the updated file has not yet been committed to the repository.

Locking and unlocking files

Although Subversion does a remarkable job of merging changed files from multiple sources, a developer occasionally may need to work more exclusively on a file. Unlike Visual Source Safe or Dreamweaver's own Check In/Check Out system, you cannot completely prevent another developer from working on the same file. You can, however, lock the file, which stops anyone else from committing changes to a file. Once the file is unlocked, others can commit their files as usual.

To lock a file, follow these steps:

1. From the Files panel, select one or more files you wish to lock.
2. Right-click (Control+click) and choose Version Control ⇨ Lock.
3. The Background File Activity dialog box displays the progress of the operation.

Dreamweaver displays a padlock icon next to the locked file on both the local and the repository views.

To unlock a file, choose Version Control ➪ Unlock.

Managing revisions

One of the primary purposes of Subversion is to keep track of all the changes made to a file and, if necessary, to allow for an older version to become the current one. Dreamweaver not only fulfills these functions with its Subversion implementation but also allows you to compare two versions of the same file or compare the current version to your local copy. To take advantage of the comparison features, you must install a third-party tool that compares files and inform Dreamweaver of its location through the File Compare category of Preferences.

To learn more about file comparison utilities and how to integrate them with Dreamweaver, see Chapter 4.

To work with different versions of a file, follow these steps:

1. From the Files panel, select a file to inspect.
2. Right-click (Control+click) and choose Version Control ➪ Show Revisions.
3. When the Revision History dialog box appears (see Figure 31-25), choose the desired operation:
   - To compare a version to the current local copy, select the version and click Compare To Local.
   - To compare two different versions, select them both and click Compare.
   - To display a selected version, click View.
   - To make a prior version the current one, select it and click Promote To Current.
4. When you're done, click Close.

FIGURE 31-25

Compare any version to your local version or promote it to the current version through the Revision History dialog box.

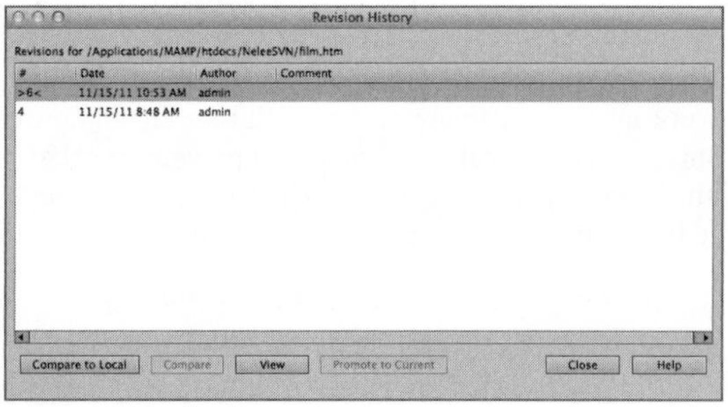

The current version of a file is listed in the Revision History with inward pointing angle brackets around the version number, like this: `>10<`.

Resolving conflicts

Although Subversion smoothly blends files from disparate sources for the most part, conflicts inevitably occur. In Subversion, one type of conflict is a direct difference between a line of code in a page checked in to the repository and the same line of code in a file that is being committed. Another type of conflict, known as a *tree conflict*, involves file management, such as renaming, moving, or deleting a file.

If Subversion detects either type of conflict, the file cannot be committed and the developer is informed of the conflict. It is up to the developer who is committing the file to make acceptable changes. Naturally, communication with the other developers is vital to making sure that the proper updates are made.

Once a conflict has been identified, the best course is the following:

1. Get the latest version of the file from the Subversion repository.
2. Make any necessary changes in the code.
3. Save your file.
4. In the Files panel, right-click (Control+click) on the files and choose Version Control ➪ Mark as Resolved.
5. Check in your file.

Summary

The expression "many hands make light work" certainly applies to website production and maintenance—but without some type of authoring management, the many hands may soon create a disaster. Dreamweaver offers both built-in and industry-standard authoring management solutions to aid in the development of websites. In addition to the precautions against overwriting files, Dreamweaver includes several other key features to help with team communication and to keep those many hands working together. For your team to get the most out of Dreamweaver, keep the following points in mind:

- For Dreamweaver's standard Check In/Check Out feature to be effective, everybody on the team must have the system engaged and in use for all file transfers.
- Metadata—information about information—about a project can be tied to any web page or web object through Dreamweaver's Design Notes feature. Again, to get the most out of this feature, it is essential that all team members use Dreamweaver's Files panel to manage their files.
- Dreamweaver includes interactive report capabilities that enable team members to quickly check the status of various HTML and workflow conditions, which can, if necessary, enable them to open a file directly for repair.
- Dreamweaver can tie into existing development projects through the WebDAV standard support.
- Subversion version-control support is built into Dreamweaver. When connection to a Subversion server is established, users can get files from the Subversion repository, make changes, and commit the files directly from within Dreamweaver.

In the next chapter, you learn about working with XML in Dreamweaver.

CHAPTER

32

Integrating XML and XSLT

IN THIS CHAPTER

- Exploring the basics of XML
- Exporting XML from templates
- Importing XML into Dreamweaver
- Building XML files
- Styling with XSL
- Incorporating XSLT fragments
- Creating client-side XSLT pages
- Dreamweaver Technique: Adding Data to an XSL Page
- Making XSLT server-side pages

XML, short for Extensible Markup Language, has quickly become a powerful force on the web and an important technology for web designers to master. XML enables designers to define the parts of any document—from web page to invoice—in terms of how those parts are used. When a document is defined by its structure, rather than its appearance, as it is with HTML, the same document can be read by a wide variety of systems and put to use far more efficiently.

Dreamweaver includes *Roundtrip XML* as a complement to its Roundtrip HTML core philosophy. Roundtrip HTML ensures that the defined tags of HTML remain just as you've written them. With XML, no fixed set of defined tags exists—XML tags can be written for an industry, a company, or just a website. Roundtrip XML permits web designers to export and import XML pages based on their own structures.

You can find XML all throughout Dreamweaver, just under the hood. The Design Notes feature is based on XML, as is the completely customizable menu system. The Third-party Tags file is pure XML and can describe any kind of tag. In fact, you can use XML to describe most anything, even HTML. This chapter explores the basics of XML, as well as the implementation of Roundtrip XML in Dreamweaver. You'll also find techniques for presenting XML data in a web page using Extensible Stylesheet Transformation (XSLT) technology; this exciting feature of Dreamweaver allows the easy display of such XML data as RSS feeds from blogs and other web services.

Understanding XML

XML is to structure what Cascading Style Sheets (CSS) are to format. Whereas Cascading Style Sheets control the look of a particular document on the web, XML makes the document's intent paramount.

Because there are almost as many ways to describe the parts of a document as there are types of documents, a set language—such as HTML—could never provide enough specification to be truly useful. With XML, you create your own custom tags to describe the page, which makes XML a truly extensible language.

XML became a W3C Recommendation in February 1998, after a relatively brief two-year study. The speed with which the recommendation was approved speaks to the need for the technology. XML has been described as a more accessible version of SGML (Standard Generalized Markup Language), the widely used text-processing standard. In fact, the XML Working Group that drafted the W3C Recommendation started out as the SGML Working Group.

What can XML do that HTML can't? Suppose you have a shipping order that you want to distribute. With HTML, each part of the document—such as the billing address, the shipping address, or the order details—is enclosed in tags that describe its appearance, like this:

```
<h2 align="center"><strong>Invoice</strong></h2>
<p align="left">Ship to:</p>
<p>J. Lowery<br>
101 101st Avenue, Ste. 101<br>
New York, NY 10000</p>
```

With XML, each section of the page is given its own set of tags, according to its meaning, as follows:

```
<documentType>Invoice</documentType>
<noTax/>
<ship-toHeader>Ship to:</ship-toHeader>
<customer>J. Lowery<br></customer>
<ship-toAddress>101 101st Avenue, Ste. 101<br>
New York, NY 10000</ship-toAddress>
```

Like HTML, XML is a combination of content and markup tags. Markup tags can be used in pairs, such as `<customer> . . . </customer>`, or they can be singular. A single tag is called an *empty tag* because no content is included. Single tags in XML must include an ending slash—as in `<noTax/>`, for example—and are used to mark where something occurs. Here, `<noTax/>` indicates that no sales tax is to be applied to this invoice.

Also, like HTML, XML tags can include attributes and values. As with HTML, XML attributes further describe the tag, much like an adjective describes a noun. For example, another way to write the `<ship-toHeader>` tag is as follows:

```
<header type="Ship To">
```

With a more generalized tag such as this one, you can easily change values, as in `<header type="Bill To">`, rather than include another new tag.

In all, XML recognizes six kinds of markup:

- **Elements:** Elements are more commonly known as tags and, as in HTML, are delimited by a set of angle brackets <>. As noted previously, elements can also have attributes set to particular values.

CAUTION
Although surrounding values with quotes is optional in HTML—as in `color=white`—quotes are mandatory in XML.

- **Entity references:** Certain characters in XML, such as the delimiting angle brackets, are reserved in order to permit markup to be recognized. These characters are represented by entities in XML. As in HTML, character entities begin with an ampersand and end with a semicolon. For example, `<Content>` is XML code to represent `<Content>`.
- **Comments:** XML comments are identical to HTML comments; they both begin with `<!--` and end with `-->`.
- **Processing instructions:** XML processing instructions are similar to server-side includes in that the XML processor (like the server) passes them on to the application (like the browser).
- **Marked sections:** XML can pass blocks of code or other data without parsing the markup and content. These blocks of character data are marked with `<![CDATA[` at the beginning and `]]>` at the end:

```
<![CDATA[If age < 19 and age > 6, then the kids are in ;
school]]>
```

  Communication between XML and HTML is greatly eased because large blocks of data can be passed in this fashion.
- **Document type declarations:** Because every XML document is capable of containing its own set of custom tags, a method for defining these tags must exist. Although a discussion of the formats of such document type declarations is beyond the scope of this book, it's helpful to know that such declarations can be made for elements, attributes, character entities, and notations. Notations refer to external binary data, such as GIFs, that are passed through the XML parser to the application.

XML documents may begin with an XML declaration that specifies the version of XML being used. The XML declaration for a document compliant with the 1.0 specification looks like this:

```
<?xml version="1.0" encoding="utf-8"?>
```

A much more detailed document type declaration (DTD), in which each tag and attribute is described in SGML, is also possible. XML documents that include these types of DTDs are labeled *valid XML* documents. Other documents that respect the rules of XML regarding nesting of tags and other matters, but don't include DTDs for the elements, are known as *well-formed XML*. Dreamweaver exports well-formed XML documents but can import either well-formed or valid XML.

Exporting XML

How do you make an XML page? You can choose File ➪ New and select XML from the Blank Page ➪ Page Type category, or you can convert an existing template-based document into XML format with one command. Currently, Dreamweaver creates its XML pages based on a template's editable regions. With this approach, the true content of a page—what distinguishes it from all other pages of the same type—can be separated and applied independently of the original web page. In other words, after the XML information is gathered from a web page, it can be imported into any other application to be displayed, read, spoken, translated, or acted upon.

To get a better idea of how to use XML, you need to understand Dreamweaver templates, which are discussed in Chapter 28.

Dreamweaver templates are composed of locked and editable regions. The locked regions are repeated for each page created from the template, whereas the content in the editable regions is added per page. The connection between XML and templates is similar to the relationship between a database form and its data. In a database, each field has a unique name, such as LastName, FirstName, and so on. When you create a database form to present the data, the placeholders for the data use the same field names. Then, when data from one record flows into the form, the information from the field goes into the areas with the corresponding field names. Likewise, each editable region has a unique name—in essence, a field name. The content within the editable region is the field's data. When the template data is exported as an XML file, the name of the editable region is converted to an XML tag that surrounds its data.

For example, Figure 32-1 shows a Dreamweaver template for a purchase order. On the left are the headings (To, Company, Address, and so on) for the information in a locked area, whereas the specific shipping data (on the right) resides in a series of editable regions, each with its own name.

When exported as XML by Dreamweaver, the resulting XML file looks like the following:

```
<?xml version="1.0" encoding="utf-8"?>
<po template="/Templates/po.dwt" codeOutsideHTMLIsLocked="false">
   <ShipDate><![CDATA[10 Oct 2002]]></ShipDate>
   <doctitle><![CDATA[
<title>Purchase Order</title>
]]></doctitle>
   <head></head>
   <Address><![CDATA[1234 AnyStreet<br>
        Anytown, USA]]></Address>
   <ShipVia><![CDATA[UPS]]></ShipVia>
   <Company><![CDATA[John's Does]]></Company>
   <To><![CDATA[John Doe]]></To>
</po>
```

Note several important items about the XML file. First, notice the use of self-evident labels for each of the tags, such as `<Company>` and `<ShipVia>`; such names make it easy to understand an XML file. Even the one tag not based on a user-defined name, `<doctitle>`, is straightforward. Second, all the data included in the XML tags is marked as a `CDATA` area; this ensures that the information is conveyed intact, just as it was entered. Finally, if you look at the `<Address>` tag data, you see that even HTML tags (here, a `<br>` tag) are included in the `CDATA` blocks. This practice enables you to carry over basic formatting from one page to the next. You can avoid this by designating just the inner content—without any of the formatting tags—as an editable region.

Dreamweaver can create one of two different types of XML tags during its export operation. The first is referred to as *Dreamweaver Standard XML* and uses an `<item>` tag with a name attribute set to the editable region's name. For example, if the editable region is named `ShipVia`, the Dreamweaver Standard tag is

```
<item name="ShipVia">Content</item>
```

FIGURE 32-1

Dreamweaver creates XML pages based on templates and editable regions. This template is now ready to be exported as an XML file.

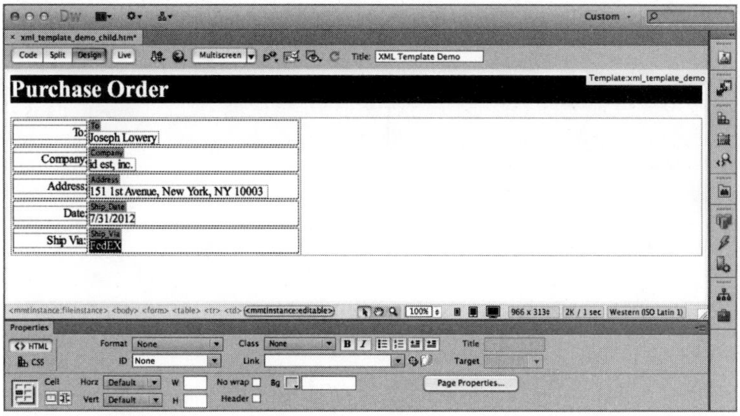

The Dreamweaver Standard XML file has one other distinguishing characteristic. The XML file is saved with a reference to the defining Dreamweaver template, like this:

```
<templateItems template="/Templates/PO.dwt">
```

When you are importing a Dreamweaver Standard XML file, if the specified template cannot be found, a dialog box appears asking that you select another template.

The other option is to use what Dreamweaver refers to as *Editable Region Name* tags. This method uses the editable region names themselves as tags. In the case of the editable region name `ShipVia`, the tag pair under this method is `<ShipVia> ... </ShipVia>`.

To create an XML file from within Dreamweaver, follow these steps:

1. Open a Dreamweaver document based on a template that has at least one editable region.
2. Choose File ➪ Export ➪ Export Template Data As XML. The Export Template Data As XML dialog box opens, as shown in Figure 32-2.
3. Choose the format for the XML tags by selecting one of the Notation options:
   - **Use Standard Dreamweaver XML Tags:** Select this option to produce `<item>` tags with `name` attributes set to the names of the editable regions.
   - **Use Editable Region Names As XML Tags:** Select this option to produce XML tags that use the editable region names directly.

   Selecting either option displays sample tags in the Sample area of the dialog box.
4. Click OK when you're finished. An Export Template Data As XML Save File dialog box appears.
5. Enter the path and name of the XML file you want to save in the File Name text box. Click Save when you're finished.

FIGURE 32-2

You can convert the editable content of any template-based page to an XML document by using the Export Template Data As XML dialog box.

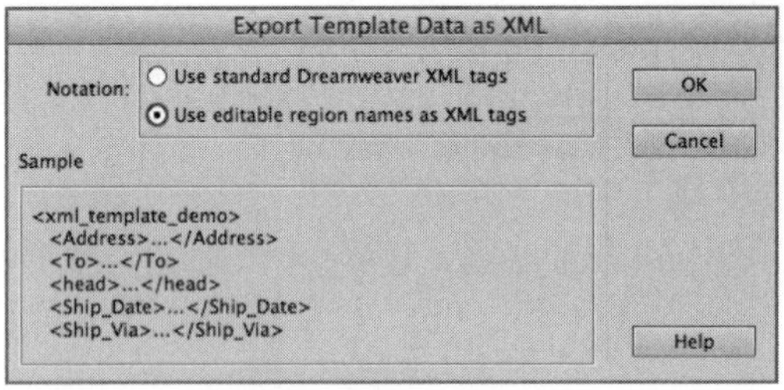

Importing XML

As part of Roundtrip XML, Dreamweaver includes an Import XML command. Like the Export XML command, Import XML works with Dreamweaver templates. The content information in the XML document fills out the editable regions in the template, much as data fills out a form in a database.

With this import capability, you can independently create and store content in an XML file and then, if you want to publish the page to the web, simply import it into the Dreamweaver template.

To be imported, XML files must follow one of the two structures used when exporting a template to XML: Standard Dreamweaver XML or Editable Region Names used as XML tags. Although it's a matter of personal preference, I find the Editable Region Names format to be easier to read and, in general, simpler to work with.

NOTE

When you're importing XML files, make sure that the XML files that you're importing have the necessary template declarations in order for Dreamweaver to find the appropriate template to format the incoming data.

How do you create a file from the XML? Naturally, you could open a template for your XML document and fill in the data by hand—but that, in a sense, defeats the purpose of automating your workflow via XML. A more efficient scenario is to use a database to accept and store content; the database entry form is easily accessible over a network or over the Internet. A report, generated by the database application, blends the content data and the XML structure, resulting in an XML file to be imported into Dreamweaver.

To import an XML file into a Dreamweaver template, follow these steps:

1. If desired, open a file based on a Dreamweaver template; otherwise, create a new blank page (you must have at least one file open before the next step).

2. Choose File ➪ Import ➪ XML into Template. The Import XML dialog box opens.

CAUTION

Any existing information in the Dreamweaver document in the editable regions is replaced by the information in the corresponding tags of the XML document.

3. Select an XML file from the Import XML dialog box.
4. Select Open when you're finished.

The XML file is imported into Dreamweaver, and the editable region placeholder names are replaced with the data in the XML document.

Styling with XSL

Whereas HTML code has some degree of built-in styling—browsers render content enclosed with `<p>` tags much differently from what's within an `<img>` tag—XML has none: It's all just data. The Extensible Stylesheet Language (XSL) specification developed by the W3C is intended to give designers the power to shape XML data. In fact, XSL has the potential to go beyond styling to actual transformation; functions within XSL can, for example, sort the XML data it is passed.

Dreamweaver embraces XSL in a major way. Dreamweaver has the power to create XSL documents to fit a variety of situations, including both server-side and client-side options. This facility opens a whole new world of possibilities for Dreamweaver users. For example, designers can include information from RSS (Really Simple Syndication) feeds right in their web pages—styled to fit into the look and feel of their site—through a very straightforward process. For intranet developers, XML reports, like those generated by Dreamweaver's own Reports system, can be presented in a suitable fashion.

XSL is actually a family of W3C specifications. In addition to the XSL standard, a separate specification covers *XSLT*, short for XSL Transformations. Many of the Dreamweaver XSL features involve XSLT functions that convert XML to HTML and CSS. Another key component under the XSL umbrella is the XML Path Language, or XPath. XPath is an expression language that allows the XML data to be selectively presented; XPath powers Dreamweaver features like the XSL Repeat Region.

Dreamweaver creates two different types of XSL content: a full XSLT page that displays HTML and transformed XML data together, and an XSLT fragment that contains only the transformed XML data. An XSLT fragment is embedded in a standard web page much like a server-side include; a feed from the Yahoo! Weather RSS service (`http://weather.yahooapis.com/forecastrss?w=2459115&u=f`), which will give you New York weather in Fahrenheit embedded in the home page of a ski resort, is a good example of how an XSLT fragment would be used. XSLT fragments are used far more frequently on the web in general, whereas XSLT pages are more often seen in intranet applications.

Including XSLT fragments

The comparison of an XSLT fragment to a server-side include (SSI) is a good one, for a number of reasons:

- Neither type of file can be viewed independently on the web because they both lack necessary HTML tags, including <html>, <head>, and <body>.
- Both require an application server for display in a browser. Dreamweaver supports ASP, ColdFusion, and PHP server models for XSLT fragments.
- You can edit either an XSLT fragment or SSI in Dreamweaver with equal ease.
- Each XSLT fragment and SSI appears to be a single entity when selected in the embedded page at design time.

Unlike SSIs, XSLT fragments have a page type all their own and can be created directly from the New Document dialog box. To create an XSLT fragment, follow these steps:

1. Choose File ➪ New.
2. From the New Document dialog box's first category, select the Blank Page category and the XSLT (Fragment) entry, and then click Create. Dreamweaver asks which data source you'd like to use for your new XSLT fragment, as shown in Figure 32-3.

FIGURE 32-3

Read the latest for any RSS feed by using the remote XML data option.

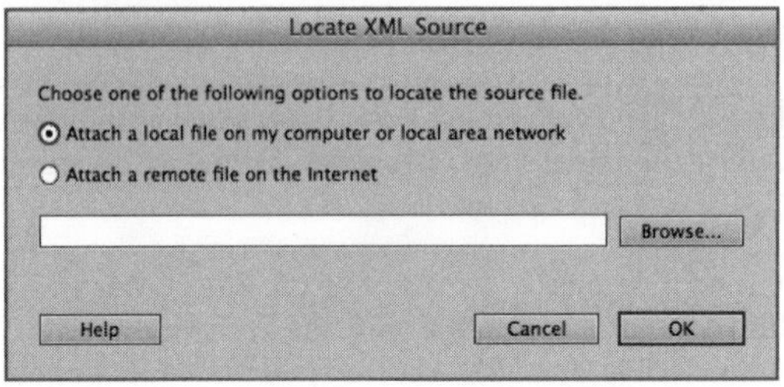

3. In the Locate XML Source dialog box, select the Attach A Local File On My Computer Or Local Area Network option if you want to incorporate data from a static XML file available on your system; use the Browse button to open the Select File dialog box or enter the path to the file by hand in the provided field.
4. If you're displaying XML data from a file on the web, choose the Attach A Remote File On The Internet option and enter the full Internet address in the available field.
5. Click OK when you're done.
6. Save the newly created document with an `.xsl` filename extension—that is, `rssfeed.xsl`.

Binding XSL data to the page

Once the fragment page is created, you're ready to create the HTML structure to hold and bind the data. You can use any standard HTML objects, such as tables and <p> or <br/> tags, to hold your data. The data itself is displayed in the Bindings panel, as shown in Figure 32-4.

FIGURE 32-4

Once your file is connected to an external XML source like an RSS feed, the Bindings panel displays the available data structure.

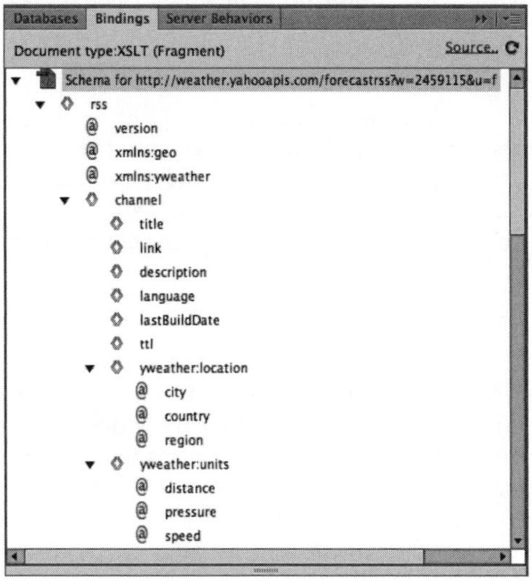

Dreamweaver provides the following visual indicators when displaying XML data:

	Child elements that occur once within a parent are identified with a double-angle bracket.
	Child elements that occur one or more times are identified with a double-angle bracket followed by a plus sign.
	Optional child elements are identified with a double-angle bracket followed by a question mark.
	Attributes of a parent are identified with an at (@) sign.

Bind data to a page by dragging an element from the Bindings panel and dropping it in the desired place or by positioning your cursor on the page and double-clicking the selected data element in the Bindings panel.

TIP

In addition to displaying XML data as text, you can also use it in a link. Select the text, data, or image you want to use as a link and then, from the Property inspector's Link field, click the Browse For File icon. When the Select File dialog box opens, select Data Sources; the XML data tree appears just like in the Bindings panel. Choose the data field you want to use as the `href` value, typically labeled `link` or `rss:link`, and then click OK twice to close the open dialog boxes. The XML data appears in the Link field wrapped in braces, like this: `{rss:link}`.

The basic code inserted by Dreamweaver for XSL data looks like this:

```
<xsl:value-of select="rdf:RDF/rss:channel/rss:title"/>
```

where the value of the select attribute is the XPath description of where the data is located in the XML file. Forward slashes represent parent nodes, much like folders in a URL.

Repeating XSL data

A common use of XSLT fragments is to incorporate results from an RSS feed onto the page. Generally, you would include a few heading elements, such as the main feed title and author, followed by a series of titles, short descriptions, and links, each concerning a particular item in the RSS feed. The layout for such a fragment often involves a table to contain the repeating data, as shown in Figure 32-5.

To display repeated data, an XSLT Repeat Region object is used. Similar to a Repeat Region server behavior, the XSLT Repeat Region object wraps the necessary code around a selection, typically one or more rows of a table. Just as you would identify which recordset to use with a Repeat Region server behavior, the XSLT Repeat Region object requires that you identify which element in the XML schema repeats. You'll remember that Dreamweaver identifies such items in the Bindings panel with a double-angle bracket and plus sign combination.

FIGURE 32-5

Use basic HTML tools such as headings, paragraph tags, and links to structure the data in an XSLT fragment.

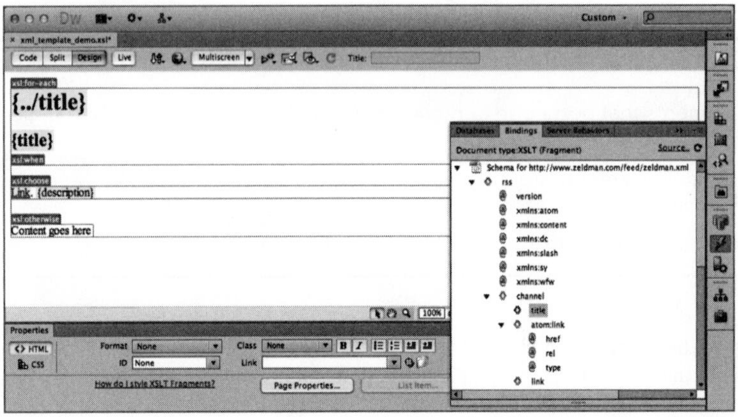

The XSL code for repeating elements is <xsl:for-each> and, when applied to a table row, looks like this example:

```
<xsl:for-each select="rdf:RDF/rss:item">
  <tr>
    <td>...</td>
```

```
    </tr>
  </xsl:for-each>
```

The `select` attribute in the `<xsl:for-each>` tag refers to the repeating element in the XML data. Dreamweaver inserts this code after you've identified the repeating item in the XPath Expression Builder (Repeat Region) dialog box.

To set an XSLT fragment area to repeat in Dreamweaver, follow these steps:

1. Select the HTML and XSL data you want to repeat. It's best to select the containing tag pair around the XSL data, such as `<tr>` or `<p>`.
2. From the Insert panel's XSLT category, choose Repeat Region.

   Alternatively, you can select Insert ⇨ XSLT Objects ⇨ Repeat Region; either approach opens the XPath Expression Builder (Repeat Region) dialog box.
3. In the XPath Expression Builder (Repeat Region) dialog box, select the element you want to repeat (see Figure 32-6).

   Repeatable elements are identified with the double-angle brackets and plus sign, +. Be sure to choose the parent repeating element of any item you want to display.
4. Click OK when you're done.

In Design view with Invisible Elements enabled, Dreamweaver displays a border around the repeated area with the label `xsl:for-each`.

FIGURE 32-6

Choose the parent repeating element with the plus sign (disclosure triangle on the Macintosh).

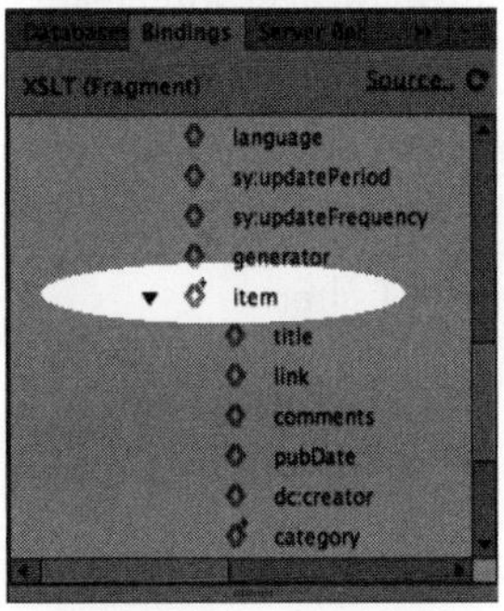

Filtering XSL data

While the XPath Expression Builder (Repeat Region) dialog box makes setting up a repeat region a simple point-and-click operation, it also permits you to establish filters for the data. You could, for example, use this feature to limit the items from the Adobe XML News Aggregator (`http://feeds.adobe.com/`) to those concerned with Dreamweaver. Filters can be applied at the same time as the XSLT Repeat Region or afterward.

To apply a filter to an existing XSLT Repeat Region, follow these steps:

1. Select any of the XML data within the repeat region.
2. From the Tag Selector, choose `<xsl:for-each>`.
3. In the Property inspector, click the lightning bolt next to the Select field.
4. When the XPath Expression Builder (Repeat Region) dialog box reopens, select Build Filter. The dialog box expands to display the filter controls.
5. Click Add (+) to start a new filter criteria. The initial filter criteria is set up to use the previously selected repeating data element in the Filter By column; your focus will be on choosing values for the Where, Operator, and Value columns.
6. Select the data element you want to filter by from the Where list. For example, if you wanted to filter by the subject field of the Adobe XML News Aggregator feed, you'd choose `dc:subject`.
7. Choose the operation you want to use in your filter from the Operator list. For string comparisons, you would select the equal sign (=) or `!=`. Other operators include <, <=, >, >=, and <>.
8. Enter the desired filter keyword or other value in the Value column (see Figure 32-7).

   If you're using a text value in your filter criteria, surround the word or phrase with single quotation marks. Dreamweaver automatically converts these to their character entity equivalents—`'`—so that the code will validate properly.
9. To add additional conditions, select either `and` or `or` from the And/Or column and repeat Steps 5–8.
10. Click OK when you're done.

Test your XSLT fragment by previewing it in the browser, and Dreamweaver will create the necessary code to display the page.

FIGURE 32-7

You can display just what you want from an RSS feed with an XSLT filter.

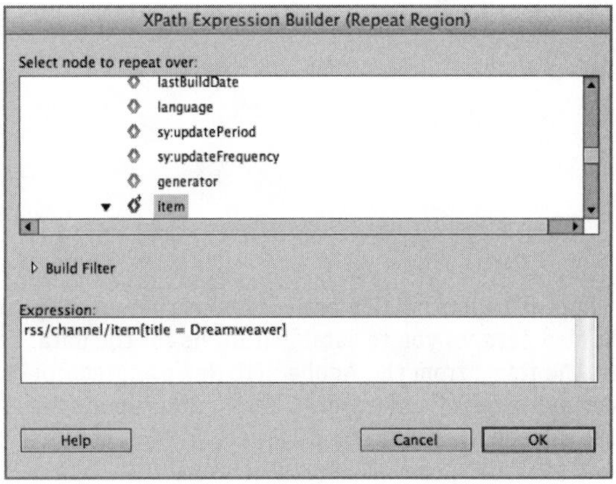

Showing XSL data conditionally

Other tools for shaping your XML data through XSL are the conditional XSLT objects in Dreamweaver. Both the XSLT Conditional Region and Multiple Conditional Region objects are used to display XML data or even standard HTML if your custom conditions are met. Unlike the filtering mechanism of the XSLT Repeat Region object, the conditional objects work with data that has already been made available to the page. You could, for example, display the optional `description` element from an RSS feed along with the Description label, but only if the `description` value exists.

The XSLT Conditional Region, when applied by itself, tests for a single condition and renders the enclosed content if the condition is met, very much like an If-Then clause in programming. In fact, the code uses the <xsl:if> tag. For example, if you wanted to display text indicating the final item from an RSS feed, you'd use code like this:


```
<xsl:if test="position()=last()">
  <p>Last item:</p>
</xsl:if>
```

The `test` attribute checks to see if the `position()` function—which refers to the current item—is the same as the one the `last()` function returns and, if so, displays the text. To apply the XSLT Conditional Region object, follow these steps:

1. Select the text, image, page object, or code you want to make conditional in either Design or Code view.
2. From the Insert panel's XSLT category, choose Conditional Region.
3. When the Conditional Region dialog box opens, enter the condition to evaluate in the Test field (see Figure 32-8).
4. Click OK.

FIGURE 32-8

Display or hide anything in an XSL fragment through the XSLT Conditional Region object.

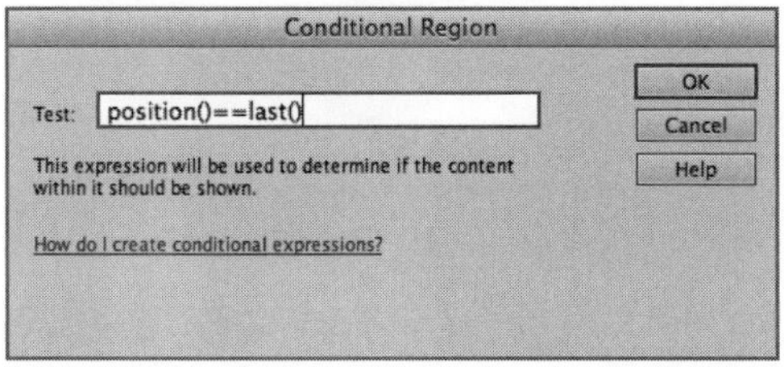

Although the XSLT Conditional Region object displays or doesn't display some code based on a single condition, the Multiple Conditional Region is much more flexible. Although the Multiple Conditional Region object initially tests a single condition, it provides alternative output leading to an either/or code output. For example, say you want to test for the final item and note it as such when it appears, but you also want to display other text—that is, `Next item:`—until it appears. In this situation, your XSL code would look like this:

```
<xsl:choose>
  <xsl:when test="position()=last()">
    <p>Last item:</p>
  </xsl:when>
  <xsl:otherwise>
    <p>Next item:</p>
  </xsl:otherwise>
</xsl:choose>
```

You can add additional condition testing by including more `<xsl:when>` tags prior to the `<xsl:otherwise>` tag. In Dreamweaver, this is accomplished by applying the XSLT Conditional Region object prior to the `<xsl:otherwise>` tag. By using the two conditional objects in conjunction with one another, you can test for as many conditions as you'd like and retain a default result.

To create multiple XSLT conditional regions, follow these steps:

1. Select the text, image, page object, or code you want to render if the first condition is true.
2. From the Insert panel's XSLT category, choose Multiple Conditional Region.
3. When the Multiple Conditional Region dialog box opens, enter the condition to evaluate in the Test field; click OK when you're done.

   Dreamweaver displays three different tabs: The `<xsl:choose>` area surrounds the `<xsl:when>`—which holds your previously selected content—and the `<xsl:otherwise>` area, which displays the placeholder text *`Content goes here`*, as shown in Figure 32-9.

FIGURE 32-9

Dreamweaver displays the content for both outcomes in a Multiple Conditional Region.

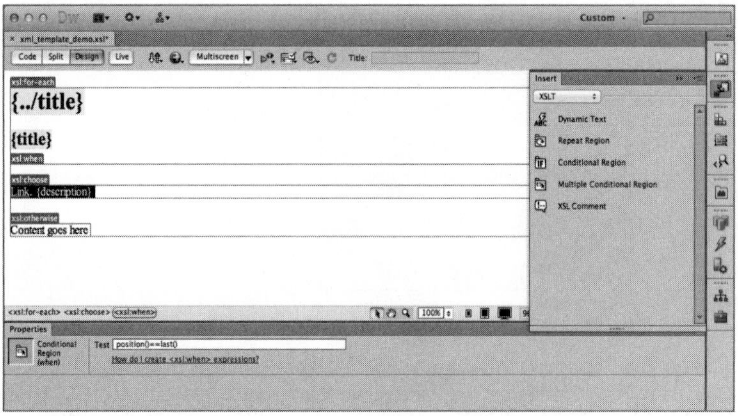

   If you just want to insert a single condition with a default result, you can stop here.

4. To add additional conditions and results, place your cursor in the placeholder content in the `<xsl:otherwise>` area and choose the `<xsl:otherwise>` tag in the Tag Selector.

5. Press the left-arrow key to move the cursor in front of the `<xsl:otherwise>` tag.
6. From the Insert panel's XSLT category, choose Conditional Region.
7. When the Conditional Region dialog box opens, enter the next condition you want to evaluate in the Test field; click OK when you're ready. Dreamweaver adds an `<xsl:when>` tag with placeholder content.
8. Repeat Steps 4–7 to add more conditional regions.

After you've created all the conditions desired, replace the placeholder text with the actual page elements or code you want rendered if the condition is true.

Styling XSLT fragments

Although you can use CSS to style your XSLT fragments, you shouldn't link to an external style sheet or embed styles within the fragment page. If you do, the CSS links and embedded styles will appear in the body of your document, along with the XSLT fragment. What's the solution? Design-time style sheets.

To refresh your memory on how to implement a design-time style sheet, visit Chapter 6.

Typically, the page intended as the receptacle for the XSLT fragment is built prior to the fragment itself, along with the CSS style sheet. To view your XSLT fragment with the desired styles, attach the same style used by the host page as a design-time style sheet. Once the design-time style sheet is in place, you can assign CSS styles to the XML data and surrounding structures, as shown in Figure 32-10.

FIGURE 32-10

Style XSLT fragments through Dreamweaver's design-time style sheet feature.

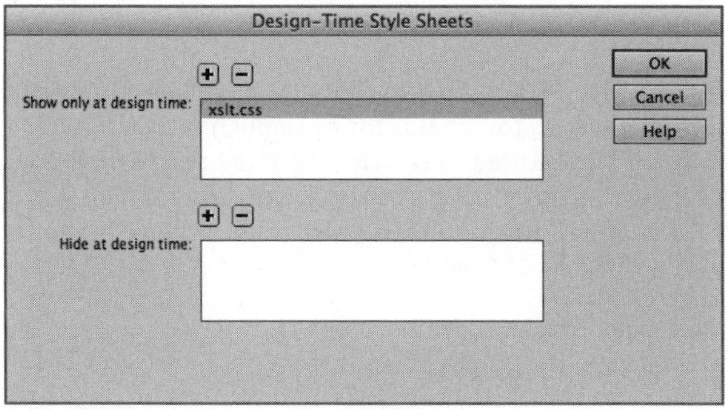

Adding XSLT fragments to web pages

Once your XSLT fragment has been completed, it's very straightforward to include it in your server model page. The actual code insertion is handled by a server behavior, XSL Transformation. To include an XSLT fragment, follow these steps:

1. Place your cursor where you'd like the XSLT fragment to appear.

2. From the Server Behaviors panel, click Add (+) and select XSL Transformation from the list.
3. In the XSL Transformation dialog box, click Browse next to the XSLT File field.
4. When the Select File dialog box appears, locate the `.xsl` file that contains your fragment and click OK. Dreamweaver automatically populates the XML URI field with the address of the XML data, as shown in Figure 32-11.
5. If you need to add any parameters to affect the XSLT fragment, click Add (+) in the XSLT Parameters area and enter the name and value of the parameter.
6. Click OK when you're done.

FIGURE 32-11

The XSLT Transformation server behavior is used to select the XSLT fragment for inserting.

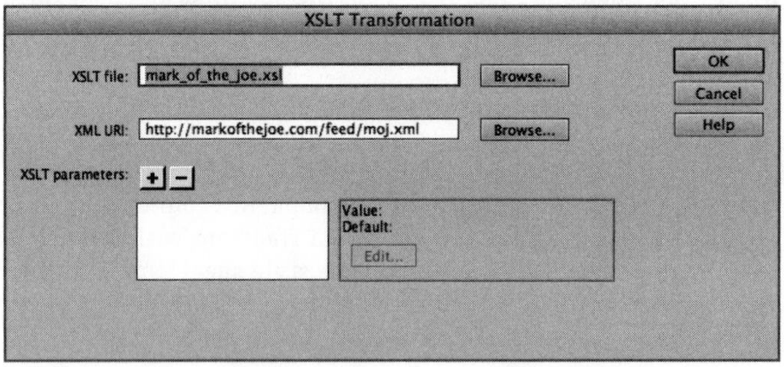

Dreamweaver displays the XSLT fragment in the page; when selected, it appears as a solid, uneditable block. Unlike with server-side includes, a custom Property inspector is not available for inserted XSLT fragments. You can preview the page in the browser to see the data within the document.

The XSLT Parameters option found in the XSL Transformation dialog boxes allows you to set up parameters to pass to the XSLT fragment. You could, for example, create an XSLT parameter named `ItemLimit` with a value of 5 if you wanted to restrict the number of XML items shown to five or fewer. To ensure that the XSLT fragment works properly with this parameter, you'd need to set a filter criteria, as described in the "Filtering XSL Data" section, where the `position()` function is less than or equal to the variable `$ItemLimit`.

Building full XSLT pages

As noted earlier, Dreamweaver gives you the option to create either an XSLT fragment or an XSLT page. Although XSLT fragments are more typically used, the full XSLT page has advantages, including the capability to transform XML data on the client-side without an application server such as ASP, ColdFusion, or PHP.

Much of the information covered in the previous XSL fragment discussion applies to full XSLT pages. XML data appears in the Bindings panel and is bound to the page in the same manner. All the objects in the Insert panel's XSLT category—including the Repeat Region and Conditional Region objects—can and should be used when crafting the XML data in an XSLT page.

Client-side pages

Dreamweaver's client-side XSL feature set is quite remarkable. With it, you can post XML data to be transformed by an XSLT page and viewed in a modern browser, without the use of server-side code. There are, however, a number of limitations:

- Only full XSLT pages, and not XSLT fragments, can be used.
- The XML file must be stored locally; you can't link to a remote XML feed.
- Both the XML and the XSLT page must be published to the same folder on the web server.
- Only a limited number of browsers can be used to view the completed page.

It's important to understand how XSLT pages interact with XML files to present the completed HTML page for the browser. Although XSL stands for Extensible Stylesheet Language, it's not an exact parallel to Cascading Style Sheets. The primary difference is that an XSLT page contains HTML and XSLT code, unlike an external CSS file, which does not incorporate any HTML. Another key point is that both the XML and the XSL files refer to one another, whereas with HTML and CSS, the only connection is the link or import code in the HTML page. The final concept to grasp is that you're actually displaying the XML file, although it is transformed by the XSLT page. All links from other pages to show the data must be to the XML file.

Here's a general overview of the workflow for applying an XSLT page to an XML file:

1. Create an XSLT page.
2. Attach the XML data to the XSLT page.
3. Bind the XML data to the XSLT page.
4. From the XML page, link to the XSLT page.
5. Publish both files to the web.
6. View the XML page.

Creating XSLT pages

Dreamweaver provides two paths to approach the initial step, creating an XSLT page. You can build a page from scratch by choosing File ➪ New Document and then selecting the Basic page category and choosing XSLT (Entire page). Or, if you have an existing HTML page you want to use to incorporate XML data, you can convert your HTML page into XSLT format.

To convert an HTML page to an XSLT page, follow these steps:

1. Open the page you want to convert in Dreamweaver.
2. Choose File ➪ Convert ➪ XSLT 1.0.

Dreamweaver automatically saves the converted file under its original name with a new `.xsl` extension. For example, `rss_feed.html` becomes `rss_feed.xsl`.

CAUTION

Neither templates nor template-derived pages can be converted to an XSLT document. You'll need to detach the template-derived page from the template before converting.

Attaching XML data to an XSLT page

Attaching XML data to an XSLT page is just as straightforward as converting the page:

1. From the Bindings panel, click the XML link in the displayed step: Please Attach XML Source Document (see Figure 32-12).
2. When the Locate XML Source dialog box opens, make sure that the Attach A Local File On My Computer Or Local Area Network option is selected.
3. Click Browse to open the Select File dialog box and locate the XML file; click OK when you've found it.
4. Click OK in the Locate XML Source dialog box to confirm your choice.

Dreamweaver parses the XML file and displays the structure in the Bindings panel.

FIGURE 32-12

Attach an XML file to an XSLT page through the Bindings panel.

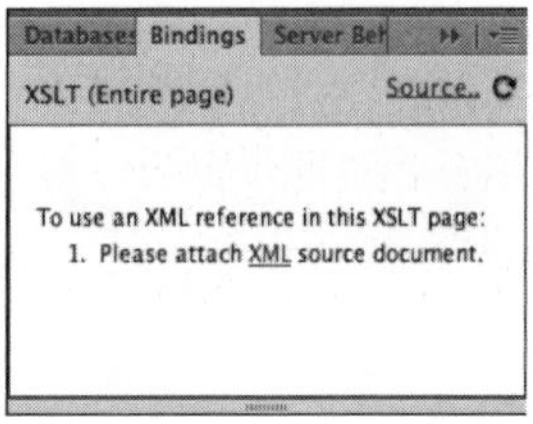

Binding the XML data

Binding the data in an XSLT page is handled in exactly the same way as with an XSLT fragment. Data is dragged from the Bindings panel onto the page or double-clicked to be inserted at the cursor position. Likewise, repeat and conditional regions are applied in the same manner as described in the previous sections, "Repeating XSL Data," "Filtering XSL Data," and "Showing XSL Data Conditionally."

Unlike with XSLT fragments, it's not necessary to use design-time style sheets because the XSL page contains the HTML, as well as the link to the CSS external style sheets. Style can be applied to XML data just like any other page element.

Linking from an XML file

All of the work so far has been centered on the XSLT page. Now it's time to shift focus to the XML document. The first action is to link the XSLT page from the XML file. Recall that the browser actually loads the XML file, which in turn calls the XSLT page to transform the data into HTML.

TIP

Client-side XSL transformations work with local XML files only. To use the data from an RSS feed, you'll need to save the data page from your browser and publish it to your own web server.

To link an XSLT style sheet to an XML page, follow these steps:

1. Open the XML file attached in the XSLT document.
2. Choose Commands ➪ Attach an XSLT Stylesheet.
3. When the Attach an XSLT Stylesheet dialog box opens (see Figure 32-13), click Browse to locate the XSLT file you've been working with.

FIGURE 32-13

Link your XML file to the appropriate XSLT style sheet.

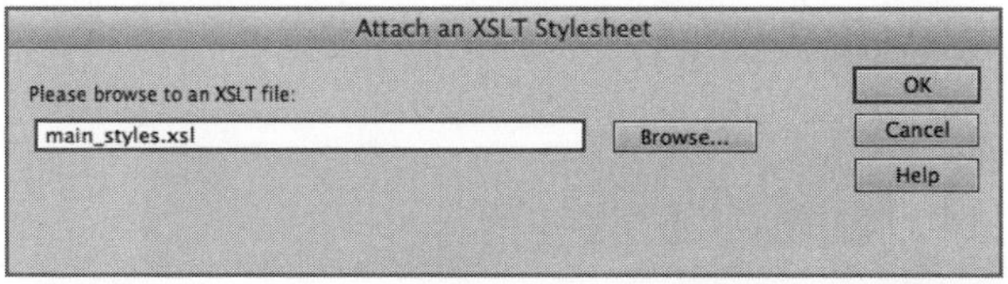

CAUTION

Remember that both the XML and the XSLT files must be in the same folder. If the XSLT file is in a separate folder, all the dependent files (including images, CSS, and includes) will not be found.

Publishing and viewing XML and XSLT files

XML files can be published to the server like any other document in Dreamweaver. Best of all, Dreamweaver is smart enough to automatically publish your XSLT files—and any files referenced in that document—if you opt to put dependent files.

It's vital to remember that you must view the XML file in your browser and not the XSLT document. Given that the XSLT page has all the visual elements, this approach might feel a bit unnatural, but it's the way it works.

Only modern browsers are capable of viewing an XML file and processing the XSLT correctly on the client-side. Among capable browsers are:

- Internet Explorer 6 and higher
- Firefox 3 and higher
- Opera 9 and higher
- Safari 3 and higher
- Chrome 1.0 and higher

Dreamweaver TECHNIQUE

Adding Data to an XSL Page

In this Technique, you convert an existing HTML page to XSLT format and then integrate data from an XML file into it.

1. From the Techniques site, expand the 32_XML folder and open the `xml_start.htm` file.
2. Choose File ➪ Convert ➪ XSLT 1.0.

   Dreamweaver converts the file and saves it as `xml_start.xsl`.
3. From the Bindings panel, select the Source link.
4. When the Locate XML Source dialog box appears, click Browse.
5. In the Locate Source XML for XSL Template dialog box, locate the `properties.xml` file in the 32_XML folder and click OK; click OK again to confirm your choice in the Locate Source XML dialog box.

   The Bindings panel is populated with the XML data schema.

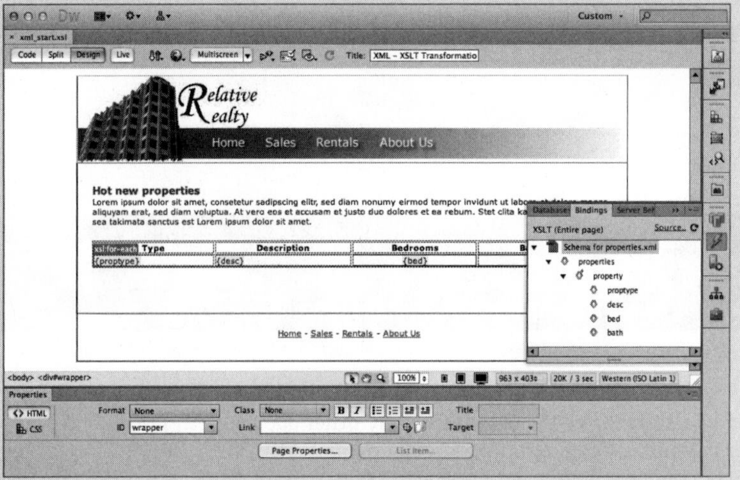

6. From the Bindings panel, drag proptype to the cell under the Type label, desc under Description, bed under Bedrooms, and bath under Bathrooms.

   The next step is to apply a repeat region so that all the XML data will be displayed.
7. Select the proptype XML data placed on the page.
8. From the Tag Selector, choose the `<tr>` tag.
9. Choose Insert ➪ XSLT Objects ➪ Repeat Region.
10. When the XPath Expression Builder (Repeat Region) dialog box opens, choose Property and click OK.
11. Save your page.

    The final step is to make the connection from the XML file to the XSLT page.

12. From the Files panel, open the `properties.xml` file in the 32_XML folder.
13. Choose Commands ➪ Attach an XSLT Stylesheet.
14. When the dialog box opens, click Browse and locate `xml_start.xsl`; click OK when you're ready.
15. Save your XML page.

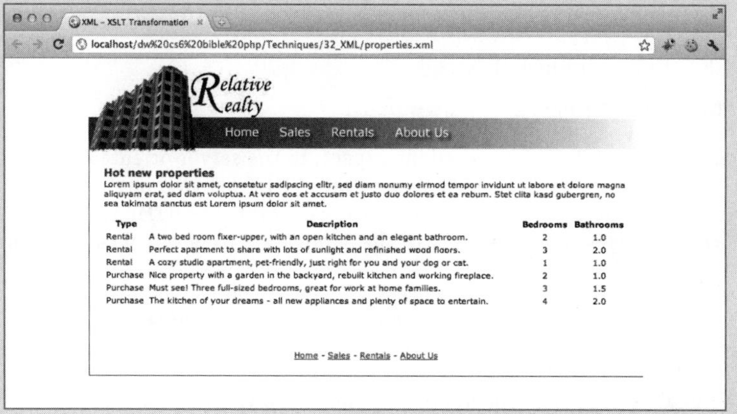

Preview the page in your primary browser by pressing F12 (Option+F12). If you're using a recent browser version, you'll see the XML data embedded in the page.

Server-side pages

Although most designers and developers working with application servers will prefer to work with XSLT fragments, they do have the option to use full XSLT pages. One advantage to taking the full-page approach is that it allows for complete separation between the server-side code and the presentation code; organizations that deploy strictly divided web teams may find this useful.

Server-side XSL transformations suffer almost none of the drawbacks seen with client-side transformation:

- Both full XSLT pages and XSLT fragments can be used.
- The XML file can be stored locally or remotely.
- Because the transformation occurs on the server-side, any browser can be used to view the transformed page.

The only similar restriction for both client-side and server-side transformations is that if a local XML file is used for the data, both must be contained in the same folder.

In Dreamweaver, server-side XSL transformations have been developed for most of the supported server models: ASP, ASP.NET, ColdFusion, and PHP. Only JSP is not supported.

The workflow for creating a server-side XSLT transformation is similar to that of a client-side transformation, with a number of key differences:

1. Create an XSLT page.
2. Attach the XML data to the XSLT page.
3. Bind the XML data to the XSLT page.
4. Remove all HTML from your dynamic page.
5. From the dynamic page, link to the XSLT page.
6. Publish both files to the web.
7. View the dynamic page.

The primary differences pertain, as you might expect, to the server-oriented nature of the page. As noted in the fourth step, you'll need to remove all HTML from your application page. This is a necessary action because the full XSLT page already contains the HTML framework—`<html>`, `<head>`, and `<body>` tags—and to leave it in the application page would cause errors.

Another difference is the manner in which the XSLT page is connected to the data. Rather than link to the XSLT page from the XML file, you apply a Dreamweaver server behavior in the dynamic page to create a connection to the XSLT file and its related XML data.

To link to the full XSLT page from the dynamic page, follow these steps:

1. With the dynamic page open, choose Window ➪ Server Behaviors.
2. In the Server Behaviors panel, click Add (+) and select XSL Transformation from the list.

   You may find the XSL Transformation box familiar; the same functionality is used when you create an XSLT fragment.
3. In the XSL Transformation dialog box, select the Attach A Local File On My Computer Or Local Area Network option if you want to incorporate data from a static XML file available on your system; use the Browse button to open the Select File dialog box or enter the path to the file by hand in the provided field.
4. If you're displaying XML data from a file on the web, click the Attach A Remote File On The Internet option and enter the full Internet address in the available field.
5. Click OK when you're done.

Before viewing it on your web server, you'll need to publish your dynamic and XSLT pages to your web server. Unlike with the client-side transformation, Dreamweaver will not automatically include the XSLT file as a dependent file. When the files have been posted, view the dynamic page to see the page with the XML data and XSLT transformations.

Summary

XML is a vital future technology that is knocking on the door of virtually every web designer. As the development tools become more common, the Roundtrip XML capability within Dreamweaver makes interfacing with this new method of communication straightforward and effortless. When you work with XML, keep the following points in mind:

- XML (Extensible Markup Language) enables content to be separated from the style of a web page, creating information that can be more easily used in various situations with different kinds of media.
- Tags in XML reflect the nature of the content, rather than its appearance.
- Dreamweaver includes a Roundtrip XML facility that makes it possible to export and import XML files through Dreamweaver templates.
- Use tag libraries to create custom XML tags and take advantage of Dreamweaver's Code Hints and Code Completion.
- XML data can be presented on the Internet with all the style of a standard web page through the use of Extensible Style Sheet Transformation (XSLT). Dreamweaver includes functionality for creating either client-side or server-side XSLT pages.

In the next chapter, you learn about customizing Dreamweaver, including how to use tag libraries.

Part VII

Extending Dreamweaver

IN THIS PART

Chapter 33
Customizing Dreamweaver

Chapter 34
Handling Server Behaviors

Chapter 35
Creating Adobe AIR Applications

CHAPTER

33

Customizing Dreamweaver

IN THIS CHAPTER

Automating web development with commands

Including custom XML tags

Modifying keyboard shortcuts

Updating Tag Libraries

Dreamweaver has a high degree of extensibility built right in, with its customizable HTML objects and JavaScript behaviors. With a tremendous number of API functions, objects, and behaviors, Dreamweaver presents a host of ways to extend its power. Here are just some of the options:

- **Menus:** The entire Dreamweaver menu system is completely customizable. You can add context menu items, rearrange the main menu, and even add completely new menus, all by modifying a single XML file.
- **Keyboard shortcuts:** Adobe makes it easy to use the same keyboard shortcuts across its product line—even extending such ease to other products—with the Keyboard Shortcut Editor. In addition to adopting the most comfortable set of key combinations, shortcuts for individual commands can be personalized.
- **Commands:** Commands are JavaScript and HTML code that manipulate the web page during the design phase, much as behaviors are triggered at runtime.
- **Custom tags:** The rapid rise of XML makes custom-tag support essential in a professional web-authoring tool. Dreamweaver gives you the power to create any custom tag and control how it displays in the Document window.
- **Property inspectors:** Custom Property inspectors go hand in hand with custom tags, enabling the straightforward entry of attributes and values in a manner consistent with the Dreamweaver user interface.
- **Custom panels:** Dreamweaver enables you to create custom panels that supplement its variety of built-in panels.
- **Translators:** Translators enable server-side and other content to be viewed in the Document window at design time, as well as in the browser at runtime.
- **C-level extensions:** Some special uses require a root-level addition to Dreamweaver's capabilities. Adobe's engineers have "popped the hood" on Dreamweaver and made it possible for a C or C++ language library to interface with it through C-level extensions.
- **Custom toolbars and objects:** The Insert panel and all other toolbars are fully extensible, enabling quick and easy access to your most frequently used Dreamweaver objects and commands.
- **Tag libraries:** Dreamweaver enables you to create, edit, and delete tag libraries.

Although a few of these extension features require programming skills beyond those of the typical web designer, most are well within the reach of an HTML- and JavaScript-savvy coder. Moreover, the Keyboard Shortcut editor employs a graphical user interface, making it accessible to all. As with behaviors and objects, the source code for all but the C-level extensions is readily available and serves as an excellent training ground. This chapter, combined with these standard scripts, provides a solid launching pad to begin carving out your own personalized version of Dreamweaver.

Adding New Commands

By their very nature, objects and behaviors are single-purpose engines. A custom object inserts a single block of HTML into the `<body>` of a web page, whereas custom behaviors add JavaScript functions to the `<head>` and attributes of one tag. Commands, on the other hand, are multifaceted, multipurpose, go-anywhere, and do-anything mechanisms. Commands can do everything objects and behaviors can do—and more. In fact, commands can even masquerade as objects.

For all their power, commands are one of the most accessible of the Dreamweaver extensions. This section describes the basic structure of commands, as well as how to use the standard commands that ship with Dreamweaver. You can also find information about how to create your own commands and control their integration into Dreamweaver.

Understanding Dreamweaver commands

When I first encountered commands, I thought, "Great! Dreamweaver now has a macro language." I envisioned instantly automating simple web design tasks. Before long, I realized that commands are even more powerful—and a bit trickier—than a macro recorder. Dreamweaver's adoption of the W3C Document Object Model (DOM) is one of the factors that make commands feasible. The DOM in Dreamweaver *exposes*, or makes available, every part of the HTML page—every tag, every attribute, every bit of content—which can then be read, modified, deleted, or added to. Moreover, Dreamweaver commands can open, read, and modify other files on local systems.

A command can have a parameter form or not, depending on how the command is written. Generally, commands are listed in the Commands menu, but by altering the `menus.xml` file (as discussed in the "Adjusting the menus.xml File" section later in this chapter), you can cause any command to appear as part of any other menu—or to not appear at all. Because one command can call another, such hidden commands are more easily modified.

My original vision of a macro recorder came true with the commands Start Recording and Play Recorded Command. Now, any onscreen action can be instantly logged and replayed—and through the History panel, even converted into a permanent, repeatable command.

So how, specifically, are commands being used? The following list describes some of the commands that have been built by web designers outside Adobe:

- **960 Grid System:** Makes it easy to design a layout using the 960 grid method. By DMXZones.
- **Replace Illegal Characters:** Switches special characters (such as ®, µ, ™, », and ©) for their character entity equivalents. By Matthew Villeneuve.

- **Add Old Browser Message:** Inserts a message that can be seen only by browsers that do not support the W3C DOM. By Rachel Andrews.
- **Replicator:** Duplicates any selected element any number of times. By the author of this book.

As is obvious from this list, commands come close to being limited only by the author's imagination.

For further evidence of just how useful commands can be, the following sections look at a few of Dreamweaver's standard commands.

The Apply Source Formatting and Apply Source Formatting To Selection commands

All the code created by Dreamweaver is structured according to the current Tag Library settings. The Tag Library identifies which codes are indented and which are on their own lines, as well as numerous other specifications regarding HTML writing. Occasionally, a web designer must work with web pages created earlier, by other designers using other programs, or even by hand. The Apply Source Formatting and Apply Source Formatting To Selection commands can rewrite the original code—of an entire web page or a selected part of the page, respectively—so that it is structured according to the current Tag Library settings and application preferences. The more accustomed your eye is to following Dreamweaver-style HTML, the more you value this command.

NOTE
You learn more about the Tag Library feature in "Customizing Your Tag Libraries," found later in this chapter.

The Apply Source Formatting and Apply Source Formatting To Selection commands are examples of Dreamweaver commands that don't display dialog boxes to gather the user's selected parameters—because there are no parameters to set. To invoke the commands, choose Commands ➪ Apply Source Formatting Or Commands ➪ Apply Source Formatting To Selection. The commands are applied immediately, with no confirmation or feedback indicating that they are complete. To verify their execution, you have to sneak a peek at your source code.

The Clean Up HTML and Clean Up XHTML commands

Dreamweaver tends to produce compact, uncluttered HTML/XHTML code, which is not always the case with other HTML/XHTML editors and hand-coded efforts. One of the most common problems is empty container tags. The resulting code is likely to resemble the following: `<p></p>`, `<strong></strong>`, and `<em></em>`.

The Clean Up HTML and Clean Up XHTML commands are custom made to consolidate redundant tags and to remove some of the code clutter that can accumulate during a page's design. In all, you have seven different cleaning operations from which to choose. Note that the Clean Up HTML and Clean Up XHTML commands are applicable only to the current page and cannot be applied sitewide.

XHTML syntax is much less forgiving than HTML; your XHTML code must be nearly perfect to work correctly. The Clean Up XHTML command fixes XHTML code syntax errors, lowercases all tag attributes, and adds (or reports) missing required tag attributes.

To use the Clean Up HTML or Clean Up XHTML commands, follow these steps:

1. Load the desired HTML or XHTML document into your Dreamweaver workspace.
2. Choose Commands ➪ Clean Up HTML (for an HTML document) or Commands ➪ Clean Up XHTML (for an XHTML document). The Clean Up HTML/XHTML dialog box appears, as shown in Figure 33-1.

FIGURE 33-1

Reduce your page's file size and make your HTML more readable with the Clean Up HTML/XHTML command.

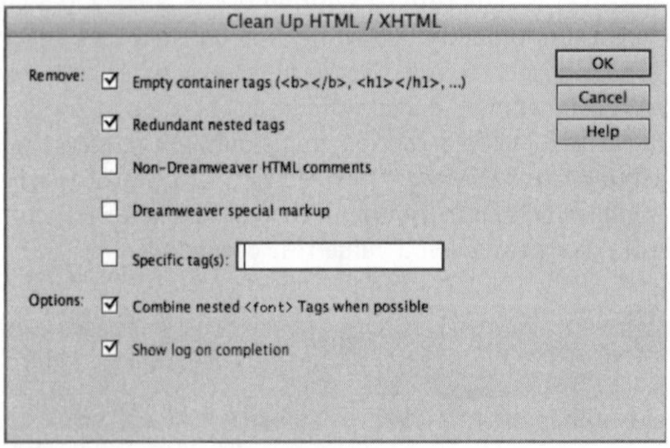

3. Choose from these options in the dialog box:
   - **Remove: Empty Container Tags:** Deletes empty tag pairs with no code between them (such as <b></b>).
   - **Remove: Redundant Nested Tags:** Eliminates superfluous tags that repeat the same code as the tags surrounding them, as shown in the following example:

     ```
     <font color="white">And the <font color="white">truth</font>
     is plain to see.</font>
     ```

   - **Remove: Non-Dreamweaver HTML Comments:** Deletes any HTML comments that were not created by Dreamweaver to, for example, mark a Library or template item.
   - **Remove: Dreamweaver Special Markup:** Clears all Dreamweaver-specific comments, such as:

     ```
     <!-- #BeginEditable "openingPara" -->
     ```

   - **Remove: Specific Tag(s):** Erases any specific tag and all its attributes. Select this option and then type the tag name or names in the text box.

NOTE

Enter tag names without angle brackets; separate multiple tags with a comma: for example, `font, blink`**.**

- **Combine Nested <font> Tags When Possible:** Consolidates `<font>` tags.
- **Show Log On Completion:** Lets you view a report of the changes applied to your document.

4. Click OK when you're finished.

Dreamweaver performs the actions requested on the current document. If you select the Show Log option, an alert displays the changes made, if any.

Recording and replaying commands

I'm a big fan of any kind of work-related automation, and I consider myself a power user of word-processing macros. The same capability is available in Dreamweaver. You save a tremendous amount of work with the capability to record onscreen actions and then replay them instantly—with the option of saving them as a command or simply pasting them into another document. Nearly every onscreen action can be replicated.

How could you use such a macro-like capability in Dreamweaver? With Dreamweaver, you can easily automate the procedure by following these steps:

1. Select the first image.
2. Choose Commands ➪ Start Recording or use the keyboard shortcut, Ctrl+Shift+X (Command+Shift+X). The cursor changes to a recording tape symbol, indicating you're in recording mode.
3. Enter the new values in the Property inspector.
4. Choose Commands ➪ Stop or the same keyboard command again: Ctrl+Shift+X (Command+Shift+X). The cursor changes back to its normal state.
5. Select another image.
6. Choose Commands ➪ Play Recorded Command.
7. Repeat Steps 5 and 6 for every image you want to change.

33

Most of the commands and onscreen moves can be replicated in this manner, but not all. The major exception is the use of the mouse. Dreamweaver cannot repeat mouse moves and selections. You cannot, for example, begin to create a drop cap by recording the drag selection of the first letter in each paragraph. You can, however, use the arrow keys and any keyboard-related combination.

For example, suppose that you have this standard list of names in your document:

```
Danilo Celic
Massimo Foti
Joseph Lowery
Al Sparber
Danielle Ugoletti
Eduordo Zubler
```

You want to change these names to a *Lastname, Firstname* format. To make this change with command recording, follow these steps:

1. Position your cursor at the beginning of the first name.
2. Choose Commands ➪ Start Recording.
3. Press Ctrl+Shift+right arrow (Command+Shift+right arrow) to select the first word. Dreamweaver highlights the first word and the following space.
4. Press Ctrl+X (Command+X) to cut the selected word.
5. Press End to move to the end of the line.
6. Type a comma and a space.
7. Press Ctrl+V (Command+V) to paste the previously cut word.
8. Press the backspace key to remove the trailing space.
9. The first line is complete, but to position the cursor to perform the recorded command again, press the right arrow to move to the start of the next line. (Because the cursor was positioned at the end of the last line, the right-arrow key moves it to the front of the following line.)
10. Choose Commands ➪ Stop Recording.
11. Choose Commands ➪ Play Recorded Command for each name in the list.

If you try to include a mouse move or selection when recording a command or playing back a recorded command, Dreamweaver issues a warning and asks if you'd like to stop recording. If you choose to continue, Dreamweaver ignores the attempted mouse move and resets the pointer in its previous position.

TIP

If you try to record your navigations around a table, Dreamweaver does not record the Tab or Shift+Tab keys. However, you can still record your table moves by using Home and End in combination with the arrow keys. To move from cell to cell, from left to right, press End and then the right arrow. To move right to left, press Home and then the left arrow. You can also move up and down columns by pressing Home or End and then either the up or the down arrow.

Recorded actions are maintained in memory, and when you issue the Start Recording command again, the previously recorded steps are replaced. You can, however, use the History panel to convert recorded steps into a command that you can use repeatedly in any document or site.

To convert recorded steps into a command, follow these steps:

1. Record a series of actions as described in the preceding set of steps.
2. Play the recorded actions at least once by choosing Commands ➪ Play Recorded Command.
3. On the History panel, the collective recorded actions are displayed as a series of steps with the label "Replay Steps Command." Select the original series of actions, as shown in Figure 33-2.

4. Click the Save Selected Steps As A Command button at the bottom of the History panel.
5. In the Save as Command dialog box, enter an appropriate name for your command and click OK.

FIGURE 33-2

Be sure to select the original series of steps in your History panel before saving them as a command.

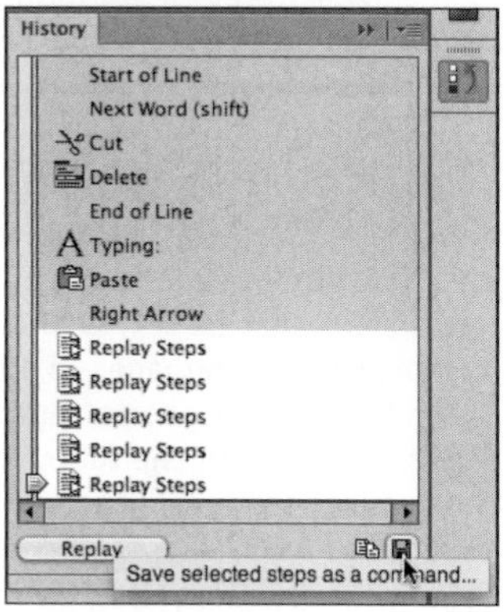

New commands saved in this manner are dynamically added to the Commands menu.

Multiuser System Customization

Dreamweaver is fully compatible with multiuser operating systems. This compatibility means that multiple users can work with a single installation of the program yet maintain their own preferences and configurations. Moreover, network administrators can maintain a group of common settings for all Dreamweaver users on the network.

To achieve such flexibility, Dreamweaver maintains customized files in a special folder for each user. These folders are stored in different locations on different operating systems. Under multiuser systems, the folders are within the specified user folder, designated by the user's ID or login name, as shown in the following examples:

- **Windows XP:** C:\Documents and Settings*User ID*\Application Data\Adobe\Dreamweaver CS6\
- **Windows Vista and Windows 7:** *Username*\AppData\Roaming\Adobe\Dreamweaver CS6\
- **Mac OS X:** Macintosh HD/Users/*Username*/Library/Application Support/Adobe/Dreamweaver CS6/

NOTE

Windows systems are shown using drive C, whereas Macintosh users use the Macintosh HD drive; naturally, the drive letter or name may be different if another system drive is used or if a Mac user renames his or her drive.

Continues

33

continued

All custom extensions installed by Dreamweaver—either by the features in the program itself (such as the History panel's Save Selected Steps As A Command feature) or by the Extension Manager—are automatically inserted in the proper multiuser folder. Folders are created on an as-needed basis; you won't see an Inspectors folder in your multiuser Configuration folder unless an inspector extension is installed.

In fact, you may need to take one additional step before any user folders are visible. Certain folders—particularly those dealing with system administration—are hidden by default in Windows and OS X operating systems. To gain access to such files, open Windows Explorer and set the Folder Options to show hidden files and folders. In OS X, hold down the Option key and, in Finder, choose Go ➪ Library.

Scripting commands

Commands, like most behaviors, are a combination of JavaScript functions and HTML forms; the HTML provides the user interface for any parameters that must be set, and JavaScript carries out the particular command. Although you can combine both languages in a single HTML file, many programmers, including those from Adobe, keep the JavaScript in a separate `.js` file that is incorporated in the HTML file with a `<script>` tag, as shown in the following example:

```
<script language="javascript" src="Clean Up HTML.js">
```

This separation enables easy modification of the user interface and the underlying code, and the sharing of the JavaScript functions.

Commands are very open-ended. In fact, only two Dreamweaver functions are specific to commands—`canAcceptCommand()` and `commandButtons()`—and neither function is required. Two other command-oriented functions, `receiveArguments()` and `windowDimensions()`, are also used elsewhere; but again, neither is required.

The `canAcceptCommand()` function controls when the command is active in the menus and when it is dimmed. If `canAcceptCommand()` is not defined, the command is always available. This function returns `true` or `false`; if `false` is returned, the command is dimmed in the menus.

You can see `canAcceptCommand()` in action in the Sort Table command. For this command to be effective, a table must be selected. Rather than require that a table be selected, the `canAcceptCommand()` function calls a subroutine, `findTable()`, which returns `true` if the user's cursor is positioned inside a table:

```
function canAcceptCommand(){
  if (dw.getDocumentDOM() == null)
    return false;
  else if (dw.getDocumentDOM().getShowLayoutView())
    return false;
  else if (findTable())
    return true;
  else
    return false;
}

function findTable(){
```

```
    var tableObj="";
    var selObj = dw.getDocumentDOM().getSelectedNode();

    while (tableObj=="" && selObj.parentNode){
      if (selObj.nodeType == Node.ELEMENT_NODE && selObj.tagName=="TABLE")
      tableObj=selObj;
    else
      selObj = selObj.parentNode;
    }
    return tableObj;
}
```

Adobe recommends that the `canAcceptCommand()` function not be defined unless at least one case exists in which the command should not be available. Otherwise, the function is asked to run for no purpose, which degrades performance.

The `commandButtons()` function defines the buttons that appear on the parameter form to the right. This expanded functionality is extremely useful when developing commands. Some commands require that an operation be enabled to run repeatedly and not just the one time an OK button is selected. As noted earlier, you don't have to declare the function at all, in which case the form expands to fill the dialog box entirely. If you do not use this standard Dreamweaver method for creating your command buttons, in most cases, you need to define them yourself.

Each button declared has a function associated with it, which is executed when the user selects that particular button. All the buttons for a command are listed in an array, returned by `commandButtons()`. The following example declares three buttons: OK, Cancel, and Help:

```
function commandButtons() {
    return new Array("OK","goCommand()","Cancel",
                     "window.close()","Help","displayHelp()")
}
```

Notice that two of the buttons, OK and Help, call user-defined functions, but the Cancel button simply calls a built-in JavaScript function to close the window. Although no limitations exist on the number of buttons a parameter form can hold, you should always strive to keep your parameter forms as simple and uncluttered as possible.

The `receiveArguments()` function is used in conjunction with `runCommand()`. Whenever `runCommand()` calls a specific command—from a behavior, object, or other command—it can pass arguments. If `receiveArguments()` is set up, that is the function executed, and the arguments are read into `receiveArguments()`. This function enables the same command to be called from different sources and have different effects, depending on the arguments passed. The `receiveArguments()` function is used extensively in menu commands and is explained more fully later in this chapter in the section "Building Menu Commands."

You can use the `windowDimensions()` function in behaviors and objects, with commands to set a specific size for the associated dialog box. If `windowDimensions()` is not defined, the size of the dialog box is set automatically. Adobe recommends that `windowDimensions()` not be used unless your parameter form exceeds 640 × 480.

The remainder of the user interface for a command—the parameter form—is constructed in the same manner with the same tools that are used for objects and behaviors. A command parameter form or dialog box uses an HTML `<form>` in the `<body>` of the file. If no `<form>` is declared, the command executes without displaying a dialog box. All the form elements used in objects—text boxes, radio buttons, checkboxes, and lists—are available in commands.

Managing Menus and Keyboard Shortcuts

Dreamweaver offers numerous ways to perform almost every task: through the Property inspector, context menus, and keyboard shortcuts, and even by entering code directly. However, in the search for ever-faster, more efficient ways of working, you may often find it desirable to take control of the menus and other command methods and make them work the way you and your team prefer them to work. If, for example, you insert a great number of AP elements and always define your links via the Property inspector, you are probably better off redefining Ctrl+L (Command+L) to Insert AP element, rather than its default, Make Link.

Dreamweaver places all menus and keyboard shortcuts under your control. Not only can you add new items, but you can also rename menu items, change their keyboard shortcuts, determine when a menu item is active or dimmed—and even add entirely new menu strips. Moreover, all this functionality is available with the context menus as well.

One file—`menus.xml`, found in the Dreamweaver CS6\Configuration\Menus folder—is responsible for menu and keyboard shortcut setup. Although you have to edit the XML file by hand to reconfigure the menus, Dreamweaver includes a Keyboard Shortcut editor for modifying the keystroke commands. Details are in the "Using the Keyboard Shortcut Editor" section later in the chapter.

Menu customization brings a whole new level of functionality to Dreamweaver. It's entirely possible for a company to create custom subsets of a program for certain departments. For example, each of several departments in a large firm might be responsible for its own section of the website. A customized version of Dreamweaver could include a predefined site and disable the Define Site commands in the Site menu. It could also offer a specialized menu for calling up Help screens, tied to the standard F1 keyboard shortcut for Help.

In addition to the fully open architecture of the `menus.xml` file, command menu items created by the History panel can be managed right in the Document window. Before you delve into the relatively complex structure of `menus.xml`, take a look at the Edit Command List feature.

Handling History panel commands

Whenever you save a series of History panel steps as a command, that command is instantly added to the bottom of the Commands menu list. Dreamweaver enables you to manage these custom added items—renaming them or deleting them—through the Edit Command List feature.

To manage History panel recorded commands, follow these steps:

1. Choose Commands ➪ Edit Command List. The Edit Command List dialog box appears, as shown in Figure 33-3.

FIGURE 33-3

Manage your recorded commands through the Edit Command List dialog box.

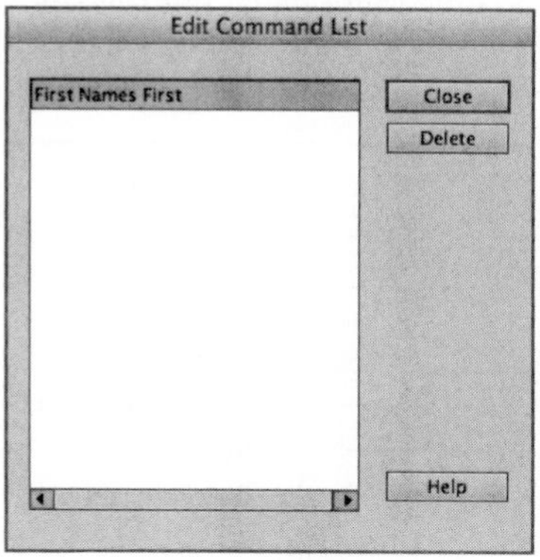

2. To remove a command, select it and click Delete.
3. To rename a command, select it and enter the new name or alter the existing one.

Using the Keyboard Shortcut editor

Whenever I'm learning a new program, one of the tasks I set for myself is to memorize the half-dozen or so essential keyboard shortcuts of the software. Keyboard shortcuts are terrific for boosting productivity—so terrific, in fact, that almost every program uses them. Although this is a good thing from a single-program user's perspective, in reality no web designer uses just one program, and having to remember the keyboard shortcuts for every program can be an absolute nightmare.

33

To put the brakes on keyboard shortcut overload, Adobe has implemented a standard Keyboard Shortcut editor for its key web products—Flash, Fireworks, and Dreamweaver. Where possible, common features share the same shortcut across the product line. For example, opening the Behaviors panel is accomplished with the same keyboard shortcut in Dreamweaver and Fireworks: Shift+F3. Dreamweaver also includes a set of shortcuts matching those from HomeSite and BBEdit to smooth your transition from those text-based editors. Best of all, you can customize any existing set of shortcuts to match the way you truly work best.

To access the Keyboard Shortcut editor, shown in Figure 33-4, choose Edit ⇨ Keyboard Shortcuts (Windows) or Dreamweaver ⇨ Keyboard Shortcuts (Macintosh).

The standard Keyboard Shortcut editor includes four standard sets of shortcuts:

- **BBEdit:** Keyboard shortcut set matching those found in BBEdit.
- **Dreamweaver MX2004:** This set uses the standard shortcuts found in Dreamweaver MX2004. These additional shortcuts are not necessarily the same as those in the Adobe Standard set because keystrokes may be added or modified for new features in the latest version.

- **Dreamweaver Standard:** The default set of shortcuts incorporating common keyboard combinations in Dreamweaver, Fireworks, and Flash.
- **HomeSite:** Keyboard shortcut set matching those found in HomeSite.

FIGURE 33-4

Use the Keyboard Shortcut editor to establish the easiest-to-remember mnemonics for your keyboard shortcuts.

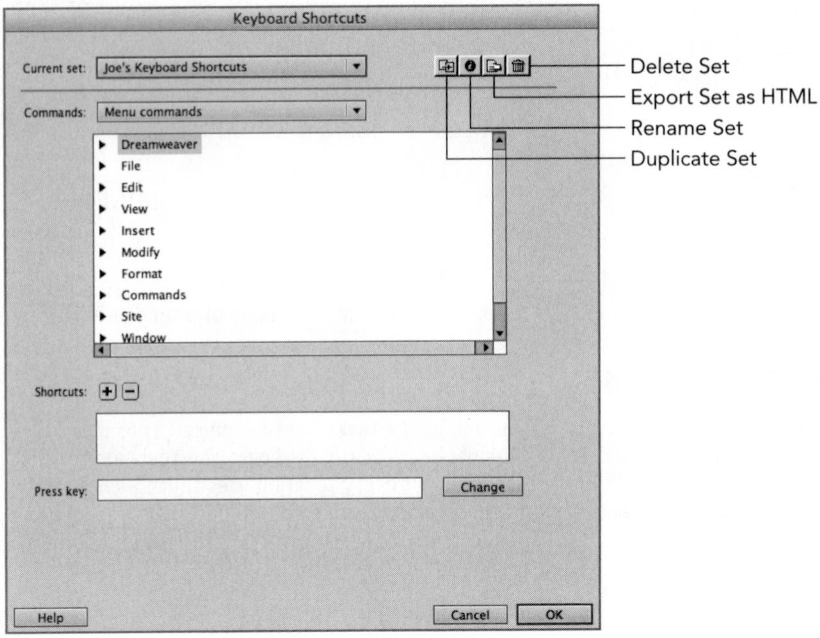

To change from one set to another, open the Keyboard Shortcut editor and choose the desired set from the Current Set drop-down list. The changes take effect immediately upon closing the dialog box; you don't have to relaunch Dreamweaver.

The standard sets are locked and cannot be altered—you can only customize a copy of one of the standard sets. Dreamweaver provides all the controls to accomplish this on top of the Keyboard Shortcut editor. The four buttons are as follows:

- **Duplicate Set:** Copies the current set (standard or custom) and appends the word "copy." The duplicate set can be fully customized.
- **Rename Set:** Renames the current shortcut set.
- **Export Set as HTML:** Saves a list of the current set of keyboard shortcuts in an HTML format that can be viewed or printed in a browser.
- **Delete Set:** Removes a keyboard shortcut set. When Delete Set is chosen, a list of all custom sets is displayed, and any set except the active one may be removed. To remove a sole custom set, select any of the standard shortcut sets prior to choosing Delete Set.

Each command has up to two shortcuts assigned to it. This facility makes it possible to retain the originally assigned keyboard shortcut and to add a more personal one.

To create a custom keyboard shortcut set, follow these steps:

1. Choose Edit ➪ Keyboard Shortcuts (Dreamweaver ➪ Keyboard Shortcuts) to open the editor. The editor might take a few moments to load your current keyboard shortcuts.

NOTE
From the Department of Pointless Nonsense, Irony Division: The Keyboard Shortcuts feature is one of the few commands without a keyboard shortcut.

2. From the Current Set drop-down list, select a standard keyboard shortcut set upon which to base your custom set.
3. Click the Duplicate Set button, type in an appropriate name for your custom shortcut set, and click OK. When the duplication is finished, select your new shortcut set from the Current Set list.
4. Choose the types of commands you want to modify from the Commands drop-down list. Dreamweaver has seven different command types in Windows—Menu commands, File panel options menu, Site panel, Code editing, Document editing, Site window, and Snippets; and four under the Macintosh system—Menu commands, Code editing, Document editing, and Snippets.
5. Select the specific command whose keyboard shortcut you want to modify. If you've chosen Menu, File panel, or Site panel from the Commands list (Windows only), click the plus (+) sign next to the menu heading containing the command. The listing expands to show the first level of menu items. If the command you want to alter is contained within a submenu, click the plus (+) sign next to the submenu. Click the minus (–) sign to collapse an expanded listing.
6. With the desired command selected, click the Add (+) button in the Shortcuts section. The cursor moves into the Press Key field.
7. Press the keyboard combination you want to assign to the command. If Dreamweaver detects a conflict with an existing keyboard shortcut, an alert is displayed beneath the Press Key field telling you the command to which that shortcut is currently assigned.
8. Select Change to confirm your choice.

   If the shortcut you selected is already in use, you can reassign it to your new choice. When you click Change under these circumstances, Dreamweaver brings up an alert dialog box warning you that the shortcut is currently assigned. It also tells you which command is using it, and asks if you want to reassign it to the command you are editing. To reassign the keystroke, click OK. To choose a new keyboard shortcut, click Cancel.

   If a command already has two shortcuts assigned to it, you select the one you want to change.
9. Click OK when you're finished to save your keyboard shortcut set.

TIP

The personalized keyboard shortcut files are stored in the Dreamweaver CS6\Configuration\Menus\Custom Sets folder as XML files. To make a keyboard shortcut set available on another system, copy the appropriate XML file to the corresponding folder in the user's Dreamweaver CS6\Configuration\Menus\Custom Sets folder. For more details on the location of the user's folders, see the "Multiuser System Customization" sidebar earlier in this chapter.

Adjusting the menus.xml file

When Dreamweaver is launched, the program reads the `menus.xml` file and builds the menu system. You can even customize `menus.xml` and reload the file from within Dreamweaver to instantly update your menu and shortcuts. The key, of course, is editing the XML file.

CAUTION

The syntax for `menus.xml` is quite complex. Dreamweaver ignores any syntactically incorrect entries and disables their corresponding menu items. So, take great care when you edit `menus.xml` to use proper syntax, and make sure you create a backup of the file *before* you begin editing.

The typical procedure for changing an existing menu item or shortcut is to open the file in a text editor (after backing up the original) and make the necessary changes. When adding menus or menu items, follow the file's syntax exactly, as described in the following sections.

Generic shortcuts

Although Dreamweaver provides a user interface for editing the keyboard shortcuts, sometimes power users must go to the source for major modifications—and the source for shortcuts is `menus.xml`. The `menus.xml` file is divided into two main sections: `<shortcutlist>` and `<menubar>`. The `<shortcutlist>` divisions are, as you might suspect, a list of keyboard shortcuts. The `<menubar>` areas are concerned with the various menu bars—in the main Document window, in the Site panel (Windows only), and in the numerous context menus. `<shortcutlist>` and `<menubar>` share several characteristics. They both follow the same basic structure:

```
<shortcutlist id="shortcutListID" [platform="win|mac"]>
  <shortcut attributeName="value" attributeName="value" ... />
  <shortcut attributeName="value" attributeName="value" ... />
  other shortcut items...
</shortcutlist>

<menubar name="menubarname" id="menubarID" [platform="win|mac"]>
  <menu name="menuname" id="menuID">
    <menuitem attributeName="value" attributeName="value" ... />
    <menuitem attributeName="value" attributeName="value" ... />
    other menuitem items...
  </menu>
  other menu items...
</menubar>
```

Shortcuts for menu items are primarily defined within the <menubar> code; the <shortcut list> is mainly concerned with those shortcuts that do not have a menu item associated with them, such as moving from one word to another. By default, Dreamweaver defines six <short cutlist> sections: DWMainWindow for the Document window menu, DWMainSite for the Site panel menu (Windows only), DWHTMLContext for the Code inspector/Code view context menu, DWServerBehaviorContext for the Server Behaviors panel context menu, DWDataBinding Context for the Bindings panel context menu, and DWServerComponentContext for the Components panel context menu.

NOTE

The key difference between the <shortcutlist> and the <menubar> sections is that although you can define new menu items or change existing ones in the <menubar> portion of the code, you can only alter existing shortcuts—you cannot add new shortcuts.

Each <shortcutlist> tag has one required attribute, the ID. The ID refers to a specific window or panel and must be unique within the <shortcutlist> section. The same ID is repeated in the <menubar> section to refer to the same window or panel. For example, the Document window ID is DWMainWindow, whereas the one for the context menu of the Server Behaviors panel is DWServerBehaviorContext. The <shortcutlist> tag takes one optional attribute, platform, which must be set to either win or mac, for Windows and Macintosh systems, respectively. (Note that in syntax statements, optional attributes are enclosed in brackets.) If no platform attribute is listed, the <shortcutlist> described applies to both platforms. Here, for example, is the beginning of the <shortcutlist> definition for the Files panel, which appears in only the Windows version of the software:

```
<shortcutlist id="DWMainSite" platform="win">
```

A separate <shortcut> tag exists for every keystroke defined in the <shortcutlist>. The <shortcut> tag defines the key used, the tag's ID, the command or file to be executed when the keyboard shortcut is pressed, and the applicable platform, if any. Shortcuts can be defined for single special keys or key combinations using modifiers. The special keys are as follows:

- F1 through F12
- PgDn, PgUp, Home, End
- Ins, Del, BkSp, Space
- Esc and Tab

Modifiers can be used in combination with standard keys, with special keys, or by themselves. A combination keyboard shortcut is indicated with a plus sign between keys. Available modifiers include those described in Table 33-1.

You can also combine multiple modifiers, as in Command+Shift+Z.

The format of the <shortcut> tag is identical to that of the <menuitem> tag, as described in the following section.

TABLE 33-1 Dreamweaver Shortcut Modifier Keys

Key	Example	Use
Alt or Opt	Alt+V; Option+V	Indicates the Alt (Windows) or Option (Macintosh) key modifier
Cmd	Command+S	Indicates the Command (Macintosh) key modifier
Ctrl	Ctrl+U	Indicates the Ctrl (Windows) key modifier
Shift	Shift+F1	Indicates the Shift key on both platforms

Menubar definitions

Each <menubar> section of the menus.xml file describes a different menu strip, either on a window or on the context menu associated with a panel. Nested within the <menubar> tag is a series of <menu> tags, each detailing a drop-down menu. The individual menu items are defined in the <menuitem> tags contained within each set of <menu> ... </menu> tags. Here, for example, is the context menu for the Server Behavior panel that allows server behaviors to be cut, copied, and pasted:

```
<menubar id="DWServerBehaviorContext">
  <menu mmstring:name="menus/DWContext_ServerBehavior"
id="DWContext_ServerBehavior">
    <menuitem mmstring:name="menus/DWContext_ServerBehavior_Cut"
command="dw.clipCut()" enabled="dw.canClipCut()"
id="DWContext_ServerBehavior_Cut" />
    <menuitem mmstring:name="menus/DWContext_ServerBehavior_Copy"
command="dw.clipCopy()" enabled="dw.canClipCopy()"
id="DWContext_ServerBehavior_Copy" />
    <menuitem mmstring:name="menus/DWContext_ServerBehavior_Paste"
command="dw.clipPaste()" enabled="dw.canClipPaste()"
id="DWContext_ServerBehavior_Paste" />
  </menu>
</menubar>
```

The <menubar> and <menu> tags are alike in that they both require a name—which is what appears in the menu system—and an ID. The ID must be unique within the <menubar> structure to avoid conflicts. If a conflict is found (that is, if one item has the same ID as another), the first item in the XML file is recognized, and the second item is ignored.

NOTE

You can put a dividing line between your menu items by including a <separator id="idname" /> tag between any two <menuitem> tags. (idname is any legal, unique XML name string.)

Numerous other attributes exist for the <menuitem> tag. The required attributes are name, id, and either file or command, as marked with an asterisk in Table 33-2.

TABLE 33-2 Menuitem Tag Attributes

Attribute	Possible Value	Description
name*	Any menu name	The name of the menu item as it appears on the menu. An underscore character causes the following letter to be underlined for Windows' shortcuts—for example, _Frames becomes Frames.
id*	Any unique name	The identifying term for the menu item.
key	Any special key or keyboard key plus modifier(s)	The keyboard shortcut used to execute the command.
platform	win or mac	The operating system valid for the current menu item. If the platform parameter is omitted, the menu item is applicable for both systems.
enabled	JavaScript function	If present, governs whether a menu item is active (the function returns true) or dimmed (the function returns false). Including enabled=true ensures that the function is always available.
command* (required if file is not used)	JavaScript function	Executed when the menu item is selected. This inline JavaScript function capability is used for simple functions.
file* (required if command is not used)	Path to a JavaScript file	The JavaScript file is executed when the menu item is selected; the path is relative to the Configuration folder.
checked	JavaScript function	Displays a checkmark next to the menu item if the function returns true.
dynamic	N/A	Specifies that the menu item is set dynamically by the getDynamicContent() function, which resides in the Menu Commands file specified by the file attribute.

TIP

The `menus.xml` file is quite extensive. You can find the main menu for Dreamweaver—the one you most likely want to modify—by searching for the second instance of its ID, `DWMainWindow`. The first instance is used by the corresponding `<shortcutlist>` tag.

You can create submenus by nesting one set of <menu> tags within another. The following example is a simplified look at the File ➪ Import commands, as structured in `menus.xml`:

```
<menu name="_File" id="DWMenu_File">
  other menu items...
```

```
    <menu name="_Import" id="DWMenu_File_Import">
      <menuitem name="_XML into Template..." />
      <menuitem name="_Tabular Data..." />
      <menuitem name="_Word HTML..." />
      <menuitem name="_Excel HTML..." />
    </menu>
    other menu items...
  </menu>
```

NOTE

If you're on a Mac and you're looking for the Word HTML and Excel HTML options under the Import menu, you won't find them. They're Windows only, which is handled by a `platform="win"` attribute included in those two `<menuitem>` tags.

Note how the `<menu>` tag defining the Import submenu is nested within the `<menu>` tag that defines the File menu.

Building menu commands

When examining the `menus.xml` file, notice that many menu items have JavaScript functions written right into the `<menuitem>` tag, such as this one for File ➪ New:

```
<menuitem name="New _Window" key="Cmd+N" enabled="true"
          command="dw.newDocument()" id="DWMenu_MainSite_File_New" />
```

When the user selects File ➪ New, Dreamweaver executes the API function `dw.newDocument()` in what is referred to as a *menu command*. Menu commands are used to specify the action of every menu item; what makes them unique is that you can use them to create and activate dynamic menus. Dynamic menus update according to user selections; the Preview In Browser list is a dynamic menu.

A menu command, like most of the other Dreamweaver extensions, is a combination of HTML and JavaScript. If the menu command is extensive and cannot be referenced as one or two functions directly in the `menus.xml` file, it is contained in an HTML file, stored in the Dreamweaver CS6\Configuration\Menus folder. Menu commands can even use a dialog box, such as standard commands for accepting user input.

TIP

You can find many examples of menu commands, written by the Dreamweaver engineers, in the Dreamweaver CS5\Configuration\Menus\MM folder.

Menu commands have access to all the Dreamweaver API functions and a few of their own. None of the seven menu command API functions, listed in Table 33-3, is required, and three are automatically called when the menu command is executed.

TABLE 33-3 Command Menu API Functions

Function	Returns	Description
canAcceptCommand()	Boolean (true or false)	Determines whether the menu item is active or dimmed
commandButtons()	An array of labels and functions, separated by commas	Sets the name and effect of buttons on the dialog box
getDynamicContent()	An array of menu item names and unique IDs, separated by a semicolon	Sets the current listing for a menu
isCommandChecked()	Boolean	Adds a checkmark next to the item if true is returned
receiveArguments()	Nothing	Handles any arguments passed by the <menuitem> tag
setMenuText()	A text string	Sets the name of the menu item according to the given function; not to be used in conjunction with getDynamicContent()
windowDimensions()	Width, Height (in pixels)	Determines the dimensions of the Parameters dialog box, such as windowDimensions(300,500)

Working with Custom Tags

With the advent of XML—in which no standard tags exist—the capability to handle custom tags is essential in a web-authoring tool. Dreamweaver incorporates this capability through its third-party tag feature. After you've defined a third-party tag, Dreamweaver displays it in the Document window by highlighting its content, inserting a user-defined icon, or doing neither depending on the Preferences selected and the attributes assigned. Third-party tags are easily selected through the Tag Selector below the Document window; therefore, they are easy to cut, copy, and paste, or otherwise manipulate. Perhaps most important, after a third-party tag is defined, you can apply a custom Property inspector that enables tag attributes to be entered in a standardized user interface.

Third-party tags can be defined directly within Dreamweaver. Just as object files use HTML to structure HTML code for easy insertion, Dreamweaver uses XML to make an XML definition for the custom tag. A custom tag declaration consists solely of one tag, `<tagspec>`, with a variety of attributes. The following list describes all of the tag's legal attributes:

- `tag_name`: Defines the name of the tag as used in the markup. Any valid name—no spaces or special characters are allowed—is possible. A tag with the attribute `tag_name="invoice"` is entered in the document as `<invoice>`.

- tag_type: Determines whether the tag has a closing tag (nonempty) and is thus capable of enclosing content or if the tag describes the content itself (empty). For example, the <invoice> tag could have a tag_type="nonempty" because all the content is between <invoice> and </invoice>.
- render_contents: Sets whether the content of a non-empty type tag is displayed. The render_contents attribute value is either true or false; if false, the tag's icon is displayed instead of the contents.
- content_model: Establishes valid placement and content for the tag in the document. The possible options are as follows:
  - block_model: Tags defined with content_model="block_model" appear only in the <body> section of a document and contain block-level HTML tags, such as <p>, <div>, <blockquote>, and <pre>.
  - head_model: Defines a tag that appears in the <head> section and can contain text—for example, content_model="head_model".
  - marker_model: You can place tags with the attribute content_model="marker_model" anywhere in the document with no restrictions on content. The marker_model value is most often used for inline tags that are placed within a paragraph or division.
  - script_model: Like the marker_model tag, script_model tags can be placed in either the <head> or the <body> section. All content within a script_model tag is ignored by Dreamweaver. This feature enables server-specific scripts to be included without alteration.
- start_string: The initial delimiter for a custom string-delimited tag; start_string and end_string must both be defined if one is declared. Lasso tags, for example, use a start_string of a left bracket ([).
- end_string: The closing delimiter for a custom string-delimited tag. The end_string for a Lasso tag is the right bracket (]).
- detect_in_attribute: A boolean value that determines whether Dreamweaver should ignore string-delimited tags used as attributes in other tags. The default is false, but for most string-delimited functions, the detect_in_attribute value should be set to true.
- parse_attributes: A boolean value that determines whether Dreamweaver should inspect and parse the attributes within string-delimited tags. By default, Dreamweaver parses all attributes; set parse_attribute to false to force Dreamweaver to ignore the attributes.
- icon: Empty tags or non-empty custom tags with render_content disabled require a GIF file to act as an icon in the Document window. The icon attribute should be set to any valid URL, relative or absolute (as in icon="images/invoice.gif").
- icon_width: Sets the width, in pixels, of the icon used to represent the tag. The value can be any positive integer.
- icon_height: Sets the height, in pixels, of the icon used to represent the tag. The value can be any positive integer.
- is_visual: Sets whether the tag is rendered in the Design view; either a true or a false value is acceptable.

- `equivalent_tag`: Sets HTML alternatives for some ColdFusion form-related tags.
- `server_model`: When included, indicates that the tag applies only on pages that belong to the specified server model. If `server_model` is not specified, the tag applies on all pages.

Here's the complete code for a sample custom tag, the Template Expressions tag (which, although created by Adobe, is technically a third-party tag):

```
<tagspec tag_name="dwtemplate" start_string="@@(" end_string=")@@"
  detect_in_attribute="true" icon="TemplateExpr.gif" icon_width="18"
  icon_height="18"></tagspec>
```

Figure 33-5 shows an example of the Template Expressions custom tags; the page is set up so that the items on the menu can be altered with template expressions.

TIP

If the content is to be rendered for a custom tag, you can easily view it in the Document window by enabling the Third-Party Tags Highlighting option in the Highlighting panel of the Preferences dialog box. Make sure that View ➪ Visual Aids ➪ Invisible Elements is enabled.

After a custom tag is defined, the definition is saved in an XML file in the ThirdPartyTags folder, in Dreamweaver's Configuration folder. If you are establishing a number of custom tags, you can place all the definitions in the same file. Adobe refers to this as the Tag DB or Database.

FIGURE 33-5

Third-party tags, such as these representing template expressions, can be displayed—and manipulated—in Design view.

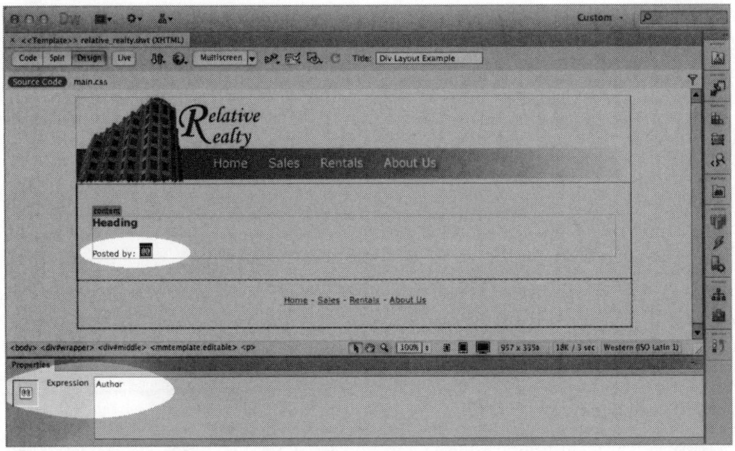

Customizing Your Tag Libraries

Dreamweaver gives you a well-designed dialog box called the Tag Library Editor that allows you to change code formatting, including tag case, attributes, indentation, and line wrapping. You can use that editor to customize every single tag you place in Dreamweaver, and you can even add additional tags if you're using a proprietary server or design XML files with commonly used tag sets.

All tag-related attributes and color code settings are stored in a tag database (the Tag Library), which is manipulated through the Tag Library Editor. Click the Tag Library Editor link in Preferences (Preferences ➪Code Format ➪ Tag Libraries) or choose Edit ➪ Tag Libraries.

Editing tag libraries, tags, and attributes

To edit the properties for a tag library, follow these steps:

1. Choose Edit ➪ Tag Libraries to open the Tag Library Editor dialog box, and select the tag library whose properties you want to set, as shown in Figure 33-6.
2. In the Used In list box, choose every type of document that should use the selected tag library. Note that the tags in the selected library are available only in the document types you've chosen.

FIGURE 33-6

You use the Tag Library Editor to customize Dreamweaver's tag libraries.

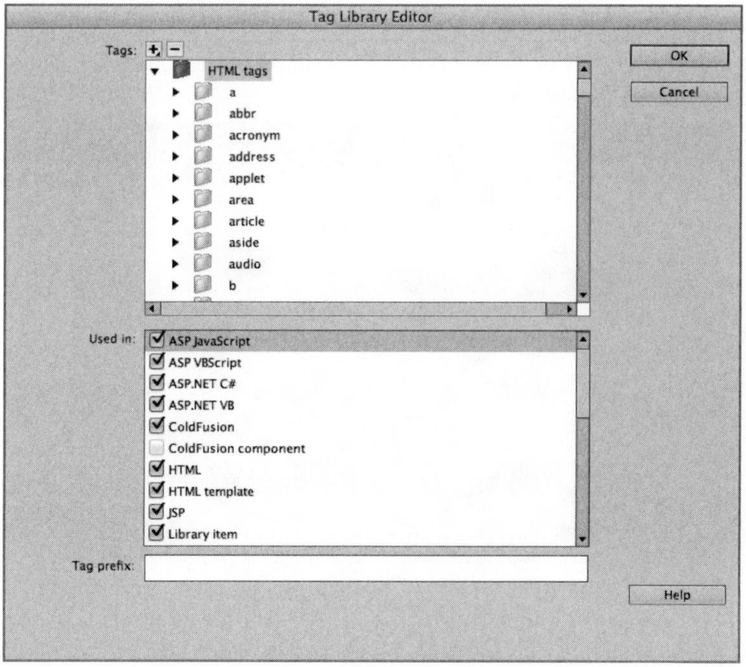

3. If the tags in the selected tag library require a prefix, enter this prefix in the Tag Prefix field. The Tag Prefix box enables you to add a prefix to the beginning of every tag in that particular library. For example, if you developed a tag library for XSL documents, you add `xsl:` as the tag prefix to add the prefix to the beginning of every tag.
4. When you are finished, click OK to close the Tag Library Editor dialog box.

To edit a tag in a tag library, follow these steps:

1. Choose Edit ➪ Tag Libraries. In the Tag Library Editor dialog box, open a tag library and select the tag you want to edit.
2. Set your desired Tag Format options:
   - **Line Breaks:** Changing the line breaks option changes where Dreamweaver places line breaks in your code. Choose between four options: No Line Breaks; Before And After Tag; Before, Inside, After; and After Tag Only. This option is great for preventing line breaks after `<td>` tags and before `</td>` tags to ensure that no unwanted whitespace shows up in your code.
   - **Contents:** This setting affects how the content inside your tags is formatted. The indentation settings are based on your code format preferences. Choose between Not Formatted, Formatted But Not Indented, and Formatted And Indented.
   - **Case:** The case settings affect how the tag and its attributes are capitalized. XHTML, for example, requires that everything be lowercase. Options are Default, Lowercase, Uppercase, and Mixed Case. Choosing Mixed Case gives you a prompt to type in exactly how you want the tag to appear. Clicking Set Default enables you to set the default for all tags, which is the same as changing your tag case preferences in Edit ➪ Preferences ➪ Code Format (Dreamweaver ➪ Preferences ➪ Code Format).

   The Preview area below the Tag Format options enables you to see exactly how your tag will be written to the page.

33

TIP
I recommend setting your default case to lowercase to comply with XML/XHTML and HTML5 standards.

To edit an attribute for a tag, follow these steps:

1. Choose Edit ➪ Tag Libraries. In the Tag Library Editor dialog box, open a tag library and select the attribute you want to edit.
2. Set your desired attribute options:
   - **Attribute Case:** This option sets the case of your attribute. Attribute Case is completely independent of the tag. Options are Default, Lowercase, Uppercase, or Mixed Case. Choosing Mixed Case enables you to enter exactly how you want the attribute formatted. Clicking Set Default alerts you to return to the Code Format category of Preferences.
   - **Attribute Type:** There are eleven different attribute types for your tag—Text, Enumerated, Color, Directory, File Name, File Path, Flag, Font, Relative Path, Style, and CssStyle. Setting the type affects how Dreamweaver asks for information when using Code Hints in Code view or the Quick Tag Editor. Choosing Color for an attribute

causes a color palette to appear if you add the attribute in Code view. Setting the Type to Relative Path gives you a Select File dialog box.

- **Values:** The Values field is used only for the enumerated attribute type and gives you a list of valid values for a particular attribute.

3. Click OK.

Creating and deleting tag libraries, tags, and attributes

The following sets of steps show you how to create a new tag library, add a tag to an existing library, or add an attribute to an existing tag.

To add a new tag library, follow these steps:

1. Choose Edit ➪ Tag Libraries.
2. Click the Add (+) button and choose New Tag Library.
3. Enter a name for your new tag library and click OK.
4. Your new tag library is now shown at the bottom of the list. You're ready to start adding new tags.

To add new tags to one of your tag libraries, follow these steps:

1. Choose Edit ➪ Tag Libraries.
2. Click the Add (+) button and choose New Tags.
3. Choose the Tag Library to add to in the list menu.
4. Enter one or more tags to add. To add several tags at one time, simply enter a comma-separated list of tags into the dialog. This method enables you to add a large number of tags very quickly.
5. Choose whether your tag requires matching end tags. Choosing matching end tags gives you tags like `<a>text</a>`. Choosing not to have matching end tags gives you tags like `<br>` and `<img>`.

To add a new attribute to an existing tag, follow these steps:

1. Choose Edit ➪ Tag Libraries.
2. Click the Add (+) button and choose New Attributes.
3. Choose the Tag Library that contains the tag you want to add attributes to from the first list menu.
4. Choose the tag you want to add attributes to from the second list menu.
5. Enter one or more attributes to add. If you want to add several attributes at one time, simply enter a comma-separated list of attributes into the dialog. This enables you to add a large number of attributes very quickly.

To delete a tag library, tag, or attribute, follow these steps:

1. Choose Edit ➪ Tag Libraries.
2. In the Tag Library Editor dialog box, select the tag library, tag, or attribute you want to delete.
3. Click the Remove (–) button. If you are asked to confirm the deletion, do so.
4. To make your deletions permanent, click OK. To discard your deletions, click Cancel.

CAUTION
After you click that OK button, your deletions are permanent. You cannot undo them, so ponder deeply before clicking that mouse or you could be forced to reinstall!

Importing a DTD or schema to create a new tag library

Dreamweaver enables you to create a new tag library by importing tags from an existing XML Document Type Definition (DTD) file or schema. In many instances, you may want to add a new tag library. If you're working on a proprietary server or a language that's not supported by Dreamweaver, you can add all the necessary tags into a new tag library.

To create a new tag library by importing a DTD file or schema, follow these steps:

1. Choose Edit ➪ Tag Libraries.
2. In the Tag Library Editor dialog box, click the Add (+) button and choose DTDSchema ➪ Import XML DTD or Schema File.
3. In the File Or Remote URL field, enter the file or URL of the DTD or schema file.
4. In the Tag Prefix field, enter the prefix to be used with the tags you're importing, to identify the tags as part of this tag library.
5. When you're finished, click OK to create your new tag library.

33

Summary

Dreamweaver's commitment to professional website authoring is most evident when you examine the program's customization capabilities. Virtually every website production house can benefit from some degree of personalization—and some clients absolutely require it. As you examine the ways in which you can make your productive life easier by extending Dreamweaver, keep the following points in mind:

- Dreamweaver includes a full range of customizable features: objects, behaviors, commands, third-party tags, Property inspectors, and translators. You can even extend the program's core feature set with the C-Level Extensibility option.
- You can use commands to affect any part of your HTML page and automate repetitive tasks.

- In addition to accessing custom commands through the Commands menu, you can configure them as objects for inclusion in the Insert panel. You can also make a command appear in any other standard Dreamweaver menu by altering the `menus.xml` file.
- To make it easy to work with XML and other non-HTML tags, Dreamweaver enables you to create custom tags complete with individual icons or highlighted content.
- You can use the Tag Library Editor to customize your Dreamweaver tag libraries.

In the next chapter, you learn how to create and use Dreamweaver server behaviors.

CHAPTER

34

Handling Server Behaviors

IN THIS CHAPTER

Using server behaviors

Altering applied server behaviors

Working with Dreamweaver's server behaviors

Adding new server behaviors

Crafting custom server behaviors

Server behaviors are the heart of Dreamweaver, the essential engine that puts the *dynamic* in dynamic web applications. Server behaviors insert server-model–specific code that handles everything from displaying dynamic data to authenticating users. Even the basic data source connection and the establishment of a recordset are, in reality, server behaviors. Without server behaviors, no dynamic capabilities would be possible in Dreamweaver.

Server behaviors are valuable for novices and veteran coders alike. They enable designers who have never heard of an ASP Request collection to gather information from a form—a procedure that utilizes the ASP Request collection—with point-and-click ease. Even serious code jockeys can appreciate the productivity potential of server behaviors, especially the capability to create their own. With the Server Behavior Builder, programmers can build a library of their custom functions, complete with fully functional dialog boxes for maximum flexibility. After these functions are crafted, you can drop any of the custom server behaviors directly onto the page—and, if need be, easily alter the parameters.

This chapter includes an overview of server behaviors, as well as basic information about their use and management. For your reference, you also find a detailed description of each of the standard Dreamweaver server behaviors. Finally, you look at ways to extend Dreamweaver's core functionality with the Server Behavior Builder.

Understanding Server Behaviors

In contrast to Dreamweaver's JavaScript behaviors—with their numerous required functions and many more optional ones—a server behavior may be as simple as one line of code. The difference, and it's a key one, is that the code is intended to be executed by the application server, not the browser.

Another difference between server behaviors and JavaScript behaviors is that server behavior code may exist outside the bounds of the HTML page. Any page with a recordset has a section of code before the opening <html> tag, and a smaller block of code after the closing </html> tag. Dreamweaver automatically places the code in the proper place—and code placement is very important on the server-side—when any of its standard server behaviors are used. Dreamweaver includes more than 25 standard server behaviors; the exact number varies for each server model. Figure 34-1 displays the available server behaviors for PHP.

FIGURE 34-1

Apply any server behavior from the Server Behaviors panel.

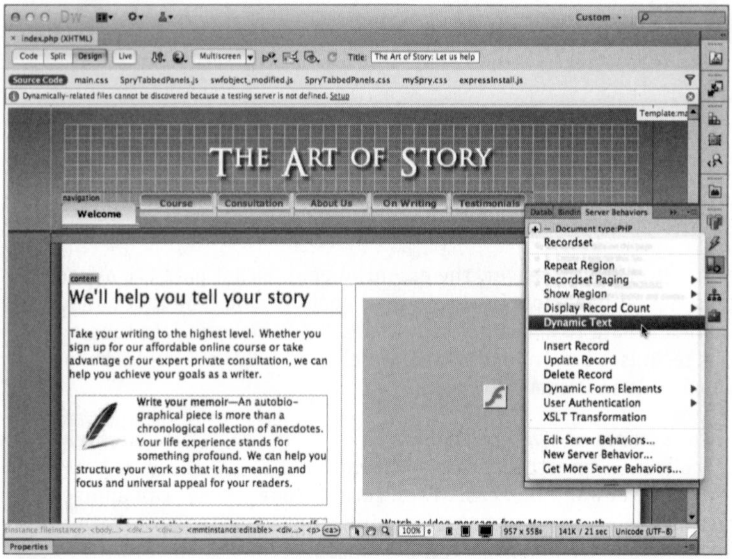

The Server Behaviors panel is the focal point for inserting, removing, and managing server behaviors. Unlike the Behaviors panel, which displays only the JavaScript behaviors attached to the selected tag, the Server Behaviors panel displays all the server behaviors included in the current page, in the order in which they were applied. Selecting a specific server behavior listed in the Server Behaviors panel highlights the attached page element, if visible in the Document window. Some server behaviors, such as Recordset, have their own Property inspector, whereas others display dynamic code as an attribute in a text or other Property inspector.

Although the simplest server behaviors can insert code without any additional user input, each built-in server behavior has a dialog box for specifying parameters. These vary in complexity from a single drop-down list to multiple-section dialog boxes with every type of input element available. As you learn in the next section, after you have inserted a server behavior, you can easily modify its parameters.

Applying and Managing Server Behaviors

If you have ever completed any web applications in Dreamweaver, you've likely already discovered how to apply and update a server behavior. The Server Behaviors panel is the primary tool for inserting, modifying, and removing server behaviors. You can display the Server Behaviors panel in several ways:

- Choose Window ➪ Server Behaviors.
- Select the Server Behaviors tab from the Application panel group.
- Use the keyboard shortcut, Ctrl+F9 (Command+F9).

The Server Behaviors panel remains available regardless of whether you are in Design view, Code view, or the split-screen Code and Design view.

Inserting and removing server behaviors

To add a particular server behavior to your page, click the Add (+) button in the Server Behaviors panel and select the desired behavior from the list. Many of the server behaviors have prerequisites—such as a recordset, form, or selected element—that must be in place before they can be installed, but these requirements vary from server behavior to server behavior. If you attempt to insert a server behavior and some precondition has not been met, Dreamweaver alerts you to the missing element; you are prevented from inserting the server behavior until all the required pieces are in place.

After you select the server behavior from the Add drop-down list, a dialog box appears to enable you to select or enter the needed parameters. Each dialog box is specific to the chosen server behavior, and they vary widely in terms of parameters offered and complexity. For information about a specific server behavior, see the corresponding section for that server behavior later in this chapter. Each section provides step-by-step explanations about completing the pertinent dialog box.

Removing an existing server behavior is simple. Select the entry for the server behavior in the Server Behaviors panel and click the Remove (–) button. Dreamweaver immediately removes all the associated code without requesting confirmation.

CAUTION
With JavaScript behaviors, if you delete a page element that has a client-side behavior attached, you automatically delete that behavior. This is not always the case with server behaviors, and it's best to always use the Server Behaviors panel's Remove (–) button before deleting any associated text, graphics, or form elements.

Editing the parameters

To modify the attributes or parameters of an inserted server behavior, double-click its entry in the Server Behaviors panel. You can differentiate between multiple applications of the same server behavior in two ways. First, the entry for each server behavior lists one or two of its key attributes in parentheses. For example, a Dynamic Text server behavior applied to the `LastName` column in the `rsMaillist` recordset is displayed as follows:

```
Dynamic Text(rsMaillist.LastName)
```

Second, you can tell which server behavior is associated with which page element by selecting the server behavior—the associated text, graphic, or other page element is also selected in Design or Code view.

When the dialog box for a server behavior reopens, you can alter any of the parameters that remain active. In some situations, as with the Go To Detail Page server behavior shown in Figure 34-2, one or more fields may be disabled and so rendered unable to be changed. If you need to alter a disabled parameter, delete the server behavior and reapply it.

FIGURE 34-2

When modifying certain server behaviors, some fields, such as the Link field in this Go To Detail Page dialog box, are disabled and cannot be changed.

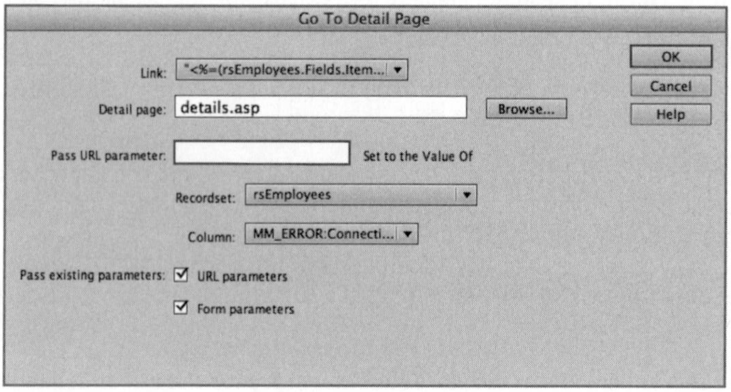

Standard Server Behaviors

Dreamweaver ships with more than 25 server behaviors, and it offers the option to add many more. The default server behaviors are geared toward handling basic web application tasks such as repeating an area and inserting records in a data source.

In the following sections, each server behavior is briefly described, along with any prerequisites. Step-by-step instructions for including the server behavior are provided; for more contextual information on using the particular server behavior, see the cross-referenced chapter.

Recordset (Query)

To create a simple recordset, follow these steps:

1. From the Server Behaviors panel, click the Add (+) button and choose Recordset (Query) from the drop-down list. The Recordset dialog box, shown in Figure 34-3, is displayed.

FIGURE 34-3

You can add recordsets from either the Server Behaviors panel or the Bindings panel through two different dialog boxes; the Simple Recordset dialog box is shown here.

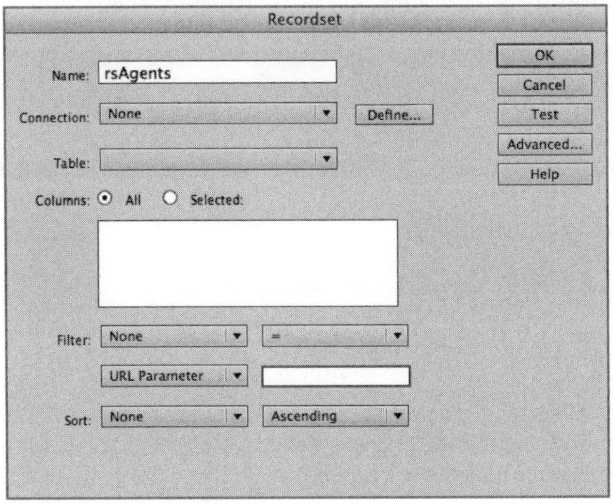

2. In the Recordset dialog box, enter an identifying label for your recordset in the Name field. It's considered good practice to prefix your recordset name with `rs`, as in `rsDBA`. This prefix quickly identifies the recordset in the code.
3. Select a connection from the drop-down list of that name.
4. If the desired connection has not been declared, click Define to open the Connections dialog box. After a connection has been selected, the available tables are shown.
5. Select a table to work with from the Tables drop-down list. The chosen table's fields are displayed in the Columns list.
6. By default, all the columns are included in the recordset. To specify certain columns, choose the Selected option and select any desired field. Shift+click to select contiguous columns, and Ctrl+click (Command+click) to select noncontiguous columns.
7. By default, all the records in the selected columns are available. To limit the recordset further, use the four Filter drop-down lists as follows:
   - Choose the field on which you want to base your filter from the first drop-down list. This list changes dynamically according to which table you've selected.

34

- From the second drop-down list, select the expression with which to compare the data from the selected column in the first drop-down list. Available expressions are =, >, <, >=, <=, <>, Begins With, Ends With, and Contains.
- Choose the type of value to compare to the selected field from the third drop-down list. Available types are URL Parameter, Form Variable, Cookie, Session Variable, Application Variable, and Entered Value.
- In the fourth input field, enter the value to compare to the selected field. Values entered are not case-sensitive.

8. To sort the data, select a column from the first drop-down list under Sort and choose either Ascending or Descending from the second list.
9. At any time, you can see what results will be returned for the recordset by clicking Test.

TIP

To see how your simple recordset translates into SQL, click the Advanced button. You can return to the original dialog box by clicking Simple on the advanced Recordset dialog box.

10. Click OK when you're finished.

For more information on defining recordsets, see Chapter 18.

Repeat Region

The Repeat Region server behavior replicates a selected page area as many times as specified. If the Repeat Region surrounds dynamic data, the record pointer advances for each repetition. A tab and highlight note the boundaries of the Repeat Region when the Invisible Elements option is enabled.

Requirements: One or more selected page elements, such as a table row or a line ending in a line break tag (<br>).

To implement a Repeat Region, follow these steps:

1. Select the dynamic data and the surrounding code you'd like to repeat.
2. From the Server Behaviors panel, click the Add (+) button and select Repeat Region from the list.

   The Repeat Region dialog box, shown in Figure 34-4, appears.
3. From the Repeat Region dialog box, choose the recordset you want to work with from the Recordset list.
4. If you want to display a subset of the recordset, enter the number of records you'd like to display in the Show Records field.
5. If you want every record in the recordset to be displayed, choose the Show All Records option.
6. Click OK when you're done.

FIGURE 34-4

With the Repeat Region server behavior, you can show some or all of the records in the chosen recordset.

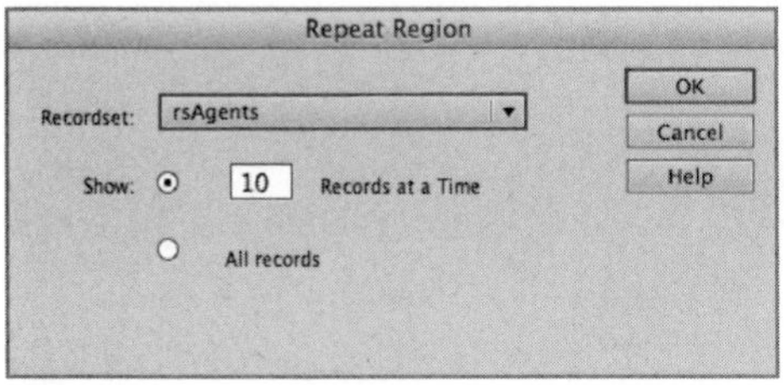

For more information on the Repeat Region server behavior, see Chapter 20.

Recordset Paging

The Recordset Paging server behaviors move the record pointer to the indicated data record in a given recordset. They are frequently used in combination to navigate through a recordset. In all, five Recordset Paging server behaviors exist; however, you insert the following four in an identical fashion:

- Move To First Page
- Move To Previous Page
- Move To Next Page
- Move To Last Page

The fifth server behavior in this category, Move To Specific Record, uses a different procedure, which is covered in the following section.

Requirements: A selected page element and at least one recordset with more than one returned row.

To use any of the four basic Recordset Paging server behaviors, follow these steps:

1. Select the text or image to which you'd like to attach the server behavior.
2. From the Server Behaviors panel, click the Add (+) button and choose the desired behavior from the Recordset Paging submenu. The appropriate Recordset Paging dialog box appears. Your selection is highlighted in the Link list, as shown in Figure 34-5.
3. Make sure that the link selected is one of those showing in the Link list.
4. Choose the recordset you want to work with from the Recordset drop-down list.
5. Click OK when you're finished.

For more information on these Recordset Paging server behaviors, see Chapter 20.

34

FIGURE 34-5

The Recordset Paging server behaviors (such as Move To Last Page) identify your selected target, which may be an image or text.

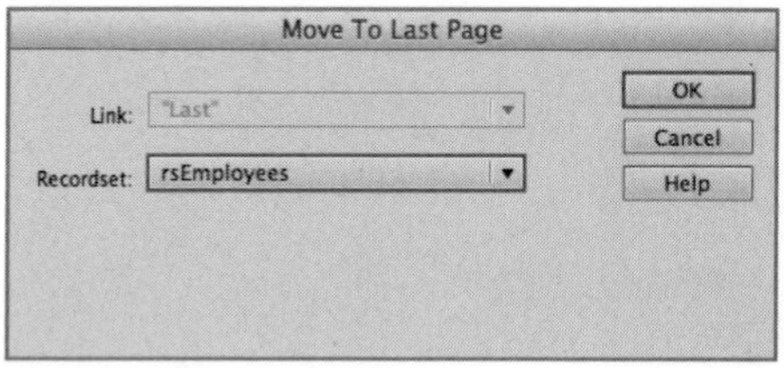

Move To Specific Record

The Move To Specific Record server behavior is used after a recordset has been created to navigate through the records. To use the Move To Specific Record server behavior (not available in ColdFusion or PHP), follow these steps:

1. Select the text or image to which you'd like to attach the server behavior.
2. From the Server Behaviors panel, choose Move To Specific Record from the Recordset Paging submenu. The Move To Specific Record dialog box is displayed, as shown in Figure 34-6.

FIGURE 34-6

An alternative method for creating a detail page uses the Move To Specific Record server behavior.

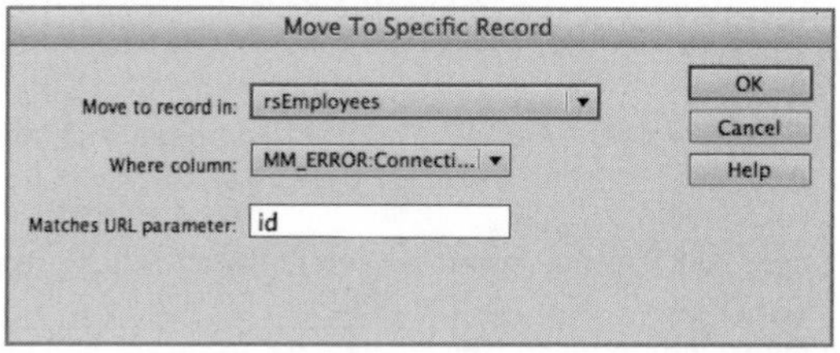

3. Select the desired recordset from the list labeled Move To Record In.
4. Choose the field referenced in the URL parameter from the Where Column field.
5. Enter the variable in the URL parameter in the Matches URL Parameter field.
6. Click OK when you're finished.

For more information on the Move To Specific Record server behavior, see Chapter 22.

Show Region

The Show Region server behavior displays an area of the screen if a particular condition is true. These are often called conditional regions. A different set of server behaviors applies for each server model.

ColdFusion and PHP:

- Show If Recordset Is Empty
- Show If Recordset Is Not Empty
- Show If First Page
- Show If Not First Page
- Show If Last Page
- Show If Not Last Page

ASP VBScript:

- Show Region If Recordset Is Empty
- Show Region If Recordset Is Not Empty
- Show Region If First Record
- Show Region If Not First Record
- Show Region If Last Record
- Show Region If Not Last Record

Requirements: One or more selected page elements and at least one recordset.

Applying a Show Region server behavior is straightforward. Just follow these steps:

1. Select the page area you'd like to show conditionally.
2. From the Server Behaviors panel, click the Add (+) button and select one of the server behaviors from the Show Region submenu. The dialog box for the specific Show Region server behavior you chose is displayed, like the one shown in Figure 34-7. The dialog boxes for all the Show Region server behaviors are identical.

FIGURE 34-7

To use any of the Show Region server behaviors, just choose a recordset.

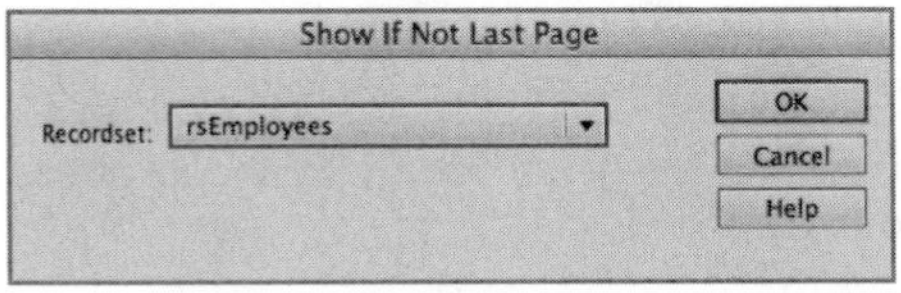

3. Select the recordset on which to base the Show Region condition from the Recordset list.
4. Click OK when you're finished.

For more information on the Show Region server behavior, see Chapter 20.

Go To Detail Page

The Go To Detail Page server behavior is used in master-detail web applications to navigate from a chosen link on the master page to a designated detail page. This server behavior passes a unique record ID via the URL query string method. The Go To Detail Page server behavior is only available with ASP VBScript.

For more on master-detail web applications, see Chapter 23.

Requirements: A selected page element and at least one recordset.

To attach a Go To Detail Page server behavior, follow these steps:

1. Select the page element—text, graphic, or dynamic data—you'd like to use as the link to the detail page.
2. From the Server Behaviors panel, click the Add (+) button and select Go To Detail Page from the drop-down list. The Go To Detail Page dialog box, shown in Figure 34-8, is displayed.

FIGURE 34-8

Specify the linking parameter sent from the master page in the Go To Detail Page server behavior.

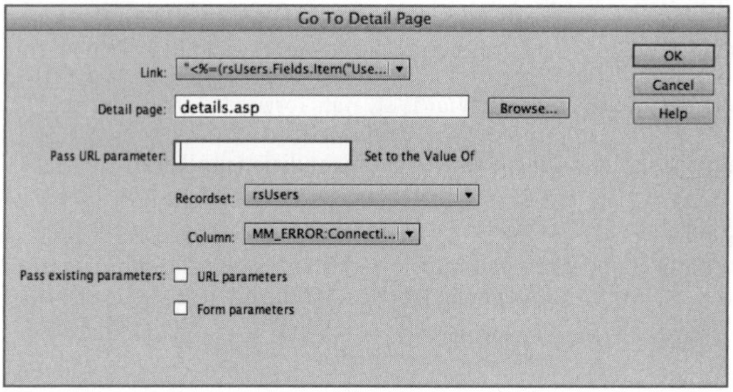

3. Make sure that the page element selected is represented in the Link field. If no selection was made, Dreamweaver creates a new Detail text link.
4. Enter the path to the detail page in the Detail Page field or click Browse to locate the file in the Select File dialog box.
5. Enter the variable name you'd like to be sent in the Pass URL Parameter field. You can use a name of your own choosing or the name of the field in the database. Whichever name you decide upon, make a note of it somewhere because you need to reference it when the detail page itself is constructed.
6. Select the recordset of the URL parameter from the Recordset list.
7. From the Column list, choose the field to which the URL parameter's value is related.

8. Unless you have preexisting URL or Form parameters to send to the detail page, leave the Pass Existing Parameters options unchecked.
9. Click OK when you're finished.

For more information on the Go To Detail Page server behavior, see Chapter 22.

Go To Related Page (ASP only)

The Go To Related Page server behavior links to a new page that conveys the form and/or URL variables previously passed to the current page.

Requirements: A selected page element and at least one recordset. The page on which the server behavior is inserted must have had form or URL values passed to it.

To attach a Go To Related Page server behavior, follow these steps:

1. Select the page element—text, image, or dynamic data—you'd like to use as the trigger for your behavior.
2. From the Server Behaviors panel, click the Add (+) button and select Go To Related Page from the list. The Go To Related Page server behavior dialog box appears, as shown in Figure 34-9.

FIGURE 34-9

The Go To Related Page server behavior can convey form values, URL values, or both to another dynamic page.

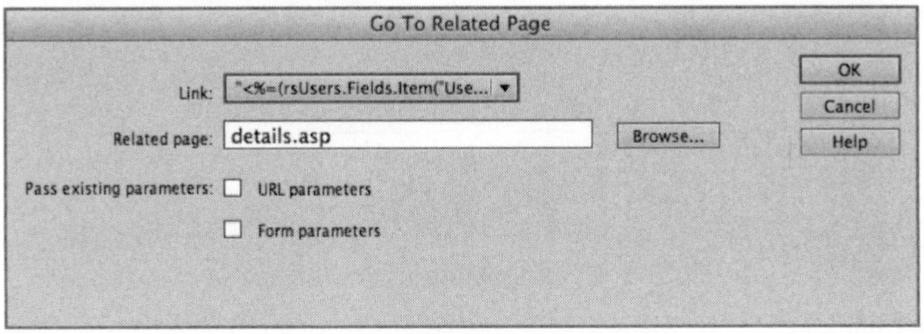

3. In the dialog box, verify that the text or code for the selected element displayed in the Link field is correct.
4. Enter the path to the target page in the Related Page field or click Browse to locate an existing dynamic page.
5. If you want to carry over values received from a query string, select the URL Parameters option.
6. If you want to pass values received from a form, select the Form Parameters option.
7. Click OK when you're finished.

For more information on the Go To Related Page server behavior, see Chapter 22.

Insert Record

The Insert Record server behavior adds a new record to a chosen table in a data source.

> **Requirements:** A form with form elements and a Submit button.

To add the Insert Record server behavior, follow these steps:

1. From the Server Behaviors panel, click the Add (+) button and select Insert Record. The Insert Record dialog box appears, as shown in Figure 34-10.

FIGURE 34-10

Users may add new data directly to a connected data source.

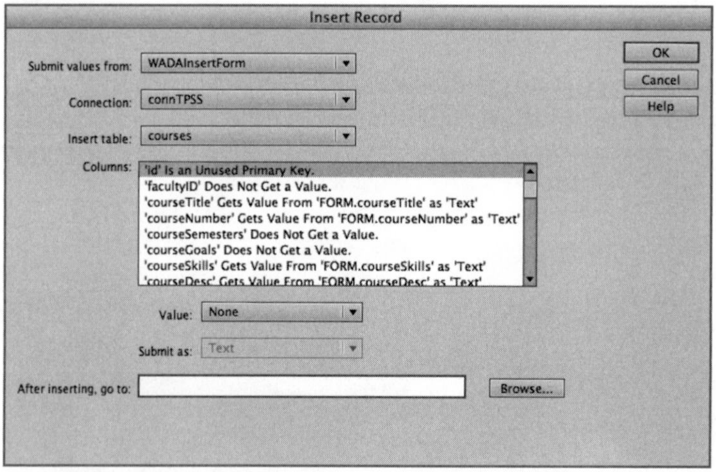

2. From the Insert Record dialog box, choose the connection from the drop-down list. If you need to establish a new connection, click Define.
3. Select the data table you want to use from the Insert table list.
4. Enter the path to the destination page in the After Inserting, Go To field, or click the Browse button to locate the file. It's important that you select a confirmation or other page to go to after the form is submitted. If you don't, no feedback is provided to the user, and no change is apparent.
5. Select the name of the form to be used from the Get Values From list. If there is only one form on the page, the form is preselected.
6. For each object listed in the Form Elements area:
   - Select the data source field into which the form object's value is to be inserted from the Columns list.
   - Choose the data source type for the data from the Submit As list. The options are Text; Integer; Double; Date; Checkbox Y, N; Checkbox 1,0; and Check -1,0.
7. Click OK when you're finished.

NOTE
Be sure to give your form fields meaningful names so you can easily choose which form field goes into each database column.

For more information on the Insert Record server behavior, see Chapter 22.

Update Record

Use the Update Record server behavior to modify existing records in a data source.

Requirements: A recordset, a form with form elements linked to the dynamic data, and a Submit button.

To insert an Update Record server behavior, follow these steps:

1. From the Server Behaviors panel, choose Update Record. The Update Record dialog box appears, as shown in Figure 34-11.

FIGURE 34-11

With an Update Record server behavior, you can modify your data source remotely.

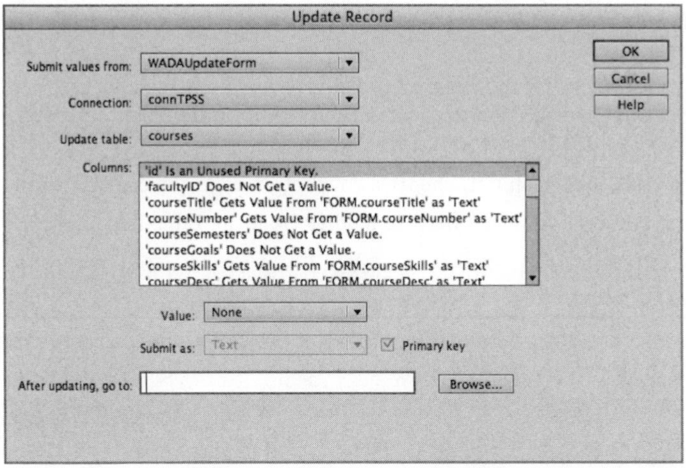

2. From the Update Record dialog box, choose the form you want to use to update your records from the Submit Values From List. If there is only one form on the page, the form is preselected.
3. Choose a connection from the drop-down list.
4. Select the data table you want to use from the Update Table list.

5. For each database field that you want to update listed in the Columns area:
   - Select the data source field into which the form object's value is to be inserted from the Columns list.
   - Choose the data source type for the data from the Submit As list. The options are Text; Numeric; Double; Date; Checkbox Y, N; Checkbox 1,0; and Check -1,0.
6. Enter the path to the destination page in the After Updating, Go To field or click the Browse button to locate the file.
7. Click OK when you're finished.

For more information on the Update Record server behavior, see Chapter 22.

Delete Record

The Delete Record server behavior is used to remove existing records from a data source.

Requirements: A recordset, a form, and a Submit button.

To attach a Delete Record server behavior to a form, follow these steps:

1. Make sure that a form exists on a dynamic page that includes at least one recordset.
2. From the Server Behaviors panel, choose Delete Record. The Delete Record dialog box is displayed, as shown in Figure 34-12.
3. PHP and ColdFusion users: Choose the desired option from the First Check If Variable Is Defined list.

   Leave the entry set to Primary Key Value if you are using a form to confirm the deletion. If you want the deletion to occur without confirmation, choose another entry from the list such as URL Parameter or Form Variable.
4. From the Connection list, choose a connection from the drop-down list.
5. Select the data table you want to modify from the Table list.

FIGURE 34-12

Maintain an up-to-date data source with the Delete Record server behavior, shown here for a PHP page.

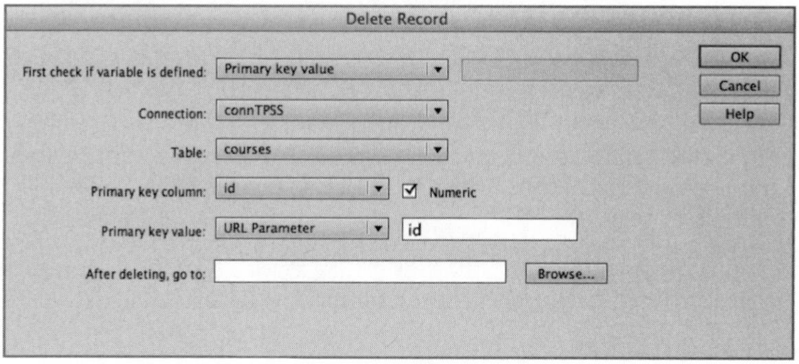

6. Select the key field from the Primary Key Column list. Dreamweaver attempts to detect whether the field is a number type, and if it is, it selects the Numeric option.
7. Choose the variable that holds the Primary Key value from that menu and enter the name of the variable in the adjacent field.
8. Enter the path to the destination page in the After Deleting, Go To field or click the Browse button to locate the file.
9. Click OK when you're finished.

For more information on the Delete Record server behavior, see Chapter 22.

User authentication

The web is all about accessing information from anywhere in the world. Sometimes, however, you need to restrict access to certain areas of your site to authorized users. Dreamweaver supplies a full complement of server behaviors to support authenticating the user against a specified data source.

Log In User

The Log In User server behavior redirects authorized users to one page and unauthorized users to another and creates a session variable for the username.

Requirements: A recordset, a form, appropriate form elements for a username and a password, and a Submit button.

To attach a Log In User server behavior to a form, follow these steps:

1. From the Server Behaviors panel, click the Add (+) button and choose User Authentication ➪ Log In User. The Log In User dialog box is displayed, as shown in Figure 34-13.
2. If there is more than one form on the page, select the form containing the username and password fields from the Get Input From Form list.
3. Select the form element used to gather the username from the Username Field list.
4. Select the form element used to gather the password from the Password Field list.
5. Choose a connection to the data source containing the table of registered users from the Validate Using Connection list.
6. Select the table of registered users from the Table list.
7. Choose the field containing the username from the Username Column list.
8. Choose the field containing the password from the Password Column list.
9. Enter the path to the page for the authorized user in the If Login Succeeds, Go To field.
10. If you want the user to proceed to the previously selected link, rather than the page entered in Step 9, select the Go To Previous URL option.
11. Enter the path to the page for the unauthorized user in the If Login Fails, Go To field.

FIGURE 34-13

The Log In User server behavior verifies that the user may be granted access.

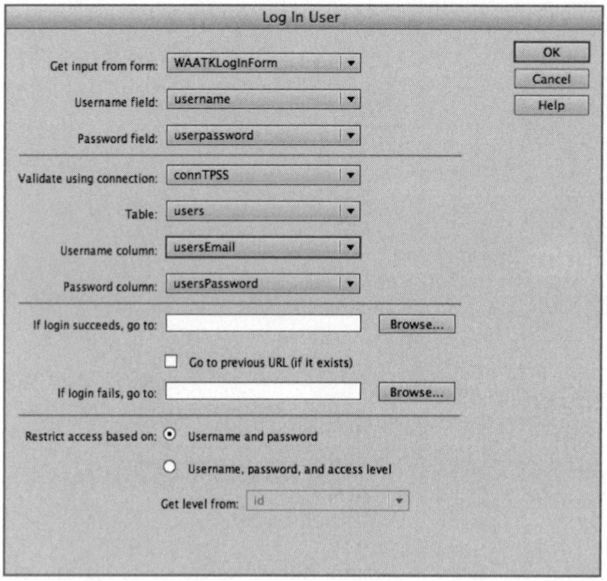

12. If access levels should be evaluated as part of the authentication:
    - Select the Restrict Access Based On Username And Password, or Username, Password, And Access Level options.
    - Choose the data source field containing the access level data from the Get Level From list.
13. Click OK when you're finished.

For more information on the Log In User server behavior, see Chapter 22.

Restrict Access To Page

The Restrict Access To Page server behavior prevents unauthorized users from viewing specific pages by checking a session variable. After it is defined, the server behavior can be copied and pasted onto another page by using the context menu commands from the Server Behaviors panel.

Requirements: A dynamic page.

To apply the Restrict Access To Page server behavior, follow these steps:

1. From the Server Behaviors panel, click the Add (+) button and choose User Authentication ➪ Restrict Access To Page. The Restrict Access To Page dialog box, shown in Figure 34-14, is displayed.
2. If you don't want to restrict admission by access levels, be sure that the Restrict Based On Username And Password option is selected.

3. To set group permissions for the page:
   - Choose the Restrict Based On Username, Password, And Access Level option.
   - Choose one or more groups from the Select Level(s) area.

FIGURE 34-14

Any dynamic page can be protected against unauthorized viewing with the Restrict Access To Page server behavior.

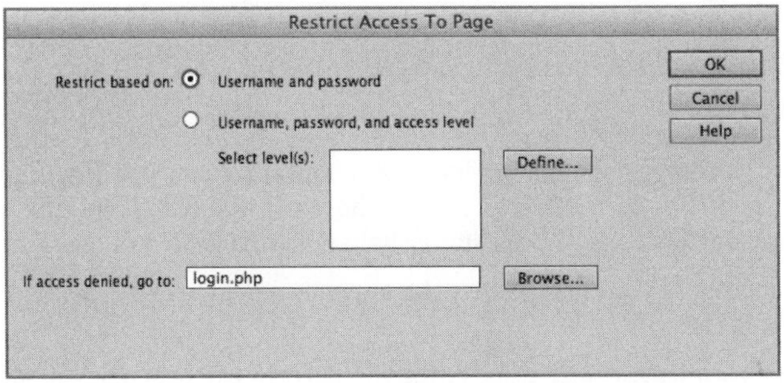

4. To add new groups to the Select Level(s) list:
   - Click Define. The Define Access Levels dialog box opens.
   - Enter the name for the access level in the Name field. The name must match a value stored in your data source in whichever column is designated for the group access levels.
   - To add additional levels, click the Add (+) button and enter another name.
   - To delete any levels, choose the level in the list area and click the Remove (–) button.
   - Click OK to close the Define Access Levels dialog box.
5. Enter the path to the file to which you want to redirect unauthorized users in the If Access Denied, Go To field. Alternatively, click the Browse button to locate the file.
6. Click OK when you're finished.

For more information on the Restrict Access To Page server behavior, see Chapter 22.

Log Out User

The Log Out User server behavior clears the username session variable established by the Log In User server behavior and redirects the user to an exit page. You can set up the Log Out User server behavior so that a user selects a link to log out or is automatically logged out when a particular page, such as one confirming the completion of an order, is viewed.

Requirements: A Log In User server behavior on another page.

To use the Log Out User server behavior, follow these steps:

1. To apply the server behavior to a specific link on the page, select that link.
2. From the Server Behaviors panel, click the Add (+) button and choose User Authentication ➪ Log Out User. The Log Out User dialog box displays (see Figure 34-15).

FIGURE 34-15

You can let the user decide when to log out by choosing the Log Out When Link Clicked option on an order confirmation page.

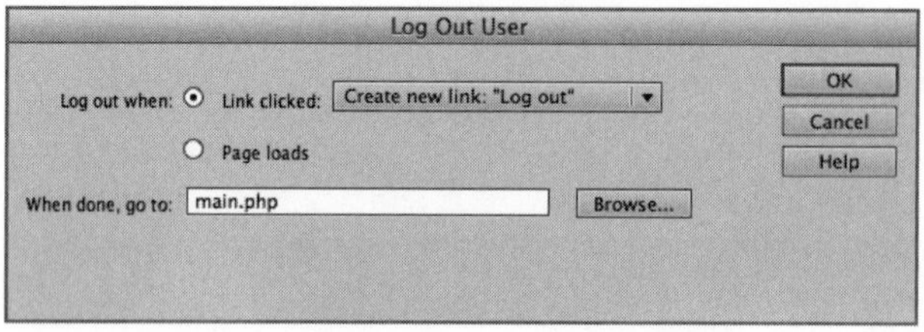

3. To trigger the server behavior with a link, choose the Log Out When Link Clicked option and make sure that your selected link is chosen in the list. If no link was preselected, Dreamweaver offers to apply the server behavior to a new link, Log Out.
4. To automatically log out users when the current page is viewed, select the Log Out When Page Loads option.
5. If you're using a link as a trigger, enter the path to the destination page in the When Done, Go To field. Alternatively, click the Browse button to locate the file.

CAUTION
Do not use the When Done, Go To option if you are automatically logging out a user when the page loads. If you do, the user never sees the current page.

6. Click OK when you're finished.

For more information on the Log Out User server behavior, see Chapter 22.

Check New Username

The Check New Username server behavior verifies that the requested username is not already in the data source, redirecting the user if it is.

Requirements: An Insert Record server behavior, a form, and appropriate form elements.

To use the Check New Username server behavior, follow these steps:

1. From the Server Behaviors panel, click the Add (+) button and choose User Authentication ➪ Check New Username. The Check New Username dialog box is displayed, as shown in Figure 34-16.
2. Select the form element that contains the requested username from the Username Field list. If a form element is called USERNAME, Dreamweaver automatically selects that entry.

3. In the If Already Exists, Go To field, enter the path to the file you want a user to see if the name the user requested is already stored in the data source. You can also click Browse to locate the file.
4. Click OK when you're finished.

FIGURE 34-16

Make sure that a requested username is not already taken by using the Check New Username server behavior.

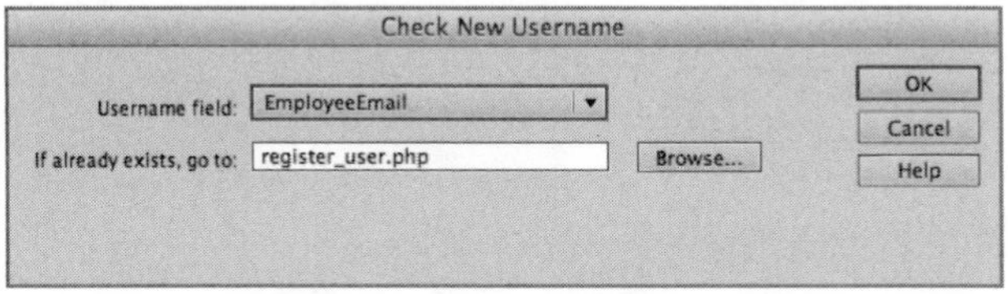

For more information on the Check New Username server behavior, see Chapter 22.

Dynamic elements

With one exception, dynamic elements in Dreamweaver refer to form elements, linked to a data source field. Data-connected form elements are typically used in web applications that update records. The single exception is Dynamic Text, which is described in the following section. Dynamic Form Elements are covered later.

Dynamic Text

Inserting a Dynamic Text server behavior is the same as dragging a field from a recordset on the Bindings panel onto the page. It's a matter of individual preference which technique you use; personally, I find dragging-and-dropping from the Bindings panel much faster and more intuitive than using the Dynamic Text server behavior.

34

Requirements: A dynamic page.

To use the Dynamic Text server behavior, follow these steps:

1. Place your cursor on the page where you'd like the dynamic text to appear.
2. From the Server Behaviors panel, choose Dynamic Text. The Dynamic Text dialog box is displayed, as shown in Figure 34-17.
3. If necessary, expand the recordset or other data source to select the desired dynamic data.
4. Choose any necessary server format from the Format list.

FIGURE 34-17

You can insert dynamic text through either the Server Behaviors panel or the Bindings panel.

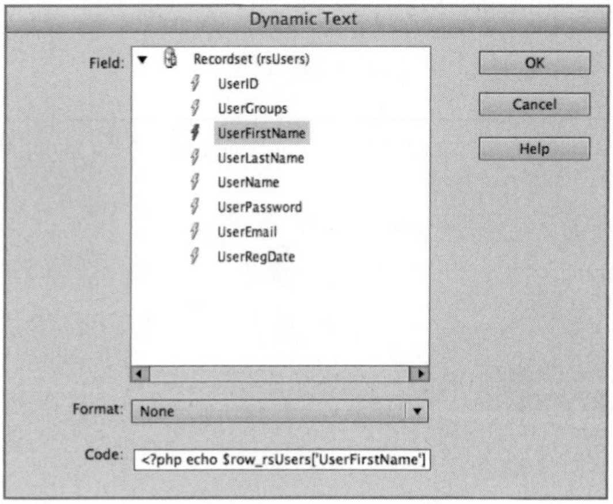

5. Enter any required adjustments to the dynamic data in the Code field. In most situations, no changes are necessary.
6. Click OK when you're finished.

For more information on adding dynamic text, see Chapter 21.

Dynamic List/Menu

The Dynamic List/Menu server behavior binds data to one or more aspects of a drop-down list. Dynamic data from a recordset is typically bound to both the values and the labels of a list or menu element; static values and labels may also be combined with the dynamic data. In addition, you have the option to dynamically set the selected value, a feature often used when updating a record.

Requirements: A list/menu form element and a recordset.

To link a drop-down list to dynamic data, follow these steps:

1. Insert a list/menu form element on a dynamic page with a recordset.
2. If you have more than one list/menu on the page, select the one you want to convert.
3. From the Server Behaviors panel, choose Dynamic Form Elements ⇨ Dynamic List/Menu. The Dynamic List/Menu dialog box, shown in Figure 34-18, is displayed.
4. Verify that the desired drop-down list is displayed in the Menu list.
5. In the Static Options box, add any nondynamic items you want to the top of the list menu. This could be something as simple as a label for the list menu or as complicated as a full URL with query strings for search pages.
6. Choose the recordset you want to work with from the Options From Recordset list.

FIGURE 34-18

Lists give the user a series of items from which to choose.

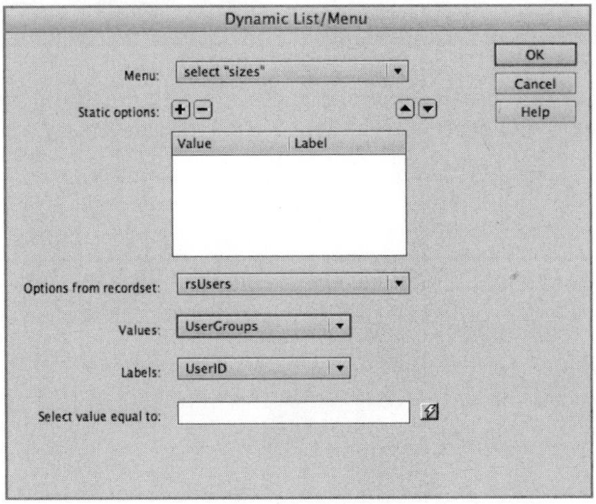

7. Choose the field from your data source containing the items you want submitted by the user from the Values list.
8. Choose the field from your data source containing the items that you want displayed to the user from the Labels list.
9. To preselect an item, enter its value in the Select Value Equal To field or use the lightning bolt icon to choose a value from the established data sources.
10. Click OK when you're finished.

For more information on the Dynamic List/Menu server behavior, see Chapter 22.

Dynamic Text Field

Unlike the Dynamic Text server behavior, the Dynamic Text Field server behavior is not just for show. The Dynamic Text Field server behavior is often used for applications that update records and may be applied to either a text field or a text area form element. According to the server model used, the data in the text field can be formatted server-side in a number of ways, such as upper- or lowercase.

Requirements: A text field or text area form element and a recordset.

To link a text field or text area to dynamic data, follow these steps:

1. Insert a text field into a form on a page with a recordset or other data source. It's a good idea to name the text field and form at this point. Although you can always change the names later, naming the elements early on avoids problems later.
2. Select the text field.
3. From the Server Behaviors panel, choose Dynamic Form Elements ⇨ Dynamic Text Field.

CAUTION
Be sure to choose Dynamic Text Field and not Dynamic Text from the Dynamic Elements submenu. If you select Dynamic Text while your text field is highlighted, the form element is replaced.

4. In the Dynamic Text Field dialog box that appears (see Figure 34-19), verify that the correct form element was chosen in the Text Field list. If necessary, choose a different text field.

FIGURE 34-19

You can make a data field editable by connecting it to a Dynamic Text Field.

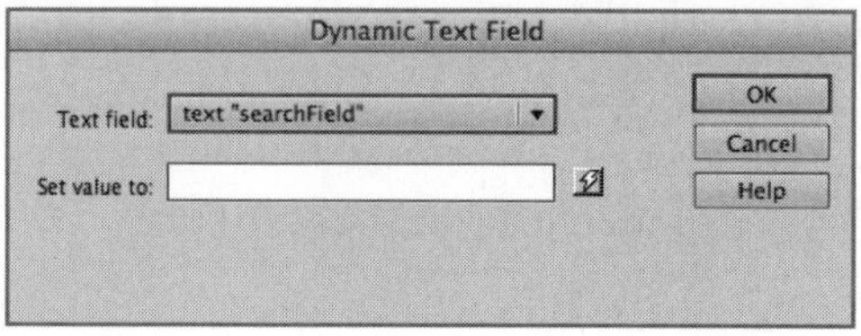

5. Click the Set Value To lightning bolt icon to display the available data sources.
6. Choose a field from the Dynamic Data dialog box.
7. If desired, you can apply a server format to the data by choosing an entry in the Format list.
8. Click OK to close the Dynamic Data dialog box and, after reviewing your choices, click OK again to close the Dynamic Text Field dialog box.

For more information on the Dynamic Text Field server behavior, see Chapter 22.

Dynamic CheckBox

Checkboxes provide users with a method of selecting one or more options in a group; a Dynamic CheckBox server behavior marks any affiliated checkbox as selected if the desired criteria are met. This server behavior is often used in conjunction with a boolean data field, also known as a True/False or Yes/No data field.

Requirements: A checkbox form element and a recordset.

To convert a static checkbox to a dynamic one, follow these steps:

1. Select a checkbox in a form on a page with a recordset.
2. From the Server Behaviors panel, choose Dynamic Form Elements ➪ Dynamic CheckBox. The Dynamic CheckBox dialog box appears, as shown in Figure 34-20.

3. Verify that your selected checkbox is correctly named in the CheckBox list.
4. Click the Check If lightning bolt icon to display the available data sources.
5. Choose a field from the Dynamic Data dialog box.
6. If desired, you can apply a server format to the data by choosing an entry in the Format list. Click OK when you're finished to close the Dynamic Data dialog box.

FIGURE 34-20

Checkboxes can depict whether a particular field of a recordset is True or False.

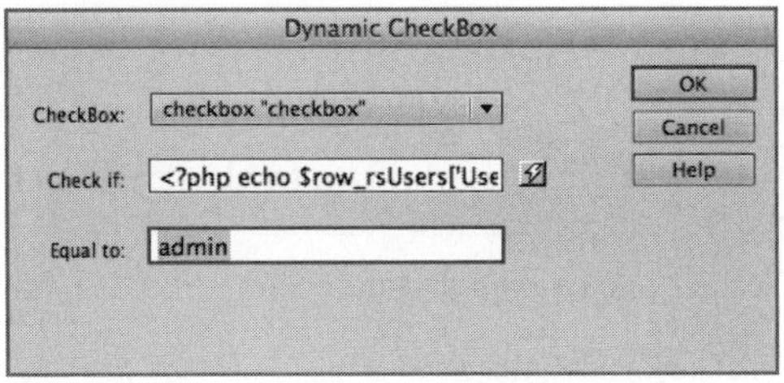

7. Enter the value expected for a selected checkbox in the Equal To field. This value is data source-dependent. For many data sources, 1 is used to represent True; for others, a -1 is used. When working with Yes/No fields from Access databases, enter **True**; be sure to capitalize the word, because lowercase does not work properly.
8. Click OK when you're finished.

For more information on the Dynamic CheckBox server behavior, see Chapter 22.

Dynamic Radio Buttons

Radio buttons are employed in a form when the designer wants the user to make an exclusive choice among a set number of options. As with the Dynamic CheckBox server behavior, the Dynamic Radio Buttons server behavior is used to mark a particular element as selected when the defined criteria are met.

Requirements: Two or more radio button form elements and a recordset.

To link radio buttons to dynamic data, follow these steps:

1. Select a radio button on a dynamic page with an available data source.
2. From the Server Behaviors panel, choose Dynamic Form Elements ➪ Dynamic Radio Buttons. The Dynamic Radio Buttons dialog box appears, as shown in Figure 34-21.
3. Verify that your selected form element is displayed in the Radio Button Group list.
4. Click the Select Value Equal To lightning bolt icon to display the available data sources.

FIGURE 34-21

Radio buttons can reflect a limited number of choices within a data source field.

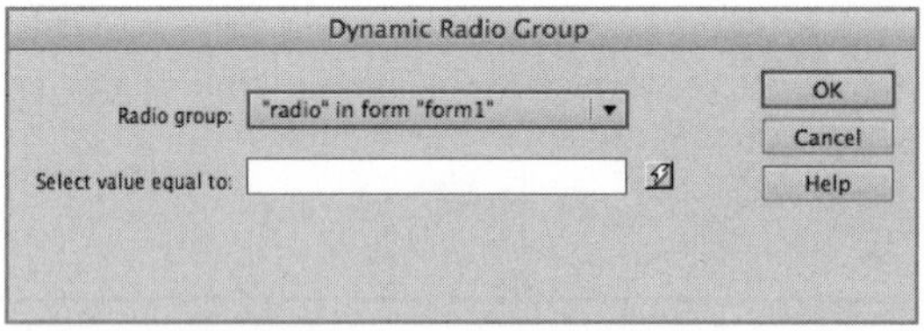

5. Choose a field from the Dynamic Data dialog box. Be sure to select a data source field with values parallel to those entered in the radio button group.
6. If desired, you can apply a server format to the data by choosing an entry in the Format list. Click OK to close the Dynamic Data dialog box.
7. When you're finished, click OK to close the Dynamic Radio Buttons dialog box.

For more information on the Dynamic Radio Buttons server behavior, see Chapter 22.

Stored procedure/command/callable

Many advanced web applications use a stored procedure application object. Stored procedures are known under a variety of names: ASP users call them *commands*, whereas PHP and ColdFusion users refer to them solely as *stored procedures*. Stored procedures are complete SQL queries that may return recordsets or other data. Stored procedures are often used for complex data source management such as inserting new tables on the fly.

NOTE

Although the current version of PHP can handle stored procedures, Dreamweaver does not at present support them for that server model.

Stored procedures are created and compiled in the data source itself, such as Microsoft's SQL Server. Because they are precompiled, they execute faster than similar SQL statements entered directly into the web application. Stored procedures, like recordsets, can be defined as a data source through either the Bindings panel or the Server Behaviors panel.

To define a stored procedure as a data source through the Server Behaviors panel, follow these steps:

1. From the Server Behaviors panel, click the Add (+) button and, for ASP, choose Command (Stored Procedure); for ColdFusion, choose Stored Procedure. The Stored Procedure dialog box for the appropriate server model is displayed; for example, Figure 34-22 shows the Command dialog box seen by ASP users.
2. In the Command/Stored Procedure field, enter a unique name.

FIGURE 34-22

Stored procedures must be included in the data source before they can be added as a data source in Dreamweaver.

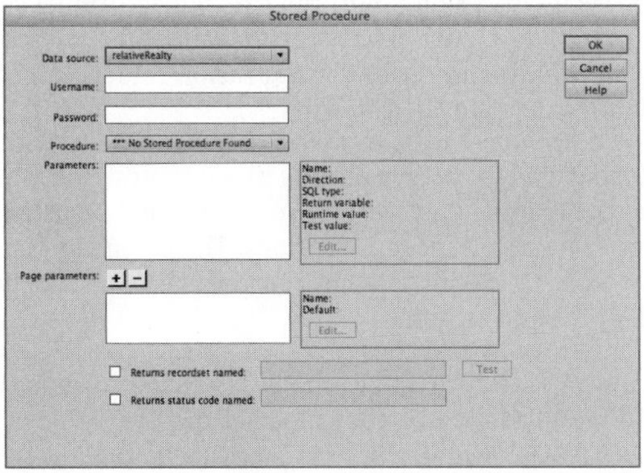

NOTE

Stored procedures and the variables necessary to use them are database- and server model-dependent. A stored procedure on SQL server is completely different from a ColdFusion stored procedure or another SQL-type database. The Stored Procedure/Command dialog box may change based on the type of database to which you're connecting, as well as the server model.

3. From the Connection list, choose the connection in which this stored procedure may be found.
4. ASP users should choose Stored Procedure from the Type list.

NOTE

The ASP Command (Stored Procedure) server behavior includes additional types: Insert, Update, and Delete. These work identically to the Prepared (Insert/Update/Delete) server behavior.

34

5. If the stored procedure returns a recordset, choose the Return Recordset option and enter a name in the Returned Recordset Named field.
6. From the Database Items area, expand the Stored Procedures list and choose the desired stored procedure. It's a good idea to click Test to be sure your connection is working properly at this point.
7. To modify the stored procedure, select any other element in the Database Items area and click the Procedure or Where button.
8. Enter any necessary variables by clicking the Add (+) button in the Variables area and entering the values under each column: Name, Type, Direction, Size, Default Value, and Runtime Value.
9. Click OK when you're finished.

Installing Additional Server Behaviors

Although Dreamweaver's standard server behaviors perform many important functions, they're just the tip of the iceberg in terms of what's possible. You can add additional server behaviors—whether created by Adobe, yourself, or a third party—at any time. Although you can transfer files to the appropriate places in the Dreamweaver Configuration folder, most custom server behaviors rely on the Extension Manager for installation.

The Extension Manager is an auxiliary program that installs files compressed in the Adobe Extension Program format; such files carry an `.mxp` file extension. To access the Extension Manager, choose Commands ➪ Manage Extensions or Help ➪ Manage Extensions. The Extension Manager displays all the extensions—including server behaviors—installed in your system. It also includes information about each extension, such as its type and creator.

The web offers numerous sources for MXP files, but perhaps the best known is the Dreamweaver Exchange, located on the Adobe site. After you've downloaded the file, you can install it by following these steps:

1. From Dreamweaver, choose Commands ➪ Manage Extensions to open the Extensions Manager.

TIP

Dreamweaver need not be open for you to install an extension—just double-click the MXP file to invoke the Extension Manager and begin the installation process. However, if you have multiple Adobe products on your system, it's better to open the Extension Manager before beginning the installation.

2. From the Extension Manager, choose File ➪ Install Extension or use the keyboard shortcut, Ctrl+O (Command+O). You can also click the Install button on the Extension Manager's toolbar.
3. Use the Select Extension To Install dialog box to locate the desired MXP file.
4. When you've located the file, click Install (Open). As part of the installation process, Dreamweaver displays the Adobe Extensions disclaimer.
5. Click Accept in the Adobe Extensions Disclaimer dialog box to continue. Dreamweaver continues to install the extension, and alerts you if a problem is encountered or if the procedure was successful.
6. Dreamweaver notifies you if the installed extension requires you to restart Dreamweaver before it can be used.

After the server behavior has been properly installed, it appears in the standard list found under the Add (+) button of the Server Behaviors panel, and it can be applied like other server behaviors. Any special requirements or directions are noted in the bottom pane of the Extension Manager.

Editing Existing Server Behaviors

One of the wonders of Dreamweaver is the capability to extend every piece of the program. This includes making new server behaviors and editing existing ones. Out of the box, Dreamweaver allows you to edit only those server behaviors you've personally created. Editing is controlled by an XML attribute in the .edml file for each individual server behavior. You can gain access to these server behaviors by changing that XML attribute.

Before you continue, please understand that many of the Dreamweaver server behaviors are extremely complex and may not work correctly if edited using the Server Behavior Builder. Instead of editing, I suggest that you create a new server behavior, and copy an existing server behavior to make sure you don't break anything beyond repair.

To show a server behavior in the Server Behavior Builder, follow these steps:

1. Locate the necessary server behavior .edml file, which is in your Configuration directory. The default location is Adobe Dreamweaver CS6\Configuration*Datasources or Server Behaviors**server model**server behavior name*.edml. For this example, open the Datasources\ASP_Vbs\Request Variable.edml file.
2. The first line of the .edml file should look like this:

```
<group serverBehavior="Dynamic Data.htm" hideFromBuilder="true">
```

3. Change hideFromBuilder="true" to hideFromBuilder="false".
4. Restart Dreamweaver.

The Request Variable server behavior is now available in the edit list of the Server Behavior Builder.

Creating Custom Server Behaviors

Dreamweaver provides a very sophisticated tool for creating custom server behaviors, the Server Behavior Builder. With the Server Behavior Builder, you can modify an existing server behavior you've created or create a new one from scratch. You can use the Server Behavior Builder in any server model configuration supported by Dreamweaver.

34

TIP

By default, you're not allowed to edit or copy the default Dreamweaver server behaviors. See the sidebar "Editing Existing Server Behaviors" to learn how to access all the built-in server behaviors.

The Server Behavior Builder breaks up any server behavior into discrete segments called *code blocks*. Each code block is surrounded by the delimiters for the particular server model: <% ... %> for ASP; <cftag> ... </cftag> for ColdFusion; and <? ... ?> for PHP. Each code block may contain one or more user-supplied parameters. The user enters the parameters in a dialog box; the Server Behavior Builder even creates the dialog box for you.

The Server Behavior Builder can also control the positioning of any individual code block. On the server-side, code is executed from the top of the page to the bottom, and it is often critical that a particular code segment follows another to be processed properly.

You have the option of modifying an existing server behavior, modifying a copy of an existing server behavior, or creating an entirely new server behavior. The process is about the same for all three methods:

1. Choose your server behavior. If it already exists, select it from the list; if it's new, give it a name.
2. Work in the Server Behavior Builder to modify and create code blocks and parameters. The Server Behavior Builder is also used for code block positioning.
3. Set up the dialog box for any parameters. The Generate Server Behavior Dialog Box command enables you to determine the type and order of any parameter elements.

To modify an existing server behavior, follow these steps:

NOTE

Make sure you've followed the instructions in the previous section so that the Server Behavior Builder can edit your chosen server behavior.

1. From the Server Behaviors panel, click the Add (+) button and select Edit Server Behaviors from the list. The Edit Server Behaviors dialog box, shown in Figure 34-23, appears.

   If you want to create a new server behavior, select New Server Behavior instead of Edit Server Behaviors and skip to Step 4.
2. From the Document Type list, select the type of code you want to modify.

FIGURE 34-23

You can create server behaviors for different server models, regardless of the server model of the current site.

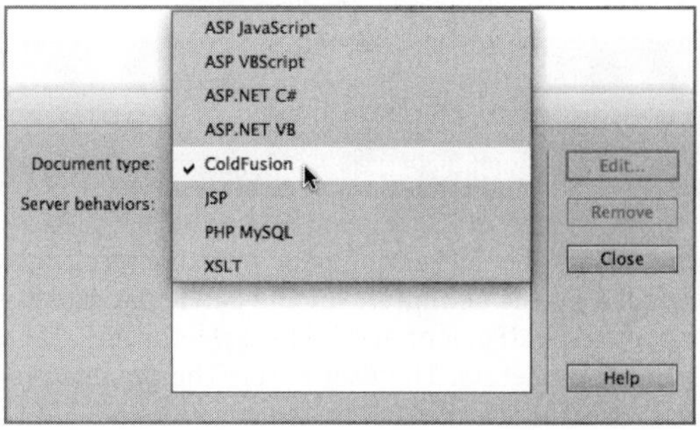

3. From the Server Behaviors list, select the specific server behavior you want to adapt. Dreamweaver posts a warning that if you are modifying a server behavior, the Server Behaviors panel may not be able to identify any instances of it already inserted into the current page. In this situation, it is strongly recommended that you choose New Server Behavior (see Figure 34-24) instead and create a different server behavior based on an existing server behavior.

   After selecting the desired server behavior, the Server Behavior Builder opens, as shown in Figure 34-25.

FIGURE 34-24

When creating a new server behavior, you can either model it on an existing one or start fresh.

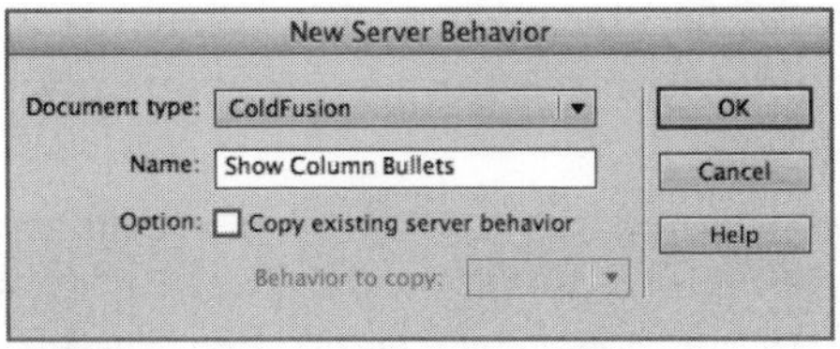

FIGURE 34-25

Dreamweaver's Server Behavior Builder offers tremendous flexibility in positioning code blocks.

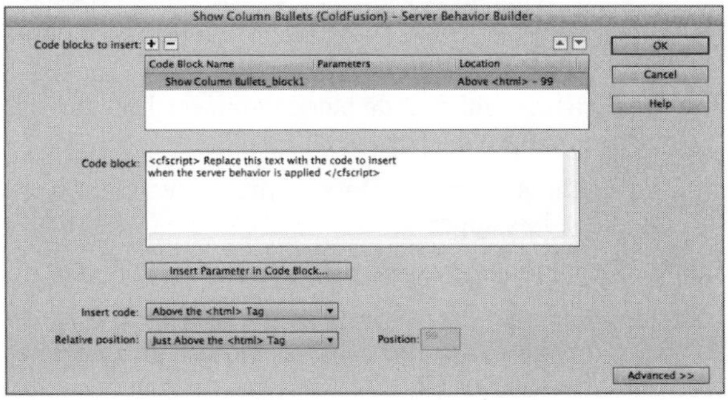

4. Highlight the code block you want to change.
5. Modify the code as desired in the Code Block area.
6. To insert a new parameter, place your cursor in the Code Block area where you want to place a variable and click Insert Parameter In Code Block.

TIP

To replace a value with a variable, select the value in the Code Block before clicking Insert Parameter In Code Block.

7. Enter a unique name for the variable in the Parameter Name field of the Insert Parameter In Code Block dialog box. Click OK when you're finished. The new parameter is inserted in the following format: `@@parametername@@`.
8. Determine the positioning of the code by first choosing an option from the Insert Code list: Above The `<html>` Tag, Below The `</html>` Tag, Relative To A Specific Tag, or Relative To The Selection.
9. If you've chosen Insert Code: Relative To A Specific Tag, select the tag name from the Tag list that appears.
10. From the Relative Position list, select the option best suited for the code block.
11. If you've chosen Relative Position: Custom Position, enter a numeric value in the Custom Position field.

CAUTION

Positioning of code blocks is very important. In particular, make sure you don't insert code that depends upon a recordset above the code that creates that recordset.

12. Repeat Steps 4 through 11 for every code block you need to modify.
13. Click the Advanced button, and choose how you want the server behavior to be displayed in the Server Behaviors panel. You can add or remove parameters to customize the display. If you don't want it to show in the Server Behaviors panel at all, clear the Identifier checkbox.
14. In the Code Block area, choose which code block you want Dreamweaver to select when it chooses from the Server Behaviors panel.
15. Click Next to proceed. If there are parameters in your server behavior, the Generate Behavior Dialog Box dialog box appears.
16. Set the position of your parameters by selecting an item in the list and using the up and down arrows.
17. Set the type of control for the parameter by choosing the down arrow next to the Display As column.

    Dreamweaver offers 17 controls to choose from:

    - Recordset Menu
    - Recordset Field Menu
    - Editable Recordset Menu
    - Editable Recordset Field Menu
    - CF DataSource Menu
    - Connection Menu
    - Connection Table Menu

- Connection Column Menu
- Text Field
- Dynamic Text Field
- URL Text Field
- Numeric Text Field
- Recordset Fields Ordered List
- Text Field Comma Separated List
- List Menu
- Checkbox
- Radio Group

NOTE
If you choose List Menu, you must manually open the created server behavior file to populate the list menu.

The Text Field control is the default.

18. Click OK when you're finished.

Dreamweaver builds the new or modified server behavior and includes it in the Server Behaviors panel.

Summary

Server behaviors are, quite literally, essential to building dynamic pages in Dreamweaver. Without the server-side code that they insert, web pages would just be static HTML. As you begin to investigate all that server behaviors can do for you, keep the following points in mind:

- Although Dreamweaver provides many of the same server behaviors for ASP, ColdFusion, and PHP, each server behavior outputs code specific to the site's chosen server model.
- The Server Behaviors panel is the primary conduit for applying, removing, and modifying server behaviors.
- After a server behavior has been inserted, you can modify the user parameters at any time by double-clicking the item in the Server Behaviors panel.
- Server behaviors often have requirements—such as forms or other server behaviors—that must be in place on the page before they can be inserted.
- Dreamweaver enables you to modify standard server behaviors. You can also create new ones based on the standard server behaviors or build them from the ground up with the Server Behavior Builder.

CHAPTER

35

Creating Adobe AIR Applications

IN THIS CHAPTER

Understanding AIR

Integrating AIR in Dreamweaver

Creating HTML and JavaScript applications for AIR

Deploying AIR applications

Computing has permeated every aspect of modern life. From checking the weather in the morning with an online service, to buying movie tickets online in the afternoon, to using a restaurant finder application on your mobile device to locate a nearby buffet—and the GPS on your phone to get there—it's a highly connected world. Adobe AIR was developed to spread the ease of rich Internet applications (RIA) to the desktop, for both the developer and the end user. AIR applications run on any platform—Windows, Mac, and Linux—and can be quickly developed using well-known web technologies, including HTML and JavaScript, or Adobe Flash and Adobe Flex.

Dreamweaver provides an excellent AIR development environment. Developers can prototype their AIR apps in Dreamweaver using HTML and advanced JavaScript, including Ajax frameworks. Once the RIA is ready for testing, it can be previewed right from within Dreamweaver and even packaged, ready to distribute.

This chapter provides an overview of AIR and then explains how to set up the AIR extension to Dreamweaver. Numerous techniques for developing HTML and JavaScript applications are provided, as well as a full explanation of how to use Dreamweaver to package your AIR application for deployment.

About Adobe AIR

If you think of Earth as a very large desktop and outer space as the web, then AIR is . . . well . . . air. Adobe AIR is positioned at the perfect balancing point between desktop applications with rich user interfaces and web applications with enormous connectivity and comparative development ease. AIR applications are built with web technologies—HTML, JavaScript, Flash, and Flex—and enjoy the same quick-to-market benefits. Likewise, web developers now have another platform on which to ply their trade, without having to learn a new skill set.

Because AIR is deployed on the desktop or on mobile devices, it has access to the local file system, which is a wonderful, yet dangerous, capability. Adobe has built in numerous security measures to make sure AIR applications have the same level of trust that desktop applications do. If an AIR app includes functionality that accesses local data, AIR asks permission to do so, right at installation time. Should the app not come from a trustworthy source, users can easily avoid any perceived risk.

AIR offers businesses many advantages:

- A single application can be deployed across platforms, so there is no duplicate development cost involved.
- The rich user interface possibilities make for engaging experiences.
- Organizations can easily create fully branded applications with full desktop capabilities.
- Content and applications developed for the web can be repurposed.
- Applications can be used anytime, anywhere—regardless of whether the end user is connected to the web.

So who is building AIR applications? Short answer: lots of people. Many large companies have recognized the power of AIR and jumped into the development pool with both feet. eBay, for example, has created a desktop marketplace, where users can place bids and, better still, be notified instantly if they've been outbid. Another large organization, Atlantic Records, created an application called FanBase that aggregates information about its musical artists and presents it in a rich and flexible interface. It's no surprise that Adobe has gotten into the AIR act with, among others, the Kuler Desktop, shown in Figure 35-1. Dreamweaver itself has hopped on the AIR bandwagon with the Dreamweaver Widget Browser, a great utility for finding, configuring, and inserting advanced web widgets from a variety of frameworks.

For more information on the Widget Browser, see Chapter 17.

AIR applications have the potential to look great and create some truly engaging experiences. One of the hallmark features of an AIR application is its ability to appear with or without the enclosing windows standard in operating systems, collectively known as the *chrome*. As you see later in this chapter, when packaging your application for AIR, you can specify to use a transparent chrome, which allows for non-rectangular interfaces, that is, the Kuler Desktop app shown in Figure 35-1.

FIGURE 35-1

Kuler for the desktop is an AIR application that gives you access to over 600,000 color themes.

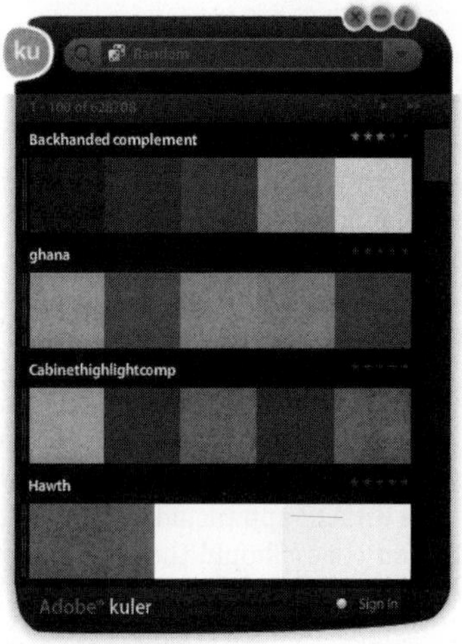

Although many AIR applications are developed with Flash and/or Flex, there's a great deal you can do with the standard web technologies of HTML and JavaScript. Let's get started exploring the possibilities by installing the AIR extension into Dreamweaver.

Installing AIR into Dreamweaver

AIR is a rapidly evolving system, and to make sure that you're always right on the cutting edge, it does not come preinstalled in Dreamweaver. Instead, you need to download and install the AIR runtime. The Dreamweaver team has also created an extension that can be used to preview AIR files and package them for deployment. In this section, you walk through the process of downloading and installing both.

To download and install AIR, follow these steps:

1. Open your browser and visit `http://get.adobe.com/air`.

NOTE
As of this writing, the current AIR version is 3.2. It is entirely possible that a later version may be available when you're reading this book. The preceding address will always get the latest version of AIR for you to install.

2. Click the Download Now badge in the middle of the screen.
3. If necessary, log in to Adobe.com.
4. Save the file on your desktop or in any convenient location.
5. Double-click the downloaded file to begin the installation process.
6. When the license agreement is presented, click I Agree to accept it and continue.
7. After installation is complete, click Finish.

The next step is to retrieve and install the Adobe AIR extension for Dreamweaver. Dreamweaver provides a command for just that purpose:

1. In Dreamweaver, choose Commands ➪ Get AIR Extension.
2. When your browser opens on the page in the Adobe site, click the Download The Adobe AIR Extension For Dreamweaver CS6 link.
3. Save the file in a convenient location.

NOTE
If you previously installed an earlier version, be sure to use the Extension Manager—accessible by choosing Help ➪ Managing Extensions—to remove it.

4. After the file has completely downloaded, navigate to its new location and double-click the `Adobe_AIR.mxp` file.
5. In the Extension Manager, accept the extension disclaimer.
6. After the installation is complete, quit Dreamweaver if it is open and restart it.

If you explore the menu system a bit, you'll discover that three new items have been added:

- **File ➪ Preview in Browser ➪ Preview in AIR:** For previewing your applications during initial testing
- **Site ➪ AIR Applications Settings:** For defining your project parameters
- **Site ➪ Create AIR File:** For packaging the AIR project

In the next section, you learn some of the ways you can use Dreamweaver to design your AIR application.

NOTE
In addition to Dreamweaver CS6 and Extension Manager CS6, you'll also need the Java JRE 1.4 or later installed to preview and create AIR applications. If your operating system is Windows, you can get the latest Java JRE at `http://java.com/en/download/index.jsp`. Mac users are best selecting Software Update (under the Apple menu) to make sure that Apple's custom version of Java is up-to-date.

Designing for AIR

Dreamweaver is an ideal environment for developing HTML and JavaScript applications for AIR. The site-oriented development situation is perfect for creating a complete AIR project. Dreamweaver's Live View uses the same rendering engine, the open source WebKit, as AIR. Therefore, WYSILVIWYGIA. Or, to spell it out, What You See In Live View Is What You Get In AIR.

Moreover, both Dreamweaver and AIR support most modern JavaScript frameworks, which open the door to a vast array of web widgets and sophisticated user interaction. Included in this collection of frameworks is Adobe Spry. As noted throughout this book, numerous Spry widgets are available as drag-and-drop objects in Dreamweaver, for layout, data, and form validation—and they can all be used in AIR.

To demonstrate how easy it is to create AIR applications in Dreamweaver, let's create the most basic web application possible—a single line of text—and then see what it would look like as an AIR app:

1. Create a new site in Dreamweaver by choosing Site ➪ New Site.
2. Set up an empty folder for your local site root.

   It's best to use a new, empty site when setting up an AIR application to avoid incorporating unnecessary files in the compiled app.
3. Create a new HTML page.
4. Enter the text **Hello World!**
5. From the Property inspector HTML tab, select Heading 1 from the Format list.
6. Save your page.

   Now you're ready to see how your incredibly sophisticated web application looks in AIR.
7. Choose File ➪ Preview in Browser ➪ Preview in AIR.

The AIR window opens instantly with the text rendered appropriately, as shown in Figure 35-2. Because no CSS formatting was applied and Dreamweaver and AIR have different defaults, the fonts in Dreamweaver and AIR may not look alike. Let's add some specific styles to address that issue.

FIGURE 35-2

Previewing your AIR application is immediate.

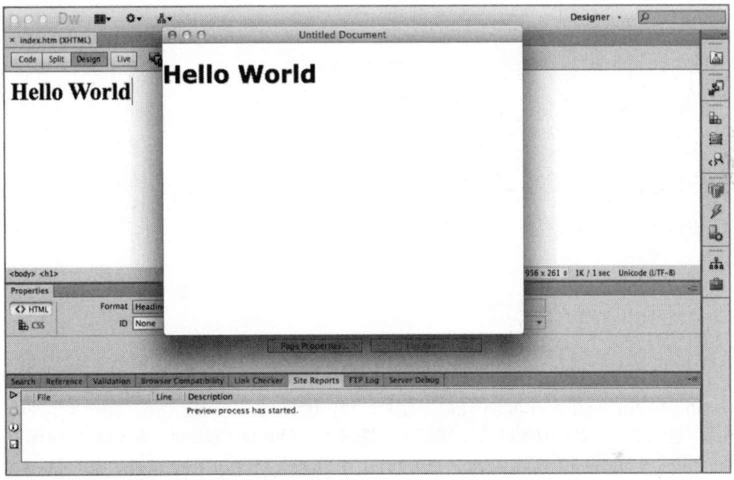

8. Close the AIR preview window and return to Dreamweaver.
9. Let's make sure your AIR application has a title and enter **AIR 01** in the Title field of the Document toolbar. Press Enter (Return).
10. Place your cursor anywhere in the `<h1>` tag.
11. In the Property inspector's CSS tab, make sure Targeted Rule is set to <New CSS Rule> and set Font to Palatino Linotype, Book Antiqua, Palatino, Serif.

    As you can see in the AIR preview shown in Figure 35-2, if you don't specify a style, you risk unexpected results. It's best to specify everything in CSS for your AIR app.
12. When the CSS Rule Definition dialog box opens, select Tag from the Selector Type list and click OK.
13. In the Property inspector, choose the following settings:

    Size: 36px

    Color: #069

    Align: Center
14. Save your file.

    If you don't save your file now, Dreamweaver will ask that you save it before previewing.
15. Choose File ➪ Preview in Browser ➪ Preview in Adobe AIR.

    Now, as evident in Figure 35-3, the Dreamweaver page matches the AIR rendering.

FIGURE 35-3

It's important to style all your content to achieve matching results.

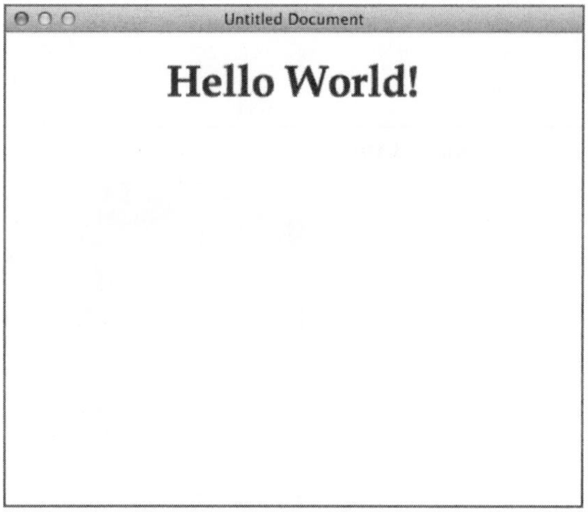

There's no limit to how you can style your AIR application in Dreamweaver. In fact, because both Dreamweaver and AIR use the WebKit rendering engine, you can achieve more advanced CSS styling than you can when building pages for the web. Unlike a standard website, your user interface will be seen only through one lens: AIR. Not only does this one-to-one correspondence eliminate the need for cross-browser testing, but it also opens the door to additional CSS properties, listed in Table 35-1.

TABLE 35-1 Additional CSS Properties in AIR

CSS Property Name	Values	Description
-webkit-border-horizontal -spacing	Non-negative unit of length	Specifies the horizontal component of the border spacing.
-webkit-border-vertical -spacing	Non-negative unit of length	Specifies the vertical component of the border spacing.
-webkit-line-break	after-white-space, normal	Specifies the line break rule to use for Chinese, Japanese, and Korean (CJK) text.
-webkit-margin-bottom -collapse	collapse, discard, separate	Defines how the bottom margin of a table cell collapses.
-webkit-margin-collapse	collapse, discard, separate	Defines how the top and bottom margins of a table cell collapse.

CSS Property Name	Values	Description
-webkit-margin-start	Any unit of length	The width of the starting margin. For left-to-right text, this property overrides the left margin. For right-to-left text, this property overrides the right margin.
-webkit-margin-top-collapse	collapse, discard, separate	Defines how the top margin of a table cell collapses.
-webkit-nbsp-mode	normal, space	Defines the behavior of non-breaking spaces within the enclosed content.
-webkit-padding-start	Any unit of length	Specifies the width of the starting padding. For left-to-right text, this property overrides the left padding value. For right-to-left text, this property overrides the right padding value.
-webkit-rtl-ordering	logical, visual	Overrides the default handling of mixed left-to-right and right-to-left text.
-webkit-text-fill-color	Any named color or numeric color value	Specifies the text fill color.
-webkit-text-security	circle, disc, none, square	Specifies the replacement shape to use in a password input field.
-webkit-user-drag	auto: Default behavior, element: The entire element is dragged. none: The element cannot be dragged	Overrides the automatic drag behavior.
-webkit-user-modify	read-only, read-write, read-write-plaintext-only	Specifies whether the content of an element can be edited.
-webkit-user-select	auto: Default behavior none: The element cannot be selected text: Only text in the element can be selected	Specifies whether a user can select the content of an element.

Because AIR is cross-platform, most differences between the operating systems are handled for you. For example, if you choose to use the system chrome for your AIR windows, they will be identical to the operating system windows.

Packaging Your AIR Application

Once you've developed your HTML and JavaScript application in Dreamweaver and tested it thoroughly, you're ready to convert it to a full-fledged AIR application. The key component of the AIR Extension for Dreamweaver is a packaging utility that gathers the indicated files, sets the window parameters, determines an icon, and creates a secure, digitally signed application.

To package an AIR application, follow these steps:

1. Open the page that will appear when your AIR application is first run.
2. Choose Site ➪ AIR Application Settings.
3. When the AIR Application And Installer Settings dialog box first opens (see Figure 35-4), enter the name you want to use for the executable file in the File Name field.

   By default, Dreamweaver uses the site name for the executable. Make sure that whatever name you choose is operating system–friendly and does not use any special characters. I also recommend that you remove any spaces, substituting underscores for them instead.
4. In the Name field, enter the name you want to appear on the installer screen.

   You're free to make this name as user-friendly as you like: There are no restrictions on special characters.
5. Enter a unique ID for your application in the ID field.

   Again, no special characters are allowed. Be sure to use only 0–9, a–z, A–Z, . (period), and - (dash).
6. Set the version of your application in the Version field.

   If you're planning to do minor and/or major upgrades, it's a good idea to use a multi-decimal system, like 1.0.0.
7. Click Browse next to the Initial Content field and locate the HTML page you want to display when your AIR application opens.
8. If you like, enter a brief description of your application in the Description field, which will appear on the installer screen.
9. Optionally, enter copyright information in the Copyright field, which will appear on the About screen for Macs. There is no equivalent screen in Windows.
10. From the Window Style list, choose the type of chrome to apply to your AIR application. The choices are:
    - **System Chrome:** Uses the standard operating system chrome
    - **Custom Chrome (Opaque):** Uses the interface elements included in your HTML page and results in a rectangular frame
    - **Custom Chrome (Transparent):** Uses the interface elements in your HTML page and applies a transparency to the edges, which can result in non-rectangular shapes
11. Set the dimensions of your application in the Window Size Width and Height fields.
12. If you'd like your application to have a custom icon, click Select Icon Images and, in the Icon Images dialog box (see Figure 35-5), choose the file and path for the four required

sizes (in pixels): 128 × 128, 48 × 48, 32 × 32, and 16 × 16. The default AIR icon is used if no custom one is defined.

Icon images must be in PNG format and stored in the current site.

FIGURE 35-4

Dreamweaver fills out many of the application and installer settings for you automatically.

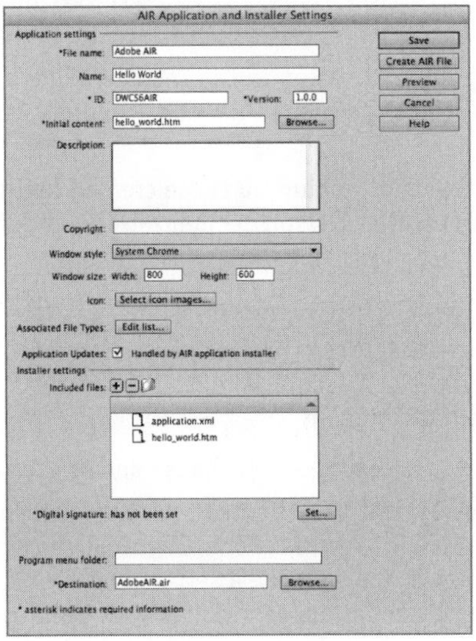

FIGURE 35-5

Set up custom images for various operating systems using PNG files at different sizes.

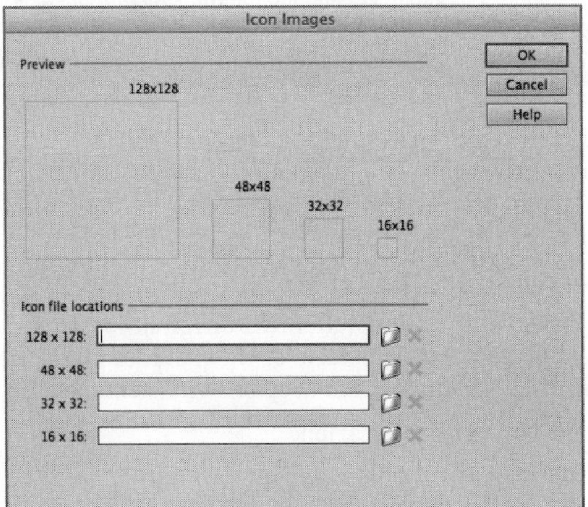

13. If you'd like to associate one or more file types to your application, click Edit List. When the Associated File Type dialog box appears, choose Add (+). In the File Type Settings dialog box, enter the name of the file type (up to 38 characters), the file extension (without a leading period), an optional description, the MIME type (that is, text/html), and the icon image locations, if custom icons are desired.
14. If you want the AIR installer to manage updates to your application, leave the Application Updates option selected. If your application is capable of managing the updates itself, deselect this option.

    That's all of the application settings; there are just a few more settings to define for the installer.
15. Add any additional files used in your application in the Included Files area. To include an individual file, click Add (+) and select the file. To include a folder, such as SpryAssets, click the folder icon.

    Make sure not to include any system files, including those created by Dreamweaver, such as any `_note` or `_mmServerScript` files. If you accidentally include these in the list, select them and click Remove (–).
16. To define your digital signature, click Set.

    The digital signature is a key piece in AIR security and a requirement for installation. When an application is digitally signed, it assures the user that the application has not been modified since it was created and signed.
17. In the Digital Signature dialog box (see Figure 35-6), choose one of the following options:
    - **Sign The AIR Package With A Digital Certificate.** Select this option if you already have a certificate or if you would like to create one. If you already have a certificate, click Browse and locate it. If you'd like to make a self-signed digital certificate, click Create and complete the dialog box that appears. Enter your password and, optionally, choose to remember it for the session. Choose the Timestamp option to ensure that the application will continue to install when the digital certificate expires.

NOTE

If you intend to distribute AIR applications publicly, it is highly recommended that you purchase a digital certificate from a known authority, such as GeoTrust. With only a self-signed certificate, the AIR installer lists the publisher as "unknown"—not a very reassuring indication.

- **Prepare An AIR Intermediate (AIRI) Package That Will Be Signed Later.** This option is viable for testing purposes only and the application cannot be installed without a full certificate.

18. If you'd like to create a subdirectory in the Windows Start menu, enter its name in the Program Menu Folder field. This option has no equivalent on the Mac.
19. If you'd like to save your application installer in a different location than the site root, click Browse and select a new path. The name of the installer is automatically supplied for you, but can be modified as long as you keep the `.air` extension.
20. Click Preview to display your AIR application.

FIGURE 35-6

All AIR applications require a digitally signed certificate for installation.

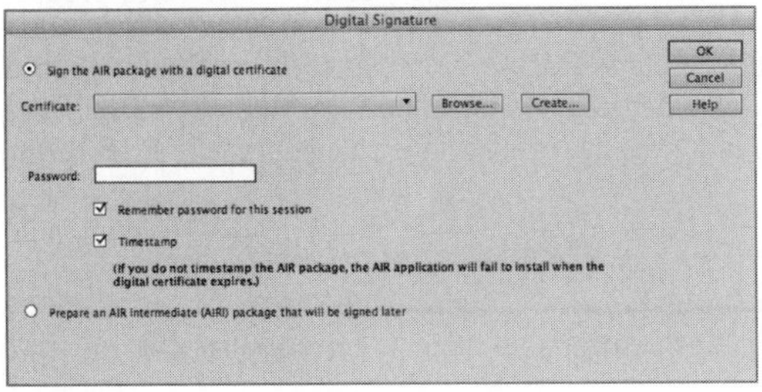

21. If you're ready to create the application installer, click Create AIR File.

    As you'll see shortly, you can also use another command to create this file once your settings are saved.

22. Click Save to store your settings and create the AIR file at a later time.

In the normal process, you would typically create a build of your AIR application and then test it. To make changes, return to Dreamweaver and add any refinements or modifications needed. If you need to add additional files, re-open the AIR Application Settings dialog box and include them.

With your settings stored, you can continue to make changes. When you're ready to create a new build of your application, choose Site ➪ Create AIR File. Dreamweaver will note that the file exists and ask if you'd like to replace it; click Yes. After a progress screen is displayed, Dreamweaver informs you whether the operation was successful and, if so, where the AIR installer file can be found.

You can double-click the AIR installer right in Dreamweaver's Files panel and it will begin the installation process, shown in Figure 35-7. Here, you can see that using a self-identifying certificate results in the publisher being listed as unknown.

FIGURE 35-7

The AIR installer lets the user know the system access level and the publisher's identity.

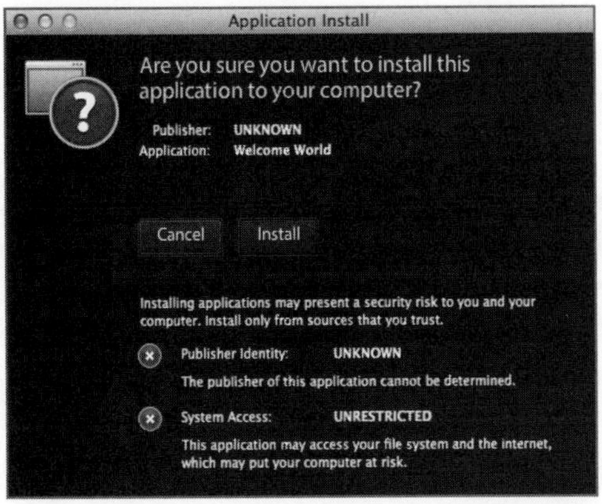

After Install is clicked, a second screen displays the name of the application and description as previously defined. It also asks if you'd like an icon placed on the desktop and if you'd like the application to start after the installation is complete; click Continue to proceed.

Next, your fully functioning desktop application is displayed, like mine in Figure 35-8. Here, I've added a Spry Accordion panel, rounded corners via WebKit's enhanced CSS styling, with transparent chrome to show them off and, of course, a lovely image to complete the Hello World application.

FIGURE 35-8

Create all manner of desktop applications, including personalized birth announcements, with Dreamweaver and AIR.

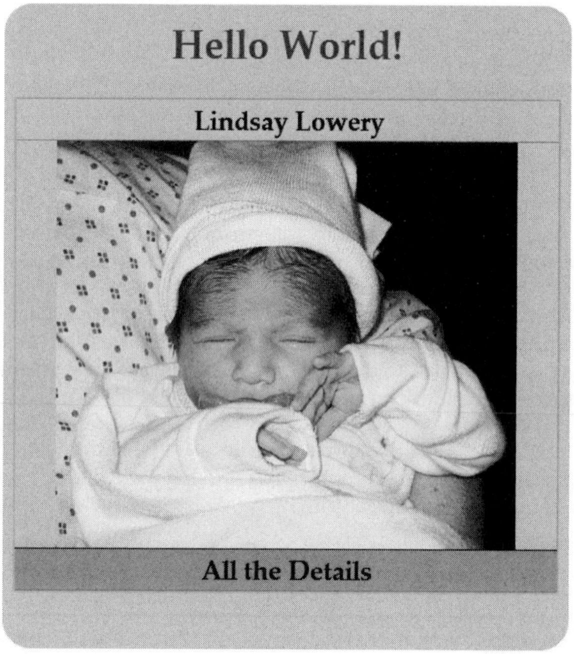

Summary

Adobe AIR is a revolutionary program that opens the door to the world of desktop applications for web developers and designers. One of the primary advantages of AIR is that standard HTML and JavaScript can be used to create the core functionality. AIR integration in Dreamweaver makes it possible for web developers to leverage their skills and create compelling desktop applications. When working with AIR in Dreamweaver, keep in mind the following:

- Adobe AIR is a cross-platform (Windows and Mac) runtime that creates desktop applications with web technologies such as HTML, JavaScript, Flash, and Flex.

- To get the latest version of AIR, you'll need to install it from the Adobe site at `http://get.adobe.com/air`.
- The AIR Extension for Dreamweaver also needs to be installed and can be reached by choosing Commands ➪ Get AIR Extension.
- Once the AIR Extension for Dreamweaver is installed, you can easily preview your applications in AIR.
- Prior to creating an AIR installer for your application, you'll need to define settings for both the application and the installer.
- All AIR applications require a digitally signed certificate, preferably by a recognized certificate authority.
- Choose the Site ➪ Create AIR File command to generate new builds of your AIR application for testing and deployment.

APPENDIX

A

What's on the Website?

IN THIS APPENDIX

Visiting the book's website

Files and programs on the website

Troubleshooting

The *Dreamweaver CS6 Bible* companion website, `http://www.wiley.com/go/dreamweavercs6bible`, contains the following:

- Code examples used in the book, including those from the Dreamweaver Techniques.
- A list of Dreamweaver extensions from the leaders in the Dreamweaver community, designed to make your work more productive. The types of extensions include behaviors, server behaviors, objects, commands, and inspectors.

Visiting the Book's Website

The website contains files that run on more than one computer platform—in this case, both Windows and Macintosh computers.

In the Configuration folder, the file structure replicates the structure that Dreamweaver sets up when it is installed. For example, objects found in the *drive*\Program Files\Adobe\Adobe Dreamweaver CS6\Configuration\Objects (/Applications/Adobe Dreamweaver CS6/Configuration/Objects) folder should be in that location for both the website and the installed program. One slight variation: In the Additional Extensions folder, you'll find the various behaviors, objects, and so on, filed under the author's name.

Files and Programs on the Website

The *Dreamweaver CS6 Bible* website contains a host of extensions and auxiliary files to assist your exploration of Dreamweaver, as well as your web page design work in general. The following sections provide a description of those files and programs.

Dreamweaver extensions

Dreamweaver is extremely extensible, and the Dreamweaver community has built some amazing extensions. In the Additional Extensions section of the website, you'll find links to tons of behaviors, server behaviors, objects, commands, inspectors, and more. The extensions are grouped according to author, and within each author's folder, they are organized by function. I've provided links so you can get the latest versions directly from the author.

Where available, extensions are packaged in an `.mxp` file, which can easily be installed using the Extension Manager. To run the Extension Manager from Dreamweaver, choose Commands ➪ Manage Extensions. Then choose File ➪ Install Extension and browse to the location of the extension's `.mxp` file.

You'll find a `ReadMe.htm` file in each author's folder, with links to the author's website and more information about his or her creations.

Dreamweaver Techniques files

One special feature of *Dreamweaver CS6 Bible* is that Dreamweaver Techniques appear in most of the chapters in the book. Each technique contains all the requisite sample HTML files and graphics files, each within its own folder. For most techniques, there is a starting file and a completed file. Open the start file to work through the technique and the final file to see how the finished file should look. To start, copy all the files in the Techniques folder of the website to your system and establish a Dreamweaver site with that folder as the local site root; the Dreamweaver Technique "Setting Up Your Site" in Chapter 4 describes the steps to accomplish this task.

Dreamweaver CS6 Bible code examples

The Examples folder on the website provides sample code used in the book. You can easily view the files through Dreamweaver or your browser without transferring the files to your system. If you do wish to transfer the files, copy the entire folder over to your system.

To incorporate the external style sheets in your websites, copy files with `.css` extensions into your local site's root folder. Then follow the instructions in the "Attaching an External Style Sheet" section found in Chapter 6.

Web resource directory

The World Wide Web is a vital resource for any web designer, whether a seasoned professional or a beginner. The companion website contains an HTML page with a series of links to resources on the web. These are links to general resources and to Dreamweaver-specific references.

Troubleshooting

If you have difficulty installing or using any of the materials on the companion website, try the following solutions:

- Turn off any antivirus software that you may have running. Installers sometimes mimic virus activity and can make your computer mistakenly believe that it is being infected by a virus. (Be sure to turn the antivirus software back on later.)
- Close all running programs. The more programs you're running, the less memory is available to other programs. Installers also typically update files and programs; if you keep other programs running, installation may not work properly.
- Reference the `ReadMe.txt`. Please refer to the ReadMe file located at the root of the website for the latest product information at the time of publication.

If you still have trouble with the website, please call the Wiley Product Technical Support phone number: (800) 762-2974. Outside the United States, call 1 (317) 572-3994. You can also contact `http://www.wiley.com/techsupport`. Wiley Publishing, Inc., provides technical support only for installation and other general quality control items; for technical support on the applications themselves, consult the program's vendor or author. To place additional orders or request information about other Wiley products, please call (800) 225-5945 or visit `http://www.wiley.com`.

Index

Symbols

" (quotes), in HTML and XML, 1033
#listnav a: style, 573, 575–576
#listnav a:hover style, 573, 577
#listnav a:link and #listnav a:visited styles, 577–578
#listnav CSS styles, 573–575
#listnav li style, 573, 574–575
#listnav ul style, 573, 574
% sign, in query strings, 771
& (ampersands)
  as field separators, 524, 525
  in query strings, 782
  code, 487
* (asterisks), in SQL statements, 701
+ (plus signs), as field separators, 524
. . . (ellipsis), query strings and, 771
= (equal signs), in query strings, 782
; (semicolons), multiple custom filters and, 830
<!-- #BeginLibraryItem> and <!-- #EndLibraryItem> tags, 971
@ signs, double, 919, 926, 938
@font-face statement, 339–340
\ (backslash), in searches, 312
©, in HTML, 970

A

<a> and </a> anchor tag pair, 381, 391
abbreviations, adding to text, 328
About view, 247
absolute positioning, 13, 402, 403
access, customer restrictions, 813–815
Access Key field (Flash), 869
access keys, defined, 382
Access Query Builder (Microsoft), 721, 723
accessibility
  Dreamweaver, 15–16
  preferences, 105–106
accessing reports, 1010–1011
Accordion Panel widgets (Spry), 661–663
acquiring. *See also* websites for downloading
  SVN files, latest version, 1026–1027
acronyms, adding to text, 328
action: attribute (<form> tag), 523
Action list, searching code and, 310–311
actions. *See also specific* actions; standard actions
  behaviors and, 449, 450
  default actions, accepting automatically, 111
  when adding behaviors, 450
active content pages, 701–702
Active Server Pages. *See* ASP (Active Server Pages)
ActiveX
  ActiveX object, 899
  embedded players and, 901
  using embed with (audio), 905
  Windows Media Player and, 903
adding. *See also* inserting
  attributes to tags, 1080
  Library items to documents, 970
  Library items to pages, 977–978
  Library items to site libraries, 968–969
  SSIs, 979–980
  tag libraries, 1080
  tags to tag libraries, 1080
<address> tag, for text styling, 327–328
addresses. *See also* e-mail addresses
  absolute addresses, 387
  address types (URLs), 387
  document-relative addresses, 387–388
Adjust Tracing Image Position dialog box, 442
administration of websites. *See also* Contribute
  Administer Website dialog box, 1017
Adobe. *See also other specific Adobe products*
  accounts, 151
  AIR-powered Widget Browser. *See* Widget Browser
  Contribute. *See* Contribute
  InContext Editing service. *See* InContext Editing
  Labs site and mini-site, 621, 622

Adobe *(continued)*
Marketplace & Exchange site, MXP extension files, 481–482
Media Encoder, 879, 880
Advanced Recordset dialog box, 721–722, 786, 793
AIR applications, 1115–1127
advantages of, 1116
basics, 1115–1117
creating, 1118–1120
CSS properties in, 1120–1121
Dreamweaver environment for, 1115, 1118
installing into Dreamweaver, 1117–1118
packaging, 1122–1126
AIR-powered Widget Browser. *See* Widget Browser
Ajax (Asynchronous JavaScript and XML)
basics, 620
capabilities, 19
limitations, 620
Spry and, 69, 619–620, 621
alert-box message, pulling data from, 465
aligning AP elements
adding elements to AP elements, 439
aligning with grids, 438–439
basics, 433
guides, 434–438
ruler, 433–434
alignment
of images, optimizing, 367–369
of objects with grids, 438–439
in tables, 498, 502–503
of text, 337
a:link , eliminating underlines and, 384
All mode (CSS Styles panel), 244–246
All Rules pane, 244, 245
Allow Multiple Consecutive Spaces option, 93
Allow Multiple Selections box, scrolling lists and, 539
alt attribute (<img> tag), 365–366
Always Show Local/Remote Files On The Right/Left option, 110–111
ampersands (&)
as field separators, 524, 525
in query strings, 782
anchor tags
<a>, attaching behaviors and, 450, 452
<a> and </a> anchor tag pair, 381
disabling underlines on, 383–384
anchors, navigating with
moving with same document, 393–394
named anchors, basic use of, 391–392
named anchors, fundamentals, 391
named anchors, inserting, 392–393, 395–396
named anchors, using in different pages, 394
null links, 394--396
and-type searches, 1013
animation
animate() function, 675
animated tooltips, displaying, 674–675
animating transitions (CSS), 285–287
CSS3 transitions, xxxiv, xxxv
AP elements. *See also* CSS-P Property inspector, AP elements and; <div> tags
basics, 106, 403–404
content, changing dynamically, 444
Drag AP Element and, 460–461
dynamically altering properties, 442
nesting, 108, 423
positioning, 404, 422–423
preferences, 106–108, 421–422
resizing, 420
selecting, 423
setting text of, 467
AP elements, creating
AP element objects, inserting, 419–420
AP elements preferences, 421–422
default characteristics, setting, 421–422
inserting AP elements, 426–427
menus for, 420–421
relative positioning, 422–423
AP elements, modifying
above and below attributes, 431
adding elements to, 439
aligning, 433, 438–439
AP Elements panel, 423, 424, 431–433
forms and, 439–440
guides, 434–438
moving, 424–425
resizing, 423–424, 425
ruler, 433–434
Appearance (CSS), Page Properties dialog box, 175
Appearance (HTML), Page Properties dialog box, 175–176
Appear/Fade effect, 474–475
Apple website, 102

applets
defined, 225
Java applets, adding, 225–227
Application bar, 50–51
application variables
defined, 809
making available, 809
applications. *See also* multipage applications; *specific* applications
mobile apps, xxxvi–xxxviii, 24,
previewing (Live View), 775–776
text from other apps, inserting into Dreamweaver, 297–298
Apply Source Formatting and Apply Source Formatting To Selection commands, 1059
applying
Repeat Regions, 754–756
Show Region server behaviors, 757–758
templates, 952
ASCII values, in query strings, 771
ASP (Active Server Pages)
ASP connections, creating, 709
ASP objects (Insert panel), 76
DSN connections with, establishing, 707–708
DSN-less connections for, 712–713
ASP Request variables, 809
ASP.NET, 701
Assets panel. *See also* Library items
dragging images from, 352–355
image previewing with, 10, 11
inserting URLs from, 385–386
Assets panel, working with templates
applying templates, 952
blank templates, creating, 951
context menu, 950–951
opening and deleting templates, 951–952
regions, mapping, 952–954
Templates category and, 949–951
asynchronous, defined, 620
Attach External Style Sheet dialog box, 254–256
Attach label tag using `for` attribute (forms), 549
attaching
existing style sheets to pages, 259
external style sheets, 254–256
XML data, attaching to XSLT pages, 1048
attaching behaviors, 450–481
adding behaviors, 452–453
basics, 450–451
Behaviors panel, 451–452
events, managing, 453–454
incorporating behaviors, 454–455
standard actions. *See* standard actions
triggering custom functions, 455
attributes
Background (CSS), 273–274
Border options (CSS), 278
Box (CSS), 277
CSS Block, 276
CSS Type, 272
defined, 76, 170
editable, making, 924–926
editable, setting, 926–928
editing, 1079–1080
Extensions attributes (CSS), 281–282
HTML, replacing, 309–311
link object, 186
menuitem tag, 1073
positioning options (CSS), 279–280
Property inspector, 78–79
Show Attributes When Inserting option, 105
on tags, modifying, 219
tags, replacing, 309–310
tags, searching, 307–309
`<tagspec>`, 1075–1077
Audacity, 909
audiences for sites, targeting, 128
audio, 897–910
`<audio>` tag (HTML), 908, 909–910
background music, 901–902
`<embed>` tag with ActiveX, 905
embedding, 898, 899–900
HTML5 players, coding, 907–910
inserting SWF files, 898
linking to audio files, 897–899
methods for incorporating, 897
podcasts, 905–907
specific plugins, targeting, 902–905
Windows Media Player, 903–904
automatic row numbering, 943–944
automating master-detail page production, 787–791
automation enhancements, 27–29
AVI video format, 887

B

<b> and <i> tags, preferences and, 93–94
Background attributes (CSS), 273–274
background music, 901–902
backgrounds
  alternating row colors, 941–943
  AP elements background color/images options, 107
  appearance, setting, 175–176
  color in forms, CSS and, 553, 554, 557
  color on WordPress sites, 833
  CSS Layout Background options, 410
  graphics for navigation buttons (lists), 567, 570–571
  images, adding, 369–372
  images or color, inserting, 431
  images vs. inline images, 370
  joining background images in frames, 604
  setting table backgrounds, 508
backslash (\), in searches, 312–313
Balance Braces command, 190
banner ads, 373–374
Base object, changing, 185
BBEdit Integration, Enabling option, 100
behaviors, 449–484. *See also* server behaviors
  activating AP elements with, 442–446
  altering parameters of, 482
  attaching. *See* attaching behaviors; standard actions
  basics, 449–450
  vs. commands, 1058
  defined, 23
  deleting, 483
  extensibility and, 25
  importance of, 449
  inserting rollovers with, 856, 857–859
  installing new, 481–482
  JavaScript, 23–24
  modifying, 483–484
  sequencing, 482–483
  setting up. *See* attaching behaviors
  Spry effects. *See* Spry effects
  updating multiple frames and, 610–611
Behaviors panel
  basics, 451–452
  vs. Server Behaviors Builder, 1084
binding
  Bind To feature, 745
  data to pages, 634–635
  defined (dynamic values and), 744
  XML data in XSLT pages, 1048
  XSL data to pages, 1038–1040
Bindings panel
  Add list, 809
  available data sources and, 10, 11
  binding XSL data and, 1038–1039
  drag-and-drop from, 10
  dynamic data and, 729, 734, 741
  dynamic text fields, creating with, 798
_blank targets, 396–397
Blind effect, 475–476
block elements, 317, 318
Block options (CSS), 275–276
<blockquote> tags, 338
<body> tags
  basics, 170, 171
  behaviors and, 452, 455
  clearing pages with, 45
  physical and logical styles and, 187–188
boilerplate.css, 418–419
boolean types, defined, 798
Border options (CSS), 278
borders
  adding to images, 366
  in framesets, manipulating, 602–603
  in framesets, setting, 605–606
  table borders, setting, 508
Box attributes (CSS), 277
box model (CSS), 410–412
box shadows, xxxiv
box-shadow property (CSS), 263, 264

 tags (break tags), whitespace and, 318
braces in code, 190
Bridge, 863–865
brightness of images, altering, 360
Browser Compatibility Check feature
  checkable browsers, 988
  compatibility errors, 988–991
  CSS Advisor site and, 996
  issues, viewing and correcting, 993–994
  page elements, excluding from checking, 992–993
  results, using, 994–996
  settings, modifying, 992
BrowserLab service, 32, 151–153

browsers. *See also* cross-browser compatibility
browser lists, 150
browser targeting, 31–32
browser window fold (guides), 437–438
capable of processing XSLT, 1049
capable of viewing XML files, 1049
checking for errors, 54–55
content in, editing. *See* InContext Editing
frameless browsers, dealing with, 612–613
Preview in Browser button, 53
preview in browser preferences, 112–114
previewing applications in (Live View), 775–776
previewing pages in, 150–151
status bars and, 469
budgets, planning sites and, 128–129
bulleted lists. *See* unordered lists
bullets, changing shape of, 564
Business Catalyst
basics, 157
integrating code, 161–164
Manage Sites dialog box and, 142
new sites, creating with, 158–159
working online, 159–161
buttons. *See also* navigation buttons, creating from lists
activating forms with, 545–547
adding, to activate Jump Menu object, 463–464
commandButtons() function, 1064–1065
Live View button, 766
Merge Cells button, 510

C

Call JavaScript action, 456
canAcceptCommand() function, 1064–1065
cascading, defined, 240
Cascading Style Sheets. *See* CSS (Cascading Style Sheets)
case sensitivity
case control options, 122–123
named anchors and, 392
targets and, 610
cells
basics, 487–488
cell wrap, 514
merging and splitting, 509–511
selecting, 497
selecting content in, 922
setting properties, 512–515
spacing and padding, 509
table header cells, 514
width and height, 514–515
centering tables in CSS, 503–504
CFForm objects (Insert panel), 76
CFML objects (Insert panel), 76
Change Property action, 457–459
<channel> tag, XML feeds and, 906
Char Width, text fields in forms and, 527
character entities, defined, 74
Character objects, 233–234
characters (regular expressions). *See also* special characters
matching character positions, 313–314
matching character ranges, 314–315
repeating characters, 313–314
Check Browser Compatibility command, 991–992
Check Browser Compatibility feature, 54–55, 268–269
Check In/Check Out system
basics, 32–33, 998–1000
enabling, 1000–1001
files and, 1001–1003
Check New Username server behavior, 817–818, 1100–1101
Check Plugin action, 458–459
checkboxes, 531–532
creating dynamic, 798–799
Dynamic CheckBox server behavior, 1104–1105
Spry Validation Checkbox, 650–652
Choose Root Folder dialog boxes, 132
chrome, defined, 1116
class selector type, 240–241, 251
classes
inserting multiple (CSS), 253–254
pseudo-classes, 251–252
Clean Up HTML and Clean Up XHTML commands, 1059–1061
clear property (images), 369
C-Level Extensibility feature, 27, 1057
client-side XSLT pages
applying to XML files, 1047
creating, 1047–1048
limitations of, 1047
linking from XML files, 1048–1049
publishing/viewing XML/XSLT files and, 1049
XML data and, 1048, 1049-50

clipping AP elements, 430
clips (video), 886–888
cloaking
  defined, 32
  site folders, 140–141
closing
  Close Tags option when coding, 116–117
  Dreamweaver, 146
  files, 146
  framesets, 599
  panels, 83, 84
CMS. *See* web content management systems (CMS); WordPress
code. *See also* validating code
  blocks, 1109–1112
  buttons for styling, 63
  code collapse, 203–205
  coloring preferences, 119–121
  copying and pasting, 298
  cross-browser compatible code, 440
  editing capabilities, 7–8
  External Code Editor option, 100
  fonts preferences, 114–116
  format preferences, 121–124
  inserting rollovers with, 856, 859–862
  integrating Business Catalyst code, 161–164
  moving, 204–205
  printing, 191
  rewriting preferences, 117–119
  sample code on companion website, 1130
  searching, 306–308
  selecting type of (Fireworks), 859
  viewing types when opening, 100
code, accessing directly, 169–235
  <body> tags, 187–188
  <head> elements. *See* <head> elements
  Code view and Code inspector, 188–190
  Coding toolbar. *See* Coding toolbar
  doctype declarations, 172–173
  HTML page structure, 170–171
  HTML5 structural tags, 191–195
  Java applets, adding, 225–227
  JavaScript. *See* JavaScript
  Live View, Related Files, and Code Navigator, integrating. *See* integrating Live View, Related Files and Code Navigator features
  Quick Tag Editor. *See* Quick Tag Editor
  Reference panel, 216–218
  Snippets panel, 214–216
  symbols and special characters, inserting, 231–234
  Tag inspector, 218–219
  Tag Library feature, 208. *See also* tag libraries
  VBScript, 227–229
  XHTML, expanding to, 171–172
code hinting
  code hints, 7, 116–117, 193, 208–210
  Code Hints tool, 208–210
  JavaScript frameworks and, 670–671
  for vendor-specific properties, xxxiii
Code inspector
  basics of, 188–190
  creating rollovers and, 862
Code Navigator, 61. *See also* integrating Live View, Related Files and Code Navigator features
Code view
  basics, 7, 42–43, 170, 188–190
  identifying Spry regions and, 632
  Inspect mode and, 410
  Open In Code View option, 100
  removing comments in, 345
  visual and text editors and, 5
codecs
  basics, 886
  changes in codec support, 895
  H.264 codec, 879
Coder workspace option, 35, 36
Coding toolbar
  basics, 60–63, 203
  Code collapse, 203–205
  code selection and highlighting, 205–206
  commenting code, 206
  CSS, separating from code, 207–208
  wrapping tags and inserting snippets, 206–207
ColdFusion
  CFForm objects (Insert panel), 76
  CFML objects (Insert panel), 76
  ColdFusion Administrator, 710–711
  ColdFusion tags, viewing, 76
  declaring ODBC data sources, 707
  DSN connections with, 708–711
  formatting time and date in, 741
  Server Debug panel, 776–778

Collapse Full Tag or Collapse Selection, 61
Collapsible Panel widget (Spry), 663–664
collapsing panel groups, 83
color
alternating row background colors, 941–943
AP elements background color options, 107
background color on WordPress sites, 833
border color options, 603
browser-safe colors, 78
Color dialog box, 332
color pickers, 78–79, 332, 333, 515
in documents, setting, 175
in forms, CSS and, 553, 554, 557
of guides, 437
of Insert panel icons, 64
inserting, 431
Kuler Desktop app and, 1116
selecting from onscreen images, 179–180
specifying for table columns/rows/cells, 515
in table borders and backgrounds, 508
text font color, adding, 330–333
of text links, 382–383
columns
column spanning, 488, 510–511
data column types, defining, 624–625
deleting, 507
File View Columns, browsing, 1007–1009
fluid grid layouts and, 416–417, 418
headings, 488–489
inserting in tables, 506–507
modifying frames and, 601–602
moving, 501
selecting, 496
setting properties, 512–515
Spry data columns, inserting into regions, 634–635
Command button (forms), 545–546
`commandButtons()` function, 1064–1065
commands
ASP users and, 1106, 1107
basics of (Dreamweaver), 1058–1061
capabilities, 26
Document window menus, 85–86
Live View Options menu, 58
meta commands, 182
vs. objects and behaviors, 1058
opening panels with, 83
Property inspector, 79
recording and replaying, 1061–1064
scripting, 1064–1066
commenting code, 206, 344–346
commenting out code, 344
comments, support for, 62
committing SVN files, 1026, 1027
Common objects (Insert panel), 64–66
compatibility (Contribute), 1015–1017
Compound selector type (CSS), 251–252
conditional operator, template expression example, 941–942
Conditional Region object (XSLT), 1043, 1047
conflicts, resolving (SVN), 1029
connecting to data sources
for ASP developers, 707–708, 709
basics, 703–705
with ColdFusion, 708, 709, 710–711
connection strings, 712–715
declaring ODBC data sources, 707
DSN basics, 705–706
managing connections, 717–718
PHP and, 712, 715–716
`Server.MapPath()` command, 713–714
connecting to Subversion servers, 1022–1023
connecting to WebDAV, 1020–1021
connection strings, specifying, 712–715
connections
Connection Speed option, 99
converting from DSN, 717
local site folder and, 130–133
preferences for online connections, 110
connectivity of Dreamweaver CS6, 5
container tags, defined, 307
content. *See also* editing table content
adding to template documents, 920–922
in browsers, editing. *See* InContext Editing
cell content, copying, 499–501
of frames, modifying, 608
marking as editable, 920–922
in templates, 915
content management systems. *See* web content management systems (CMS); WordPress
`content_model` attribute (`tagspec`), 1076
contrast in images, altering, 360

Contribute
basics, 997, 1014–1015
rollbacks with, 1018–1020
setting up compatibility, 1015–1017
sitewide administration of, 1017–1018
controls
HTML5 form controls, 552–553
input controls (forms), 523
conventions in this book, xliv–xlvi
Convert Tables To AP Divs dialog box, 984–985
copying
cell contents, 499–501
code, 298
Copy To Site function (Library items), 969
copy/paste preferences, 102–103
Microsoft Office documents' contents, 320
from Photoshop, 843–844
text, 296–297
copyright notices, Library items and, 970
countdown counter, Spry Validation Textarea widget and, 648–649
Creative Suite bundle, 839, 851–852, 863
cropping images, 357–359, 362–363
cross-browser compatibility
Browser Compatibility Check feature. *See* Browser Compatibility Check feature
compatibility errors, 988–991
converting tables, 983–984
cross-browser compatible code, 440
pages, converting older to modern, 984–985
validating code, 985–987
CSS (Cascading Style Sheets)
Advisor site, 993, 996
animating transitions, 285–287
applying for list navigation buttons, 578–579
background images, implementing with, 370
basics, 237, 238–239
browser compatibility errors and, 988–991
cascading and, 240
centering tables in, 503–504
changes in images and, 854, 855
custom selectors, defining, 240–241
customizing, 830–832
defining styles (list navigation buttons), 573–578
design-time style sheets, 288–289
Dreamweaver support for, 14–15, 20
editing and managing. *See* CSS, editing and managing
enhanced, for Spry, 639
file set-up (list navigation buttons), 571–573
for formatting dynamic data, 733
grouping properties, 239
vs. HTML, tables and, 487, 488
importance of, 237
inheritance of properties, 239–240
Layout Background options, 410
Layout Box Model visual, 411–412
layout control, 22–23
Layout Outlines, 412–413
layouts, applying, 413–414
Library items and, 968
modern CSS styling features, xxxiii–xxxv
Move CSS Rules, 62
properties in AIR, 1120–1121
Property inspector and, 76–77
rules, creating, 238, 405
separating from code, 207–208
setting height and width and, 504
Source Format Options, 123–125
specificity and, 241–242
Sprite export, 856
Style Rendering toolbar and, 59–60
styles, changing style size, 328–329
styles, creating and applying. *See* styles (CSS), creating and applying
styles, generating new. *See* styles (CSS), generating new
Styles panel, 244–248
styles preferences, 108–109
styling unordered lists with, 564–565
table-layout property, 498
CSS, editing and managing
CSS hacks, 261
CSS rules, managing, 266–268
debugging applied CSS, 268–269
print style sheets, 269–270
Styles panel Properties pane, 262–263
toggling CSS properties, 265–266
vendor-specific CSS properties, 264–265
CSS Advisor site, 993, 996
CSS for styling forms
basics, 553
highlighting, 553–554

highlighting focus, 557–558
input fields, altering, 554–555
labels and legends, changing, 556–557
lists and menus, 555–556
CSS Hacks and Filters (Wiley), 262
CSS rules
creating, 238, 405–406
CSS Rule Definition dialog box, 175, 260, 406
managing, 266–268
Move CSS Rules, 62
CSS styles and their attributes
background options, 273–275
basics of defining styles, 271
block options, 275–276
border options, 278
box options, 277
CSS Styles panel, 260–262
CSS3 enhanced styles, 263–264
extensions options, 281–282
list options, 279
positioning options, 279–280
transitions options, 282–285
type options, 271–272
CSS-P Property inspector, AP elements and
background image or color, 431
basics, 425–426
clipping AP elements, 430
<div> and <span> tags, 428, 429
ID attributes, 426
options, 425–426
overflow settings, 429–430
visibility, 428–429
z-index, 430–431
Ctrl (Command) key
cell selection and, 497
selecting multiple items and, 539
Ctrl+N (Command+N) option, 104
Current mode (CSS Styles panel), 244, 246–248
cursor:pointer property, 639
custom tags, 26–27, 1057, 1075–1077
customers
adding new, 816–817
customer access restrictions, 813–815
customer log out, 816
customer login, 812–813
relating to, 812
Customize Favorite Objects dialog box, 75
customizing. *See also* Dreamweaver, customizing
Custom Filter option, 829–830
Design Notes, 1006
multiuser operating systems, 1063–1064
panel groups, 84
server behaviors, 1109–1113
Spry widgets, 641
validation patterns (Spry), 645
WordPress sites, 830–833
workspace, 12
cutting and pasting text, 296
cutting cell contents, 499–500

D

data. *See also* dynamic form elements
appearance in HTML tables, 623
binding to pages, 634–635, 1038–1040, 1048
deleting from data sources, 807–808
display options (Spry), 626–627
dynamic. *See* dynamic data
dynamically accessed, 697
incorporating into pages, 639–641
inserting into data sources, 801–804
inserting into Spry regions, 634–635
repeating (Spry), 636–638
repeating restricted (Spry), 639–640
static data, incorporating into pages, 622
styling with XSL. *See* XSL (Extensible Stylesheet Language)
tabular data, importing, 516–518
updating records, 804–807
XML data, attaching to XSLT pages, 1048
XSL data, filtering, 1041–1042
XSL data, repeating, 1040–1041
XSL data, showing conditionally, 1043–1045
data, displaying conditionally. *See also* repeating data
basics, 751
showing/hiding page elements, 756–758
data objects
capabilities, 27–28
Insert panel, 68
for record navigation, 760–761
Data Sets
accessing, 635
incorporating Spry data into pages and, 639–641

Data Sets *(continued)*
- Spry Data Set Wizard, 623–627
- XML data, establishing Spry Data Sets with, 628–631

Data Source Name. *See* DSN (Data Source Name)

data sources. *See also* connecting to data sources
- active content pages, 701–702
- adding variables as, 808–811
- basics, 698–701
- defined, 698
- dynamic sites, setting up, 702–703
- selecting, 625

data sources, managing online
- deleting data, 807–808
- inserting data, 801–804
- updating data, 804–807

databases
- basics, 698–701
- connecting to. *See* connecting to data sources; data sources
- creating, 824–825
- searches, 725

datepicker (forms), 553

dates
- form controls and, 552
- formatting, 740–741
- inserting into pages, 342–344

<dd> tag, 580

debugging
- applied CSS, 268–269
- browser errors, 54–55
- CSS Advisor site and, 996
- embedded styles and, 207–208
- Live Code and Live View and, 198
- Server Debug panel, 776–778

decimal characters, 231, 232–233

declarations, defined, 239

defaults
- default actions, accepting automatically, 111
- default characteristics of AP elements, setting, 421–422
- default documents, 104, 149, 957
- Default Images folder, 350
- Default templates, 143

definition lists, 579–581

Delete Record server behavior, 807–808

deleting. *See also* removing
- from AP Elements panel, 433
- attributes, 1080
- behaviors, 483
- data, from data sources, 807–808
- Delete Record server behavior, 1096–1097
- frames, 608
- items from Library, 971–972
- styles (CSS), 262
- table rows and columns, 507
- tag libraries, 1080
- tags, 1080
- templates, 951–952

delimiters for code blocks, 1109

descendant selectors (CSS), 252

Description objects, aiding search engines with, 182–183

design connections, maintaining, 717

Design Notes
- basics, 997, 1003, 1004
- customizing, 1006
- disabling, 1003–1004
- heightened visibility of, 1007
- purposes served by, 1005
- reports and, 1013
- setting status with, 1005–1006
- viewing, 1006–1007

Design Time Style Sheet feature, 975

Design view
- basics, 5, 42–43
- Business Catalyst and, 163
- Spry widgets in, 641–642
- text objects in, 73–74

Designer workspace, 35, 36

designers, vs. programmers, 169

design-time style sheets (CSS), 288–289

design-time style sheets, XSLT fragments and, 1045

detail pages
- filtering recordsets, 786
- Go To Detail Page server behavior, 1092–1093
- master-detail page production, automating, 786

detail regions (Spry), 632, 634

detailed document type declarations (DTDs), 1033

development packages, all-in-one, 823

dictionaries, for spell-checking, 300

digital certificates, 1124, 1125

<dir> tag, 583
directory lists, 584
directory servers, 702
disabling
  Design Notes, 1003-1004
  underlines on anchor tags, 383–384
Discover Dynamically-Related Files list, 91
<div> object, 405
<div> tags. *See also* AP elements
  adding to fluid grid layouts, 416–417
  adding to pages, 402
  AP elements and, 428, 429
  basics, 403–404
  CSS and, 405-406, 413-414, 553, 554
  images as, 348
  inserting, 406–408
  jQuery Mobile, 683–684
  navigation buttons and (lists), 571–573
  placing, 405
  positioning content with, 22, 23
  visualizing. *See* visualizing <div> tags
<dl> tags, 580, 637-638
dockable panels. *See* panels
doctype declarations, 172–173
doctype switching, 172
_document object, 939–940
Document Object Model (DOM), commands and, 1058
Document toolbar (Design view mode)
  basics, 51–52
  browser errors, checking for, 54–55
  files, managing, 53–54
  files, previewing, 53
  multiple screen design setup, 52–53
  pages, validating, 54
  Visual Aids and the Refresh Design View buttons, 55–56
Document Toolbar (Live View mode), 56–58
Document Type Definitions (DTDs)
  creating new tag libraries and, 1081
  detailed, 1033
Document window
  basics, 40–41
  Download Indicator, 49–50
  screen size options, 47–49
  Select, Hand, and Zoom tools, 46–47
  status bar basics, 45
  switching views in, 41–44
  Tag Selector feature, 45–46
document-relative addresses, 387-388
documents
  creating new, 147–149
  maximizing, 40–41
  moving within using named anchors, 393–394
  preferences, setting, 90–92, 103–104
  Reopen Documents On Startup option, 91
Don't Rewrite Document Relative Paths option, 919-920
dot notation syntax, 731
double @ signs, 919, 926, 938
double-byte languages, defined, 93
Download Indicator, 49–50
downloading. *See also* websites for downloading
  AIR, 1117
  evaluating download times, 98
  Flash videos, 881–882
  jQuery, 672
  progressive download vs. streaming (Flash), 877, 879–880
Drag AP Element action, 442–444, 459–462
drag-and-drop
  from Bindings panel, 10
  to create framesets, 591–592
  creation of Library items, 969
  inserting dynamic text with, 731
  for text, 297
  for Word and Excel files, 320–321
dragging
  AP elements, 442–444
  images from Assets panel, 352–355
Dreamweaver, customizing, 1057–1082
  commands, adding new. *See* commands
  custom tags, 1075–1077
  extensibility of Dreamweaver CS6, 1057–1058
  keyboard shortcuts. *See* keyboard shortcuts
  menus. *See* menus, customizing
  tag libraries, 1078–1081
Dreamweaver CS6 basics, 3–34
  accessibility, 15–16
  advantages of, 3–4
  Ajax and, 19
  automation enhancements, 27–29
  CMS and, 19
  code editing capabilities, 7–8

Dreamweaver CS6 basics *(continued)*
- connectivity of, 5
- CSS layout control, 22–23
- CSS support, 14–15, 20
- extensibility of. *See* extensibility of Dreamweaver CS6
- form entry, 17
- HTML and XHTML and, 14
- integrated visual and text editors, 5–7
- interface. *See* Dreamweaver interface
- JavaScript behaviors, 23–24
- mobile app development, 24
- multimedia enhancements, 17
- multiple screen design, 18
- multiple-screen framework, 4
- new features. *See* new features, Dreamweaver CS6
- Photoshop, Flash, and Fireworks integration, 20–21
- requirements for running, xlvi–xlvii
- server behaviors, 21
- site management tools. *See* site management tools
- Spry and, 19
- table capabilities, 16–17
- team-orientation of, 9
- text and graphics support, 16
- true page representation, 5
- website maintenance tools, 8–9
- XML and XSLT integration, 21–22

Dreamweaver CS6 Bible companion website, 1129

Dreamweaver interface
- Assets panel, 10–11
- customized workspace, 12
- drag-and-drop from Binding panel, 10
- Find and Replace feature, 14
- keyboard shortcuts, 12
- layout options, 13
- plugin media preview, 13–14
- Tag Selector feature, 12–13
- text entry and, 9–10

Dreamweaver MX2004, 1067

Dreamweaver Standard XML, 1034

Dreamweaver Technique Simulation files, 134

Dreamweaver Techniques, 1130

drivers (JDBC), 709

drop-down menus
- forms, 535–538
- Spry Validation Select widget and, 649–650

Drupal, 820, 821

DSN (Data Source Name)
- ASP developers and, 707–708, 709
- basics, 697, 705–706
- ColdFusion and, 708–711
- connections, converting to DSN-less or OLE DB, 717
- declaring ODBC data sources, 707
- PHP and, 712
- setting up on Windows systems, 705–706

<dt> tag, 580

Dual Screen option, 37

DWfaq Date/Time Server Formats extension, 741

.dwr file extension, search queries and, 306

Dynamic CheckBox dialog box, 798

Dynamic CheckBox server behavior, 799

dynamic data, 729–749. *See also* dynamic form elements
- adding, 732–733
- ASP data formats, 735–737
- ColdFusion data formats, 737–738
- Dynamic Data dialog box, 890
- dynamic text, inserting, 729–731
- formatting, 733, 734–735
- integrating dynamic media, 747–748
- new data formats, 739–741
- PHP data formats, 738
- placeholders, 766, 767
- time/date formatting, 740–741
- viewing, 731–732

dynamic elements server behaviors
- Dynamic CheckBox, 1104–1105
- Dynamic List/Menu, 1102–1103
- Dynamic Radio Buttons, 1105–1106
- Dynamic Text, 1101–1102
- Dynamic Text Field, 1103–1104

dynamic form elements
- checkboxes, 798–799
- list/menus, 800–801
- radio buttons, 799–800
- text fields, 797–798

dynamic images, making, 351–352, 741–746

dynamic lists, 800–801

dynamic pages
- linking to full XSLT pages, 1052
- mapping, 129

Dynamic Related Files feature, 819

dynamic sites
multiple pages and, 781
setting up, 702–703
Dynamic Table dialog box, 754

E

echoing, defined, 528
Edit Command List feature, 1067
Edit NoFrames Content command, 613
Edit Style Sheet dialog box, 248
Edit Styles mode (CSS), 260–262
Edit Tag mode (Quick Tag Editor), 224–225
editable attributes
making, 924–926
setting, 926–928
editable optional regions, 936–937
Editable Region Name tags, 1036
editable regions
adding, 959–962
basics, 916
combining with optional regions, 936–937
content, marking as editable, 916–918
including in tables, 932–933
inserting new, 918
links in templates, creating, 918–920
locking, 920
Editable Tag Attributes dialog box, 924–925
editing
AIR applications, 1125
attributes for tags, 1079–1080
code editing capabilities, 7–8
commands on Standard toolbar, 58–59
content in browsers. *See* InContext Editing
editing preferences, setting, 92–95
font lists, 335–337
graphics within Dreamweaver, 356–357
guide settings, 437
images, 362–363
JavaScript and VBScript, 228–229
Library items, 974–975
new dynamic data formats, 739–741
ordered lists, 566–568
parameters of inserted server behaviors, 1085–1086
preferences, 92–95
server behaviors, 1109
SSIs, 981
tag libraries and tags, 1078–1079
unordered lists, 561
editing table content
basics, 497–498
cutting, copying and pasting, 499–501
inserting content, 501–502
moving through tables, 498–499
editors
BBEdit Integration, Enabling (Macintosh only) option, 100
defining for different file types, 101
External Code Editor option, 100
File Types/Editors options, 99–102
Fireworks, 102
QuickTime 7 Pro for media, 102
Reload Modified Files option and, 100
visual and text, 5–7
elements. *See also* AP elements
absolutely positioned, adding, 402
adding to AP elements, 439
Appear/Fade effect and targeted elements, 474
defined, 170
empty, 407
page elements, excluding from checking, 992–993
Show-Hide Elements action, 469–470
ellipsis (. . .), query strings and, 771
<em> tags
jQuery files, integrating and, 675
preferences and, 93–94, 325
Wrap Tag mode and, 222
e-mail addresses
administrators, 1018
Validate Form action and, 474
e-mail links, adding, 390–391
<embed> tags
with ActiveX, 905
audio parameters, 901
for inserting multimedia objects, 747
parameters, 889
Plugin object, 899
embedded styles (CSS), 243
embedding
audio, 899–900, 905
background music and, 901–902
Flash video, 879

embedding *(continued)*
video, 888
video clips, 886
empty tags, 171
enabling
Check In/Check Out system, 1000–1001
Enable Double-Byte Inline Input option, 93
Enable Related Files option, 91
<enclosure> tags, XML feeds and, 906
encoding
encoding type (<form> attribute), 525–526
Flash video, 878–879
options, 104
options, Page Properties dialog box, 178
preferences for special characters, 119
URL Encoding preferences, 119
enctype (<form> attribute), 525–526
environmental variables, defined, 979
errors
checking for browser errors, 54–55
compatibility errors, 988–991
Live View, 772
Server Debug panel and, 776–778
syntax errors, 144
events
anchor tags and, 452
behaviors and actions and, 450
managing, behaviors and, 453–454
relationship to behaviors, 449
Excel. *See* Microsoft Excel
Exceptions.xml file, 992–993
Expanded Tables mode, 16, 17, 495
export files (Fireworks), 849, 850
exporting
Export Template Data As XML dialog box, 1037
sites, without template markup, 956–957
XML, 1033–1036
expressions, templates, 934–935
extensibility of Dreamweaver CS6
C-Level Extensibility feature, 27, 1057
commands, 26
custom tags, 26–27, 1057, 1075–1077
Extension Manager, 50
Insert panel, 26
keyboard shortcuts, 1057
menus, 1057
objects and behaviors, 24–25, 1057
panels and, 26, 1057
Property inspectors, 1057
Server Behavior Builder, 25–26
Tag libraries, 1057
translators, 1057
Extension Manager, 1108, 1130
extensions
custom, 1064
Default Extension option, 104
on companion website, 1130
Extension Manager, installing MXP extension files, 482
Extensions attributes (CSS), 281–282
external style sheets
applying styles, 259–260
attaching, 254–256
templates and, 916
working with, 242–244
Externalize JavaScript command, 230
eye icon, 661
eye symbol, visibility states and, 432
Eyedropper tool, 79, 179–180

F

fading
highlights, 285–287, 478
tooltips, 675
favicons, 186
Favorites collection, images and, 353, 354
Favorites objects, Insert panel, 75–76
feed icon, 907
feeds, podcast XML feeds, 905–907
fields. *See also* text fields in forms
defined, 698
labels for, 802
<fieldset> tags (forms), 530–531, 556–557
file extensions, advanced categories of objects, 63
file fields (forms), 548
File Management button, 54
file servers, 702
File Transfer Protocol. *See* FTP (File Transfer Protocol)
file types
assigning Fireworks to, 852
defining editors for, 101–102
File Types/Editors options, 99–102

File view columns, 1007–1009
file-based data sources, 698
files
    Always Show Local/Remote Files On The Right/Left option, 110–111
    Bridge files, importing, 864–865
    checking in and out, 1001–1003
    closing, 146
    Dependent Files options, 111
    Discover Dynamically-Related Files list, 91
    on companion website, 1129–1130
    dynamically related files (WordPress), 828–830
    Enable Related Files option, 91
    image files, changing size of, 364
    linking to, 388–389
    linking to audio files, 897–899
    managing, 53–54
    opening, 144–145
    Photoshop, inserting from, 841–843
    pointing to, links and, 386–387
    previewing, 53
    reducing file size (Fireworks), 850–851
    saving, 145
    Shockwave files, adding, 874–875
    source and export files (Fireworks), 850
    SWF attributes, designating, 870–872
    SWF files, inserting, 867–870
files (SVN)
    acquiring latest version, 1025, 1026–1027
    committing, 1026
    local and repository files, viewing, 1024–1025
    locking and unlocking, 1027–1028
    repository files basics, 1023–1024
    working with different versions, 1028
Files panel
    basics, 32, 33
    Point to File feature and, 386
    server testing and, 140
filtering recordsets
    detail page recordsets, 784–786
    filter-by-URL-parameter argument, 786
    using server behaviors, 786–787
filtering XSL data, 1041–1042
filters
    CSS, 281, 282, 283–284
    defined, 700
    Filter Related Files options, 829
    filter types, 720–721
    filtering columns, 718
    search filters, 308–309
Find and Replace feature
    basics, 301–302
    Dreamweaver interface, 14
    format of text and, 304–305
    queries, storing and retrieving, 306
    regular expressions and. *See* regular expressions for Find and Replace
    searching code, advanced options, 307–309
    searching code, types of searches, 306
    searching for specific tags and attributes, 309–310
    searching for text in code, 306–307
    searching for text in content, 306–307
    searching for text relative to specific tags, 307–308
    on visual pages, 302–305
`findTable()` subroutine, 1064
Firefox, plugins for displaying video, 888
firewalls, Firewall Host and Firewall Port options, 112
Fireworks, 847–863
    basics, 20–21
    capabilities, 847
    CS6, 275
    graphic images, creating, 570
    graphics, optimizing, 850–851
    image placeholders, replacing, 853
    images, combining, 854–855
    images, editing, 851–852
    images, modifying, 847–849
    locating, 101
    rollovers. *See* rollovers
    source and export files, 850
    sprites, 854–856
fixed design, 148
Flash, 867–876
    audio, 901
    basics, 867
    integrating dynamically, 747–748
    integrating with Dreamweaver, 20–21
    MIME types, configuring, 872–873
    options for Flash objects, 870–871
    Shockwave files, adding, 874–875
    SWF attributes, designating, 870–872

Flash *(continued)*
SWF files, editing, 873–874
SWF files, inserting, 17, 867–870
SWF files, publishing videos and, 883
Flash Edit button (Dreamweaver), 873, 874
Flash video. *See also* FLV files
adding, 877–878, 885
embedding, 879
encoding, 878–879
expressInstall.swf file, 883
Flash Media Server, 883
Flash Professional CS6, 878
Flash Video Import Wizard, 879
Flash Video Streaming Service, 880
inserting, 880–883
parameters, modifying, 884
progressive download vs. streaming, 879–880
publishing, 883–884
swfobject_modified.js file, 883
video revolution, 878
flat-file databases, defined, 698
Fletcher, Mark, 195
floated images, 368–369
floating frames, 614–616
floating panels, 26
Fluid Grid Layout feature, 4, 147
fluid grids
basics, 401, 414–415
helper files, 418–419
media queries and, 415, 418
working with, 415–418
FLV files
adding, 881–883
Dreamweaver support for, 17, 20
encoding, 879
FLVPlayer_Progressive.swf, 883
FLVPlayer_Streaming.swf, 883
focus, highlighting, 557–558
:focus selectors, creating, 557–558
folders
cloaking/uncloaking site folders, 140–141
Default Images folder, 350
local site folder, 130–133
Server Folder field, 766, 768
fonts
assigning specific text fonts, 333–337
categories of, 334–335
font list, editing, 335–336
preferences, setting, 114–116
selecting, 335
text font color, adding, 330–333
text font size, adjusting, 328–330
web fonts, xxxiv–xxxv, 338–342
form fields
basics of validating, 642–643
initial values in, 797
<form> tags
attributes, 523
CSS and, 553, 554
formats
audio format support, 909
defining Fireworks as editor for, 852
of e-mail addresses, 390
file formats (Fireworks), 850
file formats (Photoshop), 841–842
files formats, Bridge and, 865
graphics, 102
HTML5 browser support for (video), 894
of text, basics of modifying, 328
validation patterns and, 645
video clip file formats, 886–887
formatting
CSS Source Format Options, 123–125
definition lists, 580
lists, 561
formatting dynamic data
ASP data formats, 735–737
basics, 733–735
ColdFusion data formats, 737–738
new data formats, 739–741
PHP data formats, 738
time/date, 740–741
forms, 521–558. *See also* dynamic form elements; Spry
accessibility, improving, 548–550
AP elements and, 439–440
basics, 522–524
building, 522, 532–535, 539–541
buttons, 545–547
checkboxes, 531–532
defined, 521
drop-down menus, 535–538
file fields, 548
<form> tag attributes, 523

Forms objects (Insert panel), 67
hidden fields, 547–548
HTML5 form elements, 550–553
implementing, 17
inserting, 524–526
jump menus, 541–544
menu values, 537–538
radio buttons, 532
Rename Form Items When Pasting option, 118
scrolling lists, 538–539
styling, with CSS. *See* CSS for styling forms
text fields. *See* text fields in forms
Validate Form action, 472–474
forms, getting values from
basics, 791–792
form and URL values, passing to related pages, 794–795
passing values, 792–794
forums (Dreamweaver), xlvii
forward slashes (/), site-root-relative addresses and, 387
`_fr` suffix, 600
frames and framesets, 587–617
basics, 587–589
content, modifying, 468, 608
controversy over, 587
creating, quick technique for, 588
frame content, targeting, 609–612
frame margins, setting, 608
Frame Property inspector, 604–608
frameless browsers, 612–613
frames, adding, 595–597
frames, deleting, 608
frames, modifying, 604–608
frames, naming, 604–605
frames, resizing, 601–602, 607–608
frames, updating, 462
frameset borders, 602–603, 605–606
frameset files, creating, 589–591
Frameset Property inspector, 600–603
framesets, closing, 599
framesets, creating visually, 591–593
framesets, creating with frame objects, 593–595
framesets, establishing, 599–600
iframes, 614–616
saving, 598–599
scroll bars, adding, 606–607
selecting, 597–598
web pages, opening into frames, 605
frameworks. *See also* JavaScript frameworks
defined, 621, 669
Dreamweaver and various, 669
FTP (File Transfer Protocol)
connecting to remote servers and, 136–138
disconnection options, 111
enhancements in Dreamweaver CS6, xxxix
FTP Log panel, 155, 156
FTP publisher, 32
FTP Time Out option, 111
FTP transfer engine, 8
Select Default Action In Dialogs After __ Seconds, 111
transferring with, 134, 154–156
`ftp://` scheme, 380
full-page refreshes, defined, 620
functions
jQuery functions, adding, 672–675
triggering custom, 455
`.fw` suffix (Fireworks), 850

G

General Preferences, 89–95
GeoTrust, 1124
`Get` method
HTTP Request Setting and, 772, 773, 774
passing parameters with, 792
Get More Behaviors menu option, 453
Go buttons (jump menus), 544
Go To Detail Page server behavior, 1092–1093
Go To Related Page server behavior, 794–795, 1093
Go to URL action, 462
gradients (CSS), 275
graphical buttons (forms), 544, 546–547
graphics. *See also* images
adjusting in WordPress sites, 833–835
background, for navigation buttons (lists), 567, 570–571
changing source files of, 848
Dreamweaver support for, 16
graphics-related objects in Common category, 65
optimizing, Fireworks and, 850–851
picking for layout guides, 178–179
wrapping around jump menus, 543–544

grids. *See also* fluid grids
aligning objects with, 438–439
grouping
declarations (CSS), 239
form controls, 530–531
properties (CSS), 239
regular expressions, 315–316
Grow/Shrink effect, 476–478
guides
for aligning AP elements, 434–438
graphics for layout guides, 178–179

H

<h1>–<h6> tags, preferences and, 94
H.264 codec, 879
hacks (CSS), 261
Hand tool, (Document window), 46
<head> elements
<meta> tags basics, 180
Appearance (CSS), 175
Appearance (HTML), 175–176
Base object, 185
basics, 173–174
built-in meta commands, 182
colors, selecting from onscreen images, 179–180
Headings (CSS), 176–177
Link object, 185–186
Links (CSS), 176
Meta object, 180–182
Page Properties dialog box basics, 174
pages, refreshing, 183–184
search engines, 182–183
Title/Encoding, 178
Tracing Image, 178–179
<head> objects, 66
<head> tags
basics, 170, 171, 180
changing bases and, 185
linking to other files and, 185–186
objects, 181
refreshing pages and, 183–184
search engines, aiding and, 182–183
headings
column and row headings, 488–489
converting paragraphs to, 294
CSS, 176–177
size of, 292, 293
Switch To Plain Paragraph After Heading option, 93
text in HTML, 291–294, 344–346
height
of AP elements, 106–107
of cells, 514–515
of images, adjusting, 364–365
of images, in source code, 349
of tables, 504, 506
helper files (fluid grids), 418–419
hidden fields (forms), 547–548
hidden objects (forms), 547
hiding
invisible elements, 95
page elements, 756–758
panels, 80–84
Show-Hide Elements action, 446
Highlight effect, 478–479
highlighting
code, 206
focus, 557–558
forms with CSS, 553–554
preferences, 96–97
hint list, 222
hints. *See* code hinting
history
Maximum Number Of History Steps option, 94
of revisions (Design Notes), 1005
History panel
basics, 29
customizing menus and, 1066–1067
Undo and Redo commands and, 298
home page, opening (WordPress), 827–828
horizontal alignment
of images, 367
of table cells/rows/columns, 513
horizontal rules, 372–373
hosted streaming services, 880
hotflash.mp3 files, 899
hotspots (Fireworks), 859–860
href attribute, 185, 892, 919
HTML (HyperText Markup Language)
Clean Up HTML command, 1059–1061
Clean Up XHTML command, 1059–1061
Code for an HTML Table (listing), 485

code searches and, 306
Dreamweaver capabilities and, 14
on Dreamweaver pages, 292
dynamic text and, 730
entering large amounts of, 445
fonts, 334
forms. *See* forms
HTML for a New Dreamweaver Page (listing), 170
Insert HTML mode, 221–222
page structure, 170–171
pages, converting to XSLT, 1047, 1050–1051
pages, merging HTML data into, 622–627
Property inspector and, 76–77
reports, outputting, 1012
rollovers and, 375
structuring data in XSLT fragments and, 1040
tables fundamentals, 485–489. *See also* tables
tags and attributes, replacing, 309–311
tags for formatting dynamic data, 733–734
Word HTML, importing, 322–324
vs. XHTML, 171–172, 1059
vs. XML, 1032
vs. XSL and XML files, 1047
HTML5
browser support for audio formats, 909
coding audio players, 907–910
form elements, 550–553
HTML5 <video> tag, 877
structural tags, 191–195
video code, 893–895
HTML5 24-Hour Trainer (Wiley), 195
HTTP request settings (Live View)
changing, 774–775
HTTP Request Settings dialog box, 772–774, 793
query strings, 770–772, 775
http scheme, 380
hyperlinks, setting appearance, 176
hypertext, defined, 170
hypertext for web surfing
address types, 387
linking to files, 388–389
links, assigning, 381
links, checking, 388–390
pointing to files, 386–387
underlines, eliminating from links, 381–385
URLs, inserting from Assets panel, 385–386

I

<i> tags, preferences and, 93–94
icons
AP element icons, 420
color of (Insert panel), 64
favicons, 186
feed icon, 907
named anchors, 393
Point to File icon, 383, 386, 393
reducing panels to, 83
ID selector type (CSS), 251
ID selectors, defining, 241
ID3 tags, 905
IDs (AP elements), 426
iframes, 614–616
Image Optimization dialog box, 841–842, 843, 847–848
Image Property inspector, 357, 363–364
Image Tag Accessibility Attributes dialog box, 349, 366
<image> tags, 363
images. *See also* Photoshop, integrating with Dreamweaver
AP elements background images option, 107
combining in Fireworks, 854–855
data columns and, 635
editing with Fireworks, 851–852
effect of texture settings, 571
joining background images in frames, 604
making dynamic, 741–746
modifying Fireworks images, 847–849
modifying Photoshop images, 845–846
modifying sliced images, 862–863
onscreen, selecting colors from, 179–180
Preload Images action, 465–466
replacing placeholders (Fireworks), 853
rescaling (Fireworks), 848
resizing Smart Object images, 845
Swap Image and Swap Image Restore actions, 471–472
Tracing Image (Page Properties dialog box), 178–179
trimming, rollovers and, 858
images, inserting, 347–377
background images, 369–372, 431
banner ads, 373–374
horizontal rules, 372–373
inline images. *See* inline images
methods for, 348–352, 355–356
Photoshop images, 842–843

images, inserting *(continued)*
quickstart method for, 347–348
rollovers, 375–377
tiling images, 371
images, optimizing and altering
alignment, 367–369
basics, 356–357
borders, adding, 366
brightness and contrast, altering, 360
cropping, 357–359, 362–363
editing, 362–363
height and width, adjusting, 364–365
Image Property inspector and, 364
image tag (<img>) and, 363
lines, sharpening, 360–361
Optimize Image command, 361–362
resampling after resizing, 359
size, reducing, 363
import method, external style sheets and, 242–243
Import XML command, 1036
importing
DTDs for new tag libraries, 1081
Microsoft Office documents, 319–320
office documents, 28–29
tabular data, 516–518
Word HTML, 322–324
XML, 1036–1037
Inconsistent Region Names dialog box, 953
InContext Editing
basics, 31, 957–958
editable regions, adding, 959–962
objects, 73
Property inspector options, 960–961
repeating page sections, 962–963
templates, basics of setting up, 958–959
Indent button, nested lists and, 582
indenting code
changing, 190
Indent Code button, 207
options, 121–122
indenting text, 316
index fields, defined, 699
_index property, template expression example, 943–944
inheritance
<form> tags and <div> tags and (forms), 553
HTML tags and, 239–240
of properties (CSS), 239–240
Init Value text box, (Text Field Property inspector), 527
initial values in form fields, 797
inline frames, 614–616
inline images
alignment options, 367–369
vs. background images, 370
basics of optimizing and altering, 356–357
borders, adding, 366
brightness and contrast, altering, 360
cropping, 357–359, 362–363
descriptions, adding, 365–366
dragging from Assets panel, 352–355
editing, 362–363
height and width, adjusting, 364–365
Image Property inspector and, 364
image tags, <img>, 363
inserting, 348–352, 355–356
lines, sharpening, 360–361
making dynamic, 351–352
naming, 364
Optimize Image command, 361–362
Relative to Document, 350–351
Relative to Site Root, 351
resampling after resizing, 359
size, reducing, 363
text, wrapping, 368–369
inline styles (CSS), 243–244
input controls (forms), 523
input fields (forms), altering with CSS, 554–555
Input Tag Accessibility Attributes dialog box, 548, 549
input types (HTML-5 forms), 551–552
<input> tags (forms), 550–551
Insert Fireworks HTML command, 862
Insert method, adding dynamic data with, 733
Insert panel, 63–76
ASP objects, 76
basics, 63–64
capabilities, 26
CFML and CFForm objects, 76
common objects, 64–66
data objects, 68
Favorites category of objects, 75–76
forms objects, 67
frame objects, 593–594
InContext Editing objects, 73
jQuery Mobile objects, 71–73

layout objects, 66–67
PHP objects, 76
Script objects, 229
Spry objects, 69–71
text objects, 73–74
XSLT objects, 76
Insert Record server behavior, 802–803, 1094–1095
inserting
absolutely positioned elements, 402
AP element objects, 419–421
AP elements, 426–427
banner ads, 373–374
Business Catalyst modules, 162
buttons, 545
dates into pages, 342–344
<div> tags, 402, 406–408
drop-down menus (forms), 536
editable regions, 918
Flash video, 880–883, 885
forms, 524–526
images. *See* images, inserting
JavaScript and VBScript, 228
Library items, 966, 969–971
Meta objects, 181
multiline text areas (forms), 528–531
named anchors, 392–393, 395–396
new items in ordered lists, 568
optional regions, 936
ordered lists, 567
properties into rules, 263
QuickTime movies, 889–893
radio buttons, 532
Refresh objects, 184
rollover images, 376
scrolling lists (forms), 538
server behaviors, 1085–1086
Show Attributes When Inserting option, 105
snippets, 206–207, 214–215
Spry Validation Checkbox widget, 651
Spry Validation Confirm widget, 654–655
Spry Validation Password widget, 653
Spry Validation Radio Group, 655–656
Spry Validation Select widget and, 649–650
Spry Validation Text Field widgets, 643–644
Spry Validation Textarea widget, 647–648
symbols and special characters, 231–234
table content, 501–502
tags and code (Insert HTML mode), 221–222
text fields in forms, 526–528
text from other applications, 297–298
text into paragraphs, 295–296
unordered lists, 562–563
Update Record server behavior, 1095–1096
URLs from Assets panel, 392–393
variables as data sources, 808–811
Inspect mode, layout and, 409–410
installing
AIR, 1117–1118
MXP files, 1108
new behaviors, 481–482
non-standard server behaviors, 1108
WordPress, 823–826
instances of templates, defined, 921
integrating Live View, Related Files and Code Navigator features
basics, 195–196
enhanced workflow with Live View, 196–197
Live Code, 198–199
Live View options, 199–200
navigating with Code Navigator, 201–203
Related Files, accessing, 200–201
interactive AP elements, creating, 442–446
interfaces
Contribute, 1014–1015
Dreamweaver CS6. *See* Dreamweaver interface
Invisible Elements
Invisible Elements panel, 95–96
repeating regions and, 929–930
iTunes, adding ID3 tags, 905

J

Java
basics, 225
Java applets, adding, 225–227
JavaScript
Ajax and, 619, 620
editing, 228–229
extracting, 230–231
freezing, 199
inserting, 228
vs. Java, 227

JavaScript *(continued)*
- null links and, 394
- rollovers and, 375
- Spry and, 621
- targeted commands, 444
- template expressions and, 938
- unobtrusive JavaScript, 230
- updating multiple frames and, 610–611
- vs. VBScript, 227–228

JavaScript behaviors
- basics, 23–24
- vs. server behaviors, 1083–1084, 1085

JavaScript frameworks, 669–694
- apps, building with jQuery Mobile. *See* jQuery Mobile framework
- basics, 669–670
- code hinting, 670–671
- frameworks, defined, 621, 669
- functions, integrating, 691–693
- jQuery, downloading, 672
- jQuery functions, adding, 672–675
- legacy web widgets, 676–678
- PhoneGap, 691–693
- web widgets basics, 669–670
- Widget Browser, 670, 678–682

JDBC (Java Database Connectivity), drivers basics, 709

joins, defined, 700

Joomla, 820, 821

JPEG format, 841

jQuery
- adding functions to pages, 672–675
- downloading, 672
- jQuery Tutorials for Designer series, 674

jQuery Mobile framework, 682–691
- basics, 24, 25, 682
- Mobile Starters, 683–685
- objects, 71–73, 685–688
- pages, 683–685
- themes, 688–691

jQuery ThemeRoller, xxxvii, 688, 689, 690–691

Jump Menu and Jump Menu Go actions, 463–464

jump menus (forms), 541–544

K

key fields, defined, 699

Keyboard Shortcut editor, 1058, 1067–1070

keyboard shortcuts
- basics of customizing, 1057, 1066
- capabilities, 12
- for changing AP elements dimensions, 424
- creating custom, 1069
- for indenting and outdenting code, 190
- Keyboard Shortcut editor, 1067–1070
- `menus.xml` file and, 1070–1072
- panels, 80, 81–83
- shortcut modifier keys, 1072
- text alignment, 337

keywords
- aiding search engines with, 182–183
- in SQL, 724

Kuler Desktop, 1116

L

La, Nick, 674

`<label>` ... `</label>` tags (forms), 548, 549

labels
- in drop-down lists, 800, 802
- in forms, 548, 556–557

Labs site and mini-site, 621, 622

languages (computer)
- tag groupings and, 213
- tag libraries and, 169
- template expressions, 938–941

languages (spoken)
- Enable Double-Byte Inline Input option, 93
- fonts and, 114
- preferences, spell-checking dictionary, 94–95
- spell-checking text in, 301

launching Bridge, 863–864

layout
- capabilities, 13
- Layout menu button, 50
- Layout objects (Insert panel), 66–67
- options (data set creation), 627
- Spry layout widgets, 657

layouts, 401–447. *See also* workspace layouts
- AP elements, activating with behaviors, 442–446
- AP elements basics, 403
- AP elements, creating. *See* AP elements, creating
- AP elements, inserting, 426–427

AP elements, modifying. *See* AP elements, modifying; CSS-P Property inspector, AP elements and
<div> tags and. *See* <div> tags
fluid grids. *See* fluid grids
Tracing Image function, 440–442
.lbi files, 971
.lck (lock) extensions, 1000
<legend> tags, 530–531
legends, in forms, 556–557
<li> ... </li> tag pair (lists), 561, 564, 567
libraries
basics, 29–30
templates and, 914
Library Item Properties panel, 971
Library items, 965–978
adding, 968–969
applying and modifying, 977–978
basics, 966–968
creating, 965–966
deleting, 971–972
editing, 974–975
inserting, 966, 969–971
Library Assets panel basics, 967–968
moving to new sites, 969
navigating with, 973
renaming, 972
vs. SSIs, 978
websites, updating with, 975–976
line breaks

 tags, 318–319
line control options, 122
in lists, 562
TD Tag option, 123
line-height property, 318
lines
horizontal, to divide web pages, 372–373
sharpening, 360–361
line-spacing, 318-319
Link Checker
basics, 32
Link Checker panel, 388, 389
link method, external style sheets and, 242–243
linking
to audio files, 897–899
dynamic pages to full XSLT pages, 1052
to other files, 185–186
to podcasts and feeds, 907
to video, 887–888
video clips, 886
XSLT pages from XML pages, 1048–1049
links, 379–398
assigning, 381
checking, 388–390
creating, 381–383
e-mail links, adding, 390–391
hypertext for web surfing. *See* hypertext for web surfing
to images, 351
importance of, 379
list creation and, 573
navigating with anchors. *See* anchors, navigating with
passing parameters and, 781–782
record navigation links, building, 758–760
rollovers and, 375
sequential navigation links example, 946–947
targeting links, 396–397
in templates, creating, 918–920
underlines, eliminating from, 383–385
updating options, 92
URLs fundamentals, 379–381
XML data as, 1039
Links (CSS), of Page Properties dialog box, 176
liquid design, 148
List options (CSS), 279
list/menus, linking to dynamic data, 800–801
lists, 559–585
bulleted, creating. *See* unordered lists
definition lists, 579–581
Dynamic List/Menu server behavior, 1102–1103
navigation buttons, creating from. *See* navigation buttons, creating from lists
nested, 581–583
ordered. *See* ordered lists
Select (List/Menu) object, 555–556
special list types, accessing, 583–584
text wraps in, 543–544
Live Code, 44, 56–58, 198–199, 410
Live View, 765–779. *See also* integrating Live View, Related Files and Code Navigator features
applications, previewing in browsers, 775–776
basics, 43–44, 56–58

Live View *(continued)*
Business Catalyst and, 163
CMS and, 819, 827, 828
entering and exiting, 768–769
Follow Links Continuously, 832
HTTP request settings. *See* HTTP request settings (Live View)
importance of, 765
Inspect mode and, 410
making changes in, 769–770
options, 199–200
page styling, 5–6
Server Debug panel, 776–778
setting up for, 766–768
true page representation and, 5
for viewing dynamic images, 743
for viewing dynamic pages, 731–732
workings of, 766
local site folder, 130–133
Localhost, for addressing local web servers, 768
locked regions, nested templates and, 947–948
locking
editable regions, 920
guides, 436
SVN files, 1027–1028
log out
customer log out, 816
Log Out User server behavior, 816, 1099–1100
logical styles, 187, 324–325
login
customer login, 812–813
Log In User server behavior, 812–813, 1097–1098
longdesc attribute (<img> tag), 365, 366
loop attribute (<audio> tag), 909

M

Macintosh
changes in Dreamweaver user interface and, xxxix
color pickers and, 333
conventions in this book for, xliv
DSN and, 705
files on website, 1129
JDBC and, 709
MAMP for, 823, 824
Wamp and, 768
workspace layouts for, 39, 40
magnification tools, 46–47
mail servers, 702
mailto: scheme, 381
maintenance tools, 8–9
MAMP, 715, 768, 823, 824
Manage Site option (Business Catalyst), 160, 161
Manage Sites dialog box, xxxix, xl, 142, 159, 160
manually inserting data into data sources, 802–803
mapping
dynamic pages, 129
inconsistent template, 952–954
margins
around boxes, 277
in frames, 608
Marketplace & Exchange site, MXP extension files and, 481–482
markup
markup elements or tags, 170
markup languages, defined, 170
XML, 1032–1033
Master Detail Page Set, 68
master pages
types of, 782
user-driven, developing. *See* forms, getting values from
master regions (Spry), 632, 634
master-detail page production, automating, 787–791
Master-Detail Page Set application object, 788–791
maximizing documents, 40–41
Maximum Number Of History Steps option, 94
measurements (guides), displaying, 435–436
media
dynamic media, integrating, 747–748
media queries, 133, 415, 418
media types, Style Rendering toolbar and, 59
multimedia enhancements, 17
plugin media preview, 13–14
QuickTime 7 Pro for, 102
types, selecting (CSS), 254–256
Media Encoder, 879, 880
Media.IO converter, 909
menu bars
menu bar definitions, 1072–1074
Menu Bar widget (Spry), 657–659
<menubar> section (menus .xml), 1070–1071, 1072

menus
accessing (Document window), 85–86
applying styles with, 257
creating AP elements with, 420–421
creating framesets with, 592
drop-down menus (forms), 535–538
jump menus (forms), 541–544
menu lists, 583–584
orientation of, 659
splitting frames with, 596
Spry Menu Bar widget, 657–659
menus, customizing
basics, 1057, 1066
History panel and, 1066–1067
menu commands, 1074–1075
menuitem tag attributes, 1073
menus.xml file
commands and, 1058
customizing, 1070–1074
customizing menus and, 1066
merging cells, 509–511
<meta> information, templates and, 916
<meta> tags, 180–183
method: attribute (<form> tag), 523
Method option, disabling query strings and, 772
Microsoft Excel, 319–321
Microsoft Office documents
content, copying and pasting, 320
drag-and-drop for, 320–321
importing, 28–29, 319–320
Word HTML, importing, 322–324
Microsoft Windows
conventions in this book for, xliv
declaring ODBC data sources, 707
files on companion website, 1129
local DSN, setting up on, 705–706
Server Debug panel with ColdFusion, 776–778
whereas WampServer, 768
XAMPP for, 823, 824
Microsoft Word
drag-and-drop for files, 320–321
Dreamweaver and, 28
HTML, importing, 322–324
web pages and, 319
MIME types, configuring (Flash), 872–873
mobile app development, 24
mobile applications, new features, xxxvi–xxxviii
mobile devices (jQuery Mobile framework), 24, 25, 71–72
mobile phones screens, 47–48
Mobile Starters (jQuery Mobile), 683–685
modifying. *See also* editing
behaviors, 483–484
jump menus (forms), 542–543
Library items, 975, 977–978
shortcuts, 1071–1072
SSI files, 978
modules, Business Catalyst, 161–164
mouse
creating framesets with, 591–592
growing and shrinking thumbnails and, 476–477
selecting entire tables with, 495–496
splitting frames with, 596–597
mouseovers, 375–377
Move CSS Rules, 62
Move To External Style Sheet dialog box, 266–267
Move To Specific Record server behavior, 786–787, 1090
moving
AP elements, 424–425
code, 204–205
guides, 435
Library items to new sites, 969
move options for HTML files, 112
text, 296, 297–298
Tracing Image, 441–442
MP3 files
embedding plugins for, 898, 900
Flash for, 901
podcasts and, 905
MPEG format, 886
multiline text areas (forms), 528–531
multimedia enhancements, 17
multipage applications, 781–818
basics, 781–782
checkboxes, 798–799
customer access restrictions, 813–815
customer log out, 816
customer login, 812–813
customers, adding, 816–817
customers, relating to, 812
data sources, managing online. *See* data sources, managing online
dynamic form elements, 797

multipage applications *(continued)*
form and URL values, passing to related pages, 794–795
forms, basics of passing information from, 791–792
forms, passing multiple values from, 793–794
forms, passing single values from, 792–793
list/menus, 800–801
master-detail page production, automating, 787–791
parameters, basics of passing, 781–782
parameters, receiving, 784–787
parameters, sending, 782–784
radio buttons, 799–800
search pages, building, 795–796
sending parameters, 782
text fields, 797–798
variables, inserting, 808–811
multiple checkboxes, validating, 652
multiple classes, inserting (CSS), 253–254
multiple conditional regions, creating, 1044–1045
multiple pages, dynamic websites and, 781
multiple Repeat Region server behaviors, 753
multiple screens, xxxvi, 4, 18, 52–53
multiple Smart Object images, 845
multiple-if template expressions, 941
multiuser operating systems, customizing, 1063–1064
MXP files, 1108
MySQL, connections, 715–716
MySQL Workbench, 721
myVersionControl, 1022

N

named anchors
basic use of, 391–392
fundamentals, 391
inserting, 392–393, 395–396
using in different pages, 394
named characters, 231, 232
namespaces (XML), defined, 622
naming
AP elements, 432
buttons (forms), 545
checkboxes (forms), 531
custom styles (CSS), 251
editable regions, 916, 917, 929
files, 146
form elements, 792
form input tags, 523–524
frames, 604–605
images, 364
inconsistent region names, 952–954
recordsets, 719
Rename Form Items When Pasting option, 118
renaming Library items, 972
repeating regions, 929
sets of radio buttons, 532
navigating. *See also* record navigation
with anchors. *See* anchors, navigating with
with Code Navigator, 196, 201–203
with jump menus (forms), 541–544
with Library items, 973
within tables, 498–499
navigation bars, 856–859
navigation buttons, creating from lists
background graphics, preparing, 570–571
basics, 569–570
CSS, applying, 578–579
CSS files, setting up, 571–573
CSS styles, building, 573–578
navigation bars basics, 569
navigation links, computing sequential, 946–947
neat forms, 529–530
nested lists, 581–583
nesting
AP <div> tags, 427
AP elements options, 108
with AP Elements panel, 432–433
templates, 947–949
New Document dialog box, 147–149, 244
new features, Dreamweaver CS6
Business Catalyst, xl–xli
CSS styling, xxxiii–xxxv
for mobile applications, xxxvi–xxxviii
multiple screens, xxxvi
program functionality, xxxviii–xxxix
New Optional Region dialog box, 934, 935
New Transition dialog box, 286
No Label Tag option (forms), 549
nodes, data sets and, 627
<noframes> tags, 612–613
nonmodal windows, defined, 302
Nonvisual Server Markup Tags option, 96
null links, creating, 394--396

numbered lists. *See* ordered lists
numbering
  automatic row numbering, 943–944
  numbering styles, ordered lists, 566, 568–569
numbers, form controls and, 552

O

object libraries, 29–30
object model, template expressions, 938–941
<object> tags
  for inserting multimedia objects, 747
  Object Tag Accessibility Attributes dialog box (Flash), 868–869
  <object> ... </object> tag pair, ActiveX, 905
objects, 1081
  AP elements objects, inserting, 419–420
  vs. commands, 1058
  conditional, 1043
  defined, 24, 25
  extensibility and, 24–25
  files extensions for advanced categories, 63
  head tag, 181
  jQuery Mobile, 685–688
  Show Attributes When Inserting option and, 105
  Show Dialog When Inserting Objects option, 92–93
  in templates, 915–916
ODBC
  basics, 714
  declaring, 707
  drivers, 714
Office. *See* Microsoft Office documents
Offscreen Rendering option, 105
<ol> tags, inserting, 637–638
OLE (Object Linking and Embedding) DB
  connections, 697, 714–715
  converting DSN connections to, 717
On2 VP6-encoded FLV files, 879
onClick function, 440
Open Browser Window action, 464–465
Open Documents feature (Coding toolbar), 203
Open In Code View option, 100
opening
  files, 144–145
  home page (WordPress), 827–828
  panels, 83
  templates, 951–952
operators, template expressions, 938–939
Optimize Image command, 361–362
<option> tags (forms)
  distinguishing lists and menus and, 555–556
  <option> ... </option> tag pair, 536
optional regions, 933–947
  alternating row colors, 941–943
  automatic row numbering, 943–944
  basic and advanced, 934–935
  basics, 933–934
  editable optional regions, 936–937
  inserting, 936
  multiple-if template expressions, 941
  properties, setting, 937
  sequential navigation links, computing, 946–947
  template expressions basics, 937–938
  template expressions language and object model, 938–941
  values in tables, computing, 944–945
orange and white feed icon, 907
ordered lists
  basics, 565–566
  editing, 566–568
  inserting, 560–561, 567
  numbering styles, 568–569
O'Reilly reference guides, 29, 217, 218, 744
orphaned files, defined, 32
Outdent button, unnesting lists and, 582
overflow settings (AP elements), 429–430

P

<p> and <h1>–<h6> tags, preferences and, 94
<p> tags, 318, 348
packaging AIR applications, 1122–1126
padding around boxes, 277, 278
Page Properties dialog box, 441
  Appearance (CSS), 175
  Appearance (HTML), 175–176
  basics, 174, 601
  Headings (CSS), 176–177
  Links (CSS), 176
  Title/Encoding, 178
  Tracing Image, 178–179
page properties, frames, 603–604
Pagebreak attribute, 281

pages. *See also* XSLT full pages, building
- adding <div> tags to, 402
- adding InContext Editing repeating regions, 962–963
- adding Spry Accordion Panel widgets, 662–663
- adding Spry Collapsible Panel widget, 663
- adding Spry Menu Bar, 657–658
- adding Spry regions, 632
- adding Spry Tabbed Panel widget, 660
- adding Spry Tooltip widgets, 665–666
- adding tables, 493–494
- adding Tracing Image, 440–441
- adding unordered lists, 562–563
- adding XSLT fragments, 1045–1046
- binding data to, 634–635, 1038-1040
- clearing, 45
- converting for browser compatibility, 983–985
- converting to templates, 923–924
- creating, based on templates, 920–922
- dates, inserting, 342–344
- dividing with horizontal lines, 372–373
- finding text on, 302–305
- Go To Related Page server behavior, 1093
- HTML, 170–171, 192–195
- HTML data, merging into, 622–627
- incorporating data into, 622, 639–641
- jQuery Mobile, creating, 683
- multiple, dynamic websites and, 781
- named anchors, using in, 394
- new, creating and saving, 143–146
- opening into frames, 605
- page elements, showing/hiding, 756–758
- passing form and URL values to, 794–795
- permission to display, 588
- placeholder pages, 143
- previewing, 49–53
- refreshing, 183–184
- removing template markup from, 955
- Restrict Access To Page server behavior, 1098–1099
- saving, 143–146, 627
- search pages, building, 795–796
- transferring with FTP, 154–156
- validating, 54

panels
- available, 81–83
- basics, 80
- customizing panel groups, 84
- displaying, 83
- extensibility and, 1057
- hiding and showing, 80–84
- Keep Focus In The Panel When Opening option, 105
- panel groups, defined, 80
- reducing to icons, 83

paragraphs
- basics of working with, 294–295
- converting to headings, 294
- copying, 296–297
- creating lists from, 560–561
- cut-and-paste, 296
- drag-and-drop, 297
- entering and pasting text, 299
- History panel, 298
- quoting text paragraphs, 338
- Redo command, 298
- Repeat command, 300
- switch to plain option, 93
- text, inserting, 295–298
- Undo command, 298

<param> tags, for inserting multimedia objects, 747

parameters. *See also* passing parameters with URLs
- altering behavior parameters, 482
- Flash, 870–871, 872, 884
- of optional regions, 937
- QuickTime plugins, 890–892
- Shockwave objects, 875
- Windows Media Player, 904

Parameters dialog box
- Flash, 872
- QuickTime, 890

parent-child relationships, 239–240

parsing responses, defined, 524

partial-page refreshes, Ajax and, 620

Partner Portal option (Business Catalyst), 160

passing parameters with URLs
- master-detail page production, automating, 787–791
- parameters, receiving, 784–787
- parameters, sending, 782–784

passwords
- password field (forms), 528
- Spry Validation Password widget, 652–654

pasting
  cell contents, 499–500
  code, 298
  copy/paste preferences, 102–103
  Microsoft Office documents contents, 320
  Paste Special command, 297, 321
  from Photoshop, 843–844
  Rename Form Items When Pasting option, 118
  text, 296–297, 299
PhoneGap, xxxvii–xxxviii, 691–693,
Photoshop, integrating with Dreamweaver
  basics, 20–21, 839, 841
  copying and pasting from, 843–844
  editing graphics and, 357, 361
  images, making dynamic, 840
  inserting files from, 841–843
  PSD files, opening, 840
  Smart Objects, 844–847
PHP
  CMS apps and, 820, 821
  connections, setting up, 716
  DSN and, 712
  MySQL and, 715
  PHP MySQL server model, 827
  PHP objects (Insert panel), 76
  WordPress and, 821
phpMyAdmin, 823, 824
physical styles, 188, 324, 325
placeholder pages, 143
placeholders
  banner ads and, 374
  images, replacing (Fireworks), 853
  MIDI files and, 902
  templates and, 915
planning web sites, 128–129
playing video, 888–889
plugins
  Check Plugin action and, 458
  Firefox, displaying video and, 888
  plugin media preview, 13–14
  Plugin object, 899, 900
  QuickTime plugins, 889, 890–892
  specific plugins, targeting for audio, 902–905
  for video playback, 877
plus signs (+), as field separators, 524
PNG, Fireworks and, 847, 850
podcasts, 905–907
pointing to files
  links, creating, 386–387
  Point to File icon, 386, 393, 919
Popup Message action, 465
`position:absolute` in `style` attribute, 615
positioning
  absolute, 13, 401, 402, 403
  of AP elements, 403, 404
  of guides, 435, 436–437
  options, 279–280
  relative, 401, 422–423
`Post` method
  HTTP Request Setting and, 772, 773
  passing parameters with, 792
`<pre>`... `</pre>` tag pair, 317, 318
preferences, 89–125
  accessibility, 105–106
  AP elements, 106–108, 421–422
  browser, 112–114
  code, customizing, 114
  code color, 119–121
  code fonts, 114–116
  code format, 121–124
  code hints, 116–117
  code rewriting, 117–119
  copy/paste, 102–103
  CSS styles, 108–109
  documents, 90–92
  editing, 92–95
  File Types/Editors category, 99–102
  general, 89–90
  highlighting, 96–97
  invisible elements, 95–96
  new documents, 103–104
  for online connections, 110
  Preferences dialog box, 89
  site, 110–112
  W3C Validator, 124–125, 986–987
  window size, 98–99
prefixes
  appended, when inserting images, 350–351
  vendor-specific, 264
preformatted text, 317–318

preload attribute (<audio> tag), 909
Preload Images action, 465–467
Preview in Browser button, 53
previewing
  AIR applications, 1119
  applications in browsers, 775–776
  BrowserLab for, 151–153
  files, 53
  images with Assets panel, 10, 11
  pages, 149–151
  Preview In Browser, 112–114
print style sheets (CSS), 269–270
printing code, 191
programmers vs. designers, 169
programs on companion website, 1129–1130
progressive download (Flash)
  adding, 881–882
  inserting, 885
  vs. streaming, 877, 879–880
properties
  adding to/removing from Properties pane, 262–263
  defined, 76
  enabling/disabling (CSS), 265
  grouping (CSS), 239
  inheritance of (CSS), 239–240
  modifying with AP Elements panel, 431–432
  optional regions, setting, 937
  toggling CSS properties, 265–266
  vendor-specific CSS properties, 264–265
Properties pane (CSS), 244, 245–246, 248, 262–264
Property inspector
  applying styles through (CSS), 253, 257
  basics, 76–79
  creating links and, 382
  CSS tab of, 248
  exploring CSS with, 248
  extensibility and, 1057
  InContext Editing options, 960–961
  for inserting e-mail links, 391
  linking to files and, 388–390
  modifying tables and, 494
  pointing to files and, 386
  table properties and, 502
PSD files, opening, 840
pseudo-classes, 251–252
pseudo-elements, 251, 252
publishing
  Flash video, 883–884
  pages, 153–156
  XML/XSLT files, 1049
Put Dependent Files option, 718
put options, 112

Q

QR code reader (AP elements), 693
queries
  media queries, 133, 415, 418
  storing and retrieving, 306
Query Builder in Microsoft Access, 721, 722
query strings
  defined, 770, 782
  disabling, 772
  Live View and, 770–772, 775
Quick Tag Editor
  <address> tag and, 327
  basics, 219–220
  Edit Tag mode, 224–225
  identifying Spry regions and, 632
  Insert HTML mode, 221–222
  Wrap Tag mode, 222–223
QuickTime
  movies, inserting, 889–893
  QuickTime 7 Pro for media, 102
  QuickTime player (audio), 900
quote marks
  in HTML and XML, 1033
  single and double in Call JavaScript behavior, 456
quoting text paragraphs, 338

R

radio buttons
  adding in Spry Validation Radio Group, 656
  Dynamic Radio Buttons server behavior, 1105–1106
  linking to dynamic data, 799–800
  providing in forms, 531, 532
radio groups
  Radio Group command, 534–535
  Spry Validation Radio Group, 655–657
ranges (character), matching, 313–314

RDS connectivity, 9
`ready()` function, 673, 674
`receiveArguments()` function, 1064, 1065
receiving parameters with URLs, 784–787
Recent Snippets button, 206–207
Record Insertion Form, 803–804
record navigation
basics, 758
data objects for, 760–762
links, building, 758–760
Recordset Navigation Bar, 760–764
recordset navigation, establishing, 762–764
recordset navigation status, 761–766
Record Update Form application object, 806–807
recording commands, 1061–1064
records
defined, 698
Delete Record server behavior, 1096–1097
Insert Record server behavior, 1094–1095
inserting in data sources, 801–803
Move To Specific Record server behavior, 786–787
Update Record server behavior, 805, 1095–1096
updating data in, 804–807
Recordset (Query) server behavior, 1087–1088
Recordset Paging server behaviors, 1089–1090
recordsets
advanced, 721, 722–724
advanced SQL statements, writing, 721–724
basics, 718
copying between pages, 726
creating simple, 718–721, 1087–1088
defined, 697
defining, 726–727
deleting, 726
filtering detail page recordsets, 784–787
navigation within. *See* record navigation
Recordset (Query) server behavior, 1087–1088
Recordset Navigation Bar, 760–764
Recordset Paging server behaviors, 758–760, 1089–1090
Simple Recordset dialog box, 784–785
using server behaviors to filter, 786–787
working with, 725–726
recursive frames, 610
redirecting users, 183–184
Redo command, 298
Reference panel, 29, 216–218
Refresh Design View buttons, 55
Refresh This Document option, 184
refreshes, full-page, defined, 620
regions. *See also* editable regions; optional regions; repeating regions; Repeat Region server behaviors
mapping inconsistent template regions, 952–954
Show Region server behavior, 1091
support for in templates, 914
regions (Spry)
basics, 631–634
repeating, 636–638
regular expressions for Find and Replace
basics, 311
grouping, 315–316
matching character positions, 313–314
matching character ranges, 314–315
repeating characters, 313–314
wildcards and, 312–313
regular expressions, reports and, 1014
related files. *See also* integrating Live View, Related Files and Code Navigator features
accessing, 200–201
defined, 828
Discover Dynamically-Related Files list, 91
Dynamic Related Files feature, 819
dynamically related files (WordPress), 828–830
Enable Related Files option, 91
Filter Related Files options, 829
integrating with Live View and Code Navigator, 196
Related Files bar, 51
relational databases, defined, 699
Relative attribute for positioning, 422–423
Relative size operator, 602
Relative to Document, inserting images and, 350–351
Relative to Site Root, inserting images and, 351
Reload Modified Files option, 100
remote servers
defined, 134
defining, 134–138
remote site folders, 130, 131
removing
applied CSS styles, 258
guides, 435

removing *(continued)*
  InContext Editing editable regions, 961–962
  properties from Properties pane, 262–263
  Remove Extra Closing Tags option, 118
  server behaviors, 1085–1086
  sites, 142
  template markup, 955–957
  Warn When Fixing Or Removing Tags option, 118
renaming
  Library items, 972
  Rename Form Items When Pasting option, 118
Reopen Documents On Startup option, 91
repairing syntax, 144
Repeat command, 300
`_repeat` object, 939–941
Repeat Region server behaviors
  applying, 754–756
  basics, 751–752, 770, 1088–1089
  implementing, 752–754
  Repeat Region object (XSLT), 1040, 1043, 1047
  vs. repeating regions, 928
repeating data. *See also* Repeat Region server behaviors
  basics, 751–752
  restricting (Spry), 639–640
  XSL data, 1040–1041
repeating elements with Library items, 965, 967
repeating regions. *See also* repeating data
  basics, 928–929
  InContext Editing and, 962–963
  modifying, 929–930
  vs. Repeat Region server behavior, 928
  Spry, 636–638
repeating tables, 930–932
replacing. *See* Find and Replace feature
replaying commands, 1061–1064
reports
  accessing, 1010–1011
  basics, 997, 1009–1010
  HTML reports, outputting, 1012
  Reports command, 997, 1010
  workflow reports, 1012–1014
repository (SVN), 1023–1025
request variables, making available, 809
requirements for running Dreamweaver, xlvi–xlvii
resampling images, 359
rescaling
  Fireworks images, 848
  Flash movies, 871–872
Reset button (forms), 545–547
Resig, John, 671
resizing
  AP elements, 420, 423–424, 425
  frames, 591, 601–602, 607–608
  graphics (Fireworks), 850–851
  tables, 504–506
resources. *See also* websites for downloading; websites for further information
  directories of, xlvii, 1130
  planning web sites and, 128–129
`respond.js`, 418
restoring deleted Library items, 972
Restrict Access To Page server behaviors, 813–814, 1098–1099
results page for page searches, 810–811
revisions, working with (Design Notes), 1005, 1006
rewriting code preferences, 117–119
rollbacks, with Contribute, 1018–1020
rollovers, 375–377
rollovers (Fireworks)
  inserting with code, 856, 859–862
  inserting with Dreamweaver behaviors, 856, 857–859
  sliced images, modifying, 862–863
Roundtrip XML, 1031–1032
rows
  alternating background colors, 941–943
  automatic numbering, 943–944
  basics, 487
  deleting, 507
  headings, 488–489
  inserting in tables, 506–507
  modifying frames and, 601–602
  moving, 501
  selecting, 496
  setting properties, 512–515
`rs--as` in `rsDBA` prefix, 719
RSS, podcast XML feeds and, 906
Rule Definition dialog box, 271, 282
rulers
  for aligning AP elements, 433–434
  guides, displaying and, 435
  moving origin, 434

rules (CSS)
basics, 239
creating, 238
CSS Rule Definition dialog box, 406
for defining <div> tags, 405–406
horizontal, to divide web pages, 372–373
managing, 266–268
Move CSS Rules, 62
Rules pane, 246, 247
Rules view, 247
style rules, viewing, 245
runCommand() function, 1065
runtime connections, maintaining, 717

S

salign attribute (Flash), 872
saving
code as snippets, 215–216
files, 100–101, 145
frames and framesets, 598–599
new pages, 143–146
pages, XML Data Sets and, 627
Save As Template command, 916, 950
Save On Launch option, 100–101
workspace layouts, 39
scale, setting (Flash), 871–872
Schiller, Scott, 901
screens
Dual Screen option, 37
multiple, xxxvi, 4, 18, 52–53
Offscreen Rendering option, 105
screen size options, 47–49
split-screen views, 189, 201
Script Property inspector, 228, 229
scripting commands, 1064–1066
scroll bars
adding to frames, 606–607
displaying, iframes and, 614
scrolling lists (forms), 538–539
search engines, aiding
with Description objects, 182–183
with Keywords, 182–183
search field, 51
search pages, building, 795–796
searching code
advanced options in Find and Replace, 307–309
HTML tags and attributes, replacing, 309–311
search filters, 308–309
text in code, 306–307
searching text. *See* Find and Replace feature
Secure File Transfer Protocol (SFTP), 134, 136
seekability of streaming video, 880
Select Image Source dialog box, 348, 349
select lists, validating (Spry), 649–650
Select tool, 46
<select> tags
inserting (Spry), 637–638
lists and menus and, 555–556
<select> ... </select> tag pair, 536
selecting
AP elements, 423
frames and framesets, 597–598
Selection menu, 211–212
table elements, 494–497
text in paragraphs, 296
selectors
advanced, 252–253
defined, 239
defining custom (CSS), 240–241
selector types, 250–252
semicolons (;), multiple custom filters and, 830
separation elements, 752
sequencing behaviors, 482–483
sequential navigation links, computing, 946–947
Server Behavior Builder
basics, 25–26, 1083
customizing server behaviors with, 1109
editing server behaviors and, 1109
server behaviors, 1083–1113
basics, 21, 1083–1084
Check New Username, 1100–1101
custom, 1109–1113
Delete Record, 1096–1097
Dynamic CheckBox, 1104–1105
Dynamic List/Menu, 1102–1103
Dynamic Radio Buttons, 1105–1106
Dynamic Text, 1101–1102
Dynamic Text Field, 1103–1104
editing, 1109
Go To Detail Page, 1092–1093

server behaviors *(continued)*
- Go To Related Page (ASP only), 1093
- Insert Record, 1094–1095
- inserting and removing, 1085–1086
- vs. JavaScript behaviors, 1083–1084, 1085
- Log In User, 1097–1098
- Log Out User, 1099–1100
- Move To Specific Record, 1090
- non-standard, installing, 1108
- Recordset (Query), 1087–1088
- Recordset Paging, 758–760, 1089–1090
- Repeat Region, 1088–1089
- Restrict Access To Page, 1098–1099
- Server Behaviors panel, 1084–1085
- Show Region, 756–758, 1091
- standard, 1086
- stored procedures and, 1106–1107
- Update Record, 1095–1096
- user authentication and, 1097

Server Behaviors panel
- basics, 21, 22, 1084–1085
- vs. Behaviors panel, 1084
- defining stored procedures through, 1106–1107

Server Debug panel, 776–778

Server Folder field, 766, 768

server models
- Show Region server behavior and, 1091
- variables for, 809

`Server.MapPath()` command, 713–714

servers
- remote servers, 134–138
- Servers category screen, 135
- testing servers, defined, 134
- testing servers, defining, 138–140

server-side includes. *See* SSIs (server-side includes)

server-side pages (XSLT), 1051–1052

session variables
- defined, 809
- making available, 809

Set Magnification, 46–47

Set Text of Container action, 442, 444–445, 467

Set Text of Frame action, 468

Set Text of Status Bar action, 469

Set Text of Text Field action, 470

SFTP (Secure File Transfer Protocol), 134, 136

SGML (Standard Generalized Markup Language), 1032

Shake effect, 479

Sharpen feature (images), 630–631

Shift key, item selection and, 539

Shockwave
- adding files to Dreamweaver, 874–875
- inserting multimedia objects and, 747
- MIME types and, 873

`<shortcutlist>` section, 1070–1071

Show Dialog When Inserting Objects option, 92–93

Show New Document Dialog Box On Ctrl+N (Command+N) option, 104

Show Region server behaviors, 756, 1091

Show-Hide Elements action, 442, 446, 470–471

showing
- page elements, 756–758
- panels, 80–84

Simple Recordset dialog box, 784–785

Simple Rollover behavior (Fireworks), 861

site cloaking, 140–141

Site Editor option (Business Catalyst), 160, 161

site management tools
- browser targeting, 31–32
- Check In / Check Out system, 32–33
- FTP publisher, 32
- libraries, 29–30
- Link Checker, 32
- templates, 30–31

Site menu button, 51

Site Setup dialog box, 130, 131, 341

site-root-relative addresses, 387–388

sites
- creating with Business Catalyst, 158–159
- exporting, 956–957
- graphics, adjusting in WordPress sites, 833–835
- Manage Sites button, 112
- preferences, 110–112
- WordPress, customizing, 830–833

sites, setting up, 127–165
- 3 steps for, 130
- basics, 127, 134
- BrowserLab for previewing, 151–153
- Business Catalyst. *See* Business Catalyst
- defining, 127, 130, 138–140
- dynamic pages, mapping, 129
- dynamic sites, 702–703
- local site folder, 130–133

local site information, managing, 142
new documents, creating, 147–149
new pages, creating and saving, 143–146
planning, 128–129
previewing, 149–151
publishing, 153–156
remote servers, defining, 134–138
site cloaking, 140–141
Site Setup dialog box basics, 130
testing servers, defining, 138–140
size
of banner ads, 373
CSS style size, changing, 328–329
of Dreamweaver headings, 292, 293
font size, adjusting, 328–330
of horizontal rules, 372
of image files, changing, 364
of images, changing, 359, 363
reducing file size (Fireworks), 850–851
Relative size operator, 602
resizing AP elements, 423–424
screen size options, 47–49
text size, changing, 60, 328–330
of thumbnails, 353, 476–477
Window Size options, 47–49, 98–99
sliced images, modifying (Fireworks), 862–863
slices
basics (Fireworks), 859–860
copying (PhotoShop), 843
Slide effect, 479–480
Smart Objects (PhotoShop)
keeping in sync, 846–847
updating, 844–846
snapping guides, 436
snippets
<script> block, inserting, 673
defined, 206–207
inserting, 206–207, 214–215
saving code as, 215–216
Snippets panel
basics, 169
code, adding with, 214–216
commenting out code with, 345
Sorenson Spark, 879
Sort Table command, 515–516
SoundManager API project, 901
source files (Fireworks), 848, 850
<source> tags, HTML5 video code, 894, 895
spaces
after periods, 316
option to allow multiple, 93
<span> tags, 258, 428, 429
spanning rows or columns, 510–511
special characters
encoding preferences, 119
inserting, 231–234
in query strings, 771
specificity of CSS rules, 241–242
speed, Connection Speed option, 99
spell-checking
dictionary preferences, 94–95
text, 300–301
spiders, defined, 612
spinner controls (forms), 552
Split view, 42
splitting cells, 509–511
sprites, 854–856
Spry
Ajax and, 619–620, 621
basics, 619, 621–622
capabilities, 5, 19
data, binding to pages, 634–635
data, incorporating into pages, 639–641
Data Sets with XML data, 628–631
enhanced CSS for, 639
HTML data, merging into pages and, 622–627
master and detail regions, 632, 634
objects (Insert panel), 69–71
repeating regions, 636–638
restricting repeated data, 639–640
Spry Data Set Wizard, 623–627
Spry Region objects, 632
Spry regions, defining, 631–633
spry:choose attribute, 638–639
spry:if attribute, 638–639
spry:region and spry:detailregion attributes, 632
static data, incorporating into pages and, 622
XML data, connecting to and, 628–631
Spry effects
Appear/Fade, 474–475
basics, 666–667

Spry effects *(continued)*
- behaviors and, 666
- Blind, 475–476
- Grow/Shrink, 476–478
- Highlight, 478–479
- Shake, 479
- Slide, 479–480
- Squish, 480–481

Spry widgets
- basics, 641–642
- form fields, basics of validating, 642–643
- Spry Accordion Panel widgets, 661–663
- Spry Collapsible Panel widget, 663–664
- Spry layout widgets, 657
- Spry Menu Bar widget, 657–659
- Spry Tabbed Panel widget, 660–661
- Spry Tooltip widget, 665–666
- Spry Validation Checkbox, 650–652
- Spry Validation Confirm widget, 654–655
- Spry Validation Password widget, 652–654
- Spry Validation Radio Group, 655–657
- Spry Validation Select widget, 649–650
- Spry Validation Text Field widget, 642, 643–646
- Spry Validation Textarea widget, 647–649
- validation custom patterns, 645
- validation widgets, using with tables, 646–647

SQL (Structured Query Language)
- advanced statements, writing, 721–724
- keywords in, 724
- statements, 700–701

Squish effect, 480–481

`src` attribute
- HTML5, 893, 908
- rollovers and, 375
- for Spry data columns, setting, 635

SSIs (server-side includes)
- adding, 979–980
- basics, 966–967, 978–979
- editing, 981
- vs. Library items, 978
- vs. XSLT fragments, 1038

standard actions, 456–474
- Call JavaScript, 456
- Change Property, 457–459
- Check Plugin, 458–459
- Drag AP Element, 442–444, 459–462
- Go to URL, 462
- Jump Menu and Jump Menu Go, 463–464
- Open Browser Window, 464–465
- Popup Message, 465
- Preload Images, 465–467
- Set Text of Container, 442, 444–445, 467
- Set Text of Frame, 468
- Set Text of Status Bar, 469
- Set Text of Text Field, 470
- Show-Hide Elements, 442, 446, 470–471
- Swap Image and Swap Image Restore, 471–472
- Validate Form, 472–474

Standard Generalized Markup Language (SGML), 403

starting Dreamweaver, 143

states
- rollovers and, 857, 858
- Spry Validation Checkbox widget, 652
- Spry Validation Confirm widget, 655
- Spry Validation Password widget, 653–654
- Spry Validation Select widget and, 650
- Spry Validation Text Field widget, 645–646
- Spry Validation Textarea widget, 648

static data, incorporating into pages with Spry, 622

status bar
- basics, 45
- Set Text of Status Bar action, 469

Status category (Design Notes), 1005–1006

Stearns, Geoff, 869

sticky settings, 491

storage with MyVersionControl, 1022

stored procedures, 1106–1107

storing search queries, 306

streaming (Flash)
- adding, 882–883
- vs. progressive download, 877, 879–880

strings, URLencoded, 771

`<strong>` and `<em>` tags, preferences and, 93–94

structural tags (HTML5), 191–192

Structured Query Language. *See* SQL (Structured Query Language)

style, importance of, 237

Style Definition dialog box (CSS), 248

Style Rendering toolbar (CSS), 59–60, 256

styles
- applying to navigation buttons, 578–579
- embedded, 207–208

list navigation buttons using CSS, 573–578
logical styles, 187, 324–325
nested unordered lists, 582
numbering styles, ordered lists, 568–569
physical styles, 188, 325
text style tags, 324–327
styles (CSS), creating and applying
applying, 242–244, 253, 256–257
basics, 248
changing styles, 258
external style sheet styles, applying, 259–260
external style sheets, attaching, 254–256
multiple classes, inserting, 253–254
new styles, generating. *See* styles (CSS), generating new
Property inspector and, 253
removing applied styles, 258
Style Rendering toolbar, 256
styles (CSS), generating new
advanced selectors, 252–253
basics, 248–250
Class selector type, 251
Compound selector type, 251–252
descendant selectors, 252
ID selector type, 251
Tag selector type, 251
Styles panel (CSS)
basics, 244–248, 260–262
Edit Styles mode, 260–262
Properties pane, 262–264
styling
Business Catalyst modules and, 163–164
text, 324–328
unordered lists with CSS, 564–565
XSLT fragments, 1045
Submit button (forms), 545–547
Subversion (SVN). *See also* files (SVN)
basics, 1021–1022
conflicts, resolving, 1029
connecting to SVN servers, 1022–1023
files, acquiring latest version, 1025, 1026–1027
files, committing, 1026, 1027
files, different versions, 1028
files, locking and unlocking, 1027–1028
local and repository files, viewing, 1024–1025
repository files basics, 1023–1024
version control system, 9
Summary for Selection pane, 247
SVN. *See* Subversion (SVN)
Swap Image and Swap Image Restore actions, 471–472
Swap Image behavior (rollovers), 861
SWF files
designating attributes, 870–872
inserting, 17, 867–870
publishing Flash videos and, 883
SWFFix, 869
Switch To Plain Paragraph After Heading option, 93
`swliveconnect` attribute (Flash), 872
symbols, inserting, 231–234
syncing Photoshop Smart Objects, 846–847
syntax, repairing, 144
system-based data sources, 698

T

tab index, defined, 382
Tabbed Panel widget (Spry), 660–661
`tabindex` attribute, 550
table properties, 502–512
adjusting, 511–512
alignment, 502–503
basics, 502
borders and backgrounds, 508
cell spacing and cell padding, 509
cells, merging and splitting, 509–511
centering tables in CSS, 503–504
deleting rows and columns, 507
inserting rows and columns, 506–507
resizing, 504–506
Table Property inspector, 502, 505
`<table>` tags, 486, 488, 501, 502, 504
tables,
adding, 486
cell columm and row properties, 512–515
cells, selecting, 497
cells basics, 487–488
changes in, Fireworks and, 863
Code for an HTML Table (listing), 487
column and row headings, 488–489
columns, selecting, 496
converting for browser compatibility, 983–984
data, importing, 516–518
defined, 698

tables *(continued)*
Dreamweaver capabilities and, 16–17
editable regions, including in, 932–933
editing content. *See* editing table content
elements, selecting, 494–497
entire tables, selecting, 495–496
Expanded Tables mode, 495
headers, 488
HTML data sources and, 623–624
HTML table fundamentals, 485
importance of, 485
inserting. *See* tables, inserting into Dreamweaver
layout objects (Insert panel), 66
modes to work with, 66
modifying basics, 494
recording and, 1062
repeating, 930–932
row headings, 488–489
rows, selecting, 496
rows basics, 487
sorting, 515–516
validation widgets, using with, 646–647
values in, computing, 944–945
tables, inserting into Dreamweaver
adding tables to pages, 493–494
methods for, 489
Table dialog box, 489–493
table width, 491–493
tabs
options, 90
Spry Tabbed Panel widget and, 660–661
switching between maximized documents with, 41
Tag Accessibility Attributes dialog box, 355, 356
Tag Chooser, 8, 212–214
Tag Completion feature, 210
Tag Editor, 213–214
Tag inspector, 8, 169, 218–219
tag libraries
Code Hints tool, 208–210
creating new, 1081
customizing, 1078–1081
extensibility and, 1057
languages included by Dreamweaver, 169
Selection menu, 211–212
Tag Chooser, 212–214
Tag Completion feature, 210
Tag Library Editor, 26–27
Tag Selector
applying styles with, 257, 295
basics, 12–13, 45–46, 217
identifying Spry regions and, 633
removing styles with, 258
removing tags and, 328
tags. *See also* Quick Tag Editor; *specific* tags
attaching behaviors and, 450, 452
attributes, modifying, 219
attributes as search filters, 307–308
Close Tags option when coding, 116–117
custom, 26–27, 1057, 1075–1077
defined, 170
editing, 1079–1080
Fix Invalidly Nested And Unclosed Tags option, 118
form input tags, 523
HTML tags basics, 170
HTML tags, for formatting dynamic data, 733–734
HTML tags, replacing, 309–311
HTML5 structural tags, 191–195
inserting with Meta objects, 180–181
italic tags (<i>) for stored data, 734
list tags, 561–562
logical tags, defined, 324
making portions of editable, 924
physical tags, defined, 324
Remove Extra Closing Tags option, 118
searching for text within, 307–308
selecting for new rules, 249–250
style tags for text, 324–327
Tag Completion feature, 210
tag pairs, 170
tag-complete areas, defined, 928
Warn When Fixing Or Removing Tags option, 118
wrapping, 206–207
in XML and HTML, 1032, 1034
<tagspec>, 1075–1077
target attribute, 185, 396
targeting frame content, 609–612
targets, 396–397
<td> ... </td> tag pair, 487
team development, 997–1029
accessing reports, 1010–1011
Check In/Check Out system. *See* Check In/Check Out system

Design Notes. *See* Design Notes
File view columns, browsing, 1007–1009
HTML reports, outputting, 1012
reports, basics, 1009–1010
SVN. *See* Subversion (SVN)
WebDAV and, 1020–1021
website administration. *See* Contribute
workflow reports, 1012–1014
Telestream Agility 2G, 880
template expressions
alternating row background colors, 941–943
automatic row numbering, 943–944
basics, 937–941
language and object model, 938–941
multiple-if template expressions, 941
sequential navigation links, computing, 946–947
Template Expressions Computing Example (listing), 945
Template Expressions tag, 1077
values in tables, computing, 944–945
templates
Assets panel and. *See* Assets panel
basics, 30–31, 913–915
content, adding, 920–922
content in browsers, editing. *See* InContext Editing
creating, 915–916
default document, changing, 957
editable attributes, making, 924–926
editable attributes, setting, 926–928
editable regions, 916–920, 932–933
InContext templates, setting up, 958–959
nesting, 947–949
Optional Region feature. *See* optional regions
pages, converting to, 923–924
removing template markup, 955–957
repeating regions and, 928–932
Template Properties dialog box, 927
Template Updating option, 919
updating, 954–955
XML and, 1034, 1035, 1036–1037
XSLT documents and, 1048
testing for browser compatibility. *See* Browser Compatibility Check feature
testing servers
defined, 134
defining, 138–140
for previewing applications, 775–776
text, 291–346
abbreviations, adding, 328
acronyms, adding, 328
<address> tag, 327–328
aligning, 337
aligning in tables, 513
of AP elements, setting, 467

 tags, 318
changing size of, 60, 328–330
code and, manipulating simultaneously, 308
color, 331–333
commenting code, 344–346
creating lists from, 561
dates, inserting into pages, 342–344
Dreamweaver support for, 16
dynamic text, inserting, 729–731
Dynamic Text server behavior, 1101–1102
entering headings, 292
Find and Replace. *See* Find and Replace feature
font color, adding, 330–333
font size, adjusting, 328–330
fonts, assigning specific, 333–337
headings, 291–294
indenting, 316
line-spacing, 318–319
Microsoft Office documents and. *See* Microsoft Office documents
modifying format, 328
paragraphs. *See* paragraphs
preformatted, 317–318
quoting paragraphs, 338
selecting, 296
Set Text Of Container, 444
Set Text of Status Bar action, 469
Set Text of Text Field behavior, 470
spell-checking, 300–301
style tags, 324–327
styling, 324–328
text editors, 5–7
text entry capabilities, 9–10
web fonts, 338–342
whitespace, controlling, 316–319
wrapping around images, 368–369
wrapping in paragraphs, 295
text fields in forms
defined, 526
dynamic, 797–798

text fields in forms *(continued)*
form controls, grouping, 530–531
inserting, 526–528
multiline text areas, inserting, 528–531
password fields, 528
text messages, including JavaScript functions or references in, 465
text objects, Insert panel, 73–74
text pattern matching system, 311
Text Property inspector, 9–10
<textarea> tags, 555
textareas, Spry Validation Textarea widget, 647–649
text-shadow property (CSS), 272, 275
<th> tags, table headers and, 488
ThemeRoller (jQuery Mobile), xxxvii, 688, 689, 690–691
themes
defined (WordPress), 821
jQuery Mobile framework, 682, 688–691
thumbnails
adding borders to, 366
growing and shrinking, 476–477
increasing size of, 353
making dynamic images, 745–746
tiling effects, 273, 371
time, formatting, 740–741
title fields
basics, 178, 382
Title text fields, 53
titles
changing (documents), 178
Title/Encoding (Page Properties dialog box), 178
toggling CSS properties, 265–266
toolbars. *See also specific* toolbars
accessing, 50
tools. *See also* site management tools
presented in panels, 80
website maintenance tools, 8–9
Tooltip widget (Spry), 665–666
tooltips, displaying animated, 674–675
<tr> ... </tr> tag pair, 487
Tracing Image function (AP elements), 440–442
Tracing Image (Page Properties dialog box), 178–179
transitions (CSS)
animating, 285–288
options, 282–285
translators
basics, 27
extensibility and, 1057
tree conflicts, 1029
triggering custom functions, 455
triggers, behaviors and, 452
troubleshooting materials on companion website, 1131
type attribute, bullet symbol and, 564
Type category (CSS), 271–272
typeface, 333–337
typos
preventing in URLs, 385–386
spell-checking text, 300–301

U

<ul> tags
inserting, 637–638
<ul> ... </ul> tag pair (lists), 561, 564
Ultimate CSS Gradient Generator, 275
uncloaking site folders, 140–141
underlines, eliminating from links, 383–385
Undo command, 298
Unicode (UTF-8), 178, 232–233
Unicode Normalization Form list, 104
unlocking SVN files, 1027–1028
unnesting
AP elements, 432
lists, 582
unordered lists
adding to web pages, 562–563
bullet shapes, changing, 564
editing, 561
inserting, 560–561
list tags, 561–562
styling with CSS, 564–565
UnsupportedPlugins.txt file, 889
Update Links option, 92
Update Pages dialog box, 975, 976, 977
Update Record server behavior, 805, 1095–1096
updating
data in records, 804–807
with Library items, 965, 967
series of pages or entire sites, 954–955
templates, 954–955
websites, with Library items, 975–976

uploading media (Flash), 883–884
URL Prefix field, 767
URLencoded strings, 771
URLs (Uniform Resource Locators)
  adding to jump menus, 543
  address types, 387
  common schemes and protocols, 380–381
  encoding preferences, 119
  fundamentals of, 379
  inserting from Assets panel, 385–386
  passing parameters with. *See* passing parameters with URLs
  URL parameters, defined, 770
  values, passing to related pages, 794–795
Use <strong> And <em> In Place Of <b> And <i> option, 93–94
user authentication server behaviors
  Check New Username, 1100–1101
  Log In User, 1097–1098
  Log Out User, 1099–1100
  Restrict Access To Page, 1098–1099
user interface, enhancements in, xxxix
user-driven master pages, 788–791
users, redirecting, 183–184
UTF-8 (Unicode) encoding, 178, 232–233
uu#sellistnav a:link, #sellistnav a:visited, #sellistnav a:hover styles, 573, 578

V

valid XML, 1033
Validate Form action, 472–474
validating code
  for browser compatibility, 985–987. *See also* W3C Validator
  CSS, 985
  HTML, 985
  site pages, 54
  Tracing Image and, 440
validating forms
  form fields, 642–646
  input, 528
  text fields, 643–646
  textareas, 647–649
validating tables, 646–647
validation widgets (Spry)
  Spry Validation Checkbox, 650–652
  Spry Validation Confirm widget, 654–655
  Spry Validation Password widget, 652–654
  Spry Validation Radio Group, 655–657
  Spry Validation Select widget, 649–650
  Spry Validation Textarea widget, 647–649
  using with tables, 646–647
  Validation Text Field widget, 642, 643–646
valign attribute, 513
value fields, Tag inspector and, 218–219
values
  in drop-down lists, 800
  in form fields, 797
  forms, getting values from, 791–794
  forms, passing values to related pages, 794–795
  in tables, computing, 944–945
van der Sluis, Bobby, 869
variables
  adding as data sources, 808–811
  application variables, defined, 809
  session variables, 809
  SSIs, 979
VBScript, 227–229
verifying code, 61
vertical alignment
  of images, 367–368
  table cells/rows/columns, 513
vertical menus, 659
video, 877–896
  clips, 886–888
  Flash video. *See* Flash video
  HTML5 video code, 893–895
  playing, 888–889
  QuickTime movies, inserting, 889–893
  video possibilities, 877
<video> tag (HTML5), 893–894, 895
View Builder in Microsoft SQL, 721
viewing
  ColdFusion tags, 76
  Design Notes, 1006–1007
  dynamic data, 731–732
  dynamic images, Live View for, 731–732, 743
  local and repository files, 1024–1025
  style rules, 245
  XML/XSLT files, 1049

views, switching, 41–44
visibility
AP elements, 428–429
of elements, controlling, 95–96, 106
heightened visibility of Design Notes, 1007
Visual Aids, 56
visual editors, 5–7
Visual Server Markup Tags, 96
visualizing <div> tags
CSS layout backgrounds, 410
CSS layout box model, 410–412
CSS Layout Outlines, 412–413
Inspect mode, 409–410
options, 408–409

W

W3C Validator
cross-browser compatibility and, 985–987
preferences, 124–125
site pages, xxxviii, 54
WampServer, 715
warnings
Check Plugin action and, 458
e-mail warnings, 391
W3C Validator, 986, 987
Warn When Fixing Or Removing Tags option, 118
Warn When Opening Read-Only Files option, 91
Warn When Placing Editable Regions Within <p> Or <h1>–<h6> Tags option, 94
WAV files, embedding plugins for, 898, 900
web content management systems (CMS), 819–836
basics, 819–821
defined, 819
support, 19
WordPress for. *See* WordPress
Web Designer Wall, 674
web fonts, xxxiv–xxxv, 338–342
web links. *See* links
web pages. *See* pages
web widgets
basics, 669–670
inserting customized, 679–681
legacy web widgets, 676–678
Widget Browser, 670, 676, 678–682, 1116
WebDAV (Web-based Distributed Authoring and Versioning)
basics, 9, 997
team development and, 1020–1021
WebKit, 4, 42
WebM video format, 887
websites
dynamic, multiple pages and, 781
team development of. *See* team development
websites for downloading
application for converting audio file formats, 909
ColdFusion, 708
custom objects, behaviors and commands, 25
Dreamweaver Technique Simulation files, 134
DWfaq Date/Time Server Formats extension, 741
feed icon, 907
Java JRE, 1118
MAMP, 768, 823
MXP extension files, 482
ODBC drivers, 705
PHP and MySQL packages, 715
phpMyAdmin, 824
QuickTime 7 Pro for media, 102
SoundManager API project, 901
Ultimate CSS Gradient Generator, 275
whereas WampServer, 768
WimpyPlayer for audio, 901
XAMPP, 823
websites for further information
Adobe accounts, 151
Adobe Labs mini-site, 620
Adobe Marketplace & Exchange site, 481–482
from the author, xlvii
banner ads, 373
CSS Advisor mini-site, 4, 268
CSS hacks, 262
Dreamweaver CS6 Bible companion website, 1129
Dreamweaver website, xlvii
Flash Video Streaming Service, 880
Flickr, 619
Google Maps, 619
HTML5 video, 895
IAB, 373
jQuery Mobile, 684
jQuery ThemeRoller, 689
MXP behavior extension files, 481